COMPANION ENCYCLOPEDIA
OF MARKETING

COMPANION ENCYCLOPEDIA OF MARKETING

EDITED BY

MICHAEL J. BAKER

London and New York

First published in 1995
by Routledge
11 New Fetter Lane, London EC4P 4EE
29 West 35th Street, New York, NY 10001

© 1995 Routledge

Typeset in Ehrhardt by
Solidus (Bristol) Limited
Printed in Great Britain by
TJ Press (Padstow) Ltd, Padstow, Cornwall

⊗ Paper manufactured in accordance with the proposed ANSI/N150
Z 39.48–199X and ANSI Z 39.48–1984

British Library Cataloguing in Publication Data

A catalogue record for this book is available from the British Library.

Library of Congress Cataloguing in Publication Data

A catalogue record for this book is available on request.

ISBN 0–415–09395–3

CONTENTS

CONTENTS

PREFACE

The *Companion Encyclopedia of Marketing* is the latest addition to the much acclaimed international series published by Routledge. With contributions covering the whole spectrum of human knowledge, Routledge Companion Encyclopedias enjoy an outstanding reputation as authoritative source and reference books. Existing or imminent volumes cover the world's major languages, the history of technology, the history of medicine, psychology, theology, archaeology, anthropology and geography. The *Companion Encyclopedia of Marketing* extends the scope of the series into modern professional practice.

Edited by Professor Michael Baker of the Department of Marketing at the University of Strathclyde, this major new reference book is intended to reflect the growing maturity of the marketing discipline.

During the past decade the need for more effective marketing has become accepted as a necessary condition for success in almost every kind of organization – manufacturing businesses, service organizations such as banks, insurance companies and airlines, and even not-for-profit institutions like charities, hospitals and universities. However, the scope, nature and practice of marketing are not well understood. Indeed, many would-be disciples of the craft and practice mistake two of its less central activities – advertising and promotion – for a concept that is concerned with the creation of mutually satisfying exchange relationships. An authoritative and comprehensive reference book such as this should do a great deal to dispel the confusion as well as provide much needed guidance on the origins, scope and practice of marketing.

As defined, 'encyclopedia' connotes the comprehensive treatment of the aspects of a subject. It follows that people turn to encyclopedias as a first point of reference to help them define a topic or issue, to establish its relationship to other associated or connected subjects, and, possibly, for guidance as to where to go for more detailed exposition. The title 'encyclopedia' also suggests a more rigorous and authoritative treatment than one would expect from a handbook, and indeed there are already several handbooks in circulation. Yet another distinguishing feature of an encyclopedia is that its emphasis is upon the accepted body of knowledge at its time of publication. Thus, while it may anticipate new trends and developments, its primary function is to summarize what is known about a subject and provide insight and understanding of it.

Given these characteristics one may identify two primary audiences for such a work – business persons and students. For both audiences the need is perceived as the same – a concise, authoritative, comprehensive and clear summary of the topic, with advice on how to apply or use the information and where to look for greater detail if this is required.

The perspective of the Editor is that 'marketing is marketing'. In other words, there is a body of knowledge and a series of generalizations that are of universal validity and so may be used to inform and enlighten any specific marketing issue and problem. It is also believed that, like medicine and engineering, marketing is a synthetic discipline. It has sound foundations in the long-established and recognized social sciences such as economics, psychology and sociology, but it differs from them in its holistic approach to understanding the nature and satisfaction of human needs. Also, like medicine and engineering, marketing embraces a body of knowledge as well as a professional practice dependent upon that body of knowledge.

The *Encyclopedia* seeks to recognize both these facets in a comprehensive and rigorous way. The work starts with an exposition and justification of the proposition that marketing is a universal discipline. This introductory chapter seeks to define the nature of the marketing concept and establish the distinction between marketing as a business philosophy, guiding an organization's direction and development, and as a business function, enhancing both efficiency and effectiveness in the execution of an organization's mission. Chapter 2 addresses the history of marketing thought in order to provide perspective and establish the origins of and linkages with other disciplines that form the basis of current marketing thinking.

Next, the *Encyclopedia* addresses the theoretical foundations that underpin and support the subject. Taken together these chapters (3–12) explore the origins, nature and functions of marketing.

Part III is concerned mainly with marketing management and seeks to define and describe the issues and tasks associated with the management of the marketing function. Chapters in this section are largely concerned with the ways and means whereby the theoretical foundations have been shaped and developed to help solve practical marketing problems.

Part IV develops the theme that the marketing manager's role is to select and integrate the available mix of marketing 'ingredients' to maximum effect. Here will be found treatment of the distinctive subfields of marketing which deal with the product, its pricing, promotion and distribution.

Part V looks at marketing in practice, examining the deployment of the marketing mix in a variety of specific contexts, such as the marketing of industrial goods and of services.

Finally, Part VI includes a number of special topics that have emerged as of particular significance and importance as we approach the millennium. Amongst these may be numbered customer satisfaction, total quality management, and marketing and the environment.

Each author has been selected on the basis that he or she is recognized internationally as an expert on the topic of his or her chapter. In order to ensure some comparability in treatment, each author was asked to ensure that his or her contribution:

- defines clearly the scope and nature of the topic;
- explains where it fits into the body of marketing knowledge;
- identifies, defines and describes the key concepts and ideas associated with the topic;
- provides a summary of current issues and potential future developments that bear upon the topic;
- suggests the most important sources of reference for further reading.

In the Editor's view they have met this specification admirably.

Michael J. Baker

THE CONTRIBUTORS

ALAN R. ANDREASEN is Professor of Marketing and Associate Dean for Faculty Affairs at the School of Business of Georgetown University, Washington, DC. He holds PhD and MS degrees from Columbia University and a BA from the University of Western Ontario. He has advised, carried out research and conducted executive seminars for a wide range of non-profit and private sector organizations and several government agencies, including the Academy for Educational Development, the Futures Group, the National Cancer Institute, the US Agency for International Development, the United Way of America, Boys and Girls Clubs of America, the American Cancer Society, the National Endowment for the Arts, and family planning and public health programmes in Egypt, Thailand, Colombia, Jamaica, Mexico, Indonesia, the Philippines and Bangladesh. He serves on the Board of Reviewers of the *Journal of Marketing*, the *Journal of Consumer Research* and the *Journal of Public Policy and Marketing*, and is past president of the Association for Consumer Research. He is the author or editor of ten books, numerous monographs and reports, and over eighty articles and conference papers on consumer behaviour and marketing strategy, and the application of marketing to non-profit organizations, social marketing, and the market problems of disadvantaged consumers.

J. SCOTT ARMSTRONG has been a Professor of Marketing at the Wharton School, University of Pennsylvania, Philadelphia, Pennsylvania, since 1968. He has also taught in Switzerland, Sweden, New Zealand, Thailand, Argentina, Japan and other countries. His research areas span forecasting, planning, education, survey research and the scientific method. He was a founder and editor of the *Journal of Forecasting* and of the *International Journal of Forecasting*. The 1989 Kirkpatrick and Locke study of scholarship ranked him among the top fifteen marketing professors in the USA. According to a publication by the Lippincott Library, he was tied for second among the most prolific Wharton faculty members during the 1988–93 period.

MICHAEL J. BAKER has been Professor of Marketing at the University of

Strathclyde, Glasgow, Scotland, since 1971. From 1978 to 1984 he was Dean of the School of Business/Strathclyde Business School, and in 1984 he was appointed Deputy Principal. He has been a Chairman of the Scottish Business Education Council, Chairman of the Institute of Marketing, and Governor of the CAM Foundation. After gaining his BA at Durham University and military service, he worked in the steel industry and then as a lecturer in marketing. He attended Harvard Business School from 1968 to 1971, where he held an appointment as a research associate and taught the Creative Marketing Strategy course; he also held a research appointment at the Marketing Science Institute. He was awarded the Institute of Marketing's Gold Medal and designated Author of the Year 1978. He is Chairman of the Senate of the Chartered Institute of Marketing (UK) and its fellowship panel. He is the author of numerous books, articles and papers.

DONALD J. BOWERSOX has been John H. McConnell University Professor of Business Administration at the Eli Broad Graduate School of Management, Michigan State University, East Lansing, since 1990. Prior to this he served for 23 years as Professor of Marketing and Logistics, and during his career he has served in various management capacities. He has served as a consultant or speaker for many major corporations and government agencies, and is frequently a lecturer at professional and trade associations. A founding member and second president of the Council of Logistics Management, he is a recipient of the Council's Distinguished Service Award. His other awards include a special commendation from the Society of Logistical Engineers, the Michigan State University Distinguished Faculty Award, and the Syracuse University Harry E. Salzberg Honorary Medallion. He has written over 100 articles and is author or co-author of twelve books, including *Logistical Management, A Managerial Introduction to Marketing, Introduction to Transportation, Physical Distribution Management, Dynamic Simulation of Physical Distribution Systems, Simulated Product Sales Forecasting, Readings in Physical Distribution Management, Leading Edge Logistics: Competitive Positioning for the 1990s* and *Logistical Excellence: It's Not Business As Usual.*

SIMON BROADBENT is a Vice Chairman of Leo Burnett, London, and a founding partner of the Leo Burnett Brand Consultancy. He has worked in advertising since 1962, after seven years at universities and ten in industry. He has a first class degree in mathematics and a diploma in statistics from the University of Oxford, and a PhD in mathematical statistics from the University of London. In industry, he worked on coal research and glass container production. He joined the London Press Exchange, now Leo Burnett, London; he was a director of their market research subsidiary, then media director, and then he ran both planning and media. He went to the Chicago office, where he was the Director of Brand Economics. He played a part in setting up the British Advertising Effectiveness Awards. He has published many papers, especially on the measurement of advertising effectiveness, and two books, on media planning and buying and on the advertising budget, as well as editing other books.

DOUGLAS BROWNLIE is Reader in Marketing at Stirling University, Scotland. Previously, he taught and carried out research in marketing subjects at the University of Strathclyde, the University of Glasgow and University College Cork, Ireland. Before moving to an academic career he worked in engineering and marketing in the steel industry. He has published on topics including technology forecasting, organizational buying behaviour, management development, strategic marketing and marketing management. In addition to contributing chapters to several books, he has presented research papers at the annual conferences of the Academy of Marketing Science, the World Marketing Congress, the European Marketing Academy, the IMP Group, the British Academy of Management and the Marketing Education Group. His current research interests include organizational ethnographies and the currency of postmodernism and critical theory in the study of marketing topics.

DAVID H. BUISSON has been Professor of Marketing and Chairman of the Department of Marketing at the University of Otago, Dunedin, New Zealand, since 1990. From 1987 to 1990 he was Dean of the School of Consumer and Applied Sciences, University of Otago. Since 1991 he has been a director of Business in the Community and a judge of the New Zealand Food Awards. He has been a trustee of the New Zealand Technology Advancement Trust and a member of the Dairy Advisory Bureau Panel. After gaining his PhD at the University of Auckland, he worked as a Research Fellow at the University of Basel, Switzerland, and as a lecturer at the University of Surrey, UK, where he was also a Leverhulme Fellow. Awarded a Harkness Fellowship, he attended the Sloan School of Management, Massachusetts Institute of Technology, as a Sloan Fellow, graduating with an SM in Management. Before moving to the University of Otago, he was an assistant director of the Division of Horticulture and Processing of the DSIR. He is a Fellow of both the New Zealand Institute of Food Science and Technology and the New Zealand Institute of Chemistry, and a Member of the Royal Society of New Zealand and the European Academy of Marketing. He consults with a number of food companies and international organizations and is the author of many papers, addresses and articles. He has wide experience in food marketing and research interests in new product development and innovation in the food industry.

ROBERT D. BUZZELL is Distinguished Professor of Marketing at the School of Business Administration, George Mason University, Fairfax, Virginia. He holds a BA from George Washington University, an MS from the University of Illinois and a PhD from the Ohio State University. From 1961 to 1983 he was on the faculty of the Harvard Business School, where he was the Sebastian S. Kresge Professor of Business Administration. He served as Executive Director of the Marketing Science Institute and later as Chairman of the Marketing Area faculty at Harvard. He was Visiting Professor at INSEAD in 1967 and taught in Harvard's International Senior Managers' Program in Switzerland in 1982–3. He is the author of numerous books, articles and papers.

KATIA CAMPO has been a Research Assistant in the Economics Department of the St Ignatius University Faculty of Antwerp (UFSIA), Belgium, since 1988. She graduated in applied economics from UFSIA in 1988. She is currently completing a doctoral study on the relationship between desire for variety and sensitivity to in-store promotions.

DAVID CARSON is Professor of Marketing at the University of Ulster, Jordanstown, Northern Ireland. He has been an active entrepreneur involved with several enterprises, and an active consultant engaged in long-term consultancies with Disneyland Paris and Stena Sea Ferries in the area of marketing strategies. He is a partner in an import/export trading company based in Ireland and operating throughout Europe. He has been editor of the *European Journal of Marketing* since 1988, and is a review board member of several international academic journals in marketing. He is the lead author of a forthcoming text on marketing and entrepreneurship. His teaching and research interests are in SME marketing and services marketing. He is primarily concerned with adapting existing marketing frameworks and exploring new approaches to marketing for use in the contexts of SMEs and services; he has published widely in these areas over many years.

EDWARD K. CHUNG teaches marketing courses at both the graduate and undergraduate level at York University, North York, Ontario, Canada, where he is a PhD candidate. He holds a BComm degree from McMaster University and an MBA from Oregon State University. Since graduating from Oregon State in 1979, he has held managerial positions in the shipping, energy and financial services industries in various parts of the world. He also operates a management consultancy practice in Toronto.

DAVID J. CLOSS is Professor of Marketing and Logistics at the Eli Broad College of Business, Michigan State University, East Lansing. He served as President and CEO of Dialog Systems Inc. and has consulted with a variety of major corporations. He has been extensively involved in the development and application of computer models and information systems for distribution operations and planning. He has written and co-written many articles and is a co-author of *Logistical Management* and *Simulated Product Sales Forecasting*. He has given numerous presentations discussing the application of information systems technology to logistics management. He is a member of the Council of Logistics Management and the Operations Research Society of America. He is also Systems Editor of the *Journal of Business Logistics*.

ROBERT G. COOPER is the Lawson Mardon Chaired Professor of Industrial Marketing and Technology Management at the Michael De Groote School of Business, McMaster University, Hamilton, Ontario, Canada. He is also

Professor of Marketing at the University, and Director of Research of the Canadian Industrial Innovation Centre, Waterloo, Ontario. He holds bachelor's and master's degrees in chemical engineering, and an MBA and PhD in business administration. He is a leading scholar and consultant in the field of new products, and has published over seventy articles and books on the topic. He is the author of the NewProd series of research studies into new product practices; his most recent book is *Winning at New Products: Accelerating the Process from Idea to Launch* (1993).

C. SAMUEL CRAIG is Professor of Marketing and International Business and Chairman of the Marketing Department at the Stern School of Business, New York University. He received his PhD from the Ohio State University. Prior to joining New York University he taught at Cornell University. He has taught marketing for executive programs in the United States as well as France, Thailand, Singapore, Greece and the former Yugoslavia. He is co-author of three books: *Consumer Behavior: An Information Processing Perspective*, *International Marketing Research* and *Global Marketing Strategy*. His research has appeared in the *Journal of Marketing Research*, *Journal of Marketing*, *Journal of Consumer Research*, *Journal of International Business Studies*, *Columbia Journal of World Business*, *International Journal of Research in Marketing* and other publications.

DAVID W. CRAVENS is Eunice and James L. West Chair of American Enterprise Studies and Professor of Marketing at the M. J. Neeley School of Business, Texas Christian University, Fort Worth, Texas. Before joining the faculty at TCU he was Professor of Marketing and Alcoa Foundation Professor of Business Administration at the University of Tennessee, Knoxville. Prior to this he was Chairman of the Department of Marketing and Transportation and Chairman of the Management Science Program. His doctorate in business administration is from Indiana University, where he also received his MBA degree. He holds a BS in civil engineering from the Massachusetts Institute of Technology. He was Director of Operatons of the Aerospace Research Applications Center (ARAC) at Indiana University, where he received the University's Distinguished Service Award. Prior to his association with ARAC, he was with International Systems and Control Inc., serving in engineering and marketing management positions. He was an Installations Engineering Officer in the USAF Strategic Air Command. He is editor of the *Journal of the Academy of Marketing Science* and associate editor of the *Journal of Strategic Marketing*.

KEITH CROSIER is Senior Lecturer in Marketing, University of Strathclyde, Glasgow, Scotland. He graduated in earth sciences and spent most of his pre-academic career in advertising management with Olivetti in London and New York. He began his lecturing career at what is now the University of Teeside after completing a master's degree at Durham University Business School. Having moved to the University of Strathclyde as a Research Fellow to study the development of 'consumerism' in the United Kingdom and stayed to take up a lectureship in marketing communications, he was appointed Director of the Honours Programme in the Department of Marketing in 1988 and Director of Teaching in 1994. He has been Visiting Professor of Advertising at Pace University, New York, and external examiner to five British universities. He is current vice charman of the Marketing Education Group and assistant editor of *Marketing Intelligence and Planning*. He is the author of contributions to three edited textbooks, two dictionaries and two encyclopedias.

PETER DART read physics at Hertford College, University of Oxford, where he was also the Organ Scholar. He joined Unilever and then worked across many markets, internationally, for some 14 years. He co-founded The Added Value Company (together with Mark Sherrington) in 1988, Europe's first marketing agency, specializing in many aspects of marketing including packaging and design research. The Added Value Company formed a sister company, Brown Inc., in 1992, which specializes in executing packaging and design. Today The Added Value Group employs almost 100 people and processes around £10 million worth of marketing and design projects.

BILL DONALDSON has been a lecturer at the University of Strathclyde, Glasgow, Scotland, since 1983 and is currently Director of the Honours Programme in the Department of Marketing. In addition to undergraduate and MBA teaching he has experience in teaching and consultancy with a number of leading companies. He is the author of *Sales Management: Theory and Practice* (1990) and has recently published several papers on customer service and the characteristics of customer-driven organizations which reflect his current research interests.

SUSAN P. DOUGLAS is Professor of Marketing and International Business at the Stern School of Business, New York University. She received her PhD from the University of Pennsylvania. Prior to joining New York University in 1978, she taught at Centre-HEC, Jouy-en-Josas, France, and was a faculty member of the European Institute for Advanced Studies in Management in Brussels. She has also taught international marketing in executive programmes in France, Belgium, Italy, Taiwan, Singapore, India, South Africa and the former Yugoslavia. A past president of the European Marketing Academy and former vice president of the Academy of International Business, she was elected a Fellow of the Academy of International Business in 1991. She is co-author of *International Marketing Research* and *Global Marketing Strategy*, and she has published over fifty articles on international marketing strategy and cross-national consumer behaviour which have appeared in the *Journal of Marketing*, *Journal of Consumer Research*, *Journal of International Business Studies*, *Columbia Journal of World Business*, *International Journal of Research in Marketing* and other publications.

PETER DOYLE is Professor of Marketing and Strategic Management at the University of Warwick, Coventry, England. Previously he has taught at the

London Business School, INSEAD and Stanford University. He has consulted and run programmes for many top international companies, including Nestlé, Hewlett-Packard, Philips, IBM, Shell, Cadbury Schweppes and Unilever. He has been voted 'outstanding teacher' on numerous programmes throughout America and Europe. He is currently Chairman of the Warwick MBA Full-Time Programme. He has published extensively on marketing strategy in such journals as the *Journal of Marketing and Research, Journal of Marketing, Management Science* and *Journal of Marketing Management*, and he has recently produced a graduate text, *Marketing Management and Strategy*.

ADEL I. EL-ANSARY is the Eminent Scholar and first chairholder of the Paper and Plastics Educational Research (PAPER) Foundation Endowed Research Chair in Wholesaling at the University of North Florida's College of Business Administration, Jacksonville, Florida. He also serves as Director of the Center for Research and Education in Wholesaling. He was the first to design and implement a curriculum in wholesaling at an American university, at the University of North Florida in 1991. He also designed and implemented a comprehensive national research programme on sales force effectiveness in wholesale distribution. He has initiated a national effort for faculty development in wholesaling, developing the *National Faculty Seminar in Wholesale Distribution* and initiating the establishment of the *American Marketing Association's Special Interest Group in Wholesale Distribution*. He has written many papers, articles and books, and co-written the book *Marketing Channels* with Louis W. Stern.

JIM FORWARD has been Franchise Development Manager of the Bass Lease Company since 1994. Having graduated in 1990 from City University Business School, London, with a first-class honours degree in business studies, he became Research Assistant to the Centre for Franchise Research at City University. He has published several articles and is currently pursuing a PhD investigating the use of franchising by small firms as a means of overcoming barriers to growth.

GORDON R. FOXALL is Professor of Consumer Research at the University of Birmingham, England, where he is Director of the Research Centre for Consumer Behaviour in the Birmingham Business School. He holds doctorates in industrial economics and business studies from the University of Birmingham and in psychology from the University of Strathclyde. He has published about a dozen books, including the best-selling *Consumer Psychology for Marketing* (co-authored with Ron Goldsmith) and the critically acclaimed *Consumer Psychology in Behavioural Perspective*. He has also written over 150 refereed papers and articles. His chief research interests are in consumer theory and innovativeness.

CHRISTINA FULOP is Professor and Deputy Director of the Centre for Franchise Research, City University Business School, London. Before and after graduating in economics and sociology at the London School of Economics, she worked in book and trade journal publishing. From 1955 to 1958 she received the Houblon-Norman Fund award of the Bank of England to investigate retail and wholesale buying methods. Between 1966 and 1968 she was a consultant and expert witness for the Registrar of Restrictive Trade Practices. In 1971 she carried out a transnational investigation into resale price maintenance for the Council of Europe. From 1977 to 1980 she was a member of the Consumer Safeguards Committee set up to monitor the merger between Tate & Lyle and Manbre & Garton. Between 1976 and 1988 she was a government-appointed member of the Milk Marketing Board. She was on the teaching staff of London Guildhall University from 1968 until 1989, and was appointed Professor in 1982. She was awarded a PhD from Brunel University in 1980. She has undertaken extensive research and consultancy into retail marketing and franchising, and has written books, articles and papers on these subjects.

LARS-ERIK GADDE is Professor of Industrial Marketing at Chalmers University of Technology, Gothenburg, Sweden, where he is also Vice Dean of the School of Technology Management. His research interests are concentrated in two areas. First, distribution systems for industrial goods; the nature of producer–distributor relationships and structural changes of distribution systems are the two principal issues in that field. Second, changes in customer–supplier relationships and industrial networks; the focus of this research programme has been to analyse the impact on company performance due to changes in purchasing strategy. He is the author of a number of articles and books.

ELS GIJSBRECHTS has been Professor of Marketing at the St Ignatius University Faculty of Antwerp (UFSIA), Belgium, since 1991. After obtaining her degree in applied economics at UFSIA in 1980, she was awarded a government research grant and obtained her doctorate in applied economics in 1984. She was appointed as a lecturer in marketing at the Catholic University of Leuven in 1985, and as an assistant professor of marketing at UFSIA in 1986, where she is now Chairman of the Marketing Department. She also holds a part-time appointment at the FUCAM (Facultés Universitaires Catholiques de Mons), where she is also co-promoter (with Alain Bultez) of the CREER research centre. She teaches several courses in marketing, including quantitative marketing, and has published a number of articles and papers in this field.

STEPHEN A. GREYSER is Professor of Marketing at the Graduate School of Business Administration, Harvard University, Boston, Massachusetts. He specializes in consumer marketing and corporate communications, and is editorial board chairman of the *Harvard Business Review*. He earned his AB, MBA and DBA degrees at Harvard. He is the author of many books, numerous journal articles and some 250 published case studies. His public policy related activities include two invited presentations to the US Federal Trade Commission and a variety of articles on consumerism and attitudes towards marketing advertising/regulation. He is a public member of the National Advertising

Review Board, the US advertising self-regulatory entity. For eight years, he served as Executive Director of the Marketing Science Institute, a non-profit research centre. He also serves on numerous corporate and non-profit organization boards. In 1993 he was voted a Fellow of the American Academy of Advertising for distinguished career achievement.

KJELL GRØNHAUG is Professor of Business Administration at the Norwegian School of Economics and Business Administration, Bergen-Sandviken. He holds an MBA and a PhD in marketing from the School, an MS in sociology from the University of Bergen, and did his postgraduate studies in quantitative methods at the University of Washington. He has been Visiting Professor at the universities of Pittsburgh, Illinois at Urbana-Champaign, California, Kiel and Innsbruck. He is also an Adjunct Professor at the Helsinki School of Economics and Business Administration. He has acted as a consultant to business and government institutions both in Norway and abroad, and over the years he has been involved in a number of research projects including a variety of marketing problems, corporate strategy, industry studies and multiple evaluation studies. His publications include numerous articles in leading American and European journals and contributions to many international conference proceedings. He is the author or co-author of fifteen books, most recently *Research Methods in Business Studies* (1995).

EVERT GUMMESSON is Professor of Service Management and Marketing at Stockholm University, Sweden. He is also on the faculty of the Swedish School of Economics and Business Administration, Helsinki, and the University of Tampere, Finland. He graduated from the Stockholm School of Economics and received his doctorate in business administration at Stockholm University. He has spent most of his career in business, including as product and marketing manager for the Swedish subsidiary of Reader's Digest and as management consultant in the PA Consulting Group. He was instrumental in launching the Service Research Centre (CTF), the first research centre in the world to focus on service management. He is a co-founder of the Quality in Services (QUIS) international conferences, the first two of which he co-chaired. In 1994, he initiated and chaired the first International Research Workshop on Service Productivity, together with EIASM, in Brussels. In 1977, he wrote the first book on services marketing in Scandinavia and he has been featured in the USA as one of the international pioneers of services marketing. His book *Relationship Marketing: From 4Ps to 30Rs* was published in Swedish in 1995 and is to be published in English in 1996.

JIM HAMILL is Reader in International Business and Academic Director of the Msc in International Marketing (Open Learning) at the Strathclyde International Business Unit, University of Strathclyde, Glasgow, Scotland. He has researched and published widely in international business and marketing. He has held visiting professorships in the USA, France and Italy, and he also has extensive experience of teaching in Singapore, Hong Kong and China. He has undertaken consultancy on behalf of the Economist Intelligence Unit, the International Labour Office and the United Nations Conference on Trade and Development. His main research interests include international market entry and development techniques, doing business in Asia, international joint ventures and strategic alliances, and crossborder mergers and acquisitions. He is author or co-author of six books and his work has appeared in *European Management Journal*, *Journal of General Management*, *Employee Relations*, *Industrial Relations Journal*, *Textile Outlook International*, *Journal of East West Business* and others.

SUSAN J. HART is Professor of Marketing in the Department of Business Organization at Heriot-Watt University, Edinburgh, Scotland, teaching marketing strategy and new product development. After working in industry in France and the UK, she joined the University of Strathclyde as a researcher. She completed her doctoral degree on the subject of product management and worked on research projects examining the contribution of marketing to competitive success and new product design and development in manufacturing industry funded by the ESRC, the Chartered Institute of Marketing and the Design Council. She works with several industrial companies in teaching company schemes and has held visiting professorships in Denmark, Spain, the Netherlands and the USA. Her current research interests are in the development of new products and innovation, the contribution of marketing to company success and marketing theory.

ROGER HAYWOOD is Chairman of Kestrel Communications Ltd, London. He has been marketing and public relations adviser to leading international companies in industries ranging from high technology to financial services and consumer products. He is a lecturer, author and broadcaster on marketing and communications and has lectured across the UK, Europe and the USA. In 1991 he was President of the Institute of Public Relations, and in 1992 he was Chairman of the Chartered Institute of Marketing; he is the first person to have held both industries' positions. He was a founding partner of the Worldcom Group Inc. in 1988, setting up the European operation and, as the first chairman, recruited partners from across the region. He was later elected chairman of the world group and doubled the size of the group in his two-year term of office. He wrote the accepted management and training guide to business communications, *All About Public Relations*, which is widely used in universities and colleges, and *Managing Your Reputation*, which is targeted at chief executives and quotes the experience of many business leaders.

ROGER M. HEELER is Professor of Marketing in the Faculty of Administrative Studies, York University, North York, Ontario, Canada. He holds a BSc in economics from the London School of Economics, and MBA and PhD degrees from Stanford University. He teaches and publishes in marketing research, research methods and international business. He has been a visiting professor at universities in Barbados, China, France, Hong Kong, Japan, New Zealand and the UK. Prior to his academic career, he worked in the automobile, airline, business consulting and steel industries.

GRAHAM J. HOOLEY is Professor of Marketing at the Aston Business School, Aston University, Birmingham, England. His prior experience includes business practice in advertising and publishing and academic appointments at the Warwick Business School, the Bradford Management Centre, the University of Maryland (European Campuses) and the University of Otago, where he was Director of the Advanced Management Programme. He has taught marketing in Europe, Australasia and South-East Asia for academic institutions, professional associations and private organizations. His research interests encompass issues in competitive positioning and strategy, the use of quantitative methods in marketing and, more recently, the development of marketing approaches in the countries of Central and Eastern Europe. He is the author of three books, five monographs and over 100 articles on marketing topics.

D. G. BRIAN JONES is Associate Professor at the School of Business, University of Prince Edward Island, Charlottetown, Canada, where he has lectured since 1988. He has been Visiting Associate Professor at the Eli Broad Graduate School of Management, Michigan State University. After completing his BComm at the University of Manitoba, he worked for IBM and General Motors. His PhD was completed in 1987 at Queen's University, Kingston, Ontario; his dissertation dealt with the history of marketing thought, which continues to be his primary subject of interest. His research has been published in the *Journal of Marketing*, the *Journal of the Academy of Marketing Science* and the *Canadian Journal of Administrative Sciences*, and has also been translated for publication in German and Japanese business journals.

MANFRED KIRCHGEORG has been Associate Professor at the Institut für Marketing at the Westfälische Wilhelms-Universität, Munster, Germany, since 1989. He joined the Institut für Marketing as a research assistant in 1985, and in 1989 he completed his doctoral thesis entitled *The Influence of Ecology on the Behaviour of Companies*; this brought him the 1990 Westfälische Wilhelms-Universität Prize for Doctoral Theses and the McKinsey Research Prize. As well as teaching at the Westfälische Wilhelms-Universität, he lectures at the Administration Academy in Münster and at the European Environment Academy in Borken. He is involved in national and international research in the field of environmental management; his main areas of interest are marketing management, environmental management, marketing research and services marketing. He is the author of numerous articles, papers and books.

PHILIP KOTLER is S. C. Johnson & Son Distinguished Professor of International Marketing at the Kellogg Graduate School of Management, Northwestern University, Evanston, Illinois. He received his master's degree at the University of Chicago and his PhD at the Massachusetts Institute of Technology, both in economics; he did postdoctoral work in mathematics at Harvard and in behavioural science at the University of Chicago. He has acted as a consultant to many major companies including AT&T, Bank of America, Ford, General Electric, IBM, Merck, Marriott and Montedison. He is the recipient of several major awards, including the Paul D. Converse Award in 1978, the Steuart Henderson Britt Award in 1983, the first Irwin Distinguished Marketing Educator Award of the American Marketing Association and the European Association of Marketing Consultants and Sales Trainers Prize for Marketing Excellence in 1985, and the Charles Coolidge Parlin Award in 1989; in 1985, the Academy of Health Services Marketing established the Philip Kotler Award for Excellence in Health Care Marketing with him as its first recipient. He has received honorary doctorates from DePaul University and the University of Zurich and Athens University. He has published many books, including *Strategic Marketing for Nonprofit Organizations*, *Principles of Marketing* and *Marketing Management*, as well as over 100 articles for leading journals; he is the only three-time winner of the Alpha Kappa Psi Award for the best annual article published in the *Journal of Marketing*.

R. W. LAWSON has worked at the University of Otago, Dunedin, New Zealand, since 1987, and was appointed Professor in 1995. He gained his BA from the University of Manchester and then worked for the UK civil service for a number of years before studying marketing at the University of Newcastle. After working at Newcastle as a teaching and research assistant for a short time, he moved to a lecturing position at the University of Sheffield. He completed his doctorate at Sheffield and specialized in the area of consumer behaviour. Much of his recent work has focused on dimensions of tourist behaviour but he has also been involved in major studies on consumer lifestyles in New Zealand and he has recently completed the manuscript for the first New Zealand text on consumer behaviour.

KAM-HON LEE is Professor of Marketing and Dean of Business Administration at the Chinese University of Hong Kong, Shatin, Hong Kong. He obtained his BComm and MComm at the Chinese University of Hong Kong, and his PhD in marketing at Northwestern University, Evanston, Illinois. He has taught in executive programmes or acted as a consultant to a variety of institutions, including the World Bank, Hang Seng Bank, Crocodile Garments, Ryoden, Coca-Cola (China), Procter & Gamble (Guangzhou), Digital Equipment Corporation, DuPont Asia Pacific Ltd, Dentsu Advertising Agency and Chinese Arts & Crafts (Hong Kong). He has published in *Journal of Marketing*, *Journal of Management*, *Journal of Business Ethics*, *World Economy*, *Interational Marketing Review*, *International Journal of Bank Marketing*, *European Journal of Marketing*, *Marketing Education Review* and other refereed journals. His research areas include cross-cultural marketing, strategic marketing and social marketing.

MALCOLM H. B. MCDONALD is Professor of Marketing Planning, Chairman of the Cranfield Marketing Planning Centre, and Director of the Institute for Advanced Research in Marketing at the Cranfield School of Management, Cranfield University, Bedford, England. He graduated in English language and literature from the University of Oxford and in business studies from the Bradford University Management Centre, and gained his PhD from Cranfield University. His extensive industrial experience includes a number of years as Marketing Director of Canada Dry. During the past fifteen years he has run seminars and workshops on marketing planning in the UK, Europe, India, the Far East and the USA. He has written 28 books, including the bestseller *Marketing Plans: How to Prepare Them; How to Use Them*, and many of his papers have been published; also, he is editor of the *Journal of International Marketing* and the *Journal of Marketing Practice*. His current interests centre around the development of computer-based training programmes in marketing and the development of expert systems in marketing.

PETER J. MCGOLDRICK is Littlewoods Professor of Retailing at the Manchester School of Management and the Manchester Business School. Previously a Senior Lecturer at the University of Manchester Institute of Science and Technology, he has taught and researched within both Schools. He is co-director of the International Centre for Retail Studies. He has worked closely with many organizations in the retailing and financial services sectors as a teacher, researcher and consultant, including Littlewoods, Makro, TSB, Argos, House of Fraser, BHS and Tesco. He has published around 150 books and papers on a wide range of topics within the fields of retail marketing and consumer behaviour, and he is editor of the Prentice Hall series in retailing. His books include *Retail Marketing* (1990), *Regional Shopping Centres* (1992), *Cases in Retail Management* (1994), *Retailing of Financial Services* (1994) and *International Retailing: Trends and Strategies* (1995).

LARS-GUNNAR MATTSSON is Professor of Business Administration at the Stockholm School of Economics, Sweden, where he heads the research and teaching programme for marketing, distribution and industry dynamics. He has also served on the faculties of the universities of Linköping, Uppsala, California at Berkeley, and the European Institute for Advanced Studies in Management in Brussels. He is a board member of the Marketing Technology Center (MTC), a founding member and board member of the European Marketing Academy and a Fellow of the Royal Swedish Academy for Engineering Sciences (IVA). His research is focused on distribution, industrial marketing and internationalization of business in a 'markets-as-networks' perspective.

HERIBERT MEFFERT has been Chairman of the Institut für Marketing at the Westfälische Wilhelms-Universität, Münster, Germany, since he founded it in 1969; this was the first institute for marketing at a German university. In 1979 he founded the Science Association of Management and Marketing to encourage contact between academic research and practical management experience. He has been a Visiting Professor in several European countries, the USA and Japan, and carried out numerous research and consulting projects. He has received many academic awards for his research in marketing management and environmental management, and in 1993 he was appointed an Honorary Professor of the University of St Gallen. Since 1995 he has been Chairman of the Verband der Deutschen Hochschullehrer für Betriebswirtschaftslehre eV. He is the author of numerous books, articles and papers, and serves on the editorial boards of several German academic journals. His areas of interest are marketing management, international marketing, consumer and services marketing, strategic management and environmental management.

KRISTIAN MÖLLER is Professor of Marketing and head of the marketing group at the Helsinki School of Economics and Business Administration, Finland. He has been a visiting research scholar at the European Institute of Advanced Studies in Management (EIASM) in Brussels and at the Pennsylvania State University, and has received three annual research grants from the Academy of Finland and a Fulbright research scholarship. During 1991–2 he served as President of the European Marketing Academy (EMAC), the leading organization for European marketing academics. He is a Research Fellow at the Institute for the Study of Business Markets (ISBM/Penn State University). He has written or edited several books, articles and papers. His research is focused on business/relationship marketing, marketing capability and business strategy, and marketing theory.

JOHN S. OAKLAND is head of the European Centre for Total Quality Management and holds the Exxon Chemical Chair in TQM at the Management Centre, University of Bradford, England. Since 1980 he has taught all aspects of quality management to thousands of organizations. He has directed several large research projects on quality in Europe, and his work on the quality management requirements of industry and commerce has been widely acknowledged and published. Following a successful industrial career, he has been called the British guru of quality management alongside Crosby, Deming and Juran in the USA and Ishikawa in Japan. His work with very large to very small companies is widely known and several international companies have publicized how they have benefited from his approach. He is the Managing Director of O&F Quality Management Consultants Ltd, which through three executive directors and some fifteen senior consultants operates across Europe, the USA and the Middle East. He is the author of several books, including *Total Quality Management*, *Statistical Process Control* and *Production and Operations Management*, and is co-author (with Les Porter) of *Cases in TQM*.

JOHN O'SHAUGHNESSY is Professor Emeritus of Business, Graduate School of Business, Columbia University, New York, and Senior Associate of the Judge Institute of Management, University of Cambridge. His early industrial background was in OR and industrial engineering but he has also been a marketing research manager, marketing manager and industrial consultant. Before going to Columbia in 1967, he was a senior lecturer at Cranfield. He has been a consultant on organization, management and marketing to a large number of firms in the USA, the UK and elsewhere. He has interests in international business, and still holds appointments at business schools in Portugal and Mexico. He is the author of ten books, including *Why People Buy* and *Explaining Buyer Behaviour*, and numerous journal articles.

STEPHEN PARKINSON is Director of the University of Ulster, Business School, Belfast. He is also Professor of Strategic Management at the University of Ulster. He was formerly Professor of Marketing at the University of Bradford Management Centre, England, and Head of the Marketing Group. He has also held positions at the University of Strathclyde and at Henley Management College. He is a consultant to several major international organizations, most recently in the area of trade marketing, distribution management and merchandising of FMCG products. He has recently been involved in attracting the Heinz Chair in Brand Management to the University of Bradford Management Centre. He is the author of *Offshore Inspection and Maintenance – The Implications of North Sea Experience* (with M. J. Baker and M. A. Saren), *Offshore Technology: A Forecast and Review* (with M. A. Saren), *New Product Development in the Engineering Industry: A Comparison Between the British and West German Machine Tool Industries, Organisational Buying Behaviour* (with M. J. Baker) and *Using the Microcomputer in Marketing* (with L. K. Parkinson). He has published many other contributions to texts in the areas of information technology in marketing, organizational buying behaviour, industrial marketing and new product development, and is also the author of a further eighty articles in professional and academic journals. He has presented papers at a wide range of international conferences. His specialist areas of interest include strategic marketing planning, industrial marketing, brand management and health care marketing.

KEN PEATTIE is a Senior Lecturer in Strategic Management within the Marketing and Strategy Group at the Cardiff Business School, University of Wales, which he joined in 1986. Before becoming a lecturer he worked as a systems and business analyst for an American paper multinational and as a strategic planner within the UK electronics industry. He is the author of *Green Marketing* (1992) and *Environmental Marketing Management: Meeting the Green Challenge* (1995), and has published widely on different aspects of marketing, strategy and management education. His main research interests focus on innovations in sales promotion and on the impact of environmental concern on marketing and corporate strategy.

NIGEL F. PIERCY is Professor of Marketing and Strategy at the Cardiff Business School, University of Wales College of Cardiff, Wales. He was recently Visiting

Professor at the M. J. Neeley School of Business, Texas Christian University. He was UK Marketing Author of the Year in 1980, 1981 and 1982. He has written some 200 articles and papers on marketing and strategic management, which have been published in journals including the *Journal of Marketing*, *Journal of Business Research*, *Journal of the Academy of Marketing Science* and *Journal of Advertising*; he is the author of eight books, including *Marketing Organization* (1985), *Marketing Budgeting* (1986) and *Market-Led Strategic Change* (1992). His research interests are in implementation and control processes, and recent projects include studies of marketing organization and information systems, marketing budgeting, marketing planning and customer satisfaction measurement.

GILLIAN RICE is Associate Professor at Thunderbird, the American Graduate School of International Management, Glendale, Arizona. Previously, she taught at the University of Michigan-Flint, West Virginia University, Concordia University (Montreal) and the State University of New York at Buffalo. She gained her PhD from the University of Bradford in 1982. She is a member of the American Marketing Association and serves as Vice President for Membership of the International Management Development Association. In 1994 she received a Visiting Professor Award from the Advertising Educational Foundation. She has published articles in journals including *International Marketing Review*, *Journal of the Academy of Marketing Science* and *International Journal of Forecasting*.

BERT ROSENBLOOM is G. Behrens Ulrich Professor of Marketing at Drexel University, Philadelphia, Pennsylvania, where he is also Associate Dean for Graduate Programs in the College of Business and Administration. Prior to coming to Drexel, he served on the faculty of the City University of New York. As an active consultant, he has worked for a broad range of industries in manufacturing, wholesaling, retailing, communications, services and real estate in the USA and abroad. He has served as vice president of the Philadelphia chapter of the American Marketing Association, on the Board of Governors of the Academy of Marketing Science, and from 1992 to 1994 as President of the International Management Development Association. He is a leading expert on the management of marketing channels and distribution systems; he is the author of nine books, including *Marketing Channels: A Management View*, *Retail Marketing* and *Marketing Functions and the Wholesaler Distributor*. He is the editor of the *Journal of Marketing Channels* and has served on the editorial boards of several other journals. His research has been published in the major professional journals, and has frequently been presented at professional conferences in the USA, Europe, Australia and New Zealand.

PHILIP ROSSON has been Professor of Marketing at Dalhousie University, Halifax, Nova Scotia, Canada, since 1988. From 1987 to 1993 he was Director of the Centre for International Business Studies, and in 1994 he was appointed

Dean of the Faculty of Management. Prior to joining Dalhousie University in 1975, he was a lecturer in marketing at Heriot-Watt University, Edinburgh, Scotland. Before embarking on a university career, he worked in marketing positions in the coal, fish and office products industries in the UK and East Africa. He gained an MA in marketing from Lancaster University and a PhD in management from the University of Bath. He has written and edited books, chapters, articles and case studies in fields such as exporting, international marketing and technology management.

JOHN SAUNDERS is National Westminster Bank Professor of Marketing and Director of the Loughborough University Business School, England. He has worked previously for the Bradford University Management Centre, the University of Warwick, the Pacific-Asian Management Institute (Hawaii) and the Hawker Siddeley Group. He holds a degree in aeronautical engineering from Loughborough University, an MBA from the Cranfield Institute of Technology and a doctorate from Bradford University. He has worked as a senior consultant with many prominent companies and institutions. His publications include several books, business games and many articles. He is editor of the *International Journal of Research in Marketing* and assistant editor of the *British Journal of Management*. He has been awarded a Fellowship of the British Academy of Management, the Chartered Institute of Marketing and the Royal Society of Arts in recognition of his scholarship.

MARK SHERRINGTON began his career in marketing in the UK with Lever Brothers. He became brand manager of their largest brand, Persil, before going on to become Marketing Director of Lever in Spain. He also ran their export detergent business, covering the Middle East and part of the Far East and South America. His final position in Unilever was as marketing coordinator for a number of product categories across Europe. In 1988, together with Peter Dart, he set up The Added Value Company, a marketing agency specializing in strategic marketing, brand development and consumer research. Their main focus is Europe but they have completed assignments for several clients in the USA, Far East and Australia. In addition to his client work, he is a regular contributor on training courses and has spoken at several major marketing seminars on strategic marketing, brands and innovation.

RAJENDRA S. SISODIA is Associate Professor of Marketing at George Mason University, Fairfax, Virginia. Before joining GMU, he was Assistant Professor of Marketing at Boston University. He has a bachelor's degree in electrical and electronics engineering from the Birla Institute of Technology and Science, Pilani, India, and an MBA in marketing and international business from the Bajaj Institute of Management Studies, Bombay. He has an MPhil and PhD in marketing and business policy from Columbia University. He has published numerous articles in conference proceedings and journals such as *Harvard Business Review*, *Journal of Business Strategy*, *Marketing Letters*, *Marketing*

Management, Marketing Research, Journal of Services Marketing, Encyclopedia of Marketing Information & Management, Telecommunications Policy, International Journal of Technology Management and *Design Management Journal*. He is on the editorial board of several journals, and is associate editor of the *Journal of Asia Pacific Business*. He is co-author (with John T. Mentzer) of *Marketing Decision Systems: Transformation Through Information Technology* (1996). His research, teaching and consulting expertise spans the areas of marketing productivity, strategic and marketing issues in the telecommunications and information industries, strategic uses of information technology in business, and the marketing of services.

N. CRAIG SMITH is Associate Professor at Georgetown University School of Business, Washington, DC, USA. He joined Georgetown in 1991, prior to which he was on the faculties of the Graduate School of Business Administration, Harvard University, USA, and the Cranfield School of Management, Cranfield University, UK. He is the author/co-author of *Morality and the Market* (1990), *The Management Research Handbook* (1991) and *Ethics in Marketing* (1993), as well as a variety of journal articles on marketing management and business policy issues. His consultancy activities encompass marketing strategy and planning and marketing ethics.

LOUIS W. STERN is John D. Gray Distinguished Professor of Marketing at the J. L. Kellogg Graduate School of Management, Northwestern University, Evanston, Illinois. Prior to joining the Northwestern faculty in 1973, he taught at the Ohio State University from 1963 to 1973 and was a Visiting Professor at the University of California, Berkeley, for the 1969–70 academic year. He served as Chairman of the Department of Marketing at Northwestern from 1977 to 1980, and as executive director of the Marketing Science Institute, Cambridge, Massachusetts, from 1983 to 1985. For the 1984–5 academic year he was the Ford Foundation Visiting Professor at the Harvard Business School. Among the awards he has received are the American Marketing Association's Paul D. Converse Award, the American Marketing Association/Richard D. Irwin Distinguished Marketing Educator of the Year Award, the *Journal of Marketing*'s Harold H. Maynard Award, the Sales and Marketing Executives–International Marketing Educator of the Year Award and the Outstanding Kellogg Professor of the Year Award.

WALTER VAN WATERSCHOOT is Professor of Marketing at the University Faculties Saint-Ignatius (UFSIA), the Catholic of the three constituent parts of the University of Antwerp, Belgium. He was appointed to this position in 1987, having been a lecturer since 1981. He attended courses in business administration at UFSIA and at CEDEP/INSEAD, Fontainebleau, France. As a doctoral student he was first enrolled at the Catholic University of Leuven and later at UFSIA, where in 1979 he defended his doctoral dissertation on consumer behaviour. He teaches principally third and fourth year undergraduate students, as well as students of the UFSIA MBA programme of which he has been the Academic Coordinator since 1990. He is the author of numerous articles and papers, predominantly on conceptual issues, and he is co-author (with Robert Bilsen) of a major Flemish marketing textbook which is now in its sixth edition.

ROBIN WENSLEY is Professor and Chairman of the Warwick Business School, University of Warwick, Coventry, England. He has previously been with RHM Foods, TI and the London Business School; he has been a visiting professor at UCLA and the University of Florida. He acts as a consultant for many major companies, and works closely with other academics and practitioners in both Europe and North America.

CHRISTOPHER WEST is Managing Director of Marketing Intelligence Services Ltd, a London-based marketing research consultancy. After graduating from the London School of Economics in 1964, he joined Shell International where he worked in the Economics and Supply and Planning departments. In 1967 he joined Eurofinance, a financial and economics consultancy located in Paris, where he produced studies of European industries for clients in banks, brokers and international organizations. He returned to the UK in 1970 to join Industrial Market Research Ltd (IMR), and commenced his career in marketing research by specializing in the assessment of business markets. He was appointed Managing Director of IMR in 1978, after the company had been acquired by AGB Research, and left in 1984 to form his own research consultancy. During his research career he has carried out assignments for a wide range of clients in Europe and North America, covering most important business sectors. Throughout the last 25 years he has written and lectured extensively on research and marketing subjects; his published works include two books, *Marketing on a Small Budget* (1975) and *Inflation – A Management Guide to Survival* (1978), and several articles in the *Harvard Business Review*, *Business Strategy Review* and the *Financial Times*.

AUBREY WILSON is a leading figure in both the commercial and academic marketing fields. He devised many of the business-to-business marketing techniques in use today, including *The Marketing Audit* for which he won the Association of European Marketing Consultants Prize. He has published eleven books on marketing topics and continues to develop new approaches for improving marketing techniques and productivity. He is a successful independent consultant and is active in education and training initiatives worldwide.

DAVID T. WILSON is Alvin H. Clemens Professor of Entrepreneurial Studies at the Smeal College of Business Administration, Pennsylvania State University, University Park, Pennsylvania, USA.

RICHARD M. S. WILSON is Professor of Business Administration at Loughborough University Business School, England. He transferred to this new post from Keele University, where he was Professor of Management and the founding

Head of the Department of Management. Prior to this, he was Professor of Management Control at the Queen's University of Belfast and previously held the Pannell Kerr Forster Chair at Nottingham Business School. His earlier commercial experience was gained in a variety of industries covering consumer goods, industrial goods and services, including employment with two US-based multinational enterprises. Among his qualifications are the Diploma in Marketing of the Chartered Institute of Marketing (of which he is a Fellow) and the Diploma of the Market Research Society (of which he is a Full Member), as well as degrees in social research, commerce, management and sociology/technology. He has written or edited some twenty-five books including *Strategic Marketing Management*, *Management Controls in Marketing* and *Financial Dimensions of Marketing*. He has contributed chapters to a further eighteen books, and has written a wide range of papers, articles and monographs on managerial topics. He acts as a consulting editor and series editor for two major publishers.

YORAM (JERRY) WIND is the Lauder Professor and Professor of Marketing at the Wharton School of the University of Pennsylvania, Philadelphia. He joined the Wharton staff in 1967, having received his doctorate from Stanford University. He is the founding director of the SEI Center for Advanced Studies in Management, which was set up in 1988. From 1983 to 1988 he served as founding director of the Joseph H. Lauder Institute of Management and International Studies, and from 1980 to 1983 as founding director of the Wharton Center for International Management Studies. He chaired the Wharton committees that designed the Wharton Executive MBA Program (1974), the Wharton International Forum (1987) and the radically new MBA curriculum (1991). He has lectured in faculty seminars and executive programmes in over fifty universities worldwide, and he is an active consultant. He is the recipient of various awards, including the prestigious Charles Coolidge Parlin Award (1985), the first Faculty Impact Award by Wharton Alumni (1993) and the 1993 AMA/Irwin Distinguished Educator Award. He is a prolific author, having written over 200 articles and monographs and ten books, and he is one of the most cited authors in marketing.

ARCH G. WOODSIDE has been Malcolm S. Woldenburg Professor of Marketing at the A. B. Freeman School of Business, Tulane University, New Orleans, Louisiana, since 1985. From 1970 to 1985 he was Assistant Professor of Marketing, Associate Professor of Marketing and Professor of Marketing at the College of Business Administration, University of South Carolina, Columbia. He is a Fellow of the American Psychological Association, and American Psychological Society and the Southern Marketing Association. He is a past president of Division 23 (Consumer Psychology) of the American Psychological Association. He has completed several empirical studies on direct marketing that have been reported in the *Journal of Direct Marketing*, *Journal of Advertising Research* and the *Journal of Marketing*. He serves as the editor-in-chief of the

Journal of Business Research, and as editor of the series *Advances in Business Marketing and Purchasing* of which the sixth volume, *Handbook of Business Marketing Management*, was published in 1994.

I THE NATURE AND SCOPE OF MARKETING

1

MARKETING – PHILOSOPHY OR FUNCTION?

Michael J. Baker

INTRODUCTION

On first introduction to a subject it is understandable that one should seek a clear and concise definition of it. If nothing else this definition should enable one to distinguish the domain of that subject from all others while also giving an indication of its scope and nature. Of course, none of us expect that a short definition will be able to encompass the complexity of a subject which, in the case of this Encyclopedia, extends to over 1,000 printed pages. This said, it does seem reasonable that persons who profess or claim expertise on a subject should be able to define it.

In this introductory chapter it will become clear that there is no scarcity of definitions of marketing and we will review a number of them. In doing so it will also become clear that views as to the scope of the subject tend to polarize in the manner implied by the title of this chapter between those who perceive marketing as a philosophy of business, or state of mind, and those who regard it as a managerial function responsible for particular activities in much the same way as production, finance or human resource management.

To throw light on this dichotomy it will be helpful first to review what is seen to be the true essence of marketing – mutually satisfying exchange relationships – and its evolution over time in parallel with stages of economic growth and development. On the basis of this review it will be argued that marketing has always been an intrinsic element of the commercial exchange process but that its importance has waxed and waned with shifts in the balance between supply and demand. Without anticipating unduly Brian Jones' discussion of Historical Research in Marketing in Chapter 2 it will be suggested that we can detect at least three major phases in the evolution of the modern marketing concept – the emergence of the mass market *ca* 1850, the articulation of the modern marketing concept *ca* 1960, and the transition from an emphasis upon the transaction to the relationship *ca* 1990. To conclude this chapter we then review specific

3

definitions of marketing to document how these have changed over time and speculate as to the possible nature and direction of future change in order to answer our opening question, Marketing – Philosophy or Function?

EXCHANGE AND ECONOMIC GROWTH

Since time immemorial humans have had to live with scarcity in one form or another. In its most acute form scarcity threatens the very existence of life itself but, even in the most affluent and advanced post-industrial societies its existence is still apparent in the plight of the homeless and the poor. Indeed, in some senses it is doubtful whether mankind will ever overcome scarcity, if for no other reason than that there appears to be no upper limit to human wants.

The use of the noun 'wants' is deliberate for early in any study of marketing it is important to distinguish clearly between 'needs' and 'wants'. Needs have been classified as existing at five levels by Abraham Maslow (1943) and his 'hierarchy of human needs' (Figure 1) is a useful starting point for a discussion of the nature of marketing. As can be seen from Figure 1, Maslow's hierarchy conceives of human needs as resting on a foundation of physiological needs, essential for existence, and ascending through a series of levels – safety, love, and esteem – to a state of self-actualization in which the individual's specification of a need is entirely self-determined. According to this conceptualization one can only ascend to a higher level once one has satisfied the needs of a lower level and the inference may be drawn that scarcity will only cease to exist once every

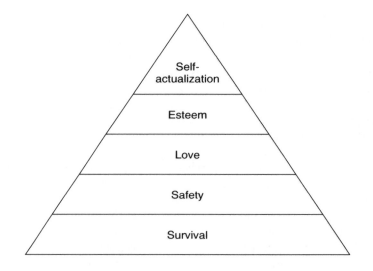

Figure 1   Maslow's hierarchy of human needs
Source: Maslow (1943: 370–96)

4

individual has attained the highest level of self-actualization.

From this description it is clear that 'needs' are broadly based and defined and act as a summary statement for a whole cluster of much more precisely defined wants which reflect the exact desires of individuals. In a state of hunger the Westerner may want bread or potatoes but the Easterner is more likely to want rice. Both of these wants are fairly basic. While they have the ability to satisfy the need 'hunger', they offer little by way of variety. The desire for variety, or choice, is another intrinsic element of human nature and much of human development and progress may be attributed to a quest for variety – of new ways of satisfying basic needs. Indeed, the process appears to be self-sustaining which prompted us to propose that a maxim of marketing is that 'the act of consumption changes the consumer' (Baker 1980). In other words, each new experience increases and extends the consumer's expectations and creates an opportunity for a new supplier to win their patronage by developing something new and better than existing solutions to the consumer's need.

Faced with an apparent infinity of wants the challenge to be faced is in determining what selection of goods and services will give the greatest satisfaction to the greatest number at any particular point in time. Indeed, the purpose of economic organization has been defined as 'maximising satisfaction through the utilisation of scarce resources'. Marketing is the function which facilitates achievement of this goal. To understand how it does this it will be helpful to review the process of economic development. Rostow's (1962) Stages of Economic Growth model provides an excellent basis for such a review.

Rostow's model is shown in Figure 2 and proposes that human societies progress from the lowest level of subsistence or survival through a series of clearly identified stages until they achieve the sophistication and affluence of the modern post-industrial state. In grossly simplified terms certain key events appear to be associated with the transition from one stage to the next.

At the lowest level of all is the subsistence economy based upon hunting, gathering and collection. Such economies are nomadic and entirely dependent upon nature for their survival. While members of such nomadic tribes may share food and shelter, and band together for safety, they are societies which are devoid of any recognizable form of commercial exchange.

With the domestication of animals and the development of primitive agriculture man begins to exercise a degree of control over his environment. At the same time new activities create new roles and the potential for the first step towards increased productivity and economic progress – task specialization. Once it becomes recognized that some people are better suited to some tasks than others then the potential for task specialization exists. For it to be realized, however, an agreed system of exchange must be developed. Indeed, it seems likely that the creation of a system of exchange was a necessary prerequisite for task specialization to flourish.

A fundamental law of economics is that beyond a certain point each additional unit of any good or service becomes worth progressively less and less to its owner

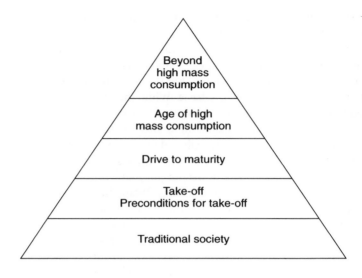

Figure 2   Rostow's Stages of Economic Growth model
Source: Rostow (1962)

(the law of diminishing marginal utility). Given a surplus of any specific good its owner will be able to increase his overall satisfaction by exchanging units of his surplus for another good which he wants. Thus hunters can exchange meat for vegetables with farmers to their mutual and enhanced satisfaction.

For an exchange to occur there must be at least two persons, each with a surplus of one good which is desired by the other. Once contact has been established between the two persons they can then negotiate an exchange which will increase their overall satisfaction by swapping units until the marginal utility of the two goods is equal (i.e. one would receive less satisfaction by acquiring one additional unit of the other person's surplus than by retaining a unit of one's own output). While this concept is easy to understand in principle, especially when discussing only one exchange, its implementation in practice poses numerous problems. To reduce these problems three additional developments are called for.

First, in order that those with surpluses to exchange can be brought together it will be helpful to set aside a specific place for the purpose – a market. Second, one needs an accepted store of value that will act as a universal medium of exchange – money. Third, because marketing is a separate task from production it will further increase productivity and add value if specialist intermediaries – merchants and retailers – come into existence to perform these functions. Clearly, markets, money and intermediaries have existed since the earliest civilization. Indeed, it would be no exaggeration to claim that the development of formal commercial exchange relationships was the foundation for civilization

6

as we know it today. It would seem that marketing is perhaps not such a recent phenomenon as many believe it to be!

The creation of markets and the development of exchange provide the preconditions for take-off. For take-off itself to occur task specialization has to be taken a stage further to what economists call the division of labour. One of the earliest and best known examples of the division of labour is provided by Adam Smith's description of the pin-making industry.

> To take an example, therefore, from a very trifling manufacture; but one in which the division of labour has been very often taken notice of, the trade of the pin maker; a workman not educated to this business (which the division of labour has rendered a distinct trade), nor acquainted with the use of the machinery employed in it (to the invention of which the same division of labour has probably given occasion), could scarce, perhaps, with his utmost industry, make one pin in a day, and certainly could not make 20. But in the way in which this business is now carried on, not only the whole work is a peculiar trade, but it is divided into a number of branches, of which the greatest part are likewise peculiar trades. One man draws out the wire, another straights it, a third cuts it, a fourth points it, a fifth grinds it at the top receiving the head; to make the head requires 3 distinct operations; to put it on is a peculiar business, to whiten the pins is another; it is even a trade by itself to put them into the paper; and the important business of making a pin is, in this manner, divided into about 18 distinct operations, which, in some manufactures, are all per- formed by distinct hands, though in others the same man will sometimes perform 2 or 3 of them. I have seen a small manufactury of this kind where 10 men only were employed and where some of them consequently performed 2 or 3 distinct operations. But though they were very poor, and therefore but indifferently accommodated with the necessary machinery, they could, when they exerted themselves, make among them about 12 pounds of pins in a day. There are in a pound upwards of 4000 pins of the middling size. These 10 persons, therefore, could make among them upwards of 48,000 pins in a day. Each person, therefore, making a tenth part of 48,000 pins, might be considered as making 4800 pins in a day. But if they had all wrought separately and independently, and without any of them having been educated to this peculiar business, they could certainly not each of them have made 20, perhaps not 1 pin in a day; that is, certainly, not the 240th, perhaps not the 4800th part of what they are at present capable of performing, in consequence of a proper division and combination of their different operations.
>
> (Smith 1970 [1776])

It seems reasonable to assume that under conditions of craft industry, where each craftsman was responsible for all the tasks associated with the production of a particular good, the number of craftsmen in a community would be approximately sufficient to satisfy the demands of that community. Indeed, the medieval craft guilds (and, more recently, trade unions) strictly controlled the number of apprentices that could be trained in the craft to ensure that a satisfactory balance between supply and demand be maintained. Clearly, the enormous increase in productivity associated with the division of labour destroyed this control and flooded the market with the product in question driving the price down and making many craftsmen redundant. One new pin factory employing 10 pin makers could match the output of 240 craftsmen and so service the needs of 240 times as many customers. As a result production became concentrated in locations possessing natural advantages associated with the product – sources of power and raw material, labour, good channels of communication – and it became necessary to employ sales persons to help sell the output into a greatly enlarged market.

Because of the enormous increase in output associated with factory production, standards of living improved substantially with a consequential increase in life expectancies and the numbers of children surviving infancy. As the size of a market is determined ultimately by the size of the population, an expanding population represented an expanding market and further fuelled the rapid economic growth associated with take-off. This growth was to receive even greater impetus with the spate of scientific and technological innovation of the eighteenth century, which gave birth to what has become known as the Industrial Revolution and formed the foundation for Rostow's fourth stage of economic growth – the age of high mass consumption.

In his original conceptualization Rostow (1962) perceived that some of the more advanced and affluent industrialized economies were approaching the limits of mass consumption. While population growth had slowed to a near steady state further improvements in productivity had created saturated markets and the potential for excess supply. John Kenneth Galbraith (1958) designated this the post-industrial society while Rostow merely termed it the Age Beyond High Mass Consumption. Eight years later, in 1970, Rostow revised his model and designated the final stage The Search for Quality – the inference being that if a static population could not physically consume more then the only way growth could be sustained would be to consume 'better'.

Elsewhere (Baker 1994) we have discussed the way in which the stages in Maslow's need hierarchy correspond closely to the stages in Rostow's economic stages model, e.g. subsistence economies are concerned primarily with physiological needs; the search for quality with self-actualization, etc. Clearly, human needs (demand) motivate supply creation and the matching of supply and demand is achieved through a process of exchange and marketing. It is also clear that these processes have existed for a very long time indeed, so why is marketing often represented as a twentieth-century phenomenon? We turn to this question in the next section but, before doing so, will summarize some of the key points that have emerged from our greatly simplified account of economic development.

First, exchange adds value and increases satisfaction. It also encourages variety and improves choice. Second, the parties to a commercial exchange are free agents so that for an exchange to occur both parties must feel that they are benefiting from that exchange. It is from these observations that we derive our basic definition of marketing as being concerned with mutually satisfying exchange relationships. Third, task specialization and the division of labour greatly increases productivity and increases the volume of goods available for consumption. In turn this increased supply results in an improved standard of

8

living and an increase in the population thereby increasing demand and stimulating further efforts to increase supply. Fourth, the concentration of production and the growing size and dispersion of the market increases the need for specialized channels of distribution and of intermediaries to service and manage them. Fifth, improved standards of living lead to a stabilization of population growth and absolute market size (demand) but accelerating techno-logical innovation continues to enhance our ability to increase supply. It was this which was to lead to the 'rediscovery' of marketing.

THE REDISCOVERY OF MARKETING

As we have seen markets and marketing are as old as exchange itself yet many people regard marketing as a phenomenon which emerged in the second half of the twentieth century – to be precise about 1960 when Professor Ted Levitt published an article entitled 'Marketing Myopia' in the *Harvard Business Review* in which he addressed the fundamental question of why do firms, and indeed whole industries, grow to a position of great power and influence and then decline. Taking the American railroad industry as his main example Levitt showed that this industry displaced other forms of overland transportation during the nineteenth century because it was more efficient and effective than the alternatives it displaced. By the beginning of the twentieth century, however, development of the internal combustion engine and the building of cars and trucks had provided an alternative to the railroads for both personal and bulk transportation. In the early years this challenge was limited because of the high cost of the substitute product, their lack of sophistication and reliability and their low availability. However, their potential was clear to see – if you owned a car or truck you had complete personal control over your transportation need and could travel from door to door at your own convenience. Henry Ford perceived this market opportunity, invented the concept of mass assembly and began to produce a reliable, low-cost motor car in constantly increasing numbers. From this time on the fortunes of the railroad began to decline so that by the 1950s this once great industry appeared to be in terminal decline.

What went wrong? Levitt's thesis is that those responsible for the management of the railroad were too preoccupied with their product to the neglect of the need that it served which was transportation. Because of their myopia or 'production orientation' they lost sight of the fact that the railroad product had been a substitute for earlier, less attractive products so that, offered a choice, consumers had switched from the old to the new to increase their personal satisfaction. It should have been obvious, therefore, that if a new, more convenient mode of transportation was developed then consumers would switch to it too. Thus, if the railroad management had concentrated on the need served – transportation – rather than their product they might have been able to join the infant automobile industry and develop a truly integrated transportation system. In other words the railroads failed because they lacked a marketing orientation.

9

At almost the same time as the appearance of Levitt's seminal paper, Robert Keith (1960) published an article in which he described the evolution of marketing in the Pillsbury Company for which he worked. In Keith's view the company's current marketing approach was the direct descendant of two earlier approaches or eras, which he termed production and sales. This three eras or stages model – production, sales, marketing – was widely adopted by what has come to be known as the marketing management school whose ideas have dominated the theory and practice of marketing for the past thirty years or more.

The essence of the production orientation – a preoccupation with the product and the company – and the marketing orientation – a focus on the consumer's need and the best way to serve it – have already been touched on in reviewing Levitt's 'Marketing Myopia'. Keith's contribution then was to propose an intermediate or transitional phase he termed the sales era. In the sales era firms were still largely production orientated but as demand stabilized supply continued to grow, resulting in fierce competition between suppliers. One aspect of this was that producers committed more effort to selling their products with an emphasis on personal selling, advertising and sales promotion – hence the 'sales orientation'.

Chronologically the production era was dated from the mid-1850s and lasted until around the late 1920s, which saw the birth of the sales era that lasted to around the mid-1950s when the marketing era commenced. This conceptualization is now seen to be seriously flawed in terms of its historical accuracy but nonetheless remains a useful pedagogical device for reasons we will return to momentarily. First, however, it will be helpful to set the record straight.

As we have noted on several occasions there has been a tendency to date the emergence of marketing to the late 1950s and early 1960s. In an article entitled 'How Modern is Modern Marketing?' Fullerton (1988) provides a rigorous analysis based on historical research.

At the outset it will be helpful to summarize the three key facets of the historical approach. First, there is 'a philosophical belief that historical phenomena such as markets are intrinsically rich and complex; efforts to simplify or assume away aspects of such phenomena are deeply distrusted' (Fullerton 1988: 109). Second, the historical research tradition emphasizes 'systematic and critical evaluation of historical evidence for accuracy, bias, implicit messages, and now extinct meanings' (ibid.: 109). The third facet of historical research is the process itself through which the researcher seeks to synthesize and recreate what actually happened in the past.

While there is considerable evidence that supports the existence of a production era there are also strong arguments to support a contrary view. Fullerton summarizes these as follows:

1. It ignores well-established historical facts about business conditions – competition was intense in most businesses, over-production common, and demand frequently uncertain.

10

2. It totally misses the presence and vital importance of conscious demand stimulation in developing the advanced modern economies. Without such stimulation the revolution in production would have been stillborn.
3. It does not account for the varied and vigorous marketing efforts made by numerous manufacturers and other producers.
4. It ignores that dynamic growth of new marketing institutions outside the manufacturing firm.

(Fullerton 1988: 111)

Each of these arguments is examined in detail and substantial evidence is marshalled to support them. A particularly telling point concerns the need for active demand stimulation and the need for production and marketing to work in tandem.

Some of the famous pioneers of production such as Mathew Boulton and Josiah Wedgwood were also pioneers of modern marketing, cultivating large-scale demand for their revolutionary inexpensive products with techniques usually considered to have been post-1950 American innovations: market segmentation, product differentiation, prestige pricing, style obsolescence, saturation advertising, direct mail campaigns, reference group appeals, and testimonials among others.

(Fullerton 1988: 112)

In Fullerton's view 'demand-enhancing marketing' spread from Britain to Germany and the USA. In the USA it was adopted with enthusiasm and Americans came to be seen as 'the supreme masters of aggressive demand stimulation', a fact frequently referred to in contemporary marketing texts of the early 1990s. Numerous examples support Fullerton's contention that producers of the so-called production era made extensive use of marketing tools and techniques as well as integrating forward to ensure their products were brought to the attention of their intended customers in the most effective way. That said, the examples provided (with one or two possible exceptions) do not, in my opinion, invalidate the classification of the period as the 'production era' in the sense that it was the producer who took the initiative and differentiated his product to meet the assumed needs of different consumer groups based on economic as opposed to sociological and psychological factors. In other words, producers inferred the consumers' behaviour but they had not yet developed techniques or procedures which would enable them to define latent wants and design, produce and market products and services to satisfy them.

Similarly, while the period from 1870 to 1930 saw the emergence and development of important marketing institutions in terms of physical distribution, retailing, advertising and marketing education, which are still important today, it does not seem unreasonable to argue that all these institutions were designed to sell more of what was being produced. This is not to deny the 'rich marketing heritage' documented by Fullerton but to reinforce the point that the transition to a 'marketing era' was marked by a major change in business philosophy from a producer-led interpretation of consumer needs to a consumer-driven approach to production.

As to the existence of a sales era (rejected by Fullerton) this seems as

11

convenient a label as any to give to the transitional period between a production and marketing orientation. In addition to the reality of a depressed world economy in the 1930s, which required large-scale producers to sell more aggressively to maintain economies of scale, the period saw the migration of many behavioural scientists from a politically unstable Europe to the safety of the USA. In retrospect it appears that it was this migration that led to the more rigorous analysis of consumer behaviour which was to underpin the emergence of a new 'marketing era'.

Combined with this greater insight into consumer behaviour were a period of great economic growth and prosperity following the Second World War, together with a major increase in the birth rate, which was to result in a new generation of consumers brought up in a period of material affluence (the baby boomers). It was this generation which sought to reassert consumer sovereignty and so initiated the change in the balance of power between producer and consumer which heralded the 'marketing era'.

Fullerton's argument that the production–sales–marketing era framework is a 'catastrophic model' 'in which major developments take place suddenly, with few antecedents' (1988: 121) is not without merit. Certainly, it could and has had the effect of disguising the evolutionary nature of marketing thought and practice. In place of a catastrophic model, or, indeed, a continuity model which tends to observe differences over time, Fullerton suggests a 'complex flux model'. Such a complex flux model has the ability to incorporate dramatic changes but it also 'stresses that even dramatic change is based on and linked to past phenomena' (ibid.). It is also neutral in the sense that it does not automatically equate development or evolution with 'improvement', leaving such judgements for others to make.

Fullerton's complex flux model embraces four eras:

1 *Setting the stage: the era of antecedents* A long gestational period beginning around 1500 in Britain and Germany, and the 1600s in North America. A period of low levels of consumption in which '75–90% of the populace were self-sufficient, rural, and viscerally opposed to change' (1988: 122). Commerce was generally discredited but its standing improved as the benefits of trade became apparent.

2 *Modern marketing begins: the era of origins* Britain 1759; Germany and USA *ca* 1830. 'This period marked the beginning of *pervasive* attention to stimulating and meeting demand among *nearly all of society*' (1988: 122). Precipitated by the Industrial Revolution and the mass migration from the countryside to an urban environment potential markets had to be created through marketing techniques and activities.

3 *Building a superstructure: the era of institutional development* Britain 1850; Germany and USA *ca* 1870 – until 1919. 'During this period most of the major institutions and many of the practices of modern marketing first appeared' (1988: 122).

12

4 *Testing, turbulence, and growth: the era of refinement and formalization* From 1930 to the present day. 'The era's most distinguishing characteristic, however, has been the further development, refinement, and formalisation of institutions and practices that were developed earlier' (1988: 122).

Fullerton's analysis reflects a growing interest in the history of marketing thought and confirms that 'modern marketing has a rich heritage worthy of our attention' (1988: 123). Whether one should substitute his conceptualization as contained in his complex flux model for the widely accepted production–sales–marketing eras model is not seen as an either/or choice. Indeed, Fullerton's emphasis on the origins and evolution of marketing thought and practice reflects the historical research approach and merits attention in its own right. By contrast the 'eras model' is seen, at least by this author, as serving a different purpose in that it seeks to distinguish between marketing as a practice and clearly present in both the production and sales eras, and marketing as a philosophy of business which shifts the emphasis from the producer's pursuit of profit as the primary objective to the achievement of customer satisfaction which, in the long run, is likely to achieve the same financial reward.

In other words the three eras model provides a convenient framework for summarizing changes in the dominant orientation of business management. Thus it is a useful, albeit over-simplified model of the evolution of modern marketing or what I prefer to designate 'the rediscovery of marketing' (Baker, 1976). In truth marketing has been around since the very first commercial exchange but there can be little doubt that until comparatively recently it has been of secondary or even tertiary importance to other more pressing imperatives in terms of increasing supply to meet the needs and wants of a rapidly expanding population. The objective of authors and teachers in using the three-stage evolutionary model has been to highlight major changes in the dominant orientation of business rather than to analyse in detail the much more complex processes which underlay and resulted in these changes. What is beyond doubt is the fact that from around 1960 onwards marketing thinking and practice has been dominated by the marketing management school of thought.

THE MARKETING MANAGEMENT SCHOOL

The marketing management school which evolved in the late 1950s and early 1960s is inextricably linked with the concept of the marketing mix and an analytical approach to marketing management following the positivist sequence of Analysis, Planning, Control. As with most major paradigm shifts no single author/researcher can claim sole credit for the new phenomenon. Among those who contributed significantly to the new school of thought were Joel Dean, Peter Drucker, Ted Levitt, E. Jerome McCarthy, Neil Borden and Philip Kotler. Dean and Drucker writing in the early 1950s paved the way but it was McCarthy's *Basic Marketing* (1960) which first promoted what came to be known as the four Ps of marketing – the idea that the marketing manager's task was to develop unique solutions to competitive marketing problems by manipulating four major marketing factors – Product, Price, Place and Promotion. This idea of a 'marketing mix' (the four Ps) was elaborated on by Neil Borden (1964), building on an earlier idea of James Culliton (1948), and confirmed by the appearance in 1967 of the first edition of Philip Kotler's best-selling *Marketing Management: Analysis, Planning and Control*. Levitt's contribution in distinguishing the essence of the marketing orientation/concept – a focus on customer needs – has already been referred to.

An authoritative review of the marketing management school is to be found in Frederick E. Webster Jnr's 1992 article in the *Journal of Marketing* ('The Changing Role of Marketing in the Corporation'). In his own words, 'the purpose of this article is to outline both the intellectual and the pragmatic roots of changes that are occurring in marketing, especially marketing *management*, as a body of knowledge, theory, and practice and to suggest the need for a new paradigm of the marketing function within the firm' (Webster 1992: 1).

While Webster's article recognizes the need for 'a new paradigm of the marketing function within the firm', in the opinion of many European scholars a much more radical reappraisal is called for which challenges the very roots of the marketing management school.

THE EUROPEAN PERSPECTIVE

One of the leading critics of the marketing management school is French professor Giles Marion. Marion's views are contained in a paper 'The Marketing Management Discourse: What's New Since the 1960s?' (1993), which is 'an attempt to describe the formalisation of ideas which make up marketing management as a school of thought' (p. 143), based upon the content of the most popular marketing textbooks (American and European).

Marion argues that 'marketing as a discipline, should show greater humility by presenting its prescriptions in a more prudent manner, and by describing more systematically the interaction between supply and demand and the organisational consequences that follow' (1993: 166). In conclusion he expresses the view that, while the normative theory of marketing management may well have had a useful impact on managerial thinking and practice 'there has been nothing new since the 1960s or even well before' (ibid.).

While Marion's critique strikes at the very heart of the marketing management school promoted by Americans it is comparatively mild compared with the trenchant criticism expressed by Evert Gummesson, a leading member of the Scandinavian School. In Gummesson's view 'the traditional textbooks do not satisfactorily reflect reality' and he proposes six objections to support his thesis (1993):

1   Textbook presentations of marketing are based on limited real world data –

14

specifically, they are largely concerned with mass marketed, packaged consumer goods.

2   Goods account for a minor part of all marketing, but the textbook presentations are focused on goods; services are treated as a special case.

3   Marketing to consumers dominates textbooks, while industrial/business marketing is treated as a special case.

4   The textbook presentations are a patchwork; new knowledge is piled on top of existing knowledge, but not integrated with it.

5   The textbooks have a clever pedagogical design; the form is better than the content.

6   The Europeans surrender to the USA and its marketing gurus and do not adequately promote their own original contributions.

In sum, Gummesson argues that US textbooks represent a colonization of thought and that this thought excludes or ignores much of the development in marketing thinking which has occurred in the fields of industrial and services marketing in Europe in the past twenty years or more. To some extent the blame must rest with the Europeans for failing to promote their ideas in the USA but the dismissive, not-invented-here attitudes of American academics who act as gatekeepers to US-based publications must also bear some of the blame.

Many of the views expressed by Marion and Gummesson are echoed in the work of Christian Grönroos (another leading member of the Scandinavian School). In Grönroos' view (1994) the majority of marketing academics and textbooks treat marketing as a subject which emerged in the 1960s and is founded upon the concept of the marketing mix and the four Ps of Product, Price, Place and Promotion (McCarthy 1960) which comprised it. As a consequence 'empirical studies of what the key marketing variables are, and how they are perceived and used by marketing managers have been neglected. Moreover, structure has been vastly favoured over process considerations' (Kent 1986).

While McCarthy's simplification of Borden's original conceptualization of the marketing mix has obvious pedagogical attractions, its application appears best suited to mass markets for consumer packaged goods underpinned by sophisticated distribution channels and commercial mass media. Indeed, this is the context or setting of many marketing courses and texts, but it is clearly representative of a limited aspect of the domain and process of marketing.

However, the concept of the marketing mix is more seriously flawed. To begin with the paradigm is a production-oriented definition in the sense that its approach is that customers are persons to whom something is done rather than persons for whom something is done. (See Dixon and Blois 1983; Grönroos 1989, 1990.) A second deficiency is that while McCarthy recognized the interactive nature of the four Ps 'the model itself does not explicitly include any interactive elements. Furthermore, it does not indicate the nature and scope of such interactions' (Grönroos 1994).

However, perhaps the major deficiency of the four Ps approach is that it

15

defines marketing as a functional activity in its own right and so creates the potential for conflict with other functional areas, discourages persons from becoming involved in marketing because it is the preserve of the marketing department and, as a result, can frustrate or compromise the adoption of the marketing concept.

Grönroos sees the four Ps as a direct development from the microeconomic theory of imperfect competition developed by Robinson and Chamberlin in the 1930s, but argues that the separation of the four Ps model from its theoretical foundations left it without roots. Indeed, Grönroos goes even further and argues that 'the introduction of the 4 Ps of the marketing mix with their simplistic view of reality can be characterised as a step back to the level of, in a sense equally simplistic, microeconomic theory of the 1930s'. This observation is largely prompted by the apparent failure of marketing academics in the USA to detect the evolution of the 'Copenhagen School's' *parameter theory*. Building upon the work of Frisch (1933), Von Stackelberg (1939), Kjaer-Hansen (1945) and Rasmussen (1955), Gosta Mickwitz observed:

> When empirically based works on marketing mechanisms show that the enterprise uses a number of different parameters markedly distinct from each other, a theory of the behaviour of the enterprise in the market will be very unrealistic if it is content to deal only with ... (a few) ... of them. We have therefore tried throughout to pay attention to the presence of a number of different methods which firms employ to increase their sales.
>
> (Mickwitz 1959: 217)

Grönroos (1994) explains further: 'The interactive nature of the marketing variables was explicitly recognised and accounted for in parameter theory by means of varying market elasticities of the parameters over the life of the product life cycle'.

At the same time that the four Ps was becoming the established 'theory' or normative approach to marketing in the USA and many other countries, new theories and models were emerging in Europe – specifically, the interaction/network approach to industrial marketing and the marketing of services (1960s) and, more recently, the concept of relationship marketing.

The interaction/network approach originated in Uppsala University in Sweden during the 1960s and was subsequently taken up in many countries following the establishment of the IMP (Industrial Marketing and Purchasing) Group. As Grönroos explains:

> Between the parties in a network various interactions take place, where exchanges and adaptation to each other occur. A flow of goods and information as well as financial and social exchanges takes place in the network. (See, for example, Håkansson 1982, Johanson and Mattson 1985 and Kock 1991.) In such a network the role and forms of marketing are not very clear. All exchanges, all sorts of interactions have an impact on the position of the parties in the network. The interactions are not necessarily initiated by the seller – the marketer according to the marketing mix paradigm – and they may continue over a long period of time, for example, for several years.
>
> (Grönroos 1994)

The network/interaction model recognizes that exchanges are not the exclusive preserve of professional marketers and may, indeed, involve numerous other members of the interacting organizations, some of whom may well have more influence and impact on the relationship than the functional specialists.

In the 1970s interest in the marketing of services developed simultaneously in the USA and Europe. But, while the four Ps framework continued to prevail in the USA, in Scandinavia and Finland the *Scandinavian School of Services* saw the marketing of services as an integral element of overall management. Grönroos and Gummesson have been strong proponents of this School and written extensively on the subject.

The interaction and network approach to industrial marketing and modern service marketing approaches 'clearly views marketing as an interactive process in a social context where *relationship building* is a vital cornerstone' (Grönroos 1994). Grönroos argues that this approach is similar to the system-based approaches to marketing of the 1950s (e.g. Alderson 1957) and contrasts strongly with the clinical approach of the four Ps paradigm which makes sellers active and buyers passive. As noted earlier, the latter emphasis tends to put exchange relationships into the hands of the professional marketers which may psychologically alienate other members of an organization from becoming involved. This is a far cry from Drucker's (1954) observation that the sole purpose of the business is to create customers!

As a consequence of rapid advances in both manufacturing (flexible manufacturing, CAD, CAM) and information technology the mass consumer markets suited to the four Ps approach have become fragmented and call for flexible and adaptable marketing approaches. In the 1980s the response to this need has been the emergence of *relationship marketing*. Grönroos refers to his own (1990) definition of relationship marketing: 'Marketing is to establish, maintain, and enhance relationships with customers and other partners, at a profit, so that the objectives of the parties involved are met. This is achieved by a mutual exchange and fulfilment of promises'. While more extended and explicit this definition is essentially similar to that proposed by Baker (1976) a number of years earlier: 'Marketing is concerned with mutually satisfying exchange relationships'. Similarly, Baker (and other authors) have argued consistently for the need to regard marketing both as a philosophy of business and a business function. As a business function responsible for coordinating and executing the implementation of a marketing plan, marketing is likely to continue to find the marketing mix model a useful one, albeit that the four Ps is an oversimplified version of the original concept. It is, of course, important to emphasize that continuing to use such an organizational and planning framework is in no way inimical to the newly fashionable emphasis on relationship marketing as contrasted to the prior emphasis on a transactional model.

Although Grönroos and others see relationship marketing as being at an early stage of its conceptual development, and there can be no doubt that its very existence has only recently been recognized in the USA, this is not to say that the practice is new. In fact, it is the very essence of the true marketing concept and can be identified as intrinsic to buyer-seller interactions since commercial exchanges were first initiated. Buyers have always looked for reliable sources of supply at a fair price as this reduces the dissonance and uncertainty of having to consider every single transaction as an entirely new decision. Similarly, sellers recognize that there are increased opportunities for long-term survival and profit if they can establish a customer franchise and repeat purchasing behaviour. That said, there can be no doubt that there are radically different interpretations of capitalism and the market economy, one of which emphasizes long-term relationships, the other the one-off transaction.

It is perhaps only with the collapse of the centrally planned and controlled command economies of Eastern Europe and the Soviet Union that the existence of two models of capitalism has come into sharper relief and focus. Based on a book by Michel Albert (1991), Christian Dussart (1994) highlights the differences between the Anglo-Saxon model of capitalism, as practised in the UK and USA, which is essentially short-term and transactionally based and the Alpine/Germanic model, which also embraces Scandinavia (and Japan), that emphasizes long-term relationships as the source of buyer satisfaction and seller profitability.

SO WHAT IS MARKETING?

At the 1993 UK Marketing Education Group Conference a group of researchers from the Henley Management College (Gibson *et al.*) presented their findings of a content and correspondence analysis of approximately 100 definitions of marketing in an attempt to answer the question 'What is Marketing?' Specifically, the authors set out to 'shed some light on the nature of the process of defining marketing, to identify strong and emerging themes, and to develop a map of the territory'. By using content analysis to evaluate the definitions collected and using these findings as input to a correspondence analysis the authors provide both a qualitative and quantitative analysis of how scholars have defined marketing over the years.

To begin with a collection of approximately 100 explicit marketing definitions were collected from textbooks, journals and institute/association publications which spanned the twentieth century. The vast majority of these definitions were academic and originated in the USA, UK and Europe. Themes were selected as the unit of assessment and five clusters were established as:

1 Object of marketing.
2 Nature of the relationship.
3 Outcomes.
4 Application.
5 Philosophy or (versus) function.

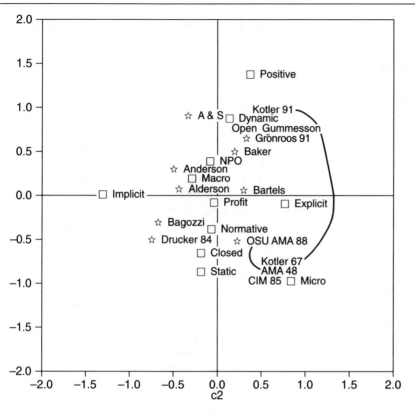

Figure 3   Marketing definitions: a map of the territory

The authors describe in some detail how each of these themes was derived and how definitions falling within them have changed in approach and emphasis over time. However, 'in order to simplify the definitions of various authors, and give more relevance to the five themes identified earlier, some of the definitions gathered and analysed for content were subjected to a process of correspondence analysis'. In essence correspondence analysis is a graphical technique which enables one to develop a two-dimensional plot indicating the degree of similarity or correspondence between rows or columns of data which have similar patterns or counts. Using the authors as rows and their perspectives on the themes as columns the map reproduced as Figure 3 was produced.

They explain:

The authors' perspectives on the original themes were constructed as dichotomies and include, first 'profit and non-profit', which related to the outcomes and application themes; secondly, 'micro and macro', which translated across to philosophy or function; thirdly, 'static and dynamic' and 'open and closed' which referred to the relationship theme and to some extent provided some insight into the

19

content and nature of the whole definition; and, finally, two additional dichotomies were included, 'positive and normative', namely, whether the definitions described what exists or prescribed what 'ought' to happen, and whether the definition was 'explicit or implicit'.

(Gibson *et al.* 1993)

Based upon both the qualitative and quantitative analyses certain conclusions may be derived.

1   Changes have occurred across all five content themes indicating significant evolution in the concept of marketing since its earliest definition.
2   The greatest change has occurred in the 'nature of the relationship' theme (i.e. between provider and user, from 'one-way narrow, discrete transactions to the recognition and positioning of relationships as a key strategy resource'). This change is also reflected in the other themes, particularly 'philosophy or function', and marks the moderation of economic explanations of consumption behaviour through the admission of concepts derived from psychology and sociology.
3   Changes in the marketing environment have resulted in a broadening and softening of the original concept and its transfer into other domains – services, not for profit, etc.
4   'Marketing' has shown itself to be adaptable, flexible, international and open. But Gibson *et al.* warn that 'this latitude has allowed ambiguity to creep into its definition and cause confusion. Definitional clarity is essential in the future'.

In conclusion, Gibson *et al.* offer three further points prompted by their analysis:

1   Marketing and its guardians continue to foster its open and innovative culture.
2   A single definition is not aimed for as its existence would probably discourage future development of the subject.
3   Nonetheless, greater rigour should be given to the formulation of definitions in future.

SUMMARY

In this opening chapter we have endeavoured to shed some light on the nature and scope of 'marketing'. As we have seen, and as is apparent from the sheer size of this Encyclopedia, marketing is a large and complex subject which covers a multitude of economic and social activities. Many of these are described in some detail in the following chapters. That said the practice of marketing is founded on a very simple philosophy, that of 'mutually satisfying (commercial) exchange relationships'.

In the 1990s 'relationship marketing' has become the dominant theme almost everywhere, despite its somewhat belated recognition in the USA. As our review has attempted to show it was ever so but, depending upon the existing balance between supply and demand at any point in time, one or other of the parties to an exchange is likely to exercise more control over the relationship than the other. If this is the producer/seller it does not necessarily mean that they are production or sales oriented and insensitive to consumer needs. Indeed, it is a truism that all successful businesses are marketing orientated – if they were not meeting and satisfying customer needs profitably they would not be successful. What matters is the state of mind of the producer/seller – their philosophy of business. If this philosophy includes a concern for the customers' needs and wants, an appreciation of the benefits and satisfactions which are looked for, a genuine effort to establish a dialogue and build a long-term relationship then this is a marketing philosophy irrespective of whether or not the organization possesses any personnel or function designated as 'marketing'.

In the chapters which follow many facets and aspects of the subject are examined and explored by internationally recognized experts. Taken together these provide a comprehensive overview of and introduction to the body of knowledge and practice of marketing. While personal perspectives may vary the core proposition remains – marketing is concerned with the identification, creation and maintenance of mutually satisfying exchange relationships.

REFERENCES

Albert, Michel (1991) *Capitalisme contre Capitalisme*, Paris: Seuil, L'Histoire Immédiate.

Alderson, W. (1957) *Marketing Behavior and Executive Action*, Homewood, Ill: Irwin.

Baker, Michael J. (1976) 'Evolution of the marketing concept', in Michael J. Baker (ed.) *Marketing: Theory and Practice*, London: Macmillan.

Baker, Michael J. (1980) 'Marketing maxims', *Advertising* 66, Winter.

Baker, Michael J. (ed.) (1994) *The Marketing Book*, 3rd edn, Oxford: Butterworth-Heinemann Ltd.

Borden, Neil H. (1964) 'The concept of the marketing mix', *Journal of Advertising Research* 4 (2).

Chamberlin, E. J. (1933) *The Theory of Monopolistic Competition*, Cambridge, Mass: Harvard University Press.

Culliton, James W. (1948) *The Management of Marketing Costs*, Andover, Mass: The Andover Press Ltd.

Dean, Joel (1951) *Managerial Economics*, Englewood Cliffs, NJ: Prentice-Hall.

Dixon, D. F. and Blois, K. J. (1983) 'Some limitations of the 4 Ps as a paradigm for marketing', *Proceedings*, Marketing Education Group Conference, Cranfield.

Drucker, Peter (1954) *The Practice of Management*, New York: Harper & Row.

Dussart, Christian (1994) 'Capitalism versus capitalism', in Michael J. Baker (ed.) *Perspectives on Marketing Management*, Vol. 4, Chichester: John Wiley & Sons.

Frisch, R. (1933) 'Monopole – Polypole – la notion de la force dans l'économie', *Nationalokonomisk Tidskrift*, Denmark.

Fullerton, Ronald A. (1988) 'How modern is modern marketing? Marketing's evolution and the myth of the production era', *Journal of Marketing* 52, January: 108–25.

Galbraith, J. K. (1958) *The Affluent Society*, Harmondsworth: Penguin.

Gibson, Helen, Tynan, Caroline and Pitt, Leyland (1993) 'What is marketing?': a

21

qualitative and quantitative analysis of marketing decisions', *Proceedings*, Marketing Education Group Conference, Loughborough.

Grönroos, C. (1989) 'Defining marketing: a market-oriented approach', *European Journal of Marketing* 23 (1): 52–60.

Grönroos, C. (1990) *Service Management and Marketing. Managing the Moments of Truth in Service Competition*, Lexington, MA: Free Press/Lexington Books.

Gronröos, Christian (1994) 'Quo vadis marketing? Toward a relationship marketing paradigm', *Journal of Marketing Management* 10.5: 1–13.

Gummesson, E. (1993) 'Broadening and specifying relationship marketing', invited paper, Monash Colloquium on Relationship Marketing, Monash University, Melbourne, Australia, 1–4 August 1993.

Håkansson, H. (ed.) (1982) *International Marketing and Purchasing of Industrial Goods*, New York, NY: Wiley.

Johanson, J. and Mattson, L.-G. (1985) 'Marketing investments and market investments in industrial networks', *International Journal of Research in Marketing* 4.

Keith, R. J. (1960) 'The marketing revolution', *Journal of Marketing* 24: 35–8.

Kent, R. A. (1986) 'Faith in 4 Ps: an alternative', *Journal of Marketing Management* 2.

Kjaer-Hansen, M. (1945) *Afsaetningsokonomi* [Marketing], Copenhagen: Erhvervsokonomisk Forlag.

Kock, S. (1991) *A Strategic Process for Gaining External Resources through Long-lasting Relationships*, Helsingfors/Vara, Finland: Swedish School of Economics and Business Administration.

Kotler, Philip (1967) *Marketing Management: Analysis, Planning and Control*, Englewood Cliffs, NJ: Prentice-Hall.

Levitt, T. (1960) 'Marketing myopia', *Harvard Business Review*, July–August.

McCarthy, E. Jerome (1960) *Basic Marketing: A Managerial Approach*, Homewood, Ill: Irwin.

Marion, G. (1993) 'The marketing management discourse: what's new since the 1960s?', in Michael J. Baker (ed.) *Perspectives on Marketing Management*, Vol. 3, Chichester: John Wiley & Sons.

Maslow, A. H. (1943) 'A theory of human motivation', *Psychological Review*, July: 370–96.

Mickwitz, Gosta (1959) *Marketing and Competition*, Helsingfors, Finland: Societas Scientarium Fennica.

Rasmussen, Arne (1955) *Pristeori eller parameterteori – studier omkring virksomhedens afsaetning*, Copenhagen: Erhvervsokonomisk Forlag.

Robinson, Joan (1933) *The Economics of Imperfect Competition*, London: Macmillan.

Rostow, W. W. (1962) *The Process of Economic Growth*, 2nd edn, New York: W.W. Norton.

Smith, Adam (1776) *The Wealth of Nations*, Andrew Skinner (ed.) (1970), Harmondsworth: Pelican Books.

Stackelberg, H. von (1939) 'Theorie der Vertreibspolitik und der Qualitätsvariation', *Schmollers Jahrbuck* 63/1.

Webster, Frederick E. Jr (1992) 'The changing role of marketing in the corporation', *Journal of Marketing* 56: 1–17.

2

HISTORICAL RESEARCH IN MARKETING

D. G. Brian Jones

INTRODUCTION

The purpose of this chapter is to review historical research in marketing. This includes not only the history of marketing thought (e.g. ideas, theories, schools of thought), but also of marketing content (the activities, practices and processes of marketing). Of course, marketing thought is often practice-driven and marketing practice is (hopefully) not thoughtless! However, this initial categorization is a useful one when reviewing the larger field of historical research in marketing (Savitt 1980).

This review includes research that deals with marketing from an historical perspective, which involves the description, analysis, or explanation of events through time (Savitt 1980: 53). An historical perspective also includes a thorough, systematic, and sophisticated awareness of change or continuity over time, and of the contexts of place, situation, and time in which change or continuity occurs (Fullerton 1987: 98). That perspective characterizes most of the research reviewed here. In some instances it was difficult to assess the extent to which a publication dealt with change or explained events through time, since it may have essentially described marketing at some point in history (rather than through time) and only implicitly was there comparison with some other era.

Historical research in marketing or, more specifically, by marketing scholars published primarily in marketing or marketing-related publications, provided the literature base for this review. The search included all of the major marketing journals, business and economics history periodicals, a computerized bibliographic search, and a survey of participants at the first three Marketing History Conferences (1983, 1985, 1987). This produced a bibliography of approximately 400 publications, including over 100 journal articles, 26 articles in books of readings, 21 books, and over 200 papers in conference proceedings (including the proceedings of the first 6 Marketing History Conferences). Because of space limitations, however, all but key citations of conference

23

proceedings and of journal articles have been omitted. It was a thorough, yet not exhaustive review of the literature. Without the relatively narrow definition of historical research in marketing used here, the bibliography could have been longer. Nevertheless, this more restricted set is thought to reflect the mainstream of historical research in marketing.

Structure and overview

The structure of this review loosely follows three themes: chronological, topical and historiographic. The first theme is, perhaps, not surprising. The discussion throughout the review follows chronologically the development of historical research in marketing, starting with a publication in 1933 by Paul Converse.

The second theme followed here is, of course, the topical one including marketing and marketing thought (referred to above) as well as methodology. Furthermore, within the history of marketing thought are works examining the development of the literature, biographies of pioneer scholars, the roles played by important organizations and institutions, the history of university teaching, and, of course, the development of concepts, theories and schools of thought. Marketing history (practices, activities and processes) includes the various marketing functions (the four Ps) and their component activities, marketing research, retailing, wholesaling, company or industry histories where the focus is on marketing, biographies of important marketing practitioners, and macro-marketing issues such as the regulation of marketing. Finally, methodology includes historiographic issues such as data sources, historical method, philosophy of history, and the justification of historical research in marketing.

Within this topical theme there are some noteworthy omissions from this review. First, many company and industry histories include discussion of marketing practices, especially histories of retailing institutions (e.g. Hower's *History of Macy's of New York, 1858–1919* (1946)). However, such histories seldom have as their primary purpose an examination of marketing. Therefore, except for some recent examples from conference proceedings and from the periodic literature, these have been excluded from this review. Also, although not that recent, Hidy (1970) presented an excellent review of such work. A second (qualified) exception is advertising history. Again, a somewhat dated bibliography and review of this topic has been published (Pollay 1979). Since then several books on advertising history have been written, although most by historians outside the marketing discipline (Pollay 1988a: 195). Therefore, the attention was restricted here primarily to the advertising history which has appeared more recently in the marketing and marketing-related literature. Finally, the history of consumption has also been reviewed more recently and quite thoroughly by a number of scholars (Rassuli and Hollander 1986a; McCracken 1987; Sheth and Gross 1988; Rassuli 1991; Smith and Lux 1993).

Therefore, the topics mentioned above will not be given the attention otherwise warranted in a complete review of historical research in marketing.

One final exception is also noteworthy. A good deal of the earliest research by marketing scholars in this century, for example, Nystrom's (1915) *The Economics of Retailing*, followed an historical perspective. However, since this research appeared before there were well recognized traditions of business and marketing history, and has also been reviewed elsewhere (Jones 1987; Jones and Monieson 1990) it has been excluded from this survey.

The final theme followed in this review is an historiographic or methodological one. In fact there is a strong correlation between the chronological development of this literature (mentioned above) and the sophistication of the historical analysis employed. So, for instance, during the 1930s when historical research in marketing began to be published, the work focused mainly on identifying and collecting historical facts – putting things on the record, so to speak. More recently some of the historical research being done is quite sophisticated in its analysis, synthesizing more sources of primary data and providing a higher level of interpretation both in the traditional story-telling approach and the social scientific approach (Jones 1993).

RECORDING THE FACTS

With the founding in 1915 of the National Association of Teachers of Advertising (NATA) leading to the formation of the American Marketing Association (AMA) in 1937, there emerged an important impetus for historical work. These first attempts formally to organize marketing scholars led naturally to reflection about the origins and development of this emerging discipline. At the same time, these events provided specialized outlets for the publication of such historical reflection. Thus, there were a number of attempts to put things on the record.

History of marketing thought

From the early 1930s to the late 1950s historical research in marketing was dominated by the study of marketing thought. During this period attention was focused on tracing the earliest literature (Converse 1933, 1945; Applebaum 1947, 1952; Coolsen 1947; Bartels 1951; Maynard 1951) and marketing courses taught in American universities (Hagerty 1936; Maynard 1941; Weld 1941; Litman 1950; Bartels 1951; Hardy 1954). The earliest historical study included in this review was Converse's (1933) 'The First Decade of Marketing Literature' published in the *NATMA Bulletin*. Converse's article was typical in its attempt to identify historically significant events. In his opinion the 'first modern books on marketing' were Nystrom's (1915) *Economics of Retailing* and A.W. Shaw's (1915) *Some Problems in Market Distribution* (Converse 1933: 1).

Other early historical studies focused on the individuals and organizations that pioneered the development of the discipline (Agnew 1941; Bartels 1951; Converse 1959b), and a series of twenty-three biographical sketches published in the *Journal of Marketing* between 1956 and 1962 was later compiled in book form (Wright and Dimsdale 1974). Bartels' (1951) article entitled 'Influences on the Development of Marketing Thought, 1900–1923' was seminal in that it was an early attempt to go beyond a simple chronicle of 'firsts'. It drew upon numerous interviews of pioneer scholars in order to examine some of the sources of early marketing ideas. Bartels' article was also the most ambitious historical analysis at that time based, as it was, on his (1941) doctoral dissertation at Ohio State University.

During the 1950s a trend began towards focusing on the history of marketing concepts (Kelley 1956; Breen 1959), theories (McGarry 1953), and schools of thought (Brown 1951). Cassels (1936) had earlier examined the influence of significant schools of economic thought on marketing, but it was not until the 1950s that marketing ideas were developed enough to warrant a retrospective. An important collection of such articles was published in 1951 under the title *Changing Perspectives in Marketing*. It claimed to be 'one of the few, if not the only one, in which a series of papers has been compiled to give historical treatment and perspective to the development of marketing [thought]' (Wales 1951: v). This included topics such as retailing, sales management, marketing research and marketing theory. Its contributors were eminent scholars in marketing – most had been recipients of the AMA's prestigious Paul D. Converse Award.

Marketing history

There was less research done during this early period on marketing history, most of which focused on the history of retailing and wholesaling (Jones 1936; Marburg 1951; Nystrom 1951; Barger 1955). Barger's (1955) book, entitled *Distribution's Place in the American Economy Since 1869*, examined the changing role of wholesale and retail sectors in the American economy from 1869 to 1950. It was a unique study of the cost and output of distribution, and of the relative importance of wholesale and retail sectors as measured by the proportion of the labour force engaged in each.

A more general history of marketing which was distinctive both in its scope of subject matter and in its historical perspective was Hotchkiss's (1938) *Milestones of Marketing*. Using the American Marketing Association's definition of marketing to guide his choice of topics, Hotchkiss traced 'the most important steps in the evolution of marketing' (p. vii) back to ancient Rome and Greece through medieval England to modern North American practices (mostly retailing, advertising, and merchandising). Only recently have marketing historians again attempted to examine the marketing practices of such early periods in history (e.g. Dixon 1979; Friedman 1984).

Another marketing history which complemented the Hotchkiss book by focusing on marketing practices of the twentieth century was Converse's (1959a) *Fifty Years of Marketing in Retrospect*. This was written as a companion to his

(1959b) study of the beginnings of marketing thought. Converse described his marketing history book as 'the story of business and particularly of market distribution as I have seen it and as I have studied it' (p. vi). In addition to marketing practices such as advertising and promotion, pricing, merchandising, and others, Converse described the changing economic conditions and technological developments during the early twentieth century which influenced such practices.

Throughout this early period historical research was mostly descriptive as marketers focused on recording the facts of marketing history and the history of marketing thought. The most prolific and perhaps the most important contributor during this era was Paul D. Converse, whose two monographs published in 1959 seemed to typify historical research in marketing to that point in time.

LAYING THE FOUNDATIONS

The 1960s was a transition period with fewer, but more in-depth, publications. A number of significant works and events laid the foundation for the growth of interest in historical research evident today. For example, during the early 1960s successive conferences of the American Marketing Association featured tracks on historical research (Greyser 1963; Smith 1965). Most of the papers published from those sessions offered justifications for doing such work and in that way may have helped to legitimate subsequent historical studies. Although there was a noticeable decline in the number of published works in the periodic literature, a number of important books were published. Four books appeared in succession on the history of marketing thought and an important collection of work on seventeenth-, eighteenth-, and nineteenth-century marketing practices.

History of marketing thought

Converse's (1959b) *The Beginnings of Marketing Thought in the United States* served as a transition point, both in time and in depth of analysis, in the history of marketing thought. One of Converse's students, Frank Coolsen, followed with a dissertation on the marketing ideas of nineteenth-century liberal economists, which was published in 1960 under the title *Marketing Thought in the United States in the Late Nineteenth Century*. Essentially, this was an expansion of some of the material in Converse's book.

Two other books on the history of marketing thought which complemented each other were Bartels' (1962) *The Development of Marketing Thought*, and Schwartz's (1963) *Development of Marketing Theory*. Bartels' book was essentially a chronology of published literature, university courses, and events that had played a role in the development of marketing thought since 1900. Schwartz was more concerned with specific theories in marketing. His was a more concentrated and rigorous follow-up to the 1951 collection edited by Hugh

27

Wales. In addition to examining the historical development of well-recognized marketing theories such as retail gravitation, regional theory, marketing functions, and Alderson's functionalist theory, Schwartz included chapters examining the potential contribution of fields such as social physics and game theory. This made the book somewhat unorthodox and may explain why it has been largely ignored by students of the history of marketing thought. Bartels' book, on the other hand, has since been updated twice (1976, 1988) and has become a staple of most doctoral seminars in North America.

In addition to those general works, there were studies of specific concepts and theories during the 1960s. Examples included Hollander's historical analysis of retailing institutions (1960, 1963a, 1966), and historical examinations of marketing management by Keith (1960), Lazer (1965), and La Londe and Morrison (1967).

During the 1960s some researchers began to integrate marketing history with the history of marketing thought. Such work went beyond the simplistic approach of earlier writings by using the history of marketing practice to interpret the development of marketing thought. An example of this was Hollander's work cited above, and more recently his reexamination of the origins of the marketing concept (1986b). That distinctive approach to historical research has recently been described by Rassuli (1988).

Marketing history

As the marketing discipline moved away from the institutional and commodity schools of thought and began to popularize marketing functions through the managerial approach, research in marketing history reflected that trend. This included historical research in advertising and promotion (McKendrick 1960; Curti 1967), product innovation (Silk and Stern 1963), and personal selling (Hollander 1963b, 1964).

A broad range of marketing history, especially in economic development, regulation, institutions, and advertising was covered in Shapiro and Doody's (1968) *Readings in the History of American Marketing: Settlement to Civil War*. As editors of this extensive collection, Shapiro and Doody stated that their objective was to 'awaken the interest of students of marketing in history and historical analysis' (1968: 12). Their book of readings and Bartels' (1962) *Development of Marketing Thought* were undoubtedly the most important publications during the 1960s. In both of those books the level of interpretation and scale of effort were unprecedented.

Ironically, as the 1960s drew to a close there seemed to be a decline of interest in historical research in marketing. The marketing discipline had been moving during the 1960s in a more quantitative, scientific direction and perhaps historical research seemed less rigorous.

THE EMERGING DISCIPLINE

The quantity and quality of historical research in marketing have grown enormously since the early 1980s. Of course, much of this work is accounted for by the Marketing History Conferences.

In 1983 Michigan State University began hosting the Marketing History Conference in an effort to provide a biannual platform for the growing number of scholars interested in the subject. At that time one of the conference organizers suggested that historical research was something marketing professors did only after they had received tenure! If this was ever true it is certainly no longer the case. The conference regularly includes the work of senior and junior faculty as well as doctoral students. Attendance has grown with each successive conference and has truly become an international gathering with the Sixth Conference (1993) participants representing five countries. There is also a regularly published newsletter, *Retrospectives in Marketing*, which is affiliated with the Conference.

Even if we exclude the 138 papers published in the Proceedings of the first five Marketing History Conferences from 1983 to 1991, the increase in the number of publications in this emerging discipline is significant. Top journals in marketing such as the *Journal of Marketing*, *Journal of Consumer Research*, and *Journal of the Academy of Marketing Science* have been regularly publishing historical research. The *Journal of the Academy of Marketing Science* recently (1990) featured a special issue on the history of marketing thought and the *Journal of Macromarketing* has specifically called for the submission of historical research. There is a new maturity in this emerging discipline and a breadth to the research evident in developments across all three major topical categories of historical research in marketing.

Methodology

If one were looking for a single publication which signalled the emergence (or rather, the revival) of history as a 'legitimate' field within the marketing discipline, it might be Ronald Savitt's (1980) 'Historical Research in Marketing' published in the *Journal of Marketing*. In substance it was a statement of the rationale and method for historical research, although in the latter, only one of a range of possible approaches. In spirit, however, it was both a symbol of the legitimacy of doing historical research by marketing scholars, and a challenge to them to do so. As a statement on method, Savitt's article initiated a much needed discussion in the marketing literature about the theory and methods of historical scholarship.

There is a wide range of methodological approaches within historiography from positivistic (e.g. Hempel 1959) to hermeneutic (e.g. Collingwood 1974: 17–40). These approaches have recently been summarized as they apply to historical research in marketing by Jones (1993). Savitt proposed what was essentially a positivistic method of historical research based on hypothesis testing (1980, 1982, 1984) and a search for causal relations (1988: 119). Kumcu (1987) has also outlined an historical method close to Savitt's in its concern with probable causes, hypothesis testing, and relative validity of laws. A more recent, and perhaps more thorough, presentation of this social scientific approach to historical research is given by Smith and Lux (1993). They discuss the ontological and epistemological assumptions of social scientific history and present a model of research design and analysis in the context of historical research into consumer behaviour.

On the other hand, Firat (1986) suggested going beyond such methods – that explanation and understanding of marketing history requires the interpretation and reflection characteristic of a hermeneutic approach. Fullerton (1987) distinguishes between the philosophy of history, which is concerned with epistemological and ontological issues, and historical method, which follows from the philosophy of history in which one believes. Fullerton's own approach to history is derived from the philosophy of German historicism (1986) which is based on assumptions very different from those of a positivistic historical method. For Fullerton, the basic elements of historical method include systematic doubt, flexible use of analytical tools, use of multiple data sources, creative and critical synthesis, and a narrative form of description (1987: 112). Consistent with the traditional approach, Stern (1990) has described the use of literary criticism as an analytical tool which complements historical method by providing additional insights when interpreting historical data.

In the echoes of those discussions about the philosophy and method of marketing history there have also been voices calling for more historical research (Savitt 1980, 1982; Fullerton 1987) and providing rationales for using marketing history in teaching (Nevett 1989; Witkowski 1989). Nevett (1991) has also described how historical method relates to marketing decision-making and offered recommendations for applying historical thinking to marketing practice. Finally, rounding out the discussion of methodology are descriptions of various data sources for historical research in marketing (Rassuli and Hollander 1986a; Pollay 1988a).

Marketing history

Until the 1980s historical research in marketing was dominated by interest in the history of marketing thought. That emphasis has since changed, with a good deal of research now being conducted on the history of marketing activities and functions such as advertising (Nevett 1982; Pollay 1985; Stern 1988; Gross and Sheth 1989), product simplification strategy (Hollander 1984a), channel relations (Marx 1985), retailers' pricing strategies (Dickinson 1988) and segmentation strategy (Fullerton 1985; Tedlow 1990; Hollander and Germain 1992).

Two recent and important historical studies of marketing segmentation

30

strategy were presented in Tedlow's (1990) *New and Improved: The Story of Mass Marketing in America* and Hollander and Germain's (1992) *Was There a Pepsi Generation Before Pepsi Discovered It?* In its subject matter Tedlow's book, in fact, goes well beyond the history of segmentation strategy. In his words the book is about 'how some of America's most important corporations have battled for dominance in key consumer product markets during the past hundred years' (1990: 4). Those corporations include Coca-Cola and Pepsi, Ford and General Motors, A&P, and Sears, Montgomery Ward. Nevertheless, Tedlow's main theme is the evolution of market structure in America from a fragmented market in the nineteenth century, to a mass market, and then to market segmentation. For example, with respect to the soft drink industry Tedlow concludes, 'there was no such thing as the Pepsi Generation until Pepsi created it' (1990: 372). It is that statement which is turned around in the title of Hollander and Germain's (1992) in-depth examination of the history of segmentation practices. They disagree with Tedlow's three-phase theory and provide detailed evidence of earlier (than those documented by Tedlow) segmentation practices as well as conceptualizations of segmentation by early marketing scholars.

Within marketing history, advertising has become a leading topic of interest. A number of individuals have contributed to this research, but the work of two authors is especially prominent. Terence Nevett has written extensively about the history of British advertising (1982, 1985, 1988a, 1988c, 1988d). Much of Nevett's work is comparative and cross cultural, for example, his study with Fullerton of societal perceptions of advertising in Britain and Germany (Fullerton and Nevett 1986), and of American influences on British advertising (Nevett 1988a), as well as British influences on American advertising (1988c). At times his work has taken on a macromarketing perspective (Nevett 1985, 1988b; Fullerton and Nevett 1986) by looking at the impact of advertising on society.

Others have also contributed to the study of British advertising history, focusing on specific companies (Ferrier 1986; Seaton 1986), professional sales promotion organizations (Legh 1986), and self-regulation in the advertising industry (Miracle and Nevett 1988).

A second individual whose work on advertising history has been prominent is Richard Pollay. During the late 1970s Pollay observed that there were very few significant sources of advertising history (1979: 8) and those had been written outside the marketing discipline. To correct that situation, he outlined an ambitious research programme for advertising history, including the justification, research method, and data sources required for such work (Pollay 1977, 1978, 1979). Having identified and developed important archival sources (Pollay 1979, 1988a), he conducted a rigorous content analysis of twentieth-century American print advertising in order to identify the portrayed values (Belk and Pollay 1985; Pollay 1984a, 1988b), the extent of informativeness (1984b), and the creative aspects of advertising strategy (1985). More recently, his work has taken on a macromarketing perspective (Pollay 1988c; Pollay and Lysanski 1990), specifically his study of the history of cigarette advertising and its impact on

31

society. This interest in the history of cigarette advertising is shared by others such as Wilcox (1991) who examined the correlation between advertising and cigarette consumption for the period from 1949 to 1985.

The complete range of methodological approaches to historical research is evident in recent studies of advertising history. Pollay's use of quantification, content analysis, and hypothesis testing is representative of the social scientific approach to historical research. In a similar fashion, Gross and Sheth (1989) performed content analysis of advertisements spanning 100 years in the *Ladies Home Journal* to investigate the use of time-oriented appeals. On the other hand, Stern (1988) has used literary criticism to examine the medieval tradition of allegory in relation to the development of contemporary advertising strategies. Nevett also used biographical data and a qualitative interpretation of advertisements to examine the development of British advertising (1982, 1983, 1985, 1988a, 1988c, 1988d).

In addition to activities and functions, three other subcategories of marketing history have attracted considerable attention. First, corporate and industry marketing practices have emerged as a popular topic of study (Erb 1985; Clark 1986; Tedlow 1990). Second, marketing systems – whole economies or systems of marketing – have also emerged during the 1980s as a significant topic for historical research (Corley 1987; Kaufman 1987; Fisk 1988; Fullerton 1988b; Speece 1990; Pirog 1991; Kitchell 1992) and is undoubtedly related to the rising interest in macromarketing (see also Hollander 1984b, 1988). Pirog's (1991) study of changes in the structure and output of the US distribution system builds on Barger's (1955) seminal work mentioned earlier in this review. Of course, an essential aspect of the history of marketing systems is the relationship between marketing and economic development (Dixon 1981; McCarthy 1988; Savitt 1988), and that fundamental importance of marketing history to the study of economic development has been used as a justification for more historical research in marketing since the late 1950s (Myers and Smalley 1959).

A third subcategory of marketing history that continues to hold interest for marketing historians is retailing. After marketing thought, retailing may have the longest consistent tradition of historical research. What we now know about retailing history, however, remains largely as scattered threads, focusing on selected firms and specific individuals. In a proposal for American retailing history Savitt (1989) agrees with Hollander's (1983; 1986a) assessment of the need for a 'synthesizing' history of retailing, one which goes beyond simple, descriptive chronology to identify patterns and integrate marketing practice with marketing thought. Examples of such an approach include Hollander's study of the effects of industrialization on retailing in the twentieth century (1980c) and his evaluation of hypothesized patterns of retail institutional evolution (1980a). The testing of hypotheses about retail institutional evolution has also been a focus in Savitt's work. Having developed specific hypotheses from McNair's wheel of retailing theory, Savitt (1984) used single-firm, total-product line data for a ten-year period to test them. Recent work by others has also contributed to the tracing of retail institutional evolution (Cundiff 1988: 149–62; Kotler 1988; Ortiz-Buonofina 1992).

History of marketing thought

It is a natural progression for any discipline to begin with isolated 'how-to' writings and university courses of instruction, then to develop concepts, theories, and eventually schools of thought. This same pattern is evident in the development of the history of marketing thought.

Recently there has been less research on the history of the marketing literature. In addition to Grether's (1976) forty-year review of the *Journal of Marketing* there have been retrospectives of other major journals in the field (Muncy 1991; Berkman 1992). Likewise there has been less research into the history of marketing teaching (Schultz 1982; Lazer and Shaw 1988). There is a need, however, to examine developments that occurred outside the USA, such as in Jones' (1992) study of early marketing courses in Canada.

There has been some renewed interest in biographical research (Jones 1987, 1989, 1993; Wright 1989; Kreshel 1990). In that connection, the third edition of Bartels' (1988) *History of Marketing Thought* is notable for its addition of biographical information about important scholars of the 1960s, 1970s and 1980s. The *Journal of Macromarketing* has recently announced a series of autobiographies of eminent scholars in marketing.

However, the development of ideas now dominates research in the history of marketing thought. For example, both Hollander (1986b) and Fullerton (1988a) have given critical historical accounts of the development of the 'so-called' marketing concept. Both scholars concluded that serious and sophisticated marketing has been practised much longer than received doctrine suggests. That conclusion was also supported by Droge, Germain and Halstead (1990). Taken together these studies also point to the value, and in some cases the necessity, of historical research in evaluating existing theory. More importantly perhaps, they have contributed to a more critical perspective and to a rewriting of the history of marketing thought. This has included an extensive reevaluation of the schools of thought from which marketing emerged as a discipline (Jones 1987; Jones and Monieson 1990) and an extension of our historical perspective beyond the twentieth century (Dixon 1978, 1979, 1981, 1982).

Another concept which has attracted recent attention is marketing productivity. Both Shaw (1987, 1990) and Dixon (1990, 1991) have done extensive work on the historical development of the concept and measurement of marketing productivity. Shaw's historical review of empirical studies concludes that marketing productivity in the USA during the past century has increased, but he points to the continuing lack of clear concepts and measures of marketing costs and effectiveness (1990: 290).

Schools of thought within the discipline have attracted increasing attention from marketing historians. Discussions of the so-called classical schools –

THE NATURE AND SCOPE OF MARKETING

institutional (Hollander 1980), functional (Hunt and Goolsby 1988) and commodity (Zinn and Johnson 1990) – have been complemented by studies of more contemporary schools of thought including consumer behaviour (Sheth and Gross 1988; Mittelsteadt 1990), macromarketing (Savitt 1990) and others (Sheth, Gardner and Garrett 1988).

The most extensive of these studies is the recent book by Sheth *et al.* (1988), *Marketing Theory: Evolution and Evaluation*, which identifies, classifies, and evaluates twelve schools of marketing thought which have emerged during the twentieth century. These include the classical schools – functional, institutional, and commodity – which most marketing historians would agree qualify as schools of thought, and nine others with which, even using the authors' criteria, some historians might disagree. The classification and evaluation of all of these schools could easily be debated, but are not essential to the historical theme which provides the bulk of the presentation. There are also some striking similarities between this book and the earlier one by Schwartz (1963) on *The Development of Marketing Theory*. Several of the 'theories' included in the latter have become 'schools of thought' in Sheth *et al.* (1988) and both books have a distinctly scientific perspective (especially evident in the form of metatheoretic evaluations of each theory or school of thought). Whereas the Schwartz book should have, perhaps, become the companion to the Bartels work, the Sheth *et al.* book will surely fill that role.

CONCLUSION

The recent growth of interest in historical research in marketing is surely a natural development in a maturing discipline. Parallel discussions about philosophies of science have focused the attention of marketing scholars on their discipline and have increased their tolerance of different methodologies and perspectives. A more mature marketing discipline has recognized the legitimacy of, as well as the need for, historical research.

At the conference level there has been widespread acceptance by the academic associations. During 1988 the American Marketing Association (AMA), Academy of Marketing Science (AMS), and Association of Consumer Research (ACR) all devoted significant portions of their conferences to historical perspectives. In addition to being the major outlet for historical research in marketing, the Marketing History Conferences have been a vital catalyst and promoter of research in the field and have served to institutionalize historical research in marketing. The success of the History Conferences (held every two years since 1983), the invisible college of marketing historians (becoming more and more visible), a regularly published newsletter (*Retrospectives in Marketing*), and a special issue (1990) in a major journal (*Journal of Academy of Marketing Science*), are all convincing evidence of the pattern Ziman has identified for the development of an academic specialty (1984: 94).

It is no coincidence that those active in marketing history tend to overlap with

34

the group of scholars working in macromarketing. Macromarketing issues, for example, economic development, tend to require a longer term perspective. Therefore, the institutionalization of macromarketing during the late 1970s through an annual seminar and subsequent publication of the *Journal of Macromarketing* has also helped to justify and stimulate historical research in marketing.

Future history?

As for the nature of future historical research in marketing, this review seems to suggest trends in some key directions. For example, we have seen a synthesis of marketing history and the history of marketing thought which, hopefully, will continue. One natural and desirable outcome of this synthesis is an increase in theory development and testing. Many marketing concepts and theories are inherently historical in nature and must be tested with historical evidence.

Another recent trend has been that of identifying and describing sources of historical data and various methodologies of historical research. A better understanding is needed of the various philosophies of history, historical methods, types of primary historical data, and how to use them. Continued efforts in this direction will help improve the quality of historical research in marketing.

Increasingly marketing historians have drawn upon business history, the history of business education, and the history of science to provide a context for historical research in marketing. This trend should be expanded to include economic, social, and political history as well as the history of economic thought and other disciplines with connections to marketing.

Finally, there is exciting work being carried out by younger scholars trained at the doctoral level in marketing history and the history of marketing thought. This next generation of scholars will ensure continued growth of interest in historical research in marketing.

ACKNOWLEDGEMENT

The author would like to acknowledge the contributions of David D. Monieson to an earlier version of this chapter which appeared in the *Journal of the Academy of Marketing Science*, Fall, 1990.

REFERENCES

Agnew, Hugh E. (1941) 'The history of the American Marketing Association', *Journal of Marketing* 5 (4): 374–9.

Applebaum, W. (1947) 'The *Journal of Marketing*: the first ten years', *Journal of Marketing* 11 (4): 355–63.

Applebaum, W. (1952) 'The *Journal of Marketing*: post war', *Journal of Marketing* 16 (3): 294–300.

Barger, Harold (1955) *Distribution's Place in the American Economy Since 1869*, Princeton: Princeton University Press.

Bartels, Robert (1951) 'Influences on the development of marketing thought, 1900–1923', *Journal of Marketing* 16, July: 1–17.

Bartels, Robert (1962) *The Development of Marketing Thought*, Homewood, Illinois: Irwin.

Bartels, Robert (1976) *The History of Marketing Thought*, 2nd edn, Columbus, Ohio: Grid.

Bartels, Robert (1988) *The History of Marketing Thought*, 3rd edn, Columbus, Ohio: Publishing Horizons Inc.

Belk, Russell W. and Pollay, Richard W. (1985) 'Images of ourselves: the good life in twentieth century advertising', *Journal of Consumer Research* 11, March: 887–97.

Berkman, Harold W. (1992) 'Twenty years of the Journal', *Journal of the Academy of Marketing Science* 20 (4): 299–300.

Breen, John (1959) 'History of the marketing management concept', in L. Stockman (ed.) *Advancing Marketing Efficiency*, Chicago: American Marketing Association, 458–61.

Brown, George H. (1951) 'What economists should know about marketing', *Journal of Marketing* 16 (1): 60–66.

Cassels, J. M. (1936) 'The significance of early economic thought on marketing', *Journal of Marketing* 1, October: 129–33.

Clark, Paul (1986) 'The marketing of margarine', *European Journal of Marketing* 20 (4): 52–65.

Collingwood, R. G. (1974) 'Human nature and human history', in Patrick Gardiner (ed.) *The Philosophy of History*, London: Oxford University Press.

Converse, Paul D. (1933) 'The first decade of marketing literature', *NATMA Bulletin Supplement*, November: 1–4.

Converse, Paul D. (1945) 'The development of the science of marketing – an exploratory survey', *Journal of Marketing* 10, July: 14–23.

Converse, Paul D. (1959a) *Fifty Years of Marketing in Retrospect*, Texas: Bureau of Business Research, The University of Texas.

Converse, Paul D. (1959b) *The Beginnings of Marketing Thought in the United States*, Texas: Bureau of Business Research, University of Texas.

Coolsen, Frank (1947) 'Pioneers in the development of advertising', *Journal of Marketing* 12, July: 80–86.

Coolsen, Frank (1960) *Marketing Thought in the United States in the Late Nineteenth Century*, Texas: Texas Technical Press.

Corley, T. A. B. (1987) 'Consumer marketing in Britain, 1914–1960', *Business History* 29, October: 65–83.

Cundiff, Edward (1988) 'The evolution of retailing institutions across cultures', in Terence Nevett and Ronald Fullerton (eds) *Historical Perspectives in Marketing: Essays in Honor of Stanley C. Hollander*, Lexington: Lexington Books.

Curti, Merle (1967) 'The changing concept of human nature in the history of American advertising', *Business History Review* 41 (4): 355–7.

Dickinson, Roger (1988) 'Lessons from retailers' price experiences of the 1950s', in Terence Nevett and Ronald Fullerton (eds) *Historical Perspectives in Marketing: Essays in Honor of Stanley C. Hollander*, Lexington: Lexington Books.

Dixon, Donald F. (1978) 'The origins of macro-marketing thought', in George Fisk and Robert W. Nason (eds) *Macromarketing: New Steps on the Learning Curve*, Boulder: University of Colorado, Business Research Division.

Dixon, Donald F. (1979) 'Medieval macromarketing thought', in George Fisk and Phillip White (eds) *Macromarketing: Evolution of Thought*, Boulder: University of Colorado, Business Research Division.

Dixon, Donald F. (1981) 'The role of marketing in early theories of economic development', *Journal of Macromarketing* 1, Fall: 19–27.

Dixon, Donald F. (1982) 'The ethical component of marketing: an eighteenth century view', *Journal of Macromarketing* 2, Spring: 38–46.

Dixon, Donald F. (1990) 'Marketing as production: the development of a concept', *Journal of the Academy of Marketing Science* 18, Fall: 337–44.

Dixon, Donald F. (1991) 'Marketing structure and the theory of economic interdependence: early analytical developments', *Journal of Macromarketing* 11, Fall: 5–18.

Droge, Cornelia, Germain, Richard and Halstead, Diane (1990) 'A note on marketing and the corporate annual report: 1930–1950', *Journal of the Academy of Marketing Science* 18, Fall: 355–64.

Erb, Lyle C. (1985) 'The marketing of Christmas: a history', *Public Relations Quarterly* 24–8.

Ferrier, R. W. (1986) 'Petroleum advertising in the twenties and thirties: the case of the British Petroleum Company', *European Journal of Marketing* 20 (5): 29–51.

Firat, A. Fuat (1986) 'Historiography, scientific method and exceptional historical events', in Melanie Wallendorf and Paul Anderson (eds) *Advances in Consumer Research*, Association for Consumer Research, 14: 435–8.

Fisk, George (1988) 'Interactive systems frameworks for analyzing spacetime changes in marketing organization and processes', in Terence Nevett and Ronald Fullerton (eds) *Historical Perspectives in Marketing: Essays in Honor of Stanley C. Hollander*, Lexington: Lexington Books.

Friedman, H. H. (1984) 'Ancient marketing practices: the view from Talmudic times', *Journal of Public Policy and Marketing* 3: 194–204.

Fullerton, Ronald A. (1985) 'Segmentation strategies and practices in the 19th century German book trade: a case study in the development of a major marketing technique', in C. T. Tan and Jagdish N. Sheth (eds) *Historical Perspectives in Consumer Research: National and International Perspectives*, Singapore: National University of Singapore.

Fullerton, Ronald A. (1986) 'Historicism: what it is, and what it means for consumer research', in Melanie Wallendorf and Paul Anderson (eds) *Advances in Consumer Research*, Association for Consumer Research, 14: 431–4.

Fullerton, Ronald A. (1987) 'The poverty of ahistorical analysis: present weakness and future cure in U.S. marketing thought', in Fuat Firat, Nikhilesh Dholakia and Richard P. Bagozzi (eds) *Philosophical and Radical Thought in Marketing*, Lexington: Lexington Books.

Fullerton, Ronald A. (1988a) 'How modern is modern marketing? Marketing's evolution and the myth of the production era', *Journal of Marketing* 52, January: 108–25.

Fullerton, Ronald A. (1988b) 'Modern Western marketing as a historical phenomenon: theory and illustration', in Terence Nevett and Ronald Fullerton (eds) *Historical Perspectives in Marketing: Essays in Honor of Stanley C. Hollander*, Lexington: Lexington Books.

Fullerton, Ronald A. and Nevett, Terence R. (1986) 'Advertising and society: a comparative analysis of the roots of distrust in Germany and Great Britain', *International Journal of Marketing* 5: 225–41.

Grether, E. T. (1976) 'The first forty years', *Journal of Marketing* 40, July: 63–9.

Greyser, Stephen (ed.) (1963) *Toward Scientific Marketing*, American Marketing Association Proceedings Series, Chicago: American Marketing Association.

Gross, Barbara L. and Sheth, Jagdish N. (1989) 'Time oriented advertising: a content analysis of United States magazine advertising, 1890–1988', *Journal of Marketing* 53 (4): 76–83.

Hagerty, J. E. (1936) 'Experiences of an early marketing teacher', *Journal of Marketing* 1 (1): 20–7.

Hardy, Harold (1954) 'Collegiate marketing education since 1930', *Journal of Marketing* 19 (2): 325–30.

Hempel, Carl G. (1959) 'The function of general laws in history', in Patrick Gardiner (ed.) *Theories of History*, Glencoe, Illinois: The Free Press.

Hidy, Ralph W. (1970) 'Business history: present status and future needs', *Business History Review* 44, Winter: 483–97.

Hollander, Stanley C. (1960) 'The wheel of retailing', *Journal of Marketing* 25, July: 37–42.

Hollander, Stanley C. (1963a) 'A note on fashion leadership', *Business History Review*, Winter: 448–51.

Hollander, Stanley C. (1963b) 'Anti-salesman ordinances of the mid-nineteenth century', in Stephen Greyser (ed.) *Toward Scientific Marketing*, Chicago: American Marketing Association.

Hollander, Stanley C. (1964) 'Nineteenth century anti-drummer legislation in the United States', *Business History Review* 38, Winter: 479–500.

Hollander, Stanley C. (1966) 'Notes on the retail accordion', *Journal of Retailing* 42, Summer: 29–40.

Hollander, Stanley C. (1980a) 'Oddities, nostalgia, wheels and other patterns in retail evolution', in R. W. Stampfl and E. Hirschman (eds) *Competitive Structure in Retail Marketing: The Department Store Perspective*, Chicago: American Marketing Association.

Hollander, Stanley C. (1980b) 'Some notes on the difficulty of identifying the marketing thought contributions of the early institutionalists', in C. W. Lamb and P. M. Dunn (eds) *Theoretical Developments in Marketing*, Chicago: American Marketing Association.

Hollander, Stanley C. (1980c) 'The effects of industrialization on small retailing in the United States in the twentieth century', in S. Bruchey (ed.) *Small Business in American Life*, New York: Columbia University Press.

Hollander, Stanley C. (1983) 'Who and what are important in retailing and marketing history: a basis for discussion', in Stanley C. Hollander and Ronald Savitt (eds) *First North American Workshop on Historical Research in Marketing*, Lansing: Michigan State University.

Hollander, Stanley C. (1984a) 'Herbert Hoover, Professor Levitt, simplification and the marketing concept', in Paul Anderson and Michael Ryan (eds) *Scientific Method in Marketing*, Chicago: American Marketing Association.

Hollander, Stanley C. (1984b) 'Sumptuary laws: demarketing by edict', *Journal of Macromarketing* 4, Spring: 3–16.

Hollander, Stanley C. (1986a) 'A rearview-mirror might help us drive forward: a call for more historical studies in retailing', *Journal of Retailing* 62, Spring: 7–10.

Hollander, Stanley C. (1986b) 'The marketing concept: a déjà-vu', in George Fisk (ed.) *Marketing Management Technology as a Social Process*, New York: Praeger.

Hollander, Stanley C. (1988) 'Dimensions of marketing reform', in Stanley Shapiro and A. H. Walle (eds) *Marketing: A Return to the Broader Dimensions*, Proceedings of the Winter Educators' Conference, Chicago: American Marketing Association: 142–6.

Hollander, Stanley C. and Germain, Richard (1992) *Was There a Pepsi Generation Before Pepsi Discovered It?*, Lincolnwood, Illinois: NCT Business Books.

Hotchkiss, George Burton (1938) *Milestones of Marketing*, New York: Macmillan.

Hower, Ralph M. (1946) *History of Macy's of New York, 1858–1919*, Cambridge: Harvard University Press.

Hunt, Shelby D. and Goolsby, Jerry (1988) 'The rise and fall of the functional approach to marketing: a paradigm displacement perspective', in Terence Nevett and Ronald Fullerton (eds) *Historical Perspectives in Marketing: Essays in Honor of Stanley C. Hollander*, Lexington: Lexington Books.

Jones, D. G. Brian (1987a) 'Origins of marketing thought', doctoral dissertation, Kingston, Ontario: Queen's University.

Jones, D. G. Brian (1987b) 'Edward David Jones: a pioneer in marketing', in Terence Nevett and Stanley C. Hollander (eds) *Marketing in Three Eras*, Lansing: Michigan State University.

Jones, D. G. Brian (1989) 'Henry Charles Taylor: a pioneer in marketing', in Terence Nevett, Kathleen Whitney and Stanley Hollander (eds) *Marketing History: The Emerging Discipline*, Lansing: Michigan State University.

Jones, D. G. Brian (1992) 'Early development of marketing thought in Canada', *Canadian Journal of Administrative Science* 9 (2): 126–33.

Jones, D. G. Brian (1993) 'Historiographic paradigms in marketing', in Stanley Hollander and Kathleen Rassuli (eds) *Marketing*, Cheltenham: Edward Elgar Publishing.

Jones, D. G. Brian and Monieson, David D. (1990) 'Early development of the philosophy of marketing thought', *Journal of Marketing* 54 (1): 102–13.

Jones, Fred (1936) 'Retail stores in the United States, 1800–1860', *Journal of Marketing* 1, October: 135–40.

Kaufman, Carol J. (1987) 'The evaluation of marketing in a society: the Han Dynasty of Ancient China', *Journal of Macromarketing* 7 (2): 52–64.

Keith, Robert J. (1960) 'The marketing revolution', *Journal of Marketing* 24, January: 35–8.

Kelley, William T. (1956) 'The development of early thought in marketing and promotion', *Journal of Marketing* 21, July: 62–76.

Kitchell, Susan (1992) 'Foundation of the Japanese distribution system: historical determinants in the Tokugawa Period (1603–1868)', in Carole Duhaime (ed.) *Marketing Proceedings*, Administrative Sciences Association of Canada Conference, 108–16.

Kotler, Philip (1988) 'The convenience store: past developments and future prospects', in Terence Nevett and Ronald Fullerton (eds) *Historical Perspectives in Marketing: Essays in Honor of Stanley C. Hollander*, Lexington: Lexington Books.

Kreshel, Peggy J. (1990) 'John B. Watson at J. Walter Thompson: the legitimation of "science" in advertising', *Journal of Advertising*, 19 (2): 49–59.

Kumcu, Erdogan (1987) 'Historical method: toward a relevant analysis of marketing systems', in Fuat Firat, Nikhilesh Dholakia and Richard P. Bagozzi (eds) *Philosophical and Radical Thought in Marketing*, Lexington: Lexington Books.

La Londe, Bernard J. and Morrison, Edward J. (1967) 'Marketing management concepts, yesterday and today', *Journal of Marketing* 31 (1): 9–13.

Lazer, William (1965) 'Marketing theory and the marketing literature', in Michael Halburt (ed.) *The Meaning and Sources of Marketing Theory*, New York: McGraw-Hill.

Lazer, William and Shaw, Eric (1988) 'The development of collegiate business and marketing education in America: historical perspectives', in Stanley Shapiro and A. H. Walle (eds) *Marketing: A Return to the Broader Dimensions*, Proceedings of the Winter Educators' Conference, Chicago: American Marketing Association, 147–52.

Legh, Faith (1986) 'Half a century of professional bodies in sales promotions', *European Journal of Marketing* 20 (9): 27–40.

Litman, Simon (1950) 'The beginnings of teaching marketing in American universities', *Journal of Marketing* 15, October: 220–3.

McCarthy, E. Jerome (1988) 'Marketing orientedness and economic development', in Terence Nevett and Ronald Fullerton (eds) *Historical Perspectives in Marketing: Essays in Honor of Stanley C. Hollander*, Lexington: Lexington Books.

McCracken, Grant (1987) 'The history of consumption: a literature review and consumer guide', *Journal of Consumer Policy* 10, June: 139–66.

McGarry, E. D. (1953) 'Some new viewpoints in marketing', *Journal of Marketing* 18 (1): 33–40.

McKendrick, N. (1960) 'Josiah Wedgwood: an eighteenth century entrepreneur in salesmanship and marketing techniques', *Economic History Review* 12: 408–31.

Marburg, Theodore (1951) 'Domestic trade and marketing', in H. F. Williamson (ed.) *The Growth of the American Economy*, New York: Prentice Hall.

Marx, Thomas G. (1985) 'The development of the franchise distributive system in the United States auto industry', *British History Review* 59, August: 465–74.

Maynard, H. H. (1941) 'Marketing courses prior to 1910', *Journal of Marketing* 5, April: 382–4.

Maynard, H. H. (1951) 'Developments of science in selling and sales management', in Hugh
G. Wales (ed.) *Changing Perspectives in Marketing*, Urbana: University of Illinois Press.

Miracle, Gordon E. and Nevett, Terence (1988) 'A comparative history of advertising self-regulation in the United Kingdom and the United States', *European Journal of Marketing* 22 (4): 7–23.

Mittelstaedt, Robert (1990) 'Economics, psychology, and the literature of the sub-discipline of consumer behaviour', *Journal of the Academy of Marketing Science* 18, Fall: 303–12.

Muncy, James A. (1991) 'The *Journal of Advertising*: a twenty year appraisal', *Journal of Advertising* 20, December: 1–12.

Myers, K. and Smalley, D. (1959) 'Marketing history and economic development', *Business History Review* 33, Autumn: 387–401.

Nevett, Terence (1982) *Advertising in Britain, A History*, London: Heinemann.

Nevett, Terence (1983) 'Blood, sweat, tears and biography', in Stanley Hollander and Ronald Savitt (eds) *Proceedings of the First North American Workshop on Historical Research in Marketing*, Lansing: Michigan State University.

Nevett, Terence (1985) 'The ethics of advertising, F.P. Bishop reconsidered', *International Journal of Advertising* 4 (4).

Nevett, Terence (1988a) 'American influences in British advertising before 1920', in Terence Nevett and Ronald Fullerton (eds) *Historical Perspectives in Marketing: Essays in Honor of Stanley C. Hollander*, Lexington: Lexington Books.

Nevett, Terence (1988b) 'Reform in Great Britain – the Scapa society', in Stanley Shapiro and A. H. Walle (eds) *Marketing: A Return to the Broader Dimensions*, Chicago: American Marketing Association.

Nevett, Terence (1988c) 'The early development of marketing thought: some contributions from British advertising', in Stanley Shapiro and A. H. Walle (eds) *Marketing: A Return to the Broader Dimensions*, Chicago: American Marketing Association.

Nevett, Terence (1988d) 'Thomas Barratt and the development of British advertising', *International Journal of Advertising* 7: 267–76.

Nevett, Terence (1989) 'The uses of history in marketing education', *Journal of Marketing Education*, Summer: 48–53.

Nevett, Terence (1991) 'Historical investigation and the practice of marketing', *Journal of Marketing* 55, July: 13–23.

Nystrom, Paul H. (1915) *The Economics of Retailing*, New York: Ronald Press.

Nystrom, Paul H. (1951) 'Retailing in retrospect and prospect', in Hugh G. Wales (ed.) *Changing Perspectives in Marketing*, Urbana: University of Illinois Press.

Ortiz-Buonofina, Marta (1992) 'The evolution of retail institutions: a case study of the Guatemalan retail sector', *Journal of Macromarketing* 12, Fall: 16–27.

Pirog, Stephen F. (1991) 'Changes in U.S. distribution output, 1947–1977: the effects

of changes in structure and final demand', *Journal of Macromarketing* 11, Fall: 29–41.
Pollay, Richard W. (1977) 'The importance, and the problems of writing the history of advertising', *Journal of Advertising History* 1 (1): 3–5.
Pollay, Richard W. (1978) 'Maintaining archives for the history of advertising', *Special Libraries* 69 (4): 145–54.
Pollay, Richard W. (1979) *Information Sources in Advertising History*, Riverside, Connecticut: Greenwood Press.
Pollay, Richard W. (1984a) 'The identification and distribution of values manifest in print advertising 1900–1980', in E. Pitts Jr. and Arch Woodside (eds) *Personal Values and Consumer Behavior*, Lexington: Lexington Press.
Pollay, Richard W. (1984b) 'Twentieth century magazine advertising: determinants of informativeness', *Written Communication* 1 (1): 56–77.
Pollay, Richard W. (1985) 'The subsiding sizzle: a descriptive history of print advertising, 1900–1980', *Journal of Marketing* 49, Summer: 24–37.
Pollay, Richard W. (1988a) 'Current events that are making advertising history', in Terence Nevett and Ronald Fullerton (eds) *Historical Perspectives in Marketing: Essays in Honor of Stanley C. Hollander*, Lexington: Lexington Books.
Pollay, Richard W. (1988b) 'Keeping advertising from going down in history – unfairly', *Journal of Advertising History* 1, Autumn.
Pollay, Richard W. (1988c) 'Promotion and policy for a pandemic product: notes on the history of cigarette advertising', unpublished paper, History of Advertising Archives, Vancouver: University of British Columbia.
Pollay, Richard W. and Lysanski, Steven (1990) 'Advertising sexism is forgiven, but not forgotten: historical, cross cultural and individual differences in criticism and purchase boycott intentions', *International Journal of Advertising*.
Rassuli, Kathleen M. (1988) 'Evidence of marketing strategy in the early printed book trade: an application of Hollander's historical approach', in Terence Nevett and Ronald Fullerton (eds) *Historical Perspectives in Marketing: Essays in Honor of Stanley C. Hollander*, Lexington: Lexington Books.
Rassuli, Kathleen M. (1991) 'An interpretation of events in the recent history of consumer research: implications for paradigms and theories', in Charles Taylor, Steven Kopp, Terence Nevett and Stanley C. Hollander (eds) *Marketing History: Its Many Dimensions*, Lansing: Michigan State University.
Rassuli, Kathleen M. and Hollander, Stanley C. (1986a) 'Comparative history as a research tool in consumer behaviour', in Melanie Wallendorf and Paul Anderson (eds) *Advances in Consumer Research*, Association for Consumer Research, 14: 442–6.
Rassuli, Kathleen M. and Hollander, Stanley C. (1986b) 'Desire – induced, innate, insatiable?', *Journal of Macromarketing* 6, Fall: 4–24.
Robins, George W. (1947) 'Notions about the origins of trading', *Journal of Marketing* 11, January: 228–36.
Savitt, Ronald (1980) 'Historical research in marketing', *Journal of Marketing* 44, Fall: 52–8.
Savitt, Ronald (1982) 'A historical approach to comparative retailing', *Management Decision* 20 (4): 16–23.
Savitt, Ronald (1984) 'The wheel of retailing and retail product management', *European Journal of Marketing* 18: 43–54.
Savitt, Ronald (1988) 'A personal view of historical explanation in marketing and economic development', in Terence Nevett and Ronald Fullerton (eds) *Historical Perspectives in Marketing: Essays in Honor of Stanley C. Hollander*, Lexington: Lexington Books.
Savitt, Ronald (1989) 'Looking back to see ahead: writing the history of American retailing', *Journal of Retailing* 65 (3): 326–55.

Savitt, Ronald (1990) 'Pre-Aldersonian antecedents to macromarketing: insights from the textual literature', *Journal of the Academy of Marketing Science* 18, Fall: 293–302.

Schultz, Quentin J. (1982) 'An honourable place: the quest for professional advertising education 1900–1917', *Business History Review* 56 (1): 16–32.

Schwartz, George (1963) *Development of Marketing Theory*, Cincinnati, Ohio: South-Western Publishing.

Seaton, A. V. (1986) 'Cope's and the promotion of tobacco in Victorian England', *European Journal of Marketing* 20 (9): 5–26.

Shapiro, Stanley and Doody, Alton F. (eds) (1968) *Readings in the History of American Marketing: Settlement to Civil War*, Homewood, Illinois: Irwin.

Shaw, Arch (1915) *Some Problems in Market Distribution*, Cambridge: Harvard University Press.

Shaw, Eric (1987) 'Marketing efficiency and performance: an historical analysis', in Terence Nevett and Stanley Hollander (eds) *Marketing in Three Eras*, Lansing: Michigan State University.

Shaw, Eric (1990) 'A review of empirical studies of aggregate marketing costs and productivity in the United States', *Journal of the Academy of Marketing Science* 18, Fall: 285–92.

Sheth, Jagdish N., Gardner, D. M. and Garrett, D. (1988) *Marketing Theory: Evolution and Evaluation*, New York: Wiley and Sons.

Sheth, Jagdish N. and Gross, Barbara L. (1988) 'Parallel development of marketing and consumer behaviour: a historical perspective', in Terence Nevett and Ronald Fullerton (eds) *Historical Perspectives in Marketing: Essays in Honor of Stanley C. Hollander*, Lexington: Lexington Books.

Silk, A. and Stern, Louis (1963) 'The changing nature of innovation in marketing: a study of selected business leaders, 1852–1958', *Business History Review* 37: 182–99.

Smith, George L. (ed.) (1965) *Reflections on Progress in Marketing*, Proceedings Series, Chicago: American Marketing Association.

Smith, Ruth Ann and Lux, David S. (1993) 'Historical method in consumer research: developing causal explanations of change', *Journal of Consumer Research* 19, March: 595–610.

Speece, Mark (1990) 'Evolution of ethnodominated marketing channels: evidence from Oman and Sudan', *Journal of Macromarketing* 10, Fall: 78–93.

Stern, Barbara B. (1988) 'Medieval allegory: roots of advertising strategy for the mass market', *Journal of Marketing* 52, July: 84–94.

Stern, Barbara B. (1990) 'Literary criticism and the history of marketing thought: a new perspective on "reading" marketing theory', *Journal of the Academy of Marketing Science* 18, Fall: 329–36.

Tedlow, Richard (1990) *New and Improved: The Story of Mass Marketing in America*, New York: Basic Books.

Wales, Hugh (ed.) (1951) *Changing Perspectives in Marketing*, Urbana, Illinois: University of Illinois Press.

Weld, L. D. H. (1941) 'Early experience in teaching courses in marketing', *Journal of Marketing* 5, April: 380–1.

Wilcox, Gary B. (1991) 'Cigarette brand advertising and consumption in the United States: 1949–1985', *Journal of Advertising Research*, August–September: 61–7.

Witkowski, Terrence H. (1989) 'History's place in the marketing curriculum', *Journal of Marketing Education*, Summer: 54–7.

Wright, John S. (1989) 'Return biography to the "Journal of Marketing": a polemic', in Terence Nevett, Kathleen Whitney and Stanley C. Hollander (eds) *Marketing History: The Emerging Discipline*, Lansing: Michigan State University.

Wright, John S. and Dimsdale, Parks B. (1974) *Pioneers in Marketing*, Atlanta, Georgia: Georgia State University.

Ziman, John (1984) *An Introduction to Science Studies: The Philosophical and Social Aspects of Science and Technology*, Cambridge: Cambridge University Press.
Zinn, Walter and Johnson, Scott D. (1990) 'The commodity approach in marketing research: is it really obsolete?', *Journal of the Academy of Marketing Science* 18 (4): 345–54.

FURTHER READING LIST

Bartels, Robert (1988) *The History of Marketing Thought*, 3rd edn, Columbus, Ohio: Publishing Horizons Inc.
Converse, Paul D. (1959a) *Fifty Years of Marketing in Retrospect*, Texas: Bureau of Business Research, The University of Texas.
Converse, Paul D. (1959b) *The Beginnings of Marketing Thought in the United States*, Texas: Bureau of Business Research, University of Texas.
Fullerton, Ronald (1987) 'The poverty of ahistorical analysis: present weakness and future cure in U.S. marketing thought', in Fuat Firat, Nikhilesh Dholakia and Richard P. Bagozzi (eds) *Philosophical and Radical Thought in Marketing*, Lexington: Lexington Books.
Fullerton, Ronald (1988a) 'How modern is modern marketing? Marketing's evolution and the myth of the production era', *Journal of Marketing* 52, January: 108–25.
Hollander, Stanley C. (1986b) 'The marketing concept: a déjà-vu', in George Fisk (ed.) *Marketing Management Technology as a Social Process*, New York: Praeger.
Hollander, Stanley C. and Rassuli, Kathleen (eds) (1993) *Marketing*, Cheltenham: Edward Elgar Publishing.
Jones, D. G. Brian and Monieson, David D. (1990) 'Early development of the philosophy of marketing thought', *Journal of Marketing* 54 (1): 102–13.
Journal of the Academy of Marketing Science (1990) 'The history of marketing thought', Special Issue (Fall).
McCracken, Grant (1987) 'The history of consumption: a literature review and consumer guide', *Journal of Consumer Policy* 10, June: 139–66.
Nevett, Terence and Fullerton, Ronald A. (eds) (1988) *Historical Perspectives in Marketing: Essays in Honor of Stanley C. Hollander*, Lexington: Lexington Books.
Pollay, Richard (1979) *Information Sources in Advertising History*, Riverside, Connecticut: Greenwood Press.
Pollay, Richard (1985) 'The subsiding sizzle: a descriptive history of print advertising, 1900–1980', *Journal of Marketing* 49, Summer: 24–37.
Savitt, Ronald (1980) 'Historical research in marketing', *Journal of Marketing* 44, Fall: 52–8.
Shapiro, Stanley and Doody, Alton F. (1968) *Readings in the History of American Marketing: Settlement to Civil War*, Homewood, Illinois: Irwin.
Sheth, Jagdish N., Gardner, D. M. and Garrett, D. (1988) *Marketing Theory: Evolution and Evaluation*, New York: Wiley and Sons.
Smith, Ruth Ann, and Lux, David S. (1993) 'Historical method in consumer research: developing causal explanations of the change', *Journal of Consumer Research* 19, March: 595–610.
Tedlow, Richard (1990) *New and Improved: The Story of Mass Marketing in America*, New York: Basic Books.

II THE THEORETICAL FOUNDATIONS

3

THE ECONOMICS BASIS OF MARKETING

Edward K. Chung and Roger M. Heeler

INTRODUCTION

If we want economic development in freedom and responsibility, we have to build it on the development of marketing.

(Drucker 1958: 259)

This chapter examines the relationship between marketing and economics. Since this is an Encyclopedia of marketing the approach will be to examine how economics interacts with the key functions of marketing, rather than the other way round. We shall explore some of the origins and central concepts of marketing thought, and their relationship with the older discipline of economics. Armed with this knowledge, we then examine how marketing works in unison with economics. Other chapters address in detail the major elements of marketing. Consequently, the following discussion offers but a necessarily brief look at important marketing concepts.

The economics foundation of marketing

The German Historical School of Economics provided much of the philosophical foundation of the discipline of marketing. Both Harvard and the University of Wisconsin, considered two of the original centres of influence in the development of marketing thought in the USA, built their marketing departments around German-trained economists (Jones and Monieson 1990). This so-called Historical School was concerned with solving real economic problems and its 'practitioner' perspective still exerts major influence on marketing scholarship today. As Bartels (1988: 186) remarks, 'economic theory has provided more concepts for the development of marketing thought than has any other social discipline'. Indeed, particularly since early marketing scholars were essentially economists, marketing was for a long time held as a branch of

47

Table 1   Economics, utilities and marketing

	Fundamental economic problems	
	Production	Distribution
Manufacturing	Form	XXX
Marketing	XXX	Time, place, possession

economics (Bartels 1988). Around the turn of the century, when the first marketing courses began to appear on American university campuses, the majority of these courses were based on the study of economics (Ferrell et al. 1991).

Inasmuch as economics 'is the study of how men and society choose ... to employ scarce production resources to produce various commodities over time and distribute them for consumption' (Samuelson 1961: 6), it is chiefly concerned with two fundamental problems: production and distribution. Where does marketing come in? According to McCarthy and Shapiro (1983), customer satisfaction is premised on four kinds of economic utilities – form, time, place and possession. Marketing provides the latter three kinds of utilities, while form utility falls into the domain of manufacturing. As depicted in Table 1, it is easy to see the role that marketing plays in addressing economic problems.

Marketing as exchange

Whereas economics emphasizes resource allocation in determining production and distribution, marketing focuses on the process of exchange which underlies this allocation (Houston and Gassenheimer 1987). Indeed, exchange has been offered as 'the defining concept underlying marketing' (Kotler and Turner 1993: 7, among others).

In a market economy, individuals enjoy a freedom to choose whom they will buy from and sell to. There is thus an exchange process for which marketing, with its emphasis on customer wants and needs, is the primary conduit. While Bagozzi (1975) identifies various kinds of exchange, he acknowledges that the 'utilitarian' or economic exchange is implicit in much of marketing literature. Underlying this concept of exchange is the idea of the 'economic man'.

Central to this notion of the 'economic man' is full and complete information, which a person uses in a rational manner to assess his or her choices and make a decision accordingly (Halbert 1964). This rational, economic being has been, for example, the predominant perspective in consumer behaviour studies until quite recently (Mittelstaedt 1990) when psychological and sociological concepts began to take hold.

In an exchange relationship, it is commonly assumed in marketing that the producer seeks to maximize profits (Anderson 1982) while the consumer seeks

Table 2 Contrasting economics and marketing

	Marketing	*Economics*
Factors of production	Little attention	Beginning point
Goals	Meet needs	Allocate resources
Success criteria	Marketers' needs met	Efficiency and fairness in allocation
Desired form of competition	Monopolistic competition	Perfect competition
Unit of analysis	Exchange	Aggregation of buyers and sellers

Source: Houston and Gassenheimer (1987)

to maximize utilities (Houston and Gassenheimer 1987). Maximization, be it profits or utilities, is of course a widely recognized economics concept. Enabling this maximization to take place is specialization, as manifested in division of labour, which has greatly affected marketing thinking (Bartels 1988). An obvious example of this is the study of marketing channels which regularly presupposes specialization of distributive functions.

Summary

Marketing owes much of its heritage to economics, and indeed emerged less than a century ago basically as *applied* economics. To this day, marketers still borrow heavily from economics in formulating their own theories and applications. Fundamental to the study of marketing are such economics-based concepts as exchange, profit maximization, utilities, specialization, the economic man and rationality.

To borrow and build upon concepts from economics, however, does not mean copying them. Table 2, adapted from Houston and Gassenheimer (1987), provides a summary of some of the contrasting features between the two disciplines.

We shall now turn to more specific areas within the marketing discipline, where the contrast depicted in Table 2 will become clearer. Inasmuch as the consumer is often the focal point of marketing endeavours, we shall next consider how economics has influenced the study of consumer behaviour.

THE CONSUMER

Positive economics can be used to analyze any form of known consumer behavior no matter how immoral, misguided or chauvinistic it may seem to be to the person conducting the analysis

(Lipsey 1966: 202)

49

As we mentioned earlier, the study of consumer behaviour was highly economics-based until recently. According to Bennett and Kassarjian (1972: 11), 'the economic theory of consumer behavior is one of the most completely refined bodies of theory in the social sciences'. Indeed, to the extent that what consumers choose to buy and what producers choose to sell reflect the economic fundamentals of demand and supply, consumer behaviour is of major concern to economists. Bartels (1988) remarks that the economic concepts of marginal utility, opportunity costs, and rationalism are some of the more popular tools that marketers have borrowed in the study of consumer behaviour. It is to the economic law of diminishing marginal utility that we shall now turn.

Choice is assumed to be universal in the economists' view of the consumer (Bennett and Kassarjian 1972), as reflected in their focus on resource allocation. Lancaster (1979: 7) notes that 'to the economist, individuals are represented in the system by their preferences . . . these preferences are, in fact, the individual's economic *persona*'. In microeconomics, the law of diminishing marginal utility[1] governs consumer choice. Essentially, the law of diminishing marginal utility suggests that an individual's enjoyment of an additional unit of a good diminishes as more and more of that good is consumed. As a result, the individual's total utility increases at a reducing rate as he or she consumes more of the product. Given that individuals are assumed to maximize their utilities (see earlier discussion), and given that an individual's resources (i.e. budget) are limited, the consumer thus faces a quandary. Of the amount of resources at his or her disposal, which goods and how much of each should the person choose?

To solve this question of choice, the economist turns to the concept of indifference curve for help (see, for example, Lancaster 1980). The indifference curve portrays the combinations of goods which give the consumer the same degree of satisfaction, or the same amount of total utility. A series of these curves form the indifference map. Thus, the individual is indifferent as to the different combinations on any particular curve. The reader will perhaps have noticed how indifference maps provide the rationale behind the technique of conjoint analysis so widely used in marketing. Colvin *et al.* (1980) present a useful example of how conjoint analysis can be used to help build an advertising strategy. Green and Wind (1975) provide more details on the technique.

Inherent in this concept of indifference are opportunity costs that an individual must face. By choosing one thing over another, the person foregoes the enjoyment that may be derived from the object not chosen. Only if the opportunity cost associated with one alternative is no greater than the total utility achieved from another alternative would the consumer be in a state of equilibrium – in this case, indifferent.

Economics is, of course, not the only discipline from which consumer researchers have borrowed concepts. Other chapters discuss consumer research, and marketing in general, through the lens of psychology and other related fields. Hence, economics does not provide the ultimate answer to the marketer's questions. But as Bennett and Kassarjian (1972: 11) point out, while the economic theory of consumer behaviour may be incomplete, 'it does make important contributions. We therefore do not wish to be guilty of "throwing out the baby with the bathwater"'. As Bartels (1988) reminds us, it is largely because of Adam Smith's notion that the objective of all economic activity is the satisfaction of consumption that led to marketing's proclamation of the consumer as king (or queen).

MARKETING STRATEGY

> Market segmentation and its counterpart, positioning, must rank as marketing's most important contributions to strategic management.
>
> (Biggadike 1981: 623)

Market segmentation involves identifying subgroups that share common properties within the total market. The objective is to discern viable target markets that the company can profitably enter. Having targeted these market segments, the marketer seeks to establish competitive advantages by positioning (which in many instances means differentiating) the company's products. This process of segmenting, targeting, and positioning represents the 'heart of modern strategic marketing' (Kotler and Turner 1993: 278).

By now, we should not be surprised to find a strong economics underpinning in this crucial area of marketing strategy. As Dickson and Ginter (1987) point out, the economics theory of monopolistic competition is the basis behind market segmentation and product differentiation. As we saw in Table 2, page 49, marketers are particularly concerned with achieving monopolistic competition. Indeed, the economics of segmented pricing provides much of the rationale behind the idea that the marketplace consists of various segments which can be appealed to differently. Essentially, in recognizing the existence of multiple segments and attempting to position its offerings accordingly, the marketer is in the process of creating what may be seen as 'mini-monopolies'. Lipsey (1966: 336) notes that in this scenario, 'the short-run equilibrium of the firm is exactly the same as that of a monopolist' – a scenario achieved by product differentiation, which involves constructing a less elastic demand curve for the firm's product. The theory of monopolistic competition predicts that more non-price competition will take place in industries characterized by monopolistic competition. Of course, non-price competition (as manifested in product differentiation) is arguably the bread and butter of marketers.

Industrial organization (IO) economists have also extensively investigated this approach to strategy. For example, Porter suggests that a firm's success depends on attaining sustainable competitive advantages, and these latter result 'from a firm's ability to perform the required activities at a collectively lower cost than rivals, or perform some activities in unique ways that create buyer value and hence allow the firm to command a premium price' (1991: 102). This is the essence of Porter's 'generic' strategies of low-cost versus differentiation, which

Table 3   Strategy and economics

Theory of monopolistic competition	
Economics	*Marketing*
Different demand functions	Market segmentation
Less elastic demand curve	Product positioning
Non-price competition	Differentiation
Sustainable competitive advantage	Market orientation
Performance	

have had considerable impact on the study of marketing strategies (e.g. see Day and Wensley 1988). This IO concept of sustainable competitive advantage is also behind marketing researchers' recent interest in the study of 'market orientation' (e.g. see Narver and Slater 1990) as a key conduit to creating superior value for customers.

Table 3 provides a synopsis of how the theory of monopolistic competition has impacted the study of marketing strategy. On the left are ideas borrowed from micro- and IO economics. On the right are marketing's version of these ideas. The final objective is to achieve superior performance.

Monopolistic competition, however, is not the only economics theory that has affected the study of marketing strategy. For example, Kerin *et al.* (1992), attempting to integrate the literature on first-mover advantage, note that marketers have been affected by the theoretical and analytical literature in IO economics, particularly in viewing a first-mover's ability to create entry barriers. Lambkin and Day (1989), seeking to develop a framework for understanding market evolution, argue that three 'forces' – the demand system, supply system, and resource environment – impact the way markets evolve. The economics concepts of complementary and substitute goods play a large role in both the demand and supply systems. Furthermore, Eliashberg and Chatterjee (1985) state that economists, investigating competition under various market structures – perfect competition, monopolistic competition, oligopoly – are traditionally concerned with the efficiencies of structures. On the other hand, marketers focus more on the conduct of the competitors. The similarity between this and IO economics' structure-conduct-performance paradigm is unmistakable. On a more fundamental level, moreover, the microeconomics assumption of profit maximization is the premise for much of the normative literature on marketing management (Anderson 1982).

At a more operational (or 'management') level, marketing is also heavily influenced by economics in the organization of marketing activities. Micro-economics has been most useful in conceptualizing the role of marketing management (Webster 1992). Transaction cost analysis (also see section on Place, page 57) can be a useful theoretical tool for evaluating whether certain marketing activities should be undertaken internally or by third parties. Ruekert *et al.* (1985) have used transaction cost analysis as their basic framework from which to build a contingency theory of marketing organization. Such an approach, for instance, has been found useful in studying the evolution of the marketing function in the developing economy of China (Heeler *et al.* 1992). Even as Webster (1992) notes that the recent shift from a transaction to a relationship focus requires marketers to go beyond the microeconomics paradigm and place increasing emphasis on relationship management, the fact that marketing is in essence an economic activity underscores the importance of economics concepts to any analysis of marketing organization.

Critical to the success of any strategy is information. Drucker's (1958) idea of entrepreneurial judo as a strategic management concept, for example, necessitates extensive information gathering and processing. And market intelligence takes a central role in promoting a 'market orientation' in an organization (e.g. Narver and Slater 1990). Thus, while economists generally assume a world of perfect information, marketers seek to actualize this assumption by engaging in market research.

PRODUCT

Individuals are interested in goods not for their own sake but because of the characteristics they possess.

(Lancaster 1979: 17)

Lancaster's 'Characteristics Approach' to analysing goods as a bundle of attributes was first published in 1966 in the *Journal of Political Economy*, and has been the cornerstone of marketing's application of multiattribute choice models (Horsky and Sen 1980). A product therefore goes beyond its physical properties and is seen as a collection of characteristics, each being preferred in varying degrees by different individual consumers. Thus, individuals react differently to the same product not because of their different perceptions of the product's properties, but because they have different preferences with respect to the bundle of attributes that the product represents.

In marketing, a product[2] can be seen as 'the needs–satisfying offering of the firm' (McCarthy and Shapiro 1983: 310). In other words, it is not so much how the product is manufactured or what other technical properties the product has, but rather how it can best satisfy the customer's needs that matters. Since, as proposed by Lancaster, a product has many different attributes, the same product is therefore capable of satisfying the different needs of various consumers.

This idea of 'bundle of attributes' is also related to the marketing concept of product (and brand) positioning. As McCarthy and Shapiro have noted, positioning usually focuses on specific product features, which is only possible if there are multiple attributes. Brand concept management (Park *et al.* 1986), a framework concerned with selecting, implementing, and controlling a brand's image over time, largely hinges on a product's ability to satisfy a multitude of needs among consumers.

Another major contribution of economics is the discipline's classification of goods into substitutes and complements. For example, marketers have been interested in the effects on a product's purchase patterns caused by stimulating demand for its complement (e.g. see Walters 1991). And as Howard (1965) notes, the concepts of substitutes and complements are also useful in planning the addition or deletion of brands.

Insofar as a marketer's job is to try to create monopolies, new product introduction takes on increasing importance as competitive products begin breaking down the differentiation walls that set the existing product apart. Because of this, marketing researchers have devoted much energy to the study of new product introduction. Pretest marketing models are among the heavily researched phenomena (for a detailed discussion, see Shocker and Hall 1986).

In the area of adoption and diffusion, marketers and economists have also been active in their research, though at different levels of analysis (Gatignon and Robertson 1989). While marketers have focused their attention mainly at the consumer level, economists have studied the phenomenon at the organizational level. Reviewing the economics literature on the subject, Gatignon and Robertson suggest that adoption of innovations, for example, may be a way to create entry barriers, and may be particularly attractive for firms in highly concentrated industries. The level of price competition is also posited by Gatignon and Robertson to have a negative impact on adoption.

PRICE

Any business transaction in our modern economy can be thought of as an exchange of money – the money being the Price – for Something. . . . The nature and extent of this Something will determine the amount of money to be exchanged.

(McCarthy and Shapiro 1983: 584)

To the economist, price is set by the market forces of demand and supply in a world of perfect competition. Indeed, the point where demand meets supply (and where marginal costs equal marginal revenues) is the 'equilibrium', where profit maximization is to be found. But as Samuelson (1961) has noted, this is applicable only in the presence of perfect competition and for certain kinds of standardized commodity such as wheat. He also indicates, however, that although other forces (e.g. imperfect competition, government interference) can and do affect prices, they do so by working through their effects on demand and supply. The forces of demand and supply not only govern market prices, but also are important determinants of quantity discounts and surcharges, which are common pricing tools in marketing. Quantity discounts appear to be intuitively appropriate, particularly in view of the conventional downward-sloping demand curve. Heeler (1989) has demonstrated that surcharges also fall into the realms of economics theory. In addition, as we shall see, imperfect information on the part of the consumer may further contribute to the existence of surcharges. Nagle points out that although economics models are abstractions and do not prescribe specific pricing actions, 'the marketer's task [of pricing] should prove less strenuous when he stands on a sound foundation of economic theory' (1984: S4). He offers three general areas of economics theory that are particularly useful in the study of pricing: the economics of information, the economics of spatial competition, and the economics of segmented pricing.

The economics of information

Pricing one's products based on buyers' perceptions of the products' values is called perceived-value pricing (Kotler and Turner 1993). In this case, price reflects value as perceived by customers. A problem may arise when, because of insufficient or inaccurate information, customers may over- or under-evaluate the value of a product. This phenomenon, for example, is quite common in the used automobile market where consumers substantially discount the value of a used car because they are unsure as to the car's condition. A related, though conceptually distinct, concept is the 'price-quality effect',[3] which suggests that lacking perfect information, consumers may infer higher quality to higher-priced products. Thus, Menon and Varadarajan (1992) suggest that this effect may cause marketers to place greater faith in information that has been gathered at high cost.

This asymmetry of information has important implications for marketing, especially when it comes to branding. A brand name is often used by consumers as the major indicator of product quality (McCarthy and Shapiro 1983). Because 'consumers should pay more of a premium for a high-quality brand' (Nagle 1984: S8), marketers who are able to create and sustain a high-quality image for their brands would reap the benefits.

In addition to asymmetrical information, economists have studied how consumers acquire information. Recognizing that 'perfect information' is not realistic in the real world, we may consider that price sensitivity is determined not so much by the actual number of competitive products (or substitutes) in the market, but by how many of these the consumer is aware. Because humans are limited in their cognitive abilities, we often do not make decisions in a systematic, comprehensive manner. This is the essence of the concept of 'bounded rationality' (see e.g. Simon 1976). As Drummond (1992: 2) puts it: 'Choice is based on intelligent guess work, the aim being to find something that "will do"'. At first glance, this may appear to contradict the basic economics assumption of rationality. But as Samuelson so succinctly points out, the 'economic man' need not be a perfect processor of limitless information, that 'he can even make most of his decisions unconsciously or out of habit ... as long as he is fairly consistent in his tastes and actions' (1961: 449).

Marketers, too, recognize that consumers do not necessarily consider (or are even aware of) all the alternatives 'out there'. The distinction between 'choice set', 'consideration set', and 'total set' of alternative products (e.g. Kotler and Turner 1993: 193) is an example of the application of the above discussion on imperfect information acquisition.

Also as a result of imperfect information, some economists posit that the fewer alternatives the consumers are aware of, the less price sensitive they will be. This has important implications for the marketer, particularly with respect to whether advertising promotes or retards price sensitivity, and consequently, consumer welfare (Kanetkar *et al.* 1992).

The economics of spatial competition

Just as marketers use spatial representations (e.g. multidimensional scaling) to analyse product positioning, economists have been using spatial competition models to study the effects of product variety on price competition since the late 1920s. Nagle (1984) suggests that these two approaches can be integrated, so that marketers may investigate not only positioning and product entry to maximize market potential, but also where (relative to the competition) to introduce the product so as to minimize potential competition from later entrants.

The economics of segmented pricing

Segmented pricing involves charging different prices to different groups of customers. Practices such as tie-ins, metering, and product bundling are examples of segmented pricing. Segmented pricing can also be seen as price discrimination (Lipsey 1966), which is a standard topic in most intermediate economics textbooks. Segmented pricing is possible because different consumers exhibit different demand elasticities for the product in question. In order for the firm successfully to implement segmented pricing, then, it would have to know, *a priori*, the factors that affect the price elasticity of different consumers. This, however, may not be a feasible task. One of the (more practical) ways to overcome this problem is by way of product bundling (Narashimhan 1984). An increasing number of companies are using discriminatory pricing, partly as a result of deregulation (Kotler and Turner 1993: 526).[4] The topic is just as popular in marketing textbooks as it is in economics texts.[5]

The contributions made by microeconomics notwithstanding, we must be cognizant of the fact that economic theory does not always fully explain human reactions towards the price element. Not satisfied with standard economics theory of the consumer, which 'omit virtually all marketing variables except price and product characteristics', Thaler (1985: 200) uses Kahneman and Tversky's (1979) 'prospect theory' as a basis to develop a new model of consumer behaviour that incorporates cognitive psychology and microeconomics. Prospect theory is an alternative to classical economic utility theory, and it posits that economic agents make choices relative to a neutral outcome or a 'frame'. People are more averse to losses than to gains, and value is judged as a proportional gain or loss rather than an absolute amount. In other words, relative to the reference point, losses are perceived as larger than gains that are equal in absolute terms.[6] Thaler thus derives his theory of transaction utility, stating that consumers gain utility not just from consumption, but also from the 'transaction' of acquiring the product, especially at a bargain price. The amount of this latter utility is directly related to the difference between the perceived special or regular prices.

It is worth mentioning that a vast literature exists on the subject of promotional discounts, in terms of both discounts to the trade (e.g. Blattberg and Levin 1987) and to the consumer (e.g. Krishna *et al.* 1991). Much of this literature has its roots in economic analysis, though other social sciences such as psychology have begun to exert increasing influence. The interested reader is encouraged to refer to the cited references for a more detailed discussion.

A discourse on the effects of economics on pricing would not be adequate without some coverage on the fundamental concept of price elasticity. Simply put, price elasticity of demand measures the impact that price changes have on demand. Demand is elastic if the ratio of change in demand to change in price is greater than one, meaning demand is responsive to price changes. It is inelastic if the ratio is less than one, signalling that price changes have limited impact on demand. For the marketer, the ability to identify (and market to) segments that are inelastic may pose profitable opportunities. In the area of adoption and diffusion, for example, it has long been posited that early adopters are relatively price inelastic (see e.g. Parker 1992 for a discussion). The interested reader is also encouraged to examine the related concepts of income elasticity and cross-price elasticity, which can be found in most economics textbooks. These concepts have significant implications for the marketer (e.g. see Bemmaor and Mouchoux 1991; Walters 1991).

PLACE

From the point of view of the economic system, the basic role of marketing intermediaries is to transform the heterogeneous supplies found in nature into assortments of goods that people want to buy.

(Kotler and Turner 1993: 541)

Goods and services in and of themselves are of limited value or meaning. The production of goods, unless somehow channelled into the hands of consumers for consumption, becomes a futile endeavour. Lipsey (1966) indicates that production and consumption are two of the fundamental problems facing economists. There is, of course, an intervening process whereby the goods produced are distributed to those who want the goods. Without a distribution system, consumers would have to travel to the orchards of the Pacific Northwest to get their apples, to the Charente region of France to get their cognac, and so on. The world of consumption would not be an overly efficient place indeed. As

57

Heilbroner (1971) has observed, the production problem and the distribution problem are two basic issues that society must address to ensure the economic survival of humans. After all, the laws of demand and supply simply would not work unless economic goods are made available.

The study of marketing, naturally, necessitates an understanding of the construct of market. We may think of a market as a place where people meet to buy and sell their products. In this everyday usage of the term, images of the farmer's market or the stock market come to mind. But market can also be seen as an economic process that facilitates the exchange of goods and services (Samli and Bahn 1992). Exchange, as we have seen, is the fundamental unit of analysis in marketing; the interaction of demand and supply is the basis of the economic process. Thus it is not enough that manufacturers produce and consumers consume. The intermediate process of bringing the two together is also of primary importance. Hence, as Jones and Monieson (1990) point out, the original scholars of marketing were basically concerned with problems of distribution.

Why do firms come together in the formation of a distribution channel? The literature on marketing channels can be divided into the design and management streams. In the design stream, the focus is on the establishment and organization of distribution channels; issues such as structure are important considerations. Should the manufacturer handle its own distribution, for instance? Or should it enlist the services of intermediaries? In this vein, vertical integration is one of those lingering topics that have been subject to much analysis by management researchers. In the management stream, the emphasis is on how best to manage a channel once it is in place; extensive investigation has been made in the topics of conflict resolution, the use of power, and so on (e.g. see Rangan et al. 1992 for a detailed discussion). The impact of economics theory would appear to be strongest on the design stream, and it is to this aspect of marketing channels that we shall now turn.

The economics idea of specialization, with its manifestation in division of labour, has greatly affected marketing thinking; the impact is particularly obvious in the area of marketing channels. Alderson (1967) suggests that attempts at maximization of productivity leads to specialization, and in turn various marketing agencies work together to form a channel for a given product. This channel, then, facilitates the exchange or flow of resources within an interorganizational network (Ghoshal and Bartlett 1990). It is to the benefit of channel members, in the interest of profit maximization, to act as a unit (Mallen 1973).

To the extent that exchange, or transaction, is the basic unit of analysis, efficient execution of this transaction requires that firms internalize those activities of exchange that they themselves can perform at a lower cost, and rely on other firms for those activities that others can provide more inexpensively. Under the transaction cost approach (TCA), minimization of transaction costs drives individual firms to participate in a channel of distribution (Williamson

1981). Essentially, TCA suggests that asset specificity and uncertainty are the two main factors guiding the choice between integrated (company-owned) or market (independent) channels. Asset specificity refers to production and distribution, as well as governance, costs. When asset specificity is high, a vertically integrated channel system may be called for. The reverse would be true when asset specificity is low. The relevance of asset specificity increases as the level of uncertainty goes up. At very low levels of uncertainty, vertical integration would not be a reasonable option, thus obviating the need to consider asset specificity at all. As observed by Rangan *et al.* (1992), the transaction cost approach is one of the most popular theories applied to the study of marketing channels. It is interesting to note, however, that even though Williamson is an economist by trade, the TCA, despite its basically economics orientation, was conceived because of Williamson's dissatisfaction with the more 'conventional' ability of economics traditions (e.g. microeconomics theory, IO economics) to address real world problems (see Williamson 1975: 248–53).

We observed earlier that economics takes as its primary interest the efficient allocation of resources (see Table 2, page 49). Insofar as the forces of demand and supply purport to lead to economic prosperity for all, questions have been raised as to the social desirability and efficiency of marketing in general, and channels in particular. This efficiency aspect, too, has been under the scrutiny of marketing scholars (e.g. see Moyer and Hutt 1978: 145–54 for a more detailed discussion). Channel 'performance', as a result, has been evaluated primarily on the basis of productivity.[7]

PROMOTION

The further a man [sic] is removed from physical need the more open he is to persuasion – or management – as to what he buys. This is, perhaps, the most important consequence for economics of increasing affluence.

(Galbraith 1972: 18)

As McCarthy, who originally coined the 'four Ps', explains, promotion is 'concerned with telling the target market about the "right" product' (McCarthy and Shapiro 1983: 43). He also indicates, however, that promotion goes beyond merely presenting information. In fact, the objective of presenting this information is 'to influence attitudes and behavior' (ibid.: 495). Thus, promotion seeks both to inform and to influence. Marketing researchers have been interested in the effectiveness of advertising and promotions, reach and frequency studies, media selection and scheduling algorithms, and many other aspects of promotion.[8] Much of this research, however, takes on a psychology bent. Indeed, as we have noticed earlier, the study of consumer behaviour has shifted away from an economics basis to a more sociological, psychological perspective. It is therefore not surprising that the 'economic man' does not much come into play in promotion decisions.

Nevertheless, this is not to say that economics does not have its impact on the topic. As we shall see, economists have written quite extensively about the efficacy of advertising.[9] It is useful at this point to address how economics and marketing converge on the information and influence functions of promotion.

Promotion as information

Economists, being concerned with the efficient allocation of resources, are understandably anxious as to the potentially wasteful practice of advertising. In Canada alone, advertising expenditure exceeded $10 billion in 1990. That was almost $400 for every woman, man, and child in the country! In the USA and other more populous nations, the figures would be that much more staggering. Defenders of expenditures on promotion (and advertising in general) argue that it serves a vital informational role. By conveying information to the consumer, advertising makes complete the economist's postulate of perfect knowledge (Backman 1968). Because there is an abundance of products in the marketplace, and since each product is a 'bundle of attributes', consumers cannot reasonably expect to have complete information with which to make purchase decisions. Producers, by promoting their products and services, provide valuable information to the consumers.

Disagreements with this view are mainly of two related varieties. First, while some forms of advertising (e.g. classified ads and department store displays) do primarily serve to convey information, much of it is to manage demand to 'insure that people buy what is produced' (Galbraith 1972: 19). The latter does not add to the economic well-being of the population, and is thus considered economic waste. Second, while acknowledging the information component of advertising, Grabowski (1974) questions the usefulness of this information. He argues that the information which producers offer may not be what is needed for consumers to make their decisions in a 'socially optimal' fashion, because manufacturers are naturally inclined to bias the information in their favour. As such, this information is neither adequate nor complete.

Promotion as influence

Regardless of advertising's effects on society's economic well-being, it plays a key role in a producer's efforts of product differentiation in a monopolistically competitive market. Comanor and Wilson (1974), for instance, report that their analysis of 36 industries shows that advertising has a substantially greater impact on demand than does relative prices. Some leading economists, such as Samuelson and Galbraith, contend that product differentiation is largely a result of advertising, a 'distortion' of consumer demand.

Galbraith (1975) sees advertising as a form of 'want creation'. In economics terms, this involves an attempt 'to shift the demand curve of the individual firm at the expense of others, or to change its shape by increasing the degree of product differentiation' (p. 30). To the extent that advertisers seek to influence consumers to buy their products instead of their competitors', this is exactly the goal. Again, questions arise as to whether this contributes to economic well-being of society. Galbraith is perhaps one of the most noted critics of advertising. He suggests that wants that are not inherent in the individual but are created by the production process are inferior, and their satisfaction is not of any economic urgency (1975). Benton (1987) agrees, noting that increased levels of consumption are not accompanied by corresponding increases in consumers' quality of life. In fact, he argues that since 'mass production requires mass consumption for ultimate success' (p. 246), industrialization has brought about a culture of consumption that has degraded human life. Advertising, being a major calibre weapon in the producer's arsenal, is thus a leading culprit of this degradation.

INTERNATIONAL MARKETING

Effective marketing not only improves the life-style and well-being of people in a specific economy, it also upgrades world markets; after all, a developed country's best customer is another developed country.

(Cateora 1993: 221)

In reviewing the relationship between economics and marketing in the context of international marketing, it is useful to delineate a macro and a micro level of analysis. Some elaboration may be in order here. By macro we mean the ways marketing operates in a macroeconomics sense; how, for instance, marketing contributes to the economic development of a nation. By micro we refer to the more conventional microeconomics issues facing the marketer; how best to meet the needs and wants of consumers, for example. We shall briefly look at each of these levels of analysis.

Macro issues

Cateora's quote (above) points out marketing's contributions from a macro-economics standpoint. In short, effective marketing facilitates economic growth. Against this backdrop, Heeler et al. (1992) have investigated the state of evolution of the organization of marketing in China. They note that (p. 252) 'a formal bureaucratic approach to marketing exists . . . (but) will certainly change as the Chinese economy evolves towards a market orientation'. But overall, while scholars such as Drucker (1958) have championed the important role of marketing in economic development, Douglas and Craig (1992: 296) lament that 'little attention has been devoted to examining the dynamics of market growth and development within different regions or worldwide'.

Micro issues

Perhaps because of more immediate applications useful to the marketing practitioner, research in international marketing has emphasized a micro-economics orientation. More precisely, research has focused on the options available to the firm. Thus, Douglas and Craig (1992) offer three key phases of global marketing strategy development: market entry, local market expansion and global rationalization. That these phases are evolutionary stages of strategy for the firm brings us back to the theories of supply and demand, and of the law of diminishing marginal utility as a basic element in the mechanism of choice (i.e. microeconomics concerns).

As we have seen, transaction cost theory has established increasing potency in shaping marketing thought. It is therefore not surprising when Rugman and Verbeke (1992) offer the transaction cost approach as an effective means of analysing international marketing strategy. They offer three major elements that comprise the transaction cost theory of international enterprise – firm-specific advantages, country-specific advantages, and internalization advantages – and demonstrate how an analysis of these elements can help evaluate strategy. For example, a firm facing 'host country-specific advantages' and 'location bound firm-specific advantages' may find the 'multinational' type of firm more appropriate than, say, the 'global' firm.

There are also other ways economics theories have impacted international marketing thought. Levitt's (1983) argument for globalization is a case in point. According to Levitt, because technology is driving the world to a point of convergence of wants, it behoves the global firm to become standardized in its offerings and marketing practices. By doing so, the firm is able to offer products of an acceptable quality at a much lower cost than competition, on account of greater economies of scale. As he remarks (p. 102), 'two vectors shape the world – technology and globalization. The first helps determine human preference; the second, economic realities'.[10]

It should be obvious that much of what concerns the domestic marketer also affects the international marketer. The problems of a broader international environment notwithstanding, the fundamental marketing principles of target marketing and the marketing mix remain cornerstones of the discipline. Cateora (1993: 9) puts it well when he writes: 'Marketing concepts, processes, and principles are universally applicable ... (but) the difficulties created by different environments are the international marketer's primary concern'.

SUMMARY

A cross-fertilization of ideas and efforts between economists and marketers will undoubtedly strengthen the scientific foundation of marketing.

(Horsky and Sen 1980: S8)

Complete volumes can be written on the many subjects that we have covered.

For the sake of our limited cognitive abilities, not to say the health of the hard disk on our PCs, we have endeavoured but a superficial level of analysis of the relationship between marketing and economics. The reference list, however, is sufficiently broad and comprehensive that the inquisitive reader may easily explore any of the topics in much greater detail. To the extent that we have raised the reader's level of consciousness as to the important lessons and concepts marketers can learn from economists, and thus enabled the reader, however superficially, to 'return to basics', this chapter has served its purpose.

We have explored the economics foundations of our discipline, relating that to the concept of exchange which is so central to the study of marketing. In the area of consumer behaviour, we have seen how the economics perspective has dominated consumer research until relatively recently. The concept of utilities, for example, is still very much a pivotal area of analysis, as is the idea that the consumer is sovereign. Another important way that economics has shaped marketing thinking is illustrated by the theory of monopolistic competition and its impact on the key marketing concepts of segmentation and differentiation. We have also examined how economics theorists have affected research and practice in various elements of the marketing mix. In addition to traditional microeconomics, we have also seen how IO economics have influenced marketing thought, particularly in the area of marketing strategy. Transaction cost theory, moreover, has become a dominant factor in the analysis of marketing channels. We would again refer the reader to Table 2, page 49, for a snapshot of some of the important contrasts between economics and marketing.

We have not investigated the impact of economics on industrial marketing. There are also other areas of convergence which we have not reviewed. This is not because we feel the relationship between economics and marketing is any less significant in those areas, but because we will be doing economics theories an even greater disservice if we attempted to be all-encompassing.

NOTES

1 Some economists choose to call it a 'principle', others a 'hypothesis'. For our purpose, we shall refer to it as 'law', following Samuelson (1961: 439).
2 Though we use the term 'product' here, the discussion is also largely relevant for services. For the sake of parsimony, we will not make the distinction between the two. Zeithaml et al. (1985) and Bitner and Zeithaml (1987) provide interesting discussions on the issues facing the service marketer.
3 Scitovsky (1944) is considered the origin of the now familiar 'price-quality' effect. Interested readers are encouraged to refer to that article.
4 It should be noted, however, that discriminatory pricing, as used in our present context, is not necessarily illegal even for regulated industries. Examples abound. For instance, airlines have been charging different fares for the same class for years and automobile manufacturers have long been offering option packages as a form of product bundling.
5 We have also seen how segmented pricing contributes to the fundamental concept of market segmentation. See page 56.

6 Winer (1988) offers a good discussion of prospect theory in the context of 'reference price'.
7 Goldman (1992) suggests that the use of productivity measurements as a proxy for channel performance may not be valid in all situations, especially in cross-cultural analyses. Whether this is so is beyond the scope of this chapter. Suffice it to say that the economics perspective of efficient allocation has indeed been the dominant paradigm in channel evaluation.
8 Lilien and Kotler (1983: ch. 14) gives a comprehensive coverage of the various decision models affecting this topic.
9 Economists generally group what marketers call promotion under the banner of advertising. Definitions may be slightly different, but the arguments still apply.
10 Levitt's paper is shown here only as an example of how economics theory affects thinking in marketing. There are others who dispute Levitt's claims that the world is homogenizing and that standardization is good. For one such counter position, the reader may wish to refer to Douglas and Wind (1987).

REFERENCES

Alderson, Wroe (1967) 'Factors governing the development of marketing channels', in Bruce E. Mallen (ed.) *The Marketing Channel: A Conceptual Viewpoint*, New York: John Wiley & Sons.

Anderson, Paul A. (1982) 'Marketing, strategic planning, and the theory of the firm', *Journal of Marketing* 46, Spring: 15–26.

Backman, Jules (1968) 'Is advertising wasteful?' *Journal of Marketing* 32 (1) January: 2–8.

Bagozzi, Richard P. (1975) 'Marketing as exchange', *Journal of Marketing* 39, October: 32–9.

Bartels, Robert (1988) *The History of Marketing Thought*, 3rd edn, Columbus, OH: Publishing Horizons.

Bemmaor, Albert C. and Mouchoux, Dominique (1991) 'Measuring the short-term effect of in-store promotion and retail advertising on brand sales: a factorial experiment', *Journal of Marketing Research* 28, May: 202–14.

Bennett, Peter D. and Kassarjian, Harold H. (1972) *Consumer Behavior*, Englewood Cliffs, NJ: Prentice-Hall.

Benton, Jr, Raymond (1987) 'Work, consumption, and the joyless consumer', in A. Fuat Firat, Nikhilesh Dholakia, and Richard P. Bagozzi (eds) *Philosophical and Radical Thought in Marketing*, Lexington, MA: Lexington Books.

Biggadike, E. Ralph (1981) 'The contributions of marketing to strategic management', *Academy of Management Review* 6 (4): 621–32.

Bitner, Mary J. and Zeithaml, Valarie A. (1987) 'Fundamentals in services marketing', in Carol Sueprenant (ed.) *Add Value to Your Service*, Chicago: American Marketing Association.

Blattberg, Robert C. and Levin, Alan (1987) 'Modelling the effectiveness and profitability of trade promotions', *Marketing Science* 6 (2): 124–46.

Cateora, Philip R. (1993) *International Marketing*, 8th edn, Homewood, IL: Irwin.

Colvin, Michael, Heeler, Roger and Thorpe, Jim (1980) 'Developing international advertising strategy', *Journal of Marketing* 44, Fall: 73–9.

Comanor, William S. and Wilson, Thomas A. (1974) 'Advertising and the distribution of consumer demand', in S.F. Divita (ed.) *Advertising and the Public Interest*, Chicago: American Marketing Association.

Day, George S. and Wensley, Robin (1988) 'Assessing advantage: a framework for diagnosing competitive superiority', *Journal of Marketing* 52, April: 1–20.

Dickson, Peter R. and Ginter, James L. (1987) 'Market segmentation, product differentiation, and marketing strategy', *Journal of Marketing* 51, April: 1–10.

Douglas, Susan P. and Wind, Yoram (1987) 'The myth of globalization', *Columbia Journal of World Business*, Winter: 19–29.

Douglas, Susan P. and Craig, C. Samuel (1992) 'Advances in international marketing', *International Journal of Research in Marketing* 9: 291–318.

Drucker, Peter F. (1958) 'Marketing and economic development', *Journal of Marketing* 22, January: 252–9.

Drucker, Peter F. (1985) 'Entrepreneurial strategies', *California Management Review* 27 (2): 9–25.

Drummond, Helga (1992) 'Another fine mess: time for quality in decision-making', *Journal of General Management* 18 (1): 1–14.

Eliashberg, Jehoshua and Chatterjee, Rabikar (1985) 'Analytical models of competition with implications for marketing: issues, findings, and outlook', *Journal of Marketing Research* 22, August: 237–61.

Ferrell, Barbara, Perreca-Smith, Louise and Glascoff, David W. (1991) 'Exchange, expectations, and the definition of marketing', in T.C. Childers, S.B. MacKenzie, T.W. Leigh, S. Skinner, J.G. Lynch Jr, S. Heckler, H. Gatignon, R.P. Fisk and J.L. Graham (eds) *1991 AMA Winter Educators' Conference: Marketing Theory and Applications, Vol.2*, Chicago: American Marketing Association.

Galbraith, John Kenneth (1972) 'The management of specific demand', in Norman Kangun (ed.) *Society and Marketing: An Unconventional View*, New York: Harper and Row.

Galbraith, John Kenneth (1975) 'The dependence effect', in Ross Lawrence Goble and Roy T. Shaw (eds) *Controversy and Dialog in Marketing*, Englewood Cliffs, NJ: Prentice-Hall.

Gatignon, Hubert and Robertson, Thomas S. (1989) 'Technology diffusion: an empirical test of competitive effects', *Journal of Marketing* 53, January: 35–49.

Ghoshal, Sumantra and Bartlett, Christopher A. (1990) 'The multinational corporation as an interorganizational network', *Academy of Management Review* 15 (4): 603–25.

Goldman, Arieh (1992) 'Evaluating the performance of the Japanese distribution system', *Journal of Retailing* 68 (1): 11–39.

Grabowski, Henry G. (1974) 'Advertising and resource allocation – critique', in S.F. Divita (ed.) *Advertising and the Public Interest*, Chicago: American Marketing Association.

Green, Paul E. and Wind, Yoram (1975) 'New way to measure consumers' judgments', *Harvard Business Review* 53, July–August: 107–17.

Halbert, Michael H. (1964) 'The requirements for theory in marketing', in Reavis Cox, Wroe Alderson and Stanley J. Shapiro (eds) *Theory in Marketing*, Homewood, IL: Richard D. Irwin.

Heeler, Roger M. (1989) 'On quantity discounts and surcharges', in G. Avlonitis, N.K. Papavasiliou and A.G. Kouremenos (eds) *Marketing Thought and Practice in the 1990s: XVIII Annual Conference of the European Marketing Academy, Vol. II*, Athens: The Athens School of Economics and Business Science.

Heeler, Roger M., Stewart, Sally, Zhi, Chang, Thomas, Huw D. and Lai, Yu (1992) 'Organization for marketing in contemporary China: using the company's creative spirit to serve society with your whole heart', *Advances in Chinese Industrial Studies* 3: 241–53.

Heilbroner, Robert L. (1971) 'The economic problem', in John R. Wish and Stephen H. Gamble (eds) *Marketing and Social Issues: An Action Reader*, New York: John Wiley & Sons.

Horsky, Dan and Sen, Subrata K. (1980) 'Interfaces between marketing and economics: an overview', *Journal of Business* 53 (3, pt 2): S5–12.

Houston, Franklin S. and Gassenheimer, Jule B. (1987) 'Marketing and exchange', *Journal of Marketing* 51, October: 3–18.

Howard, John A. (1965) *Marketing Theory*, Boston: Allyn and Bacon.

Jones, D.G. Brian and Monieson, David D. (1990) 'Early development of the philosophy of marketing thought', *Journal of Marketing* 54, January: 102–13.

Kahneman, Daniel and Tversky, Amos (1979) 'Prospect theory: an analysis of decision under risk', *Econometrica* 47, March: 263–91.

Kanetkar, Vinay, Weinberg, Charles B. and Weiss, Doyle L. (1992) 'Price sensitivity and television advertising exposures: some empirical findings', *Marketing Science* 11 (4): 359–71.

Kerin, Roger A., Varadarajan, P. Rajan and Peterson, Robert A. (1992) 'First-mover advantage: a synthesis, conceptual framework, and research propositions', *Journal of Marketing* 56, October: 36–52.

Kotler, Philip and Turner, Ronald E. (1993) *Marketing Management: Analysis, Planning, Implementation, and Control*, Canadian 7th edn, Scarborough, ON: Prentice-Hall.

Krishna, Aradhna, Currim, Imran S. and Shoemaker, Robert W. (1991) 'Consumer perceptions of promotional activity', *Journal of Marketing* 55, April: 4–16.

Lambkin, Mary, and Day, George S. (1989) 'Evolutionary processes in competitive markets: beyond the product life cycle', *Journal of Marketing* 53, July: 4–20.

Lancaster, Kelvin J. (1966) 'A new approach to consumer theory', *Journal of Political Economy* 74: 132–57.

Lancaster, Kelvin (1979) *Variety, Equity, and Efficiency*, New York: Columbia University Press.

Lancaster, Kelvin (1980) 'Competition and product variety', *Journal of Business* 53 (3, pt 2): S79–103.

Levitt, Theodore (1983) 'The globalization of markets', *Harvard Business Review*, May–June: 92–102.

Lilien, Gary L. and Kotler, Philip (1983) *Marketing Decision Making: A Model-Building Approach*, New York: Harper and Row.

Lipsey, Richard G. (1966) *An Introduction to Positive Economics*, 2nd edn, London: Weidenfeld and Nicolson.

McCarthy, E. Jerome and Shapiro, Stanley J. (1983) *Basic Marketing*, 3rd Canadian edn, Homewood, IL: Richard D. Irwin.

Mallen, Bruce (1973) 'Conflict and cooperation in marketing channels', in Louis E. Boone and James C. Johnson (eds) *Marketing Channels*, Morristown, NJ: General Learning Press.

Menon, Anil and Varadarajan, P. Rajan (1992) 'A model of marketing knowledge use within firms', *Journal of Marketing* 56, October: 53–71.

Mittelstaedt, Robert A. (1990) 'Economics, psychology, and the literature of the subdiscipline of consumer behavior', *Journal of the Academy of Marketing Science* 18 (4): 303–11.

Moyer, Reed and Hutt, Michael D. (1978) *Macro Marketing*, 2nd edn, Santa Barbara: Wiley/Hamilton.

Nagle, Thomas (1984) 'Economic foundations for pricing', *Journal of Business* 57 (1, pt 2): S3–26.

Narasimhan, Chakravarthi (1984) 'Comments on "Economics Foundations for Pricing"', *Journal of Business* 57 (1, pt 2), S27–34.

Narver, John C. and Slater, Stanley F. (1990) 'The effect of a market orientation on business profitability', *Journal of Marketing* 54, October: 20–35.

Park, C. Whan, Jaworski, Bernard J. and MacInnis, Deborah J. (1986) 'Strategic brand concept-image management', *Journal of Marketing* 50, October: 135–45.

Parker, Philip M. (1992) 'Price elasticity dynamics over the adoption life cycle', *Journal of Marketing Research* 29, August: 358–67.

Porter, Michael E. (1991) 'Towards a dynamic theory of strategy', *Strategic Management Journal* 12: 95–117.

Rangan, V. Kasturi, Menezes, Melvyn A.J. and Maier, E.P. (1992) 'Channel selection for new industrial products: a framework, method, and application', *Journal of Marketing* 56, July: 69–82.

Ruekert, Robert W., Walker, Jr, Orville C. and Roering, Kenneth J. (1985) 'The organization of marketing activities: a contingency theory of structure and performance', *Journal of Marketing* 49, Winter: 13–25.

Rugman, Alan M. and Verbeke, Alain (1992) 'A note on the transnational solution and the transaction cost theory of multinational strategic management', *Journal of International Business Studies* (Fourth Quarter): 761–71.

Samli, A. Coskun and Bahn, Kenneth D. (1992) 'The market phenomenon: an alternative theory and some metatheoretical research considerations', *Journal of the Academy of Marketing Science* 20 (2): 143–53.

Samuelson, Paul A. (1961) *Economics: An Introductory Analysis*, 5th edn, New York: McGraw-Hill.

Scitovsky, T. (1944) 'Some consequences of the habit of judging quality by price', *Review of Economic Studies* 12: 100–5.

Shocker, Allan D. and Hall, William G. (1986) 'Pretest market models: a critical evaluation', *Journal of Product Innovation Management* (3) September: 86–107.

Simon, Herbert A. (1976) *Administrative Behavior*, 3rd edn, New York: The Free Press.

Thaler, Richard (1985) 'Mental accounting and consumer choice', *Marketing Science* 4 (3) Summer: 199–214.

Walters, Rockney G. (1991) 'Assessing the impact of retail price promotions on product substitution, complementary purchase, and interstore sales displacement', *Journal of Marketing* 55, April: 17–28.

Webster, Frederick E., Jr. (1992) 'The changing role of marketing in the corporation', *Journal of Marketing* 56, October: 1–17.

Williamson, Oliver E. (1975) *Markets and Hierarchies: Analysis and Antitrust Implications*, New York: The Free Press.

Williamson, Oliver E. (1981) 'The economics of organization: the transaction cost approach', *American Journal of Sociology* 87 (3): 548–77.

Winer, Russell S. (1988) 'Behavioral perspective on pricing: buyers' subjective perceptions of price revisited', in T. Devinney (ed.) *Issues in Pricing: Theory and Research*, Lexington, MA: Lexington Books.

Zeithaml, Valarie A., Parasuraman, A. and Berry, Leonard L. (1985) 'Problems and strategies in services marketing', *Journal of Marketing* 49 (1): 33–46.

4

THE PSYCHOLOGICAL BASIS OF MARKETING

Gordon R. Foxall

MARKETING AND PSYCHOLOGY

Marketing is human behaviour. In affluent societies, it is the behaviour of buyers and managers, directed towards the fulfilment of economic objectives through consumption that is satisfying to consumers and profitable for marketers. Psychology is the science of behaviour and its application to marketing is intended to aid understanding of the activities of buyers, users and managers that contributes to the fulfilment of those objectives in more informed ways, as well as increasing academic knowledge. Marketing psychology has become an immense field of research and teaching in the last two to three decades. There are numerous textbooks on both consumer behaviour and marketing management as well as attempts to integrate what is known about consumer choice with prescriptions for marketing action. Other contributions to this Encyclopedia take these concerns further by discussing the nature of consumer behaviour and the appropriate strategic and tactical managerial decisions.

This chapter is concerned, however, with the fundamentals of both consumer behaviour and marketing response, with the basic psychological knowledge required to understand the separate activities of consumers and managers and their interactions. This knowledge is basic in the sense that it can be built upon by present and future marketing managers who wish a more elaborate picture of the specific market considerations with which they are engaged. Psychological concepts and frameworks permeate the marketing literature, implicitly and explicitly. Much of the psychology in marketing nevertheless falls short of the needs of students, marketers and researchers: it is either trivial – based on commonsense nostrums dignified with the word 'psychological' – or academically abstruse – useful for an exclusively intellectual audience but of limited applicability. Marketing knowledge requires a sure substructure of basic psychological concepts if it is to contribute either to academic or managerial goals.

Elementary marketing behaviour

There are many ways in which marketing can be approached through psychology. Social psychology, for instance, is a strong contender for special consideration, applicable as it is to the personal interactions of buyers and sellers, the structure and dynamics of groups of consumers each of whom is influenced to buy this or that product, this or that brand, or perhaps nothing at all, by the words and actions of the rest. Dynamic psychology, the work of Freud, Jung, Adler and the other psychoanalysts, might also be proposed for this role. Consumers' suppressed and repressed motives, the formation of such personality structures as id, ego and superego in the process of psycho-sexual development might be incorporated in an interpretation of consumer choice based on their supposed unconscious desires.

Cognitive psychology would certainly be an important contender. Indeed, the study of consumer behaviour in the context of marketing is dominated by theories that depict it as information processing, and has been for some forty years, since the farm economists began to view consumer choice as decision-making. Nowadays the consumer behaviour texts are replete with one or other model of the consumer as an information processor, a mechanism which takes in data from the environment and acts upon it to produce the attitudes and intentions that are held to determine purchase and consumption. Physiological psychology could also play a role. Consumers' physical characteristics which stem from genetic endowments may have an immediate effect on choice and consumption; they include body size and build, athletic prowess, some forms of disablement and sexual attractiveness. The importance of these variables is evident from the extent to which they form the basis of marketing programmes, notably advertising campaigns, and are the subject of consumer research.

All of these theoretical perspectives contribute to the superstructure of marketing psychology, but none provides the psychological basics of marketing. For one thing, the overwhelming majority of attempts to incorporate psychology into marketing concentrate on consumer behaviour rather than that of marketing managers. Although the identical cognitive decision models applied to consumers have been used by organizational behaviour specialists to elucidate managerial decision-making, what we want is a fundamental discussion of the actions of customers and managers in the same terms, something that links the two while describing them as part of the same system rather than as two apparently separate subsystems.

In seeking the psychological fundament of marketing, we are concerned with what Homans (1974) calls 'elementary social behavior'. This requires that we focus not on the characteristics of the organizations, even the groups in terms of which marketing is often discussed, but on the behaviour of the social units involved and the factors that are directly responsible for them. The aim is to emphasize the ways in which consumers and managers actually act as and where they are, rather than to derive stylized or idealized prescriptions that purport to cover every marketing problem or every situation of purchase and consumption. How do customers and managers act in the situations in which they find themselves? The search for elementary marketing behaviour, a task for description rather than prescription, should therefore propose answers to such questions as: What do consumers do – and why? What do marketers do – and why? In fact, by taking this elementary approach, we are reexamining a lot of marketing thought that has been taken for granted for decades. It is not surprising that we arrive at a novel view of why consumers behave as they do and the nature of marketing action and influence on consumer choice.

There is another sense in which the quest for the psychological foundations of marketing is one for elementary behaviour. We have argued that, as far as possible, the science and interpretation of marketing behaviour should proceed from direct description of the actions involved. This implies that – at least at a fundamental level – as few theoretical terms should intervene between description and explanation as possible. We should attempt to map out the immediate influences on consumer choice and marketing action, giving as little attention as possible to the hypothetical intervening variables that might account for the behaviour we observe. That is, an account of the psychological fundamentals of marketing should not give major prominence to the notions derived from the very behaviour they are supposed to explain: attitudes and intentions, for example, or personality traits, motives and information processing. All of these unobservables are added by the investigator to explain what has been observed. We do not object to them as such but they tend, in a search for psychological fundamentals, to obscure the simpler determinants of consumer and marketer behaviour with which we are concerned. For now, we can leave them to the textbooks of both consumer behaviour and marketing.

Costs, rewards and exchange

Consumer behaviour brings rewards and costs, almost simultaneously. The rewards are obvious and have been emphasized for decades by the marketing literature. They are the benefits gained from buying, owning and using the product or service in question. The fact that consumer behaviour is also costly is less frequently mentioned. Buyers nevertheless incur the costs of finding a suitable store, product and brand, obtaining information from marketer-dominated sources such as advertising and salespeople, buyer-dominated sources such as friends and neighbours, and neutral sources such as the Consumer Association's *Which?* magazine. They also incur costs when they make a purchase – opportunity costs, for instance: surrendering cash means that alternative products have to be foregone. Buying one thing rather than another or rather than saving may attract criticism from people who would have us dispose of our money 'more wisely'; wearing unfashionable or inappropriate clothes may invite ridicule, and so on. We can assume that consumers are constantly balancing the rewards of purchasing an item against the costs of doing

70

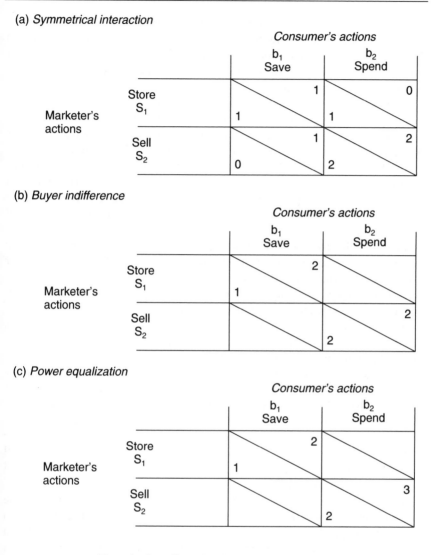

(a) *Symmetrical interaction*

(b) *Buyer indifference*

(c) *Power equalization*

Figure 1 Payoff matrices in a marketing context
Source: Foxall (1990: 81)

so, the rewards and costs of buying one product against those of buying another, the outcomes of patronizing one store against those of shopping at another, and so on.

Marketers also – perhaps more obviously – both reap rewards and incur costs as a result of supplying the marketplace with products and services that consumers might buy. Their revenues depend directly on the prices customers

71

pay, and their costs derive from their own extraction or purchases of raw materials, production, distribution, advertising, and so on. They, too, have a choice: to sell now (in which case, they are rewarded by the sale) or to retain their produce in the hope that prices will rise (in which case they must continue to pay inventory and other costs).

The interactions of consumers and marketers, their exchange behaviours, can be summarized by payoff matrices such as those shown in Figure 1. The consumer always has the choice of saving or spending on the product offered by the marketer. The marketer has the choice of selling to the consumer or storing the product for later sale. Figure 1(a) shows the payoffs available in a simple situation in which the consumer knows the brand on offer, has used and been satisfied with it in the past, and is offered it at (more or less) the prevailing market price. The marketer knows his or her costs and a sale at that price will contribute to profit expectations. If the consumer decides to save, while the marketer decides to retain the product, their gains are not as great as if an exchange takes place. However, if one party to a potential transaction either saves or stores while the other wishes to buy or sell, the former gains (e.g. interest on money that might otherwise be spent, or by holding on to an appreciating asset) while the latter loses out on the desired rewards.

This framework also allows us to speculate what will happen if the behaviours of consumer and marketer change. Figure 1(b) shows the payoffs on offer when the marketer doubles the price asked for the product. Should a transaction occur, we assume that both parties gain equally, but it is easier now for the consumer to be indifferent between buying and saving. Should he or she not make a purchase, the value of the retained spending power is greater than before. Finally – Figure 1(c) – we assume that the marketer offers a compromise: the price remains twice as high as in the first example but the marketer offers 25 per cent more of the item. If the consumer is now persuaded to buy, the seller still has a better deal than originally but a new equilibrium position is reached and exchange is once again feasible.

Real transactions are more complicated than this hypothetical example conveys. Let us concentrate on the consumer's point of view. The decision to buy or save depends not only on its likely consequence or payoff: it is also a function of the consumer's circumstances and the extent to which the situation is controlled by the consumer or the marketer. Consumer demand is determined in part by the level of satiety the individual has achieved (conversely, by his or her level of deprivation), by such state and personal variables as mood, the availability of credit or other means to pay, and his or her experience of buying and using the product in the past. Most important of all may be the immediate setting in which the transaction or act of consumption takes place. This includes the consumer's physical and social surroundings, and the norms that specify the appropriateness of certain behaviours rather than others. All of these act either to facilitate or inhibit particular acts of purchase and consumption.

At home, to give an example, one generally feels freer to choose certain consumption activities which would incur sanctions if performed elsewhere: entertainment or sleeping are obvious examples but there are doubtless others. Indeed, settings such as the home often encourage consumption: listening to the radio there is more probable than doing so elsewhere simply because it will not be interrupted or disturb anyone else; watching TV or preparing a favourite meal is more probable at home because that is where the necessary equipment is. Sometimes consumption settings are deliberately arranged to encourage purchasing: supermarkets and other retail outlets are arranged to maximize the amount of time the customer spends in them because level of purchase is a function of that time; consumers often buy books on impulse because of the way they are displayed in bookstores; the probability of visiting a speciality store such as a jeweller is greater if it is situated en route to a departmental store or other 'attractor' which the customer frequently visits; and such determinants of store atmosphere as lighting and crowding are often controlled by retailers to ensure that consumers stay and buy (Foxall and Goldsmith 1994).

Thus, in addition to the consequences of behaviour (its outcomes or payoffs), any understanding of consumer choice must take antecedents such as these into consideration. Doing so allows us to summarize the situation in which consumer behaviour occurs very simply as follows:

$$A : B : C$$

where A = antecedents,
B = behaviour,
C = consequences.

There is nothing automatic about the ways in which these variables interact. The antecedents which include the nature of the setting, the consumer and his or her experience of the product and store, and his or her personal, economic and physiological states do not make consumer behaviours such as purchase, saving or consumption inevitable: depending on their precise nature, they make one or other of these responses more likely to occur. Purchase or consumption are more probable when levels of deprivation of the product are high, when the customer is in the right mood, when he or she has the money to make a purchase or the time to consume, when social mores indicate that the act will be approved and when his or her experience of behaving like this in the past was rewarding rather than costly.

The consequences of a particular act of purchase, saving and consumption also make it more or less probable given these antecedents, but they do not make it inevitable in every circumstance. Rewards come broadly in two kinds. Some are intrinsic to the product or service itself and derive directly from its value in use. A lawnmower that cuts the grass with minimum effort and results in a smooth, even lawn that will increase the pleasure of sitting out on sunny days is usually preferred to one that churns up the garden and causes more work. We can call these direct benefits of the product the instrumental rewards of purchase and consumption. However, the intrinsic benefits of the product are not the sole

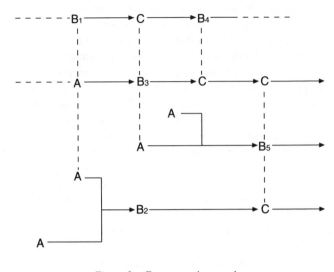

Figure 2   Consumer interaction
Source: Foxall (1990: 79)

reasons they are bought and used. Many items also provide extrinsic or expressive rewards.

Being seen to use the latest electronic lawnmower, for instance, one which is known to be expensive, exclusive, highly efficient and incorporating state-of-the-art technology may confer prestige and esteem. It provides a measure of how well one is doing, one's level of performance – not primarily as a gardener, perhaps, but as a consumer, as an earner and as a citizen. The fact that one needs such a coiffured lawn on which to hold garden parties for eminent guests is a signal to others that one is doing well. Consuming such a mower is expressively rewarding as well as instrumentally useful. Of course, the chances that one can buy and use such a machine is also decided by its costs: we have said that it is a highly expensive product; it may also require great skill to operate or entail high maintenance costs. One might have to employ a gardener to use it, though the costs of doing so would be offset to some extent – maybe entirely, depending on our income – by the social esteem this would confer. But we must remember that, in addition to the instrumental and expressive rewards of purchase and consumption, there are inevitably costs, in particular, the costs of previously buying or using the product in question may inhibit purchase. We might have been embarrassed as a result of asking naive questions in the store last time we tried to make a purchase, we might have been unable to keep up the credit repayments, or we might have been seen by our neighbours as we struggled to learn a new way of cutting the grass.

The A:B:C idea can be used to map out consumer behaviour in specific marketing settings as a dynamic process that is influenced by the setting in

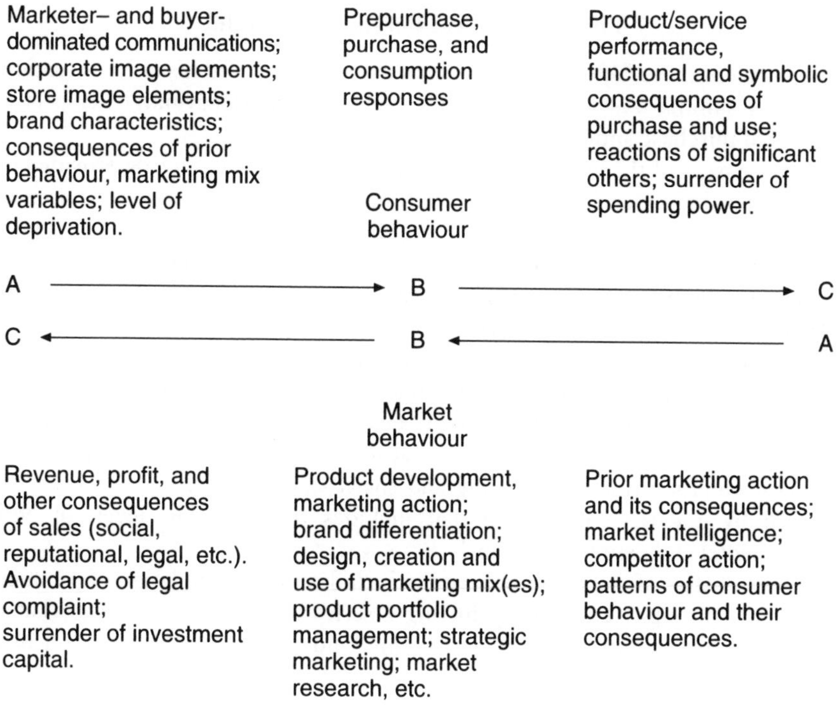

Marketer– and buyer-dominated communications; corporate image elements; store image elements; brand characteristics; consequences of prior behaviour, marketing mix variables; level of deprivation.	Prepurchase, purchase, and consumption responses Consumer behaviour	Product/service performance, functional and symbolic consequences of purchase and use; reactions of significant others; surrender of spending power.

A ——————————→ B ——————————→ C

C ←—————————— B ←—————————— A

Market
behaviour

Revenue, profit, and other consequences of sales (social, reputational, legal, etc.). Avoidance of legal complaint; surrender of investment capital.	Product development, marketing action; brand differentiation; design, creation and use of marketing mix(es); product portfolio management; strategic marketing; market research, etc.	Prior marketing action and its consequences; market intelligence; competitor action; patterns of consumer behaviour and their consequences.

Figure 3   Consumer and marketer behaviours
Source: Foxall (1990: 78)

which it occurs and the consequences it attracts. Figure 2 exemplifies the 'complex lattice of interrelated' A → B → C chains that represent consumer/marketer interactions in a retail setting. John is a consumer who enters a store (B_1), an action which is an antecedent prompt for another customer, Mary, to follow; another antecedent prompt, say an item in the store's window display, also signals the rewards that are available to Mary in the store and makes her entry (B_2) more likely. John's entry to the store is also an antecedent for a salesperson, James, to approach him and offer to help (B_3). This action also prompts another customer who is already in the store to approach another salesperson and ask for help.

A great deal of consumer behaviour in interaction with the marketing system can be portrayed in this way. The point is that consumer and marketer behaviours are mutually rewarding, each makes a set of responses on the part of the other more probable. Figure 3 portrays consumer/market interactions in this way. This basic idea indicates that the interactions involved are, in the most fundamental psychological terms, dependent on the setting variables and external rewards that shape them.

The Behavioural Perspective Model

Putting all of these factors into a model of the consumer and his or her situation, Figure 4 summarizes what has become known as the Behavioural Perspective Model of purchase and consumption (Foxall 1990).

On the basis of the levels of instrumental and expressive rewards provided by various products, services and retail outlets, we can classify styles of purchase and consumption in several ways. To simplify, note that each class of consumer behaviour can have either a low or a high level of instrumental reward and either a low or a high level of expressive reward. Figure 5 portrays the four broad classes of consumer behaviour that emerge from this analysis.

Consumer behaviours that are absolutely necessary for physical survival and the minimum level of obligation one incurs as a citizen include such activities as buying and consuming foods, paying taxes and finding a home. We can sum them up as *Maintenance* behaviours because of their essential role in providing the consumer's physical well-being and social standing. These behaviours are shaped by a pattern of reward that includes relatively low levels of both instrumental and expressive reward.

Another class of consumer behaviours includes the accumulation of products or money through saving or by buying a series of linked purchases. What is important in keeping up behaviour of this kind is frequent feedback on how

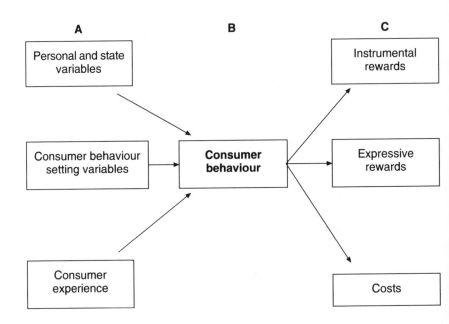

Figure 4   Simplified diagram of the Behavioural Perspective Model of purchase and consumption

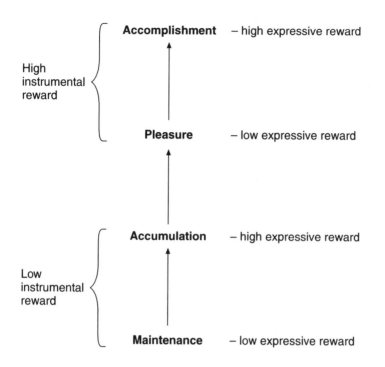

Figure 5   A hierarchy of consumer behaviours

much has been collected or accumulated so far and any bonuses that might have been added. *Accumulation* behaviour is therefore sustained by high levels of expressive reward which informs the consumer about progress to date and relatively low levels of instrumental reward.

A third class of consumer behaviour is *Pleasure*, which includes the activities involved in being entertained, playing, seeking fun, dining in restaurants. The high levels of instrumental reward that sustain this kind of behaviour are often derived from services rather than products – theatres, video tapes, hotels. By comparison with the instrumental rewards that maintain these activities, the levels of expressive reward provided are relatively low.

Finally, come consumer behaviours that are rewarded by high levels of both instrumental and expressive payoffs. Such activities as gambling in a casino or shopping for luxury and highly innovative products are included in this class, *Accomplishment*. Accomplishment is available to relatively few consumers – those who can afford to pay for the expensive products and services involved and who have been socialized by their previous experiences as consumers to seek such a pattern of reward.

A hierarchy of consumer lifestyles

The model also provides a means of classifying consumer behaviours generally in terms of the scope of the setting in which they occur and the pattern of reward that maintains them (Figure 6).

The four broad classes of consumer behaviour can be seen as a hierarchy of lifestyles which reflect the economic progress of the consumer over all or part of the consumer life cycle. The consumer life cycle consists of the sequence of stages through which the typically successful consumer may be expected to pass in the course of his or her economically active years. The cycle is confined to consumer behaviour from early adulthood onwards, when the individual is independently earning as well as spending and saving. The general sequence of lifestyles for the individual during these years is Maintenance – Accumulation – Pleasure – Accomplishment.

Maintenance is fundamental to citizenship of an affluent economic system, and represents the essential level of economic activity to which its members are first socialized. Accumulation, Pleasure and Accomplishment infer a rising level of wealth/income. Over the early and middle ranges of the consumer life cycle, the consumer typically progresses from a lifestyle concerned almost exclusively with Maintenance to those devoted in turn to the mounting acquisition of material effects, enjoyment of artistic, cultural and literary pursuits and, finally, the acquisition of status goods, self-development and other forms of fulfilment.

No consumer is ever entirely freed from the necessities of Maintenance but his or her lifestyle, given a progressive income and the sequence of obligations implied by the family life cycle, can be portrayed as a series of consumption patterns, each of which is dominated by a specific operant class of consumer behaviours.

Closed ⟵——————————————⟶ Open

Fulfilment	Status goods
Inescapable entertainment	Popular entertainment
Token-based buying	Collecting
Mandatory consumption	Routine purchase

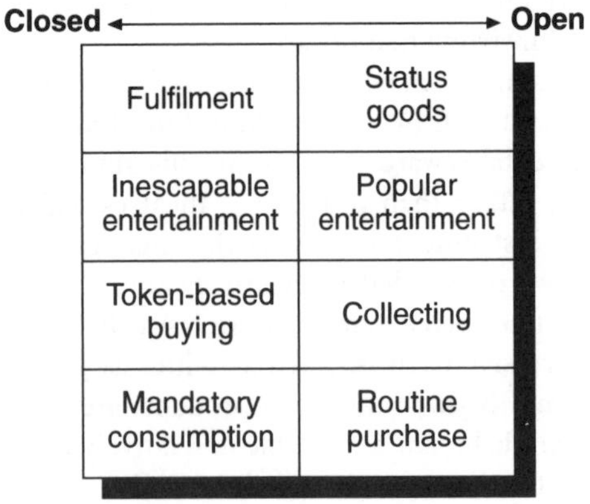

Figure 6　An integration of consumer behaviour
Source: Foxall (1992: 396)

78

We need to bear in mind that each of these four classes of consumer behaviour will also attract a different level of costs; they are not used in the definition of the classes because it is the general pattern of rewards that attracts a customer to each class but we can safely assume that total costs increase as one ascends the hierarchy and a full analysis takes this into explicit consideration (Foxall 1994).

UNDERSTANDING MARKETING MANAGEMENT

We can derive from this account of consumer choice a novel interpretation of how marketing management works. Of course, there are basically only four instruments available to marketers to attempt to control consumer behaviour – product, price, promotion and place, which together form the marketing mix. But the model proposed above suggests that a great deal of marketing activity is concerned with modifying two main variables that influence consumer behaviour. The first involves managing the scope of the consumer behaviour setting with the intention of increasing the attractiveness of the setting for the individual and reducing his or her propensity to avoid or leave it without purchasing or consuming. The second is the management of the ways in which instrumental and expressive rewards are made available to the consumer.

Management of the consumer behaviour setting

A considerable amount of managerial action in marketing can be viewed as attempting to close down the scope of behaviour settings, making the purchase of whatever the marketer offers more likely (whether this refers to spending on buying a product or consuming a service such as depositing money in a savings account) and making other responses (such as leaving the store, buying or consuming an alternative offering) less probable. Obvious examples are the provision of credit facilities for consumers who cannot afford the full cash outlay immediately, changing consumers' moods through in-store music, using advertising to promise desirable rewards contingent upon buying and using the item, and so on. Nor is this strategy of closure necessarily manipulative (in the worse sense of the word), especially in a competitive environment. Presenting the consumer with a more pleasant retail environment, for instance, or with clearer way-finding aids and more legible shopping mall designs encourages the potential buyer to stay in the marketing environment and to become an actual consumer (Foxall and Goldsmith 1994). What is the alternative? To allow consumers to find their own way around unpleasant stores where the merchandise is poorly displayed and difficult to find? Failing to compete with other marketers in order to ensure a quiet life for all? There is no doubt what consumers prefer. If closure of the consumer setting – in a competitive environment – is manipulative, it is a matter of manipulation by printed invitation.

The fact that marketing takes place within a competitive context – at least in affluent societies that ensure high levels of discretionary income, an excess of marketing capacity over demand, and thus consumer choice – means that closure strategies are limited by firms' resources. Ecological psychologists have studied the ways in which organizations use what we would call marketing and demarketing in order to respond to their ability to staff their operations. Staffing levels (both qualitative and quantitative) are one source of constraint on firms' resource bases, especially in relation to what the psychologists call over-population but which we would recognize as over-demand, but the ability to provide products of the right quality and quantity, to advertise their availability, to. price them adequately (for consumers, managers, shareowners and other stakeholders) and to distribute them efficiently also influence the extent to which firms can effect closure of the consumer setting.

Over-demand typically arises because of the density of consumers in a physical setting that interferes with the level of service available to satisfy demand. This service level is relative not only to the size of the public present in the locale but to the level of human and physical resources available to deliver the required service. More significantly, it is relative to the quality of staff and other resources and, particularly, to the implications of the quality and quantity of these resources for the delivery of a demanded level of marketing proficiency. We could suggest many examples of the ways in which marketers respond to over-demand by modifying the scope of the consumer setting in order to increase consumer satisfaction as well as marketing goals. Here are just three examples of the ways in which place has been modified to effect closure.

1 *Control of entrance of consumers into the setting.* Consumers are sometimes scheduled through an appointments system or by active demarketing such as a reduction in the volume or frequency of marketing communications. On occasion the standards required for admission are raised through a price increase or requirement that patrons (e.g. in a restaurant) wear suitable clothing. Customers might also be channelled into a holding area (such as a bar in a restaurant if a table is not immediately available). Some consumer behaviours might be banned (smoking, for instance) so that some potential customers are effectively debarred.

2 *Control of the capacity of the setting.* The size of the setting might be increased/decreased – as when airlines fly larger planes. Opening hours may be altered. Staff shortages might be compensated for by the installation of automatic teller machines.

3 *Control of the time consumers spend in the setting.* The service/product might be provided more quickly (e.g. a barber might cut hair faster or food operations in a fast food restaurant might be automated). Motorists may be allowed only thirty minutes' parking and their return prohibited for a further two hours. The flow of consumers through a service area might be controlled to ensure that bottlenecks do not occur: for example, self-service restaurants

may require consumers to place orders at one counter, obtain their purchases from another and pay at a third.

Management of rewards

There are three ways in which marketers manage the rewards system: by enhancing the effectiveness of rewards, by controlling the schedules on which rewards are presented, and by increasing the quantity or quality of rewards (Alhadeff 1982). Here are some examples.

Enhancing the effectiveness of rewards

The effectiveness of some rewards can be increased by deliberately delaying their availability to the consumer. This is an ineffective strategy when competitors can quickly step in and supply the product – there is no point in making would-be customers wait for icecreams on a hot day. But if the item in question is a service and if the marketer has been successful in closing the consumer setting there may be some scope for increasing total purchasing or consumption through delay. This is especially relevant to consumer behaviours that can be described as *Pleasure*. The consumer who has paid for a cinema or theatre seat, for instance, has entered a relatively closed setting. He or she can get up and leave at any time (though there will be costs such as the forfeiture of the entrance money, the displeasure expressed by other members of the audience who are inconvenienced, and the loss of an opportunity to see the film, play or act). Films and acts in these establishments are often scheduled, however, so that the most popular or most hyped appears last; the audience is, willingly or not, required to consume less highly demanded products such as a minor movie, new short ballets or playlets, advertisements, less well known acts, and so on. Nevertheless, they usually wait and their expectation of the major film, play or top of the bill act will actually have been increased by the interval of time. The consumer performs a series of responses, chained together so that each rewards its predecessor (watching the minor movie is a reward contingent on sitting through the ads, for example), while each signals the next and makes watching it more probable. The enjoyment of the final act is actually greater because of the anticipation that has been created, the deprivation that has been skilfully managed. Delays are not always deliberately engineered by marketers, of course. Sometimes a wait is inevitable – as when a long-haul air journey will take some hours before customers reach their destination. In the meantime the airlines often alleviate the demerits of the temporal and physical restrictions imposed by having to sit still in a passenger cabin for a long period by offering meals, movies, duty-free products and alcohol.

Another managerial strategy designed to increase the effectiveness of rewards, this time especially relevant to *Accumulation*, is the use of token-based marketing in which an ultimate reward (often instrumental) is made dependent upon the purchase or use of a series of other products (which are useful but whose primary reward in this context is expressive since they signal to the consumer how far he or she is advancing towards obtaining the ultimate product). The promotional use of such tokens as trading stamps, the presentation of encyclopedic works in monthly parts that build into a complete set, the payment of extraordinary rates of interest on long-term savings are all examples. Frequent-flyer programmes in which additional air tickets are available to passengers who accumulate high mileages are another example. Some international hotels also allow customers to accumulate points that are exchangeable for products and services. In each case, the collection of the tokens (stamps, air miles, points) is rewarded by the ultimate prize.

Scheduling of rewards

When a reward is provided every time a particular response is performed, individuals learn the required behaviour quickly – every time the switch is turned, the lights go on – but the response is quickly forgotten or extinguished once the reward ceases. Learning a response is surer when rewards are intermittent – every nth response is rewarded or a reward is given every x minutes as long as the action has occurred at least once in the period. Behaviours learned under these conditions often take longer to get into the individual's repertoire but they are performed for long periods even when all reward has ceased. Industry has long made use of these effects by making pay contingent on the amount of work done (as in piecework). They are also apparent in much consumer marketing. An example that comes under the heading of *Accomplishment* is gambling in a casino, a fairly closed setting which may be costly or inconvenient to leave once play has begun. The rewards are both instrumental (money can be won which can then be spent on other things) and expressive (the amount won over time gives accurate feedback on performance). Games of chance are scheduled in such a way that gambling is likely to persist even when nothing has been won for some time. Progressively 'stretching' the schedule of wins to responses has the effect of encouraging long periods of gaming.

Many aspects of *Pleasure* are also maintained by scheduled rewards. Take watching the television news, for instance. The 'happy news' format, pioneered in California, provides frequent rewards so that even a short period of viewing is reinforced and further viewing is made more probable. The bulletins are meant to entertain as much as they inform, presenting the audience with 'action, pace [and] an almost dizzy attempt to keep the audience from getting bored' (Tunstall and Walker 1981: 123). Stories are chosen for their entertaining and even sensational content and each gets two or three minutes' coverage in a thirty-minute broadcast, which also contains two three-minute advertising breaks and a five-minute weather forecast which is as exciting as the news items.

Increasing the quality and quantity of rewards

Marketers often increase the quality and quantity of consumers' purchases, the former by engaging in a strategy of continual product improvement, the latter by promotional deals that provide more for the same price or by reducing the price of a given amount or by refunds. Some more elaborate methods involve the creation and scheduling of information to consumers (e.g. when a product paid for now cannot be consumed for some time). Progress reports on expensive furniture that is being hand-made over a period of weeks or months, advertisements that remind consumers of the benefits of the exotic vacation they are awaiting, preparatory meetings and detailed instructions pertaining to self-improvement courses are all examples of the use of information to reward a commitment made to *Accomplishment* long before the product or service is delivered.

CONCLUSION

This chapter has shown that a fundamental model derived from the psychology of learning can account not only for consumer behaviour but also for the marketing management that is one of its chief determinants. Some researchers would prefer to include additional terms in the account – to theorize about the possible intervening influence of consumers' attitudes and intentions, their personality traits, and processes of information handling – and to conceptualize managerial behaviour in terms of similar hypothetical constructs. Well and good. As was pointed out at the beginning of the chapter, marketing has numerous links with psychological method and theory. But the point of the present account has been to present the *psychological foundations of marketing* and that has meant overcoming the temptation to elaborate.

REFERENCES

Alhadeff, D. A. (1982) *Microeconomics and Human Behavior: Toward a New Synthesis of Economics and Psychology*, Berkeley, CA: University of California Press.

Foxall, G. R. (1990) *Consumer Psychology in Behavioural Perspective*. London and New York: Routledge.

Foxall, G. R. (1992) 'The consumer situation: an integrative model for research in marketing', *Journal of Marketing Management* 8: 396.

Foxall, G. R. (1994) 'Behavior analysis and consumer psychology', *Journal of Economic Psychology* 15: 1–80.

Foxall, G. R. and Goldsmith, R. E. (1994) *Consumer Psychology for Marketing*, London and New York: Routledge.

Homans, G. C. (1974) *Social Behavior: Its Elementary Forms*, 2nd edn, New York: Harcourt Brace Jovanovich.

Tunstall, J. and Walker, D. (1981) *Media Made in California: Hollywood, Politics and the News*, New York: Oxford University Press.

FURTHER READING

Foxall, G. R. (1996) *Consumers in Context*, London and New York: Routledge.
Howard, J. A. (1989) *Consumer Behavior in Marketing Strategy*, Englewood Cliffs, NJ: Prentice-Hall.
Robertson, T. S. and Kassarjian, H. H. (eds) (1991) *Handbook of Consumer Behavior*, Englewood Cliffs, NJ: Prentice-Hall.

5

THE SOCIOLOGICAL BASIS OF MARKETING

Kjell Grønhaug

INTRODUCTION

This chapter claims that marketing is a basic social activity, and shows how the discipline of marketing has borrowed from and been influenced by sociology. Marketing has for long been recognized as a 'borrowing' discipline in particular from the social sciences (cf. Cox 1964), and is itself claimed to be a social science discipline (cf. Hunt 1991). The historical roots of marketing are embedded in classical economics (see Chapters 2 and 4). Citation analysis to determine the influences of other disciplines on marketing also show extensive borrowing from (among others) sociology (Goldman 1979).[1] The borrowing consists of concepts, theories and models, methods and techniques for doing research; of particular importance is the conceptual borrowing. Concepts are the building blocks of any theory, model or hypothesis. The concepts and how they are used (and related) guide and direct. They give focus and largely determine what is captured.

As will be demonstrated, the borrowing from sociology has had, and still has, considerable influence on marketing thinking. The emphasis here is primarily on the concepts (and perspectives) borrowed and how they have influenced marketing thinking as reflected in major marketing textbooks. The main reason for using marketing textbooks as a mirror of the sociological influences is that textbooks reflect what is taught and disseminated, and is thus believed to capture important aspects of the (sociological) impact on marketing thinking (and practice). Marketing – like other disciplines – has changed and developed over the years. This is also reflected in the borrowing from other disciplines (e.g. sociology) over time.

This chapter proceeds as follows. First, characteristics of marketing and the discipline of sociology are emphasized. In this section it is also demonstrated that marketing is a societal activity. Similarities between marketing and sociological reasoning are also discussed. The dominant focus in marketing thinking and practice and how this has influenced conceptual borrowing and use is then discussed. Next, specific concepts and ideas borrowed from sociology are emphasized. A distinction is made between concepts and ideas primarily used to characterize individuals, groups and the larger society; contributions taking relationships between social actors directly into account; and contributions focusing on change. Finally, characteristics of the borrowing from and influences of sociology on marketing are summarized and future influences from this discipline (sociology) on marketing are indicated.

MARKETING AND SOCIOLOGY

Marketing activities have a long history. Through thousands of years man has transacted goods and services to satisfy needs and enhance standard of living. As a scientific discipline, however, marketing is young, with its origin at the turn of this century (cf. Chapter 2).

Marketing as exchange

Marketing takes place in a societal context. The core of marketing as a scientific discipline relates to exchange between social actors (e.g. individuals, groups or organizations), or as claimed by Hunt:

> Marketing (science) is the behavioral science which seeks to explain exchange relationships.
>
> (Hunt 1983: 129)

(Social) exchange requires:

- the presence of (at least) two parties;
- that each party has something to offer that might be of value to the other party;
- each party is capable to communicate and deliver;
- each party is free to accept or reject an offer;
- each party believes it is appropriate or desirable to deal with the other party (cf. Kotler 1984: 8).

Exchange as a phenomenon is, however, a huge area of inquiry, and has been extensively dealt with in sociology and other disciplines. Exchange theory consists not only of one but several theories. A distinction is often made between individualistic and collective approaches to the study of exchange. Different modes of exchange have also been identified such as the market mode (i.e. exchange through markets); reciprocal exchange mode (which can be thought of as gift exchange between members of a network with reciprocal obligations); and the redistributive mode of exchange (i.e. exchange based on some principle of sharing such as blood donations; cf. Polanyi 1944).

Marketing has long been associated primarily with the market mode of exchange, where the market in a neoclassical sense is often thought of as a large number of exchange partners, with market prices yielding the necessary information and incentives. The idealized market mode of exchange is considered impersonal (as reflected in neoclassical economics) or, as stressed by Polanyi, 'it is important to emphasize the abstract and impersonal nature of market exchange' (1944: 5). In modern societies reciprocal and redistributive exchanges are also taking place. More than twenty-five years ago Codere (1968: 57) even claimed that the fraction of market exchanges of all exchanges taking place was declining.

Marketers have devoted substantial effort to study and understand exchanges. In doing so they have extensively borrowed concepts and perspectives from other disciplines. One of the first marketing scholars to recognize the limitations of 'faceless' transactions (i.e. exchange outcomes) to understand markets and marketing was Wroe Alderson. Recognized for his influential contributions on marketing thinking, he introduced the notion of an 'organized behavior system' (Alderson 1958) to capture the idea that the various actors operating in the market are more or less connected (as reflected in the recent emphasis on 'relationship' marketing). In doing so, he also saw the benefit of sociology, and claimed that 'the initial plunge into sociology is only the beginning since the marketing man must go considerably further in examining the functions and structures of organized behavior systems'.

Sociology

Sociology is one of the major social sciences. The term 'sociology' was invented by Auguste Comte, and first published in the fourth volume of his *Cours de philosophie positive* in 1838, even though the ancient roots of the discipline can be traced back to Plato and Aristotle among others. The word sociology has two stems, the Latin *socius* [companion] and the Greek *logos* [study of] – and literally means the study of the processes of companionship. The term sociology can be (and has been) defined in various ways. For example, as proposed by Giddens, 'sociology is the study of human life, groups and societies' (1993: 7).

A key point in the sociological perspective is that man does not operate in a vacuum, but is embedded in the surrounding social context. The individual forms and holds expectations about others, and because s/he is assumed to behave purposefully, expectations about others are taken into account. This basic point of departure has a distinct parallel in marketing. Marketing activities take place in a societal context. Exchange requires the presence of and access to others. Since man started transacting goods and services thousands of years ago, the importance of 'others' has been recognized. Sellers have tried to identify potential buyers, their needs and thinking in order to make transactions. Buyers have learnt about sellers and their product offerings. Through word of mouth, their own experiences and other sources of information, buyers' expectations towards sellers are shaped and their behaviour is also influenced.

The individual in context is a human being interacting with the social

87

environment. The sociological perspective tries to encompass the acting person and the acting group. The acting person is a specific human being who pursues goals, interprets experiences, responds to opportunities and confronts difficulties. As an individual in action s/he does not necessarily stay within neat boundaries of specialized activity, nor does s/he always conform to conventional expectations. For example, the seller may cheat, the buyer may shoplift, and the marketing entrepreneur may 'break the rules', change the 'social game' – and become successful.

Social organization

To capture the social influences, sociologists study how the society is organized. In doing so they often make use of the general term *social system*, emphasizing the interdependencies and interactions among social actors. The same underlying idea can easily be traced in marketing (e.g. as reflected in 'distribution systems' and 'system sales').

In their study of social organization sociologists also distinguish between different levels, for example, the micro (individual and group) level and the macro or social order level. Concepts used and phenomena focused upon vary across levels. There are, however, interactions and interdependencies between the various levels. Changes at the macro level may influence expectations and behaviour at the micro level and vice versa. For example, the automobile has dramatically changed the mobility of the individual (consumer), which has influenced shopping behaviour – and the structure of the distribution system, as reflected in the dramatic changes in the retail trade. Drop in individual fertility (e.g. influenced by a pessimistic outlook on the future) may add up to dramatic changes in demand for specific goods or services. Such demographic changes are (among others) studied by sociologists – and experienced by marketers.

Our examples so far show that there are close parallels between sociology and marketing, which are unrecognized in most contemporary marketing textbooks. We shall focus on the main concepts borrowed from sociology, how they are used and why.

MARKETING FOCUS AND SCIENTIFIC BORROWING

The author of this chapter views borrowing from other disciplines as purposeful behaviour. This borrowing is done to obtain something, for example to understand the functioning of markets and/or to improve marketing practices. On the other hand what is borrowed, and how the borrowings are used are heavily influenced by the dominant focus of the borrowing discipline (marketing).

The term 'marketing' has been used in at least three different contexts:

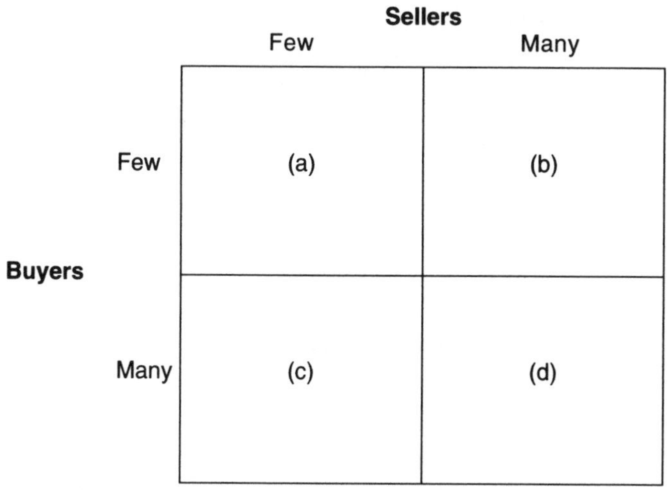

Sellers

	Few	Many
Few	(a)	(b)
Many	(c)	(d)

Buyers

Figure 1   Number of buyers and sellers

1 marketing as a management orientation or discipline;
2 marketing as a science;
3 marketing as an ideology (Arndt 1980).

According to the stated purpose, that is to capture the influence of sociology on marketing thinking as reflected in major textbooks, the first meaning of the term marketing will primarily be emphasized. As a management orientation or discipline marketing can be, and indeed until now has been, considered primarily as a business discipline. In spite of efforts to apply marketing thinking to the public sector, and in non-business and non-profit settings, there is little doubt that most marketing thinking and activities relate to business firms.

Any business firm specializes and offers a more or less limited set of product (service) offerings. The firm is dependent on its surrounding environment, in particular on the 'market' (i.e. on actual and potential customers). For the firm to survive and prosper a sufficient number of customers must be willing to buy its product (service) offerings at prices which at least cover costs, and where surplus profit is considered advantageous. Modern marketing as reflected in the majority of (American) textbooks primarily deals with mass marketing. Most textbooks are influenced by the underlying premise that generally a few firms sell to many customers (primarily individuals and households), as reflected in cell (c) in Figure 1.

Marketing situations as reflected in the other cells are also taking place (and will be discussed later). The key point here is that the situation as depicted in cell (c) reflects the dominant perspective on marketing thinking and – as will be

89

demonstrated – has influenced the borrowing from other disciplines.

The (marketing) management perspective also emphasizes the manager as an active actor, assumed to make (hopefully) wise decisions to reach goals and influence the destiny of her or his firm (organization). Due to the firm's dependence on the market, it is of crucial importance for the marketing manager to identify and understand customers as the basis for designing successful marketing strategies. This need to 'profile' customers to become effective can be traced to the borrowing of marketing from sociology, as reflected in most marketing (and consumer behaviour) textbooks.

CONCEPTS AND IDEAS

This section focuses on main concepts and ideas borrowed from sociology. The section is organized as follows. First, concepts and ideas to capture characteristics of individuals, groups and larger social segments are described. Contributions focusing respectively on relationships between actors, and contributions directed towards change are then discussed.

Individuals, groups and the larger society

Role

An important sociological concept is (social) 'role', which can be conceived as 'the bundles of social defined attributes and expectations associated with social positions' (Abercombie *et al.* 1988). For example, the role as 'mother' carries with it certain expected behaviours irrespective of the woman's feeling at any one time. Therefore it is possible to generalize about the role behaviour regardless of the individual characteristics of the people who occupy these roles. Role is sociologically important because it demonstrates how individual activity is socially influenced and thus follows regular patterns. It should also be noted that sociologists employ roles as 'building blocks' to study various social institutions (e.g. families and organizations, which are discussed later on).

In social life the individual may occupy various roles (e.g. mother or father, university professor or marketing manager) and the number occupied may vary considerably among people. The number of roles occupied by an individual needs in no way to be static; new roles may be acquired and others abandoned. The individual may also perceive two or more roles to be in conflict. For example, a person may perceive his role as employee (e.g. salesperson requiring frequent and lengthy travel) to be in conflict with his parental role as father, associated with expectations of spending much time with his child(ren).

The concept of role is a true sociological concept as it implies social relationships. For example, the role of 'husband' is primarily relevant in a household setting (e.g. in the presence of a 'wife'). The role concept has been used and has influenced marketing in various ways. The prototypical expectations associated with various roles (e.g. 'mother' and 'working woman') have been used to identify and profile target groups as the basis for designing appropriate marketing approaches. The frequently quoted roles such as 'influencer', 'decider', 'user' and 'gatekeeper' have been similarly used in organizational (industrial) buying literature as the basis for who (and how) to target – just as the focus is on 'husband' and 'wife' in the study of family (households). This somewhat 'one-eyed' perspective on how the concepts of role and relationships have been interpreted by marketing (e.g. the relationship between seller and buyer) is discussed later. However, as noted by Wallendorf (1978), so far only a fraction of the potential of role theory has been exploited in a marketing context.

Status

In any social system (e.g. group, organization or society) one may distinguish between different social positions (see discussion of social roles). Such positions can also be rank ordered, implying that positions may be lower, higher or equal in status. Sociologists have for long studied how status is achieved. Often a distinction is made between ascribed (e.g. by heritage) and achieved attributes as the basis for status (e.g. education or sports performance). The concept of status has directly (and indirectly) influenced marketing thinking. For example, the observation that things (and behaviours) may symbolize status has extensively been used to develop, introduce and communicate products. In other words, the marketer has exploited sociological insights by relating status to consumption alternatives, as reflected in Levy's seminal article 'Symbols for Sale' (1959).

Norm

The term 'norm' refers to social expectations about correct or proper behaviour. Thus norms imply the presence of legitimacy, consent and prescription. When norms are internalized they are learnt and accepted as binding the social values and guidelines of conduct relevant to the individual, the group or wider society. Internalized norms are central for social order. Deviations from norms are punished by sanctions.

The sources of norms can be found in established values, law, expectations, and accepted behaviours. Often (in most cases) norms are not written, but learnt through socialization (to be discussed later). Norms may also be more or less specific. For example, specific norms may prevail with regard to specific role behaviours.

For marketers it is of importance to know the norms in the marketplace in order to behave adequately. In marketing the concept and knowledge of norms are extensively used as input in market research to get adequate information about target groups. For example, prevailing norms may be barriers to the

91

acceptance of new products. By knowing the norms the marketer may adjust to or even contribute to change of norms. Mason Haire's well-known 'shopping list' study is an example. When instant coffee was introduced several decades ago, the acceptance rate of the new product was modest. The shopping list study exposed a sample of housewives to one of two identical shopping lists. The shopping lists were identical but for one item, coffee. One list contained 'instant coffee', while the other contained the brand name of a well-known regular coffee. The respondents were asked to describe the shopping person. House-wives (who were in majority at that time) tended to describe the shopper behind the list containing instant coffee as 'lazy' and 'not a good housewife', while women working outside the home described the shopping person as 'smart', 'modern', 'effective' and so on. Apparently the new product was conceived to be in conflict with existing norms for being a good housewife. This knowledge was successfully used to design marketing strategies to alter this aspect of the prevailing 'housewife norm'. As norms may vary across societies (and social segments), knowledge of prevailing norms represents a true challenge on an international basis. More recently marketers have also studied how norms may influence control of seller-buyer relationships.

Group

Social groups are collectives of individuals who interact and form social relationships. A distinction is often made between *primary* and *secondary* groups. The former are small groups, being defined by face-to-face interaction. The household (nuclear family) and the clique may serve as examples. The latter are usually larger groups, where each member does not directly interact with every other. Examples are unions and associations where the members (at best) interact only with a subset of other members, and where most of the communication is formalized (e.g. through newsletters). Sociological insights regarding groups have influenced marketing thinking. For example, the family (household) can be conceived as a primary group, which plays an important role in marketing thinking, primarily as a buying and consuming unit. A common observation is that buying by firms and organizations is usually carried out by a group rather than a single individual. This has led to the notion of 'the buying group' or 'buying centre', heavily influenced by sociological group insights. The focus among marketers has been on the role (position) within the buying group, identification (prediction) of who is included, their tasks and activities, and on their relative influence in purchase situations as a basis for designing effective marketing strategies.

Reference group

In forming their attitudes and beliefs and in performing their actions, people will compare or identify themselves with other people, or other groups of people.

These people are called reference groups. People can make references both to membership and non-membership groups. Reference group knowledge has influenced marketing thinking and these insights have been applied in particular to relate products or brands to groups assumed to be attractive. Research findings have demonstrated that reference group influence can be made both at the product category level (in particular for expensive goods) as well as at the brand level. For example, brands of perfume, clothes and equipment are often associated with (distant) attractive reference groups (e.g. movie stars or sports idols). Specific information about the actual reference group(s) of the target group is needed when designing such marketing strategies.

Family (household)

The notion of family (household) is extensively used by marketers. In most cases marketers use the notions of 'family' and 'household' interchangeably, indicating the Western perspective that family (i.e. the nuclear family) often coincides with household (i.e. the unit of dwelling). The family (household) is often considered as an important primary group. The family (household) can also be considered as an important social institution. The term social institution refers to established patterns of behaviour or, as suggested by Nicosia and Mayer, 'a set of specific activities performed by specific people in specific places through time' (1976: 67). Sociological insights regarding families (households) have been used by marketers both to study the relative influence of spouses (and children) on buying decisions and as a basis for studying buying decision processes, and how households (families) allocate their scarce economic resources and time.

Family life cycle

The sociological term 'life cycle' is used primarily to describe the development of a person through childhood, adolescence, mid-life, old age and death. The concept does not refer to purely biological processes of maturation, but to the transition of an individual through socially constructed categories of age and to the variations in social experiences of aging. In marketing several efforts have been made to classify people according to stages in the life cycle and, in particular, to characterize buying and consumption at the various stages. Such insights have been used to profile target groups and predict future market developments.

Social class

In most (all?) societies individuals are ranked hierarchically along some dimension of inequality (e.g. wealth, education, prestige, age, or some other characteristics; see discussion of status). Such rank ordering is the basis of social class, referring to strata of that rank ordering (e.g. 'upper', 'upper-middle', 'lower-middle' classes). In Western societies wealth, education and prestige (among others) are important characteristics to determine social class membership. Extensive research has shown that members of the various strata or social classes tend to have common characteristics (e.g. similar consumption patterns and values). Research findings demonstrate that the middle classes spend more on housing and the home, they save more and spend substantially more on education, books and art than the lower classes. (For a detailed description of findings regarding class differences, see Berelson and Steiner 1964.) Marketers have primarily used such insights to characterize consumption patterns across social classes in order to identify and characterize target groups and segment markets.

Lifestyle

Consumption patterns and values vary across social strata (and groups). Such differences are visible indicators of class position. In sociological research the lifestyle concept has been related to broad classes (e.g. to distinguish between rural and urban, urban and suburban forms of social life). In marketing the lifestyle concept has a more psychological orientation, with emphasis on identifying specific lifestyles based on detailed mapping of consumption activities, media habits, attitudes and opinions (cf. Chapter 5).

Culture

Culture has been intensively studied by both anthropologists and sociologists. Culture is a multidimensional and complex phenomenon, and for decades there has been an ongoing debate about the meaning of the concept. For example, in 1952 Kroeber and Kluckhon reviewed 164 definitions of culture. It is commonly assumed that culture includes patterns of behaviour and values, that culture is learned and shared with other people, and influences not only how one behaves, but also how one expects others to behave. How culture can be best understood and how to explain the functioning of culture, has changed over the years. For example, many anthropologists now prefer the term 'enacted' rather than learned, recognizing that people do not passively accept culture, but actively create it. In her penetrating analysis Swidler (1986) sees culture as shaping a 'tool kit' repertoire of habits, skills and styles from which people construct 'strategies of action' (p. 273). The acquisition of a repertoire of skills, habits and styles reflects that knowing how to behave in an intentionally rational (goal-directed) manner can be learned and that this knowledge is context bound, with the cultural context influencing what is conceived relevant.

Marketing has long recognized the importance of culture and has extensively borrowed research findings from anthropology and sociology. For example, cultures can be characterized according to their context of communication, often dichotomized as 'high' versus 'low' (Hall 1976). Many foreign cultures are characterized as 'high cultural contexts', characterized by dependence on non-verbal, 'hidden' insights of communication in contrast to low cultural contexts – relying more on explicit verbal communications and symbols. Such insights have been used to explain market failures and to prepare the marketer when crossing borders. Another finding from cultural research is that the cultural distance may vary considerably in importance for marketers when considering new markets to enter. Other aspects from cultural research adopted and used by marketers are differences in media structure and use, the importance of language and symbols, and variations in specific cultural values. Cultural knowledge has been used to characterize and choose markets, design adequate marketing strategies, and to understand and improve international negotiations.

Subculture

This term refers to a system of values, attitudes, behaviours and lifestyles of a social group which is distinct from, but related to the dominant culture of a society. In sociology the concept has been of most use in the study of youth and deviancy. In marketing the concept has primarily been adopted and used to study the buying and consumption activities and lifestyles of specific social groups (e.g. teenagers). Such insights have primarily been used as a basis for target group descriptions and thus to improve marketing activities and performance.

As noted above, many sociological concepts (and elements of theories) have been borrowed primarily as tools to identify and characterize target groups to improve marketing performance. Thus, even though the concepts are borrowed from a discipline concerned with social relationships, the unit of analysis in the marketing use of the concepts has been the individual acting unit (see Zaltman and Wallendorf 1977).

Marketing has also borrowed and applied sociological concepts which in a true sense capture aspects of social relationships. This has been particularly the case in situations other than mass marketing (e.g. in industrial markets), where the number of buyers is often limited (compare cells (a) and (b) in Figure 1). In so doing the unit of analysis is changed from the individual acting unit to the relationship between actors.

Relationships, power and conflict

Relationship

A relationship takes place between (at least) two actors, and the dyad is frequently used as the unit of analysis. To be considered a relationship it has to last (at least for some minimum time). A purposeful relationship assumes some flow of activities. Relationships can be of various kinds and can focus on exchange of goods, information, money and so on. The importance of relationships has long been recognized in disciplines such as sociology and anthropology – and business, but until recently has received scant attention in the marketing literature. A shift in focus is now apparently taking place, as reflected by the recent interest in 'relationship marketing' (see Webster 1992).[2] (For a fuller discussion, see Chapter 11.)

A common observation in industrial marketing is that buyers and sellers tend to enter rather long-term relationships (i.e. they tend to transact more than once, performing recurring transactions). There are several reasons for doing so. For example, it takes time, skills and economic resources to identify, negotiate with and adjust to exchange partners. Such efforts can be conceived as (partly) transaction specific investments easing future transactions. As a relationship develops information flows more easily and transaction costs are reduced. In addition to economics relationships may convey and be influenced by social values and concerns, as reflected in the notion of 'embeddedness' (Granovetter 1985).

Any transaction or relationship is guided by a contract, either explicitly or implicitly. There is a vast literature on contracts by researchers from several disciplines. Sociologists have primarily been preoccupied with the importance of 'social contracts', which can definitely deviate from legal contracts (see Blau 1964). Social contracts have important implications for marketing.

Network

The notion of 'network', often used to describe systems of relationships between actors, has a long tradition in sociology and anthropology. More recently there has been an increasing use of the network approach to understand the functioning of markets, and how firms may acquire resources, competence, access to technologies and gain competitive advantages through networking activities (cf. Chapter 11).

Conflict

When social actors exhibit purposeful behaviour (e.g. to gain market share or make money), the interests of social actors may come into conflict. For example, competition can be conceived as a conflict over the resources or advantages desired by others. The notion of conflict has been applied in several settings, for example, conflict between marketing and other functions, and between members of the distribution channel. (For an interesting discussion, see Levy and Zaltman 1975.)

Power

The study of power has a long tradition in sociology. There are several distinct perspectives of power, and the concept has been defined in many ways, for example, 'the probability that a person in a social relationship will be able to carry out his or her own will in the pursuit of goals of action, regardless of resistance' (based on M. Weber). The above definition implies that power is exercised by social actors, and involves agency and choice. Power is exercised over others and may involve resistance and conflict. Insights from sociological studies of power (and conflict) have, for example, been applied to understand and improve the functioning of distribution systems.

Learning and change

Socialization

This term is used to describe the process whereby people learn to conform to social norms, a process that makes possible an enduring society and the transmission of its culture between generations. This concept has only been modestly used in marketing, and has so far focused primarily on how children are socialized as consumers.

Social change

Sociologists have extensively studied how social systems (e.g. societies) change. This has important implications for marketing. Introduction of marketing thinking and practices to newly developing countries is, for example, assumed to enhance standards of living. Such an introduction will probably also imply dramatic social change. Characteristics of the societies may also hamper and/or alter the intended changes. Even though marketing activities are conducted to bring about changes in a societal context, few marketing studies so far have addressed the problem of social change (cf. Levy and Zaltman 1975). As society changes, marketing may change as well. For example, the explosive development in modern information technology has had dramatic effects on marketing.

Diffusion of innovations

This subject concerns how innovations (e.g. new ideas, practices or products) are spread within social systems and has been intensively studied by researchers from many disciplines, with great impact from sociology (see Rogers 1983 for an overview). Diffusion of innovations has had profound impact on marketing thinking, and researchers from the discipline have also contributed to this field. When studying diffusion of innovations, the innovation (e.g. a new product) represents something new to the potential adopter, but need not be a novelty in an absolute sense. For example, studies have demonstrated that some technologies take decades to be adopted. Diffusion of innovations is a true social phenomenon as it takes the social context directly into account. This becomes clear when looking at the elements in a diffusion process:

- the innovation;
- its communication from one individual (social actor) to another;
- within a social system (e.g. a society);
- over time.

More than 3,500 studies related to the diffusion of innovations have been conducted. Research findings show that characteristics of the innovation influence both the extent to which and how fast an innovation is diffused. For example, the perceived relative advantage has been demonstrated to have a profound effect on the propensity to adopt an innovation. A large number of studies demonstrates that the number of adopters over time follows an S-shaped curve. The time dimension for the total adoption process may, however, vary tremendously across innovation.[3]

Based on this regular pattern, adopters can be grouped according to when they adopt an innovation. Those adopting it at an early point in time, 'innovators' (or 'pioneers'), and 'early adopters' have been found to differ in characteristics and use of information sources compared to later adopters. For example, those adopting at an early stage tend to be more interested in and know more about the actual innovation, and tend to be more willing to try something new compared to later adopters and non-adopters. Research also shows that the propensity to adopt early varies across products (phenomena). Important findings from diffusion of innovations research are that later adopters tend to seek earlier adopters for advice, and that mass media information is diffused into the society via personal communication. Those adopting early and/or those who play a key role in personal communication of mass media information are frequently termed opinion leaders.

Findings from research on diffusion of innovations have influenced marketing in many ways, for example, in marketers' search for, development and evaluation of new products, marketing research and the profiling of target groups, design of marketing communication strategies, positioning of products and the 'stretching' of product life cycles.

SUMMARY AND FUTURE OUTLOOK

Marketing has borrowed extensively from sociology and much of this borrowing has been done in a mass marketing context with the prime purpose of profiling target groups as a basis for the design of more effective (mass) marketing. As other disciplines change so does marketing and more recently this borrowing seeks to capture relationships between social actors. An interesting observation is that almost no borrowing from sociology – with few exceptions – has been used to study change. This factor is surprising since marketing is primarily a dynamic phenomenon taking place in everchanging social contexts and one of its prime purposes is to effect change.

An additional observation is that the marketing discipline has been preoccupied primarily with transactions and exchanges falling within socially accepted norms, or even more restricted, visible, socially accepted market transactions (cf. Grønhaug & Dholokia 1987). In most societies many (legal) exchanges take place outside the visible, legal market (e.g. exchange of services between neighbours). Illegal exchanges also occur and in several countries the 'black economy' is estimated to constitute between 20 and 40 per cent of the gross national product. Distribution and marketing of illegal drugs and the selling of stolen goods are examples of deviant behaviour, but so far such exchanges have received only scant attention from marketers in spite of their importance. As noted by Zaltman and Wallendorf (1977) there are reasons to believe that the study of illegal exchanges can improve our understanding of marketing and its potential could be influential within legal and accepted social settings. To sum up:

- Much of the borrowing from sociology has been used as a basis for characterizing and profiling consumers and target groups (i.e. the use of the concepts have been 'one-sided', overlooking their social relational intentions as reflected in the mother discipline). This 'individualistic' perspective can probably explain the predominant influence from individual psychology as reflected in any major textbook on consumer behaviour.
- The borrowing from sociology has been applied primarily to legal, visible exchanges (i.e. only a subset of all marketing exchanges taking place). The extant work in sociology on deviant behaviour has so far been almost completely neglected.
- The borrowed concepts and ideas have mainly been used in static description and only to a modest extent to capture the dynamics of and to understand societal changes.[4]

Recent developments and changes in marketing perspectives indicate that social aspects, emphasizing relationships between social actors, will be more focused. This trend is probably only in its initial state, and is believed to continue. The influence of sociology on marketing thinking is likely to increase in the future and will probably be manifested in the following ways:

- Previously borrowed concepts (e.g. 'role', 'status' and 'group') will be applied to capture social dimensions as they were created to do, that is to capture aspects of relationships.
- Concepts and ideas to understand relationships, their initiation, changes, duration and termination will increase dramatically.
- The importance of the social context, and how it influences relationships and exchanges will be more emphasized in marketing thinking and research.
- It is also believed that dynamics and change, as emphasized in much of sociology, will have a greater impact on thinking and research in marketing in the future.

NOTES

1 An interesting observation is that there has been a considerable mutual influence between economics and sociology as reflected in the sub-discipline economic sociology (for excellent overviews, see Smelser 1963, Granovetter and Swedberg 1992).

2 An interesting observation is the recent interest in relationships and networks in American marketing thinking, without mentioning the fact that such ideas have been dealt with by European marketing scholars for almost three decades.

3 The observed S-shaped pattern allows (e.g. by using the formula) for a logistic curve to predict both rate and speed of adoption, based on observation from two points in time only.

4 This is also predominant in scholarly marketing empirical research. In spite of the dynamic character of marketing which involves time, the majority of empirical research is based on cross-sectional research designs, or experiments capturing only a limited time period between pre- and post-tests.

REFERENCES

Abercombie, N., Hill, S. and Turner, B. S. (eds) (1988) *Dictionary of Sociology*, 2nd edn, London: Penguin Books.

Alderson, W. (1958) 'The analytical framework for marketing', in D. J. Duncan (ed.) *Proceedings: Conference of Marketing Teachers from the West*, Berkeley, CA: School of Business Adm., University of California.

Arndt, J. (1980) 'Perspectives for a theory of marketing', *Journal of Business Research* 8: 389–402.

Berelson, B. and Steiner, G. A. (1964) *Human Behavior: An Inventory of Scientific Findings*, New York: Harcourt, Brace and World, Inc.

Blau, P. M. (1964) *Exchange and Power in Social Life*, New York: Wiley.

Codere, H. (1968) 'Social exchange', in D. H. Sills (ed.) *International Encyclopedia of the Social Sciences*, New York: Macmillan and the Free Press, 5: 238–344.

Cox, R. (1964) 'Introduction', in R. Cox, W. Anderson and S. J. Shapiro (eds) *Theory in Marketing*, Homewood, Ill.: Irwin.

Giddens, A. (1993) *Sociology*, 2nd edn, London: Polity Press.

Goldman, A. (1979) 'Publishing activity in marketing as an indicator of its structure and disciplinary boundaries', *Journal of Marketing Research* 16, November: 485–94.

Granovetter, M. (1985) 'Economic action and social structure: the problem of embeddedness', *American Journal of Sociology* 91 (3), November: 481–510.

Granovetter, M. and Swedberg, R. (eds) (1992) *The Sociology of Economic Life*, Boulder, Co.: Westview Press.

Grønhaug, K. and Dholokia, N. (1987) 'Consumer, markets and supply systems: a perspective on marketization and its effects', in F. A. Fuat, N. Dholokia and R. P. Bagozzi (eds) *Philosophical and Radical Thoughts in Marketing*, Lexington, MA: Lexington Books.

Hall, E. T. (1976) *Beyond Culture*, Garden City, New York: Anchor Press/Doubleday.

Hunt, S. D. (1983) 'General theories and the fundamental explanda of marketing', *Journal of Marketing* 47, Fall: 9–17.

Hunt, S. D. (1991) *Modern Marketing Theory. Critical Issues in the Philosophy of Marketing Science*, Cincinatti, OH: South-Western Publishing Co.

Kotler, P. (1984) *Marketing Management, Analysis, Planning and Control*, 4th edn, New Jersey: Prentice-Hall, Inc.

Kroeber, A. L. and Kluckhon, C. (1952) 'Culture: a critical review of concepts and definitions', *Papers of Peabody Museum* 47 (1A).

Levy, S. J. (1959) 'Symbols for sale', *Harvard Business Review* 37, July–August: 117–24.

Levy, S. J. and Zaltman, G. (1975) *Marketing Society, and Conflict*, New Jersey: Prentice-Hall, Inc.

Nicosia, F. M. and Mayer, R. N. (1976) 'Toward a sociology of consumption', *Journal of Consumer Research* 3, September: 65–75.

Polanyi, K. (1944) *The Great Transformation*, Boston: Beacon Press.

Rogers, E. M. (1983) *Diffusion of Innovations*, 3rd edn, New York: The Free Press.

Smelser, N. J. (1963) *The Sociology of Economic Life*, New Jersey: Prentice-Hall, Inc.

Swidler, A. (1986) 'Culture in actions: symbols and strategies', *American Sociological Review* 51, April: 273–86.

Wallendorf, M. (1978) 'Social roles in marketing contexts', *American Behavioral Scientist* 21 (4), March–April: 571–82.

Webster, F. E. (1992) 'The changing role of marketing in the corporation', *Journal of Marketing* 56, October: 1–17.

Zaltman, G. and Wallendorf, M. (1977) 'Sociology: the missing chunk or how we've missed the boat', in B. A. Greenberg and D. N. Bellinger (eds) *Contemporary Marketing Thought*, 1977 Educators' Proceedings, Chicago: American Marketing Association.

FURTHER READING

Blau, P. M. (1964) *Exchange and Power in Social Life*, New York: Wiley.

Coleman, J. S. (1988) 'Social capital in the creation of human capital', *American Journal of Sociology* 94, S95–120.

Dore, R. (1983) 'Goodwill and the spirit of market capitalism', *British Journal of Sociology* 34: 459–82.

Emerson, R. M. (1962) 'Power – dependence relations', *American Sociological Review* 27, February: 31–41.

Galaskiewicz, J. (1985) 'Interorganizational relations', *Annual Review of Sociology* 11: 281–304.

Granovetter, M. (1985) 'Economic action and social structure: the problem of embeddedness', *American Journal of Sociology* 91 (3), November: 481–510.

Heide, J. and John, G. (1992) 'Do norms matter in marketing relationships?', *Journal of Marketing* 56, April: 32–44.

Katz, E. and Lagarsfeld, P. (1955) *Personal Influence*, New York: Free Press.

Levy, S. J. and Zaltman, G. (1975) *Marketing Society, and Conflict*, New Jersey: Prentice-Hall, Inc.

Nicosia, F. M. and Mayer, R. N. (1976) 'Toward a sociology of consumption', *Journal of Consumer Research* 3, September: 65–75.

Polanyi, K. (1957) 'The economy as instituted process', in K. Polanyi, C. M. Arensberg and H. W. Pearson (eds) *Trade Market in Early Empires*, New York: Free Press.

Swidler, A. (1986) 'Culture in action: symbols and strategies', *American Sociological Review* 51, April: 273–86.

Wallendorf, M. (1978) 'Social roles in marketing contexts', *American Behavioral Scientist* 21 (4), March–April: 571–82.

Zaltman, G. and Wallendorf, M. (1977) 'Sociology: the missing chunk or how we've missed the boat' in B. A. Greenberg and D. N. Bollinger (eds) *Contemporary Marketing Thought*, 1977 Educators Proceedings, Chicago: American Marketing Association.

6

CULTURAL ASPECTS OF MARKETING

Kam-Hon Lee

INTRODUCTION

According to Hatch (1985), culture is 'the way of life of a people. It consists of conventional patterns of thought and behaviour, including values, beliefs, rules of conduct, political organization, economic activity, and the like, which are passed on from one generation to the next by learning – and not by biological inheritance'. Also, culture is 'governed by its own principles and not by the raw intellect, and that the differences among peoples do not reflect differences in levels of intelligence'. As such, there are many cultures in the world. In a way, there can be many cultures in a nation (Swanson 1989). It is widely recognized that theories in management and marketing are culture bound (Hofstede 1993; Tse *et al.* 1988). Marketing in one culture can be very different from marketing in a number of cultures. It becomes important to understand various issues related to launching marketing activities in a different culture.

The heart of the matter in marketing is to form a market and strike a business deal, which will bring benefits to all parties involved in the transaction. 'The marketing concept', the fundamental concept in marketing, refers to a philosophical conviction that customer satisfaction is the key to achieving organizational goals. Whether the customer is an individual or an organization, and whether the customer is nearby or in a foreign country, the challenge to the marketer is the same. Thus, the mission of marketing is to facilitate exchange and form a win-win relationship with other parties. This is no easy task when the marketer and the other parties share the same culture. It becomes even more difficult to accomplish the mission when the marketer and the other parties do not share the same culture.

This chapter will specifically examine three related issues on marketing in a different culture. First, can a marketing success in one culture be reproduced in another culture? If not, why not? If so, what are the conditions of success? Second, should a marketing success in one culture be reproduced in another culture? This is a more basic question than the first one. It examines the ethical foundation of marketing activities. Last but not the least, will cultures eventually converge? This is even more fundamental than the first two questions. When there is only one culture in the whole world, there is no need to study the cultural aspects of marketing.

CULTURE CAN POSE MARKETING PROBLEMS

First, can a marketing success be reproduced in another culture? Marketing people are supposed to be very sensitive to the changing needs of customers. Marketers know that they have to study customers' needs clearly, and deliver products which can meet those needs. When customers have different needs, marketers have to come up with different product offerings. Since customers in different cultures have minds which are programmed quite differently, it becomes important to differentiate their needs and to try to meet these needs differentially. However, even world-class marketers may not be sensitive enough to detect the differences in different cultures all the time.

Procter & Gamble (P&G) is an American giant, a model marketing company widely known to practice the marketing concept. P&G meets basic consumer needs with a strong research commitment to create products that are demonstrably better than the competition when compared in blind tests. P&G uses brand and category management systems and values market research highly, believing that it can enable the company to spot a new trend early and lead in it. Based on new liquid detergent technology and after extensive blind tests and market tests, P&G launched a new clothing detergent brand named Vizir in the early 1980s in Germany and Europe. Vizir was positioned as a complete main wash product, having superior performance in removing tough, greasy stains even in low temperature washing (Bartlett 1983).

Vizir got off to a good start all over Europe, and quickly became number one in the heavy-duty detergent category. However, in 1983 business began to weaken and the Vizir brand eventually lost about 15 per cent of its sales volume that year. In 1984 there was an additional 15 per cent sales decline. What P&G had failed to take into account was that European washing machines were at that time equipped to accept powder detergents but not liquids. When liquid detergent was added to a powder dispenser, as much as 20 per cent of the liquid was lost to a collecting point at the bottom of the machine. Thus, the product was not meeting consumers' performance expectation.

P&G changed the packages to explain better to consumers how to use Vizir, but research showed that this would not work. Subsequently, P&G managed to convince washing machine manufacturers in Europe to design liquid dispensers, but this had little impact on a market where the average machine was replaced only once every fifteen years. The next P&G attempt was to develop a retrofit system – a plastic device that fitted into existing powder dispensers and kept the liquid from leaking, while dispensing it at the same time. P&G would mail the device to consumers, free of charge, immediately after housewives told them the model number of their washing machines. However, most European machines were bolted to the wall, and the housewives were unable to see the model number; they did not know and they could not tell.

Finally, one technician in a French P&G product development laboratory invented a unique solution – a 'dosing ball' that P&G called a Vizirette. The consumer could fill the porous Vizirette 'dosing ball', place it in the washdrum on top of the clothes, and start the machine. The Vizirette would gradually dispense the detergent, with no waste. Vizir and Vizirette were subsequently introduced as a system (The Editors of Advertising Age 1989).

The story of the Vizir launch sends a strong signal to all marketers. Culture can pose marketing problems. Even when one is dealing with the most established concept in marketing (i.e. satisfying customers' needs), and even when it is implemented by a world-class marketer (i.e. P&G), it is no easy task to claim that one can move freely from one culture to another, and perform consistently well. If the story of the Vizir launch is helpful, the P&G experience in Japan is even more instructive.

MARKETING EFFORTS CAN OVERCOME CULTURAL PROBLEMS

P&G entered the Japanese market first in 1972–3. The consumer mind-set in Japan was quite unique. The primary buyer of packaged goods was the housewife. In Japan at least half the adult women were employed, but almost no Japanese mothers worked outside the home. Child-rearing was the first priority for a Japanese woman. The average family home was fifty square metres. Lack of storage necessitated several shopping trips per week and affected the structure of the distribution outlets, the market information the housewife commanded, and the relationship between shopkeeper and housewife. Thus, the market structure was quite indirect and long. Specialty and small retail stores constituted the bulk of retail outlets, commanding 72.3 per cent in 1982. There was also a close interpersonal relationship between the neighbourhood shopkeeper and the housewife. The typical Japanese customer for branded packaged goods was highly uncompromising, demanding superior quality and defining value more in terms of product performance, quality and reliability, rather than price. This attitude was even more pronounced in the area of personal hygiene. Thus, in Japan virtually all companies manufactured products to a standard of zero defects.

P&G entered Japan through a joint venture with Nippon Sunhome. They picked Cheer laundry detergent powder as a wedge to open the Japanese market for other major brands to follow. P&G followed the 'successful' formula in the USA to position and advertise 'Cheer' as an all-temperature laundry detergent powder in 1973, featured price promotions to support the advertising campaign, and went directly to the major retail chains to promote and distribute it. Cheer gained a substantial market share and managed to capture up to 12.6 per cent in the laundry detergents market in 1979. However, Cheer did not bring in profits. Also, when the featured pricing stopped in 1979 Cheer kept losing market share to different competitive brands (Kao's Wonderful, New Beads, Zab Total and Lion's Top Powder). Upon closer examination, it became clear that the three-temperature washing concept was not relevant to Japanese laundry habits. Women typically washed clothes in tap-water and occasionally the recycled family bath-water in the winter. The aggressive pricing practice only forced all players in the industry to incur substantial loss together. For example, P&G's all-temperature Cheer had been selling at 555 yens for two boxes against a suggested retail price of 800 to 850 yens for one box. Kao's New Beads large box had been selling at 400 yens against a previous resale price at 700 to 750 yens. This aggressive pricing practice antagonized all the competitors. In addition, the distribution policy through the major retail chains antagonized the wholesalers and the small retailers, who were the gatekeepers of mass distribution in Japan.

Practically all other P&G brands either failed in the test market or were preempted by competition due to a competitor's national launch of a copycat prior to the conclusion of P&G's 24-month test market period. The only exception was Pampers, which was launched in 1981 and immediately captured 85 per cent of the disposable diaper market. However, even Pampers was not completely successful. Unicharm, a relatively unknown company in Japan, introduced Moony in 1982, which was sold at a 40 per cent price premium to Pampers and managed to capture 40 per cent of the market share in 1983. In the meantime, Pampers dropped from its 1981 high of 90 per cent to its 1985 low of 6 per cent. It was quite clear that P&G could afford no more illusion. They had underestimated the sophistication level of Japanese consumers. P&G also underestimated the competitive strength of the Japanese companies. The operation in Japan was a total disaster (Yoshino and Stoneham 1990a).

It became clear to P&G in 1983 that what was best in the USA might not be good enough in Japan. This was at least true in the consumer packaged goods industry. P&G could join other well-respected packaged goods companies such as General Foods, General Mills and Colgate, who had all failed in Japan and retreated. However, P&G was convinced that Japan was a leading-edge country in the consumer goods industry, and the world leader had to be successful there. There was no other choice. If P&G could not compete with the Japanese companies in Japan, they would eventually have to compete with them in the USA. This conviction led to P&G's subsequent success in Japan, which managed to show that marketing efforts could overcome cultural problems (Yoshino and Stoneham 1990b).

The changing mentality at P&G started with the changing belief in research and development. P&G by that time believed that while American and European trends were helpful, the worldwide centre of innovation should be the Japanese consumer and competition. Thus, the R&D team in Japan was trying to develop products that would meet the needs of the Japanese consumers. While there were only 60 people in the P&G R&D group in Osaka, in comparison with Kao's 2,000 in Japan, P&G could depend on the unreserved support from the R&D group in Cincinnati. The race in R&D in the diaper product industry was instructive. P&G, Kao and Unicharm took turns to leapfrog one another in product upgrades, rendering the latest generation diaper obsolete within six months. Eventually P&G's R&D groups in Osaka and Cincinnati jointly developed the world's thinnest and most absorbent diaper, which became a clear winner over both Unicharm's Moony and Kao's Merries.

The biggest marketing challenge for P&G was to determine what advertising would work. It became clear to P&G that there was a virtual absence of side-by-side comparisons in Japanese advertising because of the indirectness of communication and the importance of harmony in Japanese culture. The tone of advertising was always friendly and never aggressive. Commercials often used background music and well-known celebrities. This author had a chance to review the P&G commercials used in Japan in the late 1970s and those used in the early 1990s. The improvement was obvious. For example, previously Pampers commercials featured an unhappy baby in an unhappy situation. Recent commercials featured happy babies in happy situations. To promote Cheer originally, P&G had merely applied the American copy to Japan, although Japanese housewives had no problems with water temperature. Recent commercials focused on the primary product benefit and dirt and odour removal.

There were commensurate changes in the distribution, manufacturing and organization areas. The whole package of changes showed that P&G was willing to take the other culture seriously, and make a commitment to invest resources to meet customers' needs. Where there is a will, there is a way, and marketing efforts can overcome cultural problems.

MARKETING POWER SHOULD RESPECT CULTURE

The examination of the ethical foundation of marketing in a different culture is equally if not more important. Should a marketing success be reproduced in another culture? Although marketing power is formidable, there should also be a limit. Limitation need not come from customers' resistance, which in fact is important in the marketplace to differentiate the capable from the less capable marketers. It will reward the capable and punish the less capable marketers. Such limitation is part of the reality in marketing interaction. However, there is another kind of limitation. It comes from company efforts to restrain the marketing power when it is appropriate for the company to do so. When customers are able to choose what would be best for themselves, consumer sovereignty can be assumed, and companies are free to exercise their marketing power to overcome the resistance and eventually manage to meet the customers' needs and conclude the deals. On the other hand, when customers are not able to choose what would be best for themselves, consumer sovereignty does not exist, and it becomes the responsibility of the company to restrain the marketing power for the sake of the public. One notable example is the case of infant formula selling in the Third World (Lee 1987).

Infant formula was developed by leading food giants in developed countries. The product was initially sold in developed countries as a substitute for breast milk. The case for infant formula is that it is available when breast milk is not (a less than 10 per cent chance), and when properly used it is an excellent alternative among all existing alternatives. In the developed and rich countries like the USA, mothers can usually afford to buy infant formula and know how to use it in hygienic conditions. Their education level is high and consumer sovereignty can be assumed. It would be enough to promote breast milk as the best choice while providing mothers a choice of settling with the 'second best' – the infant formula.

However, while infant formula is not defective in itself it is demanding. When risk conditions are present, it can be harmful to users. This became a serious issue in 1970 when the infant formula manufacturers adopted aggressive marketing efforts in developing nations (Post 1986). The problem becomes obvious when infant formula manufacturers promote heavily in a much less developed and poor country like Zambia. There are two real dangers. First, through poverty, compounded by ignorance, mothers tend drastically to overdilute the infant formula in order to make it last. As a result, infants starve and die. Second, poor hygiene causes serious troubles. Nestlé and other companies in the industry repeatedly claimed that they had no desire or intention to see unqualified consumers using their formula products. However, in 1978 at the US Senate hearings, when representatives from these companies were asked whether they had conducted any post-marketing research studies to determine who actually used their products, all representatives answered that their companies did no such research and did not know who actually used the products.

It becomes clear that the companies should be responsible for their marketing efforts. In order to guarantee that the users of infant formula products have proper information on their safe use and can make intelligent consumer choices, the companies may want to withdraw the marketing efforts or even the products from those countries. Mass marketing would certainly not be appropriate in view of the consumers' culture in such countries. If the product supply is meant to be helpful, it may be wise to do the promotion through the medical and health care system. Professionals there can exercise their judgments and make recommendations to the mothers. Nestlé's infant formula should not be regarded as an isolated case. Rather it should be regarded as an illustrative case for all kinds of first world products being sold in the Third World. There should be a similar level of sensitivity in reviewing the situation. It is important for marketing power to respect culture.

MARKETING CAMPAIGNS CAN UTILIZE
CULTURAL FEATURES

The above discussion may leave readers with the impression that marketing is the conqueror and culture is always trying to defend itself. This need not be the case. As a matter of fact, marketing campaigns can make use of the unique cultural features of the customers and the company to make a lasting impact. When a marketing programme is deeply rooted in a particular culture, the marketing programme can easily enjoy sustainable competitive advantages. In some situations, a company may 'discover' such a 'different' and perfectly compatible culture at home. The turnaround of Harley-Davidson in the American motorcycle industry is one of the most celebrated examples.

Before 1960 the motorcycle market in the USA had been mainly served by the American Harley-Davidson, BSA, Triumph and Norton of the UK, and Moto-Guzzi of Italy. Harley-Davidson was the market leader in 1959. However, in that year Honda and Yamaha entered the American market. Since the Japanese motorcycle industry had expanded rapidly after World War II to meet the need for cheap transportation in Japan, in 1959 the major Japanese producers, Honda, Yamaha, Suzuki and Kawasaki, together produced some 450,000 motorcycles, which was ten times larger than retail sales in the USA. Honda was already the world's largest motorcycle producer. These Japanese producers approached the American market in a systematic way. They started by penetrating the low end, light-weight market niche. They all placed emphasis on market share and sales volume. To realize their growth goals, the Japanese producers constantly updated or redesigned products to meet the needs of American customers; set prices at levels designed to achieve market share goals; reduced prices further when necessary; assembled full-time dealers to set up an effective distribution and maintenance network; and launched well-planned and heavy advertising campaigns. Because of scale economy and long-term strategic planning, by 1966 Honda, Yamaha and Suzuki together had 85 per cent of the US market. By 1974 apart from the Japanese producers Harley-Davidson was virtually the only company left in the market, keeping a mere 6 per cent market share (Buzzell and Purkayastha 1978).

The only option left for Harley-Davidson was to adopt niche marketing in a matured market. Harley-Davidson just concentrated on the super-heavyweight motorcycle market. However, because of the aggressive Japanese marketing efforts, even the market share in that niche had fallen from 75 per cent in 1973 to less than 25 per cent in 1980. At that time the parent company AMF was losing interest in Harley-Davidson. Early in 1981 Vaughn Beals and 12 other Harley executives wanted to take over the company through a leveraged buyout arrangement. They thought that they could do a better job and rescue the company. Subsequently, Harley-Davidson made several strategic moves that eventually led to the celebrated turnaround. In April 1983 President Reagan approved a recommendation by the International Trade Commission (ITC), raising the tariff on 'heavyweight' motorcycles (with engine displacements over 700 cc) from 4.4 per cent to 49.4 per cent for four years. The ITC's recommendation was to protect the domestic industry, and essentially the Harley-Davidson operation. Harley-Davidson made tremendous efforts to renovate the production process. They learned just-in-time manufacturing systems from the Japanese companies and adopted measures to encourage employee involvement. Production cost and product reliability were significantly improved. However, the major change and the secret of success was on the marketing side.

Harley-Davidson formed the Harley Owners Group in 1983. The acronym HOG is the affectionate name given by Harley riders to their motorcycles. Since motorcycles are often an impulse purchase, one of Harley's biggest challenges is to hold its new customers after they have bought a bike. HOG gives the new rider instant companionship through organized rides, rallies and charity runs. In 1991, with more than 155,000 members in 700 chapters worldwide, HOG is the motorcycle industry's largest company-sponsored enthusiast organization. Club members enjoy such features as a bi-monthly newsletter (*HOG Tales*), an automobile-club-type travel centre and reimbursement for motorcycle safety courses. The major attraction has been that at state, regional, national and international rallies, thousands of HOG members unite with company employees for a weekend of fun, entertainment, motorcycle demo rides and camaraderie in an atmosphere that clearly defines the 'Harley-Davidson lifestyle experience'. The rallies also give Harley executives a chance to find out what is on customers' minds.

When management celebrated Harley's 85th birthday in 1988, they arranged a party which reflected their unique way of getting close to customers. Motorcyclists were invited to participate in the event. All they had to do was to contribute US$10 to Harley-Davidson's favourite philanthropic organization, the Muscular Dystrophy Association. Starting from as far away as San Francisco and Orlando, Florida, groups of cyclists headed for Milwaukee. Each group was led by a Harley-Davidson executive, including the board chairman Vaughn Beals, and chief executive officer Rich Teerlink. Thousands of Harleys, many flying American flags, rumbled into Milwaukee on 18 June, shaking the air with the sound of their engines. Some riders had dogs, others their children. Riders wore different kinds of clothing, and they were all ages. The celebrants spent the day participating in such activities as slow races. Beals and Teerlink, among other executives, submitted themselves to the celebrity dunk tank, where they were dumped into the water by on-target baseball throwers. Music resounded all the time. At the final ceremonies, 24,000 bikers watched videotapes of their ride to Milwaukee projected on to two giant screens. As riders saw their own groups, they would shout. Thousands of Harley owners rose to their feet and burst into an unrivalled demonstration of product loyalty.

In 1989 Harley-Davidson managed to capture close to 60 per cent of the super-heavyweight motorcycle market in the USA (Rose 1990). The momentum has continued into the 1990s. The charity events and public-spirited programmes such as company reimbursement for Harley owners who took rider education classes, helped a great deal in promoting the company image. The HOG and cross-country motorcycle treks come from the root of American culture. Only Harley-Davidson can utilize these cultural features and promote nationalism in a natural way. Honda tried to form a similar group to HOG, which quite expectedly soon faded away (Fortune 1989).

CULTURE AND THE GLOBALIZATION OF MARKETS

It would not be appropriate to discuss the cultural aspects of marketing without mentioning Levitt's widely cited article on the globalization of markets (1983). In this powerful article, Levitt asserted that well-managed companies had moved from emphasis on customizing items to offering globally standardized products that are advanced, functional, reliable and low priced. Will cultures eventually converge? If so, it will no longer be necessary to examine the cultural aspects of marketing. Levitt's thesis was derived from his observation of a powerful force, technology, which was driving the world toward a converging commonality. High-tech products were standardized. High-touch products like Coca-Cola, Levi jeans and Revlon cosmetics would be the same. According to Levitt, 'everywhere everything gets more and more like everything else as the world's preference structure is relentlessly homogenized'. Levitt predicts that the global corporation will know everything about one great thing. The corporation will know about the absolute need to be competitive on a worldwide basis as well as nationally and seek constantly to drive down prices by standardizing what it sells and how it operates. Its mission is modernity and its mode price competition, even when the corporation sells top-of-the-line, high-end products. What all markets have in common is an overwhelming desire for dependable, world-standard modernity in all things, at aggressively low prices. Later in 1988, in one of the editorials he wrote for *Harvard Business Review*, Levitt created a concept called 'the pluralization of consumption' to supplement his theory of global homogenization. According to his prediction, the whole world is made up of one market segment, which consists of people with plural preferences, the new world of the heteroconsumer.

While this author enjoys reading all Levitt's writings and accepts the points he made in most of his articles, it is only appropriate to reject this contention by Levitt. If world-class marketers like P&G encountered clear cultural problems in Europe and Japan, it is quite obvious that the market is not homogenized even among the most developed countries. The case of Nestlé's infant formula is even more convincing. The economic gap between the North (those who have) and the South (those who have not) is so obvious. It is not possible to assume that people in the Third World should be approached in the same way as people in the first world. If this is still not enough, the case of

110

Harley-Davidson shows us clearly that even in the most developed marketplace in the world, the USA, culture and its consequences play a key role in marketing. Harley-Davidson depends on the cultural features to guard its market niche. No Japanese companies can reproduce the same cultural impact on American consumers. The foundation of Hofstede's (1984) seminal study on culture is the nation. As long as the national boundaries exist, and as long as there are reasons for nations to reinforce the differences between nations, the impact of culture will be here to stay.

Coca-Cola is probably the best known brand name in the world. If there is a universal standard product in the world, Coca-Cola is very likely to be one of the best, if not the best, contender. However, when the Coca-Cola company began to sell their products aggressively in China, it was clear that the reception there was atypical. Contrary to expectation, Sprite (the number two brand from the Coca-Cola company) was selling much better than Coca-Cola (the flagship) in China. Also, it was quite clear that the universal advertising copy was not at all well received in China. This led to a special advertising production for China. In the new advertising commercial that was launched in 1992, one could see the favourite Chinese images such as family ties, wedding ceremonies, Chinese New Year and the great earth. These cultural themes were clearly unique to China and the Chinese. A pop singer from Taiwan, who was best received in the mainland, was commissioned to compose and sing the theme song for that advertising commercial. This is clear evidence that consumers are not homogenized. The impact of culture is here to stay.

DYNAMIC CULTURE AND DYNAMIC MARKETPLACE

While it is unlikely that cultures will converge and form one world culture in the foreseeable future, this does not mean that cultures are stagnant. The impact of culture is here to stay, but culture itself is dynamic and changing. When the culture of a particular economy is changing, more often than not there should be commensurate changes of marketing efforts in order to enable the company and the brand to ride together with the tide. The case of Hong Kong should be instructive since it has gone through significant changes in the past several decades.

Hong Kong has been a British colony for more than ninety years. Culturally, Hong Kong has always been a Chinese society. When the Communist Party was about to take power in mainland China, many Chinese industrialists in the textile industry came to Hong Kong. They brought with them their best technicians and operators, together with money and their best equipment. In the 1950s and 1960s Hong Kong became a rapidly growing manufacturing centre with a firm base in textiles and clothing. The typical work ethic at that time was diligent and frugal, carried over from the agricultural society. Because of continued growth and prosperity, Hong Kong became quite affluent in the 1970s and well into the 1980s. In the meantime, Hong Kong people began to work more shrewdly rather than harder. They no longer feel that they are poor and even if they actually are they feel that they can become rich if they do it right tomorrow. The issue of the end of colonization in 1997 was much felt in Hong Kong, beginning in late 1982, and remains a part of daily news. Hong Kong people have been forced to reflect on their own identities. Before the issue of 1997 became real, Hong Kong people had refused to think about it, and regarded themselves as Chinese. When the changes in 1997 became a reality, Hong Kong people began to see that there is a difference between the identity of a Hong Kong person and the identity of a Chinese person. Although Hong Kong people are also Chinese, they are not Chinese in the same way as those from the mainland or Taiwan. This development is gradual but real and carries implications for marketing campaigns. It may be instructive to review the development of advertising themes for a popular soft drink in Hong Kong, since the soft drink industry may best reflect the preference of the mass society. It is about the story of Vitasoy, a soya bean milk developed in Hong Kong (Lai 1991).

The Vitasoy story began with a big idea and a little bean. Vitasoy was a milk substitute made from ground soya bean with water and sugar. It was launched as 'the poor people's milk' in the 1940s. The major theme was to deliver adequate nutrition at low cost. They promised that people would become taller, stronger and healthier. Vitasoy had always been sold at about two-thirds of the price level of leading soft drinks such as Coca-Cola. People took Vitasoy because it was thirst quenching and at the same time good for body strength. One bottle of Vitasoy met two kinds of needs. It appealed to people who were poor and frugal. This product position continued to function well in the 1950s and 1960s. However, in the 1970s this advertising theme became ineffective. Hong Kong people no longer thought of themselves as poor and malnourished. In 1974 Vitasoy decided to make a drastic change and reposition the product. They used Tetra Brik Asceptic packaging to present a new image and to make the product available in supermarkets, which had started to become a more important retail outlet than grocery stores. They raised the product price level to the ordinary price level for prestigious soft drinks, since price was no longer a concern among customers. The incremental margin would enable the company to put up more aggressive marketing campaigns. The advertising theme was changed to 'more than a simple soft drink'. The new theme created a 'fun' image and at the same time preserved the 'nutritious/healthy' image, which was still helpful to differentiate Vitasoy from other soft drinks. This advertising theme went well for more than a decade, and then went off steam. In 1988 they adopted another new theme, 'you must have been a beautiful baby'. This theme reinforced the Hong Kong identity and also enabled Vitasoy to differentiate itself from all other soft drinks which were from different countries. Since Hong Kong people at that time had begun to have confidence in their own identity, this advertising theme was timely and effective. Vitasoy has been continuously successful and the advertising themes adopted over the years have kept pace with the changing culture in Hong Kong. This is strong evidence that culture and marketing go together in a dynamic fashion. There will be no effective marketing if full attention is not paid to its cultural aspects.

CONCLUSION

Marketing theories are culture bound. Marketing success is also culture bound. When a company has developed a successful marketing formula in one culture, it is justified to try to enjoy scale economy and apply it in another culture. However, it is important to take heed and make sure that the conditions exist there to reproduce the same marketing success. Otherwise, the marketing failure can be very costly. The story of the P&G launch of Vizir is very instructive. On the other hand, the eventual success of P&G in Japan is reassuring. Good marketing efforts, even in a different culture, will pay off.

Marketing is not just profit making. When a company launches a marketing programme in a different culture, the first question that should be asked is whether the company respects the host culture. In some special situations, as demonstrated in Nestlé's infant formula case in the Third World, it may even be appropriate to adopt various demarketing measures at the expense of 'marketing success'. When a company learns to respect culture, the efforts will pay off. When the marketing programme and the culture are glued together, sustainable competitive advantages are guaranteed. The rebirth of Harley-Davidson celebrates this truth.

Although there are merits in Levitt's vision of a convergent world culture (1983, 1988), it is unlikely that this vision will become a reality in the foreseeable future. Thus, it will continue to be important to examine the cultural aspects of marketing. Levitt's thesis, in a way, reinforces the conviction that culture is developing and changing. It becomes important for the marketer to continue to study the cultural aspects of marketing even when the company is operating in the same place as before. Since culture is developing and changing, even home culture can become very different in the course of time. It becomes imperative to examine the cultural aspects of marketing whether one is operating at home or abroad.

REFERENCES

Bartlett, Christopher A. (1983) *Procter & Gamble Europe: Vizir Launch*, Boston, MA: Harvard Business School.
Buzzell, Robert D. and Purkayastha, Dev (1978) *Note on the Motorcycle Industry – 1975*, Boston, MA: Harvard Business School.
The Editors of Advertising Age (1989) *Procter & Gamble, How P&G Became America's Leading Marketer*, Lincolnwood, Illinois: NTC Business Books.
Fortune (1989) 'How Harley beat back the Japanese', *Fortune* 25 September: 93–6.
Hatch, Elvin (1985) 'Culture', in Adam Kuper and Jessica Kuper (eds) *The Social Science Encyclopedia*, London: Routledge.
Hofstede, Geert (1984) *Culture's Consequences, International Differences in Work-Related*

Values, Beverly Hills, CA: Sage Publications.

Hofstede, Geert (1993) 'Cultural constraints in management theories', *Academy of Management Executive* 7 (1), February: 81–94.

Lai, Linda (1991) 'Fortune built on a bean', *Hong Kong, inc.* 18, June: 26–47.

Lee, Kam-Hon (1987) 'The informative and persuasive functions of advertising: a moral appraisal – a further comment', *Journal of Business Ethics* 6 (1): 55–7.

Levitt, Theodore (1983) 'The globalization of markets', *Harvard Business Review* 61, May–June: 92–102.

Levitt, Theodore (1988) 'The pluralization of consumption', *Harvard Business Review* 66, May–June: 7–8.

Post, James E. (1986) 'Ethical dilemmas of multinational enterprises: an analysis of Nestlé's traumatic experience with the infant formula controversy', in W. Michael Hoffman, Ann E. Lange and David A. Fedo (eds) *Ethics and the Multinational Enterprise*, Lanham, MD: University Press of America, Inc.

Rose, Robert L. (1990) 'Harley regains lead in big-bike market', *Asian Wall Street Journal*, 7–8 September.

Swanson, Lauren A. (1989) 'The twelve "nations" of China', *Journal of International Consumer Marketing* 2 (1): 83–105.

Tse, David K., Lee, Kam-Hon, Vertinsky, Ilan and Wehrung, Donald A. (1988) 'Does culture matter? A cross-cultural study of executives' choice, decisiveness, and risk adjustment in international marketing', *Journal of Marketing* 52 (4), October: 81–95.

Yoshino, Michael and Stoneham, Paul H. (1990a) *Procter & Gamble Japan (A)*, Boston, MA: Harvard Business School.

Yoshino, Michael and Stoneham, Paul H. (1990b) *Procter & Gamble Japan (C)*, Boston, MA: Harvard Business School.

7

QUANTITATIVE METHODS IN MARKETING

John Saunders

INTRODUCTION

Quantitative methods take marketing from an art to a science, from conjecture to rigour. They have three main roles: market modelling, validation of research results and market analysis.

Market models represent market behaviour mathematically. For example, an equation can represent the relationship between sales and advertising. Managers can manipulate this on a spreadsheet to ask 'what if' questions, for example: 'What would sales be if advertising was increased by £100,000?' With financial dimensions added it could reveal the profitability of changing advertising levels or show the optimum expenditure.

Validation measures the significance of results. Market researchers often conduct surveys to find how customers respond to different treatments, such as the use of a blue or yellow wrapper on a bar of chocolate. The results could show that 32 per cent of people said they would buy the chocolate in the blue wrapper, compared with 29 per cent for the yellow wrapper. Validation uses statistical methods to measure if the difference between the 32 per cent and 29 per cent is significant. It asks if the results are significantly different or could they have occurred by chance.

Market analysis uses statistical methods to view markets. Sometimes it is a way of viewing mathematically what can be seen manually. A manager could plot sales and price and see the relationship. Alternatively, he could use statistical methods to investigate the pattern and so build a marketing model. The great value of quantitative methods in market analysis comes when markets get more complicated and the number of influences increases. There are many influences on a market so plotting sales against price often reveals little since it ignores the intervention of sales promotion, advertising, competitive intervention or economic variables. Quantitative methods can help disentangle this complexity. Techniques can look across thousands of cases where there are many influences

115

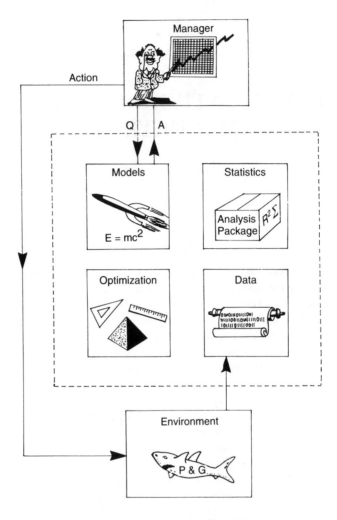

Figure 1   Managers and models
Source: Little (1979: 12)

and detect patterns that inspection would not reveal.

Market analysis methods can go beyond the automation of manual tasks and the investigation of complex models. Techniques are now available that look at markets in new ways. Their role is like an X-ray or ultrasonic scan in medicine. The doctor could look at a patient from the outside or even cut the patient open to look inside, but X-rays give a new view. The same is true of market analysis models. Markets appear in a way not seen by conventional means.

116

All three types of quantitative methods in marketing have a huge literature and are developing rapidly. There is also research by different people, who have developed their own traditions. Green *et al.* (1988) and Lilien *et al.* (1992) review the major areas considered here. The remainder of this chapter will introduce the elements of the market modelling process, statistical methods of validation, market analysis methods and some of the new computer intensive methods of market data analysis.

MARKET MODELLING

In his influential review Little (1979) showed the main components of a marketing model (Figure 1). Urban (1974) shows how other blocks help build models for managers. Each stage of a full model building and implementation process (Figure 2) is explained.

Entry

Managers rarely build the models they use. There is, therefore, a relationship between the manager and model builder. The entry stage reflects the importance of the first five seconds, minutes, hours or days of that contact. Unless trust and mutual understanding occur, any model built is likely to fail or be unused. Critical ingredients are for the modellers to understand the needs of managers and for the managers to have ownership of the model. The modeller has to listen and be concerned for the dimensions of successful models identified by Little (1970). A model should be:

1   as simple as possible – contain the necessary detail and no more;
2   robust, be relied upon to give sensible results whatever the manager inputs;
3   easy to use;

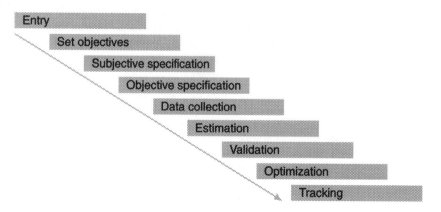

Figure 2   The market model building process

4   adaptive, so that it can accommodate new ideas or changes in the way the problem is seen;
5   complete in including all the issues that are important.

Objectives

The objectives set influence a model's design. If the objective is to forecast short-term sales, then a simple time series model will do. These predict future sales based on past sales history (see Chapter 21). More complex models allow managers to see how the marketing mix and their competitors influence sales. The output of a model could still be sales, but that would be dependent on more variables. At a higher level the models can optimize sales or determine strategy. This would influence the inputs and outputs; rather than just looking at sales, a manager may want to view contribution or profitability.

Subjective specification

Subjective specification captures the beliefs of managers and modellers about how markets behave. Table 1 contains a list devised in developing an advertising model for a major retailer (Doyle and Saunders 1990). These are worth explaining because they are generalizations that apply across most marketing variables on most occasions. The first three items express the common belief that the relationship between advertising and sales is a curve showing decreasing returns to scale, like P3 in Figure 3. Advertising effects carry over from one period to the next (Leeflang et al. 1992). The variability of marketing effects is often surprising. In the margarine market, some brands are more responsive to promotions than others. This may depend on the segments or their advertising. There are also cross-effects between competitors or, in the case of a retailer, between the sales of one merchandise and another.

Other advertising effects appear in the literature but are less reliable. It is rare to find increasing returns to scale from advertising although some believe that there is a threshold level. Saturation effects may exist at a level of sales beyond which a brand will never sell, but rarely is the dominance of a product such that these

Table 1   The subjective specification of advertising effects

1   Advertising has a small positive influence on sales.
2   It shows diminishing returns to scale.
3   Sales are not zero when advertising is zero.
4   There are lagged effects.
5   Advertising effects vary across products, brands and campaigns.
6   There are cross effects of advertising – the advertising of one merchandise will influence the sale of others.

Source: Doyle and Saunders (1990)

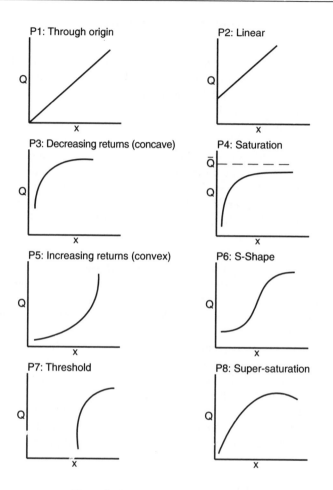

Figure 3 The shapes of market response

points are achievable. The biggest myth of all is super-saturation, where the excessive promotion of a product reduces its sales. After a review of the evidence Simon (1970) declared threshold effects 'to be a monstrous myth'.

This qualitative stage can have a big impact upon the final results given by a marketing model. An extreme case is the difference between the belief in increasing returns to scale (P5 in Figure 3) and decreasing returns to scale (P3 in Figure 3). If a model represents decreasing returns to scale for three brands, then it will suggest the optimum strategy is to spend evenly across them. In contrast, if there are increasing returns of scale the model will suggest the best strategy is to spend all the money on one brand and neglect the others.

Objective specification

Objective specification involves finding a mathematical function that is tractable and comes as close as possible to fitting the subjective specification. It is perhaps surprising to non-modellers to find out how awkward this can be. Table 2 lists some common expressions and Table 3 their relationship to the qualitative specification. The choice made depends on asking a series of questions and parsimony (simplicity):

- How many right features has the expression? No expression has all the desirable features and will always be unable to give a perfect fit to any data. The question then becomes, 'Which are the critical features?' For example, in measuring the impact of shelf space, it may not matter if the log-log expression shows that sales are zero if a product has zero shelf space. This would be quite unacceptable in an advertising model, where sales occur in periods with no advertising.
- How many of the wrong features does the expression have? An expression may have a very good fit in some ways, but be completely wrong in others. A polynomial expression is flexible but it can give ludicrous results if extrapolated. It will always show sales proceeding towards plus or minus infinity at its extremes.
- Can it be estimated? In some cases the unknown coefficients are easily estimated using regression analysis. In other cases, like the very flexible Gompertz expression, they cannot. This means more computer intensive and less familiar methods have to be used.
- Can it be optimized? The linear expression gives no optimum at all, so is quite hopeless if the aim is to use the model to allocate sales across products or media. It can guide the allocation of resources, but it gives no indication

Table 2 Common expressions

	Name	*Expression*
Linear	Simple	$Y = a + bX$
	Squared	$Y = a + bX^2$
	Square root	$Y = a + bX^{0.5}$
	Reciprocal	$Y = a + b^{1/X}$
Log linearizable	Semi-log	$Y = a + b\ln X$
	Exponential	$\ln Y = a + bX$
	Log reciprocal	$\ln Y = a + b/X$
	Log-log	$\ln Y = a + b\ln X$
Not linearizable	Little	$Y = a + (b - c).X^d/(e + X^d)$
	Gompertz	$\ln Y = a + b.c^X$
	Logistics	$Y = a/(1 + \exp(b + cX))$
	Modified exponential	$Y = a(1 - \exp(- bX^c))$

Table 3 Characteristics of specifications

Feature (Proposition)	Threshold (7)	X = Y = 0 (1)	Saturation (4)	Super-saturation (8)	Non-linear	Others
Straight (2)						Linear
Increasing (5)		Log-log				Exponential Squared
Decreasing (3)	Reciprocal Semi-log Log-log	Modified exponential	Reciprocal Semi-log	Quadratic	Modified exponential	Square root
S-shaped (6)		Log reciprocal	Gompertz	Cubic	Logistics Gompertz	
Universal			Little	Polynomial		

of when to stop. Other expressions, like the semi-log model, give simple allocation rules read direct from the equations. Others, like the non-linearizable expressions, are much harder to optimize. In reality, any expression with diminishing returns can give optima but it is much easier for some than for others.

- Has it worked before? Some expressions have gained credibility by their wide use; others have few applications. The log-log model has some deficiencies but is flexible and so used to represent the marketing mix. The simplicity of the semi-log model makes it popular in allocation problems. Using popular models reduces the chance of a gross misspecification biasing results.

In their advertising budgeting model Doyle and Saunders (1990) used a semi-log model to represent the relationship between sales of recorded music and advertising expenditure:

$$S_t = c + p\ln(P_{t-1}) + v\ln(V_{t-1}) + u_t \qquad (7.1)$$

where

S_t = sales in week t,
P_{t-1} = press advertising in previous week,
V_{t-1} = TV advertising in previous week,
c = unknown constant,
p, v = unknown elasticities,
u_t = error term and
ln = natural logarithms.

Data collection

The data available are limiting. Depending on the problem, the data can be cross-sectional or time series. Time series models (tracking models) can estimate the effect of advertising or sales promotion on sales or market share. Rarely are annual data usable, since the number of time series points needed mean the modeller would have to go back too long in order to get enough data (i.e. 24 years). Over the times the relationships between sales and the marketing mix variables must have changed and so the whole exercise made unreliable. Monthly data are more reasonable because 3 years' data, of which relationships may have been similar, give 36 time points. However, even over that time campaigns can change and there can be discontinuities in the data. There is also seasonality to contend with.

Cross-sectional data exist where data come from several places at the same time. For example, in stores, electronic point-of-sales information means it is possible to look at the relationship between sales and merchandising across a large number of outlets.

Results are biased if the data collected are inaccurate or if some time series

122

are more accurate than others. TVRs that measure television audiences are more accurate than measures of any other media so tend to show stronger results. There will always be bias due to different qualities of data, but where possible the data compared should be similar in quality. This bias suggests the media trade associations would do well to improve the quality of recording their exposure if they hope to improve the measured effectiveness and therefore desirability of using their media.

Estimation

Estimation sometimes seems the easiest of the modelling activities. Anyone with a PC can now input data and use regression analysis to get some results. Results will exist but, if there is poor specification and the methods not understood, expect GIGO (garbage in, garbage out). Estimation is an area in which a little knowledge can do a lot of damage.

Regression analysis is an indirect method because it does not explore the data for a best solution but computes a best fit to data using calculus. Equation 7.1 was estimated using regression analysis to give the following relationship:

$$S_t = 3,330 + 323\ln(P_{t-1}) + 359\ln(V_{t-1}) + u_t \qquad (7.2)$$

It shows both press and TV advertising having a similar positive effect on sales. This is an elegant approach but it needs a large number of assumptions to be made. These are embodied in the error term (u_t) in equation 7.1. Very often they are not true. Two examples will explain the situation. It assumes the data are not auto correlated, that means observation 2 does not depend on observation 1, observation 3 does not depend on observation 2, etc. This is certainly not true in much time series data where a sales promotion campaign in one period can mean that none will take place in the next. Another assumption is that of no multicolinearity; that means that the independent variables, say sales promotion and price, vary independently. This is often not true and would be the sign of bad marketing. Defy these rules and the results of regression are unreliable. In some cases artificially high elasticities occur and, in other cases, the significance of one strong variable can drive the significance of a weaker one with which it is multicolinear. These limitations do not mean the regression is unusable but it does mean the user has to understand the limitations and how to test for their presence. This is where validation is important and there is a need to understand the statistics that regression packages produce. All is not lost if the assumptions of ordinary lease squared regression, the most common form, are not true. It is sometimes possible to remove the problem by changing the specification by, say, introducing lag effects or combining multicolinear variables. It is also possible to use more advanced forms of regression that relax some of the assumptions of ordinary lease squares. Generalized lease squares regression, latent root regression and ridge regression are examples (Naert and Leeflang 1978).

In circumstances when expressions are not linearizable, direct methods of estimation are possible. There are many of these search procedures that estimate a model by searching iteratively for a best solution. The methods are usually very computer intensive but the cost of processing is declining so much that it is feasible to use them. They are not one method, but many. Some of these are like trying to climb Mount Everest by starting in the Sahara and looking at the ground immediately beneath one's feet as a way of gauging which direction would lead you to the highest point. Clearly sub-optimization, or climbing a molehill rather than Mount Everest, is a potential problem. There are ways of overcoming these problems. Breightler *et al.* (1979) review many of the procedures.

Recent years have seen creative leaps in the ways in which we can find a best answer to a problem. Some of these take lessons from nature, like artificial annealing, named after the annealing of metals. Other methods, like neural networks, model the workings of a brain in divining solutions. In the financial markets these methods have proved most impressive. Much development work is still being done and the techniques are far from universally understood or available. For a review of them see Coates *et al.* (1994).

Validation

There are three stages in the validation of a marketing model. The first stage examines the statistics describing the model. The simplest test is for face validity. This asks does the model look right? If the results show that sales decline with advertising then something is wrong. A second set of validation statistics tests the overall quality of the model. A correlation coefficient, or r-squared, shows how well the model describes the data. If r-squared is 1, then the fit is perfect; if zero, there is no fit at all. An analysis of variance (ANOVA) using the F-test is another way of doing this. It also examines the contribution of parts of a model. Student t-tests are very common and useful because they show whether an independent variable, like sale promotions, has a significant contribution or not.

Providing the first stage validation statistics for equation 7.2 gives:

$$S_t = 3,330 + 323\ln(P_{t-1}) + 359\ln(V_{t-1}) + u_t \qquad (7.3)$$

$$(24.6)^a \quad (3.2)^a \qquad (4.5)^a$$

$$r^2 = 0.93^a \qquad F(153,3) = 144^a$$

In this equation the numbers in the brackets under the equation are individual t-tests for the constant, press and TV advertising elasticities. The *a* indicates that the values are all significant at a 0.05 level. That means that there is a less than one chance in twenty of figures occurring by chance. The r^2 shows how well the equation fits the data used to build it: being close to 1.00, the result is good and 93 per cent of the variation in sales is explained. ANOVA gives the F statistic that compares the variation explained by the constant and the two elasticities (the number 3 in the brackets) against the variation remaining in the other degrees of freedom (153). The degrees of freedom are the difference between the number of estimates in the equation and the total number of observations (155 weeks of weekly data).

Second stage validation usually uses a holdout sample to see whether the model works in predicting new observations. If the data are a time series, then six months' data can be kept back and the model used to forecast it; if cross sectional, a sample of stores not used in the model and then predicted. In second stage validation, equation 7.2 (p. 123) was tested with a 12 weeks holdout sample. This showed a small 1 per cent loss in predictive accuracy compared with the model building sample.

Where data are sparse the U-method can be used. This involves (1) holding out a series of sub-sets of the data; (2) building a model without that data; and (3) seeing if that sub-set fits the model. At the extreme case, one observation is held out and the model computed as many times as there are observations. A benefit of this approach is the realization that the result of estimating this series of different models with sub-sets of data removed gives average results that approximate to a very large sample. The results from this process are jack-knife estimates.

Optimization

Optimization means using the model to find the best solution, for example, to find the best expenditure across media or allocation of shelf space to merchandise. This may be of no interest if the model is used only to guide decisions. Managers can use spreadsheets to represent and manipulate models easily, so use a model to find their favoured strategy. This works with simple problems but managers quickly hit human limitations. It is hard for people to understand complex interactions or to have the patience to search for a best of many options. There are also cases where there are just too many variables to consider or, in the case of the retailing example, too many stores and too much merchandise to manipulate manually.

If models are simple and conveniently specified, calculus can provide optimum solutions. Often this means introducing a structural equation that adds the cost of action. The model would then represent profitability. Using log-log or semi-log specifications to represent the marketing mix, decreasing returns on expenditure would show. Equation 7.2 can be interpreted very easily, the optimum allocation of advertising expenditure between the media is proportional to their elasticities: £323 on press advertising to each £359 spent on TV.

Iterative processes are an alternative if specifications are too complex for calculus. These could be the old hill-climbing techniques, integer programming – that looks at the marginal effect of spending each individual pound across media – or the more modern artificial annealing.

Nature comes to our aid in optimizing marketing models. Simulations show that, near the best solution, there is a large area where radical changes (in advertising etc.) have little impact on short-term profitability. This is not because the marketing mix variables have little impact but that at the optimum solution one pound in expenditure is balancing one pound in contributions. This insensitivity of the optimum has two assets and one liability. The assets are that unless the model is grossly misspecified and estimated naively, results tend to be similar. They also give management a great deal of room to manoeuvre since there is a whole range of combinations of variables that give roughly sales or profitability. Viewed in this way, a model provides a ball park in which the manager can play. If the issue is advertising expenditure then, without affecting profitability significantly, the manager can take a low-budget approach and sacrifice sales but keep profits up, or an aggressive approach that tends to give the same profits, but increases market share. The domain in which marketing managers make decisions is fortuitously like a plateau rather than a mountain range, where even significant deviations from the best solution can still give reasonable results. This plateau is also a liability to the optimization process. Although deviation from the best answer does not have a significant impact on profit, so flat is the surface that even slight variations in the estimated effects of the marketing mix variables can have a huge effect on the optimum solution. One year the optimum advertising expenditure may be £2 million and the next £1 million because of a slight change in elasticity. This does not mean that either answer is bad but they are both points on the plateau that, because of local variation, make them look slightly higher at one time.

Tracking

Once started, the need for the market modelling never stops. Each year companies, markets, customers and new campaigns change. This means the marketing mix must also alter. What is the best solution in one year will not be the best in another year. Tracking looks at past solutions to see if they still work. It checks deviations to see if the model needs new information. It feeds back into future model building.

Market modelling summary

Managers need knowledge both to use and to build models. The process leaves traps for the unwary but there is now considerable knowledge about what works. Some convenient conclusions come from experience. Simple methods often give answers that are as good and reliable as much more sophisticated methods. There is a need to understand the basics of the specifications and how to estimate models. Managers need to be able to ask questions and see whether results are reliable.

Market modelling looks rigid and certain but it is not. Experience and judgement play a major role and the results are useful to guide decision-making, not make decisions. Mathematics constrain the modeller like nature the engineer. The aeronautical engineer makes do with aluminium with its fatigue problems because that is the best material available for the job. The market modeller faces the same problems. All the dimensions may be understood and all desired characteristics known, but there is just no way of representing them all. A model can guide a manager away from the worst solutions and towards the best ones, but strategic decisions are the managers'.

VALIDATION MEASURES

Validation measures appear in marketing modelling (Coates *et al.* 1991), but they are also essential to empirical marketing research. They are statistical techniques used to reject or accept a hypothesis. In the tradition of logical positivism a researcher starts by setting out a hypothesis and designing an experiment to test it. Jobber and Saunders (1988) did this when investigating international questionnaire response rates where they hypothesized that questionnaires between countries would have a lower response rate than questionnaires within countries. As Table 4 shows, there were differences in the response rates within the USA and the UK and between them. It suggests that both the Americans and British are more likely to respond to domestic questionnaires (9 and 13 per cent) than international ones (6 and 5 per cent). Validation measures ask if the difference is sufficient for it not to have occurred by chance. In this case they compared sample proportions using a t-test. This shows that there is a significant difference between the British response rates (5 vs. 13) but not between the American ones (6 vs. 9). In other words, there is evidence to suggest that the British are more responsive to domestic questionnaires, but there is insufficient evidence to support the hypothesis that Americans have the same bias.

There are similar tests for other situations:

1   If samples are large (over 30), normal distribution tests see if sample scores or proportions are significant. For instance: 'Do salesmen who have gone through a sales training programme make higher commission than those who have not?' or: 'Is the proportion of people responding to a six-page questionnaire significantly less than the proportion responding to a three-page one?'

2   If samples are small (less than 30) then a t-test compares the difference between two small sample means. This is often essential where data gathering costs are high or some sample populations are small, such as industrial markets.

3   It is common to cross-tabulate survey results, say social class versus voting behaviour. A pattern may show but validation measures ask if the results could have occurred by chance.

127

Table 4   Source and destination effects on industrial mail survey
response rates

	Sent from the UK (200 mailings)	Sent from the USA (200 mailings)
Response rate from UK (per cent)	13	5
Response rate from USA (per cent)	6	9

There are many more tests and each has its role. ANOVA is a powerful tool
that evaluates the contribution of several variables. Despite the availability of
these statistics in most data analysis packages it is surprising how many
researchers still report results without referring to them. To do so is
unprofessional and stupid. Unless there is a significant difference between
results a researcher has no right to claim any findings.

Validation summary

Validation has traps for the unwary. Computer packages give the statistics but
require the user to know whether it is appropriate to use them or not. All the
statistics make assumptions about the structure of the data, the most common
one being a normal distribution. If these are not true the statistics are invalid.
If this occurs, things become more complicated and less straightforward rules
apply. Statistical packages usually give these statistics, but few understand
them.

Cross tabulations or contingency tables are particularly prone to problems
when samples are not large. The familiar chi-square test is invalid if cells contain
less than five items. This problem is overcome by collapsing groups – like
combining social classes A and B – so the numbers in each cell increase. This
can continue until the matrix is 2×2 where again the assumptions of the chi-
square statistic become unreliable. Applying Yate's correction can solve that
problem.

Given these problems, the best practice for a researcher is to examine
publications in strong journals to see what accepted practices are, understand
the methods used there, their limitations and conventions for overcoming them.

MARKET ANALYSIS

There are numerous mathematical techniques for market analysis. They can do
many things. They vary in their origin and application but are common in being
multivariate, that is, manipulating many variables at the same time. This means
they can analyse many variables and observations (say people) at the same time.

Table 5 Market analysis methods

Method	Criterion variables	Metric Criterion	Metric Predictor	Finds Groups	Typical uses
Regression analysis	Yes	Yes	Yes and no	No	Predicting sales given the mix or economic factors
Canonical correlation	Yes	Yes	Yes and no	No	Predicting more than one criterion variable
Probit and logit	Yes	No	Yes and no	No	Predicting individual buyer behaviour – will/will not buy
Discriminant analysis	Yes	No	Yes and no	No	Predicting group membership (e.g. segments)
AID[1]	Yes	No	Yes and no	Yes	Splitting items into uniform groups with different usage
Correlation analysis	No	n.a.	Yes	No	Seeing the relationship between individual variables
Factor analysis	No	n.a.	Yes	Can do	Indicating groups of similar variables
Cluster analysis	No	n.a.	Yes (almost always)	Yes	Finding groups of similar observations (e.g. segments)
Conjoint analysis	No	n.a.	No	No	Finding the perceived value of product features
MDS[2]	No	n.a.	Yes and no	Can do	Revealing how customers see markets (e.g. positioning)

Notes: 1 Automatic interaction detection
2 Multidimensional scaling

Table 6 Computer intensive methods

Method	Key features
Simulated annealing	Neighbourhood structure. Depends on a cooling schedule (like annealing metals). Improvement by random search.
Genetic algorithms	Pool of solutions (genes). Improvement by crossover and mutation (like the evolution of species).
Branch-and-bound	Tree structures. Improvement by selective search of branches of the tree.
Tabu search	Neighbourhood structure. Depends on the length of tabu list.
Neural networks	No underlying model assumed. Learns from training on a set of data (like the brain). Depends upon the architecture used.

As a result, they can provide insights which managers would be unable to gain by looking at data.

Table 5 gives some of these techniques. Green *et al.* (1988) and Hooley (1994) review them in more detail. The methods are grouped according to their dominant features, the main group being those that split variables into criterion and predictor variables and those that do not.

Methods with criterion and predictor variables

The early discussion of marketing models was mainly based on a regression analysis. It is also the first method introduced here. Variations in the approach to regression analysis discussed is typical of the variety of options that exists for each of the methods of market analysis.

Whereas regression analysis has a single criterion (or dependent) variable, canonical correlation has two or more. This can be very useful in market research where one needs to know the influences at many stages of buyer behaviour, for instance, attitude of a customer, their willingness to buy and their consumption rate of a brand. The same set of predictor (or independent) variables influences all of these. Canonical correlation examines the impact of the predictor variables on each of the criterion variables simultaneously. It can, therefore, give a much greater insight into buyer behaviour than the single criterion within regression.

Probit and logit analysis are useful when the unconstrained criterion variable

130

of regression analysis is inappropriate. In regression analysis, the criterion variable is metric, meaning it can take up any positive or negative value. Probit and logit are useful when this feature is inappropriate, for instance, when the aim is to predict whether a consumer will buy a product or not. The answer must be either yes or no, or a probability that must lie between 0 and 1. Besides being more realistic, probit and logit's constraints mean the techniques give results that look better than those from regression analysis in similar circumstances. Also, since the results have only a limited set of values, they are more reliable. Jobber and Saunders (1993) provide an example in their modelling response rates depending on questionnaire and survey design. Earlier attempts using regression analysis proved inaccurate and were not robust because they occasionally forecast response rates above 100 per cent. A logit model gave more accurate predictions and believable results are guaranteed.

Although probit and logit models allocate observations to two classes, discriminant analysis predicts the memberships of two or more groups. In marketing this can be particularly useful in understanding the membership of market segments, for instance, the difference between heavy beer drinkers in pubs, heavy beer drinkers at home, heavy wine drinkers or spirit drinkers. For a set of predictor variables, discriminant analysis finds how well they can discriminate between the groups and show which predictor variables associate with what group.

Automatic interaction detection (AID) operates quite differently from other methods of partitioning data. AID starts with a criterion variable – say, response rate to mailshots – and predictor variables search to find those that discriminate most strongly on the criteria. If the issue is response to mailshots, then the strongest predictor variable could be home ownership. If that were so, the data split into two groups; one group of home-owners and one of non-home-owners. AID would then look at home-owners and find out the predictor variable that causes the greatest difference in mailshot response amongst home-owners. This could be gender, and so AID would split the population into three groups, male home-owners, female home-owners and non-home-owners. The method would then look at non-home-owners and find the predictor variable that best works for them. In this case it could be wage earners and non-wage earners. This forms four groups. The process continues until the partitioning makes subgroups too small or no more significant differences. Although a convenient tool, AID has limitations. Its sequential approach can give poor solutions and the series of partitions of data quickly splits large data sets into very small groups. Each of the groups is identical for the predictor variables but may be too small to be managerially useful.

Non-partitioned approaches

The remaining methods of market analysis do not split the variables into criteria and predictor. Instead they view all the variables together and look at the

131

relationship between them. The most simple approach is correlation analysis that looks at the relationship between metric variables. If the correlation coefficient is 0, the variables are unrelated; if 1, they are contiguous. Correlation analysis is rarely used as the sole means of analysis. It is, however, useful before regression and other methods to remove redundant variables that waste time and invalidate the analysis.

Factor analysis, like correlation analysis, is itself often an intermediate method but has many direct and valuable uses. It does not look at the relationships between individual variables but finds sets of variables that are similar. This has very valuable uses. Where a market researcher has measured a large number of variables, they reduce to a smaller set of compound ones, called factor scores. Each of these compound variables has the advantage of being independent of the other ones and therefore ideally suited for use in regression or cluster analysis. Over the last ten years factor analysis has become fundamental to the validation of scales in market research (Churchill and Peter 1984). It is used either in an exploratory way, to find out which variables to combine, or in a confirmatory way, to see whether the expected relationship between variables is true.

Cluster analysis has one major application in marketing, the identification of market segments. Traditional *a priori* segmentation divides a market using a criterion – like age or industry – decided beforehand. In cluster-based segmentation, data on demographic, pyschographic or lifestyle characteristics of consumers are used to define similar groups. AID is another way of finding clusters. Whereas AID continually partitions the data in two, then four, then eight, cluster analysis looks at all the variables simultaneously and usually uses a hierarchical progress that starts with all consumers being individuals. Cluster analysis then searches to find a pair of consumers that are most alike and joins them to form a cluster. It then treats those two consumers as one and searches for the next pair that are most alike, then the next, then the next, until a manageable number of clusters remain. Unlike the earlier methods discussed here, cluster analysis is an umbrella name for many techniques that make different assumptions about how to measure the distance between groups, how to combine individuals that are alike or simply what a likeness means. The diversity within cluster analysis can be troublesome since it means that the answer depends on the technique used. Fortunately, there is now a sufficient case history to indicate best practices (Saunders 1994) that give reliable and meaningful results. Nevertheless, such is the openness of cluster analysis that validation of the results is of great importance. This usually means using discriminant analysis to test if the results are replicable.

Conjoint analysis has very a specific but powerful application in markets. Like multidimensional scaling (MDS) it examines perceptions and provides a way of integrating data collection with the mapping of perceptions. In this case it is usually the value of products that features, for instance, the importance

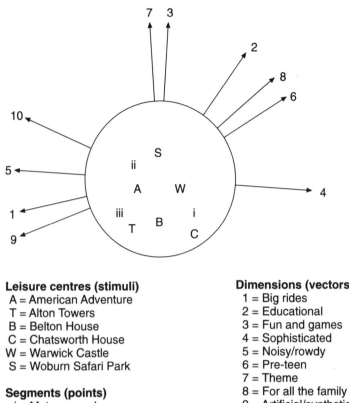

Leisure centres (stimuli)
A = American Adventure
T = Alton Towers
B = Belton House
C = Chatsworth House
W = Warwick Castle
S = Woburn Safari Park

Segments (points)
 i = Mature couples
 ii = Young families
iii = Wild young things

Dimensions (vectors)
 1 = Big rides
 2 = Educational
 3 = Fun and games
 4 = Sophisticated
 5 = Noisy/rowdy
 6 = Pre-teen
 7 = Theme
 8 = For all the family
 9 = Artificial/synthetic
10 = Good food

Figure 4   Multidimensional scaling map showing dimensions, products and segments
Source: Hooley and Saunders (1993)

of colour to selection of a hi-fi system compared with alternative sizes, prices and power output. Given a set of product features, conjoint analysis explores concepts to find the 'part worth' of each element. The power of conjoint analysis comes in being able to find out this information without resorting to an exhaustive set of permutations and combinations of the product features. Conjoint analysis gives results for each person surveyed. The conjoint results of a sample are cluster analysed to form segments. The result could show that one segment of car buyers is unwilling to pay for extra power but would be quite happy to pay for features that made the product easier to use. In contrast, another segment could be unwilling to pay for looks but happy to pay for advanced features and power.

133

Multidimensional scaling is like cluster analysis in being a range of techniques aimed at one problem, in this case the mapping of how customers perceive markets. Figure 4 shows a typical map produced by this method using information on theme parks and their features. In this figure the space is not the geographical distance between the theme parks, but the psychological space. The map shows how close the customer sees the leisure centres in his or her mind and the dimensions used. Besides visualizing markets, the maps produced by multidimensional scaling can also help position products. By knowing the location of segments, competitors and the underlying dimensions that describe their positions, managers can determine how to position their products.

Market analysis summary

The multivariate methods described here have been called the multivariate jungle (Hooley 1980). Indeed such is the variety and complexity of the methods that they can appear as dark, frightening and mysterious to people who are new to them. Also, like jungles, multivariate methods are a rich source of ideas and inspiration. They can help managers to understand complex situations and draw order from large volumes of information. Few managers are likely to be able to use these methods unaided, but they can understand what the approaches can do and some of their limitations. After being able to visualize markets in the way that multidimensional methods allow, viewing them conventionally is like using black and white when true colours are available. There was a time when their computational requirements made them inaccessible to most users, but now all are available in desk top form. The major demands they make are on data collection and understanding, not computation.

COMPUTER INTENSIVE QUANTITATIVE METHODS

The last decade has seen the emergence of new quantitative methods useful in marketing. Many of these depart radically from the traditional statistical approach to model building. Methods like simulated annealing, genetic algorithms and neural networks use inspirations from nature to search for the solutions to problems. The main use of these techniques is in the estimation and optimization of marketing models. The basic problems remain the same, but these new techniques can analyse complex problems and find better solutions than before. Although these new methods are computer intensive, computing costs are declining so quickly that they are likely to become common soon. Coates *et al.* (1994) review some of these new methods and their short description is in Table 6.

CONCLUSIONS

In the coming decade marketing managers will increasingly find themselves in a data-rich environment where the technologies and markets are changing rapidly. Quantitative methods provide a way of ordering and manipulating the large quantities of data that are available. The range is such that they could be an encyclopedia in their own right and their mathematical foundation makes it inaccessible to many of today's managers. Their importance shows in the leading marketing journals that devote as much space to developing these mathematical techniques as to other marketing problems. Without a grasp of them, a marketer is as likely to be able to make good solutions as is a navigator who thinks the world is flat. Mathematical approaches do not provide marketing answers but do give the opportunity for better grounded decision-making.

REFERENCES

Breightler, C. S., Phillips, D. T. and Wilde, D. J. (1979) *Foundations of Optimization*, Englewood Cliffs, N.J.: Prentice-Hall.

Churchill, G. A. and Peter, J. P. (1984) 'Research design effects on the reliability of rating scales: a meta-analysis', *Journal of Marketing Research* 21 (3): 360–75.

Coates, D., Doherty, N. and French, A. (1994) 'The multivariate swamp: computer intensive methods in database marketing', *Journal of Marketing Management* 10 (1–3): 207–22.

Coates, D., Finlay, P. and Wilson, J. (1991) 'Validation in marketing models', *Journal of the Marketing Research Society* 33 (2): 83–90.

Doyle, P. and Saunders, J. (1990) 'Multiproduct advertising budgeting', *Marketing Science* 9 (2): 97–113.

Green, P. E., Tull, D. S. and Albaum, G. (1988) *Research for Marketing Decisions*, Englewood Cliffs, N.J.: Prentice-Hall.

Hooley, G. (1980) 'The multivariate jungle: the academic's playground but the manager's minefield', *European Journal of Marketing* 14 (4): 379–86.

Hooley, G. (ed.) (1994) 'Quantitative techniques in marketing', *Journal of Marketing Management* (special issues) 10 (1–3).

Jobber, D. and Saunders, J. (1988) 'An experimental investigation into cross-national mail survey response rates', *Journal of International Business Studies* 19 (3): 483–90.

Jobber, D. and Saunders, J. (1993) 'A note on the applicability of the Bruvold-Comer model of mail survey response rates to commercial populations', *Journal of Business Research* 26 (3): 223–36.

Leeflang, P., Mijatovic, G. and Saunders, J. (1992) 'The identification and estimation of complex multivariate lag structures: a nesting approach', *Journal of Applied Economics* 24 (2): 273–83.

Lilien, G. L., Kotler, P. and Moorthy, K. S. (1992) *Marketing Models*, Englewood Cliffs, N.J.: Prentice-Hall.

Little, J. D. C. (1970) 'Models and managers: the concept of a decision calculus', *Management Science* 16 (3): 466–85.

Little, J. D. C. (1979) 'Decision support systems for marketing managers', *Journal of Marketing* 43 (3): 9–27.

Naert, P. A. and Leeflang, P. (1977) *Building Implementable Marketing Models*, Leiden: Martinus Nijhoff.

Saunders, J. (1994) 'Cluster analysis', *Journal of Marketing Management* 10 (1–3): 13–28.
Simon, J. L. (1970) *Issues in the Economics of Advertising*, Urban, Ill.: University of Chicago Press.
Urban, G. (1974) 'Building models for decision makers', *Interfaces* 4 (3): 1–11.

8

CHANNELS OF DISTRIBUTION

Bert Rosenbloom

In virtually any developed country around the world a vast array of products is made readily and conveniently available to millions or even hundreds of millions of consumers as well as to many thousands of industrial firms, institutions, and other organizations. Somehow, the myriad of different products seem to 'find their way' to the particular buyers who are seeking them at a given time. Whether this involves a consumer walking into a supermarket to buy a can of soup or a giant business corporation purchasing a thousand personal computers, for the most part buyers are able to have the products they want, when they want them – even though the range and diversity of their demands is almost incomprehensible and the products to meet those demands may literally come from all corners of the earth. Yet most buyers have little awareness of the enormity of the task involved in providing such a huge assortment of products. Indeed, most are rather nonchalant about it. The convenient availability of all these products is simply a given – an ordinary fact of everyday life. Yet behind this 'ordinary' process is an extraordinary set of institutions comprising the channels of distribution that have made the vast quantities and varieties of products so conveniently available to millions of consumer and industrial customers.

CHANNEL OF DISTRIBUTION DEFINED

Channels of distribution have been described in a variety of ways since marketing became a recognized business discipline in the early part of the twentieth century (Shaw 1915). Perhaps the most generally accepted definition of a channel of distribution is that it is the route taken by the title to products from the point of production to point of consumption as it passes through institutions or parties who either take the title or facilitate its transfer (Stanton 1968). Thus, according to this definition, it is the title or ownership rights in products that determines the channel of distribution rather than the physical flow of the products. Take, for example, a product that goes from the

137

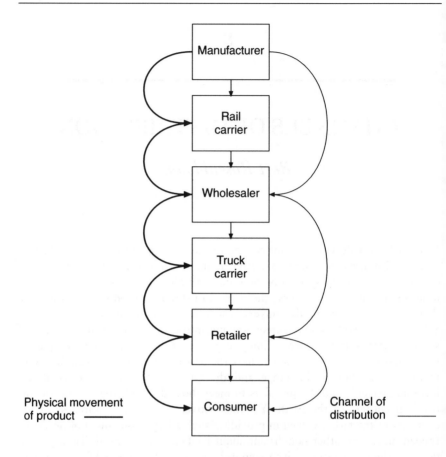

Physical movement
of product ———

Channel of
distribution ———

Figure 1   Channel of distribution based on flow of title

manufacturer via rail car to a wholesaler who in turn sends it on to a retailer via a public trucking company before it is finally sold to a consumer. The channel of distribution in this case would not include the rail or truck carriers. Instead, the channel of distribution would consist of the manufacturer, wholesaler, retailer, and consumer. This is portrayed in Figure 1. The reason for this distinction is that a trading relationship exists only among the manufacturer, wholesaler, retailer, and consumer but not between any of these parties and the rail and trucking firms. The latter are concerned merely with moving the product from point A to point B and do not take title to the product. Neither do the rail or trucking firms facilitate the transfer of the title to the product even though they, of course, facilitate the transfer of the physical product itself. The same reasoning would also hold for a public warehouse which may be called upon to store the product for a period of time in the event that the manufacturer, wholesaler, or retailer do not have sufficient space to store the product on their own premises during a given period of time.

On the other hand, an agent or broker who does not take title and normally would not take physical possession of the product would be considered part of the marketing channel. This follows because the agent or broker, by helping to bring buyer and seller together to consummate a transaction, facilitates the transfer of the title (Bucklin 1972) and thereby is very much a part of the trading relationship in the channel of distribution.

This distinction is very important for gaining an understanding of channels of distribution because it is the trading relationship involving the functions of buying, selling and transferring of title where most of the strategic marketing issues emerge. For example, a consumer goods manufacturer attempting to set up a channel of distribution for a new product would face such marketing strategy issues as identifying and selecting the appropriate kinds of sales representatives, agents, brokers, wholesalers and retailers that might be needed to make the product available to its target market, convincing these inter-mediaries to take on the product, motivating them to do an effective job of promoting it, setting the terms of the relationship such as credit, payment periods, and inventory levels, as well as numerous other tasks necessary to establish and maintain an effective trading relationship. In contrast, such tasks as providing for transportation, storage, insurance and so forth are essentially tactical or mechanical issues which, while important and perhaps challenging, are not strategic marketing issues.

So, although firms that perform solely such functions as transportation, storage and insuring may be important participants in the operation of channels of distribution, they are not members of the channel. Only those firms or organizations that are involved in a trading relationship based on the perform-ance of buying, selling or facilitating transfer of title are members of the channel of distribution.

DISTRIBUTION CHANNEL STRUCTURE

The 'form' or 'shape' that a channel of distribution takes to perform the functions or tasks necessary to make products available to final customers is usually referred to as channel structure (Rosenbloom 1991). This structure consists of all of the firms and institutions (including the producers or manufacturers and the final customers) who are involved in performing the negotiation functions of buying, selling and transferring title. Firms such as transportation companies, warehousing firms, insurance companies, and the like are usually referred to as facilitating agencies or sometimes the auxiliary channel structure because they are not involved in buying, selling or transferring title and hence, in the strict sense, are not part of the channel structure. Channel structure has three basic dimensions:

139

1   length of the channel;
2   intensity at the various levels;
3   the types of intermediaries involved.

Length of channel structure

With regard to length, channels of distribution can range from two stages where the producer or manufacturer sells directly to the final customers (direct distribution) to as many as ten stages where eight intermediary institutions exist between the producer and the final customers. With the exception of Japan, such long channels of distribution are quite rare in industrialized countries. Much more common are channel structure lengths ranging from two stages up to five stages. Figure 2 provides an illustration of typical channel structure lengths for consumer products in developed economies.

Many factors influence the length of the channel structure such as the

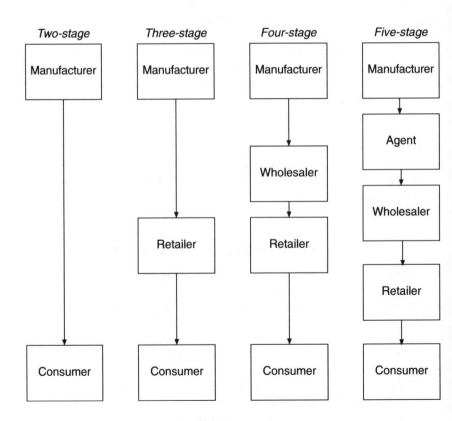

Figure 2   Examples of the length of distribution channel structure for consumer products in developed economies

geographical dispersion of customers, the size of the customer base, and their particular behaviour patterns. The nature of the product such as its bulk and weight, perishability, value and technical complexity can also be very important. For example, technically complex products often require short channels because of the high degree of technical support and liaison needed by customers which may only be available directly from the producer. Moreover, length can also be affected by the size of the manufacturer, its financial capacity and desire for control. In general, larger and more well-financed manufacturers have a greater capability to bypass intermediaries and use shorter channel structures. Manufacturers desiring to exercise a high degree of control over the distribution of their products are also more likely to use shorter channel structures because the shorter the channel, the higher the degree of control.

Intensity of channel structure

Intensity at the various levels of the channel refers to the number of intermediaries at each level. Intensity is usually described using three terms: intensive, selective and exclusive distribution. Intensive means that all possible intermediaries at the particular level of the channel are used. Selective means that a smaller number of intermediaries are used based on more thorough selection criteria, while exclusive refers to only one intermediary used at the particular level of the channel to cover a defined territory. The intensity dimension of channel structure can be portrayed as a continuum as shown in Figure 3. Although there are significant exceptions, in general, intensive distribution is usually associated with the distribution of convenience goods, selective distribution with shopping goods, and exclusive distribution with speciality goods (Bucklin 1963). Thus, inexpensive ballpoint pens, razor blades or cigarettes (convenience goods) tend to be carried by very large numbers of intermediaries, particularly at the retail level, while home appliances and apparel (shopping goods) by relatively fewer intermediaries, and speciality goods such as Rolex watches or Rolls Royce automobiles by only one dealer in a specified geographical area (territory).

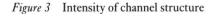

Intensive	Selective	Exclusive
All possible intermediaries	Relatively few intermediaries	Just one intermediary

Figure 3   Intensity of channel structure

141

Types of intermediaries in the channel structure

This third dimension of channel structure refers to the various kinds of intermediary institutions that can be used at the various levels of the channel. At the retail level, there may be many possibilities for some products. For example, a candy bar can be sold through many different types of retailers such as candy stores, grocery stores, drugstores, supermarkets, mass merchandisers, discount department stores and many others. For other products, such as automobiles, the choice is far more limited. It should be pointed out, however, that in recent years with the growth of scrambled merchandising, the types of intermediaries that sell various products have broadened considerably. Many hardware items, for instance, are sold not only in hardware stores but in homecentres, department stores, mass merchandisers, supermarkets, and even drugstores. Consequently, manufacturers today need to be rather broad-minded when considering the types of intermediaries to use in their channel structures. The conventional wisdom of particular products being distributed only through certain types of distributors or dealers may no longer hold.

DETERMINANTS OF CHANNEL STRUCTURE

The structure of distribution channels with regard to their length, intensity and types of intermediary institutions participating is determined essentially by three fundamental factors:

1 The distribution functions that need to be performed.
2 The economics of performing distribution functions.
3 Management's desire for control of distribution.

Distribution functions to be performed

Distribution functions, also often referred to as marketing functions or sometimes channel functions, have been described in various lists since the inception of marketing as a discipline (Weld 1917). Such functions as buying, selling, risk taking, transportation, storage, order processing, and financing are commonly mentioned. Other more generalized functions such as concentration, equalization and dispersion whereby the main functions of channels of distribution are to bring products together from many manufacturers (concentration), adjust the quantities to balance supply and demand (equalization) and deliver them to final customers (dispersion) have also been used. Other concepts of distribution functions describe them in terms of a sorting process consisting of accumulating products from many producers, sorting them to correspond to designated target markets and assorting or putting products together in conveniently associated groups to ease the shopping burden of target markets (Alderson 1957). Distribution functions have also been described in much more detailed terms whereby very specific activities sometimes unique to the particular industry or trade are presented as distribution functions (Rosenbloom 1987).

Regardless of the particular list of distribution functions one chooses to accept, the underlying rationale is the same for all of them. It can be stated as follows: distribution functions must be performed in order to consummate transactions between buyers and sellers. The reason for this is that discrepancies exist between buyers and sellers that must be overcome through the performance of distribution functions. The channel structure chosen to perform the functions reflects how the functions have been allocated to various marketing institutions such as wholesalers, retailers, agents, brokers or others.

What are the discrepancies that exist between production and consumption that must be bridged through the performance of marketing functions? Four such discrepancies have been discussed in the literature:

1 Discrepancy in quantity.
2 Discrepancy in assortment.
3 Discrepancy in time.
4 Discrepancy in space.

Discrepancy in quantity

The quantities in which products are produced to achieve low average total cost are usually too large for any individual customer to use immediately. Thus, institutions in the channel structure such as wholesalers and retailers provide a buffer to absorb the vast output of manufacturers and provide the smaller quantities desired by individual customers.

Discrepancy in assortment

Products are grouped for manufacturing purposes based on efficiencies of production while customers group products based on efficiency of shopping and consuming. In most cases, these production and consumption groupings are not inherently congruent. For example, the thousands of items a consumer finds grouped so conveniently together in a supermarket are not, of course, produced by one manufacturer. Hundreds of relatively specialized manufacturers have made those products. The supermarket retailer and many other intermediary institutions in channels of distribution have performed the functions necessary to regroup this conglomeration of products and thereby overcome the discrepancy in assortment. This enables particular manufacturers to concentrate on producing a relatively limited range of products, that when combined through distribution channels with the products of many other manufacturers, enables final customers to have wide and convenient assortments of products that greatly simplify shopping and consumption.

143

Discrepancy in time

Most products are not manufactured for immediate consumption or use. Hence, some mechanism must be available to hold products between the time they are produced and needed by final customers. Intermediaries in distribution channels, particularly merchant wholesalers and retailers, who take title to and physically hold goods until they are needed by final customers are crucial in overcoming this discrepancy in time.

Discrepancies in space

The location of manufacturing facilities for products is a function of such factors as raw materials availability, labour supply, expertise, historical considerations and numerous other factors that may have little to do with where the ultimate consumers of those products are located. Thus, the production and consumption of products can literally take place half a world apart from each other. Channel structures evolve or are consciously designed to connect distant manufacturers and users to reduce or virtually eliminate place or spatial discrepancies.

Economics of distribution function performance

Given that distribution functions must be performed to overcome the discrepancies discussed above, the channel structure must be organized to perform the functions as efficiently as possible. Two principles underlie the development and organization of efficient channel structure:

* specialization/division of labour (Stigler 1951);
* transaction efficiency (McGarry 1951).

Specialization/division of labour

The principle of specialization/division of labour underlies most modern production processes. Each worker or station in a factory focuses on performing particular manufacturing tasks and thereby develops specialized expertise and skills in the performance of the task. Such specialization/division of labour results in much greater efficiency and higher output than if each worker were to perform all or most of the tasks himself.

This two-hundred-year-old principle applies equally to distribution as it does to production. The various middlemen in channels of distribution are analogous to production workers or stations in a factory but instead of performing production tasks they are performing distribution functions. These middlemen whether they be wholesalers, retailers, agents or brokers develop expertise in distribution that manufacturers would find uneconomical to match. Moreover, many large middlemen such as mass merchandisers have economies of scale and

144

economies of scope which allow them to spread the cost of performing distribution functions over a large volume and diversity of products which would not be possible for the manufacturer.

Transaction efficiency

This concept, also called contact efficiency, refers to the effort to reduce the number of transactions between producers and final users. If many producers attempt to deal directly with large numbers of consumers, the number of transactions can be enormous. Paradoxically, by lengthening the channel structure through the addition of middlemen, the number of transactions can be

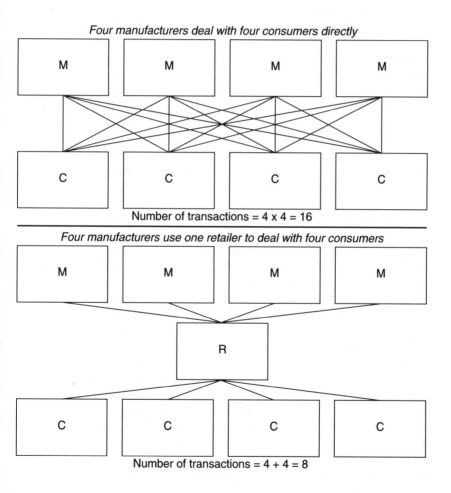

Figure 4   How the introduction of a middleman reduces the number of transactions

145

reduced and hence transaction efficiency increased. This is illustrated in Figure 4. As shown in the Figure, the number of transactions has been cut in half as a result of the introduction of the retailer into the channel structure. Given that the cost of transactions can be very high, especially if personal face-to-face meetings are necessary to consummate transactions, the reduction in contacts through the use of middlemen in the channel structure is in many cases absolutely vital for the economical distribution of products.

Management's desire for control of distribution

Even though the economics of the performance of distribution functions may imply a particular type of distribution channel structure, management's desire for control of the distribution channel may outweigh the economic considerations. In general, the shorter the channel structure, the higher the degree of control and vice versa. Further, the lower the intensity of distribution, the higher the degree of control and vice versa. For example, suppose an economic analysis based on specialization/division of labour and transaction efficiencies calls for a long distribution channel structure with a fairly high degree of intensity at the various levels. However, management in the manufacturing firm feels the need to protect the image of the product and may also believe it necessary to provide high levels of customer service. To do so the manufacturer is convinced that it needs a high degree of control and so it may opt for direct distribution or at most one level of middlemen with a very high degree of selectivity in appointing them as channel members based on their willingness to take direction from the manufacturer.

Management might also develop its distribution channel structure so as to avoid opportunistic behaviour by channel members. Such behaviour is likely to occur when channel members control major portions of transaction specific assets – the unique assets such as facilities and equipment as well as specialized expertise that make them virtually indispensable for performing distribution functions (Williamson 1975). If the channel members recognize the power of their position because of their control of the transaction specific assets, they may act in an extremely self-interested fashion to the detriment of the manufacturer. If the manufacturer wants to avoid such a situation, it may reduce substantially its emphasis on the economic considerations in the use of middlemen in the channel structure. Instead, it may decide to perform all of the distribution function itself via vertical integration, even though the cost of doing so could be significantly higher. But by vertically integrating, the manufacturer would keep all of the transaction specific assets 'in house' and therefore prevent them from falling into the hands of self-serving middlemen.

In contrast to this rather cynical view of channel member behaviour, is the partnership or strategic alliance approach to the development of channel structure (Anderson and Narus 1990). This approach stresses cooperation and mutually supportive relationships between the manufacturer and channel

146

members rather than the avoidance of opportunistic behaviour. In essence, the manufacturer seeking to develop partnerships or strategic alliances with middlemen believes that allocating significant portions of the distribution functions will enhance its degree of control of the channel because partnerships or strategic alliances require close working relationships and mutual trust between the manufacturer and its channel partners.

FLOWS IN MARKETING CHANNELS

Once a channel of distribution has been set up, a series of flows evolves which tie all of the institutions in the channel together. Eight flows were originally identified in the literature (Vail *et al.* 1952), but the following six are the most basic ones that exist in virtually all channels of distribution:

1 Title flow
2 Negotiation flow
3 Product flow
4 Finance flow
5 Information flow
6 Promotion flow

Title flow

As pointed out at the beginning of this chapter, it is the movement or flow of the title (ownership rights) in products that is the delineator of the marketing channel. The flow of the title through parties who either take title or facilitate its transfer establishes who is involved in the trading relationship of the channel rather than the mere physical handling, storing, or holding of the products. In essence, the flow of the title is a good surrogate indicator of those parties who have a stake in the channel in terms of market and financial risk. For instance, the manufacturer who sells his products through wholesalers and/or retailers is relying on these parties to make its products available to final customers. The wholesalers and retailers are giving up shelf space to the manufacturer and hence bear the opportunity costs associated with the space (Rosenbloom 1991). Yet the manufacturer's products may or may not meet the wholesalers' or retailers' sales and profit expectations. Even agents and brokers, who, by bringing manufacturers and wholesalers and/or retailers together, facilitate the transfer of title but do not actually hold the title to products nevertheless have a substantial stake in the channel because they invest time, energy, and money. In doing so, they help to establish effective and efficient trading relationships in the channel. If these relationships do not work out, the agents or brokers will not only lose their commissions but their very businesses may also be at risk.

Negotiation flow

The functions of buying and selling within the channel of distribution are carried by the flow of negotiation. For example, a manufacturer selling electronic component parts through selling agents to an industrial distributor who in turn sells those products to a computer manufacturer has initiated a vertical flow of negotiation that runs up and down the channel. A wide array of issues involving specifications, price, terms of sale, delivery schedules, returns policies, and many others will need to be negotiated not only initially to establish the trading relationship but also to keep the relationship going on a continuing basis as circumstances change.

Product flow

The flow of the product is, of course, the most obvious flow in the distribution channel. Products can flow down the channel towards the final customer through many different kinds of institutions and several possible modes of transportation before finally reaching their ultimate destinations. In many cases, the product flow may follow closely the title and negotiation flows, but as pointed out earlier, this is not necessarily the case. In fact, when agent middlemen are used and/or drop shipping is employed, the flow of title and negotiation will be quite different from the flow of the product.

Finance flow

The finance flow, sometimes termed payment flow, refers to the financial side of trading relationships in channels of distribution. Because provisions have to be made for financing inventories as products move through channels and for arranging payment for the functions performed by all of the channel members involved, the finance flow is crucial to the title and product flows. Obviously, the flows of title and product could not continue for very long if money were not made available to hold inventories and for providing payment for services rendered to the channel members.

Information flow

The flow of information refers to all of the communication necessary to conduct business through the channel. The flow of information overlaps the negotiation and promotion flows and is usually the prerequisite for the title, product and finance flows because specific information is often required to determine who owns the products, how, where, and when products are to be conveyed through the channel, and who will be responsible for holding inventory and making payment. The information flow is also very much a two-way flow both up and down the channel. Final customers communicate with retailers (or in business

148

to business situations, industrial distributors) who, in turn, pass the information up the channel all the way back to the manufacturer. Of course, many types of information flow down the channel through the various middlemen on to final customers.

Promotion flow

Although the promotion flow is at least in concept merely a special case of the information flow, it is presented separately because promotion is such a vital part of channels of distribution. Promotion in the form of such tools as advertising, personal selling, sales promotion and publicity is vital to the establishment and maintenance of all the other flows. In most cases, negotiating with channel members to carry and enthusiastically sell products and to accept the risk as well as the financial burden of holding them requires strong and effective promotion that starts with the manufacturer. The promotion effort must then be carried via the channel by all of the channel members to assist in both pulling and pushing products through the channel.

Coordinating the flows

The six flows just discussed do not automatically sequence and synchronize themselves into a coordinated mechanism for linking producers and final customers together. On the contrary, the flows if left untended can be highly uncoordinated. The communication and promotion flow may herald the arrival of products days or even weeks before they actually become available to customers via the product flow. Negotiation can bog down, stalling the transfer of both products and title. Financing and payments may fail to materialize, which can completely derail the operation of the channel. Thus coordination of the flows requires a conscious effort to manage them by some or all of the members of the distribution channel. Indeed, management of distribution channels can be viewed as the process of analysing, planning, and controlling all the distribution channel flows.

DISTRIBUTION CHANNELS AS SOCIAL SYSTEMS

In recent years the perspective used in the marketing discipline to examine channels of distribution has been broadened considerably. Once viewed only as economic systems, channels of distribution are now seen as social and political systems as well (Stern and Brown 1969). Consequently, the rules that govern channel relationships are not solely a matter of economics. In the broader social systems perspective, channels of distribution are subject to the same behavioural processes associated with all social systems. The behavioural processes of most significance in channels of distribution are power and conflict.

149

Power in distribution channels

Power refers to the capacity of one channel member to influence the behaviour of another channel member – in other words, to get the channel member to do something that he/she would not have done of his/her own volition. For example, a supermarket chain decides to place a manufacturer's new cereal product in a poor shelf location. Upon hearing of this the manufacturer requests that the supermarket provide more prominent shelf space for the product. If the supermarket responds positively to the request, it can be inferred that the manufacturer exercised power over the supermarket because it got the retailer to do something which it would not otherwise have done on its own. The source of the manufacturer's power in this case might have come from any or all of five power bases:

* reward;
* coercion;
* legitimacy;
* reference;
* expertise (French and Raven 1959).

Understanding the dynamics of how these power bases are used in the interorganizational relationships that characterize channels of distribution has become a major area of research in distribution literature. Channel analysts have been discovering that in numerous cases the politics of distribution may be just as important as the economics of distribution in the development and operation of effective and efficient channels of distribution.

Conflict in distribution channels

Since the dawn of recorded history conflict has been an inherent dimension of all social systems. Although the basis for effective and efficient operation of distribution channels is cooperation rather than conflict, because the channel is a social system, conflict is also very much a presence in the distribution channel.

Conflict is usually defined in a channels context as goal impeding behaviour by one or more channel member so that each becomes the object of the other's frustrations (Stern and Gorman 1969). Therefore it is direct, personal, and opponent centred rather than indirect, impersonal and object centred, as is the case with competition. For example, a manufacturer wants a distributor to carry only its particular brand of products and to refrain from selling other manufacturers' brands. But the distributor refuses and continues to carry other manufacturers' brands. A conflict may result from this situation because each party perceives the other to be impeding the attainment of its goals. In the case of the manufacturer, the refusal of the distributor to carry only the particular manufacturer's products reduces its ability to build market share, while from the distributor's point of view, carrying only one brand will hurt its capability for meeting the needs of its customers.

Conflict can affect distribution channel performance and therefore it is a topic of much interest in the literature. The most commonly held belief is that conflict has a negative effect on performance, but it might also have no effect or even a positive effect on performance in some circumstances (Rosenbloom 1973). Unfortunately, empirical research on the effects of conflict is still quite limited.

TRENDS IN DISTRIBUTION CHANNELS

Although there are many developments and trends that have affected channels of distribution in recent years, the following five stand out as the most basic:

1 More strategic emphasis by firms on channels of distribution.
2 Partnerships and strategic alliances gaining more ground.
3 Continued growth of vertical marketing systems.
4 Growing power of retailers in distribution channels.
5 Greater role for technology in channels of distribution.

Strategic emphasis on distribution channels

Distribution channels had been one of the relatively neglected areas of marketing but they have now come on quite strongly as a focus for strategic marketing emphasis in the 1990s. The main reason for this is that more and more firms are recognizing that superior distribution channels can help the firm to gain a sustainable competitive advantage that cannot be easily copied by competitors (Porter 1985). This pattern seems to be occurring in a wide range of industries from automobiles to consumer packaged goods to industrial equipment.

Partnerships and strategic alliances

Although not a new phenomenon, the growth in the use of partnerships and strategic alliances in channels of distribution has been accelerating rapidly during the last few years. Manufacturers are linking up with wholesalers and/or retailers in mutually supportive and synergistic relationships to achieve far more effective and efficient distribution. The same pattern is occurring in many industrial (business-to-business) channels as well.

Such partnerships or strategic alliances usually require close cooperative relationships between channel members on a continuing and long-term basis. Hence, they are the antithesis of the 'every man for himself' mentality tradition of more loosely aligned or ad hoc channel relationships.

151

Growth in vertical marketing systems

Vertical marketing systems (VMS) first described in the mid-1960s (McCammon 1965) have continued their growth through the ensuing decades and are expected to continue to grow throughout the 1990s. VMSs are divided into three categories:

1 Administrated systems whereby one channel member at the manufacturer, wholesaler, or retailer level exercises a high degree of control over the operation of the channel.
2 Contractual systems which consist of retailer cooperatives, wholesaler sponsored voluntary chains, and business format franchises.
3 Corporate systems where distribution is vertically integrated by the manufacturer (forward integration) or by a wholesaler or retailer (backward integration).

Such VMS systems create economies of scale and scope and provide a level of managerial and marketing expertise that loosely aligned traditional channels are finding increasingly difficult to match.

Growing power of retailers

Over the past decade retailers have continued to grow in average size in most developed countries. Moreover, the spate of mergers, acquisitions, and leveraged buy-outs during the 1980s accelerated the growth of large-scale retailers so that now retailers are often larger than all but a handful of the manufacturers who supply them. The growing size of retailers, along with their increased sophistication in the use of technology and modern marketing methods has dramatically increased their power in marketing channels. Consequently, channels of distribution are increasingly being dominated by giant retailers who have become 'gatekeepers' into the marketplace. As such, they are determining to an increasing extent what products enter distribution channels and in turn what products become available to consumers.

Increasing role of technology

The application of technology in channels of distribution has exploded in recent years and is accelerating rapidly. Sophisticated use of point-of-sale terminals, scanning and computerized inventory control systems, which grew so rapidly in the 1980s, are being augmented by greater use of portable and hand-held computers linked to mainframe computers or large networks of personal computers via cellular phone technology. Hence the days of clipboards and pencils to check in inventory and process orders will virtually disappear in the near future.

The use of electronic data interchange (EDI) whereby channel members are linked together in real time is another rapidly growing technological break-through. This technology enables manufacturers to schedule their production to conform to what products customers are buying as soon as they are being rung up by the retailer because the information is conveyed instantaneously from the retailer's computer to the manufacturer's.

A further technological development that is catching on in more and more instances is computerized 'salespeople' and 'consultants' whereby customers interface with the computer at the point of purchase and receive information, advice, or even plans and detailed specifications that all but the most knowledgeable human salespeople would be hard-put to match.

Finally, the potential for interactive teleshopping and computer shopping that enable customers to gain immediate access to a virtually unlimited array of products and services from around the world via an information superhighway are well on their way to becoming an everyday reality for millions of customers.

Of course, these are just a small sample of the technological developments that are affecting the structure and operation of channels of distribution in the 1990s and beyond.

REFERENCES

Alderson, Wroe (1957) *Marketing Behavior and Executive Action*, Homewood, Illinois: Richard D. Irwin.

Anderson, James C. and Narus, James A. (1990) 'A model of distributor firm and manufacturer firm working partnerships', *Journal of Marketing*, January: 42–58.

Bucklin, Louis P. (1963) 'Retail strategy and the classification of consumer goods', *Journal of Marketing*, January: 50–5.

Bucklin, Louis P. (1972) *Competition and Evolution in the Distributive Trades*, Englewood Cliffs, New Jersey: Prentice-Hall.

French, R. P. and Raven, Bertram (1959) 'The bases of social power', in Darwin Cartwright (ed.) *Studies in Social Power*, Ann Arbor, Michigan: University of Michigan.

McCammon, Bert C. (1965) 'Integrated channels in the American economy', in Peter D. Bennett (ed.) *Marketing and Economic Development*, Chicago: American Marketing Association.

McGarry, Edmund D. (1951) 'The contactual function in marketing', *Journal of Business*, April: 96–113.

Porter, Michael E. (1985) *Competitive Advantage: Creating and Sustaining Superior Performance*, New York: The Free Press.

Rosenbloom, Bert (1973) 'Conflict and channel efficiency: some conceptual models for the decision-maker', *Journal of Marketing*, July: 26–30.

Rosenbloom, Bert (1987) *Marketing Functions and the Wholesaler-Distributor*, Washington, D.C.: Distribution Research and Education Foundation.

Rosenbloom, Bert (1991) *Marketing Channels: A Management View*, 4th edn, Chicago: Dryden Press.

Shaw, Arch W. (1915) *Some Problems in Market Distribution*, Cambridge, Mass.: Harvard University Press.

Stanton, William J. (1968) *Fundamentals of Marketing*, 2nd edn, New York: McGraw-Hill.

Stern, Louis W. and Brown, Jay W. (1969) 'Distribution channels: a social systems approach', in Louis W. Stern (ed.) *Distribution Channels: Behavioral Dimensions*, New York: Houghton Mifflin.
Stern, Louis W. and Gorman, Ronald H. (1969) 'Conflict in distribution channels: an exploration', in Louis W. Stern (ed.) *Distribution Channels: Behavioral Dimensions*, New York: Houghton Mifflin.
Stigler, George J. (1951) 'The division of labor is limited by the extent of the market', *Journal of Political Economy*, June: 185–93.
Vail, Roland S., Grether, E. T. and Cox, Revis (1952) *Marketing in the American Economy*, New York: Ronald Press.
Weld, L. D. H. (1917) 'Marketing functions and mercantile organization', *American Economic Review*, June: 306–7.
Williamson, Oliver E. (1975) *Markets and Hierarchies: Analysis and Antitrust Implications*, New York: The Free Press.

FURTHER READING

Corey, E. Raymond, Cespedes, Frank V. and Rangan, V. Kasturi (1989) *Going to Market*, Boston, Mass.: Harvard Business School Press.
Dahstrom, Robert and Dwyer, F. Robert (1992) 'The political economy of distribution systems: A review and prospectus', *Journal of Marketing Channels* 2 (1), Fall: 47–86.
Hunt, Shelby D., Ray, Nini M. and Wood, Van R. (1985) 'Behavioral dimensions of channels of distribution: review and synthesis', *Journal of the Academy of Marketing Science* 13 (3), Fall: 1–24.
Journal of Marketing Channels (1991) New York: The Haworth Press.
Pellegrini, Luca and Reddy, Srinivas K. (eds) (1989) *Retail and Marketing Channels*, London: Routledge.
Rosenbloom, Bert (1991) *Marketing Channels: A Management View*, 5th edn, Fort Worth, Texas: Dryden Press.
Rosenbloom, Bert (ed.) (1993) *Wholesale Distribution Channels*, New York: The Haworth Press.
Stern, Louis W. and El-Ansary, Adel I. (1992) *Marketing Channels*, 4th edn, Englewood Cliffs, N.J.: Prentice-Hall.

9

CONSUMER BEHAVIOUR

R. W. Lawson

The fundamental basis of the marketing concept involves the matching of the skills and resources of the organization, profit or non-profit related, to the needs of the customer. Marketing management relies on an understanding of how customers make decisions and their likely reactions to the different elements of the marketing mix. In this context, consumer behaviour not only refers to the physical activity of purchasing but also to related prepurchase and postpurchase activities. Loudon and Della Bitta (1993) define consumer behaviour as 'the decision process and physical activity individuals engage in when evaluating, acquiring, using, and disposing of goods and services'.

One of the most useful applied distinctions in consumer behaviour is between consumer behaviour studied from a micro perspective and a macro perspective. At the micro level, the focus is very much on the reaction of the individual consumer with applications that are relevant to advertising managers, sales-people, or product designers of individual firms or organizations. At the macro level, consumer behaviour involves the study of the influence of consumption on the economic and social conditions within society. The collective behaviour of consumers influences our total quality of life, directing the demand and supply of products and services. The anticipation and forecasting of consumer behaviour at that level can be used for both organizational planning and product development, as well as formulation of public policy to improve the efficiency of the market system.

Research in consumer behaviour allied to the study of marketing basically stems from the 1950s. Prior to that the terminology was essentially confined to the discipline of economics. Economists had a developed series of models explaining consumer choice in terms of changing utilities, or demand prefer-ences, according to variations in price, income and quantity supplied. This approach has been relatively uninfluential within the marketing literature compared with the application of behavioural science concepts taken from psychology and sociology. Detailed reviews of the contribution of all three of these disciplines to marketing are provided elsewhere in the Encyclopedia. The

155

chapters on psychology and sociology show how concepts such as learning, motivation, perception, attitude and social groups have been applied to help our understanding of every element of the marketing mix. This chapter primarily seeks to give an overview of consumer decision-making and show how those concepts listed above may be integrated to give an understanding of the role they play in explaining decision processes of consumers. However, before considering that material in detail, it is useful to reflect on some aspects of the history of consumer research in marketing in order to appreciate the variety of approaches and the overall complexity of the subject. This historical review is not intended as a comprehensive treatise on the development of consumer behaviour but rather a framework to understand how the subject has arrived at its current status and content. It also helps to provide a platform from which to consider future developments in consumer behaviour later in the chapter.

THE DEVELOPMENT OF CONSUMER BEHAVIOUR RESEARCH

Reflecting on the literature in consumer behaviour allied closely to marketing, it is possible to discern three approximate phases of development:

- a segmentation era, primarily associated with work before the mid-1960s;
- a period from the mid-1960s through to the end of the 1970s which was dominated by the development of knowledge on consumer decision-making;
- a period of diversification and enrichment in the 1980s and 1990s.

In the 1950s and through to the mid-1960s much of consumer behaviour research involved the evaluation of consumer characteristics for market segmentation. It was at this time that consumer behaviour researchers investigated the application of personality theories and classifications of motives taken from psychology, and the family life cycle and social class taken from sociology. These were applied with very different degrees of success in cross-sectional studies of markets in order to explain variations in consumer demand for many different classes of products, and also for different choices of brands. Important contributions from this period, which are illustrative of some of the research and are still commonly referred to in the literature and in teaching consumer behaviour, include Haire (1950), Barton (1955), Martineau (1958), Evans (1959), Coleman (1960), Koponen (1960), Tucker and Painter (1961), Dichter (1964), Levy (1966), and Wells and Gubar (1966).

One of the studies from that period which has had a very profound influence on consumer behaviour and marketing is Rogers' work on the diffusion of innovations (1959, 1962). He segmented the potential market for a new product according to the time of adoption and developed a five-stage classification within which to describe potential customers – innovators, early adopters, the early majority, the late majority, and laggards. Another important facet of Rogers' work was his characterization of the adoption process. During consumers' adoption of innovations, Rogers described the individual as moving through the following series of stages in their decision to purchase:

1 Awareness.
2 Interest.
3 Evaluation.
4 Trial.
5 Adoption.

This was one of the first attempts to describe a sequential process which illustrated the stages of the consumer decision and, as will be seen in later discussion, the steps described by Rogers are typical of the framework that has been used to underpin models of consumer decision-making.

Based upon this emerging theory, the first consumer behaviour textbooks for students were published in the 1960s and the volume produced by Engel *et al.* (1968) is regarded as especially significant. Their initial edition is regarded as the first complete textbook on consumer behaviour. It helped to define the boundaries of the subject and firmly established the following as integral concepts in the study of consumer behaviour – motivation, perception, learning, attitudes, personality, social groups (especially the family), social class and culture. Further, the authors encapsulated the switch from a preponderance of segmentation research towards a focus on decision-making, and they provided one of the first, and most enduring, detailed models of the consumer decision process.

The 1968 Engel, Kollat and Blackwell model was one of a series to be developed in the late 1960s and early 1970s. Other particularly important contributions were offered by Howard (1963), Nicosia (1966), and Howard and Sheth (1969). Toward the end of the 1970s Bettman provided another substantial offering with his information processing model of consumer decision-making (1979). Taking an historical perspective on this period it is probably difficult to under-emphasize the importance of developments in attitude theory as applied to thinking and research in consumer behaviour. Approaches to the study of attitudes, particularly as represented in the work of Fishbein (1967) and its later extensions (Ajzen and Fishbein 1980), provided marketers with an easily operationalizable way of investigating and modelling consumer preferences and evaluations. If any single concept stands out as being core to the development of consumer behaviour in the 1970s, it is the theory of attitudes.

Two of the other important developments in the 1970s were the emergence of work on the family as a decision-making unit and the foundation of consumer psychographics and lifestyles as segmentation techniques. Although husband/ wife influences had been investigated earlier (e.g. Wolgast 1958), the early 1970s saw major developments in that area (particularly through the work of Davis and Rigaux 1974; Davis 1976). This work placed the investigation of family decision-making into a parallel context with individual decision-making based around the type of sequence described by Rogers. The recognition of children in the family decision process and the nature of consumer socialization also developed during this period (e.g. Ward 1974; Ward *et al.* 1977).

In the area of market segmentation, the most important developments of this period were the related concepts of psychographics and lifestyles. Retrospectively it is possible to view their development as an outgrowth of disillusionment with personality and other variables as a good basis for market segmentation. The development of mainframe computers and canned packages of multivariate techniques enabled consumer behaviour researchers and marketers to adopt what has been called a 'backwards' approach to market segmentation. Using huge questionnaires they were able to collect large quantities of data representing the activities, interests and opinions of consumers. Factor and cluster analysis techniques enabled this pot-pourri of information to be refined into apparently stable and meaningful portraits of consumer groups (Wells 1974; Mehrotra and Wells 1977).

The latest period of development and enrichment is primarily reflected in the consumer behaviour research of the 1980s and 1990s. Looking back, the dominant paradigm of the 1970s is seen to be one borrowed from cognitive approaches to psychology. In the last decade some particularly strong challenges have been made to this approach. For example, Hirschman (1986) strongly advocated humanistic modes of enquiry, and Foxall (1990) presents a radical approach to viewing consumer behaviour by drawing on alternative paradigms from behavioural psychology. Research has continued within the decision-making and segmentation frameworks established earlier, but it has also broadened and, as scientific approaches have varied, the subject of consumer behaviour has expanded with significant developments in several concepts. Illustrative of these advancements are new understandings in the role of culture (McCracken 1988), values (Kahle 1985), and language and semiotics (Umiker-Sebeok 1987). As other social and economic trends have developed which affect marketers, for example in the growth of crime rates or development of an 'underclass' in Western societies, consumer behaviour researchers have also expanded their focus to consider phenomena such as shoplifting (Cox *et al.* 1990), and the effects of homelessness on consumption (Hill and Stamey 1990).

Also emerging through the 1980s were two major and related contributions to theories of how consumers make decisions. First, there has been the evolution of an alternative 'low involvement' approach to consumer decision-making with a different set and sequence of stages to those outlined from Rogers above. Second, consumer behaviour researchers have placed an increased emphasis on the role of affective as opposed to cognitive influences. These two changes are outlined in much greater detail in the rest of this chapter, which develops the current state of thinking with regard to consumer decision-making.

CONSUMER DECISION-MAKING – THE COMPLEX APPROACH

The complex approach primarily reflects the early cognitively based theories of the subject. Starting with this approach, we can give a general overview of decision-making which can be adapted to take more recent variations into account. A good way to appreciate the overall complexities of consumer decision-making is to review one of the comprehensive models that have been proposed. One of the most popular and enduring of these models is that offered by Engel, Blackwell and Miniard (1990).[1] (See Figure 1.) As indicated above, the basis for this model was first proposed by Engel, Kollat and Blackwell in 1968 and it has been regularly revised and updated to account for new evidence about the behaviour of consumers. It should be noted that evaluations on scientific criteria (e.g. explanation, prediction, generality and heuristic power) have not always been kind to these types of comprehensive models of the consumer decision-making process. What the Engel, Blackwell and Miniard model does offer is a comprehensive illustration of the variables influencing consumers and an appreciation of the flexible and dynamic nature of the consumer decision-making process.

As can be seen, the model is arranged in four columns. The essential stages of the decision process are diagrammed in sequence down the third column. Starting from need recognition, the consumer is seen to move through search processes to evaluation of alternatives, purchase and satisfaction or dissatisfaction outcomes. These five stages reflect the same inherent hierarchy underlying the Rogers' sequence of adoption outlined earlier.

Column one is concerned with the information environment for the decision, and of particular relevance to marketers are the elements of the promotional mix that form the marketer dominated stimuli and which feed into the information processing part of the model in column two. This second column depicts the processes of perception and learning which govern the acquisition and retention of information and link with the need recognition and information search phases of the decision. Other psychological variables are defined in the alternative evaluation stage, and the model makes the central place of attitudes absolutely explicit since it can be equated to preferences governing behavioural intentions and subsequent purchase. The final column lists the influencing variables which impact on the consumer decision. Understanding how these variables impact on the decision process provides a basic rationale for their importance to market segmentation strategies.

The selection of the Engel, Blackwell and Miniard model for this review does not imply that it is the most superior approach in all situations. For example, Howard has been intensely critical of this model and also that of Bettman's in comparison to his own approach (Howard 1989: 109–21). One problem in operationalizing and actually using the Engel, Blackwell and Miniard model to help in the formulation of marketing strategy is the vagueness of the role of some

159

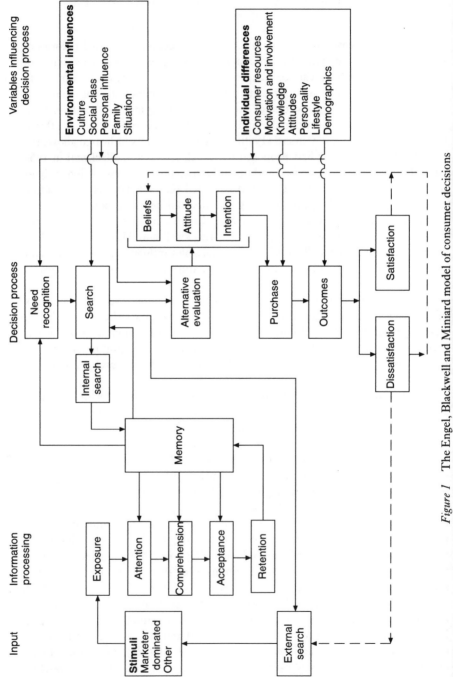

Figure 1 The Engel, Blackwell and Miniard model of consumer decisions

of the variables. The influencing variables in column four are a good example of this, since the exact nature of their relationship to the decision process is not clearly defined. The variables in both boxes in column four can impact on the decision process directly or indirectly at several stages. However, in terms of the descriptive overview for this chapter, it is the inclusion of these very variables that gives the model its appeal and helps to demonstrate the potential complexity of the interrelationships between concepts. The model provides a good starting-point from which to refine our understanding of the consumer decision process.

DIFFERING LEVELS OF COMPLEXITY IN CONSUMER DECISIONS

Since the formulation of early models of buyer behaviour, the most important developments have come in considering variations in the levels of complexity of the decision. Engel, Blackwell and Miniard believe that the same basic model described above can still be used to characterize these different levels of complexity. They argue that intensity, or degree, to which the different stages are used by consumers varies according to the task, but that the essential framework is still appropriate for all situations. However, this claim requires clarification and it is useful to consider alternative theories.

Levels of problem solving

Another of the important early contributions to consumer decision-making was made by John Howard (1963) when he defined consumer behaviour as a problem-solving exercise. Howard has retained this approach and his 1989 book is still built around this idea. He defines and describes three major types of problem solving. These categories are defined as extended, limited and routine problem solving (EPS, LPS and RPS). They reflect buying situations that essentially vary in the amount of intellectual challenge they offer to the consumer. The main determinant influencing the level of problem solving is the familiarity of the task facing the consumer.

Howard uses the same basic summary model (see Figure 2) for all three situations but adapts the complexity of the cognitive processes involved. Like Engel, Blackwell and Miniard, the overall model is still based on a hierarchy which leads through intentions to purchase. Key differences between the models, as shown in Figures 1 and 2, are Howard's inclusion of a variable to represent consumer confidence, and the recognition of direct links between information and attitudes, confidence and intentions. This allows Howard to relax assumptions about the sequence of the stages in the decision process. For example, particularly under RPS, it is possible to have a link directly from information to intention.

Extended problem solving (EPS) is seen as a form of behaviour that is appropriate when the consumer is faced with an innovation, or a first-time

161

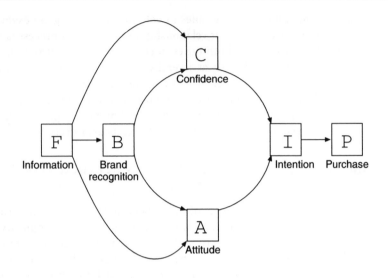

Figure 2 Howard's consumer decision model
Source: Howard (1989: 29)

behaviour, which requires the consumer to form a new product category concept. It is characterized by having two levels of choice, choice among categories and then choice between brands. In this context it would also be logical to extend the definition of EPS so that it is applicable to situations where the consumer faces a choice between non-comparable alternatives such as a holiday or a new car.

Limited problem solving (LPS) is a level of problem solving which Howard believes to be appropriate to situations where the consumer is confronted by an unfamiliar brand in a familiar product class. Consumers take in and process information to produce a cognitive response or image toward the brand, but this is completed within the context of an already existing schema or, in Howard's terminology, product hierarchy.

Routine problem solving (RPS) deals with behaviour for products and brands with which the consumer is very familiar and it is usually characterized by repeat purchasing. The buyer has an evoked set of familiar brands, and choice between brands is made on the basis of very simple heuristics, or decision rules. Typically, a consumer may apply what is known as a conjunctive decision rule. This involves fixing a minimum performance level for relevant product attributes, including price, and the consumer simply buys any brand that passes these criteria subject to availability.

A further important extension of RPS is what Howard refers to as boredom problem solving (BPS). The argument is quite simple. When a product or brand is too familiar boredom can set in. The result is that higher levels of information reinitiated search in order to provide some variety in behaviour. This is a notion that fits well with ideas on consumer motivation regarding optimum stimulation levels.

Levels of involvement

Whereas Howard's approach is essentially based on familiarity, a different but related and also more common approach considers different types of choice processes according to levels of involvement. The concept of involvement is first attributed to Krugman (1965) in explaining differences in learning from advertising between magazine and television environments. However, the concept did not make a substantial impact on thinking and teaching in consumer behaviour until the late 1970s. Even now, there exist some differences in interpretation but there is general agreement that involvement represents an intensity of interest and is a form of arousal related to a motivational state. Differences in involvement are known to be characterized by differences in overall levels of brain activity and by variations in left and right brain activity. These variations emphasize differences in the type of cognitive activities being pursued under different conditions of involvement (Petty *et al.* 1983).

Involvement is seen as having three essential dimensions. First, intensity relates to the degree of interest that the consumer experiences. It is usual to talk about high or low involvement situations, but in reality intensity of involvement is a continuum and this is reflected in the measurement scales that have been developed to assess consumer involvement (Zaichkowsky 1985). The second dimension of involvement is direction or focus. Involvement may be orientated towards the product itself, the advertising, the purchase and purchase decision, or any combination of the three. For example, in a services situation where production and consumption of the service are often simultaneous with the purchase, one may not be able to differentiate between the product and the purchase decision. The final dimension of involvement relates to its persistence. A key distinction is made between enduring involvement and situational involvement. Enduring involvement is long term and represents the ongoing personal interest that people have in particular product areas. The clearest examples of these are the consuming interests developed with pastimes and hobbies such as fishing or stamp collecting. Situational involvement is short term and normally associated only with the purchase decision. Typical examples of products which generate high levels of situational involvement are durables such as dishwashers and washing machines. The consumer may collect a lot of information on the different options and carefully evaluate the best buy for their situation, but once acquired there is little ongoing interest in the product.

Involvement is related to a consumer's values and self-concept, and varies not only across individuals but also across situations. In itself involvement embraces a number of different properties and, as a determinant of decision mode, it is

163

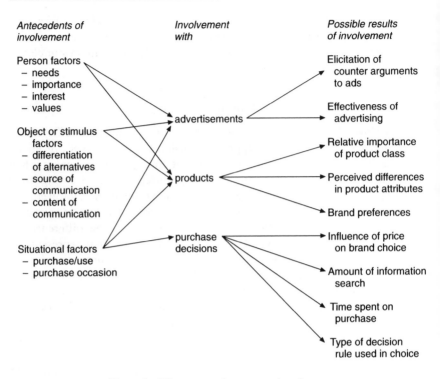

Figure 3   The nature of consumer involvement
Source: Adapted from Zaichkowsky (1986)

a much more complex notion than familiarity, or prior knowledge, which underlies variations in Howard's problem solving approach. Figure 3 gives a summary of the major dimensions of involvement. Column one describes its antecedents or influencing factors. Column two refers to the object of the involvement and column three indicates the results where differing levels of involvement have an impact on consumer decision-making.

Antecedents of involvement include a variety of variables that interact with each other to generate a degree of involvement at any particular time. Amongst the personal considerations are needs, values, experiences and interests. These interact with different products and services to produce differing levels of involvement for different individuals. The effect of the antecedents on involvement is also moderated by the ability of the consumer to find and process information.

Column two identifies the objects of involvement as discussed above, and column three in Figure 3 gives an extensive list of the results of involvement upon different aspects of consumer behaviour. However, there are two other sets of consequences that should be made clear in addition to those listed. First, in low involvement situations it is accepted that there may be very little or no evaluation of the product before purchase. Attitudes that are formed are weakly held and are primarily based on experience derived from consumption. This presents a different scenario from the previous models which identify attitude formation as a key concept leading to intentions and purchase. Low involvement is often reflected in consumers proceeding directly from need recognition to purchase with no information search or evaluation of alternatives.

A second important set of consequences relates to post-purchase behaviour and ongoing consumption. Complaints are seen as a high involvement phenomenon, while dissatisfaction with low involvement products is generally seen as resulting in brand switching. Also, brand loyalty may be viewed as a high involvement phenomenon. Indeed, the definition of loyalty may be seen to require some degree of emotional attachment which is reflected in enduring involvement. High situational involvement and a positive brand evaluation may result in a high level of brand confidence, but this need not

Table 1   Alternative views of high and low involvement consumers

High involvement view of an active consumer		*Low involvement view of a passive consumer*	
1	Consumers are information processors.	1	Consumers learn information at random.
2	Consumers are information seekers.	2	Consumers are information gatherers.
3	Consumers are an active advertising audience and as a result the effect of advertising on the consumer is weak.	3	Consumers represent a passive audience for advertising. As a result the effect of advertising on the consumer is strong.
4	Consumers evaluate brands before buying.	4	Consumers buy first. If they evaluate brands it is done after the purchase.
5	Consumers seek to maximize expected satisfaction. Consumers compare brands to see which provide most benefits related to needs and buy based on multi-attribute comparisons.	5	Consumers seek some acceptable level of satisfaction. As a result, consumers buy the brand least likely to give them problems and use few attributes.
6	Personality and lifestyle characteristics are important because the product is closely tied to the consumer's identity and belief system.	6	Personality and lifestyle characteristics are not important because the product is not closely tied to the consumer's identity and belief system.
7	Reference groups influence consumer behaviour because of the importance of the product to group norms and values.	7	Reference groups exert little influence on product choice because products are unlikely to be related to group norms and values.

Source: Adapted from Assael (1992)

equate to loyalty and may be displaced in a subsequent evaluation. Low involvement situations may be characterized by stable purchasing patterns but these are considered the result of inertia, rather than loyalty. As such it is a form of behaviour which is easily disrupted by situations such as stockouts or sales promotions.

PURCHASING WITHOUT DECISIONS

In 1979 Olshavsky and Granbois published an influential paper entitled 'Consumer Decision Making – Fact or Fiction?' They provided a synthesis of research on the prepurchase stage of consumer behaviour and concluded that, in very many cases, the prepurchase stages of information search and evaluation of alternatives were simply not present. Their argument goes far further than simply seeing routine repetitive behaviour as something which has resulted from the earlier application of some more extended process of evaluation. They conclude that at every level of consumption, from general budget allocation down to choice of individual brands, a majority of consumers do not in fact evaluate alternatives and did not therefore make decisions. It is important to realize that the evidence they quote takes into account a wide range of consumer behaviour situations, including strategic consumption decisions relating to the allocation of income across different expenditure categories, choice of retail stores, and a range of products from furnishings and household appliances through to grocery items. Purchasing without decision-making is not, therefore, to be regarded as atypical behaviour.

The notion of consumer purchasing without any explicit decision-making process is consistent with several other important contributions to consumer theory in the 1980s. For example, Zajonc and Markus (1982) have emphasized the role of affective as opposed to cognitive factors in the formation of consumer preferences. Like Krugman's initial paper on low involvement and passive learning, this is an approach which stresses how people learn through repeated exposure. Familiarity with a product is seen to be sufficient for the formation of preferences without any original cognitive justification. A good illustration of their argument is the way in which Mexican children acquire strong preferences for chili peppers in their diet despite initial aversive reactions.

The idea of consumers purchasing without decisions is also reflected in what is referred to as the 'experiential' approach to consumer behaviour (e.g. Holbrook and Hirschman 1982). The emphasis in the experiential approach is firmly placed on the symbolic nature of consumption. Consumer behaviour is seen as primarily hedonic and orientated towards aspects of pleasure and emotions rather than being associated with analytical, logical, problem solving.

The consequence of these adaptations in thinking is that consumer behaviour has become more diversified and research has incorporated more studies on consumption as opposed to inquiries solely considering the purchasing process. This has to be a positive move in an applied marketing context. Although the

Table 2   The five stages of the decision process

	Recognition	Search	Purchase	Consumption	Post-consumption
Strategic					
Central					
Generic					
Variant					

process of acquiring goods and services will always be important for marketers to understand, the long-term matching of products to customer needs has to be based on a thorough understanding of benefits sought by consumers and the way in which products are actually used. A provocative paper by Wells (1993) on the status of current research in consumer behaviour reviews a classification of consumer research developed by Johan Arndt. The classification is based on the five stages of the decision process, from problem recognition through to post-consumption activities, and the importance of the decision. (See Table 2.) Four categories of importance are considered:

1   Acquisition of strategic items. These have a 'life altering' effect and examples include a new home, a new child, or education versus employment.
2   Central budget allocation decisions. This refers to allocation of resources among important groups of products or services, for instance the choice between the vacation or the new kitchen.
3   Generic product or service decisions, or specific purchases within groups of products and services. An example may be the choice between the built-in oven or the freestanding cooker for the new kitchen.
4   Variant selection, or choice of individual brands.

Wells emphasizes that consumer researchers have spent most of their time in the bottom, left-hand corner of this chart, dealing with the early stages of low-level decisions. The work of Belk, Holbrook, Hirschman, McCracken, and others, has moved studies towards the top, right-hand corner and Wells makes a strong call for continued progress in developing research in this area which has a strong applied macro focus.

FUTURE DEVELOPMENTS IN CONSUMER BEHAVIOUR

This will first be considered in terms of research and knowledge about the subject area and then in terms of some speculative changes that may take place in the way consumers actually acquire and use goods and services.

Wind et al. (1991) provide an assessment of recent paradigm shifts in consumer behaviour which point the direction for future research and emphasize how the movement to the top right of Wells' table will change and benefit marketers' knowledge and application of consumer behaviour constructs. They summarize developments by emphasizing the seven trends listed below.

1   A move to considering more realistic units of analysis; in particular, a greater emphasis on the family buying unit and less attention to the traditional focus on the individual.

2   Consideration of assortments of products rather than individual purchase transactions; realistically, many purchases are related and it is more fruitful to look at sets of behaviours rather than single instances.

3   Examination of situation specific purchase and consumption, rather than general behaviours; recognition of this is seen to increase the validity and value of much consumer research.

4   A move from deterministic to stochastic modelling of consumer behaviour; stochastic models of brand choice have existed since the 1950s (e.g. Ehrenberg 1959) but have had little impact on traditional studies. Recently, there has been more recognition of a stochastic element in much consumer behaviour with, for example, recognition that some brand choice behaviour may be cyclical in nature.

5   A lessening of the US focus in consumer research with more cross-cultural studies and recognition of cultural variations in consumer behaviour. In part, this is seen as a response to the interest in globalization that has dominated much business and economic thinking in the last twenty years.

6   A move from a 'low tech' to a 'high tech' consumer environment; advances in computers and telecommunications are fundamentally changing the nature of consumer behaviour. They also have significant implications for methods of consumer research with the potential availability of new databases. This links closely with item four. Retail scanning technology has provided huge improvements in the databases available for modelling patterns of consumer purchases over time.

7   The use of integrated sets of research methods rather than single approaches; enhancement of software for multivariate statistics means that techniques like cluster analysis may be used more effectively with conjoint analysis or multidimensional scaling, offering more complete analyses and a better understanding of behaviour.

This review by Wind *et al.* (1991) emphasizes areas where consumer behaviour research has been relatively weak and points the directions for future developments to help marketing managers. In terms of future trends in the actual behaviour of consumers, we have to turn to considering the possible impacts of changes in the economic, ecological, social, political, and technological environments within which consumers exist. There has to be a large amount of crystal-ball gazing in any such exercise, but there are evidential trends in place which one may expect to continue. Some of the most important and most likely are outlined below.

1   The move to the high-tech environment as earmarked by Wind *et al.* will have immense impact on every stage of the consumer acquisition process. Retail scanning and eft-pos systems are obvious current examples. In the future, we may expect considerable developments in direct marketing and changes in consumer information search procedures as current business technology systems spread beyond the world of work and into the everyday home. The potential impact of home computers, modems, CDRoms, faxes, electronic mail and virtual reality is colossal. Such developments will not only allow the consumer to access information on goods, services and prices in their own home, but may also impact on other stages of the decision process. For example, we may expect expert systems to be available to help with the evaluation of alternatives. Guidance could be provided for actual decisions ranging from the contents of this week's shopping basket, to the most suitable itinerary for a round-the-world holiday.

2   Parallel with technological changes, facilitating the flow and movement of cheap information around the world, we may expect further development of cultural universals and the continued globalization of markets. This is also linked to the growth in travel and tourism, and the increased mobility of whole populations.

3   Along with increased tourism and migration we may expect other observed demographic trends to continue. Chief amongst these are the increased importance of older markets, and the questionable relevance of original family life cycle structures to marketing as alternative family forms become even more prevalent.

4   Economic recession, with continued high levels of unemployment is forecast to continue to plague Western economies. Unless there are radical shifts in thinking regarding the redistribution of wealth and work, we may expect the continued polarization of consumer segments according to wealth and ability to consume.

5   Environmental issues will have a major impact on all our lives in the future. Much discussion has taken place about the notion of sustainability. This discussion has largely been production orientated. It is difficult to see how ideas on sustainability are going to succeed until a consumption focus is imposed on the concept and consumer expectations are realistically aligned with environmental considerations. Major issues will continue to relate to packaging, energy and water usage, animal exploitation and habitat destruction.

6   Part of the environmental issue is the realization of the externalities involved and the 'true' costs of many human behaviours. As Hirschman (1991) points out, many other social problems together with their associated costs, that have increased in importance in the last thirty years, are due to consumption 'gone wrong'. These range from addictions and abuse of products through to mismanagement of credit and consequent poverty. Hirschman's call was for consumer behaviour researchers to become involved in many of these

issues. It is to be expected that marketers will also have to show more responsibility for the unplanned consequences of their actions.

Overall, the potential changes in patterns of consumer behaviour are enormous. This presents special challenges and opportunities for marketers and for students of consumer behaviour. This review has made it clear how the subject has developed primarily around an information-processing and decision-making perspective. This area of research has had many successes and will continue to be important. In terms of application, it is most relevant to the promotional aspect of the marketing mix and its success is particularly represented by the idea of involvement. Involvement has developed as an accepted theoretical construct from within the study of consumer behaviour as opposed to other concepts that have been begged, borrowed or stolen from economics, psychology, sociology and anthropology. The challenge is to develop similar levels of understanding across the whole subject area.

NOTE

1 Engel, Blackwell and Miniard have produced a slightly revised version of their model in the 7th edition of their book, published in 1993. I have chosen to remain with the 1990 version because it shows more clearly the role that attitudes have traditionally held in models of consumer choice.

REFERENCES

Ajzen, I. and Fishbein, M. (1980) *Understanding Attitudes and Predicting Social Behavior*, Englewood Cliffs, NJ: Prentice Hall.
Assael, H. (1992) *Consumer Behavior and Marketing Action*, 4th edn, Boston, MA: PWS-Kent.
Barton, S. G. (1955) 'The life cycle and buying patterns', in L. H. Clark (ed.) *Consumer Behaviour*, New York: New York University Press.
Bettman, J. R. (1979) *An Information Processing Theory of Consumer Choice*, Reading, MA: Addison Wesley.
Coleman, R. P. (1960) 'The significance of social stratification', in M. L. Bell (ed.) *Marketing: A Maturing Discipline*, Chicago: American Marketing Association.
Cox, D., Cox, A. D. and Moschis, G. P. (1990) 'When consumer behavior goes bad: an investigation of adolescent shoplifting', *Journal of Consumer Research* 17 (2): 149–59.
Davis, H. L. (1976) 'Decision making within the household', *Journal of Consumer Research* 2, March: 241–60.
Davis, H. L. and Rigaux, B. P. (1974) 'Perception of marital roles in decision processes', *Journal of Consumer Research* 1, June: 51–62.
Dichter, E. (1964) *Handbook of Consumer Motivations*, New York: McGraw-Hill.
Ehrenberg, A. S. C. (1959) 'The pattern of consumer purchases', *Applied Statistics* 8: 26–41.
Engel, J. F., Kollat, D. T. and Blackwell, R. D. (1968) *Consumer Behaviour*, New York: Holt, Rinehart and Winston.
Engel, J. F., Blackwell, R. D. and Miniard, P. W. (1990) *Consumer Behaviour*, Hinsdale, NJ: Dryden Press.
Evans, F. B. (1959) 'Psychological and objective factors in the prediction of brand

choice', *Journal of Business* 32, October: 340–69.

Fishbein, M. (1967) 'A behavior theory approach to the relations between beliefs about an object and the attitude toward an object', in M. Fishbein (ed.) *Readings in Attitude Theory and Measurement*, New York: Wiley.

Foxall, G. R. (1990) *Consumer Psychology in Behavioural Perspective*, London: Routledge.

Haire, M. (1950) 'Projective techniques in marketing research', *Journal of Marketing* 14, April: 649–56.

Hill, R. P. and Stamey, M. (1990) 'The homeless in America: an examination of possessions and consumption behaviors', *Journal of Consumer Research* 17 (3): 303–21.

Hirschman, E. C. (1986) 'Humanistic inquiry in marketing research: philosophy, method and criteria', *Journal of Marketing Research* 23, August: 237–49.

Hirschman, E. C. (1991) 'Secular mortality and the dark side of consumer behaviour: or how semiotics saved my life', in R. H. Holman and M. R. Solomon (eds) *Advances in Consumer Research, volume 18*, Provo, UT: Association for Consumer Research.

Holbrook, M. and Hirschman, E. C. (1982) 'The experiential aspects of consumption: consumer fantasies, feelings and fun', *Journal of Consumer Research* 9 (2): 132–40.

Howard, J. A. (1963) *Marketing Management: Analysis and Planning*, Homewood, IL: Richard D. Irwin.

Howard, J. A. (1989) *Consumer Behavior in Marketing Strategy*, Englewood Cliffs, NJ: Prentice Hall.

Howard, J. A. and Sheth, J. N. (1969) *The Theory of Buyer Behavior*, New York: John Wiley and Sons.

Kahle, L. R. (1985) 'Social values in the eighties: a special issue', *Psychology and Marketing* 2, Winter.

Koponen, A. (1960) 'Personality characteristics of purchasers', *Journal of Advertising Research* 1, Summer: 6–12.

Krugman, H. E. (1965) 'The impact of television advertising: learning without involvement', *Public Opinion Quarterly* 29, Fall: 349–56.

Levy, S. J. (1966) 'Social class and consumer behaviour', in J. W. Newman (ed.) *On Knowing the Consumer*, New York: Wiley.

Loudon, D. L. and Della Bitta, A. J. (1993) *Consumer Behaviour: Concepts and Applications*, New York: McGraw-Hill.

McCracken, G. (1988) *Culture and Consumption: New Approaches to the Symbolic Character of Consumer Goods and Activities*, Bloomington, IN: Indiania University Press.

Martineau, P. (1958) 'Social classes and spending behaviour', *Journal of Marketing* 23, October: 121–30.

Mehrotra, S. and Wells, W. D. (1977) 'Psychographics and buyer behaviour: theory and recent empirical findings', in A. G. Woodside, J. N. Sheth and P. D. Bennett (eds) *Consumer and Industrial Buying Behaviour*, New York: Elsevier North Holland.

Nicosia, F. (1966) *Consumer Decision Processes: Marketing and Advertising Implications*, Englewood Cliffs, NJ: Prentice Hall.

Olshavsky, R. W. and Granbois, D. H. (1979) 'Consumer decision making – fact or fiction?', *Journal of Consumer Research* 6, September: 93–100.

Petty, R. E., Cacioppo, J. T. and Schumann, D. (1983) 'Central and peripheral routes to advertising effectiveness: the moderating role of involvement', *Journal of Consumer Research* 10, September: 135–46.

Rogers, E. (1959) *The Adoption of New Products: Process and Influence*, Ann Arbor, MI: Foundation for Research on Human Behavior.

Rogers, E. (1962) *Diffusion of Innovations*, New York: Free Press.

Tucker, W. T and Painter, J. (1961) 'Personality and product use', *Journal of Applied Psychology* 45, October: 325–9.

Umiker-Sebeok, J. (ed.) (1987) *Marketing and Semiotics: New Directions in the Study of Signs for Sale*, Berlin: Mouton de Gruyter.
Ward, S. (1974) 'Consumer socialisation', *Journal of Consumer Research* 1, September: 1–16.
Ward, S., Wackman, D. B. and Wartella, E. (1977) *How Children Learn to Buy: The Development of Consumer Information Processing Skills*, Beverly Hills, CA: Sage.
Wells, W. D. (ed.) (1974) *Life Style and Psychographics*, Chicago: American Marketing Association.
Wells, W. D. (1993) 'Discovery-orientated consumer research', *Journal of Consumer Research* 19, March: 489–504.
Wells, W. D. and Gubar, G. (1966) 'Life cycle concept in marketing research', *Journal of Marketing Research* 3: 355–63.
Wind, J., Rao, V. R. and Green, P. E. (1991) 'Behavioral methods', in T. S. Robertson and H. H. Kassarjian *Handbook of Consumer Behavior*, Englewood Cliffs, NJ: Prentice Hall.
Wolgast, E. H. (1958) 'Do husbands or wives make purchasing decisions?', *Journal of Marketing* 22, October: 151–8.
Zaichkowsky, J. L. (1985) 'Measuring the involvement construct', *Journal of Consumer Research* 12, December: 341–52.
Zaichkowsky, J. L. (1986) 'Conceptualising involvement', *Journal of Advertising* 15 (2): 4–14.
Zajonc, R. B. and Markus, H. (1982) 'Affective and cognitive factors in preferences', *Journal of Consumer Research* 9, September: 123–31.

FURTHER READING

Assael, H. (1992) *Consumer Behaviour and Marketing Action*, 4th edn, Boston, MA: PWS-Kent.
Engel, J. F., Blackwell, R. D. and Miniard, P. W. (1990) *Consumer Behaviour*, Hinsdale, NJ: Dryden Press.
Howard, J. A. (1963) *Marketing Management: Analysis and Planning*, Homewood, IL: Richard D. Irwin.
Howard, J. A. (1989) *Consumer Behavior in Marketing Strategy*, Englewood Cliffs, NJ: Prentice Hall.
Kassarjian, H. H. and Robertson, T. S. (eds) (1991) *Perspectives in Consumer Behavior*, Englewood Cliffs, NJ: Prentice Hall.
Kassarjian, H. H. and Robertson, T. S. (eds) (1991) *The Handbook of Consumer Behavior*, Englewood Cliffs, NJ: Prentice Hall.
Loudon, D. L. and Della Bitta, A. J. (1993) *Consumer Behaviour: Concepts and Applications*, New York: McGraw-Hill.

10

ORGANIZATIONAL BUYING BEHAVIOUR

Stephen Parkinson

Organizations are customers for a wide range of products and services. Understanding how the organizational customer behaves when making purchasing decisions is critically important to effective marketing decisions. The study of how organizations buy (organizational buying behaviour) has evolved to meet this need.

Most of the early focus on organizational buying behaviour stressed the need to understand how customers fixed prices, determined delivery quantities and specified quality. It was assumed that these three elements determined which supplier the customer selected. Failure to meet the buyer's needs on these criteria would lead to loss of the business. These three elements relate to functional aspects of the buyer's role, commonly referred to as purchasing.

Research from the 1960s onwards has formally confirmed what many practitioners experience throughout their industrial marketing careers. Organizational buying decisions are frequently complex processes that take place over time. Typically there is a sequence of stages in the process, and there are likely to be different influences at each stage. More than one member of the organization is involved in the buying process, and each member of the buying group is likely to have different interests in the outcome. It is not sufficient when making marketing decisions to consider the role of price, quality and delivery alone. Success depends upon developing a complete understanding of how customers make buying decisions.

This chapter begins with a review of the formal tasks of organizational purchasing. The core elements of purchasing are to buy the right product at the right price at the right time. Understanding how buyers handle price, quality and delivery issues is the first stage in analysing organizational buying behaviour. The second part of this chapter discusses the nature of organizational buying decisions. It focuses on the nature of the buying process and the range of different influences on that process. This chapter has been written from the perspective of an organization wishing to sell to an organizational customer.

Organizational purchasing decisions are made to meet the objectives of an organization rather than the needs of an individual buyer. There are some problems with this definition since organizational needs and individual needs frequently overlap (for example with the purchase of a company car). However, the rationale for purchase is the distinct characteristic of the organizational buying decision that differentiates it from consumer behaviour. There are two principal determinants of supplier choice. These are the technical suitability of the product or service to meet the customer's needs, and the economic worth or value of the product or service.

Organizations buy products and services to enable them, in turn, to supply other customers with products or services. Their demand as potential customers is driven by the demand for their own products or services. Economists term this derived demand. It follows that to sell to an organization it is important to understand the influences on the demand for that customer's own goods and services.

All organizations make purchasing decisions. The scope of organizational buying behaviour includes manufacturing and service industries. It also includes public sector organizations in sectors such as transport, education, and healthcare. Primary sectors such as agriculture and extractive industries are also included. Organizational buying behaviour as a field of study also includes retailing and distribution. The potential scope of a chapter such as this is considerable. This chapter will focus primarily on manufacturing and service sectors. This is a reflection of the extent to which these sectors have been systematically analysed and researched. Although the other parts of the economy are equally important areas of economic activity, they tend to have been neglected in formal analyses of organizational buying decisions.

HISTORICAL DEVELOPMENT OF THE PURCHASING FUNCTION

Articles relating to the purchasing function can be traced back to the turn of the century (Fearon 1968). The first two books presenting an analytical view of the function appeared in 1928. However, most of the literature on purchasing has appeared from the 1950s onward. This reflects an increasing interest in the potential contribution of purchasing to organizational performance.

Economic development in many countries has led to increased specialization and therefore interdependence between organizations. When organizations no longer manufacture every part of the end product, and choose to buy components from a third party, they become dependent on the purchasing function to source that component effectively. Current trends suggest that purchasing will become increasingly important as organizations choose to concentrate on developing their core skills and competencies and supplement these with bought-in products or services as required from the most efficient supplier (Hamel and Prahalad 1993).

The traditional role of the purchasing function is to buy the right product or service, to a given specification, at the best possible price. The function is also responsible for making sure that it arrives on time to meet the organization's needs. In this traditional role the specification and delivery requirements are typically set by other functions within the organization. This leaves the purchasing function to concentrate on getting the best possible deal on price, and to ensure that the product or service is delivered on time.

Traditionally purchasing's major role has been seen as restricted to pricing decisions, negotiation and dealing with contracts. This is reflected in the relatively low status given in many organizations to the buying role (Keogh 1993). The major exception to this is in retailing where buyers have historically been recognized as one of the most important functions in the organization (Parkinson and Hogarth-Scott 1993).

Since the 1950s a succession of academics and management consultants have argued that organizations would benefit by giving purchasing a greater strategic role. They consider that bought-in materials and services are a significant proportion of total manufacturing costs in many industries (Reck and Long 1988). In such industries cost management or cost reduction can have a major and direct effect on profitability. Managing costs may be a more effective way of maintaining profitability than maintaining market share. Market share maintenance typically requires marketing expenditure, and cost reduction by definition involves reducing expenditure.

Purchasing's strategic contribution can also include improving the quality of expenditure. Purchasing is responsible for the interface between an organization and its supply markets. A professional purchasing function will identify changes in supply markets that may present opportunities or threats. For example, if a supplier is acquired by one of its major competitors this reduces the sourcing options open to the buyer. Negotiations with an alternative supplier may be more difficult because of the absence of competition. Alternative suppliers may already have contractual relationships with the organization's own competitors. In this situation purchasing may be responsible for monitoring the status of current suppliers. Where problems are anticipated alternative sources of supply may be developed to reduce dependency on a few key suppliers.

Alternatively, a new technology may offer radically improved performance over existing technologies, and give major competitive advantage to those companies which incorporate it in their own products. Purchasing's role is to scan supply markets continuously and identify technological changes that could have major implications for the organization. There is increasing evidence that much significant innovation comes as a result of the purchasing organization stimulating suppliers to develop new products or processes to meet customer requirements.

In some organizations the purchasing function has developed a broader range of supply management responsibilities (Keogh 1993). These include quality management, value engineering, value analysis and material requirements planning. It is becoming increasingly necessary for suppliers to demonstrate to such companies that they are operating to appropriate quality standards. Some purchasing organizations now have a policy of not buying from companies that do not have BS5750 or ISO9000 certification (see Chapter 51). The application of value engineering and value analysis techniques has also provided the purchasing organization with a methodology to identify systematically the specification of a specific product or service and to ensure that the company buys to that specification. Materials requirements planning disciplines have also led to the development of JIT (just in time) supply relationships with key suppliers to manage inventory levels.

Each of these professional aspects of the purchasing decision has implications for the marketing behaviour of potential suppliers. Resource management skills are growing in many organizations posing a considerable challenge for conventional marketing decisions. The purchasing organization now increasingly controls the marketplace. Marketing's challenge is to identify the requirements of customers on each of these elements and develop an appropriate response.

PURCHASING BEHAVIOUR

While it is important to understand the professional role of the purchasing function it is also important to recognize that purchasing decisions are made by individuals working in an organization. Such individuals are subject to a variety of different influences and use different criteria to make the final choice of supplier. It would be naive to ignore these behavioural influences on the buying decision.

For example, a supplier might assume that a customer will buy if the supplier's product is better than the competition in meeting the customer's technical and economic requirements. This assumption may be invalid if the customer is averse to taking risks. Another customer may be very keen to buy quickly, and be prepared to take the risk of product failure.

These influences on the buying decision are behavioural dimensions. Buyers make decisions for reasons other than economic and technical rationality. Remember the company car example from earlier? The reasons for making a decision in a particular way may be linked to a variety of factors. These include the characteristics of the purchasing company, the buying situation or the individual knowledge and experience of the buyer responsible for the final selection of supplier.

One convenient way of examining the behavioural influences on the organizational buying decision is to distinguish between the buying process and the various influences on this process. By examining the buying process, suppliers can get a feel for the range of decisions that a potential customer makes. This can enable them to anticipate what inputs are required to get the customer to consider their organization favourably.

An awareness of the influences on the buying process guides the supplier

176

towards an understanding of differences in the needs of specific customers. This can be used to differentiate products and services to meet differing requirements. A focus on influences can also be useful in tailoring communications appropriately.

THE BUYING PROCESS

The organizational buying decision can be seen as a process that takes place over time. There are several key stages in this process. However, each of these stages may not be present in every situation. The process may be extensive in some situations and relatively short in others. A variety of different models have been suggested to reflect the different stages, each with essentially the same elements. These are identification of need, specification of requirements, search for supplier, choice of supplier, purchase order, post-purchase evaluation and supplier management (Moller 1985).

Buying situations have also been classified into three categories, namely straight rebuy, modified rebuy and newbuy situations (Robinson and Faris 1967). The straight rebuy situation involves purchasing the same product or service again from the same supplier. Such a purchase will typically be made quickly and only a few people are likely to be involved in the buying process. A modified rebuy involves a change in the purchase. This could involve a new supplier or a change in specification. More people are likely to become involved in the purchasing process. Finally, a newbuy is a purchase that the organization has not made before. Typical newbuy situations involve more people than the other two purchasing situations and take longer to complete.

The concept of the buygrid has been developed to describe the interaction

Table 1   Robinson and Faris's buygrid model of organizational buying behaviour

	Newbuy	*Modified rebuy*	*Straight rebuy*
Problem (need recognition)			
Determine characteristics of needed item or service			
Describe characteristics of needed item or service			
Search for supplier			
Acquire proposals			
Evaluate proposals			
Select order routine			
Performance feedback			

Source: Robinson and Faris (1967)

177

between the buying process and the buying situation (Robinson and Faris 1967). Each of the different buyclasses (newbuy, modified rebuy and straight rebuy) can be viewed in terms of its associated buying process. This categorization provides a useful way of analysing the organizational buying decision (see Table 1).

Research can be conducted to determine how the supplier's customers identify the need to buy the product or service being offered. Do customers actually recognize the problem in the first place, or does the supplier have to create an awareness of the need? For example, it is obvious when a supply of paper runs out that it must be replaced. Similarly, components are required to keep a production line running, and must be replaced when the supply is exhausted (ideally just before). However for some products it is less obvious that there is a need. A company may be unaware of the need to improve its internal information systems. An audit of communication systems by an external supplier may reveal the extent of the problem.

Specification of requirements involves developing a description of the characteristics and quantity of the product or service that is needed. This may be done by specifying by brand name (for example, a brand of motor fuel). Alternatively, it may involve analysis of the requirement. The specification will be developed from that analysis. This process is termed value engineering. If the vendor can become involved in this process then it is possible to influence the final specification. This could involve sharing knowledge with the customer to assess the technical requirement and build a business case. In some situations the customer may simply indicate what it wants to achieve and invite the suppliers to bid against that specification (usage specification). Here the customer is relying on the expertise of the supplier to solve the problem (Dyer and Ouchi 1993).

Organizations look for suppliers in many different ways. From a supplier's perspective it is important to identify how the customer looks for alternative suppliers. It is also important to determine how many suppliers are likely to be considered. In many situations standard operating procedures specify how many suppliers must be included. This is linked to the value of the contract. The organization may insist that the purchaser obtains quotations from at least three suppliers for purchases placed with a value greater than £2,500. This may cause problems if there are only a few competent suppliers.

Evidence from a range of research also suggests that most industrial buyers do not look very far when searching for new suppliers. There is a strong tendency towards inertia. Existing suppliers are favoured over new sources of supply.

It is also important to understand which sources of information are used to find suppliers. Formal media (trade press, exhibitions and direct marketing) typically create awareness. Informal media (face-to-face meetings and personal references from other customers) are used to evaluate and choose suppliers. Some sources of information such as personal contacts are perceived as more reliable than formal contacts. This is particularly the case when considering new products or services from unknown suppliers.

When a customer creates a short list of suppliers it is important to understand the criteria that are used in choosing which suppliers to include. Often the short list is composed solely of those suppliers that the customer is currently aware of. In the straight rebuy situation the existing supplier is the only company on the short list.

In a modified rebuy or a newbuy situation the list of criteria can be extensive. Many government purchasing organizations use a formal list of criteria to shortlist suppliers. The purchasing organization regularly invites companies to register an interest in supplying a specific product or service. Suppliers that are not currently listed are evaluated and if suitable they are included in the list of qualified sources from which bids are subsequently sought. This prequalification process is mandatory for any organization wanting to supply to this sector.

Many other large organizations also adopt this approach (for example, major retailers and the major oil companies). Typical factors considered at this stage could include the financial status of the supplier, the qualifications and previous experience of the supplier, the expertise of specific personnel, location, quality standards (increasingly BS5750 or ISO9000 certification), manufacturing skills, design skills, and distribution competencies.

In some situations the customer may find that no supplier can meet their prequalification criteria. This may then lead to a process of supplier development. For example, they may assist the supplier to introduce the necessary documented processes to achieve BS5750 or ISO9000 certification. Where there is only one approved supplier the customer may choose to develop a second supplier and bring it up to an approved standard to meet its requirements, thereby creating an element of competition (Dyer and Ouchi 1993).

Choice between suppliers will be made against the specification established at an earlier stage in the buying process. The first criterion to be considered is typically the technical match between the supplier's product or service and the buyer's requirements. The quality of the match will depend on how well the customer has specified the requirement and communicated this to potential suppliers. It will also depend on the quality of the supplier's response. Both of these processes depend on the skills of buying and selling organizations. There is therefore considerable potential for misinterpretation of the requirement.

The quality of the technical solution to the customer's problem has to be evaluated against the economic case. Two competing solutions to a customer's problem may have very different technical approaches and different costs. This may require the buyer to trade off additional technical benefits against higher costs. This process may frequently involve several participants from different functional areas in the organization. Each will have his or her own criteria and seek to influence the process in different ways. In the case of straight rebuy situations the choice process will be short and the purchasing function is the only area likely to become involved. Price will be the main area for discussion between buyer and seller.

In modified buy and newbuy situations there are likely to be more people involved in the final decision. The process is likely to take longer and cover a wider range of issues. The skill of the supplier is to identify the needs of each of these members of the buying group (referred to as the 'buying centre' or 'decision-making unit') in the preparation of the business case and proposal to the customer.

The final stages in the process involve placing the order and managing the supplier's subsequent performance. Organizations differ in the extent to which they formally evaluate supplier performance and the criteria which are used. Where supplier performance is formally evaluated this can include monitoring product or service quality and delivery performance. Some purchasing organizations use performance on these criteria to make judgements about future orders.

INFLUENCES ON THE BUYING PROCESS

Many factors can influence the organizational buying process. It is important when selling to an organization to be able to identify the influences that might inhibit or facilitate the sale of specific products or services. Understanding the different influences that exist can lead to more effective market segmentation and positioning strategies. These influences have been categorized as environmental, organizational, interpersonal and individual (Webster and Wind 1972).

Environmental factors

Environmental factors include the full range of PEST factors (political, economic, social, and technical). These factors are as important to an evaluation of strategic purchasing decisions as they are to an evaluation of strategic marketing decisions. By understanding the influence of the environment on the customer the supplier is better placed to develop products and services that meet the changing requirements of the customer.

Several elements have made organizations increasingly aware of the impact of environmental factors. These include an increasing dependence on bought-in materials as a percentage of the total value added by the company, increasing shortages and uncertainties in supply markets, and a rapid rate of technical change in many sectors. These factors jointly and severally have made many organizations conscious of the strategic role which purchasing can play.

Purchasing organizations that have recognized that supply market management is an important aspect of their long-term planning, have attempted to integrate purchasing at a strategic level. Suppliers that deal with such organizations are likely to find that the levels of customer contact are senior members of the management team. Time horizons for developing collaboration are also perceived as long run rather than limited to immediate transactions.

180

The dynamics of the industries in which the organizational customer operates are a crucial aspect of the external environment. Marketing's problem is to assess how the potential customer is influenced by competition from other suppliers, the threat of new entrants, alternative substitute products, and competition from suppliers and its own customers (Porter 1985). This requires an in-depth knowledge of the customer's industries. It also requires an ability to assess how the supplier's product or service can be developed to allow the customer to compete effectively. Analysis of the customer's total business system may be required to identify the areas where the supplier can have most impact on the customer's profitability.

At one level a supplier of telecommunications equipment may offer a telephone management system to customers that allows the customer to track the costs of outgoing messages and introduce budgeting systems to control costs in different parts of the organization. It may also offer training support to improve the quality of management of incoming calls, improving the efficiency of the organization's response to its customers. Both of these services will help the potential customer to respond to its environment. Both may simply maintain the customer's current competitive situation.

In more sophisticated situations the supplier may become involved in joint product or market development activities with the customer. To do this effectively requires close collaboration over a period of time, with joint commitment of resources. To get into the relationship in the first place, the potential supplier needs to understand the end markets of the potential customer and the competitive challenges facing the customer. It is also important to understand how the supplier's product or service can influence the customer's costs or ability to differentiate itself from the competition.

This situation is typical of those facing manufacturers that are seeking to develop new markets (for example in central Europe) where manufacturing and distribution systems are rapidly changing. Recent initiatives in these markets in the retailing sector have included several joint ventures between food manufacturers and specific retail chains.

Organizational factors

Most approaches to the segmentation of organizational markets begin with an analysis of how many potential customers there are, which products they buy, how large each customer is in terms of potential buying power, where each customer is located, and which industries they serve or which services they supply.

These approaches to market segmentation are useful since they help to predict where the opportunities for the supplier are likely to arise. They also help to quantify the value of the market. Sales effort can be directed to those sectors showing greatest potential. New products and services can be developed to meet the needs of new segments. Distribution decisions can be based on an understanding of the location of potential customers and anticipated service levels.

Other aspects of the organization have also been found to be useful in marketing planning. These are essentially 'softer' elements that cannot immediately be observed from the outside, but can have a major impact on buying decisions. Such factors can be considered as aspects of the organization's culture or climate that appear to influence its response to the environment. Organizations present different personalities. Some appear to be more innovative than others. Some will take decisions faster than others. Some have a positive and open attitude to interaction with the external environment. Others do not. Each of these characteristics can have a major influence on the way in which potential customers deal with their suppliers.

Organizational markets can be segmented on these dimensions. Traditional segmentation criteria such as size and location of customer are useful in determining the potential purchasing power of the customer and how to organize the sales team. By contrast an understanding of the culture of the buying organization can indicate why an organization behaves in the way it does and can be useful in developing the sales case for a specific customer.

This can be illustrated by the purchase of new industrial products or processes. This aspect of industrial marketing has been extensively studied over the last twenty-five years (Baker 1983). Researchers have found that the economic and technical case for purchasing a new product or service is not in itself sufficient reason for many organizations to adopt it. Different organizations will take differing periods of time before they decide to buy when faced with apparently the same technical and economic advantages from buying a new product or service.

Research has established that variations in the rate of adoption of new products can be linked to variations in the structure of the organization, and general management skills, competencies and orientations. Broadly speaking organizations with flatter structures (fewer layers in the hierarchy), more open communication systems (greater lateral channels) and less frequent reporting and control cycles are likely to act faster when faced by a new product or service (to adopt or reject). Organizations with a positive attitude to the recruitment and development of staff will also exhibit greater receptivity.

From a marketing perspective it is important to recognize that different organizations in the same industry may manage their environment in different ways. In the UK offshore oil industry in the late 1970s and early 1980s companies encountered two different types of customer. One type preferred to subcontract its entire requirement to the supplier. A supplier would be commissioned to design and build an element of the offshore platform (for example the subsea production system). It would be responsible for the delivery of the system to the contracted deadline and specification. This type of customer regarded itself as being in the oil extraction and distribution business, rather than in the construction business.

Other operating companies preferred to control the whole operation from design through purchasing and construction to on site delivery and installation. The supplier became an extension of the customer's business for the period of the contract. These differences in approach reflected the history of the oil company and its preferred way of doing business.

Two segments emerged. Separate strategies were required to meet the needs of each segment. Customers that preferred to have no involvement in the delivery process bought on the basis of a design specification, price and delivery commitment. The supplier's response was typically to keep the customer informed about progress, but not become involved with the client on a day-to-day basis. When the customer took control of the supply and delivery process greater involvement was required. Typically this took the form of joint project teams, secondment of staff to the customer organization and more detailed progress reporting and checking. The supplier became an extension of the customer's organization for the duration of the contract.

Interpersonal factors

Organizational buying decisions are made by individual managers and considerable research attention has been paid in the marketing literature to who those managers are, and what their responsibilities are in the purchase of specific products or services. The marketing rationale is to identify who is likely to influence the final choice of supplier, what their needs are, and how to provide the information that they need in order to make a buying decision. A series of studies has confirmed that the involvement of different managers in the buying decision can vary considerably, almost on a company-by-company basis, even for the same products or service (Woodside 1992).

Researchers have attempted to map the nature of the buying centre for a wide range of different buying decisions. In straight rebuy situations only a limited number of staff appear to be likely to be involved, and they are likely to be relatively junior. Typically the purchasing department plays the major role. In the modified buy and newbuy situation more people become involved and they tend to become increasingly senior within the organization. Design and manufacture have a greater involvement in the specification of the requirement, purchasing takes on the role of supplier search, and general management may ultimately sanction the purchase.

Each of these members of the buying centre is likely to have different needs. The purchasing manager may be most concerned about the cost of the item, seeking to secure a source of supply at the lowest possible cost to the organization. The engineering department may be more concerned about the technical performance of the item. The manufacturing manager may be concerned about the conformance of the delivered item to specification. Finally the marketing function may be concerned about the extent to which the product enhances the appeal of the product to the customer, through cost reduction or enhanced performance.

Given that several members of the organization are likely to be involved in the final choice of supplier, attention has been focused on how choices are made. The economics literature is not particularly helpful in this respect. The theory of the firm implies that organizations make reasoned decisions about the choice of inputs based on full information about alternative consequences. While this is an elegant theory it does not reflect the realities of organizational marketing and purchasing decisions.

There has been considerable research into the criteria that are applied in purchasing decisions (Moller and Laaksonen 1985). A wide range of factors has been identified which influence choice. These include quality in relation to price, technical ability, services, location, reputation, payment terms, previous vendor history on delivery or product quality, and technical quality. An understanding of the factors that influence the final choice of supplier is clearly of immediate relevance to organizational marketing decisions.

Organizational buying decisions are also likely to be a political process with considerable potential for conflict, political persuasion and influence. The relative importance of different criteria is likely to reflect the interaction of individual managers' preferences and perceptions. Decisions are often made in a situation of partial rather than complete knowledge about the organization and its environment. They are often partial rather than complete solutions to the problem. In this situation it is difficult to generalize about the buying decision from one situation to the next.

Some attempts have been made to develop general descriptive models of the buying process that do take account of the way in which decisions are reached (Woodside 1992). In particular researchers have looked at the influence of power and methods of conflict resolution. The impact of opinion leadership within the organization has also been addressed.

Several different classification schemes have been developed to describe the roles which members of the buying centre can play. These include users, influencers, gatekeepers, deciders and buyers (Webster and Wind 1972). Each of these members of the buying centre is likely to play a different role in the purchasing decision. The classification is a useful first reminder to suppliers that there is likely to be a range of people in the organization to influence, typically with differing needs and expectations from the purchase of the product or service.

Some members of the buying centre may be able to exercise power over other members because of their relative status, or because of expertise or access to specialist information or knowledge. For a long time the information services departments of many organizations possessed considerable power and influence over the choice of computer equipment. As managers in the rest of the organization have developed their own understanding of such systems, so this power has been eroded. Today most computer suppliers have realized the importance of targeting the end user to sell computing hardware and software. Many personal computers are now specified and bought by line managers rather than by a central computing services department.

Characteristics of the buyer

Finally, some attention has been paid to the characteristics of individual members of the decision-making unit. The general knowledge and experience of the buyer influence the way in which the buyer deals with suppliers. There has been a considerable increase in the range and quality of training for purchasing management at a functional level that has implications for suppliers. Previous experience with existing suppliers and knowledge of the supply market also has an important mediating effect on the choices made by the buyer. The level of risk perceived in choosing one supplier over another has been shown to be important in understanding the behaviour of individual buyers. Personality traits such as self confidence and assertiveness appear to be less useful in the prediction of buyer behaviour (Moller 1985).

SUMMARY

Organizational buying decisions are made primarily to meet the needs of the organization. Such decisions are therefore strongly influenced by economic and technical considerations. The role of the professional purchasing manager is to make informed choices about the supply of products and services to meet the organization's needs. By taking on an increasingly strategic role professional purchasing managers have begun to exert considerable control over supply markets. Effective marketing depends on developing an understanding of this professional role and responding appropriately.

Organizational buying decisions are also influenced by a range of behavioural factors. These include the characteristics of the buying organization and the buying process. Developing an understanding of these factors can be of use in developing an industrial marketing strategy, particularly in such areas as target marketing and the development of the marketing programme.

REFERENCES

Baker, M. J. (1983) *Market Development*, Harmondsworth: Penguin Books.
Dyer, J. H. and Ouchi, W. G. (1993) 'Japanese style partnerships: giving companies a competitive edge', *Sloan Management Review*, Fall: 51–64.
Fearon, H. E. (1968) 'Historical evolution of the purchasing function', *Journal of Purchasing and Materials Management*, February.
Hamel, G. and Prahalad, C. K. (1993) 'Strategy as stretch and leverage', *Harvard Business Review*, March–April: 75–84.
Keogh, M. (1993) 'Buying your way to the top', *Mckinsey Quarterly*: 41–62.
Moller, K. E. K. (1985) 'Research strategies in analysing the adoption process', *Journal of Business Research* 13, August.
Moller, K. and Laaksonen, M. (1985) 'Situational dimensions and decision criteria in industrial buying: theoretical and empirical analysis', in A. G. W. Woodside (ed.) *Advances in Business Marketing*, vol. 1, Greenwich, Conn.: JAI Press Inc.
Parkinson, S. T. and Hogarth-Scott, S. (1993) 'Who does the marketing in retailing', *European Journal of Marketing* 27 (3): 51–62.

Porter, M. E. (1985) *Competitive Advantage*, New York: The Free Press.
Reck, R. F. and Long, B. (1988) 'Purchasing: a competitive weapon', *Journal of Purchasing and Materials Management* Fall: 2–8.
Robinson, P. J. and Faris, C. W. (1967) *Industrial Buying and Creative Marketing*, Boston: Allyn and Bacon.
Webster, F. E. and Wind, Y. (1972) *Organizational Buying Behaviour*, Englewood Cliffs, New Jersey: Prentice Hall Inc.
Woodside, A. G. W. (ed.) (1992) *Advances in Business Marketing and Purchasing: Mapping How Industry Buys*, vol. 5, Greenwich, Conn.: JAI Press.

FURTHER READING

Corey, R. (1983) *Industrial Marketing: Cases and Concepts*, Englewood Cliffs, New Jersey: Prentice Hall.
Davies, G. (1993) *Trade Marketing Strategy*, London: Chapman.
Farmer, D. (ed.) (1985) *Purchasing Management Handbook*, Aldershot: Gower.
Håkansson, H. (ed.) (1982) *International Marketing and Purchasing of Industrial Goods*, New York: Wiley.
Parkinson, S. T. and Baker, M. J. (1986) *Organizational Buying Behaviour*, Basingstoke: Macmillan.
Robinson, P. J. and Faris, C. W. (1967) *Industrial Buying and Creative Marketing*, Boston: Allyn and Bacon.
Taylor, B. and Farmer, D. (1975) *Corporate Planning and Procurement*, London: Heinemann.
Woodside, A. G. W. (ed.) (1992) *Advances in Business Marketing and Purchasing: Mapping How Industry Buys*, vol. 5, Greenwich, Conn.: JAI Press.

11

PURCHASING MANAGEMENT

Lars-Erik Gadde

THE IMPORTANCE OF PURCHASING

The role of purchasing has been changed in a very significant way during the decades after 1970. Traditionally purchasing has been considered almost a clerical function with the ultimate objective of buying as cheaply as possible. Today it is regarded as a function of major strategic importance. The main reason for the change is the increasing specialization that characterizes the industrial system as a whole. Companies have gradually concentrated their activities on more and more limited parts of the total value chain in order to enhance efficiency in operations. One consequence of this development is that manufacturing companies have become increasingly dependent on procurement of goods and components from other firms. External suppliers, therefore, have come to play an important role for most manufacturing companies. Purchased goods often account for more than half of the total costs of a company. This fact has put purchasing in focus, internally as well as externally.

Purchasing is a focus of internal interest because an increasing proportion of the resources of a company are handled within the purchasing function. If more than half of the costs of the company are determined by purchasing it must, by definition, be an important strategic function whose activities are decisive to the competitive power of the firm. Furthermore, owing to increasing specialization, technical resources are also made increasingly available to companies through their suppliers. The products and components purchased today are more technically sophisticated than before, which has increased complexity and raised the requirements on the purchasing staff. This has also been a reason for improving the status and strategic recognition of purchasing.

From an external point of view, one major consequence is that what goes on in the interface between individual companies has gained in importance. Concepts and techniques such as just-in-time deliveries, quality assurance and the zero-defect principle have more and more impact on company operations. All of this means bringing relations to suppliers into focus. It also means

187

bringing purchasing into focus, as supplier relations are mainly handled and coordinated through the purchasing department. As a whole, therefore, purchasing is of major strategic importance to a company. The changing view of purchasing is also reflected in the literature. Going back to the 'clerical' time, a representative title of a book within the profession might have been 'Handbook of Purchasing'. Such books were mainly concerned with questions regarding purchasing procedures – how much to buy, how to make inquiries, etc. The main objective of this literature was to improve purchasing efficiency. Around 1970 models of organizational buying behaviour were developed to increase the understanding of the decision-making process in the buying company and which factors determined the outcome of this process. One important contribution was the concept of a buying centre. The buying centre is an informal constellation of the members in the organization that are involved in the buying decision process. Knowledge of the behaviour and perceptions of buying centre members is an important input for the marketing strategies of selling firms. These models were thus primarily orientated at enhancing marketing effectiveness.

During the 1990s, however, titles like 'Handling Supplier Relationships' and 'Developing Partnerships' better reflect the prevailing attitudes and views of purchasing. This perspective takes the performance of both supplier and customer into consideration. The major reason behind the new perspective adopted in the literature is an alternative view of efficiency in purchasing, discussed in greater detail below.

THREE STRATEGIC ROLES OF PURCHASING

When analysing the strategic importance of purchasing three major roles can be distinguished: the rationalization role, the development role and the structural role. The role of rationalization covers the numerous day-to-day activities undertaken to affect the cost structure. Three types of rationalization may be identified. The first deals with specification of requirements of the item to be purchased. This is a major undertaking, requiring decisions including whether the item needed should be manufactured in-house or purchased from external suppliers (the make-or-buy decision) as well as the design of the item. Purchasing can contribute greatly to effectiveness in this process through cooperation with internal company functions such as R&D, design and production and a qualified awareness of the capacity and capability of different suppliers. Value analysis is a technique used in this respect, the objective of which is to reduce costs while maintaining the necessary levels of availability and product reliability.

The second type of rationalization is related to identifying the most cost-effective supplier, once the specifications have been decided. Traditionally this has been the same as finding the supplier offering the lowest price.

The third type of rationalization, finally, deals with affecting the various flows

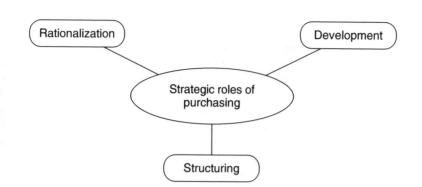

Figure 1   Three strategic roles of purchasing

associated with a business transaction. During the 1980s substantial improve-ments of efficiency in material flows decreased the need for inventories, and increased profitability. Purchasing has played an important role in these operations as changing delivery frequencies and lot sizes were important prerequisites for gaining these benefits. Material flows are not the only potential source for rationalization. Information flows provide considerable opportunities for improvements. In many cases the magnitude of information exchange is substantial and major effects can be obtained by using modern information technology.

Suppliers are important potential resources for the technical development of the customer firm. Most often that potential is only used in a passive way (i.e. the buying company waits for the supplier to develop new solutions and then decides whether or not to purchase them). A more active strategy in this respect, however, can turn the purchasing function into a major catalyst for making better use of these resources. This is what can be identified as the development role of purchasing. One reason for activating this role is the increasing specialization of the industrial system. A purchasing firm that uses components from a number of suppliers needs to coordinate component development undertaken by different suppliers with their own R&D activities. The compo-nents may even represent different areas of technology, which makes it difficult for the customer firm to develop and maintain its own knowledge of each specialized technology. A customer relying on suppliers as a source of development has to involve them early in the R&D process. This provides another advantage. Early supplier involvement makes it possible to shorten lead times in product development, which is considered one of the major competitive factors in most industries today.

Purchasing also has a structural role in that the procurement activities will affect the structure of the supplier markets. A company might choose to concentrate its purchases of a certain item on one supplier. The competitiveness

189

of that supplier is then strengthened as compared with the other potential suppliers. Another company might consider the availability of a number of alternative suppliers a major strategic aim. Such a company would probably divide its purchases among several suppliers to maintain an existing supplier structure. The actions undertaken by a firm – whether conscious or unconscious – thus, affect the structure of supplier markets in the long run, in terms of the number and location of potential suppliers. It is therefore important for a company to analyse the long-term consequences of its buying behaviour, as well as to identify and predict other trends affecting the supplier markets. A company activating the structural role of purchasing can orientate its own operations towards reinforcing tendencies beneficial to it and counteracting undesirable ones.

BASIC CONDITIONS AFFECTING PURCHASING MANAGEMENT

There are substantial disparities in the forms of purchasing management. Some of these differences are attributable to the fact that companies work under divergent basic conditions. The characteristics of supplier markets will pose certain opportunities for the procurement activities. The technology of the company will also have considerable effects. Purchasing strategies and behaviour have to be very different in mass-producing firms compared with firms manufacturing to customer specification. In this section, however, two other important conditions are discussed.

The first is external and related to the characteristics of the item being purchased. There are considerable differences between purchasing standardized raw materials and sophisticated complex machinery. The second factor is internal and deals with the way in which purchasing is organized in the buying company.

The impact of product characteristics

Some of the variability in purchasing management is explained by the characteristics of what is being procured. There are clearly significant differences between major equipment for a big turnkey project and industrial supplies for more or less immediate use. Procurement of major equipment is most often characterized by technical complexity, substantial financial investment and the fact that the products are going to be used for a long time. Therefore, negotiations preceding a purchasing decision will be extensive, including discussions of alternative designs and functions. One important issue is how the new equipment is related to the existing machinery and facilities. Availability of services, training and spare parts are other important matters. This type of procurement usually involves a large number of people and departments in the buying company. One of the major characteristics is that the choice of equipment may limit the freedom of the purchasing company for a long time.

The equipment chosen will largely determine what raw materials and maintenance supplies will be bought. Procurement of industrial supplies (for maintenance, repair and operations) is very different. Such purchases include a large number of products (fastenings, hand tools, glues and sealants etc.). They are purchased frequently, but not completely regularly, as the demand for them fluctuates. The absence of such products when they are needed can pose major problems for the purchasing company. Procurement of industrial supplies, therefore, is characterized by considerable administrative complexity. The major issue regarding these types of purchases, therefore, is to develop well-functioning order and delivery systems. Efficiency is obtained through establishing routines for purchasing as a whole, rather than carrying out each purchase in the most efficient way.

Between the extremes of major equipment and industrial supplies, there are other types of purchasing situations. One concerns raw materials and materials in different stages of processing, which are important input for many companies. Such items are often more or less standardized. They usually have a global market. Prices fluctuate in relation to the cycles of demand and supply. Expectations of changing prices, therefore, are important determinants of the timing of these purchases. Many companies buy components of various kinds for assembly operations. Procurement of components is characterized by recurring deliveries, which makes it important to take advantage of the repetitive feature to create efficiency. The need to adapt the components to each other and to the production context of the buying company is also an important determinant of these purchasing operations.

Thus, it is obvious that purchasing issues show considerable variation owing to their specific procurement characteristics. The differences can be related to technical, administrative or supplier market related reasons. Such variation is typical of purchasing in all companies, as every firm purchases various kinds of items. The major effect of this variation is that it is difficult for a company to find one best solution regarding organization and administrative routines.

Purchasing organization

There are two extremes of purchasing organization: centralization and decentralization. A centralized purchasing department provides three major advantages. One is economies of scale thanks to larger order quantities than would appear in a decentralized organization structure. The second is that it is possible to coordinate the combined activities from the purchasing company in relation to individual suppliers. The third is that centralization enhances effective allocation of resources. One example is that purchasing staff can specialize in procurement of specific items which promotes professionalism in purchasing. The major disadvantage of a centralized purchasing organization is problems with internal communication between purchasing staff and other departments (production, R&D, etc.). Especially in large companies there can be a substantial

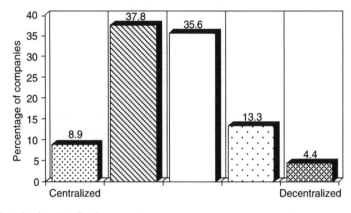

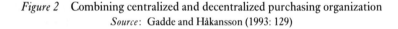

☷ Completely centralized.
▧ Centralized purchasing of strategic items, decentralized purchasing of commodities.
☐ Decentralized purchasing combined with a central purchasing department.
⠃ Decentralized purchasing combined with voluntary co-operation between various divisions.
▩ Completely decentralized.

Figure 2 Combining centralized and decentralized purchasing organization
Source: Gadde and Håkansson (1993: 129)

distance between them – both in physical terms and in attitudes. A sense of 'us-versus-them' between production and purchasing can easily arise.

These kinds of problem are better dealt with in a decentralized organization. Proponents of decentralized structures claim that purchasing should not be a specialized function, but rather an integral part of a larger context. During the last ten years the decentralized organization has gained in importance. One reason is that firms in general have turned towards decentralization. When company divisions and business units are made more and more responsible in economic terms for their operations, it is not possible to keep their major cost determinant – purchasing – under central control. The most obvious problem with a decentralized purchasing organization is the reduced professionalism of the purchasers. They become more generalists, needing competence and capability for purchasing across an extremely broad product range.

The choice between centralization and decentralization will always be a compromise. Settling for the benefits of one always means sacrificing the potential benefits of the other. For this reason purchasing will always have to put effort into eliminating the disadvantages of the organizational form that has been chosen. A decentralized organization may be supplemented with central purchasing staff, responsible for drawing up group agreements with the purpose of achieving economies of scale. A centralized purchasing organization can be supplemented with shop-floor purchasers who are responsible for acquisition of

192

specific components. This makes it possible to work with a combined approach falling somewhere between the extremes. Such intermediate types showed to be the most common forms in a study of big Scandinavian companies (Figure 2).

Traditionally, the purchasing organization of a firm has been determined by internal factors. Over time, external factors have come to play an increasing role. When purchased goods account for almost two-thirds of total costs, it is very obvious that external factors have to be considered more. The purchasing company must be organized in such a way that the exchange with suppliers is facilitated as much as possible.

STRATEGIC ISSUES IN PURCHASING MANAGEMENT

There are two major strategic issues regarding supply management in a company. One of them is how much of the input resources needed by the manufacturing company should be directly controlled (i.e. the degree of vertical integration). The other regards the nature of customer-supplier relationships (i.e. the number of suppliers used and the characteristics of the relation to individual suppliers).

The make-or-buy decision

The first issue relates to the make-or-buy decision. For every company the decision to produce in-house or to buy from external suppliers is a key strategic one. Vertical integration, historically, has been used as a strategy to secure availability of important resources. One example is automotive firms and ballbearing manufacturers that have been the owners of steelworks in order to guarantee the quality of the steel required. One main disadvantage of in-house production is that rapid changes in market demand might lead a company to be locked into obsolete technology. Another problem is that firms with a high degree of backward vertical integration might limit the prerequisites for and capability of creative thinking and development among their staff.

Over time there has been a substantial decrease in the degree of vertical integration in industry as a whole. As has already been mentioned, numerous manufacturing companies have become increasingly dependent on innovative subcontractors, who have proved able to contribute to making production as well as development work more effective. In make-or-buy analysis the loss of control has been considered a serious drawback when the degree of vertical integration has decreased. Over the years, however, manufacturing companies have identified other means for retaining control over their supply situations that do not require ownership of suppliers. There are a number of examples of more informal integration, such as strategic alliances, collaboration projects, joint investments in production tools, loans and credit guarantees. These examples of 'quasi-integration' can play the same role as vertical integration. They provide the buying company with some of the main advantages of ownership without the corresponding disadvantages.

The nature of customer-supplier relationships

The second, and more important, strategic issue is the nature of customer-supplier relationships. It is possible to identify two disparate views of what is an efficient way of managing supplier relationships. One is what can be regarded as an adversarial relationship. According to that view a customer-supplier relation is a zero-sum game (i.e. what one of the parties stands to gain, the other one stands to lose). One major issue in purchasing management, therefore, is that suppliers compete with one another. By switching from one supplier to the other, depending on the business conditions they offer, the customer will be guaranteed as low a price as possible. Using such a strategy requires the purchasing company to avoid being too dependent on individual suppliers, so that the customer always will be able to switch. Multiple sourcing, therefore, has been strongly advocated as an efficient purchasing strategy. Using a number of suppliers has also been considered an advantage in terms of handling risks (e.g. in relation to capacity problems of individual suppliers). Using this kind of procurement strategy, purchasing companies must maintain a deliberate distance in their relationship with their suppliers, which leads to an adversarial relation rather than a collaborative one. This can be called the traditional view of efficiency in purchasing.

During the 1980s a clear shift was observed in the view of what is an efficient number of suppliers. These tendencies were first observed in the automotive industry when American and European manufacturers were confronted with the supply strategies of their competitors in Japan, who relied on a more limited number of suppliers. Where Japanese firms were using 200–300 suppliers, the companies in the Western world were using 2–3,000 for a corresponding output of cars.

One example of a changing strategy is that Ford reduced its suppliers from 3,200 to 2,100 in 6 years. Changes of this type have not, however, been limited to the automotive industry. The most spectacular example is Rank Xerox which had more than 5,000 suppliers in 1981 and and just over 300 five years later. Such a strategic change contrasts greatly with what was earlier regarded as efficient purchasing. The main reason for the change is that major advantages can be obtained through cooperation with individual suppliers. Price is only one of the costs that are dependent on the purchasing behaviour. A number of other (indirect) costs can be affected, due to the nature of the relationship (see Figure 3).

To affect the indirect costs and attain the potential benefits of close cooperation requires customer and supplier to adapt to one another. Adaptations require deepened relationships, which makes it necessary to reduce the number of counterparts. Doing so will make it possible to improve considerably the

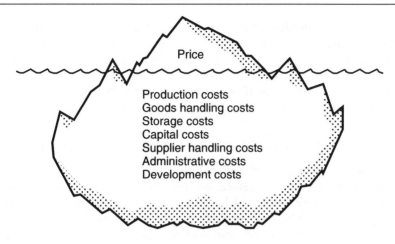

Figure 3   Costs affected by purchasing behaviour
Source: Gadde and Håkansson (1993: 47)

efficiency of relationships. According to this view a buyer-seller relationship is not a zero-sum game. Both parties will attain benefits from mutual adaptations. In terms of the strategic roles of purchasing as have been identified above, significant effects can be obtained in terms of rationalization as well as in terms of development. The change also has definite structural consequences.

Networks of suppliers

Considerable economic effects can thus be attained through developing relationships with individual suppliers. Even greater impact, however, would be obtained if the activities of the individual suppliers could in some way be coordinated. Sometimes the buying company would increase its efficiency if the supplier's supplier could be persuaded to make a certain change. Each relationship is embedded in a larger network of relationships, characterized by interdependencies of various kinds. Therefore, the performance of every relationship is contingent on a number of other relationships. Analysing and organizing suppliers and supplier markets in terms of networks provides major advantages. The best example again is the Japanese automotive industry and its reliance on a more limited number of suppliers. These firms have organized their suppliers in a hierarchical structure. Toyota, for instance, had direct contacts with only a few suppliers (less than 200). These primary suppliers are made responsible for structuring the rest of the supply network, which includes a very large number of firms (around 40,000). The way that the supplier network is organized appears to have been decisive to the strong position established by Japanese automotive firms.

Purchasing companies relying on single sourcing increase the dependence on individual suppliers. The potential for playing off suppliers to achieve a price benefit is also severely restricted. Obviously the perceptions of what is efficient purchasing behaviour must be based on different assumptions than the traditional view. We thus need to contrast that view with another way of looking at strategic efficiency, referred to as 'the alternative model'.

TRADITIONAL VIEW OF PURCHASING MANAGEMENT

Purchasing management deals with how to secure efficiency and effectiveness in purchasing operations. Therefore, an important determinant of purchasing strategy and management is which view of purchasing efficiency prevails in the buying company. The two contrasting views that have been identified are analysed below in terms of their impact on purchasing management.

According to the traditional model there is a very well-established view of how effective purchasing should be carried out (Figure 4). The first step in the decision-making process is to specify the needs to be satisfied. The next is to identify a number of potential suppliers. They are requested to submit tenders, which are then compared on the basis of various criteria. According to this view efficiency in purchasing arises from the implementation of the decision-making process. The most important determinant of this procedure is enhancing competition among the suppliers. The struggle among suppliers forces them to make improvements that also benefit the purchasing company and affects its performance. To achieve such benefits, it is recommended that customers avoid being too dependent on individual suppliers. Keeping an arm's length relationship ensures that the buyer can easily switch to another supplier offering some kind of better conditions. The

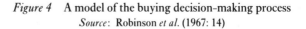

Need recognition
↓
Definition of the characteristics and quantity of item needed
↓
Development of the specifications to guide the procurement
↓
Search for and qualification of potential sources
↓
Acquisition and analysis of proposals
↓
Evaluation of proposals and selection of suppliers
↓
Selection of an order routine
↓
Performance feedback and evaluation

Figure 4   A model of the buying decision-making process
Source: Robinson *et al.* (1967: 14)

196

purchasing company will have contact with a number of potential suppliers for each item. By playing off these suppliers against each other it becomes possible to make an optimum choice. To promote competition among suppliers is thus the most important aspect of purchasing management. According to this perspective, efficiency in purchasing is attained if the price is minimized in each separate transaction. The underlying rationale is that price is the most significant cost and that other costs are not affected by a change from one supplier to another. On the contrary, there should be a great deal to be gained from such 'play-the-market' behaviour.

THE ALTERNATIVE VIEW OF PURCHASING MANAGEMENT

The alternative view is a consequence of the changing conditions described above. Today, due to increasing specialization, activities that were earlier undertaken in one and the same company are separated into different companies. This development has created a growing interdependence among companies, especially when dealing with products and components that are characterized by technological or logistical complexity. Efficiency and effectiveness in such operations can never be obtained through purchasing strategies aiming at playing off suppliers against one another. On the contrary, in complex relationships the customer has to create dependencies on specific suppliers to obtain gains in efficiency. To achieve the potential gains in performance, supplier and customer must become increasingly related. Only by mutual adaptations in technological, logistical and administrative terms can the indirect costs of the relationship be affected. This is the reason for the stand-point presented above, that purchasing organizations have to become more externally orientated. The most important organizational aspect is to relate the company to individual suppliers and to the whole network of suppliers. Thus, organizational issues are of major importance when discussing purchasing management from the alternative view. Rather than talking about purchasing organization, however, we go on to discuss various 'organizing' activities within purchasing, which leads to a more external than internal focus, and a more dynamic and developing view than the static one that often is associated with the word 'organization'.

The network approach to analysis of industrial markets is a relevant point of departure for discussing important organizing aspects of purchasing. According to this approach three important network dimensions are distinguished: activities, resources and actors. All three dimensions are essential in terms of organizing supplier relationships.

The activity structure of an industrial network is characterized by strong interdependence due to the specialization of firms. The performance of the network and the companies in the network is dependent on the efficiency of the activities *per se*, but also on the links connecting these activities. One important assignment for the customer, therefore, is to improve the coordination of its activities with those of the supplier. Linking of activities is thus an important organizing issue for improving purchasing efficiency. The development of coordinating mechanisms in transportation (just-in-time systems) and information exchange (integrated computer systems) have reduced the need for inventories and buffers.

Suppliers are providers of resources for a purchasing company. For example, a supplier can play an important role in the technical development of a customer firm. As said above, it is very difficult for a company to keep pace with rapid developments in different areas of technology. This is why a company should try to develop its resources in interaction with its suppliers, to be able to make use of their resources and competence. A second important organizing issue, therefore, is integrating customer-supplier resources. Various forms of technology transfer are relevant examples of such organizing activities. Most exchange of technology, however, takes place in the day-to-day contacts among individuals in the companies.

The third organizing issue is the need to connect the buying company to other actors, both in terms of single relationships and networks. One important prerequisite for quality in customer-supplier relationships is commitment. To attain the desired joint effects, a customer has to develop relationships of a long-term nature with an atmosphere of openness and trust. These characteristics do not evolve automatically. They have to be created, especially if previous conditions have been of an adversarial nature. Therefore, it is relevant to consider this a matter of organizing. Another important aspect is the nature of collaboration. Buyer-seller relationships relying on the alternative view of efficiency are characterized by a high degree of cooperation. For this cooperation to be successful, there is a need for a great degree of harmony in the relationship. In the same way there is a need for a certain degree of challenge. This is necessary to avoid stagnation and to secure a continuous development of the relationship. This challenge should partly be in terms of hostility and conflict since constructive conflicts promote dynamism. It is therefore an important organizing issue to create a balance between harmony and conflict in the relationship.

CURRENT ISSUES IN PURCHASING MANAGEMENT

In this final section we briefly discuss some of the major current issues in purchasing management.

The first issue is the degree of vertical integration. The question is whether the ongoing tendencies will continue or not. The basic argument for a continuing decrease in vertical integration is that the advantages provided by specialization will result in a decreasing proportion of in-house production. Design and R&D can also be expected, at an increasing rate, to be outsourced to suppliers. However, some things also speak in favour of an increasing degree of vertical integration. The argument advocating this view is that in industry today the companies in the final stages of the value chain (assemblers) are the ones that are most profitable, while those at the beginning (component producers) have financial problems, owing to heavy pressure from their customers. In the short run assembly firms have been able to improve returns thanks to disintegration. In the long run, however, it is very unlikely that independent component suppliers will be able to generate the funds needed for investments, in order to stay competitive. The only way to guarantee this is to increase the degree of vertical integration.

The divergent opinions about future integration can partly be explained by the fact that they concentrate on the formal degree of vertical integration. As discussed above, a number of forms of more informal integration, in fact, makes it possible to attain the major ownership advantages without its disadvantages. The most likely development, therefore, is continued specialization of activities, resulting in decreasing vertical integration, combined with various intermediate forms of quasi-integration based on extended supplier relationships.

The second issue deals with the nature of customer-supplier relationships. As has been argued, there are a number of good reasons for a company to develop extended supplier relationships according to the alternative view of efficiency. Most types of buyer-seller relations can be made more effective by attacking indirect costs through long-term cooperation and mutual adaptations. Sometimes, however, products from various suppliers are completely interchangeable from the perspective of the customer, sometimes the indirect costs are very small as compared to the direct costs. In such cases the purchasing firm can benefit from using the traditional view of efficiency and promoting supplier competition. It seems possible, therefore, to argue that a company aiming at purchasing efficiency should be able to behave according to both views, depending on the circumstances.

The characteristics of the business transaction determine whether the traditional or the alternative view is the most relevant one (Figure 5).

In case A in Figure 5, price accounts for most of the total cost. If switching to another supplier only causes minor problems, the best strategy seems to be to use a number of suppliers and promote competition among them to attain the lowest price possible.

Case B is a quite different situation. Suppose that the indirect costs related to purchasing are more substantial than in case A. There are always ways in which they can be influenced. In this case extensive cooperation with one of the suppliers should lead to lower costs as a whole. More extensive cooperation with a supplier might even affect the revenues of the buying company. Long-term relationships probably result in development of products and components better adapted to their functions in the products of the purchasing company. This, in turn, can be exploited in the market. Achieving these benefits requires adaptations and investments in the relationships, which creates dependencies on individual suppliers. According to the alternative model, therefore, dependency is a prerequisite for efficiency and effectiveness in purchasing.

However, using a dual approach to purchasing management is associated with

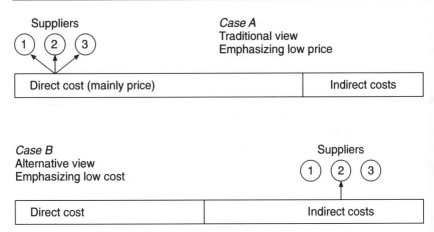

Figure 5 Traditional versus alternative purchasing strategy

major problems. Only in cases where the various supplier markets are completely unrelated to one another would it be possible for a company to behave as differently as is necessary to apply to the two different views of efficiency. Internally such a dualism would have organizational implications. It is almost impossible for individual purchasers to behave according to both views. Therefore, purchasing staff concerned with transactions and supplier markets characterized by the traditional view should be separated from those concerned with relationships of the alternative view.

On the whole, however, companies have a great deal to gain through working more in accordance with the alternative view. The traditional view, emphasizing independence and supplier competition, still has a very strong position. Most companies would therefore benefit from turning in the direction of deepened relationships. Many companies also state such ambitions in their purchasing policies. This leads to the third current issue – implementation of changes in purchasing strategy. Such changes are associated with major problems. Changing attitudes and behaviour will be required from the customer company. Purchasing staff need to act very differently and have to change completely their views of what is efficiency in purchasing behaviour. A lot of effort is required to affect prevailing attitudes. Another problem is to convince suppliers to undertake the necessary changes. If past relations have been of the adversarial type, there will be major communication problems as supplier attitudes and behaviour must also be affected.

This brings us to the fourth issue relating to organizing aspects. Traditionally, organizational structures of purchasing have mainly been determined by internal aspects. In purchasing situations characterized by the traditional view this might be a relevant point of departure. The alternative view of purchasing efficiency emphasizes the importance of individual suppliers and supplier networks. It has been shown that important determinants of effective purchasing are to link activities, to integrate resources and to connect actors. It is clear, therefore, that organizing the firm in a way that facilitates effective exchange with suppliers is the most important strategic issue. This means that purchasing management is mainly an organizing task.

REFERENCES

Gadde, L.-E. and Håkansson, H. (1993) *Professional Purchasing*, London: Routledge.
Robinson, P. J., Faris, C. W. and Wind, Y. (1967) *Industrial Buying and Creative Marketing*, Boston: Allyn & Bacon, Inc.

FURTHER READING

Axelsson, B. and Håkansson, H. (1984) *Inköp för konkurrenskraft*, Stockholm: Liber.
Blenkhorn, D. and Noori, H. (1990) 'What it takes to supply Japanese OEMs', *Industrial Marketing Management* 19: 21–30.
Blois, K. (1971) 'Vertical quasi-integration', *Journal of Industrial Economics* 20 (3): 33–41.
Burt, D. and Sukoup, W. (1985) 'Purchasing's role in new product development', *Harvard Business Review*, September–October: 90–97.
Frazier, G., Spekman, R. and O'Neal, C. (1988) 'Just-in-time exchange relationships in industrial markets', *Journal of Marketing* 52 (4): 11–27.
Gadde, L.-E. and Mattsson, L.-G. (1987) 'Stability and change in network relationships', *International Journal of Research in Marketing* 4: 29–41.
Håkansson, H. (ed.) (1982) *International Marketing and Purchasing of Industrial Goods – an Interaction Approach*, Chichester: John Wiley & Sons.
Håkansson, H. (1989) *Corporate Technological Behaviour – Co-operation and Networks*, London: Routledge.
Jansch, L. and Wilson, H. (1979) 'A strategic perspective for make or buy decisions', *Long Range Planning* 12: 56–61.
Kraljic, P. (1982) 'Purchasing must become supply management', *Harvard Business Review*, September–October: 109–17.
Kumpe, T. and Bolwijn, P. (1988) 'Manufacturing: the new case for vertical integration', *Harvard Business Review*, March–April: 75–81.
Lamming, R. (1993) *Beyond Partnership – Strategies for Innovation and Lean Supply*, Hemel Hempstead: Prentice Hall.
Miles, R. and Snow, C. (1986) 'Organizations: new concepts for new forms', *California Management Review*, XXVIII (3): 62–73.
Newman, R. (1988) 'Single source qualification', *Journal of Purchasing and Materials Management*, Summer: 10–17.
Sheth, J. (1973) 'A model of industrial buyer behaviour', *Journal of Marketing* 37 (4): 50–56.
Takeuchi, H. and Nonaka, I. (1986) 'The new new-product development game', *Harvard Business Review*, January–February: 137–46.
Webster, F. and Wind, Y. (1972) *Organizational Buying Behaviour*, Englewood Cliffs: Prentice Hall.
Westing, J., Fine, I. and Zens, G. (1969) *Purchasing Management, Materials in Motion*, New York: John Wiley and Sons.

12

RELATIONSHIPS AND NETWORKS

Lars-Gunnar Mattsson

INTRODUCTION

Most definitions of marketing relate to the general concept of exchange. To quote a well-known textbook: 'Marketing is a social and managerial process by which individuals and groups obtain what they need and want through creating and exchanging products and values with others' (Kotler 1994: 6).

We can distinguish between two, fundamentally different approaches to exchange: the marketing mix approach on the one hand, and the relationship approach, with its extended version the network approach, on the other.

In this chapter we have primarily industrial or business-to-business markets in mind, since relationship and network analyses mostly have been concerned with such markets. However, some comments will also concern recent developments in the consumer markets. We will present the relationship and network approaches. To make the points more clear comparisons with the marketing mix approach will be made.

In the relationship approach a specific transaction between a seller and a buyer is not an isolated event but takes place within an exchange relationship characterized by mutual dependency and interaction over time between the two parties. An analysis could stop at the individual relationship. However, in the network approach such relationships are seen as interconnected. Thus, the actors are also connected to each other, directly or indirectly. A specific market can then be described and analysed as one or more networks.

There are major differences between the marketing mix approach and the network approach in two respects: one concerns marketing from the firm's point of view, the other the concept of a market as an institution for coordination (or 'governance') of economic systems.

Marketing mix – a non-relationship approach to exchange

In the marketing literature one important, even dominating, view is that exchange is an outcome of the seller's marketing activities directed towards the buyer. The seller determines variables such as price, product attributes, advertising, personal selling and distribution channels. Such marketing activities comprise the seller's 'marketing mix', often symbolized by the 'Four Ps'. The seller's activities influence the buyer to react by accepting or not accepting the seller's offer. Thus, the seller acts and the buyer reacts. How the buyer reacts depends on the attributes of the buyer, for example, the buyer's needs, the buyer's financial situation, the buyer's sensitivity to differences in the seller's marketing mix variables and to differences between competing offers.

The marketing mix approach is closely related to the microeconomic theory of monopolistic competition, and to the psychological 'S-O-R' theories that link an individual's response (R) (e.g. to buy a product), to an environmental stimulus (S) (e.g. an advertisement for the product), using the attributes of the individual (O) (e.g. the individual's interests or values), as an intervening variable.

The link between the marketing mix approach and economic theories of market structure are important because they influence how firm behaviour and markets are defined.

First, the buyers are analysed and approached in an aggregated way. The buyers may, depending on similarities and dissimilarities in their response to the seller's marketing activities, be divided into market segments but not treated as individuals.

Second, the relevant delimitation of the market at the seller level includes only competitors, that is sellers offering substitutes. Thus, cooperation between complementary firms is not included in the approach.

Third, the analysis is inherently static; it refers only to transactions during one time period and not to the long-term dynamic nature of market processes.

The link between the marketing mix and the S-O-R approaches is important since it puts the seller in the active role and disregards relations between buyers and sellers. The relationship and network approaches are different in all these respects as will be demonstrated below.

RELATIONSHIPS

An exchange relationship implies that there is a specific individual dependency between the seller and the buyer and not the general dependence between sellers and buyers according to the traditional market model. The relationship develops through interaction over time and signifies a mutual orientation of the two parties towards each other. In this interaction the buyer is in principle equally active as the seller. The interaction consists of social, business and information exchange and adaptation of products, processes and routines better to reach the economic objectives of the parties involved.

How can we then explain that market transactions are framed within evolving, long-term relationships, rather than determined by the invisible hand of the market or by the attributes of competing sellers' offers in each time period? The answer to this follows four propositions about the nature of markets.

First, both demand and supply are inherently heterogeneous. Thus, the number of sellers that can potentially meet a specific demand from a specific buyer is quite limited. The heterogeneity depends partly on technical inter-dependencies in products and production systems and partly on how buyers and sellers fit in terms of their resources, organizations and strategies. The heterogeneity is to an important extent acquired through relation specific adaptations between buyers and sellers. The incumbent supplier may have adapted its product and delivery services to make them fit the specific buyer's product and production process better than offers by competitors.

Second, efficient handling of the flows of goods, services, information and payments between seller and buyer calls for development of coordination mechanisms other than those provided by anonymous market transactions. Order and delivery systems must be designed to allow for efficient production planning and high service levels. Recent emphasis on 'time-based competition', 'just-in-time deliveries', 'customized manufacturing' and the like signifies a need for mutual development by seller and buyer of routines and systems through which the individual transaction can be handled.

Third, some necessary resources for effective innovative behaviour regarding products, services and processes are controlled by a firm's suppliers and buyers. Access to communication with buyers helps to identify problems that a supplier might solve by product development. Product development by one firm requires complementary inputs of components or know-how from its suppliers. Innovative behaviour that requires cooperation between firms is more difficult to realize if the parties do not have prior knowledge about each other, acquired over time through exchange relationships.

Fourth, both buyers and sellers need to reduce uncertainty about the conditions for acquisition of inputs to, and demand for outputs from, their own production systems. Control through ownership or legally binding contracts is one way to reduce uncertainty. However, in the exchange relationship approach, social interaction by which both parties can prove their trustworthiness and their mutual commitment to the relationship is considered as a more important control mechanism.

Relationships on consumer markets

In distribution channel research, relationships between the members of the channel have always been in focus. One of the fundamental issues has been what institutional form the relationships between channel members have or should have. Should firms be linked to each other through ownership, long-term contractual agreements or only through short-term market transactions? Linked to this is the question of how power and dependency influence channel performance, channel conflicts and conflict resolution (Stern and El-Ansary 1992). It is therefore not surprising that modern approaches within institutional economics such as 'transaction cost analysis' (Williamson 1985) and 'relational contracting' (Macneil 1980) have been used to analyse different forms for exchange in distribution channels. Distribution channel researchers have made efforts to combine the two approaches (Haugland and Reve 1994).

During the 1970s relationship approaches were developed within the emergent field of consumer services marketing and thus also to consumer markets. Researchers found that service transactions often involved close interaction with the buyer during both production and consumption of the services. Large parts of the organization of the service provider were involved in the exchange. Service marketing researchers argued that planning and implementation of the marketing mix variables by a specialized marketing department could not catch the essentials of service marketing (e.g. Grönroos 1990).

During the early 1990s an emerging interest in 'relationship marketing' swept the US marketing community, as evidenced by articles both in business and academic journals. The ability to individualize mass markets, due to modern information, communication and production technology, is an important reason for this development. Databases make information available about individuals, direct marketing and telemarketing make it possible to get in contact with specified individuals, and customization of products and services is becoming more feasible. Sellers can now also more easily implement programmes to stimulate individual customers to concentrate their purchase to fewer sources and reward them for such 'loyalty'.

However, these new ideas about relationship marketing often do not involve interaction in the true sense. Only the seller has access to the databases, the seller takes the initiative in direct marketing and there is seldom a face-to-face contact between the seller and the buyer.

Research on exchange relationships

Important theoretical backgrounds for the exchange relationship approach on industrial markets are social exchange theory (Blau 1964), theories on inter-organizational behaviour (e.g. Pfeffer and Salancik 1978) and on technical systems (as referred to in Håkansson 1989 and Lundgren 1994).

The long duration and dynamic nature of seller-buyer relationships on industrial markets has been well documented by empirical marketing research (Håkansson 1989; Ford 1990). Normative analyses have also been published to show that it is good marketing policy to strive for long-term relationships with customers (Jackson 1985). In recent years the US-based research on relationship marketing has focused on the link between relationship commitment and trust (Morgan and Hunt 1994).

NETWORKS

Markets as networks

Suppose we regard the environment of the individual relationship as consisting of other relationships. Further suppose that the relationships are connected, directly or indirectly, to each other. Then we can envision the market as a network. Following the sociological definition, networks are sets of interconnected exchange relationships between actors (Cook and Emerson 1978). Exchange in one relationship (e.g. between seller A and buyer B) is conditioned by exchange in others (e.g. between A and its supplier C, and buyer B and A's competitor D). Instead of the term 'markets as networks', 'industrial networks' and 'business networks' are also used.

Exchange relationships coordinate activities performed by different actors in a production/distribution system. A network is thus a governance structure for economic activities that can be compared to coordination through a hierarchy (i.e. through a central plan) or through the invisible hand of a market. Network analyses can focus first on the individual firm (which we label the focal firm) and second on the network as such. This is equivalent to a focus in the marketing mix approach on the individual selling firm and on the market respectively.

In the network approach, the market includes both complementarities and substitutes, both cooperating and competing firms. This is in contrast to the marketing mix approach where 'a market consists of all the potential customers sharing a particular need or want who might be willing and able to engage in exchange to satisfy that need or want' (Kotler 1994: 11). This definition implies that the sellers are not part of the market, that the market consists of only one level in a value added chain and that a specific market is delimited on the basis of substitutability between offers by competing sellers.

The individual firm has a number of exchange relationships to end-users, intermediaries, suppliers and other partners. These relationships define that firm's focal network or, as we will label it here, the firm's net. Firms comprising such a net to a large extent carry out complementary activities and control complementary resources. They are predominantly positively connected to each other. Cooperation is the major mode of interaction. The important role of marketing and purchasing is to establish, maintain, develop and also, if needed, terminate relationships in the net. The nets need to have some stability in order to make efficient coordination possible. They need also to have flexibility as exchange relationships develop and new suppliers and customers are added.

Competitors also strive to develop their nets. This is a major force for change in the nets. Competitors are predominantly negatively connected to each other. They might compete for customers, suppliers or other partners. Competing firms may have customers, distributors or suppliers in common and are negatively connected to each other via those firms.

The nets are embedded in a more extended network. Nets may to some degree overlap since firms have common customers and common suppliers. Due to the dynamic features noted above, networks are constantly changing, but the changes are not independent of the network history and present network structure. Most relationships continue over many years and therefore changes in a network structure are based on considerable overall stability. Thus, both stability and change, cooperation and competition are important aspects of network dynamics.

A firm has a network position. This network position describes to whom a firm is related and the content of the relationships it has with its counterparts. The position of a firm has been influenced by its earlier exchange activities (i.e. by investment in relationships). The position at a specific time reflects the cumulative nature of the firm's marketing and purchasing activities. For example, a few years after entry into a new market the firm's efforts to develop a customer base have resulted in a network position that implies both opportunities and restrictions for its future strategic development.

Network boundaries

Since interdependencies between exchange relationships are due to both substitutes and complementarities, to both present and potential future dependencies, it is a rather subjective task to define the limits of the network that is relevant for a specific analysis. In fact defining which relationships to include and which to exclude is a creative act by the analyst. The starting-point could be one or more specific firms, a specific geographical area, a specific technology, a specific function in a value added chain, a specific project, a specific product or service from the user's point of view or a combination of such criteria. Exchange relationships that imply important present or future interdependencies, given the focus of the analysis, are then included in the network. Network studies have, for example, concerned a firm's entry into a new market, structural change in a service sector, process development in an industry, strategic alliances in two related industries, development of an infrastructural project and evolution of a new technology.

From relationships to networks

After this introduction to the network approach we can return to the discussion on individual exchange relationships and ask what is gained by including several interconnected relationships in the analysis.

Heterogeneity is an attribute at the network level. There are a great number of different combinations available in the network. However, since coordination has to cover more than one relationship, it becomes increasingly difficult to change one relationship without also changing one or more other relationships. There are thus important indirect effects in the network if one of the relationships is changed. For example, once a certain technology has become the

207

accepted norm, it is difficult to introduce any major change in one of the activities because other activities coordinated through other relationships must also then be changed.

However, network heterogeneity also opens important opportunities for new, difficult to foresee, combinations of resources that lead to innovations. Firms that belong to the same 'industry' and are thus competitors according to the traditional market model might not be close substitutes from the buyers' point of view. On the other hand, firms belonging to different industries might, due to heterogeneity between competing technologies, be potential competitors.

A fourth aspect of heterogeneity is that the allocation of activities among different actors in a specific value added chain differs and is subject to change. Suppliers and buyers may or may not use intermediaries, one buyer might decide to 'outsource' a specific component while another makes it in-house, one seller may have a systems selling strategy while another has not. Changes in the allocation of activities are a major aspect of network dynamics.

To handle flows efficiently by adaptation in one exchange relationship might not be enough. The interlinked activities that need to be coordinated cover several firms in, for example, a distribution channel or a supply system for an equipment manufacturer's production and spare parts distribution. The coordination not only involves several production and distribution units, but also service organizations such as transportation firms which also have to be included.

Adaptation of one exchange relationship between a supplier and a buyer may also have indirect effects in other ways. The buyer might be able to serve customers better. An intermediary might be circumvented.

The third aspect is uncertainty reduction. If coordination can cover several exchange relationships, uncertainty may be reduced. One example of this is when several complementary suppliers join in a systems selling project instead of submitting uncoordinated offers of the separate components. Another example is that a relationship may give access to information about third parties, such as a supplier's supplier or a buyer's customer.

On the other hand, indirect network effects on one specific exchange relationship could well increase uncertainty substantially. Entry of new competitors, development of a new technology and changing demands from other firms in the value added chain exemplify this. Explicit or implicit agreements between competitors, for example through trade organizations, strategic alliances involving several exchange relationships, development of behavioural and legal norms covering a market or an industry, are ways in which uncertainty in networks can be reduced.

Social interaction in networks may also reduce uncertainty by giving actors access to information about the wider network, perhaps also increasing mutual commitment and trust covering several interdependent relationships, for example in a distribution channel.

The fourth aspect is innovativeness. The interdependencies between resources and between activities controlled by individual firms in a network make it important to mobilize resources in several firms in order to develop something new. Some of these resources might be accessed through the innovating firm's net and some might require the establishment of relations in other parts of the network. A major emphasis in network research has been on the network interdependencies in innovation processes.

Management implications

What are the implications of the relationship and network approaches for marketing management?

First, marketing should be regarded as an investment process that is instrumental in building, developing and maintaining exchange relationships with customers and members of the marketing channel. The firm thereby develops its position in the network. Such relationships should be considered as immaterial assets for the selling firm since they give the firm access to the resources that buyers are willing to give in exchange for products and services. Marketing should thus have a long-term perspective. Marketing is a strategic activity that is crucial for the firm's development in the market and for its innovative processes. As in all investments a crucial management choice is to decide which customer relationships it wants to establish and develop. Obviously the seller must limit its commitments, both to whom it wants to be related and how strong that commitment should be.

The present position in the network is the base for future marketing activities. The position implies both opportunities and restrictions for the future. The relationship with a customer in the home market might, for example, help a supplier to start exporting as the customer internationalizes. Efforts to develop a new strategic alliance might be constrained by connections already existing between potential partners and other firms in the network.

Second, marketing must be considered as an organizational problem affecting the whole firm. Interaction with the buyer involves several functions such as manufacturing, logistics, R&D and purchasing. Adaptation processes in the exchange relationships influence all the activities and resources, not just those which traditionally belong to the marketing mix variables. The implementation of marketing activities in an organizational setting is emphasized. The role of marketing is focused on the selection and handling of relationships with individual counterparts. This will also influence the role of sales persons and the need for multi-person interaction between the seller and the buyer.

Since the firm has many relationships that are of a different nature, with different types of interdependencies and different objectives for the development of the relationship, it is important organizationally to differentiate between how different relationships are handled. This is different from the traditional 'market segmentation' idea because differentiation is based on interaction within individual relationships.

Third, marketing research, marketing planning and control should focus on individual customers and their relationships with us and with other actors in the network over time, rather than on aggregates of customers in one specific time period. Most of the market information in networks is obtained within exchange relationships and not through separate market research projects outside the ongoing commercial interaction. There is a need to systematize such information about individual relationships with customers. Such types of analyses are probably more frequent in the purchasing function's handling of supplier relationships.

The market analyses must consider how firms are connected to each other and will, depending on the specific objectives of the analysis, cut across traditional market boundaries based on geography, type of industry, or product category.

Marketing planning should start at the relationship level. Interaction with buyers and potential buyers is an important aspect of planning. This planning should include objectives and activities concerning development of the relationships. The objectives should not only be formulated for business exchange, such as sales volume and type of products, but also for social and information exchange, and for adaptation processes for products, processes and routines. Development of the individual relationships should not be hidden by aggregated data on sales, market shares and customer satisfaction. The investment nature of marketing must be considered both in the planning and in the control processes.

Fourth, marketing activities are much related to technical issues because the exchange relationships relate technically interdependent resources and activities. Technical change in individual companies – and indeed in the total economy – is dependent on exchange relationships, and thus also on marketing activities. An important objective of the interaction process between seller and buyer is to identify and solve technical problems as regards both the functioning of the present systems (e.g. 'after sales service') and the development of future products and systems. The parties might want to increase or to decrease their mutual technical interdependency. Often the seller is interested in increasing the buyer's dependence on the seller's specific technical solution by offering a system rather than individual components, a long-term service contract rather than a warranty. The buyer may or may not find such an adaptation to the seller in its own interest. The technical competence that is brought by the two parties into the interaction is an important determinant of the outcome.

As we extend the relationship approach to the network approach we broaden our management implications to concern technical interdependencies in production/distribution systems involving many firms. If those interdependencies are strong, marketing of new products and processes that are not adapted to the present interdependencies becomes much more problematic since there is a need to change the network structure in more fundamental ways. On the other hand, a more moderate technical change might serve to strengthen the present network structure.

210

Research

The markets-as-networks approach is predominantly of European origin with the major bases in Sweden and the UK (see Johanson and Mattsson 1994), and gained important inspiration from early marketing research in the USA, especially the institutional and functional approaches to marketing (Alderson 1957). The background that has been mentioned regarding the relationship approach is also valid here. We can add the sociological and organizational network analysis which has developed, much in parallel to the markets-as-networks approach. Nohria and Eccles (1992) give an overview of contemporary network research where intra- and inter-organizational subjects have been studied. There are also links with institutional economics, but the network approach is fundamentally different from transaction cost analysis (Johanson and Mattsson 1987). Recent books reporting on network research are Axelsson and Easton (1992) and Håkansson and Snehota (1995).

Network research treats a wide range of subjects in marketing. Early research focused on how the extended role of marketing, implied by the network approach, affected explanations of competitiveness of a firm and of a nation. Research on industrial purchasing, on systems selling, on the links between marketing and technical change, on internationalization processes from a network perspective and on the investment nature of marketing are other examples that have laid foundations for later research.

Issues pursued in network research in the mid-1990s are mostly focused on network dynamics. How do markets, that is networks, evolve after deregulation or after scientific developments change the conditions for technological change, which are the network effects of mergers or formation of a strategic alliance; how are the conditions for internationalization at the firm level influenced by the internationalization at the network level?

Formal economic and quantitative network analyses are still rare. The management implications of the relationship and network approaches seem to be appreciated by managers to give realistic descriptions of markets and marketing behaviour on industrial, business-to-business markets. In fact, the approaches have been developed inductively by researchers in close contact with business. However, there is still much research needed before the network-oriented planning and control instruments which have been discussed above are developed and accepted.

REFERENCES

Alderson, W. (1957) *Marketing Behavior and Executive Action. A Functionalist Approach to Marketing Theory*, Homewood, Ill.: Richard D. Irwin, Inc.

Axelsson, B. and Easton, G. (eds) (1992) *Industrial Networks: A New View of Reality*, London: Routledge.

Blau, P. M. (1964) *Exchange and Power in Social Life*, London: John Wiley and Sons.

Cook, K. S. and Emerson, R. M. (1978) 'Power, equity and commitment in exchange

211

networks', *American Sociological Review* 43 (1): 712–39.

Ford, D. (ed.) (1990) *Understanding Business Markets: Interaction, Relationships, Networks*, London: Academic Press.

Grönroos, C. (1990) 'Relationship approach to the marketing function in service contexts: the marketing and organizational behavior interface', *Journal of Business Research* 20 (1): 3–12.

Håkansson, H. (ed.) (1982) *International Marketing and Purchasing of Industrial Goods – An Interaction Approach*, London: John Wiley and Sons.

Håkansson, H. (1989) *Corporate Technological Behavior: Cooperation and Networks*, London: Routledge.

Håkansson, H. and Snehota, I. (1995) *Developing Relationships in Business Networks*, London: Routledge.

Haugland, S. and Reve, T. (1994) 'Price authority and trust in international distribution channel relationships', *Scandinavian Journal of Management* 10 (3).

Jackson, B. B. (1985) *Winning and Keeping Customers*, Lexington Ky: Lexington Books.

Johanson, J. and Mattsson, L.-G. (1987) 'Interorganizational relations in industrial systems – a network approach compared with the transaction cost approach', *International Studies of Management and Organization* 17 (1): 34–48.

Johanson, J. and Mattsson, L.-G. (1994) 'The markets-as-networks tradition in Sweden', in G. Laurent, G. L. Lilien and B. Pras (eds) *Research Traditions in Marketing*, Lancaster: Kluwer Academic Publishers.

Kotler, P. (1994) *Marketing Management*, 8th edn, Englewood Cliffs, N.J.: Prentice Hall.

Lundgren, A. (1994) *Technological Innovation and Network Evolution*, London: Routledge.

Macneil, I. R. (1980) *The New Social Contract. An Inquiry Into Modern Contractual Relations*, New Haven, CT: Yale University Press.

Morgan, R. M. and Hunt, S. D. (1994) 'The commitment–trust theory of relationship marketing', *Journal of Marketing* 58 (3): 20–38.

Nohria, N. and Eccles, R. G. (eds) (1992) *Networks and Organizations. Structure, Form and Action*, Boston, Ma: Harvard Business School Press.

Pfeffer, J. and Salancik, G. (1978) *The External Control of Organizations*, New York: Harper & Row.

Stern, L. and El-Ansary, A. (1992) *Marketing Channels*, 4th edn, Englewood Cliffs: Prentice Hall.

Williamson, O. E. (1985) *The Economic Institutions of Capitalism*, New York: The Free Press.

III MARKETING MANAGEMENT

13

MARKETING STRATEGY

Robin Wensley

INTRODUCTION

In this chapter we will consider the meaning of the term marketing strategy and the basic underlying principle of sustainable competitive advantage. We will then consider the two essential elements within such a principle: the issue of position, particularly with respect to the so-called 'strategic triangle' (the customers, competitors and the corporation), and of time, or the analysis of history. We will then consider a number of more recent developments such as the role of intermediaries in the 'enhanced' strategic triangle, the issue of market networks and inter-firm relationships, the resource-based view of the firm and, finally, the nature of business process reengineering. In conclusion, we will consider the likely future development of marketing strategy both as a field of academic study and as a practice.

THE MEANING OF MARKETING STRATEGY

Marketing strategy is now such a widely used phrase that it is difficult to remember that not long ago it was only to be found in a single chapter or even merely a section of a chapter in any marketing textbook.

Given its rapid adoption the term 'strategy' has, not surprisingly, been used rather indiscriminately and this has resulted in a profusion of definitions. Indeed Abell and Hammond (1979), in the first textbook on marketing strategy, decided not to define it because of its wide variety of meanings. Other marketers only define marketing strategy implicitly, as what is managed in their definitions of strategic marketing management.

From one perspective marketing strategy can have a broad impact on the business in terms of instilling a marketing orientation among all those in the firm: the way of thinking or philosophy of the whole organization. However, marketing strategy can alternatively be seen as dealing only with the development of competitive advantages directly associated with the marketing function

215

such as customer loyalty and distribution channel control. Hence some definitions of marketing strategy focus on a broad or philosophical approach while others prefer a narrower or functional view. In the latter case, the domain is sometimes even further restricted by sole attention to the various elements of the marketing mix rather than the more general issues of customer and channel relationships.

A further part of the confusion concerning the term 'strategy' arises out of its present use in the English language. The word strategy is derived from a Greek term which is translated roughly as the 'art of the general (or commander-in-chief)'.[1] Thus, strategy originally referred to the skills and decision-making process of the general (executive), while 'stratagem', translated as 'an operation or act of generalship', referred to a specific decision made by the executive. Over time the term 'stratagem' has fallen into disuse and, now, strategy has a dual connotation – it is both the art itself and the result or output of practising the art.

To complicate matters even further, some writers suggest that a 'strategy' implies a formal and explicitly stated logic, while others have argued that a strategy can emerge from a set of decisions and need not be explicitly stated. Mintzberg and Walters (1985) even specifically distinguished between 'deliberate' and 'emergent' strategies. Confusion, therefore, concerns the process and output of strategy as well as its domain. Some authors choose to define strategy more in terms of the explicit nature of the process involved while others focus on the content, or at least the form, of the output.

THE BASIC PRINCIPLES: SUSTAINABLE COMPETITIVE ADVANTAGE

The basic principles of marketing strategy are simply stated: to achieve persistent success in the marketplace over the competition. The firm needs to have the appropriate capabilities (broadly defined), it needs to respond to and indeed anticipate the current and changing nature of customer demand, and finally to do so in a manner which is more effective and efficient than its competitors. The overall notion of Sustainable Competitive Advantage (SCA) is often used to encapsulate this approach.

Most marketers are aware of the significant profit potential in products such as premium quality, conveniently prepared, frozen foods; computers for small business; robotic and factory automation; and genetically engineered products. However, only firms that have or are able to develop sustainable competitive advantages in these opportunities will realize these potential profits.

Many firms have been early but unsuccessful entrants to exciting markets. Some examples of firms that failed to develop a long-term sustainable advantage are Bowmar in hand-held calculators; Osbourne and Sinclair in portable personal computers; Lyons (LEO) in early large commercial computing; Texas Instruments in digital watches; Reynolds in ballpoint pens; Royal Crown in diet and caffeine-free cola drinks; and Advent in large-screen television.

Bruce Henderson, the founder of the Boston Consulting Group, emphasized the importance of understanding competition and achieving competitive advantage in the product markets:

> A Market can be viewed in many different ways and a product can be used in many different ways. Each time the product-market pairing is varied, the relative competitive strength is varied too. Many businessmen do not recognize that a key element in strategy is choosing the competitor whom you wish to challenge, as well as choosing the market segment and product characteristics with which you will compare.

> (Henderson 1980: 8)

Basis for building a competitive advantage

Methods for building a sustainable competitive advantage can be divided into three groups:

1 Advantages related to the firm as a whole.
2 Advantages residing in a functional area such as R&D, production, purchasing or marketing.
3 Advantages based on relationships between the firm and external entities.

While this categorization is somewhat arbitrary, it does illustrate how one can differentiate between a statement of business-level strategy and marketing strategy. Business strategy is concerned with the entire arena of potential advantages but the primary focus is on advantages residing in integration of functional areas within the firm. Marketing strategy concentrates on the bases of competitive advantages associated with the marketing function. In addition, marketers focus on the advantages derived from relationships typically governed by the marketing function – relationships between the firm, its customers, and the distribution channels serving those customers.

The sources of advantages which are associated with marketing often arise from activities performed by a number of functional areas within the firm and therefore cannot be seen as totally independent. However, the marketing function is typically responsible for directing the firm's resources toward satisfying customer needs. The marketing function develops long-term relationships with customers, just as the purchasing function creates competitive advantages through supplier relations. Cost- and technology-based advantages often interact with market-based advantages. Low production costs can be translated into low prices and high value delivered to customers. Unique technology advantages are translated into developing advantages in terms of cost, quality control, and/or flexibility.

Achieving sustainability in the market

Any business activity can in principle be developed into a sustainable competitive advantage. The degree to which a business activity can be used as competitive advantage is a function of the ease with which competitors can overcome the advantage. Some advantages seem to be easier to overcome than others. For example, it is difficult for one well-known firm to develop a sustainable competitive advantage over other well-known firms based on access to low-cost financial resources, because capital markets are typically very efficient in this situation. Thus, all large firms have relatively equal opportunities to raise needed financial resources. For these firms, the cost of financial resources is based on an accurate appraisal of the risk and return of the strategic investment opportunities facing the firms (Barwise *et al.* 1989). Thus, a competitive advantage possessed by a firm results in a lower cost of financial resources rather than the cost of financial resources resulting in a competitive advantage. However, businesses engaging in small, little-known product market opportunities may realize a competitive advantage from being able to secure financial resources from a large, cash-rich parent corporation. The parent corporation, based on its unique knowledge of the opportunity, will fund the business; while small, independent competitors may be unable to attract commensurate funding from a less-informed, imperfect venture capital market.

In a marketing context it is difficult to secure a sustainable competitive advantage through pricing (Buzzell and Wiersema 1981). Changes in prices are immediately recognized by competition. Competitors can respond easily to these changes, competing away any short-term advantage that might have been created. On the other hand, geographic location frequently results in a sustainable competition advantage. There are a limited number of high-density traffic sites for retail outlets selling convenience goods. Only one outlet can occupy a specific location. Thus, once McDonalds has built fast-food restaurants in the best location, Burger King and Wendy's are at long-term disadvantage when they are located in the second- and third-best sites.[2]

Two important bases of sustainable advantage related to the marketing function which have received only limited attention from a strategic perspective are customer brand loyalty and channel relationships. Reibstein outlines the strategic importance of customer loyalty in the context of consumer brands:

> Companies that have built and reinforced brand loyalty can use it as a way to reduce the threat of competition; loyal customers may resist offers from competitors – high levels of brand loyalty serve as a barrier to entry into a market by a competitor.
>
> (Reibstein 1985)

The economic value of advantages based on brand loyalty is illustrated by the sustainable premium over book value that firms have paid when acquiring brand-name consumer package goods firms. In the UK this has been illustrated in Nestlé's acquisition of Rowntrees and the interest of both General Cinema and Suchard in Cadburys.

218

In a similar vein, Corey has emphasized the sustainable, long-term nature of channel relationships as follows:

> A distribution system ... is a key external resource. Normally it takes years to build and is not easily changed ... it represents a commitment to a set of polices and practices that constitute the basic fabric on which is woven an extensive set of long-term relationships.
>
> (Corey 1976: 263)

THE STRATEGIC TRIANGLE

The conventional approach to marketing strategy is well summarized by the 'strategic triangle' popularized by Kenichi Ohmae (1982). In this triangle (Figure 1), the firm (corporation) is seen as directly interacting with both customers and competition.

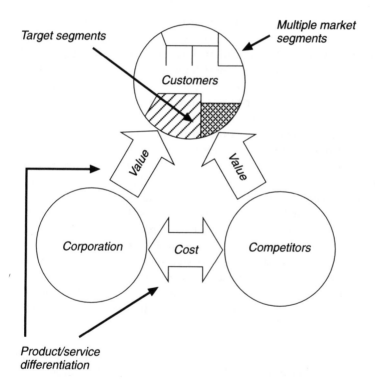

Figure 1   The strategic triangle
Source: Ohmae (1982: 92)

219

Customers

From a marketing perspective, competition takes place in a market which consists of a number of individual product markets. Each individual product market includes a group of potential customers with similar requirements and similar methods (technologies and marketing programmes) in providing products (or services) to satisfy those needs. The individual product market is therefore jointly defined by the specific product/service and the market transaction that is directly involved. In marketing strategy terms it is the most elemental unit of analysis: it is overlaid, for instance, by competitive arenas (a set of product markets within which a group of competitors 'chose' to compete) and customer clusters (a group of product markets that are used by customers in an integrated fashion).

Market segmentation

Central to the marketing approach to customers has been the notion of market segmentation as a way of characterizing a range of customer requirements without direct recourse to single individuals. The analysis of market segmentation, often defined as one of the most fundamental concepts in marketing, has a long and extended history. However, perhaps like the rest of the marketing field, it has been rather slower to recognize the competitive as well as customer basis for market segmentation

In more recent empirical work the term 'market segmentation' has generally been used to refer to a strict customer behaviour based phenomenon and the term 'market structure' to incorporate the impact of competitive reactions, but still at the customer level. In the strategic marketing area, however, market segmentation tends to be used closer to the notion of market structure and market structure itself to the network of inter-relationships between manufacturers, suppliers, other intermediaries and retailers. Kamakura and Russell (1989) set out to try and clarify this issue by using respectively the terms 'consumer segmentation' and 'elasticity structure', but unfortunately they tend to substitute 'consumer' and 'market' segmentation.

There is by now a very large body of empirical work in the general field of market segmentation, but even so there remain some critical problems. In particular:

1 We have evidence that the cross-elasticities with respect to different marketing mix elements are likely not only to be of different orders but actually imply different structures of relationship.
2 Competitive behaviour patterns which in a strict sense determine the nature of the experiment from which the elasticities can be derived, seem to be 'out of balance' with the cross-elasticity data, to use a term recently coined by Leeflang and Wittick (1993).

MARKETING STRATEGY

This raises questions about the nature and causes of this imbalance. Leeflang and Wittick are particularly interested in the notion that forms of conjoint analysis could be used to determine the underlying customer trade-off matrix which is, of course, only partly revealed in the empirical customer elasticities (because individual customers can only respond to the actual offerings that are available) and which is 'assumed' (with some degree of bias and error) by individual competitors in determining their competitive actions and reactions.

The recent empirical evidence also raises severe questions about the commonly accepted notion of customer segmentation itself. Despite various caveats in the textbooks, there is a strong tendency to present segmentation as if:

* there is little difference between customer segmentation and brand differentiation;
* 'closeness' of brands in terms of substitution can be represented in a two-dimensional diagram.

As a result of these two simplifying assumptions the notion of positioning has been given considerable emphasis (indeed in some cases, such as Ries and Trout 1985, almost exclusive concern) as a more strategic perspective on brand and product competition. Hence, it is asserted, we can make strategic statements about the positioning of the brand or product within its marketplace and leave more tactical marketing mix decisions to be taken within this strategic context.

Yet attempts to aggregate the specific evidence for cross-elasticities suggest that the patterns of interaction cannot be reduced in this way (or at least such reduction only explains a limited amount of the overall variance). This has led to the suggested use of overall indicators of competitive 'clout' and 'vulnerability' (Cooper 1991) as a better means of presenting aggregate results. However, we can argue even more radically that the search for any general form of intermediate and hence more 'strategic' representation of the market in these terms is basically flawed and that so-called 'tactical' marketing mix decisions are the very essence of practical strategy.

Competitors

It has been widely commented that marketing as both a discipline and a practice was rather slow to respond to the emergence of increased and sustained competition. Marketing remained defined for a long period primarily in terms of satisfaction of customer needs and the critical strategic role of competition was generally highlighted by economists either within the academic domain, such as Michael Porter, or working in the emerging strategy consultancies, such as Boston Consulting Group.

Nowadays, however, the issue of competitor behaviour is seen as central to marketing strategy analysis, but it is still important to distinguish between the implications of the two 'generic' forms of competitive behaviour.

221

Competition by differentiation

The basic principle of competition by differentiation was enunciated as far back as the 1930s by both Chamberlaine (in terms of his notion of 'monopolistic competition') and Robinson (in terms of 'imperfect competition'). In both cases the principle was that the individual firm or product faced a downward sloping demand curve which was distinctive from the horizontal line at the 'market price' of traditional atomistic and perfect competition. The individual firm was therefore able to make, at least to some degree, its own price–output choices independent of any competitor behaviour. What provided this isolation? The original list provided by Joan Robinson includes a number of items which would now be described as marketing factors such as branding and distribution effects.

There is, of course, a link between this notion of differentiation and the concept of market segmentation, but it is also important to appreciate their differing starting points: market segmentation starts from customers, product or service differentiation from the firm or product itself.

The crucial point in this analysis, however, is that the barriers to direct price competition are both incomplete and, to some degree, temporary. Much of the real, and anecdotal, evidence about individual firms' failure to recognize competition revolves around the extent to which they failed to see the way in which their previously 'protected' position was being eroded – either because customer tastes were changing and/or competitors had found new ways of overcoming 'barriers to competition'.

Competition by price

From an economic perspective 'traditional' competition in products or services is through price levels. With certain adjustments for the nature of accounting systems, this equates with the importance of cost competition. This traditional emphasis received a considerable boost from the popularization of the 'experience curve' effect by Bruce Henderson and others at Boston Consulting Group in the 1960s. Not surprisingly, with a bias towards areas such as electronics, much of this work established the key nature of cost competition in terms of the competitive dynamics of the industry.

Of course, the simple 'experience curve' is only a partial view of the dynamics of cost behaviour in various industries. It became recognized that issues such as 'shared' experience, as well as discontinuities in technological changes, meant that the simple experience curve model was itself only valid over a limited range: strategies were again needed which while striving for greater efficiency within the existing means of doing things also maintained a monitoring of overall effectiveness of the existing means itself.

Analysis of competitor sub-groups

Just as with customers, there are conditions under which it is more appropriate to consider either sub-groups or individual competitors, rather than to make a broad analysis of likely aggregate behaviour.

It can be argued therefore that we should look at various groups at the sub-industry level which are also apparently making the same conduct choices because they are likely to be in more direct competition with each other than with other industry members. This leads directly to the notion of strategic group analysis, which was developed most thoroughly in theoretical terms in Caves and Porter (1977) and Caves (1980).

A number of commentators including, in particular, McGee and Thomas (1986), have, however, commented on some of the confusions in the strategic group notion (including the extent to which it is 'rational' for those firms that are, in some sense, most proximate to each other, to follow exactly the same strategy and therefore increase the overall level of effective competition), as well as the problems of identifying such groups in a consistent and stable (over time) manner.

Corporation

Beyond any sub-group analysis, it is also possible to consider an analysis of individual competitors. The analysis of the individual firm or corporation uses a range of techniques. The most common are SWOT (Strengths, Weaknesses, Opportunities and Threats), and financial analysis in various forms.

SWOT analysis

SWOT (or sometimes TOWS) analysis attempts to partition the key factors influencing the strategic direction of the firm along two dimensions which are, broadly speaking, internal/external and positive/negative. The implicit assumption in the approach is that for each category there is a strategic response (Threats-Avoid; Opportunities-Exploit; Weaknesses-Compensate; Strengths-Build) and that therefore a 'balanced' strategy can result from a TOWS analysis.

Although by now an almost traditional way of presenting the initial analysis in an MBA project and similar contexts, potentially there are some major flaws:

1 To a considerable extent the internal-external and positive-negative divisions are reflections of each other so any particular factor can be located in any box within reason (it is merely a question of how it is 'presented').
2 The link between individual factors and proposed strategic action is often naive and merely semantic. In actual practice a more effective approach is to redefine the competitive domain so that negative aspects become marginalized (or indeed even positive).
3 There is a tendency to treat individual factors as distinct and uncorrelated,

when they are merely elements in a more general construct such as, say, market position. This applies not only between the boxes (see Figure 1 above) but also within individual boxes.

In summary, the form of analysis often done in SWOT is too trivial to deal with the details of strategy and particularly implementation but also involves too much detail to aid an integrated and synoptic view of higher level strategic choice.

Financial analysis

Most forms of corporate strategic analysis have to include not only a financial evaluation of the current position but also an assessment of the financial impact of future strategic choices.

Such a financial evaluation often relies on the management and financial accounting information systems within the firm but recently a number of key conceptual issues have been raised. Most important has been the development of so-called 'activity based costing' which, broadly, attempts to shift the focus of cost analysis towards individual elements in the various business activities or processes involved in the development and delivery of products and services. This follows on from earlier developments in management accounting which looked at ways of constructing management accounts so that financial perform-ance could be measured along various dimensions (such as product groups, sales territories, and key customers) as a form of strategic diagnosis.

In interpreting financial data for strategic purposes it is inevitable that two fundamental conceptual issues almost always occur at some stage: the nature of opportunity cost and the distinction between fixed and variable costs. For financial accounting purposes it is a well-established principle that the 'cost' of a particular activity should be based on adjusted, 'real', historic costs. It is also clear that for strategic management accounting purposes the costs should be an 'opportunity' cost based on alternative possible uses of the assets concerned. This inevitably leads to the difficult position that the cost of any specified activity depends on the cost of other alternatives. Indeed, strong advocates of recent developments in 'strategic management accounting' would argue that even this cost should be compared with one's competitors' costs rather than treated as an absolute figure.

In terms of the variability of costs, the simple principle is that while in the short run almost all costs are fixed, strategic analysis with its focus on the longer term tends towards a situation in which, to paraphrase the famous Keynes dictum: 'In the long run, all costs are variable'.

The problem with much strategic financial analysis is therefore to ensure that assumptions about what is fixed and what is variable which are built into the financial analysis are consistent with the actual resource choices that the firm or organization faces.

THE ANALYSIS OF HISTORY

Any analysis related to the longer term implies an appreciation of the time dimension. Hence, overlaid on the strategic triangle is the analysis of history. In a marketing strategy context we can consider the analysis of market position as the analysis of advantage alongside the issue of the characteristics of sustainability.

Market position

In explaining strategic performance in marketing terms, the notion of market position is central. Marketing strategies rarely avoid reference to 'premium positioning' or 'maintaining high value-added'.

In the simplest terms, to have (or indeed even to talk about) a position we need to have a map. To talk about market position we need to have a market map. Such maps can vary from, at the simplest, a single dimension designed to represent the price/quality trade-off, to complex multidimensional perceptual maps based on attitude research on customers.

In marketing and market research analysis the development of such maps is a large field of study in its own right, often allied with the use of conjoint analysis to try and relate particular product attributes to expressed purchase behaviour. From a strategic market perspective the key issues are the extent to which the map is stable through time and provides a reasonable guide to actual purchase behaviour.

Time stability

Little work has been done on time series rather than cross-sectional attitude data (perhaps because of lack of commercial interest and lack of public research funds), but we might expect there to be a considerable problem with time stability. This concern is reflected in some of the work on usage segmentation which suggests that the more appropriate unit of analysis is the product–use situation rather than just the product. However, since the definition of the product–use situation elements requires itself user opinions (on the appropriate use categories) rather than externally defined product categories, there remain obvious dangers of further instability.[3]

Problems of instability over time with attitude data can generate rather bizarre managerial responses. In one particular instance that we encountered it had been found that the use of sophisticated clustering routines on such data generated very different clusters (and hence 'segments') for each year of the tracking study. Hence, to produce a 'meaningful' analysis of time trends, it was decided that the relevant clusters should be fixed as those generated by the first survey and changes should only be reported within this cluster structure.

The analysis of sustainability

Recent writers and researchers on SCA have developed rather further the issue of 'sustainability' to which we referred earlier. Williams (1992) has suggested that industries can be viewed as three types in terms of the sustainability of advantages, based on what he calls the cycle speed of 'resource imitation patterns'. His primary distinction is based on the degree to which resources positions are shielded from competitive pressures and he suggests that the long-run trend in real product prices in any particular area is itself a good correlate with the degree of such imitation.[4] In terms of the central theme, the key issue is the extent to which significant changes in sustainability are predictable:

> Shifts in the characteristic rate at which an industry's products are imitated ... precede a new category of market.... Such shifts are difficult to predict and tough to adjust to. However, because sustainable resource analysis uses rates of change as benchmarks to competition, many such frame-breaking changes do not have to be unpredictable – early warnings of frame-breaking change can be had by monitoring changes in sustainability.
>
> (Williams 1992: 47)

However, beyond recommending close attention to the present as well as the past it remains unclear how far it is merely an issue of languaging to suggest that it is easier to forecast changes in sustainability if the framework of analysis based on sustainability is used.

Reed and DeFillippi (1990) focus attention on the nature of competencies that simultaneously create both advantage itself and ambiguity (which ensures imitation is difficult and hence the advantage more sustainable). They suggest that the three key characteristics of such competencies are tacitness, complexity and specificity. While these three elements are clearly important, their particular nature introduces both definitional and measurement problems when it comes to more empirical work.

Ghemawhat (1991) and others have focused attention on the nature of commitment as the key element in sustainable advantage. He suggests that analysis of sustainability relates to 'sticky factors' and then proceeds to decompose his analysis into issues of imitation, substitution, holdup (appropriation of economic value by those who are not direct owners of the relevant assets) and slack (failure to realize full economic benefits). While this development in terms of the analytical framework certainly provides for a more refined set of questions, particularly in terms of questions related to the firm and its established market, it is unclear how far the resultant questions related to new entrants become more tractable.

Analysis of investment: the issue of real options

A number of writers, particularly Myers (1984) and more recently Kogut and Kulatilaka (1992), have paid more specific attention to the directly related issue of the analysis of major investment decisions. They have recognized that such decisions have important 'optional' consequences in that they provide the base for future actions. Indeed Kogut and Kulatilaka use the term 'platforms' to describe this phenomenon. Again the basis of this insight is clearly sound: the problem lies in how operational the proposed analysis actually is. There are, for instance, severe doubts as to how far the basic framework derived in the Fisher-Black approach for financial options can be sensibly applied to such optional benefits (see Marsh *et al.* 1988) except in the case of rather specialized examples of so-called 'real' options (see Pitts 1994). The list of issues derived by Kogut and Kulatilaka also looks remarkably like the list derived by most sound *ex post* analysts of competitive advantage.

Indeed, it could be argued that the major advance represented by these writers is not the development of a new analytical structure but an emphasis towards timing any analysis at the point of a specific and major decision rather than, say, the preparation of a strategic plan. In this sense we are merely rediscovering Drucker's earlier dictum that the key concern should be the 'futurity' of current decisions:

> But even with these improved methods, decisions concerning the future will always remain anticipations: and the odds will always be against them being right. Any management decision must therefore contain provision for change, adaption and salvage ... today's managers must systematically provide for tomorrow's managers. Tomorrow's managers alone can adapt today's decisions to tomorrow's conditions.
>
> (Drucker 1961: 90)

The role of strategic intent

A key assumption in much that is written about strategy is the idea that those organizations which have maintained a consistent and central purpose or sense of direction have generally shown better performance. The most recent specific form of this behaviour is the espousal of 'strategic intent' as a key element in strategic success.

To some extent this continued emphasis clearly reflects real issues for organizational effectiveness. Any organization depends on sustaining relationships with other individuals and groups, both from the sources of key skills and talents amongst its employees to its suppliers and customers. Doubtless a crucial element in sustaining such relationships is some consistency of behaviour as well as the setting of realistic expectations.

At least to this extent, therefore, the value of some consistency in strategic intent is clear. More complex is the question of the extent to which public and prior commitment to such intents is of real value. A very active debate in the strategy field remains over the extent to which such intentions tend to emerge and be revealed much more through a sequence of actions rather than presented as a deliberate and public set of strategy statements.

227

RECENT ISSUES

Inevitably, in a field of study so closely related to the dynamics of the competitive marketplace there are always new developments. In many ways they are individual and ad hoc, but as we will suggest later they can be seen as part of a more general concern about the longer term value of the basic SCA construct.

Intermediaries: the enhanced strategic triangle

The increased strategic role of intermediaries has been widely recognized in many markets and industries. As such it has become clear that the strategic triangle to which we referred earlier should be enhanced as illustrated in Figure 2.

Intermediaries (or channels given the importance of alliteration in strategy) are to be seen as independent and self-interested agents in the market, not merely logistical channels to the end-customer. This leads to an alternative approach in addressing the earlier issue raised of the apparent imbalance between competitive behaviours and customer reactions.

Competitive behaviours revealed in the market can be seen as the joint effect of manufacturer and retailer tactics (and possibly strategies). In this sense we could use and extend the concept of 'cognitive maps' for various competitors (Porac and Thomas 1990; Hodgkinson and Johnson 1994) to maps for both key manufacturers and intermediaries such as retailers, which might help to explain the phenomenon of 'over-competition', to which Leeflang and Wittick (1993) refer.

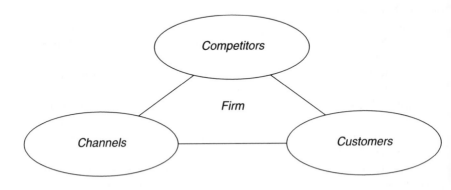

Figure 2   The 'enhanced' strategic triangle

Networks and relationships

A number of researchers and theoreticians in the marketing field, particularly those interested in innovation and industrial buyer behaviour between organizations, have started their work with the observation that relationships between firms are relatively stable and complex. This leads to a concern that the basic notion of competitive dynamics may be misleading as a characterization of such relationships. The issue is seen as one of an interacting network rather than a sequence of instantaneous and individual market transactions.

In what is still an emerging field it is difficult to summarize the perspective succinctly, although Easton (1990) provides a recent review specifically related to marketing strategy. Three main issues do, however, emerge from the current state of the work.

First, there is a danger in confusing a detailed descriptive model with a simple but robust predictive one. The basic micro-economic framework which underlies the SCA approach should not be seen as an adequate description of the analytical and processual complexities in specific situations. It is a framework for predicting the key impacts of a series of market mediated transactions: at the very least outcomes are the joint effect of decisions themselves and the selection process. In this sense the only valid criticisms of the application of such a model are that either the needs of the situation are not met by the inherent nature of the model or that the model fails to perform within its own terms.

Second, it is clear that actual relationships between firms must be seen on a spectrum between outright competition at one end and collusion at the other (Easton *et al.* 1992). At the very least such a self-evident observation raises the issue of the firm (or business unit) as the basic, and often only, unit of analysis: in certain circumstances we might more appropriately consider an informal coalition as the key unit:

> Earlier, the border of the company was seen as the dividing line between cooperation and conflict – cooperation within the company and conflict in relation to all external units. The corresponding means for coordination are hierarchy and the market mechanism. The existence of relationships makes this picture much more diffuse. There are great opportunities for cooperation with a lot of external units forming, for example, coalitions. Thus, it is often more fruitful to see the company as a part of a network instead of a free and independent actor in an atomistic market.
>
> (Håkansson 1987: 13)

Third, the recognition that there is a network of relationships is merely the first step. Approaches need to be developed for the analysis of the network. Håkansson (1987) has, for instance, suggested that the key elements of any network are actors, activities and resources. He also suggests that the overall network is bound together by a number of forces, including functional interdependence as well as power, knowledge and time-related structure.

Core competencies and the resource-based view

One set of recent perspectives on the nature of the corporation has been the 'core competencies' approach developed particularly by Hamel and Prahalad (1991). They chart out a bold and critical role for marketing in the organization: to enable management to develop 'the imagination to envision markets that do not yet exist'. Broadly speaking their emphasis is on extensive market research, speedy product development and rapid adjustment to market response.

However, most of the examples they quote are also of the 'global' (at least in terms of the developed world) market:

> HDTV,CCDs,Flat Screen Displays, Electronic Musical Equipment, Wireless Communications, Electronic Imaging, Medical Diagnosis, Camcorders, Fax Machines, ATMs, Electronic Organizers, Computer Graphics, Video-recorders, Interpreting telephones and, of course, computers themselves and cars.
>
> (Hamel and Prahalad 1991)

One is also struck by the bias in this set of examples: are we really talking of those markets which are technology dominated?

A rather broader view has developed under the general title of the 'resource-based' view of the firm (Grant 1991). Again the general emphasis is to understand the development of firm-based strategies as the exploitation of a specific and particular asset to which the individual firm has title.[5]

Business processes and socio-technical systems

More recently there has been considerable emphasis on the nature of individual business processes within organizations. In a sense this is no more than an analysis of activities in terms of specified processes rather than forms of work organization, and can be related to both forms of value-chain analysis developed by Michael Porter (1985) and also the activity-based costing framework.

Such an approach has proved to be particularly popular in the context of financial services firms and has been termed 'business process reengineering'. As a form of analysis it is most evident when considering fairly routine business systems such as customer handling and order processing. It also provides a useful framework for benchmarking activities with other different forms of organization. Its advocates make strenuous claims for its central importance in the maintenance of competitive performance and there is little doubt that it represents a useful and effective way of analysis for key business processes. Indeed it can be used to redefine the boundaries of the business by focusing solely on core processes.

However, a number of critical issues have also been raised – particularly in the extent to which the very approach can negate or ignore the people element in all such activities. Indeed, some have argued that business process reengineering can be seen to some considerable degree as the rediscovery of socio-technical systems as developed by Trist and Bamford (1951) at the Tavistock Institute of

Human Relations and elsewhere in the 1950s and early 1960s, but now without real consideration of the 'people' element (Mumford 1994).

CONCLUSION

The central analytical concept in strategic marketing – that of the pursuit of sustainable competitive advantage – has remained in place but, of course, has evolved substantially since the development of the economic analysis of imperfect competition in the 1930s. The usual forms of analysis of the firm itself alongside both its competitors and its customers fit comfortably within this overall framework.

While some of the more recent developments, such as the resource-based view of the firm, can be accommodated reasonably well within this framework, others suggest that we may be approaching a stage at which the range of issues begins to require a reappraisal of the basic concept itself.

In the longer run it may be that the implications of the 'network–relationship' perspective are much more fundamental for the more traditional economic analysis of the firm. The underlying logic of such a theoretical approach would be severely challenged if it appeared not only that the firm is not really an appropriate 'unit of analysis' in explaining micro-economic performance, but also that concepts of both competitors and customers are distinctly fuzzy as key stages in the economic development of particular commercial technologies and, finally, the cognitive frameworks actually applied by managers and executives in making strategic decisions show little relation to traditional economic ones. Only time will tell.

NOTES

1 It is important to recognize that military strategy, and relatively traditional perspectives at that, is only one source of insight into the nature of marketing strategy. Useful analogies can also be found in both sports games and evolutionary ecology as well as in more formal game theory.

2 On the other hand, in some cases even the geographic nature of the market can both change and be changed: in the UK Wimpeys have failed to build on early site choice advantages in comparison with new entrants such as McDonalds.

3 A rather naive prior hypothesis might be that by introducing two related levels of attitudes – the nature of relevant use situations and the suitability of particular products/brands within each use situation – we provide more rather than less instability. One is reminded of Frank Bass's useful dictum that forecasts based on larger numbers of input parameters are not necessarily more accurate than those based on a few.

4 Indeed he goes further in his analysis to suggest that the common concern with dynamic competition and temporary advantage may be overplayed:

On balance the research suggests that, in spite of the popular perception that markets are generally becoming more competitive, these highly isolated environments, and their strongly isolated resources, are becoming more prevalent and more important to understand.

(Williams 1992: 37)

5 The rather legalistic term 'title' is used here intentionally since given the nature of the relevant markets long-term 'ownership' of assets is too restrictive a notion. Indeed there have been interesting further developments in the view of the firm as itself a bundle of relational and other contracts.

REFERENCES

Abell, D. and Hammond, J. (1979) *Strategic Marketing Planning: Problems and Analytical Approaches*, Englewood Cliffs NJ: Prentice Hall.

Barwise, P., Marsh, P. and Wensley, R. (1989) 'Must finance and strategy clash?', *Harvard Business Review*, September–October: 85–90.

Buzzell, R. D. and Wiersema, F. D. (1981) 'Successful share-building strategies', *Harvard Business Review*, January–February: 135–44.

Caves, R. E. (1980) 'Industrial organization, corporate strategy and structure', *Journal of Economic Literature* XVIII, March: 64–92.

Caves, R. E. and Porter, M. E. (1977) 'From entry barriers to mobility barriers: conjectural decisions & contrived deterrence to new competition', *Quarterly Journal of Economics*, May: 242–61.

Cooper, L. G. (1991) 'Bridging the two traditions in scanner-data research', UCLA: Marketing Science Center Working Paper, 212, July.

Corey, R. (1976) *Industrial Marketing*, Englewood Cliffs NJ: Prentice Hall.

Drucker, P. F. (1961) *The Practice of Management*, London: Mercury Books.

Easton, G. (1990) 'Relationship between competitors', in G. S. Day, B.Weitz and R. Wensley (eds) *The Interface of Marketing and Strategy*, Conneticut: JAI Press.

Easton, G., Burrell, G., Rothschild, D. and Shearman, C. (1992) *Managers and Competition*, Oxford: Basil Blackwell.

Ghemawat, P. (1991) *Commitment: The Dynamic of Strategy*, New York: Free Press.

Grant, R. (1991) 'The resource-based theory of competitive advantage', *Californian Management Review*, 33 (3): 114–34.

Håkansson, H. (1987) *Industrial Technological Development: A Network Approach*, London: Croom Helm.

Hamel, G. and Prahalad, C. K. (1991) 'Corporate imagination and expeditionary marketing', *Harvard Business Review*, July–August: 81–92.

Henderson, B. (1980) 'Strategic and natural competition', *BCG Perspectives*, 231.

Hodgkinson, G. P. and Johnston, G. (1994) 'Exploring the mental models of competitive strategists: the case for a processual approach', *Journal of Management Studies* (forthcoming).

Kamakura, W. and Russell, G. J. (1989) 'A probabilistic choice model for market segmentation', *Journal of Marketing Research*, 26, November: 379–90.

Kogut, B. and Kulatilaka, N. (1992) 'Options thinking and platform investments: investing in opportunity', Working Paper, Wharton School: April.

Leeflang, P. S. H. and Wittick, D. (1993) 'Diagnosing competition: developments and findings', in G. Laurent, G. L. Lilien and B. Pras (eds) *Research Traditions in Marketing*, Norwell MA: Kluwer Academic.

McGee, J. and Thomas, H. (1986) 'Strategic groups: theory, research and taxonomy', *Strategic Management Journal* 7: 141–60.

232

Marsh, P., Barwise, P., Thomas, K. and Wensley, R. (1988) *Managing Strategic Investment Decisions in Large Diversified Companies*, London: London Business School, Centre for Business Strategy.

Mintzberg, H. and Waters, J. A. (1985) 'Of strategies deliberate and emergent', *Strategic Management Journal* 6: 257–72.

Mumford, E. (1994) 'Tools for change: modern miracles or dangerous disasters?', Working Paper, Manchester: MBS.

Myers, S. C. (1984) 'Finance theory and financial strategy', *Interfaces* 14 (1): 126–37.

Ohmae, K. (1982) *The Mind of the Strategist*, London: McGraw-Hill.

Pitts, A. (1994) 'Real options', Working Paper, Norwich: UEA, March.

Porac, J. and Thomas, H. (1990) 'Taxonomic mental models in competitor definition', *Academy of Management Review* 15 (2): 224–40.

Porter, Michael (1985) *Competitive Advantage: Creating and Sustaining Superior Performance*, New York: The Free Press.

Reed, R. and DeFillippi, R. J. (1990) 'Casual ambiguity, barriers to imitation and sustainable competitive advantage', *Academy of Management Review* 15 (1): 88–102.

Reibstein, D. (1985) *Marketing: Concepts, Strategies and Decisions*, Englewood Cliffs NJ: Prentice Hall.

Ries, A. and Trout, J. (1985) *Positioning: The Battle for Your Mind*, London: McGraw-Hill.

Williams, J. R. (1992) 'How sustainable is your competitive advantage?', *Californian Management Review* Spring: 29–51.

14

STRATEGIC MARKETING PLANNING

John O'Shaughnessy

Chapter 13 dealt with the nature of marketing strategy and its relationships to corporate and business strategy. This chapter centres on the strategic marketing planning process itself. It defines the rationality, role and scope of strategic marketing planning, the planning stages, the decision processes and the search and evaluation of proposed strategies.

RATIONALITY IN PLANNING

In planning we look ahead to decide what to do. The planning process itself is a systematic way of approaching the following questions:

- Where are we now and how did we get here?
- What is the future?
- Where do we want to go?
- How do we get there?
- How much will it cost?
- How can progress be measured?

There is no way to avoid planning either in personal life or in business. In our personal lives we must plan because we are required to make choices about how we will allocate our limited time and resources in the future. Similarly, as managers of organizations, we cannot just confine our decisions to improvised responses to the actions of others, like competitors and customers, but must deliberate about the future, make future commitments and coordinate our plans with the plans of others such as suppliers. All this needs to be said since planning is so frequently attacked as if it were avoidable. However, there will always be controversies over exactly what planning should be done, in what detail and how far into the future it should be carried.

Although there is never any certainty about the future, every business or organization will sensibly lean towards being more proactive than reactive. A proactive stance is one where the organization tries to forecast the future in order to influence it, that is, plan to adapt to it rather than just to surrender to it. This contrasts with a mere reactive stance where action mainly takes place in response to events with no plan to anticipate events and seek to influence them.

One ground for claiming that formal or systematic planning is likely to be more effective is because built into the procedure are rules that goals be specified and relevant options be evaluated against the evidence. Lack of thought about goals, insufficient information search to understand problems and alternative solutions, biased evaluation of proposed solutions are the factors that undermine problem-solving in business. Formal planning imposes a discipline favouring thought about goals, an extensive search for solutions (options or alternatives) and an unbiased evaluation of the evidence for each option considered.

In spite of what has been said about the need for formal (systematic) planning, there is more to planning than this. There is in fact considerable debate as to how strategic marketing planning should be conceptualized. Some writers focus on the sequence of steps to make strategic planning a logical procedure. Others claim there is a need to understand decision-making processes to deal with the problems of biased thinking and to recognize the political nature of the strategic planning process. Finally, there are those who point out that following logical procedures and processes is not enough since this is analogous to focusing on the computer program and neglecting the data itself. The focus, it is argued, should be on strategy content. All these points of view are important.

STRATEGIC MARKETING PLANNING

Organizations that undertake formal planning typically operate a hierarchy of plans. First, there is the planning that occurs at corporate level to guide the whole organization. Strategic marketing planning will get direction from such corporate-level planning, particularly over where the firm will seek its markets, on which strengths or competencies it should build a competitive advantage, and which investment objectives to adopt for what product group, whether growth, hold/defend, harvest, turnabout, or whatever.

One way to look at marketing is as a boundary-spanning activity in that marketing relates the organization to those groups beyond its boundary who use, buy, sell or can influence what is offered and/or sold. Strategic marketing planning (SMP) is planning concerned with the broad conception of how resources are to be deployed to induce those outside groups to respond favourably to the organization's offerings or to overcome resistances from such groups to the organization's marketing efforts.

Plans in marketing are typically yearly plans with some firms tying the annual plan into some, say, five-year plan: today's annual plan is the detailed plan for the immediate financial year which, if successful, is the first step to achieving the five-year plan that is reviewed and updated to reflect needed changes. The next part of this chapter considers the process of strategic marketing planning on the assumption that those concerned with corporate-level planning have set objectives, defined the firm's business or businesses, and determined investment objectives. The planning steps to be discussed are:

- setting tentative objectives for the market
- historical review and situation analysis
- interpretation of the data collected
- calculation of the planning gap (if any)
- problem diagnosis
- search for strategies
- evaluation of strategies and choice of strategy
- contingency planning.

Every organization that adopts a formal approach to planning will follow stages somewhat similar to those above. This is not surprising as they mimic the typical steps in problem solving. Thus early in the century John Dewey, the American philosopher, pragmatist and educationalist, set out six general steps to rational problem solving:

1   The setting of goals.
2   Experiencing a felt difficulty in respect to achieving those goals.
3   Defining and exploring the problem.
4   Envisaging solutions/alternatives.
5   Proposed solutions evaluated.
6   Choice/decision.

Dewey was assuming the relevant information was at hand with no need for the collection and interpretation of data collected.

Each of the stages in strategic marketing planning will now be discussed while recognizing that systematic planning, rational decision processes, political networking and, last but not least, ideas for strategy content are all essential for strategic marketing planning (SMP) to be effective.

SETTING TENTATIVE OBJECTIVES

An organization cannot set realistic, realizable objectives until it has the requisite information but, on the basis of experience, marketing management will nonetheless have tentative goals on sales volume, market share, or whatever indicators represent progress towards accomplishing the firm's objectives. What exactly these tentative goals are will be influenced by subjective estimates of what is considered reasonable at the time in relation to what resources are likely to be available.

For a manager to be able to direct an activity towards the achievement of some goal, it must be possible to imagine the goal in a way that is meaningful for guiding the activity. This is why goals purely in terms of profit are inadequate; they offer too little guidance.

HISTORICAL REVIEW AND SITUATION ANALYSIS

To develop a business or a marketing strategy an organization requires information on its past and present position. It needs to analyse information both about its environment and about itself. This is the purpose of doing a historical review and situation analysis.

A 'historical review' records and orders the historical facts about the company, or its products or one of its brands. But understanding how some situation has come about is not identical to understanding the situation as is. There is also a need for a 'situational analysis'. Whereas the historical review is a sort of developmental analysis, the situation analysis is cross sectional in that it focuses on the current situation, ignoring processes through time. In practice, the historical review and the situation analysis tend to be closely interwoven, the aim of the two of them being to:

- develop a 'reference projection' or a forecast of the future (e.g. in respect to earnings, market share and so on) assuming that current plans and practices remain unchanged.
- identify strengths, weaknesses, opportunities and threats (SWOT).
- determine the historical strengths, capabilities or competencies of the organization and corresponding competitive advantages of the firm.

A strategy is formulated with respect to some business unit or programme and is limited in its scope by what is considered relevant to that business or unit or programme. In the case of marketing planning, the minimum factors considered would be a realistic analysis of the company in terms of its markets, earnings, sales history, innovativeness, strengths and capabilities together with forecasts in respect to factors in the external environment that could affect its success.

Table 1 is a typical check list of the type of information that is collected. What information is actually collected will depend, as always, on what we believe to be relevant to the analysis. Nothing is relevant that does not relate to some definite question. New techniques for analysing data or new theories are in effect new questions or new ways of asking questions, and until these techniques and theories were introduced, certain facts were not considered relevant. However, as our understanding of marketing grows, there are changes in what we regard as relevant information.

How much information to collect is a constant problem. There is a need for a 'stopping rule' that relates to the cost and benefits of collecting more information. However, no such rule is at present sufficiently operational to be in general use.

External environment

The external environment can affect company performance; factors such as the gross national product (GNP), government legislation, tax changes and interest

Table 1   Check list for strategic marketing planning

1   External environment

Social environment:
- social movements (e.g. the consumer movement)
- sociocultural drift (e.g. working wives, lifestyles)
- agents for change (e.g. rising educational levels)
- demographic changes

Add for international markets:
- culture (values, beliefs, e.g. religious, social institutions)
- language
- form of government, ideology and stability
- foreign policy

Economic environment:
- trends in GNP
- interest rates
- levels of discretionary income
- currency fluctuations
- inflation rates
- unemployment levels
- fiscal policies

Add for international markets:
- balance of payments
- wage/price controls

Technical environment:
- government and industry spending on R&D
- technological forecasts
- patent protection

Legal environment:
- government regulation and deregulation
- tax legislation
- trademark legislation
- international trade regulations
- employment laws

2   Market

- barriers to entry
- rivalry
- substitutes from other industries
- power of buyers
- power of suppliers
- evolutionary stage
- growth rate
- demand fluctuations
- industry profitability

Table 1 continued

---

3 *Customer*

- different choice criteria
- shopping habits
- attitudes
- decision processes
- influences

4 *Competition*

- number of immediate rivals in served markets
- identity of and market shares of rivals
- strategies of competitors
- innovativeness and resourcefulness of competitors
- leadership in marketing, manufacture and technology
- relative costs
- erosion of patent protection/proprietary knowledge

5 *Company*

- trends in sales, net income and net cash flow
- thrust/core competencies
- share of served markets
- growth path
- innovativeness
- capacity utilization
- cost trends

---

rates, new technologies and demographics. A growth in national income brings with it a readiness to spend in new directions. An improved level of general education affects consumer tastes and responsiveness to different types of advertising. Shifts in the age distribution of the population make different aggregate demands on industry, and so on. All such trends have a direct impact on markets. Trends need to be identified together with their likely turning-points. Neither is easy. For example, the turn-of-the-century concept of the aeroplane was an elaborate and expensive toy with little commercial future.

Market

Information on market structure reflects Porter's (1980, 1985) five factors (discussed below) of threat of entry; degree of rivalry; substitute inroads from other industries; and the bargaining power of buyers and suppliers. Additionally, information is needed on market growth, seasonality of sales and market share trends.

Customer

Although the 'customer' could be considered under the category of 'market', it deserves to be given visibility as the customer is the major player of interest. A marketing manager would like to know all about buyers and any others who influence the buying decision: who they are, what they seek, where they buy and use the product, when they buy and use the product and how they use the product; and trends among these. Just as the successful sculptor in clay must know the behaviour of clay under different conditions, marketing managers must know the behaviour of their buyers.

Competition

The firm is seldom in the position where competition can be ignored. There are usually other companies out there with whom the firm must do battle. A firm needs to know how to evaluate threats from competitors by knowing something about their performance in the market, their capabilities and their likely intentions. Although marketers often talk about how their task is to beat competition, they will not do this just by looking at what competition is doing (although this is important) but generally by understanding the customer better than competition.

Company

To know one's own company is to know about its strengths and weaknesses as a basis for considering a vulnerability analysis and in order to develop a competitive advantage based on the firm's core capabilities or competencies.

INTERPRETATION OF THE DATA COLLECTED

Interpretation of the data collected is key since how the situation is interpreted determines what strategies appear most appropriate. All marketing strategies are based on some view of what constitutes the 'reality' or the true position of the firm in relation to the external environment as strategies are formulated on the manager's mental representation or model of that reality. When managers get the picture all wrong, the development of the cleverest of strategies is misdirected to solving the wrong problem.

No final, absolutely true interpretation can be demonstrated and some conjecture is inevitable as facts are selected, connected and put into a plausible pattern. But interpretations are far from being arbitrary since interpretations must square with the evidence. The better interpretations will be consistent with the agreed facts and account for the facts in a more coherent way: bringing the maximum number of facts into a meaningful relationship with the minimum of conjecture. Nonetheless, disagreements over what the 'facts' mean will occur as they are selected, ordered, weighted and generally interpreted against some perspective or set of presuppositions. Just as those who believe that all dreams reflect secret fears and wishes will interpret dreams in that way, so managers are also in danger of selecting from the data collected only that which suits their presuppositions. But such distortion can be reduced by making clear:

- what is really known? (e.g. actual sales);
- what is unclear? (e.g. competitor intentions);
- what is being presupposed that might be questioned? (e.g. that certain trends will persist).

We all react to the situation as perceived and perceptions can be influenced by wishful thinking. We may seek only confirmatory evidence for what we believe to be the problem and interpret ambiguous evidence to fit preconceptions. Choosing an interpretation in line with some favoured strategy is particularly common since extremely good or extremely bad experiences with a particular strategy can bias all data interpretation. In fact, if an early examination of data collected supports the preferred strategy, further analysis is apt to cease, while if it does not the analysis is likely to be carried out in much more depth.

What should be sought at this stage is an assessment of strengths and weaknesses, opportunities and threats. This is the so-called SWOT analysis. This can be followed by matching strengths against opportunities, weaknesses against opportunities, weaknesses against strengths and strengths against threats. Part of this analysis should include a 'vulnerability analysis', which aims to identify where the firm is vulnerable, such as an overdependence on a few big customers or just one industry, plus also a listing of the 'critical success factors'. Critical success factors are those which, unless done well, could lead to failure, such as the importance of distribution in the marketing of gasoline. In identifying critical success factors, we work back from the business systems needed and the necessary conditions for success.

Another part of the analysis might focus on decision weaknesses in the organization, namely, failure to anticipate, failure to learn, or failure to adapt when the information at the time suggests such failure was avoidable. It may be that all three failures occur. For example, business commentators claimed that in the 1980s IBM failed to anticipate that when it gave up leasing its computers to customers, it would lose that continuous relationship with its customers which had previously kept IBM close to its market. Similarly, it was argued that IBM failed to learn that phasing out old technology slowly, so as not to disrupt sales of its oldest machines, led to a loss in leadership as rivals rushed to fill the gap. Finally, it was pointed out that IBM failed to adapt to changes in the market when mainframe computers (the speciality of IBM) were losing their dominance.

Of course, nothing can guarantee that a decision, however well made, will turn out right. It is fallacious to assume that a bad outcome implies the decision was badly made since it may have been the most rationally defensible answer at the time. In any case, past strategies are seldom absolutely wrong or right but have different degrees of imperfection.

The various techniques, like Boston Consulting Group's (BCG's) growth market share matrix, General Electric's (GE's) business screen and Porter's work (mentioned later), plus various quantitative techniques, all help to order and bring out the implications of the data collected. These techniques can be useful in offering frameworks, analogies and models that help structure a problem situation and reduce mental overload as well as being a protection from a complete degeneration into ad hoc analysis.

CALCULATION OF THE PLANNING GAP

What do the 'facts' suggest will be the future if the firm takes no action to change current strategies? Such a prediction is known as a 'reference projection'. A reference projection is the future that can be expected in the absence of planned change. The reference projection is compared with some 'target projection' or the set of tentative goals which the firm sets for itself. The planning gap (performance gap) is the difference between the target and the reference projections:

Planning gap (performance gap) = Target projection less reference projection

The planning gaps identified will depend on which performances are of interest. At the highest level, it could be earnings per share, sales and market share, or various financial indices like return on investment (ROI). At the marketing level, it would be in terms of sales, market share, costs, market penetration or various behavioural indices like buyer attitudes.

PROBLEM DIAGNOSIS

If a firm has a large planning gap, we speak loosely of its having a problem. More accurately, the planning gap is not the problem but the symptom of one. The recognition of a problem situation is not in itself the identification of the actual problem. We do not discover a problem but diagnose one which is to make a choice about how we are to formulate the problem. This depends on what we believe would count as a solution to the difficulty encountered. Of course, some companies may define the problem as a problem of persuading the government to increase tariffs on their foreign competitors' products. Here the solution is viewed as increasing the firm's political muscle.

We cannot even understand a problem without understanding what would count as a solution, just as we cannot understand an objective without understanding what would count as the achievement of it. What all this means is that the problem that is addressed depends somewhat on which individual or group can make the problem, as they see it, count. But all management groups in a company are influenced by credible arguments and so true technical

242

expertise usually wins the day. Hopefully, it must for if the wrong problem is addressed, the wrong decisions are made and this can be more wasteful of resources than solving the right problem in an inefficient way.

THE SEARCH FOR STRATEGIES

The strategic options for closing the planning gap should not only fit the problematic situation and take account of trends and competition but should also exploit the firm's core competencies and strengths. Where the solution is other than a crisis one, there is time for more reflective planning, guided by:

- the situation as revealed by the performance gap;
- the perceived problem;
- the strengths, weaknesses, opportunities and threats identified in the historical review/situation analysis;
- current strategies and policies;
- existing capabilities or competencies.

The strategy search process should always allow for the possibility of inspiration, which may beat anything arrived at by methodical analysis.

The mental screening and evaluation of strategies can be demanding. In effect we are mentally rehearsing hypotheses about the relationship between strategies and their likely benefits – but not just benefits since strategies can have side effects which can constitute dysfunctional consequences. Thus IBM may calculate with some precision the benefits in profitable sales from introducing a personal computer that is competitively priced. More difficult to calculate is the effect on the IBM image and the dilution of that image as very upmarket. With many possible strategies and fuzzy endless chains of possible outcomes, it is not surprising that managers are apt to focus on the strategies with which their experience makes them comfortable. Unfortunately, this often means that the cards are stacked against the truly novel and imaginative solution.

A firm grows through changing the scope of its business, going into another business or broadening its technology, customer group or function served. Thus the growth option categories are:

- market penetration: same products/same markets;
- market development: same products/new markets;
- product development: new products/same markets;
- diversification and vertical integration: new products/new markets.

There are other investment objectives besides growth. There is the hold/ defend objective as well as turnaround, harvesting and divesting. The hold/ defend is common when firms see no possibility of growth or are satisfied with their current position in the market. The aim is to retain existing customers while attracting enough of the new entrants into the market to replace those that leave. In the most general terms, hold/defend strategies require the firm to keep abreast of competition by upgrading the firm's offering and matching whatever competition has to offer.

The turnabout or turnaround objective is, as the name suggests, concerned with restructuring the organization or, more simply, 'putting it on its feet' again. A firm in a situation that is ripe for a turnaround strategy typically faces persistent declines in market share, declining profit margins and working capital, increasing debt and probably high voluntary management turnover as managers become aware that the firm is in trouble.

'Harvesting' is a way of winding down a business by accepting a continuing decline in market share in exchange for an increase in net cash flow. Many a product that throws off no cash may in fact do so if all promotional support is withdrawn but perhaps not for long as competitors rush in to exploit the absence of support. It is not always possible to harvest a business, however, and some products or businesses continue to be a cash drain regardless of what support expenditure is withdrawn. In such a situation, a firm will try to divest the business. Divestment carries the notion of an orderly approach to leaving the business.

Porter argues that it is an industry's competitive structure, as reflected in the strength of just five forces, that determines the state of competition (both the rules of competition and the strategies available for competing) and ultimately the profit potential of the industry. The five forces that give rise to industry profitability are: threat of entry; degree of rivalry; pressure from substitutes; bargaining power of buyers; bargaining power of suppliers. He claims there are just three generic strategies for coping with the five forces. The first strategy is to aim at overall cost leadership to produce a cost advantage. The danger of this strategy is that some technological innovation could wipe out the cost advantage, while an obsessive fixation with cost could result in an insensitivity to changing market wants. The second strategy is that of differentiation whereby something unique is offered to the market. Given some market value in that uniqueness, it is a barrier to entry, shields the firm from rivals and substitutes, increases the dependency of customers and provides the possibility of muting supplier power through the size of its purchases. The risks associated with the strategy are either that differentiation may be imitated (the advantage is not sustainable) or that a rival's cost (price advantage) is too great to be overcome by the benefits of the differentiation. The third strategy is segmentation where overall cost leadership or a differentiated offering is applied but in this case only to a part or segment of the market.

It is not clear to many marketers that there are three distinct strategies in that it is difficult to think of product differentiation that does not appeal to just a segment of the market or, if it appeals to the whole market, it is likely to come with a price tag that many in the market are just not willing to pay. In either case differentiation implies segmentation. Porter now refers only to cost leadership and differentiation. Marketers would be tempted to say that both are paths to segmentation in that there can be price segments and there can be segments based on non-price differentiation.

EVALUATION OF STRATEGIES

Management evaluates its strategies before adoption and after implementation. In either case strategies can only be evaluated against some criteria stemming implicitly or explicitly from objectives. Evaluative criteria after implementation revolve around the strategy's effectiveness and reliability. Thus a strategy is effective if it achieves its goals, and it is reliable if it is able to do so consistently.

In evaluating strategies as a basis for adopting one, the criteria selected should help predict a strategy's effectiveness and reliability after implementation. This is seldom a straightforward process since facts are often uncertain, values and priorities among objectives often in dispute, while the stakes can be high, with the decision urgent and under time pressure. Given the many uncertainties, strategy choice is not just a matter of logic alone: proposed strategies are not ruled out by logic alone. Nonetheless, every proposed strategy should be evaluated for desirability, practical feasibility and commercial viability.

Desirability

The first step in evaluation is to think in terms of what objectives or goals are being sought. What would count as success? A common error is not to think sufficiently broadly about goals. This is because goals are typically multiple and conflicting so there is a need to establish priorities or, alternatively, set some of the goals as constraints or semi-constraints. A common reason for irreconcilable conflicts among parties to any decision lies in one party having an extremely narrow set of goals. This is not to suggest that all conflict over strategy is bad since there can be constructive as well as destructive conflict. Debate can be vigorous and sharp without polarization and this is welcome when the alternative might be 'groupthink'. With groupthink there is a collective sense of not needing outside opinions or ideas, a sense of collective certainty, invulnerability, and an illusion of unanimity. These are just the conditions leading to error arising from an inadequate consideration of goals, of alternative strategies, and the evidence for each. Under the heading of desirability we might ask the following:

1 Does the proposed strategy promote objectives? Any proposed strategy must contribute to the company's mission and goals, cohere with investment objectives and, in the case of the marketing strategy, exploit the firm's strengths and core competencies and be concerned with building customer trust and loyalty.

2 Is the degree of risk acceptable? Risk here is the probability of earning less than what is sought and the magnitude of possible losses. Measuring the degree of risk is generally a matter of judgement. There can never be any certainty of measurement, since the relationship between options (strategies) and outcomes (results) is never entirely clear when long-term consequences are influenced by unpredictable competitive actions while the wants and

245

beliefs of those in the market are often fickle. In the most general terms, it can be said that the more an organization moves away from its existing markets and core competencies, the more risky the strategy.

3   Does the strategy promote portfolio balance? There is a need for a balanced mix in a firm's portfolio of products so that, say, all the firm's offerings are not catering to stagnant markets but the firm is also backing future likely winners.

4   Is the investment required acceptable? The investment requirement has to be estimated. There are the initial entry-level costs and the costs of securing market share. Start-up or entry costs can usually be reasonably estimated but more problematic is the money needed to achieve an acceptable market share.

If a strategy is desirable there must be a strategic fit between the strategy and behaviour in the market, between strategy and internal capabilities and resources and, finally, a fit between the strategy and higher level plans since it is part of the hierarchy of plans. But even if all these 'fits' were in place, it would merely show that means suit ends. This is not enough in itself since there is a need to take account of likely undesirable side effects (dysfunctional consequences).

Practical feasibility

The problem of the feasibility of proposals receives too little attention in discussions on strategy formulation. Although it is accepted that judging feasibility involves judgement and an imaginative recreation of the likely problems encountered in implementing the strategy, the importance of experience is seldom emphasized enough. The feasibility of a marketing plan or strategy necessitates knowing about the role of product, price, promotion and distribution; knowing about the likely behaviour of customers, and competitors while knowing a good deal about the specifics of marketing like distribution possibilities.

Commercial viability

Under the heading of commercial viability, we might consider the following:

- Will the strategy yield the profit/cash flow sought? Estimates of potential payoffs can range all the way from what is little more than prophecy to predictions of sales, costs and profits based on hard evidence.
- Does the strategy contribute to minimizing likely competitive retaliation? The selection of any strategy is accompanied by the selection of rivals with whom the firm will do battle. The question arises whether the strategy minimizes the potential for competitive retaliation.
- What are the impediments to achieving commercial goals? This requires us to think about obstacles that may be in the way of success and to plan to get round them.

246

We make decisions about strategy or whatever, on the basis of beliefs about the outcomes of each option in relation to our goals. Errors occur when we do not consider the whole set of goals which interest us or we do not examine enough options or do not objectively weigh up the evidence. Weighing up the evidence can be difficult since the process can be so distorted by wishful thinking. Also when every proposed strategy seems inadequate, the quality of decision-making tends to deteriorate as anxiety tends to reduce search and analysis. In any case, evidence cannot be measured as one would a piece of wood so judgement is always involved. Of course, if no adequate strategy is forthcoming it is 'back to the drawing board' to redefine the firm's business or rethink the reasonableness of goals.

CONTINGENCY PLANNING

Behind every set of plans is a set of assumptions that needs to be realized if the plans are to be a success. Certain things are assumed to remain constant like government policy or certain trends are assumed to persist like the increasing cost of healthcare. A number of these assumptions have to do with the environment and so are constantly being invalidated by a rapidly changing environment.

Where different sets of assumptions are equally tenable, contingency plans are needed. More typically firms allow for certain of the major assumptions being invalid and have alternative plans in reserve. More and more firms see the need to develop contingency plans, just as the military have always done because the need there is so much more pressing. Monitoring the assumptions of a plan as it is put into effect is a major check on the plan's continuing validity. When assumptions are no longer valid, plans need to be revised or previously devised contingency plans put into effect. But plans in practice need to be revised all the time. Moreover, planning must affect today's decisions if it is to be treated seriously by operational managers: long-term planning should be tied to guiding today's decisions.

CURRENT ISSUES IN STRATEGIC MARKETING PLANNING

Any firm that has adopted a systematic approach to planning will have followed something like the sequence of stages discussed in this chapter. But, to repeat, following a sequence of stages is like following some computer program; it does not bring forth a successful strategy in itself as this depends on the data and ideas entering the program. The key to developing an effective strategy lies not in following a sequence of stages, though this does help, but in answering effectively the following questions:

1 What should be the content of our objectives?
2 What is the most relevant information to collect?

247

3   What is the correct problem diagnosis?
4   What strategies should be considered given our objectives?
5   What evidence is relevant to the evaluation of proposed strategies?

SMP will never be just a matter of following some formula. Current interest is no longer focused on the sequence of steps in evolving a strategy but on identifying flawed decision processes, tactics for coping with the politics arising from SMP being such a value-laden activity and, last but not least, identifying strategic options and the marketing conditions that suggest when they are most appropriate.

FURTHER READING

Certo, Samuel C. and Paul, Peter J. (1988) *Strategic Management: Concepts and Applications*, New York: Random House.
Hill, Charles W. L. and Jones, Gareth R. (1992) *Strategic Management: An Integrated Approach*, Boston: Houghton Mifflin Co.
Porter, Michael E. (1980) *Competitive Strategy: Techniques for Analyzing Your Business and Competitors*, New York: The Free Press.
Porter, Michael E. (1985) *Competitive Advantage*, New York: The Free Press.
Walker, Orville C., Boyd, Harper W. and Larreche, Jean-Claude (1992) *Marketing Strategy: Planning and Implementation*, Homewood, Il: Irwin.

15

MARKETING ORGANIZATION AND MANAGEMENT

Nigel F. Piercy and David W. Cravens

INTRODUCTION

The goal of this chapter is both to describe the structuring and positioning choices faced by management in locating marketing responsibilities in the organization and to emphasize the broader strategic significance of the choices made. Emphasis is placed on the importance of the organization of marketing for information flows and hence for market understanding inside the company; for the effective implementation of market orientation and customer orientation and marketing strategies, including the increasingly important development of relationship marketing; and, most particularly, the emergence of new organizational forms for marketing to deal with different types of marketing network and strategic alliance relationships.

Only a few decades ago marketing organization was primarily concerned with the departmentation of marketing (Weigand 1961) and the internal arrangements for the administration of functions within marketing (how to structure sales operations, advertising management, distribution; e.g. Bund and Carroll 1957). However, in recent years the marketing organization question has developed far beyond these internal administrative issues. The role of marketing in the organization is articulated as a fundamental customer-driven process, involving the entire organization (McKenna 1991a). This contemporary view of the scope of marketing has important implications for its structuring and positioning. Marketing organization has become a fundamental strategic issue concerned with intra-organizational relationships and inter-organizational alliances, and the management of critical boundary-spanning environmental interfaces.

This evolution can be traced both to rapid changes in the marketing environment and to the (partly consequent) shifting role of marketing in the modern corporation. For example, Achrol (1991) characterizes the emergent marketing environment in terms of diversity, knowledge-richness, and turbulence, which leads to flatter organizations with 'fuzzier lines of authority, extensive delegation of decision-making, and a great emphasis on teamwork'.

Further, Webster (1992) argues that continuing evolution of the marketing discipline, as well as response to environmental change, will demand the adoption of new organizational forms, including strategic partnerships and networks to replace traditional bureaucratic hierarchical organizations. Rapid environmental change and customer diversity will require the marketing organization to respond quickly to new challenges. In this future scenario, increasing attention will focus on the problems of managing strategic partnerships in marketing.

This chapter examines the full range of questions implied by the arguments above. First, we will consider the organizational 'dimensions' of marketing in terms of the impact of structure on its implementation and operation. We will then discuss briefly the conventional view of the marketing organization and examine some of the empirical evidence collected in this area. The viewpoint will then broaden to consider the imperatives leading to newer and more innovative perspectives on marketing, and hence on its organization, leading to a consideration of the new forms currently emerging and likely to develop. The chapter will conclude with a management agenda to be addressed in confronting the organizational dimensions of marketing.

THE ORGANIZATIONAL DIMENSIONS OF MARKETING

Ames (1968) distinguished the 'trappings' of marketing organization from the 'substance' of marketing. In fact, the pervasiveness and importance of organizational issues in implementing marketing have become increasingly evident in recent years.

Marketing organization and the implementation of marketing strategy

The organizational theorists' theorem that 'structure follows strategy' (e.g. Chandler 1962; Franko 1974) suggests that the implementation of marketing strategies will require the design and adoption of the appropriate administrative and organizational arrangements. For example, at the simplest level, 'going international' might lead to the development of some kind of international marketing organization – whether an export department, an international division, or simply an international sales/distribution office.

Many authorities (e.g. Hughes 1980; Bonoma 1985; Cespedes 1991) cite inappropriate and inadequate internal structures and systems as a major source of implementation failures in marketing. Moreover, the unprecedented reforming of many business firms during the last decade documents the dissatisfaction of executives with the existing structures of their marketing organizations.

Marketing organization as a determinant of marketing strategy

Additionally, marketing structures may be seen as a determinant of marketing strategy – because structure influences how organizational members perceive the environment, and represents the source of significant pressures towards maintaining the status quo in many organizations (Corey and Star 1971; Baligh and Burton 1979).

Marketing organization may actually shape the strategic choices made. Pursuing the internationalization example, not having any formal structure for international marketing may lead to the neglect of international issues in marketing strategy.

Marketing organization as part of marketing strategy

In many situations the way marketing is organized is actually part of marketing strategy. For example, Levitt (1980) suggested that if marketing success depends on competitive differentiation, then this differentiation may be based on 'anything' including the structure of the marketing organization. As will be seen below, modern claims for the potency of relationship marketing, service quality, customer care, and the like, rest in part on the ability of the organization to manage effectively the customer/organization interface.

For instance, Doyle (1994) has identified the strategic imperatives and priorities for marketing as:

- speed – in reducing 'design to delivery' cycle times;
- customization – to meet customer needs in increasingly fragmented markets;
- quality – as a basic prerequisite for competitiveness;
- information – as a source of competitive advantage;
- core focus – on real corporate capabilities;
- globalization – to spread risks and costs internationally;
- software differentiation – augmenting products with service, and the like;
- partnerships – with customers and distributors;
- innovation – for constant new products and processes;
- recognizing multiple stakeholders in the firm.

The suggestion is that these imperatives can be directly linked to how marketing will be organized for the future.

The impact of marketing organization design on strategy is illustrated by the successful housewares producer, Rubbermaid Inc. The company uses entrepreneurial teams made up of a product manager, research and manufacturing engineers, and financial, sales, and marketing professionals, to conceive new product ideas and move them from the design stage to the marketplace (Reitman 1992). Many of the products are improvements rather than totally new – such as a new mailbox design with features not available on competitors' units.

Rubbermaid's teams introduced 365 new products in 1992 with an amazing success record of 90 per cent. Organization design drives marketing strategy at Rubbermaid.

Marketing organization and market orientation

A distinction is commonly made between marketing as a philosophy or culture and marketing as a set of managed activities – strategies, systems, programmes. It is often argued that marketing organization is largely irrelevant to the former, and is concerned only with implementing the latter. New studies of market orientation suggest that for various reasons this argument underestimates the significance of the marketing organization to the culture of marketing in a company.

Kohli and Jaworski (1990) produced a widely cited conceptualization of market orientation, resting on the notion that market orientation involves the organization-wide dissemination of information and developing appropriate responses related to current and future customer needs and preferences. In fact, as will be seen shortly, one defining variable of the nature, sources and amount of intelligence and information that flows is the structure of the organization.

Parallel work by Narver and Slater (1990, 1992) adopts a view of market orientation as: customer orientation, competition orientation and interfunctional coordination. They recognize the implication that in the market-oriented company marketing specialists and departments may become less needed. However, they also note that there may be a lengthy transition for many organizations where: 'Marketing is likely to be the first function to fully appreciate the benefits of being market oriented and must demonstrate the benefits of market-driven behavior … marketing may have a key role in the development and maintenance of a market orientation' (Narver and Slater 1992). Indeed, another study links market orientation more explicitly to organizational issues in the following terms: 'Organizational actions such as the degree of market orientation are inextricably linked to the organizational structures, systems and processes created to sustain them' (Ruekert 1992). For instance, the Rubbermaid Inc new product planning process discussed earlier shows the close relationship between marketing organization and market orientation.

Marketing organization and market structure

A further relationship worth noting is between the structure and characteristics of the market (as they are understood in the firm) and the nature of the marketing organization. Howard (1968) argued that managers' perceptions of the characteristics of buyer behaviour shape a company's structure, while Corey and Star (1971) examined the impact of market segmentation on structuring marketing organization. Others have developed contingency models that examine the impact of market characteristics such as uncertainty, heterogeneity, and interdependence on the marketing organization (see below). Conversely, it has been argued that organization structure may be a major barrier to market segmentation strategy, because structure has an impact on departmental jurisdiction, 'ownership' and commitment, reward and evaluation systems, information gathering and reporting systems, and so on (Piercy and Morgan 1993).

For the moment enough has been said to establish that marketing organization provides a critical link between a company and its markets.

Marketing organization and information processing

Underpinning much of the argument above is the concept of the marketing organization as an information-processing structure. This view is important for a number of reasons: the collection and reporting of market information is determined in part by the organizational structure (i.e. 'the attentional process is determined largely by the structure of the organization', Pfeffer and Salancik 1978); the executive's understanding of the marketplace is in turn partly shaped by the way the structure focuses attention on some issues and not others and thus its impact on the process of 'environmental enactment' (Weick 1969); and, the ability of the structure to process market information will directly impact on the success of marketing in fulfilling a significant boundary-spanning role and absorbing market uncertainty for the rest of the organization (Piercy 1985).

There is perhaps no better example of how structure influences the processing of market information than the Western Union Corporation. The firm's sales and marketing executives centred their attention on the company's traditional services (e.g. telegrams), during an era of vast change in telecommunications. Fax technology dealt the final blow in the demise of Western Union. This company never faced the core issue of deciding how to compete in the telecommunications market.

Marketing organization and power

The organizational location and structuring of marketing may be linked to the power and political strength of marketing in a firm: structure represents the control of information, resources, and critical decision-making processes.

For example, marketing's power is often gauged by the functional backgrounds of top managers, and the status and influence consequently accorded to the marketing organization. In one highly successful international pharmaceuticals firm, the president, executive vice-president and divisional vice-presidents all began their careers in sales and marketing. Divisional product management groups exert strong political influence over the strategic direction of the company, and employees comment privately on the power of marketing in the company. Conversely, when popular commentators report that top management considers marketing departments 'a millstone around an organization's neck'

(Brady and Davis 1993), and that 'marketing departments are in top management's sights' (Mitchell 1993), then marketing's hidden power in the organization may be on the wane in at least some cases.

The organizational dimensions of marketing suggest that marketing organization is covertly a highly significant issue in the operation of corporate marketing. The next section will examine the conventional view of marketing organizational issues, contrast this with the reality found empirically, and then broaden the perspective adopted in the following sections.

ORGANIZATIONAL FORMS AND MARKETING

Webster (1992) points out that the normal conception of marketing organization is in the context of the large, bureaucratic, hierarchical organization, although he argues that this view is increasingly undermined by the emergence of newer organizational forms. Table 1 represents an attempt to organize these traditional and more innovative issues surrounding marketing organization. By adopting the Hofer and Schendel (1978) model of different levels of organizational strategy, we suggest that there are several levels and associated units of analysis to consider in studying the marketing organization issue. This present section will focus on marketing organization at the functional and business levels.

Functional and business level issues in marketing organization

The units of analysis here are the marketing department and its subsystems. Traditionally, interest has been in the internal structure for the marketing department:

1 Functional, to allow the employment of specialists (in advertising, sales, marketing research, and so on) reporting to the head of marketing (e.g. see Bund and Carroll 1957; Piercy 1985).
2 Product-based, to build product or brand specialization (e.g. see Kelly and Hise 1980).
3 Market-based, to reinforce a focus on markets and customer sectors or segments (e.g. see Hanan 1974; Schultz 1993).
4 Matrix structures, with programme leadership (similar to product management) drawing on resource groups (similar to functional management) to achieve both market focus and functional specialization (e.g. see Corey and Star 1971; Weitz and Anderson 1981; Piercy 1985).

The relative characteristics – advantages and disadvantages – of each of these forms are well developed in the literature and are not repeated here (e.g. see Piercy 1985 for a review). Perhaps the major developments at the marketing subsystems level consist of various suggestions for new kinds of specialists to cope with changing market situations: channel managers (Jackson and Walker 1980), marketing information systems specialists (Piercy and Evans 1994); logistics/

Table 1 Levels and focus of organizational analysis in marketing

Strategic level	Unit of analysis	Examples of major issues	Examples of new organizational forms
FUNCTIONAL	Marketing subsystems	Organizing and coordination sub-functions of marketing such as advertising, marketing research, sales operations.	Channel management. Logistics/services specialists. Information/technology specialists.
BUSINESS	Marketing department	Departmentation of marketing and internal structure of the marketing department. The integration of marketing sub-functions. Relationships with other functions.	Sector/segment management. Trade marketing. Investment specialists. Venture/new product departments.
CORPORATE	Divisional marketing responsibilities and group-wide marketing issues	Centralization/decentralization of marketing decision-making and relationships between central and peripheral marketing units.	Marketing exchange and coalition companies.
ENTERPRISE	Strategic alliances and networks	External relationships and boundary-spanning with strategic marketing partners. Marketing 'make or buy' choices.	Network organizations. Partnerships. Alliances.

service systems managers (e.g. Christopher *et al.* 1980); specialist venture groups and new product departments (Buell 1982); marketing communications managers to integrate communications internally and externally (Schultz 1992); and so on.

The departmentation of marketing itself was originally seen as an administrative mechanism to integrate customer-focused functions like advertising and sales (Weigand 1961), and as a logical progression from production orientation to marketing orientation (e.g. Kotler 1991).

However, there have been many challenges to the continued need for formally organized marketing units: hierarchic bureaucracies will dissolve in favour of networks of buyers and sellers and strategic alliances removing the need for marketing specialists (Webster 1992); market orientation and customer-driven marketing may undermine the conventional position of the marketing department (Kanter 1991; Narver and Slater 1992; Naumann and Shannon 1992); some broader organizational innovations challenge the need for a marketing department, including the development of business sector or segment-based structures (e.g. Buell 1982; Gould 1982); the growth in consumer goods firms of trade marketing organizations, where key retailer accounts are managed separately from the conventional marketing operation (e.g. Piercy 1985); the adoption of product/market structures representing different investment priorities (e.g. Hughes 1980); and, the growth of new venture and new product departments (e.g. IBM's 'Independent Business Units'; Petre 1983).

Moreover, influenced by the trend toward decentralized management, corporate level marketing units are being eliminated in many US companies, with marketing functions being placed at the business-unit and product-market levels (Hopkins and Bailey 1984). The challenge in this trend is to retain a market-driven orientation at the corporate level. Conversely, in Europe firms are confronting the tension between the desire for pan-European brand and marketing strategies, and the resulting resentment from executives in national centres when faced with reduced autonomy through the centralization of marketing (Mitchell 1994).

The status quo of the marketing organization

There has been a variety of descriptive studies of marketing organization over the years (e.g. Buell 1982; Hooley *et al.* 1984; Hopkins and Bailey 1984; Schwarz 1990), all country specific, some general and others specific to issues like account management and product/brand management (e.g. Buell 1975; Hise and Kelly 1978; Shapiro and Moriarity 1984). These studies demonstrate the diversity of organizational forms in marketing departments (Mitchell 1994). We consider two recent studies here as examples of their kind.

Tull *et al.* (1991) have examined marketing organization at the corporate level in US companies. Their findings may be summarized:

- In only one-third of the companies studied was there the degree of integration of marketing responsibilities that would be predicted by conventional marketing theories. In the remaining two-thirds marketing responsibilities were dispersed across other non-marketing organizational units.
- The reasons for this dispersal were: efficiency, span of control limitations, economy, tradition, and personality issues.
- The internal structures used were most commonly functional and product-based.
- Organizational choices were related to the environmental factors of market complexity and unpredictability, and product diversity and number (see the discussion of environmental contingencies below).

This may be compared to a UK study of marketing organization in medium- and large-sized manufacturing companies (Piercy 1986, 1992). This study suggested the following:

- The formal departmentation of marketing is far rarer than was expected and the integration of marketing functions was very limited in the sample studied.
- Chief marketing executive (CME) responsibilities were largely participative and shared.

These CME responsibilities were factor analysed to identify a number of significantly different types of marketing organization, on the basis of CME span and type of responsibility, and size of the marketing department in headcount (see Figure 1). These may be described in the following terms: the '*integrated/*

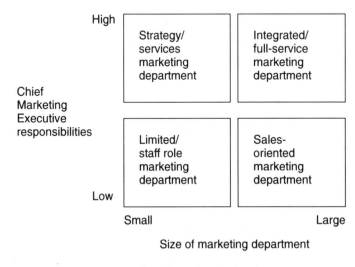

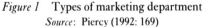

Figure 1 Types of marketing department
Source: Piercy (1992: 169)

257

full-service marketing organization', which ranked relatively highly on all responsibility factors; the *'strategy/services marketing organization'*, with high scores on product policy, corporate strategy and marketing services factors, but relatively low on the others; the *'sales-oriented marketing organization'*, which ranked high on selling responsibilities, but relatively low on the others; the *'limited/staff role marketing organization'*, which ranked lowest on all responsibility factors. It should be noted that similar classifications have been produced in the retailing sector in the UK (Piercy 1988; Piercy and Alexander 1988) and in the UK financial services sector (Piercy and Morgan 1989).

The implication of these studies is that in different ways they both undermine certain aspects of the established and conventional model of how marketing operates in the organization. Both studies suggest that the formal organization of marketing assumed implicitly by the traditional literature may be far weaker and the responsibilities of the CME far less than is normally assumed. It should be noted that these stereotypes have proved familiar and accessible to executives in identifying their own marketing organizations and the problems of marketing implementation in these different scenarios (Piercy 1992, 1994).

Perhaps the most important contribution of such empirical work is to evidence observed diversity in organizational practices, and the essential contingencies surrounding organizational choices in marketing.

MARKETING ORGANIZATION AND MARKETING CHANGE

In general terms the pressures for organizational change impacting on marketing may be summarized (after Child 1984) as: environmental change; diversification; growth or decline; technology; and human capabilities and expectations. This suggests the need to recognize pressures for change from both inside and outside the organization. Most conventional pressures for change are associated with the external marketing environment, for example:

1   The power of the marketing channel, particularly in a global marketing context, disrupts many conventional ideas about the location of strategic marketing responsibilities, as between manufacturer and distributor (Piercy and Morgan 1989) and the development of trade marketing structures (Piercy 1985), leading to the development of models of strategic marketing partnerships replacing traditional competitive models (Wortzel and Venkatraman 1991; Jap 1992).

2   Competitive and customer imperatives have led increasingly to the demand for the adoption of relationship marketing strategies (e.g. McKenna 1991b; Christopher *et al.* 1992; Gummesson 1994), as illustrated by the drastic reduction made by Xerox and other large companies in their supplier numbers, accompanied by the formation of collaborative partnerships with their remaining suppliers. Another example is the development of the

'prosumer' – the consumer actively involved in a company's new product development process (Mitchell 1994).

3 Webster (1992) describes a range or continuum of marketing relationships leading from transaction-based marketing to the network organization (resulting from multiple strategic alliances between firms producing a confederation or coalition) – which suggests the 'radical transformation' of the marketing organization, in terms of both threats to its existence and changed relationships with other functions in the firm, and the possibility that many marketing functions will be vertically disaggregated to external specialists (Achrol 1991).

However, in parallel, there are many internal organizational changes also likely to impact on the traditional role of the marketing organization, for example:

1 The advent of Total Quality Management (TQM) has raised practical questions in many organizations about the relationship between marketing and operations/production functions, even though the core of the marketing concept is central to the TQM philosophy (e.g. Morgan and Piercy 1992).
2 New information technology has changed many of the underlying assumptions that have been made about organizational structures, including those in the marketing area (Piercy 1985).
3 There have been many claims that the 'marketing concept' is an outdated paradigm, with consequent implications for the viability of a traditionally conceived marketing organization (e.g. Naumann and Shannon 1992).
4 New management approaches place more emphasis on teams, processes and change management than on formal structures. For example, Cravens *et al.* (1994a) discuss the objectives of organizational change as reducing costs, creating more flexibility and building competitive advantage around core competences.

There have been a variety of attempts to capture such pressures as these in contingency models to explain and prescribe marketing structures.

Contingency models of marketing organization

An overview suggests that the main areas of contingency to be considered in marketing organization choices are: environmental and informational; and corporate or managerial.

Environment and marketing organization

Corey and Star (1971) follow the general argument about the impact of environment on structures, to propose that market segmentation provides the primary source of internal differentiation in organizations. This leads to the critical question of how we understand market characteristics and their impact on structural choices. For instance, Weitz and Anderson (1981) proposed that the environment be analysed in terms of:

- Complexity – the number of elements in the environment relevant to the organization, such as the number of product-markets served.
- Interconnectedness – the interdependence of key elements of the environment, for example retail concentration.
- Predictability – the degree to which variation in the environment is stable and so less uncertain.

Weitz and Anderson proposed an explanatory model of marketing structuring relating these environmental and information attributes to organizational choices in the way shown in Figure 2. Their argument is that environmental complexity pushes marketing structures towards decentralization and matrix or overlay forms, while environmental unpredictability and interconnectedness create a pressure for product or programme-based structures.

A comparable analysis of environmental contingencies based on information theory can be found in Håkansson and Ostberg (1975) and Nonaka and Nicosia (1979). These analyses are particularly apposite in the context of networks and strategic alliances, because of the emphasis placed on social relationships as an

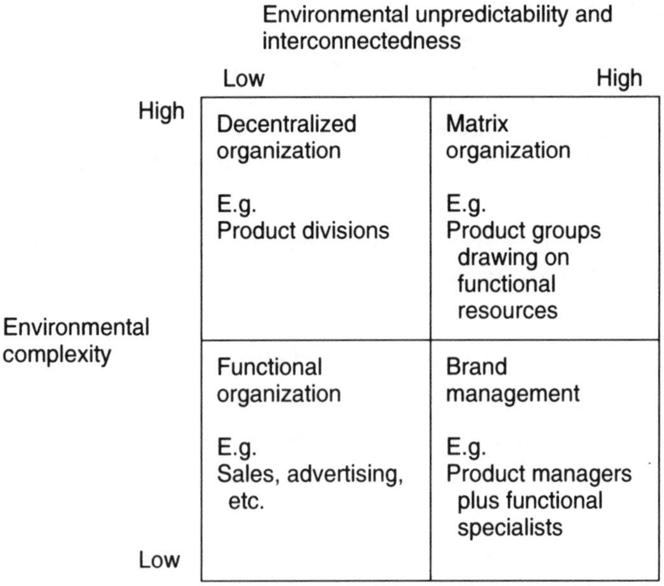

Environmental unpredictability and interconnectedness

	Low	High
High	Decentralized organization E.g. Product divisions	Matrix organization E.g. Product groups drawing on functional resources
Low	Functional organization E.g. Sales, advertising, etc.	Brand management E.g. Product managers plus functional specialists

Environmental complexity

Figure 2 Environmental characteristics and marketing organization
Source: Adapted from Weitz and Anderson (1981)

260

environmental contingency which may influence the role and form of marketing structure.

However, in addition to environmental characteristics it is necessary to recognize internal issues shaping the marketing organization – if only because managerial perceptions of environmental factors determine the impact they will have on decisions (Nonaka and Nicosia 1979).

Management and marketing organization

While influenced by environmental perceptions, there is the argument also that the departmentation and structuring of marketing involves the exercise of managerial discretion – this may be related to company history, culture, management style, marketing strategy, and so on.

It may be apposite here to consider the symptoms of structural deficiencies which may trigger managerial concern for the marketing organization issue (after Child 1984): managerial overload; poor integration; insufficient innovation; and weak control, through insufficient structural definition.

An integrative contingencies model

An attempt to integrate the various contingency approaches is provided by Ruekert *et al.* (1985). Their model of archetypal organizational forms is summarized in Figure 3. The concern here is mainly with structural characteristics (centralization, formalization and specialization), and whether activities are organized internally or externally. They identify a bureaucratic form, an organic, a transactional and a relational form.

The *bureaucratic structure* organizes marketing tasks internally, and represents the conventional functional marketing department or salesforce. The *organic structure* relates a pressure to decentralization to higher market uncertainty and leads to specialization by product or market. The *transactional form* represents the outplacement of marketing tasks, where relations with external suppliers are organized with a centralized and formal structure, such as purchase of logistics services. The *relational form* is associated with conditions of higher uncertainty where the 'spot contract' or transaction approach is replaced by a longer term relationship with an external supplier of an outplaced marketing task.

This analysis of archetypes leads attention to the development of new organizational forms in marketing.

NEW ORGANIZATIONAL FORMS IN MARKETING

Ruekert *et al.* (1985) argue that there are two fundamental questions faced when organizing marketing activities. First, when should marketing tasks be handled by the internal organization (employees) and when by external organization (external contractors). Second, how should internal or external organization be

Market versus hierarchy

	Internal organization	External organization
	Bureaucratic form	**Transactional form**
Centralized Formalized Non-specialized	• Conditions of low uncertainty, repetitive but specialized tasks • Effective and efficient but less adaptive • Examples: functional marketing organization, company/divisional sales force, corporate research staff	• Conditions of low environmental uncertainty, with repetitive but non-specialized tasks • Effective but less adaptive • Examples: contracting externally for advertising, transport, market research field work
Structure	**Organic form**	**Relational form**
Decentralized Non-formalized Specialized	• Conditions of high environmental uncertainty, with infrequent specialized tasks • Adaptive but less efficient • Examples: product management, specialized salesforce organization, research staffs organized by product groups	• Conditions of high environmental uncertainty with non-routine but non-specialized tasks • Adaptive but less efficient • Examples: retainer contract with advertising agency, continuing relationship with consulting firm

Figure 3 Archetypal organizational forms for marketing
Source: Adapted from Ruekert *et al.* (1985)

structured to achieve performance objectives. Conventionally, the precepts of organizational theory are applied to the latter question, while it is only recently that any conceptual framework has begun to emerge for the former question. This part of the chapter is concerned with the evolution of new organizational forms in marketing, both internal to the firm, but most particularly those designed to cope with new forms of environmental relationships: marketing partnerships, strategic alliances, and marketing networks of new kinds.

In various ways these partly speculative proposals reflect the general phenomenon of disaggregation and the devolution of functions from firms:

> Organizations of the future are likely to be vertically disaggregated: functions typically encompassed within a single organization will instead be performed in independent organizations. The functions of product design and development, manufacturing, and distribution ... will be brought together and held in temporary alignment by a variety of market mechanisms.
>
> (Miles and Snow 1984: 26)

The result of this process of devolution is organizational forms which have been variously characterized as 'confederations of specialists' (Webster 1992); 'networks' (Thorelli 1986); 'value-adding partnerships' (Johnston and Lawrence 1988); 'alliances' (Ohmae 1989); and 'shamrocks' (Handy 1990) – with the suggestion that they are all:

> characterized by flexibility, specialization, and an emphasis on relationship management instead of market transactions . . . to respond quickly and flexibly to accelerating change in technology, competition and customer preferences.
>
> (Webster 1992: 4–5)

The full implications of such changes for marketing are likely to be fundamental, but are not well understood or articulated at present. We can, however, track certain apparent internal organizational implications and more widespread effects as marketing networks develop.

Internal organizational implications

Some of the most significant organizational implications of environmental and strategic change in marketing, can be listed as follows:

1 Breaking hierarchies – speed and flexibility come from reducing organizational levels and numbers of employees, creating smaller business units, and empowering line management to manage key business processes (Quinn 1992; Doyle 1994).

2 Self-managing teams – critical changes will be managed by groups with complementary skills (see Katzenbach and Smith 1993), in the form of high-performance multifunctional teams to achieve fast, precise and flexible execution of programmes (Quinn 1992), possibly organized around market segments (Schultz 1993) and possibly temporary (Doyle 1994) – perhaps in the form of the 'collateral' or 'supplemental' organization like the task force for the major innovation (Huber 1984).

3 Reengineering – critical organizational processes will be radically restructured to reduce cost and increase speed and flexibility (see Hammer and Champy 1993) and to improve responsiveness to customers (Quinn 1992).

4 Transnational organizations – competing globally requires more complex structures and new skills (see Barlett and Ghoshal 1989).

5 Learning organizations – organizations will require the continual upgrading of skills and the corporate knowledge-base (Doyle 1994), leading to the adding of value for customers through knowledge feedback to create competitive advantage (Quinn 1992).

6 Account management – customer focus may be achieved by structural mechanisms (Schultz 1993; Doyle 1994).

These six factors all drive organizational change in marketing. Moreover, they are inextricably linked to how the company handles external relationships. Here strategic alliances and network organizations are leading towards the 'virtual corporation' (*Business Week* 1993; *Marketing Business* 1993) – an impermanent set of relationships to exploit a given market opportunity, which then dissolves when its purpose is achieved. These developments merit more detailed consideration.

Inter-organizational relationships

Webster (1992) suggests a number of significant changes in the role of marketing in the organization, as the focus moves from transactions to relationships and then increasingly to managing strategic alliances among independent organizations. He suggests that as traditional external boundaries between the firm and its market environment become blurred, so will traditional functional boundaries within the firm become less distinct. His argument leads to the following key conclusions:

- At the corporate level, in the network organization the marketing function will have the unique role different from the traditional, to help design and negotiate strategic partnerships with vendors and technology partners.
- At the business or SBU level, marketing managers will have new responsibility for deciding which marketing functions and activities are to be purchased in the market, which are to be performed by strategic partners, and which are to be performed internally.
- At the operating level, the emphasis will be more on relationships with customers and less on customer manipulation and persuasion. Indeed, in the USA Dickson (1994) predicts that the salesforce will become the dominant marketing organization form for companies that continue to perform the sales function internally, and there are some signs of this upgrading of the sales function in European companies also (Mitchell 1994).

The argument is that these new responsibilities and new marketing roles will demand organizational adjustments, although Webster is relatively vague about the form these may take. A more detailed description of the possible impact of networks and alliances on marketing organization is provided by Achrol (1991).

Marketing companies

Achrol has proposed two innovative marketing organizational forms as the result of environmental change: the marketing exchange company and the marketing coalition company. Both these forms are seen as 'organizing hubs of complex networks of functionally specialized firms' (Achrol 1991), and both are transorganizational systems where the critical managerial activities are boundary-spanning ones (see Figure 4).

264

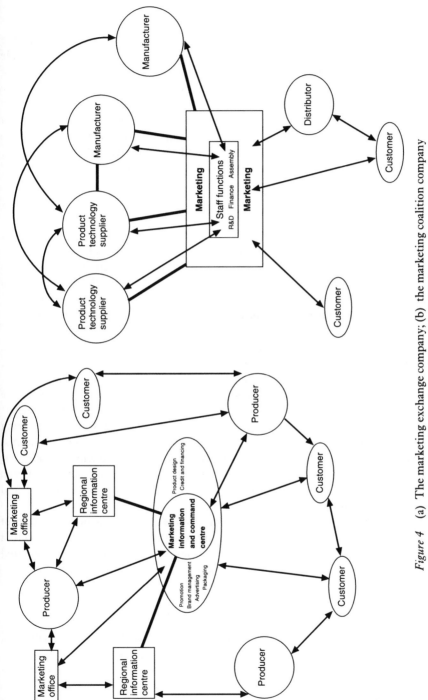

Figure 4 (a) The marketing exchange company; (b) the marketing coalition company

Source: Adapted from Achrol (1991)

The marketing exchange company

The marketing exchange company is compared to a brokerage or marketing information-based clearing-house, where the strategic core is a worldwide network of marketing offices and information centres – the 'marketing information network company'. Prototypes for this organizational form are the 'hollow corporation' (where manufacturing and other operational functions are devolved to external suppliers, and only marketing remains) and the great Japanese trading houses. Indeed, reflection suggests many similarities between Achrol's marketing exchange company, and the powerful wholesalers of the nineteenth century stimulating the entire marketing chain (Shaw 1915).

The marketing coalition company

This organizational form is conceived as the coordinating centre of a network of strategic alliances – whereas the marketing exchange company is a quasi-market, the marketing coalition company is a quasiorganization. Achrol (1991) argues this organization reflects certain key environmental changes: the trend towards a smaller in-house manufactured product component; growing recognition of the need for a climate of innovation; and the rapid growth in strategic alliances.

The critical distinction made by Achrol (1991) is that the marketing exchange company is the organizing hub for market information and complex exchanges, while the marketing coalition company is the hub for organizing a division of functions among an alliance of specialist firms. The link is that both are transorganizational entities, and that both have one central function – marketing. It is also argued that the critical managerial focus will shift from organizing internal systems to organizing boundary spanning processes. Organizational issues will thus be less about internal structure and departmental boundaries, and more about 'alternatives or substitutes for organization' (Achrol 1991): establishing productive norms of behaviour rather than hierarchical control; and developing a 'quasijudicial system' of management.

Underpinning the logic of Achrol's models is the development of networks of various kinds, to accomplish marketing tasks. Insight into the marketing organization of the future may rely on developing a better and more integrated understanding of the network organization.

Marketing networks

The network form of organization offers an alternative to the traditional hierarchy (Cravens *et al.* 1994a). The central concept is that relationships are formed among several corporate units, independent organizations and entrepreneurs. The relationships may be both vertical among members of the value-adding system, spanning from suppliers to end-users, and horizontal among actual or potential competitors. A key network characteristic is being flexible and adaptable to change. Successful networks are customer driven – guided by the needs and preferences of buyers. They differ from the traditional command and control hierarchy, displaying a flat organization form and involving interaction between network partners rather than multi-layered functions. The network members are connected via a highly sophisticated information and decision-support system, often global in scope. This system performs many of the command and control functions of the traditional organization. As a consequence of the sharing of strategic information, trust among the partners is often a vital success characteristic of strategic alliances and other network relationships.

No one form of network has evolved as the best paradigm. Importantly, networks are not always better than traditional organization forms:

> Like earlier decentralization or SBU concepts, some of these new organization modes have been touted as cures for almost any management ill. They are not. Each form is useful in certain situations, and not in others. But more importantly, each requires a carefully developed infrastructure of culture, measurements, style and rewards to support it. When properly installed, these disaggregated organizations can be awesomely effective in harnessing intellectual resources for certain purposes. When improperly supported or adapted, they can be less effective than old-fashioned hierarchies.
>
> (Quinn 1992: 147)

The motivations to form networks include rapid market and technology change and skills/resources gaps. The conditions that favour adopting a network structure are: fast technological change, shorter product life cycles, market structures where preferences are segmented, and markets that extend beyond national boundaries (Achrol 1991).

Network formation process

Networks are more likely to be launched by entrepreneurs, since the traditional vertically integrated, hierarchically organized company faces drastic changes in shifting to a network paradigm (Cravens *et al.* 1994a). The network means fewer people on the corporate payroll, different management challenges, major cultural changes, and complex collaborative relationships with other organizations.

Nevertheless, some companies are successfully transforming themselves to more flexible and adaptive organization forms. For example, Benneton (apparel) and Dell (personal computers) display several network characteristics. The most distinct example of organizational transformation, however, is the 'hollow' or 'virtual' organization, involving a core organization which coordinates relationships with a network of independent specialists.

Network classification

Two useful dimensions of classification for the new organizational forms are: first, the duration of the environmental change, and second, the type of relationship (collaboration versus transaction) among network members (Cravens *et al.* 1994b).

The volatility of environmental change has an important influence on how the organization is designed to cope with the change (Achrol 1991). In the highly volatile situation, the organization needs a flexible internal structure that can rapidly adjust to new environmental conditions. Similarly, the external relationships that exist between organizations must allow for alteration (and termination) over a short time horizon. When the competitive environment is less volatile, the inter-organizational relationships may be collaborative. The partners must commit a substantial amount of time and resources to developing the relationship, and working towards common strategic objectives.

One important organizational design issue is whether or not market segments can be distinguished (Achrol 1991). Segmented market structures enable the combination of the specialized skills and resources of other organizations using network relationships. When segments cannot be distinguished, the organization may need to rely more heavily on internal capabilities to cope with environmental dynamics and shifts in customer needs and requirements.

The second basis for classifying network organizations is the type of relationship(s) among network members. The tie may range from highly collaborative links to transactional links. Collaborative links imply an ongoing relationship between the parties, not unlike the highly relational contractual relationships discussed by McNeil (1978). Transactional links are those between parties that do not require collaboration.

The types of links between firms depend on the functions performed by the network members, the rate of environmental change, customer characteristics and requirements, market structure, technological complexity, core competency of the coordinating organization, and core competency of the network members. Since more than one type of link may be found in the network, the dominant type of link can be used in the classification of the network organization. We now examine four illustrative types of network organization (Cravens *et al.* 1994b):

1 The hollow network.
2 The flexible organization.
3 The value-added network.
4 The virtual network.

The hollow network

The hollow network is a transaction-based organizational form competing in highly volatile environments. It is designed to meet the needs of buyers that can be placed into one or more market segments (Achrol 1991). The hollow corporation is customer focused, using transactional relationships to link customers with goods and services that meet their needs. The term 'hollow organization' emphasizes that the core organization draws heavily upon other organizations (and individuals) to satisfy customer needs. Organizations competing in this situation are often specialists that coordinate an extensive network of suppliers and buyers (ibid.).

Achrol's (1991) 'marketing exchange company' (see pp. 264–6 above) is a possible design for the hollow organization paradigm. The hollow organization buffers the frequently changing environment by functioning as a marketing organization that can shift to new opportunities and sources of supply. It does not perform major research and development or production functions internally. Technology is located with network members.

The flexible organization

The flexible organization is encountered under conditions of high environmental volatility, but has intra-network links that tend to be collaborative and long term. The network coordinator is likely to be an entrepreneur or an entrepreneurial unit of an established organization. The network coordinator manages an internal team which identifies customer needs, designs products, and establishes sources of supply. The organization generates a stream of new products to satisfy a diversity of customer requirements.

One version of the flexible organization is the 'spider web' company (Quinn 1992). Its characteristics include close communications links between the nodes and the coordinating company, but each node company operates on an independent basis by performing the task(s) agreed with the hub company. The market environment for this paradigm includes fast response times, high value-added, and high risk. The coordinating company is able to leverage its expertise by linking itself with an array of node companies. 'A major driving force is customers who demand increasing flexibility and responsiveness in the supply of ever more complex products and services' (Quinn 1992: 129). Meeting these diverse requirements calls for great knowledge depth, technological competency, and response capability.

The value-added network

Companies forming value-added networks may compete in markets where preferences are diffused and segments may be difficult to define. This form of organization may utilize a global network of suppliers coupled with substantial internal operations. It differs from the virtual network in that the core organization may perform fewer of the value-added functions. Nonetheless, the core organization in the value-added network is responsible for innovation and product design.

The value-added network organization appears to fit product-market situations where complex technologies and customized product offerings are not required. Industries where this network form may be appropriate include apparel manufacturing and marketing, specialty furniture, eyeglasses, and services.

The virtual network

The virtual network is likely to be a reformed version of the traditional organization. It is a version of the 'virtual corporation' (*Business Week* 1993). The 'virtual corporation' is so named because it has a long-term orientation of adapting to meet the needs of segmented market structures, while competing in markets that experience low levels of environmental volatility. Unlike the hollow organization, the virtual network organization utilizes a substantial core competency in product innovation and production efficiency (Achrol 1991). It may perform many of the traditional functions internally, but does so in a different way. This organization form may be adopted by a traditional organization that has been reformed. It may also be used by an entrepreneur seeking to exploit a long-term growth opportunity, while hedging the risks by networking with other organizations. Low environmental volatility encourages the formation of collaborative relationships with network members and customers. Customer needs are complex and dynamic. Examples of virtual networks include General Electric, Hewlett-Packard and Motorola. Market access and technology are major drivers in these and other collaborative organizations.

Implications of network organizations

In deciding whether or how to develop or gain access to a network organization, several strategy implications should be considered (Cravens *et al.* 1994a):

1 Defining core competencies – a major reason for networking is that each member offers a core competency that the others lack. Thus, defining an organization's core competencies is an essential early step in forming networks.
2 Establishing and managing relationships – network organizations may employ transaction, collaboration or combination relationships. The network relationship may be vertical with other members of the value-added system (suppliers, producers, and marketing intermediaries), or horizontal with competitors. The latter is the most complex of the group and the most different from the experiences of most traditional organizations. These relationships are more equality based than power based.
3 Organizational culture and networks – establishing networks may impact on existing corporate cultures, particularly in international alliances. The

270

partners must be willing and able to make necessary concessions to each other.

4 Assessing network effectiveness – this issue centres on the advantage to the organization in developing a network relationship compared to not pursuing the strategic objective in question. It is useful to compare network results with expectations.

5 Staffing requirements – forming and managing the network organization calls for different managerial skills from those required in the hierarchical organization. Team-oriented generalists with the ability to manage complex projects should be effective in network situations.

THE MANAGEMENT AGENDA FOR MARKETING ORGANIZATION

In conclusion, the management agenda to be addressed in considering organizational issues in marketing includes answering the following types of questions:

1 Consider the impact of organizational structures and coordination mechanisms on the implementation of marketing strategy and on the formulation of that strategy, and what organizational arrangements imply for the firm in terms of managing the customer/company interface, in achieving market orientation, and in how people in the firm understand the marketplace.

2 In addressing the organizational dimensions of marketing, distinguish between those at the functional and business unit level, and those at the corporate and enterprise level. It will be necessary to interrelate between these levels because they are inextricably linked, but the issues at each level are somewhat different (see Table 1, p. 255).

3 Recognition should be given to the pressures for change in the marketing organization. This should include both external pressures from market and distribution channel change, and internal pressures from new technology, new management methods, and broader organizational changes.

4 The appropriateness of different organizational forms for marketing may be assessed through the evaluation of different types of market and corporate contingencies.

5 At the functional and business unit levels there are questions of the most appropriate internal structure of the marketing function or department, and more broadly the type of marketing department currently operated and that needed to achieve marketing goals.

6 The adoption of multifunctional teams in reformed organizations to guide business processes, such as new product planning, creates complex challenges in defining processes, selecting team members, determining incentives, and assessing performance.

7 At the enterprise and corporate levels the questions to address reflect broad

271

changes in the way large organizations are structured and managed, but also the process of vertical disaggregation and networking. The growing importance of relationship marketing strategies, strategic alliances, and marketing networks should be carefully evaluated in the light of proposals for new organizational forms for marketing to cope with such environmental changes.

8 Finally, the trade-off between improving organizational effectiveness and the costs of organizational change must be carefully evaluated. Redesigning the marketing organization changes the jobs and responsibilities of personnel. The new design may also require reductions in staff. Such changes are costly and should be compared to the estimated value added by the new organization.

REFERENCES

Achrol, Ravi S. (1991) 'Evolution of the marketing organization: new forms for turbulent environments', *Journal of Marketing* 55, October: 77–93.
Ames, B. C. (1968) 'Trappings versus substance in industrial marketing', *Harvard Business Review*, July–August: 93–102.
Baligh, H. H. and Burton, R. M. (1979) 'Marketing in moderation – the marketing concept and the organization's structure', *Long Range Planning* 12 (2): 92–6.
Barlett, Christopher A. and Ghoshal, Sumantra (1989) *Managing Across Borders: The Transnational Solution*, London: Hutchinson.
Bonoma, Thomas V. (1985) *The Marketing Edge: Making Strategies Work*, New York: Free Press.
Brady, John and Davis, Ian (1993) 'Marketing's mid-life crisis', *McKinsey Quarterly*, Summer.
Buell, Victor P. (1975) 'The changing role of the product manager in consumer goods companies', *Journal of Marketing* 39, July: 3–11.
Buell, Victor P. (1982) *Organizing for Marketing/Advertising Success*, New York: Association of National Advertisers.
Bund, H. and Carroll, J. W. (1957) 'The changing role of the marketing function', *Journal of Marketing* 21 (3): 268–325.
Business Week (1993) 'The virtual corporation', 8 February: 36–41.
Cespedes, Frank V. (1991) *Organizing and Implementing the Marketing Effort*, Reading, Mass.: Addison-Wesley.
Chandler, A. D. (1962) *Strategy and Structure*, Cambridge, Mass.: MIT Press.
Child, John (1984) *Organization*, 2nd edn, London: Harper and Row.
Christopher, Martin, McDonald, Malcolm and Wills, Gordon (1980) *Introducing Marketing*, London: Pan.
Christopher, Martin, Payne, Adrian and Ballantyne, David (1992) *Relationship Marketing*, Oxford: Butterworth-Heinemann.
Corey, Edward R. and Star, Steven H. (1971) *Organization Strategy: A Marketing Approach*, Boston, Mass.: Harvard University Press.
Cravens, David W., Shipp, Shannon H. and Cravens, Karen S. (1994a) 'Reforming the traditional organization: the mandate for developing networks', *Business Horizons*, forthcoming.
Cravens, David W., Shipp, Shannon H. and Piercy, Nigel F. (1994b) 'New organization forms for competing in highly dynamic environments: the network paradigm',

Conference on Relationship Marketing, Emory Business School.

Dickson, Peter R. (1994) *Marketing Management*, Fort Worth: Dryden Press.

Doyle, Peter (1979) 'Management structures and marketing strategies in UK industry', *European Journal of Marketing* 13 (5): 319–31.

Doyle, Peter (1994) *Marketing Management and Strategy*, Hemel Hempstead: Prentice-Hall.

Franko, L. (1974) 'The move towards a multidimensional structure in European organizations', *Administrative Science Quarterly* 19: 493–506.

Gould, P. (1982) 'Kellogg fattens its marketing department', *Marketing*, 14 October: 6.

Gummesson, Evert (1994) *Relationship Marketing: From 4Ps to 30Rs*, Stockholm: Stockholm University.

Håkansson, H. and Ostberg, C. (1975) 'Industrial marketing: an organizational problem?', *Industrial Marketing Management* 4: 113–23.

Hammer, Michael and Champy, James (1993) *Re-engineering the Corporation*, London: Brealey.

Hanan, M. (1974) 'Reorganize your company around its markets', *Harvard Business Review*, November–December: 63–74.

Handy, Charles (1990) *The Age of Unreason*, Boston, Mass.: Harvard Business School Press.

Hise, R. T. and Kelley, J. P. (1978) 'Product management on trial', *Journal of Marketing* 42, October: 28–33.

Hofer, Charles W. and Schendel, Dan (1978) *Strategy Formulation: Analytical Concepts*, St. Paul: West Publishing.

Hooley, Graham, West, C. J. and Lynch, James E. (1984) *Marketing in the UK – A Survey of Current Practice and Performance*, Cookham, Berks.: Institute of Marketing.

Hopkins, David S. and Bailey, Earl L. (1984) *Organizing Corporate Marketing*, New York: Conference Board.

Howard, John A. (1968) 'Organization structure and its underlying theory of buyer behavior' in S. H. Britt and Harper W. Boyd (eds) *Marketing Management and Administrative Action*, New York: McGraw-Hill.

Huber, George P. (1984) 'The nature and design of post-industrial organizations', *Management Science* 30, August: 928–51.

Hughes, G. D. (1980) *Marketing Management: A Planning Approach*, Reading, Mass.: Addison-Wesley.

Jackson, D. W. and Walker, B. J. (1980) 'The channel manager: marketing's newest aide?', *California Management Review* 23 (2): 52–8.

Jap, Sandy D. (1992) *Evolving Relationships of Retailers and Manufacturers*, Report 92–113, Cambridge, Mass.: Marketing Science Institute.

Johnston, Russell and Lawrence, Paul R. (1988) 'Beyond vertical integration – the rise of the value-adding partnership', *Harvard Business Review* 66, July–August: 94–101.

Kanter, Rosabeth Moss (1991) 'Even closer to the customer', *Harvard Business Review*, January–February: 9–10.

Katzenbach, Hon R. and Smith, Douglas K. (1993) *The Wisdom of Teams: Creating the High-Performance Organization*, Boston, Mass.: Harvard Business School Press.

Kelly, J. P. and Hise, R. T. (1980) 'Role conflict, role clarity, job tension and job satisfaction in the brand manager position', *Journal of the Academy of Marketing Science* 8 (2): 120–37.

Kohli, Ajay K. and Jaworski, Bernard J. (1990) 'Market orientation: the construct, research propositions, and managerial implications', *Journal of Marketing* 54 (2): 1–18.

Kotler, Philip (1991) *Marketing Management: Analysis, Planning and Control*, London: Prentice-Hall International.

Levitt, Theodore (1980) 'Marketing success through differentiation – of anything', *Harvard Business Review* 58 (1): 83–91.

McKenna, Regis (1991a) 'Marketing is everything', *Harvard Business Review*, January–February.

McKenna, Regis (1991b) *Relationship Marketing*, Reading, Mass.: Addison-Wesley.

McNeil, Ian (1978) 'Contracts: adjustment of long-term economic relations under classical, neoclassical, and relational contract law', *Northwestern University Law Review* 72: 854–902.

Marketing Business (1993) 'New marketing vision', January: 12–17.

Miles, Raymond E. and Snow, Charles C. (1984) 'Fit, failure and the hall of fame', *California Management Review* 26, Spring: 10–28.

Mitchell, Alan (1993) 'Transformation of marketing', *Marketing Business*, November: 9–14.

Mitchell, Alan (1994) 'New generation marketing', *Marketing Business*, February: 13–16.

Morgan, Neil A. and Piercy, Nigel F. (1992) 'Market-led quality', *Industrial Marketing Management* 21 (2): 111–18.

Narver, John C. and Slater, Stanley F. (1990) 'The effect of a market orientation on business profitability', *Journal of Marketing* 54, October: 20–35.

Narver, John C. and Slater, Stanley F. (1992) *Market Orientation, Performance and the Moderating Influence of Competitive Environment*, Marketing Science Institute Working Paper 92–118, Cambridge, Mass.: Marketing Science Institute.

Naumann, Earl and Shannon, Patrick (1992) 'What is customer-driven marketing?', *Business Horizons*, November–December: 44–52.

Nonaka, I. and Nicosia, F. M. (1979) 'Marketing management, its environment and information processing: a problem of organizational design', *Journal of Business Research* 7 (4): 277–301.

Ohmae, Kenichi (1989) 'The global logic of strategic alliances', *Harvard Business Review* 67, March–April: 143–54.

Petre, P. E. (1983) 'Meet the lean, mean new IBM', *Fortune*, 13 June.

Pfeffer, Jeffrey and Salancik, G. R. (1978) *The External Control of Organizations*, New York: Harper and Row.

Piercy, Nigel (1985) *Marketing Organisation: An Analysis of Information Processing, Power and Politics*, London: Allen and Unwin.

Piercy, Nigel (1986) 'The role and function of the chief marketing executive and the marketing department: a study of medium-sized companies in the UK', *Journal of Marketing Management* 1 (3): 265–89.

Piercy, Nigel (1988) 'The role of the marketing department in UK retailing organizations', *International Journal of Retailing* 4 (2): 46–65.

Piercy, Nigel (1992) *Market-Led Strategic Change*, Oxford: Butterworth-Heinemann.

Piercy, Nigel (1994) 'Marketing implementation: analysing structure, process and information', in John Saunders (ed.) *The Marketing Initiative*, London: Prentice-Hall.

Piercy, Nigel and Alexander, Nicholas (1988) 'The status quo of marketing in UK retailing organizations', *Services Industries Journal* 8 (2): 155–67.

Piercy, Nigel and Evans, Martin J. (1994) 'Developing marketing information systems', in Michael J. Baker (ed.) *The Marketing Book*, Oxford: Butterworth-Heinemann.

Piercy, Nigel and Morgan, Neil (1989) 'Marketing organization in the UK financial services industry', *International Journal of Bank Marketing* 7 (4): 3–10.

Piercy, Nigel F. and Morgan, Neil A. (1993) 'Strategic and operational market segmentation: a managerial analysis', *Journal of Strategic Marketing* 1: 123–40.

Quinn, J. Brian (1992) *Intelligent Enterprise*, New York: Free Press.

Reitman, Valerie (1992) 'Rubbermaid turns up plenty of profit in the mundane', *Wall*

Street Journal, 27 March, B3.

Ruekert, Robert W. (1992) 'Developing a market orientation: an organizational strategy perspective', *International Journal of Research in Marketing* 9: 225–45.

Ruekert, Robert W., Walker, Orville C. and Roering, Kenneth J. (1985) 'The organization of marketing activities: a contingency theory of structure and performance', *Journal of Marketing* 49, Winter: 13–25.

Schultz, Don E. (1992) *Integrated Marketing Communications*, Evanston, Ill.: NTC Business Books.

Schultz, Don E. (1993) 'Maybe we should start all over with an IMC organization', *Marketing News*, 25 October: 8.

Schwarz, Gordon (1990) *Organizing to Become Market-Driven*, Report 90–123, Cambridge, Mass.: Marketing Science Institute.

Shapiro, B. F. and Moriarity, R. T. (1984) *Organizing the National Account Force*, Report 84–101, Cambridge, Mass.: Marketing Science Institute.

Shaw, Arch W. (1915) *Some Problems in Market Distribution*, Cambridge, Mass.: Harvard University Press.

Staudt, T. A. and Taylor, D. A. (1970) *A Managerial Introduction to Marketing*, Englewood Cliffs, N. J.: Prentice-Hall.

Thorelli, Hans (1986) 'Networks: between markets and hierarchies', *Strategic Management Journal* 7: 37–51.

Tull, Donald S., Cooley, Bruce E., Phillips, Mark R. and Watkins, Harry S. (1991) *The Organization of Marketing Activities of American Manufacturers*, Report 91–126, Cambridge, Mass.: Marketing Science Institute.

Webster, Frederick E. (1992) 'The changing role of marketing in the corporation', *Journal of Marketing* 56, October: 1–17.

Weick, Karl R. (1969) *The Social Psychology of Organizing*, Reading, Mass.: Addison-Wesley.

Weigand, R. E. (1961) *Changes in the Marketing Organization in Selected Industries, 1950–1959*', unpublished PhD dissertation, University of Illinois.

Weitz, Bart and Anderson, Erin (1981) 'Organizing and controlling the marketing function', in B. M. Enis and K. J. Roering (eds) *Review of Marketing 1981*, Chicago: American Marketing Association.

Wortzel, Lawrence H. and Venkatraman, Meera P. (1991) *Manufacturer and Retailer Relationships: Replacing Power with Strategic Marketing Partnerships*, Working Paper 91–129, Cambridge, Mass.: Marketing Science Institute.

FURTHER READING

Achrol, Ravi S. (1991) 'Evolution of the marketing organization: new forms for turbulent environments', *Journal of Marketing* 55, October: 77–93.

Buell, V. P. (1982) *Organizing for Marketing/Advertising Success*, New York: Association of National Advertisers.

Bund, H. and Carroll, J. W. (1957) 'The changing role of the marketing function', *Journal of Marketing* 21 (3): 268–325.

Cespedes, Frank V. (1991) *Organizing and Implementing the Marketing Effort*, Reading, Mass.: Addison-Wesley.

Cravens, David W., Shipp, Shannon H. and Cravens, Karen S. (1994) 'Reforming the traditional organization: the mandate for developing networks', *Business Horizons*, forthcoming.

Håkansson, H., Wootz, B., Andersson, O. and Hangard, P. (1979) 'Industrial marketing as an organizational problem', *European Journal of Marketing* 13 (3): 81–93.

Hooley, Graham J., West, C. J. and Lynch, James E. (1984) *Marketing in the UK – A*

Survey of Current Practice and Performance, Cookham, Berks.: Institute of Marketing.

Nonaka, I. and Nicosia, F. M. (1979) 'Marketing management, its environment and information processing: a problem of organizational design', *Journal of Business Research* 25 (5): 277–301.

Piercy, Nigel (1985) *Marketing Organisation: An Analysis of Information Processing, Power and Politics*, London: Allen and Unwin.

Piercy, Nigel (1992) *Market-Led Strategic Change*, Oxford: Butterworth-Heinemann.

Piercy, Nigel (1994) 'Marketing implementation: analysing structure, process and information', in John Saunders (ed.) *The Marketing Initiative*, London: Prentice-Hall.

Piercy, Nigel and Cravens, David W. (1995) 'The network paradigm and the marketing organization: Developing a new management agenda', *European Journal of Marketing* 29 (3): 7–34.

Ruekert, Robert W. (1992) 'Developing a market orientation: an organizational strategy perspective', *International Journal of Research in Marketing* 9: 225–45.

Ruekert, Robert W., Walker, Orville C. and Roering, Kenneth J. (1985) 'The organization of marketing activities: a contingency theory of structure and performance', *Journal of Marketing* 49, Winter: 13–25.

Tapscott, Don and Caston, Art (1993) *Paradigm Shift: The New Promise of Information Technology*, New York: McGraw-Hill.

Webster, Frederick E. (1992) 'The changing role of marketing in the corporation', *Journal of Marketing* 56, October: 1–17.

Weitz, Barton and Anderson, Erin (1981) 'Organizing and controlling the marketing function', in B. M. Enis and K. J. Roering (eds) *Review of Marketing 1981*, Chicago: American Marketing Association.

16

MARKETING BUDGETING AND RESOURCE ALLOCATION

Richard M.S. Wilson

BUDGETING: SCOPE AND NATURE

Budgeting (or profit planning) is perhaps the widest ranging control technique in that it covers the entire organization rather than merely sections of it.

A budget is a quantitative plan of action that aids in the coordination and control of the acquisition, allocation and utilization of resources over a given period of time. The building of the budget may be looked upon as the integration of the varied interests that constitute the organization into a programme that all have agreed is workable in attempting to attain objectives.

Budgetary planning and control work through the formal organization viewing it as a series of responsibility centres, and attempting to isolate the performance measurement of one module from the effects of the performance of others.

Budgeting involves more than just forecasting since it involves the planned manipulation of all the variables that determine the company's performance in an effort to arrive at some preferred position in the future. The agreed plan must be developed in a coordinated manner if the requirements of each sub–system are to be balanced in line with company objectives. Each manager must consider the relationship of his responsibility centre (department or sub–system) to all others and to the company as a whole in the budgetary planning phase. This tends to reduce departmental bias and empire-building as well as isolating weaknesses in the organizational structure and highlighting problems of communication. Furthermore, it encourages the delegation of authority by a reliance upon the principle of management by exception.

Having determined the plan, this provides the frame of reference for judging subsequent performance. There can be no doubt that budgeted performance is a better benchmark than past performance on account of the inefficiencies that are usually hidden in the latter and the effect of constantly changing conditions.

There are essentially two types of budgets – the long term and the short term.

Time obviously distinguishes one from the other, and this raises the point that users of budgets should not be unduly influenced by conventional accounting periods: the budget period that is the most meaningful to the individual company should be adopted. For example, the life cycle of a product from its development right through to its deletion is in many ways a more natural budgetary period than calendar units because it links marketing, production, and financial planning on a unified basis. The actual choice of a budget period will tend to depend very much on the company's ability to forecast accurately.

Typically, however, budgets tend to be compiled on an annual basis, with this time span being broken down into lesser time intervals for reporting, scheduling, and control reasons (i.e. half years, quarters, months, and even weeks in the case of production and sales activities).

Within this framework of one year the operating budget is prepared, which is composed of two parts that each look at the same things in a slightly different way, but which both arrive at the same net profit and return on investment. These two parts are:

1 The programme (or activity) budget that specifies the operations that will be performed during the forthcoming period. The most logical way to present this budget is to show, for each marketing programme, the expected revenues and their associated costs. The result is an impersonal portrayal of the expected future that is useful in ensuring that a balance exists amongst the various activities, profit margins, and volumes – in other words, this is the plan. (See Figure 1.)
2 The responsibility budget that specifies the annual plan in terms of individual responsibilities. This is primarily a control device that indicates the target level of performance, but the personalized costs in this budget

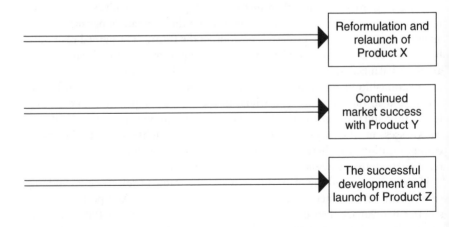

Figure 1 Programme (or activity budget)

278

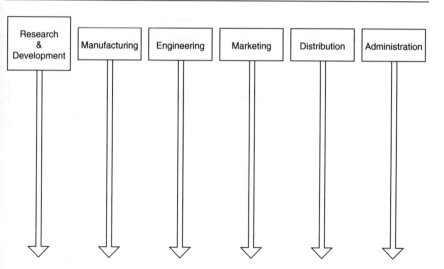

Figure 2   Responsibility budget

must be controllable at the level at which they are planned and reported. (See Figure 2.)

The significance of these two ways of dealing with the operating budget is of importance as the programme budget is the outcome of the planning phase, whereas the responsibility budget is the starting-point for the control phase. The former need not correspond to the organizational structure, but the latter must. Consequently, the plan must be translated into the control prior to the time of execution and communicated to those involved in order that no one will be in any doubt as to precisely what is expected of him or her. (See Figure 3.)

Given these two complementary aspects of the operating budget, there are two basic ways in which the budget may be prepared:

1   Periodic budgeting in which a plan is prepared for the next financial year with a minimum of revision as the year goes by. Generally the total expected annual expenditure will be spread over the year on a monthly basis on the strength of the behaviour of the elemental costs. Thus 'salaries' will be spread over the months simply as one-twelfth of the expected annual cost per month, but seasonal variations in sales will require a little more attention to be paid to marketing and production costs and their behaviour over time.

2   Continuous (or rolling) budgeting in which a tentative annual plan is prepared with, say, the first quarter by month in great detail, the second and third quarters in less detail, and the fourth quarter in outline only. Every month (or perhaps every quarter) the budget can then be revised by adding

279

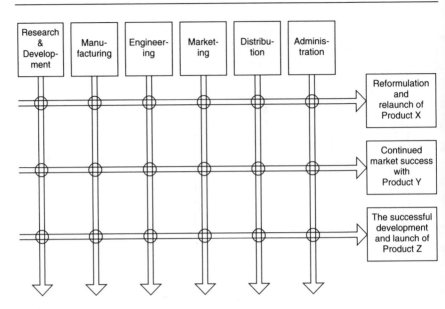

Figure 3   A simplified output budget format

the required detail to the next month (or quarter), and adding on a new month (or quarter) in such a way that the plan still extends one year ahead. Such a budgeting procedure attempts to accommodate changing conditions and uncertainty, and is highly desirable in that it forces management constantly to think in concrete terms about the forthcoming year regardless of where one happens to be in the present financial year.

Periodic budgeting will often be satisfactory for companies in stable industries that are able to make relatively accurate forecasts covering the planning period. Conversely, rolling budgeting is of greater value in the more usual cases of somewhat irregular cyclical activity amid the uncertainties of consumer demand.

LOCATING BUDGETING

It is helpful to consider the role of budgeting in relation to the broad questions contained within the management process as shown in Figure 4.

Stage One raises the question of where the organization is now in terms of its competitive position, product range, market share, financial position and overall effectiveness. In addressing this question we are seeking to establish a baseline from which we can move forward.

Stage Two is concerned with where the organization should go in the future,

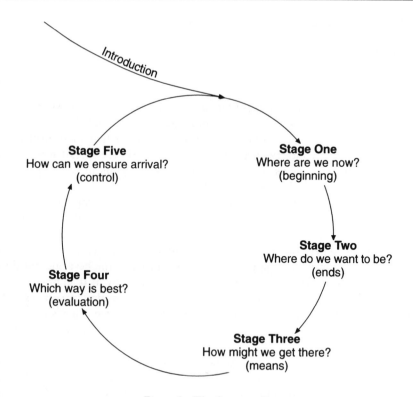

Figure 4 The framework

which requires the specification of ends (or objectives) to be achieved. While top management in the organization will have some discretion over the choice of ends, this is constrained by various vested interests.

Stage Three deals with the question of how desired ends might be achieved, which begs the question of how alternative means to ends might be identified. This strategy formulation stage requires creative inputs that cannot be reduced to mechanical procedures.

Stage Four focuses on the evaluation of alternative means by which the most preferred (or 'best') alternative might be selected. The need to choose may be due to alternatives being mutually exclusive (i.e. all attempting to achieve the same end) or a consequence of limited resources (which means that a rationing mechanism must be invoked).

Stage Five covers the implementation of the chosen means, and the monitoring of its performance in order that any corrective actions might be taken to ensure that the desired results are achieved. Since circumstances both within the organization and in its environment are unlikely to stay constant while a budget is being pursued, it is necessary to adapt to accommodate such changes.

281

Within these stages are to be found the main managerial activities of:

- planning
- decision-making
- control

The entire sequence of Stages One to Five constitutes control, within which the planning activities are to be found in Stages One to Four. At every stage it is necessary for decisions to be made, so it is apparent that these managerial activities are closely intertwined. Moreover, their links are spread across three different time dimensions which are not of equal significance: the past, the present and the future. Let us consider these in turn.

The past brought the organization (and its products, competitors, etc.) to their present positions. By gaining an understanding of how the organization arrived at its present position the managers of that organization might develop some insights to help them in deciding how to proceed in the future. However, there is no way in which the past can be influenced, so the best one can do is to attempt to learn from it instead of being constrained by it. If an organization simply continues on unchanging routes its viability is almost certain to be endangered as the environment changes but it does not. Stage One is concerned with establishing the ways in which the past brought the organization to its present position.

The present is transient: it is the fleeting moment between the past and the future when one must take one's understanding of the past and link this to the development of one's aspirations for the future. Decisions are made (with both planning and control consequences) in the present, but their impact is intended to be in the future.

The time dimension that is of major relevance in any planning exercise must be the future rather than the present or the past. There is nothing about an organization that is more important than its future and the spirit of this was aptly summarized by C. F. Kettering: 'I am interested in the future because that is where I intend to live'. The past may help us in deciding how to proceed in the future, but there is no way in which we can influence the past, so there is a limit to the amount of effort that should be applied to it as opposed to planning for the future. Nevertheless, the link between the past and the future is important as the following sequence of steps should make clear:

- We can seek to understand – on the basis of our past experience – the way in which variables of interest to us interact. This enables us to gain insights into, and an understanding of, causal relationships.
- Our understanding of causal relationships in the past gives a basis for making more accurate predictions regarding the future.
- If we are able to make accurate predictions we should be in a better position to control the outcome of events. It is in this context that budgeting can play a valuable role.

282

We can illustrate some of the roles which budgets play in organizations by reference to the characteristics of the control process highlighted above, namely: objectives, choice of inputs and outputs, predictive models and the issue of relevant alternative courses of action available to the manager.

Objectives and budgets are related in two main ways. First, a decision-maker may face reasonably clear corporate objectives such as:

1 increase the market share of the organization by 20 per cent;
2 expand into the retail/wholesale market;
3 take over certain related businesses that have an asset base of £2–4,000,000.

These general objectives will need to be further specified in the form of detailed operating goals for key decision areas. For instance, the objective of increasing market share by 20 per cent may be translated into a sales target of £10,000,000 for Division A and £15,000,000 for Division B. In this manner, a budget helps to represent and communicate the broad objectives of top management to middle management and operating personnel.

Budgets also help give form to alternative courses of action by measuring in financial terms the inputs and outputs of a particular strategy. A project or activity may begin as someone's bright idea but this cannot be implemented unless there are clear measurements of the inputs required to implement the idea and the outputs that may be expected to eventuate. A budget is a means whereby the inputs and outputs associated with a future course of action can be expressed in financial terms.

A budget also enables an organization to express estimated input–output relationships. For instance, sales budgets may be constructed using three sales estimates: £2,000,000, £2,500,000 or £3,000,000. Each of these estimates will give rise to a set of production, cash and income budgets. Having generated these three sets of budgets which, in effect, represent three different scenarios for the organization, decision-makers can determine which scenario is feasible and acceptable. Note, however, that the quality of the budget (that is, the accuracy of the budget estimates) depends on the knowledge available about the relationship between inputs and outputs. If the predictive model of the input–output relationship is erroneous the sets of budgets produced will only be of limited value.

A budget target, like a standard, expresses a desired and expected level of performance. For instance, a sales budget of £3,000,000 means the organization expects and desires to achieve £3,000,000 worth of sales revenue. Once this sales target has been specified and accepted by people within an organization it may be assigned to a particular person, such as the sales manager. This manager will then bear overall responsibility for the achievement or non-achievement of this target. Thus, at the end of the budget period, if the sales target is not achieved, the sales manager will need to account for it to the marketing director. In this way budgeting enables specific responsibilities to be assigned to particular individuals who are then held accountable for the achievement of the budget

283

target. This assignment of responsibilities for specific performance is called responsibility accounting and is widely used in many organizations.

ESTABLISHING A BASE LINE

It is usually found that enterprises – especially smaller ones – do not know what proportion of their resources are devoted to their various activities or segments, or the profitability of these allocations. Producing useful computations of segmental costs and profit contributions can readily be achieved by adopting analytical methods which, while not difficult in principle, are not widely adopted due largely to the preoccupation with manufacturing cost accounting that exists.

The fact that most companies do not know what proportion of their total marketing outlay is spent on each product, area or customer group may be due to the absence of a sufficiently refined system of cost analysis, or it may be due to vagueness over the nature of certain costs. For instance, is the cost of packaging a promotional, a production or a distribution expense? Some important marketing costs are hidden in manufacturing costs or in general and administrative costs (including finished goods inventory costs in the former and order processing costs in the latter).

Since few companies are aware of costs and profits by segment in relation to sales levels, and since even fewer are able to predict changes in sales volume and profit contribution as a result of changes in marketing effort, the following errors arise:

1 Marketing budgets for individual products are too large, with the result that diminishing returns become evident and benefits would accrue from a reduction in expenditure.
2 Marketing budgets for individual products are too small and increasing returns would result from an increase in expenditure.
3 The marketing mix is inefficient, with an incorrect balance and incorrect amounts being spent on the constituent elements – such as too much on advertising and insufficient on direct selling activities.
4 Marketing efforts are misallocated among products and changes in these resource allocations (even with a constant level of overall expenditure) could bring improvements.

Similar arguments apply in relation to sales territories or customer groups as well as to products. The need exists, therefore, for control techniques to indicate the level of performance required and achieved as well as the outcome of shifting marketing efforts from one segment to another. As is to be expected, there exists great diversity in the methods by which managers attempt to obtain costs (and profits) for segments of their enterprise, but much of the cost data is inaccurate for such reasons as:

1 Marketing costs may be allocated to individual products, sales areas or customer groups on the basis of sales value or sales volume, but this involves circular reasoning. Costs should be allocated in relation to causal factors, and it is marketing expenditures that cause sales to be made rather than the other way round: managerial decisions determine marketing costs. Furthermore, despite the fact that success is so often measured in terms of sales value achievements by product line, this basis fails to evaluate the efficiency of the effort (costs) needed to produce the realized sales value (or turnover). Even a seemingly high level of turnover for a specific product may really be a case of misallocated sales effort. (An example should make this clear: if a salesman concentrates on selling product A which contributes £20 per hour of effort instead of selling product B which would contribute £50 per hour of effort, then it 'costs' the company £30 per hour he spends on selling product A. This is the *opportunity cost* of doing one thing rather than another and is a measure of the sacrifice involved in selecting only one of several alternative courses of action.)

2 General overheads and administrative costs are arbitrarily (and erroneously) allocated to segments on the basis of sales volume.

3 Many marketing costs are not allocated at all as marketing costs since they are not identified as such but are classified as manufacturing, general or administrative costs instead.

Marketing cost accounting (or analysis) has been developed to help overcome these problems and aims to:

1 Analyse the costs incurred in distributing and promoting products so that when they are combined with production cost data overall profitability can be determined.

2 Analyse the costs of marketing individual products to determine their profitability.

3 Analyse the costs involved in serving different classes of customers, different areas, etc., to determine their profitability.

4 Compute such figures as cost per sales call, cost per order, cost to put a new customer on the books, cost to hold £1's worth of inventory for a year, etc.

5 Evaluate managers according to their actual controllable cost responsibilities.

6 Evaluate alternative strategies or plans with full costs.

These analyses and evaluations provide senior management with the necessary information to enable them to decide which classes of customer to cultivate, which products to delete, which products to encourage, and so forth. Such analyses also provide a basis from which estimates can be made of the likely increases in product profitability that a specified increase in marketing effort should create. In the normal course of events it is far more difficult to predict the outcome of decisions that involve changes in marketing outlays in comparison with changes in production expenditure. It is easier, for instance, to estimate the effect of a new machine in the factory than it is to predict the impact of higher advertising outlays. Similarly, the effect on productive output of dropping a production worker is easier to estimate than the effect on the level of sales caused by a reduction in the sales force.

As an example of how productivity analysis can be applied to segments (defined as product lines for this purpose) we might consider Table 1. Table 1 shows, for a hypothetical company, the proportion of each product line's contribution to the net profit of the whole company. Most products make some net profit after their full costs are deducted from the revenues they generate. However, two products (G and H) fail to generate sufficient revenue to cover their full costs.

Table 1 Segmental profits statement

Product	% contribution to total profits
Total for all products	100.0
Profitable products:	
A	43.7
B	35.5
C	16.4
D	9.6
E	6.8
F	4.2
Sub-total	116.2
Unprofitable products:	
G	−7.5
H	−8.7
Sub-total	−16.2

The segments could equally be sales territory or customer group, and after the basic profit computation has been carried out it can be supplemented (as in Table 2) by linking it to an analysis of the effort required to produce the profit result. (Clearly this is a multivariate situation in which profit depends upon a variety of input factors, but developing valid and reliable multivariate models is both complex and expensive.) As a step in the direction of more rigorous analysis one can derive benefits from linking profit outcomes to individual inputs – such as selling time in the case of Table 2.

From Table 2 one can see that product A generates 43.7 per cent of total

286

Table 2 Segmental productivity statement

Product	% contribution to total profits	% total selling time
Total for all products	100.0	100.0
Profitable products:		
A	43.7	16.9
B	35.5	18.3
C	16.4	17.4
D	9.6	5.3
E	6.8	10.2
F	4.2	7.1
Sub-total	116.2	75.2
Unprofitable products:		
G	–7.5	9.5
H	–8.7	15.3
Sub-total	–16.2	24.8

profits, requiring only 16.9 per cent of available selling time. This is highly productive. By contrast, product E produces only 6.8 per cent of total profits but requires 10.2 per cent of selling effort. Even worse, however, is the 24.8 per cent of selling effort devoted to products G and H which are unprofitable.

A number of obvious questions arise from this type of analysis. Can the productivity of marketing activities be increased by:

1. increasing net profits proportionately more than the corresponding increase in marketing outlays?
2. increasing net profits with no change in marketing outlays?
3. increasing net profits with a decrease in marketing costs?
4. maintaining net profits at a given level but decreasing marketing costs?
5. decreasing net profits but with a proportionately greater decrease in marketing costs?

OTHER ANALYTICAL TECHNIQUES

Any model – such as Figure 4 – is a simplified representation of a more complex slice of reality. In order to make modelling useful in resource allocation decisions it is appropriate to enquire about the effects (outcomes) that result from changing the inputs (causes) to the model on a 'what if?' basis. This is known as sensitivity analysis and is one form of experimentation. It indicates the extent to which outcomes are sensitive (i.e. subject to change) in response to variations in particular inputs and which inputs can be varied and have little impact on outputs. A model's sensitivity should correspond with the sensitivity of the real-world situation and in this sense there is a link between a model's sensitivity and its validity.

In seeking to establish causal relationships by means of experimentation it is necessary to have both 'experimental' and 'control' groups representing, say, two matched samples, or two test market locations, two retail outlets, and so on. Selected stimuli (in the form of controllable inputs) will initially be identical in both the experimental situation and the control situation, but these stimuli will be selectively and systematically varied in the former while being held constant in the latter. Assuming that the uncontrolled extraneous factors (i.e. environmental inputs) vary in the same way between the experimental and control situations, the differences in observed outcomes can be wholly attributed to the changes made in the controllable variables. Let us consider the relationship between sales and advertising for a given product. We could carry out an experiment to determine the nature of this relationship by selecting two matching market situations, one of which would be the control and the other the experimental location. Initially there would be no advertising in either marketplace, but this would be gradually introduced into the experimental location only. Prior to the introduction of advertising, with all other controllable variables being identical in each location, there would have been sales levels that accorded with existing inputs, so the introduction of a new input should be the main factor in any subsequent variation in the ratio of sales in both locations (subject to the usual tests of statistical significance). In this way it is possible to build up an awareness of the manner in which particular variables (such as sales levels or profit levels) depend on other variables (such as advertising or the interaction of cost and revenue functions). Variables of the first type are termed dependent variables and those of the second type are termed independent variables: the values of independent variables can either be determined by management or emerge from an earlier interaction of variables in which we are not currently interested, and these independent variables then interact to produce the values of the dependent variables in which we are interested.

Diagrammatically, we can portray experimentation in a systems model. (See Figure 5.)

In an experiment attempts are made to identify all the factors that affect a particular independent variable, and these factors are then manipulated systematically (insofar as it is within the firm's power to do so) in order to isolate and measure their effects on the performance of the dependent variable.

It is not possible to plan or control all the conditions in which an experiment is conducted; for example, the timing, location and duration of an experiment can be predetermined, but it is necessary to measure such conditions as the weather and eliminate their effects from the results.

The independent variable that is the subject of marketing experimentation may be the demand for one of the company's various products, or one of the

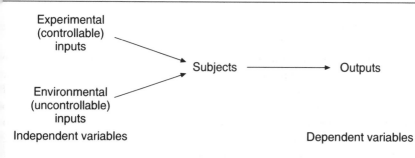

Figure 5 Experimentation

environmental factors it faces, and the dependent variable may be one of the company's objectives. Profit is a dependent variable of both the particular marketing strategy adopted and of the external conditions prevailing at the time that strategy is executed.

Because experiments are concerned with the deliberate manipulation of controllable variables (i.e. such variables as prices and advertising effort), a good deal more confidence can be placed in conclusions about the effects of such manipulations than if the effects of these changes are based purely on historical association or vague projections rather than on the basis of experimentation.

Ideas for experiments can result from marketing cost studies. The following questions are fairly representative of those that can be answered as a result of experimentation:

1 By how much (if any) would the net profit contribution of the most profitable products be increased if there were an increase in specific marketing outlays, and how would such a change affect the strategy of competitors in terms of, say, market shares?

2 By how much (if any) would the net losses of unprofitable products be reduced if there were some decrease in specific marketing outlays?

3 By how much (if any) would the profit contribution of profitable products be affected by a change in the marketing effort applied to the unprofitable products, and vice versa, and what would be the effect on the total marketing system?

4 By how much (if any) would the total profit contribution be improved if some marketing effort were diverted to profitable territories or customer groups from unprofitable territorial and customer segments?

5 By how much (if any) would the net profit contribution be increased if there were a change in the method of distributions to small unprofitable accounts or if these accounts were eliminated?

Only by actually carrying out properly designed marketing experiments can management realistically predict with an acceptable degree of certainty the effects of changes in marketing expenditure on the level of sales and profit of

289

each differentiated product, territory or customer segment in the multi-product company.

Experiments must be conducted under conditions that resemble the real-life conditions of the marketplace insofar as this is possible. It is pointless, for example, to carry out an experiment to prove that the sale of £1's worth of product X in Southampton through medium-sized retailers contributes more to profit than does the sale of £1's worth of product Y through small retailers in Leeds, if the market for product X is saturated and no reallocation of marketing resources can change the situation. This points to the danger of confusing what is happening now with what may happen in the future – ascertaining that product X is more profitable than product Y may be the right answer to the wrong question.

The style of question should be: 'What will happen to the dependent variable in the future if the independent variables are manipulated now?' If the concern is with the allocation of sales effort, the aim of an experiment may be to show how changes in the total costs of each sales team can be related to changes in the level of sales. In such a simple case, where only one type of marketing effort is being considered, this effort should be reallocated to those sales segments where an additional unit of effort will yield the highest contribution to profits.

The experiment can be designed to show which sales segment produces the highest value when the following equation is applied to each:

(Additional sales – additional variable costs)/additional expenditure

If an additional budget allocation of £1,000 to the London salesforce results in extra sales of £5,000 with additional variable costs amounting to £2,000, then the index of performance is:

$$(5,000 - 2,000)/1,000 = 3.$$

It may happen that the same index computed for the Midlands salesforce has a value of 4, in which case selling effort should be reallocated to the Midlands, provided due consideration has been given to the expected level of future demand.

As a result of the high costs involved, experiments must usually be conducted with small samples of the relevant elements. This is generally valid so long as the samples are properly determined and representative. However, it is believed by some that marketing experimentation is not a feasible means by which information can be obtained as a basis for making important decisions.

There are certainly a lot of difficulties to be overcome in planning and executing experiments, and the need to keep special records and make repeated measurements is both expensive and time-consuming. The risk is always present that the results of an experiment will not be of any value because they may not be statistically significant. A further risk is that even temporary and limited experimental variations in the marketing mix may damage sales and customer relationships both during and after the experiment.

Other problems that are involved in marketing experimentation include:

1 The measuring of short-term response when long-term response may be of greater relevance.
2 Accurate measurements are difficult to obtain – apart from the high expense involved.
3 It is almost impossible to prevent some contamination of control units by test units since it is difficult to direct variations in the marketing mix solely to individual segments.
4 Making experiments sufficiently realistic to be useful is hindered by such difficulties as the national media being less flexible than may be desired, and the fact that competitors may not react to local experimental action in the same way as they would to a national change in policy.

These problems and difficulties, while discouraging, are insufficient to discount completely the use of experimentation as a valuable means of obtaining information to increase the efficiency of marketing operations. Indeed, it is likely that the use of experimental techniques will become increasingly widespread, as has been the case with test marketing which is the best known form of experimentation in marketing.

Programming

Programming is a form of analytical modelling that is useful in allocation problems. The most widely-used technique is linear programming, which aims to determine the optimum allocation of effort in a situation involving many intereacting variables. In other words, it produces that solution which maximizes or minimizes a particular outcome in accordance with given constraints (e.g. how sales effort should be allocated among regions to maximize the level of sales subject to a maximum availability of 10,000 units of product per period, or what product mix should be sold – subject to demand – in order to give the maximum profit).

In all cases the marketing manager will be interested in making the best use of his limited resources and the constraints that exist will set the upper limit to the level of performance that is possible. The company cannot spend more on advertising each product than it has in its advertising appropriation, thus:

$$a_1 (W) + a_2 (X) + a_3 (Y) + a_4 (Z) \leq A$$

Where: $\leq$ means 'equal to or less than'
A is the total advertising appropriation
$a_1 (W)$ is the amount spent on advertising Product W
$a_2 (X)$ is the amount spent on advertising Product X
$a_3 (Y)$ is the amount spent on advertising Product Y
$a_4 (Z)$ is the amount spent on advertising Product Z

291

Similarly, a constraint exists in relation to every fixed budget or limited resource such as sales force time and warehouse space:

$$b_1(W) + b_2(X) + b_3(Y) + b_4(Z) \leq B$$

Where: B is the total available sales force time
$b_1(W)$ is the time devoted to selling product W, etc.

And:

$$c_1(W) + c_2(X) + c_3(Y) + c_4(Z) \leq C$$

Where: C equals the available warehouse space
$c_1(W)$ is the space occupied by the inventory of product W, etc.

The basis on which resources are allocated is the *marginal response*. If the expenditure on advertising of £100,000 produces sales amounting to £500,000 then the *average response* is 5/1; and if an increase in advertising expenditure of £1,000 produces additional sales totalling £10,000 this gives the measure of marginal response, which is equal to 10/1. Marginal response can thus be seen to be a measure of the value of opportunities presented.

If a company's advertising budget is set at £100,000 for a period, the optimal allocation to each of the company's products (A, B and C) is given by equating the marginal responses because this gives the situation where it will not be beneficial to reallocate funds from one product to another. The requirement is to find the best solution to the equation:

$$a_1(A) + a_2(B) + a_3(C) = £100,000$$

where $a_1(A)$ is the advertising budget for product A, $a_2(B)$ for product B, and $a_3(C)$ for product C. This is given when:

$$d\,YA/d\,XA = d\,YB/d\,XB = d\,YC/d\,XC$$

where $d\,YA/d\,XA$ is the marginal response for product A measured as change in sales/change in advertising outlay, and so on for products B and C.

Linear programming must be applied in the absence of uncertainty, which means that uncertainty must be eliminated before variables are incorporated into a linear programme. Moreover, all the relationships of problems put into a linear programming format are assumed to be linear, and this may not apply under all possible conditions. For example, costs rarely rise in direct proportion to increases in sales. But even with this discrepancy linear programming is able to indicate the best direction for allocating resources to segments. This technique can be used to determine the best (i.e. optimal) solution to allocation decisions in the following circumstances:

1   Where there is a clear, stated objective.
2   Where feasible alternative courses of action are available.

3   Where some inputs are limited (i.e. where constraints exist).
4   Where 1 and 2 can be expressed as a series of linear equations or inequalities.

DEVELOPING THE MASTER BUDGET

Most organizations are too large to permit the detailed planning of all their activities in one budget, so it becomes necessary to use a summary approach that is contained in a master budget. Essentially the master budget is a consolidated summary of all the detailed budgets showing their outcomes in terms of their contribution to overall results. Figure 6 gives one possible sequence for developing a master budget.

The sales forecast is the starting point for preparing a budget. Sales revenue, stock levels, production requirements and hence most costs and, more especially, profit, all follow from a given level of sales activity. If the sales forecast is grossly inaccurate then the entire budget plan will be wrongly balanced. A sensible approach is to acknowledge that more than one level of sales is possible, so consideration should be given to alternatives.

The sum of sales requirements plus changes in stock levels of finished goods

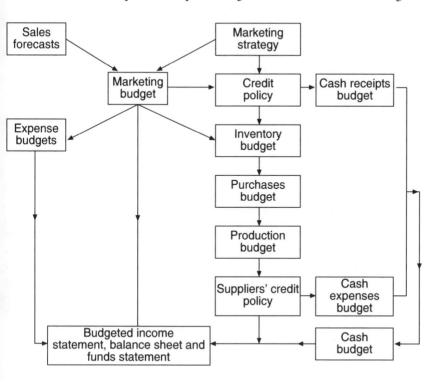

Figure 6   A sequence for budget development

293

gives the production requirements for the period being budgeted. Once it is determined, the level of productive activity becomes the starting-point for the direct materials, direct labour and indirect manufacturing costs budgets. To some extent the purchasing and manpower budgets follow from these production plans: they also depend to some extent on the purchasing and manpower requirements of other functions within the company.

A budgeted cost of sales schedule can be drawn up on the basis of the manufacturing cost of expected sales. The marketing activities necessary to achieve the expected level of sales will be budgeted in accordance with the resources and actions that are necessary to ensure that the sales forecast (in terms of volume, value and product mix) is achieved. This requires the budgeting of order-getting costs (such as advertising and selling) on the one hand, and order-filling costs (such as transport and warehousing) on the other.

Closely related to both marketing and production operations are the design and R&D functions which must be budgeted in accordance with policy requirements.

An overall administration budget can be compiled so as to include such cost-incurring items as personnel management, training, secretarial activities, general services and the directorate. Finally, a financial budget can summarize the whole package in the form of five budgeted statements:

1 Budgeted cash statement.
2 Budgeted profit and loss account.
3 Budgeted balance sheet.
4 Budgeted funds statement.
5 Capital budget.

Once the budget has been developed and implemented any deviations between actual and budgeted results will be of managerial concern for such reasons as the following:

• To highlight errors in budgeting procedures.
• To indicate the need for budget revisions.
• To pinpoint those activities requiring remedial attention.

The principles of management by exception should be applied to this process of comparison, with the focusing of attention on significant variations. However, if the budgeted level of activity differs from the actual level of activity, it will be apparent that variances of an artificial nature arise – such variances are based purely on volume rather than efficiency. This emphasizes the need for flexibility within the budgeting system: it should be able to allow for varying circumstances by recognizing and adapting to significant changes in the fundamental operating conditions of the firm. Such adaptability can be achieved by a flexible budget.

Flexible budget

In a flexible budgeting system the budget is adjusted in accordance with the level of activity experienced in the budget period. For example, a budget that is based on sales of 10,000 units during a particular period is of little value for control purposes if 12,000 units (or 8,000 units) are actually sold. The sales manager will be necessarily held responsible for the volume variance, but the level of commission, order processing/invoicing, freight and similar cost-incurring activities will tend to depend on the actual level of activity which requires that the budget be adjusted in order to show the efficient budgeted level of expenditure for the achieved level of activity.

A simple way of building a flexible budget is to start with a budget for the most likely level of activity and then to derive budgets for 5 per cent, 10 per cent, 15 per cent above and below this level.

The major advantage of the flexible budget is its ability to specify the budgeted level of costs without revision when sales and production programmes are changed. It achieves this by distinguishing between those costs that vary with changes in the level of activity and those that do not. In other words, it is based on a thorough knowledge of cost behaviour patterns.

A static budget (i.e. a fixed budget that relates to a single level of activity) can result in misleading actions. An example should make this clear: Table 3 shows the comparison of a budgeted level of 10,000 units with an actual sales level of 11,000 units. It appears that profit has improved by £300, but not all costs vary in the same way, so a flexible budget analysis is called for. This is shown in Table 4 and indicates clearly that the comparison should be between the actual level of activity and the budgeted costs, revenue and profit for that level. While profit was higher than the budgeted figure, the difference was only £20 rather than £300.

The need to distinguish fixed costs (which remain constant in total during a period) from variable costs (which remain constant per unit of output) is of paramount importance. Any costs that are neither one nor the other (i.e. semi-fixed or semi-variable expenses) can usefully be classified as mixed costs. Apart from showing the cost breakdown in some detail, Table 4 also shows the target level of activity (i.e. the fixed budget) as well as the efficiency with which the actual level of activity was attained. This information is vital to effective control.

The procedure for preparing a flexible budget is set out below, but the actual performance of the task is difficult because it must be built on a detailed analysis and understanding of cost behaviour patterns throughout the organization. In addition, there is a major educational obstacle to be overcome when first proposing to introduce flexible budgeting into an organization. All those involved in the operation must be trained to appreciate the purpose of flexible budgeting and to perform the necessary steps in the associated planning and control exercise.

295

Table 3   Fixed budget analysis

	Budget	Actual	Variance
Sales (units)	10,000	11,000	+1,000
Sales revenue	£15,000	£16,500	+£1,500
Expenditure:			
Direct	10,000	11,000	+1,000
Indirect	4,000	4,200	+200
Profit	£ 1,000	£ 1,300	+£ 300

Table 4   Flexible budget analysis

	Fixed budget	Flexible budget	Actual	Variance
Sales (units)	10,000	11,000	11,000	–
Sales revenue	£15,000	£16,500	£16,500	–
Expenditure:				
Direct	10,000	11,000	11,000	–
Fixed indirect	1,500	1,500	1,450	–50
Variable indirect	2,000	2,200	2,240	+40
Mixed indirect	500	520	510	–10
Profit	£1,000	£1,280	£1,300	+£20

Despite these major difficulties, the procedure to follow is set out in these five steps:

1   Specify the time period that is to be used. This may be, for example, daily, weekly, monthly, or four weekly, depending on the variability of the activities in question: the more variable they are, the shorter the time period should be.
2   Classify all costs into fixed, variable and mixed categories.
3   Determine the types of standards that are to be used.
4   Analyse cost behaviour patterns in response to past levels of activity. From this should come an agreed means by which a total cost figure for a given item can be accumulated at any specified level of business activity. Formulae are commonly used for this purpose: thus freight charges may be expressed as being equivalent to £500 per period plus £1.15 per unit. In this instance the fixed costs of the operation are £500 and the variable costs are £1.15 per unit, so for a sales level of 1,000 during a given period the total freight cost will be:

$$£500 + £1,150 = £1,650$$

5 Build up the appropriate flexible budget for specified levels of activity (either actual or anticipated).

SOME BEHAVIOURAL ISSUES

In many respects budgets help managers either to make sense of or give sense to organizational roles and activities. Some examples will illustrate this point.

1 Making sense of 'facts'. Budgets help managers to make sense of situations by placing particular interpretations on events, happenings and problems. For example, a report may indicate that Division A achieved sales of £500,000 in the period June–December 1994. This is a description of a state of affairs. However, we can use the budget to make another interpretation of this 'fact'. We may use it to point out that this level of sales was 50 per cent below budget which immediately colours our view of the prevailing state of affairs. By using the budget as a benchmark it is possible to assess the adequacy of a sales level of £500,000.

2 Making sense of objectives. Budgets are used to represent the aspirations of top managers within an organization and denote input–output combinations that are 'feasible' and 'desirable'. Through such representation budgets give a sense of the values and goals held by powerful individuals within organizations. In addition, changes in these values and goals will usually be reflected in budgets which play an important communications role.

3 Making sense of power and authority. Budgets give a sense of the authority and power networks within an organization by means of the top-down approach, reflecting what senior managers expect from their subordinates with respect to performance on revenue, profits, cost and other dimensions.

4 Making sense of organizational culture. Budgets are also an important means of reflecting the 'culture' or 'climate' of an organization. These concepts refer to the principal values, beliefs and social norms concerning human interaction within an organization. The culture of an organization is typically reflected in symbols, rituals, ceremonies and distinctive forms of talk, language and dress which permeate organizational life. The budget facilitates many of these characteristics.

5 Making organizations objective and orderly. Budgeted numbers and categories often exude an air of objectivity. However, this objectivity may be only skin deep for both budget numbers and categories may be manipulated to give certain impressions. For example, a sales representative might bias the estimate of next year's sales that he uses as a basis for negotiating his quota with his superior as part of 'playing the system'. Budgets also help to give a sense of order and of rational planning by their formal qualities, but it is not always the case that budgets, once compiled, are used in the control process.

In the light of these points it is possible to make a number of generalizations regarding the relationship between budgets and human behaviour in organizations:

- Budgets affect individuals' work attitudes and their level of performance.
- These individual effects are moderated or influenced by group norms, organizational and societal norms and beliefs.
- Budgets are a Janus-faced social phenomenon: there is a public, rational face and a private, political face which are both equally real and operative in organizational life.

DANGERS IN BUDGETING

Budgets drawn up along conventional (i.e. static) lines have certain fundamental drawbacks, such as:

1 They are based on assumed conditions (e.g. rates of interest) and relationships (e.g. product mix held constant) that are not varied to reflect the actual circumstances that come about.
2 They make allowance for tasks to be performed only in relation to volume rather than time.
3 They compare current costs with estimates based only on historical analyses.
4 Their short-term time horizon limits the perspective, so short-term results may be sought at the expense of longer term stability or success.
5 They have a built-in bias that tends to perpetuate inefficiencies. (For example, next year's budget is determined by increasing last year's by 15 per cent, irrespective of the efficiency factor in last year's.)
6 As with all types of budgets the game of 'beating the system' may take more energy than is being devoted to running the business.
7 The fragile internal logic of static budgets will be destroyed if top management reacts to draft budgets by requiring changes to be made to particular items which are then not reflected through the whole budget.

These typical defects are especially apparent in connection with discretionary costs, and they point strongly to the need for skill and intelligence to be exercised in tailoring a budgeting system to the particular characteristics, circumstances and requirements of each individual company.

The business environment is a dynamic one and a company must not be hindered by its budget from endeavouring to adapt to constantly changing conditions. An unduly rigid framework set up by the budgeting process can interfere with the company's well-being by preventing managers from grasping opportunities that were not predicted when the budget plan was compiled.

Conversely, of course, a budget that fails to give direction (i.e. one that is too loose rather than too rigid) cannot adequately help in coordinating corporate activities in a goal-attaining manner. Under-budgeting, which is the failure to plan ahead in a comprehensive yet flexible way, is as dangerous as over-budgeting, which is exemplified by the rigid situation suggested above in which an excessive degree of inflexibility causes the budget to become meaningless and unduly expensive.

It should be borne in mind that a budget plan represents a means to an end: it is not an end in itself. The desired end is the attainment of specified objectives. It is dangerous, therefore, to allow the budgeted targets to supersede organizational objectives. This danger can be highlighted by considering a situation in which a budget target is maintained as a major goal, irrespective of changing conditions, instead of being varied (along with other dimensions of the budget plan) in accordance with varying circumstances (subject to whatever constraints have been established) in order that the more important company objective might be achieved.

The practice whereby historical levels of expenditure are continued into succeeding periods without proper evaluation can hide – and perpetuate – inefficiencies. Past results do not necessarily reflect a desirable level of performance, so future estimates should not be based on them without a reconsideration of standards and other bases of planning by which policies are translated into numerical terms.

Finally, if budgets are used as pressure devices, the result will be resentment and thus a failure in achieving their intended purpose. One highly desirable way of overcoming suspicion and misunderstanding in budgeting is to involve all those who are concerned actively in ensuring that the company reaches its objectives – the principle of accountability planning as embodied in responsibility accounting.

FURTHER READING

Duffy, M. F. (1989) 'ZBB, MBO, PPB and their effectiveness within the planning/marketing process', *Strategic Management Journal* 10: 163–73.

Hofstede, G. H. (1968) *The Game of Budget Control*, London: Tavistock.

Mantrala, M. K., Sinha, P. and Zoltners, A. A. (1992) 'Impact of resource allocation rules on marketing investment-level decisions and profitability', *Journal of Marketing Research* 29, May: 162–75.

Mossman, F. H., Crissy, W. J. E. and Fischer, P. M. (1978) *Financial Dimensions of Marketing Management*, New York: Wiley.

Piercy, N. F. (1986) *Marketing Budgeting*, London: Croom Helm.

Piercy, N. F. (1987) *Budgeting for Marketing – Principles and Practices*, London: Allen & Unwin.

Piercy, N. F. (1988) 'The marketing budgeting process: marketing management implications', *Journal of Marketing* 52, October: 45–59.

Rayburn, L. G. (1976) *Financial Tools for Marketing Administration*, New York: Amacom.

Schiff, M. and Lewin, A. Y. (1974) *Behavioral Aspects of Accounting*, Englewood Cliffs, N.J.: Prentice-Hall.

Sevin, C. H. (1965) *Marketing Productivity Analysis*, New York: McGraw-Hill.

Shapiro, S. J. and Kirpalani, V. H. (1984) *Marketing Effectiveness: Insights from Accounting and Finance*, Boston: Allyn & Bacon.

Stasch, S. F. (1972) *Systems Analysis for Marketing Planning and Control*, Glenview, Illinois: Scott, Foresman.

Ward, K. R. (1989) *Financial Aspects of Marketing*, Oxford: Heinemann.

Wilson, R. M. S. (1981) *Financial Dimensions of Marketing: A Source Book*, vol. 1 and vol. 2, London: Macmillan.

Wilson, R. M. S. (1996) *Accounting for Marketing*, London: Academic Press.

Wilson, R. M. S. and Chua, W. F. (1993), 2nd edn, *Managerial Accounting: Method and Meaning*, London: Chapman & Hall.

Wilson, R. M. S. and Gilligan, C. T. with Pearson, D. J. (1992) *Strategic Marketing Management: Planning, Implementation and Control*, Oxford: Butterworth-Heinemann.

17

INFORMATION TECHNOLOGY AND MARKETING

Robert D. Buzzell and Rajendra S. Sisodia

INTRODUCTION

Throughout history, marketing practices and institutions have been shaped by changes in the technologies available for collecting, storing, communicating, and analysing information. To make intelligent decisions, marketing managers need accurate and timely information about sales, customers, competitors' activities, and other events in the marketplace. In this chapter we describe and evaluate trends in information technology (IT) that are affecting marketing. The evolution of IT has led to especially dramatic changes in marketing since the early 1980s. Among the key developments have been measurement of retail sales via scanning, outfitting field sales forces with laptop computers, utilization of planning software by product managers, and electronic order-entry systems.

Though these and related changes are quite recent, they represent extensions of trends that were becoming evident a generation ago. In an article in *Harvard Business Review* in 1965, John Diebold accurately foresaw many of the ways in which IT would transform managers' roles. At the same time, articles in *Business Week* (1965) and *Sales Management* (1965) described applications of computers in marketing, primarily in the areas of inventory control and salesforce reporting, while Kotler (1966) envisioned a 'marketing information and analysis centre' very much like what came to be termed in the late 1970s a '(marketing) management decision support system'.

While some marketing practitioners and scholars anticipated how IT would evolve and transform marketing practice, the changes that have taken place since the 1960s have not been easy or 'automatic'. Enormous effort, creativity, and investments have been required to realize the potential that some could envision so long ago. The changes have been cumulative, with each succeeding generation of hardware and software building on its predecessors.

In the first section of the chapter, we summarize the major developments in IT that have led to its steadily increasing use in marketing. Our review does not cover developments in mathematical modelling and methods of statistical analysis, although these analytic tools are partially dependent on IT.

In the second section, we describe and illustrate how changes in IT are affecting each of the major elements of marketing programmes: product design and development, pricing, advertising and sales promotion, sales force activities, and distribution systems. We also briefly discuss the evolution and current state of marketing decision support systems (MDSS), which aid managers in making better decisions with respect to the programme elements.

The third section explores the prospects for more fundamental modifications in marketing processes via IT-supported 'reengineering' of traditional systems.

In the fourth and concluding section, we explore prospects for future development of IT-centred applications in marketing and their implications.

KEY DEVELOPMENTS IN INFORMATION TECHNOLOGY

Increasing use of IT tools in marketing has been driven by continuing improvements in the capabilities and cost effectiveness of information processing and telecommunications systems. In both of these fields – which are rapidly converging into a single domain – the tools available to managers have become progressively more powerful, less expensive, more portable, and easier to use. In the paragraphs that follow we summarize some of the most important trends.

Trends in computer hardware and software

Processing: more powerful, smaller, and less expensive. Computer hardware systems have evolved rapidly from the earlier mainframe-based model toward one based on desktop, laptop, and notebook machines. The next step in this evolution is expected to be the Personal Digital Assistant (PDA), a hybrid device incorporating a computer, a portable telephone, and a fax machine (first-generation versions of the PDA were introduced during 1993). The development of powerful portable computers has enabled marketers to equip field sales and service personnel with greatly enhanced 'mobile computing' capabilities.

Miniaturization is also enabling manufacturers to incorporate 'computer on a chip' components into a wide variety of products. Office copiers, automobiles, appliances and other products include microprocessors that diagnose or even anticipate service requirements.

The costs of computer hardware, relative to capabilities, declined dramatically during the 1980s and early 1990s. Declining component prices reflected experience-based cost reductions as well as aggressive pricing strategies adopted by producers in order to expand their markets.

Data storage: greater capacity, easier access, lower cost. Paralleling the improvements in computer hardware, data storage capabilities are expanding and their costs are declining. Contemporary systems are designed to accommodate video images of ever-higher resolution, along with rapidly growing amounts of alphanumeric data. Compact discs (CD-ROMs) provide much greater storage capacities than earlier modes, and other technologies are also being developed.

Display: greater resolution, less bulky, and less costly. Key developments in display technology include improvements and cost reductions for so-called 'active matrix' colour liquid crystal displays (LCDs) that are used in laptop and notebook computers. Other technologies still in development include various types of flat panel displays and digital high-definition television (HDTV).

Software: easier to use, more versatile. The general adoption of graphical user interface (GUI) systems has made computers much more accessible for inexperienced users. The number and variety of applications programs, many of them specifically designed for marketing, continues to grow rapidly. Development of applications programs has been spurred, in part, by the availability of computer-assisted software engineering (CASE) and object-oriented programming tools.

Trends in telecommunications

Networks: increased capacities at lower cost. Fibre optics and digital technology are revolutionizing telecommunications networks. Telecommunications companies have already installed large amounts of fibre optic cables in their networks, and plan to extend broadband links to individual households. Concurrently, telecommunications costs have declined, due in part to privatization of state-owned systems and to the entry of new, privately-owned competing carriers.

Wireless systems: from voice to data. There has been tremendous growth in the use of wireless voice communications, and similar growth is expected in wireless data communications. Several technologies are emerging in this area, including Cellular Digital Packet Data and radio-frequency based systems.

Client-server systems and groupware

As the use of desktop and portable computers has grown, the 'architecture' of computer systems has evolved towards one in which microcomputers are linked in server-based local networks (LANs) which, in turn, are linked into wide area networks. This structure enables companies to achieve the benefits of both centralized and decentralized computing, as well as providing 'closed-circuit' communications network capabilities.

Within local and wide-area networks, there is increasing use of 'groupware', which supports collective discussion or decision-making. Teams can be assembled around specific projects, such as the Ford product development task force (see page 305). This approach will undoubtedly be more widely used in the future.

Automated information capture

An important enabling factor for the use of IT in marketing has been the development and widespread adoption of automated data collection systems. Of particular importance are bar code scanners used for measuring retail sales as well as shipments and receipts within distribution systems. A related technology is that in which magnetic stripe cards are scanned to approve credit extension and record transactions.

Electronic data interchange

A combination of several IT elements is utilized in electronic data interchange (EDI) systems. EDI is the exchange of computer data between organizations in a standard format. Efficient exchange of data requires computer systems, telecommunications networks, and (critically) standards for data format and transmission. EDI is widely used to transmit purchase orders and invoices between buyers and sellers; in some industries, such as automobiles, it has become a required method of doing business. Through 'value-added networks', EDI is now readily available to virtually all companies. As discussed later, EDI is a key element of 'channel partnerships' between buyers and sellers in a growing range of businesses.

INFORMATION TECHNOLOGY AND MARKETING PROGRAMMES

The most straightforward applications of IT in marketing are those in which IT tools are used to facilitate or improve analysis and decision-making related to the traditional elements of marketing programmes (i.e. the 'four Ps'). In this section we describe how IT is being applied to each of these areas. The changes in practice that we discuss should not be attributed solely to the adoption of IT-supported approaches; other factors, especially intensified global competition, are also influencing marketing during the 1990s.

Product design and development

Competitive pressures have stimulated managers in many companies to seek ways of accelerating and improving the methods they use to conceive, design, develop, and test new products and services. Significant applications of IT in this area include uses of computer-assisted design (CAD) systems and utilization of telecommunications among product design groups, users, and others.

CAD systems enable designers to create and readily manipulate three-dimensional images of products, which can often replace physical prototypes that are expensive and time-consuming to make. CAD systems also make it possible for designers to communicate product specifications to manufacturing, as inputs to computer-integrated manufacturing systems.

Improvements in telecommunications enable product designers in different locations to share information and coordinate their efforts by transmitting CAD images or other graphics and data. The 1994 Ford Mustang automobile, for example, was designed as a collaborative effort of design teams working in Michigan, England, and Italy (Sherman 1993).

Pricing

To the extent that utilization of IT provides managers with more accurate and more detailed marketplace information and more accurate cost data, it enables them to make better-informed pricing decisions. Data provided by scanner systems in supermarkets, for example, give consumer product marketers an improved basis for estimating the effects of price change or a temporary price reduction, taking into account the other factors affecting sales in a given time period.

A more specific application of IT to pricing that is of strategic importance in certain industries is that of 'yield management' systems. First developed by the major airlines, these systems enable managers to establish and later modify prices on the basis of past history and up-to-date reservations information for each flight. Smith, Leimkuhler, and Darrow (1992) provide a description of American Airlines' yield management system and show how it is utilized to make trade-offs between the opportunity cost of an unsold seat versus that of being unable to supply a full-fare passenger, as well as estimating the optimal level of overbooking on a given flight. Yield management systems are widely used in the hotel industry as well as by airlines. In both industries the systems have enabled companies to achieve greater average revenues per unit of capacity.

Sales force 'automation'

By the early 1980s companies that relied heavily on field sales forces had begun to experiment with using portable computers and special-purpose terminals to 'automate' sales force activities. Most of the early efforts in this area were based on special-purpose devices that enabled salespersons to enter orders from a customer location. Later, when high-capacity general purpose laptop computers became available, most companies adopted them.

In addition to order entry, IT systems are used by field salespersons for such tasks as storing customer information, scheduling, communicating with sales offices, tracking leads and enquiries, and analysing clients' problems. For large firms, equipping salespeople with computers requires a major investment: Frito-Lay, for instance, spent $40 million during 1985–6 on a system for its 10,000 route salespeople (Applegate and Wishart 1987). By the late 1980s hardware costs had declined substantially, user-friendly software was widely available, and it was clear that IT had changed the nature of field selling irrevocably. Among the benefits reported by companies that have adopted the systems are increased sales call capacity per salesperson; improved customer service; ability to roll out promotional programmes more rapidly; and reduced inventories as a result of more accurate, up-to-date information from the field.

Another impact of IT on field selling is in the area of training and product demonstrations. Videos and CDs are now widely used to communicate information about products to salespeople, dealers and users.

Advertising and promotion: micromarketing

Many of the most visible innovations in marketing practice associated with changes in IT are in the area of advertising and sales promotion. Since the 1970s there have been dramatic improvements in the databases available to marketers on individual households, businesses and institutions, and small areas. These databases are used for 'micromarketing', in which marketing programmes – especially advertising and sales promotions – are designed for and delivered to individual customers or small groups of customers. The micromarketing approach may be contrasted with mass marketing, in which standardized products and services are distributed through mass channels and supported by standardized advertising and promotion programmes.

We next discuss briefly three variations on micromarketing approaches to advertising and sales promotion: database marketing, occasion-based marketing, and local area marketing.

Database marketing

In database marketing, communications are directed to individuals, households, or organizations by name. Cespedes and Smith (1993) suggest that database marketing involves 'three Ts' – targeting messages to specific types of customers or prospects (and not others); tailoring messages to customers' interests or other characteristics; and the development of ties or long-term relationships with preferred customers.

While database marketing methods have long been employed by direct marketers such as catalogue houses and magazine publishers, improvements in IT have made the approach increasingly practical for mass marketers as well since the mid-1980s. Rapp and Collins (1990) describe numerous examples of database marketing programmes carried out by marketers of automobiles, cigarettes, alcoholic beverages, foods, personal care products, and services.

Bickert (1992) describes several types of customer databases that are used in marketing. The simplest is one that includes a company's own customers, ideally with their transaction histories. Many kinds of marketers have always had this type of information, although their ability to store and analyse the data was limited until computer systems became sufficiently inexpensive and user-friendly.

External household customer databases include customer or subscriber lists rented from direct marketers or publishers; special-purpose lists derived from public records such as automobile registrations or births; and multi-source compiled databases that are derived from a wide variety of sources. Business and institutional customer databases are derived primarily from directories, updated by periodic telephone surveys. Very large-scale databases can be stored on CD-ROMs and utilized on desktop computers or local area networks, making database marketing much easier to implement than in the past.

Occasion-based marketing

Another form of marketing communication made possible by improvements in IT is related to specific 'occasions' such as passing through a supermarket checkout lane or using an automatic teller machine. A system attached to the checkout scanner, for example, can be programmed to issue a coupon based on a shopper's purchase of the sponsor's brand or a competing brand. Other in-store systems have been tested that deliver promotional messages on a video screen attached to a shopping cart, based on the shopper's location in the store.

Local area marketing

The third form of micromarketing involves the targeting and tailoring of advertising and sales promotions to small groups of customers, or distribution outlets serving these groups, on the basis of their geographic location. In the USA this approach was first developed after the results of the 1970 Census of Population were provided on computer tapes. Several commercial firms use the Census data, supplemented by other sources, as the basis for so-called 'geodemographic' systems in which the households residing in each of many small areas are assigned to one of forty to fifty cluster types, based on demographic indicators of their lifestyles. An individual household in a given area can then be 'geocoded' and treated as if its characteristics conformed to the area's averages.

Major uses of geographic customer databases in marketing include retail store location analysis, sales territory and salesperson performance analysis, design of direct mail and telemarketing communications programmes, and design of promotional programmes for individual stores or distributors serving a given area (for examples, see Baker and Baker 1993; Castle 1993).

307

Privacy issues

Increasing use of micromarketing methods has led to growing concern about privacy issues. A 1992 survey, for example, showed that 78 per cent of US consumers were concerned about threats to personal privacy (Equifax 1992). While marketers were not the only source of these concerns, the growth in consumer databases was clearly a major factor leading to public concern and proposals for additional regulation. In 1990, when computer software producer Lotus Development announced plans to market a CD–ROM containing data on 80 million households derived in part from their credit bureau records, there was public uproar. Lotus responded by withdrawing the product, and Equifax, the credit rating agency, later discontinued sales of its data to marketers.

For some observers, unwanted telemarketing calls and faxes constituted another form of invasion of privacy; this type of communication was regulated by the Telephone Consumer Protection Act of 1991 and by various state laws. As of late 1993, there were numerous proposals for additional federal and state legislation to protect consumers' privacy. Most European countries had more stringent regulations on uses of mailing lists and telemarketing than those prevailing in the USA. Bennett (1992) summarizes the common principles of the European countries' laws, including limitations on data collection and use, security requirements, and consumer rights to access and correct their records.

Micromarketing outside North America

Most of the IT tools used to implement the various forms of micromarketing in North America were equally available to marketers in other countries. Despite this, micromarketing methods were much less widely used in Europe and Japan as of 1993 (Petrison et al. 1993). Among the obstacles to the growth of micromarketing in Japan, for example, were the lack of a standardized address system; the difficulty of coding names in Kanji characters; and regulations limiting the use of directories and lists. Despite these and similar barriers, it was expected that the use of micromarketing programmes would grow in all advanced economies in the future.

Distribution channels

Adoption of new IT-based tools has affected distribution channels in two principal ways: first, by enabling more marketers to distribute their products and services directly to end users; and second, by facilitating the formation of partnerships between vendors and customers in traditional channel systems. The latter is discussed in the section on reengineering marketing processes.

Growth in direct marketing

Advances in IT have greatly expanded the scope of direct marketing, once the almost exclusive province of mail order houses, charities, publishers, and other specialized marketers. Many mainstream marketers in both consumer and business-to-business industries have added direct marketing to their existing distribution methods, while others rely on it exclusively. Often, but not always, direct distribution is used in conjunction with database marketing programmes of the kinds described in the preceding section.

An integral element of many direct marketing systems is the use of toll-free (800 number) long-distance calling facilities, which were first introduced in the USA in 1967. Another key factor has been the rapid spread of credit card ownership, beginning in the 1970s (Sheperdson 1991). Other improvements in telecommunications that facilitate direct marketing include (Deloitte and Touche 1990):

- Growth in automatic number identification (ANI) and telephone channel capacities. ANI allows a telemarketer to match an incoming caller's identity to a customer database.
- Caller-paid (900) services.
- Interactive voice response (IVR) systems, in which callers hear a recorded menu and select from it by entering numbers on their touch-tone telephones.

Major users of direct marketing channels, in addition to traditional direct marketers, include insurance companies, long-distance carriers, major retailers and microcomputer hardware and software vendors.

No doubt the most far-reaching impact of IT on distribution channels, at least prospectively, will be via the creation of electronic marketplaces, especially home shopping systems. Cable TV-based home shopping networks play this role in a limited way already. Many believe that eventually interactive home systems will become a major form of distribution for a wide variety of goods and services. This is already the case in France where the Teletel system, which features numerous shopping and other services, had 5.6 million subscribers by 1990 (Marchand 1988). Although efforts to develop similar systems began even earlier in Great Britain (Prestel) and Germany (BTX), neither of these had reached critical mass as of 1993.

In the USA, despite numerous field tests, home shopping systems were still of minor significance in late 1993. The largest home system, CUC International's 'Shopper's Advantage', had 3.3 million subscribers (Bell 1993). It was generally expected that telephone and cable television companies would continue their efforts to develop home systems in the future, in some cases via strategic alliances and mergers.

Marketing decision support systems

The use of computer supported decision-making in marketing started in the 1960s with a focus on simulation models. The use of computers almost exclusively followed the model-building/optimization lines of research (Montgomery and Urban 1969; Kotler 1971). During the 1970s IT applications dealt primarily with improvements in marketing information systems designed to provide standardized reports to marketing managers within large firms (Choffray and Lilien 1986). Attention also centred on database management systems. The quality and availability of data were key issues in decision-making and greater attention was being given to measurement techniques. From these techniques the focus gradually shifted to managerial problem-solving and decision-making. There was an emerging trend of support systems for managers in the late 1970s which stressed that a problem-solving technology was emerging that consisted of 'people and knowledge and software and hardware . . . successfully woven into the management process' (Keen and Scott-Morton 1978).

Little (1979) suggested the need to shift from status reporting (e.g. sales, market shares) to response analysis (e.g. price and advertising elasticities). This placed greater emphasis on the embedded models and analysis tools rather than on mere reporting of data aggregated in various ways. He defined a marketing decision support system (MDSS) as:

> a co-ordinated collection of data, systems, tools and techniques with supporting software and hardware by which an organisation gathers and interprets relevant information from business and environment and turns it into a basis for marketing action.
>
> (Little 1979)

For a detailed treatment of marketing models and decision support systems see Lilien, Kotler and Moorthy (1992).

In the early 1980s Information Resources Incorporated began to popularize the optical scanner as a data collection device. It had been in use primarily as a means of speeding up store operations. This provided marketers with a large volume of timely, highly accurate data that was complete in most essential respects for the consumer packaged-goods industry. This has led, since the mid-1980s, to renewed efforts at data reduction through the greater automation of data analysis. A number of expert systems have been developed which address this need.

Expert systems for marketing

Expert systems are designed to emulate the processes used by human experts to analyse complex problems in relatively narrow domains. Starting in the later 1980s many companies came to recognize the value of expert systems to improve marketing decision-making (see Rangaswamy et al. 1987; Sisodia 1992). Some have developed expert systems around small, well-defined problems, using expert system 'shells' (relatively inexpensive and easy-to-use development tools). Other companies have incorporated intelligence into their marketing decision support systems, facilitated by the efforts of major vendors such as Information Resources Incorporated and A. C. Nielsen. The former, for example, provides systems such as PROMOTER (for the evaluation of sales promotions) (Abraham and Lodish 1987) and COVERSTORY (for the automated interpretation of scanner-derived data) (Schmitz, Armstrong and Little 1990). The latter sifts through scanner data and performs 'smart exception reporting' in the form of a brief memo giving the marketing manager the 'headlines' it was able to extract from the data.

Many companies (such as DuPont and Digital Equipment Corporation) utilize expert systems to assist in their selling efforts. Often, the expert system can provide detailed product knowledge which a salesperson may lack. Other systems are used to improve the performance of novice salespeople by providing them with the knowledge of expert colleagues. Pricing expert systems are used to generate quotes for custom orders and to assist in bidding for contracts. Expert systems are also being developed to assist in the more creative aspects of marketing, such as advertising development (Burke et al. 1990).

Most marketing applications of expert systems thus far have used rule-based approaches. Some companies are beginning to experiment with an alternative approach which utilizes *neural networks*, which are based on pattern recognition and learning. For example, some mail order companies use such systems to identify likely buyers on their mailing lists.

REENGINEERING MARKETING
PROCESSES

As business investments in IT grew steadily during the 1980s and early 1990s, many companies began exploring ways to increase the benefits they derived from these investments. Companies came to realize that, rather than using IT to automate existing methods of doing business, they could use the capabilities it provided to create new processes. This realization has impelled the burgeoning 'process reengineering' movement.

The term 'reengineering' was popularized during the late 1980s by Michael Hammer and his collaborators at the CSC Index consulting group (Hammer and Champy 1993). Hammer defines reengineering as 'the fundamental rethinking and radical redesign of business processes to achieve dramatic improvements in critical, contemporary measures of performance such as cost, quality, service, and speed' (1993: 32). Other terms used to designate process analysis and redesign include 'core process redesign' and 'process innovation' (Davenport 1993). All versions of the approach focus on processes, which Davenport defines as 'specific ordering(s) of work activities across time and place, with a beginning, an end, and clearly identified inputs and outputs' (1993: 5). Examples of processes include product development and customer acquisition. Most important business processes include activities carried out by two or more functional departments; as a result, reengineering can seldom be implemented solely within the marketing component of an organization.

Companies in a variety of industries have reportedly achieved significant performance improvements through process redesign. While process reengineering has thus far had less impact on marketing than on some other business functions, some progress has been made. Two areas in which the reengineering approach has been applied are new product development and distribution channel partnerships.

New product development

In most companies new product development is a process that involves marketing, research and development, and operations management personnel. The process is typically slow, costly, and subject to considerable uncertainty. According to Wheelwright and Clark (1992), rapid and effective new product development is increasingly the focal point of competition in many industries. Thus there are strong incentives to improve the new product development process, and some companies have made significant gains in cycle times and development costs via reengineering. One major apparel manufacturer, for instance, was able to reduce the time required for seasonal product line development by one-third (Buzzell 1993). Davenport cites similar improvements achieved by manufacturers of automobiles, power tools, pharmaceuticals, and photographic equipment. Johanasson *et al.* (1993) describe in some detail how AT&T's Power Systems Division simplified the design process for a customized product line. They also provide a step-by-step procedure for process analysis.

Channel partnerships

As noted earlier, many buyers and sellers are utilizing electronic data interchange for communication of orders, invoices, and other information. In some cases EDI serves as the foundation for 'channel partnerships' between suppliers and retailers or distributors. Buzzell and Ortmeyer (1994) define a channel partnership as 'an ongoing, non-exclusive relationship between a retailer and an independent supplier in which the parties agree on objectives, policies, and procedures for ordering and physical distribution of the supplier's products'.

One of the earliest and most widely-discussed channel partnerships was that established between Wal-Mart and Procter and Gamble in 1985 (Index Alliance 1991). Key elements of the partnership, widely emulated since by other retailers and suppliers, included:

- Frequent transmission via EDI of point-of-sale sales data, by stockkeeping unit, for the supplier's products in each of the retailer's stores.
- Agreement on a 'model stock' of the supplier's products to be displayed in each retail store.
- Authorization by the retailer for automatic replenishment of retail stocks by the supplier.
- Utilization of advance shipping notice (via EDI) and bar-coded shipping container marking to facilitate scheduling and handling of incoming shipments to stores and/or distribution centres.

A primary objective of channel partnerships is to synchronize supplier shipments and, ultimately, production, more closely with final customer demand. This is accomplished, first, by providing timely, detailed retail sales data to the supplier and second, by simplifying the processes used for ordering and physical distribution of products in the channel system. The ordering and physical distribution process is reengineered in several ways:

- IT is used to automate manual activities, including recording of sales, shipments, and receipts via scanning.
- Redundancies, such as entry of order information by both retailer and supplier, are reduced or eliminated.
- Some tasks, such as ticketing merchandise, are reassigned from one partner to the other to improve efficiency.
- Some control steps, such as checking the content and quality of incoming shipments, are eliminated or reduced to a sampling basis.

Channel partnerships have been widely adopted between retailers and domestic American apparel manufacturers, and between the latter and their upstream textile suppliers. Outside the apparel industry, channel partnerships have also been adopted by suppliers and retailers in such diverse product categories as housewares, personal care products, home furnishings and major appliances. A similar approach, called 'Efficient Consumer Response', has been advocated for the food industry (Kurt Salmon Associates 1993).

The channel partnership approach is not confined to consumer products: similar approaches have been adopted in hospital supply distribution and other business-to-business markets (Index Alliance 1991).

INFORMATION TECHNOLOGY AND THE FUTURE OF MARKETING

Several organizational changes have already been observed as a result of the use of advanced information technologies in marketing and its adjacent business functions. Some of these are:

- *Flattening of structures*: as with other functional areas, marketing is being affected by reductions in middle management ranks.

313

- *Decentralization of marketing activities*: more marketing decisions are now being made by front-line (i.e. customer contact) personnel empowered with information tools. In some companies, regional sales offices are taking over many marketing tasks.
- *Greater use of cross-functional teams*: some companies have reorganized their marketing divisions into customer-centred teams, which go beyond major account management in that they include personnel from other functional areas.

Looking to the future, two trends are apparent. First, the quality and quantity of marketing data is now such that its mere possession does not confer any competitive advantage. More important today is the quality of a company's knowledge bases (i.e. its ability to utilize its best knowledge and capabilities in every decision-making situation). Knowledge-based systems will thus become more important in the future.

Second, marketing practices will probably be significantly impacted by the development of an upgraded computing and communication infrastructure extending into the homes of individual consumers. This system is expected to be interactive (i.e. it will allow for two-way communication) and broadband (it will readily handle video, audio and other forms of information).

Marketing may be profoundly affected by this 'information highway'. Companies will be able to target more precisely their advertising, sales promotion, and personal selling efforts. They will be able to ease time and place constraints on consumers by enabling 'any time, any place' access to their offerings, and facilitating the direct delivery of goods and services. The electronic distribution channel represented by the network may be used to deliver a wider range of services.

If these changes come to pass, retailing will be broadly impacted in the process. Some retailers are already planning interactive shopping systems. For a discussion of some of the characteristics of a future information-based 'mall', see Sheth and Sisodia (1993). Marketing in this environment will involve the 'monocasting' or 'pointcasting' of communications, a high degree of customer involvement, and far greater integration between marketing and operations to deliver more customized products. It will also result in a more efficient use of marketing resources, reduced customer alienation resulting from misapplied marketing stimuli, and increased pressure to deliver greater value.

Advanced technologies allow for the creation of natural user interfaces that are likely to make future systems far more accessible to consumers than videotext systems. For example, virtual reality is a fast-improving technology that enables users to interact with computers in a natural, three-dimensional mode. While enhancing convenience, such systems will also enable buyers to make more informed purchases, since they will get immediate access to a variety of information sources.

CONCLUSION

The marketing function has made rapid strides in its use of IT capabilities. However, the potential exists for many more changes in coming years. More than all other business functions, marketing deals with variables that are intangible and difficult to measure and control. The challenge to the marketing profession has been to achieve greater precision in how it manages and measures these variables, and thus more accountability in how it expends resources on them. The use of proven marketing models, better data capture and analysis tools, and micromarketing approaches have allowed marketing to make some progress on these fronts.

Notwithstanding, the pressures on marketing remain great. Firms today spend proportionately more on the marketing function than they did in the past, as they have successfully removed many inefficiencies from other areas. Through the judicious use of IT, the marketing function can continue to increase its efficiency and effectiveness.

REFERENCES

Abraham, M. M. and Lodish, L. M. (1987) 'PROMOTER: an automated promotion evaluation system', *Marketing Science* 6, Spring: 101–23.

Applegate, L. and Wishart, N. A. (1987) *Frito-Lay, Inc.: a strategic transition (B)*, Boston: Harvard Business School Publishing Division.

Baker, S. and Baker, K. (1993) *Market Mapping*, New York: McGraw-Hill, Inc.

Bell, C. J. (1993) 'CUC International: Shoppers Advantage', Case No. 594–027, Boston: Harvard Business School Publishing Division.

Bennett, C. J. (1992) *Regulating Privacy*, Ithaca, NY: Cornell University Press.

Bickert, J. (1992) 'Database marketing: an overview' in E. L. Nash (ed.) *The Direct Marketing Handbook*, 2nd edn, New York: McGraw-Hill.

Burke, R. R., Rangaswamy, A., Wind, J. and Eliashberg, J. (1990) 'A knowledge-based system for advertising design', *Marketing Science* 9 (3): 212–29.

Business Week Special Report (1965) 'Computers begin to solve the marketing puzzle', 7 April.

Buzzell, R. D. and Ortmeyer, G. (1994) 'Channel partnerships: a new approach to streamlining distribution', Marketing Science Institute Working Paper. Cambridge, Massachusetts: Marketing Science Institute.

Castle, G. H. (ed.) (1993) *Profiting From a Geographic Information System*, Fort Collins, CO: GIS World, Inc.

Cespedes, F. V. and Smith, H. J. (1993) 'Database marketing: new rules for policy and practice', *Sloan Management Review* 34 (1): 7–22.

Choffray, J. M. and Lilien, G. L. (1986) 'A decision support system for evaluating sales prospects and launch strategies for new industrial products', *Industrial Marketing Management* 15: 75–85.

Davenport, T. H. (1993) *Process Innovation: Reengineering Work Through Information Technology*, Boston: Harvard Business School Press.

Deloitte and Touche (1990) 'A special report on the impact of technology on direct marketing in the 1990s', New York: Direct Marketing Association.

Diebold, J. (1965) 'What's ahead in information technology', *Harvard Business Review* 43 (5), September–October.

Equifax (1992) 'Harris-Equifax consumer privacy survey 1992', Atlanta: Equifax.

Hammer, M. and Champy, J. (1993) *Reengineering the Corporation*, New York: Harper Business.

Index Alliance (1991) 'Channel partnerships: an investigation', Cambridge, MA: CSC Index Inc.: 28–31.

Johansson, H. J., McHugh, P., Pendlebury, A. J. and Wheller, W. A., III (1993) *Business Process Reengineering: Break Point Strategies for Market Dominance*, New York: John Wiley & Sons.

Keen, P. and Scott-Morton, M. (1978) *Decision Support Systems: An Organisational Perspective*, Reading, MA: Addison-Wesley.

Kotler, P. (1966) 'A design for the firm's marketing's nerve center', *Business Horizons* 9 (3): 63–74.

Kotler, P. (1971) *Marketing Decision Making: A Model Building Approach*, New York: Holt, Rinehart and Winston.

Kurt Salmon Associates (1993) *Efficient Consumer Response: Enhancing Consumer Value in the Grocery Industry*, Washington D.C.: Food Marketing Institute.

Little, J. D. C. (1979) 'Decision support systems for marketing managers', *Journal of Marketing* 43 (3): 9–27.

Marchand, M. (1988) *The Minitel Saga*, Paris: Larousse.

Montgomery, D. B. and Urban, G. L. (1969) *Management Science in Marketing*, Englewood Cliffs, NJ: Prentice Hall.

Rangaswamy, A., Burke, R. R., Wind, J. and Eliashberg, J. (1987) 'Expert systems for marketing', Working Paper No. 87–107. Cambridge, MA: Marketing Science Institute.

Rapp, S. and Collins, T. (1990) *The Great Marketing Turnaround*, Englewood Cliffs, NJ: Prentice Hall.

Sales Management (1967) 'Some day, I'm going to have a little black box on my desk', 1 May (33ff).

Schmitz, J. D., Armstrong, G. D. and Little, J. D. C. (1990) 'COVERSTORY: automated news finding in marketing', *Interfaces* 20 (6) November–December: 29–38.

Sheperdson, N. (1991) 'Credit card America', *American Heritage*: 125–32.

Sherman, S. (1993) 'How to bolster the bottom line,' *Fortune* 128 (7): 14–28.

Sheth, J. N. and Sisodia, R. S. (1993) 'The information mall', *Telecommunications Policy* July: 376–89.

Sisodia, R. S. (1992) 'Expert marketing with expert systems', *Marketing Management* Spring: 32–47.

Smith, B. C., Leimkuhler, J. F. and Darrow, R. M. (1992) 'Yield management at American Airlines', *Interfaces* 22 (1): 8–31.

Wheelwright, S. C. and Clark, K. B. (1992) 'Creating project plans to focus product development', *Harvard Business Review* 70 (2) March–April: 70–82.

FURTHER READING

Blattberg, R. C., Glazer, R. and Little, J. D. C. (1994) *The Marketing Information Revolution*. Boston, MA: Harvard Business School Press.

Buzzell, R. D. (1993) 'Vanity Fair Mills: market response system', Boston: Harvard Business School Publishing Division.

Hammer, M. (1990) 'Reengineering work: don't automate, obliterate', *Harvard Business Review* 90 (4): 104–12.

Hammond, J. (1993) 'Quick response in retail/manufacturing channels', in S. B. Bradley, J. A. Hausman and R. L. Nolan (eds) *Globalization, Technology and*

Competition, Boston: Harvard Business School Press.
Lilien, G., Kotler, P. and Moorthy, S. K. (1992) *Marketing Models*, Englewood Cliffs, NJ: Prentice Hall.
Petrison, L. A., Blattberg, R. C. and Wang, P. (1993) 'Database marketing: past, present and future', *Journal of Direct Marketing* 7 (3): 27–43.

18

ENVIRONMENTAL ANALYSIS

Douglas Brownlie

INTRODUCTION

This chapter sets out to show why it is important for organizations to take a formal and systematic approach to environmental analysis. It goes on to describe such an approach and to set out how it can be used by corporate and marketing strategist alike; what benefits it brings to practising firms; what management problems are likely to be encountered; and how possibly to surmount them.

First considerations

Firms and other commercial organizations owe their existence to the market environment. Like people they are creatures of their environment and they too spend much of their life learning how to cope with the complexity, unforeseen traumas, vagaries and opportunities generated by their environment. Survival and prosperity are conditioned by the demands imposed by this environment. Thus, in the midst of an environment where frequent and major change is becoming the rule, firms must stay at the forefront of trends and issues which will affect their markets and their positions within them.

The market environment consists of the external forces that directly or indirectly influence the firms' goals, structure, plans, procedures, operations, performance, and so on. Environmental analysis is the study of these forces; the relationship between them; and their effects and potential impact on the organization.

The term environmental analysis is often used interchangeably with others such as environmental scanning, competitive intelligence gathering, external search, environmental surveillance and strategic marketing information retrieval. I use the term environmental scanning to encompass the varied information gathering, analysis and dissemination activities that firms pursue in order to keep up to date with changes in the market environment. Clearly the purpose of those activities is not merely to keep track of environmental changes.

Without environmental analysis and forecasting, there is no basis for strategic planning. Environmental scanning involves activities ranging from highly structured and regularly conducted reviews and forecasts of major trends, issues and events in the business environment, to the irregular 'tip' acquired by means of insider access to a network of private and personal contacts; by reverse engineering competitors' products; by monitoring activity at trade shows and conferences; by obtaining information from employees who used to work for competitors; or even by means of espionage.

Environmental scanning is responsible not only for generating an up-to-date database of information on the changing business scene. It also has the job of alerting management to what is happening in the marketplace, the industry and beyond by disseminating important information and analyses to key strategic decision-makers and influencers. However, the conversion of the awareness such dissemination will create into interest, and ultimately to some form of action, is a political process both overt and covert which can emasculate the most penetrating analyses – particularly where vested interests are threatened and top management support absent. It is widely appreciated that the realization of a marketing orientation is, in practice, often inhibited, not by failures of the systems, technology or methodologies of marketing, of which environmental analysis is one, but by disabling management attitudes which often express themselves as resistance to change, conservatism, suspicion and prevarication.

The tasks of gathering, analysing and disseminating information are often organized as discrete activities. The environmental analyst is likely to be a member of the corporate or marketing planning staff, or a top management aid (i.e. a decision influencer), but rarely a strategic decision-maker. Strategic decision-makers will place their own interpretations on what the expert analyst has to say. In the absence of any other intelligence gathering activity, environmental scanners will, by means of the perceived importance of the information they generate, be in an enviable position to influence strategic decision-makers' perceptions of the firm's competitive position and the options available to it. Students of history will recognize that many a bloody political intrigue was spawned by the jealously guarded and often misused privilege of proximity to the seat of power which was conferred on privy counsellors and advisors. Thus, in addition to the analytical skills demanded of environmental scanners, political skills are also important.

Management attitudes have a vital role to play in creating an organizational climate that enables the firm to operate an 'open window of perception' on the past, present and prospective business scene. Readers should understand that the methodology of environmental scanning is no simple panacea for the problems of understanding and coping with the increasingly competitive and turbulent environment of the 1990s. Methodology alone will not guarantee success and is less important than the thinking it stimulates. Methodologies can be implanted and replicated with much less difficulty than can attitudes or ways of thinking.

319

The contribution of environmental scanning

Whatever is achieved by environmental scanning will largely depend on the firm's needs and expectations. Small firms may require to be kept up to date with local regulatory and economic trends likely to have an immediate impact on day-to-day business prospects. Larger organizations will share the requirements of the small firm, but will also expect information that is broader in scope and with an orientation to the future.

Corporate level environmental scanning is likely to be charged with the responsibility of monitoring, interpreting and forecasting issues, trends and events that go far beyond the customer, market and competitive analyses which most firms perform as a matter of routine. In this context, environmental scanning will be expected to provide a broad but penetrating view of possible future changes in the demographic, social, cultural, political, technological and economic elements of the business environment. The idea is to arm strategic decision-makers with the information, analyses and forecasts they consider pertinent to the formulation of the strategies and plans. It should also provide a basis for questioning the assumptions that underpin the firm's strategic thinking and for generating new assumptions. The payoffs from formal environmental scanning can be summarized as follows:

1   Increased awareness by management of environmental changes.
2   More effective strategic planning and decision-making.
3   Greater effectiveness in governmental and legislative matters.
4   More informative and insightful industry and market analyses.
5   Improved results in foreign businesses.
6   Improvements in resource allocation.
7   More effective representation of company policies in public fora.

The scope of environmental scanning

The ability to exercise control in the firm's current product markets is derived, at least partly, from a comprehensive and reliable knowledge of customers, suppliers, competitors, regulators and investors. The successful development and upkeep of this knowledge-base is the principal task of formal environmental scanning – one to which the functions of marketing, R&D, purchasing, sales and finance can make a major contribution. However, in the long term it must do more. For instance, as the firm looks away from its existing product markets for future growth opportunities or acquisition candidates within and without its current sphere of operation, knowledge will be required of a new and unfamiliar business environment, having its own unique set of technological, economic, political and social trends. In so doing, greater demands will be made of environmental scanning.

The environment of the firm can be defined as 'those factors which are outside its control but which determine, in part, how the firm performs'. The market environment includes all those factors that exert any influence on the firm, whether directly or indirectly. Given such an unbounded definition you could argue that the rest of the world then constitutes the firm's business environment. Clearly to take such a broad view is of little practical value. The task of environmental scanning is made manageable by taking a selective and carefully considered view of the environment. It will eliminate much of the rest of the world from the firm's immediate attention.

The breadth of the view an organization chooses to take of its business environment has implications for the complexity of the tasks of environmental analysis and forecasting and thus its resource requirements. A broadly defined business mission is associated with a diversified, multi-product, multi-market firm. It would involve environmental scanning in a very broad arena of operation from which a perspective on international political and economic issues, events and trends may be called for by corporate planning. On the other hand, a narrowly defined business mission may focus the efforts of environmental scanning more on domestic issues concerning immediate events and trends in proximate product markets. Yet the firm's environmental scanning activities should cover as many relevant aspects of the business environment as available resources will permit, particularly those aspects which have an impact on the assumptions being used by the firm in its strategic planning and decision-making.

The boundaries of the market environment must be structured in such a way to enable the analyst to identify important from less important factors and to determine an appropriate time-scale for forecasting changes. One would expect there to be factors that deserve to be continuously monitored because of their immediate impact on the industry. These would include users, distributors, suppliers, competitors for customers and suppliers, workforce, government regulators, trade unions, product and process developments. The origin of such factors is known as the 'task environment'. It is defined as 'the more specific forces which are relevant to decision-making and change processes of individual organizations'.

The concept of the task environment draws the environmental scanner's eye to the immediate product and supply markets and to those factors which influence the organization's position within them. A wider view casts attention towards the remote areas of community and institutions where developments could be under way which in the longer term would impinge on the firm's position in its current product and supply markets. For instance, substitute products and processes often originate as spin-offs from technological developments that have been made by firms outwith the task environment. Clearly it is important then to look further afield than the task environment. Kast and Rosenweig (1974) divide the wider market environment into nine areas for study and analysis (see Table 1).

Table 2 outlines some of the broad social issues that firms might expect to impinge on their European activities in the 1990s. Environmental scanning would be expected to follow developments of these issues.

Table 1 Framework for analysis of the wider business environment

Cultural	Including the historical background, ideologies, values and norms of the society. Views on authority relationships, leadership patterns, interpersonal relationships, nationalism, science and technology.
Technological	The level of scientific and technological advancement in society. Including the physical base (plant, equipment, facilities) and the knowledge base of technology. Degree to which the scientific and technological community is able to develop new knowledge and apply it.
Educational	The general literacy level of the population. The degree of sophistication and specialization in the educational system. The proportion of the people with a high level of professional and/or specialized training.
Political	The general political climate of society. The degree of concentration of political power. The nature of political organization (degrees of decentralization, diversity of functions). The political party system.
Legal	Constitutional considerations, nature of legal system, jurisdictions of various governmental units. Specific laws concerning formation, taxation, and control of organizations.
Natural resources	The nature, quantity and availability of natural resources, including climatic and other conditions.
Demographic	The nature of human resources available to the society; their number, distribution, age and sex. Concentration or urbanization of population is a characteristic of industrialized societies.
Sociological	Class structure and mobility. Definition of social roles. Nature of social organization and development of social institutions.
Economic	General economic framework, including the type of economic organization – private versus public ownership; the centralization or decentralization of economic planning; the banking system; and fiscal policies. The level of investment in physical resources and consumption.

Source: Kast and Rosenweig (1974)

Table 2 Key international social issues for the 1990s

Issues	Characteristics
Low economic growth	Political instability; rising energy costs; growing unemployment; growth in international capital flows; trends to international protectionism if GATT fails; decline of basic industries; rising inflation; shortages of basic materials; falling productivity; emergence of new market economies of Eastern Europe and Far East trading blocks; increasing national indebtedness and monetary growth; falling investment.
Political uncertainty	Political fragmentation in Europe; expansion of EC; trend towards decentralizing government; growth in terrorism and armed conflict; failure of foreign and international trade policy; rise of nationalism/tribalism; regional convergence on trade and investment policy; decline of liberal democratic values; urban conflict.
Rise of the multi-locals	Large firms decentralize, downsize and form loose federations by devolving responsibility to autonomous units; growth in smaller enterprises; more cross-border networks/partnerships.
Environmentalism	Growing influence of environmentalist lobby; worldwide enactment of legislation on pollution and product liability; closer scrutiny of firms' environmental track record; growth in environmental audit requirements.
Lobby politics	Rising power and influence of lobby groups on issues such as gender, age, consumer protection, health, housing, pollution, materialism, consumer choice, representation, social responsibility, race, poverty, discrimination, access to education.
Growth of government	Closer EC and NAFTA integration and convergence brings with it more bureaucracy and democratic institutions.
Accountability and participation	Demands for greater accountability and transparency in the activities and decisions of government; greater access to local government and participation in it; greater access to information; more disclosure of information and scrutiny of decisions and activities.

INFORMATION NEEDS

Organizations subject themselves to the inconvenience and expense of strategic planning in order to acquire more control over the outcome of any chosen course of action. Thus, in accordance with Francis Bacon's dictum that 'knowledge itself is power', it could be argued that a knowledge of the business environment must precede the acquisition of any degree of control over it.

The reader is likely to have witnessed the popularization of terms such as espionage, infiltration, moles, security leaks, early warning, electronic surveillance, counter-intelligence, insider dealing, and the like. Although evocative of the anxiety and duplicity of our age, the popularization of the vocabulary of the spy lends some credence to the view that the possession of information is itself a factor endowment, and as such it should be treated as a valuable national asset. It is only one small but logical step to argue that since the gathering of information precedes its possession and dissemination, then this activity also contributes to the generation of wealth.

To the student of military strategy this view follows a familiar line of thought. History offers many examples of battles which could be said to have been fought and won on the basis of 'superior' information. In planning the deployment and employment of their armies' resources, generals rely on the intelligence provided by lines of communications which may have a political origin in their own state, but will certainly infiltrate enemy territory and institutions. By means of the intelligence so provided the general hopes to prepare himself better for the ensuing conflict and to enhance the likelihood of his victory (i.e. to gain some control over the outcome of the conflict).

In the corporate context the tasks of intelligence gathering, surveillance and monitoring are overseen by environmental scanning. The lines of communications are managed to allow a flow of information to be maintained between important elements of the business environment, the environmental scanners and the firm's strategic decision-makers. As in the military context, the corporate intelligence service will also provide early warning and careful tracking of possible environmental threats in order that a timely response is conceived and executed. Table 3 indicates corporate sources of information on the business environment. Table 4 comments on their relative importance.

Table 4 also suggests that to enhance the impact of the work of environmental scanning it should seek both the support and involvement of top management in order to implicate or consult all key decision-makers and influencers at corporate and divisional level.

In recent years the emergence of information technology has encouraged firms carefully to reexamine the purpose, structure, productivity and accessibility of their management information systems, including those governing elements of the business environment. The outcome has often been to reorganize databases and to systematize the tasks of collecting, analysing and disseminating information on the business environment. The demanding task of

Table 3 Sources of information on the business environment

Location	Types	Sources of information on business environment
Inside the company	Written	Internal reports and memos, planning documents, market research, MIS.
	Verbal	Researchers, sales force, marketing, purchasing, advisors, planners, board.
	Combination	Formal and informal meetings (e.g. working parties, advisory committees).
Outside the company	Written	Annual reports, investment reports, trade association publications, institute yearbooks, textbooks, scientific journals, professional journals, technical magazines, unpublished reports, government reports, unpublished papers, abstracts, newspapers, espionage.
	Verbal	Consultants, librarians, government officials, consumers, suppliers, distributors, competitors, academics, market researchers, industry bodies, journalists, spies, bankers, stockbrokers.
	Combination	Formal and informal meetings, membership of government working parties and advisory boards, industry bodies, trade associations.

Table 4   The relative importance of sources of environmental information

1   Verbal sources of information are much more important than written sources; 75 per cent of information cited by executives was in verbal form.

2   The higher the executive in the organization, the more important verbal sources became.

3   Of the written sources used, the most important were newspapers (two-thirds), then trade publications, then internal company reports.

4   The major sources of verbal information are subordinates, then friends in the industry, and very infrequently superiors.

5   Information received from outside an organization is usually unsolicited.

6   Information received from inside the organization is usually solicited by the executive.

7   Information received from outside tends to have a greater impact on the decision-maker than inside information.

8   The outside sources used varied according to the job of the manager. Thus, marketing managers talked more to customers.

9   The larger the company, the greater the reliance on inside sources of verbal information.

organizing a database governing elements of the firm's environment is made more so by the difficult nature of environmental information – which often possesses several of the following characteristics:

- poor structure;
- irregular availability;
- provided by unofficial sources;
- qualitative in nature;
- questionable credibility;
- ambiguous definitions;
- opinion-based;
- difficult to quantify;
- insecure methodology;
- likely to change.

THE DEVELOPMENT OF ENVIRONMENTAL SCANNING

Management systems have evolved in response to two trends: the increasing discontinuity, complexity, and novelty of the environmental challenges faced by firms; and the decreasing visibility of the future changes in the business environment. The growing impact of these trends is largely responsible for the widespread following which the strategic planning credo attracted in the wake of the Middle East oil crises of the 1970s. Those events drew attention to environmental scanning as an important element of strategic planning. They also drove developments in environmental scanning techniques and procedures, as well as in the organizational arrangements and systems which support it.

Table 5 What information do managers need on the business environment?

Market tidings

Market potential	Supply and demand consideration for market areas of current or potential interest (e.g. capacity, consumption, imports, exports).
Structural change	Mergers, acquisitions and joint ventures involving competitors, new entries into the industry.
Competitors and industry	General information about a competitor, industry policy, concerted actions in the industry, and so forth.
Pricing	Effective and proposed prices for products of current and potential interest.
Sales negotiations	Information relating to a specific current or potential sale or contract for the firm.
Customers	General information about current or near-potential customers, their markets, their problems.

Acquisition leads

Leads for mergers, joint ventures, or acquisitions	Information concerning possibilities for the manager's own company.

Technical tidings

New products, processes, and technology	Technical information relatively new and unknown to the company.
Product problems	Problems involving existing products.
Costs	Costs for processing, operations, and so forth for current and potential competitors, suppliers, and customers, and for proposed company activities.
Licensing and patents	Products and processes.

Broad issues

General conditions	Events of a general nature: political, demographic, national, and so forth.
Government actions and policies	Governmental decisions affecting the industry.

Other tidings

Suppliers and raw materials	Purchasing considerations for products of current or potential interest.
Resources available	Persons, land, and other resources possibly available for the company.
Miscellaneous	Items not elsewhere classified.

Source: Aquillar (1967)

Note: Market tidings (52 per cent) was found by far to be the most popular category of environmental information that participants looked for, followed by technical tidings (17 per cent) and broad issues (12 per cent). He also identified four approaches (i.e. undirected viewing, conditioned viewing, informal search and formal search) to the collection of environmental information and two principal sources of such information. See Tables 3 and 4.

The early evolution of environmental scanning can be traced to the mid-1960s, at which time the market environment was generally being studied only for the purpose of making economic forecasts. In more recent years has there been a wider appreciation of the need to look beyond short-term market conditions to the broad technological, economic, political, social, cultural and demographic elements of the environment.

A pioneering investigation of environmental scanning was conducted by Aquillar in 1967. In this now classic study the process of environmental scanning was originally conceptualized. In his research Aquillar found a lack of a systematic approach to environmental scanning, which is still being reported in more recent research.

Aquillar reported that the firms he had studied collected sixteen types of information about their business environment: he classified them into the five groupings displayed in Table 5. He reported that over half the environmental information that was gathered concerned market tidings; very little of the information collected concerned technical tidings and broad issues.

Aquillar identified two principal sources of information on the market environment (i.e. internal and external to the firm). Table 3 classifies sources of information according to Aquillar's scheme. Table 4 summarizes his views on the relative importance of several sources of market information. He found there to be four broad approaches to the collection of this information:

1 Undirected viewing (i.e. exposure to the elements of the business environment without there being a specific purpose in mind).
2 Conditioned viewing (i.e. directed exposure, but without undertaking an active search).
3 Informal search (i.e. collection of purpose-oriented information in an informal manner).
4 Formal search (i.e. a structured process for collecting specific information for a designated purpose).

You will observe that these approaches differ along the following dimensions: the scope of the environment to be analysed; the impetus for the analysis; the degree of active search involved; the formality of the environmental scanning process; and the task orientation of the activity.

Aquillar's study concluded that environmental scanning must be conducted in a systematic fashion. He frequently found environmental scanning effort to be fragmented and inhibited by the failure of participating managers to gather and disseminate information that users considered important. His proposals called for top management involvement in the definition and execution of analysis activities; for greater coordination and integration of these activities with strategic planning; and for greater support for these activities, not only from top management, but also from line managers.

Three broad models of environment scanning systems are available which represent increasing degrees of systematization, sophistication and resource intensity. *Irregular* systems respond to environmentally generated crises. They are found in firms where the strategic planning culture is not well established. Their emphasis is on finding solutions to short-term problems. Little attention is paid to evaluating future environmental changes.

The *periodic* model is more sophisticated, systematic, proactive and resource intensive. It entails a regular review of the task environment and some elements of the wider environment. A forward view is taken.

The *continuous* model emphasizes the ongoing monitoring of the business environment, rather than specified issues or events. It draws on the expertise of marketing, sales, purchasing, and so on. It operates a clearing-house for environmental information and uses regular information systems for analysis and dissemination. A long-term view of environmental change is taken.

The paradox of environmental scanning is that by the time sufficient information has been collected to enable a well-informed environmental analysis to be made, it may be too late for the firm to respond before the threat strikes, or the opportunity passes. Ansoff (1984) proposes an approach to strategic management that overcomes the paradox by enabling the firm to develop a timely response to partially predictable events which emerge as surprises and develop very quickly. At its heart is the continuous monitoring of the firm's external and internal environment for signals of the evolution of strategic issues which the firm considers able to influence its operations. Ansoff's approach is driven by strategic issues rather than the conventional elements of the business environment. Issue-driven approaches to environmental scanning have also been developed by Nanus (1982) and Murphy (1989).

Ansoff's solution to the paradox is that instead of waiting for sufficient information to accumulate, the firm should determine what progressive steps in planning and action are feasible as strategic information becomes available in the course of the evolution of a threat or opportunity.

PROCEDURES AND PITFALLS

The environmental scanning procedures of an organization will evolve over time as its commitment to them and experience of them change. It is unrealistic for a firm that is about to embrace environmental scanning for the first time to expect to operate a foolproof system from the outset: several technical and managerial constraints will impede the progress of environmental scanning efforts. The provision of top management support throughout the evolutionary period helps to ensure that a viable system emerges from early efforts, which are likely to be directed towards the installation of a system modelled on an ideal scanning procedure such as that shown in Table 6. An established strategic planning culture also helps to expedite matters by providing a receptive organizational climate.

Top management involvement in the commissioning of the environmental scanning system should focus on the definition of the following system parameters:

Table 6 A typical sequential model of the ideal scanning procedure

1 *Monitor* broad trends, issues and events occurring in the firm's task environment. This can be complemented by means of identifying a core list of relevant publications and assigning them to volunteers who report important articles to environmental scanning for further study. Selected areas of the remote environment should be reviewed from time to time. External consultants may be employed.

2 *Identify* trends which may have significance for the firm. A scanning team of senior executives should determine and implement the criteria by means of which relevance is established. Weak signals may not be amenable to screening in this way.

3 *Evaluate* the impact of significant trends on the firm's operations in its current product markets. Those having a significant impact will either be threats or opportunities. Line managers should participate in the evaluation.

4 *Forecast* the possible future directions of the significant trends and examine the new opportunities and threats they appear likely to generate.

5 *Evaluate* the impact of these threats and opportunities on the firm's long-term strategies.

1 The boundaries of the task and business environment.
2 The appropriate time horizon for future studies.
3 The allocation of responsibility for environmental scanning.
4 The degree of formality circumscribing environmental scanning.
5 The use of environmental analyses in strategy making.

Defining boundaries

To define the boundaries of the firm's environment in terms of concrete measures is a very difficult, open-ended task for all but the smallest of one-product firms servicing a local market. Nevertheless, the environmental scanner needs practical guidelines to enable relevant environmental information to be separated from the irrelevant.

Such guidelines can be developed in consultation with members of the top management team responsible for the formulation of long-term strategies and plans. The user and the analyst can define the terms of reference and objectives of environmental scanning assignments. In this way an operational definition of a target zone of the environment is at least possible, using as a reference point the needs of the strategists for environmental data. Of course the definition will depend on the position and abilities of the members of the environmental analysis team, their past experience in environmental scanning projects and success in the application of the various research and forecasting techniques.

There are no hard and fast rules for making the distinction between relevance and irrelevance. The nub of the problem is one of achieving a balanced view of the scope of the firm's environment. To avoid misdirecting effort to peripheral and irrelevant issues it must not be too wide in scope. Neither should it be a narrow, data-dependent, eonometric but relevant, if myopic, view. Clearly the problem will be exacerbated in diversified organizations possessing several relevant environments.

Appropriate time horizon

Given the difficulty experienced by organizations in defining boundaries, it is not surprising that they tend to focus on familiar environments – preferring to study remote environments on an ad hoc basis, perhaps with the assistance of consultants. A similarly conservative view is often taken of the appropriate time horizon for future studies to be conducted by environmental scanning. Divisional management tends to prefer shorter time horizons, while corporate management tends to take a longer view.

The time horizon should in theory be determined by the investment cycle of the industry and the nature of the product or service provided. For example: in the oil industry a scanning term of twenty-five years is not unusual; in the fashion industry a period of four years is more appropriate. Therefore the time horizon of environmental scanning should exceed the duration of the firm's strategic plans. If the firm operates a policy of waiting to see what the industry leaders get up to, then environmental scanning activities may be easily resourced. However, there is every chance that they will provide a narrow, reactive view, which is biased towards the short term.

Responsibility for environmental scanning

The responsibility for environmental scanning can be allocated in three different ways. First, line managers in functions such as purchasing, sales and marketing can be asked to undertake environmental scanning in addition to their other duties. These managers are likely to be able to provide information on the business environment and should, therefore, contribute in some way to any environmental scanning system. However, this approach suffers from disadvantages: the demotivating resentment line managers may feel towards this additional imposition on their time, especially when no allowances are made, resources provided or training given; the requirement for specialist analytical, research and forecasting skills which line managers are unlikely to possess; the possibly incompatible mentalities of the roles they are asked to play – creative and far-sighted visionary on one hand and hard-headed operator on the other.

The second approach is for environmental scanning to be made part of the strategic planner's job. This division of labour of strategic planning leads to specialization which may also have some drawbacks, but environmental scanning cannot easily be abdicated to technical specialists. They do not have to answer for the results of business unit performance, and often do not understand the technical requirements of the unit's business. Most importantly, such specialists do not have a system for defining, measuring and interpreting a business's environment more accurately than its own management can. It may then be desirable for both planners and line managers to be involved in environmental scanning.

Ansoff (1984) argues that the need for this involvement is seldom more critical than when making the choice of environmental analysis and forecasting techniques. In his view this choice is too important to be left to the environmental analyst, as is often done in practice. He argues that the user of the output of environmental scanning has an overriding duty to exert influence on the choice of technique, if actionable information and understanding are desired. Knowledge of the applicability of a technique is more important to the strategist than knowledge of the details of the technique's execution. The details of environmental analysis and forecasting techniques can readily be found in a voluminous literature on the subject (see Brownlie and Saren 1983; Brownlie 1994).

The third approach is to establish a separate organizational unit that is responsible for conducting regular and ad hoc scanning at all levels, and for channelling the results to those in the firm to whom they may be relevant. General Electric in the USA is known to operate such a unit and to fund its activities by charging recipients for the environmental information provided by scanning. Where large amounts of data are collected and analysed it has proved useful to establish a special team whose task is to make recommendations for action to top management, based on the environmental analysis.

This approach may represent a theoretical ideal. However, combinations of the first two approaches are most popular with all but the very large diversified firms who can afford to underwrite the operation of a separate unit. Combinations often operate by means of a temporary scanning team, set up on an ad hoc basis to oversee the study of the impact of a controversial environmental trend, issue or event on various areas of the firm's operations.

The team membership may consist of both line (divisional) and general (corporate) management: line managers consider the product market, while top managers scan the wider environment. Line managers may even be temporarily seconded to a staff position for the duration of the study, often as part of on-the-job training for general management. They will often be closely involved in determining the impact of environmental changes on areas of the firm's operations in which they are experienced. Consultants, either internal or external, may be used where the impact of environmental change is likely to threaten the vested interests of line managers in some way.

There is no clear agreement about the best way to assign responsibilities for environmental scanning. Every organization will experience unique circumstances that merit taking a particular approach, which an off-the-shelf environmental scanning system may be incapable of embracing. Attempts to implant an ideal approach to environmental scanning in such a fashion are likely to contribute to inflated and ultimately unfulfilled expectations, and frustration. Researchers agree that firms should involve managers of various levels in environmental scanning activities and that it takes time for those activities, and the system which integrates them, to be assimilated effectively into the corporate culture. However, if environmental scanning is to become an effective contributor to the firm's strategic decision-making, then organisational commitment and integration are vital.

Clearly attention should be given to the quality of communications between environmental analysts and managers. Formal management education and training provides ways of forming managers with analytical skills, which may serve as a basis for communication with analysts. Conversely, analysts familiar with the needs of managers will be more able to communicate with strategy-makers. Job rotation may also improve communication. The top manager who has previously served as a member of an environmental analysis unit should find it easier to communicate with analysts. For general managers the range of desired skills is too broad, making it virtually impossible for one person to acquire them through job rotation in one lifetime. Intermediary advisors or consultants can also be used to improve communications, particularly in organizations where the career of the strategy-maker is very different from that of the analyst – as is the case where a government minister is a politician and the analyst a civil servant.

Whatever the means by which responsibility for environmental analysis is assigned, I argue that those responsible should still undertake the following tasks:

1   Monitoring of trends, issues and events in the business environment and studying their possible impacts on the firm's operations.
2   Development of the forecasts, scenarios and issues analyses that serve as inputs to the firm's strategic decision-making.
3   Provision of a destination to which environmental intelligence can be sent for interpretation, analysis and storage.
4   Construction of a means of organizing environmental information so that a library or database on environmental developments can easily be accessed.
5   Provision of an internal consulting resource on long-term environmental affairs.
6   Dissemination of information on the business environment by means of newsletters, reports and lectures.
7   Monitoring the performance of environmental analysis activities and improving it by applying new tools and techniques.

Degree of formality

Who should be responsible for environmental scanning is not the only difficult decision to be made. The degree of formality to be applied is also a matter for top management concern. The view taken by the organization will depend on the extent to which top management feel it necessary to be able to exert some control over the day-to-day activities of environmental scanning. Control may

Table 7   Attributes of a formal approach to environmental scanning

- Environmental trends, events and issues are regularly and systematically reviewed.
- Explicit criteria have been established that can in turn be used to evaluate the impact of environmental trends.
- Scanning activities are guided by written procedures.
- Responsibility for scanning activities has been clearly assigned.
- Scanning reports, updates, forecasts and analyses are documented in a standardized format.
- Such documentation is generated on a regular basis and disseminated to predetermined personnel according to a timetable.
- The application of formal techniques such as delphi studies and multiple scenarios.

be a problem where responsibility for these activities is devolved to line managers whose own regular responsibilities are likely to take precedence over what they may consider to be marginal 'blue sky' and 'ivory tower' exercises. This problem is likely to be exacerbated where no formal system for collecting, analysing and disseminating environmental information has been agreed. The lack of commitment and scepticism which line managers will often express about environment analysis can only be dealt with by means of education, training and involvement. They have to understand the need for better informed planning and decision-making, and the role that environmental scanning has to play in making this possible. In order to appreciate these requirements they also have to understand the forces acting on the firm in its environment and the strategies it has for dealing with them.

Yet some organizations are content to take an informal approach to environmental scanning, relying on key executives in sales, marketing, purchasing and finance to keep abreast of changes in the business environment through newspapers, trade literature, conferences, exhibitions and personal contacts. Others prefer to organize their efforts into a series of structured and planned activities for which specified staff bear responsibility. The difference is readily one of degree. Table 7 indicates the attributes likely to be possessed by a formal approach to environmental scanning.

Larger firms are more likely to take a formal approach to environmental scanning. This is not surprising given that such firms are also more likely to take a broad view of their business environment, competing as they will do in a number of markets with a number of products. The informal approach is not only the prerogative of the small, one-product firm. Diversified companies may prefer to take an informal approach to such scanning activities as long-term forecasting, the generation of alternative scenarios, issues analyses and the management of weak signals. These activities demand a degree of creative thinking that can best be stimulated in an informal environment – even if the output of the process is subjected to a more formal treatment.

Environmental scanning and strategy-making

In determining the composition of the environmental scanning unit, top management should also take care to clarify the role of the participating analysts, in order to foster realistic expectations of the contribution they are able to make to strategy formulation. The pursuit of unrealistic expectations can have a debilitating impact on environmental scanning. Such unrealistic expectations are most likely to be held by both analysts and strategists while introducing a formal environmental scanning procedure to a firm for the first time. Fortunately, experience of environmental scanning puts analysts and strategists in a better position to judge each other's contribution realistically, but some unrealistic expectations may still persist. Analysts cannot realistically expect strategy-makers always to make full use of their analyses, or to apply their recommendations completely and without question; they should rarely have the power to prescribe strategy. Where analysts tend to have such expectations, the reality of their engagements with strategists may be one of impotence rather than influence. In such circumstances the unfulfilled expectations of the analyst can easily become a source of alienation, misunderstanding and ill-feeling, only serving to weaken communications and impede the impact of environmental analysis on strategy formulation – a position made worse by the lack of any demonstrable, direct effect of such analyses on strategy formulation. Similarly, top management's desire to delegate strategy-making to the environmental scanning unit should be treated with caution. The careful deflation of any heroic expectations will contribute to improved communications and understanding.

The data and analyses generated by environmental scanning are only one of several inputs to the strategy-making process. Its major contribution is to identify environmental trends, issues, events or signals that should trigger the reconsideration and, perhaps, revision of the strategic plans. Consequently, there is every chance that environmental scanning will have an important hand in initiating strategy changes. Indeed, where a staff unit for environmental scanning exists, the occurrence of such a trigger is likely to lead to a request from strategists for environmental scanning to conduct a specific study of the related issue or trend.

The indirect use of environmental analyses in strategy-making is at least possible, by virtue of the quality of its work. However, its direct use requires an enabling mechanism directed to the translation of the output of environmental analyses into specific recommendations or even a plan for implementing strategy changes. Once again communication difficulties must be surmounted. The problem is not merely that a thorough understanding of environmental analysis demands skills similar to those of the analysts, which strategy-makers are unlikely to possess. The vocabulary, assumptions, processes and techniques employed by the analysts will also be alien to them. One answer is not to leave the task of translation only to the environmental analysts. They may also be unfamiliar with the arcane terminology, skills, outlook and expectations of the strategists and their peers. The use of specially convened action teams, staffed by advisers or consultants, is often recommended as a translation mechanism. The best solution is one that brings analysts and strategists closer together as often as possible.

CONCLUSION

Environmental scanning can make an important contribution to the survival and prosperity of the firm. The increasingly turbulent and unpredictable market environment of the 1990s will convince more and more organizations of the need systematically to scan and analyse their market environment. This is not an easy task. The organization must expect to encounter many technical and managerial problems, particularly in enabling environment scanning to contribute fully to the formulation of business strategy. Reading this chapter is no more than a first step.

REFERENCES

Ansoff, H. I. (1984) *Implanting Strategic Management*, New York: Prentice Hall.
Aquillar, F. S. (1967) *Scanning the Business Environment*, New York: Macmillan.
Brownlie, D. T. (1994) 'Environmental scanning', in M. J. Baker (ed.) *The Marketing Book*, 3rd edn, Oxford: Butterworth-Heinemann.
Brownlie, D. T. and Saren, M. A. (1983) 'A review of technology forecasting techniques and their applications', *Management Bibliographies and Reviews* 9 (4).
Kast, F. E. and Rosenweig, J. E. (1974) *Organisation and Management: A Systems Approach*, 2nd edn, Maidenhead: McGraw-Hill.
Murphy, J. (1989) 'Identifying strategic issues', *Long Range Planning* 22 (2): 101–5.
Nanus, B. (1982) 'QUEST – quick environmental scanning technique', *Long Range Planning* 15 (2): 39–45.

FURTHER READING

Brownlie, D. T. (1994) 'Environmental scanning', in M. J. Baker (ed.) *The Marketing Book*, 3rd edn, Oxford: Butterworth-Heinemann.
Diffenbach, J. (1983) 'Corporate environmental analysis in large US corporations', *Long Range Planning* 16 (3): 107–16.
Makridakis, S. (1990) *Forecasting, Planning and Strategy for the 21st Century*, New York: Free Press.
Stubbart, C. (1982) 'Are environmental scanning units effective?', *Long Range Planning*, June: 139–45.
Taylor, J. (1992) 'Competitive intelligence: a status report on US business practices', *Journal of Marketing Management* 8: 117–25.
West, J. and Olsen, D. (1989) 'Environmental scanning, industry structure and strategy making: concepts and research in the hospitality industry', *International Journal of Hospitality Management* 8 (4): 283–98.

19

MARKETING AND PUBLIC POLICY

Stephen A. Greyser

This chapter treats the marketing and public policy territory of the field of marketing, with particular emphasis on its evolution over the past forty-plus years.

THE 'OLD DAYS': MARKETING AND THE LAW

In the period after World War II, the operating model of marketing and public policy was generally equated with 'the legal aspects of marketing'. The focus was on anti-trust and issues of competition. The major application areas were market concentration and price discrimination. In addition, false advertising remained an issue, having surfaced as part of the anti-advertising sentiments that had arisen during the Depression.

Reflecting these elements are the major topics treated in the American Marketing Association's *Journal of Marketing* in the post-World-War-II period. In the late 1970s, for the book *Marketing Research and Knowledge Development*, a five-yearly content analysis of the major marketing journals was undertaken (Myers *et al.* 1980: 82–3).

In 1947 articles on retail price maintenance (now no longer a meaningful issue) and false advertising were among the major topics in the *Journal of Marketing*, as were the implications of the Robinson-Patman Act in 1952. Not until 1967 (in our quinquennial analysis) did public policy emerge again – in the *Journal of Marketing*'s treatment of government impacts on marketing. Five years later, in 1972, as activism, particularly consumerism, had begun to emerge, articles addressed consumerism and unit pricing.

An analogous trend was found in marketing textbooks. Extensive sections on public policy did not meaningfully appear in textbooks until the mid-1970s onwards. By then the traditional module on marketing and the law had been replaced by a full section – typically termed 'the new environment of marketing' – encompassing law, government, consumerism, and public policy (Myers *et al.* 1980: 91).

THE FORK IN THE ROAD: HIGH-WATER MARK IN THE 1970s

In my view the late 1960s and 1970s can be characterized as a period of burgeoning activity and interest in public policy and marketing – by the government itself via a reinvigorated Federal Trade Commission (FTC), by marketers in response (mostly defensive), and by marketing academics as well. The high-water mark of the decade-plus of increased regulation in the wake of Ralph Nader's *Unsafe at Any Speed* (1972) came just prior to the defeat of comprehensive consumer regulation legislation in the late 1970s. By then the cost/benefit-fuelled trend to deregulation was discernible, and the view of the FTC as a 'national nanny' came to transcend its praised role as a consumer protector.

As noted, the late 1960s and 1970s constituted a period of growth in protection-oriented public policy initiatives in a number of new areas of consumer concern. These are detailed elsewhere, notably in several papers from a 1989 Notre Dame conference on marketing and advertising regulation at the FTC.[1] Of all the developments in this decade, perhaps the most significant to marketing academics was the rapid recognition of consumer behaviour specifically, and marketing generally, as relevant disciplines for the public policy community itself. In an early personal conversation with FTC Commissioner Mary Gardiner Jones, she said: 'By my appointment, I am an expert in marketing and consumer behaviour. But in truth, our FTC staff has no one trained in either'. (She hired Murray Silverman for her own staff.)

The 1971 FTC hearings on Modern Advertising Practices represented a major opportunity for the FTC Commissioners and senior staff to absorb much about how marketers and advertisers actually conducted marketing and advertising. The research and literature of the economic and social issues involved in advertising were synthesized in a major Marketing Science Institute monograph (Pearce *et al.* 1971). A coterie of consumer behaviour professors (mostly in annual single file) took up residence as visiting consultants at the FTC. William Wilkie at the Bureau of Consumer Protection was the first resident professor with the FTC staff, followed later by Harold Kassarjian and others (Murphy 1990).

Very quickly, and significantly, the legal basis for what consumers thought shifted from what competing experts thought consumers thought to competing experts interpreting empirical data on what consumers themselves said they thought. Indeed, both consumer research consultants and consumer research professors (sometimes the same person) flourished in an age of empiricism. A new generation of aspiring marketing scholars found a wide range of public policy topics to explore – alas, often using the traditionally readily available students as their subjects, who in turn would render the real-world validity of many of their findings questionable.

By this time the application of behavioural sciences research to marketing, which was in its early stages by 1960, had reached a mature state. This clearly became a very salient dimension of the marketing and public policy arena. In my view, a major – perhaps the major – contributor to the growth in interest in consumer behaviour research was its potential for applicability to public policy issues. Many of today's leading public policy professors are primarily trained in consumer behaviour rather than in economics, as had been their predecessors.

A TIME OF REMISSION

If the 1970s constituted a period of almost hyperactivity in the marketing and public policy realm in the USA, the 1980s were largely a time of remission. Government initiatives shrunk. Marketers' interest declined sharply in the absence of 'feeling the pressure', and activism generally waned (at least until it became rather chic to be 'green'). Helping to maintain academic interest in the public policy field were the advent of the *Journal of Public Policy and Marketing* and the start of the series of American Marketing Association conferences in the field.

LOOKING AHEAD

In answer to the question, what of the 1990s? – I see a tremendous potential for growth in the marketing and public policy territory, and have written so long before the 1992 US election of a Democratic administration and its consequent likelihood of a pendulum shift in Federal regulatory activity. We have witnessed regulatory initiatives in food labelling (regarding nutrition information) and in the tobacco industry.

More specifically, consider some key changes that have been taking place in the marketplace itself. We have undergone a technological revolution in communications, on the one hand enabling consumers to gain much more control of their media environment (via the remote button), and at the same time enabling greater audience targeting than marketers have enjoyed via TV in the past.

In the wake of this change in mass communication, we have witnessed a huge increase in direct marketing – via telephone and mail. Telephone marketing is arguably more amenable to deceptive selling than is the national advertising that has been the traditional regulatory focus on commercial communication. (Of course consumers themselves can easily control this channel of marketing too – via hanging up the phone and using the wastepaper basket more often.)

We have seen the rapid growth of ethnic populations such as Hispanics and Asians in the USA, for many of whom English is not their first language. One key consequence is increased potential for marketplace fraud.

We have experienced the growth of the services sector – where it is often inherently more difficult to determine what constitutes satisfactory performance for consumers compared to a provider's promise. For example, it is much easier for a consumer to judge that a can-opener opens cans or that a washing machine washes clothes clean than it is for the same consumer to assess his or her satisfaction with a hotel room promising a superior experience or with one's 'personal banking' experience. The potential for services marketers – even when well intentioned – fuelling the promise-performance gap that creates discontent with marketing is much higher in my view than it is for product marketing.[2]

A key dimension of today's public policy scene is that issues appear to be driven much more by consumer problems than by philosophy or ideology. This seems particularly true at the state level in the USA.

One other major change involving marketing in the public arena has occurred over the past twenty years, and actually increased during the 1980s. This change is the great interest in marketing on behalf of not-for-profits and social causes. Reflecting broader and deeper interest here is MSI's current research competition, chaired by Paul Bloom, on Using Marketing to Serve Society. The main headings in the competition are instructive as to the breadth of the issues here:[3]

1   Understanding the social consequences of consumer/buyer behaviour, including responses to risky consumer behaviour, social tradeoffs (e.g. price premiums for perceived socially beneficial attributes), and problems of vulnerable segments.
2   Improving business responses to social needs, including being effective *and* ethical, and evaluation of campaigns encouraging socially beneficial behaviour.
3   Improving public agency responses to social needs, including assessing policy proposals, and improving the marketing knowledge of public agencies.

The increase in both the practice and study of what is called social marketing has broadened the definitions of marketing and its impacts on behalf of society.

TWO WORLD VIEWS

Let me offer some closing thoughts on marketing and public policy. These are not new – but I believe they still pertain in attempting to resolve regulatory issues in marketing. Some twenty-five years ago my late senior colleague Raymond A. Bauer and I published an article in the *Harvard Business Review* entitled 'The Dialogue That Never Happens', which posited that two different views of the consumer world – two different conceptions of the marketplace and marketing's role in it – serve to explain the communications gap between business, especially marketers on the one side, and both regulators and critics of marketing on the other (Bauer and Greyser 1967). This is pertinent today because I not only think the gap remains but also believe that research, even well-designed and executed research, can go only part-way to bridge the gap. For example, the two mindsets explain why marketers consider advertising properly to be persuasive while regulators focus on information as advertising's proper role.[4]

Consider five key words or phrases: competition, product, consumer needs, rationality, and information. Let me compare the typical regulator's view (recall that the vast majority of marketing regulators are still drawn from the ranks of lawyers and economists) with the typical business view. The regulator focuses on competition in terms of price (and typically cost-based price), whereas the business view of competition is one of product differentiation (to help escape from price competition) with price based on value for the customer.

Regulators tend to see a product only in terms of its primary function. In contrast the business view of differentiation is dominantly through secondary characteristics, since primary ones are largely generic to a category and often only 'me too' for a given brand.

Consumer needs are seen by regulators as corresponding closely (or directly) with primary function (e.g. a car is for transportation). However, the business view is that consumer needs encompass any desire on which the product can be differentiated, certainly including psychological differentiation (e.g. in terms of self-image).

To the regulator, rationality is the efficient matching of product to consumer needs. Business people, particularly marketers, are more agnostic: any consumer decision that serves the customer's own perceived self-interest constitutes rationality.

Finally, information to the regulator is whatever facilitates the fit of a product's proper function with the customer's needs, already defined rather narrowly as a marketer would see it. Marketers more broadly consider information to be whatever truthfully puts forward the attractiveness of the product in the consumer's eyes. And honest persuasion is a legitimate element of our society.

NOTES

1 See notably Jones, Mary Gardiner (1990) 'The Federal Trade Commission in 1968', in Murphy, Patrick E. and Wilkie, W. L. (eds) *Marketing and Advertising Regulation*, Notre Dame, Indiana: University of Notre Dame.

2 For the conceptualization and assessment of the 'promise-performance gap', see Greyser, S. (1989) 'Services and satisfaction keys to the '90s agenda', *Mobius* Fall. Also Greyser, S. A. and Diamond, S. L. (1974) 'Business is adapting to consumerism', *Harvard Business Review* September–October.

3 MSI (1992) *MSI Call for Proposals*, Cambridge, Massachusetts: Marketing Science Institute.

4 For more explanation, see Greyser, S. A. (1983) 'Advertising as information *and* persuasion in the marketplace', presentation to Federal Trade Commission, May.

REFERENCES

Bauer, Raymond A. and Greyser, S. A. (1967) 'The dialogue that never happens', *Harvard Business Review*, November–December.
Murphy, Patrick E. (1990) 'Past FTC participation by marketing academics', in Patrick E. Murphy and W. L. Wilkie (eds) *Marketing and Advertising Regulation*, Notre Dame, Indiana: University of Notre Dame.

Myers, J. G., Massy, W. M. and Greyser, S. A. (1980) *Marketing Research and Knowledge Development*, Englewood Cliffs: Prentice Hall.

Nader, Ralph (1972) *Unsafe at Any Speed*, New York: Grossman.

Pearce, M., Cunningham, S. M. and Miller, Avon (1971) (under the supervision of R. D. Buzzell and S. A. Greyser) *Appraising the Economic and Social Effects of Advertising*, Cambridge, Massachusetts: Marketing Science Institute.

20

MARKETING RESEARCH

Christopher West

MARKETING RESEARCH AND THE MARKETING KNOWLEDGE-BASE

Organizations use many types of resources to function. One of the most valuable, but often the least understood, is their knowledge-base. Management is unable to take informed decisions without knowledge and the quality of that knowledge may be all which distinguishes a successful from an unsuccessful organization. Knowledge, like skills, resides primarily in employees, but can also be collected in databases, reports, patents, plans, budgets, memoranda and a variety of other documents. The knowledge-base covers all aspects of the organization's activities – products, technology, human resources, finance, sales and marketing – and is a wasting asset requiring constant updating, improvement and extension to keep pace with changes in the operating environment.

Nowhere is the need for detailed, accurate and up-to-date knowledge more evident than in the marketing function. Markets have two characteristics which distinguish them from the other environments in which companies operate.

1 They are invariably dynamic and are tending to become more so in response to the increasing pace of technical development, competitive pressure and a continual uplift in customers' expectations
2 Change is caused by a wide diversity of factors, most of which are beyond the control of any single supplier.

Marketing therefore operates in an inherently unstable environment and it is all too easy for companies to lose touch with conditions in the markets they service. Furthermore, in the quest for growth, or even to defend existing market positions, the problem tends to be exacerbated by the fact that companies continually need to do something new. They develop new strategies, launch new products, target new markets and initiate new service packages – all of which push them into increasingly unfamiliar marketing territory.

The antidote to these conditions is a marketing knowledge-base which is

343

updated and extended in line with the development of the business. Marketing knowledge is created from a number of inputs. Experience and expertise are critical, as are experimentation and analysis, but the key dynamic ingredient is marketing information derived from sources within the marketplace itself, notably customers, competitors and distributors. Marketing research is the marketing service which collects, analyses and interprets marketing information.

USERS OF MARKETING RESEARCH

The mainstream users of marketing research are all types of commercial organizations who require information which will assist them to improve the quality of their marketing decisions. Suppliers of raw materials, manufacturers, distributors, suppliers of professional and other services are the main initiators of marketing research surveys. They are sometimes joined by organizations and institutions who participate indirectly in the marketing process or who need to observe what is happening in markets for purposes other than marketing management. Trade associations commission research on behalf of their members. Government agencies with a marketing mandate, such as tourist boards, commission research to obtain the data they require to direct their promotional activity. Television channels, newspapers, the trade press and exhibition organizers commission research to demonstrate the effectiveness of their media as promotional vehicles and, in some instances, to obtain editorial copy.

Some confusion arises from the fact that the survey techniques used by marketing researchers are also used to obtain information which has no marketing application, unless a very liberal definition of marketing is adopted. Opinion polls, which provide a substantial income stream to research companies, are arguably part of the information input required by political parties to market themselves to the electorate; research into attitudes towards government policy forms a basis for government marketing strategies. Investigations into housing conditions, community health or wage and salary levels is in reality social and political research which has little, if any, connection with marketing.

INFORMATION FOR MARKETING PLANNING

Like many sciences, or pseudo-sciences, market research is plagued with impenetrable terminology. Terms such as perceptual mapping, psychographics and behavioural research, while all worthy in their own right, disguise the fact that most market research is devoted to providing information which will solve the most basic marketing problems – what should I sell, how much of it can I sell, what do I have to do to sell it, where do I sell it and what prices can I achieve? There is a host of more esoteric problems which research can tackle, but it tends to concentrate on the provision of three broad groups of information:

344

1 Market measurement.
2 Customer research.
3 Competitor analysis.

Even within this relatively simple framework, research can help to solve a wide diversity of marketing problems and the following paragraphs outline only the most common research applications.

Market measurement

A primary requirement for business planners is to set achievable sales targets and to show how these can be achieved. The quantitative element of a basic marketing plan for a product or service will show the planned sales progression (in volume or value), the customer groups that are to be targeted and the distribution channels that are to be used. To do this it is essential to know the total volume of sales that the market is absorbing (or is capable of absorbing) and the structure of the market. Sales data need to be broken down by product type or product category and the structural data need to show the channels through which products are distributed and the relationship between channels and customer groups. Sales targeting also requires detailed information on the customer base – who are the purchasers of the product or service, how large is each purchasing group and what relationships exist between the products purchased and the types of purchasers.

Tracking data, which monitor the progress of sales, in total, by customer group, by brand and by supplier, permit planners to assess the impact of their marketing and promotional strategies on a continuous basis.

Forecasts are essential for planning future business. Information on how markets are expected to develop in the future enables planners to assess the attraction of the market, set forward budgets and allocate marketing promotional resources in the light of the yield they could be expected to achieve. Surveys of buyers' intentions can provide a strong, though far from infallible, indication of short-term market performance. Longer term projections rely on an analysis of trend data and the relationship between demand and general economic variables such as consumer expenditure and industrial investment.

Customer research

Customer strategies that will achieve the sales targets which have been set are a core component of marketing and promotional activity. Detailed analysis of the customer, be it an individual or an organization, therefore represents a major task for marketing research. If, in essence, marketing is devoted to providing what the customer wants, market research is there to define what that is. Customer research is designed to provide marketers with an understanding of

345

product and service requirements, customer behaviour, attitudes, purchasing preferences and purchasing procedures.

Market research is at its most valuable when assessing the potential demand for new products since this is where the unknowns are greatest and risk is high. The use of research for conceptual evaluations of customer needs and the testing of prototype designs replace gut feel with more tangible evidence of what will sell. This process extends to modifications to existing products to take account of changing customer requirements and to the definition of the services which customers require in support of their product purchases.

The analysis of customer behaviour is most concerned with the factors that determine customer choice of product and supplier. Understanding the interaction between price, product quality, product features and a host of service considerations such as delivery, installation and customer advisory services is critical to success in any marketplace. The weighting of product and supplier selection criteria shows how product and service packages should be constructed and also supplies a key input to the definition of promotional messages.

It is also essential to know the extent to which suppliers are meeting customers' expectations and this has given rise to customer satisfaction research to provide a numerical measurement of supplier performance. Image research is closely allied in that it shows customers' perceptions of suppliers. Perceptions can be equally as powerful as reality in determining supplier acceptance and research can highlight changes in image which need to be engineered in order to improve the chances of success.

Customer research is commonly used to define discrete segments of a market which lend themselves to separate marketing approaches. It is rarely easy to be all things to all men and marketing effectiveness can be improved by targeting specific market segments with the products, services and marketing messages they find most acceptable. Segments can be defined by parameters such as geography, demographics, taste, attitudes and buying practices, but research is required to show whether the segments are sufficiently different and homogeneous to support separate marketing approaches.

Research into customers' purchasing intentions is used to compute short-term forecasts of demand for products and to predict the success of new products. The accuracy of the results tends to be higher in industrial and professional markets where there is a close correlation between stated purchasing intentions and actual behaviour, but surveys of consumer purchasing intentions can also provide a valuable input to short-term forecasting models.

The study of the effectiveness of individual marketing communication and promotional techniques provides planners with guidelines for the allocation of their marketing expenditure. The effect of advertising, direct marketing, sales promotion, exhibitions and public relations is usually studied indirectly by testing recall and customers' reaction to content such as copy, images and venues. The real effectiveness of advertising, namely the effect on income, is difficult to establish, though a number of models are available to compute the

346

relationship between advertising expenditure and sales. The effectiveness of below-the-line expenditure is normally apparent in the form of response and take-up rates and does not need to be established by research.

Media research is an important component of communications research, which is devoted to analysing newspaper and journal readership and radio and television audiences, poster viewing and cinema audiences. To be fully effective media research should be allied with research into purchasing decision-making, so that the relationship between those responsible for purchase decisions and media audiences can be demonstrated.

Other aspects of marketing activity which can be pre- and post-tested by studying customer reactions include the use and effectiveness of distribution channels, packaging, merchandising and perhaps, most importantly, pricing. Pricing decisions are critical to the success of all marketing strategies and customer research can provide valuable insight into the acceptability of pricing proposals before they are activated in the marketplace.

Competitor analysis

The widespread adoption of customer research by suppliers of consumer and industrial products and suppliers of professional services has resulted in noticeable similarities in product and service strategies. Reductions in differentiation in customer strategies has heightened interest in competitor strategies, which tend to be aimed at improving market share.

In order to compete it is essential not only to identify the competition but also to understand their resources, their strategies, their strengths and weaknesses as perceived by customers, the threat they pose to other suppliers and their vulnerabilities to attack. Detailed knowledge of competitors has never been easy to acquire and marketing history is littered with examples of successful businesses that have been brought down by competition which was either unknown or known but undervalued. There are also countless examples of opportunities missed through failures to capitalize on competitors' weaknesses.

Keeping abreast of competition is becoming increasingly difficult as the pace of change in markets accelerates. Competitive tension is being heightened by powerful forces which are driving existing competitors to be more aggressive and at the same time attracting new competitors. Deregulation, reductions in trade barriers, radical political realignments and the increasing globalization of supply all create new opportunities but at the same time threaten those who fail to appreciate that the competitive environment is changing and that previous competitive boundaries have been blurred.

The most basic information requirement is a map which plots the competitive environment and shows who the competitors are, where they are, where they have come from and the resources they deploy. A typical competitor information profile will cover:

347

- ownership and organizational structure;
- financial history;
- financial resources;
- key decision-makers and their track records;
- staff resources;
- production resources and locations;
- product lines and portfolios;
- patents, licences and other unique assets;
- markets and segments serviced;
- distribution channels used;
- export activity and countries supplied;
- sales and marketing activities.

The profile can be extended by probing each competitor's image, reputation, strengths and weaknesses among customers.

MAJOR RESEARCH FORMS

The market research industry has responded to the information requirements of its clients in a variety of ways, each reflecting the difficulty and cost of acquiring the information and the extent to which clients require information which is proprietary to themselves and not shared with others. The main research forms are:

- Continuous consumer panels.
- Retail audits.
- Ad hoc surveys.
- Omnibus surveys.
- Syndicated surveys.

Continuous consumer panels

Continuous consumer panels are used to collect information regularly, normally month by month, from standing panels of customers selected to be representative of households or specific groups of individuals. They are best suited to the collection of information on purchases that are made regularly and record simple data, such as products or services purchased, brands purchased, the source of purchase, prices paid and the receipt of any incentives or special offers with the purchase.

Retail audits

Retail audits collect similar data to that recorded on consumer panels but the source of the data is a sample of retail outlets rather than customers. Electronic data collection techniques are moving retail research more towards censuses than samples, though far from all retailers are prepared to cooperate with agencies on this research. Clearly what passes through retail outlets should agree with purchases made by customers and the main differences between consumer panel and retail audit data lie in the ways in which the data can be structured and analysed.

Retail audits and consumer panels are both used to provide quantitative information which tracks purchasing trends. Neither seeks information that explains the trends which are observed. Both obtain high degrees of accuracy and produce detailed information by covering large samples of respondents. They are costly to mount and are viable only because the resultant data is sold to large numbers of clients.

Ad hoc surveys

Ad hoc surveys cope with research requirements which arise sporadically. Each survey is custom designed to meet specific information needs or to solve one of a wide variety of marketing problems. The main advantage of ad hoc surveys is that the client obtains the precise information that is required and retains proprietary control over it. Panel and retail audit data can be customized by means of special analysis, which is also the proprietary property of the client who commissions it, but the amount of tailoring that can be achieved is limited by the type and structure of the initial data that are collected.

Ad hoc surveys fall into two groups, which also reflect two major divisions in the research business. These are quantitative and qualitative research. As the name implies, quantitative research records what is happening by quantifying requirements and the patterns that arise in the market. Qualitative research seeks to understand why consumers behave the way they do and to describe the alternative patterns of behaviour that can exist.

Omnibus surveys

Omnibus surveys are regular research exercises carried out weekly, monthly or quarterly with defined samples of respondents such as motorists, mothers with young children or a general sample representative of the population as a whole. Clients use omnibus surveys as a vehicle for carrying questions they want answered, but which do not justify the cost of a specially mounted ad hoc survey. An omnibus questionnaire can carry two to three questions from ten to fifteen separate clients. Each client receives an analysis of the responses to the questions he has placed and pays a fee for each question asked.

Syndicated surveys

Syndicated surveys are ad hoc research programmes with the cost shared by a group of clients who wish to participate. Shared cost means that clients gain the benefit of research programmes many times larger than they could afford on their own. The disadvantage is that competitors have access to the same data. Syndicates can either be 'closed', meaning that a predetermined group of clients buys the research and no further sale is permitted, or 'open' meaning that anyone can buy the research.

DATA COLLECTION METHODS

Quantitative and qualitative survey techniques are well defined and are common to all branches of market research. The essence of all surveys is the collection of information:

- from existing published (or secondary) sources;
- directly from participants in a market.

Secondary research

The information age has been characterized by an ever growing corpus of published information on industries and markets of all types. The sources of information are as diverse as the industries they cover though there is a growing tendency to collect data into computerized databases (such as Textline, Dialog, Infoline and Nexis) which are available on-line for efficient and rapid searching.

Secondary (or desk) research is still an undervalued research technique, often relegated to the role of providing clues which will verify data collected by primary research techniques. However, if used properly desk research can make a significant contribution to the basic information required for market analysis. The depth and quality of information available varies considerably from market sector to market sector and from country to country but a diligent search can be expected to yield data on:

- Population size, structure into geodemographic groups and growth.
- The structure of distribution and the importance of various channels.
- Total sales, imports and exports of products.
- Imports and exports by origin and destination.
- Products available and their specifications.
- New product launches.
- Sources of supply.
- New contracts and successful bidders for outstanding contracts.
- List prices.
- Advertising expenditure by product, industry sector and supplier.
- New market entrants.
- Staff movements.
- Financial performance of suppliers.

The sources of published information are too numerous to list in their entirety and the process of source identification is a skill which takes time to acquire.

Researchers are assisted by the existence of a number of 'sources on sources', such as Marketsearch, Findex, Predicasts, the Research Index and Reports Index, which collectively list most of the data that are available.

Much published information is available free of charge or at very low cost. The main disadvantage is that the sources can be highly fragmented and the data collection process can be time consuming. There is, however, an increasing trend to publish research reports on specific products, industries or activities which bring together the data available from secondary sources and are designed to provide researchers with comprehensive overviews of markets. These reports, also available at relatively low cost, provide the useful function of predigesting and harmonizing information and commonly add an element of primary research to support the data obtained from secondary sources.

Primary research

Primary research techniques are used to collect original data from participants in markets. They can be directed at all types of respondents who possess information that has value to those designing and running marketing strategies. The targets include:

* customers;
* distributors – retail, wholesale and specialist;
* specifiers and advisors;
* designers;
* suppliers.

The most frequent target for survey research is the customer – the person buying for his or her own consumption or on behalf of the organizations that employ them. The major primary research techniques currently in use for marketing research are:

* personal (face-to-face) interviews;
* telephone interviews;
* group discussions (focus groups);
* mail/fax questionnaires;
* diaries;
* electronic data collection techniques;
* hall tests;
* observation techniques.

All of these involve direct contact with respondents using a questionnaire or an interview guide and sometimes requiring display material or samples of the product being researched.

The interview

Whether carried out face-to-face or by telephone the interview is the most common market research technique. It seeks information on respondents' actions, reactions, preferences, perceptions or requirements. It can be carried out in a variety of locations of which the most common are the street, the home, the place of work or a specific venue associated with the research topic such as a shop or an airport. The live contact between the interviewer and the respondent permits not only data collection but also the verification of responses and the introduction of supplementary questions to probe the unusual or unexpected. An advantage of face-to-face interviews is that they can be set up to permit subjects to be explored in depth – in which case they are called 'depth personal interviews'.

As telephone ownership has become universal, telephone research has tended to displace personal interviewing, largely because it is quicker, can be controlled better and is less expensive. The telephone is ideally suited to the collection of small amounts of highly structured information from samples that are scattered over a wide geographical area. It is unsuitable for individuals who are unlikely to respond well on the telephone, such as children, or those that are difficult to reach by telephone, such as residents in old people's homes or farmers; nor can it be used when material needs to be displayed to the respondents. The telephone can be less intrusive than personal interviews but can also be unwelcome during the evenings when respondents are most likely to be at home. For business research the telephone can be the most acceptable method of data collection because it requires the least time commitment by respondents. The main disadvantages of telephone research are the lack of visual contact, which means that respondents' reactions cannot be observed, and the relative ease with which respondents can refuse to cooperate.

Group discussions

Group discussions are face-to-face interviews carried out with a collected group of respondents. Though difficult and expensive to organize, they yield massive amounts of qualitative information enhanced by the fact that participants argue and debate between themselves. The moderation of such events is a skilled process but, done well, a few groups of six to eight participants can reveal far more about customers' requirements or attitudes than the equivalent twelve to sixteen interviews. Groups can only be used with respondents who can be brought together physically, commonly in specialist facilities with video, sound recording and viewing capability. This is rarely a problem with consumer groups where there are usually enough qualifying respondents living in the catchment area of the facility, but it can become more problematical for specialist respondents such as purchasing officers or surgeons. Part of the added cost of group discussion research arises from the fact that participants are commonly remunerated for the time they have devoted to take part in the group.

Mail questionnaire

The mail questionnaire, which is either posted or handed out to respondents for completion and returned to the researcher, is a low-cost research technique still used in social research but of declining importance in market research. They have a value in extracting information from respondents who are difficult to contact by other methods, such as executives constantly on the move, or in situations where respondents can be identified but where an interview on the spot is not feasible, as in traffic surveys for example. The main problem with mail surveys is the lack of control over the response. Response rates tend to be low and it is difficult if not impossible to demonstrate that those who choose to reply are typical of the universe as a whole. The most extreme example is the guest questionnaire placed in hotel bedrooms which is invariably completed only if the guest has experienced a problem. In business research, faxing questionnaires injects an element of urgency which can be missing in postal surveys. Faxed questionnaires are also as effective as the telephone in their ability to reach the targeted respondent (a major weakness in mail surveys which too often end in the post-room wastebin along with 'junk mail'). Unfortunately, domestic fax ownership is too low for this technique to be effective for consumer surveys.

Diaries

Diaries are used in surveys that seek to track respondents' actions over a period of time. The diary is in effect a questionnaire on which the respondent records his or her purchases daily, weekly or monthly, depending on the nature of the survey. Diaries are placed with respondents at the commencement of the survey and collected once the diary period is completed. Diaries can run for a fixed calendar period or can be completed once a target number of transactions or events are recorded.

Electronic data collection

Electronic data collection has come into its own with the spread of computers and information technology. The most basic form of automation in research is the computerization of questionnaires for administration by telephone (Computer Aided Telephone Interviewing – CATI) or face-to-face (Computer Aided Personal Interviewing – CAPI). These sophisticated programmes display the questionnaire on a screen, capture the responses via the keyboard, verify each response (to ensure that it is compatible with other responses given), insert the correct skip patterns and prepare the data for analysis. The associated management system holds a file of potential respondents and ensures that the quotas of different respondent types are maintained. The set-up costs of CATI and CAPI surveys are high, which generally means that they are employed only in large-scale surveys. They are also less effective for surveys in which a high proportion of the questions are open ended, requiring the entry of large numbers of verbatim comments.

At a higher level, EPOS and stock control systems which collect point-of-sale and stock information have proved to be of considerable value in tracking the flow of products through distributors. The analysis of tapes obtained from retailers and wholesalers has replaced physical store checks for many product groups.

Electronic meters are widely used in television audience research to collect viewing statistics. Current versions record the times a representative sample of sets are switched on and off, the channels tuned and, via a sensor system, the number of individuals watching the set. These data are collected automatically through a telephone link to a central computer for overnight analysis. The use of meters for other measurements which lend themselves to mechanical analysis, such as the use of vehicles, have been explored but not as yet implemented.

Hall tests

Hall tests are employed largely in new product development programmes when samples of the products need to be shown or tested on a large sample of potential buyers. They comprise a physical set-up in a hall located in or near a shopping precinct. Respondents are recruited to visit the hall, test the product and record their reactions.

Observation techniques

Observation techniques encompass a wide range of research approaches ranging from measured reactions to products or advertising material to recording the ways in which customers shop, handle products or behave. Observation is a physical, as opposed to a reported, record of customer actions and can therefore be more accurate. Unfortunately the situations in which customers can be observed are often artificial and their actions may differ from those occurring in real life.

Questionnaires

The questionnaire, however applied, is the general workhorse of all market research activity. The use of a questionnaire ensures that the research is carried out consistently and that the results are collected in a format.which facilitates analysis. The format of the questionnaire to be used depends on the type of data to be collected, the number of interviews to be completed and the method of analysis. Large quantitative surveys generally deploy short, highly structured questionnaires which are suitable for machine analysis. Qualitative surveys are normally based on small numbers of interviews using a long, unstructured questionnaire which is likely to be analysed by hand. Questionnaires generally incorporate one or more of the following types of question:

- dichotomous questions (yes/no);
- multiple choice questions (giving a list of possible responses);
- semantic scales (scales based on words such as excellent, average, poor);
- scaling questions (numerical importance or rating scales or Likert scales);
- open-ended responses.

Questionnaires can be either unstructured (in which all the questions are open-ended checklists), fully structured (in which all questions are multiple choice or scaling questions), or semi-structured (a mixture of the two). Fully structured questionnaires assume that the full range of responses is known in advance and to achieve this may require preliminary, unstructured research. There is nothing worse than to design a questionnaire with multiple options only to find that a high proportion of respondents opt for the 'others' category.

Sampling

All forms of survey research rely on the fact that the activities, requirements or attitudes of any given universe can be described by analysing a small sample of that universe. This in turn requires that the sample be representative of the universe and is structured to reflect the various types of individuals or units that make up the universe. The prime determinants of the size of sample required depends on the homogeneity of the universe and the level of detail required in the final analysis. Samples of several thousand, structured by income group, life-style or region are regularly used to represent national populations of tens of millions, but if the analysis is required by fine breakdowns of consumer type the numbers can increase dramatically. Sample numbers are also affected by the characteristic of the product being surveyed. Products or services purchased frequently by a high proportion of individuals, such as food and drink, can be researched using relatively small samples. Products or services purchased infrequently, such as automobiles or consumer durables, may require large samples simply to identify customers that have made a purchase within the recent past.

Sampling is an exact science but in market research it is usually practised pragmatically. The true random sample, in which all units of the universe have an equal chance of appearing in the sample, is rarely practised – mainly because it is too costly to implement. The most common approach is the quota sample in which quotas are set for respondents fulfilling certain criteria. Individuals are then screened to determine whether they fit one of the quotas and interviewing proceeds until the quotas are filled. Geographically random samples are feasible using telephone interviews but are commonly abandoned in favour of random locations, which concentrate interviewing in specific parts of the territory.

A major concern of researchers is to ensure that the sample contains no bias which might make the results of the survey unrepresentative. Bias can occur from the way in which the sample is structured or the way in which it is selected, either of which can favour particular members of the population. The over-representation of some groups of the population and the under-representation of others will lead to results which do not represent the population as a whole. The sample design strategy must seek to eliminate or at least minimize these problems.

Geodemographic and lifestyle data

Knowledge of the structure of the consumer universe, and therefore the types of sample that need to be drawn, has been considerably enhanced by the development of geodemographic and lifestyle information. Traditionally, the primary segmentation of consumers was by socio-economic group implying that the requirements and expenditure patterns of high income, managerial grades and other key groups were reasonably homogeneous. This system worked reasonably well for years, though the category into which a respondent fell could not normally be determined until they were interviewed. It was then shown that the type of residence and its location, as defined by postcode, was not only a more effective predictor of purchases but was also more accessible. Thus, geodemographic group has become more widely used as a basic structure for sampling. Similarly, lifestyle research has shown that definitions such as age, marital status, size of family can be replaced by descriptors which take account of the aspirations and perceptions of individual consumers. 'Yuppies' and 'empty nesters' have distinct expenditure patterns which are unique to them and enable suppliers to apply a more relevant segmentation approach to their marketing.

Analysis

The final stage in the research process is the analysis of findings and recommendations. In large-scale quantitative surveys this is normally under-taken mechanically using survey analysis packages. Qualitative surveys, for which the samples are smaller, are generally analysed by hand. The output, be it tables or qualitative description, is reported to the research user in a report which interprets the findings and draws conclusions. The report is the prime record of what has been done and the outcome from the research.

THE ANALYSIS OF INDUSTRIAL MARKETS

By far the highest proportion of research expenditure is spent on the analysis of consumer markets. However, there are important applications for market research in the analysis of industrial markets where the risks attached to poor decision-making are as high if not greater than in consumer goods marketing.

Outside certain specialist sectors such as pharmaceuticals, marketers of industrial goods and services have rarely been consistent users of market research. This is partly because of the size and structure of the market environments in which they operate and partly because the marketing process tends to be more direct, giving the vendor substantially higher exposure to his customers than is normally the case in consumer markets.

Industrial markets are considerably more complex than consumer markets. The main causes of complexity lie in the fact that specifying and purchasing are rarely in the hands of a single individual and that the criteria by which suppliers are selected and evaluated take into account a wide range of technical and commercial considerations as well as the emotional factors that operate so powerfully in consumer markets. Buyers of industrial products have a heightened need to be seen to have made a good decision, as their jobs are at stake as well as their professional esteem. All of this points to an increased need for market analysis to provide marketing and sales staff with a firm foundation for decisions. However, in most industrial markets the number of potential customers is a fraction of the customer base for consumer products. There are exceptions such as office equipment and telecommunications which are sold into very large industrial universes, but the norm is small customer universes in which it is theoretically easier to gain in-depth knowledge of practices and requirements. An industrial salesforce calling regularly on clients can easily be persuaded that it understands the market in which it is operating. This is rarely true, since purchasers of industrial goods and services have a number of good reasons to bias the information provided to suppliers and any sense of complete understanding is usually misplaced.

Despite their added complexity, industrial markets are researched in much the same way as consumer markets. The key differences lie in sampling procedure, which is substantially more complex, and in the need to employ research staff who can understand the technicalities of the businesses being researched. The research techniques are virtually identical, though there is a tendency to use more qualitative approaches to provide a deeper understanding of customer requirements, buying procedures, supplier evaluation criteria and the performance of suppliers.

INTERNATIONAL RESEARCH

As markets develop globally there is a growing requirement for global information. Research can be carried out in most, if not all countries and research services are available on a global scale either through multinational research groups or independent local research companies. Whereas, some years ago, market research would have been an alien concept in certain cultures, increasing use has made it acceptable everywhere.

Given the enormous differences in culture, lifestyle and the patterns of purchases, research surveys are surprisingly similar in approach and structure worldwide. When defining international surveys the problems are more of adaptation to suit local conditions in each country than the adoption of completely different approaches. Some of the more obvious differences in research in different countries are:

1   In many countries the demand for continuous research programmes is insufficient to justify their establishment and this type of data is therefore unavailable.
2   The quality of secondary information sources can vary considerably from country to country; as a general rule they are good in the industrialized countries but weak in the developing world.
3   The quality and recency of demographic information on individual consumers and industry varies substantially from country to country.
4   The usefulness of telephone research is obviously dependent on the quality of the telephone service and the incidence of telephone ownership. There are also cultural barriers to collecting information by telephone – in Japan for example.
5   Data which are willingly given in some countries are regarded as strictly confidential in others.
6   In many countries products are not purchased in standard packages, which may make it difficult to track the volumes of purchases.
7   Structures of distribution can vary significantly from country to country and this must be reflected in the research approach.

National surveys that examine markets in a single country are rarely problematical. However, multinational surveys seeking comparable results in two or more countries do generate problems. Such surveys need to be planned with considerable care to ensure that recorded differences in attitude and approach reflect market conditions and not differences in survey approach. There is an increasing trend towards international surveys which are set up, analysed and reported centrally but with fieldwork carried out separately in each market. These have the major advantage of a common approach and harmonized analysis and are generally less costly than a series of individual country surveys. There has also been some use of centralized telephone interviewing into a number of national markets regarded as suitable for a telephone approach. To be effective this demands a supply of linguists and an ability to work round the clock to take account of time differences.

WORKING WITH RESEARCH COMPANIES

Over the last decade there has been a continual trend amongst research users to outsource their research requirements from professional agencies rather than undertake studies themselves. This has brought advantages such as anonymity, objectivity and cross-fertilization as well as cost savings, but it also means that in order to get the most from their budgets clients require skills in working with outside agencies. The three elements of the research programme that are key to ensuring a successful outcome are:

1 the research brief;
2 the agency proposal;
3 liaison during the research.

These are most applicable to ad hoc research. Where data are being purchased off the shelf, as is commonly the case with continuous or syndicated surveys, there is less interaction with the research agency and the findings can be viewed in advance to ensure that they are what is required. Even then, if special analysis of the data is required, the following guidelines may prove important.

The research brief

A survey is only as good as the initial brief. If users fail to set out what they require it is unlikely that the right result will be obtained. A good briefing document flows naturally from the planning process which results in the need for a survey being defined and should contain at the very least:

- background information (the company, its record, its association with the business to be considered in the survey);
- the nature of the problem to be tackled by the research;
- the product or service to be researched;
- relevant internally available information on the market;
- thoughts on the best research approach;
- time and budgetary constraints.

This document should be sent to a shortlist of companies thought to be capable of carrying out the project, together with an invitation to quote and a time scale within which the quotation is required. If requested the client should agree to a meeting in which the research requirement is explained in more depth.

The proposal

Those invited to quote should respond with a proposal which will be the basis for selection of the research agency to be used. At its simplest, in situations where the client has provided a very precise specification of what is required (number of interviews, interview type, interview length, sample methodology and analysis routines), the proposal will contain the agency's credentials, a response to any questions raised in the brief, suggestions for improving the project or reducing costs and a fee. Where the brief does little more than outline the problem the proposal needs to be much fuller and should contain:

- the objectives of the research;
- the information to be sought;

359

- the research approach, the types of research techniques to be deployed and the numbers of interviews and group discussions;
- the cost;
- the time the survey will take to complete;
- the research team and their qualifications;
- any related experience the agency has.

It should be borne in mind that some agencies write better proposals than research documents, but the content, format, presentation and amount of thought provided in the proposal should give a reasonable guide to the ability of the agency.

Controlling the research process

Once the agency has been chosen there are some simple ground rules for ensuring that the survey runs smoothly. The client should follow the following procedures.

1 Meet the research team and brief them personally to ensure that they all understand what is required.
2 Pass over all information that is relevant and non-confidential; there is no point in asking research staff to regenerate what is already in existence.
3 Obtain frequent progress reports.
4 Do not change the research specification midway through the research project.
5 Receive an oral presentation of the findings once the data have been analysed, but prior to a report being written.
6 Ensure that the research team interpret their findings and specify what they see as the solution to the client's problem.

CONCLUSION

Research is a complex, time-consuming and costly process which must be used effectively. It is essential to recognize when additional data can enhance the quality of decision-making, but it is equally essential to know when research is an expensive luxury, the cost of which cannot be justified. The results of too many research projects have languished unused on marketing managers' shelves, acting as a discouragement for further expenditure. The application of simple specification rules will help to ensure that expensive mistakes are avoided and that research will make its rightful contribution to the efficiency and effectiveness of the marketing process.

FURTHER READING

Baker, M. (1991) *Research for Marketing*, London: Macmillan.
Birn, R., Hague, P. and Vangelder, P. (eds) (1991) *A Handbook of Market Research Techniques*, London: Kogan Page.
Bradley, U. (1987) *Applied Marketing and Social Research*, London: John Wiley.
Chisnall, P. (1991) *Marketing Research*, London: McGraw-Hill.
Dutka, Alan (1993) *AMA Handbook for Customer Satisfaction*, Lincolnwood Ill.: NTC Business Books.
Hague, P. (1990) *The Industrial Marketing Research Handbook*, London: Kogan Page.
Malhotra, N. K. (1993) *Marketing Research: An Application Orientation*, Englewood Cliffs, NJ: Prentice Hall.
Moroney, M. (1992) *Facts From Figures*, London: Penguin.
Sutherland, K. (ed.) (1991) *Researching Business Markets*, London: Kogan Page.
Worcester, R. and Downam, J. (eds) (1986) *Consumer Market Research Handbook*, Netherlands: Elsevier.

21

THE MARKETING AUDIT

Aubrey Wilson

Every company, without exception, has locked within its operations resources that are either unused, underused or wrongly used. These resources could take many forms – physical, administrative, know-how, image, customers, skills, markets, brands, R&D are just a few. They have in common that their potential in terms of their contribution to marketing is not known or not always fully appreciated by their owners.

The marketing audit is a relatively simple, low-cost technique that enables a company to identify and exploit these possessions – thereby yielding usually low-cost, often no-cost, techniques, which when released into the marketing activity will materially improve the company's position. Lack of timely and detailed knowledge is caused partly by familiarity with the organization and its markets, but above all because the pressure of everyday events prevents standing back and taking an objective look at the company.

The marketing audit should not be confused with the market audit. The market audit is, as implied in its title, a quantification and qualification of markets (i.e. size, structure, trends, shares). The marketing audit is an analytical tool for identification, evaluation, measurement, motivation and action for improved performance. It gives a marketing profile for the audited company and it provides a method of assessing marketing effectiveness in a number of functions. The results of such examinations indicate where action is required to improve marketing. Properly conducted, the marketing audit highlights clearly where an organization stands along a scale ranging from no marketing to total sophistication. However, the major purpose is to give clear guidelines to top management on how to respond to a low or mediocre position or to improve further a satisfactory performance by introducing better marketing motivation and action.

Audits, which are commonplace in business, are almost invariably after-the-fact studies. The marketing audit provides evaluation and analysis before the actions are decided upon and is designed to ensure that all resources, even those with no apparent contribution to make to marketing but nevertheless impacting

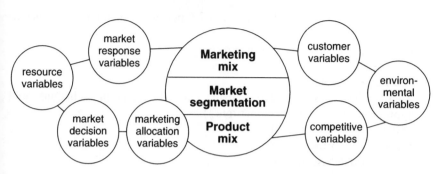

Figure 1   The marketing audit

on it, are fully employed to release their maximum potential. The audit technique, as applied to marketing, provides a simple, logical, coherent and structured approach to a business activity to which objective scrutiny is not normally applied.

Conventionally, audits tend to be introduced when a company's marketing activities are perceived as not wholly effective. This is usually demonstrated by the firm losing market shares or by declining profit or a loss. Recently, however, the audit is being adopted for regular periodic use – in fact as a benchmarking technique rather than as a damage limitation exercise.

It should be clear that the marketing audit is as much concerned with the overall marketing strategy of the company as with tactical considerations. It can investigate the successes, failures and potential of the three main components of strategy – segmentation, marketing and product mix – and the variables which the strategy influences or controls. See Figure 1.

TECHNIQUE

The audit method is based on extracting and interpreting information already in the company. It does not seek original external facts and therefore no market or other research, which can be expensive and time consuming, is involved. Any lack of data identified does or can lead to appropriate action for obtaining recent, detailed and better information.

The audit commences with the collection and study of the company's documentation. This usually comprises the following, but for the individual organization there may also be specific items:

• Organization chart (official and informal).
• Corporate/market/profit plan/budgets.
• Sales analyses.

363

- Job specifications of marketing and sales personnel including the sales or order office.
- Catalogues and brochures (own and competitors').
- Press releases.
- Salesforce costs analyses.
- Media advertising and direct mail material (including schedules and appropriations (own and competitors')).
- Other marketing costs analyses.
- Salesforce reporting formats.
- Customer database formats.
- Enquiry records.
- Pricing forms including discount structure.
- Sales analyses (home and export).
- Salesforce's, agents' and distributors' performance assessment forms.
- New product search reports and evaluations.
- List of journals and publications received.
- List of external statistics regularly received.
- Guarantee claim record.
- Credit note analyses.
- Complaints analyses.
- Service record formats.
- Agency contracts.
- Terms of business.
- Costing and pricing formats.
- Training programmes for sales and/or marketing people – content and frequency.
- Details on any market research and customer satisfaction undertaken or bought in during the last one or two years.

Even at this early stage of the process, recommendations can arise. The lack of up-to-date competitor literature is a frequent omission that is easily rectified. Indeed, a recommendation would be to create a dossier for all important competitors comprising their literature, every reference found in trade and other press (there are commercial services which will undertake this task), annual reports, relevant extracts from salesmen's reports and all other contacts and sources. Within a very short space of time a picture emerges of the competition and, indeed, of competitive scenarios.

Another example of how the collection of documentation can lead to early recommendations is whether 'terms of business', often devised many years ago, are appropriate for today's conditions. For example, a clause stating the contract shall be read under English law may not be acceptable to European Union customers. Statements such as: 'Goods manufactured by us and which are shown to our satisfaction to be defective' no longer fit today's ethos of customer care.

As can be appreciated, the key aspects of documentation collection are:

identification of what is not as well as what is available; whether the documentation yields useable information; whether those who provide it are acknowledged; whether it is demonstrated to them how that information is to be used. Those who provide input, most particularly the salesforce, can be greatly demotivated if they perceive the documentation to be pure bureaucracy, with no practical application or benefit to the person involved in input.

IDENTIFYING RESPONDENTS

The first step in the audit proper is to identify who within the organization will be able to provide information. The company's structure schematic, as well as any informal networks which can be traced, will give an indication of who should be consulted. This can be amended as the programme proceeds. The personnel needed are those who can provide information because of their knowledge, experience and activities. Substantially, the lists will be drawn from marketing and sales functions, but it is not unusual for other departments to be included such as servicing, R&D, production, personnel and finance.

Typically, respondents will include a stratum of top and middle management and, where appropriate, 'sharp end' personnel such as field sales, servicing engineers, order office staff, and even reception and telephone operators. An example of the value of the contribution of this last, apparently unlikely, group can be found in a professional service firm where a conversation with the telephonist revealed a problem with strong negative image connotations. She complained that in a large and rambling building it was difficult to locate professional staff who lacked the discipline to notify her when they were away from their offices and where they could be contacted. This caused clients to be forced to wait while a search was made and the aggravation caused often led to irritation being directed against the operator as well as the missing member of staff. Apart from the obvious effect on clients the problem also inflamed inter-personnel relations which in turn led to a further deterioration in service. The resolution of the problem was simple. Given that discipline could not be imposed an internal paging system was introduced. The interesting aspect of the situation was the total unawareness of top management that any problem existed.

A CHECKLIST APPROACH

The most efficient way to conduct an audit is to develop a specially designed checklist, or to adopt or adapt any of those which are available in published form.[1] Apart from imparting discipline into the information gathering process, the checklist ensures that the same ground is covered in the same way if the audit is used for benchmarking each time a check is taken.

Since the essential tool of the auditor is the checklist, the questions must be structured while also being free-ranging. They should cover every significant

365

aspect of a company's marketing activities. Conventionally, but not exclusively, they will embrace some twenty-eight subjects. See Appendix, page 376. However, as with documentation, individual companies may have areas which are specific to them.

The core of the technique, indeed one of the principal skills required, is to select the subjects to be investigated and the questions to be posed and to devise supplementary questions which will yield the information (or conversely any lack of important information) required.

In using a typical preprepared checklist, the first stage is to eliminate all sections which are irrelevant. A company manufacturing advanced technical products would have no interest in non-differentiated (commodity) marketing (Appendix, item 26). Companies which do not export could ignore an export list (Appendix, item 5). Service companies are not concerned with physical distribution (Appendix, item 21). Of the list in the Appendix, typically some ten to fifteen subjects could be abandoned at once.

It is now necessary to study each of the remaining lists and remove any irrelevant questions. Asking questions about 'brand' visibility for a company that does not have branded products is obviously unnecessary (although in parenthesis it should be said that a question as to whether they should have brands will need to be asked). Similarly probing appropriations for direct response campaigns when this particular marketing tool is not part of the 'mix' of course eliminates this and other enquiries related to direct mail. Typically 30–40 per cent of the questions in any one list will be abandoned, making the final selection far less daunting and more manageable.

The supplementary questions

As important as the basic questions are, the supplementary questions which the original answer engenders will be critical. The following conversations are a precis of actual interviews.

Q	'Which directories, yearbooks and buyers' guides do we appear in?'
A	'*Kompass, Printers Year Book, Printing Trades Directory, Printing Portfolio* and about six Yellow Pages.'
Q	'What do these entries cost us?'
A	'Without checking I would say in the region of £50,000 a year.'
Supplementary question	'Can you trace any business directly to these insertions?'
A	'No.'
Supplementary question	'How do you justify continued use of these media?'

A	'All our competitors appear in them and if we don't it could affect us badly.'
Supplementary question	'Have any of your competitors dropped out?'
A	'I'm not sure. We don't monitor this and we don't keep out-of-date copies.'

From this exchange the recommendations are clear, namely to substantiate the statement which implied non-appearance would lead to loss of business and to establish the level of new and discontinued competitor entries and their market performance over, say, the past five years and then take the appropriate decisions.

Another example leading to a recommendation was:

Q	'How many days in the working year do the salesmen actually spend visiting customers?'
A	'Average (taken after reference to records) 152.'
Supplementary question	'Taking 222 days as a typical year of available days, what happens in the missing 50 days?'
A	'Administration matters, making appointments, order progress chasing in the plant.'
Supplementary question	'Which of these activities could someone with equal but different skills undertake for them?'
A	'Perhaps appointment making and progress chasing, possibly some administration.'
Supplementary question	'What would one extra call per sales person per week increase the annual call rate to?'
A	'Across the whole salesforce about 650 per annum.'
Supplementary question	'On the basis of current conversion of calls to orders can you give me a feel for how many extra orders 650 calls would produce?'
A	'Assuming the quality of calls remained the same, about 125 orders.'
Supplementary question	'What is the average value of an order?'
A	'There is a big variation, but at a guess, about £500.'
Supplementary question	'If the extra orders then represent perhaps over half a million of additional business would this offset the cost of having someone else lift part of the non-selling burden?'

The recommendation would be to analyse the average daily/weekly order intake and values to see if extra days gained at the cost of having someone else take over non-selling work would justify such a policy.

A last example relating to demonstrations can be given.

Q	'What is the conversion rate of enquiries to orders?'
A	'About 1:6.5.'
Supplementary question	'Can you break that down to show the conversion rate between enquiries to orders and enquiries to demonstrations to orders?'
A (after consulting records)	'Demonstration to order is about 1:3.'
Supplementary question	'If you were to increase the number of demonstrations would that ratio be maintained?'
A	'Probably drop slightly.'
Supplementary question	'Given improved conversion would it not be a better sales platform to "sell" demonstrations instead of machines?'

The recommendation was to change the sales platform to seek to obtain demonstrations. Since it is more difficult to get prospects to the factory it was recommended that a demonstration caravan should be fitted out to take on to customer sites.

A critical supplementary question to every response must always be 'how do you know?' The answer must be interpreted in terms of validity of the source and its timeliness.

OBTAINING THE INFORMATION

The above sequences occurred in a one-to-one personal interview but there are other ways, none so satisfactory, but worthy of consideration, which can be adopted.

Self-analysis

The self-analysis or self-completed questionnaire technique calls upon the chosen personnel to answer a series of questions. While a narrative response is always preferable and should be encouraged, most busy respondents prefer a structured response where they only have to tick, eliminate or score. When scoring is invoked each question should be weighted to arrive at a final score.[2] A simple rating of each issue does not give an accurate result unless the importance of the questions in relationship to each other is allowed for. That is, scoring high on an issue such as 'accessibility of the marketing department' and scoring high on 'punctual delivery' does not make them of equal importance. Similarly and unfortunately scoring high on an unimportant (to the customer) issue does not cancel out scoring badly on an important issue. Thus, it is very necessary to weight each question to enable the grossed-up score to have immediate relevance to the issues involved and to influence the final score.

Table 1 Advantages and disadvantages of self-analysis

Advantages	Disadvantages
The method can be quick and is cheap.	The wrong respondents may be chosen or be self-selected.
It forces the consideration of key issues in a logical sequence.	It is difficult for respondents to be totally objective.
Self-analysis is generally more acceptable where criticism of the marketing operation is inherent.	Some of the answers are on a semantic scale and it is not always possible to place a real meaning on the chosen answers or on the scale interval.
It does not imply an imposed solution.	The respondents may attempt to answer questions where their knowledge is inadequate, lacking or out of date.

The auditor has to make a trade-off between the advantages and disadvantages of the self-analysis approach before making a decision to adopt it. See Table 1.

Self-analysis plus independent evaluation of the analysis

This technique follows the self-analysis method and the resulting questionnaire is then used for discussion between the respondents and the analyst. Each answer is discussed and probed. In particular, facts are called for to support the opinions expressed. In order to avoid the suspicion of a predetermined and/or imposed solution, possible courses of action arising out of the point in question are sought from the respondent. This is essentially an iterative process in which

Table 2 Self-analysis plus independent evaluation

Advantages	Disadvantages
Inherent biases and ambiguities in the self-completed questionnaire can be probed.	The interrogation technique can create hostility unless handled with sensitivity.
It is a process of forcing 'second thoughts' or reconsideration of the original answers, particularly those which are given impulsively or without cross-reference.	Under questioning the respondent may feel, particularly where the evaluation is showing a fairly low level of marketing effectiveness, that they are being subjected to unfair or even prejudiced criticism.
It challenges conventional wisdom, folklore or unsubstantiated statements.	The interrogation itself may imply lack of belief in the original self-completed questionnaire.

values and actions are examined, but without comment by the analyst. (See Table 2.) The final appraisal is drawn up by the analyst, which can (but does not have to) be submitted to the respondent for further comment and perhaps correction or change. Such corrections and changes are themselves part of the evaluation process.

Mail interrogation

Mail interrogation can be undertaken on the self-analysis basis, but with the questioning recycled via correspondence so that the respondents have time to think about what is required of them and do not feel pressured. The process not only gives the respondents time to consult and to prepare replies, but the interviewer also has time to reflect on the formulation of the questions as each cycle of the enquiry is developed. See Table 3.

Table 3   Mail interrogation

Advantages	Disadvantages
Relatively cheap and total coverage in that all departments or companies in the group can be dealt with at the same time.	For the process to be completed rapidly it is necessary that the respondent should in fact reply quickly, which may not be particularly easy to achieve when people are pressed with other work, travelling, or resent the work involved.
Question formulation, reply and evaluation can receive careful consideration.	Communication by mail tends to be less clear, whereas in a personal interview questions can be explained more fully.
The respondent feels in control of the situation.	———

Visits and interviews

This approach is for the analyst to undertake the audit by straight interviewing techniques using semi-structured or unstructured methods. The respondent has no prior knowledge of the questions to be asked and therefore the replies tend to be more spontaneous, but at the same time it is possible for the analyst to ask for validation of views given. Moreover, by visiting the respondent it is possible to examine and observe some types of marketing activity and to arrive at a view on attitudes and activities. Visits and interviews can either be single interviews with a designated respondent whose job specification and activity can be checked at the interview for his or her ability and authority to deal with all the points to be raised. Alternatively, the visit can be for multiple interviews, with all the personnel involved. This enables the entire questionnaire to be covered in one meeting and also ensures that comments made are within the knowledge of everyone involved in the marketing process. See Table 4.

Table 4   Visits and interviews

Advantages	Disadvantages
Cross-evaluations and checks can be made.	Respondents may answer with more consideration for their colleagues' attitudes and reactions than the interviewer or the purpose of the interview.
Taken in groups, respondents, far from feeling at a disadvantage, feel at an advantage over the interviewer, and therefore are more inclined to cooperate.	Answers may be withheld or given defensively where respondents feel they may be criticized by their colleagues.
Group dynamics apply and modification of views (not simply consensus) will occur, which is of considerable value.	There may be resentment at inclusion/exclusion in the group chosen.

Method choice

The final choice of method(s) will depend upon the structure of the company and the units to be audited and to some extent on the numbers and types of personnel to be involved in the process. There can be no one approach which will work in all circumstances. Experience indicates that the personal interview either one-to-one, or as a group, has many advantages in terms of time and yield. Working in groups enables a Delphi approach to be adopted when each member can hear the advocacy for and against a particular opinion and as a consequence and if needs be to modify his or her views. However, while suggestions for actions should be welcomed, care must be taken not to get into the stultifying position of arguing about them. It is the job of the auditor to decide what are the implications of the information. An action plan created by a committee is going to be the antithesis of quick movement and decisiveness.

An important psychological point must be considered. The audit and questioning process can well disturb respondents who may regard the whole process as a personal performance assessment leading perhaps to some disadvantage. Before any meeting takes place, or at the very beginning of a meeting, the purpose of the audit must be explained to respondents – that it is the contribution of their knowledge, experience and ideas which is sought and that the interview is not a performance review. It is vital to obtain their enthusiastic cooperation. Thus, the purpose and outcome of the audit need to be completely understood by respondents.

MECHANICS

Once the questioning is complete the auditor must then evaluate the yield in terms of the actions which are required. The examples given above are indicative of the types of recommendations which can emerge. A typical audit for a company with say a £12m turnover should generate about 70–80 action points most of which, as has been indicated, could be introduced at low cost.

In terms of mechanics of the information-gathering stage it has been found that the best way to administer the questionnaire is to note responses in three different coloured pens or using three different symbols. Replies are noted using one colour. Any responses which would lead to a recommendation should be circled in another colour or marked with the appropriate symbol. Those replies which require further investigation, perhaps later during the interview, carry the third identification. As with all good interviewing, respondents should not be interrupted when they are providing relevant information, but only when discrepancies or contradictions that occur or the answers themselves raise new points. These are better dealt with separately, probably at a different part of the interview or at the end when any clarification can be sought. By adopting this method when the interview notes are interpreted the recommendations will stand out for transfer to the report, using the notes as a justification for the recommendation.

It is recognized that not all the recommendations can be implemented within the resources and time span available, so it may be necessary to place an order of priority on the introduction of changes or activities that are deemed necessary. To this end it is advisable to extract all action points for categorization into priority groups with an indication of, at the very least, the time implied by such terms as 'at once', 'short-term'. Without this and, on their own, time designations of this type have no real meaning. It is also useful to classify recommendations by likely cost implications, so that no-cost and low-cost measures can be initiated without budget changes or authorization. This alone should ensure the removal of one possible blockage to progress. It is well worth stating that any recommendation that can be adopted without cost or disturbance becomes a priority and has a high implementative value.

WHO SHOULD DO THE AUDIT?

It is essential that whoever conducts an audit should be totally unbiased and neutral. It is asking too much of a person to expect them to remain objective when reporting on a situation that may reflect on themselves or on their department or activity. There is certainly no technical reason why a member of the firm should not conduct the audit provided the desiderata can be met. The use of internal personnel carries the great advantage that they know a great deal about the company, its organization, personnel, markets, systems, opportunities and threats, thus learning-curve costs are not incurred. This very knowledge can unwittingly produce its own biases, which is something to be resisted, however difficult that may be.

Using an external consultant for the most part avoids the problem of lack of objectivity, but the advantage of familiarity with the organization is lost. However, while these factors might balance themselves out the one advantage the external consultant brings is the cross-fertilization of ideas and solutions which can occur between widely different industries. A recommendation successfully adopted by a travel agency was found, with modifications, to be applicable to a leading-edge electronics designer.

It is not possible to designate which is the best solution – both have their advantages and disadvantages. One feasible compromise is to have internal staff trained by an experienced external consultant using a hands-on approach. Hence, the first audit is conducted by the consultant, using the internal staff member as assistant and explaining the thinking behind the questions and how the recommendation emerges. On a second audit the consultant and staff member act as a partnership, undertaking some sections together and other parts alone. The consultant checks, amends and expands the internal staff member's sections, again explaining any changes. On a third audit the staff member leads with the consultant acting as assistant, with an occasional touch on the tiller. The consultant also edits the final report and again, as before, always explains any changes introduced.

Such a sequence will give the internal auditor confidence, help him or her identify their own biases and subjectivities and clearly demonstrate both technique and the wide-ranging thinking necessary to produce really creative recommendations.

THE REPORT

The report will tend to be quite daunting in size but must be capable of being handled easily and quickly. The format should follow the headings of the subjects audited and each item should comprise:

- Situation analysis – the auditor's understanding of the activities and performance.
- Recommendation for a course of action.
- Justification for the recommendation made.

In order to assist rapid implementation it is always advisable to extract the recommendations alone and restate them in the briefest form in a separate document or as an appendix. They must be cross-referenced to the body of the report, so that it is possible to consider the situation and justifications without allowing them to obscure the recommendation itself.

The last action of the audit is to place a date for initiation and completion of each activity, to decide who is responsible for carrying it through and who is to monitor progress and satisfactory completion. This point requires extra emphasis. Completing an audit does not automatically imply that the appropriate actions will be taken. To be certain that the marketing resources will be fully realized it is important to ensure that every action decided upon is allocated to an individual or group, that the time for its completion is scheduled and promulgated and that someone monitors that the task is satisfactorily completed by the due date. Allocate, schedule and monitor are the key words for guaranteeing action.

There are some basic rules which apply:

1 Peer pressure is better than instruction. If everyone knows what everyone is supposed to be doing and by when, the activity is more likely to get completed.
2 Volunteers are better than conscripts. In making recommendations, although not the task of the auditor to carry them out, it is helpful if he or she can weld together a team to implement the suggestions. However enthusiastic volunteers may be, it is obvious that they must have the skill to undertake the task.
3 While time recommendations are important relative to starting and completing, the likelihood of enthusiastic cooperation is greater if those who have accepted the tasks can set their own schedule. This way there can be no question that the requirements were unreasonable.

A format (see Figure 2) circulated to all those involved ensures that the whole action plan is known to everyone.

The marketing audit is not a substitute for action, nor should it be permitted to delay decision-taking. The auditor should keep this thought foremost in mind when undertaking the work. The audit process can be summarized as follows:

• Collect documentation.
• Decide the subjects for investigation.
• Devise or adopt a question checklist.
• Delete all non–relevant questions.
• Auditor answers all questions within his or her capability and recommends courses of action.
• List others who need to be consulted to complete audit.
• Decide whether to take individual replies or operate as a group.
• Identify which questions will be asked of which persons (for individual responses).
• Decide how response will be taken (i.e. personal interview, advance notice of questions and personal interview, written request and written response) (for individual responses).
• Conduct interviews.

Action Plan

Period   Date of issue

Target group	Objective	Activity/Media	Budget	Respon-sible	Plan dead-line	Time schedule											
						Jan	Feb	Mar	Apr	May	Jun	Jul	Aug	Sep	Oct	Nov	Dec
		Total															

Figure 2

- Analyse yield.
- Suggest courses of action with justification arising from the responses.
- Extract all action points and categorize according to urgency, likely cost, ease of implementation.
- Allocate each task by name, schedule it by date or elapsed time, agree monitoring procedure.

APPENDIX

Subjects for consideration

1 Marketing strategy and planning.
2 Product/service range.
3 The service element in marketing.
4 Company performance.
5 Export marketing.
6 Marketing information: systems and use.
7 Market size and structure.
8 Future market.
9 The salesforce and its management.
10 Support staff's role in marketing.
11 Cross-selling and internal marketing.
12 The agency system.
13 Non-personal promotion: methods and media.
14 The distributive system.
15 The buying process.
16 Analysing lost business.
17 Introducing new products/services.
18 User industries.
19 Key customer marketing.
20 Competitive climate.
21 Physical distribution and packaging.
22 Industry contacts.
23 Pricing.
24 Images and perceptions.
25 Quality in marketing.
26 Non-differentiated products and commodities.
27 Service businesses.
28 Product/service financial information.

NOTES

1   The Further Reading list gives details of some published checklists.

2   A weighting and rating system relating to ease of entry to new markets and which can be adapted for any subject will be found in Wilson, Aubrey (1991) *New Directions in Marketing*, Chapter 3, London: Kogan Page.

FURTHER READING

These titles all contain checklists.

Alles, Alfred (1988) *Exhibitions – Key to Effective Marketing*, London: Cassell.
Anderson, A. G. (1986) *Marketing Your Practice*, Chicago: American Bar Association.
Bittleston, J. and Shorter, C. B. (1982) *Book of Business Check Lists*, London: Associated Business Programmes.
Brand, Gordon T. (1972) *The Industrial Buying Decision*, London: Associated Business Programmes.
Brill, S. and Maister, D. H. (1984) *99 Questions. A Management Work Book*, supplement to *The American Lawyer*, November.
Davidson, J. P. (1990) *Essential Management Check Lists*, London: Kogan Page.
Godferoy, G. H. and Robert, C. (1993) *The Outstanding Negotiator*, London: Piatkus.
Hitchcock, E. B. (1981) *How To Sell Effectively Through Manufacturers' Agents*, New York: Frost & Sullivan.
Kotler, Philip and Bloom, P. N. (1984) *Marketing Professional Services*, Englewood Cliffs: Prentice Hall.
McDonald, M. (n/d) *Handbook of Marketing Planning*, Bradford: MCB Publications.
Maister, David (1993) *Managing for the Professional Service Firm*, New York: Free Press.
Martin, W. B. (1991) *Managing Quality Customer Service*, London: Kogan Page.
Melkman, A. (1979) *How to Handle Major Customers Profitably*, Farnborough: Gower.
Mendelsohn, Martin (1980) *How To Evaluate A Franchise*, London: Franchise Publication.
Ornstein, Edwin (1972) *The Marketing of Money*, Farnborough: Gower Press.
Ornstein, Edwin and Nunn, Austin (1980) *The Marketing of Leisure*, London: Associated Business Programmes.
O'Shaughnessy, J. (1984) *Competitive Marketing*, London: Allen Unwin.
Reed, Richard C. (ed.) (1980) *Win-Win Billing Strategies*, Chicago: American Bar Association.
Shaw, W. C. (1981) *How To Do A Company Plan*, London: Business Books.
Stapleton, J. (1989) *How To Prepare A Marketing Plan*, Farnborough: Gower.
Walmsley, John (1989) *The Development of International Markets*, London: Graham & Trotman.
Wilson, Aubrey (1973) *Assessment of Industrial Markets*, London: Associated Business Programmes.
Wilson, Aubrey (1984) *Practice Development for Professional Firms*, Maidenhead: McGraw-Hill.
Wilson, Aubrey (1992) *Marketing Audit Check Lists*, Maidenhead, London: McGraw-Hill.
Wilson, Aubrey (1993) *The Industrial Marketing Researchers Check List*, London: Department of Trade and Industry.
Wilson, M. (1980) *Management of Marketing*, Farnborough: Gower.
Winkler, J. (1989) *Winning Sales and Marketing Tactics*, London: Heinemann.

22

SALES FORECASTING

J. Scott Armstrong

This chapter focuses on sales forecasting. The main issue addressed involves predicting the amount of a product people will purchase, given the features of the product and the conditions of the sale. Sales forecasts are vital to the efficient operation of the firm. They are used to help investors make decisions about investments in new ventures, and aid managers on such decisions as the size of a plant to build, the amount of inventory to carry, the number of workers to hire, the amount of advertising to place, the proper price to charge, and the salaries to pay salespeople. Profitability depends on:

1 having a relatively accurate forecast of sales;
2 assessing the confidence one can place in the forecast;
3 using the forecast properly in the plan.

IMPORTANCE OF FORECASTING

Marketing practitioners believe that sales forecasting is important. In Dalrymple's (1975) survey of marketing executives at US companies, 93 per cent said that sales forecasting was 'one of the most critical' or 'a very important' aspect of their company's success. Furthermore, formal marketing plans are often supported by forecasts (Dalrymple 1987). Given its importance to the profitability of the firm, it is surprising that basic marketing texts devote so little space to the topic. Armstrong *et al.* (1987), in a content analysis of 53 marketing textbooks, found that forecasting was mentioned on less than 1 per cent of the pages.

Forecasting deserves more attention because research over the past three decades has produced surprising and useful findings. As a result, current sales forecasting practices are out of date at most firms. This chapter summarizes what has been learned about approaches that are helpful and those that are not. The chapter first provides a brief overview of forecasting methods. These methods are then discussed in the context of direct and causal approaches to sales forecasting. Particular attention is given to new product forecasting. This is followed by a discussion of how to select appropriate methods. The impact of improved data is considered. Finally, it describes how to assess uncertainty, and how to gain acceptance of forecasting methods and of forecasts.

FORECASTING METHODS

What forecasting methods are available? Forecasting methods differ in several ways. We describe them here in terms of how they process information. They may use either subjective or objective processes to analyse information. Also, some methods use information other than the variable of interest; of particular importance here is the use of causal information. Finally, some causal methods use classifications whereas others use relationships. These factors allow us to describe methods using a forecasting tree (see Figure 1). We describe each method briefly and summarize some of the more important findings about each. Makridakis and Wheelwright (1989) provide details on how to apply these methods.

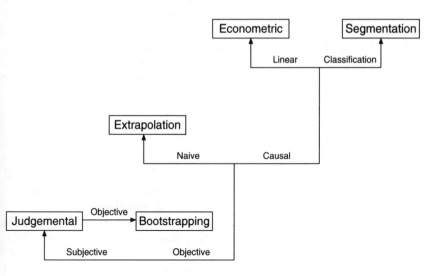

Figure 1 Forecasting methodology tree

Judgement

Judgemental forecasting methods process data subjectively. Judgement is the most popular method used by marketers for making important forecasts. It is especially appropriate when marketers lack data, such as when they are

379

forecasting for new products. When few forecasts are needed, judgement offers an inexpensive approach. When data are available, judgemental forecasting is typically less accurate than other methods.

The accuracy of judgemental forecasts can be improved through the use of structured methods. The Delphi procedure is one such method. Delphi is an iterative survey procedure in which experts provide forecasts for a problem, receive anonymous feedback on the forecasts from other experts, and then make another forecast. (For a summary of the evidence on the accuracy of Delphi versus unstructured judgement, see Armstrong 1985: 116–20.)

Bootstrapping

Bootstrapping converts judgemental methods into objective procedures. One way to do this is to obtain protocols of experts, whereby the expert describes the process as he or she makes forecasts. This process is then converted to a set of rules that is used to make forecasts. Another approach is to create a series of situations and to ask an expert to make forecasts for each. These judgemental forecasts are then regressed against data that the experts used to make their forecasts. This method provides estimates of how the experts relate each variable to sales volume.

Once developed, bootstrapping models offer a low-cost procedure for making additional forecasts. They almost always provide an improvement in accuracy in comparison to judgemental forecasts, although these improvements are typically small (Armstrong 1985: 274–84).

Extrapolation

Extrapolation methods use only historical data on the series of interest. The most popular and cost effective of these methods are based on exponential smoothing, whereby the more recent data are weighted more heavily. Gardner (1985) provides a review of research on exponential smoothing methods.

Interestingly, judgemental and quantitative extrapolation methods provide forecasts of roughly equal accuracy in many situations (Lawrence et al. 1985). The quantitative extrapolations have a small advantage when the data are ample and changes are expected to be large (Armstrong 1985: 393–401). Judgemental methods are preferable when there have been large recent changes in the sales level and where there is relevant knowledge about the item to be forecast (Sanders and Ritzman 1992). More important than these small gains in accuracy, however, is the fact that the quantitative methods are often less expensive. When one has thousands of forecasts to make every month, the use of judgement is not cost effective.

Empirical studies have led to the conclusion that relatively simple extrapolation methods perform as well as more complex methods. By simple methods, we mean that the functional form is simple, generally either linear or multiplicative.

For example, the Box-Jenkins procedure, one of the more complex approaches, has produced no measurable gains in forecast accuracy relative to simpler procedures (Makridakis *et al.* 1993). Although distressing to statisticians, this finding should be welcome to managers.

Quantitative extrapolation methods have two related shortcomings. First, they make no use of management's knowledge of the series. Second, they assume the causal forces that have affected the historical series will continue over the forecast horizon. The latter assumption is typically false, but problems arise only when the causal forces are contrary to the trend in the historical series (Armstrong and Collopy 1993). While such problems may occur only in a small minority of cases in sales forecasting, their effects can be disastrous. One useful rule is that trends should be extrapolated only when they coincide with management's expectations based on causal forces.

Econometric methods

Econometric methods can relate directly to planning. They can include marketing mix variables as well as variables representing key aspects of the market and its environment. Econometric methods are appropriate when one needs to forecast what will happen under different assumptions about the environment, and what will happen given different strategies. Econometric methods are most useful when:

1 strong causal relationships with sales are expected;
2 these causal relationships can be estimated;
3 large changes are expected to occur in the causal variables over the forecast horizon;
4 these changes in the causal variables can be forecast or controlled, especially with respect to their direction.

If any of these conditions does not hold (which is typical for short-range sales forecasts), then econometric methods should not be expected to improve accuracy.

Segmentation methods

Segmentation, like econometric methods, uses causal factors to forecast sales. However, it does this by grouping the various actors according to the causal variables (e.g. low-, middle-, and high-income customers). Segmentation avoids some assumptions often made by econometric models, such as that a variable has constant elasticity over its range. However, because separate analyses may be conducted for each segment, the method requires large sample sizes. Based on the few validation studies that have been done (Armstrong 1985: 412–17), segmentation is more accurate when a substantial amount of data are available and when the data are otherwise subject to problems with interactions (e.g. a relationship between sales and price is affected by another variable, such as advertising) and nonlinearities (e.g. the effect of price on sales varies depending on whether the price is above or below the reference price).

DIRECT APPROACHES TO SALES FORECASTING

Many firms try to forecast sales directly (i.e. by using trends over time), with little explicit attention given to causal factors (Dalrymple 1987). This approach is inexpensive and easy to understand.

Extrapolation methods are widely used for short-term forecasts of demand for inventory and production decisions. Exponential smoothing has been one of the most cost-effective extrapolation methods. When the data are for time intervals shorter than a year, it is generally advisable to use seasonal adjustments, given sufficient data. When the historical series involve much uncertainty, the forecaster should use relatively simple models (Schnaars 1984) and dampen the forecast as the horizon increases (i.e. forecast smaller changes from the most recent value; see Gardner and McKenzie 1985).

Intentions-to-buy studies have been widely used to forecast sales, especially for proposed products. Potential consumers are provided with a description of the product and the conditions of sale, and then are asked how much they would buy. Eleven-point rating scales are popular for this approach. The typical scale also has verbal designations such as 0 = 'No chance, almost no chance (1 in 100)' to '10 = Certain, practically certain (99 in 100).' Intentions surveys are useful when all of the following conditions hold:

1 The event is important.
2 Responses can be obtained.
3 The respondent has a plan.
4 The respondent reports correctly.
5 The respondent can fulfil the plan.
6 Events are unlikely to change the plan.

These conditions imply that intentions forecasts are more useful for short-term forecasts of business-to-business sales.

The technology of intentions surveys has improved greatly over the past half century. Useful methods have been developed for selecting samples, compensating for nonresponse bias, and reducing response error. Dillman (1978) provides excellent advice for designing intention surveys. Despite significant improvements, response error is typically the most important cause of errors (Sudman and Bradburn 1982). Improvements in this technology have been clearly demonstrated by studies on voter intentions (Perry 1979). Still, as shown in the review by Kalwani and Silk (1982), the correspondence between intentions and sales is often not close.

As an alternative to asking potential customers about their intentions to purchase, one can ask experts to predict sales. For example, Wortruba and

Thurlow (1976) discuss how opinions from members of the salesforce can be used to forecast sales. One can also ask distributors or marketing executives for sales forecasts. Experts, however, are often subject to biases. Sales people may try to forecast on the low side if the forecasts will be used to set quotas. Marketing executives may forecast high in their belief that this will motivate the salesforce. One useful strategy is to include experts who are expected to have different biases.

CAUSAL MODELS TO FORECAST SALES

Instead of forecasting sales alone, one can forecast the factors that cause sales. This includes the environment along with the actions of customers, competitors, and intermediaries. Forecasts of these elements can then be combined to provide an overall sales forecast. Causal models are advantageous in that they can be more directly related to decision-making. On the other hand, they are more expensive to develop and maintain. Typical causal elements for sales forecasting are shown in Figure 2.

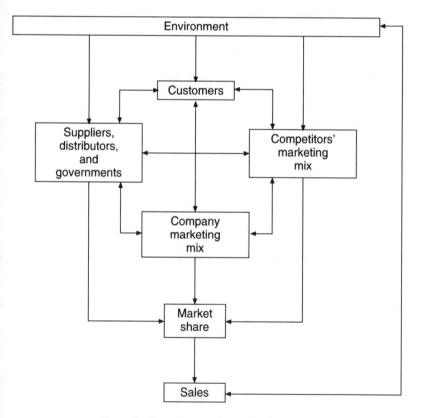

Figure 2 Causal approach to sales forecasting

The breakdown of the problems into the elements of Figure 2 is useful for thinking about the decisions. However, it should only be used for forecasting if one has good information about each of the components and understands how each relates to sales. Given the necessary information, the breakdown should allow for a more effective use of the information. If not, decomposition of the problem is likely to reduce forecast accuracy because an error in a multiplicative element is translated to the overall sales forecast. Furthermore, errors in the same direction will be compounded. Thus, an overestimation of 10 per cent in each of 2 elements would lead to a 21 per cent error in the sales forecast (i.e. 1.1 times 1.1 equals 1.21).

The breakdown of Figure 2 assumes a series of models to represent each component. It is not recommended that all of the factors be incorporated into a single-equation model, such as a regression equation. This is because one is unlikely to be able to find sufficient relevant data by which to estimate the parameters of the model. Furthermore, various statistical problems such as collinearity and interactions make it difficult to estimate relationships. Instead, each component should be handled separately. To obtain sales, one simply multiplies market share times the market size.

Environmental forecasts

Interestingly, there exists little evidence that more accurate forecasts of the environment (e.g. population, the economy, social trends, technological change) lead to better forecasts of behaviour by consumers, competitors, and inter-mediaries. However, improved environmental forecasts are useful when large changes are likely, such as the adoption of free trade policies, reductions in tariffs, economic depressions, natural disasters, and wars.

One key to better environmental forecasts is to use quantitative causal models. Econometric models provide more accurate forecasts than those provided by extrapolation or by judgement when large changes are involved (Armstrong 1985, chapter 15, summarizes evidence on this). Important findings that aid econometric methods are to:

1 Base the selection of causal variables upon forecasting theory and knowledge about the situation, rather than upon the statistical fit to historical data (e.g. do not use the R^2 of the fit data).
2 Use relatively simple models (e.g. do not use simultaneous equations; do not use models that cannot be specified as linear in the parameters).
3 Use variables only if the estimated relationship to sales is in the same direction as specified a priori.

The last point is consistent with the underlying theme to base forecasting methods on theoretical reasoning, not on statistical criteria. Consistent with this viewpoint, leading indicators, a non-causal approach to forecasting that has been widely accepted for decades, does not seem to improve the accuracy of forecasts

(Diebold and Rudebusch 1991). Fortunately, it is often possible to obtain published forecasts of environmental factors. These may be adequate for many purposes.

Customers

One should know the size of the potential market for the given product category (e.g. how many people in region X might be able to purchase an automobile); the ability of the potential market to purchase (e.g. income per capita and the price of the product); and the needs of the potential customers. Separate examination of each of these factors can help in forecasting demand for the category.

The choice of a forecasting model to estimate customer response depends on the stage of the product life cycle. As one moves through the concept phase to the prototype, test market, introductory, growth, maturation, and declining stages, the relative value of the alternative forecasting methods changes. For example, intentions and expert opinions are vital in the concept and prototype stages. Later, judgement is useful as an input to quantitative models. Extrapolation methods may be useful in the early stages if it is possible to find analogous products (Claycamp and Liddy 1969). In later stages, extrapolation methods become more useful and less expensive as one can work directly with data on sales or orders. Econometric and segmentation methods become more useful after a sufficient amount of actual sales data is obtained.

Company

The company sets its own marketing mix. This reduces the need to make forecasts of its actions. However, sometimes the policies are not implemented according to plan because of changes in the market, actions by competitors, or a lack of cooperation by those in the firm. Thus, it may be useful to forecast the actions that will actually be taken (e.g. if we provide a trade discount, what will be the average price paid by the final consumers?).

Intermediaries

What actions will be taken by suppliers, distributors, and the government? One useful prediction model is the naive or random walk, whereby we assume that the future is the same as the most recent past. This model is surprisingly difficult to improve upon. Nevertheless, it is not appropriate when large changes are expected. In such cases one can use structured judgement, extrapolate from analogous situations, or use econometric models.

Structure typically improves the accuracy of judgement, especially if it can realistically mirror the actual situation. Role playing is one such structured technique. It is useful when the outcome to be predicted depends on the interaction among different parties. For example, Armstrong and Hutcherson (1989) asked subjects to role play the interactions between producers and distributors. In this disguised situation, Philco was trying to convince super-markets to sell its appliances through a scheme whereby customers received discounts based on the volume of purchases at selected supermarkets. A short (less than one hour) role play of the situation correctly predicted the supermarket managers' responses for nine of twelve two-person groups. In contrast, only one of thirty-seven groups was correct when two-person groups made predictions without benefit of formal techniques.

Econometric models offer a much more expensive approach to forecasting the actions by intermediaries. This approach requires a substantial amount of information. For an example, see Montgomery (1975), which presents a model to predict whether a supermarket buying committee would put a new product on its shelves. This model, which used information about advertising, supplier's reputation, margin, and retail price, provided reasonable predictions for a hold-out sample.

Competitors

Can we improve upon the simple, 'naive', forecast that competitors will continue to act as they have in the past? Surprisingly, little evidence exists that we can. These forecasts are difficult because of the interaction that occurs among the key actors in the market. Because competitors have conflicting interests, they are unlikely to respond truthfully to an intentions survey.

A small-scale survey of marketing experts suggested that the most popular approach to forecasting competitors' actions is unaided expert opinion (Armstrong et al. 1987). However, because the 'experts' are usually those in the company, this may introduce biases related to their desired outcomes. For example, brand managers are generally too optimistic about their brands.

Market share

Can we do better than the naive model of 'no change'? For existing markets that are not undergoing major change, the answer seems to be no (Brodie and de Kluyver 1987). This is true even when one has excellent data about the competitors (Alsem et al. 1989). However, causal models should improve forecasts when large changes are made, such as when promotions are used to increase sales. Causal models should also help when a firm's sales have been artificially limited due to production capacity, tariffs, or quotas. Furthermore, contingent forecasts are important. A firm can benefit by obtaining good forecasts of how its policies (e.g. a major price reduction) would affect its market share.

NEW PRODUCT FORECASTING

New product forecasting is of particular interest in view of its importance to decision-making and the large errors that are typically made in such forecasts. Tull (1967) estimated the mean absolute percentage error for new product sales to be about 65 per cent. Shocker and Hall (1986) provide an evaluation of pretest market models, which have gained wide acceptance among business firms. Wind *et al.* (1981) contains a collection of papers on the topic.

When the new product is just a concept, heavy reliance is usually placed on intentions surveys. Intentions to purchase new products are complicated because potential customers may not be sufficiently familiar with the proposed product and because the various features of the product affect one another (e.g. price, quality, and distribution channel). Furthermore, producers are often considering several alternative designs for the new product. In such cases, potential customers are presented with a series of perhaps twenty or so alternative offerings. For example, various features of a personal computer, such as price, weight, battery life, screen clarity, and memory, might vary according to rules for experimental design (the basic ideas being that each feature should vary greatly, and that the variations among the features should not correlate with one another). The customer is forced to make trade offs among various features. This formal procedure is called 'conjoint analysis' because the consumers consider the product features jointly. This procedure is widely used by firms (Cattin and Wittink 1982). An example of a successful application is the design of a new Marriott hotel chain (Wind *et al.* 1989). This use of conjoint analysis to forecast new product demand can be expensive because it requires large samples of potential buyers, the potential buyers may be difficult to locate, and the questionnaires are difficult to complete. Respondents must, of course, understand the concepts that they are being asked to evaluate. Although conjoint analysis rests on good theoretical foundations, little validation research exists in which its accuracy is compared with the accuracy of alternative techniques such as Delphi.

The use of data from experts is different from that supplied by consumers. When an expert is asked to predict the behaviour of a market, there is no need to claim that this is a representative expert. Quite the contrary, the expert may be exceptional. When using experts to forecast, one needs few experts, typically only between five and twenty (Hogarth 1978). Perhaps the most surprising finding is that experts with modest expertise about the item to be forecast are just as accurate as those with high expertise (Armstrong 1985: 91–6 provides a review of this evidence). This means that it is not necessary to purchase expensive expert advice. It is generally wise to use some experts who are not involved with the products in order to avoid biases (Tyebjee 1987). The accuracy of expert opinions is comparable to forecasts based on consumer intentions, and each approach contributes useful information with the result that a combined forecast is more accurate than either one alone (Sewall 1981).

Once the new product is on the market, it is possible to use extrapolation methods. In particular, much attention has been given to the selection of the proper functional form to extrapolate early sales. The diffusion literature posits an S-shaped curve to predict new product sales. That is, growth builds up slowly at first, becomes rapid as word-of-mouth and observation of use spread, then slows again as it approaches a saturation level. A substantial literature exists on diffusion models. As a rough measure, from 1984 to 1991, the *Social Science Citation Index* listed 1,887 articles that used 'diffusion' or some variant in their title or keywords, and about a third of these were related to business. Despite this, Collopy *et al.* (1994) found no well-designed empirical comparisons of diffusion models against alternative forecasting methods. In Rao's study, simple extrapolations were more accurate than diffusion models, but the situations did not lend themselves ideally to forecasting with diffusion models.

SELECTION OF THE BEST METHOD

Assume that you were asked to predict annual sales of consumer products such as stoves, refrigerators, fans, and wine for the next five years. What forecasting method would you use? As indicated above, the selection should be guided by the stage in the product life cycle and by the availability of data. But general guidelines cannot provide a complete answer. Because each situation differs, you should consider more than one method.

Given that you use more than one method to forecast, how should you pick the best method? One of the most widely used approaches suggests that you select the one that has performed best in the recent past. This raises the issue of what criteria should be used to identify the best method. Statisticians have relied upon sophisticated procedures for analysing how well models fit historical data. However, this has been of little value for the selection of forecasting methods. Instead, one should rely on *ex ante* forecasts from realistic simulations of the actual situation faced by the forecaster. By *ex ante* we mean that the forecaster has only that information which would be available at the time of an actual forecast.

Traditional error measures, such as mean square error, do not provide a reliable basis for comparison of methods (for empirical evidence on this see Armstrong and Collopy 1992). The Median Absolute Percentage Error (MdAPE) is more appropriate because it is invariant to scale and is not overly influenced by outliers. For comparisons using a small set of series, it is desirable also to control for degree of difficulty in forecasting. One measure that does this is the Median Relative Absolute Error (MdRAE), which compares the error for a given model against errors for the naive, no change, forecast (Armstrong and Collopy 1992).

One can avoid the complexities of selection simply by combining forecasts. Considerable research suggests that equally weighted averages are accurate compared with any other weighting scheme (Clemen 1989). Such an approach produces consistent, though modest improvements in accuracy, and it reduces the likelihood of large errors. Combining seems to be especially useful when the methods are substantially different. For example, Blattberg and Hoch (1990) obtained improved sales forecasts by equally weighting judgemental forecasts and forecasts from a quantitative model.

The selection and weighting of forecasting methods can be improved by using knowledge about the item to be forecast, which is referred to as domain knowledge (Collopy and Armstrong 1992). Domain knowledge can be formulated, along with a consideration of the features of the data (e.g. discontinuities), to enable improvements upon the equal weighting strategy. This should be welcome news to marketing practitioners who suspect that their domain knowledge is valuable.

ESTIMATING CONFIDENCE INTERVALS

In addition to improving accuracy, forecasting is also concerned with assessing uncertainty. Although statisticians have given much attention to this problem, their efforts generally rely upon fits to historical data as a way to infer forecast uncertainty. Forecasters are advised to ignore measures of fit (such as the standard error of the estimate of the model) because they have little relationship to forecast accuracy. Rather, you should simulate the actual forecasting procedure as closely as possible, and use the distribution of the resulting *ex ante* forecasts to assess uncertainty. So, if you need to make two-year-ahead forecasts, save enough data to be able to compare accuracy for a number of two-year-ahead, *ex ante* forecasts.

Quantitative studies tend to have confidence intervals that are too narrow. Some empirical studies have shown that the percentage of actual values that fall outside of the 95 per cent confidence intervals is substantially greater than 5 per cent, and sometimes greater than 50 per cent (Makridakis *et al.* 1987). This occurs because the estimates ignore various sources of uncertainty. For example, discontinuities might occur over the forecast horizon. The forecast errors are usually asymmetric, so this makes it difficult to estimate confidence intervals. One possibility is to examine separate distributions of errors for forecasts that exceed or fall short of actual sales. While loss functions can be asymmetrical (the cost of a forecast that is too low may differ from the cost if it is too high), this is a problem for the planner, not the forecaster.

Judgemental forecasts also suffer from overconfidence (Fischhoff and MacGregor 1982). To a large extent, this is because forecasters typically do not get good feedback on their predictions. When they do, they can be well calibrated. For example, weather forecasters are well calibrated. When forecasters say that there is a 60 per cent chance of rain, it rains 60 per cent of the time (Murphy and Winkler 1977). This suggests that marketing forecasters should try to ensure that they receive feedback on the accuracy of their forecasts. The feedback should be relatively frequent and it should summarize the results in a meaningful fashion. Another procedure that helps to avoid overconfidence is for the forecaster to make a written list of all of the reasons why the forecast might be wrong (Koriat et al. 1980).

IMPLEMENTATION

There are two key implementation problems. First, how can you gain acceptance of new forecasting methods, and second, how can you gain acceptance of the forecasts themselves?

Acceptance of new forecasting methods

The diffusion rate for new methods is slow. Exponential smoothing, one of the major developments for production and inventory control forecasting, was developed in the late 1950s, yet most firms have yet to adopt it (Dalrymple 1987). Adoption may slow because there are many steps involved. Techniques are first developed and tested. Then they are reported in the literature. They are later passed along via courses, textbooks and consultants. The process takes many years. In the future, the latest methods will be incorporated into expert systems that can be sold as software packages.

Acceptance of forecasts

The most valuable forecasts are typically for situations that are subject to significant changes. Often, these involve bad news. For example, Griffith and Wellman (1979), in a follow-up study on the demand for hospital beds, found that the forecasts from consultants were typically ignored when they indicated a need that was less than that desired by the hospital administrators.

One way to gain acceptance of forecasts is to get decision-makers to decide in advance what decisions they will make given different possible forecasts. Typically, this is a difficult exercise. The use of scenarios offers an aid to this process. Scenarios involve writing detailed stories of how decision-makers would handle situations that involve alternative states of the future. Decision-makers project themselves into the situation and they write the stories in the past tense. (More detailed instructions for writing scenarios are summarized in Armstrong 1985: 38–45.) Scenarios are effective in getting forecasters to accept the likelihood of certain situations.

Firms often confuse forecasting with planning, and they may use the forecast as a tool to motivate people. That is, they use a forecast to drive behaviour, rather than making a forecast conditional on behaviour. (One wonders if they also change their thermometers in order to influence the weather.) One way to avoid this problem is to gain agreement on what forecasting procedures to use, rather than to gain agreement on the forecasts themselves. The resulting forecasts would then be used without further review. Such an agreement on process is difficult to achieve in most organizations.

THE QUALITY OF DATA

Forecasting methods are dependent upon the available data. Intentions data have been especially important for sales forecasting. Although the technology for intentions surveys has been improved, it is still difficult to relate intentions to behaviour. Also, intentions data are often expensive. To get representative results about the intentions of the customers, you need large samples, often numbering a few hundred from each segment for which you need forecasts.

The existence of scanner data means that, for existing products, more emphasis can be placed on behavioural data (which tend to be good predictors of future behaviour) and less on intentions (which are not as good). With the advent of scanner data, we now have behavioural information that is detailed, accurate, timely, and inexpensive. The accuracy of the forecasts should improve, especially because of the reduction in the error of assessing the current status. (Historically, not knowing where you are starting from has been a major source of error in predicting where you will wind up.) Scanner data can also help in conducting low-cost field experiments by varying key features such as advertising or price to see how they affect sales. The outcomes of such experiments should aid forecasting.

CONCLUSIONS

The basic findings about sales forecasting methods can be summarized as follows. First, methods should be selected on the basis of empirically tested theories, not statistically based theories. In addition, domain knowledge should be used. When possible, the methods should use behavioural data, rather than judgements or intentions to predict behaviour. Quantitative methods are usually more accurate than judgemental methods and they are often less expensive. But for the many important cases that require judgement, a heavy reliance should be placed on structured procedures such as Delphi, role playing, and conjoint analysis. When making forecasts in highly uncertain situations, the trend should be dampened over the forecast horizon. Finally, complex models have not proven to be as accurate as relatively simple models.

Overconfidence occurs with quantitative and judgemental methods. In addition to ensuring good feedback, forecasters should explicitly list all the things that might be wrong about their forecast.

Planning and forecasting are often confused. The forecast should be free of political considerations in a firm. To help ensure this, emphasis should be placed on agreeing about the forecasting methods, rather than the forecasts. Also, for important forecasts, decisions on the use of the forecasts should be made before the forecasts are made. Scenarios are helpful in guiding this process.

REFERENCES

Alsem, K. J., Leeflang, P. S. H. and Reuyl, J. C. (1989) 'The forecasting accuracy of market share models using predicted values of competitive marketing behavior', *International Journal of Research in Marketing* 6: 183–98.

Armstrong, J. S. (1985) *Long-Range Forecasting: From Crystal Ball to Computer*, New York: John Wiley.

Armstrong, J. S., Brodie, R. and McIntyre, S. (1987) 'Forecasting methods for marketing', *International Journal of Forecasting* 3: 355–76.

Armstrong, J. S. and Collopy, F. (1992) 'Error measures for generalizing about forecasting methods: empirical comparisons', *International Journal of Forecasting* 8: 69–80.

Armstrong, J. S. and Collopy, F. (1993) 'Causal forces: structuring knowledge for time series extrapolation', *Journal of Forecasting* 12: 103–15.

Armstrong, J. S. and Hutcherson, P. (1989) 'Predicting the outcome of marketing negotiations: role-playing versus unaided opinions', *International Journal of Research in Marketing* 6: 227–39.

Blattberg, R. C. and Hoch, S. J. (1990) 'Database models and managerial intuition: 50% model + 50% manager', *Management Science* 36: 887–99.

Brodie, R. J. and de Kluyver, C. A. (1987) 'A comparison of the short-term accuracy of econometric and naive extrapolation models of market share', *International Journal of Forecasting* 3: 423–37.

Cattin, P. and Wittink, D. R. (1982) 'Commercial use of conjoint analysis: a survey', *Journal of Marketing* 46: 44–53.

Claycamp, H. J. and Liddy, L. E. (1969) 'Prediction of new-product performance: an analytical approach', *Journal of Marketing Research* 6: 414–20.

Clemen, R. T. (1989) 'Combining forecasts: a review and annotated bibliography', *International Journal of Forecasting* 5: 559–83.

Collopy, F., Adya, M. and Armstrong, J. S. (1994) 'Principles for examining predictive validity: The case of information systems spending forecasts', *Information Systems Research* 5: 170–9.

Collopy, F. and Armstrong, J. S. (1992) 'Rule-based forecasting: development and validation of an expert systems approach to combining time-series extrapolations', *Management Science* 39: 1394–414.

Dalrymple, D. J. (1975) 'Sales forecasting: methods and accuracy', *Business Horizons* 18: 69–73.

Dalrymple, D. J. (1987) 'Sales forecasting practices: results from a U.S. survey', *International Journal of Forecasting* 3: 379–91.

Diebold, F. X. and Rudebusch, G. D. (1991) 'Forecasting output with the composite leading index: a real time analysis', *Journal of the American Statistical Association* 86: 603–10.

Dillman, D. A. (1978) *Mail and Telephone Surveys*, New York: John Wiley.

Fischhoff, B. and MacGregor, D. (1982) 'Subjective confidence in forecasts', *Journal of Forecasting* 1: 155–72.

Gardner, E. S., Jr. (1985) 'Exponential smoothing: the state of the art', *Journal of Forecasting* 4: 1–28.

Gardner, E. S., Jr. and McKenzie, E. (1985) 'Forecasting trends in time series', *Management Science* 31: 1237–46.

Griffith, J. R. and Wellman, B. T. (1979) 'Forecasting bed needs and recommending facilities plans for community hospitals: a review of past performance', *Medical Care* 17: 293–303.

Hogarth, R. M. (1978) 'A note on aggregating opinions', *Organizational Behavior and Human Performance* 21: 40–6.

Kalwani, M. and Silk, A. J. (1982) 'On the reliability and predictive validity of purchase intention measures', *Marketing Science* 1: 243–86.

Koriat, A., Lichtenstein, S. and Fischhoff, B. (1980) 'Reasons for confidence', *Journal of Experimental Psychology: Human Learning and Memory* 6: 107–18.

Lawrence, M. J., Edmundson, R. H. and O'Connor, M. J. (1985) 'An examination of the accuracy of judgmental extrapolation of time series', *International Journal of Forecasting* 1: 25–35.

Makridakis, S., Chatfield, C., Hibon, M., Lawrence, M., Mills, T., Ord, K. and Simmons, L. (1993) 'The M2-competition: a real-time judgmentally based forecasting study', *International Journal of Forecasting* 9: 5–22.

Makridakis, S., Hibon, M., Lusk, E. and Belhadjali, M. (1987) 'Confidence intervals: an empirical investigation of the series in the M-competition', *International Journal of Forecasting* 3: 489–508.

Makridakis, S. and Wheelwright, S. C. (1989) *Forecasting Methods for Management*, New York: John Wiley.

Montgomery, D. B. (1975) 'New product distribution: an analysis of supermarket buyer decisions', *Journal of Marketing Research* 12: 255–64.

Murphy, A. H. and Winkler, R. (1977) 'Can weather forecasters formulate reliable probability forecasts of precipitation and temperature', *National Weather Digest* 2: 2–9.

Perry, P. (1979) 'Certain problems in election survey methodology', *Public Opinion Quarterly* 43: 312–25.

Rao, S. (1985) 'An empirical comparison of sales forecasting models', *Journal of Product Innovation Management* 4: 232–42.

Sanders, N. R. and Ritzman, L. P. (1992) 'The need for contextual and technical knowledge in judgmental forecasting', *Journal of Behavioral Decision Making*: 39–52.

Schnaars, S. P. (1984) 'Situational factors affecting forecast accuracy', *Journal of Marketing Research* 21: 290–7.

Sewall, M. A. (1981) 'Relative information contributions of consumer purchase intentions and management judgment as explanators of sales', *Journal of Marketing Research* 18: 249–53.

Shocker, A. D. and Hall, W. G. (1986) 'Pretest market models: a critical evaluation', *Journal of Product Innovation Management* 3: 86–107.

Sudman, S. and Bradburn, N. R. (1982) *Asking Questions: A Practical Guide to Questionnaire Design*, San Francisco: Jossey-Bass.

Tull, D. S. (1967) 'The relationship of actual and predicted sales and profits in new-product introductions', *Journal of Business* 40: 233–50.

Tyebjee, T. T. (1987) 'Behavioral biases in new product forecasting', *International Journal of Forecasting* 3: 393–404.

Wind, Y., Mahajan, V. and Cardozo, R. N. (1981) *New Product Forecasting*, Lexington, MA: Lexington Books.

Wind, J., Green, P. E., Shifflet, D. and Scarbrough (1989) 'Courtyard by Marriott: designing a hotel facility with consumer-based marketing', *Interfaces* 19 (1): 25–47.

Wortruba, T. R. and Thurlow, M. L. (1976) 'Sales force participation in quota setting and sales forecasting', *Journal of Consumer Research* 8: 162–71.

23

MARKET SEGMENTATION

Yoram (Jerry) Wind

All markets are heterogeneous. This is quite evident from the proliferation of popular books describing the heterogeneity of the US market. Consider, for example, *The Nine Nations of North America* (Garreau 1982), *The Nine American Lifestyles* (Mitchell 1983) and *Latitudes and Attitudes: An Atlas of American Tastes, Trends, Politics and Passions* (Weiss 1994). When reflecting on the nature of markets, consumer behaviour and competitive activities, it is obvious that no product or service appeals to all consumers and even those who purchase the same product may do so for diverse reasons. Effective marketing and business strategy therefore requires a segmentation of the market into homogeneous segments, understanding of the needs and wants of these segments, design of products and services that meet those needs and development of marketing strategies to reach effectively the target segments. Thus focusing on segments is at the core of organizations' efforts to become customer driven; it is also the key to effective resource allocation and deployment. Following such a market segmentation strategy would allow the firm to increase its profitability, as suggested by the classic price discrimination model which provides the theoretical rationale for segmentation.

Since the early 1960s segmentation has been viewed as a key marketing concept and has been the focus of a significant part of the marketing research literature. Until recently the concept of segmentation (as articulated, for example, in Frank *et al.* 1972) has not been altered. Similarly, the fundamental approaches to segmentation research have not changed greatly (Wind 1978), despite the publication of a number of increasingly sophisticated research and modelling approaches for segmenting heterogeneous markets.

Yet the recent advances in information technology and the trend towards globalization are introducing a discontinuous change to the segmentation area. The revolution in information technology and strategy makes possible the creation of databases on the entire universe and enormous advances in database marketing and innovative distribution approaches. It has also facilitated much of the development in flexible manufacturing with the consequent emergence of mass customization. These changes are leading to the creation of 'one-on-one marketing' or segments of one. The globalization of business expands the scope of operations across tens of countries and requires a new approach to local, regional and global segments.

These changes require not only an appraisal of what we know about segmentation, what works and what does not work, but also a review of the segmentation area as part of an entirely new marketing and management paradigm.

Therefore the purpose of this chapter is to introduce the reader to both the 'best practice' in the segmentation area and the likely new developments in this critical field. These observations are based on advances in marketing concepts, marketing science research and modelling tools, generalizations from empirical studies, successful practices of leading firms and the conceptual implications of operating in the global information age. This discussion of the best segmentation practices and likely advances encompasses five areas:

1   Use of segmentation in marketing and business strategy.
2   Decisions required for the implementation of a segmentation strategy.
3   Advances in segmentation research.
4   Impact of operating in the global information age on segmentation theory, practice and research.
5   Expansion of segmentation to other stakeholders.

The chapter concludes with a set of critical issues that provide the guidelines for a research agenda in this area.

USE OF SEGMENTATION IN MARKETING AND BUSINESS STRATEGY

Conceptually any market and business strategy should be based on understanding, meeting and even exceeding the needs of target segments. Figure 1 clearly illustrates the centrality of segmentation by suggesting that at the core of any strategy is the understanding of the needs of target segments. This provides the guidelines for the development of products and services and their associated positioning which could meet the need of the target segments. These products and services as positioned to meet the needs of the target segments provide the foundation for the rest of the marketing strategy and the processes, resources and other activities of the firm.

In support of the value of segmentation, there are numerous published and unpublished case studies. For example, Gensch et al. (1990) provide compelling evidence of the positive consequences of segmentation of electrical equipment buyers. In a one-year test segmentation applied in two of three geographic districts resulted in sales increases of 18 per cent and 12 per cent – while sales declined 10 per cent in the district in which segmentation was not applied and 15 per cent for the industry. The firm reports continuous market share increases

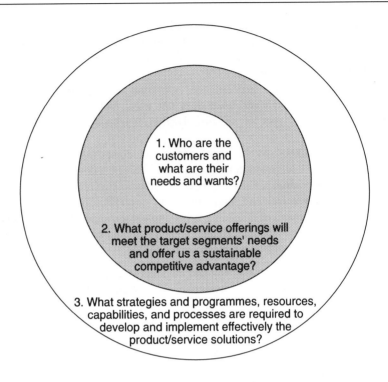

Figure 1 Customer-driven strategy questions

from the segmentation approach. This is not an isolated case. The popular business press and the conference circuit are full of anecdotal cases in which creative segmentation has paid off. In fact a growing number of firms do use segmentation as the basis of their marketing strategy.

Yet despite the general acceptability of segmentation and its value, too many firms are not segmenting their markets effectively and are not basing their strategies on the needs of target segments. The experience of the more successful firms in consumer and industrial markets alike suggests, however, that effective segmentation is a must. The likelihood of a positive response to the firm's offerings is increased, the cost of reaching customers and chances of new product and service failure are reduced.

In order to determine whether a firm uses an effective segmentation strategy, it may help if a segmentation audit is undertaken. Table 1 presents such an audit, which was developed for a large computer manufacturer. In scoring the audit it is important to note that effective segmentation requires a positive answer to each question. Any lower score on any of these dimensions requires correction.

Practice	Completely describes us	Somewhat describes us	Does not describe us at all	Do not know
1 Our business strategies recognize the need to prioritize target segments.				
2 Our marketing plans include specific plans for each of the selected segments.				
3 We have specific product offerings for each target segment.				
4 We have a process for updating the information on our segments on an ongoing basis.				
5 Our segments are unique to the US, and are not developed across countries.				
6 We have an effective process for implementing segmentation research.				
7 We have an effective process for implementing segmentation strategies.				
8 We have P&L reports and accountability by segment.				
9 We have detailed information about segments, including: • Current size of segment • Potential size of segment • Key business needs of the segment • Information systems needs of the segment • Their prioritized needs/benefits sought • Their prioritized preference for product and service features • Demographic characteristics of the segments • Product/system ownership and usage • Competition's strength in each segment • Perceived positioning of each competitor by the members of the segment				
10 Information about the target market segments are incorporated effectively into the following strategies: • Positioning • Product and service offerings • Pricing • Promotion • Advertising • Distribution • Salesforce				

DECISIONS REQUIRED IN IMPLEMENTING A
SEGMENTATION STRATEGY

Effective segmentation strategy requires answers to five sets of questions:

1 How to segment the market?
2 What research procedure to use to develop a segmentation strategy?
3 What segment(s) to target?
4 How to allocate resources among the segments?
5 How to implement the segmentation strategy?

Segment identification decision

This decision involves the determination of which set of variables – basis – to use for segmentation of the market. Should we segment on product usage patterns (e.g. users vs. non-users or heavy vs. light users)? Should we segment based on benefits sought (e.g. product performance vs. convenience vs. price sensitivity)? Should we use some other measure of consumer response to marketing variables (e.g. likelihood of buying a new product concept, response to price promotion, participation in a loyalty programme)? The 'best practice' in this area suggests three propositions:

1 An effective basis for segmentation should allow one to differentiate among segments based on their response to marketing variables. Thus buyers vs. non-buyers or price sensitive vs. non-price sensitive are possible bases for segmentation. Age, sex, marital status, psychographic characteristics or other general characteristics of the consumer are not good bases for segmentation since they do not assure differential response to marketing variables.
2 The selected basis for segmentation should be directly related to the strategic purpose of the segmentation effort. In general, there are two reasons for segmentation:
   • A general segmentation of the market which allows the organization to organize itself around the selected target segments. As increasing numbers of companies shift from a product management organization to a market-driven organization or a matrix organization of product by market, it is critical to identify relatively stable and large segments which could serve as strategic business units. Examples of such segments, in the case of a financial service firm, are the delegators – consumers who prefer to have a money manager take complete control over the management of their financial affairs, and the electronic DIY – who prefer to do it themselves using direct computer trading. To reach these two segments effectively the firm needs quite distinctly different strategies. Members of each of these strategic segments share some common financial/investment needs. Yet each of these segments may still be quite

398

heterogeneous with respect to other needs and, thus, could benefit from further sub-segmentation into more homogeneous groups.

• Specific segments for specific marketing and business decisions. For example, in the introduction of a new product, a focus on the segment that has the highest likelihood of buying the product. In the launch of a new on-line electronic shopping service, a focus on those with access to computers and who are likely to use an electronic shopping service. Other specific segments can be developed for each of the marketing mix decisions. Consider, for example:

• For positioning:
  Product usage
  Product preference
  Benefits sought
  A hybrid of the variables above

• For new product concepts (and new product introduction):
  Reaction to new concepts (intention to buy, preference over current brand, etc.)
  Benefits sought

• For pricing decisions:
  Price sensitivity
  Deal proneness
  Price sensitivity by purchase/usage patterns

• For advertising decisions:
  Benefits sought
  Media usage
  Psychographic/lifestyle
  A hybrid (of the variables above with or without purchase/usage patterns)

• For distribution decisions:
  Store loyalty and patronage
  Benefits sought in store selection

• For general understanding of a market:
  Benefits sought (in industrial markets, the criterion used is purchase decision)
  Product purchase and usage patterns
  Needs
  Brand loyalty and switching pattern
  A hybrid of the above variables

3 To gain a better understanding of the various segments and their character-istics, it is critical to profile the segment's key discriminating characteristics. These include the complete segment profile on demographic, psychographic, product usage, perceptions and preferences, attitudes and the like. In the case of industrial (business-to-business) segmentation, these variables should include both the characteristics of the organization and each of the

Table 2 Variables commonly used as basis for segmentation and as descriptors of segments

Basis for segmentation (or descriptors)	Descriptors of segments
Organizational	**External**
• Share	• Socioeconomic, political environment
• Trial	(culture, technology, economic,
• Purchase/adoption	political, regulatory, legal)
• Source loyalty	• Behaviour towards competitors
• Price sensitivity	• Etc.
• Customers of key competitors	
• Etc.	**Organizational**
	• Industry type (e.g. SIC)
Buying centre	• Size
• Buying process	• Degree of centralization
• Information search	• Capabilities (technical, financial, etc.)
• Criteria/benefits sought	• Geographic location (country, region,
• Negotiation style	city, etc.)
• Application	• Etc.
• Decision	
• Post-purchase evaluation	**Buying centre**
• Etc.	• Size
	• Composition
Individual	• Buying situation
• Awareness	• Influence
• Knowledge	• Consensus among the members
• Perceptions, preferences, attitudes	• Buying process
towards the brand	• Buying organization and policies
• Preference	• Relations with suppliers
• Recommendation	• Etc.
• Purchase	
• US age	**Individual**
• Loyalty	• Demographic (age, sex, family life
• Etc.	cycle, income, education, social
	class, etc.)
	• Psychographics (personality, lifestyle,
	activities, interest opinions, etc.)
	• Etc.

key members of the relevant buying centre. Table 2 identifies a list of variables commonly used as a basis for segmentation and as segment descriptors. It is important to note that variables not used as a basis for segmentation can become descriptors of segments that are developed based on other bases.

Selecting a research programme

The quality of a segmentation programme depends largely on the quality of information. Segmenting any market requires information on the characteristics

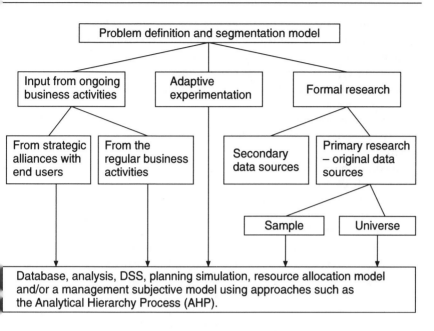

Figure 2   Selecting a segmentation research programme

of the market including:

- The size and growth of the market.
- The criteria buying centres use in making their buying decisions (including the benefits they seek and problems they try to solve).
- The perceptions of preference for, attitudes towards and usage of the products and services of the firm and its competitors.
- The demographic characteristics of the members of the buying centre and the organization in the case of business-to-business markets.
- The psychographic (lifestyle, personality and other psychological and attitudinal) characteristics.
- Reaction and sensitivity to the marketing actions of the firm and its competitors.

To collect data on these variables and to analyse and interpret them requires a research programme. Historically, segmentation research centred on customer surveys. Yet there are a number of additional approaches that should be considered.

Figure 2 outlines the range of options. Formal primary research and especially surveys on a sample of customers and prospects have been the most common approach to segmentation research. Recent developments of databases on the entire universe have changed the nature of segmentation research. Consider, for example, the pharmaceutical industry in which a number of firms are developing databases on the entire industry – 400,000-plus physicians, 7,000 hospitals and thousands of managed care organizations.

A second type of formal research includes secondary data analysis using geodemographic data which can be used both for segmentation research as well as for experimentation.

Adaptive experimentation is another approach which could yield insights into the characteristics of various market segments and their response to marketing activities.

The third approach is input from ongoing business activities. In this case, we include both data on the market response to various strategies and insights gained from strategic alliances with customers. This latter approach is especially critical in the new product development area when the firm works closely with its customers on the development of new products and service.

Best research practice would include using a number of these approaches, integrating the resulting data in a database, continuously updating the database and having it as part of a decision support system (DSS).

Selecting target segments

Having segmented a market it is often not desirable to pursue all segments. Thus, a critical decision is the selection of target market segments. All segments have to meet four conditions: measurability (ability to measure the size and characteristics of the segment); substantiality (having a minimum profitable size); accessibility (ability to reach and serve the segments); actionability (ability to implement strategies to serve the segments) (Kotler 1991). Beyond these requirements, the selection of target market segments requires answers to the following questions:

- What is the likely response to the firm's offering, including response to the positioning of the firm's products and services?
- What is the size of the segment in terms of the revenues and profits it is likely to generate?
- Can the segment be reached (via controlled media and distribution or via a self-selection strategy)?
- What are the current and likely competitive activities directed at the target segment?
- What are the likely costs of reaching effectively the target segment?
- What is the likely impact of changes in relevant environmental conditions (e.g. economic conditions, lifestyle, legal regulations, etc.) on the potential response of the target market segment?
- Do we have the required offerings and competencies effectively to develop, reach and serve the selected segments?
- How many segments can you manage effectively?

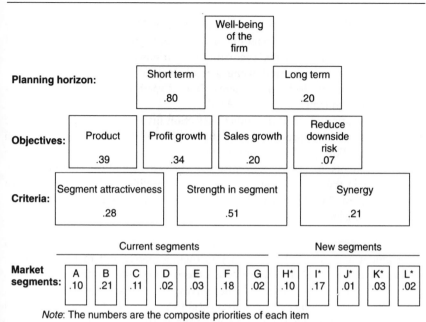

Note: The numbers are the composite priorities of each item

Figure 3 An illustrative output of an analytic hierarchy process (AHP) designed to select a portfolio of market segments

These and related criteria often require information that is not always available from market research. Consequently, a decision support framework is needed to aid managerial decision-making. This framework should utilize both managerial experience and available data. At the minimum it should include: identifying relevant criteria; evaluating the segments on the selected criteria.

Following the logic of product and business portfolio analysis, a portfolio of current and potential market segments can be constructed (Wind and Robertson 1983). Figure 3 illustrates a portfolio of segments in which each segment is evaluated on its attractiveness, on the firm's expected strength in the segment and on synergy. The first two criteria are the same dimensions used in the GE/McKinsey portfolio matrix. These dimensions can be based on a single criterion or represent a composite of multiple criteria. For example, segment attractiveness could include such factors as the segment's size and growth, risk factors and the cost of reaching the segment. Segment strength could include such factors as current and expected share in the segment and expected profitability. The specific criteria and their relative weights can be determined by management judgement and marketing research input.

The segment selective process illustrated in Figure 3 utilized the analytic hierarchy process (AHP). The AHP (Wind and Saaty 1980; Saaty 1992) is a measurement approach and process that helps quantify management subjective judgements. The essential steps in implementing an AHP include: setting up the decision problem by the relevant management group as a hierarchy of interrelated decision elements; evaluating the various elements of the hierarchy by pairwise comparisons and using a mathematical method to estimate the relative weights of decision elements. The *Expert Choice* software greatly facilitates the implementation of an AHP.

The application of AHP to segment selection involves bringing together the key executives and presenting to them all available marketing research information. This provides input to the deliberation and evaluation of the various segments, in a pairwise comparison, against each of the chosen criteria. The results in the prioritization of the segments are illustrated in Figure 3. An examination of this illustrative hierarchy suggests a number of segmentation related conclusions:

- Management established three criteria (segment attractiveness, strength in segment and synergy) which vary in their importance with respect to the firm's ability to achieve their four objectives (profit, profit growth, sales growth and downside risk). The objectives, in turn, vary in their importance under short- or long-term conditions (not shown in the figure). The overall importance of the four objectives, assuming an 80/20 weight for short versus long term is presented in Figure 3. The seven current segments when evaluated against the three criteria (segment attractiveness, strength and synergy), which in turn are weighted by their importance to the accomplishment of the four objectives (weighted by their importance for the short- and long-term well-being of the firm), suggest that three of the segments – D, E and G – are not very attractive and should be considered as candidates for deletion, or at least destined to receive no incremental resources.
- Five new segments were identified. When evaluated on the three criteria, two of the segments – H and I – were viewed as candidates for inclusion in the portfolio and three – J, K and L – as candidates for deletion.
- As a result of the process, a new portfolio of segments was established with segments A, B, C, F, H and I.
- The outcome also suggests how much resources to allocate to each segment. Since the dimensions included in the hierarchy encompass both the expected benefits from each segment as well as the cost of reaching them and risk, the priorities can be used as a rough guide for resource allocation. This would lead to the following allocation: A = 11 per cent, B = 24 per cent, C = 13 per cent, F = 21 per cent, H = 11 per cent and I = 20 per cent.

Another example for a portfolio of segments pursued by a firm is a recent advertisement by Citibank which identified products and services for six segments. These segments were:

- Planning for retirement: tax deferred investments make more sense than ever.

- Retirees: don't ignore the new tax law.
- When leaving a job: be certain to protect your retirement fund.
- Paying for college: start a fund early and invest regularly.
- Home equity/borrowing: a great strategy for a host of reasons.
- Small business owners: a long-term strategy is crucial.

Allocating resources among segments

The selection of target segments and the allocation of resources among segments are interrelated and iterative decisions. For example, in the preceding section, AHP was utilized to select a portfolio of segments. It also provided guidelines for resource allocation among the segments. Allocation of resources typically involves not only the allocation among segments, but also the allocation of resources to the various marketing mix variables – products, price, distribution, promotion and advertising.

The basic problem of resource allocation is to decide on the mix of resources that generates optimal response (sales, profitability, etc.). How, for example, should sales persons currently covering a market be allocated across segments to optimize their return? Estimating and modelling the sales response of each segment to the various marketing resources is critical. The more innovative resource allocation models have been developed in the context of designing optimal product lines. These approaches, which are typically based on conjoint analysis studies among current and potential customers, have been applied to a wide range of situations including computers, telecommunications products and services, pharmaceuticals, etc. (Green and Krieger 1985). In the cases in which empirically based market response functions are not available, management's subjective judgement, using either decision calculus methods (Little 1979) or the AHP (Wind and Saaty 1980), can be employed.

The disguised AHP example outlined in Figure 3 included, in its original application, a lower level focusing on various marketing strategy options. This allowed management to generate the marketing programmes best suited for reaching the selected segments. A similar application, but for a consumer service, was reported by Dunn and Wind in 1983. The complexity and importance of the resource allocation decision suggests the advisability of employing a methodology such as the AHP that incorporates managerial judgement, empirical data derived from both econometric market response models and experiments, consumer studies and decisions models.

Implementing a segmentation strategy

The most difficult aspect of any segmentation project is the translation of the study results into marketing strategy and programmes. No rules can be offered to assure a successful translation and, in fact, little is known (in the published literature) on how this translation occurs.

405

Informal discussions with executives and observations of 'successful' and 'unsuccessful' 'translations' suggest a few generalizable conclusions on the conditions likely to increase successful implementation.

1 Involving all relevant decision-makers (e.g. product managers, new product developers, advertising agency, sales management, etc.) in the problem definition, research design, strategy generation and evaluation.
2 The segment characteristics should be rich enough to provide the basis for innovative product positioning and product, pricing, communication and distribution decisions.
3 The segment characteristics should also provide guidelines for the generation of creative executions of the selected strategy.
4 Recognizing the non-marketing orientation of product management, it is desirable to shift the responsibilities for segmentation strategy to segment-driven managers and teams.
5 Since information on media and distribution reach is rarely linked to market response functions, it is critical to develop data that link market response to media and distribution systems and use 'self-selection' strategies. (Members of a target segment self-select the message which is designed to appeal to them from a general media.)

ADVANCES IN SEGMENTATION RESEARCH

Many of the papers published in *Marketing Science* and the *Journal of Marketing Research* offer advances in segmentation research and modelling. Yet the key segmentation research and modelling centre around six sets of 'tools'.

Classification

The classification of methods for segmenting the market is especially critical for clustering-based segmentation approaches and for hybrid designs. A clustering-based segmentation design involves determining the number, size and characteristics of the segments based on the results of clustering of respondents on a set of 'relevant' variables. Benefit, need, and attitude segmentation are examples of this type of approach. Significant advances have been made in the clustering area.

Hybrid segmentation design includes those cases in which a priori segmentation design such as product purchase or usage, loyalty or customer type is augmented by some cluster-based segmentation on variables such as benefits sought. Hybrid designs are especially common in business-to-business segmentation.

Approaches such as macro and micro segmentation (Wind and Cardozo 1974) and sequential clustering (Peterson 1974) are often used in practice. Sequential clustering, for example, clusters on some market-based demographics followed by attitude (or benefit) clustering within each demographic segment. In both cluster-based design and hybrid design, the size and other characteristics (demographics, socioeconomic, purchase, etc.) of the segments are estimated.

Discrimination

Discrimination methods employed to establish the profile of the segments commonly use multiple discriminant analyses or regression analysis. Such statistical methods are often augmented with graphic packages that graphically display the profile of the segments.

Simultaneous evaluation of number of segments, profile and desired positioning for a set of product and service offerings

This is one of the areas receiving the attention of academic researchers and typically involves sophisticated multidimensional scaling and multivariate statistical analyses. Consider, for example, the work on simultaneous determination of the size of the segment and the segment's preferences for various products and their positioning. Such studies often result in joint space maps and the output of logit and nested logit models to the simultaneous estimation of segment size, choice and incidence probabilities which apply simultaneously to segmentation and market structuring. See, for example, Bucklin and Gupta (1992) and other approaches such as Grover and Srinivasan (1987).

One of the most interesting developments in this area is the componential segmentation approach. This model was proposed by Green and De Sarbo (1979) and shifts the emphasis of the segmentation model from the partitioning of a market to a prediction of which person type (described by a particular set of demographic and other psychographic attribute levels) will be most responsive to what type of product feature. The componential segmentation model is an extension of conjoint analysis and orthogonal arrays to cover not only product features but also person characteristics. In componential segmentation the researcher is interested in developing, in addition to parameter values for the product stimuli, parameter values for various respondent characteristics (demographic, product usage, etc.).

In a typical conjoint analysis approach to market segmentation, a matrix of subjects by utilities is developed. This matrix can serve as the input to the determination of the profile of some a priori segments (e.g. product users versus non-users) or alternatively as the input to a clustering programme which would result in a number of benefit segments. In componential segmentation, the same design principles which guide the selection of (product) stimuli are applied also to the selection of respondents. For example, in a study for a new health insurance product, four sets of respondent characteristics were identified on the basis of previous experience and management judgement: age, sex, marital status and current insurance status. Employing an orthogonal array design, one screens respondents to select those who meet the specific profiles specified by the design. Each respondent is then interviewed and administered the conjoint analysis task for the evaluation of a set of hypothetical health insurance products (also selected following an orthogonal array design).

Having completed the data collection phase, the researcher would have a matrix of averaged profile evaluations of the product stimuli by the groups of respondents. This data matrix is then submitted to any number of componential segmentation models, which decompose the matrix into separate parameter values (utilities) for each of the levels of the product feature factors (comprising the stimulus cards) and separate parameter values (saliences) for each of the levels of the customer profile characteristics (describing the respondents) which indicate how much each profile characteristic contributes to variation in the evaluative responses.

Given these two sets of parameters, the researcher can make predictions about the relative evaluation of any of the possible product features by any of the respondent types. The results are used with a simulation to estimate: for each respondent segment the frequency of first choices for each of the considered new product combinations; for each new product combination the frequency of first choices across segments.

Componential segmentation offers a new conceptualization of market segmentation in that it focuses on the building blocks of segments and offers simultaneously an analysis of the market segment for any given product offering and an evaluation of the most desirable product offering (or positioning) for any given segment. The concept and algorithm of componential segmentation can be extended to cover not only two data sets (product feature and respondent characteristics) but three or more data sets by adding, for example, the components of usage situations and distribution options.

Database management

Database management involves the creation, management and access to databases and its incorporation in a decision support system. The interest in this area is increasing especially from management, yet the field is still in its infancy.

Simulation and optimization

Simulation and optimization are at the core of models for selection of a target portfolio of segments. These models are typically based on conjoint analysis studies. Among the most powerful of these approaches is flexible segmentation. In contrast to a priori segmentation in which the segments are determined at the outset of the study and clustering-based segmentation in which the selected segments are based on the results of the clustering analysis, the flexible segmentation model offers a dynamic approach to the problem. Using this approach one can develop and examine a large number of alternative segments, each composed of those consumers or organizations exhibiting a similar pattern of responses to new 'test' products (defined as a specific product feature configuration). The flexible segmentation approach is based on the integration of the results of a conjoint analysis study and a computer simulation of consumer choice behaviour.

The simulation model in a flexible segmentation approach uses three data sets:

1   Utilities for the various factors and levels for each respondent.
2   Perceptual ranking or rating of the current brands on the same set of attributes.
3   A set of demographics and other background characteristics.

The active participation of management is also requisite to design a set of 'new product offerings' (each defined as a unique combination of product features – specific levels on each factor included in the conjoint analysis study). Management participation can be on a real-time basis in which managers interact directly with the computer simulation. Alternatively, management can specify in advance a number of plausible new product concepts or react to a number of 'best' product combinations.

The consumer choice simulator is based on the assumption that consumers choose the offering (new product or existing brand) with the highest utility. The simulator is designed to establish: the consumer's share of choices among the existing brands, which can be validated against current market share data if available; the consumer's likely switching behaviour upon the introduction of any new product. This phase provides a series of brand-switching matrices. Within each matrix management can select any cell or combination of cells as a possible market segment (e.g. those consumers remaining with brand i versus those who switched to new brand j, etc.). Once the desired segments (cell or cell combination) have been selected, the demographic, lifestyle, product purchase and usage and other relevant segment characteristics can be determined by a series of multiple discriminant analyses which can be incorporated in the simulation.

Some of the more significant developments in the segmentation area in the last decade have been the advances in simulation and optimization procedures and associated user-friendly software. The developments by Green and Krieger (1991, 1994) greatly facilitate the task of selecting an optimal (or close to optimal) set of segments.

Linking segmentation findings with management subjective judgements

Given the complexity of the decisions which a portfolio of segments has to target, it is helpful to use a framework and methodology that captures management's subjective judgement while allowing the incorporation of findings from various segmentation studies. The analytic hierarchy process (AHP), as illustrated in Figure 3, is ideally suited for this task.

Addressing the problems

In addition to methodological advances in these six areas, some of the more interesting advances in segmentation research and modelling are those developed to address three of the criticisms of segmentation research – that it has too narrow a focus, that it is static and deterministic and that it is poorly integrated with strategy. The advances in addressing these problems are briefly discussed below.

Too narrow a focus

This criticism encompasses five areas that can be addressed using specific advances in research and modelling.

1 The traditional focus on 'one segment per customer': the assignment of individuals to mutually exclusive and collectively exhaustive segments is too narrow. This problem can be overcome by the use of overlapping clustering – a relatively new clustering procedure that allows for an individual to belong to more than one segment. For a discussion of this method, see Arabie *et al.* (1981) and Chaturvedi *et al.* (1994).

2 One segmentation scheme fits all: this problem of trying to fit one segmentation scheme for all marketing decisions can be solved by employing the flexible segmentation approaches or by developing a number of segmentation schemes and linking them.

3 Neglect of sub-segments: with the exception of segments of one, most segments are heterogeneous. It is important to recognize this and augment the basic segmentation with additional sub-segmentation. This is the concept underlying hybrid segmentation models and is increasing in its popularity. In this context it is also helpful to develop a hierarchy of segments. A byproduct of this research is the development of measures on the segmentability of each market (and the degree of homogeneity of selected segments).

4 Individual as the unit of analysis: most segmentation studies use data on individuals. However, few decisions are made by a single individual. Most households and industrial (business-to-business) decisions are made by a buying centre. An important advance in segmentation research is the shift in the unit of analysis from individuals to buying centres. Recognizing the heterogeneity within a buying centre, the use of key informants as representative of the buying centre is often not appropriate. A better approach would be to identify all the members of the buying centre and

410

collect the information on a subset of the buying centre members. This allows an assessment of the level of consensus among members of the buying centres. The level of consensus as well as the composition of the buying centres can be used as a basis for, or descriptors of, segments. Choffray and Lilien (1978) demonstrate critical differences in decision criteria among members of buying centres for industrial heating and cooling equipment. In addition, Wilson *et al.* (1991) describe and test the best ways to combine the preferences of individuals and buying centre members when trying to determine how the buying centre is most likely to act.

5   The segmentation of the month: the segmentation area has not escaped other management fads and has had its share of 'segment of the month' promise and advocates. To avoid this trap, there has been some progress in theory-driven segmentation. Also of help is to keep the focus on market response variation as bases for segmentation and to include all other variables as segment descriptors.

Static and deterministic perspective

A major limitation of many of the segmentation studies is their neglect of the dynamic aspects of segmentation. Static/deterministic segmentation tends to ignore segment change and market dynamics; ignoring such changes often has several consequences. (See Johnson and Lilien (1994) for a conceptualization and model-based approach to deal with segment dynamics). To address this issue one can do the following:

- Define bases for segmentation that focus on change.
- Monitor changes in segment composition over time.
- Focus on strategies that will change segment membership (from non-users to users, light to heavy users).
- Incorporate competitive actions and reactions, since the desirability of a segment depends not only on the segment's characteristics and our own strategies but also on competitive actions and reactions.

A second major weakness of much of the segmentation research is the missing stochastic component. To solve this problem there have been a number of efforts to introduce stochastic components to estimates of segment size and characteristics. Some attention has also been given in the academic world to fuzzy clustering (see, for example, Wedel and Steenkamp 1991).

Poor integration with strategy

To address the problem that segmentation studies are often not reflected in the resulting strategy, a number of actions can be taken. These include:

1   Analyse the results of all studies such as copy, concept, product, distribution

411

and other marketing studies at the segment level.

2   Avoid infrequent and expensive large base-line segmentation studies and instead include in all marketing and business studies a segmentation analysis.

3   Link the segmentation to positioning and its associated marketing mix strategies. Specifically recognize the interdependence between the two. Given a positioning, what is the best segment(s)? Given a segment, what is the best positioning(s)? Having fixed on a segment/positioning, it is critical to develop a marketing strategy that will meet the needs of the selected segment and reflect the target positioning.

4   Carry the segmentation efforts to the salesforce level by encouraging each sales person to segment his/her market. In addition, segmentation can also be very helpful in segmenting the salesforce.

5   Carry through the segmentation strategies to the business and corporate level by focusing on a portfolio of segments and by using the portfolio of segments as the core of the business and corporate strategy.

SEGMENTATION IN THE GLOBAL INFORMATION AGE

The information revolution, which has been receiving enormous coverage in the business and popular media and has been the subject of an increasing number of scholarly studies, has captivated the imagination of scholars, managers and the population at large. This revolution is greatly affecting the ways in which firms are managing their operations and is likely to change dramatically the way in which business is conducted. Information strategy is at the heart of most recent efforts to reengineer and reinvent the corporation and is leading to the creation of a new management and associated marketing paradigm.

In the new management and marketing paradigm (Wind 1994), information is having a profound effect on: (a) the nature and quality of management decisions; (b) the nature of business strategies; (c) the creation of innovative communication and distribution systems.

Management decisions

Management decisions are affected by the advances in the development and management of databases (on the entire population) and their linkage to decision (and executive) support systems (DSS/ESS), which in turn can include expert/ knowledge based systems. In this context, many advances in segmentation research and modelling can be incorporated in the DSS and much of our knowledge of segmentation can be developed as rules for a knowledge-based system that could help management to select target segments.

Some of the advances in this area include the ability to have 'live' databases in which one can update on an ongoing basis the customer database. Consider, for example, Citibank, which is developing an interactive intelligent decision-support system to guide all interactions with the customer; for example, the delivery of a direct mail or telephone sales message will be targeted by the system which will also coordinate a number of customer interactions to create a 'dialogue' to follow the consumer with the appropriate interaction at each point of contact of the consumer with Citibank such as subsequent telephone enquiry, while using an ATM, when meeting with a bank teller, when receiving the statement. This system is based on a new relationship model with household and not only on the traditional banking focus on accounts.

Data mining

Other interesting developments are in data mining (Lewinson 1994). This term refers to a number of pattern recognition models using either neural nets or fractal technology to discover patterns in the data. These methods have been employed commercially to identify segments of customers most likely to buy a given product (in banking, for example) and to the identity of customers most likely to leave (cellular telephones, for example). These approaches, although intriguing, are still in their infancy and require further validation.

Whereas the Citibank example illustrates future development, much of the work today relies more on the traditional geodemographic segmentation based on consensus and other data. An example of this type of effort is the Claritas Prizm lifestyle segmentation. This segmentation divides the USA into 62 clusters. These clusters are further divided into 15 groups that vary with respect to the type of location – rural, town, suburb or urban – and with respect to level of affluence. The Prizm lifestyle clusters can be related to any target group of interest.

Information strategies

Information strategies are relatively recent additions to the traditional set of marketing strategies. One of the early and most effective information-based strategies was the 'capture the client' strategy of America Hospital Supply's direct link between hospital computers and AHS computers, eliminating the need for human interaction in the straight rebuy case. 'Capture the clients' strategies such as the direct computer link between P&G and Walmart are increasing in popularity.

New communication and distribution options

Information technology is also changing dramatically the nature of the communication and distribution options. Electronic shopping via kiosks, CD-ROM or online are being developed at a much faster pace than was ever expected (see, for example, Rangaswamy and Wind 1994). For a more general

413

discussion of impact of information technology on marketing see Blattberg *et al.* (1994).

These changes affect all aspects of our lives and are altering the concept of segmentation. In the new marketing paradigm the traditional mass market is being replaced with segments including, at the extreme, segments of one. In a breakthrough book, *The One to One Future*, Peppers and Rogers (1993) present a vision of their one-to-one paradigm which includes and focuses on:

- Share of customers not share of market.
- Collaborating with customers to create products and relationships.
- Customizing products, services and promotional efforts for each customer.
- Economics of scope.
- Engaging the customers in dialogues – the interactive individualization of media is here.

The shift to segments of one requires both a rethinking of the segmentation concept as well as the development and utilization of sophisticated databases, marketing analysis, modelling and strategy. The trend towards such developments is inevitable and is accompanied by another discontinuous trend – the globalization of business.

Globalization

Increasing numbers of industries are global. To succeed in this environment firms have to shift from a domestic perspective to considering the world as the arena of operations both with respect to the consumer markets for products and services as well as for the resources markets for raw material, R&D, manufacturing, human and capital resources.

The globalization of industries is also accompanied by trends towards regional economic integration – the European Union, NAFTA and the various other efforts for regional integration in Asia and Latin America. The implication of these developments for segmentation is that management has to consider portfolios of segments that include:

- global segments;
- regional segments;
- segments within specific countries.

Added to this complexity is the need to consider as the unit of analysis not just countries but countries by mode of entry, since the risk and attractiveness of a country depend on the mode of entry. The selection and implementation of a portfolio of segments which includes global segments, regional segments and segments within countries (by mode of entry) requires a significant amount of information on all relevant markets around the world. The creation and maintenance of such a data/knowledge base is not a trivial undertaking and is one of the major obstacles to the development of global segmentation strategies.

Creation of processes for the development and maintenance of country, regional and world databases is a high priority undertaking for all global firms. Yet the development of effective segmentation can take place even without such databases if the firm will proceed in an iterative bottom-up and top-down segmentation. This process involves three bottom-up steps:

1 Segmentation of the market in each country (by mode of entry).
2 Examination of the resulting segments in all the selected countries to identify common segments across countries – clustering of country segments.
3 The creation of a global portfolio based on various clusters of segments.

The resulting portfolio of segments should be compared to a desired (top-down) conceptual portfolio of segments. The comparison and contrast of the two portfolios should be driven by the concept of global operation which balances the need to develop strategies that best meet the needs of the local markets (given the idiosyncratic market, competitive and environmental conditions), while at the same time trying to achieve economies of scale and scope by focusing on cross-country segments in a number of markets. The AHP framework and methodology can and has been used in this context to help make such decisions, even in the absence of the needed 'hard' market data. As data become available, both from the firm's own experience and from other sources, the data can be integrated in a database and used as input to the AHP process.

The segmentation of global markets offers enormous opportunities but is still one of the neglected areas of segmentation. It does offer intellectual and methodological challenges and is critical from a management point of view. The literature presents scattered examples of global segmentation. See, for example, the proposed segmentation based on multinational diffusion patterns (Helsen *et al.* 1993). However, the opportunities for breakthrough research in this area and especially as it relates to the information revolution are staggering.

EXTENDING THE SEGMENTATION CONCEPT

In the marketing literature, in practice and in the discussion so far, segmentation has been limited to 'customer' markets. Yet the concept applies to all heterogeneous populations and can and should be extended to the other stakeholders in the firm – all those who have a 'stake' in its survival and growth.

Consider, for example, the firm's own salesforce. Most large firms employ thousands of sales people who vary considerably in their performance. The 20/80 rule often applies to them as it does to the customers (i.e. 20 per cent of the salesforce often accounts for 80 per cent of the profits). In multi-product firms, different sales people often tend to sell different mixes of products. They differ in their family life cycle stages and hence have different financial and time needs (some are still worried about college education for their kids while others are single, etc.). These and other differences among the sales persons of any firm suggest that the traditional approach, in which a single sales strategy and compensation is employed, is suboptimal. To benefit fully from one's salesforce, it is critical to segment it.

The segmentation of the salesforce based on needs, benefits sought, expertise, perceptions and preference or any other relevant characteristics could lead to the identification of homogeneous segments and the design of separate strategies towards them. In fact in any situation where management relies heavily on a salesforce a dual marketing strategy should be developed – one for the (target segments of) customers and a corresponding one for the (segments of the) salesforce. Obviously these two strategies should be coordinated and integrated. Furthermore, a segmented strategy towards compensation is also desirable. To implement it while avoiding discriminatory practices requires the use of a compensation system with a number of options relying on a self-selection strategy in which the various sales people could select the option most appropriate for their needs. While the segmentation of the salesforce and the resulting segmented strategies are likely to meet with considerable resistance, future research needs to address whether the benefits outweigh the difficulties and cost involved.

Similarly, a segmentation strategy can benefit the firm's dealings with its other stakeholders. Wind (1978) described a segmentation of security analysts and portfolio managers that led to better understanding by a firm of the criteria used in the evaluation of firms in their industry and the perceptions of the given firm and its competitors. Following a segmentation/positioning study, a strategy was developed to meet the needs of a target segment of security analysts that resulted in a spectacular increase in the P/E ratio of the given firm.

Other stakeholders such as suppliers, customer service personnel, competitors, government agencies and the firm's own shareholders are often heterogeneous. In all of these cases, understanding the key segments and selecting desired target segment(s) can greatly enhance the firm's effectiveness. In fact, as the cost of doing business in today's environment increases, a segmented strategy may be essential for any organization concerned with the return of their marketing investments.

ISSUES AND ASSOCIATED RESEARCH AGENDA

In the author's introduction to the *Journal of Marketing Research* special issue on segmentation research (Wind 1978) the following conclusions were presented:

> Market segmentation has served as the focal point for many of the major marketing research developments and the marketing activities of most firms. Yet, too many segmentation researchers have settled on a fixed way of conducting segmentation studies. This tendency for standardization of procedures is premature and undesirable. Innovative approaches to segmentation have been offered in the past few years, and further work on the new conceptual and methodological aspects of segmentation should be undertaken.
> Of particular importance seems to be research on the following areas:

1 New conceptualizations of the segmentation problem.
2 Reevaluation and operationalization of the normative theory of segmentation with emphasis on the question of how to allocate resources among markets and products over time.
3 The discovery and implementation of new variables for use as bases for segmentation (i.e. new attitudinal and behavioral constructs such as consumption-based personality inventories and variables which focus on likely change in attitude and behavioral responses to the marketing variables) of the markets for products, services and concepts.
4 The development of new research designs and parallel data collection and analysis techniques which place fewer demands on the respondents (i.e. data collection which is simpler for the respondent and data analysis procedures capable of handling missing data and incomplete block designs).
5 The development of simple and flexible analytical approaches to data analysis capable of handling discrete and continuous variables and selected interaction at a point in time and over time.
6 Evaluation of the conditions under which various data analytical techniques are most appropriate.
7 The accumulation of knowledge on successful bases for segmentation across studies (product, situations, and markets).
8 Undertaking external validation studies to determine the performance of segmentation strategies which were based on findings of segmentation studies.
9 Designing and implementing multitrait, multimethod approaches to segmentation research aimed at both the generation of more generalizable (reliable) and valid data.
10 Integration of segmentation research with the marketing information system of the firm.
11 Exploring alternative approaches to the translation of segmentation findings into marketing strategies.
12 Studies of the organizational design of firms which were successful and unsuccessful in implementing segmentation strategies.

Review of some of the issues and current advances in segmentation research indicates that despite the great advances in the management of and research practice of segmentation, numerous frontiers still require creative and systematic study.

(Wind 1978)

The basic conclusions and their related research agenda are still valid. Despite the advances in academic research during the past sixteen years, we still do not have satisfactory solutions to the issues raised in the 1978 research agenda. The changes in the business environment and especially the implications of operating in a global information age do suggest, however, the need to add a few additional items to the research agenda. These include:

1 Reconceptualization of segmentation problems in light of the impact of operating in the global information age.
2 Development of expert system/knowledge-based systems to help management to select and manage the portfolio of segments. Such systems would ideally be incorporated in an effective decision support system. Key to this is the development of a set of rules summarizing our current understanding of market segmentation. These rules can reflect the empirical generalizations

in this area and can be aided by appropriate meta-analyses.

3   Development of the processes and organizational architecture required to assure effective adaptation and management of segmentation. This includes adoption of the segmentation concept as the foundation of all marketing and business decisions (as outlined in Figure 1) as well as the development of guidelines for effective management of segmentation.

Addressing these newer challenges and continuing building our knowledge concerning the items identified in the 1978 research agenda would be critical to our ability to increase the value of segmentation. Continuous innovation and improvement in segmentation research and modelling for generating and evaluating segmentation strategies is essential. However, real progress in this area requires rethinking the role of segmentation in the global information age and concentrated efforts by management to develop and implement innovative and effective segmentation strategies.

The obstacles to effective segmentation are not methodological, nor even the lack of data, but rather the ability and willingness of management to undertake a segmentation strategy and establish the processes and resources required for successful implementation. The concept of segmentation, once adjusted to reflect the impact of the information revolution and the globalization of business, is sound and valid. It is the practice of segmentation that is fraught with problems. These problems are solvable but the solutions require revision and alteration to most of the current approaches used to segment markets. If we have the conviction and courage to reexamine the traditional segmentation concept and approaches, we shall be able to increase significantly the worth of our segmentation efforts in creating value to our customers and other stakeholders.

REFERENCES

Arabie, Phipps, Carroll, J. Douglas, DeSarbo, Wayne S. and Wind, Jerry (1981) 'Overlapping clustering: a new method for product positioning', *Journal of Marketing Research* 18: 310–17.

Blattberg, Robert, Glazer, Robert and Little, John (1994) *The Marketing Information Revolution*, Harvard: Harvard Business School Press.

Bucklin, Randolph E. and Gupta, Sunil (1992) 'Brand choice, purchase incidence, and segmentation: an integrated modeling approach', *Journal of Marketing Research* XXIX, May: 201–15.

Chaturvedi, Anil, Carroll, J. Douglas and Green, Paul E. (1994) 'Market segmentation via overlapping K-centroids clustering', Working paper, Pennsylvania: Wharton School, University of Pennsylvania, May: 1–21.

Choffray, Jean-Marie and Lilien, Gary L. (1978) 'A new approach to industrial market segmentation', *Sloan Management Review* 19 (3), Spring: 17–30.

Frank, Ronald, Massy, William and Wind, Jerry (1972) *Market Segmentation*, Englewood Cliffs, NJ: Prentice Hall.

Garreau, Joel (1982) *The Nine Nations of North America*, Boston: Houghton Mifflin.

Gensch, Dennis, Aversa, N. and Moore, S. (1990) 'A choice modeling market information system that enabled ABB Electric to expand its market share',

Interfaces 20, January–February, 6–25.

Green, Paul E. (1977) 'A new approach to market segmentation', *Business Horizons* 20, February: 61–73.

Green, Paul E. and DeSarbo, Wayne S. (1979) 'Componential marketing in the analysis of consumer trade-offs', *Journal of Marketing* 43: 83–91.

Green, Paul E. and Krieger, Abba M. (1985) 'Models and heuristics for product line selection', *Marketing Science* 4, Winter: 1–19.

Green, Paul E. and Krieger, Abba M. (1991) 'Segmenting marketing with conjoint analysis', *Journal of Marketing* 55, October: 20–31.

Green, Paul E. and Krieger, Abba M. (1994) 'An evaluation of alternative approaches to cluster-based market segmentation', Working paper, Pennsylvania: Wharton School, University of Pennsylvania.

Grover, Rajiv and Srinivasan, V. (1987) 'A simultaneous approach to market segmentation and market structuring', *Journal of Marketing Research* 24, May: 139–53.

Helsen, Kristiaan, Jedidi, Kamel and DeSarbo, Wayne S. (1993) 'A new approach to country segmentation utilizing multinational diffusion patterns', *Journal of Marketing* 57, October: 60–71.

Johnson, Brent and Lilien, Gary L. (1994) 'A framework and procedure for assessing market segment change', Penn State ISBM working paper, Penn State University, University Park, PA.

Kotler, Philip (1991) *Marketing Management*, Englewood Cliffs, NJ: Prentice Hall.

Lewinson, Lisa (1994) 'Data mining: tapping into the mother code', *Database Programming and Design*, February: 50–6.

Mitchell, A. (1983) *The Nine American Lifestyles*, New York: Macmillan.

Peppers, Don and Rogers, Martha (1993) *The One to One Future*, New York: Doubleday.

Peterson, Robert A. (1974) 'Market structuring by sequential cluster analysis', *Journal of Business Research* 2, July: 249–64.

Rangaswamy, Arvind and Wind, Yoram (1994) 'Don't walk in, just log in! Electronic commerce on the information highway',Wharton School Working Paper, February.

Saaty, Thomas L. (1992) *Decision Marketing for Leaders*, Pittsburgh: RWS Pittsburgh Publications.

Wedel, Michel and Steenkamp, Jan-Benedict E.M. (1991) 'A clusterwise regression method for simultaneous fuzzy market structuring and benefit segmentation', *Journal of Marketing Research* XXVIII, November: 385–96.

Weiss, Michael (1994) *Latitudes of Attitudes: An Atlas of American Tastes, Trends, Politics and Passions*, Boston: Little Brown and Company.

Wilson, Elizabeth J., Lilien, Gary L. and Wilson, David T. (1991) 'Developing and testing a contingency paradigm of group choice in organizational buying', *Journal of Marketing Research* 28, November: 452–66.

Wind, Yoram (1978) 'Issue and advances in segmentation research', *Journal of Marketing Research* XV August: 317–37.

Wind, Yoram and Cardozo, Richard N. (1974) 'Industrial marketing segmentation', *Industrial Marketing Management*, March: 153–65.

Wind, Yoram and Saaty, Thomas L. (1980) 'Marketing applications of the analytic hierarchy process', *Management Science* 26, July: 641–58.

Wind, Yoram and Robertson, Thomas (1983) 'Marketing strategy: new directions for theory and research', *Journal of Marketing*, Spring: 12–25.

Wind, Yoram and Dunn, Elizabeth (1987) 'Analytic hierarchy process for generation & evaluation of marketing mix strategies', in Gary Frazier and Jagdish Sheth (eds) *Contemporary Views on Marketing Practice*, Boston: Lexington Books: 111–31.

24

POSITIONING

Graham J. Hooley

INTRODUCTION

Positioning refers to the place in the market that a company, product or service occupies relative to others in that same marketplace. It is defined in terms of the target customer groups the offerings are aimed at and the differential advantage or uniqueness created and offered to that target. There are two similar types of positioning: company competitive positioning; and product or brand positioning.

A company's competitive position relates to how it attempts to build its overall competitive advantage in the marketplace. Competitive position is the totality of offer and image of the company relative to competing companies. In UK food retailing, for example, Marks and Spencer (M&S) occupy an 'up-market' position competing on the basis of quality and gourmet appeal while Aldi competes primarily on the basis of low price. Both have a clear (but different) view of their target customers and both have a clear (but different) basis on which they attempt to create their uniqueness.

Company positioning is generally based on the combination of price, quality and, increasingly, service positioning. Low price positions are clearly targeted at the most price conscious customer groups. 'Bargain', 'budget', 'economy' and 'super economy' positionings typically, but not always, signal lower quality products at lowest prices. Higher quality positions are, again typically but not always, associated with higher prices at the 'luxury' or 'premium' end of the market. Higher price can be used as a quality signal to indicate a high-quality product. Service positionings concentrate on the less tangible aspects of product, on service in choice, delivery, use and after sales care as a means of differentiation for service demanding customers.

Where company position is well developed the full range of the company's offerings benefit, or suffer, from that positioning. For example, new products or extended product ranges offered with the St Michael (Marks and Spencer) brand benefit from the good-quality positioning enjoyed by M&S. Similarly customers shopping for food items in Aldi can be confident that the prices charged will be, if not the lowest, very close to the lowest available in any major food shop.

Product or brand positioning is more concerned with a particular offering and how that is received by customers and potential customers relative to other, competing, brand offerings. In cases where company positioning is strong (well defined) such as in food retailing the brand positioning might be affected by it. When the H.J. Heinz company purchased the Weight Watchers brand in 1978 it was to exploit the strong weight control association's position in the minds of consumers. Within a decade Heinz had 60 frozen food items and 150 non-frozen food items on the market under the Weight Watchers brand (see Aaker 1991).

Positioning is closely related to two key concepts in marketing: market targeting; and product differentiation. Decisions on these two aspects of marketing are at the heart of competitive strategy development. Without a clear idea of the position aimed at it is difficult if not impossible to take coordinated decisions on the rest of the marketing mix. Indeed, defining the competitive positioning aimed for often dictates the most effective combination of other elements of the marketing mix.

KEY CONCEPTS AND IDEAS

There are a number of central ideas and issues in positioning. First, positioning is concerned with long-term strategy rather than short-run tactics. Positions take time to create and are not just produced by short-term advertising campaigns. They offer a sustainable means of differentiation and creation of a competitive advantage. Well-crafted positions are sustainable, defensible and further exploitable. That said, positions may be managed to evolve and change over time as markets develop, mature and die.

Second, positioning is in the mind of the customer (see Ries and Trout 1981). It is what the customer believes about the company, product or service. This is generally brought about by a combination of reality (the tangible features of the product, its pricing, the distribution channels and the type and levels of service built into the product) and image (created through advertising, PR, promotions and so on). Therefore it is crucial that position be defined from the customer, rather than the company, perspective. Note that some of the 'tangible' features, such as price and the channels chosen for distributing the product, may also serve to reinforce (or clash with) the image created through promotion.

Third, positioning is essentially benefit based. Strong positions translate features of the company or product (such as an ability to produce at low cost) into benefits of value to the target customers (such as low relative price). Effective positions not only convey a clear image to the customer but also offer clear reasons (benefits) for buying what the company has to offer.

Fourth, because positioning is benefit based, and because different customers are often seeking different benefits in buying and using essentially the same

421

products and services, the position a particular product occupies in the mind of one customer may be different from the position it occupies in the mind of a different customer. In segmented markets it is clearly important to understand the position the company and its offerings occupy in the minds of all relevant market segments.

Finally, positioning is a relative concept. Products and brands only occupy positions relative to competing products and brands. A price level in isolation from competition is neither 'bargain' nor 'premium'. Similarly quality and service levels can only be judged relative to what is offered by the competition.

A number of alternative bases for establishing product and brand positions have been suggested (Wind 1982). These include product features (e.g. notebook-size computers), the benefits those features convey (portability), specific use occasions (when travelling away from home or office), particular user groups (professionals who work in a variety of locations) or directly against alternatives (more versatile).

EFFECTIVE POSITIONING STRATEGY

For positioning to be effective requires four main conditions to be met (see Arnold 1992; Hooley and Saunders 1993):

1 There must be a clear view of the target market and customers aimed for. Given that the same position in a market may be viewed differently by different customers, it is essential that the impact of the positioning on all the key targets be understood and also that the impact on non-target segments be anticipated.

2 Similarly, the benefits on which the positioning is built must be important to the target customers aimed at. Clearly a low-price positioning when aiming for a segment that is not price sensitive does not make sense. The benefits of features built into the positioning must be ones which are attractive to the target customers.

3 The positioning should build on real strengths of the company and/or its brands. Ideally, these strengths or the combination of core competences used to create the strengths should be unique to the company. This 'asset-based' approach (see Davidson 1987), using the company's assets to best effect to create competitive positions, ensures that they are both defensible and sustainable in the face of competitive attack.

4 Finally, positions should be communicable. They should be capable of being communicated to the target market. This often means that they should be simple and uncomplicated, amenable to translation into attractive and creative advertising or other communication means.

CURRENT ISSUES IN THE DEVELOPMENT OF A POSITIONING STRATEGY

Positioning strategy involves three main phases: identify where you are currently positioned; decide where you wish to be positioned; and implement the strategy to get you there. Each are discussed in turn below.

Identifying current product positions

A starting-point for developing a positioning strategy is to understand the position the product currently occupies in the minds of the customer and potential customer. Whether this has been pursued overtly or not, the product will occupy some current place in the market. There have been a great many research approaches over the years to identify product positions. There are typically, however, several stages in a positioning study.

1 *Identification of the competitive set.* The first step involves identifying which other offerings are considered as alternatives (see Lehmann and Winer 1991). This may be product form competition (e.g. for Diet Pepsi that would include other diet colas such as Diet Coke); product category competition (other soft drinks including non-diet forms, 7-Up, Ir'n Bru); generic competition (other beverages including beer, milk, tea, coffee); or budget/ need priority competition (other foods such as a hamburger or even entertainment such as a visit to the cinema). Identifying the competitive set can be done from a company perspective by looking for substitute products that can serve the same function or, and more usefully, by directly asking customers what alternatives they consider when making a purchase. Note that the competitive set could be scenario specific. It may depend on the purchase or usage context. Thus for one use (e.g. thirst quenching) one competitive set may be important, while for another (e.g. socializing with friends) a different set might be appropriate.

2 *Identification of relevant product dimensions.* Once the competitive set has been defined the next issue is to identify the bases on which customers select between the various alternatives open to them. Central to this is identifying what product benefits are important to them. This information is best obtained through the use of qualitative research techniques such as group discussions. Projective techniques such as Kelly's Repertory Grid, brand personality research, free association and picture interpretation can also be useful. The result should be a comprehensive listing of product benefits and/or features used by customers to compare the alternatives in the competitive set. Again it should be noted that benefits sought are likely to be dependent on the usage context or scenario. When purchasing a pen as a gift for someone else different factors might be important than when buying for one's own use.

423

3   *Estimation of relative importance of attributes.* Not all features will be equally important to all customers. Step three seeks to identify what is important and how important it is to each customer/group. This is best done through quantitative research, ranking or rating attribute importance on importance scales or by points allocation methods (e.g. 'divide 100 points across the features giving most points to the features you consider most important'). Note that at this stage it is important to segment the market if differences in importances arise. Indeed, this is a very powerful way of segmenting markets (benefit segmentation).

4   *Identify positions of competing products on the important attributes.* The fourth step attempts to find where the competitors sit on the various dimensions important to the segments under study. Again, quantitative research using a representative sample is the most appropriate approach. Techniques such as semantic differential scales or Likert scales can be used to elicit brand attribute data. It is important to identify differences in perceptions between various respondents. In addition to differences in importances, noted above, within importance (benefit) segments there may be different views of the market and competing offerings.

5   *Identify customer requirements.* On the same dimensions customer requirements can be identified. This may be achieved by asking customers to rate their 'ideal' brand. Alternatively ideals may be inferred by asking respondents to rank in preference order the alternatives available (a technique known as 'unfolding'; see Green *et al.* 1989). Again, at this stage it is possible that there will be differences in requirements (despite possible similarity in importances and in perceptions found previously). Hence it is important to look for market segments based on different requirements and preferences.

6   *Putting it all together.* Finally, there is a need to put all the above data together in a way that encapsulates the data and facilitates understanding of the results. This can be accomplished through the use of multidimensional scaling techniques (see Green *et al.* 1989) to produce brand maps. The maps summarize the dimensions that are important to customers, the current positions of competing offerings on those dimensions and the location of customer requirements on those dimensions. This can form the basis for deciding on the positioning strategy to adopt (see Figure 1).

In Figure 1, six competing brands were identified in the competitive set (Brand 1 to Brand 6 on the diagram). Two dimensions were found to be important to customers when selecting between alternative brands (price and durability). Three distinct market segments were identified requiring different combinations of the price/durability features (Segment 1 to Segment 3).

Brands 5 and 6 compete directly with each other for sales in Segment 1. Both brands offer the combination of durability at a low price required by the segment. Segment 3, on the other hand, prefers a non-durable brand, but again at a low price. Brands 1 and 2 both serve this segment but neither offer exactly

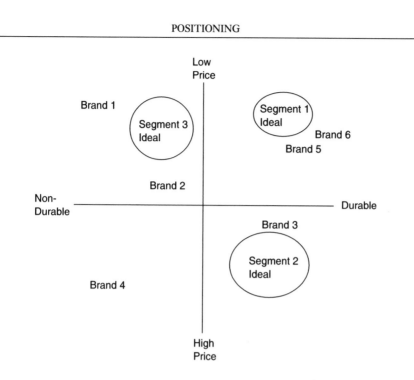

Figure 1   A hypothetical brand map

what the segment requires (Brand 1 is too non-durable, while Brand 2 is not low enough in price). Brand 3 appeals to Segment 2 offering a durable product at an average to high price. Finally, Brand 4 appeals directly to no segment being seen as high price and non-durable, a combination no segment is looking for.

Deciding where you wish to be positioned

Once the current positions of the various competitors and the locations of customer ideal requirements have been identified the company is ready to decide which positioning to aim for. The decision encapsulates two key decisions:

1   The selection of target market (and hence of target competitors).
2   The definition of competitive advantage, or points of difference with the competitors (see Hooley and Saunders 1993).

The decisions are made on the basis of market segment attractiveness and current or potential strength in serving the market segment (see Figure 2).

A number of factors affect the attractiveness of alternative target market segments. Market factors include the size and growth rate of the segment, the stage of industry evolution (stage of PLC), predictability of the market, price elasticity, cyclicality and seasonality of demand and the bargaining power of

425

		Market segment attractiveness		
		Unattractive	Average	Attractive
Current and potential company strengths in serving the segment	Weak	Avoid	Avoid	Avoid
	Average	Avoid	Avoid	Lesser targets
	Strong	Lesser targets	Secondary targets	Prime targets

Figure 2 Target market selection

customers. Economic and technological factors include barriers to entry and exit, bargaining power of suppliers, level of technology utilization, investment required and margins available. Competitive factors include competitive intensity, quality of competition, threat of entry, threat of substitution and degree of current differentiation. Wider (macro) environmental factors include exposure to national and international economic fluctuations, exposure to political and legal factors, degree of market and industry regulation, social acceptability and physical environment impact.

Other factors affect current and potential company strengths in serving a particular target market. Current market position is indicated by relative share of the market, rate of change of share of market, existence of exploitable marketing assets and the existence of unique and valued products and services. Economic and technological position concerns cost structure relative to competitors, capacity utilization and technological capability. The wider capability profile includes management strength and depth, marketing strength and degree of forward, backward and horizontal integration.

The most attractive market positions are therefore those which combine attractive market segments with strong current or potential company strengths. Where these combinations do not exist positionings are selected that trade off on one or other factor. The strong evidence from the literature on competitive success (see Saunders 1993) is that companies are well advised to pursue less attractive markets where they still enjoy clear strengths over competitors in preference to possibly more attractive markets where their strength or potential strength is only average. Markets where the company is at a competitive disadvantage (weak) should be avoided.

Implementing the positioning strategy

Positioning strategy depends on the selection of a target market and the creation of a complete offering to attract and satisfy that target better than the competition. Having identified current position and decided on the position to be aimed for there are several main strategy alternatives.

Reinforce existing position

Where the existing position is a favourable one (i.e. the position is close to what the target market want and is distinct from competing offerings) the strategy may be one of reinforcing that position. In the example shown in Figure 1, page 425, this strategy could be appropriate for Brand 3 if it seeks to serve Segment 2. This strategy may be achieved by continuing with similar product configurations and similar communications.

The position to be reinforced may not necessarily be a leadership one. In car rental Avis successfully positioned as number two in the market behind Hertz with the slogan 'because we're number two we try harder', appealing to the customer on the basis of the plucky underdog, striving to give a higher level of service than a complacent market leader. When Hertz eventually retaliated, however, the positioning backfired to some extent. The retaliation was 'for years Avis have been telling you we're number one. Here's why'.

Incremental repositioning

Where customer wants are changing or expected to change, or the technology for delivering customer satisfaction is developing, movement from current positions may become inevitable. Such changes may be incremental or radical. An example of incremental repositioning is the washing powder Persil. For half a century Persil has been a market leader in the UK, continuously being adapted to meet changes in washing habits and customer requirements. Product reformulations and communications modifications have attended customer usage changes from hand to machine washing, top-loading to front-loading washing machines, and more recently lower temperature washing. This incremental repositioning has enabled Persil to retain its market leadership position in the face of strong competitive attacks.

Where the physical product is close to what customers want there may be a need for image re-engineering to change the image to draw that closer to what target customers want. Brand 1, for example, may be equally as durable as Brand 2 but past communications have failed to convey that to target customers. A promotional campaign using advertising, PR and other communications tools may help to change the image and make Brand 1 closer to what Segment 3 is looking for.

Radical repositioning

Where the position is not favourable (too far from target customers – Brand 4), or too indistinct from competitors (Brands 5 and 6) then more drastic repositioning may be required. This could mean physical re-engineering of the product to make the offer closer to what customers want. In the case of Brand 4 there is an obvious need to improve on the durability of the brand if it is to appeal to Segment 2, or a dramatic reduction in price (together, presumably, with a commensurate reduction in costs) if it is to appeal to Segment 3.

Radical repositioning may mean attacking a completely new market segment. Lucozade, the carbonated glucose drink, was originally positioned as an energy provider to children when ill. Parents administered it almost as a medicine. More recently, however, in an attempt to enter more attractive segments of the market, the drink has been repositioned as an energy source for fit and healthy adults. The advertising campaign featuring superfit athletes such as decathlon gold medallist Daley Thomson signalled this repositioning most effectively. The comparison between Thomson (arguably at the time of the advertisements the fittest man in the world) and sick children could hardly be more stark.

Repositioning may appeal to new values not currently addressed in the market. Hellmann's mayonnaise was sold in the UK primarily as an accompaniment to salad dishes. The market was highly seasonal (summer period dominant) and the product competed with salad cream and other salad dressings. A strong advertising campaign in the mid-1990s attempted to reposition the brand as a suitable accompaniment to a variety of dishes that could be served throughout the year including high recall advertisments promoting use at Christmas as an accompaniment to turkey dishes.

Competitor depositioning

Where position is a favourable one but competitors are encroaching and gaining ground the strategy may be one of attempting to displace the competition. By the early 1990s the traditional dominance of butter as a 'yellow fat' for spreading on bread had been seriously eroded by margarine brands. The launch of butter-grade margarines such as Krona in the early and mid-1980s were so successful that major attempts were made by butter marketers to convince the public that margarine was no real substitute ('no buts – it's got to be butter').

FUTURE DIRECTIONS FOR POSITIONING

A number of trends in marketing can be identified and their impact on positioning predicted. First, in most markets both domestic and international competition is increasing apace. That means that positioning will need to be sharper to help differentiate one offer from another and ensure that the various offerings are more closely targeted at specific market segments.

The customers of the future will be more highly educated and have far greater choice due to the increased levels of competition. Consequently, they are less likely to be influenced by image-based positionings where products do not live up to their promises. Customers will demand increased levels of service and quality at ever more competitive prices. Positionings for the future will be based more on reality than image.

At the same time advances in manufacturing technology, and the continued take up of Total Quality Management (TQM) techniques are leading to a degree of quality convergence in the physical aspects of many product offerings. This makes it increasingly difficult to differentiate on the basis of the physical, or core product (see Levitt 1986). Differentiation, and hence positioning, is likely to depend increasingly on the augmentations and additional services of value that can be built into product offerings.

Finally, we should note that the tools and techniques available to the marketer are becoming ever more sophisticated. Through direct mail marketing, for example, it is now possible to target highly focused campaigns at more tightly defined customer groups. Mail order marketers in particular now maintain sophisticated databases detailing prior purchases and relating them to socio-economic, demographic and other data. This again will lead to more closely targeted positioning. Ries and Trout (1981) announced fifteen years ago that 'the positioning era cometh'. It is still here and will be even more pronounced in the fragmented markets of the twenty-first century.

REFERENCES

Aaker, D. A. (1991) *Managing Brand Equity: Capitalising on the Value of a Brand Name*, New York: The Free Press.

Arnold, D. (1992) *The Handbook of Brand Management*, London: Economist Books Ltd.

Davidson, H. (1987) *Offensive Marketing*, 2nd edn, Harmondsworth: Penguin Books.

Green, P. E., Carmone, F. J., Jnr and Smith, S. M. (1989) *Multidimensional Scaling: Concepts and Applications*, Boston: Allyn and Bacon.

Hooley, G. J. and Saunders, J. A. (1993) *Competitive Positioning: the Key to Market Success*, London: Prentice Hall International.

Lehmann, D. R. and Winer, R. S. (1991) *Analysis for Marketing Planning*, 2nd edn, Boston: Irwin.

Levitt, T. (1986) *The Marketing Imagination*, New York: The Free Press.

Ries, A. and Trout, J. (1981) *Positioning: The Battle for your Mind*, Maidenhead: McGraw-Hill.

Saunders, J. (ed.) (1993) *The Marketing Initiative*, London: Prentice Hall International.

Wind, Y. J. (1982) *Product Policy: Concepts, Methods and Strategy*, Reading, Mass: Addison-Wesley Publishing Co.

IV THE MARKETING MIX

25

THE MARKETING MIX

Walter van Waterschoot

INTRODUCTION

In 1953 Neil Borden coined the term 'marketing mix' in his presidential address to the American Marketing Association. Borden had been inspired by James Culliton who, in the preceding decade, had pictured the marketing executive as somebody combining different ingredients. The term 'marketing mix' referred to the mixture of elements useful in pursuing a certain market response. The metaphor not only suggested the availability of a wide range of possible ingredients, as well as the numerous ways in which these elements could be combined, but also the fact that different amalgamations produce different results, with some preferable to others. The expression reminds one of many other types of combination with similar characteristics – not every mixed grill is as delicious as another and not every drink can be combined successfully with another.

NATURE AND SCOPE

The concept of the marketing mix refers to the set of 'controllable demand-impinging instruments that can be combined into a marketing program used by a firm (or any other organization) to achieve a certain level and type of response from its target market' (van Waterschoot and Van den Bulte 1992: 88). By definition instruments are concerned that more or less directly influence demand to a greater or lesser extent, like the price of a product or the way in which it is advertised. The price of a product will exert a greater or lesser immediate impact on demand, depending among other things on the type of product and on the type of market. Private demand for basic telephone services offered by a state monopolist will not be very much influenced by the price charged. Industry demand by car manufacturers for exhaust pipes, delivered by one specific supplier out of a greater number, will be rather price sensitive. Advertising may hardly be able to raise demand in either case. If a supermarket chain uses television advertising to announce a temporary discount on a major brand of beer during a particular week, its sales may rise very markedly that same week. Advertising may also influence demand indirectly by creating and sustaining a brand image, as in the case of many Coca-Cola advertisements.

However, not all marketing instruments are also marketing mix instruments. For example, marketing research – if carried out properly and if its information value exceeds its costs – is often a useful marketing instrument, without belonging to the marketing mix. The reason is that marketing research does not directly influence demand. Customers will not start buying more of a brand for the mere reason that its producer or distributor increases his marketing research budget or employs more competent research personnel or hires a more skilled research agency or starts using more appropriate research techniques. Adequate marketing research will only influence demand indirectly (e.g. by helping to (re-)specify product characteristics better to match customer needs and desires). Such improved product characteristics make part of the marketing mix, since they directly influence demand to a greater or lesser extent. The marketing research efforts that gave rise to the ameliorated product characteristics have only affected demand in an intermediate or indirect way and therefore by definition do not belong to the marketing mix.

Next to exerting a direct effect, the demand impinging element should also be controllable to be a marketing mix instrument. Fine weather fosters coastal tourism, but is not a marketing mix instrument. However, the distinction between controllable and non-controllable elements, is not always obvious and lack of control does not necessarily imply lack of influence. Controlling over a variable means being able to establish its value. Influence over a variable means having some but not complete control of it (Ackoff 1981: 174). A country's birth rate, for example, is an important but uncontrollable demand impinging element for a manufacturer of baby clothes. If, however, government measures such as birth premiums can significantly raise demand and if government measures are highly dependent on company lobbying, then the birth rate can be called susceptible to influence. As the example suggests, controllable (marketing mix) variables may be used to influence crucial, but uncontrollable environmental elements.

The traditional target groups at which the marketing mix is directed consist of an organization's intermediate and ultimate buyers. Conceptually, however, the marketing mix need not limit itself to these groups, but may and often should also serve to relate an organization to any of its so-called 'transactional publics', consisting of 'those individuals, organizations and institutions with which the corporation interacts directly' (Ackoff 1981: 90). Examples are suppliers, investors, creditors, government and regulatory agencies, competitors and the press.

Like the marketing concept itself, the mix idea applies not only beyond mere consumer publics, but also beyond business organizations. To realize some of its manifold aims such as heightening environmental awareness and provoking environmentally favourable behaviour, as well as to gain financial support from ecologically minded individuals, an environmentalist organization like Greenpeace has a set of instruments at its disposal that – notwithstanding its own peculiarities – is similar to strictly commercial marketing mixes. Greenpeace mainly and successfully tries to generate free advertising or publicity. Their direct non-violent actions – like steering a small inflatable craft between the harpoon guns of whalers and their prey – yields them spectacularly wide media exposure. Their marketing programme towards the general public further relies on personal mailings and sales of Greenpeace merchandise via mail order as well as via a small set of specialized shops in major cities.

Marketing mix instruments are typically combined in order to provoke a certain type and level of demand, which an organization deems worthwhile in pursuing its ultimate objectives. In the realization of these ultimate objectives, demand creation constitutes an intermediate goal. An organization may, for instance, try to maximize its long-term profits. It might therefore stimulate demand by developing a high-quality product with unique features, which focuses on a segment of affluent buyers willing to pay a high price, preferably buying in specialized upper-class boutiques and probably reading advertisements in exclusive magazines. Mix instruments, however, are not only apt to encourage demand but also to discourage it – an approach called 'demarketing' (Kotler and Levy 1971). In 1993 – due to a continuous oversupply of practitioners – organizations of Belgian doctors visited secondary schools in order to discourage school-leavers, or at least some of them, from studying medicine.

FOUR GENERIC FUNCTIONS

For exchange to come about, it is essential that there are at least two parties believing that it is appropriate or desirable to deal with one another and being free to make, accept or reject an offer. Moreover, each of these parties must possess something that might be of value to the other and each must be capable of communication and delivery (Kotler 1972). The latter condition summarizes the four fundamental or generic functions that marketing mix instruments have to fulfil.

Obviously, exchange or demand creation is not possible if one does not have any object or service at one's disposal that might be of value to the other party. So a primary function of the marketing mix consists of configuring something that is valued by the prospective exchange party. Since the idea behind a potential exchange is to gain from it in some way or another, a second function consists of determining the offers and sacrifices that need to be made by the prospective exchange party. The previous two functions would not allow any exchange if no communication could take place. The respective parties need to be informed about one another's intentions and requirements and perhaps be persuaded about the attractiveness of the other party's offering, or even about entering into such an exchange relationship. This third fundamental function consists of bringing the offer to the attention of the prospective exchange party and influencing its feelings and preferences about it. Even now no exchange would come about if the respective parties were unable actually to deliver the object or service that is exchanged for some higher valued object or service. Here arises a fourth fundamental function of placing the offer at the disposal of the prospective exchange party.

The marketing discipline considers these four mix functions as generic, in the sense that they have to be fulfilled, for exchange to come about (see Table 1, left-hand column). This necessity follows from the marketing discipline's realistic market assumptions, which would be called impure by economists because of the supposed lack of instantaneous transactions and perfect knowledge (Houston and Gassenheimer 1987: 15). Consequently, poor execution of any of these functions will bring about poor exchange results or worse results than those that could potentially have taken place. However, if any of these functions is not carried out, no exchange can take place, no demand can be created, fulfilled or maintained.

THE MULTIPLE FUNCTIONS OF MIX INSTRUMENTS

In practice, numerous marketing mix instruments exist. Out of an endless theoretical list of mix instruments a specific actual combination has to be chosen, taking into consideration its expected effects. A fundamental observation is the fact that any instrument predominantly serves one of the four generic functions mentioned previously, but at the same time it also contributes – be it to a lesser extent – to the fulfilment of the three other functions (see Table 1). Take, for example, the choice of the type of retail outlet. If a certain brand is exclusively for sale in upper-end shops, then this choice predominantly takes part in the availability function. At the same time, however, the first generic function is also affected, since shopping in a highly esteemed outlet fills needs such as prestige and dominance. Due to the relatively low density of such shops, however, transportation costs will be higher in terms of monetary expenses, time and effort and as such act upon the price function. Finally, the communication function is influenced, since the choice of the particular type of sales outlet strengthens or weakens the image of the product itself. A brand that is only for sale in a very limited set of exclusive shops will be perceived differently from a brand that is available in any mass distribution outlet, even if the objective product characteristics were identical.

To the previous example numerous others can be added. Any specific marketing mix instrument affects all four generic marketing mix functions, but predominantly one of them. Vice versa, any generic marketing mix function is served by any specific marketing mix instrument or hampered by it. Since in actual applications several specific instruments contribute to the fulfilment of all four generic functions, coordination becomes of the utmost importance. The

Table 1 Relative importance of diverse marketing mix instruments in the fulfilment of generic marketing functions

Generic function	Product instruments	Price instruments	Distribution instruments	Communication instruments
Configuration of something valued by the prospective exchange party	xxxxx	x	x	x
Determination of the compensation and sacrifices to be brought by the prospective exchange party	x	xxxxx	x	x
Placing the offer at the disposal of the prospective exchange party	x	x	xxxxx	x
Bringing the offer to the attention of the prospective exchange party and influencing its feelings and preferences about it	x	x	x	xxxxx

Source: van Waterschoot and Van den Bulte (1992: 89)

instrumental choices should be made in such a way that the different elements not only reinforce one another's positive effects and neutralize one another's negative effects with regard to one generic function, but also with regard to all four such functions simultaneously. Moreover, each generic function actually consists of a set of specific subfunctions that require specific instrumental goals. Communication, for example, presumes amongst other things the creation of awareness, knowledge, preference and conviction.

THE FOUR P CLASSIFICATION

In the development of a new body of thought, such as marketing throughout the twentieth century, the making of listings and taxonomies is one of the primary tasks. Typically, early taxonomies are not developed in an inductive way on strictly logical grounds as a derivation from existing theory (Hunt 1991). Rather they are made in a deductive way. Known elements, supposedly belonging to the investigated population, are inventoried and grouped into classes on the basis of their similarity. In this way early writers on the marketing mix tried to itemize the large number of controllable demand impinging instruments. Frey (1956) and Borden (1964) adopted a checklist approach. Other authors developed more succinct and convenient classifications that could be easily memorized (Frey 1956; Howard 1957; McCarthy 1960; Lazer and Kelly 1962). Of the many developed schemata, only McCarthy's has survived and has become the 'dominant design' or 'received view'.

The McCarthy typology has become known as the Four P classification of the marketing mix, since it distinguishes four classes of items under four headings beginning with the letter P: Product, Price, Place and Promotion. Although McCarthy only named these classes without defining them, they roughly correspond to the four previously mentioned generic marketing mix functions.

The first class contains instruments that mainly – although not exclusively – aim at the satisfaction of the prospective exchange party's needs such as product variety, product quality, design, features, brand name, packaging, sizes, services, warranties and return.

The second class comprises instruments that mainly – although not exclusively – fix the size and the means of payment exchanged for the goods or services. Examples are the list price, discounts, allowances, the payment period and credit terms.

The third class holds instruments that mainly – although not exclusively – determine the intensity and manner of how the goods or services will be made available. Examples are the choice of distribution channels, the coverage of existing outlets and location of outlets.

The fourth class of instruments in the McCarthy typology is a hybrid one. Whereas the three previous classes nicely correspond to the three cited generic functions, McCarthy's fourth P only roughly corresponds to the fourth generic function. Indeed this fourth P is typically subdivided into four classes, of which only the first three exclusively encompass instruments that mainly aim to bring the offer to the attention of the prospective exchange party and to influence feelings and preferences about it. These three subclasses are Advertising, Personal Selling and Publicity. Traditional definitions are the following:

Advertising: any paid form of nonpersonal presentation and promotion of ideas, goods, or services by an identified sponsor.

Personal Selling: oral presentation in a conversation with one or more prospective purchasers for the purpose of making sales.

Publicity: nonpersonal stimulation of demand for a product, service, or business unit by planting commercially significant news about it in a published medium or obtaining favorable presentation of it upon radio, television, or stage that is not paid for by the sponsor.

(Alexander 1960)

The fourth P of the McCarthy typology, however, also encompasses a residual fourth subcategory, which serves as a catch-all to host all marketing mix instruments that do not find a place in any other category. In contrast with the three previously mentioned typical communication subclasses, only the fourth subcategory of McCarthy's fourth P consists of promotion instruments in the strict sense of the word. A traditional description of this (sales) Promotion category is the following:

Those marketing activities, other than personal selling, advertising and publicity, that stimulate consumer purchasing and dealer effectiveness, such as displays, shows and exhibitions, demonstrations, and various nonrecurrent selling efforts not in the ordinary routine.

(Alexander 1960)

THE PECULIAR NATURE OF PROMOTION INSTRUMENTS

A fundamental drawback to the traditional promotion concept is its negative definition. Instead of defining promotion in a residual way it should be defined positively. Current marketing literature contains sufficient elements to compose such a definition. One important view is that promotion concerns activities directed at inducing potential exchange partners to consummate immediate exchange. For example, a price reduction may cause a customer to take direct action, whereas the same customer may hesitate or postpone his purchase in its absence. Another important view concerns the nonroutine, short-duration element of promotion instruments. It stresses that a price reduction can be considered as promotional to the extent that this reduction is of a temporary nature. In fact, the first view is structurally linked to the second. If people are not convinced of the exceptionality of a price reduction it becomes unlikely that it will provoke an immediate purchase.

Interpreting promotion instruments as inducements implies that they are not identical to the communication category of the marketing mix. Communication

439

Table 2 An improved classification of the marketing mix

Marketing mix				Communication mix		
	Product mix	Price mix	Distribution mix	Mass communication mix	Personal communication mix	Publicity mix
Basic mix	*Basic product mix* Instruments that mainly aim at the satisfaction of the prospective exchange party's needs.	*Basic price mix* Instruments that mainly fix the size and the way of payment exchanged for the goods or services.	*Basic distribution mix* Instruments that mainly determine the intensity and manner of how the goods or services will be made available.	*Basic mass communication mix* Non-personal communication efforts that mainly aim at announcing the offer or maintaining the awareness and knowledge about it: evoking or maintaining favourable feelings and removing barriers to wanting.	*Basic personal communication mix* Personal communication efforts that mainly aim at announcing the offer or maintaining awareness and knowledge about it; evoking or maintaining favourable feelings and removing barriers to wanting.	*Basic publicity mix* Efforts that aim at inciting a third party (persons and authorities) to favourable communication about the offer.
	e.g. product characteristics options, assortment, brand name, packaging, quantity, factory guarantee.	e.g. list price, usual terms of payment, usual discounts, terms of credit, long-term savings campaigns.	e.g. different types of distribution channels, density of the distribution system, trade relation mix (policy of margins, terms of delivery, etc.), merchandising advice.	e.g. theme advertising in various media, permanent exhibitions, certain forms of sponsoring.	e.g. amount and type of selling, personal remunerations.	e.g. press bulletins, press conferences, tours by journalists.

Promotion mix	Product promotion mix	Price promotion mix	Distribution promotion mix	Mass communication promotion mix	Personal communication promotion mix	Publicity promotion mix
	Supplementary group of instruments that mainly aim at inducing immediate overt behaviour by strengthening the basic product mix during relatively short periods of time.	Supplementary group of instruments that mainly aim at inducing immediate overt behaviour by strengthening the basic price mix during relatively short periods of time.	Supplementary group of instruments that mainly aim at inducing immediate overt behaviour by strengthening the basic distribution mix during relatively short periods of time.	Supplementary group of instruments that mainly aim at inducing immediate overt behaviour by strengthening the basic mass communication mix during relatively short periods of time.	Supplementary group of instruments that mainly aim at inducing immediate overt behaviour by strengthening the basic personal communication mix during relatively short periods of time.	Supplementary group of instruments that mainly aim at inducing immediate overt behaviour by strengthening the basic publicity mix during relatively short periods of time.
	e.g. economy packs, 3-for-the-price-of-2 deals; temporary luxury options on a car at the price of its standard model.	e.g. exceptionally favourable price, end-of-season sales, exceptionally favourable terms of payment and credit, short-term savings campaigns, temporary discounts, coupons.	e.g. extra point of purchase material, trade promotions such as buying allowances, sales contests; temporary increase of the number of distribution points.	e.g. action advertising, contests, sweepstakes, samples, premiums, trade shows or exhibitions.	e.g. temporary demonstrations, salesforce promotions such as salesforce contests.	e.g. all measures to stimulate positive publicity about a sales promotion action.

Source: Van Waterschoot and Van den Bulte (1992: 90)

creates awareness, provides knowledge and motivates use desires, whereas promotion amplifies and accelerates the decision to buy. Persuasive communication is used to overcome a lack of awareness or appreciation (information barriers), or a lack of credibility (credibility barriers), or even to change the preference structure of prospects (Beem and Shaffer 1981). In contrast to these three 'barriers to wanting', promotion tackles 'barriers to acting' such as physical and psychological inertia barriers, risk barriers, or competitive barriers from close substitutes (ibid.: 16–18).

Notwithstanding the previous observation, some communication instruments also possess a promotional nature, such as supermarket advertisements which announce a temporary price discount. In other words, there is a typical overlap between some promotional tools and some communication instruments. A similar overlap occurs between other promotional tools and the rest of the marketing mix. Whereas trade shows and exhibitions are clearly of a communicative nature, other typical promotions are not. Coupons, for instance, essentially represent a specific form of price reduction. Economy packs form another promotion example where communication is not the most important issue, but rather where the product aspect is, since economy packs offer a larger quantity of the product at the original price. In the same vein trade promotions typically intensify the distribution effort, without communication being the major aspect.

THE FOUR P CLASSIFICATION REVISITED

The very existence of promotion instruments indicates that the list of four generic mix functions described earlier is incomplete. Direct inducement or provocation is in some situations a necessary condition for the exchange to take place. Hence, promotion represents a 'situational' or 'complementary' marketing function (van Waterschoot and Van den Bulte 1992: 88). As a result, McCarthy's Four P classification is improved by systematically and explicitly combining the idea of four generic marketing mix functions, with a 'situational' or 'complementary' marketing mix function (see Table 2).

The columns of Table 2 represent a classification of the marketing mix variables on the basis of the generic function they primarily fulfil. Vertically, the marketing mix variables are subdivided according to the criterion of whether the instruments are basic to the consummation of an offer or whether those instruments are more complementary. This supplementary mix actually contains the elements fulfilling the previously mentioned 'situational' function that is usually found in the promotion mix. However, this mix is now defined in a positive and not in a residual manner and not limited to the narrow domain of communication instruments, but spread out over all the major classes of marketing instruments. The promotional mix can be positively defined as follows:

contains demand-impinging instruments that have no power of themselves but can, during relatively short periods of time, complement and sustain the basic instruments of the marketing mix (namely product, price, distribution, and communication) for the purpose of stimulating prospective exchange partners (commonly referred to as target market(s)) to a significant degree of desirable forms of immediate, overt behaviour.

(van Waterschoot and Van den Bulte 1992: 89)

Desirable forms of immediate, overt behaviour usually consist of straight buying. However, other forms of overt – or visible – behaviour also exist, such as information gathering. Many promotional activities and actions in business marketing and direct marketing are aimed not at stimulating immediate purchase, but at moving the prospect one step forward in the buying process. Free sampling, clearly a promotional activity, is used to induce trial use, not buying.

EXPLICATIONS AND EXTENSIONS

Throughout the years a number of alternative marketing mix classifications have been formulated, often to reflect the peculiarities of a specific field of application. In most instances this adaptation was realized by adding one or more Ps to McCarthy's mnemonic Four P list. In instances where an explication of a subcategory of instruments is concerned, such an addition – although conceptually not strictly necessary – is defensible on pedagogical grounds. In instances where an extension outside the boundaries of the marketing mix is concerned, no conceptual justification exists. Despite the indisputable relevance of the managerial issues behind the added Ps, the extension of the mnemonic list mainly serves as an eyecatcher. In further instances, the proposed names of the new categories are not appropriate as a result of the obligatory P. The subsequent paragraphs summarize the main examples of such explications and extensions.

Occasionally, a separate fifth P is added to denote People, Personnel or Personal selling. In this way a collective noun is provided to stress the importance of all types of selling and servicing efforts which are being carried out by any person within the organization. In applications where sales efforts are of a typically high strategic value – as for example in the case of service marketing – no fundamental objection can be made to this explication, although there is no conceptual necessity since the provision of services belongs to the P of the (service) Product, and sales efforts form part of the P of Promotion. In retail marketing, as well as the supplementary P of People a further P is often added to denote the Presentation of merchandise as well as the store layout. Again an explication is involved that is defensible on pedagogical grounds, but which is not necessary from a conceptual or classificatory point of view, since the generically rooted Four Ps also hold these elements.

In service marketing Ps have also been added to represent Participants,

Physical evidence and Process (Booms and Bitner 1981). The Participants in a service marketing situation can significantly improve or harm the quality of the execution of service. However, the activities of the personnel carrying out the service conceptually belong to the first P of Product, encompassing all instruments which aim primarily at want fulfilment. Insofar as the clients are meant by Participants, the addition becomes conceptually incorrect, since the marketing mix groups demand impinging elements and not the actual demand constituting elements. The Physical environment where the service is provided, together with tangible elements which are used to support the service, obviously influences demand. Where these elements are under the control of the marketer, they form part of the Product or Place instruments. If these elements cannot be controlled by the manager, they are by definition not marketing mix variables. The same remark also holds for the procedural elements of servicing, meaning that a separate P for Process is not really necessary.

With regard to the persuasion of the public outside the most typical target groups, Kotler (1986) has introduced the concept of 'megamarketing', denoting the art of supplying benefits to parties other than target consumers and intermediaries like agents, distributors and dealers – parties such as governments, labour unions and other interest groups that can block profitable entry into a market. Specific instruments in this context are Public Relations and Power. Public relations try to influence public opinion, mainly by means of mass-communication techniques. Power on the other hand addresses itself to 'influential industry officials, legislators, and government bureaucrats to enter and operate in the target market, using sophisticated lobbying and negotiating skills in order to achieve the desired response from the other party without giving away the house' (Kotler 1986: 120). The term power is not appropriate in this instance. Power refers to the ability of the marketer to get some other party (consumer, distributor, government) to do what the latter would not otherwise have done (buy, search for information, give a permit) (Stern and El-Ansary 1992: 268). Marketing mix instruments – if properly combined – are capable of developing a certain amount of power. Calling one instrument category, applied in a specific context, Power, implies a linguistic distortion to make the instrument fit a mnemonic row.

CRITICISM OF THE MARKETING MIX CONCEPT

In spite of the immediate and widely spread acceptance of the marketing mix concept, it has been criticized in several respects. Van den Bulte (1991) summarized these criticisms under nine headings. The following reflects Van den Bulte's inventory, together with our personal assessment.

The marketing mix concept is accused of applying to micro issues only, because it takes the stance of only one exchange party, namely the seller or the 'cake mixer' or the 'channel captain' rather than the consumer or society at large. Indeed, the channel captain perspective typifies the marketing discipline as a whole, except for those fields where social goals dominate from the outset, as in the case of true charity marketing. The marketing mix concept cannot be criticized in this respect, since the usefulness of a known and classified set of demand impinging instruments – even if suggested by the specific metaphoric expression – is not by its own nature limited to channel captain applications, but applies to any exchange situation.

A second criticism concerns the concept's limited managerial use in an organizational context, because of its attributed 'lack of attention to the internal tasks of the marketing function, like disseminating information to all people involved in or affected by marketing activities, human resources management, and developing incentive and control systems' (Van den Bulte 1991: 11). Also this point of criticism results from unrealistic expectations about a basic and powerful but at the same time limited concept. The marketing mix concept has not been developed to encompass guidelines for internal organization and communication. On the other hand, a clearly defined and classified set of demand impinging instruments contributes to a sound organization of commercial efforts. The existence of the concept and the corresponding classification should be seen as a necessary, but at the same time insufficient, condition for theoretical and practical development.

Valuable research has been conducted regarding interactions and interdependencies between mix variables. The mix concept is criticized because the hypotheses cannot be derived from the metaphor itself. This criticism can again be countered quite easily: the mere inventory of a set of instruments cannot be supposed to encompass a theory about the interactions amongst them. The classification of these instruments, however, to some extent, can. Empirical investigation and theory building rely heavily on the way such instruments are classified. The classification itself, however, cannot be anything more than a solid tool for theory building and empirical investigation, which it cannot replace.

A fourth point of criticism accuses the marketing mix concept of a mechanistic view on markets. The market is often described in terms of response curves, depending on a certain 'parameter' or 'marketing decision variable' or on the entire mix. In this way the optimization problem upon which the concept of the marketing mix focuses is solved. Modelling the relationship between commercial instruments and market response serves analytical and forecasting purposes. Forgetting the limitations and assumptions of the model or technique represents an undeniable risk, which cannot be attributed to the marketing mix as a concept. Models – whether they are of a stimulus-response or of an interactive type – suppose a sound marketing mix concept and classification, but the characteristics of the former should not be attributed to the latter and vice versa.

A fifth point of criticism comes very close to the previous one. The concept is accused of having a one-way (stimulus-response) character, which impedes marketing from shifting its focus from exchange as an isolated act towards the

445

richer concept of exchange relationships. The marketing mix concept in no way conflicts with an idea of interaction. Indeed, its instruments and their categorization perfectly fit such approaches, as they also fit the idea of an exchange relationship. An exchange relationship supposes, for example, a more pronounced quality and service accent than a mere one-time exchange.

The concept's poor market orientation also follows from the suggested view of the customer as someone to whom something is done – by the cake mixer – and not as someone for whom something is done. The stimulus-response approach that is attributed to the marketing mix is at the same time criticized for proposing to lump individuals into a market of homogeneous respondents. Presence or absence, as well as degree of market orientation, depends on factors like market structure, power balance between parties, organizational structures and procedures, personal attitudes, corporate culture, business mission and business goals. However, to blame the mix concept for causing a lack of market orientation is intellectually not correct. This basic, but by its very nature limited, concept is a factual device in any market approach.

The mix concept is also criticized for implying a view of the firm (or any exchange-seeking party in general) – perhaps suggested to some people by the picture of the independent cake mixer – as being a rather self-sufficient social unit having access to a considerable resource base. Except for manufacturer-distributor links, the concept would remove resource dependency between social units. As a result the different bridging strategies – such as bargaining, contracting, cooption, joint programmes, licensing, integration, trade associations and government action – are issues that would not be taken into consideration. Once again this is an example of unjustified criticism, resulting from unrealistic expectations. Also here the argument can be turned round. Interorganizational 'bridges' will influence the specific marketing mix choice. As such an argument is given not against but in favour of a clear concept and classification.

A further point of criticism concerns the concept's supposed reactive attitude towards the environment.

> Traditionally, marketing mix proponents have myopically considered the transactional environment to be composed of customers and dealers only, putting all other social units into the category 'contextual', hence lumping them together into faceless environmental forces. Thus blinding themselves, they have not taken into consideration the fact that the links with some transaction-environmental units and the activities these deploy can be changed through lobbying, legal action, public relations, issue advertising, strategic partnering and so on. Finding a way to control or influence variables that were previously considered to be beyond discretion, is often the cornerstone of great marketing creativity and the gateway to superior profitability.
>
> (Van den Bulte 1991: 18)

This citation contains a major and well-expressed lesson in marketing management. Marketing practice and marketing theory have been putting too much emphasis on their traditional public, but there is no logic in blaming the mix concept for it.

Finally, critics accuse the mix concept of possessing a mechanistic and rational-economic neoclassical view of markets and firms, and stripping out the institutional and social supports to market processes such as attraction, trust, friendship, power and interdependency. As a result the marketing mix would be 'rendered impotent before many strategic management problems' (Van den Bulte 1991: 20). In this case the criticism also concerns actual marketing practice as well as the conceptual development that has taken place at an instrumental, tactical and strategic level; the criticism does not hit the mix concept itself.

CONCLUSION

The mix metaphor has gained usage spectacularly quickly as a result of its expressiveness, liveliness, compactness and therefore memorability. Equally imaginative has been McCarthy's pragmatic grouping of the instruments. His Four P classification also received acceptance speedily and easily, presumably as a result of its strong mnemonic appeal. The Four Ps have even become synonymous with the marketing mix. The mnemonic row, however, has too often been used as a means of explication of submixes or in order to draw the attention to marketing aspects that were not always mix issues. Over the years the limitations of the original mnemonic approach have become apparent, amongst other things as a result of the increased importance of promotion instruments in marketing practice. Consequently, the Four P classification, with its inherent negatively defined Promotion category within the communication family, has been contested by many authors. Its adaptation, based on modern insight into promotion, significantly improves the original scheme.

The marketing mix concept itself is as elementary, powerful, and at the same time limited in marketing thinking as the alphabet in the use and development of language. It is therefore unjustified to blame the mix concept for the peculiarities of the overall discipline. In the same way the concept cannot be blamed for the limitations of the metaphor, which contributed so significantly to its popularity and understanding. The marketing mix concept forms a fundamental building block in theory and practice. A clearly defined, named and classified concept is a necessary, but at the same time insufficient, condition for successful theory building and practical implementation. Marketing theory should concentrate its attention on measuring, explaining and predicting the isolated as well as the combined effects of the mix instruments, as a solid basis for actual practice in diverse fields and circumstances.

REFERENCES

Ackoff, R. L. (1981) *Creating the Corporate Future: Plan or Be Planned for*, New York: John Wiley.

Alexander, R. S. (1960) *Marketing Definitions: A Glossary of Marketing Terms*, Chicago: American Marketing Association.

Beem, E. R. and Shaffer, H. J. (1981) *Triggers to Action – Some Elements in a Theory of Promotional Inducement* (Report 81–106), Cambridge, MA: Marketing Science Institute.

Booms, B. H. and Bitner, M. J. (1981) 'Marketing strategies and organization structures for service firms', in J. H. Donnelly and W. R. George (eds) *Marketing of Services*, Chicago: American Marketing Association proceedings.

Borden, N. (1964) 'The concept of the marketing mix', *Journal of Advertising Research* 4, June: 2–7.

Frey, A. W. (1956) *The Effective Marketing Mix: Programming for Optimum Results*, Hanover, NH: The Amos Tuck School of Business Administration, Dartmouth College.

Houston, F. S. and Gassenheimer, J. B. (1987) 'Marketing and exchange', *Journal of Marketing* 51, October: 3–18.

Howard, J. A. (1957) *Marketing Management: Analysis and Decisions*, Homewood, IL: Richard D. Irwin, Inc.

Hunt, S. D. (1991) *Modern Marketing Theory: Critical Issues in the Philosophy of Marketing Science*, Cincinnati, OH: South-Western Publishing Company.

Kotler, P. (1972) 'A generic concept of marketing', *Journal of Marketing* 36, April: 46–54.

Kotler, P. (1986) 'Megamarketing', *Harvard Business Review* 64, March–April: 117–24.

Kotler, P. and Levy, S. L. (1971) 'Demarketing, yes, demarketing', *Harvard Business Review* 49, November–December: 71–80.

Lazer, W. and Kelly, E. J. (1962) *Managerial Marketing: Perspectives and Viewpoints*, rev. edn, Homewood, IL: Richard D. Irwin, Inc.

McCarthy, E. J. (1960) *Basic Marketing: A Managerial Approach*, Homewood, IL: Richard D. Irwin, Inc.

Mason, J. B., Mayer, M. L. and Wilkinson, J. B. (1993) *Modern Retailing: Theory and Practice*, 6th edn, Homewood, IL: Richard D. Irwin, Inc.

Payne, A. (1993) *The Essence of Services Marketing*, London: Prentice Hall International.

Stern, L. and El-Ansary, A. (1992) *Marketing Channels*, London: Prentice Hall International.

Van den Bulte, C. (1991) *The Concept of the Marketing Mix Revisited: A Case Analysis of Metaphor in Marketing Theory and Management*, Ghent, Belgium: The Vlerick School of Management, University of Ghent.

van Waterschoot, W. and Van den Bulte, C. (1992) 'The 4P classification of the marketing mix revisited', *Journal of Marketing* 56, October: 83–93.

26

PRODUCT POLICY

Susan J. Hart

INTRODUCTION

Central to the marketing concept is the notion of an exchange between two parties which delivers satisfaction to both. The media through which this theoretical, mutual satisfaction is derived are those products and services offered by the supplier to the customer. Thus, products and services must be seen as central to marketing strategy if they are to deliver satisfaction to the customer and profit to the supplier. However, two factors affect this issue: the need to manage the exchange relationships over time and the nature of customer satisfaction. These two factors are interrelated, in that the needs and wants of customers are themselves dynamic, not static. As customers and markets become familiar with the array of products and services available in a given product market, their needs evolve, become more sophisticated and discerning. It follows, therefore, that the nature of the exchange (product and/or service in return for money) will also have to change. This changing complexion of products and services offered is the core of 'product policy'. If no change occurs, the product or service offering will become quickly out of tune with customer requirements and will meet with less success. This contention reveals the link between product policy and marketing strategy since the adaptation of the products and services offered by companies to customers to effect long-term growth and profitability is what is understood to be the essence of marketing strategy. Consequently, marketing strategy and product policy are intimately related, and address the central question of managing the firm's destiny.

While the optimal approach to product policy may well be to start with customer needs and design products and services as 'bundles of satisfaction', the reality of most companies is that of having to manage existing products for maximum profits which can be invested into the design and development of products and services of the future. In other words, firms must begin with their current resource base – current manufacturing capabilities and technologies, current management skills, current products and customers. Accordingly, the

449

objective of this chapter is to explore the key issues involved in constructing a product policy which delivers 'bundles of satisfaction' to customers and delivers profits for reinvestment and renewal for the future.

First, the role of the product in marketing strategy is examined, showing how products are central to concepts of competitive strategy such as cost leadership and differentiation. The ensuing discussion underlines the necessity of differentiating products based on market needs. Second, the association between market needs, product characteristics and benefits and competition is considered. Third, the concept of change in products is presented via the concept of the product life cycle, together with its oft-cited criticisms. Finally, methods for diagnosing the strategic value of current products to a company are discussed.

THE ROLE OF THE PRODUCT IN MARKETING STRATEGY

At the heart of competitive marketing strategy are products. The most basic of strategic choices expounded by Porter (1980) to achieve competitive advantage are lower cost and differentiation. The former is to offer a comparable product to the marketplace at a price which is lower than, or near to that of the competition. The low price is sustainable due to efficiencies in design, production and marketing which provide acceptable returns to the company. On the other hand, differentiation's aim is to offer a superior, or unique product to the customer, charging a premium price. The superior, or unique product is achieved via product quality, special features or after-sales service. Each of these two basic strategies have products at their centre. The cost leadership strategy will largely depend on offering standardized products to customers who have a need for a particular type of product. The differentiated strategy depends on the existence of groups of customers who have different requirements for which they are prepared to pay. Thus, Porter's basic strategies are akin to the options developed and used by marketers: undifferentiated, differentiated and focus or niche strategies. The first two are explained above, while the third involves choosing one major market segment and concentrating efforts in order to tailor the company's offering closely to its particular needs. It is, in short, a specialized form of differentiated marketing. From the marketer's point of view, however, the chosen strategy should be aimed at satisfying customers, so that the basic product is viewed in terms, not of its characteristics, but of the benefits customers will derive from its purchase.

Delivering customer satisfaction or 'selling benefits' is something of a truism unless translated into tangibles which can be acted upon by management. Since the benefits sought by customers vary, not only in relation to the type of product in question, but also in relation to the type of customers and their individual perceptions of those products, a definition of 'benefits' is extremely elusive. The economic rational model tends to view benefits in terms of price and performance, both of which are taken to be objective. Where this rational model dominates thinking, there is a marked tendency to emphasize high production volumes and low costs as the key elements in competitive success. An understanding of the more subjective motivations that condition customer choice (as well as the so-called objective ones) has led to product differentiation as a basic competitive strategy, where products are designed to be different according to those attributes – benefits – which will deliver 'satisfying experiences'.

An example of these two strategies is seen at the lower end of the small car market. The cheapest models typically have 900cc engines, no radio and no head restraints. In contrast, other models include 1100cc engines, come ready fitted with radios, special coachlines and are given distinctive names. Base products are stripped of added value and are sold purely on the basis of price and often the past performance of the company. Those products which do not foster the popular image attempt, through minor product characteristics, to portray more personalized products with added value.

The question of the relative success rates of either strategy ultimately depends on whether the target markets perceive the extras supplied by some companies as real benefits which deliver satisfaction or prefer the low price-no extras option. Thus companies must learn how to define products in terms of customer benefits. Manufacturing companies can choose among a battery of product characteristics in order to define their product range. These character-istics are specific in terms of the raw materials and technologies used in their production. Yet management has to decide which of these characteristics are considered most important by the customer if it is to produce a competitive range of products.

Failure to devote time to this carries the risk of emphasizing the creation of subjective differences between competitive products through service and promotional effort on the assumption that small differentiating features will be considered of value to customers.

The home laundry market in major developed economies serves as a prime example of this. Washing powders are produced in 'traditional' and 'concen-trated' form. There are detergent- and soap-based powders as well as both biological and enzyme-free brands. There are 'environmentally friendly' and more harmful products, as well as original and replacement packaging. In addition, there are powders developed to preserve brightness of colour in washed clothes. There are, on top of this diversity, liquid versions of most of the major brands, sold complete with their dispensing systems which are independ-ent of the design of washing machines. Some liquids and powders have built-in fabric softeners, while an entire range of independent fabric softeners is also marketed by the industry's main players – in both standard and concentrated form. In addition, one manufacturer also markets a fabric softener for use in tumble-driers.

Surely it is reasonable to question how much control can be exerted over this range, how easy or profitable it is to develop or sustain these differences? If differences can be created through developing user-relevant product character-istics, then the constant need to invent producer-defined differences will be reduced. What are the implications of all this? Quite simply, that in making the development of products an activity related to user benefits, the old adage of delivering quality and value cannot be overlooked as it is the basis for a sharper edge to competitive marketing. All this means is that marketing is not solely concerned with market research, advertising and selling techniques, but also extends to the core of corporate strategy: products.

USER NEEDS

Having established that products are the business of marketing as much as promotion, advertising and selling, we have to return to the unanswered question of how to relate user needs, benefits and product characteristics. Starting with user needs, Rothwell *et al.* (1983) developed a way of classifying needs which is helpful to management.

Need elements

Need elements indicate the overall price and specific performance characteristics required by customers. Thus they define the characteristics a product must contain. However, many characteristics will be assumed to exist if the product is to be considered at all. King (1987) categorizes needs into three types:

1 Basic needs: those which a customer will assume the product satisfies. A consumer expects that a vacuum cleaner will clean carpets.
2 Articulated needs: those which a consumer can express readily. These are often met by at least one current solution, or are easily imagined as being met. For example, a consumer might imagine a vacuum cleaner that shampoos a carpet.
3 Exciting needs: those that will 'delight and surprise' a customer. These are usually unmet by current products available and customers might find them difficult to imagine or articulate, for example, some customers might be excited by a vacuum cleaner that distributed anti-stain solution and fibre conditioner.

Returning to the example of the small car, any intended distinctive features, such as coachlines, only enter into the equation when there is no anxiety over the steering, the brakes or the engine.

Need intensity

Need intensity specifies the relative importance that customers attach to any given element. Some car models may have coachlines but do not come fitted with

452

head restraints – which may be more important to the buyer. These are also known as 'importances'.

Need stability

Need stability describes the degree to which an element remains unchanged over time. This gives an indication of the longevity of the characteristic designed.

Need diffusion

Need diffusion assesses how widely the element is felt throughout the population. This allows managers to evaluate whether there is an adequate amount of demand for the development of profitable characteristics.

The need elements, if satisfied, constitute a benefit to be derived from purchasing the product. Together, the need elements and intensity are combined, giving an idea of the configuration of the characteristics required by the product if it is to deliver benefit. However, product characteristics will not always be surveyed individually to evaluate their potential benefit. The purchaser of a TV set is not so much interested in the nature of the electronics behind the screen as in the quality of the sound and picture those electronics deliver. Ultimately, it is the product quality that turns product characteristics into customer benefits.

Quality is a multi-faceted term which has become a key issue in management today, covering many areas of a company's operations. However, in relation to product policy, that is the configuration of a company's product or service offering over time, product quality describes the link between customer needs and differentiating features. In order to render the notion of product quality more actionable, Garvin (1984) has broken it down into eight characteristics:

1 *Performance*: The primary operating characteristics of a product. Taking the small car as an example, traits such as acceleration, cruising speed, kilometres per litre and comfort would apply. However, there is no direct association between performance traits and the 'best' quality product because the importance attached to individual traits may vary among customers.

2 *Features*: The 'bells and whistles' will, in our car example, refer to the 'trim', added to spice up the basic product. Sunroofs, interior materials used, radios fitted, 'go-faster' stripes are all extras, which for some customers may add to the perceived quality, but which are secondary to the basic product on offer.

3 *Reliability*: The extent to which we can count on the product. How many times has it failed to start this winter? Two measures are applied: (a) how long did the car last before it first failed to start; and (b) how long is the average time between mornings when it has failed to start.

4 *Conformance*: This is related to the extent to which a product matches pre-established specifications. Do the kilometres per litre figures hold in various types of driving conditions? Does the service interval adequately reflect the engine's needs?

5 *Durability*: Reflects the economic or physical life of a product. How long will the car last in terms of years, mileage or usage?

6 *Serviceability*: Describes the speed of repair, an important element in the product's quality image. (Not only are the drivers worried about the car breaking down, but also about the time it takes to repair the car.)

7 *Aesthetics*: Refers to more subjective elements, since how the product looks, feels, sounds can often be a question of personal judgement.

8 *Perceived quality*: Describes yet another subjective element which is often affected by advertising or other products produced by the company.

Already emphasized is the need to strike a balance between the physical characteristics of a product and the needs that they satisfy. These two elements are two sides of the same coin, the substance of which is the quality of the product in question. It is important in formulating product policy that both the 'needs' and the 'physical characteristics' be taken into consideration, since product policy is the basis upon which a company's products and services will compete in the market over time. The usefulness of Gavin's classification of quality elements is that it combines these two elements and can be used to formulate a foundation upon which to consider how products and services might compete.

Given the classification, it is possible to compete on quality in a number of different ways. For example, one company might compete on price-and-performance, while another might compete on features such as aesthetics or perceived quality.

Further, to become a quality leader in a market does not require being first on all eight dimensions of quality. For example, Boesendörfer has a reputation for high-quality pianos, emphasizing the hand-crafted distinctive feel. The Japanese company Yamaha has emphasized automation, resulting in a consistent product with regard to workmanship and performance. Competing on different bases allows companies to spread the manufacturing responsibility in such a way that excellence on one quality dimension does not impede excellence on another.

Finally, the effectiveness of the dimensions of quality is likely to change throughout the life of the product. This holds not only because 'the act of consumption changes the consumer' but also because product and process technologies change. It is not surprising, therefore, that in mature markets, firms tend to give greater attention to the features, aesthetics and perceived quality dimension. Our earlier example of the home-washing market exemplifies this. So, in considering the way in which products will compete in the market, product policy is as much concerned with the dimensions of the products as well as their dynamics.

In fact, the phenomenon of dynamic change in products is described by the biological metaphor of a life cycle where products are born, move through a phase of sales growth into maturity (market saturation) and eventually become moribund (fewer sales) and die. The term product life cycle or PLC has been coined to describe this sales pattern, and is the subject of the next section.

THE PRODUCT LIFE CYCLE

The concept of the product life cycle is depicted in Figure 1, where the four phases of introduction, growth, maturity and decline in terms of sales over time can be seen.

One of the earliest exponents of this concept was Theodore Levitt (1960) whose article 'Marketing Myopia' describes the way in which product life is limited by the emergence of new ways of delivering satisfaction of market need(s) provided by alternative products and technologies. The classic product histories he cites are the American railroad, superseded by road and air transport and the Hollywood film industry, threatened by television. The underlying point is that while market needs remain stable, the way in which those needs are satisfied is changed with development in technologies. Other examples include the replacement of vinyl records with compact discs.

In each of these examples, the dying products were once growth products which became mature and diffused throughout their respective markets. The value of the concept of the PLC lies in the concomitant realization that satisfying needs is a lasting endeavour, current products will not satisfy customers forever, the only certainty is the advent of change itself. In addition, different stages of the life cycle demand different approaches to both products and their marketing, which is described below.

At the introduction stage, a product will require heavy investment, largely in the form of the new product launch and promotional campaign. In addition, despite the fact that the launch of the new product may be confined to one or

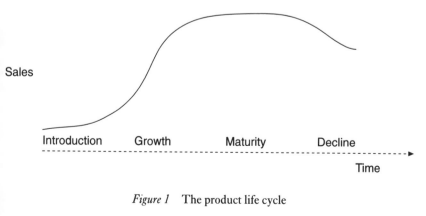

Figure 1   The product life cycle

455

two variations, design and development will continue in order to keep the advantages of the new product ahead of the competition, demanding more investment.

During the growth stage the drive for improvement will increase quality and technical performance differentiation of competitive products. Promotion costs are still high, but as sales are growing quickly in this stage, the volume sold, combined with the improvements to manufacturing, marketing and distribution that accompany the growing experience of the product, means that profitability of the product is also increasing.

At the maturity stage, a company may market several product variations, which are differentiated in superficial, rather than fundamental ways. With the product type now well diffused through the market, many customers have tried the early versions of a product, and, learning from this what improvements are required, are ready to trade up to enhanced versions. Although the manufacturing cost base for mature products is likely to be based on efficiency, overall product profitability may begin to get squeezed as the market, familiar with the product, begins to seek out products not only improved, but at a lower price. Manufacturer experience, coupled with incipient over-capacity in a given industry make the lower price achievable.

At the decline stage product sales begin to fall away. Decreasing values make larger capital investment in the product hard to sustain. The result is that companies de-invest, in terms of manufacturing plant and product variants. Finally, they will begin to withdraw marketing support, leaving a basic product variation to sell at its own pace to only the most loyal of customers. The profit curve that accompanies the PLC is shown in Figure 2.

These phases describe the cycle of a product within an industry that is experiencing the same cycle at an aggregate, for example, the 'personal hi-fi' market can be seen to have passed through three of the stages: introduction, growth and maturity, the current phase. The earliest models were produced by a limited number of suppliers – Sony being the chief developer – and

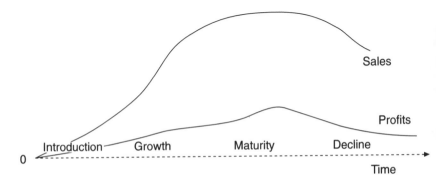

Figure 2   The profit curve that accompanies the PLC

456

commanded high prices to recoup development costs and capitalize on novelty in the marketplace. Within three to four years, several competitors had entered the market, prices were beginning to fall, while the first companies strove to introduce improvements and extend their first-mover advantages to customers ready to trade up. Thus personal hi-fis that could record were launched, versions for use underwater were introduced. In the current mature stage, a host of manufacturers compete, the product's price is a fraction of that of the originals and the early entrants have moved on to new endeavours.

The value of the PLC to businesses is that it provides knowledge of the likely competitive situation of products over time and gives clues as to the likely profitability of these products. Thus, managers can see the financial risks of having too many products at any one stage of the life cycle. The PLC is not without its critics, however, among whom Dhalla and Yupseh (1976) have been widely quoted. In their view the major limitations of the PLC are both conceptual and pragmatic. The conceptual limitations are: as products are not living, a biological metaphor is inappropriate, since products can be managed to confound any inevitable demise; it is a misplaced concept for brands whose purpose is to extend a product's life by creating consumer loyalty and preference, within which managers can introduce and delete many product varieties; the whole business of fitting sales to a predetermined curve are merely 'sterile exercises in taxonomy'.

In short, argue Dhalla and Yupseh (1976) it is a dependent variable determined by marketing actions, not an independent variable to which marketing plans should be adapted. The practical limitations relate to the fact that there are no clear definitions of the four stages, thwarting the determination of a product's position in its PLC. Hence, the PLC cannot be used as a planning tool. In addition to these criticisms, the PLC ignores the important variables of markets and technologies, both of which have the power to upset a predictable sales pattern. A new technology can wipe out the 'satisfaction' delivered by a previous technology, while markets can quickly turn away from established and preferred products, as in the case of CFC-aerosol sprays where environmental damage caused by CFC has caused manufacturers across many product markets to develop aerosols without CFC.

A final shortcoming is the extent to which the PLC is foreshortened in some industries, leaving no time for either a high-price strategy in the early months or perfecting product quality. In the electronics industry, for example, new products have to be introduced at optimal quality and at a price consistent with current applications and solutions. This apparent contradiction is the result of extremely short PLCs, due to the high levels of technological competition.

In view of this, somewhat stiff, criticism, the PLC is a weakened concept. It is, however, a persistent concept in the business world which retains validity. It is a powerful indicator of the need for a number of alternative products in a company's range and finally, it keeps to the fore the inevitability of change.

In providing these perspectives, however, the PLC still has to be considered product-by-product. In reality, all but single-product companies have to consider their products as a collection or portfolio of products within their respective markets. The development of analytical frameworks to take account of these dimensions is epitomized by the Business Portfolio, developed by the Boston Consulting Group.

The Business Portfolio

The Business Portfolio is reproduced in Figure 3. Four types of product are identified requiring four different types of marketing strategy. Products experiencing high market share in growth markets are stars: these are competitively attractive products achieving high sales in expanding markets. While they require high investment, both for marketing and redevelopment, they are largely profitable, due to buoyant market conditions. If investment is appropriately managed, these products will become cash cows in the future; if not, they will become dogs when the market is no longer growing. The cash cow is the established product, with a high market share in a market that is no longer growing. Volumes are high in a large market, contributing healthy profits, hence the label. Where market growth is high, but market share is low, considerable investment would be required to turn the product into a star. This is a difficult situation because the low market share does not return much profit for such investment. If improving the competitive position is deemed inappropriate, deletion of the product would be advised. Dogs have weak competitive positions in low-growth markets. They have little chance of increasing market share and are not very profitable. This said, where a dog has a relatively strong position

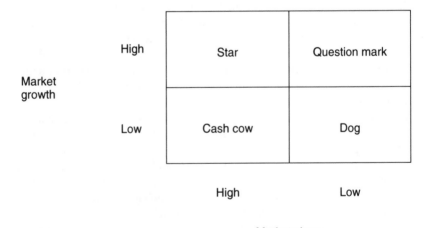

Figure 3   The Business Portfolio
(Boston Consulting Group, see Hedley 1977:11)

in a segment of the market, there may be enough cash return on the product to warrant its classification as a cash dog which can be sustained until such time as returns become unacceptable. The value of using a diagnostic tool such as this is in deciding upon the strategic use of resources. As can be seen, the market share, indicative of competitive position, indicates the amount of investment required and the amount of revenue returned by each type of product in the portfolio. Thus it gives theoretical insights into cash flow. It follows then, that, whatever the strategic orientation the company takes in relation to product policy in terms of differentiation, there must be a balance of cash generating and cash absorbing products in the firm's portfolio.

Like many models designed to facilitate marketing management, the Business Portfolio has been criticized on a number of counts. Firstly, it ignores many factors in the external environment which have a bearing on product decisions. Technological change, legal requirements, social trends and political pressures all have a bearing on current product performance and new product potential. In addition, there will be instances where, despite high market share and growth, price competition may erode profits. Alternatively, the benefits of scale production that are supposed to accumulate with the 'cash-cow' product can be obliterated by production-technology innovations which reduce the costs of short production runs.

As with most management models, it is necessary to treat them, not as prescriptions for strategy and outcome, but as aids to decisions which further understanding of the company's present position and future options. The Business Portfolio is one of several analytical frameworks that have been developed, in some cases by major companies. For example Shell's Directional Policy Matrix (Figure 4) is based on the company's competitive capabilities and prospects for sector profitability.

| | | Prospects for sector profitability | | |
		Unattractive	Average	Attractive
Company's competitive capabilities	Weak	Disinvest 9	Phased withdrawal 6 Custodial	Double or quit 3
	Average	Phased withdrawal 8	Custodial 5 Growth	Try harder 2
	Strong	Cash generation 7	Growth 4 Leader	Leader 1

Figure 4 Directional Policy Matrix

459

Table 1   Ansoff's vector matrix

Product market	Present	New
Present	Market penetration	Product development
New	Market development	Diversification

Similarly, the Business Assessment Survey, developed with General Electric, uses 'industry attractiveness' and 'business strengths' to develop another three-by-three matrix. These models offer similar ways to structure management's thinking about its current and future products. Ultimately every company could tailor the concept of portfolio analysis to suit their particular industries, products and markets; paying special attention to the dimensions used and their measurement. Further reading on how to design portfolios can be found in Wind and Mahajan (1981).

A final conceptual tool to be described in this chapter, is how to formulate product policy in terms of future growth. Ansoff's famous vector matrix is based upon the consideration of the implications of change in both the product (technology) and the product market.

1 *Market penetration*: the company increases sales for its present products through aggressive selling, promotion and distribution.

2 *Market development*: the company increases sales by taking its present products into new markets.

3 *Product development*: the company increases sales by developing improved products for its current markets.

4 *Diversification*: the company increases sales by developing new products for new markets.

The first three strategies capitalize on at least one of the current core strategic variables, building upon the common thread of the business. The common thread is composed of:

1 The product-market scope – a specification of the industries where the company consolidates its position.

2 The growth vector – an indication of the direction the company takes in relation to its current product market position.

3 The competitive advantage – an identification of properties of the product-market that will yield strong competitive position.

Of vital importance here is that maintaining a common thread is not a straight choice set against breaking with tradition. Product penetration is the least risky option, while diversification is the most risky. However, as is intimated by portfolio analyses, companies should not regard these as discrete directions but rather as options from which an appropriate mix should be chosen, in order to supply the company with a product portfolio which yields enough profits for future investment in products.

FUTURE PERSPECTIVES OF PRODUCT POLICY

Product policy is at the centre of marketing, at both strategic and operational levels. It is intimately related to strategic planning, competitive strategy and positioning. Several concepts useful for managerial guidance in product policy matters have been explained in this chapter, but a current move has been to question the extent to which methods such as these suffocate the entrepreneurial spirit in management which is so essential to create and maintain vibrant businesses (Hayes and Abernethy 1980). In addition, it has been argued that these analytical methods do not focus enough on how to gain competitive advantage (Wensley 1983). In the last analysis there are two essential options to product policy: make products of a comparable quality to competitors more cheaply and offer it at a lower price, or, make a better product for which a higher price can be demanded (Baker 1992). Focusing product policy on these options and channelling resources to realize their potential is a future challenge for practitioners and academics alike.

REFERENCES

Ansoff, H. I. (1965) 'Corporate strategy: an analytical approach to business policy for growth and expansion', Maidenhead: McGraw-Hill.
Baker, M. J. (1992) *Marketing – An Introductory Text*, 5th edn, Basingstoke: Macmillan.
Day, G. S. (1986) *Analysis for Strategic Market Decisions*, West Publishing Co. (General Electric Business Screen).
Dhalla, N. K. and Yuspeh, S. (1976) 'Forget the product life cycle concept', *Harvard Business Review*, January–February: 102–12.
Garvin, D. (1984) 'What does product quality really mean?', *Sloan Management Review* 26 (1), Fall.
Hayes, R. and Abernethy, W. (1980) 'Managing our way to economic decline', *Harvard Business Review*, July–August.
Hedley, B. (1977) 'Boston Consulting Group approach to business portfolio', *Long Range Planning* 10 (1).
King, R. (1987) 'Better designs in half the time: implementing QFD in America', Methven, MA: GOAL 1 QPC.
Levitt, T. (1960) 'Marketing myopia', *Harvard Business Review*, July–August: 45–57.
Porter, M. E. (1980) *Competitive Strategy: Techniques for Analysing Industries and Competitors*, New York: The Free Press.
Rothwell, R., Schott, K., Gardiner, P. and Pick, K. (1983) 'Design and the economy', London: The Design Council.
Wensley, R. (1981) 'Strategic marketing: betons, boxes or basics', *Journal of Marketing* 45, Summer: 173–82.
Wind, Y. and Mahajan, V. (1981) 'Designing product and business portfolios', *Harvard Business Review* 59 (1).

27

NEW PRODUCT DEVELOPMENT

Robert G. Cooper

NEW PRODUCTS: THE KEY TO CORPORATE PROSPERITY

New product development (or product innovation) is one of the riskiest yet most important endeavours of the modern corporation.[1] Countless companies owe their success today to successful new products: Glaxo in the UK with its anti-ulcer pharmaceutical, Zantac; Apple in the USA with its Macintosh computer; Lego in Denmark with its plastic blocks, to name a few. Today new products account for a staggering 40–50 per cent of company sales or turnover. (Here a product is defined as 'new' if it has been on the market by that firm for five years or less.) The figure has been going up dramatically (see Table 1).

New products have a similar impact on corporate profits. In the period 1976–81 new products contributed 22 per cent of corporate profits. This had grown to 33 per cent for the next five-year period (1981–6). By 1995, it was estimated, the figure would rise to 46 per cent. That is, profits from new products accounted for almost half of corporate profits (Page 1991).

R&D expenditures are also impressive: the USA is the largest spender with R&D expenditures amounting to $138 billion annually, or about 2.9 per cent of GDP (in the USA, however, 49 per cent has been for military work) (*R&T Mgmt* 1991). In Japan and Germany R&D spending is also about 2.8 to 2.9 per cent of GDP (but much less is military – private industry finances 71 per cent of Japanese and 64 per cent of German R&D spending).

Table 1 Percentage of company sales by new products

Year	Company sales by new products %	Source
1976–81	33	(Booz–Allen and Hamilton 1982)
1981–6	40	(Booz–Allen and Hamilton 1982)
1985–90	42	(Page 1991)
1995	52	(Page 1991)

Certain industries, noted for their growth and profitability in recent decades, spend heavily on R&D. For example, office products and services, including computers, business machines and software averages 7.9 per cent of sales on R&D in the USA; and electrical and electronics products (which includes instruments and semiconductors) averages 5.5 per cent of sales on R&D (*Business Week* 1991). This quickening pace of new product development has a number of drivers (Booz-Allen and Hamilton 1982):

1 Technology advances: the world's base of technology and know-how increases at an exponential rate, making possible products not even dreamt of a decade or so ago.

2 Changing customer needs: marketplaces are also in turmoil, with market needs and wants and customer preferences changing regularly.

3 Shortening product life cycles: within a few years of launch, sometimes even months, the new product is superseded by a competitive entry.

4 Increased world competition: globalization of markets has created significant opportunities for the product innovator: the world product targeted at global markets. It has also intensified competition in every domestic market. Both factors have speeded up the pace of product innovation.

All four drivers are likely to remain, perhaps intensify, in the next decade or two, meaning that product innovation will be even more critical to corporate prosperity in the years ahead.

HIGH ODDS OF FAILURE

While product innovation is critical to long-term success, the hard realities are that the great majority of new products are failures: most never make it to market; and those that do face a failure rate on launch somewhere between 25 and 45 per cent. These figures vary, depending on what industry and how one defines a 'new product' and a 'failure'. Some sources cite the failure rate at launch to be as high as 90 per cent. But these figures tend to be unsubstantiated, and are likely wildly overstated. According to one thorough review, the true failure rate at launch is about 35 per cent (Crawford 1979).

Note that these failure rate figures only describe new products that were launched, but do not include the majority of new product projects that are killed along the way and long before launch, yet had considerable time and money spent on them. The attrition curve of new products tells the whole story. A recent investigation reveals that for every 11 new product concepts, 3 enter the development phase, 1.3 are launched and only 1 is a commercial success in the marketplace (Page 1991). Further, an estimated 46 per cent of all the resources allocated to product development and commercialization by US firms are spent on products that are cancelled or fail to yield an adequate financial return (Booz-Allen and Hamilton 1982).

463

WHAT ARE 'NEW PRODUCTS'?

How does one define a 'new product', 'innovativeness' or 'newness'? There are many different types of new products. Newness or new products can be defined on at least two dimensions:

1 New to the company, in the sense that the firm has never made or sold this type of product before, but other firms might have.
2 New to the market or 'innovative': the product is the first of its kind on the market.

Viewed on a two-dimensional map, six different types or classes of new products have been identified (Booz-Allen and Hamilton 1982):

1 New-to-the-world products: these new products are the first of their kind and create an entirely new market. This category represents only 10 per cent of all new products. Well-known examples include the Sony Walkman, the first home VCR (developed by Philips) and 3M's yellow Post-It Notes.
2 New product lines: these products, although not new to the marketplace, nonetheless are quite new to the particular firm. Reckitt & Colman's UK launch of an adult soft drink line, Robinsons Aquiesse, is a new product line to the firm, but in a well-established market with many competitors. About 20 per cent of all new products fit into this category.
3 Additions to existing product lines: these are new items to the firm, but fit within an existing product line the firm makes. They may also represent a fairly new product to the marketplace. Hewlett Packard introduced its LaserJet 4, a more advanced version of its laser printers (more features, scalable fonts) within the LaserJet line; its added performance made it somewhat novel or 'new to the market'. Such new items constitute about 26 per cent of all new product launches.
4 Improvements and revisions to existing products: these 'not-so-new' products are essentially replacements of existing products in a firm's product line. They offer improved performance or greater perceived value over the 'old' product. These 'new and improved' products also make up 26 per cent of new product launches.
5 Repositionings: these are essentially new applications for existing products, and often involve retargeting an old product to a new segment or for a different application (e.g. the repositioning of aspirin or ASA from a headache/fever reliever to a blood clot, stroke and heart attack preventer). Repositionings account for about 7 per cent of all new products.
6 Cost reductions: these are the least 'new' of all new product categories. They are new products designed to replace existing products in the line, but yield similar benefits and performance but at lower cost. They represent 11 per cent of all new product launches.

Most firms feature a mixed portfolio of new products. The two most popular types, additions to the line and product improvements or revisions, are common to almost all firms. By contrast, the 'step-out' products – new to the world and new-to-the-firm product lines – constitute only 30 per cent of all new product launches, but represent 60 per cent of the products viewed as 'most successful'. Many firms stay clear of these two more innovative categories: 50 per cent of firms introduce no new-to-the-world products, and another 25 per cent develop no new product lines. This aversion to 'step-out' and higher risk products varies somewhat by industry, with higher technology industries launching proportionately more products that are innovative (Kleinschmidt and Cooper 1991).

THE NEW PRODUCT PROCESS

The conception, development and launch of a new product is a process. This new product process begins with an idea and, all going well, culminates with a commercially successful new product in the marketplace.

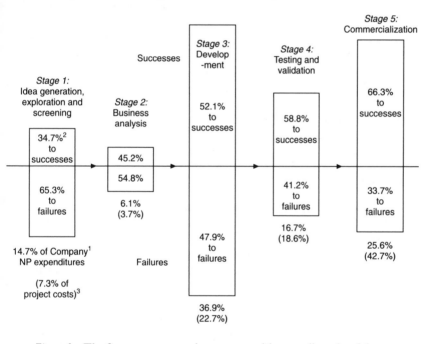

Figure 1 The five-stage new product process with expenditure breakdowns

Source: Booz-Allen and Hamilton (1982: 12).

Notes

1 14.7% of all the monies that firms spend on product innovation go to this first stage, idea generation.

2 Of the money spent on idea generation, only 34.7% goes to successful new products.

3 In a typical project, only 7.3% of project costs go to this first stage.

465

The new product process, like most processes in companies, can be flow-charted and described schematically. Although models differ, there are essentially five main stages or phases (see Figure 1). Here is a simplified, somewhat normative, description of the new product process (Booz-Allen and Hamilton 1982; Cooper and Kleinschmidt 1986), complete with a resource allocation breakdown.

Idea generation, exploration and screening

This first stage generates the idea and performs an initial culling (screening out) of the poor ideas. Ideas can arrive from many sources, both inside and outside the firm. Common external sources of ideas include: customers and lead users; competitors; trade shows and conferences; trade publications; universities, consultants and private inventors. Internal sources of ideas include company employees, most often in technical positions (R&D, engineering) and marketing/sales positions. Idea generation may be proactive (for example, the result of activities such as holding brainstorming groups with customers or employees, or undertaking preliminary or exploratory technical research in new fields) or simply reactive (ideas are sent in by employees or requests are made by customers). Ideas can also be 'technology push', where a technical discovery (for example in a laboratory) opens up new possibilities: Post-It Notes involved the serendipitous discovery of a glue that would not stick; or 'market pull', where a customer need or an unfilled demand is identified and technical solutions are sought.

The source of new product ideas does not seem to have a major or consistent impact on the new product process or new product success. There are some tendencies however:

- The great majority of all successful new products are market derived (a figure of 75 per cent is often quoted). But then just about 75 per cent of all failures are also market derived!
- Lead users are an excellent source of new product ideas (Von Hippel 1988). Lead users are particularly innovative customers, who often experiment with or redesign existing products to meet their needs better. Ideas derived from customers of all types also seem to do better than internally generated ones, on average (Cooper and Kleinschmidt 1993a).
- There are mixed views on technology push ideas. The greatest innovations have been technology push, even technological breakthroughs. Nylon, the laser, radar, early computers and others were largely technology-driven projects, often with little idea of ultimate market demand or market requirements. Against this is the fact that success rates tend to be much lower here, perhaps because technology push projects fail adequately to build in the needs of the customer (Cooper and Kleinschmidt 1993a).

Stage one also sees initial attempts to qualify and screen projects. Some

466

companies have developed rigorous screening, selection and prioritization tools to help choose new product projects, barely at the idea stage, on which to focus resources.

The typical company spends about 15 per cent of its total product innovation expenditures on this first stage (Booz-Allen and Hamilton 1982). Note from Figure 1 that 65 per cent of this expenditure goes towards unsuccessful projects, the message being that much exploration must be done to uncover a few worthwhile projects. On a per project basis, this first stage accounts for about 7 per cent of the total project costs.

Business analysis – build the business case

This second stage – the critical homework phase – ideally defines the product: it determines the target market and positioning strategy, benefits to be delivered, product requirements and perhaps even detailed product specifications. This stage also provides justification for the project, most often in the form of financial analysis.

Activities that might occur in stage two include a variety of marketing, technical, production and financial tasks. Marketing tasks can involve:

- desk research or secondary research – accessing published information, library (key word) searches, a search through company materials (e.g. existing market studies, competitive analysis files) and inputs from company salespeople and technical service people.
- focus groups with potential customers or users to scope out the product requirements and determine level of market interest.
- detailed market research (for example, personal interviews or discussions with customers) to determine exactly customer needs, wants and require-ment as input to the final design of the product. Positioning studies, to identify possible positioning strategies, may also be undertaken.
- concept tests with customers, where a representation of the product is presented to potential customers (e.g. a concept statement, a drawing, a storyboard, a dummy spec sheet) and potential customers' reactions – interest, liking, preference and purchase intent – are gauged. Concept tests help to assess likely market acceptance and possible positioning strategies.
- competitive analysis, involving a thorough review of competitive products, competitive strategy (and pricing), and competitive results (e.g. share and profits).

Technical activities also occur during stage two, usually designed to assess (and sometimes prove) technical feasibility (that the product can indeed be developed) and manufacturing feasibility. Such technical work varies by industry but could include: library research and a thorough technical literature search; conceptual work to identify possible technical routes or solutions; very preliminary development work (e.g. some lab work; computer modelling; initial design work) to probe feasibility and identify technical risks; development of an R&D plan (complete with a schedule and spending estimates); and legal (patent), environmental, health and safety assessments.

Manufacturability is also an issue in stage two, where a detailed manufacturing appraisal may be undertaken: this determines the likely production route, possible manufacturing costs and throughputs and capital equipment and expenditures needed.

Given the results of these marketing, technical and manufacturing analyses, a financial analysis is conducted during stage two to help justify the project prior to opening the door to a full-scale development project (stage three).

Given all these vital activities in stage two, one might expect it to be quite expensive. Quite the contrary, this stage receives the least resources, typically only 6.1 per cent of total expenditures and 3.7 per cent of the total project cost. This low level of spending on this homework phase may explain why the remainder of the new product process is problematic for too many projects, and why so many new products fail. Indeed, there is considerable evidence that firms which spend more time and money on these stage two homework (or pre-development) activities have much higher success rates (Cooper and Kleinschmidt 1988).

Development

The development and initial testing of a prototype product is the major objective of stage three. This phase tends to be dominated by technical work, as scientists, engineers, software writers or other technical professionals translate the product as defined in stage two into reality. This stage is most costly, accounting for 36.9 per cent of company spending, and 27.7 per cent of spending on a per project basis. This is also a hit-and-miss stage, with almost half (47.9 per cent) of development expenditures going to unsuccessful projects, perhaps the result of a rather weak and underfunded business analysis stage (stage two).

Marketing work also continues during stage three, as the product should be constantly checked by the marketplace to ensure that the evolving product satisfies the customer. Progressive companies make the customer an integral facet of this development phase by building rapid prototypes and seeking immediate customer reaction, and by including a number of customer checks throughout the development phase as the new product takes shape. This iterative rapid-prototype-and-test approach stands in marked contrast to traditional schemes, which see the R&D department develop the product, and only much later (following development) is it exposed to the customer via customer tests.

Testing and validation

Phase four is where the product, its production and its marketing are tested and validated. Although some inhouse or alpha testing usually takes place as part of development (stage three), much more extensive inhouse testing remains to ensure that the product meets its specifications and requirements, and performs as expected. These inhouse tests are typically technical ones, and are undertaken in controlled or laboratory settings.

Customer tests of the product come next. These are designed to prove that the product really does work under live (or real world) conditions, and in some cases, to establish purchase intent – that the product does delight the customer. These tests, called field trials, customer tests, beta tests or user preference tests, are often conducted at selected and representative users' premises (home, office or factory) and can extend over a long period of time.

The production process can be tested during phase four. Here trial, pilot or test production methods are used to prove (and debug) the manufacturing process and to confirm costs and throughputs.

Some companies also include test market activities in phase four. Test markets can be conducted for both industrial and consumer goods and services. Here, the product is sold to a limited number of test customers: for example, in a limited geographic area; or through a limited number of stores, distributors or sales offices. A test market is an experiment to determine market acceptance of the new product (e.g. expected sales or market share). Test markets can also be used to test alternate strategies: for example, two different pricing or positioning strategies. Unlike customer tests or trials (above), which test only the product, the test market tests the entire strategy: the product, positioning, price, promotion and sometimes the distribution.

Frequently repurchased consumer goods can be subjected to another customer test, called a simulated (or pre) test market. Various market research firms have developed novel methodologies which provide a simulated shopping experience: the potential customer is exposed to the product (e.g. via an advertisement) and is then allowed to 'shop' for the product in a simulated shopping environment. The consumer decision (whether they buy the new product or not) together with their reaction to the product after several weeks of use enables the research firm to make very predictive estimates of trial and repurchase rates, hence market share. These pre-test market techniques have proven to be considerably less expensive, much faster, more controlled and almost as predictive as a full test market.

Phase four, testing, is a moderately expensive stage, accounting for 16.7 per cent of company expenditures on product innovation, and 18.6 per cent of expenditures on a per project basis. By this point in the process, many of the would-be losers have been culled out, so that for the first time in this process, the majority of expenditures goes to winners (58.8 per cent of spending is spent on successful projects by this stage).

Commercialization

The final stage witnesses the commercialization of the product. This includes the startup of full-scale production (or the transfer of production from batch or limited production to the plant).

Market launch or roll-out occurs concurrently, and the various elements of the launch plan are implemented: advertising, promotion, the salesforce effort.

On a per project basis, commercialization is by far the most expensive of all stages, amounting to 42.7 per cent of project spending. But most projects do not reach this stage, so as a percentage of all company spending on innovation, commercialization accounts for only 25.6 per cent.

This high figure (42.7 per cent of project costs) is a reflection of the substantial market launch costs for many products, especially consumer goods (Procter & Gamble spends about $100 million to roll out a new brand in the USA). Additionally, capital costs can be substantial, especially if a new plant or new production equipment are required.

GO/KILL DECISION POINTS

Throughout the new product process are a set of go/kill decision points which follow or precede each stage. These are the culling points, where poor projects are weeded out of the process. Several important decisions points include:

- Initial screening, which follows the generation of the idea and precedes the business analysis. It marks the decision to spend significant resources on the project.
- The 'Go to Development' decision, which precedes stage three and signals a full-fledged development project. It is often based on a full financial and business analysis, the result of efforts in stage two.
- The launch decision, which precedes the last stage, commercialization, and opens the door for a full launch and production start-up.

Additionally, some companies build in a final point following launch, which signals the end of the project and where a retrospective analysis is undertaken: 'what happened and what can we learn?'

Project evaluations are among the weakest facets of the entire new product process (Cooper and Kleinschmidt 1986). Formal evaluations often do not take place at all, especially from the development phase onwards: the project gets a life of its own. When undertaken, these go/kill decision points are plagued by vague, inconsistent and sometimes even no decision criteria. Often the wrong decision-makers are involved (e.g. marketing makes the decision without the involvement of R&D or production).

To correct these deficiencies and to ensure that resources are devoted to the right new product projects, some companies have developed a formal set of decision points or 'gates', complete with required deliverables, 'criteria for Go', and a multifunctional group of decision-makers to ensure that only the best projects proceed to the next stage.

The three main formal approaches to project evaluation or making go/kill decisions are (Cooper 1993):

1 Benefit measurement techniques, which capture qualitative facets of projects, and include methods such as checklists, scoring models and sorting techniques.
2 Economic models, which include a variety of financial methods.
3 Portfolio approaches, which consider the totality of projects underway and attempt to allocate resources to the most appropriate subset of projects.

Economic models are the best known, and include a variety of standard methods such as payback period and discounted cash flow (internal rate of return and net present value). Today's computer-based spreadsheets enable DCF methods to be easily combined with sensitivity analysis in order to identify key risks and possible downside losses. While popular for new product evaluation, note that financial/economic methods are often very unpredictive: financial data are both limited and unreliable, especially in the earlier (pre-development) stages of the project.

Checklists are simply lists of qualitative criteria thought to be important in project selection. Criteria often include mandatory items such as strategic alignment, technical feasibility, existence of a customer need and meeting company legal, safety and environmental standards. Such mandatory items are called 'must meet' criteria and are used as 'knock out' or initial culling criteria. Highly desirable characteristics (or 'should meet' items) can be handled via a scoring model, where the project is rated on a number of characteristics (for example, using 0–10 scales), which are then added to yield a project score. Desirable characteristics that enhance the attractiveness of a project include various elements of product or competitive advantage, synergies with the firm's resource base, market attractiveness, and the existence of a project champion. Often, weights are applied to the criteria to reflect the fact that some scoring criteria (such as product advantage) may be more important than others (such as synergy with the plant). Checklists and scoring models have proven to be particularly effective for making gross distinctions between good and poor projects, especially for the first few gates, that is, near the beginning of the project where financial methods are unreliable.

Portfolio models are used to prioritize projects, to allocate resources among competing projects and find use in combination with the two approaches above. Recent developments in portfolio models have improved their user-friendliness, and a handful of firms have adopted them. In one scheme, a four quadrant plot of all new product projects is developed, with 'probability of success' plotted against 'value to the company'. This plot provides a visual representation on key

471

dimensions to enhance the effectiveness of the resource allocation decision (Roussel *et al.* 1991).

WHY NEW PRODUCTS FAIL

The new product process described above provides an idealized view of product innovation. Reality is very different: new products fail at an alarming rate; and new product management is often deficient. As a result, many studies have probed the causes of failure so that management can then take corrective action (Hopkins 1980; Cooper 1993). Here are some major reasons for new product failure:

1 *A lack of a market orientation*: inadequate market analysis, a failure to understand customer needs and wants and insufficient attention to the marketplace are consistently cited as major reasons for new product failure. Managers confess to a serious misreading of customer needs, too little field testing or overly optimistic forecasts of market need and acceptance. Management often falls into the trap of deciding in advance what the marketplace wants without asking that market what its priorities are. Another common mistake is to assume that because a product may be adequate in the eyes of the designers or R&D department, the customers will see it the same way.

Many firms omit critical marketing tasks, especially those in the early phases of a project. Detailed market studies (to determine customer needs and wants and to assess likely market acceptance) and test markets (to test the launch plan and determine market penetration) are most often omitted – in about three-quarters of projects, according to some studies (Cooper and Kleinschmidt 1986). Moreover, preliminary market assessment and detailed market studies are poorly executed. Finally, marketing actions receive a disproportionately small share of the total resources spent on projects: 32 per cent of funding (most of which goes to the market launch); and only 16 per cent of the effort (measured in person-days) (Cooper and Kleinschmidt 1988).

2 *Moving too quickly or too slowly*: the penalties of moving too slowly, or too fast, stem both from technical problems and also from flawed planning, organization or control (Hopkins 1980). Numerous new product failures result from not moving quickly enough, given a limited window of opportunity. In some cases there is a shift in customer preferences during the development cycle; in others the competitor moves more quickly with a new product, and seizes the market opportunity.

The need to move quickly to market – the fast-paced company – has created yet another set of timing problems: rushing a product through the process, and cutting corners to do so. Shortcuts are taken with the best intentions, but too often result in disaster. Key steps and stages are often skipped (or handled too quickly), such as market studies, prototype testing and field trials, with inevitable results: serious quality problems; the need for

472

product redesign once into production; and marketing and sales weaknesses.

3 *Poor quality of execution*: errors of omission and of commission abound in the new product process, and reveal a process very much in trouble. Key actions, often considered central to success, are arbitrarily omitted, so that the typical new product process is very much a truncated or incomplete one (Cooper and Kleinschmidt 1986). Certain pivotal activities are noticeable more for their absence than presence: detailed market studies, test markets and pre-commercialization business analysis are left out of the majority of projects. Quality of execution is rated as 'mediocre' across a broad spectrum of actions, some of the weakest areas being initial screening, preliminary market assessment, detailed market studies, business/financial analysis, pre-commercialization business analysis, production start-up and market launch.

4 *Not enough homework*: three themes above – inadequate market analysis, moving too quickly, and poor quality of execution – all point to weaknesses in the homework or business analysis phase, specifically those actions that precede the Development phase. The homework simply does not get done: typically the project moves from idea through a rather superficial definitional and homework phase right into a full-scale development: a 'ready, fire, then aim' approach. The pre-development activities receive a relatively small proportion of the total resources – 7 per cent of the money and 16 per cent of the effort for a typical project – and are also plagued by serious omissions and poor quality of execution (Cooper and Kleinschmidt 1986, 1988).

5 *A lack of differentiation*: too many new products are reactive efforts – a 'me too' product which lacks differentiation, fails to provide superior benefits or to deliver customer value, and meets a competitive brick wall. The failure to do one's homework, responding to competitive moves, a lack of willingness to seek customer input, and the desire to move quickly too often leads to a reactive, 'copy-cat' product as the easy solution. Such 'me too' products provide the firm with no competitive advantage and are one of the most popular ways of failing.

6 *Technical problems*: a common cause of new product failure is technical problems in design and production (Hopkins 1980). Difficulties in trying to convert from laboratory or pilot plant scale to full-scale production are common, while manufacturing glitches and product quality problems frequently arise. In many cases, it is a failure to conduct the earlier phases more thoroughly – technical research, design, engineering – before moving to the commercialization phase. At other times, the technical problems stem from a lack of understanding of the customer's requirements – for example, trying to develop the 'perfect product' – one that is simply overengineered (and too costly) when compared to what the customer wanted.

7 *No focus, too many projects and a lack of resources*: a lack of resources, particularly from certain functions in the company (e.g. marketing) and for specific activities in a project (e.g. the upfront or pre-development stages) plagues too many new product projects. This lack of time, money and people is the root

cause of many errors of omission and poor quality of execution, which in turn have such serious consequences for new product results. Why this lack of resources? In some firms senior management has simply starved product innovation: management has grossly underestimated the resource requirements for an effective new product programme. In most firms, however, it boils down to not enough focus and hence too many projects for the available resources. The result is that scarce resources are dissipated across many fronts and that the truly deserving projects are under-resourced.

NEW PRODUCT SUCCESS FACTORS

The quest for new product success has led to numerous studies into what makes winners and what distinguishes successful new products from unsuccessful ones. Here are the more important success factors and/or lessons uncovered by these success/failure studies:

1 A differentiated product that delivers unique benefits and superior value to the customer is a key success factor. Product superiority separates winners from losers more often than any other single factor, according to many studies (Maidique and Zirger 1984; Cooper and Kleinschmidt 1987; Cooper 1993). Note that product superiority is defined in the eyes of the customer, not in the eyes of the R&D, engineering or even marketing departments. Product superiority is based on an indepth understanding of customer needs and wants as well as competitive product weaknesses.
2 A strong market orientation – a market-driven and customer-focused new product process – is critical to success. This finding is supported in virtually every study of product success factors: a thorough understanding of customers' needs and wants, the competitive situation and the nature of the market is an essential component of new product success. To be successful, a market orientation must prevail throughout the entire new product project:

   - idea generation – seeking ideas from customers; understanding customers' problems.
   - the design of the product – using market research, not just to check for market acceptance, but to determine users' needs, wants and preferences.
   - during the development phase of the project, constant and continuing customer contact via frequent rapid-prototype-and-test iterations.
   - as part of testing – building in customer tests and test markets.
   - the launch – based on a solid marketing plan.

3 More pre-development work – the homework – must be done before product development gets underway. Studies show that the quality of execution of the pre-development steps – initial screening, preliminary market and technical studies, market research and business analysis – is closely tied to the product's financial performance. Successful projects have over 1.75 times

as many person days spent on pre-development steps as do failures. These initial screening, analyses and definitional stages are critical to success, so managers must resist the temptation to skip over the upfront stages of a project, moving an ill-defined and poorly investigated project into the development phase (Cooper 1988).

4 Sharp and early product definition is one of the key differences between winning and losing at new products. How well the project is defined prior to entering the development phase is increasingly cited as a key success factor (Cooper and Kleinschmidt 1990). This definition includes:

- specification of the target market: exactly who the intended users are.
- description of the product concept and the benefits to be delivered.
- delineation of the positioning strategy.
- a list of the product's features, attributes, requirements and specifications (prioritized: 'must have' and 'would like to have').

5 Successful new products feature the right organizational structure, design and climate. Product innovation is not a one-department show. A cross-functional project team, with core team members drawn from various functions in the firm and led by an empowered, committed champion is a fundamental key to success (Larson and Gobeli 1988). Similarly, organizational climate – one that supports and rewards entrepreneurial behaviour – facilitates successful innovation.

6 Top management support is a necessary ingredient for getting the product to market. Top management can muster the resources and cut through the organizational bureaucracy to get the project done. In successful firms, top management's main role is to set the stage for product innovation to occur, to be a 'behind the scenes' facilitator, and not so much to be an actor, front and centre. Top management commits to internal product development as a source of growth; they develop a vision, objectives and strategy for product innovation that is driven by corporate objectives and strategies (Booz-Allen and Hamilton 1982). They make available the necessary resources and ensure that these resources are not diverted to more immediate needs in times of shortage. They commit to a disciplined game plan to drive products to market. Senior management empowers project teams, and supports committed champions by acting as mentors, facilitators, 'godfathers' or sponsors to project leaders and teams – acting as 'executive champions'.

7 Market attractiveness and synergies with the firm are two important success drivers. New products aimed at attractive markets – high growth, high need markets, high margin markets and markets which lack strong, dominant competitors – fare better. Synergies are also important to success: marketing synergies, where the product sells to the firm's existing customer base, via the firm's existing salesforce and channel system; and technological synergies, where the product can leverage inhouse technical and production skills and resources. Both elements – market attractiveness and synergies – can be

used as project selection criteria in order to make sharper project selection decisions and yield better focus.

8 A well-conceived, properly executed launch is central to new product success. The best products in the world will not sell themselves, hence the need for a strong marketing effort, a well targeted selling approach and effective after sales service. A well integrated and properly targeted launch does not occur by accident; it is the result of a fine-tuned marketing plan, properly backed and resourced and proficiently executed.

9 Completeness, consistency and quality of execution make the difference between winning and losing. Certain key activities – how well they are executed, and whether they are done at all – are strongly tied to success (Cooper and Kleinschmidt 1990). These activities include undertaking preliminary market and technical assessments early in the project, carrying out a detailed market study or marketing research prior to product design, performing a detailed business and financial analysis and executing the test market and market launch in a quality fashion.

One solution is to treat product innovation as a process. Design a formal new product process and engineer into this process quality assurance approaches: for example, introduce check points in the process that focus on quality of execution, ensuring that every action in this process is executed in a quality fashion; and design quality into the process by making mandatory certain key activities that are often omitted, yet are central to success.

10 Companies that follow a multi-stage, disciplined new product process fare better. A number of companies have implemented formal new product processes or disciplined 'stage-gate' systems (Cooper and Kleinschmidt 1991) and have reaped the benefits.

A stage-gate system is a conceptual and operational model for moving new product projects from idea through to launch (Cooper and Kleinschmidt 1993b; Cooper 1993). It is a blueprint or road map for managing the new product process to improve efficiency and effectiveness. Operationally the scheme breaks the new product process into a series of multi-functional stages comprised of multiple, parallel activities; each stage is preceded by a gate or decision point. This stage-gate process is not unlike the idealized process described above, except that it is more rigorous, formal and disciplined. The stage and gate format leads to names such as 'gating' or 'stage-gate' or 'toll-gate' systems.

CYCLE TIME REDUCTION IN PRODUCT INNOVATION

Speed has become the new competitive weapon. Speed yields competitive advantage; it means less likelihood that the market or competitive situation might change; and it means a quicker realization of profits. But speed is only an interim objective – a means to an end; the ultimate goal is profitability. Often attempts to reduce cycle time end up costing the firm both time and money. Here are some ways that progressive firms use to reduce cycle time in product innovation:

- Do it right the first time: build in quality of execution at every stage of the project. The best way to save time is by avoiding having to recycle back and do it a second time. Quality of execution pays off not only in terms of better results, but via reducing delays (see item 9 above).
- Homework and definition: doing the upfront homework and getting clear project definition, based on fact rather than hearsay and speculation, saves time downstream: less recycling back to get the facts or redefine the product requirements; and sharper targets to work towards (see items 3 and 4 above).
- Organize around a multi-functional team with empowerment: multi-functional teams are essential for timely development: 'Rip apart a badly developed project and you will unfailingly find 75 percent of slippage attributable to "siloing" or sending memos up and down vertical organisational "silos" or "stovepipes" for decisions, and sequential problem solving', according to Peters (1988). Sadly, the typical project resembles a relay race, with each function or department carrying the baton for its portion of the race, and then handing off to the next runner or department (see item 5 above).
- Parallel processing: the relay race, sequential or series approach to product development is antiquated and inappropriate for the 1990s. Given the time pressures of projects coupled with the need for a complete and quality process, a more appropriate scheme is a rugby game or parallel processing. Here, activities are undertaken concurrently (rather than sequentially) so that more activities are undertaken in an elapsed period of time. Parallel processing demands the use of a cross-functional team approach.
- Prioritize and focus: the best way to slow projects down is to dissipate the firm's limited resources and people across too many projects. By concentrating resources on the truly meritorious projects, not only will the work be done better, it will be done faster. But focus means tough choices: it means killing other and perhaps worthwhile projects. And that requires good decision-making and the right criteria for making go/kill decisions (see item 7 above).
- Keep it simple: find opportunities for unbundling products and projects. For example, instead of a project where three inventions are required, break it into three separate new product projects: introduce three successively better generations of products. The experience here is: project complexity doubles and triples the cycle time; so work to reduce the complexity of projects.
- Use flow-charting: that is, map out each and every activity in a project (or in your NPP), and remove the time-wasters. Any NPP can be accelerated by shortening each stage (Rosenau 1988). Sensible shortcuts (omitting the unrequired) are obvious timesavers.
- Use planning tools: utilize critical path planning and project management software (e.g. Microsoft Project, On Target, MacProject, Harvard Project Manager). Look for opportunities for undertaking tasks concurrently, or for beginning one task before another ends.

- Add flexibility to the process to ensure greater speed. Overlap stages; bring activities forward into an earlier stage, especially long lead time activities; and have multiple gate approvals.
- Deadlines must be regarded as sacred if speed is the objective. Time-based innovation is impossible without a discipline adherence to deadlines. Delays are dealt with via extra input of effort and resources, not by postponement.
- Have flexible funding: that is, set aside envelopes of money (or resources) so that one does not have to wait for a new budget year for money to start a promising project.

NOTE

1 This chapter focuses on physical or tangible products as opposed to new service products. Although obvious differences exist, there are also many similarities between the two, and indeed many of the concepts and methods explained in this chapter also apply to new service products.

REFERENCES

Booz-Allen and Hamilton (1982) *New Product Management for the 1980s*, New York: Booz-Allen and Hamilton Inc.

Business Week (1991) 'R&D statistics', *Business Week, Special 1991 Issue* 25 October: 173–208.

Cooper, R. G. (1988) 'The new product process: a decision guide for managers', *Journal of Marketing Management* 3 (3): 238–55.

Cooper, R. G. (1993) *Winning at New Products: Accelerating the Process from Idea to Launch*, 2nd edn, Reading, Mass: Addison-Wesley.

Cooper, R. G. and Kleinschmidt, E. J. (1986) 'An investigation into the new product process: steps, deficiencies and impact', *Journal of Product Innovation Management* 3 (2): 71–85.

Cooper, R. G. and Kleinschmidt, E. J. (1987) 'New products: what separates winners from losers', *Journal of Product Innovation Management* 4 (3): 169–84.

Cooper, R. G. and Kleinschmidt, E. J. (1988) 'Resource allocation in the new product process', *Industrial Marketing Management* 17 (3): 249–62.

Cooper, R. G. and Kleinschmidt, E. J. (1990) *New Products: The Key Factors in Success*, Chicago: American Marketing Association.

Cooper, R. G. and Kleinschmidt, E. J. (1991) 'New product processes at leading industrial firms', *Industrial Marketing Management* 10 (2), May: 137–47.

Cooper, R. G. and Kleinschmidt, E. J. (1993a) 'New product success in the chemical industry', *Industrial Marketing Management* 22 (2): 85–99.

Cooper, R. G. and Kleinschmidt, E. J. (1993b) 'Stage gate systems for new product success', *Marketing Management* 1 (4): 20–9.

Crawford, C. M. (1979) 'New product failure rates – facts and fallacies', *Research Management*, September: 9–13.

Hopkins, D. S. (1980) *New Product Winners and Losers*, Conference Board Report number 773, New York: The Conference Board.

Kleinschmidt, E. J. and Cooper, R. G. (1991) 'The impact of product innovativeness on performance', *Journal of Product Innovation Management* 8: 240–51.

Larson, E. W. and Gobeli, D. H. (1988) 'Organizing for product development projects'

Journal of Product Innovation Management 5: 180–90.

Maidique, M. A. and Zirger, B. J. (1984) 'A study of success and failure in product innovation: the case of the U.S. electronics industry', *IEEE Trans. in Engineering Management* EM-31, November: 192–203.

Page, A. L. (1991) *PDMA New Product Development Survey: Performance and Best Practices*, Chicago: PDMA Conference, Chicago, 13 November.

Peters, Tom (1988) *Thriving on Chaos*, New York: Harper & Row.

R&T Mgmt (1991) 'Year end R&D numbers', *Research & Technology Management* 34 (6), November–December: 6.

Rosenau, M. D. Jr. (1988) 'Phased approach speeds up new product development', *Research and Development* 30 (11), November: 52–5.

Roussel, P., Saad, K. N. and Erickson, T. J. (1991) *Third Generation R&D, Managing the Link to Corporate Strategy*, Cambridge, MA: Harvard Business School Press.

Von Hippel, E. A. (1988) *The Sources of Innovation*, New York: Oxford University Press.

FURTHER READING

Boznack, R. G. and Decker, A. K. (1993) *Competitive Product Development: A Quality Approach to Succeeding in the 90s and Beyond*, Burr Ridge, IL: Irwin.

Crawford, C. M. (1993) *New Products Management*, 4th edn, Homewood, IL: Dow Jones Irwin.

Gruenwald, G. (1993) *New Product Development: Responding to Market Demand*, 2nd edn, Lincolnwood, IL: NTC Business Books.

Moore, W. L. and Pessemier, E. A. (1993) *Product Planning and Management: Designing and Delivering Value*, New York: McGraw-Hill.

Rosenau, M. D., Jr. (1993) *Faster New Product Development: Getting the Right Product to Market Quickly*, New York: Amacom.

Rosenthal, S. R. (1992) *Effective Product Design and Development: How to Cut Lead Time and Increase Customer Satisfaction*, Burr Ridge, IL: Irwin.

Rothwell, R. (1972) 'Factors for success in industrial innovations', in *Project SAPPHO – A Comparative Study of Success and Failure in Industrial Innovation*, Brighton: SPRU, University of Sussex.

Rothwell, R. (1976) 'Innovation in textile machinery: some significant factors in success and failure', *SPRU Occasional Paper Series* (2), Brighton: SPRU, University of Sussex.

Rothwell, R. (1976) 'The "Hungarian SAPPHO": some comments and comparison', *Research Policy* (3): 30–8.

Rothwell, R., Freeman, C., Horseley, A., Jervis, V. T. P., Robertson, A. B. and Townsend, J. (1974) 'SAPPHO updated – project SAPPHO phase II', *Research Policy* (3): 258–91.

Scheuing, E. E. (1989) *New Products Management*, Columbus, OH: Merrill Publishing Co.

Souder, W. E. (1987) *Managing New Product Innovations*, New York: Lexington Books.

Urban, G. L. and Hauser, J. R. (1993) *Design and Marketing of New Products*, 2nd edn, Englewood Cliffs, NJ: Prentice Hall.

Wheelwright, S. C. and Clark, K. B. (1992) *Revolutionizing Product Development: Quantum Leaps in Speed, Efficiency and Quality*, New York: The Free Press.

Zangwill, W. I. (1992) *Lightning Strategies for Innovation: How the World's Best Firms Create New Products*, New York: The Free Press.

28

PRODUCT LIFE CYCLE MANAGEMENT

Peter Doyle

This chapter explores two related issues essential to developing marketing strategies. First, it examines how markets evolve over time – how they start, grow, reach maturity and eventually decline. This involves reviewing the concept of the product life cycle and examining the broader underlying market dynamics which shape the behaviour of both customers and competitors. While we show that there is no standard product or market 'life cycle', there are common evolutionary processes which influence markets over time.

Second, the chapter describes how an understanding of this process of change in a market should influence marketing strategy. By anticipating developments in buyer behaviour, competitive activities and emerging technologies, managers can reposition their businesses and proactively change products and marketing policies to strengthen their competitiveness and improve their financial performance. Finally, the chapter explores the strategic issues facing businesses in different competitive positions. It looks at the forces which should determine the different marketing strategies of the pioneers of the industry, those seeking to challenge the market leader, and those companies aiming at niche positions within the larger market.

CYCLES OF CONFUSION

The concept of a product life cycle has had a major impact on the marketing literature. Every textbook has a chapter on the subject and numerous articles have appeared on it. It has also influenced many of the popular management techniques such as the Boston Consulting Group matrix and the McKinsey portfolio.

Figure 1 shows the popular representation of the theory. The theory postulates that a product has a life cycle (usually described by an S-shaped sales curve), which can be divided into four stages: introduction, growth, maturity and decline. The slow introductory phase reflects the difficulty of overcoming buyer inertia and stimulating trial of a new product. Rapid growth then occurs

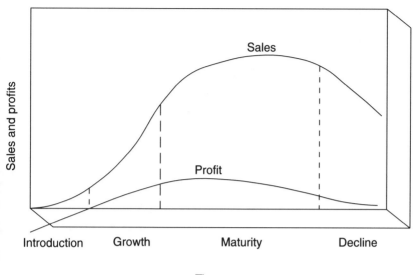

Figure 1   The product life cycle

as many new buyers are attracted once the product is perceived as successful. Saturation of the product's potential buyers is eventually reached, causing the rapid growth to level out to the underlying rate of growth of the relevant target market. Finally, decline will set in as new substitute products appear.

From this product life cycle theory it has then been common to draw implications for marketing strategy, the marketing mix and the organization of marketing (e.g. Levitt 1965). The main recommendations are summarized in Table 1. It is argued that in the introduction stage the strategic objective should be aggressively to develop the market, focusing on the most innovative customers and seeking to preempt competition. As the product moves into the growth stage new competitors enter, the initial product has to be enhanced with features and line extensions, prices have to be cut and distribution intensified now that a mass market is emerging. As the market for the product matures profit margins fall, competition is intense and the organization has to shift from a focus on marketing to one on efficiency and cost control. Finally, in the decline stage, the future is bleak and the business should seek to milk the product for cash. This cash is then pushed into new products and the product life cycle is repeated.

Despite the popularity of the product life cycle, there is unfortunately no evidence that most products follow such a four-stage cycle. Nor is there any evidence that the turning-points of the different stages are in any way

Table 1 Product life cycle: implications for marketing

	Introduction	Growth	Maturity	Decline
Characteristics				
Sales	Low	Fast growth	Slow growth	Decline
Profit	Negative	Rapid rise	Falling margins	Declining
Cash flow	Negative	Moderate	High	Moderate
Strategy				
Objective	Aggressive entry	Maximize share	Boost profits	Milk product
Focus	Non-users	New segments	Defend share	Cut costs
Customer targets	Innovators	Early adopters	Majority	Laggards
Competitor targets	Few, preempt	Growing number	Many	Declining
Differential adv.	Product performance	Brand image	Price and service	Price
Marketing mix				
Product	Basic	Extensions and enhancements	Differentiation, variety	Rationalize range
Price	High	Lower	Low	Stabilizing
Promotion	High	High	Falling	Low
Advertising forms	Awareness	Brand performance	Loyalty	Selective
Distribution	Selective	Intensive	Intensive	Rationalize
Organization				
Structure	Team	Market focus	Functional	Lean
Focus	Innovation	Marketing	Efficiency	Cost reduction
Culture	Freewheeling	Marketing led	Professional	Pressured

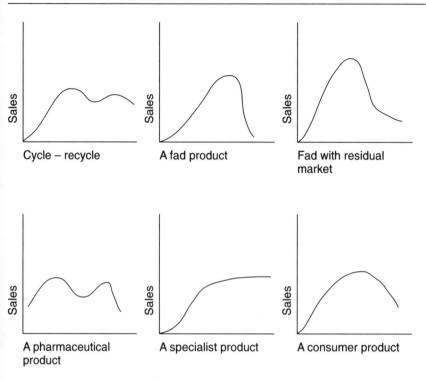

Figure 2   Alternative product life cycle patterns

predictable. On the contrary, the shapes of the sales curves appear to be completely idiosyncratic. One review of life cycles identified sixteen different patterns in addition to the S-curve. Some of the more common curves found in empirical studies are illustrated in Figure 2. Similarly, the turning-point from maturity to decline can occur after a few months (e.g. the hula hoop) or not be evident after several generations (e.g. Scotch whisky). If the shape and length of the product life cycle are so irregular and unpredictable, the concept would appear to have little utility for market planning and decision-making.

Part of the problem with the product life cycle concept is that it has never been properly defined. What does 'product' mean? Some studies use the total industry sales (e.g. computers); others use product forms (e.g. notebook computers); still others use brands (e.g. Apple Mac). Each 'product' has quite a different life cycle: one can be in long-term decline while another exhibits rapid growth.

To see the managerial implications of these differences it is useful to show how they relate to one another (Table 2). Market analysis starts not with the product but with the needs of customers. A need is a basic requirement of

Table 2   Alternative product life cycle concepts

Concept	Definition	Typical length	Examples
Need	Basic underlying requirement	Indefinite	Transportation, calculating
Demand	Specific solution to a need	Very long	Car, computer
Technology	Current state-of-the-art	Short	Composite engine, 16-bit computer
Product	Product with specific technology	Shorter	4-wheel drive car, 16-bit pc
Product form	Variant of product	Very short	Open-top, 4-wheel drive, 16-bit notepad pc
Brand	Manufacturer's offer	Long	Honda Civic, IBM pc, Coca-Cola

customers. For example, customers have needs for transportation, calculating power or energy. Such needs may persist and grow over centuries and indeed may never have a decline stage.

Next, at one level of disaggregation, we have a *demand* for a specific solution to the need. This is sometimes called a demand-technology life cycle. For example, the demand for transportation was once met by a coach and horses, now it is met by a car. The electronic computer has replaced the mechanical comptometer. The life cycle of these broad product solutions, while shorter than the need curve, can be extremely long.

Next is the *current technology* curve. While the demand curve represents a broad technological solution (e.g. internal combustion engine, electronics) beneath this curve are a whole series of incremental technological changes which obsolete previous processes. For example, 16-bit technology replaces 8-bit; ceramic filters replace copper; fibre optic cables replace wire. Technology curves can be quite short and are certainly getting shorter.

At the next level of disaggregation managers make choices. A *product* curve is a category of offer incorporating current technology. For example, companies offer four-wheel drive cars or a 16-bit personal computer.

Next, line extensions or alternative *product forms* normally appear such as open-top four-wheel drive cars or 16-bit notepad computers. Both product and product forms may exhibit short life cycles due to changing tastes and technology.

Finally, there is the *brand* product life cycle. This is the distinctive offer of a specific business. The brand life cycle can be long or short depending upon the marketing strategy. Unilever believes that, by incorporating the latest technology and adapting the product and product form to changing market conditions, the brand can have an indefinite life. Brands such as Persil, Coca-Cola, Range Rover and many others last for generations because they change the technological, design and service content of the offer while still retaining the brand values.

For managers to talk of a product being at the declining stage can therefore be highly misleading. First, sales are often resuscitated by new uses and new markets. Second, for every declining product there are almost invariably rapidly growing technologies, product forms and brands. For example, total sales of tea have been declining for generations, but within this total sales of some product forms such as herbal and instant teas have been showing explosive growth in recent years.

Weaknesses of the product life cycle

To summarize, for the following reasons, the product life cycle is not of much use for marketing strategy.

Undefined concept

There is no agreement about the level of aggregation to which the concept is supposed to refer. Needs, demands, technologies, product categories, forms and brands have quite different driving forces.

No common shape

However products are defined there appears to be no standard curve. An S-shaped curve appears to describe only a minority of products. The actual sales development is shaped by both outside events and by the strategies of competitors.

Unpredictable turning-points

While most products and brands do peak eventually, there is no way of predicting when the turning-point will occur. For some it is a matter of months, for others it may be generations.

Unclear implications

Even where a life cycle pattern can be identified the implications are not clear. For example, the growth phase may or may not be associated with high profit margins. If barriers to entry are low and industry competition is fierce (e.g. as in some areas of electronics), rapid growth can be accompanied by very low profits. By contrast, if there are low exit barriers and little competition, the

485

decline stage can be exceptionally profitable (e.g. the foundry supplies business).

Not exogenous

The product life cycle is often the result of management actions rather than being caused by outside events. Many managers have been taught to think that the product life cycle is inevitable. When sales have plateaued, rather than looking to upgrade the technology and search for new opportunities, management have defined the business as a cash cow and sought to 'diversify' into other businesses. In these situations the product life cycle becomes a self-fulfilling concept.

For example, Foseco was the leader in supplying linings to steel refractories around the world – a £300m-a-year business. The linings were fibrous boards installed inside the furnaces. A small competitor entered with a cheaper spray-based alternative. Foseco, with its strong reputation and marketing capability, could easily have responded to this threat by adopting the technology. In fact, they were given the opportunity to acquire the competitor. Instead management had identified their business as a 'cash cow' and so declined to invest. The result was that the competitors rapidly took over the market. Spray linings became a high-growth business as the steel companies substituted from board. Foseco refractory profits collapsed. A few years later an ailing Foseco was acquired by Burmah Castrol.

Product oriented

The core concept of marketing is that the business should seek to meet the needs of customers rather than focus on selling its products. The product life cycle is a production rather than a marketing orientated concept. By focusing on the product managers fail to understand those factors which shape the business's ability to satisfy the needs of its customers in competitive markets. The fortunes of the company are not tied to its products but to five other primary forces which determine its ability to maintain a competitive advantage. These forces are:

- the changing requirements of customers;
- the objectives and strategies of competitors;
- the attractiveness of the market to new competitors;
- the emergence of new technologies which can replace existing solutions;
- the performance and power of those companies supplying resources, raw materials and components to the business.

These are the drivers which obsolete the product. A product will die if the needs of its customers change, if competitors come up with better offers, if new technologies permit cheaper or superior solutions, or if suppliers to the firm choke off its ability to satisfy the market profitably. Therefore it is better to tune

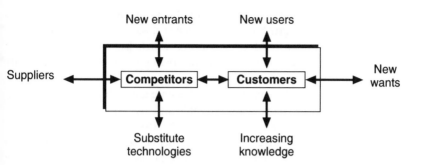

Figure 3   The Business Portfolio
(Boston Consulting Group, see Hedley 1977:11)

managers into concentrating on the causes of change rather than the consequences of it. In this way they can more effectively anticipate developments in the market and create product strategies which adapt to these opportunities.

MARKET DYNAMICS

Just as there is no uniform, predictable product life cycle, so there is no standard pattern of market evolution. However, there are common processes which shape markets. By analysing these processes managers can anticipate how markets and competition will develop. From this analysis they can develop strategies both to capitalize on these changes and to influence these forces of change. Such processes affect each of the following five 'actors' in the industry. (See Figure 3.)

Customers

As a market evolves certain changes can be anticipated among customers. First, the level of demand changes. Sales are a function of the number of buyers and the frequency with which they buy. In the initial stages, growth can be extremely rapid because of the number of new buyers being attracted to the market. Eventually this pool of available non-users diminishes, the market becomes saturated and sales slow as they become largely a function of repeat purchasing. A second change to be anticipated is that customers' expectations will progress. The primary function of the product comes to be accepted as the 'norm' offered by all competitors. Customers look for additional attributes which add new benefits to the product.

For example, in the early 1980s doctors hailed Squibb's revolutionary new hypertensive drug, Capoten, which eventually sold over £1bn a year. Subsequently, twenty competitors entered the market. The new products were not superior in the primary function of lowering blood pressure but they began to offer additional desirable attributes such as lower dosage and fewer side effects. Today the market leader is Merck's Vasotec which has the attribute that a patient needs to take it only once a day rather than the two or three times daily required by Capoten.

Finally, three factors cause customers to become increasingly price sensitive. First, customers become more knowledgeable and are willing to shop around. Second, there are more competitors to choose from. Third, as the market develops, more price sensitive customer segments have to be penetrated to maintain growth. Innovative customers tend to be less price sensitive because they attach a high value to the new product, later customers have to be attracted by lower prices.

While evolutionary processes in the market push towards slower growth and falling prices, both can be postponed or forestalled by firms making product or market innovations. By innovative repositioning, the firm can meet new needs, offer new attributes or create new markets. Such innovations have fuelled resurgent growth and maintained high prices in many markets such as those for bicycles, icecream, alkaline batteries and industrial lubricants.

Competition

Evolutionary processes also lead to certain expected changes in the behaviour of current competitors in the market. First, the intensity of competition will initially be low because the rapid rate of growth makes competition a non-zero sum game – all can grow. But later, as the market slows and firms have added to capacity, competition for customers becomes increasingly intense. Second, during the latter part of the growth phase, the more aggressive competitors begin to pursue repositioning strategies that put them into direct competition with firms which were previously in different strategic groups.

For example, up to the mid-1980s, IBM and Apple did not compete head-on. IBM dominated the mainframe market, Apple the emerging PC market. Then in 1984 IBM, concerned about the slowing growth in the mainframe market and the expanding purchases of PCs by its customers, launched its own PC. With this new direct clash between the two leaders competition massively increased, producing a rapid shake-out of the weaker players.

A third change is that during the growth stage winning strategies begin to emerge and industry leadership tends to become established. The winners are those that have aggressively built market share in the early stages, moved down the experience curve and built economies of scale in operations and marketing. As the industry matures they have lower unit costs and powerful marketing and distribution systems. The leaders are then hard to dislodge unless a competitor can introduce radically innovative products or marketing strategies.

New entrants

A market is pioneered by one or two companies. However, a rapidly growing market automatically attracts new competitors – often in large numbers. Sometimes there is an interval in which patents, lack of technical expertise and uncertainty about the market's potential, act as barriers to entry. But this interval is now very short in most industries. Less than one year after Apple launched the first personal computer, it had ten competitors; eight years later it had five hundred. Speciality chemical companies expect their new products to be copied within six months.

Today all well-managed companies are scouring the environment for growth markets that might utilize their capabilities. As the market's potential becomes less uncertain, large firms will seek to enter the market. Sometimes they will establish their own businesses, more often they will acquire one or more of the pioneers. Existing competitors have to compete not only with local entrants but global competition increasingly becomes the pattern.

As the market enters its mature phase, the number of new entrants sharply reduces and companies begin the exit. Slow growth normally triggers a shake-out and the number of competitors declines. The survivors are increasingly those who have pursued the winning strategies of achieving high market shares, broad product lines and global markets. Consequently, managers in innovative businesses must appreciate that their lead time is always short and that soon they will be challenged both by small, nimble followers and large, resource-rich giants. If they are to survive, their technological edge must be matched by strategy to build share rapidly and create a viable brand.

Substitute product and technologies

Over time managers should expect substitute products and technologies to threaten their position in the market. A substitute is anything that meets the same customer need. Concrete can be a substitute for steel in building a bridge, high fructose corn syrup can substitute for sugar, acrylic for nylon. Several factors increase the threat from substitutes as the market evolves.

First, competitors in adjacent industries are attracted by the growth and profit to be made in the market. For example, commercial banks once dominated the financial markets, but in the last decade they have lost share. On the commercial side the banks have lost share to securities firms. On the retail side they have lost share to building societies and non-banks such as ATT and Marks & Spencer who now offer services such as credit cards and investment funds.

Second, needs in the market change, making old technologies less appropriate. For example, today's customers find making a special trip to a bank for a routine transaction a chore. A new bank First Direct attracted nearly half a million customers by offering telephone banking. Unlike old rivals, First Direct has no branches, all the functions and transactions are available through a seven-day, twenty-four-hour telephone service.

Third, progress in adjacent technologies is likely to eventually threaten current solutions. For example, new plastics which are light and strong increasingly substitute for steel in car manufacturing. Finally, the government can influence the position of substitutes through regulations, quotas and subsidies. For example, environmental regulations are forcing the wind-down of many packaging and chemical products and stimulating the creation of new substitutes.

In these situations management have to decide whether to beat the emerging substitutes or to modify their strategies and incorporate the new products and technologies. The answer will depend upon an analysis of which alternative best meets the needs of customers and of the trend in the relative price-performance ratios.

Supply relationships

Entrepreneurial firms depend upon suppliers and subcontractors to facilitate growth. During the initial stages of the market obtaining suitable supplies may be a constraint on growth. Those early competitors that can access efficient suppliers or have the resources to integrate backwards can lever important competitive advantages.

Suppliers can limit the potential of a company to exploit its capacity for innovation. Porter (1980: 27–8) suggests a supplying group is powerful where the following conditions apply in the market:

- It is dominated by a few suppliers and is more concentrated than the industry to which it sells.
- It is not obliged to compete with other substitute products for sales to the industry.
- The industry is not an important customer of the supplier group.
- The supplier's product is an important input to the buyer's business.
- There are high switching costs in moving away from the products of the supplier group.
- The supplier group poses a credible threat of forward integration.

In general supplier power diminishes as the market grows. Nevertheless control and power over suppliers can offer a sustainable competitor advantage. For example, Marks & Spencer's long-term relationship with its suppliers, its skill in influencing their design and processes, and its ability to negotiate strongly with them have been central to the company's sustained position as Europe's leading retail firm.

THE EVOLUTION OF MARKETS

These five key components are affected by evolutionary forces. For convenience, these developments can be divided into four phases.

The emerging market

A new market is triggered by an innovation. This innovation may be a new product that is superior to earlier ones; a new marketing concept that creates a new set of customers; or a process innovation that dramatically cuts costs or increases the availability of a product.

For an innovation to succeed it has to offer benefits that customers perceive as superior to current solutions. The customers who perceive this benefit first and who can act on this perception are called innovators. Innovators are normally not price sensitive because they value the benefit highly and do not want to wait for competition to bring prices down. The central marketing task at this stage is to segment the market with the aim of identifying those buyers most likely to benefit from the performance or the promise of the new product. Typically some potential customers will benefit hugely, others perceive very little benefit at all. The former are the ones to target.

For example, when Rolm (now part of Siemens) invented the electronic PABX (the telephone switching system used by an office or company), the primary benefit was that it allowed companies to economize on long-distance call costs. For the top two per cent of companies with very large long-distance call bills, the savings averaged over £100,000 a year. On the other hand, for most companies, with more modest long-distance bills, the savings were minimal. Rolm's initial strategy was therefore to identify and target the former segment.

At the beginning sales growth is normally slow, buyers have to be informed about the innovation and to be persuaded of its benefits. Uncertainty, high switching costs and the lack of established distribution and service infra-structures also restrain buyers. Barriers to adoption are more easily broken down when the new product has the following characteristics:

- a major performance advantage which is easily demonstrated;
- the cost of switching into it is low;
- the cost of product failures is limited;
- support requirements are small;
- buyers in the segment have the resources to change.

Once the innovators begin to adopt the product, the market may grow very fast, fuelled by the penetration of the large non-user group.

Competition is initally weak. The pioneer's main competition comes from the older technology. New entry is temporarily forestalled by barriers which include:

- patents;

491

- lack of technical know-how;
- uncertainty about what customers want;
- lack of expertise in sourcing supplies and parts;
- shortage of risk capital.

Unfortunately for the innovator, such barriers to entry tend to crumble very rapidly. Movements of personnel, the spread of knowledge and the adaptability of aggressive, fast followers soon erode the leader's temporary monopoly. Within a year there are likely to be several new entrants in the market.

The high growth phase

The high growth phase is characterized by the expansion of the market to new customer segments and new uses. These are stimulated by the spread of knowledge about the product beyond the innovator group, the reduction of uncertainty about standards and switching costs and the inevitable decline in prices. As prices fall, the new product becomes increasingly attractive to customers who only perceive a modest advantage in it.

The number of competitors often grows to strikingly high numbers. For example, in the motor cycle industry, at its peak, there were 136 manufacturers in the UK alone and an estimated 700 worldwide. They were attracted by the rapid growth and profitability of the market. In addition, the development of a strong infrastructure of subcontractors and distributors facilitates entry. Prices generally fall rapidly as experience and scale economies lower unit costs and competition increasingly forces most of these gains to be passed on to the customer.

In the later stages, as the growth rate begins to slow, competition for market share intensifies. The leading players begin to develop global ambitions and to broaden their product lines, pushing them into markets and segments occupied by other strong competitors. Companies which have not developed strong market positioning strategies or achieved low cost structures begin to see their profit margins falling and more are forced to exit the market.

The mature phase of the market

Market maturity occurs when the number of new users and new uses dry up. The marketing focus then has to switch from attracting non-users and creating new uses to maintaining or gaining market share. Since current users are more experienced, price and service becomes more important. Difficulties in finding new uses for the product and additional attributes to differentiate it at this stage of market, heightens the drift towards commodity status.

Competition has normally become fierce. There will be excess capacity, the market has become zero-sum and the inroads of international competitors all tend to increase the pressures on companies. Two other factors amplify these pressures on margins. Dealers become more powerful. They can play off alternative suppliers and may introduce their own brands. Second, it is harder for competitors to reduce costs because most of the scale economies and experience curve effects have already been obtained. The shake-out of marginal competitors then usually proceeds rapidly through amalgamations, takeovers and bankruptcies.

At the late stage of maturity the market may consolidate around a handful of large competitors who effectively create barriers to entry. These barriers centre around the scale economies they possess, the high capital requirements, the advantage of established brand names and the implicit threat of sharp retaliation newcomers may face. Markets that have matured into this oligopolistic pattern include the oil industry, the supermarket sector and the detergents business.

While internal competition in the industry may become more constrained, competition from substitute technologies is likely to grow over time. For example, continual improvements in plastics and composites add to the problems of steel producers seeking to maintain volume. Such companies then face the dilemma of a vain attempt to fight off the threat or a substantial investment in acquiring and adapting to the substitute technologies.

The decline phase

A new stage is reached when the market enters a period where volume looks set for permanent decline. This occurs when the pool of potential new users and new uses has dried up, when substitute products have demonstrated clear superiority or when buyers' needs change.

Characterizing the market as 'in decline' can be a dangerous mistake. Many markets have developed new sources of growth after entering what appeared to be the decline phase. Resurgent growth can be created by new products, new users and new uses. The motorcycle market declined by 50 per cent in the 1960s, then exhibited explosive growth as new, younger customers bought it as a fun product rather than as a cheap form of transport. Nylon has been written off many times, but instead, as Figure 4 illustrates, new uses have continually fuelled resurgent growth.

Even if the decline phase looks certain, the strategic implications are not clear. The usual recommendation from advocates of product life cycle theory or portfolio concepts such as the Boston Consulting Group's matrix, is to divest from the market. But, in practice, such a view can be a costly oversimplification. Many markets in decline can be highly profitable and substantial cash generators for a very long period if managed properly (e.g. the cigarette market). Further, today there are many more declining markets than in the past. Slower world economic growth, rapid technological change and a fast-changing environment make the management of declining industries an important issue for most firms. The appropriate strategy depends upon how the evolutionary process affects the pattern of declining demand and the intensity of competition.

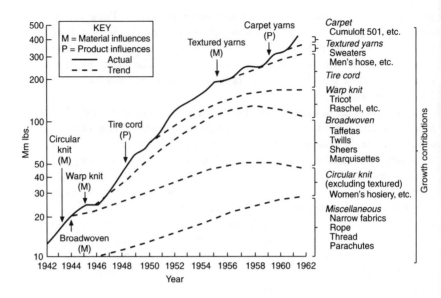

Figure 4   Extending the market: the case of Nylon
Source: Yale (1964: 33)

A market does not decline in a homogeneous pattern, rather the more innovative segments leave the market for new alternatives leaving behind customer groups who are reluctant or unable to change. Often these remaining customer groups are conservative and price inelastic. This occurs where, perhaps because of habit, the product is perceived as important to them. Other factors may be a lack of acceptable alternatives, if it is not seen as a major cost element in the budget, or if past long-term advertising has built up strong brand loyalties. In these situations, the remaining competitors may be able to push up prices to offset the decline in volume.

Whether this is possible depends upon the intensity of competition. Factors which may damp down competition allowing the survivors to earn reasonable returns are:

- when there are only a small number of large, evenly-balanced competitors remaining in the market;
- if general agreement exists that the market will continue to decline so that costly battles to win market share look unattractive;
- if significant non-price differences exist between competitive products so that they are not perceived as commodities;
- if exit barriers are low so that it is not too costly for competitors to leave the market as prospects decline;

- if fixed costs are relatively low so that total costs decline in line with volume.

In some markets (e.g. heavy chemicals) these conditions are clearly not present. Here fixed costs are high, there are major international competitors pursuing varying strategies, plants are highly specific and buyers regard the product as a commodity. In such markets the decline stage is often characterized by intensive competition, ruinous price wars and large losses.

Porter (1980: 267–73) identified four strategic options available to the business in the decline phase.

1 *Leadership.* The firm invests in acquisitions and other market share building strategies to rationalize and dominate the market. This is a high-risk strategy only justifiable if management are convinced that the resulting market structure will allow the firm to recover its late investment.
2 *Niche.* The firm focuses on a segment which is more robust and price insensitive than the mass of the market. Again this may be a difficult strategy since the remaining competitors are likely to target such a segment.
3 *Harvest.* Here the firm seeks to optimize cash flow rather than market share. Harvesting strategies involve cutting costs, raising prices and rationalizing the range of products, customers and channels. This strategy is most attractive if the firm has been a strong player in the market. If it has not been recognized as an industry leader, the harvesting strategy will normally lead to a rapid collapse of volume thereby eliminating any gains to be obtained from the strategy.
4 *Divest.* Here the business is sold off to maximize its net investment recovery. This strategy is only likely to be profitable if a decision is made early in the decline phase. If left until later, or after the business has been harvested, it is not likely to find much interest in an acquisition.

Choosing the right strategy depends upon analysing the strength of the firm's competitive position and assessing the evolutionary processes affecting the market. If the firm has a strong position and the decline phase is expected to be steady and without bruising price wars, the attractiveness of a leadership or niche strategy is enhanced. On the other hand, if the company has no marked advantage, if no robust niches are apparent, and if the products are seen as commodities, rapid exit may be the best alternative. The earlier the oncoming decline phase is recognized and the better the evolutionary characteristics are understood, the more options are available to management.

FORMULATING MARKETING STRATEGIES

The marketing strategy that management should adopt depends upon three factors. First, what is its competitive position – is it a market leader or a challenger? Second, what is its strategic objective? Is it seeking market dominance or merely to carve out a profitable niche? Third, at what stage is the market? Is it in its early growth stage or does it look to be in late maturity? If the company is the one to create the market through a significant innovation, it has the opportunity to gain first mover advantages. These include image advantages, customer loyalty, higher margins and economies of scale and experience. But these advantages are far from assured. There are numerous examples of the pioneer being quickly caught up and disappearing from the scene. The evidence suggests that to exploit an innovation the pioneer has to move both quickly and substantially to push into the main markets and to capture a significant market share. Such requirements are costly and difficult problems for the smaller company.

. As the market moves from growth to maturity the strategy has to change from aggression to defence. Recently marketing academics have found the writings of the military strategists such as Clausewitz (1908) and Liddel-Hart (1967) illuminating for discussing the defensive options open to companies seeking to maintain the leadership positions they have built up. Such options include offensive defence, position defence, flanking defence, mobile defence, etc. Kotler and Singh (1981) have written the best known summaries of these military analogies applied to marketing.

If the company is not the innovator but a later entrant seeking to challenge the pioneer, different strategies will apply. Attacking a leader is easier when it is pursued at the early stage of a market's evolution. This is particularly the case when the pioneer has not aggressively expanded the market beyond the small innovatory niche. At the early stage of the market the two most effective strategies for the challenger are to seek new market segments or new attributes.

If the challenger is attacking at the maturity stage of the market, there are again military analogies to draw on. Kotler and Singh (1981) describe frontal, flank, encirclement, guerrilla and by-pass attack strategies.

SUMMARY

Managers have to understand that markets are highly dynamic. Today customer requirements, competitive activity and technological solutions are impermanent and in constant flux. The product life cycle is too simple a model for predicting the nature of these changes. Instead management have to assess the six underlying evolutionary forces which shape the behaviour of markets.

Successful competitive strategies are based on anticipating these evolutionary forces and using them to advantage. Most pioneers need to appreciate that their advantage is shortlived and that the strategic window they create must be rapidly and decisively exploited and then vigilantly defended. Newcomers find the odds stacked against them when they attack an effective market leader. A successful leader is rarely overtaken by a head-on strategy. Instead success usually depends upon further innovation in identifying new market segments and additional attributes not yet identified or exploited by the leader.

Market evolution is characterized by competitors crossing into each other's strongholds. Competition increases both in intensity and scope. This makes it difficult for companies pursuing single-niche strategies. Over time, high value niches become attractive to larger companies searching for new avenues of growth.

REFERENCES

Clausewitz, C. Von (1908) *On War*, London: Routledge.
Kotler, P. and Singh, R. A. (1981) 'Marketing warfare in the 1980s', *Journal of Business Strategy*, Winter: 30–41.
Liddell-Hart, D. H. (1967) *Strategy*, New York: Praeger.
Porter, Michael E. (1980) *Competitive Strategy: Techniques for Analyzing Your Business Competitors*, New York: The Free Press.
Yale, Jordan, P. (1964) 'The strategy of Nylon's growth', *Modern Textiles Magazine*, February: 33.

FURTHER READING

Buzzell, R. D. and Gale, B. T. (1987) *The PIMS Principles: Linking Strategy to Performance*, New York: The Free Press.
Doyle, P. (1994) *Marketing Management and Strategy*, Hemel Hempstead: Prentice-Hall International.
Levitt, T. (1965) 'Exploit the product life cycle', *Harvard Business Review*, November: 81–94.

29

PACKAGING AND DESIGN

Peter Dart

Marketing is about the process of adding value. The more successful one brand is over the competition in adding value provides flexibility and leverage – either to make more profit from a price premium or to make more profit by selling more at a lower relative price, or, in the most successful cases, to do both (i.e. sell more than the competition at a higher price).

There are many constituents that go towards 'added value': the reputation of a brand – how long it has been around, its heritage; its performance and effectivity; its image, caused mostly, but not solely, by advertising and other forms of communication. By image we mean how the brand feels to the users personally, together with what the users think it will say about themselves as viewed by other people.

In this chapter about packaging it is asserted that as media get more difficult, more fragmented and more expensive, the role that packaging can play in adding value to a brand has increased significantly. The trick, of course, is to add more packaging value than cost, and hence be able to charge a price premium and make an increased profit. This chapter is about practical advice, not theory, and it has been organized under the following ten key themes.

PACKAGING PROVIDES ONE OF THE MOST FERTILE AREAS IN THE MARKETING MIX FOR ADDING MORE VALUE THAN COST

The easiest area to consider regarding 'adding value' is surface design, in the sense that if a label or pack has to be printed with something, the ink may as well show something excellent; the best it can possibly be. The corollary is also true: if the surface design is ineffective then it is a constant dampener on the brand's rate of sale; a lead weight that prevents the brand from flying high. The cost is only the once-off cost of developing a superb design; the variable on-cost of such a design can be zero or thereabouts – and so value is added.

Trade brands, especially in the UK, have certainly recognized the importance of design in recent years. A glance through the 1994 edition of *British Packaging*

NOW reveals that around a third of the 250 or so examples chosen are 'brands' of UK retailers. They have recognized the mechanism of added value through design, albeit that they normally want to get increased volume at a lower price as their competitive position versus traditional brands.

Traditional brands have therefore not only got to get the most effective possible surface designs, they have also got to look for other ways to add value, and this can only come from structural innovation, a topic considered in its own right (see pp. 500–1).

The key point to recognize is that most categories are now looking at how to add more structural value: whether it is an easy opening lid on a tin can, an easy to open and close 'stopper' on a cardboard liquid package, a tear-tape to get into a packet of biscuits more easily, or ice-cream packaging that actually keeps the product cold out of the freezer.

What's more, if most companies are moving into more functional packaging innovation, there are a number of consequences: first, better do it faster than the rest of the category to gain competitive advantage; and second, better be sure that it really will be possible to earn a return via a higher price or an increased volume, or both. Otherwise moves like 'easy-open' cans, while giving instant and excellent added value for the consumer, if not charged for, and copied across the category, simply lead to erosion of category profitability.

PACKAGING AND DESIGN PROVIDE AN EXCELLENT MECHANISM FOR CHANGING CATEGORY RULES

Marketing is about creating brand norms that provide safe, secure and shorthand mechanisms for consumers to make quick, confident choices. Brand leaders try to own the high ground in a market, appealing to most people most of the time and trying to capture the combination of the most important needs/ benefits in the market: 'Ivory liquid is gentle on your hands and it washes more plates per penny'. 'Lever 2000 is a family deodorant soap that's gentle on your skin'.

Just as the biggest brands are trying to control their category and continually judging a carefully planned evolutionary approach to brand development and range extensions, the new challengers in the category want to make their presence felt in no uncertain terms. They have something new to offer and therefore have to say it in a new way as well, to gain attention and to be convincing about their new idea.

Packaging offers a superb vehicle for expressing newness and changing the 'rules' of the category. In several markets, most ice-cream was sold in rather large plastic tubs until Haagen Däzs came along with a much smaller tub which was cardboard not plastic. Admittedly the product was excellent – but the nature of the packaging caused a fundamental reappraisal of the premium ice-cream market. And the well-judged size and shape made it extremely tempting to eat individually.

Pet food is sold in tin cans or paper sacks. Several years ago Pedigree Petfoods introduced some new super-premium brands of petfood in small flexible aluminium trays. They changed the category rules and created a new subcategory at a price/feed premium of over 200 per cent.

In Germany, as in most countries in Europe, there is a large edible fats (butter and margarine) market, where for years brands like Rama dominated and created the design rules of the category. Lätta was a healthy half-fat spread (that tasted excellent) and launched a new (more dairy-like) design into the market (it had originally been launched into the Swedish market). It was a credit to Unilever that they marketed both the brand that created the category norms, Rama, and the brand that challenged them, Lätta.

In France the Personal Products Division of Unilever noticed in the late 1970s that men were becoming far more confident in personal grooming and that they demanded a new generation of more sophisticated products to meet their needs. Current brands of aftershave and deodorant lacked the spirit of their new-found confidence. Axe (Lynx in the UK) changed the rules of the male deodorant market and created a new subcategory of male body spray. The key ingredients were the shape of the can, the colour (black), the contrast in finish between can and cap and the surface graphics.

So in conclusion, packaging and design play vital roles in both creating and challenging the category rules, as new generations of consumers and new competitors fight to gain and regain the initiative.

INNOVATION IN MARKETING AS A WHOLE OFTEN FINDS ITS BASIS IN PACKAGING

Apart from 'adding value', one of the other buzz words in marketing today is innovation. Or in other words introducing new and creative ideas that better satisfy consumer needs. Today it is not only legitimate, it is essential to consider such consumer parameters as novelty, fun, secondary uses and user interaction. We have moved on from a world where we are satisfied by the traditional basics of products. It is not enough to wipe on a liquid window cleaner with a cloth: today we expect it in a trigger pump spray with refill docking mechanism to save money longer term. It is not enough to have a plain bar of soap in the shower: today we expect something that opens, closes, dispenses, hangs conveniently and does not expel its contents if the nozzle is inadvertently left open.

Innovation is many different things. Most often it translates itself as a representation of already existing or known parameters. One of the richest sources of innovative inspiration is to combine seemingly uncombinable things. In fact, they can seem so uncombinable that the opportunity may have been dismissed as impossible. For decades dentists in the USA have been telling their patients that the two best substances to clean their teeth were baking soda and peroxide (bleach). And these two ingredients could not possibly live together (they were too reactive). So, end of story.

Unilever persevered, however, with a packaging-led solution to the problem (opportunity). They invented a two-cavity bottle with a pump mechanism that combined the two ingredients at the point of dispensing. Terribly easy in hindsight, but it took a lot of internal energy and some considerable packaging innovation skill to invent exactly the right container.

For years hospitals and medical institutions have been using very small plastic capsules to hold just a few millilitres of a drug or other vital medical substance. This packaging form provided the starting point for Elizabeth Arden to launch its time capsules containing the new generation of anti-ageing ceramides. The packaging form presented the ceramides in exactly the right way: scientific, almost medical, precious, expensive, measured dosage, and with good branding and other balance points to add the necessary degree of cosmetic attractiveness. Other brands have now copied the Arden initiative. Packaging has created a whole new sector.

Packaging has given birth to many other highly innovative ideas in recent years. Müller Yoghurt redefined the meaning of yoghurt and how to eat it with its famous duo-cavity pack. A more expensive, more space inefficient, more factory complex, more trade unfriendly, more wasteful pack – but one that was entirely new and relevant to consumers who were keen to buy a new way of thinking about and individualizing their consumption of yoghurt.

Refills, systems, secondary usage containers, easier to open, easier to store, directable, concentrated, dilute, beer that comes out with a head (as if from draught), pumps, air sprays, microwavable, small portions, big portions – the world is exploding with packaging innovation. And as the pace hots up consumers are demanding more, better, faster than ever before.

BRAND POSITIONING IS KEY: UNDERSTAND POSITIONING BEFORE YOU IDENTIFY THE ROLE OF PACKAGING AND DESIGN

In chapter 30 the point is made that one of the most crucial tasks for any brand's manager is to be clear (and right) about a brand's positioning:

* Is the brand differentiated?
* Is there a clear reason why consumers should buy it?
* Does it satisfy functional and emotional needs?
* Does the brand deliver its promise consistently?

These are some of the most basic marketing questions – and yet they are the ones most frequently ignored by marketers. Successful brands have (or at least once had) clear positionings.

In many cases the packaging will replicate or emphasize the brand's overall positioning, and this is the most frequently occurring relationship. A clear view about positioning means a clear brief to the designer and in turn a creative solution that fits the brand. Body Shop packaging underlines the positioning as earth friendly, straightforward, 'under-marketed', reusable, not wasteful. Sheba petfood comes in small flexible trays that look valuable and almost humanistic and the graphic design looks indulgent and special. The packaging clearly and correctly encapsulates the brand positioning.

Some categories are much more complicated and it will be necessary to understand the packaging as a constituent part of a total communication mix. In these situations it is vital to analyse other communication media such as television advertising in coming to a conclusion about the exact role of packaging. In the beer/lager market, for instance, whereas television will often be used to give a brand a distinctive identity and personality (satisfying the emotional part of the positioning), packaging will communicate authenticity, product values, origins, heritage (satisfying the more functional part). Similarly compare the packaging/advertising mix for Campari and Malibu.

In some brands of cosmetics, the role of television and packaging are complementary with their own distinctive roles. Take Chanel, for instance. The equilibrium achieved by advertising and packaging allows both media to push their individual role to the limit.

All too frequently these complementary roles are not discussed sufficiently, with the respective talents of packaging design and advertising not being combined at an early enough stage. It is, after all, a crucial decision whether the packaging should attempt to 'be the total brand' or, alternatively, play a clearly defined role of emphasis of just one or two specific aspects.

UNDERSTAND YOUR BRAND'S PACKAGING AND DESIGN EQUITIES AND ENSURE THEY ARE PROTECTED

Branding was invented to communicate something specific to a potential purchaser. Early producers of pottery would invent their own special mark to single out their pottery from that of the competition. Over one hundred years ago pioneers of modern branding such as William Hesketh Lever 'branded' various different types of soap with names such as Sunlight and Lifebuoy. Not only were the names deliberately unusual, but the way in which they were written was also unique.

The crucial point is that such a name, styled in such an individualistic way, would allow the brand to be protected by law. In other words there was a solid foundation on which to build the credibility and goodwill of the brand.

Looking around the world today, it is remarkable how companies differ in the importance they place on registering and protecting their brand names and associated 'get-up' (distinctive features). Some have centralized departments that monitor and control the use of brand names and, through ensuring total consistency, make it as difficult as possible to be imitated (especially by trade brands).

Other companies appear to have lost sight of the fact that a consistent use of a brand name, logo style and associated marques or features is the most important legal protection that they can have to ensure their ownership. There are few controls and brand managers around the world appear to have considerable freedom to add their own personal preferences to the brand's basic identity. It is not surprising that the imitators have had such a field day.

There is another crucial point here, beyond the legal one, which has to do with consumers and how they recognize the brands to which they have become loyal or semi-loyal. We know that in the supermarket consumers do not have time to consider every purchase from a fundamental point-of-view. Most often, with limited time, they pick the brands they know. The recognition is produced by a familiar combination of brand name, logo style, colouring and other symbols or features that have come to equal the brand. So it is essential to review whether the heartland 'brand' design is as strong as it should be. Dove cleansing bar does a great job of communicating a name, a unique style, a colour and a symbol clearly and effectively. Pedigree dogfood uses a distinctive typeface, with a 'rosette' symbol in red, on a yellow-gold background. McDonald's uses its famous M symbol, together with a red and yellow colour scheme.

Some brands can be recognized by a symbol alone, although not all great brands have great symbols (Coca-Cola has a famous typeface but not a famous symbol) and not all great symbols are attached to great brands. It is important to note that symbols do not need language to communicate and so they travel around the world. For example, in China the Woolmark is a widely understood and valued symbol.

Finally, it is important to be aware of what the consumer sees as the equities of a brand. This is often completely different from what the brand manager believes that the consumer sees. Change what is important to the consumer at your peril. On the other hand why hold on to design 'clutter' if it has no consumer value?

A checklist of possible packaging and design equities would include the following:

- the shape of the container (e.g. Toilet Duck);
- a distinctive opening device (e.g. Grolsch);
- the packaging material (e.g. Ferrero Rocher);
- the packaging material finish (e.g. Absolut vodka);
- any other distinctive physical features (e.g. the shape of the capsules in Elizabeth Arden time capsules, ceramides);
- the colour of the packaging (e.g. Marlboro);
- the logo style (e.g. Coca-Cola);
- the use of a symbol (e.g. Woolmark);
- the use of a personality (e.g. Colonel Saunders);
- any other surface design feature, possibly more abstract (e.g. the simplicity and elegance of Chanel).

SEE THE ENVIRONMENT AS AN OPPORTUNITY NOT A CONSTRAINT

There is no doubt that there is a clear trend in most of the world today towards more environmentally friendly packaging. There are many manifestations:

- Less bulk: simply using less material.
- Removal of secondary packaging: why sell toothpaste in two containers when it is perfectly OK sold in one?
- Concentration: concentrated detergents now use less than half the packaging material compared to before.
- Reusable: many products are now sold in a 'first time' box/tin/jar, which can then be replenished via a 'refill' pack.
- Secondary usage (especially important in developing markets): design the packaging for its original purpose and for a secondary purpose (e.g. a storage jar).
- Recyclable: design the material and its construction so that it can be collected back in and either reused directly or reprocessed.
- Bulk or home delivery: the ultimate non-use of packaging, but not yet commonplace.

There are other manifestations which involve clever new materials, more space-efficient shapes and so on – and in some markets, in some countries, there is a certain competitive advantage to be had in being rated as 'environmentally friendly'.

There is no point in the marketer ignoring these environmental trends. They should not be viewed as constraints but rather as challenges and opportunities. The new rules and new sensitivities will apply to everyone, so the race is still on to do it better, cheaper and more effectively than the competition. Innovation in environmentally sensitive packaging will be a key area in which to gain competitive advantage in the future.

IT IS NOT ENOUGH TO BE INDIVIDUALLY EFFECTIVE: PACKAGING ALSO HAS TO WORK AT THE POINT OF SALE

The point has already been made (on page 498) that packaging has a vital role to play at the point of purchase. Far too much emphasis is given to the design process as to how a pack looks and feels individually, and not nearly enough emphasis to the need to stand out and communicate in store. These objectives are not alternatives: they are both crucial. Consideration must be given to impact and display value, as well as the detailed and more subtle features of the individual pack. There are a number of points that should be taken into account:

- How will the packaging look in a mass display? Will the colour form a 'block' of colour to stand out effectively (e.g. Kodak film)?

- Will the design structure work in a mass display? The OXO logo works well on a box and in combination where all the letters join up: OXOXOXOXO.
- Will the mass effect stand out from competition? If everyone else is coloured, then is it better to be white? If the category language for cooking oil is yellow, what will consumers think of red (a real example from Italy)?
- Will the packs stack neatly and be space efficient for the shop? Some cans fit one into the other – they are far more easy to stack than ones that do not have this feature.
- Will the brand name and/or sub-brand and/or variety be clearly and unmistakably recognizable, not only from a couple of centimetres but also a metre or so? This is especially true about brands that offer a wide range of varieties.

There are two golden rules: truly understand the trade/selling arena first, before the packaging is designed or changed. Second, judge and test the new designs in a selling arena as well as individually.

EFFECTIVE PACKAGING IS ONE OF THE MOST DIFFICULT PARTS OF THE MIX TO PROGRESS IN COMPANIES: IT CONCERNS ALMOST EVERY DISCIPLINE

Most of the headings considered in this chapter make points about the substance of packaging itself. In large corporations, however, the key to developing great packaging lies in how the resources of the organization are utilized. This is because, unlike, say, advertising, packaging development can impinge on almost every department, especially if it involves physical structure. There are a number of key process requirements:

- Understand the role and expertise of all the various disciplines involved (e.g. production, packaging development, distribution, supply chain, customer marketing, consumer marketing, PR).
- Ensure senior manager sponsorship for the changes or developments that are proposed.
- Involve everyone at an early stage and establish a 'teamwork' *modus operandi*.
- Be clear about objectives, responsibilities, time scales, costs and record them regularly in writing.
- Establish clear leadership of the team so that the pace and direction of activities can be judged.

The more organized and systematic the process, the easier it will be to be innovative and creative. When all the key players are involved and confident about proposed changes, then it is far easier to take more adventurous and courageous decisions.

USE SUPPLIERS AND OUTSIDE ADVISORS FOR NEW IDEAS AND INDUSTRY EXPERIENCE

The experts are often involved far too late in the process. The world is changing very fast. Artwork can now be sent around the world at the touch of a button. The top design companies working with the best clients have computerized interaction so that design can be appraised simultaneously and amended by agency and client in collaboration.

New materials such as polymers and laminates are appearing faster and faster; new ways of opening and closing; longer-life storage; more efficient distribution; more cost-effective use of materials; more environmentally friendly materials: 'Should I move away from steel and into aluminium? Or vice versa? Is paper better than plastic? If plastic is better, can I make it look like paper? Should I have a budget for a widget or a gadget?'

There are three broad streams of expertise: the suppliers of the packaging (sometimes including the suppliers of the packaging production equipment); the agencies and consultants who develop the physical packaging and the surface graphics; and the agencies and consultants who research and help clients judge whether new ideas are more effective from a consumer and customer point-of-view.

The suppliers have a perspective across a broad range of industries and will be able to offer guidance on trends and preferences. They have their own innovation processes and are often on the lookout for breakthrough ideas themselves. They can sometimes be persuaded to channel their new ideas into an exclusivity deal with a top customer.

The packaging/design agencies form an extensive industry around the world, with over a thousand separate companies in operation. Again it is important to do one's homework before deciding on exactly who to work with. A possible list of questions could be:

- Do I need physical development or surface graphics, or both?
- Do I need a high level of creativity and design flair?
- Do I need purely packaging advice, or marketing as well?
- Do I need international expertise, with the ability to translate languages and work cross-border?
- Do I need specific expertise in one particular category (e.g. food, ice-cream, cosmetics)?
- Do I need an agency with full digital capability that can send me artwork, in colour, instantly?
- Is a high level of confidentiality/security important?
- Is this a job to try out someone new, or do I need the confidence of one of my regular suppliers?

The marketing and research agencies who will help a client to evaluate both current packaging and future ideas is the other crucial outside source of expertise. Some experts in the industry have stated that research is unnecessary. However, the writer of this chapter has the opposite view with the usual caveat that research should not dictate a decision – rather research informs and shapes a decision. Many sensitive and reliable techniques have been developed using audit, qualitative and quantitative research. The best processes are often when packaging/design agency, marketing/research agency, other suppliers and client all work together as a team.

AN INTERNATIONAL POINT: THE WORLD IS GETTING SMALLER AND BRANDS NEED TO HARMONIZE CROSS-COUNTRY BOUNDARIES

Some of the most successful designs are managed on a global basis, both from a legal and a consumer point-of-view. Kodak is the same colour yellow throughout the world. McDonald's M can be recognized in Tokyo and Tahiti. The Woolmark stands for pure new wool in China and Barlaston, where Wedgwood make china, and are famous for their Wedgwood blue, which is extremely popular in Tokyo. Satellite television, global sponsorship, increasing trans-global production, an increasingly mobile and knowledgeable consumer, and the need to produce goods more cost effectively are some of the influences upon multinational companies to work towards global harmonization.

The problem of a global image has been less difficult for companies in sectors such as cosmetics and luxury goods (where such an image has been part of the brand's prestige from the very beginning), than in more mundane sectors such as food, detergents, functional personal products or paper products. Here, multinational companies were often organized on a country-by-country basis, with each local unit arguing the case for why they should be different from everyone else. This led to a massive proliferation in packaging and design, making it virtually impossible to centralize sales, production or communication.

For most sectors the key objective should be 'glocalization'. This means adopting a global approach, a global vision and global harmonization wherever it is common sense so to do, but at the same time being sensitive to the local culture in such areas as (obviously) language, recipe fine tuning (e.g. sweetness, strength of flavour), perfume note/strength and cultural insensitivities.

Achievement of localized packaging needs strong global leadership with the ability and power to direct the global process, while being sensitive and aware of local needs. The key is that the former precedes the latter, and not the other way round.

507

SUMMARY

Most fastmoving consumer goods (FMCG) companies spend considerable sums of money in variable packaging costs, sometimes many times more than the amount spent on theme advertising. As marketing becomes more competitive, it is imperative that companies renew their focus and commitment.

REFERENCES

Booth-Clibborn, E. (1993) *British Packaging Now*, Internos Books Ltd.

FURTHER READING

Coleman, Lipuma, Segal & Morrill, Inc (1994) *Package Design and Brand Identity*, Rockport Publishers.
Harckham, A. W. (1989) *Packaging Strategy – Meeting the Challenge of Changing Times*, Technomic Publishing Company.
Olins, W. (1989) *Corporate Identity*, London: Thames and Hudson.
Paine, F. A. (1981) *Fundamentals of Packaging*, Leicester: Brookside Press Ltd.
Pynor, R. and Booth-Clibborn, E. (1991) *Typography Now: the next wave*, Internos Books.
Wozencroft, I. (1992) *The Graphic Language of Neville Brody*, London: Thames and Hudson.

30

BRANDING AND BRAND MANAGEMENT

Mark Sherrington

Marketing has come to be seen as the central business discipline. The marketing function acts as a sort of 'gearbox', making a profitable connection between a company's core competencies and the needs of the market. For most marketers brands are the cogs in the gearbox. Brands and brand marketing lie at the heart of business and many of the world's best known companies, Unilever, Procter and Gamble, Mars, are structured around their brands.

Companies become attractive take-over targets and the value of their stock rises because of the strength of their brands. Some have even gone as far as putting a balance sheet value on their brands to reflect this. Branding is most commonly associated with consumer goods companies, but in fact the notion of branding has now gone well beyond this narrow view. Service industries have discovered and exploited the power of branding. Where previously they relied on their corporate name to differentiate themselves in the market they have now developed brands and sub-brands. Indeed, in every industry the importance of the corporate brand itself has been recognized and much of the theory of branding in consumer goods and services has been applied to corporations and many other organizations, even charities. If one understands brands one understands that Oxfam is as much a brand as Coca-Cola.

So what is a brand, what are the features of great brands and what is their value to companies and consumers? Let us take consumers as our starting-point, as any good marketer would do, and look at the history of brands.

THE VALUE OF BRANDS TO CONSUMERS – AN HISTORICAL PERSPECTIVE

The act of marking a product with a device that signifies its origins is branding and the value to consumers is that it assists and simplifies choice. When in Roman times artisans signed or in some other way identified their produce they branded it and in so doing they helped consumers to pick out their products if they had been given a recommendation by a friend (the most powerful form of

509

advertising), or find them again if they had tried them, appreciated them and wished to repeat the experience. Branding for consumers represents the mark of a given level of quality and value that helps them choose between one product and another. Even in Roman times consumers were required to make so many purchase decisions and, like any sensible consumer, did not want to risk a bad experience (a poor quality chariot?); branding had real utility for them as a simplifier of choice.

In more recent times Lord Lever branded his soap in order to provide his target consumers with a way of recognizing it from the many, poorer quality alternatives. He even advertised the soap to gain widespread acclaim for it, using the advertising to imply values that went beyond the mere cleansing characteristics. He implied that a certain type of person used Sunlight Soap which made you feel a certain way, thereby endowing it with outer directed and inner directed emotional values to add to the established functional cleaning values. Unfortunately, this was no help to him if the shopkeeper, upon whom many customers relied for advice, recommended a competitive brand, and while the retail trade operated in this way the power of brands was restricted. The advent of the self-service supermarket signalled the start of the golden age of brands since the consumer had to rely on them more and more to guide their choice.

Thus, the fundamental driving force behind brands is that they have utility for consumers. Life would not only be duller, it would be a good deal more complicated without brands. Imagine how long the weekly grocery shop would take if everything came in unmarked brown packages?

THE VALUE OF BRANDS TO COMPANIES

Brands also have utility for the company. Consumers' loyalty to a brand based on their experience of it gives the brand protection against new rivals. This loyalty will decay if in reality the brand is no better than its competitors, but that may take some time during which the company can rebuild its competitive advantage.

The other advantage of brands is that they allow companies to target different groups of consumers, or segments of the market, with different branded offerings. Not everyone has the same needs, outlook on life or budgets. In every market, even water, particular groups of consumers can be persuaded to pay more if they believe they will get more. Developing more than one brand enables a company to segment a market and target different consumers. As long as they add more value than cost for these new segments, they will increase their overall profitability. It also enables the company to defend itself from competitors seeking to do the same. This use of different brands to segment and dominate markets is very evident in areas such as detergents, confectionery and petfoods, where companies like Unilever and Mars have a large portfolio of brands competing in the same product category but aimed at different groups of consumers.

The development of a portfolio of discrete brands has further advantages for the company. It enables them to insulate the problems of one product from the rest of the range (as Johnson & Johnson were able to do during the Tylenol product tampering scare in the USA) and it can allow them to sell off brands (as SmithKline Beecham were able to do with Marmite). However, there is a limit to the number of brands a company will want to have since each brand has a fixed cost in terms of the investment needed to differentiate it and communicate its uniqueness. Heinz has predominantly gone down the road of developing one 'umbrella' house brand, while companies such as Ford and Kellogg have a house brand with various sub-brands. The advantages and disadvantages of different approaches to brand structures is returned to below.

By developing a range of brands to cover different consumer segments a company can be well positioned to benefit from changing consumer needs. Silk Cut was a small part of Gallagher's portfolio for many years before concerns over smoking generally, and tar content in particular, made it one of the company's major profit earners. This leads on to consideration of brands as a means of resource allocation within a company. Competing companies are themselves the mechanism whereby scarce resources are allocated to the best performing areas in a capitalist economy. Brands perform the same function within a company. Resources can be taken from an underperforming brand and directed at a growth brand to achieve higher returns. The Boston Consulting Group developed a model that enables a company to group sectors or brands into four quadrants ranging from 'Star' to 'Dog' as a way of deciding strategic investment priorities.

THE VALUE OF BRANDS – A SUMMARY

- Brands have value to consumers as a way of identifying a given and consistent level of quality that simplifies choice.
- This builds consumer loyalty, which provides a company with a degree of profit protection over time.
- Developing a portfolio of brands can enable a company to target different consumer segments, thereby increasing share and profit, and providing a defence against competition.
- Some companies will seek to dominate their market through one house brand and a range of products or sub-brands. This gives economies of scale but carries risks if an individual product fails.
- Brands are a means whereby finite investment resources are allocated within a company.

THE FEATURES OF GREAT BRANDS

Value performance

Behind every great brand is a great product. So much has now been written about the clever use of advertising to hype marginal benefits and develop brand personalities that will inflate consumer demand that the real product perform- ance is often neglected. Every great, durable brand either has or has had for a significant part of its history a demonstrable and well-recognized product advantage. Mercedes may now sell many cars on the basis of what they say about the purchaser, but the fact is that for many years they were a better engineered car compared to any of an equivalent price, and it is this reputation, jealously maintained through successive product improvements, that provides the foundation for customer loyalty. As noted above, this loyalty will decay over time if Japanese cars continue to erode or even overtake the product lead Mercedes have enjoyed, but it is this well-earned reputation that sustains sales in the face of tough competition, and all other values are based on it.

To go further, Mercedes are excellent value for money, which shows the foolishness of those who talk about 'value brands' when they mean lower value. All brands are bought because their consumers believe them to be best value. Consumers have different hierarchies of needs and different budgets, which allow for different brands in a market. However, consumers have also learnt that market competition usually ensures you get what you pay for. There are of course many subtleties of positioning but in essence there is a value curve in any market and to be a great brand you have to be on it or at least in the 'combat zone'. A simple example for the car market is given in Figure 1, showing how

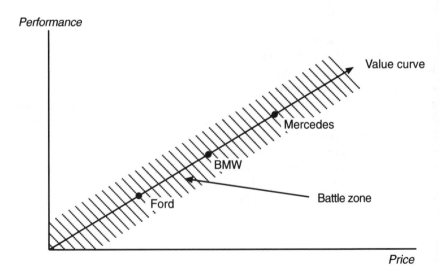

Figure 1   The value curve ('You get what you pay for!')

512

Ford, BMW and Mercedes are positioned on the value curve.

As shown in Figure 1 each brand is successful, each offers great value (i.e. for a given price each gives the best value performance where performance is the summary of all the characteristics a consumer looks for in a car). Based on past reputation a brand may, for a limited period, operate below the line, but only because at some point in its history the brand operated above the line, which is to say that for a given price it gave the customer more. It is upon this competitive advantage, current or past, real or perceived, that its brand credentials have been built.

Highest common factors

For the purpose of explaining the value curve, the idea of performance being an aggregate of what people look for in a car was used, the implication being that consumers then have the choice to buy different amounts. In reality consumers are often asked to make trade-offs between possible benefits. One can either have the personal service of a small airline company at a higher price or the convenience of a large airline carrier at a lower price. These trade-offs are what allow brands to adopt different positioning targeted at different consumers with different needs, attitudes and budgets. However, the big durable brands stay big by keeping most of the people happy most of the time. In other words, they offer consumers a higher common factor between two or more conflicting benefits. To use the airline example, British Airways tries to convey the convenience of the big airline with the service one would expect only from a smaller carrier, the overall proposition being 'The world's favourite airline'. Apple computers offer leading-edge technology that is easy and fun to use. Many detergent brands including Persil and Fairy offer tough cleaning yet with care for the item they are used upon.

In this way the big brands will try to dominate the high ground of the market. Smaller brands will then position themselves on one of the dimensions (e.g. the best efficiency but at the expense of care, or the most care but at the expense of efficiency). The new entrant will try and change the rules by introducing a new dimension (e.g. a deodorizing perfume, or care for the environment). Big brands react to this by relaunching to include the new benefit. However, if, in functional terms, there is a real trade-off between existing benefits and the new one (better care for the environment can only be delivered at the expense of cleaning efficiency, to take the example above) then the new brand can successfully defend its new positioning in the market and the market ground rules will have changed.

Spiritual reward

Life is not all about rationality and functionality. People seek experiences that make them feel better about themselves, and outward expressions that

513

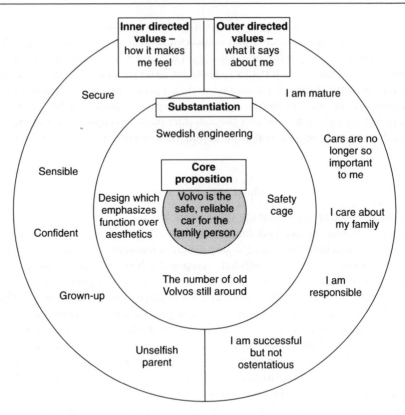

Figure 2 Volvo brand proposition

communicate their self-worth to others. In a way not to be overly exaggerated brands help us in this. A mother will reassure herself that she is doing the best for her family by buying brands that reinforce this (OXO or Persil) and will want that brand to communicate this to her family and friends. The successful businessman will want to reward himself and communicate his success to his peers through purchase of a Rolex watch. These are the so-called inner directed and outer directed values that brands can deliver. In their own small way they nourish the soul.

As already outlined, these values spring from, and work symbiotically with, the product values. Persil's caring values originally came from its soap-based formula, which made the clothes not just clean but nicer to wear. Mercedes' status values came from the fact that the company did indeed offer better engineering and more comfort for those with the means to afford it. These non-functional values, like the functional ones, are intrinsic to the brand and are reinforced by the other people that use the brand and what they say about it. They can of course be amplified by advertising and other forms of promotion.

The brand value, its distinctive competitive advantage, is referred to as its positioning. There are many different ways to express this, such as the way you would expect a consumer to describe the brand to a friend. Figure 2 demonstrates another useful approach. The centre circle contains the summary of the brand proposition; the next layer shows the various things in the brand that substantiate the proposition at a functional level; the outer layer contains the non-functional values that come from the substantiation (i.e. what the brand says about the purchasers and how it makes them feel).

Distinctive added value

The essence of a great brand is therefore its ability to target this rounded package of functional and non-functional values at particular groups of consumers. At the heart of the brand is a core set of beliefs that represent its distinctive proposition to its target consumers, which is supported by the tangible things that substantiate the proposition, and the intangible, that is inner and outer directed values.

What distinguishes the brand from the commodity is that it has added values. In functional terms these values add cost, since extra performance adds manufacturing cost. However, the skilful manufacturer, by focusing on and understanding the needs of the target customers better than the competition, can create functional advantages so unique that they command a price premium. In other words, more value than cost is added. This value is further increased through the unique non-functional attributes that the brand offers.

This added value must be communicated to consumers in a distinctive way. How do you know that the unique properties of a Rolex watch are relevant to you, that its expensive craftsmanship and style will reward you and signify your success to your friends, if you and they cannot recognize it from any other watch? The basis of this recognition lies in the product itself – its visual identity. Experiments show that consumers only have to be able to see the smallest fraction of a famous brand's logo or some other aspect of its design to be able to recognize it. Just the combination of colours in thin stripes will tell you that the computer is an Apple; just the glimpse of the 'd' in Dunhill will tell you that the belt or tie is made by Dunhill. Marlboro have invested a huge amount of advertising and sponsorship money to ensure that the colour red will conjure up the brand in your mind. Great brands have evolved very distinctive liveries to ensure that the added value they offer is instantly recognized.

Coherent brand mix

With real product performance plus the intangible values that come from this, and distinctive packaging design as the foundation blocks, brands can also use the other elements of what is called the 'brand mix' to communicate the total proposition. Two have already been touched on.

515

First, price is part of the brand mix since it works in conjunction with the other elements to determine the value equation. Second, there is promotion which covers all aspects of paid-for advertising as well as free support from opinion formers such as the press, and sales promotion – although not so much the tactical money-off sort but rather promotional schemes that make a statement about the brand (e.g. the chance to win tickets to a rock concert from Pepsi).

The place you see a brand and indeed the people you see using it also communicate the proposition. This explains why Rodeo Drive in Hollywood, St Honoré in Paris and Bond Street in London command such high rent premiums from the luxury goods brands who have shops there, and also why marketers will 'seed' the brand with aspirational figures to gain acceptance from the masses. These Six Ps of the brand mix – product, packaging, price, promotion, place, people – are all employed consistently and coherently by the great brands to communicate and reinforce their competitive advantage.

Summary

- Great brands are based on performance and value. Even if over time their performance advantage has been competed away, a great brand will have residual consumer loyalty based on perceptions of superior product performance and value. This reputation is durable but not everlasting.
- Brands attempt to dominate the high ground of a market by offering the highest common factor between conflicting benefit areas (e.g. hi-tech but easy to use, efficient but caring).
- Based on functional advantages brands develop inner and outer directed values (how they make you feel and what they say about you). These added values, both functional and non-functional, separate brands from commodities.
- It follows therefore that strong brands can command a price premium or at the very least a higher volume for an equivalent price.
- Great brands develop very distinctive visual identities that act as the summary of their brand proposition (i.e. their added values).
- Brands use all aspects of the brand mix consistently and coherently to communicate their proposition.

This summary can also be expressed as a very practical checklist for a brand.

1 Does the brand have performance that is recognized as superior by its target consumers in blind (unbranded) product trials?
2 Are those performance advantages closely aligned to what consumers say are the key parameters upon which they make purchase decisions?
3 Does the brand have a personality which the consumer sees as motivating in the context of the product category (a loving mother for a range of baby products, a successful sportsperson for a high performance car)? Note that

in small research groups this can be tested by asking consumers to describe the brand as a person if it came to life.

4 Does the consumer believe the brand is purchased by other consumers that they regard as aspirational?

5 Does the brand charge a price premium and/or have a significant volume share lead over other brands in its market segment (at least a 2 to 1 sales advantage)?

6 Does it have a significantly higher loyalty profile (e.g. a greater proportion of its consumers who chose it in more than three out of their last five purchases in the case of grocery category, or a higher propensity to repurchase in the case of a consumer durable)?

7 Is the brand instantly recognizable among its target consumers through just small portions of its visual identity?

8 Is every aspect of its brand mix communicating all or at least a significant part of its proposition? Note that brands can use different aspects of the mix, even different media, to emphasize certain values.

If the answer to any of these questions is negative then the brand may still continue to deliver profit but it is living on borrowed time.

HIERARCHY OF BRAND INFORMATION

It has been established that a brand is a bundle of values that makes it distinctive and this distinction is communicated through a bundle of elements known as the brand mix. Within the values there is a hierarchy that will vary with each brand (the intangible or non-functional elements are more important for a perfume, and the tangible or functional elements are more important for a parachute). So it is with the elements within the brand mix. Figure 3 sets out a fuller list of

Product		Examples		
		Country of origin	Germany	UK	France
Packaging		Manufacturer/ corporate brand	VW	ICI	LMVH
Price					
Promotion		Brand	Golf	Dulux	Moët & Chandon
Place (distribution)		Sub-brand/ descriptor	Gti	Gloss finish	Medium-bodied
People (users)		Product	5-door small car	Indoor and outdoor paint	Champagne

Figure 3   Hierarchy of information

517

elements (but by no means comprehensive) that in total communicate the brand. Examples are given that expand on the product related, 'from where', part of the brand information.

In the case of the car the specific descriptor or sub-brand (see Brand Structures, page 521) Gti is more important than Golf, which is in turn more important than VW. The country of origin also plays a role, since other brands of cars have established a reputation for Germany as a source of reliable, well-engineered cars. German origin is part of what distinguishes the Golf Gti from other rivals made in, say, Japan or Italy, since for cars, as for many other product categories, the countries themselves have brand identities.

In the case of the paint the primary focus is on Dulux. That it is 'Gloss finish' and for indoor/outdoor use is quite important information but probably only after the brand choice has already been made. The corporate brand, ICI, has a role in the hierarchy of information but the country of origin, the UK, is not important at all.

For the wine its French origins are vital, as is the fact that it is a champagne. However, its parent brand LMVH is not really relevant at all and Moët & Chandon is not as important a part of the brand proposition for this wine as Gti is for the car, or Dulux is for the paint.

Thus, there is a hierarchy of brand information that must be understood through research and reflected through other elements of the mix such as packaging design and advertising. Over time the hierarchy can be changed through the actions of the brand owner and the attitudes of consumers. Australia has been made a feature of some beers, but Germany is no longer relevant to cameras because consumers have become more interested in electronic rather than optical features.

BRAND RANGE EXTENSION

A variant of a brand is the provision of extra choice within the same product category that essentially leaves the core brand proposition untouched, for example the addition of a new peach flavour to an ice-cream brand. The intrinsic values of the ice-cream remain the same but you can now enjoy a new peach flavour if you happen to like peaches. Where the new product within the brand range is addressing different needs, and in so doing changes the way people see the brand, this is a range extension. The addition to the ice-cream brand of a new line of flavours based on alcoholic drinks for eating on special occasions and called 'After Hours' would make quite a difference to the way one would view the 'parent' brand which had been originally positioned as, for example, the most fun ice-cream for children.

Range extensions can therefore be aimed quite close to the original or parent brand, perhaps just to a new segment within the same product category, or can carry the brand into a new category altogether. The two golden rules are that the brand must have values that in part or whole are relevant to the new segment

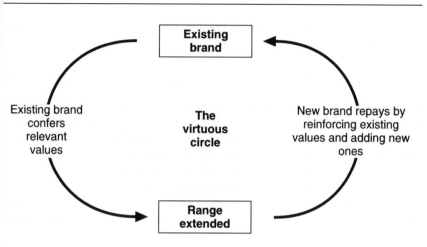

Figure 4   Brand range extension

or market, and that the new range extension enhances or adds back to the core brand. Since brands are now regarded as valuable assets for a company, financial analogies in branding are often used. The core brand values, carefully nurtured over many years, are often referred to as the 'brand equity' and represent a sort of 'capital account'. As well as ensuring that the parent brand core equity has relevance for the new segment, the new range extension should repay the capital account and build the total brand equity. Good examples of range extensions or 'equity stretch' that obeyed the golden rules are Marks and Spencer foods and Mars ice-cream; bad examples are Cadbury's Smash (instant potatoes) and Levi suits.

The decision to range extend an existing brand rather than exploit a new opportunity through launching a different brand is a cost-benefit analysis. Studies have shown that significant savings can be made in launching a range extension compared to a new brand since the extension needs less advertising to establish its credentials. Success rates too can be higher for the range extension as consumers are less resistant to try a new product from a name they trust. However, this line of thinking can be dangerous. Companies can be tempted into underestimating the investment needed and overestimating the relevance of the parent brand values to the new market. Despite the risks and costs it can still be better to launch a new brand. Unilever have been able to develop a very profitable global shampoo brand, Timotei, based on care, where they might have been tempted to try and seize the same opportunity with their Pears brand, which had similar credentials but was seen as old-fashioned in a sector that demanded modernity. Procter and Gamble, on the other hand, were able to do the reverse by using the Vidal Sassoon brand and its salon credentials to establish 'Wash & Go', where new brands from competitors had failed to overcome consumer scepticism that just one product could successfully clean and condition hair.

BRAND STRETCH AND LIMITS TO RANGE EXTENSION

Warning notes have been sounded about range extensions that fail to live up to the core brand values and thereby risk killing the original brand. In reality there are few examples of this because most range extension has occurred on well-established brands which can withstand even quite big failures (witness the disastrous Coca-Cola relaunch which resulted in consumers demanding the return of the original). On the positive side range extensions can revitalize tired brands by clearly demonstrating the core values of the brand and establishing new ones. Dunhill, having started as a range of tobacco products including a well-crafted lighter, has developed into a global luxury goods brand for men covering clothing, watches and even a successful fragrance. In research the technique of asking consumers to react to the use of a brand on many different types of products is used to disclose what consumers really think about the brand. One study revealed that crunch was the core property of a potato crisp rather than its potato taste since consumers were able to relate to it as a biscuit more easily than they could as a new oven chip.

As well as revealing the core values, these types of study also show the degree of stretch in a brand. In principle any brand can extend into any market if one has the time, commitment and money to invest, but its inherent elasticity will tell you how long, how hard and how much it will take, and can help show the steps on the way. (See Figure 5.) The Dunhill brand moved from lighters to

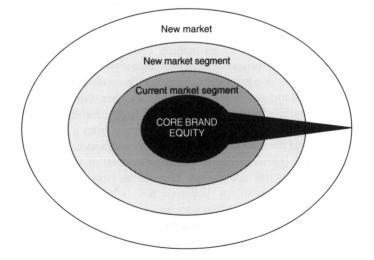

Figure 5 As a brand moves further from its currrent market segment it stretches its equity. Brand elasticity varies and can be enhanced over time with successive moves

520

accessories such as pens and cufflinks, then to belts and ties, a blazer and eventually a full range of menswear. Through range extension Dunhill was able to find a higher order of brand values, such as British craftsmanship and style, on which to build its brand, rather than remain locked into smoking requisites. Lucozade was able to develop energy from a health drink to launch a new range of isotonic sports drinks. However, where a brand becomes so closely associated with the product characteristics of its category its elasticity can be low. It is harder to see Ford as a range of consumer electronics than it is, for example, to see Sony as a car.

BRAND STRUCTURES

When range extending a brand the issue of brand structure needs to be carefully considered. There are two questions that must be addressed. The first is what to call the new range extension. Should it just be given a descriptor, e.g. 'Heinz Baked Beans', where 'Baked Beans' is the descriptor, or a sub-brand, e.g. 'Ford Scorpio', where 'Scorpio' is a sub-brand. 'Scorpio' is a sub-brand because it is a new name that means nothing in the context of cars, although it may start to suggest certain things, and so gives the opportunity to add new values, in this case values relevant to the luxury executive car market. There is an option in between, the 'ownable descriptor' (e.g. 'Heinz Big Soup'). 'Big Soup' is semi-descriptive of what it is but still offers the vehicle whereby Heinz can segment the market and offer new values, in this case a more male-orientated soup that can be a meal in itself. By dint of the fact that different companies have successfully employed different approaches (Heinz, Kellogg, Unilever and others have employed all three), each route is viable but each has different implications.

The descriptor does not allow for much that is new to be said about the brand. Heinz Baked Beans conjures up nothing new about Heinz. On the other hand, if one's experience of the product is good it translates instantly into an enhanced view of Heinz. Ford needed to say something different to make the brand appropriate to a successful business executive wanting to trade up to a more prestigious car such as a Mercedes or BMW. Scorpio afforded Ford the opportunity to position a new car for these consumers. However, a good experience of a Scorpio does not instantly transfer back into an enhanced view of Ford as a brand. The consumers, by having a sub-brand to refer to, can tell their friends that while the Scorpio is a great car they are still not sold on Ford generally.

The test of the relationship between the range extension and the parent brand is whether the name of the range extension is sufficient in itself to allow consumers to get what they want. Ask for baked beans and you may or may not get Heinz; ask for a Scorpio and you will get only the Ford Scorpio. The ownable descriptor operates somewhere in the middle. Leaving aside retail copies, 'Frosties' will get you Kellogg's Frosties. The experience of it will also

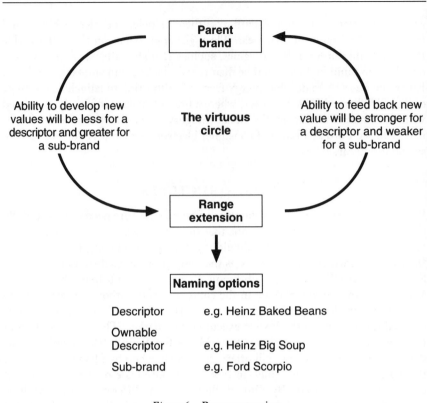

Figure 6   Range extension

feed directly back into Kellogg and add to the core equity of the child values which the range extension embodies. The consumer will say 'Frosties' but will visualize 'Kellogg's Frosties'.

The decision of which option to take (and it must be noted that there are 'shades of grey' between the three options outlined) will therefore depend on how appropriate are the values of the parent brand to the new segment or market, whether the range extension needs to be able to express new values on the one hand, and the degree to which one wants those new values to feed back into the parent brand on the other.

The second question to be addressed in brand structures follows from the analysis used to determine the name for the range extension. What weight in communication and especially the packaging should be given to the parent brand and the range extension? This refers back to the idea of a hierarchy of information. The options range from full endorsement where the parent brand is most prominent (e.g. 'Kodak Gold'), to recessive endorsement (e.g. 'Lexus, the Luxury Car from Toyota') where the sub-brand is most prominent, with options in between. The key factor is the relevance of the parent brand values.

Where they are wholly appropriate, as in the case of Kodak, the manufacturer is only too keen to see positive product experience feed directly back into the parent brand (and make savings in marketing costs since sub-brands need more support than descriptors). Where the parent values are not wholly relevant the manufacturer will allow the parent brand to take a back seat and the sub-brand to develop new values which will slowly enhance the parent brand.

Corporate branding adds another dimension to the issue of brand structures. There are many examples where the brand structure falls into several tiers, the corporate brand, parent brand, sub-brand, with possibly even product descriptors and country of origin. The principles are the same in arriving at the hierarchy of brand information. To a certain extent the decisions rest on consumer attitudes but the brand owner can make choices about how to manage these attitudes through use of the brand mix which will in total communicate the overall brand proposition.

RANGE EXTENSION AND BRAND STRUCTURES – A SUMMARY

- A range extension is where the new addition to the range changes the core values of the parent brand.
- The values of the parent brand should be relevant in part or whole to the new segment or market and the range extension should reinforce and enhance the parent brand's core values or 'equity'.
- Range extending rather than launching a new brand offers cost savings and a lower risk of failure but, while riskier, a new brand can give higher returns if the parent brand values do not fully stretch to the new market opportunity.
- Different brands have different elasticities, that is the ability to stretch their core values to exploit new segments or markets. The elasticity can be changed and improved over time depending on commitment, investment and the sequence of moves made.
- Choosing whether to give the range extension a descriptive name or a sub-brand name depends on the appropriateness of the core brand values and the degree to which the extension is required to feed new values back to the parent. This also determines the weight to put behind the parent versus the range extension in the information hierarchy.

BRANDING IN SERVICE INDUSTRIES

Quite deliberately the emphasis up to this point has been on consumer goods brands since the theory of branding has largely been developed in this area. In service industries the historical approach has been to rely on the corporate brand with simple descriptions of services beneath it. However, the acquisition of a range of service brands by companies such as BET in the area of industrial services or Sears in retail, has required the brand owners to address the branding issues more seriously. Sears has a number of retail brands (including four in the UK just in the area of womenswear) which need to be positioned and developed. Furthermore, sub-brands have been used within service brands just as in consumer goods brands to target particular consumer groups, for example McDonald's 'Happy Meals' or 'McPizza'.

There are two key differences about branding in service sectors. First, the brand mix is significantly more complex. Consider retail where the brand proposition is conveyed by a very wide range of factors such as store ambience, range stocked, display, returns policy, opening hours and many more. Second, the importance of the various elements and the hierarchy of information, is often very different. Advertising is an important part of consumer goods branding as a means to communicate brand values and generate trial, but in retail it is relatively less important since consumers can experience the total offering just by walking into the store. Probably the most important element in the brand mix in any service industry is staff. In most cases they are the brand for consumers and are therefore the single most important means by which brand values are communicated. Interestingly, Marks and Spencer have built one of the most successful retail brands in the world with no advertising but they do have a widely admired staff loyalty.

Thus, in many ways brand development is more complex in service companies than in consumer goods companies. The difficulty of this task is often increased by the fact that the marketing department has a more limited role, with its remit being in the 'marketing services' of research and promotions, while product development, the key part of marketing, is made the responsibility of other functions.

BRAND MANAGEMENT

Returning to consumer goods, the brand management system that most companies employ was developed by Procter and Gamble in the USA. A typical organizational structure is illustrated in Figure 7.

Each brand will have a brand manager who will get involved with every aspect of the company's operation which has a bearing on the brand. This is virtually every other area since, as has been outlined above, the brand mix incorporates everything from product development to sales and distribution. The brand manager has been likened to the managing director of their particular brand, responsible for everything from strategic development to bottom-line profitability. Thus the brand manager will look at the organization as depicted in Figure 8.

The analogy of marketing as the gearbox of the business holds true for the brand manager who will work with the full range of the business functions and will employ a wide range of external help and information to create forward energy behind the brand.

In truth this model of brand management is breaking down and was never

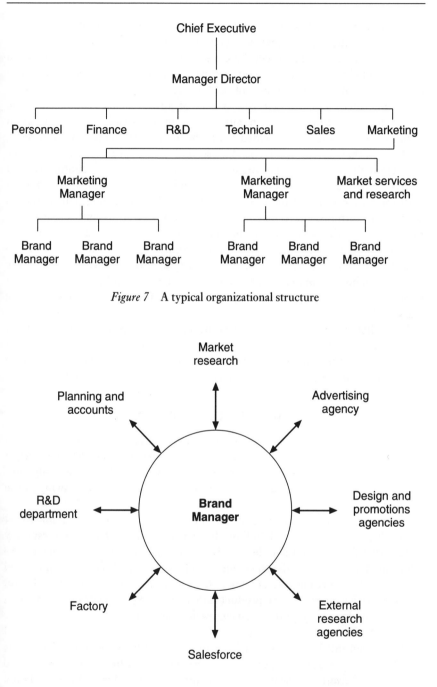

Figure 7　A typical organizational structure

Figure 8　Brand manager's role within an organization

appropriate for one-brand companies. As noted above, this includes many service companies, where a matrix structure is used with more than one function owning the decisions that affect the development of the brand. However, even for the multi-brand consumer goods companies the traditional role of the brand manager is changing. In the first place the brand is too important to be left to brand managers alone. Their role is one of advocacy, using their intimate knowledge of all aspects of the brand to make business cases for the allocation of finite resources that are decided by the board against competing cases being made by other brand teams. In the second place, many brands are now international, global even, and brand management has become another type of matrix involving multinational as well as multi-functional teams. In common with most aspects of business the new order in brand management is one of continually forming and reforming project teams geared to innovation events through which the business and the brands attempt to fulfil agreed strategies. To ensure that there is still good stewardship of the brand in these more complex international business structures many companies have appointed very senior franchise or brand group managers to be responsible for formulating strategy that is then implemented by local brand teams across several geographic markets.

Nevertheless, brand management is increasingly the prime responsibility of the chief executives, since it is they who are ultimately responsible to shareholders for maximizing the return on assets employed and the brand(s) are one of the company's most important assets, second only to its people.

THE FUTURE OF BRANDS

Brands probably reached their zenith in terms of prominence and numbers in the 1980s. Since then there has been a 'market correction' and the 1990s began with some sections of the business press announcing, almost certainly prematurely, the death of brands. A number of factors lie behind this swing of the pendulum.

First, in the 1980s bull market many brands were guilty of adding more cost than value. They have been found out by consumers who, in more recessionary times, have shown themselves less willing to pay the premiums demanded. The addition of some gold to the label, and 'Gold' to the brand name, did not mean that the value equation had genuinely been improved for consumers. Behind every great brand is a great product and behind every declining brand is a product which no longer offers real competitive advantage.

Second, the retail trade in many areas has been growing in strength and sophistication and developing 'own label' products. These retail branded products have been promoted at the expense of the weaker brands, which in many cases have been delisted from the major stores altogether. This trend will almost certainly continue but it is of course merely the replacement of one brand, the manufacturer's brand, with another, the retailer's. The fundamental value of brands to consumers and the principles of brand management remain the same.

Third, the emphasis has switched to global brands and bigger umbrella brands. The latter reflects the trend towards range extension of existing brands rather than the development of new brands for the reasons, largely to do with cost saving, outlined above. The world is probably 'over-branded' and there will be continued consolidation behind fewer global brands with wider product ranges (Macrae 1991).

Against this trend is the emergence of new brands in many sectors such as financial services and indeed well beyond the traditional business world. For to understand brands is to understand that anything is a brand which is distinctive, well differentiated, and has competitive advantage in that it meets consumer needs, both functional and non-functional, better than alternatives. Charities are brands, the Louvre in Paris or the British Museum in London are brands, even the Pope is a brand. In the world of business, the structure and ownership of brands may change but brands will remain for one basic reason – consumers want them and value them as simplifiers of choice. Back in Roman times when the artisans branded their products they were effectively saying 'I made this, I'm proud of it, you can trust it and I will stake my reputation on it'. This is useful information if you are a consumer.

REFERENCE

Macrae, C. (1991) *World Class Brands*, Reading, MA: Addison-Wesley Publishing Co. Inc.

FURTHER READING

Cowley, D. (1991) *Understanding Brands By 10 People Who Do*, London: Kogan Page Ltd.
Interbrand (1990) *Brands: an International Review*, London: Gold Arrow Publications with Interbrand Group plc.
Jones, J. P. (1986) *What's in a Name? Advertising and the Concept of Brands*, Aldershot: Gower.
King, S. (1984) *Developing New Brands*, Letchworth: Garden City Press.
Levitt, T. (1986) *The Marketing Imagination*, London: Collier Macmillan.
Nilson, T. H. (1992) *Value-Added Marketing, Marketing Management for Superior Results*, Maidenhead: McGraw-Hill.

31

PRICING

Katia Campo and Els Gijsbrechts

PRICING: CONCEPTS AND ISSUES

Price is traditionally defined as 'the number of monetary units a customer has to pay to receive one unit of that product or service' (Simon 1989). However, many marketers now advocate the use of a broadened price definition that reflects the complexity and multifaceted character of the price concept (e.g. Zeithaml 1988). For the consumer, price is more than the objective monetary value charged by the manufacturer or retailer. It also comprises non-monetary components (e.g. time) and risk (see Zeithaml 1988; Murphy and Ennis 1986): consumer behaviour is not only guided by the objective price but also by price perception. Perceptions may deviate substantially from objective prices and can have both a negative and positive component (price as a sacrifice or loss, and price as a quality indicator, see Buyer behaviour, page 533). For the manufacturer or retailer, price also performs several (conflicting) functions: it is an important component of the marketing mix and in this sense an instrument to boost demand or respond to competitive threats, but also a major determinant of profit margins.

The multidimensional character of price should be taken into account for the pricing of products and services. Pricing involves the determination (and adjustment) of a price structure and price levels, as well as decisions on short-term price changes. According to Rao (1984) pricing is one of the most important marketing mix decisions, price being the only marketing mix variable that generates revenues, and that has an immediate and direct effect on buyer behaviour. In practice however, pricing decisions are often made arbitrarily or merely on the basis of cost-related criteria, with limited or no pricing research to guide them. As a result, prices often fail to capture the value realized by other marketing mix instruments (Nagle 1987).

A more effective, goal-oriented approach to pricing is needed, which explicitly takes the role of price as a marketing mix instrument and as a profit generator into account. The purpose of this chapter is to provide a framework

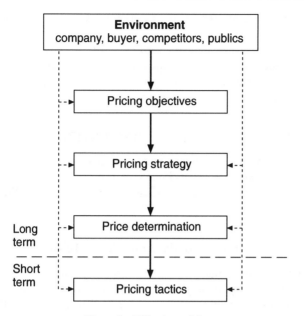

Figure 1 Effective pricing
Source: Nagle (1987) and Morris and Calantone (1990)

for effective, goal-oriented pricing, and to highlight the major aspects and factors influencing the pricing decision. Additional information can be found in Monroe (1990) and Nagle (1987), and in review articles on the topic (Monroe and Della Bitta 1978; Rao 1984; Gijsbrechts 1993).

Figure 1 provides a schematic overview of the steps involved in effective price decisions. Obviously, thorough analysis of the environment is a prerequisite for proper strategy selection. Company goals and costs, buyer behaviour, character-istics of competitors and of other publics may strongly affect relevant pricing options and are discussed below (see pages 530–7).

Environmental analysis is a building block for the specification of pricing objectives, which must – as well as being consistent with the environment – be attainable and operational. (For a summary of the most important pricing objectives see page 537.)

The next step is to specify which pricing strategies may enable one to obtain the objectives, and to select the alternative most appropriate for the pricing environment. (For a discussion of the major types of strategies see pages 538–9.)

To implement the selected strategy, a price structure and price level(s) have to be determined. The different approaches and techniques that can be used for price determination and strategic price changes have been summarized (pages 539–44). A discussion on the impact of short-term price adjustments concludes this chapter and concentrates mainly on price promotions, the most important class of price tactics.

It goes without saying that the process just described is not a purely chronological one. As the dotted lines in Figure 1 indicate, environmental characteristics influence each subsequent step and feedback loops within one decision period and over time are bound to occur.

ANALYSIS OF THE PRICING ENVIRONMENT

To be effective, pricing objectives and strategies must be in line with the characteristics of the environment. Four important characteristics are discussed here: company characteristics, buyer behaviour, competitive conditions, and the influence of other publics.

Company goals, strategies and costs

Pricing objectives and strategies have to be consistent with company goals and overall marketing strategy. Company goals are 'general aspirations toward which all activities in the firm, not only pricing, are directed' (Nagle 1987). For a discussion of the different types of company objectives we refer to Kotler (1991) and Nagle (1987), and Lewison and DeLoizier (1986) for retailers. (The impact of company goals on pricing objectives and strategies is discussed on pages 537–8.)

To achieve the selected goals, a global strategy has to be developed. Since price is an important component of a firm's marketing mix, the pricing strategy must be part of an overall market strategy, and take interrelationships with other marketing instruments into account. First and foremost, the pricing strategy must be adjusted to the product's (perceived) value and cost characteristics (e.g. dynamic effects), and its relation to other products in the line (demand, costs). Other relevant characteristics (especially for the planning of pricing tactics) are the perishability and purchase frequency of the product (durable versus consumer goods; see Simon 1989). Advertising may affect price sensitivity (negatively or positively) and reinforce the effect of a price promotion. Finally, the product's distribution influences consumer price perceptions as well as the practicability of segmented pricing strategies (see Nagle 1987 for a more detailed discussion). A number of these issues will be taken up below.

Price is not only an important marketing mix instrument, it is also a major determinant of a firm's profits and cashflows. To analyse the profit implications of a pricing decision, cost information is indispensable. Not all costs are relevant, however: according to Nagle (1987) only forward-looking, incremental and avoidable costs must be taken into account for pricing. Monroe (1990) gives a detailed discussion of the different cost types, and the ways in which they can be measured and forecasted. Traditional methods for profit evaluation on the basis of cost and price information are break-even and contribution margin analysis. Break-even analysis determines the sales volume that is needed to cover variable and fixed costs at a given price level. To be profitable, the price must at least generate the break-even sales volume. The contribution margin consists of the difference between price and unit variable costs: if negative, selling the product at the given price level would lead to a loss; if positive, at least some of the fixed costs can be covered. Consequently, costs set a price floor: to be profitable, price must be equal to or greater than unit variable cost in the short term, and equal to or greater than unit total cost in the long term. In this respect it is important that unit (variable) costs are not static, but often decline as accumulated production volume increases (see pages 535–6), and that the profitability analysis is more complicated in the case of product line pricing because of shared costs and interrelated demand.

A fourth group of company characteristics that influence the pricing decision are the type of company and type of buyer. With regard to company type, a distinction should be made between manufacturers and retailers, because they may face substantially different pricing problems. Manufacturers often have to take two prices into account: the selling price to the wholesaler or retailer, and the resale price to the ultimate consumer. The resale or final consumer price determines final demand, but is not under the direct control of the manufacturer (see pages 536–7). Retailers only have to set final consumer prices, but often face very complex pricing problems because of huge assortments, cross-product effects, and difficulties in assessing the impact of individual prices on the store's overall price image. The following discussion concentrates mainly on the manufacturer's pricing decision. Important differences for retailer pricing will be indicated where appropriate.

In addition, a distinction should be made between two types of buyers: consumers and businesses. The corresponding pricing decisions are termed consumer pricing and industrial or business-to-business pricing. Specifics of industrial pricing will not be treated here. For more information one should refer to Monroe (1990), and Akintoye and Skitmore (1992).

Buyer behaviour

Price-volume relationship

Price is an important determinant of demand and sales volume. According to the economic theory of buyer behaviour the price-volume relationship is negative: higher prices will generate lower demand. The magnitude of the sales reduction (increase) for a given price increase (reduction) reflects the price sensitivity of the consumers. In economics, price sensitivity is measured by price elasticity: the percentage change in sales due to a one per cent price change.

The price sensitivity of consumers varies considerably between products, and may change over time. Product-related factors that reduce price sensitivity are believed to be (Nagle 1987): the unique value of a brand, the difficulty of comparing substitutes, the use of price to signal quality, payment of costs by someone else (wholly or partly) and sunk investments in assets for which the product is used. Conversely, price sensitivity tends to be stronger for products that have high prices, are easy to stock, are used in combination with other products to produce a single benefit, or for which many substitutes are widely available. For most products, price sensitivity increases over the product life cycle (PLC) as competitive offers become more standardized, are perceived as closer substitutes, and as consumers become better informed. However, empirical investigations have demonstrated that this is only true for the decline stage of the PLC (Simon 1979). More information on the factors that affect price elasticity dynamics can be found in Nagle (1987) and Parker (1992).

Price perceptions

Estimated price-volume relationships provide a direct link between actual price levels charged and company results; as such, they seem a practical and valuable basis for decision-making. By treating the consumer as a black box, however, they ignore the complexity of the role of price in the potential buyer's decision process. Closer attention to the variety of phenomena and reactions on the part of consumers uncovers important implications for strategic and tactical pricing.

A first point of interest is the distinction between real prices and perceptions: rather than exclusively concentrating on 'objective' or factual prices, decision-makers should be concerned with how these prices are perceived and evaluated.

To start with, recent studies on consumer price knowledge unequivocally point at low awareness levels for specific item prices of frequently purchased consumer goods (Dickson and Sawyer 1990; McGoldrick and Marks 1987; Krishna et al. 1991). This lack of price knowledge concerns regular as well as promotional prices. Many reasons may account for the incompleteness of price information, such as the complexity of the offer (variety of brands and package sizes, at different prices in different stores); the time pressure during a shopping trip, and the limited absolute (differences between) prices in many consumer goods' product classes. In any case, these findings suggest that managers cannot take consumer awareness of actual prices for granted.

Numerous sources further suggest that 'customers' response to prices are based on much more than rational calculations' (Nagle 1987), and that price perception/evaluation relies on convenient and simple decision processes. It is widely believed that consumers build up an 'acceptable price range' for a given product or product class, characterized by an upper and a lower price limit (see Rao and Sieben 1992). The upper bound (reservation price) identifies the price above which a product is considered 'too expensive' and stems from the negative role of price in the decision process (monetary loss). The lower bound specifies a price level below which consumers are suspicious of quality, or worry about the (lack of) social status signalled by the product. This lower boundary illustrates that price can be viewed as an asset, and thus play a positive role in the buying process.

Considerable research has investigated the relationship between price and product quality. Studies analysing the link between actual prices and objective quality have come up with mixed results. On average, the relationship is positive but fairly weak; it is also highly variable among product classes (see e.g. Rao and Monroe 1989; Tellis 1987). As to the link between price and perceived quality, evidence suggests that consumers sometimes use price as a quality indicator. Whether such inferences are made depends on the availability of other cues (e.g. brand name), and on the degree of prior knowledge (on true product characteristics and price).

It is further believed that consumers, in evaluating specific observed prices, confront the actual price of an item with a 'reference price', and that the distance between the two affects the probability of purchase of the particular item. The notion of a reference price is now widely accepted, and a variety of conceptual and operational definitions have been put forward. An important distinction is that between external and internal reference prices. External reference prices, as the term suggests, are provided by 'observed stimuli in the purchase environment' (Mayhew and Winer 1992). Internal reference prices, in contrast, are standards or benchmarks stored in consumer memory. A variety of such internal standards may be used. A common view is that the internal reference price(s) reflect(s) the consumer's perception of a 'normal', 'fair' or 'appropriate' price for an item under the circumstances considered. The formation of internal reference prices is shown to be based not only on past prices and currently observed price levels (e.g. external reference prices) but also on expectations concerning future price evolutions, and is strongly influenced by the purchasing context (see e.g. Nagle 1987).

For retailers, it is not only important how consumers perceive prices of individual items and brands, but also how the store as a whole is viewed (expensive versus cheap). Though store price images have been shown to affect strongly store traffic and performance, fairly little is known about how they are formed (e.g. impact of nonprice cues; first impressions tend to persist; focus on a few products as exemplars of the store's total price level).

Psychological aspects of pricing

It has become clear by now that consumers can encode and evaluate price information in different ways. The extent to which potential buyers are aware of prices, as well as the way they perceive them, evaluate them, and use them to 'update' reference prices, will depend on many factors, and exhibits 'rational' as well as seemingly 'irrational' features.

Consumers can 'encode' information on actual item prices in absolute terms (amount to be paid), but also in relative terms. Consumers' awareness of absolute versus relative prices is found to be closely linked to their 'processing goals' (for direct or later use: Mazumdar and Monroe 1990; brand choice or purchase quantity: Krishnamurthi and Raj 1988, 1991).

Psychological 'peculiarities' further affect not only how item prices are recorded, but also perceived. For one thing, price endings may significantly affect price perceptions (odd prices, see e.g. Nagle 1987; Schindler and Wiman 1989). Another phenomenon that decision-makers should bear in mind is the 'relative' evaluation of price cuts. The same absolute price discount is perceived as less important when it constitutes a smaller percentage of the item's normal price, and the further a brand's price is from the average price level in the category (in either direction), the less sensitive consumers tend to be to price changes to that item (Monroe 1990).

The formation and dynamic adjustment of reference prices is also subject to 'specific' psychological processes: for example, a minimum price change (threshold) is needed for a reference price adaptation to occur (Lattin and Bucklin 1989; Monroe 1990), and the presentation order of observed prices affects the presence and magnitude of the adjustment. In the context of price discounts, the impact of externally provided reference prices on a consumer's internal price standard is shown to depend on whether this external reference is seen as plausible or implausible.

Finally, the evaluation of a price offer will strongly depend on its 'mental framing', that is, on whether they are presented as 'gains' or as 'losses' (see e.g. Diamond and Sanyal 1990). In a similar vein, it is found that price increases tend to entail a stronger (negative) reaction than discounts of the same magnitude (positive immediate sales effect).

Consumer heterogeneity

So far we have emphasized the complexity of consumer reactions towards prices, and the psychological factors affecting the role of price in the decision process. An even more important observation is the enormous heterogeneity in price reactions among potential buyers. This heterogeneity is already apparent at the level of price awareness and knowledge. In addition, consumers may evaluate prices differently, because they are more or less informed about prevailing prices and product characteristics (they have different search costs); or because they attach more or less importance to the negative role of price (they have different reservation prices). Also, transaction costs (e.g. costs of shopping) strongly vary among consumers, causing differences in willingness to pay for specific items on given purchase occasions (Tellis 1986). Decision-makers should recognize these differences, and positively 'exploit' consumer heterogeneity in the development of pricing strategies and tactics.

Competition

The results of the pricing strategy will not only depend on consumer response, but also on the reaction of competitors. Competitive behaviour varies considerably with market structure, intensity of competition, and the existence and nature of significant competitive advantages.

Market structures can be classified according to the number of sellers and the degree of product differentiation (see Kotler 1991; alternative classifications can be found in Simon 1989). These characteristics affect the pricing decision in two ways. First, the number of sellers (available substitutes) and the degree of product differentiation influence the price sensitivity of consumers. Second, the intensity of competition depends on the number of competitors, and the threat of substitute products (see Porter 1980 for other factors), and determines the likelihood of competitive reactions to pricing decisions. Competitors' prices are therefore more directive for own pricing decisions in markets with many undifferentiated competitors.

Market structure and intensity of competition change over the PLC as new competitors enter the market and products become more homogeneous. Competition intensifies in most cases, and becomes especially severe in the maturity and decline stage, because sales growth can now be accomplished only at the expense of the competitors' sales volume.

Intense competition implies an increased likelihood of competitive reactions to pricing decisions (adjustments in price and/or other marketing mix variables). Besides market structure, the distribution of market shares, the sources and types of competitive advantages and the marketing goals and strategies of competitors affect the likelihood and nature of competitive reactions (Porter 1980). Competitive retaliation may attenuate pricing effects, and sometimes provoke real price wars (prices are continually reduced, even to unprofitable levels). The analysis of competitive behaviour is therefore a prerequisite for effective pricing. On the one hand, potential competition warrants attention: the use of non-myopic, entry deterring strategies turns out to be particularly rewarding in new product settings (see also pages 543–4). On the other hand, insight into reaction patterns of current market players is indispensable. Competitive response behaviour can be investigated in several ways, for example by means of competitive response profiles (Porter 1980), reaction matrices (Lambin et al. 1975), or game theory (Moorthy 1985).

Substantial deviations from competitors' price levels are only feasible through significant competitive advantages. Information on the different types of competitive advantages, their sources, measurement, and associated market strategies can be found in Aaker (1992) and Day and Wensley (1988). The most important competitive advantages for pricing relate to costs and unique product values.

Cost advantages exist when the product can be produced and/or distributed

535

at a lower unit cost than competitors; they result from superior skills or resources (e.g. location: see Stern 1986), or from learning. The learning effect is usually represented by the experience curve, which implies that 'each time cumulative production volume of a product doubles, unit costs fall by a constant percentage, the learning rate' (Simon 1989: 125). A pricing strategy that exploits these cost dynamics is experience curve pricing (see page 538).

Unique product value results from (tangible or intangible) product characteristics that are valued by consumers and differentiate the product from its substitutes (Nagle 1987). Unique product value reduces the price sensitivity of consumers, thereby enabling the firm to set prices above the competitors' level without experiencing a considerable decrease in demand.

Retailers may find it especially hard to obtain sustainable competitive advantages, because costs cannot easily be reduced, competitive stores often sell the same or highly similar products, and many other differentiating characteristics can easily be copied (Berman and Evans 1986).

Other publics

In addition to buyers and competitors, a number of other publics influence pricing decisions. The most important are government (legal constraints), distribution channels and suppliers. Other individuals, groups or institutions may have an impact on the pricing decision (e.g. financial institutions, workforce) but are not discussed here.

A number of government laws set legal constraints to competitive pricing behaviour, consumer pricing and (the control over) retailer pricing. In the USA competitive pricing behaviour is mainly restricted by the Sherman Anti-trust Act. Similar regulations are in effect in Europe. Prohibited or restricted pricing practices are price fixing, the exchange of price information among firms to fix prices, and predatory pricing. Important legal constraints on consumer pricing are the restriction of price discrimination, and the Federal Trade Commission's regulations against deceptive pricing. More detailed information is provided in Nagle (1987) and Monroe (1990). Control over retailer pricing by the manufacturer is severely restricted by the amendment to the Sherman Act concerning Resale Price Maintenance (see Sheffet and Scammon 1985; Fabricant 1990). This regulation prohibits agreements by which a manufacturer can enforce a minimum resale price on the retailer. Information on other laws that restrict retailer pricing can be found in Berman and Evans (1986), for example, minimum-price laws, unit pricing legislation, bait-and-switch advertising.

In addition to legal constraints, manufacturers have to take into account the impact of the distribution channel on final prices and price perceptions of consumers (available substitutes, price/quality image of the store, retailer promotions). Characteristics of the distribution channel also determine the success of competitive and segmented pricing strategies.

536

From the distributor's perspective, the costs charged by the manufacturers and their actions to gain control over final consumer prices (e.g. suggested resale prices) are important factors in the pricing decision (see e.g. Berman and Evans 1986).

PRICING OBJECTIVES

Environmental analysis provides crucial input for the specification of operational and attainable pricing objectives, which are in line with company goals and strategies and exploit the possibilities offered by the marketplace. Many pricing objectives can be pursued and these can be classified as:

1   Profit-oriented objectives (e.g. profit maximization, profit satisfaction, target return on investment).
2   Cost-oriented objectives (e.g. recover investment costs over a particular time period, generate volume in order to drive down costs).
3   Demand/sales-oriented objectives (e.g. sales growth or maintenance, market share growth or maintenance, use price of one product to sell other products in the line, build traffic).
4   Competition-oriented objectives (e.g. be price leader, discourage entry by new competitors, discourage others from lowering prices).

Companies may pursue more than one pricing objective: in that case, pricing objectives should be mutually consistent, and priorities (or interrelationships) clearly defined (Monroe 1990). Managers (especially retailers) often concentrate on cost-oriented pricing objectives, because these can easily be translated into rules of thumb that simplify the pricing problem (see page 541). In doing so, however, they disregard opportunities for profitable pricing based on factors other than cost (see pages 538–9).

Other examples of pricing objectives and their classifications can be found in Morris and Calantone (1990), and Berman and Evans (1986) for retailers. Of particular relevance to us is the typology suggested by Tellis (1986). Tellis distinguishes three major pricing objectives. Companies can:

* exploit consumer heterogeneity and the presence of various market segments;
* take competitive position as a basic asset for the pricing strategy;
* concentrate on opportunities offered by product line pricing.

Although these different objectives are not mutually exclusive, they indicate 'key' points of interest in pricing, and provide a basic framework for positioning the variety of pricing strategies described in literature and practice.

PRICING STRATEGY

A myriad of pricing strategies have been put forward by marketing academics and practitioners. Which of these are feasible in a given problem situation depends on two main factors (Tellis 1986; Nagle 1987): the characteristics of the environment (in particular those of the target market, see pages 531–4); and the objectives of the company (e.g. following Tellis: segment, competition, or product line oriented priorities). Some typical pricing strategies are highlighted below.

Segmented or differential pricing strategies charge different prices to alternative consumer segments to take advantage of their differences. Because 'straight' price discrimination may cause legal problems and consumer segments are not always easy to identify, many of these strategies rely on self-selection. In *peak-load pricing*, lower prices are charged in off-season periods, an example would be off-season sales for fashion goods. *Price skimming* refers to a strategy of introducing new products at a high price level, which is gradually reduced in later periods. Both strategies have a time-based pricing scheme that exploits consumer differences in willingness to pay. In *random discounting*, a product's regular price is maintained at a high level, but temporary price cuts are offered at random points in time. The idea behind this strategy is to make consumers with low levels of price knowledge pay the full price, while allowing price sensitive consumers, who will 'search' for bargains, to profit from the price cut. In some situations, more *direct price discrimination* schemes can be used, based on consumer identity or market membership. Examples are the use of different price rates for children, students, adults and new members, or price dumping. A strategy that has gained increased attention is the use of *price-quantity discounts*, where the consumer is offered more advantageous purchase conditions if he buys larger product quantities (see e.g. Dolan 1987).

So far we have looked at cases where the pricing regime is primarily linked to consumer characteristics. Other strategies crucially rely on competitive differences in order to be successful. In *price signalling* a company offers its low-quality product at a high price, hoping that non-knowledgeable consumers will take this elevated price level as a quality indicator. Obviously, this strategy only works if at least some competitors follow an 'honest' strategy (low quality and price, or high quality and price). *Geographic pricing* becomes an issue when the company serves geographically distant markets, and transportation constitutes an important component of transaction costs. Depending on the competitive conditions in those markets and on the threat of entry, it may be more profitable to charge *uniform delivered prices* in all markets; to adopt an *FOB* strategy (customer pays for transportation cost); or to settle for an in-between strategy (*zone pricing*). *Experience curve pricing* as well as *penetration pricing* refer to the introduction of new products at low prices to preempt competition, gain economies of experience more rapidly (in case of experience curve pricing), or stay in business in the price-sensitive segment (in case of penetration pricing).

538

A number of strategies are relevant for multiproduct companies, offering a line of products. *Premium pricing* implies that lower quality versions in a line of substitute products are priced below cost, but that this 'loss' is made up for by the premium charged for superior versions. This strategy is particularly useful when demand is heterogeneous (consumers differ in their quality requirements and willingness to pay), and when joint economies of scale exist for products in the line. In *image pricing*, the same product is marketed under a different name (with a different positioning strategy) and at a different price level, so that consumers who attach a lot of importance to the positive role of price (quality or status signal) would buy the higher priced version. *Price bundling* refers to a situation where two or more products are marketed in a single package for a special price. This strategy may be used for 'imperfect substitutes' (for instance, season tickets for a theatre) as well as for complementary items (e.g. packages of options on automobiles); it may be pure (products only available in bundle) or mixed (separate item purchase is still possible). A rationale for price bundling is demand asymmetry: consumers vary in their preferences and reservation prices for different items. *Complementary pricing* is adopted when in a line of complementary products some are sold at a very low price, while a premium is charged on other items. Typical variants are 'loss leadership selling' by retailers, 'captive pricing' and 'two-part pricing' for services (see Tellis 1986).

A variety of other strategies are described in the literature which are variously related to the ones discussed here. As pointed out, each of these strategies will be more or less appropriate depending on specific environmental conditions and company objectives; also, a number of strategies may be combined. Ultimately, the success of a pricing strategy will strongly depend on how it is carried out: – on the cost and accuracy of implementation, and the exact price levels charged within the framework of the suggested strategy. It is this issue of price determination that is taken up next.

IMPLEMENTATION OF PRICING STRATEGIES: PRICE DETERMINATION AND ADJUSTMENT

To implement the pricing strategy, a (general) price structure and specific price level(s) have to be determined. In addition, effective pricing is a dynamic process, responding to significant changes in the environment, and to the threat of competitive reactions.

Price structure

A pricing strategy outlines the basic 'principles' to be adopted. Within the confines of these principles, a price structure specifies how the characteristics of a product will be priced and lays the foundation on which price levels will be set (Stern 1986). It determines:

- which aspects of each product or service will be priced;
- how prices will vary for different customers in the case of differential pricing strategies, and for different products or services in the case of product line pricing;
- time and conditions of payment.

More information on these issues can be found in Nagle (1987); Dada and Srikanth (1987); Day and Ryans (1988); Lal (1990); Monroe (1990); Morris and Calantone (1990).

Price structure is an important component of an effective price policy: it provides the pricing flexibility that is needed for a successful implementation of differential and product line pricing strategies, and for a quick and effective instrument to respond to competitive threats (Stern 1986). Guidelines for the development of a strategic price structure can be found in Monroe (1990) and Morris and Calantone (1990).

Methods and techniques for setting price levels

Numerous methods and techniques have been developed for determining price levels. Rather than enumerating all the available techniques, we shall indicate the major approaches and illustrate each approach by one or more specific techniques.

Optimization methods

Optimization methods attempt to derive the optimal price level analytically or numerically. In general, the derivation of optimal prices involves:

1. The specification and estimation of demand and cost functions; recent contributions also include competitive response functions in the optimization approach (see pages 543–4).
2. The selection of a pricing objective, in most cases profit maximization.
3. Derivation of optimal prices by means of mathematical optimization techniques.

A prominent example of this class of pricing methods is the traditional microeconomic pricing model (see e.g. Simon 1989; Monroe 1990). An example of an optimization model for retailers can be found in Feichtinger et al. (1988).

Some important limitations of the optimization approach are the use of simplifying assumptions to keep models tractable, the focus on profit maximization and difficulties in obtaining the necessary information to calculate optimal prices. To solve these problems more complex models and alternative pricing methods have been developed. A review of extensions to the traditional economic pricing model can be found in Nagle (1984). A class of pricing techniques that tries to avoid or reduce measurement problems are the rules of thumb that will be discussed next. Simulation and perceived value pricing techniques (pages 541–2) attempt to limit the use of simplifying assumptions and to derive prices on the basis of more realistic relationships (e.g. taking psychological pricing effects into account).

Rules of thumb

In many cases, optimization methods cannot be applied because the necessary information is not available or is too costly to obtain. To solve this problem, a number of rules of thumb have been developed. Most of these rules are cost based, because cost information is more readily available for most companies.

Markup or cost-plus pricing is one of the most widely practised pricing heuristics, especially by retailers (Berman and Evans 1986). A second cost-based pricing rule is target return pricing (see Kotler 1991 for examples). Both techniques are easy to apply and require only cost information, but they ignore price-volume relationships, dynamic cost effects and competitive reactions.

A third rule of thumb that is more competition oriented is going-rate pricing. In this case the firm bases its price largely on competitors' price levels. Going-rate pricing mainly attempts to maintain competitive (price) position, and is not based on a thorough analysis of competitive conditions and behaviour. Demand relationships and cost differences are also ignored.

The main advantages of these pricing rules consist therefore in their ease of use and low information requirements. They are not likely to yield optimal or near optimal price decisions, since important pricing determinants are ignored.

Simulation techniques

Like optimization methods, simulation techniques first specify and estimate demand (and cost) relationships, subsequently select pricing objectives, and finally determine the price(s) that best meet the objectives. Both methods differ, however, in the way 'optimal' prices are derived. Whereas optimization methods make use of mathematical optimization techniques to calculate the optimal price, simulation methods estimate and compare results for various pricing scenarios. The scenario that gives the best results provides the (near optimal) price.

Simulation is often used in combination with conjoint analysis, a technique for estimating utility functions for existing or new products (see Goldberg et al. 1984 for an example). The estimated utility functions can be used to simulate choice behaviour of consumers, and to estimate the market share or sales volume at different price levels. To evaluate profit implications, the demand relationship must be combined with a cost function (see e.g. Kohli and Mahajan 1991). Simulation and conjoint analysis can also be applied to more complex pricing problems, such as product line pricing (Dobson and Kalish 1993). Limitations of conjoint analysis for preference modelling are discussed by Green et al. (1981).

Perceived value pricing

Perceived value pricing sets price level(s) in relation to the product's value as judged by consumers. Like simulation, this pricing technique concentrates mainly on the demand side of the pricing problem, but can take cost and profit implications into account.

The first step of the procedure consists of the estimation of perceived value. Monroe (1990) defines perceived value as the weighted sum of acquisition and transaction value. Acquisition value consists of the ratio of perceived benefits to perceived sacrifice, and the transaction value is the difference between the reference and the actual price. In this way, the perceived value reflects the multifaceted character of price, and the buyers' perceptions.

The next step consists in the determination of the price level. Price can be set above, below or equal to perceived value, depending on costs, pricing objectives and strategy (see Nagle 1987). Various methods can be used to determine specific price levels (see e.g. Nagle 1987; Kijewski and Yoon 1990; Monroe 1990; Kortge and Okonkwo 1993).

Important advantages of perceived value pricing are that psychological pricing effects can be incorporated into the pricing decision, and that the method can be used for different pricing objectives and strategies. Disadvantages are that 'the' perceived value is difficult to estimate, especially for new products. Moreover, value perceptions may vary considerably among consumers, and even over usage situations.

Limitations of price setting methods

In addition to the disadvantages indicated in the previous paragraphs, the price-setting methods already described have some common limitations. First, they implicitly assume that the manufacturer has direct control over final consumer prices while in reality control over consumer prices is restricted by Retail Price Maintenance regulations (see page 536). Manufacturers can only suggest resale prices, base selling prices on retailers' pricing policy and the target consumer price, or try to obtain dealer/retailer cooperation (e.g. by means of trade discounts, special promotions or trade deals: see Lal 1990; Monroe 1990). Second, most methods do not explicitly take cross-product effects into account. This severely limits their usefulness for product line pricing and retailer pricing. In recent years, efforts have been undertaken to incorporate cross-product effects in traditional pricing methods. Examples are optimization models for product lines (see e.g. Oren et al. 1984; Reibstein and Gatignon 1984; Dobson and Kalish 1988); simulation models for product lines (e.g. Dobson and Kalish 1993); and perceived value of product bundles (e.g. Yadav and Monroe 1993). Third, most methods cannot be used for planning of short-term price changes. Approaches specifically tailored to the problem of sales promotion planning are, for example, Allaway et al. (1987), and Dhebar et al. (1987). Tactical price

542

decisions are further discussed later in this chapter (see pages 544–6). Finally, the previous methods are myopic in the sense that they rely on stable cost and demand functions, and largely ignore competitive reactions.

Dynamic pricing models

The methods and techniques for setting price levels already discussed determine an optimal or satisfying price level at a given point in time. In reality, though, several price determinants are not static, but change in a more or less predictable and uniform way (e.g. experience curve and product life cycle phenomena). Some of the strategies discussed under pricing strategy make use of these dynamic effects to increase profits (e.g. skimming strategy), obtain competitive advantages (e.g. experience curve pricing) or preempt competition (e.g. penetration pricing).

Dynamic pricing models explicitly take cost and/or demand evolutions into account and determine an (optimal) price path, rather than one (optimal) price level. Models including cost dynamics predominantly concentrate on experience curve effects. Most dynamic demand models are based on the diffusion model developed by Bass (1980). A review of diffusion models is given in Parker (1992) and Horskey (1990). Dynamic pricing models are further discussed in Simon (1989) and Gijsbrechts (1993). For the determination of the optimal price path, analytical solutions can be derived by means of optimal control theory (see Dolan and Jeuland 1981). Because of the complexity of such derivations, simplifying assumptions are usually needed to keep the models tractable. Clarke and Dolan (1984) therefore suggest an alternative procedure that makes use of simulation techniques.

Another limitation is that the pricing methods already considered do not explicitly take competitors' reactions to price decisions into account, although their impact, especially in mature and declining markets, may be considerable. To incorporate competitive dynamics into the pricing model, demand and cost relationships have to be supplemented with a competitive response model. The dominant approach to modelling competitive behaviour is based on game theory (see Moorthy 1985 for the basic concepts and applications to price competition).

A distinction can be made between models that determine competitive reactions to:

1 General changes in competitive conditions (e.g. entry of new competitors: see Eliashberg and Jeuland 1986; threat of entry or copying: see Nascimento and Van Honacker 1988).
2 Price information or price decisions, in particular.

In the latter case, the reaction models used may be simple response functions (competitors react to price actions with a change in their own price), or multiple reaction functions (all marketing mix instruments could be used to retaliate).

Also, available models differ in their assumptions on the amount of price information available to companies.

A comprehensive review of analytical models of competition is given by Eliashberg and Chatterjee (1985). More recent references can be found in Griffith and Rust (1993). Examples of models that combine dynamic and competitive effects are Rao and Bass (1985); Dockner and Jorgensen (1988); Coughlan and Mantrala (1992).

PRICING TACTICS

Pricing strategy versus pricing tactics

Some confusion exists in the pricing literature on the distinction between pricing strategies and pricing tactics. In this chapter we adhere to the viewpoint of van Waterschoot and Van den Bulte (1992), and Morris and Calantone (1990), who state that pricing strategies determine long-term price structure and price levels, and their evolution over time in response to long-term changes in the environment. Pricing tactics consist of short-term price decisions (mostly price reductions from the normal or long-term level) to induce immediate sales increases or to respond to short-term changes in the environment.

Part of the confusion stems from the fact that the same set of instruments and actions can serve both strategic and tactical purposes. For instance, this is true for the use of price deals. From a strategic point of view, temporary price cuts can be used as a legal way of price discrimination (e.g. in a random discounting strategy). The aim of this strategy is clearly to increase long-term sales. At the same time, price deals and sales promotions in general, can be used temporarily to support various pricing strategies (e.g. to eliminate stocks), and thus serve as a tactical instrument.

Price promotions

The measurement of sales promotion effects has generated a great deal of interest in recent years. While a variety of promotional activities is available, the bulk of sales promotion actions take the form either of a straight price cut, or a more indirect price reduction (e.g. in the form of a coupon or extra quantity). Typical of such price promotions is their temporary character; nevertheless, they may generate effects that extend over a longer period of time. In this section, we summarize findings on the immediate as well as long-term effects of promotional actions.

Concerning the short-term effects of promotional price cuts, the literature is fairly unanimous: sales promotions, and in particular price deals, create a dramatic boost in the sales of a brand. Promotional elasticities tend to be much larger (in absolute value) than regular price effects (see Bolton 1989; Bemmaor and Mouchoux 1991), and they are certainly more pronounced than immediate advertising impacts (Sethuraman and Tellis 1991). A large portion of the observed sales increase stems from brand switching. These switching effects appear to be asymmetric: recent findings suggest that dominant, manufacturer, higher priced (and often higher quality) brands attract a large portion of other brands' buyers during promotional periods, but that the reverse is not true. Price promotions may induce product class sales effects, mainly as a result of sales displacement (e.g. purchase acceleration, or purchase postponement when a deal is anticipated). If observed, however, the magnitude of such effects is generally low.

Blattberg and Neslin (1989) emphasize the importance of interaction effects between price promotions and other marketing mix activities. Experimental studies point to a considerable increase in the impact of a price cut when supported by point-of-purchase promotional signals or advertising announce-ments (see e.g. Inman et al. 1990; Bemmaor and Mouchoux 1991). Also, the form of the advertisement or display is deemed important: presenting advertised prices as a reduction from regular prices tends to increase the impact of the discount (Cox and Cox 1990). Apparently, insight into the psychological aspects of the consumers' decision process vis-à-vis prices pays off.

While the immediate impact of price cuts on sales of the promoted brand is clearly positive, long-run implications are more complex. In general, sales promotion activities could enhance repeat sales and build consumer franchise. According to Jones (1990), temporary price reductions have about the weakest positive long-term effects of any below-the-line activity since they appeal to rational (financial) arguments rather than building brand image or franchise. While the evidence on positive long-run implications on brand sales is limited, there are indications that price deals lead to purchase acceleration and stockbuilding, followed by sales dips in the post-promotion period. In other words, sales promotions may partly 'borrow sales from the future'. More importantly, frequent price cuts may reduce the consumer's willingness to buy the product at the regular price (perhaps as a result of a downward reference price adaptation), and eventually damage product image (to the extent that a price-quality inference is made). Several authors emphasize that these negative effects jeopardize the long-run profitability of price deals from the point of view of the individual brand (Hardy 1986; Jones 1990).

So far we have concentrated on price deal implications for the promoted brand. For multiproduct manufacturers, and especially for retailers, additional impacts are worth noting. First, the switching effects towards the promoted brand may cause (unwanted) cannibalization of more profitable non-promoted items. On the other hand, some studies reveal significant positive effects of price promotions on the sales of complementary items (e.g. Walters 1988; 1991). From the retailer's point of view, the profitability of price promotions strongly depends on their ability to attract new customers to the store (see e.g. Walters and McKenzie 1988; Mulhern and Leone 1990). Evidence on traffic building capacity of price cuts is still inconclusive; so far interstore brand substitution seems to be limited.

In the long run, retail promotions may be useful in creating barriers to entry (Walters 1988), and in increasing store competitiveness. Closely related to this is the impact of sales promotions on the store's price image, which, as already mentioned (pp. 531–4), is a major determinant of store patronage. To date, however, only fragmented insights are available on how store price images are formed, and more research is needed in this area.

Overall, the impact of price promotions on brand sales, product line sales, and store performance seems to be a multifaceted and tricky issue. The nature and impact of promotional effects varies widely from case to case. The recent literature, however, has succeeded in providing: more theoretical insights into the economic rationale behind price cuts and their behavioural underpinnings (for an overview of models dealing with this issue, see Gijsbrechts 1993); and empirical evidence on factors affecting the magnitude of promotional elasticities. Consumer characteristics (e.g. loyals versus variety seekers), product type (e.g. perishability), promotional activity in the product class or in the retail environment, all seem important determinants that interact in a complex way. The lesson to be drawn is that managers interested in profit should not engage in promotional tactics too hastily, but carefully analyse the characteristics of the market setting in which they operate.

CONCLUSIONS

In recent years marketing scholars as well as practitioners have increasingly recognized the importance and the complexity of the pricing decision. To be effective, pricing must be the outcome of a systematic and goal-oriented process, in which characteristics of the internal and external environment are carefully researched; and pricing strategies, structures, regular price levels and temporary deviations are set to exploit fully the possibilities offered by this environment.

Recent marketing publications contribute to effective pricing by shedding more light on the intricacies of consumer and competitor reactions, by describing a range of possible pricing strategies and the rationale behind them, and by offering measurement instruments and methods for assessing price impacts and levels. Yet, a lot remains to be done. Future contributions should continue to evaluate empirically the consumer's price sensitivity and competitor's reactions in a variety of (dynamic) settings. Also, the role of the retailer and the issue of multiproduct pricing seem to be undervalued to date. Above all, there appears to be a need for the development of managerial guidelines, such that the 'state-of-the-art' in pricing finds its way to practice.

REFERENCES

Aaker, D. A. (1992) Strategic Market Management, New York: John Wiley.
Akintoye, A. and Skitmore, M. (1992) 'Pricing approaches in the construction industry', Industrial Marketing Management 21: 311–18.

Allaway, A., Mason, J. B. and Brown, G. (1987) 'An optimal decision support model for department-level promotion mix planning', *Journal of Retailing* 63 (3): 215–42.

Bass, F. M. (1980) 'The relationship between diffusion rates, experience curves, and demand elasticities for consumer durable technological innovations', *Journal of Business* 53 (3, pt 2): S51–S67.

Bemmaor, A. C. and Mouchoux, D. (1991) 'Measuring the short term effect of in-store promotion and retail advertising on brand sales: a factorial experiment', *Journal of Marketing Research* 28, May: 202–14.

Berman, B. and Evans, J. R. (1986) *Retail Management: A Strategic Approach*, New York: Macmillan.

Blattberg, R. and Neslin, S. (1989) 'Sales promotion: the long and the short of it', *Marketing Letters* 1 (1): 81–100.

Blattberg, R. and Wisniewski, K. (1989) 'Price induced patterns of competition', *Marketing Science* 8 (4): 291–309.

Bolton, R. (1989) 'The relationship between market characteristics and promotional price elasticities', *Marketing Science* 8 (2): 153–69.

Clarke, D. G. and Dolan, R. J. (1984) 'A simulation analysis of alternative pricing strategies for dynamic environments', *Journal of Business* 57 (1, pt 2): S179–S200.

Coughlan, A. and Mantrala, M. (1992) 'Dynamic competitive pricing strategies', *International Journal of Research in Marketing* 9 (1): 91–108.

Cox, A. D. and Cox, D. (1990) 'Competing on price: the role of retail price advertisements in shaping store price image', *Journal of Retailing* 66 (4): 428–45.

Dada, M. and Srikanth, K. N. (1987) 'Pricing policies for quantity discounts', *Management Science* 33 (10): 1247–52.

Day, G. S. and Ryans, A. B. (1988) 'Using price discounts for a competitive advantage', *Industrial Marketing Management* 17 (1): 1–14.

Day, G. S. and Wensley, R. (1988) 'Assessing advantage: a framework for diagnosing competitive superiority', *Journal of Marketing* 52 (2): 1–20.

Dhebar, A., Neslin, S. A. and Quelch, J. A. (1987) 'Developing models for planning retailer sales promotions: an application to automobile dealerships', *Journal of Retailing* 63 (4): 333–64.

Diamond, W. D. and Sanyal, A. (1990) 'The effect of framing on the choice of supermarket coupons', *Advances in Consumer Research* 17: 488–93.

Dickson, P. and Sawyer, A. G. (1990) 'The price knowledge and search of supermarket shoppers', *Journal of Marketing* 54, July: 42–53.

Dobson, G. and Kalish, S. (1988) 'Positioning and pricing a product line', *Marketing Science* 7 (2): 107–25.

Dobson, G. and Kalish, S. (1993) 'Heuristics for pricing and positioning a product-line using conjoint and cost data', *Management Science* 39 (2): 160–75.

Dockner, E. and Jorgensen, S. (1988) 'Optimal pricing strategies for new products in dynamic oligopolies', *Marketing Science* 7 (4): 315–34.

Dolan, R. J. (1987) 'Quantity discounts: managerial issues and research opportunities', *Marketing Science* 6 (1): 1–23.

Dolan, R. J. and Jeuland, A. P. (1981) 'Experience curves and dynamic demand models: implications for optimal pricing strategies', *Journal of Marketing* 45 (1): 52–62.

Eliashberg, J. and Chatterjee, R. (1985) 'Analytical models of competition with implications for marketing: issues, findings, and outlook', *Journal of Marketing Research* 22, August: 237–61.

Eliashberg, J. and Jeuland, A. P. (1986) 'The impact of competitive entry in a developing market upon dynamic pricing strategies', *Marketing Science* 5 (1): 20–36.

Fabricant, R. A. (1990) 'Special retail services and resale price maintenance', *Journal of Retailing* 66 (1): 101–18.

Feichtinger, G., Luhmer, A. and Sorger, G. (1988) 'Optimal price and advertising policy for a convenience goods retailer', *Marketing Science* 7 (2): 187–201.

Gijsbrechts, E. (1993) 'Prices and pricing research in consumer marketing: some recent developments', *International Journal of Research in Marketing* 10 (2): 115–51.

Goldberg, S. M., Green, P. E. and Wind, Y. (1984) 'Conjoint analysis of price premiums for hotel amenities', *Journal of Business* 57 (1, pt 2): S111–S132.

Green, P. E., Carroll, J. D. and Goldberg, S. M. (1981) 'A general approach to product design optimization via conjoint analysis', *Journal of Marketing* 45, Summer: 17–37.

Griffith, D. E. and Rust, R. T. (1993) 'Effectiveness of some simple pricing strategies under varying expectations of competitor behavior', *Marketing Letters* 4 (2): 113–26.

Hardy, K. (1986) 'Key success factors for manufacturers' sales promotions in package goods', *Journal of Marketing* 50, July: 13–23.

Horsky, D. (1990) 'A diffusion model incorporating product benefits, price, income and information', *Marketing Science* 9 (4): 342–65.

Inman, J. J., McAlister, L. and Hoyer, W. D. (1990) 'Promotion signal: proxy for a price cut?', *Journal of Consumer Research* 17, June: 74–81.

Jones, J. P. (1990) 'The double jeopardy of sales promotions', *Harvard Business Review* 68, September–October: 145–52.

Kijewski, V. and Yoon, E. (1990) 'Market based pricing: beyond price performance curves', *Industrial Marketing Management* 19: 11–19.

Kohli, R. and Mahajan, V. (1991) 'A reservation price model for optimal pricing of multiattribute products in conjoint analysis', *Journal of Marketing Research* 28, August: 347–54.

Kortge, G. D. and Okonkwo, P. A. (1993) 'Perceived value approach to pricing', *Industrial Marketing Management* 22: 133–40.

Kotler, P. (1991) *Marketing Management: Analysis, Planning, Implementation, and Control*, London: Prentice Hall.

Krishna, A., Currim, I. S. and Shoemaker, R. W. (1991) 'Consumer perceptions of promotional activity', *Journal of Marketing* 55, April: 4–16.

Krishnamurthi, L. and Raj, S. P. (1988) 'A model of brand choice and purchase quantity price sensitivities', *Marketing Science* 7 (1): 1–20.

Krishnamurthi, L. and Raj, S. P. (1991) 'An empirical analysis of the relationship between brand loyalty and consumer price elasticity', *Marketing Science* 10 (2): 172–83.

Lal, R. (1990) 'Manufacturer trade deals and retail price promotions', *Journal of Marketing Research* 27, November: 428–44.

Lambin, J. J., Naert, P. A. and Bultez, A. V. (1975) 'Optimal marketing behavior in oligopoly', *European Economic Review* 6: 105–28.

Lattin, J. M. and Bucklin, R. E. (1989) 'Reference effects of price and promotion on brand choice behavior', *Journal of Marketing Research* 26, August: 299–310.

Lewison, D. M. and DeLoizier, M. W. (1986) *Retailing*, Columbus, Toronto, London: Merrill Publishing Company.

McGoldrick, P. J. and Marks, H. (1987) 'Shoppers' awareness of retail grocery prices', *European Journal of Marketing* 21 (3): 63–76.

Mayhew, G. E. and Winer, R. S. (1992) 'An empirical analysis of internal and external reference prices using scanner data', *Journal of Consumer Research* 19, June: 62–70.

Mazumdar, T. and Monroe, K. B. (1990) 'The effects of buyers' intentions to learn price information on price encoding', *Journal of Retailing* 66 (1): 15–32.

Monroe, K. (1990) *Pricing: Making Profitable Decisions*, New York: McGraw-Hill International Editions.

Monroe, K. B. and Della Bitta, A. J. (1978) 'Models for pricing decisions', *Journal of Marketing Research* 15, August: 413–28.

Moorthy, K. S. (1985) 'Using game theory to model competition', *Journal of Marketing Research* 22, August: 262–82.

Morris, M. H. and Calantone, R. J. (1990) 'Four components of effective pricing', *Industrial Marketing Management* 19: 321–9.

Mulhern, F. J. and Leone, R. P. (1990) 'Retail promotional advertising', *Journal of Business Research* 21, November: 179–94.

Murphy, P. and Ennis, B. M. (1986) 'Classifying products strategically', *Journal of Marketing* 50, July: 24–42.

Nagle, T. (1984) 'Economic foundations for pricing', *Journal of Business* 57 (1, pt 2): S3–S26.

Nagle, T. (1987) *The Strategy and Tactics of Pricing: A Guide to Profitable Decision Making*, Englewood Cliffs, N.J.: Prentice Hall.

Nascimento, F. and Vanhonacker, W. (1988) 'Optimal strategic pricing of reproducible consumer products', *Management Science* 34 (8): 921–37.

Oren, S., Smith, S. and Wilson, R. (1984) 'Pricing a product line', *Journal of Business* 57 (1, pt 2): S73–S99.

Parker, P. M. (1992) 'Price elasticity dynamics over the adoption life cycle', *Journal of Marketing Research* 29, August: 358–67.

Porter, M. E. (1980) *Competitive Strategy*, New York: The Free Press.

Rao, A. and Monroe, K. B. (1989) 'The effect of price, brand name and store name on buyers' perceptions of product quality: an integrative review', *Journal of Marketing Research* 26, August: 351–7.

Rao, A. R. and Sieben, W. A. (1992) 'The effect of prior knowledge on price acceptability and the type of information examined', *Journal of Consumer Research* 19, September: 256–70.

Rao, R. C. and Bass, F. M. (1985) 'Competition, strategy and price dynamics: a theoretical and empirical investigation', *Journal of Marketing Research* 22, August: 283–96.

Rao, V. R. (1984) 'Pricing research in marketing: the state of the art', *Journal of Business* 57 (1, pt 2): S39–S60.

Reibstein, D. J. and Gatignon, H. (1984) 'Optimal product line pricing: the influence of elasticities and cross-elasticities', *Journal of Marketing Research* 21, August: 259–67.

Schindler, R. and Wiman, A. (1989) 'Effects of odd pricing on price recall', *Journal of Business Research* 19, November: 165–77.

Sethuraman, R. and Tellis, G. J. (1991) 'An analysis of the tradeoff between advertising and price discounting', *Journal of Marketing Research* 28, May: 160–74.

Sheffet, M. J. and Scammon, D. L. (1985) 'Resale price maintenance: is it safe to suggest retail prices?', *Journal of Marketing* 49, Fall: 82–91.

Simon, H. (1979) 'Dynamics of price elasticity and brand life cycles: an empirical study', *Journal of Marketing Research* 16, November: 439–52.

Simon, H. (1989) *Price Management*, Amsterdam: Elsevier.

Stern, A. (1986) 'The strategic value of price structure', *Journal of Business Strategy* 7, Autumn: 22–31.

Tellis, G. J. (1986) 'Beyond the many faces of price: an integration of pricing strategies', *Journal of Marketing* 50, October: 146–60.

Tellis, G. J. (1987) 'Consumer purchasing strategies and the information in retail prices', *Journal of Retailing* 63 (3): 279–97.

van Waterschoot, W. and Van den Bulte, C. (1992) 'The 4P classification of the marketing mix revisited', *Journal of Marketing* 56, October: 83–93.

Walters, R. (1988) 'Retail promotions and retail store performance: a test of some key hypotheses', *Journal of Retailing* 64 (2): 153–81.

Walters, R. (1991) 'Assessing the impact of retail price promotions on product substitution: complementary purchase, and interstore sales displacement', *Journal of Marketing* 55, April: 17–28.

Walters, R. G. and McKenzie, S. B. (1988) 'A structural equations analysis of the impact of price promotions on store performance', *Journal of Marketing Research* 25, February: 51–63.

Yadav, M. S. and Monroe, K. B. (1993) 'How buyers perceive savings in a bundle price: an examination of a bundle's transaction value', *Journal of Marketing Research* 30, August: 350–8.

Zeithaml, V. (1988) 'Consumer perceptions of price, quality and value: a means-end model and synthesis of evidence', *Journal of Marketing* 52, July: 2–22.

FURTHER READING

Akintoye, A. and Skitmore, M. (1992) 'Pricing approaches in the construction industry', *Industrial Marketing Management* 21: 311–18.

Blattberg, R. and Wisniewski, K. (1989) 'Price induced patterns of competition', *Marketing Science* 8 (4): 291–309.

Gijsbrechts, E. (1993) 'Prices and pricing research in consumer marketing: some recent developments', *International Journal of Research in Marketing* 10 (2): 115–51.

Monroe, K. (1990) *Pricing: Making Profitable Decisions*, New York: McGraw-Hill International Editions.

Monroe, K. B. and Della Bitta, A. J. (1978) 'Models for pricing decisions', *Journal of Marketing Research* 15, August: 413–28.

Morris, M. H. and Calantone, R. J. (1990) 'Four components of effective pricing', *Industrial Marketing Management* 19: 321–9.

Nagle, T. (1984) 'Economic foundations for pricing', *Journal of Business* 57 (1, pt 2): S3–S26.

Nagle, T. (1987) *The Strategy and Tactics of Pricing: A Guide to Profitable Decision Making*, Englewood Cliffs, N.J.: Prentice Hall.

Rao, V. R. (1984) 'Pricing research in marketing: the state of the art', *Journal of Business* 57 (1, pt 2): S39–S60.

Simon, H. (1989) *Price Management*, Amsterdam: Elsevier.

Stern, A. (1986) 'The strategic value of price structure', *Journal of Business Strategy* 7, Autumn: 22–31.

Tellis, G. J. (1986) 'Beyond the many faces of price: an integration of pricing strategies', *Journal of Marketing* 50, October: 146–60.

Walters, R. (1991) 'Assessing the impact of retail price promotions on product substitution: complementary purchase, and interstore sales displacement', *Journal of Marketing* 55, April: 17–28.

Zeithaml, V. (1988) 'Consumer perceptions of price, quality and value: a means-end model and synthesis of evidence', *Journal of Marketing* 52, July: 2–22.

32

CHANNEL MANAGEMENT

Bert Rosenbloom

INTRODUCTION

No less of a management guru than Peter Drucker has said that channels of distribution should be 'a major concern to every business and industry'. He goes on to say that:

> To be able to anticipate changes in distribution channels and in where customers buy (and how, which is equally important), one has to be in the marketplace, has to watch customers, and non-customers.
>
> (Drucker 1990)

What Drucker is saying, in effect, is that channels of distribution cannot be ignored or left to their own devices if firms expect them to serve their target markets effectively and efficiently. Rather, channels of distribution need to be managed if they are to achieve the firm's distribution, marketing, and corporate objectives (Cespedes 1988). If channels are not managed the distribution of goods and services will be left largely to the competitive forces of the marketplace, as each firm in the channel attempts to maximize its own returns. Although this may result in effective and efficient distribution channels in some cases, for the most part this is not a good state of affairs for firms that want to exercise some influence over how, when and where their products and services are distributed.

Yet channel management, the analysis, planning, organizing and controlling of the firm's channels of distribution, can be a complex and challenging undertaking (Rosenbloom 1995). Not only can there be many elements or issues to consider, but there are also the problems stemming from the inter-organizational setting of channel structure. That is, channels of distribution by their very nature consist of independent business organizations such as manufacturers, wholesalers and retailers as well as agents and brokers who, although 'linked' together in a trading relationship to form channels of distribution, are nevertheless still independent businesses. As such, each has its own objectives, policies, strategies and operating procedures, which may or may not be congruent with those of the other members of the channel (McVey 1960). Moreover, in most cases, in a channel of distribution there are no clear organization structures, superior/subordinate relationships, or lines of authority so typical of management in single-firm intraorganizational settings. Hence, managing a channel of distribution, and especially gaining a high degree of control of the channel, is frequently more challenging than managing within the intraorganizational setting of a single firm (Cespedes and Corey 1990).

PERSPECTIVES FOR CHANNEL MANAGEMENT

Channel management can be viewed from two basic vantage points:

1 From the producer or manufacturer looking 'down the channel' towards the market.
2 From the retailer (or other final reseller) 'up the channel' back to the producer or manufacturer.

Although either of these perspectives is a valid one for examining the subject of channel management, the first one (from the producer or manufacturer looking down the channel towards the market) is by far the most commonly used perspective in the literature of channel management. Indeed, virtually all modern analysis and research on the subject is from this vantage point. This is probably because channel management is generally regarded as a subset of the larger field of marketing management, which has almost universally been treated from the perspective of the producer or manufacturer (Kotler 1988). Consequently, our discussion of channel management will be from the producer/manufacturer perspective.

BASIC AREAS OF CHANNEL MANAGEMENT

Channel management viewed from the perspective of the producer or manufacturer looking down the channel towards the market can be divided into six basic decision areas (Rosenbloom 1995):

1 Formulating channel strategy.
2 Designing the channel structure.
3 Selecting the channel members.
4 Motivating the channel members.
5 Coordinating channel strategy with the marketing mix.
6 Evaluating channel member performance.

This chapter is organized around a discussion of each of these areas of channel management. Figure 1 provides a schematic overview of these decision areas.

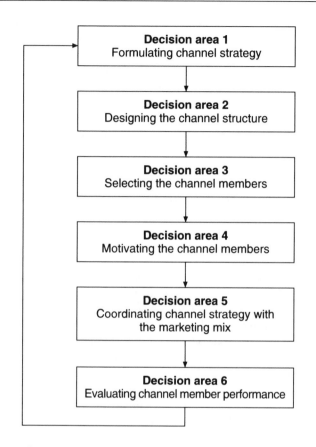

Figure 1   Major decision areas in channel management

Formulating channel strategy

Channel strategy refers to the broad principles through which the firm seeks to achieve its distribution objectives. Distribution objectives are usually set in terms of how, when and where the firm plans to have its products made available to its target markets. If the firm places heavy emphasis on distribution for gaining a competitive advantage, then the achievement of distribution objectives and hence the formulation of channel strategy can become a key strategic tool for the firm (Abell and Hammond 1979). For example, an automobile manufacturer that wants to improve on the experience that customers have when shopping for cars may set a distribution objective in terms of improving the customer service level provided by its independent dealerships. This may involve a substantial investment by the manufacturer in dealer education and training programmes aimed at changing the culture and operating procedures of its dealers towards a more customer-oriented focus. Indeed, the manufacturer may believe that superior customer service by its independent dealers is crucial to its long-term profitability or even its very survival. In this case, channel strategy that seeks to effect such an improvement in dealer service would unquestionably be seen as a key strategic issue for the manufacturer.

Distribution objectives that seek to help differentiate products through very selective or exclusive distribution (often the case with prestige or luxury products); or that provide a novel means of making products available (such as through direct marketing) not available from competitive manufacturers; or that seek to offer much faster response times for customers through superior systems and technology, are all examples of methods which raise channel strategy to a level of strategic importance. In short, if the firm looks to channel strategy as a major means for gaining a sustainable competitive advantage (Porter 1985) by achieving higher levels of target market satisfaction via distribution, then it will be of strategic importance in helping the firm to achieve its long-term goals and objectives.

On the other hand, many distribution objectives, while important, may not be of strategic significance. For example, distribution objectives relating to the availability of products at a level consistent with competitors, those involving terms of sale, and geographical coverage of territory, for the most part would probably not be of vital strategic concern. Of course, there may be exceptions to this. For instance if the geographical coverage objective involved setting up distribution channels in new foreign markets, then indeed this distribution objective could be of strategic importance.

In any case, channel strategy, whether involving the pursuit of distribution objectives at the strategic level or at a lower operational level, is still an area that needs to be given high priority if any of the following four conditions exist:

1 Target markets (customers) demand a strong emphasis on distribution.
2 Competitive parity exists in other marketing mix variables.
3 Competitive vulnerability exists because of distribution neglect.
4 Opportunities for synergy exist through distribution strategy.

Target market demand and channel strategy

Modern marketing management is, of course, based fundamentally on customer orientation. Marketing managers therefore need to focus on the demands of their target markets and attempt to develop the best marketing mix of product, price, promotion and distribution variables to satisfy those demands more effectively than the competition. Channel strategy (along with logistics) comprises the distribution variable of the marketing mix. If customers in the target market have needs and wants that can best be addressed via channel strategy, management must adapt to meet these requirements. Such responses can range from making products more widely available to customers (e.g.

Woolite tripled its sales by selling the product through supermarkets as well as department stores), all the way to creating an entirely new dealer organization (as Honda motors did in the USA to establish a luxury car identity for its new Acura division). In short, if customers can be served better through changes in channel strategy, then marketing managers must remain as alert to this need as they would be to the need for changing strategies in the other marketing mix variables.

Competitive parity and channel strategy

From a competitive standpoint, it is becoming increasingly common for competitive parity to exist among firms in the products they offer, the prices they charge and the promotional messages they convey (Cravens 1988). Such competitive parity in the product, price and promotional variables of the marketing mix has grown even more pronounced with the growth of global competition in recent years. Faced with this situation, more and more firms are focusing on the distribution variable in the marketing mix, and particularly the channel strategy component, as a means for standing out from the competition. What these firms have discovered is that channel strategies that serve target markets effectively and efficiently are not easily copied by competitors. This is because channel strategies and decisions are long term in nature and require substantial planning, development and investment to create a combination of organizational and human resources that result in superior channels. The superb franchised channel system developed by McDonald's is perhaps the world's best known example of the long-term competitive advantage of having superior channels of distribution.

Distribution neglect and channel strategy

Of the four variables of the marketing mix, distribution, particularly channel strategy, has been neglected in relation to product, price and promotion strategies. With the exception of the logistical aspects of distribution, relatively little systematic attention has been given to the strategic questions of how, when and where, products and services should be made available to target markets. Instead, conventional thinking and evolutionary developments have characterized changes in channel structures rather than carefully formulated channel strategies. In fact, bold and innovative approaches to distribution are rather rare. But when they do occur they tend to stand out. Timex watches, the first watchmaker to sell watches through mass market channels, Haynes, with its L'eggs pantyhose, the first firm to sell hose through supermarkets and drug stores, and Dell Computers, the first to sell personal computers via mail order, are some of the best known examples of bold and innovative channel strategies that had apparently been overlooked by competitors.

Synergy through channel strategy

In recent years the terms partnership and strategic alliance have been heard with increasing frequency in connection with channel strategy (Anderson and Narus 1990). The reason for this is that firms at various levels of the channel are seeking synergies by linking themselves more closely with other channel members. Manufacturers of consumer products such as Proctor & Gamble are developing strategic alliances with giant retailers such as Wal-Mart. Manufacturers of industrial products are forming partnerships with industrial distributors in an effort to meld their distinctive capabilities into a more effective and efficient distribution system than would be possible with traditional, more loosely aligned or 'arms length' channel relationships. By working closely together and with mutual commitment to each other spelled out, opportunities to create synergy are enhanced because each firm is more aware of the other's strengths and weaknesses while dysfunctional tendencies or working at cross purposes are reduced. Thus, as more manufacturers learn that synergistic relationships can be built by developing partnerships or strategic alliances with their channel members, an emphasis on the channel strategies needed to create such relationships will increase.

Designing the channel structure

Having considered the overall strategic role of channel strategy in the firm, management then needs to turn its attention to the task of designing the firm's channels of distribution. Channel design is the process of developing new channels where none had existed before, or making significant modifications to extant channels (Rosenbloom 1995). The process of channel design can be broken down into four basic stages or phases:

1 Setting distribution objectives.
2 Specifying the functions that need to be performed by the channel.
3 Considering alternative channel structures.
4 Choosing an 'optimal' channel structure.

These stages are depicted in Figure 2.

Setting distribution objectives

As alluded to in the previous section on channel strategy, distribution objectives refer to what the firm would like its channel strategy to accomplish in terms of how, when and where its products and services are provided to its target markets.

At the stage of channel design, distribution objectives need to be stated explicitly so that they can be made operational. Usually this means expressing the distribution objectives in quantifiable terms such as the following: within

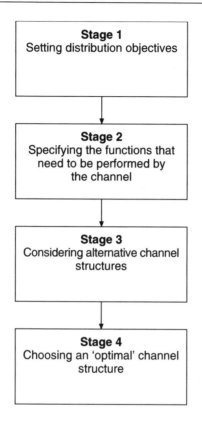

Figure 2 Stages in the channel decision process

eighteen months we would like to have **XYZ** cereal available in 90 per cent of the supermarkets in which consumers of this product are likely to shop.

Distribution objectives must also take into account the firm's broader marketing and corporate objectives so that there are no inconsistencies. A manufacturer of a prestigious product, for example, would have to pay close attention to whether distribution objectives which seek to broaden the availability of its products would detract from the exclusive image of the goods.

Specifying the functions

Making products and services available to final customers how, when and where they want them can involve a great deal of work. The various activities, tasks or functions needed to perform this objective have to be specified at this point. Such tasks can range from providing 'simple' transportation for products all the way to the development of sophisticated electronic data interchange (EDI) systems for linking the manufacturer's and channel member's computers together for instantaneous information transmittal (Rosenbloom 1987). Management must therefore try to be as comprehensive and precise as possible in spelling out just what functions need to be performed to attain the distribution objectives.

Alternative channel structures

The form or shape that the channel of distribution takes to perform the distribution functions is the channel structure. Unless a direct channel structure from manufacturer to final customer is used, the structure will include some combination of independent intermediaries such as wholesalers, retailers, agents and brokers.

Management needs to be concerned with three dimensions of channel structure:

1 Length of the channels.
2 Intensity at the various levels.
3 The types of intermediaries involved.

With regard to length, in developed countries management usually has only three or four options for the distribution of consumer goods ranging from direct up to possibly three levels of intermediaries. In channels for industrial products, the range of choice for levels in the channel is usually even less.

The intensity dimension, which refers to the number of intermediaries to be used at each level of the channel, is usually characterized as: intensive – where as many intermediaries as possible are used; selective – where the number of intermediaries to be used is limited through more careful selection; and exclusive – where only one intermediary is used in a given geographical territory.

With regard to the types of intermediaries to be used at each level in the channel structure, this can vary quite widely depending upon the industry in question.

Decisions involving any of the dimensions of channel structure, particularly those of intensity and type of intermediary, should be guided by channel strategy and the distribution objective being pursued to avoid channel structures that are inappropriate to the strategy and objective. For instance, if a firm's objectives and strategy stress high levels of attention and service for final customers, this would generally be far more difficult to attain with an intensive distribution structure than with a more selective one because the very large numbers of channel members involved in intensive distribution would be harder to monitor and control than a small group of carefully chosen ones.

Choosing an optimal structure

In practice it is not possible to choose an optimal channel structure in the strictest sense of that term. However, it is possible to choose an effective and efficient channel structure that can meet the firm's distribution objectives.

Many different approaches have been suggested over the years for choosing such a channel structure. Very formal management science approaches, financial capital budgeting methods, distribution cost analysis techniques, and relatively recently, transactions cost analysis (Dwyer and Oh 1988) have all been offered as means for choosing channel structure. For the most part, these methods have not found much use in practice. Much more common are judgemental and heuristic approaches that rely on managerial judgement augmented by some data on distribution costs and profit potentials. Sometimes these judgemental, heuristic-type approaches are made more formal, through explicit identification of criteria to be used in choosing a channel, along with weighting and scaling techniques for ascertaining the relative importance of criteria and to provide a general scheme for scoring various channel structure alternatives.

Of course, in the process of applying its best judgement, management also needs to takes into consideration a number of key variables that are usually relevant when choosing channel structure. The most basic of these are:

• market variables
• product variables
• firm variables
• intermediary variables
• behavioural variables
• external environmental variables.

The location of final customers, the numbers of customers and their density, together with their patterns of buying behaviour, would all be key market variables.

Such factors as bulk and weight, unit value, newness, technical vs non-technical and perishability are product variables that are frequently important.

The financial capacity of the firm, its size, expertise and desire for managerial control are some of the most important firm variables.

Cost, availability and services provided are indicative of significant intermediary variables which management needs to consider.

Factors such as the potential of particular channel structures to reduce conflict, while maximizing power and communications effectiveness are critical behavioural variables for management to consider.

Finally, variables such as economic conditions, socio-cultural changes, competitive structure, technology, and government regulations can all be important environmental variables to consider when choosing channel structure.

Selecting the channel members

The selection of intermediaries who will become channel members can be viewed as the last phase of channel design (choosing the channel structure), or as an independent channel management area if selection is not undertaken as part of an overall channel design decision. In any case, the selection of channel members essentially consists of four steps:

1 Developing selection criteria.
2 Finding prospective channel members.
3 Evaluating the prospective channel members against the criteria.
4 Convincing prospective channel members to become actual channel members.

Developing selection criteria

Each firm should develop a set of selection criteria for selecting channel members that is consistent with its own distribution objectives and strategies. Obviously then, there is no universal list of selection criteria which would be applicable for all firms under all conditions. As a general rule, however, there is a basic guiding principle or heuristic that most firms can use which can be stated as follows: the more selective the firm's distribution policy, the more numerous and stringent the criteria used for selection should be and vice versa (Pegram 1965).

Thus, the list of criteria for a firm practising highly selective distribution might include such factors as the prospective channel member's reputation, competing product lines carried and management succession. A firm using very intensive distribution might use little more than one criterion consisting of the ability of the prospective channel members to pay the manufacturer for the products it ships to them.

Finding prospective channel members

The search for prospective channel members can utilize a number of sources. If the manufacturer has its own outside field salesforce, this is generally regarded as the best source because of the salesforce's knowledge of prospective channel members in their territories.

Other useful sources include final customers, trade sources, advertising and trade shows. Usually, a combination of several of these sources is used to find prospective channel members whether they be at the wholesale or retail levels.

Assessment against criteria

Once the group of prospective channel members has been identified, they need to be assessed against the criteria to determine those who will actually be selected. This can be done by an individual manager (such as the sales manager) or by a committee. Depending upon the importance of the selection decision, such a committee might well include top management even up to and including the chairman of the board if the selection decision is of great strategic importance. For example, when Goodyear Tyre and Rubber Company selected Sears Roebuck and Company to sell its tyres, Goodyear's board chairman was heavily involved in the decision because it would have long-term strategic implications for Goodyear.

Converting prospects to actual channel members

The key issue of concern here is to recognize that the selection process is a 'two way street'. Not only do producers and manufacturers select retailers, whole-salers, or various agents and brokers, but these intermediaries also select producers and manufacturers. Indeed, quite often it is the intermediaries, especially large and powerful retailers and wholesalers who are in the 'driver's seat' when it comes to selection. Consequently, the manufacturer seeking to secure the services of quality channel members has to make a convincing case that carrying its products will be profitable for the channel members. Given the sophistication of today's retailers and wholesalers, owing to the excellent computerized information systems they use, manufacturers must make their case very carefully and thoroughly to win the acceptance of such channel members.

Motivating the channel members

Motivation in the context of channel management refers to the actions taken by the manufacturer to secure channel member cooperation in implementing the manufacturer's channel strategies and achieving its distribution objectives (Rosenbloom 1990). Because the manufacturer's efforts to motivate channel members take place in the interorganizational setting of the marketing channel, the process is often more difficult and certainly less direct than would be the case for motivation in the intraorganizational setting of one firm.

Motivation management in the marketing channel can be viewed as a sequence of three steps:

1 Learning about the needs and problems of channel members.
2 Offering support for channel members to help meet their needs and solve their problems.
3 Providing ongoing leadership.

Although the stages in the motivation process are sequential, the process is also iterative because of the continuous feedback from stages two and three. This is shown in Figure 3.

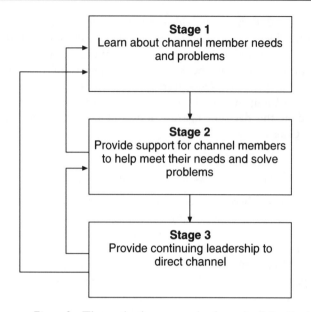

Figure 3   The motivation process in channels of distribution

Learning about channel members' needs and problems

As mentioned earlier, channel members as independent businesses have their own objectives, strategies and operating procedures. But also as independent businesses they have their own needs and problems, which might be quite different from those of the manufacturer (Wittreich 1962). Hence, if the manufacturer seeks strong cooperation from the channel members, it is incumbent on that manufacturer to discover the key needs and problems of channel members in order to be able to help meet those needs and solve those problems. This is not a simple or straightforward task for the manufacturer because the range of needs and problems of channel members can be legion. Small retail channel members may be overburdened with inventory, lack modern information systems, need better managerial skills and newer ideas for competing against giant retailers. On the other hand, giant retailers may face problems of how to reduce costs to operate profitably on razor-thin gross margins while being forced to carry larger and larger inventories as wholesalers disappear from the channel and new products proliferate. At the same time, wholesale channel members may be in desperate need to find ways of competing successfully against power-buying retailers and customers who seek direct sales from the manufacturers. This list could go on and on for different channel members in particular industries, times and circumstances.

How does the manufacturer discover the particular needs and problems of channel members that need addressing? Basically, by taking a proactive rather than a reactive approach where the manufacturer merely waits for the information about channel members to somehow flow in through the 'grapevine'. Effective proactive methods include:

* in-house research on channel members;
* outside research;
* channel member advisory committees.

In-house research of channel members consists of the manufacturer applying the same research capabilities used to gather information about final customers to channel members in order to learn about their needs and problems.

Outside research of channel members can be used by firms who do not have an in-house research capability, or by those firms that do but want to avoid the possibility of bias that can creep into in-house research.

A channel member advisory committee consists of representatives from wholesale and/or retail level channel members and key executives from the manufacturer meeting on a regular basis (such as twice a year) in some neutral location. This type of close interaction between the manufacturer and channel members can foster the kind of candid dialogue needed to uncover channel member needs and problems which may not emerge in the normal course of business.

Offering support for channel members

Offering support to channel members to help meet their needs and solve their problems can be done in a variety of ways, from an informal 'hit or miss', ad hoc approach through to formal and carefully planned partnerships and strategic alliances.

The ad hoc approaches, also called cooperative support, are the most common in loosely aligned traditional channels. Basically, advertising dollars, promotional support, incentives, contests and a host of other ad hoc activities are offered by the manufacturer to 'jump start' the channel member's efforts to push the manufacturer's products or to 'firefight' a particular need or problem.

Partnerships and strategic alliances, in contrast, represent a more substantial and continuous commitment between the manufacturer and channel members. Support provided by the manufacturer is based on extensive knowledge of the needs and problems of the channel members and tends to be carried out on a longer term basis, with specific performance expectations that have been carefully worked out by the manufacturer in conjunction with channel members.

Providing continuing leadership

Even a well-conceived motivation effort, based on a thorough attempt to understand channel member needs and problems, together with a carefully articulated support programme still requires leadership on a continuing basis to achieve effective motivation of channel members. In other words, someone has to be in charge to deal with the inevitable changes and unforeseen problems that arise such as new forms of competition, technological developments and government regulations. While the manufacturer cannot always assume the leadership role and immediately deal with any problems, it is important that support should be available to provide direction and input over the long term instead of only while a new motivation programme is being developed and then quickly left to the channel members to deal with on a day-in-day-out basis.

Coordinating channel strategy with the marketing mix

Channel management does not, of course, take place in a vacuum. All the other variables of the marketing mix are also in operation: hence, channel strategy needs to be coordinated with the marketing mix. Such coordination should help reduce strategies and actions in the four areas of marketing mix that work at cross purposes. Ideally, good coordination should enhance the effectiveness of the firm's overall marketing mix strategy by creating synergies among the marketing mix variables rather than the debilitating incongruencies that can result from neglecting this important issue.

To achieve such coordination, management needs to be aware of and sensitive to the many possible interfaces and relationships of channel strategy with product, price and promotional strategies. A few of these are discussed below.

Product strategy and channel management

Product strategy is often dependent on channel strategy because some key product strategies interface with channel strategies in ways that can spell the difference between success or failure for both (Rao and McLaughlin 1989). For example, the successful introduction of new products relies heavily on strong channel member support in stocking, displaying and promoting the product. Product strategies implemented during the various stages of the product life cycle have significant implications for channel management. In the maturity stage, for instance, when competitive products fight especially fiercely for shelf space, the right channel strategy is critical in helping to keep the manufacturer's products on the channel members' shelves. Other major product strategies such as product differentiation, product positioning, product line extension and brand strategies are also dependent on channel strategy for their implementation.

564

Pricing strategy and channel management

Pricing strategy is related to channel management because pricing decisions need to take into account channel factors if the manufacturer expects strong cooperation from the channel members. Although costs, market demand and competitive factors are obviously crucial in developing pricing strategy, so too are channel factors. In other words, most manufacturers do not have the luxury of being able to ignore the views of channel members when formulating pricing strategies. Clearly, such factors as the profit margins available to channel members, the different prices charged to various classes of channel members, prices of competitive products carried by channel members, special pricing deals, meeting various price points, changing pricing policies, the use of price incentives and 'grey market' pricing are all factors of major concern to many channel members. Thus, the manufacturer needs to make sure that it knows something about the expectations of channel members for these and other relevant pricing factors before embarking on any pricing strategy. What should not be forgotten is that when it comes to securing the services of channel members, the manufacturer must 'buy' those services from them (Warshaw 1962). The margins on the sale of its products are, in effect, the price charged by the channel members. If the manufacturer does not meet the price being sought by the channel members, in the long run they will not continue to offer their services.

Promotion strategy and channel management

Promotion in the form of both push and pull promotion strategies interfaces extensively with channel management. This is because many promotions undertaken by the manufacturer require strong channel member support and follow-through to work successfully. For example, major advertising campaigns frequently require large point-of-purchase displays in the store, special deals and merchandizing campaigns require channel members to stock up on extra inventory, contests and incentives call for participation from retailers and wholesalers.

Gaining channel members' cooperation and follow-through in promotion is not something that happens as a matter of course. On the contrary, very substantial effort is needed to sell the channel members on the value of any promotional campaign from their perspective before they will enthusiastically participate in presenting it to final customers. Moreover, a growing body of research shows that manufacturers need to develop carefully planned promotional programmes that are sensitive to the channel members' concerns to gain their continuous and long-term cooperation in promotional programmes (Curhan and Kopp 1988). Ad hoc, quick fix type promotions that are not part of a carefully planned channel strategy for gaining channel member cooperation in promotion programmes tend to be ineffective and costly relative to the results achieved.

Evaluating channel member performance

The evaluation of channel member performance is necessary to assess how successful the channel members have been in implementing the manufacturers' channel strategies and achieving distribution objectives.

Evaluations require the manufacturer to gather information on the channel members. The manufacturer's ability to do this will be affected by:

- degree of control of channel members;
- importance of the channel members;
- number of channel members.

Usually, the higher the degree of control, the more information the manufacturer can gather and vice versa.

With regard to the importance of channel members, if the manufacturer relies heavily on them for the distribution of its products, it will tend to put more effort into evaluation than those who do not rely heavily on independent channel members.

Finally, when large numbers of channel members are used such as in intensive distribution, evaluation tends to be much more cursory than when smaller, more carefully selected channel members are used. The actual performance evaluation essentially consists of three steps:

1 Developing performance criteria.
2 Evaluating channel members against the performance criteria.
3 Taking corrective actions if necessary.

Developing performance criteria

Although a wide variety of performance criteria can be used to evaluate channel members, by far the most commonly used ones are:

1 sales performance;
2 inventory maintenance;
3 selling capabilities;
4 attitudes;
5 competitive products handled;
6 growth prospects.

Of course, this list can be supplemented to fit the particular circumstances of the manufacturer. The relative importance of each criterion may also vary considerably based on the policies of a particular manufacturer.

Evaluating channel members against criteria

The use of a list of criteria to evaluate channel members can be done in an informal, judgemental fashion or by using a more formal quantitative approach.

In the former approach, criteria are used as a general benchmark of what the manufacturer is seeking. Channel members are then assessed against this list based on qualitative managerial judgements.

In the latter approach, formal weighting schemes can be developed to specify precisely the importance of criteria relative to each other. Formal scoring systems such as a scale of one to ten can then be used to rate each channel member against each criterion. It is then possible to arrive at an overall quantitative performance index for each channel member by multiplying the criteria weights by the scores and adding up the results.

Taking corrective actions

The management purpose behind evaluation is not only to monitor performance but also to take the necessary actions to improve the performance of those channel members who are below the standards. Thus, an integral part of the evaluation process is to have a set of preplanned steps to be taken to help channel members to meet or exceed performance expectations. Termination of the relationship with the channel member should be the very last step in this preplanned corrective process.

TRENDS IN CHANNEL MANAGEMENT

In recent years some significant developments in channel management have occurred. Perhaps the most basic and important ones are:

1 An increasing emphasis on developing channel strategy.
2 Growth of partnerships and strategic alliances.
3 Heavy emphasis on managing to reduce costs of distribution.
4 More and more emphasis on technology.
5 Broadened behavioural perspectives used in managing channels.

Emphasis on channel strategy

More and more companies are 'discovering' channel strategy as an important area of focus for gaining long-term competitive advantages. At both the corporate and marketing levels, firms are finding it increasingly difficult to sustain competitive advantages through product, pricing, or promotional strategies and so they are looking to channel strategy as a viable alternative. In short, distribution channel strategy has become a valuable strategic competitive tool.

567

Growth in partnerships and strategic alliances

Partnership or strategic alliances in the context of channel management refer to the establishment of close working relationships between the manufacturer and key channel members to create mutual advantages and synergy. In contrast to traditional, loosely aligned channels, partnerships and alliances link the manufacturer and channel members more formally and closely and explicitly spell out the mutual expectations of all parties. In other words, the channel operates as a team instead of a collection of independent businesses. As a consequence of this trend, much more stress on channel management will be needed to create and nurture these partnerships and alliances.

Cost reduction emphasis

Over the past decade there has been a tremendous emphasis in many industries on cost reduction through mergers and acquisitions to create economies of scale, re-engineering to develop more rational organizations, flattening out of organizations to reduce layers of management and downsizing to increase productivity. While not exactly parallel, the same type of thinking has begun to permeate channel management because a much greater emphasis is being placed on finding ways to reduce the costs of distribution through superior management of distribution channels.

Increased emphasis on technology

Closely related to the distribution cost reduction trend is the greatly increased focus on technology for enhancing distribution effectiveness and efficiency. Telecommunications and computer technology have, of course, been at the forefront of this technological emphasis. From a channel management standpoint, this growing role for technology means that executives involved in channel management will need more in-depth knowledge of technology and, even more importantly, insight into how it can be gainfully applied to improve the effectiveness and efficiency of distribution channels.

Broadened behavioural perspective

Until about twenty-five years ago distribution channels were viewed only as economic systems and virtually devoid of social interactions and processes. Over the last two decades the behavioural approach, which takes a broader perspective of channels by viewing them as social systems as well as economic systems, has grown substantially (Stern 1969). Thus, such basic issues as the use of power and the management of conflict in channels of distribution are approached from a behavioural perspective using the concepts and methods of the behavioural sciences instead of just economic analysis. Those involved in channel management need to be aware of this broadened perspective on social systems because it provides an enhanced set of tools for channel management.

REFERENCES

Abell, Derek F. and Hammond, John S. (1979) *Strategic Market Planning Problems and Analytical Approaches*, Englewood Cliffs, N.J.: Prentice Hall.
Anderson, James C. and Narus, James A. (1990) 'A model of distributor firm and manufacturer firm working partnerships', *Journal of Marketing*, January: 42–58.
Cespedes, Frank V. (1988) 'Channel management is general management', *California Management Review*: 98–120.
Cespedes, Frank V. and Corey, E. Raymond (1990) 'Managing multiple channels', *Business Horizons*, July–August: 67–77.
Cravens, David W. (1988) 'Gaining strategic marketing advantage', *Business Horizons*, September–October: 44–54.
Curhan, Ronald C. and Kopp, Robert S. (1988) 'Obtaining retailers' support for trade deals: key success factors', *Journal of Advertising Research*, January: 51–60.
Drucker, Peter (1990) 'Manage by walking around – outside', *Wall Street Journal*, 11 May: A12.
Dwyer, F. Robert and Sejo, Oh (1988) 'Transaction cost perspective on vertical contractual structure and interchannel competitive strategies', *Journal of Marketing*, April: 21–34.
Kotler, Phillip (1988) *Marketing Management Analysis, Planning, Implementation and Control*, 6th edn, Englewood Cliffs, N.J.: Prentice Hall.
McVey, Phillip (1960) 'Are channels of distribution what the textbooks say?', *Journal of Marketing*, January: 61–5.
Pegram, Roger (1965) *Selecting and Evaluation of Distributors*, New York: The Conference Board.
Porter, Michael E. (1985) *Competitive Advantage Creating and Sustaining Superior Performance*, New York: The Free Press.
Rao, Vithala R. and McLaughlin, Edward W. (1989) 'Modeling the decision to add new products by channel intermediaries', *Journal of Marketing*, January: 80–8.
Rosenbloom, Bert (1987) *Marketing Functions and the Wholesaler-Distributor: Achieving Excellence in Distribution*, Washington, D.C.: Distribution Research and Education Foundation.
Rosenbloom, Bert (1990) 'Motivating your international channel partners', *Business Horizons*, March–April: 53–7.
Rosenbloom, Bert (1995) *Marketing Channels: A Management View*, 5th edn, Fort Worth, Texas: Dryden Press, Harcourt Brace Jovanovich.
Stern, Louis W. (1969) *Distribution Channels: Behavioral Dimensions*, New York: Houghton Mifflin.
Warshaw, Martin R. (1962) 'Pricing to gain wholesalers' selling support', *Journal of Marketing*, July: 50–6.
Wittreich, Warren J. (1962) 'Misunderstanding the retailer', *Harvard Business Review*, May–June: 147–59.

FURTHER READING

Boedecker, Karl A. and Morgan, Fred W. (1980) 'The channel implications of product liability developments', *Journal of Retailing*, Winter: 59–72.

Butanay, Gul and Wortzel, Lawrence H. (1988) 'Distribution power versus manufacturer power: the customer role', *Journal of Marketing*, January: 52–63.

Calantone, Roger J. and Gassenheiner, J. B. (1991) 'Overcoming basic problems between manufacturers and distributors', *Industrial Marketing Management*, Winter: 215–21.

Cespedes, Frank V. (1992) 'Channel power: suggestions for a broadened perspective', *Journal of Marketing Channels*, Spring: 2–37.

Dahlstrom, Robert and Dwyer, F. Robert (1992) 'The political economy of distribution systems: a review and prospectus', *Journal of Marketing Channels*, Fall: 47–86.

Hardy, Kenneth G. (1986) 'Key success factors for manufacturer's sales promotions', *Journal of Marketing*, July: 13–23.

Narus, James A. and Anderson, James C. (1986) 'Turn your industrial distributors into partners', *Harvard Business Review*, March–April: 66–71.

Rosenbloom, Bert and Anderson, Rolph (1985) 'Channel management and sales management: some key interfaces,' *Journal of the Academy of Marketing Science*, Summer: 97–106.

Rosenbloom, Bert (1995) *Marketing Channels: A Management View*, 5th edn, Fort Worth, Texas: Dryden Press, Harcourt Brace Jovanovich.

Shipley, David D. (1984) 'Selection and motivation of distribution intermediaries', *Industrial Marketing Management*, October: 249–56.

Stern, Louis W. and El-Ansary, Adel I. (1992) *Marketing Channels*, 4th edn, Englewood Cliffs, New Jersey: Prentice Hall.

Sutton, Howard (1986) *Rethinking the Company's Selling and Distribution Channels*, New York: The Conference Board.

33

LOGISTICS AND PHYSICAL DISTRIBUTION

Donald J. Bowersox and David J. Closs

Logistics describes the activities required to plan and move items from a material or manufacturing source to the point of consumption. In the past logistics referred to military activities that provided food, clothing, supplies and equipment to troops in the field. Generals understand well the importance of sound logistics in effective military operations. These activities include transportation and storage of supplies and equipment as well as personnel transportation.

While the role of logistics has not always been as visible and well defined for commercial and non-profit enterprises, individual transportation, storage and customer service activities were still performed. However, top management did not always understand the importance and competitive impact of integrated logistics. Wide acceptance of enterprise operating philosophies such as just-in-time, total quality management, customer satisfaction and customer responsiveness enhances the role of logistics in achieving the enterprise mission. A well-planned logistics effort is necessary for timely shipment arrival, undamaged product and satisfied customers. Both the professional and popular press recognize logistics' role in serving customers effectively.

Simply stated, customers desire nine rights in any transaction:

1 the right product;
2 the right quantity;
3 the right quality;
4 the right place;
5 the right time;
6 the right form;
7 the right price;
8 the right packaging;
9 the right information.

Logistics plays a major role in delivering these rights to customers.

This chapter describes logistics and its role in achieving customer satisfaction for the enterprise. The discussion describes activities required to achieve the logistics mission and logistics' role in firm strategy. The first section offers a formal definition of logistics and discusses its role as a component of the marketing mix. The second section describes the logistics value chain flows, objectives and activities. The value chain represents the institutions, inventory and information flows required to serve customers effectively and efficiently. The third section discusses current issues in logistics. Strategies used by leading-edge logistics firms to achieve their mission and sustain an overall competitive advantage are illustrated. The chapter concludes with a summary and suggestions for further study.

A CLOSER LOOK AT LOGISTICS AND WHAT IT DOES

This section reviews a definition of logistics and describes some of the managerial activities involved. The role of logistics relative to the other elements of the marketing mix is also discussed.

The Council of Logistics Management, the major logistics professional organization, defines logistics as 'the process of planning, implementing and controlling the efficient, effective flow and storage of goods, services and related information from the point of origin to the point of consumption for the purposes of conforming to customer requirements'. A few comments regarding this definition are appropriate.

First, logistics includes the actions required to design (plan), manage (implement) and measure (control) the activities of the firm when moving materials or finished products to customers. The design or planning activities include the selection of distribution parties and carriers. The parties include wholesalers, distributors, retailers and third party service providers necessary to offer service at the level demanded by customers. The carrier design decision includes the selection of modes (rail vs truck vs combination) and specific carrier operators. The managerial aspect of logistics includes scheduling and execution of activities to respond to customers and facilitate shipments. Management or execution activities include order processing, selection and shipment. Measurement includes monitoring activities to ensure performance both satisfies customers and deploys firm resources effectively. Typical measures include customer service level, cost, productivity, asset utilization and quality.

Second, while logistics has historically focused on goods movement, current definitions broaden the scope to include services and information since customers typically require that goods, services and related information arrive concurrently. Examples of product-related services and information include order and shipment documentation, manuals, warranty information and invoices.

Third, logistics includes product movement and storage from point of origin to point of consumption. This scope specifically encompasses the movement of raw material and components from suppliers to manufacturing sites and movement of finished product to distribution facilities and ultimately to customers.

While logistics has been defined as a discipline of its own, it is important to note that logistics is also a critical component of the firm's marketing capability. The contribution of logistics to the firm's marketing efforts is discussed below.

A firm's marketing mix is defined as the combination of product, price, promotion and place that provides superior value to customers. The product is the physical good or service desired by the customer. In general, logistics offers timely delivery of the place component. A firm must make many place-related decisions when developing a marketing strategy. Some of these decisions include:

1 Which wholesalers or distributors to use?
2 How large a geographic area to serve?
3 What type of retailers to use (if any)?
4 Whether to make inventory to stock or to order?
5 How should information technology support inventory movement and allocation activities?

Make to stock means inventory is produced to forecast or plan in anticipation of customer demand. Make to order involves custom production. The right product, price and promotional mix is useless without dependable and timely product availability (place). Timely availability means that the customer can purchase a product at the desired location or arrange delivery when and where desired. For a customer, availability or timely delivery of a shirt or pair of pants is as important as the right price or colour.

LOGISTICS VALUE CHAIN

The logistics value chain is a conceptualization that views all activities required to meet objectives as a single process linking an enterprise with its customers. The value chain could represent a single vertically integrated firm controlling all activities from raw material procurement to retail sales which is typical of the petroleum industry.

Alternatively, the value chain could involve a number of firms including material suppliers, manufacturers, wholesaler, retailers and carriers. Figure 1 illustrates the value chain and its flow in the form of inventory and information. The information flow consists of sales activity, forecasts and orders which must be refined into deployment, manufacturing and procurement plans. As products and materials are procured, a value-added inventory flow is initiated which ultimately transfers ownership of finished product to customers under the terms and conditions of sale. Thus, the logistics process is not viewed in the context of traditional functions such as transportation and warehousing but ideally in terms of two interrelated flows:

573

Value-added inventory flow

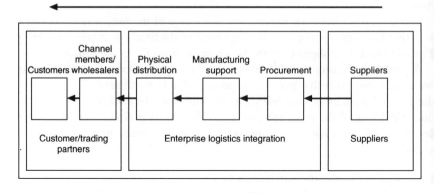

Information requirements flow

Figure 1   Integrated logistics operations

1   information flow;
2   inventory flow.

Two observations are in order prior to discussing each flow in detail. First, the logistics process illustrated in Figure 1 is not limited to for-profit business firms, nor is it unique to manufacturing firms. For example, the American Red Cross uses logistics extensively to support day-to-day blood collection operations and periodically for disaster relief. Product must be collected from donors (blood donors or goods contributors), stored in a warehouse and delivered when and where needed. The need to coordinate requirements and physical fulfilment occurs in all businesses and public sector organizations.

Retailers and wholesalers typically link physical distribution and procurement activities since no change in product form is typically required. Nevertheless, wholesalers and retailers are key contributors to logistics value added. Wholesalers develop assortments of products from multiple manufacturers allowing retailers to purchase desired product combinations in smaller quantities. Retailers make a broad range of product conveniently available to customers. All societies and organizations require some elements of logistics regardless of their political structure and degree of economic development. Logistics is universal to growth and survival.

A second observation is that normal value-added inventory flow towards customers must sometimes be reversed. Product recall capability is a critical competency to accommodate increasingly rigid quality standards, product expiration dates and responsibility for hazardous materials. Reverse logistics is also necessary due to the increasing number of laws prohibiting disposal and encouraging recycling of containers and packaging materials. Reverse logistics does not usually enjoy the scale economies characteristic of initial outbound movement. However, reverse movement capability is a social responsibility that must be accommodated in logistical system design. A significant reverse logistics requirement is the need for maximum control when a potential health or liability exists (e.g. spoiled or tainted product). In this sense, a recall programme is similar to a maximum customer service strategy that must be executed on a zero defect basis without concerns for cost. Johnson & Johnson's response during the Tylenol crisis was a prime example of maximum control customer service. Thus, operational requirements of reverse logistics range from lowest total cost, as in returning bottles for recycling, to maximum performance solutions for critical recalls. The important point is that sound logistics strategy cannot be developed without careful evaluation of reverse logistics requirements.

VALUE CHAIN FLOW

As previously discussed, the logistics value chain includes both inventory (physical) and information flow. The participants, components and activities involved in each flow are discussed.

Logistics operations are concerned with movement and storage of materials and finished products. Logistics operations begin with the initial shipment of materials or component parts from a supplier and are finalized when manufactured or processed product is delivered to a customer. From the initial material or component purchase, logistics adds value by moving inventory closer to the market and making it available in assortments and quantities desired by customers. Material gains value as it is transformed into finished product or moves closer to the market. For firms using assembly processes, work-in-process inventory must also be moved to support manufacturing operations. The cost of each component and its movement becomes part of the value added. The final and only meaningful value added occurs when final ownership is conveyed to customers when and where specified.

For large manufacturers logistical operations may include thousands of movements, which ultimately culminate in the delivery of assembled products to an industrial user, retailer, wholesaler, dealer or other customer. For large retailers logistical operations may commence with the procurement of products for resale and terminate with consumer pickup or home delivery. For hospitals logistics begins with procurement and ends with full support of patient surgery and recovery. The significant point is that regardless of the size and type of enterprise, logistics is essential and requires continuous management attention. For better understanding, it is useful to divide logistical operations into three operating areas:

1 physical distribution;
2 manufacturing support;
3 procurement.

Figure 1 illustrates the integrated logistics operations of an enterprise and extends the integration through the entire value chain.

Physical distribution describes product movement to customers. Physical distribution links a logistics value chain with its customers by providing the time and place utility of the marketing mix. All physical distribution systems have the common characteristics of linking manufacturers, wholesalers and retailers into value chains that make product available throughout the marketing channel.

Manufacturing support concentrates on managing work-in-process inventory as it moves between manufacturing stages. The primary manufacturing related logistics responsibility is facilitating a master production schedule and arranging timely material and component availability. Thus, the overall logistics concern is not how production is performed, but ensuring that materials and components arrive in a timely manner and that finished goods are released for shipment. The difference between manufacturing support and physical distribution is that the former serves customers and therefore must accommodate market uncertainty. Manufacturing support generally involves moving materials under enterprise control. The uncertainties introduced by random customer ordering and erratic demand characterizing physical distribution are not typical of manufacturing support.

Procurement involves the purchasing and arranging for inbound movement of materials, parts and/or finished inventory from suppliers to manufacturing or assembly plants, warehouses or retail stores. Depending on the situation, the acquisition process is commonly identified by different names. In manufacturing acquisition is typically called purchasing. Government acquisition has traditionally been termed procurement. Retailers and wholesalers often use the term buying. In many circles the total process is referred to as inbound logistics. Acknowledging that differences do exist concerning acquisition situations, procurement is used here to represent all types of purchasing. Procurement is concerned with availability of the desired material assortments where and when required. Whereas physical distribution is concerned with product shipments, procurement is concerned with inbound materials timing, sorting and assembly. Under most marketing situations involving consumer products, such as a grocery manufacturer who ships to a retail food chain, a manufacturer's physical distribution directly interfaces with retailer procurement. Although similar or even identical transportation requirements may be involved, degree of managerial control and risk relative to the implications of performance failure vary substantially between physical distribution and procurement.

Within a typical enterprise, the three logistical operations overlap. Viewing each as an integral part of the value-adding process creates opportunities to capitalize on unique characteristics of each while facilitating overall performance. The prime concern of integrated logistics is to coordinate overall value-added inventory movement to reduce redundancy and waste. A total logistics perspective must provide integrated management of materials, semi-finished components and finished products moving between suppliers, manufacturers, wholesalers and customers of the enterprise. In this sense, logistics is concerned with strategic management of total movement and storage.

Information comprises the second key flow in the value-added chain. Information communicates customer and replenishment requirements, provides order status updates and initiates physical activities to process orders. Replenishment orders resupply wholesalers and distributors from suppliers or manufacturing plants. With lower cost information technology and increasing demands for reduced operating uncertainty, logistical operations can use enhanced information flow as a primary means to increase value added. Value is enhanced through information accuracy, timelines and appropriateness, thus reducing the personnel, capital and inventory resources required to accomplish the logistics mission.

There are two primary information flows that drive logistics operations:

1 Planning and Coodination Requirements.
2 Operational Requirements.

Planning and Coordination Requirements systems drive capacity, logistics, manufacturing and procurement requirements planning. Based on business and product forecasts, Planning and Coordination Requirements systems time phase product needs to determine which products are needed where and when. The requirement plans can then be used to plan facility and manufacturing capacity requirements and product replenishment schedules. Accurate and timely Planning and Coordination Requirements systems reduce uncertainty, thus limiting the need for anticipatory actions and extensive safety stocks. Safety stocks are buffer or just-in-case inventories maintained to cover situations such as excessive demand or extended delivery times.

Operational Requirements systems initiate and control customer and replenishment orders. While Planning and Coordination Requirements systems are designed to anticipate product demands without being overly speculative in terms of inventory movement, Operational Requirements systems initiate physical activities to satisfy customer demand after it has actually been experienced. The operating activities include order entry and management, warehouse operations, inventory control, transportation and invoicing. These activities represent the day-to-day work of logistics. The Operational Requirement system, typically termed the order processing and shipping system, is the backbone of most firms' information systems.

The combination of the two systems forms total logistics information flow. Planning and Coordination Requirements systems manage the firm's production and inventory capacity while Operational Requirements systems fulfil customer demand. When a firm operates in a make-to-order environment, the systems coincide since it is not necessary to maintain anticipatory inventory. When the firm operates under a make-to-stock strategy, the logistics information system must rationalize conflicts between facility and operating capacities, inventory levels and customer demands.

VALUE CHAIN OPERATING OBJECTIVES

When designing and administering logistics systems, each firm and its value chain partners must simultaneously strive to achieve six conflicting operational objectives. These objectives are the primary determinants of logistical performance and include:

1 rapid response;
2 minimum variance;
3 minimum inventory deployment;
4 movement consolidation;
5 total quality;
6 life-cycle support.

Rapid response concerns the firm's ability to satisfy customer requirements in a timely manner. Demands may be in the form of special product requests, quick delivery or product status information. Information technology increases the potential to postpone logistical decisions to the last possible moment and then helps facilitate rapid delivery of required inventory. Examples of such information technology applications include the use of point-of-sale (POS) data to drive replenishment of retail inventory. In the past retail replenishment was based on forecasts, which included substantial uncertainty resulting in significant safety stock. The ability to track daily retail sales and rapidly respond with the exact replenishment assortment reduces safety stock needs. Rapid response introduces the capability to shift operational emphasis from anticipatory planning based on a forecast to a response-based operation based on actual sales. Since inventory in a response-based system is typically not positioned until customer requirements are known, little tolerance exists for operational failure. Rapid response eliminates inventories traditionally required to satisfy anticipated customer requirements.

Minimum variance is the second objective. Variance is any unexpected disruption of logistics system operations. For example, order receipt delays, manufacturing disruptions, damaged goods or demand surges all result in operating variances that must be identified and resolved. Logistics variance results in stockouts or requires safety stock to reduce stockouts. Variance can be both internal and external to the enterprise. External variance is the more difficult to identify and costly to resolve. An example of internal variance is the inconsistency in order-processing time due to delays correcting or validating order information. A major form of external variance is deviations in transit time as vehicles are delayed by traffic, weather or equipment breakdowns.

All aspects of logistics system operations have variance potential. The traditional solution for resolving variance was to deploy safety stock or use high-cost premium transportation. Reliance on such traditional high-risk and costly practices has been replaced by exacting forms of logistics process control. Rather than maintaining safety stock just in case, a preferred solution is to identify and eliminate the source of the uncertainty. To the extent that variances are minimized, logistics productivity is improved. Thus, the second logistics performance objective is to minimize variance.

The third objective, minimum inventory, focuses on asset commitment and relative turn velocity. Asset commitment is the value of inventory deployed throughout the logistics system. Turn velocity refers to the rate of inventory usage over time. For an average retail food item, the distribution channel maintains about fifteen weeks of supply, which includes inventory located at the manufacturer through finished items on the retail shelf. This implies the total value chain 'turns over' inventory approximately 3.5 times per year (52 weeks/ 15 weeks). High turn rates mean that assets devoted to inventory are being effectively utilized. Conversely, low turns suggest that excessive inventory is being held by manufacturers, wholesalers and retailers. The objective is to reduce inventory deployment as low as possible while meeting desired customer service goals and achieving the lowest total logistics cost. Concepts like zero inventory have become increasingly popular as managers seek to reduce inventory deployment risk. Operational deficiencies in a logistics system are often not apparent until inventory is reduced to the lowest level. For example, high inventory levels often mask the operating problems caused by variances in processing or transportation cycle time. While the goal of eliminating all inventory is attractive, it is important to remember that inventory can and does provide some important logistics benefits including decoupling demand and supply. Inventory can also provide improved return on investment through manufacturing or procurement economies of scale. To achieve the minimum inventory objective, the logistics system design must control inventory commit-ment and turn velocity for the entire enterprise as contrasted to each business location. The extension of enterprisewide inventory management to a total value chain requires cross-organizational planning and cooperation. Managing inven-tory deployment for the total value chain reduces duplication and wasted effort caused by poor communication between partners.

The fourth logistics objective is to achieve maximum movement consolida-tion. Transportation is the largest logistics expense. In general, transportation cost increases with distance and product susceptibility to damage. Transporta-tion cost per unit of weight decreases as shipment size increases. Many logistical systems use high-speed, small shipment transportation such as air express to provide premium service at a high cost. Maximum movement consolidation can help to reduce transportation expense. Consolidation can be achieved by aggregating multiple smaller shipments into one large quantity for linehaul (i.e. long distance) movement. The linehaul shipment is then split for delivery to customer destinations. Although there is usually some expense for local distribution, there is substantial cost saving from the consolidated linehaul move. Maximum consolidation requires innovative programmes to group small shipments for movement. Such programmes must be facilitated by arrangements that transcend the overall value chain.

The fifth logistics objective is to seek continuous total quality improvement. Total quality management (TQM) is a major commitment throughout industry. A defective product or poor service detracts logistics value added. Once a product is moved closer to the customer, logistics expenses for storage and transportation cannot be recovered for damaged or incorrect product. In fact, when product or service quality fails either prior to or within the logistics system, the logistical process typically needs to be reversed and then repeated. Logistics itself must perform to demanding quality standards. The management challenge of achieving zero defect logistical performance is magnified by the fact that logistics activities are performed across a vast geography at all times of day and night. The quality challenge is further magnified by the fact that most logistical work is performed without supervision. Repeating a shipment as a result of incorrect content or in-transit damage is far more costly than performing it right the first time. Logistics is a prime component in achieving continuous TQM improvement.

The final logistics objective is life-cycle support. Few items are sold without some guarantee that the product will perform as advertised over a specified period. In fact, some products, such as copying equipment, derive the majority of their profits from after market sales and service of supplies and parts. The importance of life-cycle support varies directly with the product and customer. For firms marketing consumer durable or industrial equipment, the commitment to life-cycle support constitutes a demanding operational requirement as well as one of the largest costs of logistical operations. The life-cycle support capabilities of a logistical system must be carefully designed. As noted earlier, reverse logistical competency, given worldwide attention to environmental concerns, requires the ability to recycle ingredients and packaging materials.

LOGISTICS ACTIVITIES

While it is appropriate to consider the logistics process as an integrated value chain, it is also useful to reflect on the major activities used to accomplish the logistics mission. Traditional organizations incorporate four logistics activities:

1 Customer service;
2 Transportation;
3 Inventory management;
4 Distribution operations.

Even though many firms have integrated the logistics process with other internal functions and externally to suppliers and customers, these activities remain the heart of the logistics value chain. Each activity is described.

Customer service is the primary interface between the firm and its customers from an order fulfilment perspective. Customer service includes order taking and change, order status enquiry handling and often customer problem resolution. While the historic customer service focus has been order taking and change, other customer service considerations are receiving increased attention. Order taking excellence is expected as the norm. However, a key service determinant is often a firm's ability to offer responsive and flexible service tailored to meet each customer's needs at the lowest possible total cost. For example, customers expect the firm's customer service activity to be capable of providing accurate information regarding product availability, delivery time, product substitution, pricing and product customization options.

Transportation controls product movement from manufacturing sites to distribution facilities and from distribution facilities to customers. The responsibilities include selecting carrier mode (air, rail, truck), carrier scheduling, routing and freight payment. In addition to managing the firm's shipping activities, transportation is responsible for monitoring carrier performance. Logistics is responsible for improving transportation service levels while simultaneously decreasing overall cost. The transportation management objective is to minimize expenses associated with all movements from suppliers to the final customer. While there are not many fundamental advances in transportation technology or modal offerings, advanced transportation carriers do offer customized services that can provide value to customers. Examples of such value-added services include electronic scheduling, billing and invoicing, consolidation with other shippers and product storage. Transportation is responsible for monitoring the service offerings of carrier (or other third-party service providers) and evaluating ways effectively to incorporate new services into the overall value chain.

Inventory management is responsible for monitoring inventory levels and requirements at manufacturing plants and distribution facilities. The inventory management objective is to maintain enough inventory to satisfy customer demands while minimizing total asset deployment. Historically, inventory management has focused on establishing the necessary safety stock to meet desired service level. The focus today is to identify information technology applications that can reduce operating uncertainty and thus safety stock requirements. Leading edge logistics firms gather information regarding customer demands, customer marketing plans, delivery times and replenishment cycles so that improved knowledge can reduce inventory requirements.

Distribution operations is responsible for the physical facilities and activities that take place at the distribution facilities used by a firm. The facilities include the buildings, offices, communications equipment, storage racks and material handling equipment such as forklifts. The activities include product receipt, storage, order selection and shipment. The distribution operations objective is to minimize expenses for receiving, storing and shipping product from a distribution facility. The historical operations focus has been to minimize the variable cost associated with handling or moving a product through a distribution facility. However, minimum variable cost is not the only objective. A more comprehensive focus is to reduce assets required to support logistics while simultaneously increasing operating flexibility. Reduced assets implies removing distribution facilities and handling equipment off a company's books. Operating flexibility is necessary to accommodate both larger, time-critical orders and smaller, less service-sensitive orders. While some firms attempt to service both types of orders through the same facility, others improve flexibility while using fewer assets through the employment of third-party service providers such as public or contract warehouse operators.

While management of each activity must focus on cost reduction, the major objective must be minimization of total cost for providing coordinated logistics services that meet desired customer service levels. In this sense, the cost-to-cost trade-off between each activity must be evaluated to identify potential performance improvements. For example, use of air freight as the transport mode may increase transportation expense but may also decrease total logistics cost by reducing inventory management and distribution operating expenses. Logistics management is responsible for identifying the trade-off that can provide comparable or enhanced customer value added while reducing total logistics expense.

CURRENT ISSUES AND FUTURE DEVELOPMENTS

Logistics has responded to efforts to improve enterprise competitiveness through six enhancements in strategy and practice. Each is described and illustrated.

Value chain integration

Value chain integration refers to the coordination of planning and operating activities throughout the distribution channel including suppliers, manu-facturers, distributors and retailers. Value chain integration implies that channel organizations apply a total systems perspective. For example, without integra-tion, each channel organization manages its own inventory. This independent approach means that inventory for each channel participant is designed to protect against the uncertainty introduced by independent action of the other organizations in the channel. Specifically, under the independent management scenario, a retailer managing inventory must provide a safety stock to allow for the possibility that the distributor may be out of stock. Since the distributor would have to do likewise, distributor safety stock is necessary. Since uncertainty exists at all interfaces within a channel, multiple inventory safety stocks are required unless operations are coordinated.

The value chain integration scenario coordinates overall channel inventory management by transferring information and assigning agreed-to responsibility among channel members. The organization that accepts overall inventory management responsibility uses the shared information to reduce each channel member's uncertainty. Less uncertainty reduces the need for safety stock at each channel level. With the coordination offered by value chain integration, channel members can provide comparable service to customers with less inventory. Lower inventories reduce expenses by reducing investment or working capital needs.

In addition to inventory reduction, value chain integration reduces redundancy and increases coordination in other areas such as transportation, packaging, labelling and documentation. A review of the information processing and product handling activities performed by each channel member often identifies redundancies and non-value-added actions. Value chain integration improves channel effectiveness by removing redundancies and assigning specific responsibilities to the channel member that can best perform the action. Effective value chain integration requires accurate activity-based costing and refinements to the compensation system for channel members.

Performance measurement

A second enhancement is a strong focus on performance measurement. Cross-organization measures are required to monitor current performance and identify improvement opportunities. The range of performance measures include customer service, cost, productivity, asset deployment and quality. Typical service measures focus on order fill rates, order cycle time, and customer responsiveness. Cost measures include transportation and handling expenses measured in amount per order or amount per kilo. Cost measures also focus on the profitability of individual products or accounts by tracking logistics expenses required to serve specific segments. Productivity measures monitor utilization for facilities, equipment and labour. Asset deployment and quality measures include inventory turnover, service quality and damage.

Measurement systems must combine both performance targets specified by management and information systems to track, analyse and report performance. Performance can be tracked using real-time monitoring technologies such as bar-coding, scanning, radio frequency communication and on-board computers. These technologies facilitate product tracking and data collection by effectively recording movement without excessive paperwork. The data collected are then evaluated to identify past performance problems and to anticipate future problems.

Information technology

Extensive application of new information technology capabilities is another enhancement characteristic of best practice logistics organizations. Technologies

583

include processing, storage and communications hardware as well as extensive advanced software applications. From a performance perspective, information technology must provide accurate, available, flexible, integrated and timely systems.

Information technology facilitates operations in two ways. First, it permits faster performance of order receipt, handling, selection, shipment and invoicing. Faster performance reduces order cycle time from the customer's perspective and reduces clerical labour and errors, thus reducing cost. Rapid communications also reduces demand and lead time uncertainty, thus reducing the need for safety stocks. Second, information technology facilitates planning and evaluation of alternatives using decision support applications. Identification and evaluation of alternatives improves the speed, accuracy and comprehensiveness of logistics decisions.

Communications

Improved real time communications between sites and distribution channel partners is another logistical best practice enhancement. Information transfers include day-to-day tactical information such as orders and inventory status. It also includes longer term strategic information such as product development and marketing plans. While such information could be communicated via mail, such exchange is neither fast nor consistent enough significantly to improve logistics operations. Historically, information exchanges were costly and error prone. However, using electronic data interchange (EDI) it is now possible to exchange instantaneously both tactical and strategic information. Examples of such exchanges include orders, inventory status, shipment notification, invoices, payments, development and marketing plans. Rapid accurate communications reduce delays and increase decision certainty, resulting in lower asset and financial risk. For example, many of the mass merchandisers use satellite communications to report daily item sales allowing for rapid and accurate store replenishment.

Globalization

The fifth logistics best-practice enhancement is the ability to support global operations. While not all firms operate internationally, firms are increasingly realizing that global business will impact their competitiveness and growth potential. Global sourcing can reduce material expense through the use of lowest cost suppliers. Global marketing enhances potential growth by opening up new customers and regions. While globalization might offer significant opportunities, a firm must accommodate a number of logistics challenges if they elect to source or market outside their primary geographic area. The challenges involve extended transport distances, increased documentation and increased customer diversity. Longer transport distances increase both transportation cost and uncertainty. Global operations means documentation must accommodate local requirements for customs, carriers, invoices and insurance. Global operations must also accommodate customer diversity in the form of technical characteristics, packaging and languages. These challenges place significant demands on logistics operations. However, enhanced potential for growth may outweigh the cost of logistic complexity. Therefore, leading-edge logistics organizations are learning to operate effectively in a global environment.

Time-based strategies

A final change being implemented by leading-edge logistics firms is the ability to exploit time-based logistics strategies. Examples of time-based logistics strategies include just-in-time (JIT), quick response (QR), continuous replenishment (CR) and profile replenishment (PR). Time-based strategies shift coordination activities between value chain members to reduce performance cycle lengths and to increase inventory velocity.

Just-in-time is a time-based strategy that schedules material arrival to coincide with production requirements. The major driver of a JIT process is a manufacturing schedule that is relatively fixed. There is a subtle difference between JIT, which is manufacturing focused, and the remaining time-based strategies, which are market focused. The market-focused strategies must react to changes and uncertainties in market demands which typically have significantly more uncertainty than a manufacturing schedule.

Quick response is a cooperative effort to provide merchandise supply closely matched to consumer buying patterns. QR is driven by monitoring retail sales for specific products and sharing information across the value chain to guarantee the right product assortment will be available when and where it is required. Information sharing facilitates the QR process between retailers and manufacturers. A typical QR arrangement operates as follows. Orders from retailers are sent to manufacturers via EDI. The manufacturer can then plan the most effective and efficient way to satisfy requirements. The planned fulfilment is communicated to retailers in advance of product arrival so that labour and deliveries can be scheduled. This closed loop or engineered cross-organizational working arrangement reduces uncertainty, total cost and inventory assets required to perform logistics and typically improves service performance.

A continuous replenishment strategy is an extension of QR that eliminates the creation of replenishment orders. The CR goal is to create a supply chain arrangement so flexible and efficient that retail inventory is continuously replenished. Using a daily transmission of retail sales or warehouse shipments, the manufacturer assumes the responsibility to replenish retail inventory in the required quantities, colours, sizes, and styles.

The profile replenishment (PR) strategy extends QR and CR by giving manufacturers the right to anticipate future requirements based on their overall knowledge of what is important to a merchandise category. A 'profile' is the

585

combination of sizes, colours and associated products that typically sell in a merchandise category. Given profile responsibility, the manufacturer can eliminate retailer efforts to track sales and inventory levels for fast-moving products.

These time-based strategies illustrate how the coordination of logistics throughout the value chain can shift responsibilities to the channel partner which can perform it most efficiently and remove redundant activities. For example, a manufacturer may take inventory management responsibility for wholesalers and retailers since information technology can offer total inventory visibility which significantly decreases uncertainty. Another example is the elimination of retailer activities, such as invoice verification, by improving manufacturer invoice accuracy. Time-based strategies reduce process delays and cycle times resulting in lower logistics cost.

CONCLUSION

This review of logistics and its role suggests three conclusions. First, logistics is a significant component in the engine driving economic development. Logistical management plans, performs and monitors the movement of product from the suppliers through value-adding stages ultimately to consumers. On average logistics consumes about 11 per cent of the gross domestic product and employs approximately 20 per cent of a nation's workforce. While the cost and magnitude of logistics operations is significant, the logistics performance in most developed countries is even more impressive. While there are occasional out-of-stocks, it is rare that customers cannot be satisfied through product substitution or alternative sourcing. On the other hand, inadequate logistics systems in underdeveloped economies significantly contribute to poor availability and relatively high product cost on retail shelves.

Second, increased demand and globalization will continue significantly to challenge logistics operations and management. Customers demand more specialized products and services from a wider range of sources resulting in need for logistics systems that can handle more product variations through alternative distribution. These demands increase logistics system complexity since it is no longer the case that customers are willing to purchase standardized products. Logistics capability must provide assortments in a number of different package configurations from a number of retail formats. The combinations dramatically increase logistics operating complexity. Global logistics must support global procurement and marketing across diverse geographical areas. This support increases product diversity, distance and documentation requirements, all of which increase the complexity of logistics.

Third, logistics expertise can contribute to a substantial competitive advantage for high-performance firms. Strategies such as value chain integration, performance measurement, information technology applications, communication advancements, global operations and time-based competition can position firms to provide more time or service value to customers at a lower total cost. Since these strategies cannot be duplicated readily by competitors, logistics can provide a sustainable source of competitive advantage.

NOTE

Some of this material is adapted from the forthcoming text: Bowersox, D. J. and Closs, D. J. *Logistical Management*, 4th edn, Boston: McGraw-Hill.

FURTHER READING

Bowersox, D. J. (1990) 'The strategic benefits of logistics alliances', *Harvard Business Review* 68 (4): 36–45.
Bowersox, D. J. and Closs, D. J. (forthcoming) *Logistical Management*, 4th edn, Boston: McGraw-Hill.
Bowersox, D. J., Daugherty, P. J., Droge, C. L., Germain, R. N. and Rogers, D. S. (1992) *Logistical Excellence: It's not Business as Usual*, Burlington, MA: Digital Press.
Stalk, G., Evans, P. and Shulman, L. (1992) 'Competing on capabilities: the new rules of corporate strategy', *Harvard Business Review* 70 (2): 57–70.

34

WHOLESALING: THE ROLE OF MARKETING INTERMEDIARIES[1]

Adel I. El-Ansary and Louis W. Stern

WHOLESALING DEFINED

The focus of this chapter is on the functions of specialist markets and intermediaries between producers and organizational buyers (i.e. wholesaling). Wholesaling is concerned with the activities of those persons or establishments which sell to retailers and other merchants, and/or to industrial, institutional, and commercial users, but who do not sell in significant amounts to ultimate consumers.

Of course, accepting this definition as the gospel truth means that every sale made by every organization to anyone but an ultimate consumer is a 'wholesale transaction'. This would include every manufacturing firm (with the exception of the small amount of sales made through factory outlets to household consumers) as well as sales made by such diverse organizations as hotels, insurance companies and accounting firms when they deal with 'industrial, institutional, and commercial' users in booking rooms, arranging pension plans, or preparing annual reports. Therefore, almost all organizations (except those dealing with ultimate consumers) are engaged in wholesaling and their transactions are classified as wholesale transactions.

RATIONALE FOR THE EMERGENCE OF MODERN WHOLESALERS

The wholesaler's functions are shaped by the vast economic task of coordinating production and consumption, or, in Alderson's words (1971: 20), of matching heterogeneous demands for assortments at various levels within distribution. Thus, wholesalers aid in bridging the gap between periods and places in which goods are produced and those in which they are consumed or used.

The sorting process of wholesalers is the key to their economic viability. It frequently happens that the quantities in which goods are produced or the

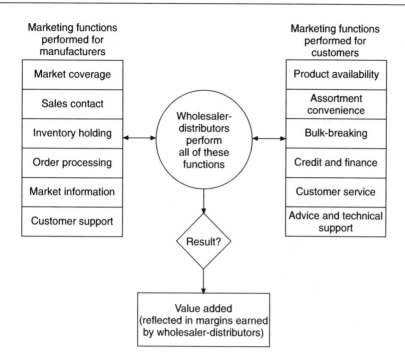

Marketing functions performed for manufacturers

Market coverage

Sales contact

Inventory holding

Order processing

Market information

Customer support

Wholesaler-distributors perform all of these functions

Result?

Marketing functions performed for customers

Product availability

Assortment convenience

Bulk-breaking

Credit and finance

Customer service

Advice and technical support

Value added (reflected in margins earned by wholesaler-distributors)

Figure 1   Value added by wholesaler-distributors through the performance of marketing functions
Source: Rosenbloom (1987: 26)

characteristics with which they are endowed by nature do not match either the quantities in which they are demanded or the characteristics desired by those who use or consume them. Channel intermediaries (e.g. wholesalers and retailers) essentially solve the problem of the discrepancy between the various assortments of goods and services required by industrial and household consumers and the assortments available directly from individual producers. In other words, manufacturers usually produce a large quantity of a limited number of products, whereas consumers purchase only a few items of a large number of diverse products. Middlemen reduce this discrepancy of assortments, thereby enabling consumers to avoid dealing directly with individual manufacturers in order to satisfy their needs.

Wholesalers may participate in the performance of any or all of the marketing flows (i.e. ownership, physical possession, information, financing, risk taking, negotiating, ordering and payment). However, the rationale for a wholesaler's existence boils down to the 'value adding' functions he performs for the suppliers and customers he serves as illustrated in Figure 1. His economic justification is based on just what it is that he can do for his clientele, whether

they are retailers, institutions (e.g. hospitals, schools, restaurants), manufacturers, or any other type of business enterprise. For example, in the case of
industrial goods needed in the assembly of a given product (e.g. transistors for
radios), it may be less costly for the purchasing organization to place the burden
of handling, owning, storing, delivering and ordering the goods on a wholesaler
rather than having to order in very large lots directly from the manufacturer,
especially if the goods will have to be held for a considerable period before they
are used up in the production process.

THE STRUCTURE OF WHOLESALING

Wholesaling may be characterized as a sector of the economy in which the degree of
specialization has constantly increased. In fact, as depicted in Table 1, the
institutional variety in wholesaling is almost overwhelming. Such a variety offers
buyers and sellers many channel choices, as dictated by such considerations as size,
market segmentation, financial strength, services offered and chosen method of
operation. It also makes possible a high degree of marketing flow or functional
shiftability, whereby any of the functions performed at the wholesale level of
distribution may be shifted from one type of agency to another.

Table 1   Types of operation, wholesale trade

Merchant wholesaler
Wholesale merchants or jobbers
Industrial distributors
Voluntary group wholesalers
Importers
Exporters
Cash-and-carry wholesalers
Retailer cooperative warehouses
Terminal and country grain elevators
Farm products assemblers
Wholesale cooperative associations
Petroleum bulk plants and terminals

Manufacturers' sales branches and offices
Sales branches (with stocks)
Sales offices (without stocks)

Agents, brokers and commission merchants
Auction companies
Import agents
Export agents
Selling agents
Merchandise brokers
Commission merchants
Manufacturers' agents

Source: US Dept of Commerce, Bureau of Census (1990: A–10–A–11)

Table 2 Summary of wholesalers' participation in the marketing flows

	Physical possession	Ownership	Promotion	Negotiation	Financing	Risk	Ordering	Payment
Merchant wholesalers								
Full-function or service wholesalers	High	High	High	High	High	High	High	High
Limited-function wholesalers								
Drop shipper (desk jobber)	None	High	Low	High	High	High	High	High
Cash-carry wholesalers	High	High	Low	High	None	Low	High	High
Wagon (truck) jobbing	Low	Low	Low	High	Low	Low	High	High
Rack jobbers (service merchandise)	High	High	High	High	High	High	High	High
Converters	Low	High	Low	High	High	High	High	High
Wholesaler-sponsored (voluntary) chains	High	High	High	High	High	High	High	High
Retailer-sponsored cooperatives	High	High	High	High	High	High	High	High
Functional middlemen (agents and brokers)								
Brokers	None	None	High	Low	None	None	High	Low
Manufacturers' agents	None	None	High	None	None	None	High	Low
Selling agents	None	None	High	High	None	None	High	Low
Commission merchants	High	None	High	High	High	High	High	High

From a channel analysis perspective, it is important to understand what specific roles the various wholesaling institutions and agencies assume, so that when a channel is designed or adjusted the appropriate kind of organization can be included. An essential piece of information in this regard is whether a wholesaler participates in all or only a few of the marketing flows (physical possession, ownership, promotion, negotiation, financing, risking, ordering and payment). That is, assuming a manufacturer's or a retailer's perspective for the moment, what is it that one could expect to receive from a wholesaler in the way of services performed? Clearly, the more services performed, the higher the wholesaler's compensation will have to be from the channel as a whole. Table 2 produces a summary of the flows participated in by the variety of wholesaling enterprises.

An examination of Table 2 indicates that full-function merchant wholesalers participate in all the flows while brokers and manufacturers' agents participate in only a few of them. Therefore, if a manufacturer were to 'employ' full-function merchant wholesalers, the functional discount granted to them would have to be considerably more than the commission he would have to pay to manufacturers' agents or brokers for selling his products to end-users. But when a manufacturer does not use a full-function wholesaler he does not 'save' the discount, because he must assume all of the services the wholesaler would have provided. This is why the discount is called 'functional'. It is granted for these wholesalers to compensate them for the cost incurred in the performance of these functions.

SELECTING AND USING WHOLESALERS

It is an old axiom of marketing that it is possible to eliminate wholesalers (or any middlemen, for that matter) but impossible to eliminate their functions. The major question facing a manufacturer is whether, by vertically integrating (that is, by establishing his own sales branches and warehouse facilities), he can perform the functions more efficiently and effectively than a wholesaler. This question is a cause of considerable controversy in formulating marketing channel strategy.

The likelihood is that the cost of marketing through wholesalers is not going to be vastly different from the funds a firm would have to expend on its own to obtain the same services. If this is so, then what accounts for the large amount of direct selling that goes on? Why is vertical integration of wholesaling functions so popular, especially among large manufacturing and retailing firms?

The answer lies not only in efficiency considerations but mainly in effectiveness considerations. The fact that a given type of wholesaling firm participates in a number of marketing flows gives some idea about the potential for a division of labour in the channel. But the crucial question from a management perspective is to what extent (i.e. how heavily) and with what level of quality does the firm participate? To answer this question, we must first examine what it is that wholesalers can, ideally, provide. Then, we will juxtapose this description against a hard-nosed assessment of the orientation of many wholesalers.

How can wholesalers serve suppliers?

Ideally, wholesalers have a great deal of potential as channel partners for suppliers. From an operational perspective, suppliers of both industrial and consumer goods may rely on wholesalers for several key reasons:[2]

1   Wholesalers have continuity in and intimacy with local markets. Being close to customers, they are in a position to take the initial steps in the sale of any products – identifying prospective users and determining the extent of their needs.
2   Wholesalers make possible local availability of stocks and thereby relieve suppliers of small-order business, which the latter can seldom conduct on a profitable basis. Also, they tend to have an acute understanding of the costs of holding and handling inventory in which they have made major commitments.
3   Within their territories, wholesalers can produce suppliers with a salesforce that is in close touch with the needs of customers and prospects. Also, because a wholesaler represents a number of customers, prospects and suppliers, he can often cover a given territory at a lower cost than the manufacturer's own sales representative.
4   Wholesalers perform financial services for suppliers by providing volume cash markets through which they can recover capital that would otherwise be invested in inventories.

The economic role of the distributor (or wholesaler) is to transfer marketing costs from the manufacturer into his own business. This is achieved through the performance of critical marketing functions by the wholesalers on behalf of the manufacturers they represent.

From the point of view of the manufacturer, the performance of these functions shown in Table 3 by wholesalers must be evaluated in determining the type of wholesaling establishment to use. Such evaluation must always be conditioned by the nature of the ultimate market for the goods in question. Therefore, manufacturers must equally examine how well does each wholesaler-distributor perform functions viewed as critical by their customers as shown in Table 4.

How can wholesalers serve retailers?

Manufacturers are interested in getting retailers to promote and sell their own brands in the lines of products they produce. On the other hand, wholesalers have a strong vested interest in building up their retail customers as merchants

Table 3 Marketing functions performed by wholesaler-distributors for manufacturers

Market coverage function
Markets for the products of most manufacturers consist of many customers spread over large geographical areas. To have good market coverage so that their products are readily available to customers when needed, manufacturers can call on wholesaler-distributors to secure the necessary market coverage at reasonable cost.

Order processing function
Many customers buy in very small quantities. Yet manufacturers both large and small receive a number of small orders from thousands of customers. By carrying the products of many manufacturers, wholesaler-distributors' order processing costs can be absorbed by the sale of a broader array of products than that of the typical manufacturer.

Sales contact function
The cost to manufacturers of maintaining outside salesforces is quite high. If manufacturers' products are sold to a large number of customers spread out over a large geographical area, the cost to manufacturers of covering all customers with their own salesforce can be prohibitive. By using wholesaler-distributors to cover all or a substantial portion of their customers, manufacturers may be able to reduce significantly the costs of outside sales contacts because their salesforces would be calling on a relatively small number of wholesaler-distributors rather than the much larger number of customers.

Market information function
Wholesaler-distributors are usually quite close to their customers geographically and in many cases have continual contact through frequent sales calls on their customers. Hence, they are in a good position to learn about customer product and service requirements. Such information if passed on to manufacturers can be valuable for product planning, pricing, and the development of competitive marketing strategy.

Inventory holding function
Wholesaler-distributors take title to and usually stock the products of the manufacturers whom they represent. By so doing, they can reduce the manufacturers' financial burden and reduce some of the manufacturers' risk associated with holding large inventories. Moreover, by providing a ready outlet for manufacturers' products, wholesaler-distributors can help manufacturers to better plan their production schedules.

Customer support function
Besides buying products, customers need many types of service support. Products may need to be exchanged or returned, set up and adjustment may be required, as well as repairs and technical assistance. For manufacturers to provide all such service directly to large numbers of accounts can be very costly and ineffective. Instead, wholesaler-distributors can be used by manufacturers to assist them in providing these services to customers.

Source: Rosenbloom (1987: 73)

of assortments of multiple brands in multiple lines of products. Hence, it is quite likely that, particularly in the case of smaller retail establishments, an individual wholesaler will be able to supply a large part of the retailer's requirements for merchandise. It is in the wholesaler's interest to spend considerable effort and resources on training, stimulating and helping retailers

Table 4   Functions performed by wholesaler-distributors for customers

Product availability function
Probably the most basic marketing
function offered by
wholesaler-distributors to their
customers is providing for the ready
availability of products. Sometimes this
even includes fabricating operations,
assembly and set-up of products. Because
of the closeness of wholesaler-
distributors to their customers and/or
their sensitivity to their customers' needs,
they can provide a level of product
availability that many manufacturers
would be hard put to match.

Assortment convenience function
Closely related to the previous function is
the wholesaler-distributors' ability to
bring together from a variety of
manufacturers an assortment of products
that can greatly simplify their customers'
ordering tasks. So customers, instead of
having to order from dozens or even
hundreds of manufacturers, can turn to
one or a few general line or specialty
wholesaler-distributors who can provide
them with all or most of the products
they need.

Bulk-breaking function
Quite often customers do not need large
quantities, or even if they do at times they
may need only small quantities of
products in a given order. Many
manufacturers find it uneconomical to
sell directly to small order customers and
so they establish minimum order
requirements to discourage small orders.
By buying from manufacturers in large
quantities and breaking these bulk orders
down into the smaller quantities desired
by customers, wholesaler-distributors
provide customers with the ability to buy
only in the quantities they need.

Credit and finance function
Wholesaler-distributors provide their
customer with financial assistance in two
ways. First, by extending open account
credit on products sold, their customers
have time to use products in their
businesses before having to pay for them.
Second, by stocking and providing ready
availability for many of the items needed
by their customers, wholesaler-
distributors significantly reduce the
financial inventory burden their
customers would bear if they had to stock
all of the products themselves.

Customer service function
Customers often require many types of
services such as delivery, repairs,
warranty work. By making these services
available to their customers,
wholesaler-distributors can save their
customers considerable effort and
expense.

Advice and technical support function
Many products, even those that are not
considered technical, may still require a
certain amount of technical advice and
assistance for proper use, as well as advice
on how they should be sold.
Wholesaler-distributors, often through
the use of trained outside salesforces, are
able to provide this kind of technical and
business assistance to customers.

Source: Rosenbloom (1987: 74)

595

to become better merchandisers. Therefore, high-performance wholesalers become highly knowledgeable in retail merchandise management. In this respect, the benefits to the retailer derived from relying on wholesalers may be described as follows:

1 Wholesalers can give their retail customers a great deal of direct selling aid in the form of price concessions of featured items, point-of-sale material and cooperative advertising, all of which are frequently generated by specific suppliers for wholesalers to pass along to retailers.
2 Wholesalers can often provide assistance in planning store layout, building design and material specifications.
3 Wholesalers can offer retailers guidance and counsel in public relations, housekeeping and accounting methods, administrative procedures and the like.

In the toy industry, for instance, many retailers prefer to make a significant proportion of their total annual toy purchases from wholesalers rather than from manufacturers for the following reasons:

1 In many instances reorders are filled more quickly.
2 Wholesalers guarantee the sale (any items not sold can be returned for full credit).
3 Defective products are replaced promptly.
4 The wholesaler extends long-term credit.
5 The percentage of markup by working through a wholesaler is more than offset by decreased inventory costs and improved service.

Obviously, the foremost advantage for many retailers in relying on wholesalers is the fact that the latter buy in large quantities, break bulk to suit the convenience of their customers, and then pass along the savings effected both in cost and transportation. These savings are frequently very favourable when compared with the costs of obtaining merchandise directly in small lots from distant points. Thus, by using wholesalers, independent retailers can avoid diluting the energies of their often overtaxed executive staffs. Furthermore, these retailers obtain access through wholesalers to a large group of products of small manufacturers that might not otherwise be available to them. Even for large establishments, reliance on wholesalers allows conversion of deadweight store space, formerly devoted to merchandise storage, into profit-making selling or customer service space. For example, although supermarket and discount chains can buy at the same price as a rack jobber or service merchandiser, the latter's hold on the market comes from knowing precisely what to buy and minimizing the handling and inventory costs of a variety of non-food products, such as health and beauty aids, tapes and records, hardware and sporting goods. Even for the more mainstream grocery items, managers of large chains operating in widely scattered areas have found it beneficial to get some of their supplies from wholesalers.

How can wholesalers serve the business user?

Although many of the advantages to the business user from relying on wholesalers are exactly the same as those mentioned for retailers, some additional factors are briefly discussed here. The short lead times on deliveries made available through wholesalers are especially important to industrial users. Flexibility in production scheduling can generally be achieved if production planners know that speedy local deliveries can be forthcoming. This factor is especially important for just-in-time (JIT) inventory scheduling. Just-in-time is requiring industrial distributors to work more closely with manufacturing customers in planning inventory needs. The manufacturers are paring the number of distributors from which they buy in order to make closer planning more workable. The introduction of just-in-time is requiring distributors to hold larger inventories, thus pressuring profit margins. However, just-in-time represents a great opportunity for many distributors who are capable of capitalizing on it.

Demands by customers for rapid delivery are expected to increase in the 1990s. A study of future trends in wholesaling reports that 'the durable wholesaler-distributors' customers are expected to place a greater value on the frequency and speed of delivery, principally because of the increased focus on just-in-time inventory requirements and the manufacturers' increased attention to productivity' (Arthur Andersen 1987: 35).

In addition, many types of wholesalers provide unique forms of technical assistance that are relatively costly to duplicate elsewhere, except in situations where a buyer can purchase in very large quantities. For example, machine tool and accessories wholesalers often have specialists on their staff who are available to help customers with problems pertaining to the selection and use of tools and parts. It is not unusual to find such technically trained persons as metallurgists, chemists, draftsmen and mechanical and civil engineers employed by wholesalers for this purpose. In data processing, wholesalers called value added resellers (VAR) have emerged who package computer software with computing equipment to solve specific problems for specific industries (e.g. inventory control for autoparts dealers). Even managerial assistance is being increasingly provided to business users by wholesalers. For example, one electronics distributor analyses the stockkeeping methods of one of his industrial customers and recommends revised delivery schedules, prearranged items, packs suitable for assembly line use and standardized item identification. The customer was able to reduce the possession costs on his stock by 15 per cent of its value.

Business users and retailers alike must be concerned with the overall or ultimate cost of the goods they purchase, handle and store – not merely with the price at which such goods are obtained. When adequate accounting is made, it can often be found that the ultimate cost of dealing with wholesalers is less than the ultimate cost of dealing directly with manufacturers, even though the quantity discounts made available by the latter are not generally available when wholesalers are used as suppliers. This ultimate cost concept can justify the use of wholesalers in situations where they might not otherwise appear to be economical.

Recognition of the ultimate cost concept by both wholesalers and their customers has led to a phenomenon called systems selling.

> Systems selling is a broad, inconclusive term that may be used to describe any form of cooperative contracting relationship between an industrial distributor and his customer for the ordering and distribution of low-value, repetitively used items for maintenance, repair, or operating (MRO) purposes, or for use in manufacturing original equipment.
>
> (Hannaford 1976: 139)

Wholesalers offer such purchasing systems in order to alleviate the high cost and paperwork facing firms seeking to acquire a wide variety of items, ranging from power tools and welding supplies to lamps, electronic equipment and hardware. The major means employed by wholesalers' system selling arrangements to solve these problems include:

1 Shifting the bulk of customer's on-premises MRO inventory back to the stocking wholesaler.
2 Providing for automatic and semiautomatic ordering of these items on an as-needed basis.
3 Providing one-day delivery of the ordered items (Hannaford 1976: 139).

A HARD-NOSED ASSESSMENT

Most of the preceding description of what a wholesaler can do for suppliers, retailers, and business users provides optimistic pictures. However, the channel analyst should approach the selection of wholesalers as channel partners with a great deal of caution.

Over the past forty years, the position of wholesalers has been significantly threatened with regard to the marketing of consumer goods. Relatively few wholesalers have been successful in meeting the challenges head on. Although there have also been changes in the marketing of industrial goods, it appears that wholesalers have, from a managerial perspective, shown greater adaptability and innovativeness in their approaches to industrial goods suppliers and markets than they have in their approach to consumer goods. To obtain a realistic perspective of wholesaling, it is important to delve briefly into developments in both sectors of the economy as they have affected wholesalers.

Consumer goods

Retailers have been particularly active in revolutionizing physical distribution practices. They have taken advantage of large-volume purchasing, warehousing and delivery operations by forming mass merchandising chain organizations. To a large extent, as the chains grew and prospered, wholesalers were quickly relegated to meeting the needs of small businesses. Because there are still tens of thousands of small manufacturers and retailers in existence, many wholesalers of consumer goods have continued to serve an economic purpose, but to a shrinking portion of the market.

On the other hand, those wholesalers who saw the writing on the wall and tried to secure the marketing and physical distribution advantages of large-scale retail chain operations while permitting local ownership of individual retail units have succeeded handsomely. They formed voluntary (wholesaler-sponsored) chains, franchised systems and administered systems in order to gain efficiencies in purchasing, advertising, warehousing, accounting, inventory control and virtually every other business function. They also permitted themselves to become part of retailer-sponsored cooperatives.

Beyond those consumer goods wholesalers who have formed vertical marketing systems, there are those who have been successful without changing their corporate organization. Some have restricted their activities to a limited range of products and have sought market niches that do not require high sales volume to be competitive. In groceries, drugs, hardware and jewellery, specialty wholesalers have been able to develop a substantial volume of business. For example, in the grocery trade, such firms supply products like frozen foods, dairy products, fancy or gourmet foods, bread and baked goods and beverages.

A good example is service merchandisers or rack jobbers. They have been particularly effective because they focus on supplying value-added services listed in Table 5. The more successful specialty wholesalers, like rack jobbers, have been able to serve both large suppliers and large buyers, thus severing the wholesalers' traditional dependence on small-scale retailing.

On the other hand, there have also been a number of general- or full-line consumer goods wholesalers who have achieved viability. Their route to success has been to improve their management and marketing practices, particularly by creatively utilizing advanced information-processing technology. Excellent examples are formed in the wholesale distribution of pharmaceuticals (i.e. wholesaler distributors who sell pharmaceuticals, over-the-counter drugs and toiletries to small, independently owned drugstores). Leading wholesalers have adopted innovative electronic data-processing procedures that have brought efficiencies to pharmacists' handling of inventories. For example, a clerk in a drugstore can alert a hand-held computer to a product's identity simply by waving a small wand across a code on a shelf label. Then the clerk can feed the computer an order from that particular item, and the machine relays it over telephone lines directly to the wholesaler distributor's warehouses. Electronic systems have helped drugstores not only eliminate errors and reduce clerical expenses but also keep inventories down because the wholesaler can deliver within twenty-four hours. The wholesalers also sell customized shelf labels and stickers for each product, priced to the druggist's specifications. They can pack items in the order in which the merchandise will be placed on shelves. The

599

Table 5   Services offered by service merchandisers (rack jobbers)

Merchandising services
Recommend type, brand and amount of merchandise to stock.
Design a plan for the rotation of goods, especially high-risk
  seasonal items.
Develop merchandise 'planograms' for stores.
Prepare ad mats that customers can use in local newspapers.

Computer services
Track customers' sales and gross profit by category.
Print price labels and conduct other paperwork.
Provide tailor-made information upon request.

Salesperson's services
Check merchandise at the back of the store after it arrives from
  the warehouse to ensure that the customer receives exactly
  what has been ordered.
Serve as a store consultant by helping managers plan and execute
  promotions.
Plan the rotation of merchandise.
Advise on in-store display techniques.
Conduct in-store order writing.
Stock shelves and keep them orderly.

Warehouse and delivery services
Receive shipments from manufacturers.
Separate and warehouse shipments.
Select, label and box merchandise for individual stores.
Deliver merchandise to stores.

Source: Takeuchi (1980: 12). Adapted and reprinted by permission.

wholesalers also provide retailers with management information reports, which measure sales and markups for groups of products in each store.

The wholesalers have set up computerized accounts-receivable programs that enable pharmacists to offer charge accounts to preferred customers – something most small businesses cannot handle without investing in processing equipment of their own. The pharmacists can also check a patient's drug allergies or provide customers with records of drug purchases for submission with their tax returns.[3]

Industrial goods

Manufacturers of many types of industrial goods tend to be more engineering oriented than marketing oriented. They prefer to allocate resources to research and production rather than to distribution, which they know has historically delivered a much lower return on investment. Given this orientation, it is not surprising that they frequently turn 'troublesome' marketing problems over to distribution specialists. This is one of the reasons that industrial distribution, in contrast with consumer goods, has been a particularly viable sector of wholesaling over the years.

The situation involving industrial distribution is particularly intriguing because in some respects it is generally a microcosm of the dynamics of distribution. Industrial distributors are frequently viewed as a special class of merchant wholesaler.

An industrial distributor sells primarily to manufacturers. He stocks the products he sells, has at least one outside salesperson as well as an inside telephone and/or counter salesperson, and performs a broad variety of marketing channel functions. The products stocked include: maintenance, repair and operating supplies (MRO items); original equipment (OEM) supplies, such as fasteners, power transmission components, fluid power equipment and small rubber parts, which become part of the manufacturer's finished product; equipment used in the operation of a business, such as hand tools, power tools and conveyors; machinery used to make raw materials and semi-finished goods into finished products.

On average, industrial distributors are as small as the wholesalers serving retailers, but the median size is increasing as the number of distributors declines and as the market expands. The increase in size means that more firms are able to adopt electronic data processing for inventory control, order processing and other administrative matters.

The distributor's importance in the marketing channel for industrial goods is growing for a variety of reasons:

1   The desire of manufacturers to shift more physical distribution responsibilities to distributors as a result of inflationary cost pressures.
2   The tendency of a number of products (e.g. bearings) to become commodities, which permits distributors more control over the relationship with the customer because of the diminishing importance of brand names for such products.
3   The increased value that distributors are adding to products by performing special services, such as assembly and submanufacturing, for their customers (Webster 1984: 198).

From the supplier's perspective, industrial distributors have become more capable in fulfilling their major responsibility in the channel. That is, their job has been primarily to contact present and potential customers and to make the product available – with the necessary supporting services, such as delivery, credit and technical advice – as quickly as is economically feasible. In this respect, they may have discouraged the kind of integration of wholesaling functions so prevalent in consumer goods channels. In fact, it is much easier for the industrial goods manufacturer to go 'direct' than it is for the consumer goods manufacturer. In consumer goods the major problem for wholesalers is the backward vertical integration of retailers into wholesaling. In industrial goods, the problem is one of manufacturers integrating forward. While such integration is occurring, the problem for wholesalers appears to be more acute relative to consumer goods.

One of the ways in which industrial distributors have maintained and even increased their importance in the marketing channel is by doing something some of their counterparts selling consumer goods have also done (i.e. they have specialized their operations).

Another way in which industrial distributors have enhanced their role in the marketing channel is the formation of distributor chains. Individual entrepreneurs have either acquired or established multiple outlets. As a result, they have been able to secure significant economies of scale by establishing one highly sophisticated inventory, purchasing and distribution system.

The formation of distribution chains is critical for serving national accounts in the hospitality, health care, and fast food industries. Some of the advantages that distributor chains have over small, privately owned, single-warehouse firms are as follows:

1   Inventory power. Chain inventories are not only deeper and cheaper but also broader and more diversified.
2   Large, linked warehouses. Such warehouses permit adding highly sophisticated computerized systems, purchasing in quantity, and stocking in depth which result in lower warehousing costs per outlet.
3   Quantity discounts.
4   Multiple brand coverage.
5   Private labelling. This movement is particularly strong for such product lines as bearings, electrical motors and equipment, and MRO supplies.

From a potential customer's perspective, the chains incorporate many of the attributes that are important to industrial customers in choosing a source of supply. They are able to keep delivery promises, offer a better discount structure, maintain an efficient phone order system, provide stock breadth and depth, offer technical services, enact appropriate sales procedures (e.g. regular sales calls), maintain a strong assortment of brand names, offer quick delivery time and provide quality assurance. Indeed, because of their capabilities, they have created serious policy questions for manufacturers seeking to employ both independent and chain distributors in their channels. Some of these questions are as follows:

1   Can we afford to offer exclusives to independents? to chains? If we offer them to independents, is there any way to protect existing exclusives and still sell to chains?
2   How do we sell to chains? De we need separate salesforces, one for chains and one for independents?
3   Is our volume to chains large enough to permit us to withdraw our branch warehousing support to independents?

4 Should we help independents to pool?
5 How large a reduction in price are we willing to grant chains for assuming the entire warehousing burden?
6 Do we want to provide private labels?
7 What kind of discounting structure should we employ?

CONCLUSION

The significance of the wholesaler's role in a channel of distribution is defined by the efficiency of his sorting function, whereby he helps match the heterogeneous output of suppliers on the one hand with the diverse needs of retailers and industrial and business users on the other. There have been increased pressures on wholesalers to prove their economic viability in this respect.

The wholesaler-distributor continues to face market, technological, financial and organizational forces of change. In order to remain a viable force in the distribution channel in the twenty-first century, wholesalers must devise strategies to deal with forces of change projected well into the future. These include:

- Competitive threats from relatively newer forms of competition such as catalogue and warehouse chains.
- Dramatic rise in mergers and acquisitions to achieve diversification, increase market share, enter new territories and achieve economies of scale.
- Continued decline in gross margins accompanied with rising customer service standards including order fill rates, electronic order entry and just-in-time inventory management.
- Doubling of technology expenditures with emphasis on the use of new supplier and customer communication techniques such as videotext and electronic data interchange.
- Rising need for externally generated capital necessary to compensate for the decline in internally generated funds and to finance capital expenditures for new technology investment in information systems, marketing, and logistics.
- Transitioning from family-owned and managed corporation to professionally managed, publicly held, and perhaps foreign-owned corporation (Arthur Andersen 1987: 12–16).

NOTES

1 This chapter is based in its entirety on Louis W. Stern and Adel I. El-Ansary (1992) *Marketing Channels*, 4th edn, Englewood Cliffs, New Jersey: Prentice Hall: 106–48.
2 Many of these points have been made in more detail by Richard M. Hill (1963), *Wholesaling Management*, Homewood, Ill.: Richard D. Irwin: 10–14. See also

Webster, Frederick E. Jr (1984) *Industrial Marketing Strategy*, 2nd edn, New York: John Wiley and Sons, Inc.: 194–204.

3   See Raymond Corey (1985) 'The role of information and communications technology in industrial distribution', in Robert D. Buzzell (ed.) *Marketing in an Electronic Age*, Boston, MA: Harvard Business School Press: 29–51.

For more information about EDI systems, see Louis W. Stern and Patrick J. Kaufmann (1985) 'Electronic data interchange in selected consumer goods industries: an interorganizational perspective', in Robert D. Buzzell (ed.) *Marketing in an Electronic Age*, Boston, MA: Harvard Business School Press: 52–73.

REFERENCES

Alderson, Wroe (1971) 'Factors governing the development of marketing channels', in William G. Moller, Jr. and David L. Wilemon (eds) *Marketing Channels: A Systems Viewpoint*, Homewood, Ill.: Richard D. Irwin.

Arthur Andersen and Company (1987) *Facing the Forces of Change: Beyond Future Trends in Wholesale Distribution*, Washington D.C.: Distribution Research and Education Foundation.

Hannaford, William J. (1976) 'Systems selling: problems and benefits for buyers and seller', *Industrial Marketing Management* 5, June: 139.

Rosenbloom, Bert (1987) *Marketing Functions and the Wholesaler-Distributor: Achieving Excellence in Distribution*, Washington, D.C.: Distribution Research and Education Foundation.

Takeuchi, Hirotaka (1980) *A Note on Wholesale Institutions*, Boston, MA: Harvard Business School: 9-581-011.

US Department of Commerce, Bureau of Census (1990) *1987 Census of Wholesale Trade*, Subject Series, Report WC87-5-1, Washington, D.C.: US Government Printing Office.

Webster, Frederick E. Jr. (1984) *Industrial Marketing Strategy*, 2nd edn, New York: John Wiley and Sons, Inc.

35

RETAILING

Peter J. McGoldrick

RETAILING: DEFINITION AND SCOPE

Originally defined as 'the sale of goods in small quantities', a better working definition of retailing is: 'the sale of goods and services to consumers for their own use'. This distinguishes retailing from the supply of goods, in quantities large or small, to industrial buyers. It also recognizes the adoption of retailing terms and concepts by a wide range of services providers. For example, banks and other financial services providers use the term 'retail' to differentiate their consumer and their corporate activities (McGoldrick and Greenland 1994).

As the marketing of services is considered in Chapter 47, the focus of this chapter is upon the sale of goods to consumers. The principal types of institution involved in retailing are examined, as are the major functions of retailing. Attention is given to the trends in retail internationalization and to the threats/opportunities of non-store retailing. First, consideration is given to how retailing has evolved, and the key role it now plays within the 'marketing channel'.

EVOLUTION OF RETAILING

The growth of power

Retailing has always been a major component of economic activity. In Great Britain alone there were a quarter of a million retail businesses in 1990, with a total turnover of £132,704m, employing 2.5 million people (Central Statistical Office 1993). On a wider scale, there were 3.3 million retail enterprises in the EC, employing 13 million people (Eurostat 1993). Such expressions of scale cannot alone capture the major changes that have taken place, as retailing has switched from a more passive to a highly proactive role within the overall marketing process.

Many of the revered concepts of marketing, including the marketing mix,

605

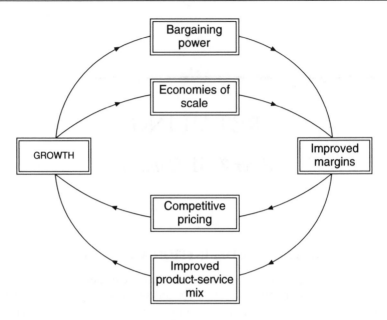

Figure 1   The retail growth cycle

originated in a period when the manufacturer was truly 'king'. Post-war product shortages focused attention upon production, which gave way to an emphasis upon branding as shortages diminished. Inevitably, retailing tended to be depicted as just part of the marketing channels, largely controlled by manufacturers. The last two decades have seen retailers grow in size and sophistication, often exceeding that of their largest suppliers.

Figure 1 depicts in outline the growth cycle of powerful retailers. Growth enhances bargaining power and helps in the achievement of other economies of scale. The improved margins thus gained may be used to achieve further growth, through competitive pricing and/or a product-service mix which offers superior value to customers. As the growth cycle continues, major retailers have invested in better management and superior information systems. Their power has been increased further by the development of retailer brands, extensive advertising and sophisticated trading environments.

Many large retailers have subsumed the roles traditionally ascribed to wholesalers, increasing further their dominance of the marketing channel. It is now equally appropriate to present a view of consumer goods marketing that is retailer driven (McGoldrick 1990). Within this alternative view, manufacturers may be depicted as part of the 'channels of supply', with only limited power to influence the marketing strategies of major retailers. Large-scale retailers have truly evolved from shopkeeping to strategic marketing.

Theories of retail change

Given the dynamic nature of retailing, several theories have developed to explain aspects of evolution and change. Two of the most influential are the Wheel of Retailing and the Retail Life Cycle. These and other theories of retail change are discussed in detail by Brown (1987).

The Wheel of Retailing suggests that new types of retailers tend to enter as low-price, low-margin, low-status operators. Over time they acquire more elaborate facilities, incur higher operating costs and cease to be as price competitive. Eventually they mature as higher-cost, higher-price retailers, vulnerable to newer types who enter at the first phase of The Wheel. Many examples can be found of retail types and individual companies that have evolved in this way, including department stores and supermarkets. The process has been ascribed to various influences, including a shift away from the aggressive management style of the founders, the attraction of the up-market segments, a preference amongst leading retailers for non-price forms of competition, and possible 'misguidance' by suppliers of elaborate equipment and fitments. It is also possible that the boom-recession cycles within most advanced economies contribute to the process, encouraging trading-up during the boom years and encouraging new forms of price competition during recessions.

The Retail Life Cycle concept derives from the better known Product Life Cycle, elaborated in Chapter 28. Retail institutions and formats appear to be moving from innovation to maturity with increasing speed. Davidson *et al.* (1976) estimated that the city centre department store took some eighty years to mature, whereas the home improvement centre in the USA took only fifteen years. Figure 2 shows the four main phases of the retail life cycle, illustrating that the life cycle phase for any given retail format may differ greatly between the countries of Europe.

TYPES OF RETAIL ORGANIZATION

The growth of retailer power and influence has stemmed largely from the concentration of trade into the hands of fewer, larger enterprises. This section looks first as this process of concentration, involving the shift of trade from independent to multiple retailers. Consideration is then given to symbol retailing, franchises and cooperatives.

Independents and multiples

The term 'multiple' signifies more than one outlet but different data sources use different definitions (e.g. at least two, five or ten outlets). Table 1 provides a breakdown of three sectors of GB retailing, showing the dominance of the large multiples in the food sector particularly. In that sector, the five largest

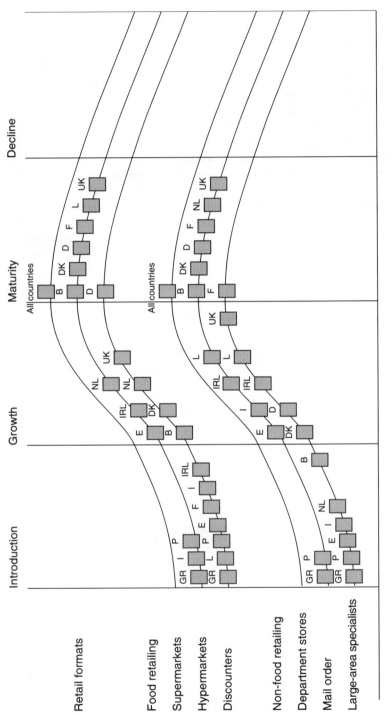

Figure 2 Retail life cycles in EC countries
Source: Eurostat (1993: 20)

Table 1 Share of multiple retailers: GB

Sector (1990 data)	Single outlet retailers %	Small multiples (2–9) %	Large multiples (10+) %
Food retailers	16.8	6.9	76.3
Clothing, footwear	22.5	20.2	57.3
Household goods	37.4	17.3	45.3
All retailers	26.9	11.7	61.4

Source: Central Statistical Office (1993)

Table 2 Contrasting retail structures: EC

Country (1988–90 data)	Number of outlets	Outlets per 10,000 inhabitants	Employees per outlet
Portugal	173,300	175	2.1
Greece	175,000	174	1.9
Italy	929,700	161	2.6
Belgium	127,800	128	2.1
Spain	454,850	117	3.2
Denmark	48,100	94	4.2
Luxembourg	3,520	93	5.1
Eire	29,300	84	4.5
France	461,800	82	4.5
Germany	439,000	70	5.4
Holland	95,000	64	6.7
United Kingdom	348,200	61	8.7
12 countries	3,285,570	96	4.0

Source: Eurostat (1993)

organizations alone account for 41.5 per cent of trade, compared with 18.6 in household goods, 36.3 in clothing and footwear (Central Statistical Office 1993). In the retail sector as a whole, large multiples increased their share by 9.6 per cent between 1982 and 1990, to the detriment of the smaller retail businesses.

Retail structures contrast markedly across the different countries of Europe. Table 2 expresses two measures of 'shop density', showing the UK to be highly concentrated in terms of shops per 10,000 inhabitants, or in terms of employees per outlet. The first five countries in the upper portion of Table 2 have more, smaller outlets than average for the EC. This can be ascribed to the family-based structure of many retail enterprises, laws protecting small retailers and the importance of tourism.

Not all small stores are independently owned; the convenience store or 'c-store' format has been developed by multiples, voluntary groups and franchisers. Definitions of the convenience store vary somewhat but the Advertising Association (1993) suggested the following criteria:

- self service;
- 1,000–3,000 sq. ft selling area;
- parking facilities;
- open seven days a week for long hours;
- wide range but limited brand choice, including groceries, toiletries, some medicines, alcohol and stationery; some also offer video hire, take-away foods and petrol.

It was estimated that there were 7,000 c-stores in the UK in 1993, including those developed on petrol forecourts.

Voluntary groups

One response of independent retailers and wholesalers to the growth of the multiples has been the formation of 'voluntary', 'symbol' or 'affiliation' groups. Within this form of contractual chain, a group name is utilized and the retailers are normally required to buy a given proportion of their merchandise through the group. The organization typically provides buying and other marketing services, including special promotions, advertising and frequently own brands. The group is therefore able to achieve some of the buying power and economies of scale characteristic of major multiples. Table 3 summarizes the structure of voluntary chains and buying groups in the UK, showing their particular significance in the chemists sector, where the Unichem, Numark and Vantage groups predominate.

Euromonitor estimates for 1995 show a great diversity in likely percentage penetration within the total retail trade of other European markets:

Belgium	13	Norway	20
Denmark	36	Spain	4
Finland	42	Sweden	39
Netherlands	30	Germany	35

Table 3 Voluntary and buying groups: UK

Sector	Outlets	Sector share (%)
Confectioners, newsagents and tobacconists	12,000	19
Chemists	11,000	76
Food trade	10,500	12
DIY/hardware	6,500	10

Source: *Retail Monitor International* (1993, February: 112)

This type of affiliation appears well suited to areas of low population densities but the voluntary groups are under pressure from the multiples in many countries.

Franchises

Franchising, in various forms, has a long history both in Europe and in the USA. Its fastest growth as an element of retail structure occurred through the 1980s. From 2,600 franchised units in the UK in 1980, the number grew to 18,600 by 1991, of which 4,075 could truly be classified as retail outlets (*Retail Monitor International* 1993). Franchising can take many different forms, notably the following:

1 The manufacturer-retailer franchise: common in the sale of cars and petrol.
2 The manufacturer-wholesale franchise: for example, franchises to bottle Coca-Cola or Pepsi-Cola.
3 The wholesaler-retailer franchise: includes some voluntary groups, discussed above.
4 The business format franchise: typical in fast food or car hire.

The benefits of franchising can flow from achieving the best of both worlds in business, combining the power, sophistication and reputation of a large organization with the energy, motivation and commitment of the independent owner-manager. For well-conceived and well-managed business formats, franchising has proved to be a powerful vehicle for expansion, as in the cases of Body Shop, Benetton and Seven-Eleven Japan (Sparks 1994).

Cooperative societies

There is essentially one cooperative movement in the UK but its retail activities have been fragmented into a large number of relatively autonomous societies. This fragmentation has been a major reason for the decline in the share of retail trade held by the cooperatives, in spite of the potential for buying power and

Table 4 UK cooperative societies

Year	Societies	Outlets	Turnover £m	% of all retail sales
1983	129	6,433	4,300	5.4
1986	100	5,208	4,989	4.7
1989	81	4,671	6,249	4.4
1992	62	4,637	7,238	4.2

Source: Co-operative Union (1993 and earlier) *Co-operative Statistics*, Manchester: Co-operative Union.

economies of scale within the movement as a whole. The cooperative share of UK retail sales fell from 5.6 per cent in 1982 to 4.2 in 1992.

Table 4 summarizes trends within the movement. Whereas 231 individual societies existed in 1977, this had fallen to 62 by 1992; significant mergers have occurred since then. Rationalization of outlets has continued and the societies have developed strength in discounting and neighbourhood retailing.

In some countries of Europe, the cooperatives hold a far higher share of retail sales. In Switzerland the two major cooperatives, Migros and Co-op Schweiz, held 27 per cent of all retail sales in 1988, 38 per cent of the food trade. The cooperatives also held over 20 per cent of the food trade in Denmark, Finland, Sweden and Norway. Again, this illustrates the great diversity of retail structures across Europe.

MAJOR RETAIL FORMATS

The type of organization that owns or manages a store is not always obvious to the consumer. Other, more striking characteristics of shops serve to differentiate one format from another in the minds of shoppers. A retail format can be defined along a number of different dimensions, including:

single store	– group of stores
in-town	– out-of-town
large	– small
innovative	– mature
food	– non-food
specialized	– generalized
niche	– commodity
high added value	– discounter

This section examines briefly shopping centres, retail parks, superstores, hypermarkets, department stores, variety stores and a number of formats that use the term 'discounter'.

Shopping centres and retail parks

The term shopping centre is normally applied to a coherent, planned and controlled group of retail establishments, as distinct from the more random grouping of a shopping district. In Europe the most typical location for shopping centres is still within existing town centres; the out-of-town centre is a relatively recent phenomenon. Whereas out-of-town centres developed from the 1920s in the USA, some fifty years elapsed before they started to make an impact in the UK.

The differences between the USA and European development patterns can be ascribed in part to differences of economics, geography and demography. Most of all, the more restrictive planning regulations within most European

Table 5 Shopping centre construction

| | Space under construction (million sq. ft) | | |
| | Shopping centres | | Retail parks |
	In-town	Out-of-town	
September 1988	13.8	5.1	7.0
March 1990	22.8	13.0	6.2
December 1991	12.5	6.6	2.7
June 1993	4.8	3.6	3.5

Source: Hillier Parker May & Rowden – regular analyses of schemes 'in the pipeline'.
Note: Many UK sources measure space in square feet; one square metre is equal to 10.76 sq. ft.

countries have served to limit developments out-of-town. The planning debates revolve around a range of economic, environmental and social issues, summarized in McGoldrick and Thompson (1992)

The move out of town has been described as three 'waves' of development (Schiller 1992). The first comprised the superstores, selling mostly food and limited ranges of non-food items. The second wave of decentralization involved bulky goods, such as DIY, carpets, furniture, large electrical items and garden centres. The third wave involved clothing and other comparison shopping, representing the most direct threat to existing town centres. The decision by Marks & Spencer to develop out of town, both within major new centres and in freestanding schemes with food superstore partners, was a major element of this third wave.

Table 5 analyses the shopping centre space under construction over a five-year period. All such development became muted by the long recession but the in-town developments remained significant. The late 1980s saw the development of four especially large out-of-town centres in the UK, each in excess of one million square feet. Situated in Tyneside, South Yorkshire, West Midlands and Essex, each represented a full alternative to the traditional town centre.

The development of retail parks is also depicted in Table 5. These more utilitarian groupings of 'retail sheds' are also termed 'retail warehouse parks'. They offer convenient access and car parking arrangements but lack the indoor malls and many of the other comforts of the new, out-of-town shopping centres. The first such scheme opened in the UK in 1982; by 1990 there were 214 in operation. They involve far lower development costs than the major, full-service shopping centres, which typically include extensive leisure and catering facilities. The trading format of the retail park has proved fairly resilient to adverse economic conditions and their development has continued, shifting the balance away from traditional town centres.

Department and variety stores

In most new shopping centres developers seek to ensure that they attract key 'anchor tenants' in the form of major department and variety stores. Ironically, the market shares of both these retail formats have tended towards decline in most European countries.

According to the International Association of Department Stores, a department store must have at least 2,500 sq. metres of space (26,900 sq. ft). Furthermore, it must offer a product range that is both wide and deep in several product categories. The Association estimates that there were around 960 such stores in the EC in 1990, a slight decline from 1,112 in 1980. Table 6 summarizes the changes in market share, showing decline in France, Germany and the UK. Spain is one of the few countries within which this format is growing, the leading operator being El Corte Inglés. In the UK the leading department store retailers are John Lewis, Debenhams and House of Fraser/Harrods, each with around 20 per cent of the sector share.

Many European variety stores were founded in the 1930s by department store operators, in order to offer a lower priced, lower service and lower assortment format. Examples include Prisunic by Printemps and Priminimé by Bon Marché. In the UK there are few such links between the department and variety store sectors and variety stores hold a relatively strong 6.2 per cent of retail trade, compared with 2.1 per cent in France and 1.1 per cent in Germany.

Many variety stores have traded up and diversified. Department stores, on the other hand, have tended to withdraw from some product ranges in the face of specialist, lower priced competition. Accordingly, the distinction between the department and variety formats has become blurred.

Superstores and hypermarkets

Whereas the supermarket format has reached maturity in most countries (Figure 2), the superstore and hypermarket formats have been claiming increased share in most countries. Being situated mostly outside traditional shopping centres, they tend to enjoy greater accessibility by car, greater economies of scale and the

Table 6 Department store shares

| | % share of retail trade | | |
	1970	*1980*	*1990*
France	3.4	2.9	1.9
Germany	11.0	7.2	5.6
UK	5.5	4.7	4.0

Source: Tordjman (1993: 150)

Table 7 Hypermarkets and superstores in Europe

	Number of outlets (1990)		% share of total retail sales
	Hypermarkets	Superstores	
Belgium	70	30	3.0
France	851	n.a.	29.0
Germany	643	1,013	12.2
Italy	103	25	1.5
Netherlands	40	339	14.0
Spain	116	n.a.	19.0
UK	645	1,050	16.7

Source: Retail Monitor International (1992, September: 49)

benefits of being purpose built. Superstores form the 'anchor stores' of retail warehouse parks and of many partnership schemes, such as the Marks & Spencer–Asda partnership at Owlcotes, near Leeds.

In Britain a superstore is defined as having at least 25,000 sq. ft of selling space; a hypermarket has at least 50,000 sq. ft. Some sources use the near equivalent metric measures of 2,500m^2 and 5,000m^2 respectively. Comparisons between countries encounter great difficulties as these thresholds vary considerably. In some cases, the terms imply large stores selling primarily groceries; in others, the terms are used with more flexibility to describe any large-scale, specialist format, offering a strong depth of assortment, trading on one level and providing ample car parking. Having noted these caveats, Table 7 offers a comparison of penetration within seven countries of Europe. In all European markets, as in the USA, this format is forecasted to continue its growth, the rate of which depends upon regional saturation and planning restrictions.

Discounters

Like so many of the descriptive terms in retailing, discounter is regrettably imprecise. As the Wheel of Retailing suggests, many new concepts have entered by offering prices at levels below existing competition (i.e. by discounting). Accordingly, the term 'hard discounter' has been adopted in some countries to distinguish between new, deep discount formats and other, more mild manifestations of price competition.

In the context of food retailing, Tordjman (1993) distinguished between the key financial and operational characteristics of discounters and hypermarkets, as shown in Table 8. This demonstrates the ability of the format to produce reasonable net margins through the strict control of operating costs. As Figure 2 depicted, the discount food format is in growth within most countries but has reached maturity in Germany.

615

Table 8   Discounters and hypermarkets compared

Typical key indices	Discount supermarket	Hypermarket
Store size: m²	600	6,000
Number of lines	1,000	35,000
Stockturns per year	40	22
Gross margin % of sales	14.5	16.0
As % of sales:		
Labour	5	7
Distribution	2	3
Property	1	2
Other costs	3	2
Net margin as % of sales	3.5	2.0
Asset turnover (times)	7	9
Return on investment (%)	24.5	18.0

Source: Tordjman (1993: 85–6)

Table 9   Penetration of food discounters in Europe

Country	Leading food discounter	% share of food trade	
		Leader	All discounters
Belgium	Aldi	8.0	16.0
Denmark	Netto	5.4	12.0
Germany	Aldi	12.7	22.0
Spain	Dia/Dirsa	5.0	8.0
France	(various)	—	2.0
Italy	(various)	—	2.0
Netherlands	Aldi	4.8	6.7
United Kingdom	Kwik Save	7.0	10.0

Source: Eurostat (1993: 21)

Table 9 summarizes the shares held by food discounters in eight European countries, showing where appropriate the leading operator. According to A.C. Nielson studies, some 38 per cent of UK households visited a discounter for some grocery purchases in the first 3 months of 1993, compared with 26 per cent in 1991.

The concept of the warehouse club represents the most recent addition to hard discounting in Europe. These clubs started to develop from 1982 in the USA; by 1991 there were around 500 units, typically with in excess of 100,000 sq. ft space. The first such unit opened in the UK in 1993, after massive opposition from major supermarket chains. Warehouse clubs charge a membership fee to customers, which ensures selectivity and generally greater loyalty. A wide range of mostly packaged foods and non-foods is offered in sparse surroundings, usually in large or multiple packs. Price comparisons are therefore difficult but the low gross margins, coupled with the 'subsidy effect' of the membership fee, provide an attractive proposition for the more price conscious shoppers.

RETAIL FUNCTIONS

Given the enormous breadth of activities that comprise retailing, it is possible here to provide only a glimpse of its major functions. A more comprehensive treatment is provided in the chapters of McGoldrick (1990) and the case studies of McGoldrick (1994). The emphasis here is to:

1 indicate the role of each function within the overall process of marketing consumer goods;
2 outline the significance of each function within the strategic mix and within the value chain of retailers.

Each element of the value chain can serve to increase value, real or perceived. Most elements incur costs but can contribute to the process of differentiation. For comprehensive discussions of strategic planning in retailing, see Johnson (1987).

Location

Store location decisions are probably the single most crucial elements of retail marketing strategy. They represent long-term investment decisions which, if incorrect, are very difficult to change. While good locations cannot alone compensate for a weak overall strategy, a poor location is a very difficult deficit to overcome. Bad location decisions also undermine the asset value of the retail organization; such stores are difficult to sell.

The retail location decisions must address macro and micro issue; they are often depicted in three stages (Brown 1992):

1 Search – identifying geographical areas that may have market potential.
2 Viability – evaluating the turnover potential of the best available sites.
3 Micro – examining the detailed features of the shortlisted sites.

Clearly, not all location decisions pass through this sequence and a great deal of intuition and executive judgement is still applied. A number of more systematic techniques are available to assist decision-makers.

1 Checklists – very detailed lists of factors relevant to location evaluations have been evolved and are widely used. The factors include many aspects of the population within the catchment area, competition (existing and potential), accessibility by car and by foot, and the specific costs of developing a store on that site.
2 Geographic information systems – can provide detailed analysis of many

617

checklist factors, such as income, employment and expenditure profiles within specified localities.

3   Analogue methods – extrapolate the performance of a site under consideration, based upon analogous sites already in operation.

4   Regression models – help to forecast turnover by modelling the influence of location factors which contribute to, or detract from, the turnover of existing stores.

Product selection and buying

The buying function represents the main interface between retailers and other members of the supply chain. Accordingly, many suppliers create specialist sales teams to serve key retail accounts, developing a close knowledge of the organization and the individuals involved. In some retail organizations, individual buyers have extensive autonomy within their specific product category; in others, the buying team is the norm, which typically includes selectors, merchandisers, technologists and quality controllers.

Numerous criteria must be considered by retail buyers, not least of which are the projections of sales and profitability. Product selection is also a key element of differentiation and buyers are becoming increasingly proactive in sourcing items that will help to provide a competitive edge. Buyers must also consider the capabilities of the supplier, in terms of volume, flexibility and reliability.

In the USA the Robinson Patman Act limits the scope of major retail buyers to obtain better terms, purely on account of their buying power. Such legislation has been considered but not implemented in the UK. Accordingly, large retailers can demand a wide range of additional benefits, analysed by the Office of Fair Trading (1985).

Retail brands

A significant manifestation of retailer power has been the ability of major retailers to develop their own brand product ranges. These are defined as: products sold under a retail organization's house brand name, which are sold exclusively through that retail organization's outlets.

The name may be that of the retailer, for example Tesco, or a name closely linked with the company, such as Marks & Spencer's St Michael brand. From time to time grocery retailers have also launched ranges of 'generics', a low-priced, plain label variant upon the own brand concept.

Retailer brands have been especially important within grocery retailing. The three leading grocers in the UK, J. Sainsbury, Tesco and Safeway, derived 53, 42 and 36 per cent of their turnover respectively from their own brands in 1992. Table 10 summarizes own brand across Europe. Such brands are not restricted to grocery sectors; with 100 per cent own brands, Marks & Spencer has been described as 'a manufacturer without factories'. This company is totally

Table 10 Grocery own labels in Europe

% of market	1980	1990
UK	22.0	30.5
Germany	15.0	24.0
Netherlands	n.a.	24.0
France	11.2	20.0
Belgium	n.a.	16.0
Spain	1.8	8.9
Italy	n.a.	5.0

Source: *The Grocer* (1993, 8 May: 39)

involved in the specification, design and quality control processes.

Motives for developing retailer brands vary, as does the positioning of the ranges. Generally, retailers are seeking to reinforce their images, generate better margins and improve competitiveness, in terms of price and/or differentiation.

Pricing

Since the abolition of resale price maintenance in most areas, the control of retail prices has shifted largely from manufacturers to retailers. This now represents one of the most complex elements of retail management. Whereas 100 products could represent a fairly wide assortment for a manufacturer, a retailer may be responsible for pricing 10,000 or more items. Compounding upon this complexity is the fact that many multiples differentiate prices between branches. As each store serves a different market, why not differentiate in response to local market conditions?

Retailers conduct or obtain audits of competitors' prices in order to help determine their own price levels. In the retailing of wide product assortments, such as groceries, the perceptions of consumers concerning price levels are of crucial importance. Retailers are able to determine which products are 'known value items', items for which shoppers have high levels of price awareness, and ensure that these items are priced very competitively. In other areas of retailing, notably clothing and footwear, extensive use is made of prices such as £49.95, which are thought to create a lower price perception. Conversely, if the price is intended to signal a prestige purchase, round numbers such as £220 tend to be preferred.

Pricing is also used widely as a promotional tool, usually in conjunction with advertising and in-store support. Short-term special offers, often heavily subsidized by manufacturers, are a feature of many retail sectors. Seasonal sales are also used extensively to clear lines, to generate additional turnover and as a response to the promotional activities of others.

Table 11 Media advertising expenditures

£M	1988	1992
Tesco	6.3	26.8
Texas	13.4	22.6
M.F.I.	18.3	21.1
Comet	11.6	19.6
B & Q	18.5	18.2
Woolworths	16.9	17.7
Sainsbury	9.6	16.9
Currys	12.6	16.5
Safeway	6.5	15.4

Source: Economist Intelligence Unit (1993a: 26)

Advertising

Advertising is the theme of Chapter 38 so here it will suffice to emphasize the financial and strategic importance of advertising to retailers. Expenditure by UK retailers grew from £285m in 1985 to £523m in 1992 (Economist Intelligence Unit, 1993a). Table 11 shows a few of the major spenders, although it should be recognized that some of this expenditure is subsidized by manufacturers, in the form of 'cooperative advertising' deals.

Retailers have many ways of communicating with their own regular customers, both in-store and by mailings sent to account or store card holders. Major objectives of media advertising are therefore to attract new customers, or to increase the visit frequency/expenditure of more marginal customers. Some retailers also make use of sponsorship as a promotional vehicle, which can avoid much of the 'clutter' in conventional media advertising. For example, the first year of the Littlewoods Cup sponsorship attracted over 300 minutes of BBC or IBA transmission time.

The selling environment

The in-store environment offers retailers numerous opportunities to influence the purchasing patterns of shoppers. The overall design and atmosphere of a store creates/reinforces an image, as well as affecting mood states and shopping behaviour. 'Atmospherics' has been defined as: 'the conscious designing of space to create certain effects in buyers' (Kotler 1973). An atmosphere includes the many visual aspects of a store, the sounds, scents and textures. Experiments have shown how various colours or different types of music can affect customer behaviour. The smell of fresh bread is commonly used by supermarkets; some retailers are now experimenting with the use of more subtle aromas.

In that most retailing environments invite self-service, the detailed allocation of selling space has become an important science. Major retailers tend to use computer models both to optimize and to visualize space allocation. They aim to achieve a balance between the desire to maximize impulse purchasing, the need to offer a wide range, the need to hold adequate stock and the need to offer a convenient and pleasant shopping environment.

Human resources

With around 13 million people employed in retailing in Europe (Eurostat 1993), 2.5 million in Great Britain (Central Statistical Office 1993), it is clear that retailing is a 'people business'. Retailers also face the challenge that their lowest paid staff interface directly with their customers. Imagine how images of cars or chocolates would change if customers dealt directly with assembly-line workers, rather than receiving these images through carefully crafted advertisements.

In retailing, the shelf packers, cleaners and checkout operators all represent key components of the service experience. This highlights the need for careful selection and training; overall, the need for an effective human resource function (see Marchington 1994). Large retail chains also have the challenge of communicating their mission, values and expectations to a large and geographically dispersed staff.

There are of course some retail contexts within which staff hold highly creative selling roles. In the retailing of fashion goods, cars or other major durables, the sales staff are expected to combine extensive product knowledge with the skills of personal selling; further elaboration is provided in Chapter 40.

Information and logistics

Although logistics is the theme of Chapter 33, a summary of key retail functions would be incomplete without this vital component. The logistics role is largely unseen by most customers, becoming more apparent when it fails to maintain stock levels. Out-of-stock conditions may cause not only the immediate loss of item sales, but also undermine customer loyalty by increasing the need to shop elsewhere. The efficient management of the supply chain is therefore a key strategic function.

The benefits of electronic point-of-sale (EPoS) equipment to supply chain management are starting fully to be realized. Post-News (1993) identified the main benefits from the integration of EPoS and automatic reordering systems, estimating the likely extent of the changes.

Increase in stock availability	(to 95 per cent)
Reduced inventory levels	(by 20 per cent)
Improved stockturns	(by 17 per cent)
Improved choice for customers	(by 10 per cent)

EPoS equipment also offers direct benefits to customers in terms of faster service and itemized receipts. Further service enhancement is being provided by the integration of electronics payment systems, accepting credit or debit payments and, in the latter case, offering customers the facility to request cash back.

INTERNATIONALIZATION OF RETAILING

In spite of the power and sophistication of large-scale retailers, the process of internationalization has been slow and painful. In addition to the legal, linguistic and logistical problems, it is difficult to export even the most successful of retail concepts into other markets. As noted earlier, competitive structures differ greatly and there are still major differences in consumer tastes and preferences (Brown and Burt 1992).

Difficult or not, the internationalization of retailing is gaining pace. Figure 3 summarizes the major facets of this process, including the arrival of foreign competition and entries into foreign markets. A view of internationalization should also recognize the flow of know-how and the import/export of retail concepts. International product sourcing has a long history in some companies but is becoming more widespread; for some retailers, it has facilitated the development of branches abroad. Table 12 summarizes the international activities of certain European retailers that derive a relatively large proportion of turnover from operations outside their home market.

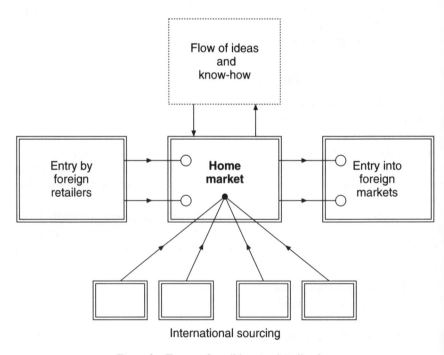

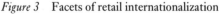

International sourcing

Figure 3   Facets of retail internationalization

622

Table 12 International retailing in the EC

Company	Country	International turnover (MU ECU)	% of total turnover	Main activity
Ikea	S	2,138	76.2	Furniture
Delhaize le Lion	B	5,283	72.4	Food
Tengelmann	D	12,656	55.7	Food
Ahold	NL	4,548	50.6	Food
Otto Versand	D	3,602	45.9	Mail order
Vendex	NL	2,808	35.3	Department store/food
La Redoute	F	879	35.0	Mail order
Metro	D	6,036	35.0	Department store/food
Promodes	F	5,506	34.4	Food
Carrefour	F	3,414	31.1	Food
Dixons	UK	726	30.6	Electrical

Source: Eurostat (1993: 27)

Motives for internationalization

The pressures towards and reasons for internationalization are diverse, but may be summarized as 'push', 'pull' or 'facilitating' factors.

1 'Push' factors, including the maturity or saturation of home markets, domestic trading restrictions, unfavourable economic conditions, rising costs, adverse demographic changes and imitation of trading styles.
2 'Pull' factors, including more enlightened corporate philosophies, perceptions of growth opportunities abroad (niche or underdeveloped markets), established bridgeheads in other countries and imitative 'bandwagon' effects.
3 'Facilitating' factors, including the lowering of political, economic and perceived barriers between countries, the broader vision of senior management, an accumulation of expertise, the ability to assess other retailers' international moves and the improvement of communication technologies.

The particular mix of these factors often determines the most appropriate route to internationalization. Also relevant is the availability of capital, the level of understanding of market needs within other countries, and the compatibility of the domestic trading format(s) with those needs. It is clear that retailers have sometimes adopted the wrong approach to internationalization. There are several examples of leading retailers in domestic markets running into difficulties abroad.

Entry strategies

A number of alternative approaches are available, including the following.

1 Self-start entry, the chain being built up from scratch, or developed through organic growth from a very modest initial acquisition. Examples include Woolworths development in the UK and Laura Ashley in the USA.
2 Acquisition, providing a quick entry route but at cost, not least because companies available for acquisition may well be in financial difficulty. The approach has been used by many UK retailers, including the acquisition of Kings supermarkets and Brooks Brothers menswear in the USA by Marks & Spencer.
3 Franchising, avoiding much of a risk and demands upon capital; especially appropriate where a retailing concept can be readily exported. Notable examples include Italian manufacturer/franchiser Benetton, with over 6,000 outlets in over 80 countries.
4 Joint venture, reducing time, cost and risk of entry by working with a partner already familiar with the market. In spite of their benefits at the outset, many joint ventures/partnerships have been terminated, having not met expectations.
5 Concessions (shops in shops), a relatively low cost/risk approach to exploring new markets, used for example by Burton in Spain and elsewhere.

Cross-border alliances have become a major element of international retail cooperation and expansion in recent years. There are four main types, purchasing led alliances, development alliances, skills based alliances and multifunction alliances. Within this last category may be included the development of the European Retail Alliance (ERA) and Associated Marketing Services (AMS), linking retailers across Europe and opening opportunities for many forms of cooperation, including purchasing, sourcing, logistics, product development, promotion and political lobbying.

The internationalization of retailing has produced very diverse styles of operation, ranging from global to multinational. Global retailers such as Benetton vary their format very little across national boundaries, achieving the greatest economies of scale but showing the least local responsiveness. Multinationals, on the other hand, tend to develop or acquire a diversity of formats internationally, usually achieving rather lower benefits from integration.

A middle course may be termed 'transnational' retailing, whereby the company seeks to achieve global efficiency while responding to national needs, opportunities and constraints. Some of the more recent developments by Marks & Spencer could best be described as transnational, recognizing that even the most successful retail formats within the domestic market may require adaptation to suit markets abroad.

NON-STORE RETAILING

In conclusion of this chapter, it is appropriate to mention potential and existing forms of non-store retailing. This category includes itinerant traders, a category for which little information is available, traditional 'home shopping' and various forms of electronic shopping.

Home shopping

In that telephone ordering has largely replaced the posting of orders, the term 'mail order' is giving way to 'home shopping'. In spite of numerous predictions that home shopping would take over a large share of retail trade, its role in Europe is still fairly modest. In Germany it holds the largest share, around 4.7 per cent of retail trade, the sector being dominated by Otto Versand and Quelle. This compares with 2.7 and 2.5 per cent in the UK and France respectively. In Italy and Spain home shopping holds a very small share of less than one per cent.

The structure of home shopping in the UK is highly concentrated, as Table 13 illustrates. Great Universal Stores (GUS) alone holds 37.3 per cent of the market, followed by Littlewoods and Freemans. The sector has been the target of international acquisition, Grattan being sold to Otto Versand and Empire being acquired by La Redoute. Although holding a relatively modest share, the Next Directory represented a significant departure from traditional catalogues. Its style and design illustrated that home shopping could be targeted towards younger, more affluent shoppers. In response, major operators introduced 'specialogues', designed for specific needs and groups.

Catalogues are not of course the exclusive domain of non-store retailers. Many retailers send or make available seasonal or specialist catalogues to their customers, to encourage preselection at home and to generate more store visits.

Table 13 Home shopping in the UK

Company	% share of market
GUS	37.3
Littlewoods	22.1
Freemans (Sears)	13.2
Grattan (Otto Versand)	10.6
Empire (La Redoute)	5.8
N. Brown	4.2
Fine Art	3.9
Next Directory	2.3
Other	0.6

Source: Verdict (1993) *Verdict on Home Shopping*, London: Verdict

The catalogue showroom represents a hybrid retail format, allowing selection at home from an extensive catalogue but usually requiring collection from a store. The advantage over conventional home shopping is that the item can be obtained without delay. Catalogue showrooms also display some of the seasonal or higher value items, allowing inspection before purchase. The format is well developed in the Netherlands and the UK, where the largest operators are Argos and Index (Littlewoods).

Electronic shopping

Although logically a sub-set of home shopping, forms of electronic or teleshopping merit special attention, representing an area of future development in retailing. Existing offering systems include the following:

1 Videotex services – combining telephone transmission and television screen display of 'pages' of information. Experimental systems have used the Prestel system but with little commercial success; that technology is old and not especially user friendly (Economist Intelligence Unit 1993b). However, major advances are being made in the quality of images that can be transmitted down telephone lines.
2 Shopping channel – delivered by satellite or cable, thus providing high quality picture and sound, but usually requiring telephone ordering. Many such channels have failed in the USA but the QVC channel grew to a customer base of three million by 1992; it started satellite broadcasting in Europe in 1993.
3 Interactive cable television systems – allow the customer to access more detailed information about specific products. J.C. Penney's 'Teleaction' claimed to be the first commercial system of this type in the USA.

Projections for the future of home shopping present many possibilities, including videophones, compact disc and multi-media. It is also possible that the technology of virtual reality, currently used to visualize kitchen layouts by some retailers, could be used at home to simulate the experience of browsing a store and touching the goods. With the history of failures and withdrawals from teleshopping, it is not surprising that most retailers are waiting for more widespread adoption of the relevant, home-based technologies. Only one thing is certain, technological developments, both in-store and out of store, will continue to be a major driving force for change in this dynamic sector called retailing.

REFERENCES

Advertising Association (1993) *Marketing Pocket Book 1994*, London: NTC Publications.

Brown, S. (1987) 'Institutional change in retailing: a review and synthesis', *European Journal of Marketing* 21 (6): 5–36.

Brown, S. (1992) *Retail Location: a Micro-Scale Perspective*, Aldershot: Avebury.

Brown, S. and Burt, S. (1992) 'Retail marketing: international perspectives', *European Journal of Marketing* 26 (8/9).

Central Statistical Office (1993) *1990 Retailing*, London: H.M.S.O.

Davidson, W. R., Bates, A. D. and Bass, S. J. (1976) 'The retail life cycle', *Harvard Business Review* 54 (6): 89–96.

Economist Intelligence Unit (1993a) 'Annual review of retailing', *Retail Trade Review* 26, June: 6–29.

Economist Intelligence Unit (1993b) 'Home shopping', *Retail Business* 421, March: 4–9.

Eurostat (1993) *Retailing in the Single European Market*, Brussels: Statistical Office of the European Community.

Johnson, G. (1987) *Business Strategy and Retailing*, Chichester: John Wiley.

Kotler, P. (1973) 'Atmospherics as a marketing tool', *Journal of Retailing* 49 (4): 48–64.

McGoldrick, P. J. (1990) *Retail Marketing*, London: McGraw-Hill.

McGoldrick, P. J. (ed.) (1994) *Retail Management Cases*, London: Pitman.

McGoldrick, P. J. and Greenland, S. J. (1994) *The Retailing of Financial Services*, London: McGraw-Hill.

McGoldrick, P. J. and Thompson, M. G. (1992) *Regional Shopping Centres*, Aldershot: Avebury.

Marchington, M. (1994) 'Adding value through the human resource function: the case of food retailing', in P. J. McGoldrick (ed.) *Retail Management Cases*, London: Pitman.

Office of Fair Trading (1985) *Competition and Retailing*, London: O.F.T.

Post-News (1993) *Electronics in Retailing*, Stoke-sub-Hamdon: Post-News.

Retail Monitor International (1992), London: Euromonitor, September: 49.

Retail Monitor International (1993), London: Euromonitor, February: 112.

Schiller, R. (1987) 'Out-of-town exodus', in E. McFadyen (ed.) *The Changing Face of British Retailing*, London: Newman Books, 64–73.

Sparks, L. (1994) 'Seven-Eleven Japan Co. Ltd: from licensee to owner in eighteen years', in P. J. McGoldrick (ed.) *Retail Management Cases*, London: Pitman.

Tordjman, A. (1993) *Evolution of Retailing Formats in the E.C.*, Jouy-en-Josas: Groupe HEC.

36

DIRECT MARKETING: MODELLING CUSTOMER-MARKETER RELATIONSHIPS IN INTEGRATIVE MARKETING COMMUNICATIONS

Arch G. Woodside

INTRODUCTION

According to the Direct Marketing Association (*Direct Marketing Magazine* 1993): 'Direct marketing is an integrative system of marketing that uses one or more advertising media to effect a measurable response and/or transaction at any location, with this activity stored on database'. About two-thirds of all advertising in the USA, Canada, UK, and other developed nations include one or more ways for viewers, listeners, or readers to respond directly to receive additional information or to buy the product/service being promoted. In the USA this two-thirds amounts to $142 billion in 1991 (*Direct Marketing Magazine* 1993). Direct response mechanisms include telephone numbers, coupons, reader service (bingo) cards, free-standing-insert coupons and telefax numbers.

Most direct marketing strategies include combinations of three or more advertising vehicles to achieve a measurable response from prospects. For example, a television commercial might include the offer of a free brochure if the viewer telephones the toll-free number on the screen, or completes and mails a postcard. Thus, an effective communication process usually involving more than three media needs to be designed to complete the planned exchange:

- television to make the offer;
- the telephone and postcard mailing response media;
- the brochure;
- the computer to create/store/retrieve the customer-product-firm database;
- the marketer reply medium to send the brochure (often via mail) to the customer;
- people to process responses, stuff envelopes, and/or talk on the telephone;

- the products/services in the brochure (a product is always a communication medium as well as combination of attributes that provides benefits).

Given the impact of combining, that is, integrating multiple media, to make direct marketing strategies effective, it should not be surprising that direct mail expenditures represent less than 20 per cent of the total direct marketing expenditures. However, to say that direct marketing is much more than direct mail misses the really important point: the use of multiple media needs to be integrated well to make direct marketing work.

Integrated marketing communication (IMC) programs include designing and implementing a dynamic, interactive, marketer-customer system that incorporates multiple media, measured customer responses, and immediate access and use of customer databases. For many details of why IMC programs are needed and how to design them see Roman (1988); Rapp and Collins (1988); Schultz *et al.* (1993); Shepard (1990). Thus, several advocates have made compelling cases for IMC programs.

In this chapter the major opportunities and problems with direct marketing and IMC programs are reviewed briefly. Next, a model of the early stages in customer-marketer information search and responses in integrative marketing communications is described; some research findings related to the model are reviewed. Finally, based on the discussion of the model, direct marketing implications for designing and implementing effective IMC programs are offered. The aim here is to start to detail all the important small, and big, behavioural steps that need to be integrated and assessed in interactive systems known as direct marketing.

MAJOR OPPORTUNITIES/BENEFITS AND PROBLEMS WITH DIRECT MARKETING STRATEGIES AND IMC PROGRAMS

Both opportunities/benefits and problems are associated with designing and implementing effective direct marketing strategies and IMC programs. Substantial increases in marketing effectiveness and efficiency have been documented in case studies of IMC programs (see monthly issues of *Direct Marketing Magazine*, the industry trade publication in the USA). Unfortunately, the problems that always occur with starting and running IMC programs receive little attention in the literature. Three major opportunities and benefits gained from an effective IMC program are described; two major problems that almost always occur with designing/implementing IMC programs are then discussed.

Opportunities and benefits

Building close, long-term relationships with customers

Effective direct marketing and IMC programs permit the building of long-term, close relationships linking the marketer and customer; this feature of direct marketing is the most important benefit of effective IMC programs. The marketer is able to respond to customers individually through the marketer's IMC program. Thus, the first two sustainable strategic advantages (Peters and Austin 1985) can be achieved via effective IMC programs: creating and maintaining an obsession with customers (the second is constantly to innovate). Individual service designed to meet the personal needs of a customer with whom the marketer communicates by name is a useful description of relationship marketing. Relationship marketing is achieved by effective direct marketing and IMC programs.

A well-designed and implemented IMC program prevents relationships from going stale. Levitt (1983) points out that relationships tend to grow stale without continual attention:

> The sale merely consummates the courtship, then the marriage begins. How good the marriage is depends on how well the relationship is managed by the seller.... The natural tendency of relationships, whether in marriage or in business, is entropy – the erosion or deterioration of sensitivity and attentiveness.... A healthy relationship requires a conscious and constant fight against the forces of entropy.
>
> (Peters and Austin 1985: 82)

The argument might be offered here that dramatic increases in marketing costs will occur from designing and implementing an IMC program. Contrary to this conventional wisdom, decreases in total marketing expenditures often occur from effective IMC programs for two reasons. First, because of technological advances in using computers and databases, data handling and customer contact costs continue to fall. Second, with an effective IMC program, marketers start spending substantially less money on trying to reach prospects who will never buy or who become unprofitable customers. Also, such improved allocations of marketing funds result in higher net returns per dollar spent because specific marketing actions can be targeted to reach customers most likely to buy. Thomas Roger, a US producer of software for direct marketing, offers the following example: 'We tell people, "you can mail 1,000 letters, or you can use one of these [IMC database] systems and mail 100 letters and get the same results"' (quoted from Bulkeley 1993). Thus, contrary to conventional wisdom, embracing direct marketing and an IMC system need not and should not substantially increase marketing costs.

Using 'frequency marketing' to increase sales to best customers

We know that all customers are not alike: for both consumer and industrial firms, 5 per cent of a firm's customers often provide more than 20 per cent of total sales and more than 30 per cent of net profits (see Dubinsky and Ingram 1984; Dwyer 1989). This knowledge is leading more firms to create and maintain 'frequency marketing' (FM) programs.

Frequency marketing is 'to identify, maintain, and increase the yield from best customers, through long-term, interactive, value-added relationships' (*Colloquy* 1991).[1] A firm's best customers (e.g. the customers above the 90 percentile in total purchases among all customers in a firm's customer base) are usually the most sensitive to the firm's new product offerings, special promotional offerings of the firm, and tend to buy products from the firm that provide the highest contribution to overhead and profits (for a detailed example see Woodside and Soni 1991). Even though very few customers are loyal one hundred per cent of the time, an enterprise can often capture a larger share of the available business among its best customers by creating frequency marketing programs. Frequent traveller membership programs among airlines are early examples of such FM programs.

Often, it is cheaper and more profitable to persuade established customers (especially best customers) to respond to a specific marketing action than it is to bring in new customers. James Pisz, the national direct response manager for Toyota Motor Corporation in the USA, estimates that it is 'three-to-five times more expensive to attract a new customer than a repeat customer' (quoted in Bulkeley 1993). Pisz uses a computer workstation to locate best customers among a seven-million US customer database. When Toyota dealers plan 'tent sales', Pisz provides mailings to local area residents who have bought new Toyotas three years before.

Certainly an enterprise needs to design/implement marketing strategies to attract new customers. The point here is that most firms do not have explicit strategies directed toward their best customers; FM programs are made possible by well-developed direct marketing and IMC programs.

A pre-emptive competitive strategy by Mighty Dog provides a packaged-product example of initial steps towards an FM strategy (*Direct Marketing Magazine* 1992). In 1992 Mighty Dog wanted to defend its brand and market share against a larger competitor about to launch a national campaign for a new dogfood entry (Heinz's Reward). The problem was that Reward's spending levels could not be matched. The strategy was to use a targeted mailing to pull known Mighty Dog households out of the market prior to Reward's roll-out. Mighty Dog wanted dog owners to stock up on their product before Reward's campaign hit.

Mighty Dog sent a direct mail piece to 526,291 households, the majority of which came from Mighty Dog's own database of names generated from previous promotions. Tactics included timing the mailing to be in consumers' homes two

LYNCHBURG COONHUNTERS CLUB
P.O. Box D

LYNCHBURG, TENNESSEE

December 19, 1991

Dr. and Dr. Jerome D. Wilson
North Hills Court
Rural Route 2, Box 467-C
Hodges, South Carolina 29653

Dear Dr. and Dr. Wilson,

Well it's a shame you couldn't make it down for the coonhunt this year, because we sure had a good time. And like I said in my note to you, we didn't hurt your property much at all since the dogs went off in the other direction and never did circle back to your place. When they finally did tree a coon, it was the only one we saw the whole hunt. There was quite a discussion as to who's dog actually did the treeing, since the commotion was so loud and two or three of the dogs sound just about alike.

Well I finally settled the question by declaring everybody's dog a winner, which seemed to satisfy everybody except Roger, but he calmed down after a spell. And after a little Black Label.

It was a clear night, but a bit chilly and we were glad we had our long handles on. There were a few out=of=towner Tennessee Squires along this year, and I tried to take a picture of the whole group. Unfortunately I had some camera trouble. By the time I got it working most everybody had gotten tired and left, including the dogs, and the few that were still hanging around weren't very cooperative as you can see.

What with these hunts getting bigger every year, Dr. and Dr. Wilson, I sure hope you can figure a way to join us one of these times. Just drop me a line if your plans look hopeful, and I'll be glad to add your name to the list.

Cordially yours,

Bill Weaver

Bill Weaver

Figure 1   Jack Daniel's 'Tennessee Squire' letter

632

weeks prior to the Reward launch and to deliver ten time-sensitive, computer personalized, sequentially dated coupons to the user households. The direct mail package included $5 worth of Mighty Dog coupons and the chance for consumers to purchase a personalized dog bowl and blanket once they had sent in the appropriate number of UPC symbols from Mighty Dog Products.

A total of 6.7 per cent of the coupons distributed were redeemed. Premium redemption was 13 per cent: 71,000 households redeemed the UPS symbols for either the bowl or blanket. Mighty Dog used coupon values forcing high-purchase commitment (saving $1 on 10 cans) and attracted known customers to complete a program of having enough UPC symbols to redeem for a personalized bowl or blanket.

Mighty Dog's market share increased 0.5 per cent during the first two weeks of the promotion. The promotion minimized Mighty Dog's market share loss (only 0.2 per cent) to Reward, in the first 8 weeks.

The 'Tennessee Squires' is an FM customer association, 'club', founded by Jack Daniel's to create brand loyalty among the firm's best customers. Each member of the club receives a deed to a small plot of land owned by the distiller, invitations to local raccoon hunts, updates on 'municipal' business, a Squire card, and a certificate of membership.

The letter shown as Figure 1 helps create and maintain a strong sense of being a Tennessee Squire, 'belonging' to the club, and probably helps to maintain top-of-mind awareness and preference for Jack Daniel's whiskey among club members.

Note the informal, very enjoyable reading in the letter, for example: 'we didn't hurt your property much at all since the dogs went off in the other direction and never did circle back to your place'. Accompanying the letter was an out-of-focus, colour photograph showing twenty-four club members, one child, and four coon-hunting dogs. The photo explains the sentence in Figure 1, 'Unfortunately I had some camera trouble'. (The club members are posed with no rifles in the photograph, a thoughtful tactic given the negative connotations that might come to mind with drinking alcohol and guns.)

Note that the letter ends with a personal reference to the Wilsons in the last paragraph. This illustrates the individual, personalizing feature of effective FM programs and direct marketing.

Jack Daniel's started the Tennessee Squires in 1957; the club predates all airline frequent traveller programs. By 1993, 80,000 US households included one or more Tennessee Squires. In other mailings, members of the Tennessee Squires receive new product information and how-to-consume product information (e.g. brief, lovely poems to offer as toasts when 'sipping' Gentleman Jack Rare Tennessee Whiskey).

Assessing performance and building forecasting models

Advertising budgets and other marketing expenditures are much easier to justify to senior management when sales can be linked directly, and accurately, to money spent. Therefore, a major benefit of direct marketing is that a performance tracking system can be created continually to monitor relationships with customers, including how customers respond to specific advertising executions. Thus, the term measurable response, in the DMA definition of direct marketing, is particularly noteworthy.

Rapp and Collins (1987) present a strong case for designing a measurable response into almost all advertising executions, including image advertisements:

> Most advertisers of products, services, and establishments who devote their advertising to building their favorable awareness can, at the very least, incorporate a direct-response element as an index of performance. Inviting a direct response of some sort can measure comparative creative impact, comparative positioning effectiveness, and comparative media performance.
>
> (Rapp and Collins 1987: 7)

Performance tracking systems can be developed at different levels of sophistication, for example, from low (Stage 1) to high (Stage 5):

Stage 1: One-time conversion studies.
Stage 2: One-time true experiments.
Stage 3: Continual monitoring and relationship-building.
Stage 4: Continual monitoring/relationship-building with true experiments.
Stage 5: Continual monitoring/relationship-building, true experiments, with forecasting models of consumer response functions.

Stage 1: One-time conversion studies

In Stage 1 the performance of advertisements and advertisement placements in competing media vehicles in delivering inquirers (prospects) is measured for an advertising campaign. The conversion power of advertising and advertisement placements is measured; conversion is the proportion of inquirers who convert into buyers.

Also, revenues and the net profits associated with each advertisement and placement can be monitored. Conversion rates can be tracked by surveying inquirers to learn if they purchased the brand or service, for which they requested information.

CPI, RPI and ROI are index values of performance often used to compare impact in direct marketing campaigns. CPI is cost per inquiry, calculated by dividing all costs assignable to a particular advertisement placed in a given media vehicle (e.g. advertising space cost and expenses in fulfilling the prospect's inquiry, including fulfilment literature expenses) by the total number of

Table 1 Revenue and cost analysis of advertising in competing magazine vehicles

Category	Magazine	Revenue per inquiry (RPI) $	Cost per inquiry (CPI) $	CPI as a percentage of RPI
Life cycle	Magazine X	240	49.51	20.6
	Magazine Y	35	15.16	43.3
Food	Gourmet	256	14.28	5.6
	Bon Appetit	89	6.60	7.4
Women's service	Family Circle	159	7.60	4.8
	Ladies Home Journal	105	4.18	4.0
Regional focus	Southern Living	237	5.99	2.5
	Texas Monthly	227	18.15	8.0
Travel related	Travel & Leisure	446	12.27	2.8
	N. G. Traveler	180	7.59	4.2

Source: Woodside and Soni (1990: 63)

Table 2 Profitability analysis of advertising by magazine vehicles

Category	Magazine	Advertising total cost $	Total tax revenue[1] $	Net profit to state and local governments $
Life cycle	Magazine X	24,856	10,843	−14,013
	Magazine Y	12,524	2,602	−9,922
Food	Gourmet	26,616	42,947	16,331
	Bon Appetit	29,934	36,293	6,359
Women's service	Family Circle	91,480	172,292	80,812
	Ladies Home Journal	30,108	68,059	37,951
Regional focus	Southern Living	46,968	166,564	119,596
	Texas Monthly	21,581	24,184	2,603
Travel related	Travel & Leisure	38,516	125,994	87,483
	N. G. Traveler	32,396	69,158	36,762
Total		$354,979	$718,936	$363,957

[1]Estimated using 9 per cent of total revenue.
Source: Woodside and Soni (1990: 63)

inquiries generated by this advertisement placement.

RPI is the revenue per inquiry, calculated by dividing the revenues to the advertiser from the advertisement placement by the total number of inquiries generated by this placement. ROI is return on investment, calculated by dividing revenue net of assignable costs by assignable costs.

A tracking system developed by the state of Louisiana for assessing advertising performance for attracting tourist visitors provides details of such a Stage 1 tracking system (see Woodside and Soni 1990). In the Woodside and Soni (1990) report, the conversion proportion of visitors-divided-by-inquirers for advertisements placed in 1987 in *Southern Living* magazine was very high (0.46) compared to the conversion proportion from advertisements in *Bon Appetit* (0.11).

However, conversion rates are only one measure of performance. Similar to a medical doctor examining a patient, multiple-method measurements should be included to assess well-being, that is, advertising performance. Tables 1 and 2 are examples of RPI, CPI, and profit measures of performance for the 1987 Louisiana advertising campaign. Note in Table 2 that profits associated with the *Bon Appetit* ads are positive. Thus, the Louisiana advertisement 1987 performance associated with *Bon Appetit* might be judged to be fairly good, even with the low conversion rate. (Magazines X and Y are not named in Tables 1 and 2 because of their poor profit performance for the advertiser.)

Data evaluation is a critical issue in Stage 1, and other stages, in performance monitoring. Managers looking at the study, and evaluating the evaluation, should ask: how are the data variables defined in the study? What are the details of the procedures with which the data were collected? What factors were controlled and not controlled in obtaining the data? What are the statistical properties of the data? In what direction will data problems bias the results (Clarke 1993: 41)?

In several respects, data evaluation of the 1987 Louisiana study led to the conclusion that the data look satisfactory. The study was designed to achieve a high response rate (52 per cent) for the questionnaire sent to inquirers; the data included questions on buying competing brands (i.e. visiting other states); and the questionnaire and cover letter did not reveal the sponsor of the study (to reduce sponsor identity biases in responding to the questions). Most conversion research studies on tourism report very high overall conversion rates, for example above 45 per cent. Such reports make the advertising expenditures look very good, even if the estimates are unrealistic (i.e. invalid estimates of reality). One reason such high conversion rates are estimated is often that multiple attempts are not made to reach non-respondents in sampled households. Non-respondents are usually different from respondents in surveys – not in their demographic profiles but in their product use profiles (see Woodside and Ronkainen 1994).

Stage 1 performance evaluations have two major shortcomings:

1 Relationship marketing is not done.
2 The basic issue of advertising effectiveness (does advertising cause sales?) is not adequately answered.

A major shortcoming with Stage 1 performance tracking is that no long-term relationships are developed with inquirers. After the inquiry is 'fulfilled' by sending some literature, possibly a brochure or an information kit which might include a video or offers for additional information, that is the end to the relationship. No additional contacts with the customer by the marketer are attempted; the marketer discards the names, addresses and other information provided by the inquirers. Hard to believe, isn't it? Yet many marketers using direct marketing do only Stage 1 performance evaluation. They do not attempt additional 'sales calls' by telephone, personal visits, or through the mail other than a one-time response to the customer inquiry. Almost all state travel offices in the US and Canadian provincial tourism agencies do Stage-1-type perform-ance evaluations of their advertising programs, even though they are marketing a high-ticket service (average expenditures in a state by overnight, visiting travel parties are typically above $1,000).

Stage 1 tracking does not answer the basic question: how many sales (how much revenue was gained) because of the advertising? As a research tool, Stage 1 research is unscientific in learning valid answers to cause-and-effect relation-ships, even if customers respond favourably when asked whether seeing the advertising and receiving the literature requested influence them to buy (would you accept a medical report that a new drug works well because patients report that they felt better after taking the pill containing the new drug?). Scientific research to learn cause-and-effect influence requires a direct comparison of results between two equal groups, one exposed to a treatment (say, advertising) and one not exposed. Such comparisons are known as 'true experiments' (see Banks 1965).

Stage 2: True experiments

Doing true experiments to estimate cause-and-effect relationships between advertising and sales are more sophisticated than conversion research studies. While Stage 1 conversion studies may provide useful information of the relative performance of alternative advertising executions and media vehicles, they cannot answer the more basic questions: did the advertising cause sales beyond what would have occurred without it? Did the sales performance of the new advertisement beat the sales performance of the old advertisement?

Stage 2, true experiments, provides useful answers to the question of whether advertising does cause sales. True experiments involve the creation of two, three, or more, equal groups of subjects (e.g. prospects) and the exposure of one group to treatment A, a second group to treatment B, and other groups to other treatments. Treatment A might be a new advertisement; treatment B might be the standard advertisement often used by a firm. The executives in the firm want to know if the new advertisement performs better than the standard one in generating inquiries, new customers, sales and profits. Equal groups are created by randomly assigning a sample of subjects (say, 20,000) from a representative population to each group in the study (10,000 to group A and 10,000 to group

B). Demographic and buying behaviour characteristics of the groups can be checked to ensure that the random assignment has worked to create two or more groups which do not differ (see Banks 1965 for details). Treatment A might be tested against treatment B, where treatment B is no advertising, that is, one group of subjects is assigned randomly to be exposed to advertisement A and the second group is exposed to no advertising. This test is designed to examine how much impact is caused by advertising exposure versus no exposure: thus, how much, if any, does advertising cause sales?

True experiments are used in medical research to test the effectiveness of new drugs versus a placebo (sugar pills) in double-blind designs, that is, the administrators of the drug and the patients receiving either treatment A versus treatment B do not know which of the treatments are being administered. Thus, care is taken to avoid false reports of impact often made because subjects know they are being tested.

True experiments are known as split-run tests in advertising and direct marketing. A 'split-run' is an old newspaper term referring to splitting a publication run by removing an advertising or newspaper section, and adding a second advertising or newspaper section.

Split-run testing and other forms of true experiment can be used in testing the cause-and-effect influence of advertising versus no advertising, newspapers versus television, station A versus station B, magazine X versus Y, appeal M versus R, headline T versus U. Here is one example (from Caples 1974: 279) of split-run testing two headlines: the copy and illustrations were identical in both advertisements except for a change in headline wording:

Headline of Ad A: Save one gallon of gas in every ten
Headline of Ad B: Car Owners! Save one gallon of gas in every ten

Ad B pulled 20 per cent more inquirers. While the sales results were not in this test, most likely ad B pulled more total sales orders than ad A.

John Caples' (1974) book continues to be the best source to learn about true experiments, and wisdom, in advertising, including a famous quotation:

> I have seen one mail order advertisement actually sell, not twice as much, not three times as much, but 19½ times as much goods as another. Both advertisements occupied the same space. Both were run in the same publication. Both had [the same] photographic illustrations. Both had carefully written copy. The difference was that one used the right appeal and the other used the wrong appeal.
>
> (Caples 1974: 11)

David Ogilvy makes a telling observation about direct marketing in the Foreword to Caples' (1974) book:

> Experience has convinced me that the factors that work in mail order advertising work equally well in *all* advertising. But the vast majority of people who work in [advertising] agencies, and almost all their clients, have never heard of these factors. That is why they skid helplessly about on the greasy surface of irrelevant brilliance.

They waste millions on bad advertising, when good advertising could be selling 19½ times as much.

In 1993 Don Schultz reported that most advertising agencies are still unable to embrace direct marketing and IMC programs. Unfortunately Ogilvy's observations about advertising agencies still hold true as we enter the mid-1990s. Schultz (1993) reports two problems that many advertising agencies perceive about direct marketing: it has less style and is less profitable (for the agency) compared to placing image advertising on television.

Workable solutions to transform advertising from image communicating to integrated marketing communications have to be started in client firms – not with their advertising agencies. Advertising and marketing managers need to insist on creating relationship marketing strategies with customers (i.e. IMC programs) because:

1   IMC programs are more effective than image advertising.
2   IMC programs provide the hard evidence demanded by senior management on how much advertising and marketing cause sales.
3   Most advertising agencies will not do it unless they are forced to do it.

The real problem is that many advertising and marketing managers lack the knowledge/ability (they do not know how to do it) and conviction (they do not really believe in it) needed to create IMC programs; we return to this issue in the next section of the chapter.

The single, best technical reading on true experiments in marketing continues to be Banks (1965). Banks offers detailed numerical examples of simple true experiments, as well as sophisticated research designs to test cause-and-effect relationships. The book is out of print but well worth finding because it provides the readable technical training needed by advertising and marketing managers.

Stage 3: Continual monitoring and relationship-building

Two important features of relationship marketing are:

1   Creating unique products/services for distinct groups of customers in a firm's customer database.
2   Communicating the offer only to these distinct groups.

For example, Cindy Lay used her personal computer to find 1,400 Southern women who buy Anne Klein dresses only on sale. Evaluating their past purchases, she discovered that when they waited until the second markdown, they 'cost me an additional $75 per person'. So before the first markdown period ended, she spent $850 to notify these customers of a 'special sale' on the clothes they wanted. The two-day event increased volume on the dresses by 97 per cent in a normally slow period (Bulkeley 1993). Ms Lay is the director of market

639

research for Proffitt's Inc., an Alcoa, Tennessee, department store chain that has recently created an IMC program.

All firms in some industries have transformed themselves into relationship marketers by creating such IMC programs: direct marketing, financial investment firms (e.g. Fidelity Investments); credit card companies (e.g. American Express); airlines for customers in their frequent flyer programs (e.g. Delta Airlines); direct marketing, clothing companies (e.g. L. L. Bean); mail order seed companies (e.g. Burpee). Some firms, and whole industries, have yet to start IMC programs (e.g. marketing departments in state and Canadian provincial governments, most banks, many department stores).

With an IMC program, most marketers are able to keep and use a customer database of the complete buying history of each customer. Customer demographic and lifestyle information can often be included in such databases. Individual customer account databases usually begin by including the following information: how many years the customer has been buying from the company; what was purchased each year; how the customer responded to each marketing communication to reach this customer; customer complaints and how the firm responded; the total dollar amount purchased by the customer per year; and how frequently the customer buys each year.

The SALES model developed by Pareto, a Cincinnati-based database marketing company, is an example of a database system to provide department store marketers with the capability to target customers with unique buying histories to receive marketing communications especially designed for them. The SALES model is based on five key indicators of customer activity and value. Sales data are processed through the SALES model and customer/department summary entries are created. For each unique relationship between a customer and a department in the store, a numeric indicator value is computed ('A Database' 1991). The indicators are:

S Sales history (sales volume for this customer in this particular department).
A Across department (cross-buying in other departments).
L Last purchase (last purchase in days in this department).
E Extent of the relationship (how long a customer).
S Shopping frequency (frequency of buying in this department).

Here is an example using the SALES model. If a retailer decides to invite 1,000 of its best customers to a special preview of the men's autumn suit selections, these customers can be selected by criteria based upon the entries in the SALES model for the menswear department. A typical selection criteria might be to select all customers:

1 in the top 20 per cent for sales history in menswear (S);
2 in the top quartile for buying across departments (A);
3 in the top 20 per cent for last menswear purchase in days (L);

DIRECT MARKETING

Table 3 Sales system: women's wear

Name	Account number	S	A	L	E	S
Joe Smith	1434528	8	2	7	3	7
Melanie Jones	1417076	4	1	4	9	3
Carrie Loftus	1381154	6	4	8	6	6

Source: *Colloquy* (1991: 13)
Note: The example above illustrates three partial database entries from the SALES system for a particular department. Melanie Jones has a 4 under the first S (sales history), which indicates that she falls somewhere between the 40th and 49th percentile in 'sales history' (year to date spending in this department). The 1 under A indicates that she falls into the lowest of four equal-sized groups in terms of 'tendency to buy across departments'. The 4 under L indicates that she falls somewhere between the 40th and 49th percentile in terms of 'days since the last purchase in this department'. The 9 under E indicates that Melanie is one of the customers with the longest 'history of purchase activity in this department'. She falls at or above the 90th percentile in terms of 'extent of relationship' with the women's wear department. Finally, the 3 under the second S indicates that she falls somewhere between the 30th and 39th percentile in terms of 'frequency of purchase' in this department.

4   in the top 30 per cent for extent of relationship (E);
5   in the top 40 per cent for menswear shopping frequency (S).

The first criterion (the first S requirement) selects the biggest spenders in the department for the year. If the count turns up less than 1,000 customers, the criteria for an indicator may be revised, and the selection computer run made a second time. Table 3 is a summary of entries in the customer database in the SALES model.

The biggest problem in creating the customer database needed for relationship marketing is that firms' management information systems (MIS) are programmed only to meet the needs of the finance and accounting departments. For example, banks generally have customer account databases for each product: mortgages, car loans, savings and credit cards, savings accounts. The databases may even identify the same customer differently – without a middle initial, for example, or last name first. Marketers want one customer database that includes all details of the firm's relationship with each customer.

The most workable solution to this problem is not in trying to transform a firm's existing MIS to a complete customer database. Given the substantial decreases in costs of customer database software programs and computer workstations, the faster and most workable solution is to create a customer database from scratch – by selecting from several high-quality spreadsheet programs; and using a workstation or personal computer with the necessary hard drive memory. A critical point in relation to this approach is that now is the time for the marketers to develop finger-tip computer capability to mine their own customer database on their own personal computers.

641

For years, marketing gurus have been preaching the merits of 'mining' corporate databases. But the databases used for billings, deposit records and installment-plan payments usually have been inaccessible except to the programmers who maintain them. Marketers designing direct-mail campaigns have had to stand in line to ask programmers to search for particular types of customers. Now the marketing experts themselves [programmers not needed] can get at the data. High-end PCs with two-gigabit hard drives – 20 times larger than the 100 megabyte drives most home users buy now – can hold several million customer names on hardware that costs about $10,000 now. The software to manage such data starts as low as $15,000.

(Bulkeley 1993)

Thus, given that the marketers are willing to invest some time, they are personally now able to have the technical capability and wisdom to create and handle a customer database to fulfil the two major benefits of direct marketing:

1 relationship marketing including forecasting net profit contributions of marketing tactics using customer response functions and financial data;
2 hard-evidence measuring of how much advertising and marketing influences sales.

Before the 1990s low-cost approaches for high-quality relationship marketing (IMC) programs were not widely available. The situation has finally changed. The best technical introduction to customer database management and relationship marketing is likely to be Clarke (1993), which provides the marketer with basic training and wisdom of handling databases to make better marketing decisions.

Stage 4: Continual monitoring/relationship-building with true experiments

Stage 4 includes true experiments (Stage 2) in relationship marketing programs (Stage 3). Thus, Park Seed, a mailorder seed company, might test a special high-price bulb offer designed to be purchased by the firm's best customers (identified using a SALES-type software program) by randomly assigning a randomly selected sample of best customers to two groups: one group receiving the special offer (treatment A), and the second group not receiving the special offer (treatment B). Note that two types of randomization are used:

1 Random selection to achieve representativeness of the sample to the population of best customers.
2 Random assignment to achieve equality between the two groups on all variables so that only the marketing offer (treatment A versus B) is available to explain any difference in sales response.

Quasi-experiments can also be performed in Stage 4 IMC programs. Quasi-experiments look at changes in customer responses to the presence and absence of marketing offers through time, without equivalent test and control treatment groups. They do not meet the two requirements of true experiments for testing cause-and-effect relationships, but examining database relationships between marketing actions and customer responses through time provides useful information, even when true experiments are not planned. Customer response models can be considered and tested to learn which models, if any, are useful for explaining responses among some groups of customers to particular marketing actions. The best, advanced, reading on quasi-experimentation is Cook and Campbell (1979); Banks (1965) is helpful preparation.

Stage 5: Continual monitoring/relationship-building, true experiments with forecasting models of customer response functions

Stage 5 relationship marketing is what Shepard (1990) means by 'The New Direct Marketing'. In Stage 5 the marketer uses the customer database, develops and tests customer response functions, and does financial payback ('what if') sensitivity analysis of different marketing strategies and tactics. For example, with useful customer response models developed from insight and tested using the database, a catalogue company might examine the question of what if its business was built on the assumption of three catalogue mailings to customers per year instead of two? Instead of using a third catalogue mailing, what would be the net contribution to profit if the firm spent the available marketing funds on attracting new customers? A lifetime value analysis of new customer marketing can forecast useful answers to this question, based on the valid customer response functions. Shepard (1990) is a useful introduction to Stage 5 relationship marketing.

Equation 1 is an illustration of a customer response model. In this model, unit sales for product X are influenced by four variables: price of the product; advertising; customer annual household income; age of household head. The two marketing variables are advertising and price. The model was developed, and tested against other possible models from data in the firm's customer database.

Equation 1: unit sales =
$$320\,[1 + ((1/250{,}000)\,(\text{advertising})^{1.5})\,((1/12)\,(\text{price})^{-0.9})] + (.065)\,(\text{income}) + (.86)\,(\text{age}).$$

This hypothetical model indicates that increasing advertising has a positive influence on unit sales; increasing price has a negative influence; increases in income have a positive effect; and increases in age have a positive effect. Unit sales forecasted from Equation 1 can be used with revenue and cost of goods sold equations to forecast net contribution for different prices and advertising combinations.

Equation 2: revenue = (unit sales) (price).

Equation 3: COGS = ($8.00) (unit sales).

If the firm wants to consider the impact on net contribution of 4 prices at each

643

of 3 levels of advertising, then 12 (4 prices by 3 advertising) combinations of specific prices and advertising expenditures can be included in Equation 1 in a computer spreadsheet program to forecast sales for each combination. Equations 2 and 3 can then be used to estimate the net contribution for each pricing-advertising mix.

Airlines, mailorder seed companies, credit card companies, and many firms in several industries are now using such customer response functions to provide specific forecasts of results of specific marketing actions.

Problems with direct marketing strategies and IMC programs

Two major problems almost always occur in designing and implementing IMC programs:

1 Not planning and coordinating deeply enough even to accomplish Stage 1 direct marketing. This problem includes:
    * marketing team members refusing to contact new customers (i.e. not responding to inquiring prospects who reply to an advertising offer);
    * no follow-up to learn if prospects have received the information they requested and to prompt purchase;
2 The advertiser's and marketer's lack of knowledge and technical ability, in modelling customer/marketer information search and relationships in IMC programs.

Not planning and coordinating deeply enough

Two independent studies confirm that about 20 to 40 per cent of customer requests for product/service information offers in direct response advertising go unanswered. The conclusion would be reasonable that some (more than a few) marketers refuse to fulfil customer requests for the information offered in the marketer's own advertising.

In one five-year study, Performark researchers, pretending to be potential customers, mailed in thousands of reader-response cards, the kind found in business and trade publications with offers of more information on goods and services. They responded to solicitations from hundreds of companies selling industrial products costing at least $5,000.

> What happened? It took an average of 58 days for the requested pamphlets or brochures to arrive. Nearly one out of four inquiries went unanswered. Only one in eight generated a follow-up call by a sales representative, and those contacts came an average of 89 days after Performark's initial indication of interest.
>
> (Gibson 1993)

The President of Performark, Joseph Lethert, reports: 'The problem is sales and marketing aren't working together. No one has responsibility for making sure prospects are converted to customers'. Too often marketing people blame

644

the salesforce for not pursuing leads, while salespeople are loath to share information about their customers (Gibson 1993).

Similar findings are reported in a second study of business-to-business and consumer marketers responses to inquiries (Woodside *et al.* 1991). Acting as customers, inquiries were sent to 90 direct marketers (47 business and 43 consumer firms). After 8 weeks, 25 per cent of the business marketers and 28 per cent of the consumer marketers had yet to respond in any manner. However, the proportion of responses did vary according to media used to make the inquiry: overall, 80 per cent of the marketers responded to telephone inquiries; 80 per cent to direct mail inquiries, but only 60 per cent responded to reader-response inquiries. Follow-up calls after responding to the inquiries were made by only 34 per cent of the business marketers and 25 per cent of the consumer marketers.

Thus, besides many advertising agencies not supporting direct marketing and IMC programs (see Schultz 1993), many advertising and marketing team members within firms with active IMC programs fail to implement the program and/or fail to design in IMC steps for effective relationship marketing. One specific example serves to illustrate the problem: in 1984 the sales manager of an office furniture distributor in Greenville, South Carolina, did not want area customers (recently buying furniture) interviewed for the company's customer newsletter. Photographs of the customer executives using the product were always run with the news stories and the newsletter is direct response advertising for the company. The sales manager reasoned that too many persons in companies who would not be buying might call him and tie him up on the phone. This problem was not occurring in the other four company sales territories participating in the program. The Greenville sales manager also reported, 'I know all customers in the Greenville-Spartanburg area and they know me, there's no reason for sending them a newsletter or advertising to them'.

Part of this first problem is that a database had not been created to store each marketing contact attempt and customer response within each customer's file record. Unfortunately, most companies in Stage 1 direct marketing are probably not operating an on-line customer database that includes marketing contacts (plus second follow-up contacts to learn if prospects received the information requested and whether or not they would like help in their buying decisions) and customer responses.

Part of the solution to this serious problem is to create and use daily an on-line customer/marketer computer database to help to build up and maintain relationships with new and established customers. With the continuing decrease in the costs of software, data handling and storage, this solution is feasible in the 1990s. Given that relationship marketing includes knowing the customer by name and the nature/quality of current contacts and responses with this customer, storing such information in the heads of a few persons and on paper is inadequate for designing active marketing strategies and building valid marketing response models. Monitoring the execution of planned marketing contacts with customers (including follow-up calls) and customer responses can occur systematically with an on-line customer/marketer database.

To make on-line entries and analysis of such databases and to achieve widespread acceptance and enthusiasm for IMC programs requires senior executives (including the CEO) to be technically competent in personally handling the database, understanding customer response functions and what if, sensitivity and analyses of marketing moves. Thus, the time has come to discard the old solution to problems of failing to deliver the literature offered and not following up on inquiries by 'educating sales people on the importance of direct marketing'. The new solution is in leadership by behavioural example from the CEO and other executives in contacting customers and hands-on ability in handling a computer-based customer/marketer database.

Lack of knowledge and skills for modelling customer/marketer IMC relationships

Until the mid-1980s creating and running an effective and efficient IMC program (and achieving Stage 5) was difficult to accomplish for three reasons. First, low-cost help, including computer software programs and PCs, was unavailable for managers to develop and test explicit and useful market response models for estimating how much marketing actions affect customer responses. As discussed, this problem now has been eliminated.

Second, skill-building books and manuals were not widely available for combining useful marketing response models and financial spreadsheet analysis into decision models (to forecast net contribution impacts of alternative marketing actions). With the availability of skill-training books such as Shepard (1990) and Clarke (1993), this problem now has been eliminated. The unique moment of the mid-1990s is captured well by Clarke:

> Developments in the fields of statistics, mathematical marketing models, and marketing research have advanced by slow increments over the years to provide finally a meaningful, critical mass of useful knowledge. Parallel developments in computer technology, computer software, and commercially available software, which have advanced at a fantastically rapid rate, have converged to provide an analytical capability for marketing managers that could only have been dreamed of ten years ago. In terms of both power and accessibility, these developments have the potential to greatly expand the manager's knowledge of how the marketplace works, as well as to explode old myths and increase the manager's ability to exploit his or her knowledge.
>
> (Clarke 1993: 5)

This second problem includes not fully describing, understanding, and modelling the search and choice processes involved in customer/marketer IMC programs. For example, the substantial possibilities are not included usually in such models that customer requests for information offered in advertisements may not be fulfilled and customers may not receive or notice they have received the information requested and sent to them. This issue is discussed more fully in the next section.

Third, illusion of knowledge may be the last major obstacle for advertisers and marketing managers to overcome. All successful marketing managers have an intuitively insightful model (of customer responses) for making decisions and implementing actions.

> The result is that most marketing managers base their decisions on conceptual models of the marketplace that are part fact and part imagination. Like Christopher Columbus, who died believing that the island of Cuba was the east coast of Asia, the misconceptions of marketing managers will never be corrected by monitoring the same data in the same way as they have in the past.
>
> (Clarke 1993: 6)

The goal is not to replace marketing imagination with database decision models but to combine them to achieve better decisions.

MODELLING CUSTOMER/MARKETER INFORMATION SEARCH AND RELATIONSHIPS IN INTEGRATIVE MARKETING COMMUNICATIONS

Effective IMC programs require deep understanding and database entries of the multiple give-and-take responses between the customer and marketer. Figure 2 is an overview of two-way responses that may occur in using direct marketing for starting an IMC program with customers. Figure 2 is intended to be a model of the sequence of steps that often occur in direct marketing and to emphasize the many possibilities for reoccurring communication breakdowns/failures. The model is intended to be relevant for both business and consumer marketing. The steps in the model and some research findings related to these steps are summarized in this section.

In Figure 2, this direct marketing model begins by asking whether or not the customer is exposed to an advertisement that includes a direct response offer. Prior media steps, such as vehicle distribution and customer exposure to the vehicle, are described in the Advertising Research Foundation's model for evaluating media (see ARF 1961; Phelps 1993).

Mere exposure effects of advertising

Given that customer exposure to an advertisement containing a direct response occurs (box 1), the advertisement may have an influence even if the customer does not notice it (boxes 2 to 3). Thus, including box 3 in the model is to include the hypothesis supported by empirical evidence that mere exposure can influence attitude and purchase choices (see Krugman 1965; Zajonc 1980; Fazio *et al.* 1989; Petty *et al.* 1991). Thus, the sequence of moving through boxes 1–2–3–5–7–15 is to indicate the peripheral route to persuasion described by

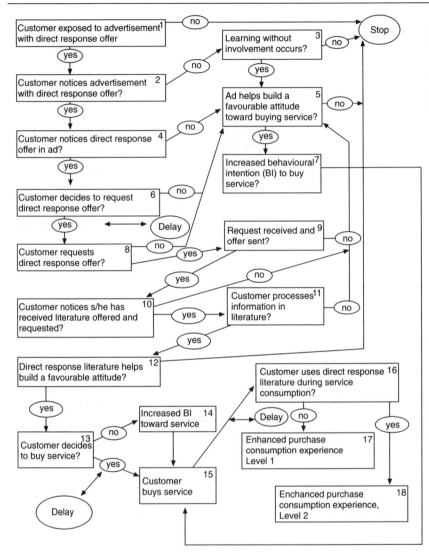

Figure 2 Model of customer/marketing information search and use of direct response advertising

Petty and Cacioppo (1986), and the possible impact of perception without awareness (Bornstein and Pittman 1992).

The central route to persuasion

The central route to persuasion described (Petty and Cacioppo 1986; Petty *et al.* 1991) applied to direct marketing is reflected in the customer noticing and being motivated to request the direct response offer (linking of boxes 4 and 6), or increases in customer awareness of the advertising affecting favourable attitude toward the brand (linking of boxes 4 and 5).

$TOMA_a$ and $TOMA_b$ linkage: to box 5 and beyond

Image advertising effects are accounted for in the model by linkage between boxes 4 and 5, as well as the mere exposure effect. $TOMA_a$ is the customer's top-of-mind-awareness for an advertisement in a product category. Shares of $TOMA_a$ for different brands in different product categories are reported in one issue each month in *Advertising Age* from monthly US household surveys sponsored by Gallup and *Advertising Age*. Unaided $TOMA_a$ by brand is measured by asking sample members to name the advertising that first comes to mind from all they have seen, heard or read in the previous thirty days. The hypotheses are supported empirically that: increasing $TOMA_a$ is associated with increasing $TOMA_b$, top-of-mind-awareness toward the brand. $TOMA_b$ is associated positively to building preference (box 5), intentions (box 7) and sales (box 15) (Woodside and Wilson 1985).

The customer direct-response route to persuasion

Rapp and Collins (1987) emphasize that advertisements can and should, 'do double-duty by inviting a [direct] response from your best prospects while increasing general awareness of your product or service'. The authors then advocate that 'advertising a high-price, high-involvement product should focus first on getting a response from prime prospects rather than on creating an image. Then, convert that response to a sale by providing powerful linkage [the fulfilment literature]'.

The active noticing of a direct response offer is a central route to persuasion that may lead to deciding to request the offer in the advertisement, for example request a free catalogue or brochure offered in a television commercial, magazine or newspaper advertisement (linking boxes 4 and 6). Note in Figure 2 that a delay is indicated between boxes 6 and 8: customers may decide to request the direct response offer but never get around to doing so. Advertisers sometimes attempt to limit the delay by reducing the effort and time necessary for the customer to respond. Such attempts include placing a telephone number in the advertisement, sometimes toll-free, using free-standing-inserts (FSIs), and suggesting in a magazine advertisement that a number be circled on the reader-service card to respond. There are systematic differences in buying behaviour according to the mode customers use to request information (Manville 1987; Woodside and Soni 1988). For example, when advertising a high-involving service such as vacation destination travel, the proportion buying the service (visiting the destination) varied from a low of 0.26 (reader-service card inquirers), to 0.36 (direct-response coupon inquirers), to 0.43 (toll-free telephone inquirers).

Marketers' responses to customer inquiries

According to the DMA, direct marketing is 'an interactive system'. Thus, two-way customer/marketer communications are planned for implementation. However, as described earlier, substantial numbers of marketers do not fulfil requests made by customers to offers included in the advertisements. Thus, the marketing activity of getting back to the customer (boxes 8 to 9 to 10) has to be built in and actively monitored in the IMC program. This first fulfilment step is often sub-contracted out by the advertiser or the advertising agency to a 'fulfilment house'. Such a marketing strategy has the advantage of bringing in the expertise of fulfilment experts, but also increases the need for careful coordination and attention to customer requests.

Unfortunately, in most directing programs, little attempt to gain information and to build a relationship (i.e. bonding) are designed into the initial linkage of customer response and marketer fulfilment. As a test of this proposition, make ten telephone calls in response to television commercials and magazine advertisements and record the number of questions asked by the person fulfilling your request beyond asking for your address. Also record persuasive attempts to encourage readership included in the fulfilment package. Also record whether or not the advertiser calls you back to learn if you received the fulfilment linkage and to ask for your order. The proposition is that most marketers are missing the opportunity to build relationships with new customers at the first moment-of-truth, even for high-price products and services.

Customer use of fulfilment materials

What happens after customers receive the fulfilment literature they request? Customers vary considerably in how they process fulfilment literature: some are not aware of receiving it; some do not report ever requesting it when later asked; and some do use the materials extensively for making buying decisions.

In our study, 45 per cent of inquirers, who were sent the literature they requested, did not report either asking for nor receiving the literature (Woodside and Soni 1991). Thus, customers may not process (notice, look at, or read thoroughly) information they request and receive: reaching box 11 (Figure 2) is not a certainty. Monitoring this step in the direct marketing process is necessary to ensure customer usage of fulfilment literature.

> Great advertising creative work that results in high inquiry rates is not good enough; the direct-response offer may have to be even better to get through the second level of clutter – all the competing advertising brochures and catalogs being received by the inquirer.
>
> (Woodside and Soni 1991: 36)

Customer information processing of the fulfilment materials may often be helpful in convincing the customer to buy (box 13) and her/his purchase choices (box 15). Note that a delay is shown between box 13 and 15 to indicate that the effects of direct marketing fulfilment on buying behaviour may be long term and not immediately visible in one advertising campaign. Monitoring the impact of direct marketing on sales should include assessing the effects over several time periods beyond the immediate advertising-and-buying time frame.

The term 'enhanced purchase consumption experience' is used in box 17 to express the proposition that the customer's experiences in using the product or service are affected by processing the fulfilment literature before purchase versus not requesting, receiving, or processing such literature.

In some industries, customers may refer to the fulfilment materials while using the product or service (box 18). For example, consumers buying seeds and plants using mail order may refer to their catalogues for planting information and recipes for preparing vegetables grown; vacation travellers may refer to destination 'visitor guides' during a planning phase to learn about places to visit, things to do and products to buy during their visit. In one tourism advertising study of visitors to Prince Edward Island in Canada (Woodside *et al.* 1993), total dollar purchases more than doubled among customers using fulfilment literature while on their visit compared to expenditures using the literature only before visiting (comparing sales results between box 17 and 18).

Limitations

For many customer-marketing interactions, the model summarized in Figure 2 is a simplification of the first stages in an IMC program. Multiple two-way contacts may occur between the customer and marketer before the first purchase-sale. In the US office furniture industry for example, customer response to a direct mail or newspaper advertisement is often followed by several telephone conversations and four to seven personal sales calls and customer visits to the marketer's showrooms – all before the first purchase. The recent and long-term history of interactions with many established customers may exist only in the long-term memories of one or two persons in the marketing firm, with no computer database yet developed for such relationships in many firms.

However, some firms (including some office furniture marketers) and entire industries have accomplished IMC programs with long-term customers that meet the DMA definition of direct marketing. Handling a database built on such long-term interactive systems, and estimating customer response functions to marketing actions in such systems, are more than a possibility. Such interactive systems and the use of decision models for sensitivity analysis is now more than the future promise of direct marketing. However, building and using computer databases for forecasting net contribution effects of marketing decisions is still time-consuming, not inexpensive, and requires management science expertise.

The good news is that the high-performing, low-price computer software and hardware tools and modelling skill-training, have become available in the 1990s.

DIRECT MARKETING IMPLICATIONS FOR DESIGNING AND IMPLEMENTING EFFECTIVE IMC PROGRAMS

In 1986 Stan Rapp predicted:

> When the light of a new day dawns on January 1, 1990, I believe that all service companies and many product manufacturers will be spending as much time and money maximizing their relationships with known customers as they now do on their brand-image advertising to the world at large.
>
> (Rapp and Collins 1990: 57)

The review here of some of the empirical studies in direct marketing indicates that this prediction has not come to pass. However, substantial strides have been made in achieving the opportunities and benefits of direct marketing by some marketers.

The transformation from the illusion of knowledge into marketing wisdom is now occurring in many IMC programs because of:

1 advances in computer software/hardware tools in creating and handling databases;
2 marketers' use of customer response functions in decision models for 'what if' analyses.

The model and empirical findings described here of the initial stages in customer-marketer, direct marketing interactions indicate that monitoring of each of the multiple points-of-contact needs to occur for an IMC program to be useful.

Transforming marketing away from image advertising towards relationship marketing – that is, an effective, working IMC program – requires technical computer software and skill-training by marketers, including the CEO and CMO (chief marketing officer). The tools and skill-learning materials are now available. Creating and using decision models from such IMC programs will enable marketers to justify their marketing strategies and tactics with hard evidence; senior management continues to demand nothing less. In conclusion, may this recommendation be made: that the transformation should take place before the year 2000.

NOTE

1 *Colloquy* is a free quarterly newsletter published by Frequency Marketing Inc., P. O. Box 3920, Milford, Ohio 45150; telefax: 513-248-9084.

REFERENCES

ARF (1961) *Toward Better Media Comparisons*, New York: Advertising Research Foundation.
Banks, Seymour (1965) *Experimentation in Marketing*, New York: McGraw-Hill.
Bornstein, Robert F. and Pittman, Thane S. (1992) (eds) *Perception Without Awareness*, New York: Guilford Press.
Bulkeley, William M. (1993) 'Marketers mine their corporate databases', *The Wall Street Journal*, 14 June: B6.
Caples, John (1974) *Tested Advertising Methods*, Englewood Cliffs, NJ: Prentice Hall.
Clarke, Darral G. (1993) *Marketing Analysis and Decision Making*, 2nd edn, South San Francisco, CA: The Scientific Press.
Colloquy (1991) 'Calling all Tennessee Squires', Milford, OH: *Colloquy*, Frequency Marketing, Inc., October: 3.
Colloquy (1991) 'A database designed especially for department stores', Milford, OH: *Colloquy*, Frequency Marketing, Inc., October: 12–13.
Cook, Thomas D. and Campbell, Donald T. (1979) *Quasi-Experimentation*, Chicago: Rand McNally.
Direct Marketing Magazine (1992) 'Trend setters', November: 41.
Direct Marketing Magazine (1993) 'Direct marketing . . . an aspect of total marketing', April: 2.
Dubinsky, Alan J. and Ingram, Thomas N. (1984) 'A portfolio approach to account profitability', *Industrial Marketing Management* 13, February: 57–62.
Dwyer, Robert F. (1989) 'Customer lifetime valuations to support marketing decision making', *Journal of Direct Marketing* 3, Autumn: 8–15.
Fazio, R. H., Powell, M. C. and Willliams, C. J. (1989) 'The role of attitude accessibility in the attitude-to-behavior process', *Journal of Consumer Research* 16: 280–8.
Krugman, Herbert (1965) 'The impact of television advertising: learning without involvement', *Public Opinion Quarterly* 29: 349–56.
Levitt, Theodore (1983) *The Marketing Imagination*, New York: Free Press.
Manville, Richard (1987) 'Does advertising – or product 'publicity' – pull more inquiries? Which ones are more valuable?', *BPAA Communicator*, New York: Business and Professional Advertising Association.
Peters, Tom and Austin, Nancy (1985) *A Passion for Excellence*, New York: Warner Books.
Petty, Richard E. and Cacioppo, J. T. (1986) *Communication and Persuasion: Central and Peripheral Routes to Attitude Change*, New York: Springer/Verlag.
Petty, Richard E., Unnava, Rao and Strathman, Alan J. (1991) 'Theories of attitude change', in Thomas S. Robertson and Harold H. Kassarjian (eds) *Handbook of Consumer Behavior*, Englewood Cliffs, NJ: Prentice Hall.
Phelps, Stephen P. (1993) 'A media evaluation model for the 21st century', in Esther Thorson (ed.) *Proceedings of the 1993 Conference of the American Academy of Advertising*, Columbia, MO: School of Journalism, University of Missouri-Columbia.
Rapp, Stan, and Collins, Tom (1987) *Maxi-marketing*, New York: McGraw-Hill.
Rapp, Stan, and Collins, Tom (1990) 'Special report: the great marketing turnaround', *Direct Marketing Magazine*, October: 57–60.
Roman, Ernan (1988) *Integrated Direct Marketing*, New York: McGraw-Hill.
Schultz, Don E. (1993) 'Why ad agencies are having so much trouble with IMC', *Marketing News*, 26 April: 12.
Schultz, Don E., Tannenbaum, Stanley I. and Lauterborn, Robert E. (1993) *Integrated Marketing Communications*, Chicago: NTC Business Books.
Shepard, David (1990) *The New Direct Marketing*, Homewood, IL: Business One Irwin.

653

Woodside, Arch G. and Wilson, Elizabeth J. (1985) 'Effects of consumer awareness of brand advertising on preference', *Journal of Advertising Research* 25, August–September: 41–8.

Woodside, Arch G. and Soni, Praveen K. (1988) 'Assessing the quality of advertising inquiries by mode of response', *Journal of Advertising Research* 28, August–September: 31–7.

Woodside, Arch G. and Soni, Praveen K. (1990) 'Performance analysis of advertising in competing media vehicles', *Journal of Advertising Research* 30, February–March: 53–66.

Woodside, Arch G. and Soni, Praveen K. (1991) 'Direct-response advertising information: profiling heavy, light, and nonusers', *Journal of Advertising Research* 31, December: 26–36.

Woodside, Arch G., Brose, Frederick C. and Trappey, Randolph J., III (1991) 'Assessing performance of business-to-business and consumer direct marketing fulfillment strategies', working paper, New Orleans: Freeman School of Business, Tulane University.

Woodside, Arch G., MacDonald, Roberta and Trappey, Randolph J., III (1993) 'Effects of knowledge and experience on purchasing behavior and consumption experiences', working paper, New Orleans: Freeman School of Business, Tulane University.

Woodside, Arch G. and Ronkainen, Ilkka A. (1994) 'Improving conversion research studies', in J. R. Brent Ritchie and Charles R. Goeldner (eds) *Travel, Tourism, and Hospitality Research*, 2nd edn, New York: Wiley.

Zajonc, Robert B. (1980) 'Feelings and thinking: preferences need no influences', *American Psychologist* 35: 151–75.

37

MARKETING COMMUNICATIONS

Keith Crosier

WHAT IS 'MARKETING COMMUNICATIONS'?

The familiar 'Four Ps' mnemonic reminds us that products (or services) need to be made available in the right place, offered at the right price and backed by the right kind of promotion, if they are to be successful in today's crowded and noisy marketplace.

Here, we are concerned with the last of those four variables in the marketing equation, for 'promotion' and 'marketing communications' are in practice virtually interchangeable terms. The task of promoting a product or service is essentially a matter of selecting, deploying and controlling a marketing communications mix within the broader framework set by the marketing mix. Since experts disagree about the number of ingredients it contains and how those should be defined, the working definitions which follow have been formulated specifically to emphasize both the close family similarities and the strategically important differences among seven varieties of marketing communication activity.

1 *Advertising* communicates via a recognizable advertisement placed in a definable advertising medium, guaranteeing exposure to a target audience in return for a published rate for the time or space used.
2 *Publicity* communicates via a news release to definable news media in the hope of secondary exposure to a target audience through an editorial mention earned by the newsworthiness of the subject matter.
3 *Packaging* communicates via display, guaranteeing exposure to a potential customer at the point of sale but not normally to a wider target audience.
4 *Personal selling* communicates person to person via a sales pitch by a sales representative to a prospect, or by a sales assistant to a customer, guaranteeing exposure to a selected individual within a target market.
5 *Direct marketing* communicates person to person but through an intervening channel, such as the post (a mailshot or mailing), door-to-door delivery (a

mail drop), the telephone (telemarketing) or a fax line (no specific description yet), guaranteeing exposure to a selected individual within a target market. For many years, the only form of direct marketing in use was direct mail.

6 *Sponsorship* communicates via explicit association of a product or service with an entity, event or activity, in the expectation of secondary exposure to a target audience through identification during associated media coverage.

7 *Sales promotion* communicates via a variety of promotions not encompassed by any of the definitions above, each aiming for exposure to a target audience and some furthermore offering an incentive to respond actively.

Several of these activities may be prefixed by the description direct-response if reply facilities are incorporated, to collect data for mailing-list building or to win an order immediately. The term 'mail order' may be used to describe initiatives with the second of those two objectives. Typical examples of direct-response marketing communications are advertisements specifying free-call or local-charge telephone numbers, or mailshots including pre-paid reply coupons, but there are many other possibilities.

Two of our seven working definitions are subject to a certain amount of misuse in practice. Sales promotion initiatives are often described loosely as 'promotions', inviting confusion with other elements of the broader 'promotion' within the Four Ps. Publicity can be used to describe what is actually advertising, though there is a fundamental and obvious strategic difference between the two. Unfortunately, in three major languages, the word for advertising is in fact a version of 'publicity'. It is therefore wise to make sure that vocabulary is being accurately used if a key decision is going to be made.

Some readers may be surprised not to find *public relations* in this version of the marketing communications mix. It is deliberately excluded because it is an expression of corporate strategy rather than marketing strategy and hence belongs outside the marketing discipline, let alone within marketing communications. Indeed, it is itself a prolific user of three ingredients of the latter mix: advertising, publicity and sponsorship.

WHAT IS KNOWN ABOUT HOW MARKETING COMMUNICATION WORKS?

The seven definitions above all beg the crucial question how the activities described actually 'communicate' with the target audiences, and the answer is by no means straightforward.

Practitioners around the world are liable to respond with one member or another of a family of hierarchical models of marketing communications effect. The progenitor first appeared in an American textbook on the psychology of selling published in 1925. It has since been widely adopted as an explanation of advertising effect, and can just as logically be applied to the other elements of the marketing communications mix. It is the famous 'AIDA', a mnemonic to remind us that sales pitches, advertisements and the rest are forces that can move a target audience sequentially through states of Awareness, Interest and Desire to eventual Action. Successors, the best known of which are DAGMAR and the Hierarchy of Effects, both published in 1961, increased the number of steps and used different labels to describe them but did not increase the sophistication of the original in any other way. The problem is that such so-called 'models' provide an intuitively reasonable explanation of what may happen in certain stereotypical situations, but no explanation at all of how or why it does. Though their conceptual shortcomings were eloquently summed up by an influential academic critic more than thirty years ago, they are as frequently encountered today as they were then.

Fairly thorough discussions of this unduly influential paradigm and some theoretically superior alternatives have been published by Crosier (1995) and McDonald (1992) but no single text can be recommended as a complete synopsis of current thinking. Notably absent from typical marketing textbooks is any serious analysis of the contribution that might be made by information processing theory or by the discipline of semiotics, which approaches the subject from the direction of the audience's decoding rather than the originator's encoding. Readers wishing to discover the state of the art with respect to the mechanism of persuasive marketing communication will need to consult the collection of papers on a 'How Advertising Works Project' published by the American *Advertising Research Foundation* (1991) and screen recent issues of the American *Journal of Advertising Research* and the British *Admap* and *International Journal of Advertising*. Despite strong traditions of relevant empirical research in France and the Netherlands, no correspondingly influential journals seem to exist in either language. Little has been written on the subject in the context of marketing communications mix elements other than advertising.

A crucial but concealed drawback of the popular hierarchical model is the powerful influence it exerts in practice on the way campaign effectiveness is assessed. In an ideal world, this process would consist of comparing results recorded by appropriate measures of performance with specific criteria derived from explicit objectives. However, only in the obviously special case of direct-response initiatives is the process generally so controlled. Otherwise, inspection of case histories shows that both objectives and measures are very often based on the unsatisfactory hierarchical model in one guise or another, though seldom overtly.

Four surrogate criteria are especially common: awareness, recall, attitude and sales. Ready-to-use measures are widely available in each case. Established tests of unprompted and prompted awareness are used to demonstrate that attention has been gained, sometimes offered as evidence that the campaign was 'effective' regardless of other, unstated objectives it may have been meant to achieve. Likewise, equally common measures of recall may be used to test for a somewhat higher-level response, on the grounds that memory indicates a degree of interest in the proposition. A variety of tried and tested attitude scales borrowed from psychology are used to measure desire to engage more actively with the communicator in some way, on the grounds that one common definition of attitude is a 'predisposition to act'. Lastly, measurement of post-hoc sales movements correspond to the highest level hierarchical response, action, or the lack of it. Of course, it may in truth be virtually impossible to separate the effect of communications initiatives from many other controllable and uncontrollable variables in the cause-effect equation, and there may be a considerable time lag in practice before lower level responses are converted to action, but the assertion is regularly heard that this particular surrogate variable is the only 'real' test of effectiveness.

While it is perfectly logical that a model of effect should be used as the basis for measurement of effectiveness, the point is that AIDA and its derivatives are inadequate for the purpose. Readers interested in pursuing this vital issue further could begin with the comprehensive review of European and American empirical research by Franzen (1994).

PLANNING THE MARKETING COMMUNICATIONS CAMPAIGN

Given the degree of uncertainty about effect and effectiveness just noted, it is obviously essential that practitioners plan their actions methodically, at the very least.

The outcome, a formal marketing communications plan, is a document for the guidance of those charged with the responsibility for converting general objectives into an operational campaign. Whether the recipient is an in-house specialist or one of the rapidly proliferating intermediaries specializing in a particular ingredient of the marketing communications mix, it is important to notice that the purpose is to provide guidance about implementation by explaining the predetermined broad strategic framework, not to present a ready-made prescription. Accordingly, the template overleaf provides for transmission of the essential background information needed for that second-phase decision-making.

Context

With reference to Table 1, it is vital that the profile of the product or service in section 1 specifies the benefits that can be delivered to potential customers. Narrow-minded concentration on the technical specifications of the offering runs counter to the very principle of marketing orientation, but happens all too often in practice. Likewise, the description of the target audience needs to provide a 'psychographic' profile, if it is to realize its full potential as a key factor in the development of the communication strategy. It should explain what is known about the audience's lifestyles, aspirations, reference group affiliations and so on. An example of such psychographic profiling in practical use, in

Table 1　The format of a marketing communications plan

1　CONTEXT　Explains who and what the plan is about.

* *Raw materials*

  The product or service
  specification: what does it do?
  benefits: what does it offer?
  developments: what next?

  The company
  specification: what do we do?
  identity: who do we believe we are?
  image: how do we want to be seen?

  The audience
  demographics: where are they?
  psychographics: who are they?

  The market
  structure: what is it?
  competition: who are we up against?
  dynamics: what forecasts?

* *The marketing mix*
  What potential effect on strategies?

* *Imperatives*
  precedents: what is traditional?
  mandatories: what is compulsory?

2　OBJECTIVES　Explains what the plan is meant to achieve.

* *Goals*
  What are the general longer-term aims?

* *Targets*
  What are the specific aims within the timescale?

* *Criteria*
  What are the benchmarks of performance?

3　BUDGET　Explains how proposed initiatives will be paid for.

* *Appropriation*
  How much money is available to spend?

* *Allocations*
  How will it be spent?

* *Contingency*
  What if?

* *Control*
  How will budget-holder's performance be evaluated?

4　STRATEGY　Explains how objectives are to be achieved.

* *Message*
  What do we tell the target audience?

* *Creative*
  How do we say it?

* *Vehicle*
  Which delivery systems do we use?

5　PROGRAMME　Explains when initiatives will happen.

* *Timescale*
  How long have we got?

* *Schedule*
  What happens when?

6　IMPLEMENTATION　Explains who is to put the plan into action.

* *Authority*
  Who can approve or disapprove?

* *Responsibility*
  Who coordinates action?

* *Delegation*
  What will be subcontracted?

* *Procedures*
  Who will keep track, and how?

Britain, is the commercially available ACORN Lifestyles system for segmenting target markets.

When considering the marketing mix, the strategically crucial fact that all four of the Four Ps have the potential to transmit messages about the organization and its offering, not just the one labelled 'promotion', should always be kept in mind. The practical issue raised concerning imperatives is that the execution of a marketing communications plan can in practice be constrained by precedents set in previous campaigns and by non-negotiable requirements set at a higher level in the organization.

Objectives

Part 2 of the plan is perhaps even more crucial. While it is self-evidently useful to set goals and targets, such potential performance indicators too frequently remain implicit in practice and the process of measurement becomes, as we have already seen, a questionable process of 'testing' effectiveness by reference to surrogate criteria.

Budget

Without a clear answer to the question posed about the 'appropriation' available, the rest of the plan will become somewhat academic. Many textbooks cite a potentially bewildering variety of procedures for deciding how much should be spent on advertising, the general principles of which can be transferred to other elements of the marketing mix. The fact is, however, that most are fairly unsophisticated and suffer from critical weaknesses if applied on their own. Research surveys have repeatedly shown over the years that marketing managers typically rely on one method, or two at most, and that the least sophisticated options dominate practice. Space does not permit further elaboration here, but interested readers can find a full account in two textbooks by the internationally acknowledged expert on the subject, one written for American practitioners (Broadbent 1988) and the other from a British perspective (Broadbent 1989).

Strategy

The content of part 4 of the plan will vary considerably according to the particular pattern of deployment of the marketing communications mix, which will in turn directly affect the budgetary allocations required in section 3. It is therefore important to identify the criteria which should guide decisions among the available options.

Space does not permit discussion of more than the five most crucial of those, which are considered in the next section. The delegation decision to be made in part 6 is also sufficiently crucial to demand a section to itself, which follows thereafter.

DEPLOYING THE MARKETING COMMUNICATIONS MIX

This decision is essentially a matter of striking a balance among target, message, cost, measurement and control.

Some target audiences are more effectively reached by one kind of marketing communications initiative than by another. For instance, business executives might be relatively easily reached by a well-constructed advertisement in an appropriate magazine or newspaper but would probably miss positive publicity in a daytime radio discussion programme. Prudent marketing managers will therefore base their choices on reliable target audience research data, perhaps drawing upon the accumulated experience of the professional consultancies that have proliferated in all branches of the marketing communications discipline over the past decade.

Sometimes the nature of the message will have more influence than the specification of the target audience. A simple, brash claim would lend itself to poster advertising, for example, while the communication of a complex argument could best be accomplished by a well-constructed mailing to a carefully chosen list.

Thus, reaching a target audience of business executives might come down to a choice between direct mail and press advertising, in which case the decision-maker will want to know about the relative cost of the two options. The facts are straightforwardly accessible in practice, but susceptible to change over time and variable from country to country to the extent that it would be rash to offer even broad generalizations here.

Cost is only half of the cost-effectiveness equation, of course, and prudent decision-makers will make sure to compare the availability and reliability of procedures for the measurement of effectiveness, as discussed in an earlier section. A few options offer the prospect of clear cut and very direct assessment of results, direct-response press advertising being an obvious example. In the case of some others, such as television advertising, long-established and well-understood tests are available, but there can be heated debate among experts about the interpretation of the results obtained. In yet other cases, a total absence of accepted measurement techniques demands a virtual act of faith, sponsorship being at present the most obvious case in point.

A quite separate consideration is the degree of control a user can exert over the outcome. The definitions offered earlier are careful to speak in terms of 'exposure' to target audiences, which is fairly routinely achieved by all the ingredients of the marketing communications mix. If the initiative is well designed, active attention may be engaged but the key strategic issue is the extent to which the outcome is the intended one.

This kind of control is high in the case of advertising, for instance. Users buy the right to fill blocks of space or time with messages and graphics exactly to their own specification, within the law and various codes of practice, and the advertising media have a duty to ensure that no distorting influences occur.

However, the price of that control varies from high to very high. The situation is exactly reversed in the case of publicity. It costs comparatively little to disseminate a news release, but those who choose that option are repeatedly frustrated by outright rejection or significant distortion. The perfect right of editors to use information to suit their own purposes rather than the supplier's is the potentially high penalty of low cost.

It is clear, then, that strategic decisions concerning deployment of the marketing communications mix demand careful trading-off among these five key criteria, and many less crucial ones besides.

Explicit identification of one of the Four Ps with strategies for communication tends to divert attention from the fact that the other three also have the potential to transmit a message about the organization and its product or service.

It is not hard to imagine a situation in which, for instance, the visibly basic features of a product are at odds with the up-market claims being made for it in an advertising campaign. Similarly, it is easy to picture the damage done to a quality offering by an ill-judged sales promotion initiative. Marketing managers repeatedly ignore the fundamental truth that the 'positioning' of a product or service in the audience's mind is decided by the audience itself, on all the available evidence. Even if these two of the Four Ps are in harmony, the product or service still needs to be offered to its potential customers in a location which is in keeping with the perceived and promoted image. Otherwise, the audience may come to its own conclusions about an apparently up-market product on the shelves of an unarguably down-market discount store. Even if three out of four deliver a consistent message, the remaining one, price, can destroy the whole position.

The issue is synergy, of course. If all four elements of the marketing mix are pulling the marketing communications cart in the same direction, the outcome will potentially add up to more than the sum total of the parts. If they are all pulling in different directions, the outcome is all too easy to predict: countersynergy. In between, luck will have a dangerous role to play. It is clearly in the best interests of managers with responsibility for marketing communications to pay close attention to the messages sent out by the activities of others in the organization and, if possible, to make sure that they can exercise some degree of influence over marketing mix decisions.

DELEGATING CAMPAIGN MANAGEMENT

Section 6 of the marketing communications plan directs attention to decisions about the subcontracting of campaign development and execution.

In the particular case of advertising, it is known that the responsibility for development and execution of the campaign strategy outlined in the marketing communications plan is routinely delegated to advertising agencies in most advanced economies: in Britain, for example, less than a quarter of total annual advertising expenditure is not transacted in this way. Until the 1980s it was also normal to entrust the management of campaigns involving other elements of the marketing communications mix to so-called 'full service advertising agencies'. Since then, specialist intermediaries in sales promotion, direct marketing, sponsorship and packaging have proliferated. There is no reason to suppose that marketing managers are less willing to use their services, in which case responsibility for strategy implementation will nowadays not only be delegated but also shared among several intermediaries.

Very recently, a breed of generalist marketing communications agencies has begun to develop, threatening to reduce the traditional full-service advertising agency's role to provider of one specialist service among many and starting a reversal of the trend towards multiple delegation. For reasons too complicated to explain here, those newcomers are sometimes described as 'through-the-line' operators.

Responsibility is delegated because the implementation of marketing communications strategy has become a far more complicated process than it once was. For instance, advertising media options have been both increasing in number and changing in nature in every decade in the second half of the century, while developments in direct marketing are currently happening at a frenetic pace. Even the most sophisticated marketing managements would find it virtually impossible to keep abreast of prices and availability across the marketing communications mix, month-by-month, let alone maintain quality control and verify that every initiative had been executed as planned.

Even if an organization were prepared to recruit a marketing communications staff large enough to contend with such a challenge, there are three more reasons for delegation. First, the salaries commanded by many of the experts in the typical disciplines would be an excessive operating overhead. Second, because marketing communications campaigns are normally discrete events rather than continuously developing activities, it is unlikely that a single marketing division would be able to keep a variety of costly specialists fully employed throughout the year. In engineering terms, it would be paying for significant periods of machine downtime. Third, few organizations could provide the atmosphere, stimulation and motivation enjoyed by specialists working in an agency on projects for several clients. These facts explain why it has become normal to buy a share in the collective skills of established expert service providers, rather than to try providing the required expertise in-house.

The penalty of delegation is, of course, loss of control. The client provides the agency with a brief; the agency provides the solution. The client may require the agency to justify its particular campaign proposals but will in the end have to concede that it has delegated responsibility to what it accepted in the first place as the expert. Therefore, it is vitally important that the client exercises as much control as is practically possible. This can be achieved in two main ways: by taking great care over the selection of collaborators and by delivering the right kind of guidance in the briefs given to them. Unfortunately, neither process is typically carried out efficiently in practice.

There is no great practical difficulty in setting up a systematic procedure for the selection of an expert collaborator, which makes the many case histories of ineptitude and disappointment all the harder to understand. Space does not permit us to go through one in detail here, but a specimen framework is offered by Crosier (1994).

As for the brief, the structure of a marketing communications plan (Table 1) provides a usable framework. Constructing one will be a relatively simple matter of deciding which components are properly part of the brief and which are more internal concerns. However, it is important to recognize that the process of briefing is a matter of offering guidance, not giving orders; clients must beware of dogmatism, which can only have a stultifying effect on their agency's response to the brief. Furthermore, the amount of detail to be provided is an issue: too little will leave too much room for inference and interpretation, perhaps counterproductively; too much will obscure the wood with trees. Striking the right balance is not straightforward. The professional association representing the clients of advertising agencies in Britain has suggested that 'a good brief will be as short as possible but as long as is necessary', implying that brevity should be the main aim. The recipient can always ask follow-up questions, after all.

REFERENCES

Advertising Research Foundation (1991) *ARF Seminar: Breakthrough Marketplace Research for Bottom Line Results*, New York: Advertising Research Foundation.

Broadbent, S. (1988) *The Advertiser's Handbook for Budget Determination*, New York: Lexington Books.

Broadbent, S. (1989) *The Advertising Budget: The Advertiser's Guide to Budget Determination*, Henley-on-Thames, England: NTC Publications for the Institute of Practitioners in Advertising.

Crosier, K. (1994) 'Promotion', in M. J. Baker (ed.) *The Marketing Book*, 3rd edn, Oxford: Butterworth-Heinemann.

Crosier, K. (1995) 'Marketing communications', in M. J. Baker (ed.) *Marketing: Theory & Practice*, 3rd edn, London: Macmillan.

Franzen, G. (1994) *Advertising Effectiveness: Findings from Empirical Research*, Henley-on-Thames, England: NTC Publications for the Advertising Association.

McDonald, C. (1992) *How Advertising Works: A Review of Current Thinking*, Henley-on-Thames: NTC Publications.

FURTHER READING

Corstjens, J. (1990) *Strategic Advertising: A Practitioner's Handbook*, Oxford: Butterworth-Heinemann.

DeMooij, M. (1994) *Advertising Worldwide: Concepts, Theories & Practice of International, Multinational & Global Advertising*, 2nd edn, Hemel Hempstead, England: Prentice Hall.

Griffin, T. (1993) *International Marketing Communications*, Oxford: Butterworth-Heinemann.

Rijkens, R. (1992) *European Advertising Strategies*, London: Cassell.

Smith, P. R. (1993) *Marketing Communications: An Integrated Approach*, London: Kogan Page.

Wilmshurst, J. (1993) *Below-the-Line Promotion*, Oxford: Butterworth-Heinemann.

38

ADVERTISING

Simon Broadbent

INTRODUCTION

Advertising is paid-for communication to more than one person, intended to inform or to change behaviour.

This chapter is about 'traditional' media advertising (i.e. in television, newspapers and magazines, radio and outdoor). It is part of 'integrated communications', which also include direct and database marketing, consumer sales promotions such as coupons, trade promotions, public relations, sponsorship and events. These are discussed elsewhere; they also use media advertising and share many of the procedures described below. The distinction between the different sorts of communication is becoming increasingly hard to make and in practice it is hardly necessary to do so.

Whether small or substantial sums of money are involved, an individual advertisement – or certainly its underlying idea – is basically the work of a very small team, often only one or two people. The fact that an idea can affect the fortunes of a large company, but could have been a bath-time inspiration, is one of the romantic appeals of advertising.

We have already started discussing 'advertising' as though it were a uniform commodity. For simplicity the word will continue to be used and other generalizations will be made, but the variety of advertisements is one of the most striking aspects of the subject. The product, service or cause advertised may only just be launched – or we may have grown up with it. The advertiser may be a person, a company or a government. An appeal in your local newspaper for a lost puppy, the announcement in your national newspaper of a bank's interest rate, and a multi-million expenditure on a television campaign for a household-name grocery brand – all of these are advertisements.

Planning and buying advertisements can be methodical; indeed it should be. This does not mean it has been automated – far from it. Advertising was defined, before television, as 'salesmanship in print'. Salespeople can be trained but must have hunger, flair and good judgement. So it is with advertising people.

ADVERTISING STATISTICS

Data

The reason for advertising is usually to defend or to increase sales volume and profit. Total spend on advertising is of course the sum of many separate decisions, but broadly varies with business and consumer confidence, with consumers' expenditure and with the level of profits which businesses are making.

Data for your country is collected by your local organizations. Table 1 shows as an example some UK expenditure.

A lot of advertising is 'classified', often placed by individuals or small businesses; it appears in directories or on classified advertisement pages in newspapers. The rest is called 'display'. Display expenditure in 1991 came from the broad sectors shown in Table 2.

Table 1 Total advertising expenditure in the UK including production costs and agency commission

	At current prices £m	At 1985 prices by RPI £m	% of GNP
1985	4,608	4,608	1.50
1986	5,321	5,145	1.63
1987	6,055	5,622	1.69
1988	7,044	6,235	1.77
1989	7,827	6,426	1.79
1990	7,885	5,914	1.65
1991	7,577	5,368	1.53

Source: Advertising Association, London

Table 2 UK expenditure on display advertising 1991

Sector	%
Consumables (drink, household goods, pharmaceuticals, food, toiletries and cosmetics, tobacco)	36.9
Durables (leisure equipment, automobiles, household appliances and equipment, wearing apparel)	19.6
Retail	14.4
Services (entertainment, vacations, travel, transport, publishing)	11.2
Financial	9.1
Industrial (institutional, agricultural, office equipment)	6.5
Government	3.2

Table 3   Division of total UK 1991 advertising expenditure
between the media

Medium	£m	%
Newspapers and magazines		
display	2,893	38.2
classified	1,923	25.4
TV	2,303	30.4
Outdoor and transport	267	3.5
Radio	149	2.0
Cinema	42	0.6

Such numbers are available in much more detail, on the assumption that full rate-card costs were paid, which is rarely the case for large advertisers. They indicate the sizes of several important sectors not fully dealt with here, for example business-to-business, corporate, recruitment, political and charity advertising. Manufacturing categories are also reported separately: in 1991, £332m on new motor cars, £10m on training shoes, £1.6m on disinfectants and so on. Spend by individual campaign and by the media used are similarly estimated.

The largest UK advertising company in 1991 was Procter and Gamble; the Rover Group was twenty-fifth; International Distillers and Vintners was fiftieth. Tesco Stores was the largest brand; W.H. Smith was twenty-fifth; TV *Quick* magazine came in fiftieth.

The money spent by the advertiser mostly goes to media owners, who provide the time (on television and radio) and space (in newspapers, magazines and outdoor sites). In 1991 advertising contributed 62 per cent of total newspaper revenue and 50 per cent for periodicals, as well as nearly all television income.

A smaller part of the advertiser's money goes to those employed to plan and make the advertisements. The numbers shown in Table 1 are gross (i.e. they estimate the total spend by manufacturers, including commission paid to agencies and production costs, although they exclude other overheads). The way advertisers pay their agencies is in flux. Once it was normal for agencies to keep the commission paid by media owners, at 15 per cent of the gross, but other arrangements now exist, for example different commission rates or fees.

In 1991 the largest advertising agencies each handled over £100m in 'billings' (i.e. what their clients spent in the media at rate card). For an agency around twenty-fifth in size, £20 to £30m is typical. The last ten of the top fifty agencies each had about £15m billings. There are many smaller agencies, each billing a few million. Table 3 demonstrates how total UK expenditure in 1991 was divided between the media.

International comparisons

As a percentage of gross domestic product (GDP), expenditure on advertising in the UK is relatively high: 1.20 per cent in 1990. This compares with 1.36 per cent in the USA; 1.56 per cent in Spain; 0.89 per cent in Japan; 0.85 per cent in Germany; 0.78 per cent in France; and 0.62 per cent in Italy.

The business is truly international, with very similar practices across the developed world. Staff move with little difficulty from country to country, though intimate knowledge of the local language and customs are necessary for fine-tuning.

Some campaigns are also international, since big ideas cross borders easily. Deliberately aiming at international campaigns provides the advertiser with central control and some economies. If it is clumsily done, it may result in mid-Atlantic advertisements, written by committee and truly satisfying no one.

PEOPLE INVOLVED

The following description sounds complicated only because it covers several possible organizations of the work. It is a disadvantage if the particular route followed is actually complex. Decisions should be taken by the smallest number of people possible – both on the advertiser's side and by his partners. Tiers of executives may exist in large companies, some of whom can say 'no' but cannot give final approval. This dilutes the work and adds time and cost.

You may be the only person responsible. You can plan and write your own small advertisement, send it to the paper with your cheque, and sit back. But for companies this is rarely sensible.

There is a wide choice open to advertisers, not only concerning who to employ, but how to organize the choice. The simplest decision is to pass all the work to a single company, a full-service advertising agency. At the most complex, the advertiser can mix and match, doing part in-house and using *à-la-carte* several agencies or suppliers as well. This is practical only if the advertiser has sufficient experience and time, both to brief out and to coordinate, and in addition to keep standards up to the best available. Otherwise what looks like clever buying may ultimately add expense.

Whatever the organization, advertisers need to maintain a good level of advertising skills. They may not have to master all the detail of how the process works, but they need to know enough not to be blinded by suppliers. They are responsible for spending millions of their companies' money and should be professional about it, neither overtrustful and naive, nor oversuspicious and self-contained.

Appointing an agency is a costly business – on both sides. It is sensible for an advertiser to keep himself informed about what is available (i.e. to meet other advertising agencies than the one employed, to consider other media buying arrangements and to talk to consultants about all sides of his business). But continuity has considerable value and frequent changes of partner spell trouble. This is not only because of the time spent in getting new suppliers up to speed, but because of the way advertisements work on consumers: some novelty helps but constant change is inefficient.

The advertiser

There are no willing advertisers, only marketers who know no better tool. Advertising is usually controlled by the marketing director, but in a company where it is a major expense, the CEO and board may pay particular attention to it. The finance director or budget committee may also be directly involved though their grasp of the subject is sometimes tenuous.

The advertiser orchestrates the range of communications touched on above. These work more efficiently if they are seamless. The structure to ensure this, which also balances the spend between the different activities, is the subject of current debate.

Day-to-day matters may be under a brand manager, but in mature companies it is understood that advertising will have long-term effects; it is argued that it is unwise to alter strategy as fast as personnel change. So a brand manager may have little influence, much as he wants to make a mark.

The advertising agency

The norm was once the 'full-service' advertising agency and this is still the most usual supplier. It is a business in its own right, with its own version of a factory, a salesforce, research and development and so on. It handles all the necessary jobs, though parts may be sub-contracted. It is legally responsible for the financial commitments to media for carrying the advertisements.

The full-service agency has two essential functions: creative and media. The creative department includes 'writers' or copywriters, and 'art directors'. Put simply, writers write copy (the words in a newspaper or magazine advertisement or outdoor) and scripts (the words and directions in a television or radio commercial). Art directors look after the appearance of the advertisement. Normally, the two work as a team; what people are going to do and say in the advertisement, and how it is directed or laid out are hard to separate.

The media department includes 'media planners' and 'media buyers'. Again the two work together as a team or may be the same person. The two main jobs are to recommend which media to use and to deal with media owners about price – remember that rate cards are complex and often negotiable.

There are two other functions of the agency which concern the advertiser. The first is account management. The advertiser works directly with an account director or manager who adds his own experience and ideas, and may be an all-rounder who does a lot of the work himself. He also coordinates all the work in the agency, represents the advertiser to the agency and vice versa.

The second function in a large agency is account planning or, sometimes, research. The agency which handles a number of advertisers builds up expertise in understanding consumers. Part of the input into an advertising idea are insights into what consumers think and feel; it is important to have a general understanding of how they react to advertising. The planners represent these consumer views and contribute to advertising strategy. They take part in briefing creatives and work with them in advertisement development. A researcher in an agency may also function as the advertiser's research department: designing, buying (or carrying out) and interpreting consumer research.

Naturally the advertiser and agency employ others who administer the business, keep accounts, control the production of advertisements, coordinate with distribution partners, manage client consumer databases, ensure advertisements meet legal and industry codes, program computers and make coffee, but they are not further described here.

Media

The media services just outlined have in some cases shifted outside the full-service agency. Some advertisers have decided to give the work to specialist firms, called 'media independents' (i.e. independent of the other functions). In turn, some of these now also offer creative services which they have in-house or buy from creative specialists or 'boutiques'. Advertisers, and even agencies, may also make use of these services. This decision depends largely on how media recommendations are evaluated: is media a commodity, bought by the yard, and cost is all that matters? Alternatively, there are advantages in having media under the same roof as planning and creative departments. There are qualitative aspects of the advertisement-target-medium interaction of which advantage can be taken and which may outweigh crude cost considerations.

Media departments and independents are serviced by the representatives of media owners, who compete for the business. Large advertisers will also meet these salesmen, who try directly to influence them. They may also have in-house media coordinators.

Research

Advertisers usually buy directly their own research into marketing and advertising. In addition to data used for several marketing purposes (sales audits, panels and surveys), they may purchase tracking studies, or usage and attitude surveys, in which there is a major advertising component. They or the agency often commission creative development research or pre-tests specifically about advertisements. An evaluation of media performance may also be bought, usually into the prices paid by the media buyer, but also about media planning.

THE ADVERTISING PROCESS

In this section is an outline of how an advertising campaign is put together. The alternative organizations outlined above are not dwelt upon. Whoever is responsible, the work has to be done. Also a brief may be queried or modified, mistakes may have to be put right, this may be the first time the team tackles the job or it may be a routine; such comments are not repeated below.

The job begins when the advertiser approaches the agency. This starts a two-way process: the advertiser knows the marketing objectives but is usually not ready to write or to sign off a creative brief. It is a dialogue between advertiser and agency which produces the best advertising brief.

Strategy

There are three essential inputs to the marketing strategy which are also used in planning advertising. First is information about the product – its content, performance, price, distribution, comparison with competition and so on.

Second, who are the purchasers and consumers – both existing and others targeted? What is their behaviour, their understanding of the product and of competitors, their attitudes, beliefs and so on? These facts and decisions are used in some ways more intensively in planning advertising than in planning product improvements, distribution policies and other marketing decisions. Because advertisements are so public, and can be so effective, advertising decisions can lead other parts of the marketing mix. After all, marketing begins by deciding what the consumer will buy, which depends on how you sell. Deciding what to say about yourself is a good discipline in setting priorities.

The final introductory comment is the most important. We have to decide what job the advertisements have to do. Exactly how is exposing an advertisement going to change or reinforce a person's behaviour or beliefs?

Further, we have to decide why the investment in advertising is likely to be worthwhile. What is the economic value of the activity? Is the return looked for in the short term, and do we want clear evidence? Or, are we mainly contributing to branding, so facilitating other marketing activities, and expecting indirect and long-term effects which may be hard to identify?

Not only do we need objectives in the marketing sense, we need a theory to connect communication with action. This is a tall order. 'How advertising works' has been the subject of hundreds of books and papers. There is no general theory, though much effort has been spent in searching for one. There are as many ways as there are campaign strategies, individual brand situations and of course advertisements.

It matters whether sales are already increasing naturally, are static or are falling. It is not always practical to aim at increasing or 'conquest' sales; often it is more realistic to reinforce existing behaviour, to defend the territory. It matters whether or not we have 'news' to announce. It matters whether our

672

product has real, discernible advantages over competitors or whether we are selling what is virtually a commodity.

As examples, here are a few common ways in which advertisements may work. Often the most important is to 'add value' which helps to turn a 'product' into a 'brand'. There are many kinds of added value: explaining the consumer benefit of a property of the product, giving it a personality, and so on. This is a slow job, in contrast to expectations for some advertising effects. A brand is worth more than a product because of all the associations attached to it. The reader will not need to be reminded of the very large sums paid for some companies, well above the value of their fixed assets, because of the brands they own. Advertisements are not all that create brand equity, but they are often a major part.

As well as this usually fundamental job, advertising often brings a brand to the front of mind of consumers who buy among a repertoire. Such reminders typically create 'blips' in the plot of sales over time, just after a burst of advertising.

Straightforward communication is often the purpose of advertising, when we have news about the product to put across or coupons to distribute.

By reassuring retailers about the rate of sale of the brand, advertising often helps salespeople in getting and holding distribution in today's competitive retail environment. Display, shelf footage, other aids at the point of sale may similarly be assisted. We do not see as frequently as we used to 'As seen on TV' but the message is still relevant.

It is often overlooked that advertising can encourage the manufacturer's own employees, for example by setting standards for counter staff and others in touch with the public.

The last two points are examples of the apparent target – the purchaser – being no more important than another target – retailers, our salesforce, shareholders, the financial community, opinion leaders and so on.

Budget setting

Deciding whether to advertise at all is hard. The question should be approached methodically, as set out in the rest of this section. The answer will be yes only if communication to a reasonably large target is desirable. Advertising agencies are sometimes criticized for not advertising themselves enough. But if their target (or yours) is only a few hundred people then an advertisement may be an inefficient way to reach them.

This point is illuminated by the famous postcard comparison. You can hardly pay less than 30p each to print and send a postcard to 1,000 people, at a total cost of £300. Though the media cost of a 30-second television spot is large, it may work out at only £5 per thousand (to which you may add 10 per cent to 20 per cent production cost). If you buy 20 cms by 3 columns in the *Daily Mail* you will pay around £6,000 media cost plus production, but there are over 4,000,000 adult readers so for 1,000 readers you pay £1.50 or so. Thus, in one

673

sense television and newspapers are cheap: you pay only about £6 or less than £2 per thousand people reached. In another sense they are expensive: a sizeable investment is needed.

This example makes two other points. You will have to judge (or decide after an experiment) how to compare the effect of reading a postcard with the effect of seeing an advertisement. Second, your cash flow restrictions, and the actual amount you need to spend, matter as much as calculated efficiencies.

Deciding how much to spend behind a brand, for example for the coming year, is also not an easy decision. No formula is adequate, though rules of thumb are much used. Most advice on the subject consists of methods which suggest a budget; but these should not determine it. No method takes into account every one of the factors which should properly be considered. This is done by a procedure which is recommended below.

There are cases where the decision is not worth much trouble – when the budget is a very small part of overall costs or a small sum in itself. Then commonsense will do, plus perhaps one of the following methods.

It is advisable to consider separately three parts of the overall spend on advertising. First, on media, including agency commission, usually the largest part and which is the subject of the rest of this section. Second, on production, which has its own section below. Finally, there are other costs, which will vary according to the conventions of the firm (e.g. overheads, staff directly attributable to the advertising function, related research and so on).

The budget is not decided by a detached, abstract procedure. It depends on the task to be done, the effects expected, the creative idea and even production costs. The process below will lead to a suggested expenditure. This may well change as creative development proceeds, or as other circumstances alter.

Reviews

The process is preceded by four reviews. This sounds onerous, but in fact the information should already have been collected. First, what are the brand's objectives, including the advertising objectives? Often these are summed up as the task we have to do, but as well as immediate jobs the objective should include the company's vision, or long-term goals. Second, what have your budgets been in recent years and how were they decided and modified? Third, a history and forecast of the category in which we compete is required. Thus, we review what competitors spent, how they fared and how they are likely to affect us next year. Fourth, what have we learned, and what do we estimate, about the effects of our advertisements? It is because this last item is usually so uncertain that the overall job is hard.

After the reviews, one or more of the methods below should be used to give suggestions about what to spend. The following is not a complete list of ways of indicating a sum of money. Nor will they normally agree, though they will bracket a range.

Task method

Many companies say they use the task method. That is, an amount of advertising exposure to the target is first decided, deemed to be sufficient to achieve the task. The cost of this exposure is then worked out. For example: 'We need six opportunities to see a 30-second commercial in order to create awareness of our product improvement; this costs X'. It is not always clear that the immediately defined task is all that our communications are needed for, nor that six exposures will work and four are not enough, but the method is understandable and with experience and commonsense works reasonably well.

Ratio to sales

Another common method is to set a ratio to sales. This means that the spend on advertising is in a fixed ratio to sales revenue, or to sales volume, often based on a category average. For example, 'two per cent of gross revenue'.

It is of course necessary to define precisely the terms used, and also to decide on the ratio (the problem has not been solved, only restated). You must not compare your actual spend and factory-gate revenue with a competitor's spend reported at rate card and his sales at retail level. Because of economies of scale for large brands, and because the desire to grow small brands leads to investment and aggressive marketing spends, the ratios for large brands are usually less than for small ones.

Brand history review

You will discover how this works in your own category if you use the third recommended method: brand history review. This may be part of one of the initial reviews you should start with; it pays particular attention to what you and competitors have spent, how well or badly you have done, and what connections there may be between spend and copy on the one hand, sales volume on the other (allowing for other factors which affect sales).

After the initial reviews, and with one or more suggested budgets, you finally choose how much to spend. Decide whether the suggestion is too much – in the light of your financial targets. Decide whether it is enough – given your view of its effects and your volume targets. If the answers are incompatible, decide what has to give way: your cash limits, your volume (which has a financial effect, of course), your long-term goals. Compromise is normal, as in all budgeting.

Creativity and the creative brief

This chapter will not teach you to write advertising copy, draw storyboards or lay out press advertisements. Part of the work should be methodical; craft skills can be learned. But making effective advertisements depends on being noticed, fresh, believable, motivating – and many other words which are summed up as 'creative'. Although the aim – to be effective – is simply stated, someone has to decide how.

There is plenty of dubious advice, and there are even more offputting recipes, about being salient, involving, credible, memorable, linked to the brand and so on. It is still a job which some people are consistently better at than others.

The work has also to be doubly relevant. That is, both meaningful to the viewer or reader in the target, and also meeting the advertising objectives which have been agreed as part of the marketing strategy. The latter is ensured at the beginning by the way the creatives are briefed; during development by creative research; after exposure by evaluative work.

The brief may consist of a document, but is normally expanded by discussion. It may be summed up by two questions: Where are we? Where do we want to be? That is, a description of the product or service; its competitors; its purchasers and users and what they think and feel. Then, the role for advertising and what it is we want to communicate, which may be facts and emotions, with an explanation of why these are believable and desirable, plus how the recipients will be different after exposure. There may be a summary: the advertising proposition, with its supporting evidence. There will also be an indication of the possible budget and perhaps of the media likely to be used. If the work is not a totally new project, there may also be guidelines about details in the advertisement, learned from experience.

Developing and pre-testing

After writers and art directors have some work to show, initially in rough form, their ideas go through internal screening, by peers, department heads, account managers, planners and so on.

It has been reasonably estimated that the difference in value between an ordinary and a great advertisement is higher than most media budgets, and much more than anything spent in pre-testing (as research at this stage is often and intimidatingly called). Hence it has been argued that methodical estimation of likely effects deserves serious time and money. On the other hand, it has also been shown that such estimates are dubious – for the reasons given below. Advertisers may well like to have, but should not expect, over-literal or precise forecasts of how a campaign will perform in the field after an assessment of a crude exposure of one advertisement.

Because of the expense, finished work is not normally used in development research, and this is only one of the reasons why it requires judgement and involves risk, particularly when the finished work will look very different from the rough. In addition, the exposure of the rough advertisement is necessarily in circumstances unlike natural viewing and reading. Finally, its effect is usually judged by the answers to questions, rather than by the way it influences behaviour.

Too often, pre-testing is seen as a simple pass-or-fail technique. It has even been presented as a sales forecast. Because of the weaknesses of the techniques, neither of these views is recommended. Nevertheless, early work is often seen by representatives of the target group. Research is carried out, directed by the advertiser or by the planner, among small groups of target consumers. This may be done at the 'concept stage', that is, when the stimuli are strategic statements written to be explained to consumers, without any 'added values'; or they may be actual advertisements (i.e. 'executions' or 'treatments') though in rough form. Several different and well-publicized systems are available.

Pre-testing is controversial. There is a lot of money riding on decisions at this stage, not to mention egos and careers. The technical decisions crystallize some of the key questions about advertising. Who is it aimed at (who is in the sample)? How does it work (what is the idea or model behind the particular measurements made)? Can it be judged in the short term (is one exposure enough – if not, how many)? Can what consumers say be taken literally (how rational and verbal are the true responses to advertising)?

Here some well-worn controversies may flare up: 'Trust me: I'm an Art Director', versus a businessman's need for reassurance and often for quantification; 'Small works of art at someone else's expense' versus the need for marketplace effectiveness. Undoubtedly some very successful campaigns have gone ahead despite apparently damning findings at this stage (less publicized, vice-versa). Although conflicts occur, they are not necessary. After all, creativity and effectiveness are not antonyms: one is the means and the other is the end. One is stimulus, the other is response. When the partners (advertiser, agency, research) respect and trust each other, mutual understanding and compromise will determine the outcome.

More importantly, guidance can improve some work. Research should be seen more in its diagnostic role. That is, not 'this ad is good, that is bad', but 'this ad seems to work because . . ., that one has these problems which might be solved if . . .'.

Advertisements at an early stage of development can often be improved by sensitive, usually qualitative, research. We most want to know about communication – do consumers take out what we think we have put in? Sensitivity is exercised not only in the interpretation of respondents' answers; it also has to be used in working with the writer of the advertisement. Creatives should want to understand how people will react, and should see the consumer's interpreter as a partner in the creative act.

Production

Once rough advertisements or advertising ideas have been agreed, they must be turned into the form from which the media will reproduce them. A television or cinema script and storyboard are shot on film or videotape and edited. A radio script is recorded, and also edited. A magazine or newspaper rough is typeset and illustrated.

677

These are not mechanical procedures, though a lot of technology is involved. The quality which can be added in the process can be critical to the effectiveness of many advertisements. Financial prudence here does not consist in saving as much money as possible, but in spending only what is needed to get the job properly done.

Making a television or cinema commercial has a lot in common with making any film. In cost per second, the commercial often exceeds the feature film. This is partly because of the diseconomies of the small scale, partly because extreme care is taken to get this fragile vehicle in shape for its precious cargo, the impressions which may be costing hundreds of thousands of pounds to communicate.

Specialists in film production are required to plan and direct the film, often a producer from the advertising agency as well as independent people hired by the day. Production often takes months from start to finish though actual shooting may last only a day or two. Preplanning, as well as talent, is vital. It is at the early stage (as well as when the writer starts with the words 'Open on a cast of thousands lining a Pacific beach') that costs are best explained and determined. The shooting schedule is planned, the cast, location and props are selected.

When the film has been shot, time is needed to produce cuts of the right length, to record voice and music tracks, to add special effects and so on. Copies are supplied to the TV stations on broadcast-quality tape.

Producing a radio commercial is much less complicated, and less costly. Voices, music and sound effects are recorded in a studio on individual tracks, then edited and mixed to make the finished commercial.

Equally careful technical work and judgement are required to lay out and set press advertisements. Generally illustrations are required, which means that a photographer or illustrator is briefed to produce the artwork. Typesetting is done separately and then the two elements – pictures and words – are combined in a 'mechanical', which is the final definition of how the advertisement should look. Colour film separations of the finished work are made, and sent to the various media for printing.

The media brief, media planning and buying

An essential part of the advertising plan is how the message will reach the target. Wise expenditure requires decisions about effectiveness as well as cost negotiation and much practical detail.

A full description of the media available, their costs and what they can do is not given here. Changes are frequent, in ownership of the media, their content and the audiences they reach. The number of different media is increasing, but the time people choose to give to reading and viewing changes little. Hence individual audiences fragment into smaller numbers. Expert and up-to-date advice is essential. Forecasting is part of the skill.

The currency at this stage is media research – the syndicated data about how people are exposed to the different media. Because there are many different users of these data, both buyers and sellers, the design of this research is often shared through joint decision-taking and the specification is then put out to tender.

The advertiser is not really buying the transmission of a commercial or the printing of millions of newspapers. He is buying people in his target seeing the screen during the transmission, or reading his advertisement in the paper. Only careful interpretation of media research can estimate these numbers. They vary, of course, by channel, by TV programme, by time of day, by time of year, by individual publication, by position and size of advertisement, and so on. A medium can deliver only people with open eyes and ears in front of the advertisement. After that we are back to creative skills.

Evaluating the campaign

This step naturally comes at the end. However, for most brands it is also the beginning of another cycle. Knowing what advertisements have done – or not done – has already been stressed as an aid in planning and budgeting. Although we can hardly ever know exactly what our work has achieved, we always learn from trying to find out.

First, we need to have agreed how our advertisements are expected to have their effect. The advertiser and agency must work on common ground: what it is they look for and how it will be measured. The variety of possible effects was indicated above in the section on strategy.

Many of the comments made about controversy in development research apply at this stage also. When we carry out consumer research, whether qualitative or quantitative, we again have to take care in the interpretation of how respondents answer, which usually needs specialist skills. For example, high awareness of the advertisements themselves tells us little about the relevance or persuasiveness of their content.

As well as such 'soft' data, there is now the possibility of 'hard' data: sales or other behaviour, either observed as it fell, or in some planned test. Unfortunately, sales data, even in an experiment, usually fail to give unequivocal answers. Sales are always influenced by factors other than our advertisements, and these have to be allowed for statistically. Worse, the effect of advertising is a construct: what we observe less what would have happened without advertising, or different advertisements, or more or less spent. Time also enters disturbingly: we have to ask ourselves whether enough time has passed to predict effects over several years, which may include the larger part of the results we hope for.

An objective of advertising research is to measure the brand equity which, as stated above, is often the most important reason for investment in advertising. There is as yet no agreed way to do this; some methods at least indicate lower estimates for this value.

ADVERTISING AND SOCIETY

Advertising, public opinion and the economy

We are all exposed to hundreds of advertisements each day. Most of them are for products and services we are not at that moment interested in. We filter many of them out as not worth conscious thought; others we look to for entertainment. Only a very small proportion get real attention.

From these facts it follows, first, that advertisements are part of Western 'culture' in the broad sense. We grew up with them, most of us take them for granted, we have learned to cope with them and to use them for our own purposes. Second, we are genuinely unaffected by most of them, and the advertiser accepts this: the nature of mass media is such that much is apparently 'wasted'. Most people say 'Advertising does not affect me', and they are broadly correct. This is quite consistent with advertising's efficiency as a means of communicating with specific target audiences.

The pervasiveness and blatantly commercial nature of advertisements is distasteful to some. There are also those who exaggerate what they see as manipulation and the advertisers' misuse of this power. Thus, as well as 'never making me buy anything', it is claimed that advertisements 'create unnecessary wants and discontent' and 'force people to buy products' of which the critic disapproves.

In the latest UK Advertising Association survey of attitudes to advertising, it comes low on the list of 'things in most need of immediate attention and change', scoring 4 per cent. This compares with education at 32 per cent, the government at 30 per cent, bringing up children at 12 per cent, and so on.

There is a small arena, in politics and economics, where the general effects and desirability of advertising is debated. Reference to facts in such debates is less frequent than it should be. In a free society, advertising is an important tool in the competition which is the invisible hand guiding production. It is a shop window, displaying what is freely available. It speeds up innovation and encourages mass production and competitiveness which lower prices.

People are well aware that they are being sold to and they make up their own minds; they use advertising both for information and entertainment. Advertising provides massive subsidies for television and for nearly all publications, themselves valued products and sources of information.

Advertising controls

Marketers should be aware that their liberties are under threat. This is no exaggeration. The industry argues that freedom of speech must apply to commercial communication, subject to no more laws than other messages (about libel, for example). The Trade Descriptions Act and other legislation apply to advertising as well as to business generally.

680

Advertising is largely self-regulated. Despite the theoretical weaknesses of self-policing, its advantages over government rulings are agreed by a majority. The UK Advertising Standards Authority, the Independent Television Commission and the Radio Authority operate clearance systems so that advertisements under development can be discussed in advance of production. The press is less formal.

The Advertising Standards Authority also deals with complaints by the public about print and cinema advertising. In 1991 it received 10,610 complaints, of which it pursued 4,203; 67 per cent of these complaints were upheld (i.e. it was held that the advertisements were not 'legal, decent, honest, truthful' and therefore they were changed or dropped). In addition, the Authority carries out its own monitoring. It may check whether claims can be substantiated or whether particular parts of the Code of Advertising Practice were violated, such as for cars, tobacco products, alcohol and products for children. These findings are also reported.

NEXT STEPS

Associations

Each country has equivalents of the following UK trade associations, which can be contacted for information and reading lists. The Advertising Association deals with matters common to the two following bodies, and to media owner groups, which all belong to it but also have their own interests.

The Advertising Association, Abford House, 15 Wilton Road, London SW1V 1NJ. Tel: 0171-828 2771

The Incorporated Society of British Advertisers, 44 Hertford Street, London W1Y 8AE. Tel: 0171-499 7502.

The Institute of Practitioners in Advertising, 44 Belgrave Square, London SW1X 8QS. Tel: 0171-235 7020.

FURTHER READING

Broadbent, Simon (1989) *The Advertising Budget*, Henley-on-Thames: NTC Publications Ltd for the Institute of Practitioners in Advertising.

Bullmore, Jeremy (1992) *Behind the Scenes in Advertising*, Henley-on-Thames: NTC Publications Ltd.

Cowley, Don (ed.) (1989) *How To Plan Advertising*, London: Cassell/APG.

Hedges, Alan (1988) *Testing To Destruction*, London: Institute of Practitioners in Advertising.

Jones, John Philip (1986) *What's In A Name?*, Lexington, MA: Lexington Books.

McDonald, Colin (1992) *How Advertising Works*, Henley-on-Thames: The Advertising

Association in association with NTC Publications Ltd.
White, Roderick (1988) *Advertising, What It Is and How To Do It*, 2nd edn, Maidenhead: McGraw-Hill in association with the Advertising Association.

39

SALES PROMOTION

Ken Peattie

DEFINING SALES PROMOTION

Within the field of marketing communications the term 'sales promotion' is frequently used as a 'catch-all' term encompassing those elements which cannot be classified as advertising, selling or public relations (PR). Sales promotion can be defined as:

> 'marketing activities usually specific to a time period, place or customer group, which encourage a direct response from consumers or marketing intermediaries, through the offer of additional benefits'.
>
> (Peattie and Peattie 1994: 534)

Sales promotions are often referred to as being 'below-the-line'. The line in question originally denoted whether or not communications efforts were channelled through advertising agencies. The line has become something of an anachronism with the trend towards integrated marketing communications agencies, and with an increasing tendency for sales and PR to be treated as separate functions. Advertising is still referred to as being 'above-the-line', and 'below-the-line' has now become synonymous with sales promotion.

The everyday vocabulary relating to promotion in marketing is full of inconsistencies. For simplicity and brevity, the word 'promotion' will be used here to refer to a sales promotion, rather than its broader context of marketing promotion.

THE ROLE OF SALES PROMOTION

Sales promotions are all around us. If you pick any form of breakfast cereal from the supermarket shelf the chances are that the box will contain extra product, a free gift, or will have printed on it a recipe, puzzle, competition entry form or a token to collect. Coupons and free samples tumble through our letter boxes, or are tucked inside the periodicals that we buy, and it is difficult to walk through a retail district and avoid seeing the word 'Sale' somewhere.

People commonly associate sales promotions with 'special offers' which provide customers with an additional incentive to purchase, usually by a reduction in price or an increase in the quantity of product offered. Such offers are an important part of sales promotion, but our definition takes a wider perspective in terms of the parties that promotions can be targeted at, the responses that can be sought and the benefits that can be offered.

Promotions can be targeted at three distinct groups:

1 *Consumers.* Most promotions targeted at consumers are designed to provide them with an incentive to purchase, and to provide a reason for buying the promoted brand rather than its competitors. These are known as 'pull' promotions. Consumers vary in terms of their responsiveness to a promotion for a particular product. Some consumers will remain brand loyal regardless of promotional activities; others will allow usual brand loyalties to be overridden by attractive promotions; while others will frequently switch among brands to take advantage of different promotions. As well as influencing brand choice, promotions can affect the timing and volume of consumers' purchasing. Brand-loyal consumers may stockpile while their preferred brand offers a promotion, and brand switchers may stockpile while any brand is being promoted. Responsiveness to promotions can form a basis for market segmentation, and it can be valuable for marketers who are thinking of running promotions to understand what proportion of the market is likely to change its purchasing behaviour in response to a promotion, and whether that response will involve brand switching, stockpiling or both.

2 *Retailers and other external marketing intermediaries.* Trade or 'push' promotions involve offering intermediaries incentives such as special discounts (known as allowances), gifts, contests, marketing information or extra product to gain their enthusiasm and shelf space. Other trade promotions involve providing management training and assistance, point-of-sale displays, trade shows and inventory control assistance.

3 *The salesforce.* The salesforce of a company is frequently the target of promotional contests aimed at improving its performance and adding a 'fun' motivational challenge into its work. Around three-quarters of companies use such contests, which are usually linked to the achievement of sales goals.

It would be unwise for a marketer to plan a 'pull' promotion without first considering what must be done to encourage intermediaries and the salesforce to provide the necessary support. Therefore one promotional campaign may have elements aimed at each of the three groups.

A common and quite logical assumption is that the response which any sales promotion seeks from its target will be an increase in sales. Despite the fact that most promotions are sales orientated, this is a rather narrow and potentially misleading view. Promotions, like all marketing activity, ultimately aim to generate profitable sales to satisfied customers, but the direct responses that they may aim for are many and varied. A promotion might seek to get a customer to consume a free product sample, to visit a retail outlet, to fill in an enquiry coupon or to explain why they like a product in twelve words or less.

The benefits which different promotions offer to their targets also vary widely. A fundamental distinction can be made between value increasing, and value adding promotions. Value increasing promotions alter the basic 'deal' (the relationship between the product and the price) by increasing the quantity or quality of the product on offer, or by lowering its price. The price can be altered directly, through a sale or discount, or indirectly through the use of a coupon or a refund offer. Such promotions emphasize a rational economic view of consumers and assume that they are relatively aware of prices, and are willing and able to change their consumption behaviour in search of a better deal.

Value adding promotions leave the product/price relationship intact, and instead add something extra into the total product offering. This 'something' could be a premium, an entry into a competition or an extended guarantee. Value adding promotions can offer their targets benefits which are less tangibly economic than the extra value that comes from getting more product for less money. Some promotions provide the customer with benefits in terms of simplifying the buying process or reducing the risks associated with purchase. The distribution of product catalogues, or allowing a product to be tested, provides customers with information which can help them make their purchase decisions with confidence. Another increasingly popular form of promotion involves a proportion of the purchase price of a product being donated to charity by the manufacturer. While this provides no direct material advantage to the consumer, it provides them with the psychological benefits that come from knowing that one payoff of their consumption has been a contribution to a worthy cause.

THE DEVELOPMENT OF SALES PROMOTION

The traditional stronghold of promotions is among fast moving consumer goods (FMCG) markets, and packaged foods in particular. In recent years promotions have become a major feature in a more diverse range of markets, including financial services, consumer durables and the marketing of charities. The 1980s witnessed widespread growth in expenditure on promotions. Although estimates concerning the costs of promotions vary widely, reflecting the different definitions of sales promotions used, it is fair to say that in a wide range of markets sales promotion expenditure comfortably exceeds that on classic brand image advertising. A number of factors are behind the growth in promotions:

1 Growing doubts about the cost effectiveness of advertising, in the face of rising prices and increased advertising 'clutter': a lack of conclusive evidence to link advertising directly to consumer preference and buying behaviour,

and apparent consumer hostility towards advertising have fuelled these doubts. The advent of videos and television remote controls which allow adverts to be 'zapped' has also eroded television advertisers' confidence in their ability to reach their target audience.

2 Sales promotions have acquired new-found 'respectability' through greater use by market leaders and increasing professionalism among sales promotion agencies.

3 Increased impulse purchasing, particularly for FMCG products: according to the American Point of Purchase Institute, some 80 per cent of all purchase decisions are now made in-store, and can therefore be influenced by in-store promotions.

4 Planning time horizons have been shortened, reflecting increasing market volatility and rivalry, and accelerating product life cycles. The development of advertising campaigns which build and nurture the desired image for a brand is a slow and painstaking process. The more immediate boost offered by promotions is attractive to marketers under pressure to improve market share and sales volume in the short term.

5 Micro-marketing approaches: in response to fragmenting markets, promotions can provide more tailored and targeted communication than mass media.

6 Declining brand loyalty: caused by widening choice, narrowing perceived differences between brands and, in FMCG markets, retailers' own brands becoming increasingly credible.

7 A 'snowball' effect in some markets, with companies feeling obliged to match rivals' sales promotion activity, or risk losing market share and competitive position.

8 Affordability: national mass media have become prohibitively expensive for many companies, particularly during recessionary squeezes on marketing budgets. Promotions allow national coverage at a lower cost, cost sharing with co-promoters and can even be self funding.

TYPES OF SALES PROMOTION

There is a very wide range of marketing activities that seek to gain response from consumers and marketing intermediaries by providing them with additional benefits, and which therefore could be classified as a form of promotion. The most common forms of promotions can be categorized as follows.

Price-based value increasing promotions

Discount pricing and sales

Discounting is a widely used form of promotion in a range of markets. It is only effective where the additional sales volume will compensate for the lost revenue, and in markets where a reduction in price will not be interpreted as a reduction in quality. Discounts are a relatively expensive form of promotion in that they provide a price reduction for all consumers, regardless of their price and promotion sensitivity. Discounting also carries with it the danger that it will undermine the consumer's expected reference price, so that they come to expect discounting and will resist a return to 'normal' prices.

Money-off coupons

Coupons are a very popular form of promotion, particularly in FMCG markets. Coupons can be delivered by direct mail, in stores, as inserts in publications, or on packages. The traditional disadvantages of couponing are in the logistical effort of the redemption handling process, losses due to misredemption and consumer resistance to the need physically to clip and carry coupons. New technology may overcome all of these problems with innovations such as bar-code scanning for coupons, and 'smart cards' for consumers which store information about coupon entitlements.

Refunds

'Cashback' offers have become an increasingly popular way of reducing the cost to consumers of relatively expensive items, without eroding the reference price in consumers' minds. Consumers receive a refund by mailing in their proof of purchase and, unlike discounting, this will only benefit those consumers who are price sensitive enough to follow through the refund application process.

Improved payment terms

Interest free credit and 'buy now, pay later' offers make purchase easier for consumers, and may reduce the real cost of purchase, while allowing the price to stay constant. Special payment terms are popular for relatively expensive consumer durables such as cars and domestic appliances.

Product-based value increasing promotions

Product samples

Samples are frequently used to encourage product trial for items such as foods, drinks and toiletries. There are various methods of delivering samples, including direct mail, inserts within publications or packages, or sampling points inside stores. Sampling is a relatively expensive form of promotion, which often involves a high degree of wastage. It can also be difficult to assess its effectiveness, since there is no way to establish whether those who receive

687

samples later go on to purchase (unless the sample is accompanied by a coupon).

Multipacks and multibuys

Offers of 'three for the price of two' are a useful means of getting consumers to stock up on a particular brand. Banding multiple product units or complementary products together can now be accomplished electronically through the use of EPOS systems, rather than physically.

Increased product quantity

Goods such as packaged foods and bottled drinks can offer so many per cent extra for free. The marginal cost of the extra product is usually relatively small for the producer, as long as their packaging processes are easily customized. There is a danger of a 'reference quantity' effect in markets such as canned beers where extra product is so frequently offered that it can become expected by consumers.

Improved product quality or features

Major consumer durables such as cars or new homes are often marketed with additional free features such as a car stereo or a free fitted kitchen.

Tangible value adding promotions

Valued packaging

This is a relatively unusual type of promotion, used in food and drink markets and occasionally for other forms of product that need to be contained in use. Typical valued packaging offers involve selling audio-cassettes in storage boxes, tea bags in tea caddies or cookies in cookie jars.

Premiums

Premiums are free gifts which can be supplied in or on packages, or in the mail. Self-liquidating premiums require the consumer to mail in money to cover the cost of providing the item. A typical in-pack premium might involve a free mug packaged up with two jars of coffee.

Gift coupons

Collecting gift coupons is a relatively unfashionable occupation, but petrol companies and cigarette manufacturers still make extensive use of them.

Opportunity-based value adding promotions

Competitions

Competitions are a very versatile promotional tool that can be aimed at consumers, intermediaries or the salesforce. Selecting the right prize can help to reinforce the brand's image. The limited number of winners and known cost of prizes generally make competitions a very cost effective form of promotion, and one which can appeal to a wide range of consumers.

Promotional information

A great deal of promotional activity involves providing prospective customers with information which assists their purchasing process. The information provided can also be put into an entertaining and informative format which reinforces the image of the brand and its advertising. Some companies issue information with little direct 'selling' message, which aims to educate consumers and hopefully make them likely to discern in the company's favour. Examples include financial service providers issuing beginners' guides to investment videos, and hi-fi manufacturers issuing guides to hi-fi and music.

Guarantees

Extended guarantees for major consumer durable purchases are a useful way of reducing the perceived risk associated with purchase.

Product buyback and exchange schemes

Buyback and exchange schemes are an alternative means of reducing the perceived purchase risk used in a range of consumer durable markets such as cars, televisions and audio products.

Clubs

Clubs are a good method of developing a long-term relationship with a customer and are useful for encouraging customer loyalty. These have proved popular in service industries such as air travel and hotels, and in the marketing of products to children.

PROMOTIONS AND THE REST OF THE MARKETING MIX

Although promotions are often referred to as a subset of marketing communications, it would be more accurate to consider them as a customization of other mix elements. Each mix element offers different benefits to customers (see

689

Figure 1   Satisfaction chain

Figure 1). To increase the desirability of the total product offering, sales promotions can provide additional benefits which:

- Enhance the product offering's utility by enhancing quality, or adding extra tangible benefits.
- Improve affordability by increasing the quantity offered, decreasing the price or easing the payment terms.
- Improve accessibility by gaining access to distribution channels and through extras such as free delivery.
- Support the advertising, sales and PR effort to boost the product's visibility and credibility through eye-catching and newsworthy promotional materials, and by creating subjects for advertising campaigns or discussions with customers.

Promotions are usually temporary customizations of the marketing mix, but some promotions become permanent features, such as the Miss Pears beauty contest which has been running since 1932. Some would argue that such permanence turns a marketing activity from a promotion into a different element of the marketing mix. This is rather a moot point, but it illustrates the difficulties of drawing clear and consistent boundaries around the whole field of sales promotion. Exactly where the borderline is between promotional pricing and ordinary pricing, or between promotional events and public relations is impossible to say.

Figure 2 illustrates how sales promotions interface with the other mix elements, represented as an expanded 'Nine Ps'. The emphasis placed on value increasing promotions means that it is the relationship with the product and with pricing that gains the most attention. However, promotions offer

690

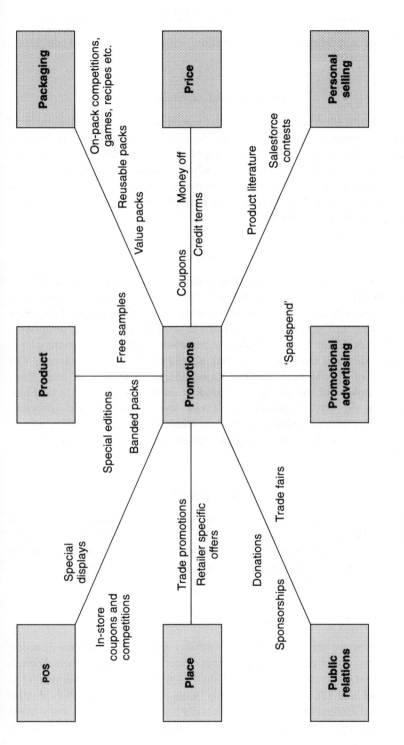

Figure 2 Promotions and the marketing mix: an integrated model

considerable opportunities for integration with other forms of marketing communication.

Promotions and advertising

Promotions and advertising have frequently been portrayed as rival methods of marketing communications. This rivalry represented the competition between the agencies that serviced the different types of campaign rather than any form of marketing logic. In fact advertising which features promotions has been proven to be particularly effective in communicating to consumers and to enhance a company's image. Promotions have also proved to be most effective when supported by advertising.

Promotions and selling

Promotions targeted at distributors and retailers are very important in FMCG markets to support the efforts of the salesforce to introduce new products, to gain shelf space and encourage intermediaries to 'push' products. Temporary auxiliary sales staff may also be necessary to support a particular promotion, such as a trade fair or a seasonal sale. Promotions can play an important part in supporting the sales efforts of industrial, as well as consumer, marketers. The negotiation of special deals for key customers, participation at trade fairs, product samples and the provision of product information all play a vital part in reducing the buyers' perception of risk and helping to win contracts. Promotional gifts as humble as calendars, pens and mugs all play a part in communicating, and in keeping the promoter's name at the potential purchaser's fingertips.

Promotions and PR

Promotional events such as trade fairs and product launches form a major area of crossover between sales promotion and PR. Such events will provide potential customers with extra benefits such as entertainment, refreshment, promotional gifts and information and may provide opportunities for product trial or participation in a competition.

Promotions and the place of purchase

Manufacturers are very aware that the visibility and location of their products within a retail outlet can be crucial to their success. This makes them keen to develop posters, special dispensers and shelf cards to be used by the retailer at the point of sale (POS). However, only some 25 per cent of POS display materials that are sent to retailers are eventually used. This relatively low success rate is caused by a failure to plan POS materials with the retailer's needs in mind. The result is displays that are unsuitable for the retail environment, that are too bulky, or are too difficult for the retailer to set up correctly.

PROMOTIONS AS A MEANS OF COMMUNICATION

Although it would be misleading to think of promotions simply as a form of marketing communications, promotions do have an important role to play in communicating with the marketplace. Communicating effectively requires the marketer to develop the right message, select an appropriate media, and accurately target the campaign. When it comes to targeting, promotions are more flexible than advertising, which essentially presents one message at a time to the entire audience (a 'shotgun' approach). Promotions have the ability to communicate different messages to different customer groups, perhaps through the offer of a variety of prizes in a competition or through customized electronic catalogues held on computer disk being sent to different types of customer.

In terms of persuasion, the direct response orientation has been focused on the 'action' phase of Strong's classic AIDA model (1925) when discussing communications capabilities. In fact, promotions work effectively during each phase of this communication process:

1 *Attention*: promotions are undoubtedly attention grabbing. Words such as 'Extra', 'Free', 'Win' and 'Special' all help promoted products to stand out on supermarket shelves, which can contain over 35,000 different products jostling for the consumer's attention.

2 *Interest*: promotions can inject novelty and even fun into the most familiar or mundane of products, and the most habitual of purchases.

3 *Desire*: encouraged by the offer of additional benefits, and by promotions which reinforce the desirability of a product, for example by offering it as a desirable competition prize.

4 *Action*: promotions differ from advertising (with the exception of direct response advertising) in seeking a direct response. The responses which a promotion might try to generate, include encouraging consumers to:

- accelerate their purchase timing of a brand;
- select a brand for their initial purchase;
- stay loyal to a brand;
- switch brands;
- replace a consumer durable;
- overcome their previous objections to a brand and sample it;
- gather information about a brand.

TACTICAL AND STRATEGIC DIMENSIONS OF PROMOTIONS

The majority of promotions are of the value-increasing type, with coupons and discounting being particularly popular. Such price-orientated promotions will

693

clearly only be effective while they are on offer. Their popularity has led to an overemphasis on the rational economic dimensions of promotions, and the emergence of a conventional wisdom that regards them as tactical weapons whose results are short term in nature. Any longer term effect of promotions was generally held to be negative in terms of potentially devaluing a brand in the minds of consumers, or creating post-deal resistance to the 'normal' selling price.

As a tactical weapon, promotions can be an effective and swift response to competitors' advertising campaigns or new product introductions. Responding with a new product or advertising campaign may take months or even years. Promotions can be put into place in a matter of weeks, particularly since previous successful promotions can often be taken 'off the shelf', given a fresh theme and relaunched. This can allow a company to regain the initiative in the short term, while more strategic responses are developed. Promotions can also be an effective remedy in situations which otherwise appear disastrous. Following a 55-day strike, company executives at United Airlines feared that it would take 7 months for lost market share to be regained. Instead, an offer of half-price flight coupons devised by their marketers restored their market share in only eleven days.

During the 1980s many companies began to take a less tactical and more strategic approach to the management of sales promotions. This was partly a response to the growing proportion of the marketing budget being invested in promotions, and partly a result of the development of integrated marketing communications strategies, which used each form of communication in a coordinated, and hopefully synergistic, way. Companies became aware that promotions which are managed effectively and avoid simple price cutting can contribute to the strategically important tasks of building up the image of a brand, nurturing brand loyalty and building market share.

SALES PROMOTION PITFALLS

Although careful investment in sales promotions has been proven to be a flexible and effective way of generating competitive advantage, the use of promotions is not without potential risks and drawbacks. Sales promotion as a marketing activity has often drawn criticism from marketing commentators. Some critics have suggested that overuse is training customers to buy products only on promotion, while others claim that promotional overkill is desensitizing consumers to their benefits. It is certainly the case that any promotional tool must be used with care, since overuse tends to blunt effectiveness. There is also the concern that emphasizing promotions leads marketers to focus on short-term tactical issues instead of longer term strategy. The question of whether the growing importance of promotions is a symptom or a cause of waning brand loyalty and shortening marketing planning time horizons is very difficult to answer. However, it is clear that many of the promotions that are growing in popularity, such as on-pack coupons, clubs, or those which require the collection of purchase proofs, are aimed at producing rather than overcoming brand loyalty.

Promotions have definite limitations. They will neither compensate for fundamental weaknesses in the rest of the marketing mix, nor revive the fortunes of an outdated brand, and overuse can be counterproductive. Unless carefully managed, promotions can also present serious risks to the marketing strategy and the business as a whole. Advertising, with its fixed upfront costs, is often considered riskier than promotions, whose costs are generally more spread out and related to sales volume. However, while misconceived advertising dents credibility and wastes communications budgets, a bungled promotion can also incur significant 'clean-up' costs. This was vividly demonstrated by the fallout from a mismanaged competition run by Pepsi-Cola in the Philippines, which has cost the company an initial £8 million, has led to them facing over 22,000 lawsuits, and has provoked riots, death threats against company executives and grenade attacks on Pepsi lorries.

Since discounting and couponing are the dominant forms of sales promotion, the key problems associated with promotions are the danger of sparking price wars, the effects of discounting on consumers' reference prices, and the costs of coupon fraud. However, each different form of promotion brings its own particular potential pitfalls which must be carefully avoided. Competitions involving gamecard promotions require careful attention to printing accuracy and security to prevent the problems of excessive prize awards that have befallen the likes of Esso and Beatrice Foods. Coupons, giveaways and buyback schemes all require accurate estimates of the potential response. If such promotions are unexpectedly successful in attracting customers, they can result in significant financial losses. Misjudging the extent or timing of consumer response can also lead to stock-outs and subsequent customer dissatisfaction. The mechanics of returning mail-in premiums are usually dealt with by specialist handling houses. Although this arrangement is usually very effective, there have been instances where handling house delays and failures have occurred. These cause consumer dissatisfaction and reflect badly on the promoter.

Promotions generally encounter problems for one of four reasons:

1 A failure to apply the type of rigorous planning and control processes afforded to advertising campaigns.
2 Time pressure leads to poor decision-making and mistakes.
3 A tendency for the implementation and evaluation of promotions to be delegated too far down the organization.
4 A failure to integrate the promotion with other elements of the marketing strategy and mix.

MANAGING AND PLANNING SALES PROMOTIONS

Although tactical promotions may have to be organized almost immediately, promotions benefit greatly from thorough planning. Any plan for a sales promotion should be drawn up with reference to the overall marketing strategy, which in turn will reflect the environmental opportunities and threats facing the business and the internal organizational realities of corporate strategy, resources and politics. An ideal situation is to have a specific corporate communications strategy which seeks to divide the marketing tasks and resources between the different forms of marketing communications in a cost effective and co-ordinated way. This slightly idealized situation is reflected in a model summarizing the sales promotion planning process shown in Figure 3.

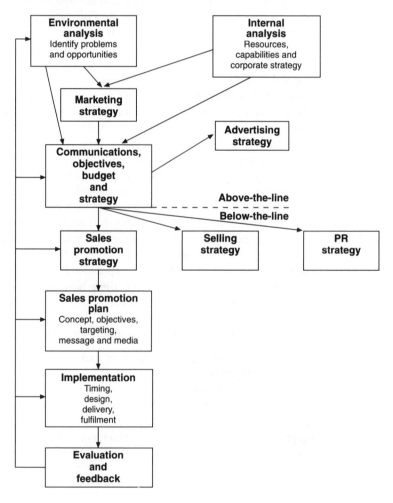

Figure 3   The sales promotion planning process

696

Once the overall sales promotion objectives and budgets have been set, the sales promotion plan will usually be divided into a series of campaigns. Each campaign will aim to fulfil specific objectives, and will use one or more type of promotion, each with its particular underlying concept, marketing message and means of reaching its target.

In addition to the obvious objectives of increasing sales or encouraging product trial, promotions can pursue a wide range of strategic and tactical objectives including:

- Creating awareness of, or interest in, the product.
- Overshadowing a competitor's promotional or other activities.
- Deflecting attention away from price competition.
- Reinforcing advertising themes.
- Developing a relationship with customers or intermediaries.
- Gathering marketing information.

To develop a promotion which will meet its objectives, it is important for the marketer to select the appropriate form of promotion, to apply it correctly in terms of geographic area and product variants (sizes or models), to offer benefits which appeal to the target in both nature and scale, and finally to time the launch and duration of the promotion to maximum effect.

The planning and implementation of a promotion will frequently be supported by a sales promotions agency. Such agencies resemble advertising agencies in many respects. They operate on a fee basis for their creative input, with 'account handlers' representing the interests of each client. Agencies provide clients with impartial advice about which form of promotion will best suit their needs. They will also be able to supply or arrange all the artwork, design, prizes and premiums that are needed to bring a promotion to fruition. The tactical origins of promotions have been reflected in a tendency for them to be sought and supplied on an ad hoc basis. The increasing trend towards strategic promotions has led to more sales promotions agencies working with clients on a retainer basis. It has also led to the emergence of an increasing number of agencies supplying integrated marketing communications services instead of just advertising, sales promotions or direct mail.

SELECTING AN APPROPRIATE PROMOTION

With the bewildering array of different types of promotion available, selecting an appropriate type can be a daunting task. The choice of promotional tool will be influenced by a number of factors:

1 *Marketing problem to be addressed.* A free sample is an excellent way of stimulating product trial, a money-off coupon is useful for prompting past customers to repurchase, a sale can help to smooth seasonal demand fluctuations, while a competition can help to generate a database of

customers at whom to target future promotions.

2   *Stage in product life cycle.* The marketing challenges faced by a particular product will frequently reflect its life-cycle stage. Products being introduced will require consumer promotions aimed at gaining product trial such as sampling programmes, and trade promotions aimed at getting channels to stock and display the product. More mature products may need to rely on price promotions and trade promotions aimed at generating salesforce and retailer enthusiasm for a familiar product and ensuring that channels are protected.

3   *Nature of the product.* Different promotions suit different types of product. An offer of 10 per cent extra free is a logical choice for packaged goods, but would look very strange in a hairdressing salon.

4   *Target consumer groups.* Different types of promotion appeal to different types of people. The likely success of any form of promotion will be influenced by the profile of the target market in terms of factors such as age, sex, nationality, socioeconomic grouping and ethnic origin.

5   *Geography.* The cultural acceptability of, and legal restrictions on, different forms of promotion vary between different countries. Such differences need to be taken into account when attempting to plan a promotion for an international brand on an international scale.

A FOCUS ON TRADE PROMOTIONS

A key choice in planning sales promotion strategy is whether to target consumers to stimulate demand, or whether to invest in trade promotions aimed at intermediaries. During the last decade retailer mergers, increasingly centralized buying and retailer access to marketing information from electronic point-of-sale (EPOS) systems have all shifted power away from producers towards retailers. Many products now rely heavily on retailer support, and increasing trade promotions reflects their importance in maintaining good channel relationships.

Trade promotions need to offer retailers or other marketing intermediaries benefits in terms of direct financial incentives or some means of improving their own performance. Retailers will tend to favour those promotions which aim to increase the volume of a product sold overall, as opposed to those which will encourage the switching of purchases from one brand to another. They will only be interested in supporting brand-switching promotions which are likely to encourage switching away from brands that they do not carry, or which offer them improved margins on the promoted brand. Trade promotions can aim to:

*   encourage or reward sales efforts from intermediaries;
*   support the introduction of new or revised products;
*   increase or maintain floor or shelf space for products;
*   encourage stocking up by intermediaries;

- gain acceptance for special displays outside normal shelf locations;
- gain access to new sales outlets;
- insulate intermediaries from temporary sales downturns or pressure on margins;
- reduce excess inventories and increase revenue;
- create a basis for joint retailer/producer advertising;
- reinforce communication to, or education of, intermediaries.

Many products such as cars, hi-fi, cosmetics, jewellery and domestic appliances need to be actively 'sold' to consumers by retailers or dealers, and the skills and knowledge of their salespeople will be a key determinant of marketing success. It is clearly in the interests of both manufacturers and intermediaries to ensure that the staff selling the products are knowledgeable and well trained. This has led to an increasing emphasis on sales training by manufacturers. Such training can be provided by the manufacturer's sales representatives or, as is increasingly popular, through the use of training video tapes.

Trade shows are another form of promotion which, usually on an annual basis, allow manufacturers to display and demonstrate their products to current and potential future buyers. Trade shows are a popular forum for introducing new products. In a short space of time they can provide access to most major customers or channels, and allow feedback on products and potential sales leads to be gathered. The marketing effort at such shows is usually backed up by a range of other promotions, including free gifts, catalogue distribution and competitions open to those visiting a given stand.

EVALUATING THE EFFECTIVENESS OF SALES PROMOTIONS

An important final step in the management of promotions is to monitor and evaluate their effectiveness. In terms of measurability the direct nature of the consumer response makes their short-term effect on sales easier to measure accurately than for advertising, particularly with the advent of information from EPOS systems.

The monitoring of the effect of promotions on sales can be attempted by a number of techniques:

1 *Monitoring sales data by time periods.* Breakdowns of sales, possibly on a weekly basis, covering before, during and after the promotion can help to identify its effect on sales.

2 *Monitoring sales data by matched markets.* For promotions run on a geographic basis it can be useful to compare sales for areas where the promotion ran against comparable areas in which it did not.

3 *Comparison with sales forecast.* Where sales trends for a market can be made quite accurately by using historical sales data, it is possible to project the likely sales pattern for the brand and compare this with the actual pattern produced by the promotion.

4 *Comparisons by channel*. Where a promotion was run through specific channels, results can be compared to those for channels in which it was not.

Longer term or non-purchasing responses can be more difficult to evaluate and are unfortunately often ignored as a result. As well as measuring the impact on sales, it is quite possible to measure other dimensions of consumers' response to a promotion. This can be done through personal interviews, telephone surveys, postal questionnaires or 'scratch' response cards.

THE FUTURE FOR SALES PROMOTION

Despite the criticisms aimed at sales promotion by many within the field of marketing, as the new millennium approaches there is every indication that promotions will continue to grow in importance. Consumers are faced with an ever increasing range of products and brands from which to choose. In many markets the differences between brands are also becoming increasingly slim, with any innovations which yield competitive advantage being rapidly imitated by the pack of brands chasing the market leaders. It is therefore not surprising that many consumers are abandoning previous brand loyalties to experiment and to take advantage of brands which differentiate themselves through the offer of additional benefits.

A number of trends bode well for the future growth of sales promotion. Technological advances in packaging and information processing are making it possible to target additional benefits at consumers and to the trade more accurately and cost effectively than ever before. The increasing trend towards the sharing of promotions with retailers and other manufacturers has opened up whole new worlds of opportunity for companies to target new customers and to offer new benefits to entice previous purchasers back towards the brand.

The view of sales promotion is also maturing to recognize its effectiveness, flexibility, brand-building potential and strategic importance. Instead of being viewed as a tactical 'bolt-on extra' which is added into the marketing mix as a defensive move in times of difficulty, promotions are being viewed increasingly as an integral part of the marketing mix. In the future, effective use of sales promotion will continue to be an important factor in determining the competitive success of a wide range of brands.

FURTHER READING

Cummins, Julian (1989) *Sales Promotion: How to Create and Implement Campaigns that Really Work*, London: Kogan Page.
Davies, Mark and Saunders, John (1992) 'The double delight of sales promotion', in Whitelock *et al.* (eds) *Marketing in The New Europe and Beyond, Proceedings of the 1992 MEG Conference*, Salford.
Engel, James F., Warshaw, Martin R. and Kinnear, Thomas C. (1991) *Promotional*

Strategy: Managing the Marketing Communications Process, 7th edn, Homewood, Illinois: Irwin.

Peattie, Ken and Peattie, Sue (1993) 'Sales promotion: playing to win?', *Journal of Marketing Management* 9 (3).

Peattie, Sue and Peattie, Ken (1994) 'Sales promotion', in Michael J. Baker (ed.) *The Marketing Book*, London: Butterworth-Heinemann.

Quelch, John A. (1989) *Sales Promotion Management*, Englewood Cliffs, NJ: Prentice Hall.

Robinson, William A. and Schultz, Don E. (1982) *Sales Promotion Management*, Chicago: Crain Books.

Shimp, Terence A. (1990) *Promotion Management and Marketing Communications*, 2nd edn, Fort Worth: The Dryden Press.

Strong, E. K. (1925) *The Psychology of Selling*, New York: McGraw-Hill.

Toop, Alan (1992) *European Sales Promotion: Great Campaigns in Action*, London: Kogan Page.

40

PERSONAL SELLING AND SALES MANAGEMENT

Bill Donaldson

INTRODUCTION

One of the conflicts in marketing management which presents difficulties for both academics and practitioners is the problem of resolving the conceptual nature of strategic decisions with the reality of day-to-day operations. Nowhere is this conflict more apparent than with issues in personal selling and sales management. While it is necessary to focus on what the business is and where it should be, vital to target markets and match resources to fulfil customers' expectations and essential to be customer oriented, businesses must sell today's output to survive. The front line of revenue generation is the salesforce. This chapter will briefly review the traditional role of personal selling and sales management and focus on the changes in this important area concerned with the organization, motivation and evaluation of the salesforce. This is a wide-ranging subject and could conceivably involve types of selling, characteristics of salespeople, interaction and behavioural theory, time and territory management with issues of recruitment, selection, training, leadership, motivation and many more aspects of what constitutes managing the sales function. The content is, by necessity, limited to a few of these important issues and the additional reading list is intended to give the interested reader more comprehensive coverage of the subject.

THE IMPORTANCE OF PERSONAL SELLING

Personal selling is the personal contact with one or more purchasers for the purpose of making a sale. To be effective, marketing management needs to integrate personal selling with other promotional elements, with other organizational functions such as distribution and production and with the customer and competitive structures prevailing in the market. The importance of personal selling is such that expenditure on the salesforce usually exceeds the budget for all other marketing activities added together, with the possible exception of promotion in fast-moving consumer goods companies. The role of personal selling has two interrelated functions – information and persuasion. The information role is part of a two-way process whereby information about the company's product or offer needs to be communicated to existing and potential customers and, in the reverse direction, customers' needs are correctly interpreted and understood by management. Salespeople impart knowledge about the product or service which provides benefits to customers and also a range of information on promotional support, finance, technical advice, service and other elements which contribute to customer satisfaction. Salespeople are also the face-to-face contact between purchasers and the company and for good reason are referred to as 'the eyes and ears of the organization' since senior management's customer contact may be limited.

A second role that salespeople must fulfil is persuasion. The importance of correctly identifying customers' needs and market opportunities can never be overstated. Nevertheless, in competitive markets prospective customers are usually faced with an abundance of choice. As a result, adoption of the marketing concept can be no guarantee of competitive advantage. Purchasers will have to be convinced that their needs have been correctly identified by the company and that the offer provides benefit over any other firm. Salespeople are part of this process through persuasion and service.

The most significant difference between selling and other elements in the marketing effort is the personal contact. The need for this personal contact will vary depending on such factors as the scale of risk, size of investment, type of customer, frequency of purchase, newness of product and many other factors. In some situations the information or persuasion role can be achieved by impersonal means of communication, particularly advertising. Advertising is impersonal, indirect and aimed at a mass audience, whereas selling is individual, direct and much more adaptable. With advertising the message is more limited, cheaper per contact but unidirectional, relying on a pull approach rather than personal selling which is two-way, but employs a push strategy and is relatively expensive per contact.

TYPES OF PERSONAL SELLING

In most exchanges, except direct response campaigns, it is unlikely that a sale can be made without first establishing a personal contact. This is the primary role of personal selling. While selling skills are always important, it is worthwhile to distinguish between different types of selling such as transaction and relationship selling and between new business and service selling. In the case of one-off transactions, salesmanship is often the reason a sale is made or not and therefore gives rise to hard-sell techniques. In some cases these techniques seem to be the opposite of marketing, as characterized by double glazing, timeshare and second-hand car salespeople where customer dissatisfaction and post-cognitive dissonance levels are unacceptably high. In these direct selling situations the task of the salesperson is to provide prospective buyers with information and other benefits, motivating or persuading them to make buying decisions in favour of the seller's product or service. In other situations, salespeople are involved with regular rather than one-off customers where repeat business is both the aim and the norm and it is more appropriate to think of exchange as a continuing relationship, not merely that of making a sale. This form of exchange is characterized by buyer and seller being known to each other, by business being lost rather than won and by forms of joint cooperation in the exchange relationship.

It is also important to distinguish between new business selling and maintenance selling. In a new business situation the salesperson has to identify worthwhile prospects, identify the influences and decision-makers within the buying unit and, by establishing a relationship based on identification of customer needs, problem solving and shared values, build up a rapport with prospects and customers. This type of salesperson has to match their offer to the buyers' real needs and motivate the prospect to change. Further, this change has to materialize into an initial order and, finally, the salesperson has to convert the initial purchase into repeat ordering behaviour. This is a time-consuming, difficult job. Most salespeople are employed to sell existing products to existing customers. This type of selling, service selling, requires different skills and a different approach to that of the new business or development salesperson. Here the task is to consolidate existing customers, to preserve and expand the volume of business these customers do and maintain inertia in the buyer-seller exchange relationship. Service salespersons know their customers very well, know their customers' business, have access to a number of personnel in the buying organization and seek to maintain the status quo and continue the favoured buyer-supplier relationship. A salesperson's tasks might include taking orders, product display, advice to distributors, advice to users and specifiers, after-sales service, complaint handling, collecting payment, stock management, training customers' staff and many other activities. To assist sales management to identify the salesperson's role, selling has been categorized into four types – serving existing customers or trade selling; specification selling; technical selling; and new business development (Newton 1969). In another classification, nine different categories of selling were identified, based on the perceived degree of difficulty, ranging from simple delivery and order taker to selling major contracts (McMurry 1961).

THE ROLE OF SALES MANAGEMENT

Sales management is the management process of directing strategy, organizing tactics and implementing policies which fulfil the firm's sales, marketing and corporate objectives. This is achieved by means of influencing subordinates to be more efficient and effective. The job of the sales manager is not to sell but to achieve sales through subordinates. Managing a salesforce is different to selling. Put simply, sales managers need to establish the role salespeople can be expected to perform, the tasks to be accomplished and the means to achieve their sales objectives.

Three problems hamper sales managers. First, there is the high cost of personal selling. In 1992 the average cost of a salesperson in the UK was £38,000 per annum (*Financial Times* 1993). Second, only about 20–30 per cent of a salesperson's time is spent face to face with customers (other time is spent in driving, administration, call preparation, merchandising). Third, customer buying is changing, becoming more professional, efficient and increasingly automated and centralized. There may be a danger that with the passage of time and maturity in product markets the salesforce may become courtesy callers rather than salespeople and this is an expensive resource for this purpose. An amusing way to describe salespeople is to refer to them as inter-organizational boundary spanners, but this is exactly what they are and what makes their management both challenging and difficult. As a result, increasing the productivity of salespeople is a necessary and important managerial activity.

ORGANIZATION AND DEPLOYMENT OF SALESPEOPLE

Having decided on the role salespeople will play, management must select and organize individuals into an effective salesforce by deciding first on the type and structure of organization, second, on how best to recruit and train salespeople and third, how to lead and motivate their sales team.

Direct salespeople versus independent agents

The high proportion of marketing expense accounted for by direct sales costs, the relatively fixed nature of these costs and the low face-to-face selling time has encouraged a reappraisal of how salesforces operate. One important decision is whether to use manufacturers' representatives (agents) or to employ a direct salesforce. Management have traditionally been wary of acknowledging this choice, instead preferring to alter training and remuneration or to change deployment or other features when problems arise. There is some evidence that contracting out the sales function, similar to the trend to subcontract many non-core activities, may be a viable alternative to the high cost of a national direct salesforce. Traditionally, agents have been used where the market is new such as exporting, where the company has lacked adequate resources or where tradition has encouraged this practice (e.g. printing and publishing). However, a salesforce of service callers has become something of a luxury item and serious consideration should be given to using highly motivated independent agents. The independent agent whose survival and prosperity depends on sales performance may be a realistic alternative. Such people can be used where a number of complementary products are sold to the same customer as with computer software, the food broker or financial services. The agent requires less training, will already have established a relationship with customers and prospects and is only paid when sales are made. Supervision, recruitment and training costs will be much less and turnover in personnel will be significantly lower. They are also unlikely to transfer to the competition. As markets extend yet fragment the local knowledge of an agent may be a significant advantage if it brings continuity and greater customer knowledge.

Generally, a direct salesforce would be preferred where there is high investment, specialized products and a need to control the selling situation because of uncertainty in the market or environment in which the company operates. If sales performance is difficult to evaluate and non–selling activities such as technical advice and goodwill are likely to be important then a direct salesforce is more likely.

Structure of the salesforce

A second management task is to decide how to deploy salespeople to achieve the best, most productive result. There are six concepts to be borne in mind when designing an organizational structure:

1 Organizational structure should be marketing oriented.
2 Organizations should be designed for activities not people.
3 Clearly defined responsibility and maximum possible delegation of authority to subordinates.
4 A reasonable span of control.
5 Organizations should be stable yet flexible.
6 Organizations should be balanced and coordinated in the activities to be performed.

Inevitably there will be some conflict between organizational and sales objectives and between management and individuals as to the best way to organize selling effort. The salesforce organization will achieve best results where duplication of effort is eliminated, where internal conflicts are minimized and where cooperation is maximized. This is not easy. The sales manager must:

- set clearly defined objectives;
- specify the role of salespeople and the tasks to be performed;
- group activities into specific jobs with clear authority and responsibility;
- assign personnel to these jobs;
- provide effective coordination and control.

Geographical specialization

This is the traditional and most widely used type of sales organization. In this type of structure each salesperson is responsible for all tasks, all products and

706

all existing and prospective customers within a geographical area. It is most appropriate in larger rather than smaller organizations, where there is a widely spread customer base rather than only a few, where regional variations are more important than national standards and where personal contact between buyer and seller is frequent rather than occasional. The advantages of a geographical split are likely to be that travel time and expense is lower. Each salesperson can build good customer and area knowledge, which itself is a motivating factor in that salespeople manage their territory. There is less confusion since multiple calling on a single customer is avoided, customers know who is the point of contact. Additionally, management control and evaluation is more easily administered. These advantages are important but the complexity of today's selling job and the dynamics of the business environment may require specialization. The need to specialize in product or customer, the need to use experts to meet customers' needs and the problem of using low-level personnel for key management decisions does exist. Further, while control is straightforward, overhead costs may rise as more layers of management evolve.

Product specialization

A company with product lines which differ in technical complexity, end users and profitability would benefit from product specialization, with each salesperson attaining the necessary expertise in product knowledge to handle different customer requirements more effectively. Companies who take over or merge with others sometimes continue to operate separate salesforces. Also, the case for expertise with a new product may require specialist development salespeople. With this type of organization problems do arise concerning duplication of effort and multiple calling on one customer. This requires management to promote cooperation between salespeople with minimum conflict and confusion as to who does what job.

Market specialization

This type of sales organization is not yet popular in UK industry but there has been a trend for some industries to organize by customer or prospect. Implementation of the marketing concept would suggest that the most appropriate form of specialization is that based on the customer. Where market segmentation policies can be applied it is sensible to operate the salesforce specializing on the respective segments. Grouping of customers into suitable classifications means salespeople can develop customer expertise and implement marketing policy and programmes. In dynamic, innovative markets the information exchange process may require this form of specialism. In other cases, too much specialization will result in excessively high selling costs.

Combined methods

The advantages and disadvantages of the three previous methods encourages many firms to seek systems of organization which combine the benefits of specialization with reduced selling costs. The increasing complexity of the selling job in dynamic, changing markets gives impetus to this organizational dilemma. The problem still remains of how to deploy salespeople to achieve sales objectives. Several more recent developments in salesforce organizational structure must be considered:

Key account selling

A newer form of market-based organization may split customers into key accounts, different channel members or by industry type. In several markets, particularly food, DIY and household goods, there is no doubt that the disproportionate effect of major customers' control on the market necessitates specialist sales treatment. This in turn affects the job to be done by salespeople on the ground at branch level. A separate merchandising salesforce may be used to call on branches rather than to sell to buyers. In some markets such as office equipment a junior salesforce establishes contact and evaluates prospects. In 1991-2 Kraft General Foods PLC reduced their UK salesforce from just under 300 to a mere 24. The traditional sales role of calling on individual supermarket accounts at local level was replaced in favour of a small number of account managers dealing with the head offices of the major supermarkets and the major wholesale chains. This combination of key account selling and boosting inside sales and customer service was considered to be the most appropriate organization for the company in the 1990s.

Telesales

The application of the 80/20 rule can also mean that large numbers of customers account for a relatively small proportion of sales. An inside salesforce or telemarketing operation may be used to complement the outside salesforce for specific tasks. The most obvious advantage of telemarketing is the ability to target specific contacts quickly at much lower cost than a personal sales call. Telemarketing can be used both to prospect, qualify and service accounts, and as an order-taking vehicle. Customers who are small, marginal or geographically remote can be handled more efficiently than in person. Telemarketing can be used:

- as a low-cost substitute for personal selling. One estimate suggests that five to six personal calls can be replaced with 30 long telephone calls at one tenth the cost (Stone and Wyman 1986).
- to supplement personal selling calls.
- to reinforce a direct mail campaign.

• to offer guidance and advice on product usage or as a complaint vehicle for customers.

Team selling

Based on successful implementation in 'high tech' selling and 'big ticket' items, a recent development has been the emergence of team selling whereby the salesperson is supported in negotiations by technical, operations and financial specialists, or others, as appropriate. This approach has extended to other markets as the advantages of relationship building between supplier and buyer, or intermediary, become apparent. For example, Procter and Gamble, recognizing that 80 per cent of sales come from a number of key accounts, have developed business teams whose sole responsibility is to sell the whole product range for one key customer. In some cases this team has offices within their customer's head office.

Information technology (IT)

A related but separate issue has been the impact of IT on sales operations. The ability to obtain, store, analyse and retrieve large amounts of information quickly and cheaply has given innovative sales organizations a competitive edge. It enables the firm to collect data from dispersed and diverse sources such as prospects, customers, distribution channels, company sources and salespeople themselves. If relevant information can be drawn together, formatted, stored, retrieved and manipulated into meaningful sales support information that is relevant, timely and cheap then salesforce productivity will improve. This applies not only in administration and reporting but in assisting in routing, call scheduling and other forms of time management.

Salesforce size

It should now be accepted that problems in sales management are complex and solutions seldom permanent. In determining salesforce size the temptation to look for a simple, universal formula should be avoided. The type of sales organization will affect the size of the salesforce, particularly the degree of specialization considered appropriate. The nature of the selling task between development and service selling will be fundamental. Other aspects of the selling task will be affected by the time required to be spent on activities such as:

• demonstration/presentation
• negotiating on price
• explaining company policy
• providing information on competitors and customers
• dealer support programmes

709

- stock checking
- display work
- complaint handling
- credit problems
- prospecting for new business
- report writing

These activities should be part of the salesperson's job description, being included to reflect their importance to the firm. This importance will in turn affect whether six or sixteen calls per day are possible. Questions about salesforce size will also depend on company objectives, company resources and on competitive or other environmental factors. Neither can issues of salesforce size be divorced from the form of organization, the method of specializing and territory allocation.

The traditional approach to determining salesforce size was based on one of three methods. The workload method is a composite figure made up from the total work time available, the allocation of this time to sales tasks and the time spent with each customer or prospect, usually on the basis of size of sales revenue per account. This is the most commonly used technique in UK sales management. With this approach each salesperson should have a similar workload in terms of size of accounts, number of calls and travel time. It is rarely the case that accounts can be distributed evenly so that travel time in some areas will eventually be much greater than in others. Other weaknesses in this approach may be that larger accounts are not necessarily those with the highest future potential. If potential is used these may not be the most profitable if costs of servicing the account are higher or a less profitable product mix is taken. The most serious problem is the simplistic assumption that quantity equals quality. Each account and each salesperson will be different in quality, a factor not incorporated in this method. Put simply different call frequencies (and time per call) may yield higher sales and profits.

A second method is to base size on an estimate of sales potential for the company's products (sales forecast) based on management objectives and a desirable market share. If each salesperson performs to their job description an average productivity level per person can be calculated. Some allowances should be made for the loss of someone leaving, say 10 per cent per annum. Part of the problem with this method is the accuracy in estimating each variable, particularly average productivity. The accuracy of such an average is influenced by the effects of someone leaving, the lead time for a replacement to become established and the effects of cross-selling between salespeople in different areas. It assumes a rather static market position when most companies will experience growing or declining sales productivity and perhaps regional variations within an overall sales forecast.

In order to overcome weaknesses in both previous methods, the incremental method is suggested. Intuitively this makes good business sense since the

710

salesforce should be expanded as long as additional sales revenue exceeds additional costs. The difficulty of estimating incremental revenues and costs can be quite daunting. This formula oversimplifies the economics of selling by assuming the product mix is uniform, that extraneous factors can be correctly assessed in advance in each area, that the costs of selecting, recruiting and dismissing salespeople can be accurately predicted and that other forms of promotion such as advertising have an equal effect on all prospects. It is unlikely these assumptions will prevail. The simplicity of sales responding to personal selling effort where all other factors are constant is simply not tenable. The dynamic nature of markets coupled with economic growth or decline patterns, distort the calculations of the effectiveness of salespeople in terms of a sales response function. Seasonal, cyclical and competitive fluctuations create market uncertainty with a possible danger of overstaffing leading to cost inefficiencies. Companies may compound these problems by adding salespeople as long as profits are positive. The important weakness here is that salespeople become the result of sales rather than the creators of sales. Further, it fails to take account, or alternatively dismisses the effects of differing abilities, knowledge, skills and aptitude of salespeople.

As a result of weaknesses in these traditional approaches management should consider methods which combine good organizational practice with sound territory planning and which incorporate flexible management and lean organizational structures. These are considered next.

TERRITORY MANAGEMENT

One aspect of sales management and a key determinant of organization, performance and control is territory management. It would be wrong to isolate organization, especially salesforce size, from territory management or to suggest that suitable territories can be determined and evaluated without studying other determinants of performance such as salesperson ability, distribution, economic conditions or marketing effectiveness. Nevertheless, sales territories are established to facilitate effective salesforce operations. This is achieved by allocating a number of present and potential customers within a given area to a particular salesperson. The benefits of sales territories are:

- more thorough coverage of the market;
- clearer definition of an individual's responsibilities;
- more specific performance evaluation;
- reduced selling expense;
- better fit between sales resources and customer's needs;
- improved job clarity for the salesperson.

To establish sales territories management must decide on the basic unit, evaluate the number of accounts and sales potential, analyse salesperson workload, design the basic territories and assign salespeople to these territories.

The optional territory design is achieved where:

- territories are easy to administer;
- sales potential is relatively easy to estimate;
- travel time and expense are minimized;
- equal sales opportunity is provided across customers and prospects;
- workload is equalized.

The aim of good territory design is to make more effective use of salespersons' time. The most significant improvements can be achieved through salespeople being more disciplined and professional by better planning of work, less calling on unqualified or unimportant prospects, more use of the telephone, including making appointments, and more systematic paperwork. Various attempts have been made to model the territory allocation problem. CALLPLAN (Lodish 1971), SCHEDULE (Armstrong 1976) and PAIRS (Parasuramun and Day 1977) are three such models. Computer software packages are now available, based on these original concepts, which can assist with salesforce time management problems. Whatever model is used, research confirms that the most significant factor in territory sales performance is to put the effort where sales potential is greatest. Territory design on the basis of anything other than potential (e.g. workload, historical rule of thumb) will be less efficient (Ryans and Weinberg 1979).

RECRUITMENT

Many sales management problems could be eliminated or at least mitigated if a successful sales type could be found. This would imply that successful salespeople are born, have acquired the necessary skills or possibly have been self-taught by experience. The sales manager's task is to find such people. Some of the best books on selling show that many are still searching for this formula. Other books on personal selling present formal lists of attributes that people should or must have while others suggest the mysteries of the super salesperson are to be found in personality and psychological characteristics (Lamont and Lundstrom 1977).

Sales situations are often unique or, at the very least, vary by type as outlined above. The various roles, complex tasks and variety of situations which can occur require some adaptability by individuals to any list of principles of selling which may be put forward. Not least, the problem of the measurement of personality and psychological traits is complex. The nature of the job (new business versus service calling) may mean that entirely different characteristics are needed to be effective in different situations (Greenberg and Greenberg 1980). A unidimensional approach will be inadequate and better explanations have yet to be found between the fit of certain jobs and the personality of individuals and vice versa. The evidence on the characteristics of successful salespeople is inconclusive and contradictory. Indeed the basic premise that

712

there is an ideal sales personality may be unsound. Should not the characteristics of buyers rather than salespeople be examined for a better explanation of sales performance? Sales managers, like marketing managers, must respond to changes in supply, demand, or the framework in which business is conducted. People operating at the interface or boundary between different units in a dynamic environment need a wide range of skills from strategic problem solving and profit orientation to highly developed communication capabilities. The modern salesperson has had to acquire more qualities, more skills and a more flexible approach. Unfortunately for sales recruiters people who have these skills may consider selling as low in status and unable to provide them with the necessary levels of job satisfaction.

In a marketing context, personal selling facilitates the matching of product offerings with buyer requirements. An important dimension of selling ability is the individual's competence in matching and influencing the variety of needs and behavioural complexities of the buyer. The factors that determine job success are not necessarily the intellectual dimensions which most selection devices are designed to measure. Instead, the result reflects a match between the prospect's and the salesperson's personalities and the knowledge, judgement and persuasive powers of both parties. Salespeople are 'made' rather than 'born'. This does not mean that personality and physical characteristics are no longer important in the type of salesperson employed but that such characteristics need to be cultivated and channelled by training, leadership and other forms of motivation.

TRAINING

Traditionally salespeople have been trained in simplified sales processes usually seen as a series of sequential steps beginning with making the initial contact, arousing interest, creating preference, presenting a specific proposal, closing the sale and retaining business. It is seldom the case that this form of stylized process operates in reality and, while useful as a pedagogical tool, the process does not relate to the reality of most exchange situations. Further, salespeople rarely conform to the popular stereotype. Today salespeople are better trained and qualified, professional sales teams are used and there is increasing use of technology. There are fewer, larger customers, more tasks to be performed such as merchandising and service support, improved purchasing and supply management and increasing levels of competition across industries, especially internationally. To respond to these changes requires enlightened sales management. Increased sales, reduced costs and achieving a more profitable product and customer mix are the three ways to improve salesforce performance. At the individual salesperson level, performance can be improved by first increasing the number of calls. While such improvement, by definition, is finite, various studies in the USA and UK show that higher call rates equate with

713

higher performance. Second, most salespeople are also aware of the importance of controlling costs and try to improve on this dimension but again the improvement is limited and finite. Third, the allocation of effort between products and customers can be changed. Training can contribute to all three of these areas but it is in the third area that the main differences in performance can be found. It is interesting to note that sales managers estimate that on average the difference between an average salesperson and the top salesperson is about 20 per cent – so quality matters (Ingram *et al.* 1992). Training should aim to get salespeople to work smarter, not just harder. Basically, quality improvement in sales performance can be achieved in one of three ways. These are by improving message content, by more effective communication and by development of interpersonal relationships.

MOTIVATION OF SALESPEOPLE

At any one time ability and technique may make the difference as to whether a sale is won or lost but the key factor in sales performance over time is motivation. The motivation problem is how to get salespeople who operate on their own, away from head office, in a hostile environment, geographically distant, at a relatively high cost, to do their job well in the way management wants it to be done. Motivation is the amount of effort a salesperson expends on each of the activities or tasks associated with their job. Salespeople respond to stimulus and sales managers can influence this process. Various theories of motivation are suggested as relevant to salesforce problems: Maslow's Hierarchy of Needs (Maslow 1970); Herzberg's Motivator-Hygiene theory (Herzberg 1966); and Vroom's Expectancy theory (Vroom 1964). Space does not permit coverage here and the interested reader is recommended to consult the selected references for this chapter, in particular Churchill *et al.* (1991).

The motivation of salespeople is neither easy nor straightforward but there is no doubt that it has great significance on sales performance. Part of the complexity of this problem is the multiplicative nature of the variables which impact on performance such as aptitude, role perception and the components of motivation itself. The problem is compounded by the individuality of the selling job since the nature of the task, the individual's perception of each element and the prospect's reaction to sales stimulii are all variable. The problem of industry-specific contexts, the type of selling and the characteristics of individuals all hamper the search for definitive solutions and create unique problems. To prescribe a management solution requires a selection of factors or influences to be considered which can then be adapted to the particular circumstances. Some of the factors that affect motivation include:

1   *The job itself.* If a salesperson does not find the job challenging or interesting there will be a motivation problem. Compared with many jobs this problem will be less for salespeople than, for example, an assembly-line worker. Sales

managers should be careful that excessive routines, job simplification or too strict a discipline do not demotivate staff. Part of the attraction of the job is the freedom of action which is permitted. This autonomy combines with a variety of tasks and their perceived importance.

2 *Accuracy and feedback.* A problem already identified is that sales tasks and sales effort have an indirect rather than a direct effect on sales performance. Missionary selling is particularly prone to this difficulty. For others, organizational complexity or dual effort may confuse the sales process and its effect on performance. Nevertheless accurate and timely feedback for salespeople has a positive effect on job performance and job satisfaction.

3 *Motivated people.* Salespeople who have drive and a need for achievement will have higher sales performance. Demirdjian (1984) suggests that motivation can be expressed as a function of a salesperson's economic needs, social needs and self-actualizing needs.

4 *Participation.* There is a greater commitment and involvement when salespeople take an active part in decision-making. The use of management by objectives or similar schemes can have a positive effect on salesforce motivation.

5 *Being part of the company.* As with participation, so involvement is increased by salespeople who are committed to their company, colleagues and supervisors. This belief extends to the products being sold (task importance) and that sales effort will make a contribution to the company's prosperity and the prosperity of other employees.

6 *Morale.* Motivation is affected by morale. Morale is difficult to define but is a mix or sum of a person's feelings towards their job, pay, other employees, conditions of work, competitors and other factors. Good morale by itself is not sufficient to motivate but poor morale can be a demotivating factor.

7 *Discipline.* Views on the correct amount and type of discipline vary but it is a factor to be considered. Too strict a discipline can discourage people but little or weak discipline can lead to a situation of anarchy. A fair code of actions not allowed (e.g. dishonesty), of areas requiring improvement (e.g. late reports, poor appearance) and areas of freedom (e.g. call patterns) should be established. Generally negative factors are weak motivators.

8 *Monetary rewards.* Remuneration is the most important reward used to motivate salespeople. The variety of payment plans in operation, even within similar industry and sales situations, suggests that management do not understand the effect of payment on their employees' motivation.

9 *Good management.* Although management practices are a difficult concept to measure with the necessary degree of precision to make conclusions on sales motivation and performance, it should be recognized that they do have a combined impact. Factors such as goal setting, evaluation, control, coaching, understanding and know-how contribute to individual salespeople's motivation.

The importance and complexity of motivation and its effect on performance has led to the idea of the motivational mix which represents the combination of factors to be considered, including remuneration, financial incentives, non-financial incentives, leadership, management controls and the salesperson's personality (Donaldson 1990). These factors, individually and collectively, influence an individual's motivation to work and, ultimately, their job performance. The individual may respond, positively or negatively, to the different factors which management can deploy to motivate the salesforce. The quest for understanding the components of motivation and its impact on performance should at least lead to some tentative formula for improving salesforce motivation. Before doing this, it is first necessary to restate and highlight the problems created by a lack of motivation. One problem is that sales will be lower. Enthusiasm, drive and hours worked will be less if individuals are not fully motivated. These factors directly affect sales performance. A related problem is that sales staff turnover will be higher, especially among better performing salespeople who are more able (and motivated) to find work elsewhere. A lack of motivation not only results in less hours being worked but often higher expense claims, more give-aways to customers and higher mileage. Lower motivation often coincides with indiscipline or 'bad mouthing' to other colleagues or customers. As in most occupations the importance of minor complaints becomes magnified, diverting management time to peripheral issues. Conditions to avoid which may exacerbate the problem include poor working environment, poor reporting procedures, unfairness in rewards, lack of promotion opportunity, lack of individual involvement and participation, no incentives, a disproportionate number of older salespeople and poor communication between subordinates, supervisors and top management.

A more positive approach is to take actions which will increase motivation. Such actions involve the elements in the motivational mix previously described. Among the most vital are likely to be:

1   *Status enhancement.* Acknowledgement of a job well done, a more prestigious title, a management training course, an above average pay increase are not only important in themselves but as recognition of effort and a stimulus to greater effort.

2   *Positive communication.* People are less motivated if they have negative views about the job, the company or their performance. If these views are accurate the cause of dissatisfaction must be corrected via product, price, distribution policies or organizational and managerial changes. If the views are inaccurate then management must improve their communication message. This can be done by measuring existing levels of satisfaction through a complaint procedure, suggestion box, formal survey, exit interviews (leavers) or by keeping close to employees. Whatever the technique or approach, good two-way communication is vital for effective management of the salesforce.

3   *Individual recognition.* Salespeople exist in an environment of relative

isolation. It follows that they will be sensitive to the distance between themselves and control of the operation. They require not only rewards for work done but frequent and positive acknowledgement of their perform- ance.

4 *Ability to handle rejection.* In the course of doing the job salespeople will inevitably get many rejections, rebuffs and lost sales. To overcome these negatives, especially in newer recruits, management must train salespeople to handle and expect rejection. These problems relate to an individual's role perceptions and, in particular, role conflict and ambiguity.

5 *Group involvement.* Since salespeople operate on their own, fostering team spirit, camaraderie and group involvement is part of the management task.

6 *Availability and understanding.* As with any employee individuality is important. At any one time salespeople may face personal problems such as health, finance, marital difficulties and so on. These can only be treated on an individual basis.

The formula for the management of motivation is first, give status rewards. Second, pay particular attention to role problems and rejection handling, especially for new recruits. Third, arrange frequent communication, both individually and via regional or team meetings. Fourth, provide coaching and training for sales staff, including special assignments for older, more experi- enced staff. Finally, stay close to subordinates – be available and understanding.

EVALUATION OF SALESFORCE PERFORMANCE

At one level evaluation of salespeople is easy – they either make target or they do not. The problem with the link between sales effort and sales response is that it is neither simple nor direct. Most companies do conduct some form of evaluation but few do this in a formal way which assesses the causes as well as the outcomes. Part of the problem with evaluation is that it is far from easy and if done properly it is time-consuming, costly and downright difficult. At the individual salesperson level evaluation is necessary to identify above and below average performers, to identify possible candidates for promotion or dismissal, to identify areas of weakness in the meeting of sales objectives. For management, evaluation is necessary to assess the efficacy of sales management practices such as territory deployment, recruitment, training, remuneration and so on. Finally, evaluation is necessary to modify the sales tasks in line with customer and company needs so that sales plans, and assessment of these plans, are against the most appropriate criteria for improved sales performance. A good salesforce evaluation programme should be realistic and fair. It should be positive and contribute to motivation and improved job performance. It should be objective, involve salespeople themselves and be economic in cost and time to administer. These aims inevitably conflict. Accountants, operational researchers, behaviour- ists, management scientists, economists and many other disciplines have tried to find better and more accurate measures of sales performance with varying degrees of success. It appears that evaluating salespeople is still something of an art struggling to be a science. Before commenting further on evaluation it is worthwhile to reconsider the unique problems of the selling job.

- Salespeople have inadequate or incomplete information about their job, especially concerning the needs and preferences of customers and customer organization.
- Salespeople usually work alone and independently without direct supervision. Although considered by many to be an advantage this independence creates other problems of role clarity.
- Salespeople operate in an inter-organizational boundary position which creates role conflicts.
- The sales job is demanding in terms of the degree of innovation and creativity required. There is no one right approach.
- The job requires adaptability and sensitivity from salespeople to the needs of customers, frequently met by different degrees of antagonism, hostility and aggression.
- Sales decisions may have to be made quickly requiring decisiveness and mental alertness.
- Individual sales performance evaluation lacks direct observation of inputs – only outcomes are assessed.
- Evaluation is often inferred and subjective, people biased.
- Salespeople have little control over the conditions in which they operate.

As a result of these peculiarities traditional systems of evaluation fail to measure the complete job. Evaluation has relied on inadequate definition of the necessary inputs to achieve the desired outputs. That is, the use of sales, call rates or other easily assessed measures are preferred to the more difficult quality dimensions of the job. The quality measures are often the most important. Further, most sales managers place an over-reliance on subjective factors. Seemingly contrary to the first point, many managers evaluate salespeople on selected personality traits or qualities. These characteristics are seldom proven measures of quality in sales performance. More likely they are factors considered by managers to have made themselves successful when they were selling. Evaluation will be a greater motivation if used in a positive rather than a negative way. It is incumbent upon sales managers to improve their evaluation procedures. Ways in which this can be done include the systems approach (Henry 1975); the sales management audit (Dubinsky and Hansen 1981); and the company-focused approach (Ryans and Weinberg 1981).

In the review by Churchill *et al.* (1985) of the many studies which have been conducted on the evaluation of salesperson performance, they uncovered 116 separate studies, listing 1,653 possible associations. The only certain conclusion of this meta analysis is that there is no one variable which has a significant influence on salesperson performance. In these studies, with few exceptions, on average only 4 per cent of variation in salesperson performance could be explained by a single predictor variable. The answer must therefore be sought from multiple predictor relationships and causes. Although these studies are only partial explanations of salesforce performance they do provide some help for the bemused but enlightened sales manager. First, solutions must be sought within the relevant context of the sales job. Service calling and development selling, organizational and individual customers, industrial, consumer or service selling can be so varied as to require separate, perhaps unique, analysis. In the complex trading situations now encountered, the use of sales volume or value is itself incomplete if not inadequate. Further, the mix of hard and soft data, quantitative and subjective, cause real assessment problems. The search goes on. Multiple determinants of sales performance are a better explanation but no single factor, or single set of factors, provides an adequate and satisfying explanation of salesperson performance. Personal characteristics, aptitude and skill will be important but sales managers need to concentrate not only on improving these attributes via training but also on relating them to the buyers and needs of the market. The right people, experience, skill and role clarity do matter but only when matched to the prospect. This confirms what successful salespeople and sales managers already know but few seem able to achieve.

SUMMARY

The importance of personal selling to the achievement of company marketing objectives, and to the efficiency of the exchange process, must not be underestimated. Salespeople provide information on their products and ser-vices, use persuasion and salesmanship to obtain and sustain a competitive advantage and are responsible for building a relationship between a supplier and its customers. These activities are fundamental to both customer satisfaction and the competitiveness of the firm. Sales managers should be clear as to whether salespeople are employed to win new business or service existing customers. While these tasks are not mutually exclusive, they do require different skills and perhaps separate organizational solutions. The job of the sales manager is to achieve sales targets through subordinates. This involves decisions on whether to employ direct salespeople, use independent agents, or a combination of both. They must decide and manage a suitable sales structure on the basis of geographic, product or customer specialization, or by a combination of these methods. The use of key account salespeople, telesales, team selling and information technology should be used in an efficient combination to ensure that the productivity of the salesforce is maximized. Various ways of determining salesforce size can be recommended but by recruiting the most suitable people, training them effectively and, most of all, motivating them to work to their full potential, salesforce performance and company prosperity will be enhanced.

REFERENCES

Armstrong, G. M. (1976) 'The schedule model and the salesman's effort allocation', *California Management Review* XVIII (4), Summer: 43–51.

Churchill, G. A., Ford, N. M., Hartley, S. W. and Walker, O. C. (1985) 'The determinants of salesperson performance: a meta analysis', *Journal of Marketing Research* XXII, May: 103–18.

Churchill, G. A., Ford, N. M. and Walker, O. C. (1991) *Sales Force Management*, 3rd edn, Homewood, Illinois: Irwin.

Demirdjian, Z. S. (1984) 'A multidimensional approach to motivating salespeople', *Industrial Marketing Management* 13 (1), February: 25–32.

Donaldson, Bill (1990) *Sales Management: Theory and Practice*, London: Macmillan.

Dubinsky, A. J. and Hansen, R. W. (1981) 'The sales force management audit', *California Management Review* XXIV (2), Winter: 86–95.

Financial Times (1993) 22 April.

Greenberg, H. M. and Greenberg, J. (1980) 'Job matching for better sales performance', *Harvard Business Review*, September–October: 128–31.

Henry, P. (1975) 'Manage your sales force as a system', *Harvard Business Review*, March–April.

Herzberg, F. (1966) *Work and the Nature of Man*, Cleveland: World.

Ingram, T. N., Schwepker, C. H. and Hutson, D. (1992) 'Why salespeople fail', *Industrial Marketing Management* 21: 225–30.

Lamont, L. M. and Lundstrom, W. J. (1977) 'Identifying successful industrial salesmen by personality and personal characteristics', *Journal of Marketing Research* XIV, November: 517–29.

Lodish, L. M. (1971) 'CALLPLAN: an interactive salesman's call planning system', *Management Science* 18 (4) Part II, December.

McMurry, R. N. (1961) 'The mystic of super salesmanship', *Harvard Business Review* 39, March–April: 113–22.

Maslow, A. H. (1970) *Motivation and Personality*, 2nd edn, New York: Harper & Brothers.

Newton, D. A. (1969) 'Get the most out of your sales force', *Harvard Business Review*, September–October.

Parasuraman, A. and Day, R. L. (1977) 'A management-oriented model for allocating sales effort', *Journal of Marketing Research* XIV, February: 22–33.

Ryans, A. B. and Weinberg, C. B. (1979) 'Territory sales response', *Journal of Marketing Research* XIV, November: 453–65.

Ryans, A. B. and Weinberg, C. B. (1981) 'Sales management: integrating research advances', *California Management Review* 24 (1), Fall: 75–89.

Stone, B. and Wyman, J. (1986) *Successful Telemarketing: Opportunities and Techniques for Increasing Sales and Profits*, Lincolnwood, Ill.: NTC Business Books.

Vroom, V. (1964) *Work and Motivation*, New York: Wiley.

FURTHER READING

Anderson, E. (1985) 'The salesperson as outside agent or employee: a transaction cost analysis', *Marketing Science* 4, Summer: 234–54.

Bagozzi, R. P. (1980) 'Performance and satisfaction in an industrial sales force: an examination of their antecedents and simultaneity', *Journal of Marketing* 44, Spring: 65–77.

Behrman, D. N. and Perrault, W. D. (1984) 'A role stress model of the performance and satisfaction of industrial salespersons', *Journal of Marketing* 48, Fall: 9–21.

Buzzotta, V. R., Lefton, R. E. and Sherberg, G. M. (1982) *Effective Selling Through Psychology*, Cambridge, Mass: Ballinger.

Carlisle, J. A. and Parker, R. C. (1989) *Beyond Negotiation: Redeeming Customer-Supplier Relationships*, Chichester: Wiley.

Drucker, P. F. (1973) *Management: Tasks, Responsibilities, Practices*, New York: Harper Row.

Kotler, P. (1988) *Marketing Management Analysis, Planning, Implementation and Control*, 6th edn, Englewood Cliffs: Prentice Hall.

Lidstone, J. (1986) *Training Salesmen on the Job*, Aldershot: Gower.

Newton, D. A. (1989) *Sales Force Management: Text and Cases*, 2nd edn, Homewood, Illinois: Irwin.

Rackham, N. (1987) *Making Major Sales*, Aldershot: Gower.

Weitz, B. A. (1981) 'Effectiveness in sales interactions: a contingency framework', *Journal of Marketing* 45, Winter: 85–103.

41

PUBLIC RELATIONS

Roger Haywood

WHAT IS THIS PUBLIC RELATIONS BUSINESS?

Virtually every one of the Fortune 500 and *The Times* Top 1000 companies utilizes formalized public relations in its operations – defined as having a senior executive with public relations responsibilities, according to studies by such bodies as the Public Relations Society of America and the Institute of Public Relations of the UK. Yet this management function barely existed, outside some Western governments and their military forces, before the 1950s.

This chapter explores the role of public relations within organizations – particularly commercial companies, though the principles apply to any body (or individual) with relations with various groups of people. For example, trade unions, charities, government departments and professional bodies all use public relations techniques to improve communications. This section also looks at the inter-relationship of public relations with marketing, finance, human resources and other company operations.

However, it is helpful to appreciate the relatively short history of public relations as a formalized business discipline. For example, it has not always been universally understood. It continues to evolve. It has often been practised with an informal or unstructured approach – in much the same way as marketing was some decades earlier in its development.

All this has been changing. Public relations has been developing its own body of theory and case experience. Both practical and learned books have been published on the craft. Professional bodies have become well established. In the USA public relations has been offered as an academic course in many universities. The same development, though coming from a later start, has been noted in countries such as Australia, Canada, Germany, India, the Netherlands and the UK.

How did public relations achieve such universal acceptance, certainly within sophisticated commercial operations? This was probably part of the growing education of the consumer: this led to the consequent demand for better information; the desire for choice; the need to understand products and services offered; indeed, the desire to approve the organization behind the commercial offer. Public relations became the organized link between the company and its publics. Both marketing and public relations have grown as a result of what could be described as commercial democracy operating in the court of public opinion.

Not corporate 'image' but personality that counts

Public relations helps both to define and project the 'personality' of the organization to the audiences that it depends on for success.

One view of public relations describes the craft as the projection of the personality of the organization. The corporate personality is what the organization is, reflects what it believes in, determines where it is heading. But, above all, the personality can be developed and controlled by the management, to become the central factor in the building of the corporate reputation. Perhaps, the most satisfactory practical description of public relations is that it is the management of corporate reputation.

Just as we can anticipate how someone with a developed and balanced personality will behave, we should be able to predict how high profile corporations will handle themselves.

A useful working definition of public relations is – those efforts used by management to identify and close any gap between how the organization is seen by its key publics and how it would like to be seen.

Of course, there are many other factors that are essential to success, above all, marketing itself. The best public relations will not compensate for weaknesses in production, quality, service or personnel and many other important business areas. Indeed it is likely that an active public relations policy will expose rather than hide such weakness.

The official definition of the craft by the Institute of Public Relations (1994) describes it as the planned and sustained effort to establish and maintain goodwill and mutual understanding between an organization and its publics.

Some definitions of public relations only cover 'mutual understanding'. This is not satisfactory for they focus on the knowledge of the publics but not necessarily their opinions and attitudes. Clearly, information is only part of communications, as communications is only part of public relations. For what the company does is as important as what it says.

Marketing is defined by the Chartered Institute of Marketing (1994) as the management process responsible for identifying, anticipating and satisfying customer requirements profitably. Implicit in this definition is the need to create the best business environment within which these products or services can be sold and supported. It is not unreasonable to extend this to the creation of goodwill between the organization offering the products and services and the purchasers of these – this is the normal situation within an information democracy.

HOW DOES PUBLIC RELATIONS WORK WITHIN THE ORGANIZATION?

Organizations can win the reputation they wish; whatever they do, they will get the one they deserve. Current public relations practitioners do not see themselves as publicists but as custodians of the public reputation of the organizations they represent. Their craft may involve publicity functions but it should also include the responsibility for advising on and helping develop the stance the organization takes towards issues – strategic policymaking. Public relations professionals are concerned with the relations between the organization and the diverse publics (sometimes called audiences) that can affect any aspect of its operations.

If the organization is to win the goodwill and support of those publics upon whom it depends for success, then what it does matters as much as what it says. Its attitude to these publics will shape their attitudes to the organization and its products and services. Therefore, true public relations starts before communications and should be all about company policy – and not just the brands.

This might seem to be true for marketing overall, but it has not always been the case. In Europe, for example, until well into the 1990s, Unilever believed the corporate reputation should be carried almost entirely by the brands. The company felt it could afford to remain virtually anonymous to the public. More recently, as with many major corporations, it has realized that the organization behind the brands is important – marketing presents and develops the brands and their values while, in a sense, the corporate public relations is 'marketing the company'.

This was brought to the forefront by the detergent wars when claims and counterclaims on product performance and damage to clothes as well as worries about dermatological hazards made the public deeply concerned about the corporate philosophies behind those famous brands. A similar shift in public focus towards the men and women in grey suits that ran the corporations happened when IBM ran into trouble; when Pepsi-Cola challenged Coca-Cola; when Ford and General Motors faced major legal challenges over product safety that brought their corporate policies under scrutiny.

MARKETING AND PUBLIC RELATIONS HAVE DIFFERENT RESPONSIBILITIES

'Marketing public relations' can be one of the most powerful and effective influences within the broader craft of marketing. It should work in harmony not only with other marketing communications disciplines such as advertising and sales promotion but with other elements of public relations targeted at those audiences that are not always considered part of the marketing responsibility – for example, employees, shareholders, suppliers, factory neighbours and government.

Is public relations part of marketing, as might be suggested by such phrases as 'public relations and other marketing disciplines'? Yes and no. Yes, because marketing is concerned about relations with important publics such as customers, potential customers, wholesalers, distributors, retailers. No, because marketing is focused on marketing audiences and public relations has the broadest responsibilities across all the activities of the corporation. The exception to this is in those rare companies where marketing is made responsible for all relations with all corporate audiences.

The chairman or the CEO/chief executive are not always happy to delegate relations with groups that they view as their personal responsibility – such as shareholders – to the marketing discipline.

Companies like American Express and Boeing have developed effective methods to ensure the coordination of the public relations and the marketing efforts, while keeping each separate with its own performance and reporting responsibilities. Of particular importance is to ensure that the marketing-support public relations truly supports marketing, while being integrated into the larger public relations programme.

THE QUALITY OF CORPORATE REPUTATION AFFECTS COMMERCIAL SUCCESS

However these responsibilities may be allocated, the success of all business activities – including marketing, sales and, therefore, profit – are dependent on how the company is regarded. Corporate reputation can be the most valuable asset. To quote George Washington, a little out of context: 'With public opinion you can do anything – without it, nothing.'

The principles involved in building good relations with the public the company serves and private relations are the same, believed Lord Forte, founder of the major international hotels, catering and leisure group: 'Reputation and respect can only be built on foundations of honesty and trust. Honesty can conceivably get you into trouble but it remains the best policy. Anything less can destroy in a day what may have taken years to achieve.'

ATTITUDE IS A VITAL FACTOR IN MOST DECISIONS

Attitude is a critical factor in virtually every decision. In business there is an understandable pressure to focus only on the tangible factors that make business sense – for example, is the price competitive; are the working conditions acceptable; will this earn the right return for the shareholders; might the factory neighbours accept this planning application?

Most of the audiences upon which every company depends for business success are not in business with the company. They may have a very different agenda; employees may be looking at security or career options; shareholders comparing investments for their pensions; local politicians seeking a vote-winning business/community alliance.

One aim in many public relations programmes will be to win the hearts and not just the minds of these key audiences. Sometimes managers rely too much on logic and believe all decisions are made on a rational basis alone. The factor they may overlook is that decisions can be influenced by opinions and attitudes. One of the prime functions of public relations is to manage company policies and associated communications to build the regard in which the organization is held.

When Exxon ran a tanker aground in Alaska and failed to react decisively, one of the first measures of the impact was a collapsing share price. Why? This was long before any real damage to the trading position could be calculated. It was simply that the public liked neither pollution nor cynicism.

When British Airways explained to its staff that customers were number one – and trained them in how to make their travellers feel that they were number one – sales soared. Customers liked being treated as if they mattered. In many cases, this approach proved to be more important to flyers than the ticket price.

The attitudes of the key publics to any organization are shaped largely by the attitudes of the organization towards them. It is easy to test such attitudes. Would the public expect Ford knowingly to sell a dangerous vehicle? Or Shell to compromise marine safety by cutting down on crew training, or Dow to put the health of employees at risk through poor environmental health policies? Or Forte deliberately to mislead its shareholders? Positive or negative, the feelings such possibilities arouse indicate an appraisal of these companies' attitudes to the audiences concerned. Public relations should be the central function in presenting corporate attitudes to important publics.

POLICY MUST BE DECIDED – AND SUPPORTED – FROM THE TOP

Public relations is an essential top management responsibility – not an optional extra, nor a mechanical function that can be delegated to administrators.

International businessman, Lord Hanson, built one of the world's largest and most diversified corporations over the course of his career, starting from virtually nothing. Effective public relations was central to this; indeed, many journalists rated him as a great personal practitioner. He has commented that the basis of good public relations, as he saw it, was to do it yourself:

> Do not delegate the key elements. Let advisers set up the procedures – but never let them become the spokesman for your organization. That is the job that senior executives must undertake themselves. Creative people may be able to develop great advertising for you, but this principle should not be applied to public relations. This is essentially a personal skill and a senior responsibility.
>
> (Lord Hanson quoted in Haywood 1994: 7)

Public relations must be a two-way activity – listening to what the public thinks, as well as projecting the organization's messages. It follows that public relations efforts can only be effective where the aims of the organization are compatible with the aims of the public. The concept of the hidden persuader in public relations is nonsense.

Sir Denys Henderson, when chairman of ICI, one of the largest chemical manufacturing companies in the world, oversaw a dramatic reorganization of its operations when the bioscience activities were successfully separated out as Zeneca; this bold move created two distinct and buoyant companies able to concentrate in their different markets. Public relations was an essential element in smoothly and efficiently completing the complex and far-reaching changes that had an impact on all stakeholders in the company. Integrity in communications, he believed, was central as was the basic need to be honest. As Sir Denys Henderson explained:

> The most skilful use of 'smoke and mirrors' can disguise fundamental problems for no more than a limited period. In the end, there must be substance behind the promise – truth will undoubtedly out, regardless of any camouflage efforts by the most expert 'spin doctor'. Management has to accept responsibility not only for the success or otherwise of the message but also for the facts behind it. It is for this reason that I view the professional management of communication as an essential tool for business success.
>
> The ability to communicate key messages, with fluency and integrity, is a vital skill which managers must acquire if they are to succeed in today's complex, ever-changing business world. The audiences to be addressed may well cover employees, customers, shareholders, politicians, local communities and the general public, often, both at home and across the world. The different concerns of each group must be met sensitively. The relevant messages, whether good or bad news, must be communicated with consistency, clarity and honesty. An evasive, inarticulate introvert is unlikely to be successful.
>
> (Sir Denys Henderson quoted in Haywood 1994: 8)

Any failure of the directors to be on top of communications could be most damaging. Should the company experience difficult times, it is likely that shareholders or statutory bodies might become interested in how the public relations aspects of key issues were being considered at board level, as they unfolded.

Critical questions on public relations can have been asked when problems arise; companies that do not review their corporate communications at board level are taking a risk. Yet with proper planning, the review of a responsibly run programme takes little time. Indeed, the fact that the board signs off policy may be one vital element in ensuring that the programme is responsibly run.

When Sir Adrian Cadbury, chairman of the UK Committee on the Financial Aspects of Corporate Governance, was gathering evidence, he confirmed that communications, particularly investor public relations, was an essential and integral element within proper corporate governance, as was well appreciated by the City of London.

When it was subsequently published in 1993, the *Code of Best Practice on the*

Financial Aspects of Corporate Governance specifically required that the board should have a formal schedule of matters for decision to ensure that control of the company was firmly in its hands. This referred, of course, to financial matters where communications were central. In addition, the Code also said that it was the board's duty to present a balanced and understandable assessment of the company's position. Again this focused on financial communications.

Mobil, the US oil and petroleum corporation, ran a very successful word-of-mouth campaign to change public attitudes – supported by some skilful media relations. The CEO and other senior executives projected their philosophies through a planned series of public speeches to key audiences across the USA, often business leaders but also including political and community groups judged to be opinion leaders.

The responsibilities of directors are extending steadily to encompass all aspects of corporate communications. However, few companies have written communications policies and fewer publish these. Such policies can be an invaluable way to help define the responsibilities of the board and senior executives.

COMPANIES GAIN THE SUPPORT THEY DESERVE

The ideal reputation for the organization will not be earned by accident. It will be won through application, direction and commitment. Therefore, managers should ensure that the public relations implications of all company operations are considered in all appropriate policies and plans.

Ideally, the mission statement (or the corporate objectives) will include an appropriate commitment to the development of the corporate reputation. This will also need to be reflected in all business and marketing plans. As an illustration, marketing may be all about satisfying customer needs profitably, but it also has a responsibility to develop and reinforce the reputation of the organization. A suitable statement in the marketing plan about the reputation objective will help avoid the adoption of unacceptable sales techniques or promotional activities – for example, those that may be better for short-term results than they are for the longer term perceptions among those who matter.

Despite fluctuating fortunes, IBM, as an illustration, follows policies that reflect its belief in behaving properly. People relate to such decent values. Being well regarded by the public creates a good reputation. People like to buy from and work for those that have good reputations. Companies that people like to deal with have an advantage over those who are not popular. If IBM products and prices are as good as its promised services and proven values, it will have a competitive edge. Companies with shorter term horizons may risk being more cavalier with customers, but those with long-term aims need the goodwill of those who can make or break them – as IBM proved when they traded through the difficult times.

MAKE THE POLICY SHAPE COMPANY BEHAVIOUR

Many companies are choosing to define and publish their mission. They make a formal commitment against which individual managers and employees can measure their own performance or, indeed, direct their staff, peers or even their bosses when standards appear to be in conflict with some of the points in the mission statement. One of the weaknesses of some corporate mission statements is that companies will tend to write them to be broad enough to cover most eventualities; this means they do not have quite enough focus.

One helpful recommendation might be to start with a general mission statement but to refine it over a period of time. Certainly no company should be publishing the identical mission statement year after year in, for example, the annual report unless they are convinced that this is the definitive version. It can always be improved and the sharper the focus of the mission statement, theoretically, the sharper the focus of the organization. Similarly, corporate aims can be shaped over time to become measurable objectives.

APPRAISAL OF REPUTATION SHOULD BE ON BOARD AGENDA

The only satisfactory reporting method must be for public relations to be a regular and routine board item. Directors should not just be concerning themselves with communications when there is a problem. Perhaps winning a good company reputation is a little like building a good marriage – it requires constant work, through the good times and the bad. When problems strike, it may be too late to apply remedial treatment. Effective relations between the organization and its various publics require constant attention.

It may not be necessary for the board to become involved in the detail but each director must be comfortable that he has a good overview. Public relations strategy might be reviewed once or twice a year with brief progress reports in between. A strategy review paper presented to the board might cover the following areas:

1 *Objectives*. What is to be achieved over the coming period to support the mission statement or corporate objectives? Aims for the communications efforts may be acceptable. However, could these be quantified, to identify a specific point that should be reached over an agreed period of time?
2 *Strategy*. What tone of voice is being adopted to achieve these objectives? Do all the elements support this and how do they combine into an overall plan? Is each activity complementary? Can any be extended to reach broader audiences and improve cost effectiveness?
3 *Perceptions*. How is the company seen? What are the attitudes of those whose goodwill the company needs for success? (Every so often these must be identified by research, but interim reviews should note the observations of public relations, marketing, sales, personnel and other professionals in contact with prime audiences.)

4 *Messages.* How do directors wish the company to be seen? What gaps are there between reality and perception? Is the company communicating in the way that will win support – and behaving in the way that will win support? Are all the communications activities reinforcing these agreed messages?

5 *Tactics.* What communications methods are to be used? How will these relate to other corporate activities? Who is directing and implementing the programme? What are the company contingency plans, proposed to deal with the unexpected?

6 *Initiatives.* Are there special events of which directors should be aware – such as the preview of the new corporate video, the launch of the new sponsorship? Are these on strategy and, if so, how can these be best tied in to the broader company business timetable?

7 *Calendar.* What are the major activities in the corporate calendar that have public relations implications? What are the plans to support these? Is the programme scheduled realistically to coordinate such events with any new communications initiatives?

8 *Concerns.* What issues might the communications professionals wish to discuss? Are there areas of policy where the directors' views and support are essential? Will members of the board be expected to participate in functions? If not, might these be enhanced if they did?

9 *Competition.* Are there public relations activities by competitors that should be discussed? How is their public relations effectiveness, say in the tone of media coverage, in comparison with yours? Is this competitive position improving?

10 *Appraisal.* How effective is the programme overall? What performance criteria are set so that the effectiveness can be appraised and the direction fine tuned? What are the achievements to date, ideally measured against the objectives that were set?

11 *Management.* How is the competence of those charged with managing the function? Do directors have any commendations or concerns that should be voiced? How are consultants or other advisers performing? Any changes that need considering?

12 *Resources.* What is the total cost of the activity proposed – including staff time? Does anything require additional company resources – such as regional seminars, factory open days, wholesaler briefings? How well prepared are the communications team to handle any crisis that may arise?

EFFECTIVE MARKETING DEMANDS EFFECTIVE PUBLIC RELATIONS

Public relations as a marketing support technique is well understood. Indeed, the craft has come of age over recent years. This success has sometimes overshadowed other important areas of influence. For example, public relations is less often seen as a strategic approach to undertaking business – in effect, creating the environment within which the marketing efforts can be most successful.

Major business successes have been built on the strength of effective public relations. Brand awareness and loyalty can be more credibly developed through communications channels. For example, McDonald's identified public relations as central to the business strategy originally developed by the founder of the company, the late Ray Kroc. His policy, continued by the company, was to make a significant commitment to local community relations, consistently year after year, market by market, to build a deep consumer trust in the business. For McDonald's, public relations is not an option. As senior executives have commented, the payback is there for all to see.

Get the corporate projection right and the company will have the business environment in which to thrive with the right products, service, prices and people. Get it wrong and, whatever the quality of the rest, the company may not survive. So, where does public relations fit in and how does it relate to marketing?

A CENTRAL AIM OF MARKETING MUST BE TO BUILD REPUTATION

Public relations is an essential element in the building of goodwill. Any marketing plan that does not consider public relations is likely to be dangerously deficient. One MORI survey confirmed that goodwill towards the company is closely linked to public perceptions of product quality – a central element in marketing. Some 70 per cent of a sample of the general public believed that reputable companies do not sell poor quality products.

Also, shoppers are more likely to try something new from a trusted name. Such an advantage, built through marketing techniques (including relevant public relations and advertising), can be very significant in sales and market share terms.

Other studies have demonstrated the direct relationship between familiarity and high regard. All such evidence confirms the importance of the brands as well as the company behind the brands. The credibility of public relations as a communications technique which tends to be trusted by consumers can be important in the marketing mix – and certainly able to justify its own significant proportion of the spend.

However, does that mean that public relations is part of marketing? Certainly not. Is finance part of personnel? Or production part of sales? However closely they need to relate, each has separate responsibilities. Of course, public relations has a crucial role to play in supporting (and sometimes leading) marketing, but these are different disciplines with distinct responsibilities. The critical decision that management must make is where should public relations report?

USE MARKETING PUBLIC RELATIONS TO BUILD TANGIBLE ASSET VALUE

The goodwill of a company may well be its largest single asset. With consumer goods companies, this goodwill is often represented as the value of the brands. In recent years there has been much debate about whether these should be shown on the balance sheet.

The Accounting Standards Committee in the UK suggested that a brand value should be written off against profits over an agreed period of twenty or more years. Of course, this makes no sense as major brands like Buick, Burberry, Marlboro, Stella Artois or Tide may be of vastly increased value and some of these have been around for fifty or more years. Of course, in some cases it becomes difficult to separate the brand value from the company – particularly where the same name is in use, such as BMW, Campbells, Electrolux, Firestone, Hoover or Olivetti.

Consider the commercial value that brands can have and, therefore, the potential return on the marketing effort that can build those brands. Nestlé bought Rowntree Macintosh for a sum in excess of £2.5 billion in 1988 when the physical assets represented only 20 per cent of this price. The balance was to pay for marketing expertise, distribution capability and the range of brands. In other words, Nestlé were prepared to pay five times as much as the assets to acquire these brands and the mechanics that had been perfected for delivering the brands to the market. Similar deals carried out in the late 1980s valued companies at four or five times the asset value.

SEPARATE MARKETING PROMOTION FROM CORPORATE PROJECTION

Whatever company policy, it is still important that the public relations keeps the brand statements separate from the values of the company. Ideally there should be two public relations programmes, promoting the products and projecting the corporation – separate but coordinated.

The marketing approach to the corporation can put a fresh perspective on the management of this important asset, the company name. Sometimes companies can create a whole aura around an organization. The statement that 'We try harder' was credible and worked hard for Avis around the world.

In the business-to-business sector, European agrochemicals leader Scheering created an interesting example. The company recognized that many of its products were seen as damaging to the environment. Through a skilful mix of public relations, technology, new products, customer service and marketing the company repositioned itself under a theme, Green Science. The result was better credibility, an enhanced reputation and an award for excellence from the Chartered Institute of Marketing in the UK. Even more important Scheering won for itself a stronger commercial competitive position.

INTEGRATE CUSTOMER RELATIONS AND CONSUMER PUBLIC RELATIONS

Good public relations can not only build brand loyalty, it can reinforce customer relations efforts, backing both the salesforce and customer services operations.

In the car rental industry, Hertz built a world brand using marketing and public relations policies that were consistent around the world, even where local management were resistant to global branding. Public relations was used to promote the customer experience.

The thinking was that a Coca-Cola-type brand spelled consistency wherever it was developed. Business travellers and holidaymakers alike were more reassured at the prospect of hiring a car which would be prepared to conform to the same high standard – and provided on comparable terms through identical payment methods. Above all, the customers' relationship with the company would be recognized, even if this was the first time they had visited Manhattan, Madras or Madrid. Local variations may be attractive in food, fashion or shopping but not in car rental.

Avis later fought this challenge through similar harmonizing of operations, plus an appealing, impertinent challenge to the leader – effectively, 'we're number two so we have to try harder'. A decade later number three in the Europe market merged some ten or so operations – one owned by Volkswagen and one by Renault – to form Europcar. Various old brands were dropped, such as Inter-rent and Godfrey Davis. Coordinated public relations, working within a clear marketing framework, across all operating markets helped project the new offer and establish the new brand with customers.

DEVELOP PUBLIC RELATIONS STRENGTHS AS INSURANCE

The best laid marketing plans can sometimes be devastated by factors that are outside the control of marketing management. Confidence in products has been shaken by health, safety or pollution scares which often attract wide news coverage. A couple of angry shareholders at an annual general meeting have been known to attract more attention than the announcement of a massive new production facility. A few neighbours have been influential in stopping planning permission for extensions to factories.

Public relations for the company, its values and aims will be important, but this will be most effective if it is consistent with the messages projected through marketing.

An historical problem with mercury pollution at one site created poor local media coverage for international chemical giant, Rhône-Poulenc. Under an enlightened management, the company developed possibly some of the finest environmental policies in the industry and called in professional public relations resources to improve community relations. These joint initiatives were so successful that, with the full cooperation of local communities, the company has

733

since invested over £50 million on that site in new research and manufacturing facilities. Community relations was essential to enable the products to be properly marketed; a poor community reputation is equally damaging to sales.

A chicken production facility jointly owned by a leading feed company and a large retailer had such a smell problem that local residents successfully blocked planning permissions for extensions which would have created many new jobs. The problems could not be solved by technical improvements alone. The goodwill and support of the local people had to be won through a public relations programme to show the company listened and acted vigorously to end the nuisance and become a good neighbour.

Cargill corn milling plants have been threatened with closure through complaints from neighbours over smells. When Union Carbide suffered the tragic accident at Bhopal in India, planning permissions for many factory developments at locations around the world were blocked, even where the processes were unrelated to the chemicals involved in the Bhopal incident. With both companies, technical improvements were successfully introduced in parallel with effective communications to win community support.

In all these cases the product marketing could not solve the problem and sales were threatened by issues remote from the normal responsibilities of the marketing function.

CONSIDER LEADING MARKETING COMMUNICATIONS WITH PUBLIC RELATIONS

Some marketing campaigns will be led by advertising. Everyday products of limited news value and which are frequently bought may need the strength of advertising to lift them above competition, stress their special features and benefits, remind the purchaser of their brand values. Examples might include soft drinks, coffee and most grocery products. Public relations may be used in support to reach both trade and consumer audiences. Coca-Cola has an active involvement in soccer, for example.

Yet many products and services can best be supported with public relations, with this discipline taking the lead. This will be particularly relevant where the product or service has a broad interest because it is new or affects the quality of our lives, for example.

Philips, the Netherlands-based electronics company, used public relations to launch a sophisticated energy management system for business premises. The Canadian mushroom industry developed a public relations approach into which the advertising was designed to fit. First Direct, Europe's first telephone home banking service established its position of strength almost entirely through public relations.

Marketing professionals will be making the decisions on which discipline will play which role. However, a useful exercise is to ensure that the advertising, sales, promotion and public relations professionals identify the balance and the priorities for each craft. Of course, advertising and public relations should not be viewed as competitive but should be run as complementary, reinforcing communications techniques. Therefore, liaison between the advertising and public relations must be close and effective.

ENSURE THAT PUBLIC RELATIONS AND ADVERTISING WORK TOGETHER

Coordination will only be possible if marketing management brings the advertising and public relations people together and establishes mutual understanding and trust. It is essential to get all elements in the marketing mix working together. This puts a special onus on the client for there are usually quite powerful personalities at work heading up the advertising agency, public relations consultancy, marketing, research house design company, sales promotion specialists and so on. The loudest or most powerful should not dominate the others.

Once the budgets have been agreed, there should be no competition for expenditure between advertising and public relations. The effective coordination of advertising and public relations could be assisted by following these ten simple suggestions:

1 Involve both disciplines in the marketing planning.
2 Define complementary public relations and advertising objectives.
3 Allocate separate and firm budgets to each.
4 Agree responsibilities and planned activities.
5 Establish practical routines for coordination.
6 Have regular joint liaison sessions.
7 Get public relations/advertising to present their campaigns to each other.
8 Arrange for them to make a joint presentation to the organization's management.
9 Ensure regular exchange of all documents/information.
10 Insist that all parties work together this year – or they might not get the chance next.

GOOD PUBLIC RELATIONS CREATES THE RIGHT BUSINESS ENVIRONMENT

Public relations alone cannot win orders, generate profit or reduce costs. However, used skilfully, public relations can substantially enhance the effectiveness of marketing, helping to develop the goodwill of the key corporate audiences. In essence, along with other communications disciplines, it can create the business environment within which the marketing offer can be presented.

To paraphrase the famous McGraw-Hill advertisement: I know your company, you have a good reputation, your products and services are well regarded. What is the proposition you wish to put to me?

FURTHER READING

Bell, Quentin (1991) *The PR Business*, London: Kogan Page.

Bernstein, David (1986) *Company Image and Reality: A Critique of Corporate Communications*, London: Cassell.

Bing, Richard and Bowman, Pat (1993) *Financial Public Relations*, 2nd edn, Sevenoaks: Butterworth Heinemann.

Black, Sam (1989) *Introduction to Public Relations*, London: Modino.

Black, Sam (1989) *Exhibitions and Conferences from A to Z*, London: Modino.

Bowman, P. (1989) *Handbook of Financial Public Relations*, Sevenoaks: Butterworth Heinemann.

Cadbury, Sir Adrian (ed.) (1993) *Code of Best Practice on the Financial Aspects of Corporate Governance*, London: Gee & Co.

Connelly, John (1992) *Dealing with Whitehall*, London: Century Business.

Ellis, N. (1988) *Parliamentary Lobbying*, Oxford: Heinemann.

Haywood, Roger (1991) *All About Public Relations*, 3rd edn, Maidenhead: McGraw-Hill.

Haywood, Roger (1994) *Managing Your Reputation*, Maidenhead: McGraw-Hill.

Howard, Wilfred (ed.) *The Practice of Public Relations*, 3rd edn, Sevenoaks: Butterworth Heinemann.

Institute of Public Relations (1994) *Professionalism in Practice*, London: Institute of Public Relations.

Jefkins, Frank (1992) *Public Relations*, 4th edn, London: Pitman.

Olins, Wally (1990) *The Corporate Identity*, London: Thames and Hudson.

Patterson, B. (1992) *Lobbying: an Introduction*.

Phillips, David (1992) *Evaluating Press Coverage*, London: Kogan Page.

Ross, Dina (1990) *Surviving the Media Jungle*, London: Pitman.

Stone, Norman (1991) *How to Manage Public Relations*, Maidenhead: McGraw-Hill.

White, Jon (1991) *How to Understand and Manage Public Relations*, London: Century Business.

42

EXHIBITIONS

Gillian Rice

TYPES OF EXHIBITIONS

Exhibitions are important arenas where marketing opportunities occur. An exhibition is defined as:

> a facilitating marketing event in the form of an exposition, fair, exhibition or mart . . . whose primary objective is to disseminate information about, and display the goods and services of competing and complementary sellers who have rented specifically allocated and demarcated areas or 'booths', clustered within a particular building(s), or bounded grounds; and whose audience is a selected concentration of customers, potential buyers, decision influencers, and middlemen.
>
> (Banting and Blenkhorn 1974)

Exhibitions, expositions, trade fairs or trade shows (all terms are used interchangeably) are a form of direct marketing. Most exhibitions are regularly occurring events lasting between one day and several weeks. A particular industry's trade show often brings together most of that industry's buyers and buying influences under one roof for the express purpose of shopping. There are also permanent exhibits or marts. Here, potential customers and distributors can view new displays at any time or make appointments with an exhibitor. Examples are the Merchandise Mart in Chicago which displays household and office furniture and the InfoMart in Dallas which focuses on computer and communication equipment.

There are several types of exhibition which need to be evaluated by the prospective user. Exhibitions can be classified according to geographical reach, market coverage and whether or not they are consumer or trade oriented.

GEOGRAPHICAL REACH

Exhibitions are held at the local, regional, national and international levels. Local exhibitions are relatively small-scale events intended to attract participants from the immediate vicinity. Some local events are mobile exhibitions that

737

firms organize to travel around the country. The participants (usually pre-selected and invited) are from an immediate local area for each stop of the mobile exhibit. Regional exhibitions are often regional offshoots of national shows and are defined in the USA as drawing a minimum of 40 per cent of their attendance from within 200 miles of the show site. Examples are the Nepcon shows. Nepcon West, one of the largest of the electronic component shows occurs several times a year in different geographic regions of the USA. The Machine Tool Builders Association also sponsors a series of regional exhibitions each year. International exhibitions such as the Frankfurt Book Fair and the Paris Air Show have as their exhibitors and visitors firms from many countries. The American Textile Machinery Association operates two shows worldwide: the European show is held every four years in different cities and the US show is held every two years in Greensville, South Carolina.

Historically, exhibitions have been a major marketing medium for the dominant exporting countries. Germany, for example, has utilized international trade fairs to build its position as one of the world's leading exporters. More than half the world's major exhibitions are held in Europe. Brussels, Barcelona and the National Exhibition Centre in Birmingham, England, which are medium-sized European exhibition sites, have larger international audiences and exhibitors than even the largest American centres.

MARKET COVERAGE

There are both specialized (vertical) shows and shows which have broad appeal (horizontal shows). Vertical shows promote a single or related industry category to a specialized professional clientele, sometimes by invitation only. Examples are the fire prevention equipment fair in Ostrava and Interpack, the world's largest packaging exhibition. There are many examples of vertical shows serving the computer, information handling and communications industries: computer shows for the medical industry, for the legal profession, for the financial community and so on. Trade fairs have become increasingly specialized and certain centres have achieved international status as the focal point of a particular industry.

In contrast to vertical shows, 'horizontal' shows have many product categories with broad appeal. Examples include trade fairs held in Hannover and Milan. The annual Hannover Fair attracts about half a million visitors and over five thousand exhibitors from more than forty nations. Other fairs which are not restricted to particular industry categories include the Poznan International Fair in Poland, the Bucharest International Fair and the Cairo International Fair.

CUSTOMER ORIENTATION

Some exhibitions are intended for business customers (manufacturers, whole-salers, retailers) whereas others are consumer exhibitions open to the general public. The latter often feature products and services associated with specific themes or activities. Manufacturers and retailers showcase their newest merchandise to consumers by creatively displaying products in booths designed to inform and persuade (Barczak *et al.* 1992). Most medium and large cities offer an array of highly targeted consumer events such as camping shows, pet shows and home improvement shows. As well as these vertical shows, there are horizontal consumer shows such as the annual Canadian National Exhibition in Toronto.

ROLE OF EXHIBITIONS IN MARKETING STRATEGY

Exhibitions are used in various aspects of marketing strategy. They have three major roles: selling, relationship building and marketing research.

Selling

Exhibition activities related directly to selling include identifying new prospects, selling to new and current customers, servicing current customers at the show as well as developing exhibition-related strategies that will encourage follow-up sales after the show. A visit to a booth by a prospect is comparable to a sales call. Yet an exhibition has the following advantages for selling products and services (Dudley 1991):

1   Sales staff meet a large number of customers in a short time
2   These customers are in a buying frame of mind.
3   It is a cost-effective way of meeting a large number of responsive buyers.

Relationship building

Exhibitions are events where firms can develop a network, maintain relationships and establish a presence in the market. At international shows firms can find local agents, distributors and joint venture partners. In some market contexts it is also important to meet with government officials. Trade shows are microcosms of the industries they represent, with a multitude of buyers and sellers, service providers, partners, industry and regulatory bodies all gathered in one place to do business so that for the duration of the show, the show almost becomes the market (Rosson and Seringhaus 1995). Trade shows are therefore ideal places to network with others in the industry.

Market research

Like relationship building, marketing research is an activity indirectly related to selling. At exhibitions firms can learn about the latest technologies. Through observation, surveys and focus groups conducted during the show, information can be gathered about competitors, distributors, existing customers and potential customers. A firm can build a mailing list, test new products and find new applications for existing products.

EXHIBITIONS AS COMMUNICATION TOOLS

The first two roles of selling and relationship building are ways of communicating with customers. A firm's complete marketing communications programme consists of advertising, personal selling, public relations and sales promotion. Dudley (1991) explains how exhibitions share common attributes with each of these programme components. As an advertising tool, exhibiting uses specific media (shows) to convey messages to target audiences. Exhibiting has the added advantage of being a form of direct marketing and can generate an immediate response from the audience. As a sales promotion tool, exhibiting is versatile and provides excitement and urgency. Exhibiting is also often exploited as a public relations activity to enhance corporate image.

Trade shows efficiently deliver integrated messages about products and services because the exhibition format utilizes a variety of coordinated personal and non-personal information sources (Barczak et al. 1992). Personal sources are staff members in the booth, special show events like seminars and receptions, and live demonstrations. The trade show environment is action oriented, ideal for demonstrations by exhibitors. Seeing products in action attracts the attention of show visitors and spurs them to ask questions. Providing visitors with hands-on experiences of product usage enhances their learning and the probability of them remembering the exhibit. Non-personal information sources include booth signage and pictures, product displays and samples, film and videos, and sales literature.

IMPORTANCE OF EXHIBITIONS FOR DIFFERENT TYPES OF FIRMS

The relative importance of exhibitions as a marketing tool differs for different types of firms. Research by Lilien (1983) and Faria and Dickinson (1986) shows that exhibitions are of greatest importance to firms with the following characteristics: relatively high amount of sales and market share; a moderate number of product lines, selling through middlemen; and technically complex products for which many people are involved in the purchase. Consumer product manufacturers that sell to retailers participate in shows because of the large and geographically dispersed audience they must reach. However, industrial firms tend to have high field expense ratios and generally allocate proportionately more funds to trade shows than do consumer goods firms (Browning and Adams 1988). Trade shows are especially important in industrial markets because the products are often more complex and have high purchase value. These characteristics contribute to high levels of perceived risk and investment. Also, it is common that firms use flexible and modular manufacturing strategies, constantly update products, and tailor them to customer demands. Trade shows are useful in helping managers to position their products and learn more about customers' delivery, service and price criteria. In particular, a firm can reach specifiers and influencers in the decision process who are not regularly seen by the salesforce.

EXHIBITIONS AS A TOOL FOR EXPORTING

The efficiency of exhibitions in delivering a high quality target audience is particularly important in an overseas context where it is even more expensive to communicate with a customer or a potential customer and where other forms of promotion may be restricted. Participation in trade shows is likely to vary according to the firm's commitment to international business. For example, a passive exporter may take advantage of unsolicited orders obtained from overseas buyers attending shows in the exporter's country. Active exporters will travel to participate in trade shows in foreign countries, in search of potential customers and to learn about competition on a global scale. Research suggests that the impact of attending trade shows overseas may be greater for new exporters. After trade fair participation 60 per cent of new exporters and 42 per cent of experienced exporters increased their marketing efforts (Rosson and Seringhaus 1991).

DEVELOPING AN EXHIBITION STRATEGY

When carefully planned, exhibitions can be one of the most cost-effective components of the marketing programme. Developing an exhibition strategy involves setting objectives, choosing an exhibition, setting a budget, pre-show activity, booth design and location, staffing, special in-booth promotions and specific activities for attracting and holding the attention of visitors, post-show activity, and evaluation of the strategy's effectiveness. The following highlights certain aspects of strategy development.

Setting objectives

Objectives need to be targeted and measurable and should be put in the context of the firm's overall marketing strategy. These written objectives should be used to define the exhibition strategy.

Managers should segment the market according to the requirements of customers and be adaptable to these varying needs when developing strategy. Selling and relationship building strategies for different customer segments (potential customers, new customers and established customers) can be planned in advance. For example, the objectives and strategy pursued with respect to

741

potential customers may be quite different from the objectives sought when furthering relationships with long-term customers.

Selecting an exhibition

For the choice of an exhibition, decisions include geographic location (local, regional, national, international) and market coverage (horizontal or vertical) as well as customer orientation. A good decision requires knowledge of market targets and understanding of the special features, benefits, costs and opportunities at particular shows. The decision needs to be made at least a year in advance in order to accomplish the necessary arrangements.

Exhibition audiences tend to be heterogeneous at large-scale horizontal and international events. Research studies imply that firms that participate in vertical shows are more successful and are more satisfied with their performance (Gopalakrishna and Williams 1992; Kerin and Cron 1987). Because a vertical show attracts visitors from a specific industry, almost all visitors can be potential leads. In contrast, a horizontal show, like Comdex in the USA, attracts visitors from several industries having an interest in computer technology and equipment. Exhibits are thus more likely to attract a larger number of 'window shoppers' rather than serious potential leads.

Managers should make decisions concerning government or industry association assistance, that is, whether to participate in the show by having a booth or being part of a sponsored pavilion. This decision will depend on the firm's resources and prior trade show experience. Governments and business organizations, like trade associations, promote trade shows extensively. All twelve developed countries in a study by Seringhaus (1987) offered trade fair programmes as part of their export promotion programmes. For example, the US Department of Commerce promotes American firms' attendance at overseas trade shows. In addition, state, county and municipal authorities also help firms to attend international fairs and often organize group exhibits. Governmental assistance to firms participating in trade shows can ease the burden facing many new or expanding exporters by helping them to overcome operational and resource-based barriers to exporting (Rosson and Seringhaus 1991). For example, at the huge international fair at Nuremburg, as well as other overseas shows, many British toy firms go under the auspices of a joint venture scheme between the British Toy and Hobby Manufacturers' Association (BTHMA) and the British Overseas Trade Board.

Trade shows have their own promotional organizations. For example, at all Hannover fairs, US pavilions (which include booths for many US exhibitors) are organized and managed by Hannover Fairs USA, the marketing and communications office for Hannover fairs. The office provides exhibitors with extensive assistance, including training workshops and promotional activities (Tesar 1988).

742

Staffing the booth

It is often the quality of the staff that determines the success or failure of a trade show exhibit. Salespeople working the booth must establish personal contact with visitors and screen out 'casual' visitors so as to generate good leads. Body language and dialogue as well as knowledge are important to a salesperson's success (Wiesendanger 1990).

Bello (1989) found that personal in-exhibit sources are a much more utilized source of information than are personal out-of-exhibit and non-personal sources. His research also suggested that show audience members were more interested in gaining technical information than in getting transactional information. Studies by the Trade Show Bureau in the USA emphasize that the salesperson's knowledge is most often the critical issue of importance for visitors. A survey of computer industry decision-makers revealed that at trade shows they prefer to speak to technical and engineering personnel (Gibson 1991). This preference is particularly strong when the primary interest of visitors is to learn about new products or when complex products are involved. In order to be effective, a booth must be staffed by personnel trained to deliver the firm's technical message.

The location of the exhibition also has an impact on staffing. For cultural reasons, use of female executives may be unwise in some situations. In shows outside of the USA it is often the norm for top managers to participate in the show, in contrast to the American practice of having middle managers at the booth. A European multinational firm is likely to have the heads of its own foreign subsidiaries in the USA, Asia, or South America on hand to speak directly to potential buyers coming from their parts of the world. The intercultural, interpersonal contact that upper-level managerial peers form at trade fairs can have implications for long-term business relationships. Since trade shows are especially important to the marketing strategies of European firms, the calibre of a firm's staffing as well as of its display, reflects its position in the industry. Firms that are not represented, or appear in limited capacity, risk losing market share. In the USA, while it has not been traditional to send upper-level management to trade shows, a survey of 100 chief executive officers from 500 major US corporations found that 82 per cent had visited at least one company exhibit in 1989 (Konopacki 1990).

Pre-exhibition activity

This includes public relations activity as well as identifying prospects in advance and sending them special invitations. Such an invitation can be the most influential factor in a prospect's decision to attend the exhibition.

743

Special in-booth promotions

For subsequent interaction between visitors and booth personnel to be successful, that is resulting in qualified sales leads, certain information must be gathered by both suppliers and customers at the show. Relationship development is a dynamic process and opportunities for follow-up by the exhibitor are crucial. The busy, complex nature of the exhibition environment may necessitate special strategies to ensure the information is obtained. For example, Everett (1989) described how one company offered a customized monogrammed pen to everyone who completed a detailed questionnaire about projected product requirements. Delivery of the pen occurred after two weeks. If the questionnaire revealed that the person was 'qualified', delivery of the pen was done by a company salesperson, thus giving the company an additional contact with a potential customer. Non-qualified visitors received their pens by mail.

Trade show participation is too expensive to be left to the formal exhibit alone. The real value of shows often lies in 'behind the scenes' negotiations. The atmosphere at European shows is designed to encourage people to spend significant amounts of time in the booths they visit, thus lengthening interactions. Most stands (the European term for booths) have their own seminar rooms, conference rooms and lounges; drinks, snacks and even entire meals may be served to visitors.

Seminars and lectures arranged by a firm at a trade show can enhance the relationship development process between suppliers and customers. Many potential benefits hinge on a company's ability to develop a strong relationship with customers in the course of educating them. At the CeBIT fair in Hannover, the world's leading fair for office, information and telecommunications technology, lectures have two purposes: as a forum for the exchange of information between professionals and as a vehicle for the presentation of product information aimed at a particular target group, such as systems packages for lawyers, architects and retailers.

Post-show activity

Information collected at an exhibition should be consolidated into the exhibiting firm's marketing information system. Leads uncovered must be pursued while the exhibit and any exhibition discussions are still fresh in the visitor's mind.

Evaluating exhibitions

There is a lack of useful and meaningful measures of the effectiveness of trade show performance. Often, managers cannot easily identify the return on their investment nor can they relate performance to their specific trade show objectives.

Exhibitors' purposes vary and therefore firms use different evaluation techniques. There is probably no single criterion against which the effectiveness of all kinds of exhibitions can be measured precisely, because exhibitions are not homogeneous with respect to objectives and strategies. Another complicating factor is that some objectives for participation are qualitative and some are quantitative. Bonoma (1983) has thus described trade shows as an inherently 'sloppy' marketing problem.

To aid exhibitors in show evaluation, exhibition organizers provide statistical information on show attendance. In the USA the Business Publications Audit of Circulation Inc. audits registered attendance at trade shows. It provides detailed statistical information which enables measures such as 'audience quality', 'audience activity', and 'exhibit effectiveness' to be calculated. Exhibit effectiveness includes the total number of visitors attracted by a display and the cost per visitor reached (Bellizi and Lipps 1984). Research is also conducted by the exhibition industry itself on various shows and on the memorability of individual exhibits.

Research studies on exhibition effectiveness suggest ways to proceed for the evaluation task. For example, Kerin and Cron (1987) used subjective measures of managers' satisfaction with exhibition performance. Gopalakrishna and Williams (1992) focused on an objective measure, that is the generation of leads at the show (in particular, lead efficiency), as a basis to assess trade show performance. It is important to recognize, however, that generating leads is not the ultimate objective of most firms' participation in exhibitions; rather the conversion of leads into profitable sales is what counts. As the authors emphasize, evaluating exhibition effectiveness is further complicated by the fact that sales are not necessarily a direct consequence of the show alone. To improve evaluation of trade show sales, therefore, a good lead tracking system is essential.

Furthermore, Rosson and Seringhaus (1991) note that exhibiting has results which cannot be captured solely through leads and sales measures. These results include a learning experience which influences a firm's future marketing efforts. They demonstrate both subjective and objective measures of exhibition effectiveness. These include sales (achieved on site, within twelve months and committed future sales) as well as the extent to which an exhibition helped a firm to achieve its stated objective. The extended period for measurement of sales is particularly appropriate for situations in which buyers and sellers interact over a period of time. Although results can occur quickly, they are more likely to occur after some extended time. The majority of sales may occur not at the show but several months after exhibiting. The trade show environment itself, lasts for only a short time.

CURRENT ISSUES AND POTENTIAL FUTURE DEVELOPMENTS

The most prominent issues in the further development of exhibitions as a valuable element of marketing strategy concern the difficulties of evaluating exhibitions, the impact of technological change and globalization on exhibitions and the need for more information about the worth of exhibitions.

Evaluation difficulties

While exhibitions are believed to be cost effective and have many marketing communications benefits, there is an important issue yet to be resolved by industry specialists, managers or researchers. This issue concerns the method of measuring the effectiveness of an exhibition. As participation costs for exhibitions increase, this issue gains in importance. The emphasis on effectiveness measures such as the number of leads/contacts made, cost per lead/contact, amount of literature distributed and sales achieved suggests that most managers view trade shows as merely an extension of personal selling done in mass fashion (Bonoma 1983). Instead, the evaluation of exhibitions should acknowledge their additional roles as tools for relationship building and marketing research.

Impact of technological change

Technologies such as video and computers have for some considerable time enhanced presentations and product demonstrations at exhibitions. Questions can be raised concerning the impact on exhibitions of the merging of technologies along with the continuing development of the information industry. For example, what changes will occur in:

1 The decision to use exhibitions rather than some other communications media?
2 How exhibitions will be used (booth design, activities at the exhibition and so on) in response to developments in technologies such as telecommunications, robotics and virtual reality?

Impact of globalization

Along with the increasing globalization of business in general, globalization of the exhibition business is expected to continue. National shows are more likely to be international events, attended by exhibitors and customers from around the world.

The 1980s was a period of extensive growth in the exhibition business. This growth occurred in terms of the number of exhibitions held in the USA, the Far East, Asia, Africa and Latin America. China and Singapore, in particular, saw substantial growth in their exhibition industries during the period. International exhibitions are important to developing countries where such events are viewed as valuable economic development tools.

Economic reforms in Eastern Europe spawned a proliferation of smaller, provincial fairs in outlying cities to supplement the well-known international trade fairs. Leipzig was traditionally a significant centre for East–West trade. It is now one of the exhibition centres in unified Germany and is attempting to strengthen its competitiveness by offering a series of specialized fairs, focusing on industries such as construction and tourism.

Wherever exhibitions are located, they are used by participating firms in the same way for the same purpose. Yet logistical issues and the idiosyncrasies of individual markets and regions necessitate special attention to international exhibitions (Dudley 1991). For example, at the huge shows in Europe, higher level personnel are involved and many visitors arrive at shows ready to order products. European firms also allocate a significantly greater percentage of their annual marketing budgets to trade shows than do American firms (Schafer 1987).

The environment of international shows is different; since these are attended by exhibitors and visitors from many countries, opportunities exist for social interaction to take place in a multicultural environment. With respect to purchasing behaviour (by consumers or businesses), culture makes a difference in problem identification, in the objectives motivating choice and in negotiation of terms. At an exhibition, understanding different cultures and the likely purchasing strategies of the various visitors to a booth is essential for success. Staffing should include salespeople responsible for territories from the countries of the foreign buyers attending the exhibition. Language capabilities of staff are important, as well as having literature and audio-visual displays in appropriate languages.

Need for information

There is a dearth of impartial and publicly available information on how firms manage the exhibiting process and how this process might be improved. Many studies have been conducted by industry specialists working for organizations like the Trade Show Bureau and the International Exhibitors Association, but these bodies are in the business of promoting the exhibition industry. As an area of academic research, exhibitions suffer from a distinct lack of attention, even though the importance of exhibiting is widely acknowledged. The emphasis in the 1990s on networks and relationship marketing is encouraging more study of exhibitions and their role in firms' marketing strategies.

REFERENCES

Banting, P. M. and Blenkhorn, D. L. (1974) 'The role of industrial trade shows', *Industrial Marketing Management* 3: 285–95.
Barczak, G. J., Bello, D. C. and Wallace, E. S. (1992) 'The role of consumer shows in new product adoption', *The Journal of Consumer Marketing* 9 (2): 55–67.
Bellizi, Joseph A. and Lipps, Delilah J. (1984) 'Managerial guidelines for trade show effectiveness', *Industrial Marketing Management* 13: 49–52.

Bello, D. C. (1989) 'Buyer-based management of a major promotion medium: trade shows', in P. Bloom *et al.* (eds) *AMA Educators' Proceedings Enhancing Knowledge Development in Marketing*, Chicago: American Marketing Association.
Bello, D. C. and Barksdale, H. C. (1986) 'Exporting at industrial trade shows', *Industrial Marketing Management* 15: 97–206.
Bonoma, T. V. (1983) 'Get more out of your trade shows', *Harvard Business Review*, January–February: 75–83.
Browning, J. M. and Adams, R. J. (1988) 'Trade shows: an effective promotional tool for the small industrial business', *Journal of Small Business Management*, October: 31–6.
Dudley, J. W. (1991) *Successful Exhibiting*, Holbrook, MA: Bob Adams, Inc.
Everett, M. (1989) 'Using a carrot to qualify your prospects', *Sales & Marketing Management*, June: 91.
Faria, A. J. and Dickinson, J. R. (1986) 'What kinds of companies use trade shows most – and why', *Business Marketing*, June: 150–5.
Gibson, M. M. (1991) 'Who do you want to talk to in a trade show booth?' *Business Marketing*, February: T8.
Gopalakrishna, S. and Williams, J. D. (1992) 'Planning and performance assessment of industrial trade shows: an exploratory study', *International Journal of Research in Marketing* 9: 207–24.
Kerin, R. and Cron, W. L. (1987) 'Assessing trade show functions and performance: an exploratory study', *Journal of Marketing* 51: 87–94.
Konopacki, A. (1990) 'CEOs attend trade shows to grab "power buyers"', *Marketing News*, 15 October: 5–18.
Lilien, G. (1983) 'A descriptive model of the trade-show budgeting decision process', *Industrial Marketing Management* 12: 25–9.
Rosson, P.J. and Seringhaus, F. H. R. (1991) 'International trade fairs: firms and government exhibits', in F. H. R. Seringhaus and P. J. Rosson (eds) *Export Development and Promotion: The Role of Public Organizations*, Boston: Kluwer Academic Publishers.
Rosson, P. J. and Seringhaus, F. H. R. (1995) 'Visitor and exhibitor interaction at industrial trade fairs', *Journal of Business Research* 32: 81–90.
Schafer, J. (1987) 'German trade fairs open foreign markets for US products', *Marketing News*, 8 May: 13.
Seringhaus, F. H. R. (1987) 'Export promotion: the role and impact of government services', *Irish Marketing Review* 2, Spring: 106–16.
Seringhaus, F. H. R. and Rosson, P. J. (1994) 'International trade fairs and foreign market involvement: review and research directions', *International Business Review* 3 (1).
Tesar, J. (1988) *Trade Shows: Opportunities to Sell. A Case Study of Hannover Fair CeBIT*, Denver: Trade Show Bureau.
Wiesendanger, B. (1990) 'Are your salespeople trade show duds?' *Sales & Marketing Management*, August: 40–6.

FURTHER READING

Bello, D. C. and Barczak, G. J. (1990) 'Using industrial trade shows to improve new product development', *The Journal of Business and Industrial Marketing* 5 (2): 43–56.
Exhibitions Round the World 1992–3 (1992) Dallas, TX: Trade Winds, Inc.
Motwani, J., Rice, G. and Mahmoud, E. (1992) 'International trade shows as export promotion tools: macro and micro perspectives', *Review of Business* 13 (4): 38–42.
Rice, G. (1992) 'Using the interaction approach to understand international trade shows', *International Marketing Review* 9 (4): 32–45.

Tradeshow Week Data Book International Edition (1993) New Providence, NJ: R.R. Bowker.

Webster, V. J. (1993) *Trade Shows Worldwide*, 7th edn, Detroit, MI: Gale Research, Inc.

43

CUSTOMER CARE AND SATISFACTION

David Carson

INTRODUCTION

Customer care and satisfaction are often overused and abused terms in marketing. Many aspects of marketing activity appear to give priority to the philosophy of customer care and satisfaction but in fact often pay little more than lip-service to it. Why should customer care and satisfaction have such high profiles and why should there be such an apparent deficiency in performing to promises and achieving expectations? In answering these questions it is useful to consider customer care and satisfaction in the broader context of marketing as a whole.

Marketing can be considered as having a fundamental philosophy which is based around the customer/consumer – indeed this philosophy is the essence of marketing. In meeting the requirements of the customer the management of marketing activity must be organized in such a way that it is customer oriented as well as organizationally efficient. On the bases of these two concepts, a customer-oriented philosophy and efficient management organization, marketing activity itself will be performed.

This chapter will consider the scope and nature, body of knowledge, and current issues and future development of customer care and satisfaction in relation to its origins; the organization and management of marketing activity, and the relevant aspects of marketing activity. The chapter will conclude with a comment about future development in customer care, by describing a fully integrated concept of customer care based on contemporary marketing management thought.

ORIGINS

Customer care and satisfaction have their foundations in the fundamental concepts of marketing. As already stated, the philosophy of marketing is essentially that of customer orientation. The evolution of this philosophy can be traced over many years and is well documented as beginning with a production oriented era, which gave way to a sales oriented era which in turn led to the marketing oriented era of more recent times.

This marketing orientation puts the customer at the core of thinking and activity. In many organizations the philosophy is manifested in terms such as: 'everything an organization does is with the customer in mind'; 'the customer is the focus of everything we do'; 'what the customer wants is paramount'. In striving to achieve this philosophy marketing practitioners seek to satisfy every whim of their customers. Indeed, some writers suggest that many companies have developed a 'marketing mania' whereby they have become obsessively responsive to such customer whims.

Today more enlightened companies encompass the philosophy of marketing orientation by concentrating on 'looking after' their customers and 'maximizing' their satisfaction. Thus it is easy to see the essential foundation of a sub-philosophy centred around the concepts of customer care and satisfaction.

The origins of customer care and satisfaction stem from attempts by marketers to enhance the dimensions of after sales service. Originally, after sales service was provided primarily, if not solely, as a necessity to support certain products. These were products that required regular maintenance or occasional repair. This after sales service was largely seen as a necessary and integral part of the product itself. Companies did not sell certain types of machinery or equipment without the recognition that such products automatically required servicing. Similarly, the sale of spare parts and process equipment often came under the umbrella of after sales service.

As marketing decision-makers became increasingly aware of the advantages of providing good after sales service, so the concept of incorporating such service into the total product package began. In order to gain maximum impact from such incorporation this concept was marketed as 'added value'. That is, the product benefited from the added value of a range of things over and above after sales service. Also, since added value could literally mean add-ons to 'basic' products, the concept of added value spread to a wide range of products and marketing variables in a variety of marketing circumstances. In the early stages of the development of this concept the enhancement of a product through added value was viewed as providing something beyond the minimum or standard version of a product. Later this was to lead to the concept of 'core' and 'peripheral' dimension of customer care. An additional benefit provided by added value, from a company perspective, was the enhancement of brand image.

The advantages to be gained from providing and marketing added value products soon led to marketers incorporating the total package into a fully integrated sales programme. Such programmes offered a multiplicity of variations for product purchase.

Of course, most of this development of after sales service towards customer service, and thereby greater customer satisfaction, did not occur in isolation from market changes and trends. Throughout this development the marketing environment was subjected to increased competitive activity. Such competition occurred because of a variety of factors. From a consumer perspective there was a general increase in demand stoked by greater affluence and higher disposable income. Such affluence required greater variety and choice and as consumers became more confident in making discernible decisions, consumer sophistication demanded more custom-made variations to products.

In responding to these consumer requirements marketers were in effect behaving in the enlightened way of the marketing orientated firm. Thus began the emergence of the customer-led firm which placed an emphasis on customer care and satisfaction rather than simply perfecting a stand-alone product for sale. There is a general recognition that consumers who are striving for satisfaction do not simply look for the end product or service but also draw satisfaction from the completeness of the service interaction and transaction.

An obvious area of development of customer care has been in the arena of services. Because of the intangible characteristics of services it is obvious that aspects of customer care that focus on these will greatly enhance the impact of a service. A similar circumstance prevails with the widening of the marketing concept beyond the confines of commercial transaction and into non-profit sectors.

Currently, much of the development of customer care activity is closely linked with improvements in 'quality', both throughout an organization and also in terms of the total marketing package across all of an organization's marketing variables.

Today the guiding concept of customer care and satisfaction, indeed of marketing, is 'value', incorporating the ideal product in the ideal use – that is, a 'complete' product in use.

The importance of customer care and satisfaction is underlined by the fact that most major texts in marketing now contain chapters specifically on the topic, or at least frequent references to the concepts in relation to customer service, consumer behaviour and aspects of marketing activity such as the areas of communications and selling.

SCOPE OF CUSTOMER CARE

What are the significant variables of customer care? Indeed, what is the scope of customer care activities? Chaston (1990) outlines the variables of customer care as:

1   The product knowledge and interpersonal skills of the employees who interact with the customers.
2   The type of service required by the customers and their perception of how the organisation fulfils their expectations on quality.
3   The organisational structure of the company, which determines the efficiency with which services [products] are delivered at all phases from the point of initial

contact through to the customer's post-purchase evaluation of the service [product] received.

(Chaston 1990: 145)

Customer care and satisfaction transgress all aspects of marketing, whether it be in consumer markets or industrial markets, inter- or intra-industry. However, it is in the area of services marketing that most progress and attention has been given to customer care and satisfaction. Much of this attention began with the notion of perceiving service as a product and also the notion of the 'service package' and 'value added' services. These issues will be explored later in this chapter.

Many authors have volunteered a variety of definitions of customer care. One of the most current and comprehensive descriptions is provided by Clutterbuck (1988): 'Customer care is a fundamental approach to standards of service quality. It covers every aspect of a company's operations, from the design of a product or service to how it is packaged, delivered and serviced.' This emphasizes the importance of attention being given to every element of the exchange process from design and production through to delivery and service back-up. Indeed, Christopher (1986), when discussing the dimensions of logistics and marketing processes argues that:

Customer service is the thread that links the logistics and marketing processes, because in the end, the output of the logistics system IS customer service. The skill lies in managing the twin arms of marketing and logistics in such a way as to maximise the value added through customer service whilst still seeking a cost advantage.

Essentially, as Peters and Austin (1985) state, customer care 'all boils down to perceived and appreciated and consistently delivered service and quality to customers'.

These statements serve to assist appreciation of the 'concept' of customer care, but what are the actual parameters of its scope of activity? Many terms have been used both by authors and companies to label customer care activity, such as customer service, product quality, service quality and after sales service. These terms appear to have different meanings in different companies and different situations. To clarify these terms for the purpose of this discussion and to emphasize the complete definition of customer care as an all-encompassing term, these four aspects are explained as follows:

1 *Customer service*. Generally includes advice and information for customers regarding the technical specifications of a product or service and after sales back-up arrangements and procedures. To emphasize this point Christopher (1986) writes that 'ultimately customer service is determined by the interaction of all those factors that affect the process of making products and services available to the buyer'.

2 *Product quality*. Relates to standards and measures set to ensure a product conforms to specifications and is therefore fit for its purpose and safe to use.

3 *Service quality*. Refers to the company/customer interface and relationship,

753

focusing on the customer's experience during the process of the transaction.

4 *After sales service*. Covers after sales enquiries and complaints, together with repair and maintenance procedures.

All of these aspects form part of the total customer care package which is about adopting a caring attitude through being helpful, friendly, concerned and reassuring. The aim is continuously to satisfy customer requirements and comply with expectations. In this context customer care applies to all aspects of marketing.

Customer care can incorporate anything that an organization does for and on behalf of its customers. What form this takes will depend on a multiplicity of factors, such as the nature of the product or service, the industry, the competition and the expectation of consumers. Consequently, customer care may be found somewhere between a whole range of general parameters. For example, minimum aspects of care may be sufficient to satisfy customers, or alternatively, maximum levels of care may be necessary in order to be competitive. Customer care may be deemed poor but the differentiation of the product may more than compensate for this. Alternatively, excellent care may be a core requirement for some products or services. Equally, simple care may be all that is necessary for some situations, while sophisticated care may have been developed as a significant marketing differentiation. Whatever the scope and nature of customer care, two things are likely to be constant: it is determined by management and judged by customers and consumers in terms of expectations.

CUSTOMER EXPECTATIONS AND SATISFACTION

The scope of customer care marketing activity will encompass customer experience from the pre-purchase, through the purchase period and end with post-purchase follow-up. A company's pre-purchase activity will consist of building customer awareness and desire through attractive and efficient information flow and distribution. It will strive to balance changing customer expectations and requirements while ensuring ease and flexibility of enquiry and diminution of anxiety. Pre-purchase customer care establishes the first bridgehead in organization/customer relationships and serves as a 'draw' in encouraging and enticing the customer towards purchase. The purchase period of customer care is most obviously linked with the core product or service in an integral way. In addition to the product aspects of customer care there is considerable requirement for efficiency in processing orders and in the overall order management cycle, paying attention to small details and meeting customer demands in ways which are entirely compatible with the customers' expectations and requirements both in terms of function and time. It is here that organization/customer interface and relationship is bonded by the mutually beneficial negotiations. The post-purchase customer care activity will focus upon efficient follow-up and full completion of the product or service transaction. In the longer term this follow-up will concentrate either on reliable continuous servicing or on persistent maintenance of awareness. The eventual object will be to entice the customer back for further purchases.

In the marketing of customer care it is important to position the term 'satisfaction' in terms of a company's experience and previous trading activity in its marketplace. Thus, it is important to distinguish between customer expectations that relate first to satisfaction and are seen as predictors or probabilities of what is likely to happen during a transaction and, second, expectations viewed as desires or wants based on what will actually be offered (Lewis 1993). It is the latter part of this distinction to which the term satisfaction most relates in this discussion.

How can customer care fully encompass customers' expectations that stretch across the whole scope of customer experience as outlined above? Swan and Combs (1976) argue that there are two dimensions to customer expectations, 'instrumental' expectations and 'psychological' expectations about a product or service performance. These expectations relate both to quantifiable factors which can be measured using 'hard' data and to qualitative factors which can be measured using 'soft' data. Hard data are those which relate to quantifiable issues such as performance and reliability. Such issues are tangible and therefore relatively easy to measure by both the company and the customer. However, it is more difficult to measure customer care in relation to the qualitative elements of customer relations. These 'soft' issues can be described as those concerned with descriptions of and knowledge about customer feelings, perceptions, expectations and requirements. These are more difficult to measure because they are intangible (Carson and Gilmore 1989).

DIMENSIONS OF CUSTOMER CARE

The interrelationships between quantitative hard standards and qualitative soft standards can be seen in Figure 1. This model illustrates the range of factors that can be included in the complete definition of customer care. These elements range from the hard, tangible aspects such as packaging, to the soft, intangible aspects such as the degree of courtesy and consideration experienced by the customer.

Many of these aspects of customer care are difficult to measure and evaluate by both customers and companies. An examination of the nature of the characteristics upon which they can be evaluated allows classification of goods or services into three categories (Darby and Karni 1973; Nelson 1974). These classifications are 'search' properties, 'experience' properties and 'credence' properties. Search properties are those which a consumer can determine prior to purchasing a product, for example, packaging, price, and so on. Experience properties are those such as courtesy, ease of contact, dependability, and as such can be discerned only after purchase or during consumption. Credence

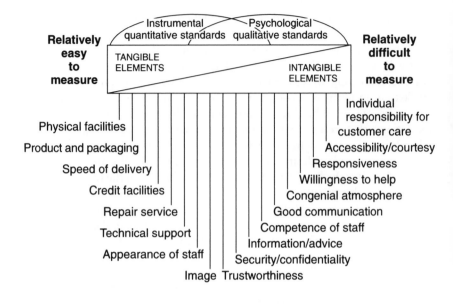

Figure 1 Dimensions of customer care
Source: Carson and Gilmore (1989–90: 52)

properties are those qualities or attributes which consumers may find impossible to evaluate even after purchase and/or consumption, perhaps because they do not have the knowledge or skill to do so and therefore have to rely on the professional credence of the supplier.

In the dimensions model shown in Figure 1, there are relatively few elements which can be described as having search qualities. Those which may contain search properties are those which are part of the instrumental 'hard' dimension of customer care. In fact, it can be argued that the majority of elements listed in Figure 1 contain more experience and credence properties than search properties. Indeed, experience and credence qualities have been described as those which are less absolute, more conditional, less concrete and more intangible than search qualities. Consequently, this makes the evaluation of experience and credence qualities more difficult for consumers and for companies.

It is argued that the variables in the dimensions model which primarily have experience and credence properties are also those which are part of the psychological 'soft' dimension of customer care. For example, courtesy and responsiveness of staff can be evaluated only through experiencing these dimensions. Similarly, security and confidentiality must have an inherent credence to be accepted. Where there are more search qualities in evidence not only is it easier for the customer to evaluate the quality, but also it is easier for the producer to determine, offer and standardize those qualities. This is manifested in dimensions such as credit facilities, product and packaging, speed of delivery, and comparisons between competitive offerings. Thus, there is a tendency by management to concentrate on the instrumental standards and a corresponding difficulty in defining and measuring psychological standards. In the case of 'hard' instrumental standards, which are primarily tangible, management can identify customer expectations by various quantitative methods and can therefore set appropriate specifications, rules or procedures to allow for those requirements. In this respect, many companies will have data on aspects such as the time period customers perceive to be reasonable in waiting for delivery of the product just purchased, or how long they would be prepared to wait for it to be repaired after a breakdown. Similarly, management can set standards relating to a product's fitness for use, performance, safety and reliability. Further, it can set procedures for what the company should do if the product breaks down.

MEASURING CUSTOMER CARE

When quantitative measures have been applied to determine less definite areas such as the number of staff required at any point on a shop floor, or in any service situation, they have been less successful. In this case quantitative measures alone are not sufficient because they fail to take into account the inherent psychological dimensions which relate to the customer's expectation evaluation in terms of experience and credence qualities. It is acknowledged that some companies, such as airlines and hotel chains, have used quantitative techniques in measuring relatively intangible service dimensions – for example, in check-in waiting time, baggage labelling, toilet cleaning and telephone answering. These are all duties which may have relied on intuitive behaviour on the part of service personnel in executing the tasks. However, by stipulating rigid procedures and minimum performance standards, these companies have considerably improved their service offerings. Thus, for example, telephones are required to be answered within a given time period, or waiting at check-ins reduced to stated efficiency levels.

Total customer care should also attempt to take account of customers' feelings, perceptions and requirements in respect of a product or service. This is particularly important where the qualitative psychological dimensions are dominant in the transaction and where customers rely heavily on experience and credence qualities. However, where such qualities are difficult to define, customers will be influenced strongly by the customer contact personnel and to a lesser extent the environment in which the contact takes place. To summarize, consideration of the elements illustrated in the Figure 1 model suggests that the instrumental 'hard' dimensions can be implemented mainly through suitable rules and procedures, whereas the psychological 'soft' dimensions of customer care are determined by an emphasis on perceptions, attitudes and behaviour of customer contact staff.

BALANCED CUSTOMER CARE

A good customer care package will benefit from consistency in performing the tasks and balancing the performance across all the dimensions. Consistency is crucial in maintaining standards of performance. This is particularly so with regard to the soft intangible dimension of customer care. Because of the 'personal touch' aspect it is easy to have high variances in standards of performance if due care and attention to consistency are neglected. Concentration on the instrumental dimensions may improve the customer care offering, but much of the improvement will be negated by the neglect of the psychological dimensions. Companies can provide better 'balanced' customer care in two ways. First, they can improve the environment where the transaction takes place and, second, apply marketing concepts internally, particularly amongst customer contact staff.

One of the initial steps is to ensure that management pay sufficient and continuing attention to the processes of meeting customer needs. This attention should extend to the environment within which the product or service is transacted. Indeed, as Bitner (1992) stresses, 'Research in organisational behaviour suggests that the physical setting can influence employee satisfaction, productivity, and motivation.' The same physical settings will have a similar impact on customers' satisfaction with the product or service. The environment lends itself to highlighting the instrumental and largely tangible elements of customer care illustrated in Figure 1, for example physical facilities, such as modern efficient equipment, appearance of staff, and so on. Similarly, many companies go to considerable effort to show tangible evidence of some or more of the tangible variables. For example, companies in financial services provide secluded booths for private interviews, thus giving the impression of confidentiality. Similarly, in retailing the introduction of new technology has speeded up transactions and redesigned stores have improved the customers' shopping environment by implying more responsiveness and a calmer atmosphere. However, it is not enough to focus only on an efficient environment, it is also important to balance this with the personal touch dimensions.

One way of achieving a balance between the personal touch and modern efficiency is to focus on the 'soft' psychological dimensions of customer care. Obviously, because of the characteristics of face-to-face interaction, front-line company staff can have a major influence upon the perceived service quality and customer care in general. Each individual in a company, irrespective of level or function, has an important role to play in the customer's perceptions of the product or service. Many writers refer to this as the 'people factor'.

INTERNAL CUSTOMERS

If management does indeed determine customer care then what procedures will management address in maintaining and developing aspects of customer care?

The core essence of management determined customer care is that of genuine and comprehensive marketing orientation incorporating both internal and external dimensions.

In an attempt to improve perceptions of staff towards customer care, some companies have tried schemes which involve treating their employees as customers, that is internal marketing training. Berry (1981) describes this as 'viewing employees as internal customers, viewing jobs as internal products and then endeavouring to offer internal products that satisfy the needs and wants of these internal customers while addressing the objectives of the organisation'. Internal marketing is important in that it recognizes that customer service is not just the responsibility of front-line staff. The concept of internal marketing involves the application of marketing principles to 'selling the staff' on their role in providing customer satisfaction.

MARKETING ACTIVITY: CORE AND PERIPHERAL PRODUCT

What are the key component parts of customer care? What is the scope of customer care marketing activity? Much of the explicit focus of customer care and satisfaction lies outside the 'core' of marketing activity. Obviously there is an implicit dimension of customer care and satisfaction in all aspects of marketing activity. As a consequence, the 'tangible' aspects of marketing, primarily the core product, represent the broader aspects of customer care in terms of meeting customer needs, perceptions and expectations. The 'core' aspects of customer care focus on the customer/organization interactions and as a consequence are primarily people related and 'intangible' in nature. It is this dimension which sometimes leads to the perception that the concepts are primarily about the 'customer service package' (Shostack 1977; Grönroos 1990; Normann 1991).

This service aspect is easily accepted in the wide area of service marketing. It is in service industries that most concentrations of customer care improvement and development can be found. Indeed, some might argue that customer care represents the core of service marketing activity. It is in services marketing that concepts such as 'total service offering' and 'quality of services' can be found.

In addition to the core customer care will have a 'peripheral' dimension. This peripheral aspect can be substantial and can consist of a wide range of factors and activities. It is here that the little added extras and attention to detail can be provided that will complete a good customer care programme. Peripheral aspects can often be provided by other marketing variables other than people dimensions.

It is an established view that peripheral aspects of the customer care package will eventually evolve into meaningful core aspects in themselves. Therefore, as a company enlarges and expands the level of customer care around added peripheral aspects these will be viewed by customers as integral and standard to the customer care package. Thus, after a period of time a company would actually disappoint customers by withdrawing these aspects which had become part of the actual core of customer care.

MARKETING ACTIVITIES: OTHER MARKETING VARIABLES

In all marketing variables customer care will require attention to be given to interaction points at various stages of the transaction. Customer care at these interaction points will be efficient, friendly and stimulating, designed to avoid or at least solve problems, to prevent passive customer periods and to encourage active customer involvement. In its entirety a customer care programme will create a unique ambience, appearance and atmosphere surrounding an organization and its customers.

The four actual marketing variables of most significance to customer care in creating this ambience are as follows:

1 *Product or service.* This will obviously be the core of customer care activity in terms of its range, choice and variety, and provide scope for customization and personalization to suit the individual customer.
2 *Communication materials.* These will include any literature which is designed to create and stimulate awareness through customer orientated information flows. This information will focus on customer care dimensions of product use, availability and delivery, and price/value perceptions.
3 *Sales incentives.* These will play an important role in customer care. They may be tangible, covering such things as samples and trials or tests, price discounts and give aways, and intangible, such as extra service or extended service.
3 *Positive public relations.* This will play a significant role in customer care, both in terms of its scope and spread and the degree of activity. Public relations will enable customers to be informed and to feel they belong to an organization.

In marketing activity in general, customer care and satisfaction will be of a prime concern in all aspects of marketing communications, sales incentives and motivations, quality improvements and value added dimensions.

TQM AND TOTAL SYSTEMS

Much of the internal marketing concept has been superseded by new and wider approaches, such as total systems and total quality management (TQM). A total systems approach requires an organization to incorporate what it does as a cohesive whole. That is, all departments and functions must be viewed as a coordinated grouping of activities whereby the sum of the whole operation is greater than the sum of the individual component parts. Total quality management adds another dimension by evaluating and improving the quality of all operations within an organization in a cohesive and coordinated fashion. The effect of these types of 'systems' upon an organization's customer care performance is obvious, since they will contribute significantly towards the overall marketing orientation of the organization. By improving the quality of an organization's performance the efficiency and end products of a firm's offerings will be passed on directly and indirectly to its customers. But the external dimensions of customer care must be addressed in a way which is compatible with internal improvements.

RELATIONSHIP MARKETING

The external management of customer care must focus upon building stronger links and cementing closer relationships between an organization and its customers. The essence of this focus is on communication. Good customer care communication signals efficiency and flexibility from a customer perspective and is manifested in the quality and ease of contacts with an organization. Thus, consistent customer care will be provided at all stages and all areas of contact. An organization will not only be aware of its core contact personnel, but also its peripheral contact points, as well as its first and last contact points. A weakness in any one of these contact points may result in damaging the expected customer care performance. The concentration of any customer care contact point should be on establishing sound one-to-one interactions between company personnel and the individual customer at a personal level. Customers must feel that they are not only known but are individually important to an organization.

IMPLEMENTATION OF CUSTOMER CARE

How can management improve customer care through internal marketing orientation? Internally, organizations will strive to engender a culture of customer orientation. Such an orientation will be wide ranging in its approaches to doing business and measures of performance which are designed to motivate and stimulate good customer relations. Thus systems of management procedure and administration are structured in such a way as to be customer friendly, efficient and flexible, from the beginning to the end of transactions. Key aspects of good performance competence are measured through accountability and responsibility for satisfying customers and establishing and maintaining good customer/organization relationships. Performance at key management positions within an organization will be crucial in internal marketing activity – by applying the principles of marketing in terms of appreciating the requirements of other departments and servicing them to their satisfaction, while at the same time marketing themselves to other departments in terms of their own performance requirements. Any commitments undertaken by staff must be followed through. Guarantees and promises must be met. Tasks must be completed. In other words good customer care relies as much upon the implementation performance of an organization as it does upon stated objectives and plans.

Equally, the success of a customer care programme will be determined by the efficiency of staff performance in their tasks. Thus, good customer care programmes will place much credence upon accountability and responsibility of staff towards the task performance. The level and range of accountability and responsibility will be dependent upon the overall staff competencies and skills. Customer care cannot be left in the hands of incompetent or inefficient staff. There is a clear implication therefore that successful customer care programmes are highly dependent upon the personnel required to perform and implement them. Like any other management function customer care may require sound training and staff development if the function itself is to be maintained at a satisfactory level and if it is to be developed.

FUTURE PERSPECTIVES OF CUSTOMER CARE

Customer care will continue to evolve along with marketing developments, which in turn will be heavily influenced by environmental changes and pressures. Future perspectives in customer care will reflect new perspectives in marketing. Some of these new perspectives have already been alluded to, principally relationship marketing. Sheth (1993) includes relationship marketing as one of ten emerging marketing strategies. Two others that may have most impact upon customer care and satisfaction are network marketing and customer focused quality. Relationship marketing and networking are debated elsewhere in this text. However, it is useful to consider both together with the dimension of quality from the specific perspective of customer care. Relationship marketing is implicit to network marketing and also to the notion of marketing competencies.

MARKETING COMPETENCIES

There is an increasing recognition of the fact that managers should have competence in their relevant functional area. It is also widely recognized that developed management competencies are the key to improved management performance. These issues are no less relevant in the context of customer care. Management and staff must have appropriate competencies for successfully implementing customer care packages. What is meant by management competencies and which are appropriate for customer care?

Boyatzis (1982) suggests that a competence is an underlying characteristic of a person which consists of an effective mix of motives, traits, skills, aspects of one's self-image or social role, or body of knowledge used by an individual. From a management perspective it can be considered that competence is the ability to use knowledge and skills effectively in the performance of a specific task. Competencies may embrace a more tangible set of attributes: ability to make sound judgements, creativity, willingness to take risks, decisiveness, high energy level, ability to take initiative, results orientation, tenacity, integrity, adaptability, resilience, ability to deal with detailed information and lateral thinking. The list can be inexhaustible in terms of human traits. When applied to the marketing concept and in particular to customer care the focus is upon those competencies which are most appropriate to performing effective customer care. Assuming that customer care personnel have a 'common sense' knowledge of the marketing concept, then it is a matter of concentrating on enhancing appropriate competencies for the task. There are two competencies which can be deemed most appropriate for customer care – knowledge and communication.

Any manager or member of staff must possess and develop knowledge of the company's products or services in the context of the total customer care package. In addition, customer care requires a sound knowledge of customer expectations, desires and satisfactions and a knowledge of how to translate these to the transaction and interaction processes of customer care. Clearly, this requires considerable and compatible competency in communication in order to maintain a mutual understanding between company and customer. In addition, experience and judgement can be added as key factors towards effective customer care. Sound judgement in decision-making is essential, but this will only be achieved by the effective mix of knowledge and communication and these will be immensely enhanced by meaningful experience competency. By focusing upon these aspects of competency, management can enhance and develop its overall customer care performance.

NETWORKING

As well as developing competencies, management must take full cognizance of good networking. These competencies will be naturally enhanced by good networks, since they revolve around meaningful 'personal contacts'. The personal contact network defines any relationship, either direct, in terms of a particular impact upon the company/customer interface, or indirect in that it may lead to further contact through and with other people. The density, reachability and diversity of a personal contact network will have considerable bearing on the impact it has on customer care.

The network most appropriate for customer care is one that reflects aspects of marketing. Thus, people who are involved in the company/customer interface represent the richest sources of personal contact, for example, buyers, gatekeepers, store managers, office administrators, and so on. These are important people from both the perspective of the company and of its customer. By proactively nurturing and enhancing the relationship network with all of these individuals a person with customer care responsibility will perform more effectively.

QUALITY

Quality is a much abused term in all aspects of business and in marketing particularly. When marketers talk of improving quality the focus has traditionally been on improving the features of the product or service. While this is a wholly acceptable objective, it displays a myopic view of the total marketing effort (Gilmore and Carson 1993). Marketing is not just concerned with the product dimension, it must also maintain a balance with decisions on price, promotion, distribution, and not least customer care. Thus, fundamental to the consideration of quality improvement in customer care is the wider consideration of improving, in a balanced way, the same aspects of quality across the whole spectrum of customer care related activities. This chapter alluded earlier to aspects of quality in total quality management and total marketing systems. Quality consistency was also considered across the full range of customer experience in relation to a company, from pre-purchase through to post-purchase and everything in between. Clearly, dimensions of quality are integral to the whole concept of customer care. Therefore how can management hope to perform and improve effective customer care across such a wide range of activities?

FULLY INTEGRATED CUSTOMER CARE

The ultimate answer to effective customer care is a fully integrated package of activities and decision-making functions. This means focusing on key factors and linking these together into such an integrated package. The key factors drawn from this overview of customer care are:

1 Wide consideration of all marketing functional variables – variables which include product or service, advertising, promotion, personal selling, delivery, order processing.
2 Identification and enhancement of key marketing competencies and personal contact networks – concentration upon knowledge, communication, experience, and judgement; in addition, the nurturing and development of personal contacts at all aspects of customer care influence.
3 Consistent and balanced delivery of key customer care activities – consideration across the whole spectrum of customer care activities (outline in Figure 1).
4 A consistent and balanced perspective on the customer/company interface – acknowledgement of all aspects of the interrelationships between customers and a company, particularly in relation to hard instrumental and soft psychological dimensions.

By combining all four of these factors under clear and precise customer care objectives and policies an organization will perform customer care with an

764

impact which will have a lasting effect on its customers and provide maximum satisfaction.

SUMMARY

This chapter has attempted to outline the important factors of customer care and satisfaction. It has considered these from the perspective of organizations providing customer care and at the interface between companies and their customers. There are many important issues not debated here which specifically influence customer care. Most significantly are customer satisfaction from the perspective of consumer and buyer behaviour; sociological and psychological aspects of marketing; relationship marketing and networking; and the total marketing environment. All of these aspects are covered elsewhere in this volume and should be taken into account when reading and understanding this chapter.

This chapter has focused upon the key issues of customer care to provide the reader with an appreciation and understanding of the scope and activities of this function, its importance in modern marketing and its growing influence.

REFERENCES

Berry, L. L. (1981) 'The employee as customer', *Journal of Retail Banking* 3 (1), March: 33–40.

Bitner, M. J. (1992) 'Servicescapes: The impact of physical surroundings on customers and employees', *Journal of Marketing* 56, April: 57–71.

Boyatzis, R. E. (1982) *The Competent Manager: A Model for Effective Performance*, New York: J. Wiley.

Carson, D. and Gilmore, A. (1989) 'Customer care: the neglected domain', *Irish Marketing Review* 4 (3): 49–61.

Chaston, I. (1990) *Managing for Marketing Excellence*, Maidenhead: McGraw-Hill.

Christopher, M. (1986) 'Reaching the customer: strategies for marketing and customer service', *Journal of Marketing Management* 2 (1): 63–71.

Clutterbuck, D. (1988) 'Developing customer care training programmes', *Industrial and Commercial Training*, November–December: 11–14.

Darby, M. R. and Karni, E. (1973) 'Free competition and the optimal amount of fraud', *Journal of Law and Economics* 16, April: 67–86 in A. Parasuraman, V. A. Zeithaml and L. L. Berry (1985) 'A conceptual model of service quality and its implications for future research', *Journal of Marketing* 49, Fall: 41–50.

Gilmore, A. and Carson, D. (1993) 'Enhancing service quality: A case study', *Irish Marketing Review* 6: 64–73.

Grönroos, C. (1990) *Service Management and Marketing. Managing the Moments for Truth*, Massachusetts: Lexington Books.

Lewis, B. R. (1993) 'Service quality measurement', *Marketing Intelligence and Planning* 11 (4): 4–12.

Nelson, P. (1974) 'Advertising as information', *Journal of Political Economy* 81, July–August: 729–54 in A. Parasuraman, V. A. Zeithaml and L. L. Berry (1985) 'A conceptual model of service quality and its implicatons for future research', *Journal of Marketing* 49, Fall: 41–50.

Normann, R. (1991) *Service Management and Marketing*, Chichester: J. Wiley and Sons.

Peters, T. J. and Austin, N. (1985) *A Passion for Excellence: The Leadership Difference*, New York: Random House.

Sheth, J. N. (1993) 'Emerging marketing strategies in a changing macroeconomic environment', *Journal of International Marketing* 1 (2): 9–14.

Shostack, G. L. (1977) 'Breaking free from product marketing', *Journal of Marketing* 41, April: 73–80.

Swan, J. E. and Combs, L. J. (1976) 'Product performance and customer satisfaction', *Journal of Marketing* 40, April: 25–33.

FURTHER READING

Bateson, J. E. (1989) *Managing Services Marketing. Texts and Cases*, Chicago: The Dryden Press.

Christopher, M., Payne, A. and Ballantyne, D. (1991) *Relationship Marketing: Bring Quality, Customer Service and Marketing Together*, Oxford: Butterworth Heinemann.

Zeithaml,V. A., Parasuraman, A. and Berry, L. L. (1990) *Delivering Quality Service. Balancing Customer Perceptions and Expectations*, New York: The Free Press.

44

DEVELOPING AND IMPLEMENTING A MARKETING PLAN

Malcolm H. B. McDonald

OVERVIEW

The overall purpose of marketing planning and its principle focus is the identification and creation of sustainable competitive advantage. It is a logical sequence and a series of activities leading to the setting of marketing objectives and the formulation of strategies and tactics for achieving them, together with the associated financial consequences. It is necessary because of the complexity caused by the many external and internal factors that interact to affect an organization's ability to achieve its objectives. There are two outputs from the process of marketing planning:

1 The strategic marketing plan, which covers a period of between three and five years.
2 The tactical marketing plan, which is the detailed scheduling and costing out of the specific actions necessary to achieve the first year's objectives in the strategic marketing plan.

The strategic marketing plan is a model of a unit's position in its market relative to competitors and contains a definition of market needs, the objectives to be achieved, the strategies to achieve the objectives and the resources required to achieve the desired results.

The marketing planning process starts with financial objectives, moves on to the marketing audit stage, then to the setting of draft marketing objectives and strategies for a three- to five-year period. At this stage other functional managers get involved to ensure that the organization is capable of resourcing the market's requirements. Strategic marketing plans are then finalized and tactical marketing plans are prepared. Headquarters will often consolidate all of these into corporate plans. At the start of the organization's fiscal year the tactical marketing plan is implemented and measured, until the whole process starts again. Thus, it can be seen that the process is continuous. The degree of formalization of the process depends on an organization's size and complexity, but the process is universally applicable, irrespective of circumstances.

THE IMPORTANCE OF MARKETING PLANNING

All organizations operate in a complex environment, in which hundreds of external and internal factors interact to affect their ability to achieve their objectives. Managers need some understanding, or view, about how all these variables interact and they must try to be rational about their decisions, no matter how important intuition, feel and experience are as contributory factors in this process of rationality.

Most managers accept that some kind of formalized procedure for planning the organization's marketing helps sharpen this rationality so as to reduce the complexity of business operations and add a dimension of realism to the organization's hopes for the future. This is born out by research into the efficacy of marketing planning, which has shown that the main effects within organizations are:

- the systematic identification of emerging opportunities and threats;
- a preparedness to meet change;
- the specification of sustainable competitive advantage;
- improved communication among executives;
- a reduction of conflicts between individuals and departments;
- the involvement of all levels of management in the process;
- a more appropriate allocation of scarce resources;
- consistency of approach across the organization;
- a more market-focused orientation across the organization.

These effects have made a major contribution to commercial success, according to the research of: Thompson (1962); Leighton (1966); Thune and House (1970); Kollatt *et al.* (1972); Ansoff (1977); McDonald (1984) and Greenley (1987).

WHAT MARKETING PLANNING IS

The contribution of marketing to business success in manufacturing, distribution or merchanting activities lies in its commitment to detailed analysis of future opportunities to meet customer needs and a wholly professional approach to selling to well-defined market segments those products or services that deliver the sought-after benefits. While prices and discounts are important, as are advertising and promotion, the link with engineering through the products is paramount. But such a commitment and activities must not be mistaken for budgets and forecasts, which have always been a commercial necessity. The process of marketing planning is concerned with identifying what and to whom sales are going to be made in the longer term to give revenue budgets and sales forecasts any chance of achievement. Furthermore, the chances of achievement are a function of how good an organization's intelligence services are; and how well suited their strategies are in relation to the identified market opportunities.

Marketing planning is a logical sequence and a series of activities leading to the setting of marketing objectives and the formulation of plans for achieving them. It is a management process. Conceptually, the process is very simple. Marketing planning by means of a planning system is, *per se*, little more than a structured way of identifying a range of options for the company, of making them explicit in writing, of formulating marketing objectives which are consistent with the company's overall objectives and of scheduling and costing out the specific activities most likely to bring about the achievement of the objectives. It is the systematization of this process which lies at the heart of the theory of marketing planning.

Marketing planning, then, is a managerial process, the output of which is a marketing plan. There are two principal kinds of marketing plan:

- the strategic marketing plan;
- the tactical marketing plan.

THE STRATEGIC MARKETING PLAN

The strategic marketing plan covers three or more years. It is the written document which outlines how managers perceive their own position in their markets relative to their competitors (with competitive advantage accurately defined), what objectives they want to achieve, how they intend to achieve them (strategies), what resources are required, and with what results (budget).

Three years is the most frequent planning period for the strategic marketing plan. Five years is the longest period and this is becoming less common due to the speed of technological and environmental change.

THE TACTICAL/OPERATIONAL MARKETING PLAN

The tactical marketing plan is the detailed scheduling and costing out of the specific actions necessary for the achievement of the first year of the strategic marketing plan. The tactical plan is usually for one year.

Research by McDonald (1984) into the marketing planning practices of organizations, shows that successful ones complete the strategic plan before the tactical plan. Unsuccessful organizations frequently did not bother with a strategic marketing plan at all, relying largely on sales forecasts and the associated budgets. The problem with this approach is that many managers sell the products and services they find easiest to sell to those customers who offer the least line of resistance. By developing short-term, tactical marketing plans first and then extrapolating them, managers merely succeed in extrapolating their own shortcomings. Preoccupation with preparing a detailed marketing plan first is typical of those companies that confuse sales forecasting and budgeting with strategic marketing planning.

THE CONTENTS OF A STRATEGIC MARKETING PLAN

The contents of a strategic marketing plan are listed below.

1 Mission statement
2 Financial summary
3 Market overview
   • market structure
   • market trends
   • key market segments
   • gap analysis
4 Opportunities/threats
   • by product
   • by segment
   • overall
5 Strengths/weaknesses
   • by product
   • by segment
   • overall
6 Issues to be addressed
   • by product
   • by segment
   • overall
7 Portfolio summary
8 Assumptions
9 Marketing objectives
   • strategic focus
   • product mix
   • product development
   • product deletion
   • market extension
   • target customer groups
10 Marketing strategies (Four Ps, positioning/branding)
   • product
   • price
   • promotion
   • place
11 Resource requirements
   • budget

Explanations of the terminology used in this contents list follow (see p. 772 onwards).

THE CONTENTS OF A TACTICAL MARKETING PLAN

The contents of a tactical marketing plan are as follows:

1 Overall objectives
 • Overall objectives – these should cover the following together with a few words of commentary/explanation:

| Volume or value | Last year, | Current year estimate, | Budget next year |
| Gross margins | Last year, | Current year estimate, | Budget next year |

 • Overall strategies – new customers, new products, advertising, sales promotion, selling, customer service, pricing.
2 Sub-objectives, strategies, action/tactics.
 • Sub-objectives – more detailed objectives should be provided for products or markets or segments or major customers, as appropriate.
 • Strategies – the means by which sub-objectives will be achieved should be stated.
 • Action/tactics – the details, timing, responsibility and cost should also be stated.
3 Summary of marketing activities and costs.
4 Contingency plan – it is important to include a contingency plan, which should address the following questions:
 • What are the critical assumptions on which the one-year plan is based?
 • What would the financial consequences be (i.e. the effect on the operating income) if these assumptions did not come true? For example, if a forecast of revenue is based on the assumption that a decision will be made to buy new plant by a major customer, what would the effect be if that customer did not go ahead?
 • How will these assumptions be managed?
 • What action will be taken to ensure that the adverse financial effects of an unfulfilled assumption are mitigated, so that the same forecast profit results at the end of the year? To measure the risk, assess the negative or downside, asking what can go wrong with each assumption that would change the outcome. For example, if a market growth rate of 5 per cent is a key assumption, what lower growth rate would have to occur before a substantially different management decision would be taken? For a capital project, this would be the point at which the project would cease to be economical.
5 Operating result and financial ratios, to include:
 • Net revenue
 • Gross margin
 • Adjustments
 • Marketing costs
 • Administration costs
 • Interest

771

- Operating result
- Return on sales (ROS)
- Return on investment (ROI)

6 Key activity planner – a summary of the key activities, indicating the start and finish. This should help considerably with monitoring the progress of the annual plan.

7 Other – there may be other information, such as sales call plans, which might usefully appear in the one-year marketing plan.

Mission statement

This is the first item to appear in the strategic marketing plan. The purpose of the mission statement is to ensure that the *raison d'être* of the unit preparing the plan is clearly stated. Brief statements should be made which cover the following points:

1 Role or contribution of the unit – for example, profit generator, service department, opportunity seeker.

2 Definition of business – for example, the needs the unit satisfies or the benefits provided. Do not be too specific (e.g. 'we sell milking machinery') or too general (e.g. 'we are in the engineering business').

3 Distinctive competence – this should be a brief statement that applies only to the unit preparing the plan. A statement that could equally apply to any competitor is unsatisfactory.

4 Indications for future direction – a brief statement of the principal things the unit would give serious consideration to (e.g. move into a new segment.)

Financial summary

This section is designed to give a bird's eye view of the unit's total marketing activities. There should be a quantitative summary of performance (Table 1). Unit managers should give a summary of reasons for good or bad performance. They should use constant revenue $(t - 1)$ in order that the comparisons are meaningful. Make sure the same base year values are used for any projections provided in later sections of this system.

Table 1 Quantitative summary of performance

	Three years ago	Two years ago	Last year
Volume/turnover			
Gross profit (%)			
Gross margin (£000)			

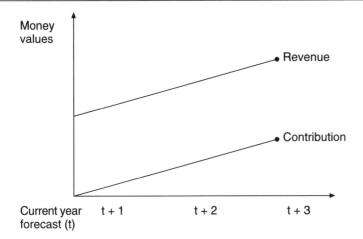

Figure 1   Summary of financial projections over three-year planning period

Next, there should be a summary of the financial projections. Its purpose is to summarize for the person reading the plan the financial implications over the full three-year planning period. It should be presented as a simple diagram along the lines shown in Figure 1. This should be accompanied by a brief commentary.

Market overview

This section is intended to provide a brief picture of the market before descending to the particular details of individual market segments, which form the heart of the marketing plan.

This section is based upon the segmentation of markets, dividing these into homogeneous groups of customers, each having characteristics which can be exploited in marketing terms. This approach is taken because it is the one which is often the most useful for unit managers to be able to develop their markets. The alternative, product-orientated approach is rarely appropriate, given the variation between different customer groups in the markets in which most organizations compete. The market segmentation approach is more useful in revealing both the weaknesses and the development opportunities than is an exclusively product orientation.

While it is difficult to give precise instructions on how to present this section of the marketing plan, it should be possible to present a market overview which summarizes what managers consider to be the key changes in their markets. In completing this section, unit managers should consider the following:

1   What are the major products, markets (or segments) which are likely to be

able to provide the kind of business opportunities suitable for the organization?

2 How are these changing (i.e. which are growing and which are declining)?

This section should be brief and there should be some commentary by the unit manager about what seems to be happening in their market. It is very helpful if unit managers can present as much of this information as possible visually (i.e. bar charts or pie charts, product life cycles).

Opportunities and threats, strengths and weaknesses, issues to be addressed

To decide on marketing objectives and future strategy, it is first necessary to summarize the unit's present position in its market(s). In respect of the major products and markets (segments) highlighted in the previous section, the position must now be summarized in the form of a number of SWOT analyses. The word SWOT derives from the initial letters of the words strengths, weaknesses, opportunities and threats. In simple terms:

* What are the opportunities?
* What are the present and future threats to the unit's business in each of the segments which have been identified as being important?
* What are the unit's differential strengths and weaknesses *vis-à-vis* competitors? In other words, why should potential customers in the target markets prefer to deal with the unit preparing the plan rather than with its competitors?

Finally, there should be a summary, by major segments, of the key issues that have to be addressed in the planning period. These key issues will be clear from the SWOT analyses.

Portfolio summary

This is a summary of the previous SWOT analyses that makes it easy to see at a glance the overall competitive position and relative importance of each of the segments to the unit preparing the marketing plan. This is best done by drawing a diagram in the form of a four-box matrix which shows each of the important product/market segments described earlier. An example is shown in Figure 2.

From Figure 2 it can be seen that the horizontal axis reflects the scores in the strengths and weaknesses analysis and that the vertical axis quantifies the attractiveness to the organization of each of the important segments contained in the plan. The circle sizes are relative to the current turnover in each. The dotted circles indicate sales in three years' time.

Thus, some segments are becoming less attractive, some more, while in some the unit is becoming stronger against competitors, in others, less.

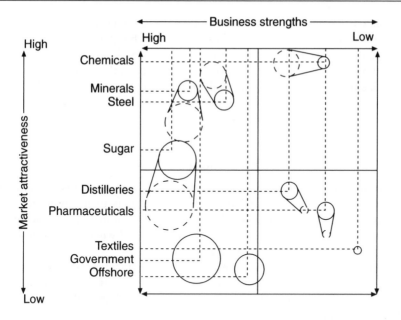

Figure 2   Portfolio summary – four-box matrix (directional policy matrix)

In the bottom left box, strengths are high, but the markets are less attractive, probably because of a lack of growth. The unit should probably seek to maintain these and manage them for sustained earnings.

In the top left box, strengths are high and the markets are attractive, probably because they are growing fast. The unit should probably invest heavily in these markets and seek to increase market share.

In the top right box, we have low strengths, but the markets are attractive. Here, the unit should probably invest selectively in order to improve its competitive position.

Finally, in the bottom right box, the unit has low strengths and the markets are not attractive. In such cases, it should probably manage these markets for profits.

This matrix, which is sometimes known as the directional policy matrix, gives a clear indication of the kind of marketing objectives and strategies that should be set for each segment shown.

Assumptions

The unit should now highlight the assumptions which are critical to the fulfilment of the planned marketing objectives and strategies.

Key planning assumptions deal in the main with outside features and anticipated changes which would have a significant influence on the achievement of marketing objectives. These might include such things as market growth rate, the organization's costs, capital investment and so on.

Assumptions should be few in number and relate only to key issues such as those identified in the SWOT analyses. If it is possible for a plan to be implemented irrespective of the assumptions made, then those assumptions are not necessary and should be removed.

Marketing objectives

Following the identification and statement of key strengths, weaknesses, opportunities and threats, and the explicit statement of assumptions about conditions affecting the business, the process of setting marketing objectives is made easier, since they will be a realistic statement of what the unit desires to achieve as a result of market-centred analysis.

As in the case of objective setting for other functional areas of the business, this is the most important step in the whole process, as it is a commitment on a unit-wide basis to a particular course of action which will determine the scheduling and costing out of subsequent actions.

An objective is what the unit wants to achieve. A strategy is how it plans to achieve it. Thus there are objectives and strategies at all levels in marketing. For example, there can be advertising objectives and strategies, pricing objectives and strategies, and so on.

However, the important point about marketing objectives is that they should be about products and markets only, since it is only by selling something to someone that the unit's financial goals can be achieved. Advertising, pricing and other elements of the marketing mix are the means (the strategies) by which the unit can succeed in doing this. Thus, pricing objectives, sales promotion objectives, advertising objectives and so on should not be confused with marketing objectives.

If profits and cash flows are to be maximized, each unit should consider carefully how its current customer needs are changing and how its products offered need to change accordingly. Since change is inevitable, it is necessary for units to consider the two main dimensions of commercial growth (i.e. product development and market development). Marketing objectives are concerned with the following:

- Selling existing products to existing segments.
- Developing new products for existing segments.
- Extending existing products to new segments.
- Developing new products for new segments.

Marketing objectives should be quantitative, and should be expressed where possible in terms of values, volumes and market shares. General directional terms such as 'maximize', 'penetrate' should be avoided unless quantification is included.

The marketing objectives should cover the full three-year planning horizon and should be accompanied by broad strategies (discussed in the following section) and broad revenue and cost projections for the full three-year period.

The one-year marketing plan should contain specific objectives for the first year of the three-year planning cycle and the corresponding strategies which will be used to achieve these objectives. At this point, it is worth stressing that the key document in the annual planning round is the three-year strategic plan. The one-year plan represents the specific actions that should be undertaken in the first year of the strategic plan.

Marketing strategies

Marketing strategies should state in broad terms how the marketing objectives are to be achieved, as follows:

- The specific product policies (range, technical specifications, additions, deletions).
- The pricing policies to be followed for product groups in particular market segments.
- The customer service levels to be provided for specific market segments (such as maintenance support).
- The policies for communicating with customers under each of the main headings such as salesforce, advertising, sales promotion, as appropriate.

The following summarizes some of the marketing objectives and strategies that are available to managers.

Objectives

1 Market penetration.
2 Introduce new products to existing markets.
3 Introduce existing products to new markets (domestic).
4 Introduce existing products to new markets (international).
5 Introduce new products to new markets.

Strategies

1 Change product design, performance, quality or features.
2 Change advertising or promotion.
3 Change unit price.
4 Change delivery or distribution.

5 Change service levels.
6 Improve marketing productivity (e.g. improve the sales mix).
7 Improve marketing administrative productivity.
8 Consolidate product line.
9 Withdraw from markets.
10 Consolidate distribution.
11 Standardize design.
12 Acquire markets, products, facilities.

Resource requirements

Finally, units preparing the plan should provide financial projections for the full planning period under all the standard revenue and cost headings as specified by the organization. It will be obvious from all the foregoing, that the setting of budgets becomes not only much easier, but the resulting budgets are more likely to be realistic and related to what the whole company wants to achieve rather than just one functional department.

The most satisfactory approach would be for marketing directors to justify all their marketing expenditure from a zero base each year against the tasks they wish to accomplish. This is possible if the procedures described above are followed, as a hierarchy of objectives is built up in such a way that every item of budgeted expenditure can be related directly back to the initial corporate financial objectives. For example, if sales promotion is a major means of achieving an objective in a particular market, when sales promotional items appear in the programme, each one has a specific purpose which can be related back to a major objective.

Doing it this way not only ensures that every item of expenditure is fully accounted for as part of a rational, objective and task approach, but also that when changes have to be made during the period to which the plan relates, such changes can be made in such a way that the least damage is caused to the company's long-term objectives.

The incremental marketing expense can be considered to be all costs that are incurred after the product leaves the factory, other than costs involved in physical distribution, the costs of which usually represent a discrete subset.

There is no textbook answer to problems relating to questions such as whether packaging should be a marketing or a production expense, and whether some distribution costs could be considered to be marketing costs such as, for example, insistence on high service levels results in high inventory carrying costs. Only common sense will reveal workable solutions to issues such as these.

Under price, however, any form of discounting that reduces the expected gross income, such as promotional discounts, quantity discounts, royalty rebates, and so on, as well as sales commission and unpaid invoices, should be given the most careful attention as incremental marketing expenses.

Most obvious incremental marketing expenses will occur, however, under the heading 'promotion', in the form of advertising, sales salaries and expenses, sales promotional expenditure, direct mail costs, and so on.

The important point about the measurable effects of marketing activity is that anticipated levels should be the result of the most careful analysis of what is required to take the company towards its goals, while the most careful attention should be paid to gathering all items of expenditure under appropriate headings. The healthiest way of treating these issues is a zero-based budgeting approach.

THE MARKETING PLANNING PROCESS

Figure 3 (a) depicts the relationship between the marketing planning process and the output of that process – the strategic and tactical marketing plans. Figure 3 (b) shows the same process in a circular form, as this indicates more realistically the on-going nature of the marketing planning process and the link between strategic and tactical marketing plans.

THE MARKETING AUDIT

It will be seen that a marketing audit appears as a step in the marketing planning process. An audit is the means by which a company can understand how it relates to the environment in which it operates. It is the means by which a company can identify its own strengths and weaknesses as they relate to external opportunities and threats. It is thus a way of helping management to select a position in that environment based on known factors.

Expressed in its simplest form, the purpose of a corporate plan is to answer three central questions:

1 Where is the company now?
2 Where does the company want to go?
3 How should the company organize its resources to get there?

The audit is the means by which the first of these questions is answered. An audit is a systematic, critical and unbiased review and appraisal of the environment and of the company's operations. A marketing audit is part of the larger management audit and is concerned with the marketing environment and marketing operations.

Any company carrying out an audit will be faced with two kinds of variables. First, there are variables over which the company has no direct control. These usually take the form of what can be described as environmental, market and competitive variables. Second, there are variables over which the company has complete control. These are known as operational variables.

This indicates how an audit should be structured. That is to say, in two parts:

779

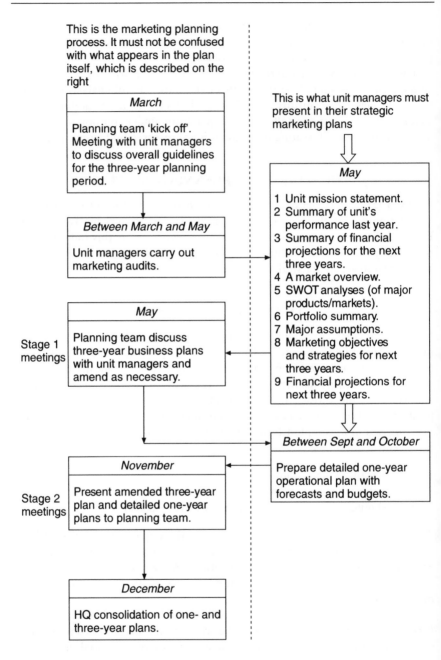

This is the marketing planning process. It must not be confused with what appears in the plan itself, which is described on the right

March
Planning team 'kick off'. Meeting with unit managers to discuss overall guidelines for the three-year planning period.

Between March and May
Unit managers carry out marketing audits.

Stage 1 meetings

May
Planning team discuss three-year business plans with unit managers and amend as necessary.

Stage 2 meetings

November
Present amended three-year plan and detailed one-year plans to planning team.

December
HQ consolidation of one- and three-year plans.

This is what unit managers must present in their strategic marketing plans

May
1 Unit mission statement. 2 Summary of unit's performance last year. 3 Summary of financial projections for the next three years. 4 A market overview. 5 SWOT analyses (of major products/markets). 6 Portfolio summary. 7 Major assumptions. 8 Marketing objectives and strategies for next three years. 9 Financial projections for next three years.

Between Sept and October
Prepare detailed one-year operational plan with forecasts and budgets.

Figure 3(a) The marketing planning process

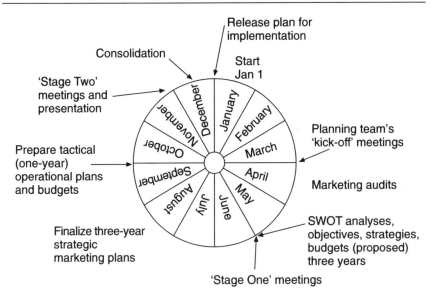

Figure 3(b)   Strategic and operational planning cycle

1   External audit
2   Internal audit

The external audit is concerned with the uncontrollable variables, while the internal audit is concerned with the controllable variables. The external audit starts with an examination of information on the general economy and then moves on to the outlook for the health and growth of the markets served by the company and competitor activities in those markets.

The purpose of the internal audit is to assess the organization's resources as they relate to the environment and *vis-à-vis* the resources of competitors.

MARKETING PLANNING SYSTEMS

The degree to which organizations need formalized systems for marketing planning depends on size and complexity. In small companies top management tends to have an in-depth knowledge of both the technology and the market, hence they have a clear view of their comparative strengths and weaknesses. There is often also a shared understanding between top and middle management of the logical framework of ideas within which they are all working.

In large organizations and in those operating in complex product and market situations, a more formalized approach via operating manuals, procedures and processes is more necessary, because of the sheer size and complexity.

781

In all cases, however, research has shown that the process is universally applicable. All that varies is the degree of formality in its systematization.

Relationship between marketing planning, business planning and corporate planning

Marketing planning is based on markets, customers and products.

Business planning involves the other corporate resources that must be brought to bear on the identified markets.

Corporate planning usually involves applying business planning to several different units of the business aggregate.

Table 2 depicts marketing planning and its place in the corporate planning cycle. If marketing is a major activity in an organization, as in the case of consumer goods companies and many service organizations, it is usual to have a separate strategic and tactical marketing plan. In other cases, the marketing elements are incorporated into business plans for all the other organizational functions at the same time as marketing objectives and strategies are set. Often, these business plans get incorporated into a corporate plan, which will contain long-range corporate objectives, strategies, plans, profit and loss accounts, and balance sheets.

One of the main purposes of a corporate plan is to provide a long-term vision of what the company is or is striving to become, taking account of shareholder expectations, environmental trends, resource market trends, consumption market trends, and the distinctive competence of the company as revealed by the management audit. What this means in practice is that the corporate plan will contain the following elements:

* Desired level of profitability.
* Business boundaries:
  – what kinds of products will be sold to what kinds of markets (marketing).
  – what kinds of facilities will be developed (production and distribution).
  – the size and character of the labour force (personnel).
  – funding (finance).
* Other corporate objectives, such as social responsibility, corporate image, stock market image, employer image.

Such a corporate plan, containing projected profit and loss accounts and balance sheets, being the result of the process described above, is more likely to provide long-term stability for a company than plans based on a more intuitive process and containing forecasts which tend to be little more than extrapolations of previous trends.

In contrast, the headquarters of one major multinational company with a sophisticated budgeting system used to receive 'plans' from all over the world and coordinate them in quantitative and cross-functional terms such as numbers of employees, units of sales, items of plant, square feet of production area, and

782

Table 2 Marketing planning and its place in the corporate planning cycle

Step 1	Step 2 *Management audit*	Step 3 *Objective and strategy setting*	Step 4 *Plans*	Step 5 *Corporate plans*
	Marketing audit Marketing	Marketing objectives, strategies	Marketing plan	
	Distribution audit Stocks and control; transportation; warehousing	Distribution objectives, strategies	Distribution plan	Issue of corporate plan, to include corporate objectives and strategies; production objectives and strategies; long–range profit and loss accounts; balance sheets
Corporate financial objectives	**Production audit** Value analysis; engineering development; work study; quality control; labour; materials, plant and space utilization; production planning; factories	Production objectives, strategies	Production plan	
	Financial audit Credit, debt, cash flow and budgetary control; resource allocation; capital expenditure; long-term finance	Financial objectives, strategies	Financial plan	
	Personnel audit Management, technical and administrative ability, etc.	Personnel objectives, strategies		

so on, together with the associated financial implications. The trouble was that the whole complicated edifice was built on the initial sales forecasts, which were themselves little more than a time-consuming numbers game. The really key strategic issues relating to products and markets were lost in all the financial activity, which eventually resulted in grave operational and profitability problems.

In summary, strategic and tactical marketing planning has been shown to make a vital contribution to an organization's long-term financial health.

REFERENCES

Ansoff, H. I. (1977) 'The state and practice of planning systems', *Sloan Management Review* 18 (2).

Greenley, G. (1987) 'An exposition into empirical research into marketing planning', *Journal of Marketing Management* 3 (1).

Kollatt, D. J., Blackwell, R. D. and Robeson, J. F. (1972) *Strategic Marketing*, New York: Holt, Reinhart and Winston.

Leighton, D. S. R. (1966) *International Marketing Text and Cases*, New York: McGraw-Hill.

McDonald, M. H. B. (1984) 'The theory and practice of marketing planning for industrial goods in international markets', PhD, Cranfield: Cranfield Institute of Technology.

Thompson, S. (1962) 'How companies plan', AMA Research Study, Chicago: American Marketing Association.

Thune, S. and House, R. (1970) 'Where long-range planning pays off', *Business Horizons* 7 (4).

FURTHER READING

Leppard, J. and McDonald, M. H. B. (1987) 'A reappraisal of the role of marketing planning', *Journal of Marketing Management* 3 (2).

McDonald, M. H. B. (1989) *Marketing Plans: How To Prepare Them; How To Use Them*, Oxford: Butterworth-Heinemann.

V MARKETING IN PRACTICE

45

COMMODITY MARKETING

David H. Buisson

Trade in commodities is probably the world's largest business and each year it continues to grow. Fully 70 per cent of the world's 125 largest economies depend on primary commodities for more than half their export earnings. Constant change, progressively fiercer competition and the rise in the number of large transnational companies is changing the nature of world commodity markets – increasing the marketing role as an element of the business. This chapter examines the role of marketing in relation to world trade in commodities or undifferentiated world products.

WHAT ARE COMMODITIES?

A commodity can be broadly defined as 'an item suitable for trade' that can assume many different forms and characteristics which render it suitable to be bought and sold for commercial purposes (Gordon-Ashworth 1984). Primary commodities are described as goods in or near to their first stage of transformation (ibid. 1984). However, Brown (1975) offers an alternative definition: those commodities which are products of the land – whether they are extracted from, grown on or raised on – can be considered primary commodities while they remain in an unprocessed or partially processed state. Products which are harvested or fished from bodies of water are also primary commodities until they have undergone substantial transformation. If the product has undergone some processing, but with only minor inputs which do not change its essential characteristics, it can still be considered a primary commodity. Many commodities do undergo some processing before they are first exchanged internationally. (For example, rubber in its unprocessed state straight from the tree has to undergo a transformation process to make it solid rubber, the final commodity which is bought and sold.)

In more recent times many new innovative products in various industries such as chemicals, plastics, electronic products, semiconductors and salmon were differentiated products. With economies of scale, learning by doing, oligopolistic exploitation of these advantages, low cost mass producers and international competition, these products have been rendered essentially manufactured commodities in world markets. As Rangan and Bowman (1992) state even though such products are loosely characterized as commodities, in reality it is the product market combination that one usually refers to in making such a characterization. Regardless of whether the product is corn or computers it is the market dynamics that distinguish a commodity. Most managers recognize the early warning signs of commoditization – increasing competition, availability of 'me too' products, the customer's reluctance to pay for features and services accompanying the product, and pressure on prices and margins in general. Steadily and deliberately as the market transforms into a commodity, many buyers begin to perceive the product and its suppliers to be homogeneous, and price becomes the predominant buying criterion.

Thus a commodity market is one where the company has minimum advantages in terms of differentiation and cost. Commodity products are those where the customer has no particular requirement to buy from a particular supplier, and will readily purchase other origin products almost entirely on the basis of comparative pricing.

When a product is in a commodity situation, the conventional market theory is to differentiate the product by adding value in packaging, convenience, or in the delivery system. This is not possible with many commodity products such as metals, crude petroleum product, and agricultural products such as grains. However, traditional commodities of the past such as chicken have been successfully moved from a commodity position to a differentiated product to the extent that chicken is now a branded product with the marketing opportunities that affords (Thomas and Koonce 1989; Jereski 1985).

Commodity products cover a wide range of product options from raw materials through partially processed products to manufactured goods. For the purpose of this chapter manufactured commodities will only be considered where they add to the understanding of the marketing of primary commodities. Commodities will be treated as basically primary commodities which are traded in a relatively standardized state with minor if any differentiating features. Consideration will be given to the immense marketing pushes occurring today to differentiate traditional commodities.

THE DEVELOPMENT OF COMMODITY MARKETING

The trading of commodities involves huge, worldwide markets. All countries produce some primary products, in particular primary commodities are the single most important contributor to trade in 75 per cent of developing countries if mineral fuels are excluded.

Some commodities are traded widely but others, because of high transportation costs, are largely traded regionally compared with internationally. For example, timber from Canada is mainly sold within Canada and the USA, but increasingly to Japan and Asia.

The development of the marketing of commodities requires a brief consideration of the history of commodity trading. The importance and value of commodities reflects marketing developments in the past, current activities today and developments underway for the future.

In 1938 the top three commodities traded were cotton, coal and crude petroleum. Cotton was the commodity with the highest value of $600 million annually in 1938. By 1977 the situation had changed dramatically and the three most traded commodities were crude petroleum, petroleum products, and coffee with cotton having fallen to twentieth place, a situation which has continued through the 1980s and into the 1990s. Agricultural commodities are the major primary commodities produced though not traded internationally.

The role and importance of nations has also changed considerably since the turn of the century. In the 1930s the UK and colonies were the most important traders, accounting for over 50 per cent of world trade of wool, rubber, tea and tin, and over 30 per cent of wheat, butter, beef, lamb, mutton, rice and flour. However, following the outbreak of World War II primary commodity trade changed. The severe foreign exchange regulations radically changed the ways in which primary commodities were distributed and marketed. In the UK and USA governments bought in bulk from producer organizations and distributed to the final consumer. Exporters were faced with one or two large buyers and the effect on marketing was the replacement of private merchandising with almost complete government control. The private merchandising system was not fully in place and commodity marketing developed until 1956.

The greatest trend since post World War II has been the decline in real prices of commodity goods compared with manufactured goods. The long-term decline is mainly the outcome of falling long-term production costs as a result of intensified competition in the world economy, including competition generated by more advanced country exporters.

Price decline is continuing to be a dominant trend but primary commodity exports still account for the bulk of foreign exchange earnings for many less developed countries (LDCs). For the majority of LDCs most export earnings come from sales of three or less primary commodities. For example, in 1990 Burundi, Ghana and Zambia received 70 per cent of their export earning from one primary commodity. The fall in primary export earnings in real terms has greatly added to the indebtedness of LDCs. The problem for these countries is further exacerbated by import barriers from developed countries which make it harder for LDCs to sell their primary commodities and therefore reduce their debt.

The high volatility of prices is also contributed to by the rigidities of supply caused by the very nature of the commodities such as dependence on weather conditions or long gestation periods of investments (e.g. a coffee tree has to grow for five years before a crop can be harvested). These supply rigidities are very often reinforced by inappropriate domestic policies which insulate domestic from international price movements (Fischer 1991).

From a demand perspective, technological progress, low population growth and the increasing availability of substitutes more desired by consumers has impacted significantly the demand for some commodities. Demand for coffee is nearly saturated in terms of per capita consumption; artificial substitutes for sugar have taken increasing shares of the markets as consumers demand diet products; demand for oil has decreased as nations have exploited their own alternative fuels such as gas; and demand for raw materials like copper or cotton are sensitive to growth of industrial output.

Agricultural policies, most notably in the USA, EU (European Union) and East Asia (including Japan and South Korea), have impacted significantly trade in agricultural commodities. Subsidies for agricultural production and export have contributed to increased world supply and lower prices. Protectionism has reduced demand and contributed to price volatility and to the need to differentiate products to circumvent non tariff trade barriers. These have all distorted international commodity markets to varying extents. Marketing monopolies in both producer and consumer countries have also markedly distorted trade.

In 1990 there were three principal consuming markets for commodities. The USA was the biggest importer of coffee, sisal, sugar and lead. The UK imported the most meat, dairy products, tea and zinc. Western Europe was the largest importer of petroleum, wheat, cotton, vegetable oils and seeds, wool, rubber, copper, tobacco, cocoa, jute and maize.

TRADING IN COMMODITIES

Although the trading of primary commodities is essential to the functioning of the world economy, there are a number of problems that must be addressed in order for the system to operate efficiently. Four of these important problems will be discussed here. First, the perceived declining terms of developing countries' trade has a negative influence on international commodity policy. Second, the high dependence of developing countries' economies on primary commodities means they are greatly affected by price reductions. Therefore the developing countries are much more vulnerable as their export portfolios are highly concentrated on primary commodities. For example, in 1987 twelve developing countries relied on one primary commodity for 90 per cent of their income and 23 developing countries relied upon crude petroleum and petroleum products for 50 per cent or more of their export earning. In comparison, only one developed country (Iceland) relied on one primary commodity (fish) for more than 50 per cent of its export earnings. Another problem is that manufactured goods have caused particular problems for the economies of developing countries. Hence, price stabilization has formed a recurrent objective of international commodity controls. The fourth problem is that without careful planning and control the supply of some primary commodities may be depleted if demand increases.

To overcome some of these problems a number of world commodity controls have been developed with some form of control being applied to most commodities impacting the marketing of them. Two main types of commodity control exist. The first are international commodity agreements between governments and producer organizations. The most clearly defined of these have been applied to tin, wheat, sugar, rubber, coffee, cocoa and tea. The principal aim of international commodity agreements has the main emphasis on balancing supply with demand resulting in an increase in export earnings to the producers. The most common form of control mechanism has been some form of quantitative restriction on exports, used in conjunction with either international or national stock control policies (Gordon-Ashworth 1984). The second type are international cartels described as 'arrangements between producers or traders with the aim to control production and distribution to their common advantage'. Crude petroleum (OPEC), copper, mercury, bauxite, uranium and iron ore are notable cartels which have varied in strength over the years with increasing disintegration over recent times.

These controls, while they have their advantages, do bring up several issues for debate. Agricultural protectionism policies, especially in Europe, cause problems for other overseas exporters. The Common Agricultural Policy (CAP) of the EU is a significant obstacle as the EU represents the largest world market for agricultural goods. This policy effectively excludes competition from more cost-efficient nations. The EU also creates instability in world markets by dumping surplus products as subsidized exports and through variable import levies. For example, levies rise when world prices fall, thus restricting demand when world supplies are plentiful. The effect of these protectionist policies is damaging to the protecting nations (higher consumer prices) and to developed agricultural exporters, such as New Zealand, and to developing nations. The tariff escalation policies aim to deter exporters from attempting to differentiate or add value to their products, thus maintaining them as commodities. These policies dictate that the tariff increases, as further processing is done. Thus, the tariff varies inversely with value added resulting in exceptionally high rates of protection. This denies countries the opportunity effectively to increase their income by adding value where they have a comparative advantage in growing or processing.

Primary commodity producers in LDCs have particular problems in that they have limited bargaining power in relation to large transnational companies and therefore find it difficult to improve their share of the final price. There are two alternative strategies to overcome this problem. The first strategy attempts to reduce the concentration in trade and increase marketing. This requires producers to increase their marketing efforts with the aim of increasing the number of buyers or to stimulate competition between existing buyers. An alternative strategy is to endeavour to increase the price elasticity of supply. This could be achieved by establishing a single marketing board for each commodity in each country and would mean that the producers are acting as a monopoly to counterbalance the power of transnational companies. However, the ability to increase price is still limited in the case of many countries due to relatively weak market positions. Their power ultimately depends on their ability to market directly to the final consumer. LDC producers are at a great disadvantage with transnational corporations in processing and marketing products because these organizations have certain monopolistic advantages which make it difficult for the LDCs to develop independently their own effective marketing strategies. The major problems facing the LDCs is that they have limited access to relevant market information, they have no cheap transport and they face many obstacles from intra-firm agreements of transnational companies.

Several world organizations have attempted to aid LDCs in the marketing of commodities. For example, UNCTAD established the Integrated Programme for Commodities (IPC) which aimed 'to establish within the context of the IPC a framework of international cooperation in the field of marketing and distribution of LDCs' commodity exports, with the objective of increasing their export earnings'. Only a few producer associations were formed and they had limited success. They resulted in improved information sharing, promoted the harmonization of marketing policies and established cooperative marketing but did not succeed in raising prices.

MARKETING OF COMMODITIES

An integral part of the process of selling commodities is the marketing process. This has been defined by Rowe (1965) as the process of:

> transferring supplies of the commodity from the producing units, whether these be individuals or small or large corporations, to the processors or manufacturers in the consuming countries. Marketing thus involves physical processes of collection from the actual producers, transport within the producing country to the ports, ocean shipment, stockholding, and distribution within the consuming countries.
>
> (Rowe 1965: 32)

This process is often aided by a commodity exchange defined as 'an organisation usually owned by member traders, which provides facilities for bringing buyers and sellers of specified commodities or their agents, for promoting trades in these commodities' (AMA Committee on Definitions 1963: 15). The marketing of commodities is an intricate process with the main structure and principles of marketing being much the same for all commodities, though varying in detail for specific commodities. Ownership of the goods is transferred many times during the process and the price must be determined for each exchange. Buyers usually satisfy their requirements through issuing tenders or through placing 'spot' orders with commodity merchants or brokers. Most transactions take place directly between commodity manufacturers and food or non-food manufacturers, but merchant traders sometimes act as agents or commission brokers. Some countries have government-controlled marketing boards which act as the sole buyers and sellers of the commodity. For example, the Cocoa Marketing Board in Nigeria guarantees minimum prices for the growers and aims to reduce exploitation.

Buyers choose suppliers on the basis of the products being within specification and delivered at specified times. Buyers who are exposed to the open world commodity market are particularly sensitive to variations in commodity prices and wish to avoid the risk of holding higher-priced stocks on a falling market.

Manufacturers who have the option of procuring commodities by tender or spot purchase sometimes derive higher value from direct contractual linkages with producers. These provide assurances of reliable supply, consistent quality and service. Contracts also enable buyers to make requests for limited special features, such as delivery schedules. Premiums of up to 5 per cent over free market prices can be obtained for some commodities under such contractual arrangements. Government buyers are particularly prevalent in this increasingly used type of exchange for commodity purchase.

Price determination is critical for commodity buying and selling. Prices in all markets for commodities tend to be uniform once allowances are made for differences in quality and in transport and distribution costs. The world market price reflects the demand and supply conditions over the world as a whole, both immediately and in the foreseeable future. Rivalry in tendering and spot commodity markets is based largely on price competition.

Price fluctuation is a problem with the marketing of primary commodities. The prices of all primary commodities, without an organized control scheme, would fluctuate dramatically. With most commodities supply and demand are continually changing and this can greatly affect prices. In general, in the short term, final consumer demand is inelastic due to slow changes in consumers' tastes and supply is inelastic since producers cannot rapidly increase or decrease their output. The effect of this is that prices tend to fall very considerably if supply is even slightly larger than demand, and rise sharply if it is even slightly smaller. In the long term, prices are affected by changes in final consumption, demand and current production. In the long term final demand is inelastic for small price changes but may alter if the price change is sufficiently large. The commodities most affected by price changes are those which have competitive substitutes. For example, during World War II tin shortages dramatically raised the price and therefore the demand for substitute metals increased. However, after the war when tin supplies increased and it became a moderately low priced commodity demand for tin did not increase as consumers were used to substitutes. Generally a continued low price is needed to prevent the development of artificial substitutes. A sustained price change can lead to large changes in production capacity, but usually only in response to large and prolonged price changes. One problem is that short-term price fluctuations often mask long-term trends. Thus, production is likely to be increased or decreased too much causing further oscillations in price. These price changes greatly affect the economies of exporting countries, hence the desire to move out of the commodity pricing trap.

THE FUTURES MARKET

Commodities face rapidly fluctuating prices depending on the output, exports, political and climatic conditions and the world economy. Many producers and users in the marketing system attempt to minimize these swings in value because of the lack of financial ability to withstand these price and earning risks. The market mechanism established to stabilize commodity prices or earnings uses the futures market as the market instrument to protect against price fluctuation beyond one's control. This is done by trading some of the output in advance of its actual production at prices known at the moment of trade. By choosing the quantity agreed to be delivered at a fixed price, the producer is able to alter the price and earnings distribution in a desirable way, but leave the price and earnings distribution for the rest of the market unchanged.

Futures exchanges exist throughout the world. The most notable are the Chicago Board of Trade, operating principally in agricultural products; the Coffee, Sugar and Cocoa Exchange in New York; the New York Cotton Exchange; and the London Metal Exchange, which is the world's premier exchange for commodity metals such as aluminium, copper, zinc, lead, nickel and silver.

Futures contracts can be exchanged through traders or brokers in an extremely wide range of commodities based on agricultural, metallurgical and petroleum products in exchanges based all over the world with those listed above tending to be price setters. Delivery of the commodity is possible on many futures markets but is optional and seldom occurs in practice. The usefulness of the futures market in protecting traders against adverse price changes depends on the convergence of cash and futures prices as the contract approaches maturity.

Futures markets can protect both producers and processors alike from price changes, but they also have a role in price determination in that the market takes account of information about the conditions of supply and demand and provides estimates of future prices based on this information.

To assist trading, transactions in various commodities are standardized: for wool the standard contract is 2,500 kilos; for live cattle 10,000 kilos liveweight; copper 25 tonnes; gold 250 grams; cocoa 25 tonnes; EU wheat 100 tonnes; fuel oil 100 tonnes.

The disadvantages of a futures market is that it is possible for people who have no direct interest in a particular commodity to operate in the relevant futures market. However their presence is considered to make a more efficient market (Campbell and Fisher 1991). The futures market, while not engendering any loyalty to a particular product or producer, plays a valuable role in risk transfer, equity financing, market intelligence, price discovery and forward pricing. In theory at least, a futures market should result in more stable prices. There are, however, other ways to organize these functions and activities, in particular in food commodities. Today, many commodities appear to be marketed efficiently without the benefit of futures trading. Kohls and Uhl (1990) conclude that marketing costs are reduced by the costs of risk for a net increase in operational efficiency for the food industry. Whether this is true of the metals commodity market is open to debate. The commodities futures markets are much criticized, but play a necessary and important role in price determination and price stabilization in the marketplace. It is, however, extremely difficult to look at a pricing strategy for commodities in such a marketplace.

MARKETING INFORMATION

Marketing information is critical for success in exporting commodities. Accurate information is particularly important when predicting future demand and supply and future prices. The amount and quality of information readily available varies among commodities largely because of differences in trading practices. For example, if the commodity is sold at an auction (e.g. tea) or on an exchange (e.g. sugar and coffee) then information on sales is generally available daily. However, if the commodity is sold on a long-term contract or intra-firm (e.g. bauxite and jute) information on sales is not easily obtainable by outsiders. There are a number of secondary sources of published information which provide useful information. These include information from government departments, international commodity study groups and major trading firms' publication of marketing information and forecasts, information from the Food and Agricultural Organization and the World Bank, and material from specific trade journals. However, this type of information is not really detailed enough to serve as an effective aid to decision-making, thus compounding the problems of marketing commodities.

To obtain business, commodity traders need excellent sources of information about production levels, the level and specifications of stocks, forthcoming orders from manufacturers, and changes in price support levels and subsidies.

ORGANIZATION FOR MARKETING COMMODITIES

Commodity marketing of agricultural products, in particular, is characterized by marketing by producer cooperatives or by marketing boards. Marketing boards are potent marketing agencies with the combined powers of cooperatives, marketing orders and bargaining associations. They are common worldwide such as the New Zealand Dairy Board; the Australian Wheat Board, and also operate in Canada, France, England and Africa.

Marketing boards are essentially producer-controlled organizations with government monopoly powers over a broad range of farm production and

795

marketing activities. The chief functions of these operating boards have been outlined by Kohls and Uhl (1990) as:

1 Collective bargaining and price negotiation, acting as a single agent for all producers of the commodity.
2 Sole marketing agent for the commodity, with broad controls over all aspects of marketing, including the ownership of storage facilities.
3 Sponsorship of market intelligence activities and market research.
4 Producer pooling arrangements to divide receipts among farmers.
5 Settling production and marketing controls and quotas.

The argument in support of such boards is that marketing regulation is very important in commodity trading to exploit market power, thus maximizing producer returns. References to orderly marketing, weak selling, destructive competition, market premiums and the need to extract the most from the market are the arguments for those advocating regulations to achieve coordinated and disciplined marketing of agricultural commodities.

The marketing power most readily exploited by these boards is that arising through preferred access to a restricted and higher priced market under quota and access restrictions. Such quotas exist for commodities in many markets such as agricultural quotas into the EU, cheese and beef quotas into the USA, and the butter quota into the UK. The entitlement or quota to sell, usually a maximum quantity, in a market where trade and domestic policies maintain prices above international levels is valuable. These quotas exist widely in the commodity trade and distort the traditional marketing process of a product.

With global changes and increasingly open access of some markets, calls have been made for the abolition of such marketing boards on the grounds that the regulations and marketing structures emphasize a marketing objective of maximizing farm gate prices rather than profit maximization in the marketplace through allowing a series of suppliers to compete in a marketplace (Hussey 1992).

Commodity markets are shrinking relative to consumer products. A new era in food demand and marketing has already commenced. There are no longer principally generic markets for products such as dairy products, meat or wool. Instead there is an increasing diversity of markets for products derived from these raw materials with product form, packaging, and methods of retailing differing between markets. While there has been a trend from commodity to consumer products in the agricultural marketing of some countries, it is questionable whether it has matched the rate of market change. The tendency of monopoly sellers or marketing regulations to restrict product range and to innovate more slowly than competitive sellers is being used as the argument for changing the monopoly selling status of marketing boards (Hussey 1992).

PROMOTION OF COMMODITIES IN THE MARKET

As commodity markets reach saturation and competing products develop, the role of market boards is to promote the product. These operate domestically in many countries and play a significant role in promoting commodity products. Organizations such as the National Livestock and Meat Board of the USA, the Ontario Milk Marketing Board of Canada and the Danish Dairy Board of Denmark widely promote sales of their products domestically and increasingly internationally.

International commodity producers have bonded together as competition from alternative products or declining consumer demand is evident. These 'commodity' groups funded by producers generically promote the product. Notable examples are the International Wool Secretariat and the International Coffee Organization, both based in the UK. The argument of effectiveness of generic promotion can be considered in contrasting these two products.

The International Wool Secretariat conducts wool promotion on behalf of the growers of its member countries (Australia, New Zealand, Uruguay and South Africa) using the 'Woolmark' symbol. It promotes wool in the major wool-consuming markets around the world, principally in Western Europe, the USA and Japan. An important distinction between wool and other commodities subject to generic promotion is that, for the most part, wool is not directly the object of consumer choice. Promotion is typically directed at increasing the demand for final products in which wool is an attribute. In a study on the effectiveness of such generic promotion Dewbre and Beare (1992) showed that wool promotion, prices and household income were all statistically significant variables in household level wool-in-apparel demand. The conclusions of this study were that such expenditures were profitable and stimulated demand for wool but the question remains as to whether there is an increasing or decreasing response to further promotional expenditure.

In a review of the role of promotion of the International Coffee Agreement (Greer and Chattalas 1989) it was concluded that despite the many advertising themes and campaigns the critical areas of theme appropriateness, setting of objectives, continuity, potential for synergy between generic and brand campaigns, and evaluation have received inadequate attention. The Promotion Fund had ignored many opportunities such as decaffeinated coffee, had not developed cooperation between the commodity producing nations and largely capitalist consuming countries and had the misconception that promotion is mainly a capitalist-colonialist tool used for the exploitation of their national markets.

Generic promotion of a commodity has the unique potential to help smooth out the devastating effects that demand instability can have on commodity industries. Promotion would tend to stabilize third world economies since price alone has not proved to be a sufficient stabilizer of demand and revenue. Promotion would make demand more predictable and consequently more dependable for market development than price stabilization alone.

The effectiveness of generic advertising from a commodity perspective has come under increasing scrutiny recently. Collectively generic commodity advertisers spend significant amounts, with the likelihood that as new mandatory check-off programmes such as for beef, pork and milk in the USA become mandated, the total value will increase significantly. Despite the large sums spent and the apparent willingness of producers to support the programmes, little is known about the economic impacts of generic advertising. The impacts of generic advertising on middlemen and producers either are not addressed or are inferred from retail impacts. Inferences about producer level impacts based on measurement at the retail level may be misleading, especially if middlemen possess the market power (Wohlgenant 1991).

Through advertising initiatives, commodity groups are attempting to promote the marketing of their product. Conventional marketing wisdom perceives in getting a product to market first. Hence there is a belief that generic advertising is not a prudent way to spend money. It is generally agreed that new techniques are needed to evaluate generic advertising and its effectiveness (MacDonald and Gould 1992). Success cannot be measured by profit and loss as in the case of private companies.

Results of a major study on the catfish industry in the USA (Zidack *et al.* 1992) suggest that the generic advertising programme increased producer returns both at the wholesale and farm levels of the market. It was concluded that despite industry concentration at the wholesale level, it appears that farmers could benefit from promotional programmes aimed at shifting retail demand. Results suggested that commodity promotion programmes did not have to be big to be effective, even limited budget programmes could increase demand and be profitable, especially if supply is inelastic.

The results of international and domestic studies highlight the critical need for careful allocation of funds to ensure that they are used in the most efficient manner possible. In particular with commodities, because markets are dynamic, subject to rapid change due to changes in relative prices, income, new products and other factors, advertising programmes must be routinely assessed to determine their effectiveness and to provide guidance for future funding decisions.

CURRENT AND FUTURE DEVELOPMENTS IN COMMODITY MARKETING

As commodity markets change, producers are attempting to differentiate their product. Traditionally firms operating in the commodity sector have tended to focus their efforts on a specific segment of the sector. The implicit demarcation according to Hudson (1990) between the production and processing subsectors has been commodity processing (i.e. the killing of livestock, the milling of grain). Firms involved in activities which impact the commodity prior to processing are

Input-oriented goods and services

Output-oriented goods and services

Figure 1 A traditional view of competitiveness focusing on the production sector
Source: Hudson (1990: 184)

in the production subsector and firms involved after processing are in the processing subsector. Firms in the production subsector view commodity producers as the primary consumers of the goods and services they provide, while firms in the processing subsector focus on the final consumers.

Hudson (1990) depicts the view of competitiveness in the agribusiness industry focusing on the production sector. As depicted in Figure 1 the producer is the central focus of the firm and the emphasis is on surrounding the producer with goods and services which are either inputs associated with commodity production (feed, seed and fertilizer; machinery and equipment; financing; and production information), or outputs associated with commodity marketing and distribution (marketing services; commodity processing; market information; and transportation).

Commodity firms with a view to competitiveness strive to surround the commodity producer using vertical coordination to control the various spokes of the wheel in Figure 1. Hudson (1990) cites numerous examples that illustrate the application of this perspective. This perspective is changing with firms aggressively pursuing contractual arrangements for the production and procurement of commodities. The common thread identified by Hudson (1990) is the merging of the production and processing sectors towards a strategy of vertical coordination. Strong evidence of this is seen in the USA and increasing evidence in New Zealand, Australia and Denmark.

Advances in technology, increasing concern by consumers over diet, and an expanded demand for convenience, have created a two-tier processing sector: commodity processing and further processing. With this two-tiered structure we have commodity firms and value added firms. Some firms specialize in either commodity or value added processing and other firms in both activities. Commodity marketers are likely to consider the perspective shown in Figure 1 and utilize a generic strategy of cost leadership to survive. Such firms will differ largely by their geographic location and the services which they offer producers. An approach being utilized increasingly is one of a cost leadership strategy augmented by a move to achieve differentiations through service to customers.

However, Hudson (1990) predicts that as the focus on consumers continues to characterize the food and agribusiness sectors, new relationships within the vertical production marketing channel will evolve. Both commodity processors and value added processors will seek further control of the activities between production of commodities and the final consumer product, and an increased blurring of the commodity and value added sector will occur. These changes will become increasingly important in shaping the future of commodity marketing. Goldberg (1985) suggested that 'a systems approach to each major commodity system has to be developed in order to position a firm or a nation in its global food setting'. To survive as a commodity marketer in the future will require a close evaluation of position and involvement in the food chain.

Commodity bundling – the grouping of products and services so that when combined they form a unique marketing offering – has potential for the marketing of traditional commodities. It is a familiar approach in many industries, yet the strategic and structural implications are not well developed. Lawless (1991) discusses the potential advantages of commodity bundling resulting in lower costs or increased benefits at a higher cost, based on products that could be loosely defined as manufactured commodities. Such strategy has the potential to be used increasingly by commodity marketers to differentiate their product. For example, the New Zealand Dairy Board offers strong technical support, pilot scale facilities and training with sales of milk proteins in the USA. It also tailors commodity production to meet tight customer specifications. The vulnerability of commodity trading has led producers to differentiate their commodity offerings by reducing buyers' risk. They do this by guaranteeing delivery schedules, volumes and product specifications.

Commodities have been successfully differentiated. Poultry products traditionally were considered relatively homogeneous and undifferentiated products at both farm and retail level. Branding and brand advertising is now relatively common for eggs and usual for chickens. The success of branded chickens such as Perdue, Tysons and Holly Farms attests to the ability to differentiate a commodity. Adverse market conditions, unique among food processors, of slim profit margins, feed prices that are variable on an hourly basis and the distribution problems of a fresh product – all that conspire against the creation of a brand – were overcome. Tysons succeeded in dispelling the commodity image of the industry by marketing and distributing a wide variety of new processed products in what the industry called value enhanced products. These value enhanced products allow processors to differentiate their offerings from those of their competitors as well as making profits less susceptible to fluctuation in raw material costs, improving profit stability (Thomas and Koonce 1989).

Strategies of differentiating through value enhancement are being made, for example, by the New Zealand Dairy Board for milk powder in new forms of convenient packaging for industrial users or in reducing dust problems through the use of new powder-forming technologies. Branding strategies are being developed, for example the ENZA brand of the New Zealand Apple and Pear Marketing Board allowing it to sell apples of equivalent quality sourced worldwide, rather than simply from New Zealand. Branded merino wool in its commodity state is being sold as Merino Gold out of Australia. Branding and differentiation strategies will eventually move many commodities into differentiated product markets changing commodity marketing in some products as we know them. Developments in meat, many fruit and vegetable and some parts of the cereal sectors are clearly directed towards a differentiation strategy.

The future will see increasing differentiation of commodity products, a shrinking of the commodity markets for many products, increasing vertical integration of the commodity processing and value added sectors of the food industry reducing the need for commodity marketing, and increasing competition in what remains of the traditional commodity markets. The commodity market will remain distorted through marketing control, protectionism, and the particular nature of trading of commodities on the futures market or using commodity brokers. The results of the Uruguay GATT round may in years to come significantly change commodity marketing. The challenge is to look for and take opportunities to use marketing concepts to differentiate and stimulate markets for commodity products in an often very distorted marketplace.

REFERENCES

AMA Committee on Definitions (1963) *Marketing Definitions: A Glossary of Marketing Terms*, Chicago: American Marketing Association.
Brown, C. P. (1975) *Primary Commodity Control*, London: Oxford University Press.
Campbell, K. O. and Fisher, B. S. (1991) *Agricultural Marketing and Prices*, Melbourne: Longman Cheshire.
Dewbre, J. and Beare, S. (1992) 'Measuring wool promotion response with household survey data', in H. W. Kinnucan, S. R. Thompson and H. S. Chang (eds) *Commodity Advertising and Promotion*, Ames: Iowa State University Press.
Fischer, B. (1991) 'From commodity dependency to development', *OECD Observer* 169, April–May: 24–7.
Goldberg, R. A. (1985) 'A concept of a global food system and its use by private and public managers', *Agribusiness* 1 (1): 5–23.

Gordon-Ashworth, Fiona (1984) *International Commodity Control*, New York: St Martin's Press.
Greer, T. V. and Chattalas, M. J. (1989) 'The role of the promotion fund of the International Coffee Agreement', *International Marketing Review* 6 (3): 47–61.
Hudson, M. A. (1990) 'Toward a framework for examining agribusiness competitiveness', *Agribusiness* 6 (3): 181–9.
Hussey, D. (1992) *Agricultural Marketing Regulation: Reality versus Doctrine*, report prepared for the New Zealand Business Roundtable, Wellington: New Zealand Business Roundtable.
Jereski, L. K. (1985) 'The wishbone offense: branding a commodity', *Marketing and Media Decisions* May: 80–4, 176.
Kohls, R. L. and Uhl, J. N. (1990) *Marketing of Agricultural Products*, New York: Macmillan Publishing Company.
Lawless, M. W. (1991) 'Commodity bundling for competitive advantage: strategic implications', *Journal of Management Studies* 28 (3): 267–80.
MacDonald, A. and Gould, P. (1992) 'Generic advertising: a commodity perspective', in H. W. Kinnucan, S. R. Thompson and H. S. Chang (eds) *Commodity Advertising and Promotion*, Ames: Iowa State University Press.
Rangan, V. K. and Bowman, G. T. (1992) 'Beating the commodity magnet', *Industrial Marketing Management* 21: 215–24.
Rowe, J. W. F. (1965) *Primary Commodities in International Trade*, London: Cambridge University Press.
Thomas, J. G. and Koonce, J. M. (1989) 'Differentiating a commodity: Lessons for Tyson Foods', *Planning Review* September–October: 24–9.
Wohlgenant, M. K. (1991) 'Distribution of gains from research and promotion in multistage production systems: the case of the US beef and pork industries', unpublished manuscript cited in Zidack *et al.* (1992).
Zidack, W., Kinnucan, H. and Hatch, U. (1992) 'Wholesale and farm level impacts of generic advertising: the case of catfish', *Applied Economics* 24: 959–68.

FURTHER READING

Araim, A. S. (1991) *Intergovernmental Commodity Organisations and the New International Economic Order*, New York: Praeger.
Breyer, R. F. (1931) *Commodity Marketing*, New York: McGraw-Hill.
Hughes Hallett, A. J. and Ramanujam, P. (1990) 'The role of futures markets as stabilisers of commodity earnings', in L. A. Winters and D. Sapsford (eds) *Primary Commodity Prices: Economic Models and Policy*, Cambridge: Cambridge University Press.
Kolb, R. W. and Hamada R. S. (1988) *Understanding Futures Markets*, Glenview: Scott Foresman and Company.
Nappi, C. (1979) *Commodity Market Controls*, Lexington: Lexington Books.

46

BUSINESS MARKETING

Kristian Möller and David T. Wilson

Business marketing includes the development and marketing of products and services to business markets. Business markets are local and international markets for products and services purchased by businesses, government and institutions (like hospitals), for consumption (e.g. production process materials, office supplies, consulting services), for use (e.g. machinery, office equipment), or for resale.

Business marketing has important differences from consumer marketing. The customers of business marketers are organizations buying with different motivations from customers purchasing for their own or family's needs. The organizational buyer is acting for many others in the organization and is governed by a set of purchasing policies that define the rules of buying whereas the consumer buyer in most cases acts alone and is not governed by a set of buying policies and a formal procedure.

Organizational buying behaviour, described in Chapter 10, forms a key requisite for both the understanding and managing of business marketing. An important aspect of business marketing is doing business through long-term customer/supplier relationships. The principles of working through relationships and networks are portrayed in Chapter 12. An increasing part of the contemporary business marketing scene draws its sources and marketing strategies from international markets and firms (see Chapter 50).

We describe business marketing through the following key phenomena and concepts:

1 Types and characteristics of business markets illustrated through types of products, services, and customers.
2 Competitive and cooperative relationships.
3 A discussion of segmentation and positioning a product in a competitive business market.

CHARACTERISTICS OF BUSINESS MARKETS

Business markets are any market in which one organization sells goods or services to another organization. We envisage a broad view of industrial or business markets including all markets except the transactions between an organization and the final consumer. When Procter and Gamble (P&G) sell product to channel members such as distributors and chain stores or when they sell to the government they are acting as business marketers but when they sell to consumers they act as consumer marketers. Our broad definition is narrowed for the purposes of this chapter to describe the marketing of goods and services between 'for-profit' organizations.

What defines industrial markets?

Industrial markets include the industries that are in the value chain from producer to consumer ranging from agriculture, forestry, mining and fisheries to construction and manufacturing. They include services such as transportation, communication, banking, finance, insurance and public utilities. In order to place a can of tuna in the hands of a consumer, the value chain would include catching and processing the tuna, making cans for the processor, paper for labels, distributors, advertising and trucking the brand to market. Figure 1 describes a simplified value chain linking some of the many key elements that must be accomplished to bring a can of tuna to a consumer.

Consumer and industrial markets differ along a number of major dimensions. Buyers tend to be fewer in number than in consumer markets and a few buyers may control a large proportion of the volume in the industry. Industrial markets tend to be geographically concentrated. For example, more than 50 per cent of the industrial buyers in the USA are concentrated in 7 states. Figure 2 describes examples of the range of industries representing business marketing customers.

From an economic perspective industrial markets tend to be derived demand markets. The sale of tyres to automobile producers is dependent upon total car sales. At the market level, industrial demand is inelastic as the total demand for goods and services is not greatly affected by price changes. A drop in the industry price for tyres will not increase demand because the lower tyre cost to the auto producer will not change the final price of the car to the consumer enough to stimulate consumer demand.

A major difference between consumers and industrial buyers is size. An individual consumer usually represents a small portion of any seller's total sales whereas frequently an industrial buyer is a large portion of a seller's total sales. If the consumers are unhappy or dissatisfied they have limited direct power to pursue their grievances but an unhappy industrial buyer may have a great deal of power to force the seller to rectify the situation.

Product and technical knowledge between buyer and seller tend to be equal or may favour the buyer in industrial markets but knowledge generally favours

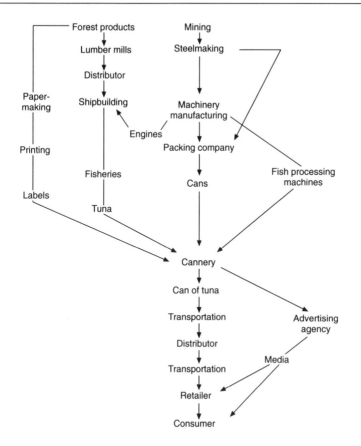

Figure 1   A simplified value chain to deliver a can of tuna to a consumer

the seller in consumer markets. Combining the knowledge differences that a professional buying organization possesses with the purchasing power differences of buyers and sellers often makes the industrial buyer equal or stronger than the seller. This scenario is quite different from the consumer market where the seller is more powerful and knowledgeable than the consumer.

The policies and procedures of professional purchasing force industrial buyers to be very deliberate in their purchasing process. The diversity of organizational interests that must be accommodated in many purchases dramatically influences buying behaviour in the industrial market.

Buying behaviour in business and consumer markets differs widely. In the consumer market, although one member of a household may act as a buyer for another member of the household, they are not guided by a policy manual as in the business market. The firm's rules for buying, combined with the interaction

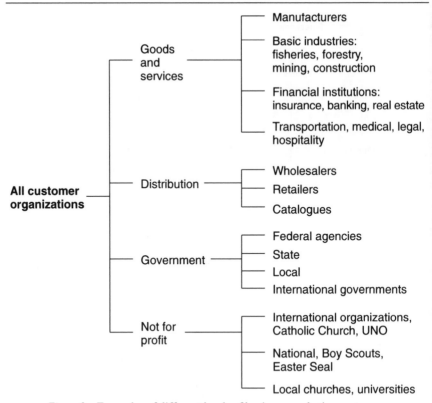

Figure 2   Examples of different levels of business marketing customers

of strong departments who may have a stake in the purchase, make industrial buying more complex than consumer purchases. Buying a new packaging machine may involve not only the interests of production engineers concerned with maintenance but also industrial engineers concerned with productivity, marketing concerned about the quality of the package, and management who may be concerned about the machine's impact on the workers. This level of complexity creates purchasing situations that tend to make personal selling the main communication tool in many industrial marketing situations.

At a simple level, both industrial and consumer marketers use the same marketing tools: advertising, promotion, salespeople, product, channels and price. The factors that describe industrial and business markets discussed above shape how the business marketer uses marketing tools and technology. At one end of the spectrum are consumer-like products such as fax machines and small copiers where there is a large dispersed market. The marketing programme for these consumer-like products approaches a consumer marketing programme in concept and execution. At the other extreme is a market with very few buyers such as the commercial aircraft market which requires a targeted marketing programme.

The traditional assumption in industrial markets has been that an adversarial relationship generates the lowest price purchases. Most buying firms have several suppliers compete against each other for shares of the purchase which helps the buyer negotiate the best purchase terms. Today many firms are moving to a cooperative model which assumes that by cooperating with a single source of supply, a lower total cost of acquiring the goods or services results. This lower total comes from containing other costs in the manufacturing process such as inventory costs being offset by just-in-time delivery. Buyer–seller relationships are dramatically reducing the number of suppliers any one firm uses. Some have reduced their supplier base from 1,500 suppliers to 300 to 400 suppliers who supply all of their needs in goods and services.

TYPES OF BUSINESS MARKETING RELATIONSHIPS

Classification of the different forms of marketing relationships helps to reduce the complexity of business markets into a few basic types. In Table 1 a distinction is made between market-based transactions, short- and long-term relationships, and buyer–seller partnerships. Transactions refer to business marketing exchanges where the competitive market forces (number of buyers and sellers and homogeneity versus differentiation of products/services) determine not only the price level and terms of delivery, but also the success of competing business marketers. The above situation can be called traditional or competitive marketing. It relies on identifying the target markets through segmentation and then positioning the product according to the competitors' offerings. These practices form the platform for planning and executing a marketing programme based on the marketing mix approach (see Chapters 23, 24, 25).

Table 1 Types of marketing relationships

Marketing relationships	Influencing forces	Characteristics
Transactions and repeated transactions	Market forces Competition	Sellers' market Buyers' market
Short-term and long-term relationships	Competition Interdependence Mutual goals	Balanced command
Partnerships (J-I-T, R&D, market entry, channels)	Interdependence Mutual goals Competition	Balanced Unbalanced

Source: Webster (1992)

807

Short-term and long-term buyer-seller relationships are characterized by more complex interaction between the marketer and customers. These interactions can be composed of social, economic, legal, technical, informational, and procedural relations. In the implementation phase, considerable effort to gain a contract needs to be given – for example, establishing an annual supply contract for important components such as different memory chips in PCs or a large maintenance order contract for mining machinery. Through established relationships, companies become interdependent; consequently, changing a supplier might involve considerable switching costs. Because of this interdependency, negotiations and transaction conditions between the marketer and customer become influenced.

In short-term relationships, the goal is to win a contract. In addition to competitive marketing practices the emphasis is on negotiations and bargaining behaviour. In this area, salespeople are the prime influence on the outcome. The organization of marketing and purchasing is often based on group interaction. Marketing or selling centres, as well as buying centres represent interfunctional forms of managing the dyadic marketing and purchasing relationship. Creating the customer relationship demands skills and activities which we refer to as relationship marketing.

In long-term business relationships (which we define as relationships ranging from several to tens of years) the focus shifts from establishing a dyadic contract to developing and managing the customer relationship. Long-term relationships create many new issues such as how to make the relationship effective and efficient, how to maximize benefits while minimizing risk, how to solve the inevitable conflicts which may occur. These issues form the content of relationship management.

Market forces still influence the relationship. Depending on the balance of the interdependence a customer relationship can be dominated either by the seller or the buyer.

The distinction between long-term business relationships and partnerships is often blurred. A key characteristic in marketer-customer partnerships is their intentional character. Both parties seek mutual benefits by cooperating and sharing information and resources. Examples of these business partnerships are J-I-T supply relationships, joint market operations, sharing distribution networks, and R&D cooperation.

In partnerships each party approaches total dependence on the other. Trust and cooperative management replace market control. Management of the relationship generally includes multiple level interaction between the participants involving representatives from several functions. Task forces and joint management groups are often employed for establishing the partnership and for monitoring the performance of activities. Relationship marketing has expanded into relationship management. In the next section we discuss competitive business marketing and conclude by dealing with relationship marketing and the management of a portfolio of customer relationships.

MARKET OFFERING AND COMPETITIVE TARGET MARKETING

The unique features of business markets that are described above make the developing global competitive advantage a challenge for business marketing managers. The customer and the selling organization are linked together through the market offering of the selling firm. The challenge is to create a market offering that provides differentiated value to the buyer that cannot be readily copied by competitors. When this occurs the selling firm has a sustainable competitive advantage.

The market offering of a firm may be conceptualized as having four components. The physical component is the actual physical representation of the product or service. For example, a computer has a keyboard that can be described by a set of engineering specifications which can be translated into a physical entity. A service company such as Federal Express creates the physical aspects of its service through the distinctive dress of its uniforms, trucks, airplanes and tracking software.

Technology is an increasingly important part of the market offering. Interactive technology represents the technology through which we interact with the product. We may interact with a computer to use a word processing program through the strokes of a keyboard or we can give directions to the program using a mouse and a windows program. The facilitating technology is more complex for the windows word processing program than the keystroke version of the program.

People represent all of the individuals with whom the buyer's firm interacts in acquiring the product or service. People from such diverse groups as sales, order entry, service, installation and accounts all impact on the performance level of the attributes sought by the customer. People are an important part of the business firm's market offering.

Company attributes are the fourth part of the market offering. These attributes go across all of the products or services that the firm offers. In a broad sense they represent the reputation of the firm in the marketplace.

The market offering connects the firm to the customer. The customer can be conceptualized as having a hierarchy of expectations that are based on needs and expressed in the benefits expected from the market offering. A marketing offering which matches the customer's needs leads to satisfaction and to the ultimate goal of creating customer value. Value is the provision of superior benefits at a price that the customer considers to be less than the benefit package is worth. Value is usually seen within the context of competitive marketing offerings.

Sellers use resources such as plant, capital and people to create capabilities, which in turn create a superior market offering. The firm's market position determines the ease with which it can manage the market offering in a market. A strong market position enhances the likelihood of success for a new market

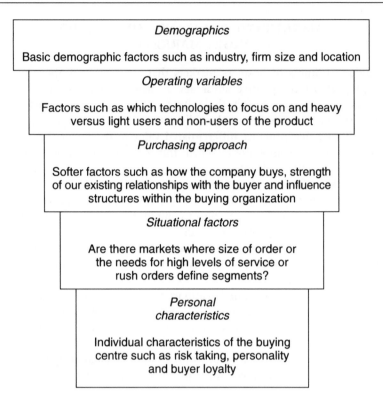

Figure 3   Important segmentation variables for business markets
Source: Bonoma and Shapiro (1983)

offering from the firm. A weak market position will probably require considerable resources to gain a market position and achieve success.

Both buyers' and sellers' interactions are coloured by their experiences and
perceptions of the marketplace. The market offering is the connection that joins
buyers and sellers. A successful business marketer needs to focus on markets that
will be most receptive to the market offering.

In order to make the best match of market offerings to customer needs we
begin by structuring the market. The goal of business market segmentation is
to get beyond the basic segmentation criteria that divide markets on such
mundane divisions as SIC code or size of firm. These are good fundamental
criteria but we need to go beyond the basic criteria to find ways of segmenting
the market that provide richer insight into the customer and their needs.
Bonoma and Shapiro (1983) suggest a nested set of factors for segmenting
business markets. Figure 3 presents their variables and a brief description of
each variable. The segment structure is matched with groups of products to

create a product/market matrix. Products in this instance means market offering. The objective is to prioritize the cells in the matrix and develop a unique marketing programme for the top priority cells.

Because of the special characteristics of business markets marketing programmes tend to focus more on the sales and channel decisions than on mass media issues. Although price is important it is not usually the most critical attribute in supplier selection. More detailed discussion of the marketing mix variables is available in other sections of this book.

The segmentation becomes more micro the further one goes into the nested segmentation criteria. Demographic descriptors allow us broadly to segment markets at a macro level. We enrich the segmentation by considering operating variables such as the rate of usage. When we segment on the basis of personal characteristics such as innovativeness and risk taking we are operating at a micro level. In selecting marketing targets we probably define these targets using segmentation criteria at several levels in the nest hierarchy.

We target markets that offer us the best set of opportunities available within the possible set of markets available to us. The selection of the target markets is a function of both the fit with our capabilities and the size of our resource base that constrains the size of the set of markets in which we can effectively compete.

MANAGEMENT OF CUSTOMER PORTFOLIO

Business marketers can have a very diversified customer base. For example, personal computer manufacturers like IBM and Apple have business end-users who vary from small one-person businesses to large-scale customers who can place orders and service contracts for thousands of PCs, purchasing through a mix of distribution channels (computer stores, direct mail order operations and various general retailers). Customers can vary in their purchasing expertise, buying strategy, supplier loyalty and potential profitability. To be successful a business marketer needs to resolve two key issues:

1 How to manage a portfolio of different customers.
2 How to manage a particular customer relationship.

While all marketers must manage a portfolio of customers and manage individual customer relationships, business/industrial marketers face a wide variety of buying situations. Earlier we discussed the differences between the consumer and business buying and marketing. These differences influence the portfolios available to be managed. Buyers have led the drive to create relationships which limit a marketer's portfolio choice if the buyer does not seek his/her firm as a partner. A current major trend is for buyers to reduce the number of suppliers that they use, which limits the marketer's ability to make choices about firms who may be in their portfolio. Some sellers may face constrained choices if suppliers do not see them as potential partners.

811

Consumers do not usually form long-term relationships with their suppliers. Consumers may be brand loyal but generally they maintain an arms-length relationship and not the close interwoven relationship that sometimes exists in business markets. In most cases a consumer, even a brand loyal one, can easily switch from one supplier to another. This may not be the case in the business market situation where switching costs may be high, thus limiting the buying firm's motivation to end a relationship. A great deal of the customer contact in consumer markets is through advertising, which is an impersonal media. In business markets the contact tends to be through individuals, which is a more personal media. At the individual customer level, consumer marketers seldom have the complex day-to-day interactions with the customer that characterize many business marketing situations.

The number and type of customers that a firm has can be viewed as assets as they influence directly volume and margins which in turn influence profits. The efficient management of a customer portfolio refers to the development and maintenance of customer relationships to ensure stable long-term profitability. Management time and other scarce resources need to be allocated carefully between potential and current customers to ensure both current and future cash flows.

Customer portfolio (CP) management involves two basic levels: strategic level portfolio management which focuses on the allocation and acquisition of strategic resources and concerns key customer types; and operational management of major customer types. Strategic CP management is discussed by Campbell and Cunningham (1983, 1985); the essence is depicted in Table 2 which shows a classification system for customers based on their present and future importance to the firm.

Tomorrow's customers represent firms that the marketer is especially trying to gain. They may be customers with a high reference value or access to distributors in new export markets or customers in new product application areas which have been opened up as a result of technical development. Technological leaders are generally important potential customers because supplying them offers a vehicle for developing the marketer's own product technology. Today's special customers are firms that either buy an important share of products or have become a partner with the business marketer. Examples of these special customer relationships are just-in-time supply partnerships, product or process development relationships, marketing and distribution oriented cooperation. Because the development and maintenance of special relationships may require considerable resources, the direct revenue from this kind of customer can be low or even negative. Successful relationships return the investment in developing the relationship through increment revenue gained from improved production technology, customer know-how, distribution capability, or gaining market access.

Today's regular customers represent the established 'mainstream' customers of the producer. They are an important source of revenue but do not generally

Table 2 Life cycle classification of customer relationships

Criteria for classification of customers	Customer categories			
	Tomorrow's customers	Today's special customers	Today's regular customers	Yesterday's customers
Sales volume	Low	High	Average	Low
Use of strategic resources*	High	High	Average	Low
Age of relationship	New	Old	Average	Old
Supplier's share of customer's purchases	Low	High	Average	Low
Profitability of customer to supplier	Low	High	Average	Low

*The technical, marketing and production resources devoted to developing future business rather than maintaining existing business.
Source: Campbell and Cunningham (1983).

request special services or attention. They can generally be nurtured through the marketing system. Yesterday's customers refers to customers whose demand is decreasing or small, who do not possess any special resources of interest for the marketer and who represent declining sectors.

By classifying its customers into the four life cycle categories the business marketer can respond to the essential issues of customer portfolio management. Each firm needs to develop its own portfolio to fit its customer base. Do today's customers, both special and ordinary, provide enough profit for developing tomorrow's products and customers? Are yesterday's customers taking an unwarranted share of resources compared to their contribution? Do we have enough of tomorrow's developmental customers in the relationship-creating process to ensure future competitive advantage and profits?

At a more operational level the portfolio approach can be employed for analysing and managing the relationships with various types of regular customer. This is relevant when the regular customer base, being fairly large and diverse, can be classified according to criteria relevant to their buying responses. For example, one group might be served through special distributors, another with independent sales representatives and a third might prefer closer contacts with the sales persons and technical service people. Sometimes customers can simply be dichotomized into the ones preferring a 'hands off' competitive supply relationship and those opting for a more interactive relationship requiring relationship marketing.

MANAGING A CUSTOMER RELATIONSHIP

Relationship management has been depicted as a five-stage process involving the initiation, development, maintenance and closure of a business relationship

(Ford 1990). The basis for the management of a relationship lies in understanding its dynamics.

1 In the pre-relationship stage the actors evaluate each other's business potential with the help of available internal and external information. Interest is often triggered by the seller's marketing activities or the buyer's problems with current suppliers. If a large gap between the partners exists because of cultural or technological distance, the relationship may terminate despite the partners holding common views in other areas.

2 In the early stage the marketer begins negotiations, which may take the form of large investment projects, major equipment purchases or systems sales. Then the marketer sends sample deliveries or delivers small-scale orders. Parties begin building interactive opinions about business practices, the products and services in question, as well as the representatives of the counter organization. If the buyer perceives problems or feels that the cultural distance is too wide, the process may be aborted. The development of the exchange relationship is also dependent on the availability of other customers/suppliers and on their relative attractiveness.

3 Commitment increases in the development stage, as the relationship becomes strong due to increased volume of business or expansion of the relationship to other projects. Generally both parties have to adapt or change their products, procedures and organizations in order to maximize the relationship potential. Because these changes are often costly, the partners refrain from making adaptations unless they see the potential for long-term profits.

4 Commitment between the parties characterizes the long-term phase of the relationship. In complex relationships (e.g. J-I-T) commitment may lead to extensive adaptations to business processes resulting in considerable switching costs if either party leaves the relationship. Conversely, parties that trust each other generally take the benefits of the relationship for granted. The management of a routine relationship becomes an institution, demanding less resources than in the development phase. This lack of interest in the management of the relationship causes the marketer to ignore the buyer's new demands, creating dissatisfaction and making the relationship vulnerable to competitive entries.

5 The final stage describes those rare yet stable institutionalized relationships. These relationships flourish only in industries or markets where competition is low and both parties are complacent. However, this situation is vulnerable to the opening of new competition in the market.

These five stages cover the full life cycle of a customer relationship and portray a complex and deep relation. Obviously many business relationships are not so complex and can also end at any stage.

Relationship management presumes skills beyond mastering the ordinary competitive marketing programme (a combination of product, price, distribution and marketing communications solutions) but does not make them in any way obsolete. Relationship management is based on close scrutiny of potential new customers, investigating their demands, preferred management techniques, previous and existing supplier history, and the key persons or buying centre responsible for the target business. This knowledge guides the development of a marketing strategy that offers to do business in the way in which the potential customer prefers. The marketing team relates to the buying centre and is able to understand its needs. Partners need to learn each other's business culture.

Managing the development of a relationship presumes communication and negotiations skills and a strong motivation to understand the customer. Expertise in problem solving helps to prevent conflicts. Clearly defined goals, conflict resolution techniques, incentive and monitoring practices which are related to the defined objectives, and especially mutually agreed ways of handling setbacks and financial losses are powerful means of successful relationship management.

A marketer should be able to evaluate both the revenue potential and the level of involvement needed to retain a customer, together with investments necessary to generate the potential revenue. The expected net profits should be compared to other alternatives. In practice this is difficult as future revenues depend on how both parties manage the relationship. However, this basic economic goal of the relationship should be a strong guiding factor of relationship management.

FUTURE DIRECTIONS IN BUSINESS MARKETING

Business marketing is going through a rapid development period, with several issues needing our attention as marketers. The management of customer portfolios needs better tools. This concerns the development of databases that allow the integration of customer characteristics (their purchase histories, buying policies and practices, buying centre membership, evaluation criteria) and management information system data (revenue per customer types and per major accounts, sales objectives, development type objectives). Management needs information systems that facilitate the strategic management of the customer portfolio, the operational management of customer segments and individual major customers. Integrated and concerted use of various customer-related activities on two levels is a closely related management issue. First, many large manufacturers are utilizing a growing number of marketing channels to deal with different customer types. National account management, own sales representatives, telemarketing, direct mail, retail stores, distributors, dealers and value-added resellers, and increasingly also electronic communication systems are employed jointly. To avoid conflicts, coordinating these 'hybrid marketing systems' to achieve efficiency must be the goal of business marketing in this time of change (see Moriarty and Moran 1990).

A second level of coordination concerns the various activities that form the customer relationship. Generally several functions (marketing and sales, R&D,

quality management, technical service) are involved in the development of a complex business relationship. Today's marketer must find an organizational solution for coordinating the business activities, people and communications targeted to a major customer. Account management and the marketing centre concept are paving the way. Integrated use of marketing communication channels forms another challenge for business marketers. The rapid development of telecommunications and forms of electronic data interchange (EDI) are rapidly changing the ways in which buyers and sellers communicate and interact.

Databased marketing is changing how firms relate to their customers. The development of large databases permits the seller to 'know' the customer in depth. Detailed information about key contacts and sales and service histories can be readily accessible to anyone contacting the customer. Using these databases, customized marketing programmes can be developed which are tailored to fit the need profile of the customer. Although database marketing is just developing in business markets it promises to have a major impact on the way in which firms relate to each other.

Although organizational buying behaviour is covered elsewhere in this book the emerging paradigm of buyer and seller relationships sums up many of the changes in organizational marketing. The total quality movement powered the development of single sourcing by buyers. Time to market drives concurrent engineering and expands the scope of buyer-seller relationships. These close relationships alter the ways in which firms sell and buy; the marketing programme designed to convince a potential customer to buy is not appropriate for the partner in a single-source relationship. The reward and motivation of salespeople and buyers is important as they must change from adversarial to cooperative behaviour. Firms will develop traditional marketing programmes for transaction customers and relationship programmes for partner customers. This is an era of exciting change and challenge for all business marketers. The future winners will be those firms who master the basics and can build the sophisticated organization which can react to the rapid change in products and customers.

REFERENCES

Bonoma, Thomas V. and Shapiro, Benson P. (1983) *Segmenting the Industrial Market*, Lexington, Mass: Lexington Books.

Campbell, Nigel C. G. and Cunningham, Malcolm T. (1983) 'Customer analysis for strategy development in industrial markets', *Strategic Management Journal* 4: 369–80.

Campbell, Nigel C. G. and Cunningham, Malcolm T. (1985) 'Managing customer relationships. The challenge of deploying scarce managerial resources', *International Journal of Research in Marketing* 2(4): 255–62.

Ford, David I. (ed.) (1990) *Understanding Business Markets*, London: Academic Press.

Moriarty, R. T. and Moran, Ursula (1990) 'Managing hybrid marketing systems', *Harvard Business Review* 68 (6): 146–55.

FURTHER READING

Axelsson, Bjorn and Easton, Geof (eds) (1992) *Industrial Networks: A New View of Reality*, London: Routledge.

Haas, Robert W. (1992) *Business Marketing Management: An Organization Approach*, Boston: P.W.S. Kent.

Håkansson, H. (ed.) (1982) *International Marketing and Purchasing of Industrial Goods: An Interaction Approach*, New York: Wiley.

Hutt, Michael D. and Speh, Thomas W. (1992) *Business Marketing Management: A Strategic View of Industrial and Organization Markets*, Orlando: The Dryden Press.

47

MARKETING OF SERVICES

Evert Gummesson

This chapter deals with the unique characteristics of services and their consequences for marketing. However, all companies depend on both goods and services, and many of the lessons learnt in goods marketing are also applicable to services and vice versa. The chapter does not deal with issues that are accepted as generally applicable to all types of marketing, for example segmentation or market research techniques.

The presentation is structured around the following themes: the emergence of services marketing; unique characteristics of services; different types of services and the service perspective; the expanded marketing mix approach versus the relationship marketing approach; the role of marketing and the customer in the service production and delivery process; the significance of service development, service design and re-engineering for marketing; service quality and service productivity as a basis for marketing; the organization of services marketing; the importance of infrastructure for services marketing; and, finally, thoughts on the future of services marketing.

THE EMERGENCE OF SERVICES MARKETING

Since the mid-1970s the interest in services marketing has grown and continues to grow in the 1990s. Its emergence has also met with resistance, 'There is no such thing as services marketing,' said one American professor to his PhD students in the late 1960s. There are still people who advocate that services marketing is the same as goods marketing and that services are just peripheral to goods. 'We can't live on cutting each others' hair,' is such a statement. No, but we cannot live better on selling scissors to each other. Haircuts and scissors are complementary; both create value for the customer but they provide their services differently. Services and goods are sometimes substitutes. Products can be designed in such a way as to diminish the need for services. For example, modern maintenance-free small copiers, which are bought off the shelf, are little dependent on services.

'Goods are wanted because they are able to perform services,' stated Norris (1941) quoted in Abbot (1955). Levitt (1972) has claimed that everybody is in service. A long-term trend in management thinking goes in the direction of these statements. Services are gradually replacing goods as the vantage point for the customer offering. At the beginning of the 1990s private and public sector services constituted approximately two thirds of the economic activities in the industrialized world. Goods will always be necessary, but can be seen as one of several ingredients in a total package. It is a matter of providing an offering which is characterized by benefits and value to the customer, customer satisfaction and customer perceived quality.

The development of services marketing is the outcome of contributions from scholars and practitioners in many countries. They represent different schools of thought, but due to international cooperation, services marketing thinking has converged towards certain issues which will be dealt with in this chapter. Particularly influential contributions have come from the UK, France, Scandinavia (The Nordic School of Services) and USA. Among the earliest adopters of the new service thinking were Scandinavian Airlines (SAS) and British Airways (BA).

UNIQUE CHARACTERISTICS OF SERVICES

Certain unique traits are ascribed to services, and to some extent these require different marketing practices from those used in goods marketing. Four characteristics of services are usually given. The first three characteristics are *intangibility* (as opposed to the tangibility of goods); *perishability* (cannot be stored); and *heterogeneity* (difficult to standardize).

Although these give some guidance to the marketing of services, the fourth characteristic – *inseparability* (or *simultaneity*) – more distinctly captures the essence of services. It states that services are partly produced and marketed at the same time and by the same people, that the customer is partly involved in the production and delivery process, and that the customer partly consumes the service during its production. In conclusion, services marketing cannot be dealt with in isolation from other functions of the firm or in isolation from the personal contact with the customer. Services marketing has to be approached as an integral part of a total management process.

TYPES OF SERVICES AND THE SERVICE PERSPECTIVE

Goods marketing and services marketing – rather than being two clearly delimited types of marketing – could be approached as two perspectives on the marketing of the same offering. Traditional marketing theory lacks a service perspective, but the recent developments in services marketing have contributed to set this imbalance right.

The traditional classification into service companies (hotels, airlines, hospitals, banking, insurance) and manufacturing companies is gradually losing importance. If more than 50 per cent of a company's output is services, official statistics usually refer it to the service sector; if it is the other way around it is classified as a manufacturing company. This classification is not operational from the point of view of marketing. Marketers have to understand the total offering and treat both the goods part and the service part on their own unique terms and not let one suppress the other. Manufacturing companies are also heavily involved in services such as installation, maintenance, transportation, consulting and finance. Even if the services do not necessarily account for the major share of a manufacturer's revenue, they may be a strategic necessity. They are used to differentiate a company from the competition and may thus constitute its marketing edge. Service companies need products to perform their services (e.g. aircraft) and to make them more attractive (e.g. a selection of wines during a transatlantic flight).

Within services, different marketing practices may be required, depending on the characteristics of a specific service and its target customers. Some services are primarily consumer services whereas others are producer services (i.e. they are sold to other organizations).

Services can be mass produced or customized. Some services are simple to perform, while others require unique skills and long training. The latter are referred to as professional services, rendered by individual specialists in knowledge-based organizations, such as hospitals or management consulting firms.

Moreover, work inside an organization – traditionally labelled administrative routines, office work or white-collar work – is gradually being treated as internal services, delivered to internal customers. Computer support, property maintenance and internal mail are examples of internal services that are often assigned to profit centres, sometimes to incorporated subsidiaries. These have to sell their services on the internal market and the internal customers have the option of outsourcing the service. The internal suppliers enter into a competitive situation and have to develop their marketing skills.

The public sector is primarily a service sector. Deregulation (or more realistically, re-regulation) and privatization of public services have become internationally accepted policies during the 1980s. In many service areas private alternatives are offered in competition with previous government monopolies. This requires a dramatic change in government agencies having to learn how to deal with the citizen as a customer with a choice.

Public services are largely non-profit services. This creates a unique situation in the relationship with the customer/citizen; for example, the connection between payment and delivery is not direct as 'payment' is handled via the tax system. There are also other types of non-profit organizations such as voluntary organizations and educational institutions for whom fund raising becomes an important part of their marketing.

Other classifications have also been proposed, based on generic features, for example high and low contact services. Without further elaboration, it is obvious that such diversity within services needs a contingency marketing solution in each specific instance. Knowledge of the conditions of a particular service industry and its markets is necessary in order to design a proper marketing plan and marketing organization.

EXPANDED MARKETING MIX VERSUS RELATIONSHIP MARKETING

To explain differences in the approach to services marketing, two vantage points will be used. They are partly overlapping but are also different.

The reigning approach to marketing management is the marketing mix theory, mostly described as the Four Ps: *product, price, promotion* and *place*. In a service context, *product* refers to the service and its design and production. *Pricing* of services can be different from pricing of goods which has to do with the difference in tangibility, industry tradition, etc. *Promotion* partly occurs during the service production process, partly through traditional promotion channels such as personal selling and advertising. *Place* represents the distribution and availability of the service. For many services, for example telecom services and certain financial services, it is a matter of applying information technology in the distribution; for others, the physical proximity of a service-producing unit to the local market is an absolute necessity.

The marketing mix approach has been criticized for being incomplete and manipulative, not properly considering the needs of the customer. The marketing concept postulates that once you know your customers, through market research or otherwise, you can design, price, promote and distribute a product that matches these needs and become a success in the marketplace. The seller is considered the active party and the customer has to be persuaded to buy. The empirical base of the marketing mix theory is mass manufacturing of standardized consumer goods. It has never become particularly successful for services as it disregards their unique features. In order to overcome some of its deficiencies, the Four Ps have been expanded into Seven Ps, adding the following three 'service Ps' (Booms and Bitner 1992): *participants* (the service provider's employees and the customers who participate in the service delivery and thus influence its quality and the present and future purchases); *physical evidence* (the environment of the service organization and all the physical products and symbols used in the communication and production process); and *process* (procedures, mechanisms, flows of activities and interaction that form the service production and the contact with the customer).

Kotler (1986) has suggested two additional and general Ps, *political power* and *public opinion formation*. He further refers to them as megamarketing, thereby implying that marketing takes place above the market proper. For example, services are often produced in heavily regulated markets and there might be a need to change regulations in order to open up a market. Lobbying becomes an important marketing activity.

As an alternative to the marketing mix approach, the core of services marketing can be seen as relationships, networks and interaction. This approach is referred to as relationship marketing, a term that has gained rapid acceptance since the early 1990s (Gummesson 1994). Although the addition of the 'service Ps' incorporates relationships and interaction into the marketing mix theory to some extent, relationship marketing provides somewhat different lenses and the outcome of the marketing is different. Relationship marketing emphasizes a long-term interactive relationship between the service provider and the customer and long-term profitability. It recognizes that both the customer and the seller can be active parties. They should see each other as equal partners and both must find the relationship rewarding; it is a win-win relationship. Ritz-Carlton Hotels express this approach in their motto: 'We Are Ladies and Gentlemen Serving Ladies and Gentlemen'.

It is particularly obvious in the relationship approach that services marketing cannot be isolated from the service management process. It is more appropriate to speak of marketing-oriented management than of marketing management. The following four sections will show how marketing is embedded in the management process.

THE SERVICE PRODUCTION AND DELIVERY PROCESS

Service production and delivery are most often a simultaneous process and the terms production and delivery are therefore used as synonyms. Four aspects of the generic service production process and its significance for marketing will be described below.

1 *Interaction between the service provider's contact person (the front line) and the customer* (for example between doctor and patient, advertising agency and product manager, passenger and flight attendant). The customer is a co-producer. The quality of the service is enhanced if both the customer and the service provider are knowledgeable. The contact is sometimes extremely intense and intimate and includes enormous stakes for the customer (such as in surgery or counsel in a divorce case). The shared experience can cement or prevent long-lasting relationships. Other service encounters can be trivial but regular, such as taxi and postal services, but because of the repeated need for these services, they are assessed as important by the customer. All such contacts provide face-to-face marketing opportunities.

2 *Interaction among customers.* Customers partly produce the service between themselves if the seller provides a service arena: the right systems, the right environment, and the right staff. An obvious example is a dance restaurant. If the customers refuse to dance with each other, no service will be produced. The choice of segmentation variables therefore becomes important. The

interaction among customers is sometimes non-existent, for example when services such as cleaning are performed on the customer's premises. The waiting time for a service may be dependent upon other customers who want the service at the same moment; queues can be viewed as other customers blocking access to a service.

3   *Interaction between the customer and the provider's physical environment, equipment and products.* The marketing director of a hamburger chain stated that his most important marketing staff were a group of architects who design the restaurants. They influence the visibility of the restaurant through the architecture of the building and the signs, attract the desired customer segments through the right interior decoration, affect the number of customers that can be seated. The physical access is important; the service operation must be conveniently located for the customer. Information technology reshapes services and replaces human activity with machines. The physical environment is also perceived as evidence of the price class and of the professionalism of the service provider.

4   *Interaction between the customer and the provider's system.* The first three types of interaction constitute the part of the service production system which is visible to the customer. From a marketing point of view, systems should be customer friendly. Aspects of access to the system are important, such as location and opening hours. Systems sometimes scare away customers (for example, the withdrawal of money from an automated teller machine may be difficult for old people). One strategy is to create seamless services (i.e. services which consist of a well integrated flow of events rather than a set of loosely connected discrete events). A number of systems-related questions that affect the marketing of services can be raised, such as: What should the customer do and what should the service provider's employees do? What should the 'high-tech, high-touch' ratio be (i.e. what should be automated and robotized, and what should be carried out by human beings)? How does the replacement of employees with information technology affect the marketing and the customer relationships?

The description above is based on situations where the customer interacts with the service provider during part of the production and consumption phase. This interaction is referred to as the service encounter or moment of truth. Due to the customer's involvement in the process, these encounters are an essential part of the service organization's marketing. They provide natural opportunities for the provider to influence the customer and for the customer to assess the provider.

There are exceptions to the interactive production of services, for example, the courts, military defence and road maintenance. We only interact with these service providers in rare cases, but they provide ongoing services to all citizens.

SERVICE DEVELOPMENT, DESIGN AND RE-ENGINEERING

As marketing is an integral part of the service delivery, it must be designed into the service from its very conception. This is often not done properly and marketing and sales are assigned the task of promoting impossible services, which are neither in demand nor offer opportunities for profits. Services must be designed in minute detail. It takes an average of twelve years from the conception of a pharmaceutical substance to the actual launch on the market. During this period the future medication goes through a rigorous design process. The major portion of this process consists of tests on human beings. Only one in four thousand compounds will be approved for sale. Although this may be an extreme, pharmaceutical companies are accustomed to the fact that lead time from idea to market is considerable. Cutting down time to market, however, is an essential competitive strategy.

A major problem with services is that they are often launched without having been properly tested and properly designed. There is no general methodology for designing services; there is no profession called service designers. During the 1980s efforts began to be made to find generally applicable service design methods. As the service part of an offering may be interactive with customers, a different type of design methodology is needed than is used for designing buildings, engines or drugs. The drawings and specifications must show activities and processes; they become 'dynamic drawings', a special type of flowchart. Such methodologies have gradually emerged, the best known being service blueprinting (Shostack 1987).

The novelty of the service flowchart is that it shows the service delivery process not only from the perspective of the provider, but also from the perspective of the customer. It shows the interaction between the provider and the customer as well as interactions inside the organization; the latter being behind the customer's line of visibility. Weak links – fail points – can be revealed in the service process. In doing these drawings the service designer must understand customer logic as well as provider logic. Unfortunately, service design is often governed by provider logic where computer programming, legal considerations and bureaucratic rigidity may rule. Moreover, service design needs to be integrated with the design of physical products such as buildings, motor vehicles or computer keyboards.

Adjusting existing services to changing preferences among consumers, changing competition, new segments or new needs and lifestyles, is sometimes referred to as re-engineering of services. If the design of a service is inadequate, the provider's personnel as well as the customers have to live with this every day. It creates frustration, low quality and low productivity, and consequently the design does not support long-term customer relationships. The feedback process from the front line to the management is most essential, but is often hampered by departmental and hierarchical boundaries.

824

SERVICE QUALITY AND SERVICE PRODUCTIVITY

The field of service quality was developed during the 1980s and most contributions came from services marketers. Within this quality tradition marketing becomes a matter of influencing customer perceived quality through designing and managing the services operations in such a way that the services are favourably perceived. Quality is often used as synonymous with customer satisfaction.

Grönroos (1990) makes a distinction between what is actually delivered (technical quality) and how it is delivered (functional quality). Both these qualities (Qs) refer to the outcome of the service delivery process, the customer experiences as compared to the expectations. Further the image of the providers and their services affect perceived quality. Perceived quality can be influenced by managing expectations, experiences and image, areas where marketing is engaged.

Even if the marketer represents a customer-oriented perspective, the internal management of service quality – the sources of quality – must not be neglected. In their Four Q model of service quality Grönroos and Gummesson (Grönroos 1990) have added two Qs, *design quality* and *production and delivery quality*. Design quality refers to how well the offering is designed, with the support of drawings, specifications, flowcharts or whatever means are used. Production and delivery quality refers to how well the offering is produced as compared to the design. Low production and delivery quality results in delays, the need to correct errors, missed sales opportunities, and disruptions in customer relations.

There is not necessarily a match between quality in fact and quality in perception (Townsend 1990). For example, waiting time on a telephone may be one minute but is perceived by the customer as five minutes.

Active proponents for quality as a basis for services marketing are Zeithaml *et al.* (1990). They are best known for Servqual, which includes five quality dimensions, the gaps model and a technique for measuring customer-perceived quality. The five customer-related quality dimensions are as follows:

1 *Tangibles.* Special mention is made of equipment, consumer goods, people and communication materials. Including people is logical but, at the same time, people are very much the carriers of the quality dimensions below. Personal appearance and clothes are important aspects in the perception of quality.

2 *Reliability.* The provider's ability to keep promises and perform the service dependably and accurately. Studies suggest that customers consider reliability the most important dimension; it is also closely linked to the core service.

3 *Responsiveness.* Refers to the provider's willingness to help the customer and deliver prompt service. It includes recovery, the ability of the provider to correct errors and do so with a minimum of inconvenience to the customer.

4 *Assurance.* This includes the knowledge, courtesy and credibility of the service provider's personnel. Pleasant behaviour is often promoted as the key

to customer relationships but has sometimes been turned into artificial smiling and superficial quality, thus failing to deal with the root causes of a problem.

5 *Empathy*. The ability to put oneself in the position of others, to adopt their perspectives and give caring, individualized attention. It includes availability, language that communicates and the avoidance of internal industry jargon.

Even if lists such as this can act as a guide, each company needs to define those dimensions that are specific to their current situation. For example, for a railway company security and punctuality are keys to 'reliability'. In the dimension 'tangibles', one could specify quality features used in evaluating goods which emanate from quality management in manufacturing, such as performance, durability and aesthetics. Moreover, computer software, which is at the heart of many services, has its own quality management systems and dimensions. Caution should be used in ranking the dimensions as they are supportive of each other and all contribute to the quality of the total offering.

The gaps model defines gaps between the customers' expectations and management's perception of their expectations; between management's perception of the customers' expectations and the design of the service; between the design and the actual service that is produced; between the actual service produced and the communication directed towards the customer; and finally between the expected service and the perceived service. Expectations, though, are not precise; there is a tolerance zone between the desired service and the adequate service, within which the customer remains satisfied.

International and national quality awards are becoming increasingly frequent and they also include services. The model for most of these prizes is the Malcolm Baldrige National Quality Award, which was established in the USA in 1988. It excludes non-profit and government services. The Baldrige Award allocates 30 per cent of the possible points to issues concerning customers and marketing. Service companies that have won the prize (including 1992) are Federal Express (postal services), AT&T (its telephone card operation) and Ritz-Carlton (hotel chain).

ISO9000 (BS5750) certification becomes a necessity for services marketing if organizational buyers require it in order to include a company in its list of suppliers. ISO9000 is not primarily a quality system – even if it is often presented as such – but a tool for standardization of contract provisions in order to facilitate purchasing. A special instruction on services has been added to the original documents.

While service quality established itself during the 1980s, service productivity is still in its infancy at the beginning of the 1990s. Service quality improvements are assumed to influence favourably the profitability of the service firm. There is a lack of empirical evidence to justify this assumption, which also assumes a favourable influence on service productivity. Service productivity is to some extent inherent in service quality, for example in the strategy of 'doing it right the first time'. The rework of services that have gone wrong not only disturbs the customer's perception of quality, but also lowers productivity, thus increasing the costs of the provider and reducing its competitiveness.

MARKETING ORGANIZATION IN SERVICE FIRMS

In the section on service production and delivery, two roles of the marketing organization were identified: the customers and the contact (front line) personnel. An original contribution of services marketing is to see customers as part of the organization; they are sometimes even called part-time employees. The other two generic roles of the service organization are support functions and management. Support functions – sometimes referred to as the back office or backstage – are, for example, the kitchen of the restaurant, repair of the car rental company's vehicles and maintenance of the computer systems.

The task of management is to provide a platform for the front line and the support functions. Managers may also assume the roles of both support and contact personnel; for example, the hotel manager who fills in on reception when there is a queue. They may want to be visible to the customers part of the time; for example, to chat with regular guests in the restaurant, thus reinforcing the relationship with them. Management should delegate authority and make sure that operating conditions are known throughout the organization. The behaviour of contact personnel, interaction between customers, physical environment and systems can only partly be improved by the front-line and support functions. An important task for management is to contribute to continuous improvements by initiating major systems and resource changes.

The marketing and sales departments – which are populated by full-time marketers – are unable to handle more than a limited portion of services marketing. Staff cannot always be in the right place at the right time with the right customer contact. As a consequence of the embeddedness of marketing in all functions of the service operation, everyone else becomes part-time marketers. A company should identify where the full-time marketers would be superior in fulfilling the marketing tasks and where the part-time marketers would be superior; organize one or several marketing and sales departments; recruit, train and motivate part-time marketers; and design the service production system to support marketing activities.

Empowerment of front-line employees to deal with customers without delay is becoming an increasingly important marketing strategy. For example, the employee who can correct mistakes and handle claims quickly and smoothly without having to refer the issue back to a manager reinforces the positive relationship with the customer and also improves productivity. Empowerment requires enabling employees to take responsibility and work more independently.

Internal marketing is a means to empower and enable employees. It is a new concept that has emerged from services marketing, but the term is now used in all types of organization. Internal marketing is based on the notion that in service firms, where so many people have direct customer contact, it is essential that all employees represent the company well. As part-time marketers, they should understand the company mission, the organization, the services that can be provided. They should behave in a way that creates positive rapport with customers and a long-term relationship. In internal marketing, know-how from external marketing is applied to the 'employees market'. The purpose is to communicate new information in order to enhance knowledge, influence attitudes and motivate employees.

Large service companies are often heavily decentralized because of the need for local presence, for example, a retail chain or a firm of accountants. Growth is a matter of multiplying a well-defined business concept to more sites. Franchising has proved to be a viable concept for rapid growth. It unites the best of two worlds: large-scale strategic strength and small-scale closeness to the customer. Examples of large franchise operations are The Body Shop (1,000 shops in 1995) and McDonald's (15,000 restaurants in 1994).

SERVICE INFRASTRUCTURE

A well developed service infrastructure provides an environment amenable to service delivery and marketing. Traditionally, infrastructure is focused on manufacturing with many basic services, such as goods transportation and postal services, being ancillary to goods. The public service sector is in itself an infrastructure that caters for basic needs such as defence, education and health care.

Infrastructure is gradually being more focused on providing favourable conditions for services. This is partly caused by the growth in information technology. Telecom and computer services are in themselves expanding, but they also provide a new communications infrastructure. For example, global reservation systems for airlines, railways, car rentals and hotels are made possible through computers, data highways, databanks and new telephone systems.

The regulations between countries, prohibiting free movement of labour and capital over borders, have limited internationalization of services. The current trend of deregulation and privatization as well as transnational alliances such as the European Union (EU) and the North American Free Trade Agreement (NAFTA; with USA, Canada and Mexico) will dissolve some of these restrictions.

General changes in society as well as private initiatives can change the service infrastructure for whole countries, regions or towns. Examples are the Eurotunnel between England and the European continent and the bridge between Denmark and Sweden.

If EuroDisney outside Paris – which was opened in 1992 – can survive financially, it is large enough to become an infrastructure in itself with its theme park, hotels and convention centres. It is likely to attract other theme parks and hotels to the area as well as retailing and taxi services. Simultaneously, a transportation infrastructure is necessary for EuroDisney to attract visitors. Thus, it has its own station which is connected both with a local Paris train and the high-speed services to Brussels and London; it has a bus service to Charles de Gaulles airport. Destination marketing is emerging as a special type of marketing, closely connected with services and infrastructural developments.

THE FUTURE OF SERVICES MARKETING

During the 1980s services marketing established its own identity. Moreover, it has become a driving force in the development of marketing thinking in general. Going back to the early 1800s the gross national product and employment were dominated by agriculture. Gradually manufacturing took over. Services were referred to as residuals, and later as intangibles and invisibles. Beginning in the 1960s, we have slowly entered into a service society, where services constitute the major portion of economic activity. Consequently, it is natural that services should have become the focal point for the new marketing, just as agricultural marketing was surpassed by the marketing of manufactured goods.

Services marketing has contributed with new approaches and concepts. The interactive production and marketing of services with customer involvement has become better understood. Relationship marketing, in part inspired by service thinking, will establish itself during the 1990s and provide a new general framework for marketing. Service quality has developed its own approach to marketing while service productivity is still not well established. The interaction and causal connections between service quality, service productivity and profitability need to be further understood. Systematic service design is yet little understood and little applied, but may be the most important area for future development. The concept of the part-time marketer has emerged in services and shows that marketing is deeply embedded in the whole service management process. Internal marketing has become a household word in marketing in general, although the concept was generated within services marketing. The deregulation and privatization of government monopolies will continue. Information technology will provide new services and new ways of performing traditional services.

Some of the tenets of services marketing may have face validity but lack depth. The understanding of the real nature of services and their relationship with goods is still limited. Although services marketing has come a long way, there is need both for basic research and further development of hands-on techniques.

REFERENCES

Abbott, Lawrence (1955) *Quality and Competition*, New York: Columbia University Press.

Booms, Bernhard H. and Bitner, Mary J. (1992) 'Marketing strategies and organisation structures for service firms', in James Donnelly and William R. George (eds) *Marketing of Services*, Chicago: American Marketing Association.

Grönroos, Christian (1990) *Service Management and Marketing*, New York: Macmillan/Lexington Books.

Gummesson, Evert (1994) *Relationship Marketing – From 4Ps to 30 Rs*, Stockholm: Stockholm University, School of Business.

Kotler, Philip (1986) 'Megamarketing', *Harvard Business Review* March–April: 117–24.

Levitt, Theodore (1972) 'Production line approach to service', *Harvard Business Review* September–October.

Shostack, G. Lynn (1987) 'Service positioning through structural change', *Journal of Marketing* 51, January: 34–43.

Townsend, Patrick L. (with Gebhardt, Joan E.) (1990) *Commit to Quality*, New York: Wiley.

FURTHER READING

Bateson, John E. G. (1989) *Managing Services Marketing*, Orlando, FL: The Dryden Press.

Berry, Leonard L. and Parsuraman, A. (1993) 'Building a new academic field – the case of services marketing', *Journal of Retailing* 69 (1), Spring: 13–60.

Congram, Carole A. and Friedman, Margaret L. (eds) (1991) *Marketing for the Service Industries*, New York: American Management Association, Amacom.

Cowell, Donald (1984) *The Marketing of Services*, London: Heinemann.

Eiglier, Pierre and Langeard, Eric (1987) *Servuction*, Paris: Ediscience/McGraw-Hill.

The International Journal of Service Industry Management (1994) 5 (1).

Lovelock, Christopher (1991) *Services Marketing*, Englewood Cliffs, NJ: Prentice Hall.

Normann, Richard (1992) *Service Management*, London: Wiley.

Payne, Adrian (1993) *The Essence of Services Marketing*, New York: Prentice Hall.

Quinn, James Brian (1992) *The Intelligent Enterprise*, New York: The Free Press.

Vandermerwe, Sandra (1993) *From Tin Soldiers to Russian Dolls. Creating Added Value through Services*, Oxford: Butterworth-Heinemann.

Zeithaml, Valerie A., Parasuraman, A. and Berry, Leonard L. (1990) *Delivering Quality Service*, New York: The Free Press.

48

FRANCHISING

Christina Fulop and Jim Forward

WHAT IS FRANCHISING?

The term franchising encompasses a wide variety of business relationships and is often used interchangeably with the term licensing. However, the distinguishing feature of business format franchising, with which this chapter is concerned, is that it entails a more integrated relationship between the parties involved compared to other forms of licensing. As a business format it has been increasingly utilized as an alternative method of distribution and of business expansion over the last forty years.

In business format franchising (hereafter simply referred to as franchising) the licensor (i.e. the franchisor) does not only grant permission for the licensee (i.e. the franchisee) to sell the franchisor's branded products or services. The franchisor should also provide a proven method of operating, support and advice on the setting up of the franchisee's business and ongoing support. The franchisee has invariably to pay an initial fee to the franchisor, some type of ongoing fee, and a marketing/advertising levy. Although the two parties work together, and combine their efforts with the aim of creating a successful business formula, the franchisor and the franchisee remain legally distinct.

HISTORY AND DEVELOPMENT OF FRANCHISING

Business arrangements similar to franchising as we know it now seem to have been in existence as far back as the Middle Ages. The more modern origins of franchising began in the USA and specifically with the establishment of the Singer Sewing Machine Company in the latter half of the nineteenth century. The relationship between Singer and the outlet owners of its network, which sold sewing machine spare parts and undertook repairs, bore certain resemblances to modern day franchising, including branding the outlets with Singer signage.

Second generation franchising, which is a term used interchangeably with business format franchising, began in the USA in the late 1940s and early 1950s. For the first time franchising was applied as a distinct way of starting a new business as opposed to merely a way of distributing an existing product.

Franchising thrived in the USA during the rapid post-war economic expansion of the 1950s and early 1960s. From the few franchisors who could be identified in 1946, by 1960 there were over 700. During this period many businesses that have since become household names were established, such as McDonald's, Holiday Inn, Budget Rent-a-Car. Franchising was first established in the UK in 1955 when J. Lyons & Co. Ltd. purchased the master franchise rights for the UK from the American operation Wimpy hamburger restaurants. However, during the late 1960s two factors inhibited the growth of franchising.

The first factor was the widespread prevalence of pyramid selling schemes in both countries. Pyramid selling, which was essentially the selling of distributorships, resulted in highly publicized and substantial financial loss for many investors. Its adverse effects were eventually addressed in the UK in the Fair Trading Act 1973, which, *inter alia*, aims to regulate such schemes. Franchising was associated with pyramid selling because this is how such schemes were described in order to mislead potential investors. As a result, franchising acquired a damaging stigma which slowed down appreciably its rate of growth.

The second factor is attributable only to the USA. In the late 1960s the US economy began to slow down which adversely affected the expansion of franchising. On the other hand, it had the effect of stimulating many American franchisors to consider moving into foreign markets, including the UK. Since that time franchising has spread throughout the world where it is present in varying stages of development in some 140 countries, many of which have mature franchise communities (Mendelsohn 1992).

In the UK during the 1970s and 1980s franchising grew rapidly and gained acceptance. The main impetus to the development of franchising has been from newly emerging businesses which have utilized this method of marketing goods and services as a means of financial expansion with less risk. In recent years too a growing number of large well-established companies have entered franchising as a means of developing their businesses. These firms have had varying degrees of success, because the decentralized organization and operating methods implicit in the franchising concept and its implementation is usually alien to or difficult to reconcile with the centralized decision-making, management and culture of a corporate concern.

Although franchising is found mainly in the retail and service sectors, it is also utilized by manufacturers in order to secure outlets for their products, and by wholesalers not only to obtain outlets for products but also to enable them to make more economic use of storage and distribution facilities. Some established retail chains have introduced franchising alongside their managed outlets in order to achieve a more rapid rate of market penetration than would have been possible through their company-owned operations alone; to raise capital by converting existing branches; and to improve the performance of some of their marginally profitable outlets by converting them to franchising.

The main source of statistics on franchising in the UK are the annual surveys commissioned by the British Franchise Association (BFA) since 1984 and sponsored by National Westminster Bank. These surveys are valuable to the understanding of the scope and growth of franchising. On the other hand, they have certain limitations. For example, the response rates are low, and a much higher proportion of respondents are BFA members, who tend to be the more long-established franchises, than non-members.

The estimated turnover of business format franchises is estimated to have risen between 1984 and 1991 from £0.84bn to £4.8bn, and is forecast to rise to £10.3bn by 1996, equivalent to just under 3 per cent compounded growth per annum. Although franchising grew steadily between 1984 and 1990, there followed a slight decline in 1991 due to the recession. The number of franchise systems increased between 1987 and 1991 from 253 to 432 (BFA 1991).

Unfortunately it is not possible to compare accurately the scope of franchising in the UK with that of the USA. American franchise statistics, for instance, include the sales turnover from the company-owned outlets within a franchise system, and also the turnover of automobile dealers and petrol retailers, whereas UK figures do not include any of these categories. Similarly, although franchising in the UK does not seem to be as developed as in France, where it is estimated to generate £10bn turnover annually and there are some estimated 675 franchise operations, it is difficult to make a meaningful comparison with that country – and indeed other countries – due to differences in definitions and the varying methods of data collection.

In which business sectors is franchising found?

In the USA where franchising is further developed than elsewhere at least 65 categories of franchised business sectors have been identified, several with numerous sub-classifications. These range from the ubiquitous fast food operations, car rentals, printing and duplicating services, hotel and motel chains, employment and temporary help services to travel agents, vending operations and sales training. In the USA franchising has also penetrated into such professional and financial services as pharmacists, opticians, accountants and insurance brokers. In the UK the BFA's membership covers 46 business classifications, with an additional 38 sub-classifications. Many of these business sectors are the same as those which have been successfully franchised in the USA but also include parcel delivery services, driving schools, many forms of home improvements, playgroups and milk delivery.

WHY FRANCHISING HAS DEVELOPED

Franchising has expanded over the past forty years as a preferred marketing and distribution channel option over alternative business formats due to: the advantages it offers to both franchisor and franchisee; developments in the socioeconomic environment; and the role of interested third parties.

Franchisor perspective

The prime motivation for franchising is usually lack of capital or, alternatively, unwillingness to take on the risk of borrowing. Since franchisees provide the capital that is invested in the outlet expansion should be achieved with a lower capital input from the firm; some of the business risks are passed from the firm to the franchisee; there is the potential for more rapid growth than would otherwise be possible; the franchisor needs fewer staff than if the outlets were all company-owned; and the relatively lower capital investment of the franchisor should lead to high returns on capital employed. Furthermore, franchising should enable firms to acquire some of the characteristics of a small business operation at outlet level (e.g. local knowledge, extended opening hours, flexibility). Moreover, franchisees who have invested their own wealth in the business are generally highly motivated individuals, which should lead to improved outlet performance when compared to outlets operated by company managers. It should also prove easier to attract quality franchisees than quality managers because of the benefits connected to owning your own business. Where a firm may have found itself unable to afford the required calibre – or specific expertise – of an outlet manager franchising may help to solve its staffing problems.

Franchisee perspective

A person may choose to become a franchisee rather than an independent small business person because they wish to gain the beneficial combination of a large and small business.

Although franchisees have to be prepared to relinquish some independence, in return they receive 'opportunity and support' which considerably reduces the risk inherent in establishing a new business. This is because the small firm has the freedom to operate in a controlled, assisted and supported environment, while at the same time gaining the benefits of a brand name, professional management, and the economies of scale of a larger organization. Finally, the franchisee has a business which, hopefully, can be sold on at a profit.

Impact of socioeconomic influences and third parties

Several environmental factors have facilitated the expansion of franchising. In particular, the shift in the economy towards the service sector – where franchising is concentrated – has been a stimulus, together with the fact that the input of a committed and highly motivated franchisee encourages a high quality of service.

Furthermore, the prevalence of an 'entrepreneurial culture' since the 1980s has given a further impetus to franchising, because it represents an easier and less risky entry into business. A high incidence of unemployment has also made a great deal of redundancy money available for the purchase of franchises. Moreover, franchising has benefited from the increased interest in the expansion of small firms by central government. The European Community (EC) has also acknowledged the value of franchising for the survival and health of the small business sector, and as a means of stimulating the creation of small businesses in less well commercially developed areas of the EC. As a consequence, in 1988 franchise agreements were exempted from the normal EC competition legislation (Mendelsohn and Harris 1992).

British banks also take a very positive view of franchising because the failure rate amongst franchisees is lower than among other small businesses and hence represents a lower risk. As a result franchisees receive preferential funding treatment. The approval of the banks has helped franchising gain increased respectability within the UK. Lastly, the efforts of the BFA, the trade association of franchisors, has helped to raise the profile and image of franchising, and to improve standards.

THE DOWNSIDE OF FRANCHISING

Franchising has many advantages for the franchisor and the franchisee, but it is not an easy concept to manage. Although the franchisee may bring motivation, commitment and initiative, together with an input of capital to a business, these assets may be offset somewhat by the expense and difficulty of ensuring in such a decentralized operation the maintenance of uniform standards of service and a consistent public image across the network. Franchisees can be highly motivated but can also be very demanding of senior management time and effort. To some degree this is due to the fact that the business of the franchisee is legally separate from that of the franchisor. As a consequence, compared to managed outlets, the scope for issuing commands is limited. Essentially, a franchise is a partnership – albeit an unequal one – and the difficulties of coping with the complexities of this arrangement, and the potential for conflict that may ensue, has sometimes led to the failure of franchised operations.

For the franchisor the biggest challenge is to manage successfully the relationship with the franchisee in all its aspects. For the franchisee the most important concerns are the quality of the franchisor, how well the business concept has been tested, and how well the franchisor will fulfil its ongoing responsibilities to its franchisees.

WHAT MAKES A BUSINESS FRANCHISABLE?

By no means all businesses are suitable for the introduction of the franchise format. There are some specific criteria that need to be taken into consideration in order to establish whether the basic ingredients for franchising a business exist. These comprise:

- that the products and/or services offered should already have been proven in practice. This is to ensure that franchisees are confident they are buying into a viable business.
- that the product/service is distinctive, and backed by a brand name or trade mark already well known in the business sector of the potential franchisor. This enables franchisees to be offered a valuable commercial asset they would otherwise have difficulty in acquiring.
- that the processes and systems the franchisor needs to pass on to the franchisees must be simple, easy to learn and capable of being put into operation within a short time. This is to ensure successful replication and the projection of a consistent image across all the outlets.
- that the margin must be adequate to provide both the franchisor and the franchisee with an acceptable level of income and return on investment.

In addition:

- a mechanism must have been built up to provide the franchised network with ongoing support and assistance, and the development of the business.
- an adequate supply of franchisees must be available, and be consistent with the business plans of the potential franchisor.

COMPONENTS OF A FRANCHISE SYSTEM

The major components of a franchise system comprise: the pilot operation, the franchise contract, franchise manual, franchisee selection, and ongoing support. Since franchise systems are more heterogeneous than might be first thought, it will be appreciated that there will be some variations in these components. It is also necessary to point out the intensive input which is required at the very early stages of developing a system, particularly in regard to time, manpower and other resources.

The 'pilot'

At least one pilot operation is an essential component in the development of a franchise before beginning to sell franchises. As in any test marketing exercise, its purpose is to emulate the proposed franchised outlets as closely as possible to gain an accurate indication of their likely performance; to identify problems in order to take the necessary steps to overcome them; and, not least, to determine whether it is worthwhile to continue with the development of the franchise system. Although 'pilots' do provide valuable information they are unlikely to test two of the most significant factors in a franchised business, namely, the franchisee and the franchisee/franchisor relationship, because they are usually operated by company employees.

Franchise documents

The two key franchise documents are the manual and the contract. The manual contains detailed advice and guidelines to the franchisee on how the business should be operated. The contract defines the formal relationship between the franchisor and the franchisee, and is comprehensive and specific in terms of the obligations of franchisees. (See pages 838–9 for the effect of the contract on the franchisor/franchisee relationship.) The contract specifies, for example, the three financial charges which the franchisee pays to the franchisor: the 'initial fee', which is mainly to cover the costs of the franchisor in setting the franchisee up in business; the ongoing 'management service fee', and the 'levy' contribution towards advertising and marketing. Both the latter are calculated as a percentage of the franchisees' sales turnover. The management service fee varies widely from 5.5 per cent (catering and hotels) to 9.6 per cent (vehicle services) depending on the degree of support provided, and profit margins. Franchisors may also, or alternatively, place a mark-up on goods supplied to franchisees. Some franchisors use this as their main source of income and charge a very low management service fee. On average the various ongoing charges collected by franchisors in 1991 accounted for an estimated 8.9 per cent of franchisees' turnover (BFA 1991).

Franchisee selection

The selection procedures employed to recruit the first franchisees are especially important to the subsequent success of a franchise operation. In order to overcome their initial lack of experience of franchisee selection franchisors are recommended to draw up a profile of 'ideal' franchisees. In practice this is difficult to accomplish in the early stages of a franchise, but as time goes on franchisors tend to learn from experience which attributes they are looking for in a franchisee. Other aspects of franchisee recruitment which require to be considered include if, and where, to advertise for franchise applicants and the screening procedures to be used. (See also pages 839–40 for characteristics of existing franchisees.)

Ongoing support

The final ingredient of a franchise is to determine the type and quantity of ongoing support required by the franchise network. Support may encompass many different aspects of the operation such as assistance provided by the franchisor's field staff, the laying on of training programmes for franchisees, the development of new products and systems, and the updating of manuals. Not least, support includes the continuous monitoring of the marketplace for the benefit of the franchisees and the franchise.

FRANCHISOR/FRANCHISEE RELATIONSHIP

The major topics that are the subject of debate in franchising revolve around the franchisor/franchisee relationship since this is one of the key determining factors in the success or otherwise of the business. These aspects of the relationship include: the relative independence of franchisees when compared to other small businessmen or women; the characteristics of franchisees; and whether franchisee protection should be via legislation or self-regulation.

The contract is often considered the pivotal factor in inhibiting the independence of franchisees and in leading to conflicts. Also, that its bias in favour of the franchisor enables the latter to hold the balance of power in the relationship. Notably, it is pointed out that the contract obliges the franchisee to put into operation any changes made to the operating manual over the period of the franchise, and that the franchisee signs the franchise contract before they see the franchise manual in detail.

Nevertheless, there is an opposing view to the above which maintains that the specific nature of the contract is unavoidable if uniformity is to be achieved across the system. Such homogeneity is seen as an advantage not only for the franchisor, but as beneficial to all franchisees, because it diminishes the likelihood of wide variations in service and offering which may well lead to dissatisfied customers, and penalize all franchisees, not only those who breach the rules. Termination clauses are also sometimes regarded as unfair to franchisees. However, there is again an opposing view that such clauses may be necessary to ensure uniformity of standards and service across the network and thereby the success of the franchise.

The contract may not, in fact, be a reliable guide to the extent of the franchisees' independence. In practice, there appears to be a difference between formal independence (as expressed in the contract) and operational independence (as experienced in the course of the relationship). Furthermore it is not only franchisees who relinquish some of their independence, franchisors also do. This is because they are dependent upon their franchisees to operate as stipulated, to implement changes in the operation, and not to bring the franchisor's name into disrepute. With a company-owned network this dependence on a person who is not an employee would not exist. Due to the interdependence, therefore, of the franchisor and the franchisee both parties have to accept some trade-off in terms of loss of independence in return for the advantages they receive.

The extent to which the contract inevitably leads to conflict in the franchisor/ franchisee relationship has also been closely examined. While there is always likely to be some degree of conflict in such a complex relationship compared with that of a company-owned network this does not emanate from the clauses of the contract alone. It is also neither necessarily destructive nor unwelcome. Some franchisors actively welcome the continual dialogue that is the essential feature of a franchise, and the forthright and critical comments of their franchisees. Nevertheless, one sign of unhealthy conflict within a system is often taken to be the existence of a franchisee association. Generally such associations are established when a significant proportion of franchisees are dissatisfied with the franchisor and hence seek to lobby the latter *en masse*. Indeed, when the relationship is strained, and sometimes when it is not, a franchisor may form a consultative committee with franchisees in order to pre-empt the formation of an association and create a 'tension management' device.

In practice most franchisees seem prepared to renew their contracts, and express little desire to change the content of the contract. There is also some evidence that franchisees are able to negotiate certain clauses with their franchisor prior to signing. That most franchisees do not seem to hold the view that the contract is detrimental to them may be because few have been threatened by franchisors with contract clauses. In reality, the contract appears to have little bearing on the relationship because experience has shown that management by persuasion and example, rather than by threat, seems more likely to lead to channel cooperation. The franchisor's non-coercive sources of power include the training programme which – if formal, authoritative, and detailed – will influence the franchisee to operate in line with the franchisor's guidelines. Similarly, if the franchisees are happy that they are receiving adequate support from the franchisor they are easier to control.

The characteristics of franchisees

Interest in the characteristics of franchisees has been generated from two sources. First, those who are concerned with the study of small business are curious as to the background, characteristics and motivations of franchisees. Second, many franchisors are quick to attribute the failure of, or problems with, franchisees as being a direct result of poor selection. Consequently, they are keen to identify the characteristics of the 'ideal' franchisee applicant.

The major socioeconomic characteristics of franchisees which have been identified include: on average they are better educated than other small business people; on the whole franchisees are slightly younger than other small business people, although there appears to be a clear link between cost of the franchise and age; they are 'upwardly mobile' in their aspirations and past employment history; and the spouse of the franchisee is involved in the franchise.

Apart from these outward manifestations of the characteristics of franchisees there exists little agreement on the 'ideal' profile. For example, there is no general consensus on whether franchisors should try to avoid applicants with past experience in the same type of business. One reason advanced for rejecting such people is that they will already have preformed ideas about the running of that business which may conflict with the franchisor's management and operational systems, and lead to poor performance within the network. There is also the view that franchisors may prefer to take on inexperienced franchisees and then provide comprehensive training, because this will help franchisors to exert more power over them. However, a more practical reason why many franchisors seem to prefer to take on inexperienced people as franchisees is that they are provided with such a high level of support as to render previous experience unnecessary.

On the other hand, some franchisors actively look for franchisees with previous business experience because although they teach franchisees about their particular operation, they do not consider it their role to teach general business skills. Moreover, with the extension of franchising into professional and financial services, there is likely to be a greater emphasis on the recruitment of qualified people and those with related business skills.

A further characteristic which is sometimes considered desirable is prior sales and marketing experience in the belief that franchisees with such experience will outperform those without and learn more quickly.

Since there exists such a diversity of views on the attributes of the 'ideal' franchisee, and this may well be a reflection of the diversity of types of franchise format, franchisors have little alternative but to ensure the recruitment of franchisees whose personal and business characteristics are compatible with the mission of the parent organization.

Franchisee protection: self-regulation or legislation?

Although franchising is generally acknowledged as being beneficial to the creation of small businesses and employment, nevertheless concern has been expressed that franchisees are insufficiently protected both in the negotiations leading up to the signing of the franchise contract and during the ensuing relationship.

At present in the UK – unlike in the USA and several other countries – there is no legislation specifically aimed at the protection of franchisees. Although the EC Block Exemption regulation governs the structure of franchises this is to allow a franchise to operate in ways which would otherwise infringe EC competition legislation. Apart from the BFA's voluntary Code of Ethics, which in any case is only applicable to its members, the franchisor/franchisee relationship in this country is governed by general business legislation. The issue has, therefore, arisen as to whether self-regulation is sufficient to protect franchisees, or whether there is a case for legislation.

Those who believe that self-regulation provides insufficient protection propose the introduction of specific franchise legislation to ensure that before signing the contract franchisees are provided with adequate and comprehensive information on which to base their decision. The second area where there is a demand for legislation is to curtail the ability of franchisors to include and enforce 'unfair' contract clauses, particularly in terms of renewal, termination, assignment, goodwill, and conflict resolution.

The purpose of regulation, whether through self-regulation or by legislation, is to encourage franchisors to behave in a manner which is not 'unfair' to franchisees. Legislation tends to be favoured by those who view the franchisee as being significantly disadvantaged *vis-à-vis* the franchisor (Terry 1991). On the other hand, supporters of self-regulation regard voluntary Codes of Ethics as an equally efficient means of 'policing' franchising with the added advantage of avoiding the additional costs and barriers to entry which legislation may cause. They also point out that the small occurrence of unscrupulous actions by *bona fide* franchisors does not warrant legislation, and that dissatisfied franchisees have existing avenues of seeking redress.

Legislation aimed at inducing appropriate disclosure of information prior to the signing of the franchise contract is prevalent in the USA. France has also introduced trade mark licensing disclosure laws which include franchising and seek to achieve this aim. In the USA there are two methods of attempting to ensure that the contents of the disclosure document are appropriate. The first requires a franchisor to register their disclosure document with the state authorities for approval on a continuous basis. The second, included in American Federal legislation, lays down guidelines on the information which should be included in a disclosure document, but no registration of the document is necessary.

Those who oppose the introduction in the UK of widespread legislation fear that it will lead to some of the undesirable consequences which have followed legislation in the USA. These have included: higher costs; in many instances the disclosure of less information rather than more as intended; and some evidence that it has acted as a barrier to entry and helped to slow down the rate of expansion of franchising. In order, therefore, to avoid these possible hindrances to the growth of franchising, the opponents of legislation maintain that the UK should retain self-regulation, and continually strive to improve it. They also argue that prospective franchisees have an obligation to investigate thoroughly any business proposition before entering the relationship.

In Australia the establishment of a 'mandatory' Code of Practice may herald a practical answer to the self-regulation versus legislation dilemma. This 'mandatory' Code was introduced after Australia had experimented with, and had experience of operating franchising systems over two decades under a variety of legislative, quasi-legislative and non-legislative regimes. The Code was the proposal of a 'Task Force' that had been set up to investigate how franchisees could be protected without inhibiting the growth of ethical franchising. The successful implementation of a 'mandatory' franchising Code of Practice may offer a compromise solution that satisfies both the proponents and opponents of legislation as it is possible that it will provide franchisees with an adequate degree of protection without hindering the expansion of franchising.

THE FUTURE

There are a number of influences – some favourable, some unfavourable – which are likely to affect and shape the franchise industry in the future.

The most important factor will be the changing health and structure of the economy. As would be expected, the growth of franchising is directly related to the buoyancy or otherwise of economic activity. The rapid rate of expansion of franchising that took place during the 1980s may well not be repeated should the economy fail to expand at a commensurate rate during the remainder of the 1990s.

On the other hand, certain structural changes such as the continuing expansion of the tertiary sector are likely to stimulate franchising in the service and retail sectors. Furthermore, the already competitive environment in these sectors will intensify with the entry of new trading formats, and compel many established firms to achieve a better performance from their outlets. This may accentuate the existing development that has led some firms which have hitherto relied upon other forms of third-party distribution such as dealers, licensees or tenants to adopt franchising as a preferred option. The conversion of these looser distribution arrangements into franchises facilitates a higher degree of support and control, which results in better quality and more uniform customer service, more consistent operational standards across the network, and not least improved performance at outlet level with reduced operating costs. Similarly, the willingness by an increasing number of mature organizations to develop their businesses through franchising is likely to persist as a means of assisting them in the implementation of their diversification and/or market penetration strategies, the need of some of them to recruit qualified and skilled staff, and the need of other such firms to maximize the potential output of the outlet.

There is also scope for franchising to penetrate further in the UK – as has already occurred in the USA – into such professional and financial services as opticians, accountants, insurance brokers, pharmacists and estate agents. To a large extent the expansion plans of the growing number of multiples in these sectors will depend on the recruitment of highly qualified staff to operate their outlets. Conversely, the increasingly competitive environment in many of these sectors may make many professionally qualified people who would formerly have set up in business by themselves consider franchising as an alternative option which provides them with the opportunity to gain the benefits of working under the umbrella of a large organization, while still operating as a small business.

Ever since franchising started to develop rapidly, there has been a movement by franchisors into foreign markets. This trend is likely to accelerate as an increasing number of franchise systems reach maturity in their domestic markets. In particular, US franchise systems will increasingly seek out other markets, of which the UK will probably continue to appear the most attractive because of the common language and the idea of creating a 'bridgehead' to continental Europe. The French, who have more franchise systems than the UK, are also increasingly entering the UK and other EC markets. Thus, while British franchisors will be seeking to develop abroad, they will also face the potential threat of foreign competition.

A further stimulus to international franchising is likely to emanate from the growing number of retailers who do not operate franchising in their domestic market but who utilize franchising as a mode of entry into overseas markets where population size or per capita expenditure may be insufficient to support a major programme of expansion but warrant the introduction of a small number of stores. Such firms also employ the franchise format as a means of test marketing in foreign countries prior to establishing a full-scale operation, thus helping to lessen the financial risk of moving abroad. Finally, a more unusual development which should lead to the expansion of international franchising is its increasing recognition as a means of contributing to the establishment of marketing and distribution networks in the territories formerly known as the USSR and Eastern Europe, and in 'developing' countries (Mendelsohn 1992).

REFERENCES

BFA (1984–92) *The NatWest-Franchise Survey*, Henley-on-Thames: British Franchise Association.

Mendelsohn, M. (1992) *The Guide to Franchising*, 5th edn, London: Cassell.

Mendelsohn, M. and Harris, B. (1992) *Franchising and the Block Exemption Regulation*, Harlow: Longman.

Terry, A. (1991) 'Policy issues in franchise regulation: the Australian experience', *International Journal of Franchising and Distribution Law* 6 (2): 77–90.

FURTHER READING

Burt, S. (1995) 'Temporal trends in retailer internationalisation', in P. J. McGoldrick (ed.) *International Retailing: Trends and Strategies*, London: Pitman.

Commission of the European Community (1991) *Towards a Single Market in Distribution*, Brussels: Commission of the EC: Com (91).

Fitzgerald, R. (1991) *Franchising Task Force*, Final Report to the Australian Minister for Small Business and Customs, December, Canberra: Dept of Industry, Technology and Commerce.

Forward, J. and Fulop, C. (1993) *Issues in Franchising: An Analysis of the Literature*, London: NatWest Centre for Franchise Research, City University Business School.

Forward J. and Fulop, C. (1993) 'Elements of a franchise: the experiences of established firms', *Service Industries Journal* 13 (4): 159–78.

Sanghavi, N. (1991) 'Retail franchising as a growth strategy for the 1990s', *International Journal of Retail and Distribution Management* 19 (2): 4–9.

Sibley, S. D. and Michie, D. A. (1982) 'An exploratory investigation of co-operation in a franchise channel', *Journal of Retailing* 58 (4): 23–45.

Stanworth, J. (1991) 'Franchising and the franchise relationship', *The International Review of Retail, Distribution and Consumer Research* 1 (2): 175–99.

Stern, L. W. and El-Ansary, A. (1988) *Marketing Channels*, 3rd edn, New Jersey: Prentice-Hall.
Stern, P. and Stanworth, J. (1988) 'The development of franchising in Britain', *NatWest Bank Quarterly Review*, May: 34–48.

49

EXPORTING

Philip Rosson

INTRODUCTION

Companies around the world are increasingly engaged in marketing to foreign customers as well as those at home. As a result, world exports grew from $314 billion in 1970 to $3.4 trillion in 1990, almost eleven times. This chapter provides an overview of the important activity of exporting. The focus is largely on manufactured products, since the international trade in commodities is dealt with in Chapter 45. Although the marketing of services is covered in Chapter 47, some mention of services exporting is made here.

Exporting is a strategy for business expansion. Any strategy that takes a company into a new area is demanding and risky, and exporting is no exception. The extant literature is largely concerned with company readiness for export involvement; market selection, entry and penetration activities; and the process of internationalization.

Exporting defined

Exporting is defined here as: where a company located in country A makes sales of its products and/or services in other countries, supplied from its operations in country A. Two facets of exporting which distinguish it from domestic marketing are implied in this definition: first that exported products/services move across national borders and second that exporters deal with foreign customers at some distance. When companies move their products or services across national borders, a variety of new issues are encountered. Documentation is one example. Movement across a border and into the market will be halted unless the correct documents accompany the export product/service. A second example is selling prices: will these be quoted in the currency of the exporter, the importer, or in the currency of some third nation? Since the risk of non-payment is often higher overseas than at home, another issue concerns the terms of sale that should apply. These are some of the more important matters that companies must deal with from the very first export order. The early literature on exporting tended to concentrate on such issues. Fortunately, the development of an operational capability in these and other areas is not too difficult. A variety of service companies such as freight forwarders, banks and customs brokers can provide assistance to the exporter. The literature in this area is largely descriptive and experiential, with few studies of company practices.

Since exporters supply overseas customers with products/services from their home location, they are usually several steps removed from foreign customers. A sales and supply 'separation' results and provides a major challenge for exporters. Although some sales separation may exist between suppliers and customers at home, because of greater proximity and cultural similarity, these are less acute than those experienced in exporting. Intermediaries, partners and/ or sales subsidiaries located in the foreign market help to reduce the sales and supply separations but add another managerial complication for the exporter. These questions are more strategic in focus and have attracted research attention. This strand of the literature is more conceptual and empirical than the former, with considerable attention paid to company practices, especially as these relate to export performance.

A further distinctive feature of exporting which is not apparent from the definition above, is that government usually plays a more direct role in exporting than in domestic marketing activities. Given the importance of exports to the economic well-being of most nations, governments are very active in the promotion of exporting and in the development of an increased capability among companies.

Exporting research

Exporting (and the more general activity of international marketing dealt with in Chapter 50) has attracted more limited attention from researchers than might be expected given the contribution of exports to gross national product in many nations. This situation prompted the editor of a leading marketing journal to state that international marketing has a 'stepchild' status in the marketing literature (Wind 1979). Although the level of activity has increased in recent years, the complexity and cost involved in exporting research constrains the amount of empirical work undertaken. The body of knowledge that currently exists is dominated by results from North American and European studies. Although Japan is a leading export nation and one from which many lessons might arguably be learned, relatively little empirical research at the company level has been published in English. This is not the case for Hong Kong, Korea, Singapore and Taiwan, where an increasing number of export studies are being undertaken. This is also true for Latin America. As far as other regions are concerned – Africa, the Middle East, Asia, Eastern and Central Europe – with notable exceptions, little is known about company export behaviour.

INVOLVEMENT IN EXPORTING

Four generic strategies exist through which companies can expand their operations (Ansoff 1988). Market penetration is often the easiest to accomplish, since expansion involves no new products or markets. Where existing products are introduced to new markets, a market development strategy is pursued. A product development strategy seeks growth through offering new products to existing markets. A diversification strategy involves both new products and markets and is therefore a riskier expansion strategy. Exporting should be seen as a particular type of market development strategy, where products/services that have proven themselves at home are subsequently sold in markets located overseas. Although this pattern of development characterizes a majority of companies, for others exporting is a factor from establishment. Some specialist products/services face such restricted demand that they must be exported from the very start. Still other companies are established explicitly to export, because knowledge of, and contacts in a foreign market provide the company's competitive advantage. For the majority of companies however, exporting is a way to develop incremental sales for proven products/services.

Two streams of research have investigated the involvement of companies in exporting. Some researchers have examined the barriers that prevent companies from exporting while others have studied the factors that motivate companies to begin exporting. A second group has sought to understand export involvement by contrasting exporters with non-exporters.

Export barriers and motivators

In most countries, a minority of companies are involved in exporting. Numerous factors that inhibit greater export participation have been identified. One classification identifies motivational, informational, and operational/resource-based barriers. Motivational barriers deter serious investigation of foreign markets by many companies and include: a buoyant or large home market; the perceived higher costs and risks of transacting business overseas; and the burden of documentation requirements. A lack of adequate information on foreign markets is a second barrier for companies, which seldom possess data on the demand for their products overseas and/or fail to understand how these data might be accessed. Operational factors also deter many companies. Exporting requires additional resources – whether for working capital or additional staff – and marshalling these is another barrier to export involvement by companies (Cavusgil 1983).

Factors motivating companies to begin exporting have also been examined. The reasons companies provide to explain initial exporting are many but fall into either 'proactive' or 'reactive' categories (Czinkota 1982). Examples of the former include: unique products, exclusive market information, economies of scale, and profit advantage. Reactive reasons for exporting include: unsold inventories, saturated domestic markets, and excess capacity. Studies suggest that companies more often begin exporting for reactive rather than proactive reasons. The initial foray into exporting is frequently serendipitous (an unsolicited enquiry/order arrives from a foreign buyer or intermediary) or a way of dealing with unfavourable conditions (production capacity is seriously underutilized). A minority of companies start exporting because it is suggested by a corporate strategic planning exercise.

Exporters and non-exporters

Another substantial stream of enquiry has examined whether there are discernible differences between exporters and non-exporters. This research has practical implications for both companies and government, for if it were demonstrated that exporters do have 'different' characteristics, such information could:

1 help companies decide whether they should venture overseas;
2 permit government export promotion programmes to be targeted to appropriate companies.

This stream of research began with a study of Wisconsin manufacturing companies (Bilkey and Tesar 1977; Cavusgil *et al.* 1979) and has been carried forward by its originators (e.g. Cavusgil and Naor 1987) and many others (e.g. Dichtl *et al.* 1990; Reid 1981). The studies typically examine relevant industry, company and management factors and have generated profiles that are often markedly different for exporters and non-exporters. For example, exporters have been found to be in more technology-intense industries, to be larger, to spend more on R&D, and to have younger, better educated and more cosmopolitan managers. Unfortunately, these findings are not consistent across studies, making it difficult to generalize and to use such information for diagnostic purposes. Some researchers attribute the inconsistent findings to the differing study approaches and methods employed. Others argue that the findings reflect reality. A good illustration is provided by Bonaccorsi (1992) who demonstrates that, in contrast to the results of many US studies, company size does not explain the export involvement of Italian companies and theorizes why this should be so.

COMPANY EXPORT DECISIONS

Once a decision has been made to expand into international markets, companies face several issues. These are reviewed below, following discussion of the overriding matter of the company internationalization process.

The company internationalization process

A prevailing view in the literature is that companies internationalize their operations in a logical and incremental manner. Thus, expansion first takes place in nearby (geographic, cultural or psychic) markets, through the low-cost, low-involvement method of exporting. Over time, as knowledge and experience is developed, more distant markets are entered. Further, as sales grow to a sufficient level, exporting is replaced by more direct and local operations such as sales subsidiaries and foreign direct investment. The genesis of this view developed from research conducted at Uppsala University into the internationalization of four Swedish industrial companies (Johanson and Wiedersheim-Paul 1975), and was reinforced by later empirical (Luostarinen 1980) and conceptual work (Johanson and Vahlne 1977). A merit of the theory is that it treats export decisions in a systemic fashion, through its consideration of the linkages between company resources, export markets, entry methods and operations.

Although this view of international development is widely held, the theory was based on limited empirical research and has come under increasing challenge as the results of more studies have been reported. For example, the notion that managers' experiential knowledge leads them to enter more and distant foreign markets is not supported by research on European forest products companies (Sullivan and Bauerschmidt 1990). Turnbull's (1987) study of market operating methods found that British companies used a combination of methods to serve single European markets, rather than the dichotomous structures implied by the stages theory. These and other studies (Andersen 1993) suggest that the widely accepted Uppsala theory of internationalization should be treated with caution.

Rather than seeking out such general theories to explain company export behaviour, emphasis is increasingly focused on 'middle-range' theories. Reid (1983b), for example, has argued that company- and market-specific factors explain the arrangements that are made to handle exports. This view is echoed by others and approaches of this kind are reflected in the discussion of market selection and entry methods below.

Which export market?

The choice of foreign market is the first major decision for the company that is expanding internationally. For a number of reasons, this decision tends not to be handled well. It was noted earlier that many companies begin exporting in response to an unsolicited order or enquiry. When this is so, the choice of market is made for rather than by the exporter. Although this saves time and the expense of market analysis, the exporter might forego much better market opportunities. The position can be more serious since filling an unsolicited order might commit the company to a foreign intermediary as well as a market. In some cases then, the separate decisions: first, to export; second, to a given market; and third, through a given intermediary, are collapsed into one. A further influence can also mean that optimum market choices are not made. Government export support programmes (see below) often encourage companies to take part in trade missions or trade fairs to specific countries or regions. Participation in such activities again leads the company to markets that have been chosen by others. While government trade departments target the best markets for given industry sectors, there is no guarantee that individual companies will be well served. Thus, export orders might be filled as a result of participation in an event of this kind, but better markets may be overlooked in the process.

Even when smaller companies make their own market choices, their behaviour is at variance with textbook models. Despite a surfeit of data on most markets and a variety of analytical methods, most companies consider only a few markets. This stems from their inadequacies and preferences. Knowledge of, and access to information is one problem, as is the fact that most companies are ill-equipped to undertake or interpret quantitative market analysis. Company practices are also heavily influenced by a preference to enter markets which are geographically, culturally and psychically close. As a result of these factors, a restricted and fairly obvious list of markets is usually considered by management (i.e. the process is non-systematic; Papadopoulos and Denis 1988). Recognizing this situation, simpler but systematic foreign market selection procedures have been proposed (Walvoord 1980; Papadopoulos 1987).

Which market entry method?

Figure 1 shows the major alternatives that exist for foreign market entry and operations. Emphasis is placed here on the more common methods, with the special cases of trading companies, consortia and franchising described separately below.

With a market chosen, the new exporter must decide how entry will be effected. This is an important matter since it determines how the company's products/services will be marketed abroad. Key questions for companies include the resources available for market entry and development, the amount of control required over foreign marketing, and the degree of risk that can be tolerated. Studies in a number of countries indicate that new exporters of products most frequently choose one of the following methods: commission-based foreign agents/brokers/representatives, foreign distributors and company sales visits. These methods do not require much investment of money or managerial time, and involve limited risk. Exporters give up some control when they employ agents and distributors to represent their interests in foreign markets. This is not the case when markets are developed through company sales visits. However, this approach can be expensive if frequent and distant travel is required. In contrast, agent and distributor usage involves limited expense

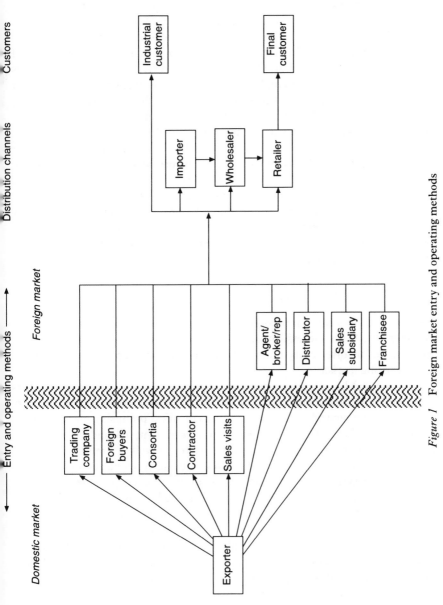

Figure 1 Foreign market entry and operating methods

beyond start-up, communication and visit costs. If a suitable agent or distributor is appointed, the exporter benefits from immediate access to prospective customers in the market in question. Direct selling through company sales visits is often employed when there are relatively few customers for their products/ services in the foreign market and these are easily identified (e.g. rail cars).

Because of a very limited literature, the foreign market entry practices of service companies is less clear. One difference in services is that foreign agents and partners are sometimes employed to deal with non-tariff barriers that favour local service businesses. Another difference involves the use of local partners to produce and deliver the service, the former function not needed for product exports. At the same time, many of the same principles guide the choice of entry method for services as products. For example, the greater knowledge, lower uncertainty and less risk faced by service companies which followed clients into foreign markets led them to use higher involvement entry methods than companies going it alone overseas (Erramilli and Rao 1990).

Choice of foreign market entry method often involves selection of a company to carry out the marketing task. The limited literature suggests that this is another area of weakness, with exporters carrying out only the most rudimentary of checks on prospective partners prior to their appointment.

Managing exporting operations over time

Following the first move into foreign markets, a variety of fresh challenges face management. With success, thoughts inevitably turn to further development; whether this involves entry into additional markets or adaptation of marketing in the existing market.

An issue that has attracted attention concerns the number of foreign markets that should be entered and the speed of entry. A market concentration strategy is said to be pursued when a company enters the most promising market(s) first, followed by others only when success has been achieved and resources are available. In contrast, a market spreading strategy involves simultaneous entry into as many markets as possible, followed by later emphasis on the most profitable markets. Factors favouring one approach over the other have been identified by Hirsch and Lev (1973), and expanded on by Ayal and Zif (1979) and Piercy (1982). The former authors' findings show that both strategies are pursued by companies, for different reasons and with varying results. The concentration strategy is more suitable for risk-averse companies; it requires smaller initial investment in marketing, and subsequently leads to more diversified and stabilized exports than the spreading strategy.

Another issue faced by companies that have achieved a level of success in a market is whether marketing adaptations should be made. A company's initial export operations are usually based on its domestic market experience, with only essential changes made to the product/service, promotion, distribution and price (Cavusgil and Kirpalani 1993). Over time, as the company seeks to strengthen its position in the foreign market through satisfying more fully customer needs and preferences, these aspects of foreign marketing are likely to see greater change. Indeed, companies sometimes develop new products/ services for particular foreign markets. An important element in the process of adaptation is change in the method of market operation. Ford *et al.* (1982) describe the experience of British companies in establishing overseas sales subsidiaries and find some support for the internationalization theory. However, other research is less supportive. Okoroafo (1990) argues that changes in operating method can be either incremental or non-incremental, and identifies factors that explain company substitution patterns. A study of 139 changes in international operating methods led Calof (1993) to conclude that no one theory explained the behaviour of the companies involved.

The emphasis of the exporting literature is almost exclusively on growth. The Uppsala theory of internationalization, for example, only considers expansion of foreign activities. However, not all companies are able to develop their foreign operations along these lines; many withdraw from export markets, while others continue less than successfully. Few studies focus on negative export experiences but those that exist are instructive. Companies are vulnerable in the initial stage of exporting, with internal (preparation, commitment) and external (exchange rate shifts, competition) factors often leading to failure (Welch and Wiedersheim-Paul 1980). Other research indicates that a substantial proportion of companies discontinue exporting, and that attitudes are more important than economics in explaining their decisions (Roy and Simpson 1981). Even among experienced exporters, success is often elusive, forcing management to think more in terms of experimentation or consolidation rather than expansion and/or greater involvement (Rosson 1987).

ROLE OF GOVERNMENT

Three types of export barrier have already been referred to. Programmes and initiatives have been established by government to help companies to overcome these barriers, including: motivation – advertising and local seminars highlighting the benefits of export involvement; information – market reviews and overseas visits that enable the assembly of timely and inexpensive foreign market data; and operational/resource – export financing and trade fair participation on a cost-shared basis. Although governments recognize that companies need assistance to compete in world markets, the level and nature of export support varies quite markedly. Canada, for example, spends proportionately more than the UK, while Sweden supports marketing activities in contrast to South Korea's emphasis on financing and guarantees. Despite the fact that national governments make large expenditures in this area, the impact of such export support is seldom well documented. Assistance programmes are clearly useful, but precisely how useful is difficult to determine. Programme evaluations usually reveal positive benefit/cost ratios. However, studies at the company level

Table 1   Export assistance: providing organizations and approaches

Providing organization(s)	*Loose coordination*	*Integrated, strategic*
Government	Coordination attempted between different federal and other levels of government. No strategic view of overall export promotion effort (e.g. Australia, Canada).	Industry sector and company export plans are developed, monitored and evaluated (e.g. France).
Government/private sector	Restricted government involvement. Chambers of commerce, industry associations and export councils cooperate in offering assistance (e.g. The Netherlands, Italy).	Partnership approach to achieve trade policy and/or jointly developed objectives. Sharing of resources to promote exporting and achieve goals (e.g. Sweden, UK).
Private sector	Chambers of commerce and industry associations provide export assistance to member companies (e.g. Germany).	Ties to chambers of commerce and industry associations are obligatory. Exporting subjected to strategic planning approach (e.g. Austria).

produce equivocal results, export programmes being viewed positively in some quarters, and critically in others.

In the developed world, export assistance programmes reveal certain common elements. These programmes: focus on small and medium-sized companies; offer forms of assistance that vary by export stage; provide support across the full spectrum of foreign market involvement. Because of these common elements, there are many similarities in the assistance that is extended to companies in the industrialized world. However, these same services are executed in quite a different manner from country to country. Export assistance is provided by government in some countries, the private sector in others, and a mixture of the two in still others. There are other differences too: assistance to companies is loosely coordinated in some countries whereas a more integrated and strategic approach is employed elsewhere. Table 1 describes six 'models' of assistance.

Although some developing countries have become important exporters of manufactured products, many more have similar aspirations. Accordingly, export promotion organizations have been formed in many countries and charged with the responsibility for developing and diversifying exports. Many of these organizations have been established with the assistance of the International Trade Centre (ITC) of the United Nations Committee on Trade and Development/General Agreement on Tariffs and Trade (UNCTAD/ GATT). Created in 1968, the ITC is the focal point in the UN organization for assisting developing countries with trade promotion. ITC works with these countries to develop more effective trade institutions, strategies and operations. As in the developed world, a variety of organizational export promotion arrangements and approaches exist. Although export promotion has been studied from a macro standpoint in the developing world, the effectiveness of the programmes delivered to companies – the micro standpoint – is generally not well documented (Seringhaus 1993). An exception is Brazilian research that shows that government incentives may stimulate companies to export but not prepare them for sustained foreign marketing (Christensen *et al.* 1987).

Export promotion has evolved into a comprehensive instrument for trade stimulation in the developed and developing world. The following types of government export promotion are generally considered acceptable under the GATT:

1 Provision of market research information.
2 Support for participation in international trade missions and trade fairs.
3 Establishment of trade promotion offices overseas.
4 Investment in R&D leading to exportable products.
5 Provision of exporting financing and insurance.
6 Rebate of indirect taxes on exports.
7 The establishment of free-trade zones.

Other methods for stimulating exports – direct government subsidies to support exports, for example – are viewed as subsidies and are in contravention of the GATT. Three books provide a perspective on this subject area: Cavusgil and Czinkota (1990) principally focus on developments in the USA, whereas Seringhaus and Rosson (1990, 1991) are more international in their coverage.

SPECIAL EXPORTING TOPICS

In this section, a number of special exporting topics are addressed. Among these are the topics of franchising and countertrade that are dealt with more comprehensively in Chapter 48.

Trading companies

Trading companies have a long history of involvement in international commerce. The earliest trading companies were European, date back to the thirteenth century and include such organizations as the Hanse, the British East India Company and the Compagnie Français de l'Afrique Occidentale. Trading companies such as Mitsui and C. Itoh (sogo shosha) were established in the 1870s when Japan decided to end its dependence on foreign traders. Socialist countries have historically used state trading companies to channel exports to foreign markets. Trading companies have also played a critical role in the internationalization of domestic industries in other countries, including Brazil and South Korea (Cho 1987). Given the success of trading companies in developing exports for smaller companies in many countries, it was hoped that passage of the 1982 Export Trading Company Act would produce similar results in the USA. For a variety of reasons, however, this has not transpired (Terpstra and Yu 1992).

Trading companies vary in their ownership, purpose and functions. In most countries, they are privately owned while in other countries they are seen as important to trade development and are publicly owned. Some trading companies have existed for many years as major players in specific commodity trades, whereas others have been founded by multinationals as an adjunct to normal operations. A majority of trading companies focus on export and import functions and have an industry sector and/or geographic region focus. Some, however, are involved in more complex international business forms, such as countertrade, mega-project development and joint ventures (Amine 1987). For the beginning exporter, however, it is the foreign marketing capability that is of greatest interest. Either on a commission or merchant basis, trading companies develop export sales for companies and deal with the associated risks and uncertainties. This is attractive to many companies since they are able to expand their market coverage internationally while engaging only in domestic transactions.

Consortia

For companies that are new to exporting, an alternative to the use of a trading company is participation in an export consortium. Export consortia (groups or cooperatives) come into being when companies voluntarily decide to combine and centralize their export activities so as to achieve greater strength. The main benefits result from better and more extensive selling and promotion, lower costs and more professional management (Organization for Economic Cooperation and Development 1964). Other benefits include greater visibility, enhanced attractiveness to foreign partners, skill and resource sharing, economies from joint use of export facilities at home and abroad, and risk and cost spreading. Export consortia help overcome the resource deficiencies and risk concerns associated with exporting and, in so doing, create stronger and more viable entities. However, the fact that consortia are collaborative organizations means that questions surface. Who will lead/manage the consortium? How will decisions be made? How will sales be allocated and profits shared?

Research indicates that the job of the consortium manager is a challenging one, involving not only the development of group trust and cohesion, but also the execution of a strategy for successful foreign market penetration (Welch and Joynt 1987). As well as the choice of consortium manager, critical to operational success are organizational factors such as: the size of the group, the extent of product diversification, complementarity among members, and legal and financial provisions (Lanzara *et al.* 1991).

In overall terms, consortia account for a small portion of total export sales. Although holding out great potential, relatively few smaller companies have embraced this form of exporting. In large measure this stems from the preference most companies have for autonomy. Companies only cooperate if there is some compelling reason that outweighs all other factors or if an outside change agent, such as government or a private sector organization with a vested interest, forces the issue.

Countertrade

Countertrade is a form of trade where the buyer pays for those products/ services received either wholly or partly with products rather than money. Buyers principally use countertrade when they lack the cash to pay for their purchases or where the cash is non-convertible. Sellers principally become involved in countertrade activities as a means of exporting to countries that face foreign exchange shortages.

Increased demands for countertrade have been experienced since the global debt crisis in the mid-1970s. Due to a lack of reliable data, estimates of the importance of countertrade to world trade vary widely. However, countertrade is generally held to account for 10 per cent of world trade. The main forms of countertrade are barter, counterpurchase, buy-back, switch trading, and offsets. Counterpurchase deals are most frequently used, involving the signing of two separate contracts which specify the products/services to be exchanged. Offsets are also very important and frequently employed in defence and other high value sales. For example, where one country purchases aircraft from another, a condition of the contract may require that part of the aircraft be built in the buying country.

Specialized intermediaries are frequently used by companies in countertrade contracts and these are often located in neutral, strategic cities such as Vienna and Zurich. Some trading companies have expertise in this area. Governments in the developed world officially frown on countertrade but recognize that it is an inevitable feature of modern trade. Similarly, most companies would prefer to sell on a cash basis but many have been forced to deal on a non-cash or part-cash basis. Okoroafo (1993) provides a review of this method of exporting from both a country and company perspective.

Capital projects

Depending on its level of economic development, 20–30 per cent of a country's gross domestic product is accounted for by fixed capital investment (e.g. power generating plants, transportation systems). In developed countries, such investment is primarily financed by national governments and private businesses and, for a number of reasons, it is difficult for foreign companies (i.e. exporters) to supply goods and services to the resulting projects. In developing countries the situation is different. The local supply of engineering, construction and project management services and industrial equipment is generally poor in relation to demand, and funding – usually provided through aid or loan programmes – requires a call for tenders. Consequently, it is estimated that 60–75 per cent of the market for international capital projects is concentrated in developing countries (The World Bank 1990).

The market for international capital projects can be segmented according to the nature of the project, its size and the execution structure. These criteria help companies to focus their efforts, for skill, experience and capability in a given project field must be demonstrated to be seriously considered, as must the staff and resources to undertake a project of a specific size. As in other areas, the capital project exporter will most often be seeking foreign business based on its domestic market experience. The large scale of much capital project work means that a relatively small number of companies will be seen as capable of executing the contract. Small companies interested in such contracts must form a consortium or joint venture to be viewed as credible competitors. Whichever approach is taken, very large contracts frequently require home government political and financial support as well as concerted marketing effort by the bidding company. A variety of execution structures exist, including the following contracts:

1 government-controlled;
2 project management;
3 turnkey;
4 product-in-hand;
5 market-in-hand;
6 build, operate, transfer (or BOT).

These execution structures involve a different allocation of tasks and responsibilities between the buyer and supplier, that is to say, the supplier's responsibility and the supply of goods and services increases, whereas the managerial and technical capability required of the buyer decreases, from (1) to (6).

Exporting in the capital project field – often of services – is essentially the same as elsewhere. A company must assess its capabilities, match these to potential markets and search out projects, promote the company overseas, secure local agents/partners, position itself to bid, submit a winning proposal and execute the contract well. For smaller companies, the development of databases of planned projects and suppliers by agencies such as the World Bank, has made the market search and promotion functions somewhat more easily managed than in the past. In several respects, however, the capital projects field is still particularly demanding of exporters, requiring an understanding of the capital project cycle, sources of bilateral or multilateral project funding, an ability to work with government agencies at home and abroad, and, perhaps, a greater willingness to collaborate with other companies through consortia or other arrangements (Dhawan and Kryzanowski 1978).

Franchising

Franchising has been a major engine of economic growth in recent decades. Although product and tradename franchising still dominates, business format franchising is growing the most quickly. Under the latter arrangement, a franchisor provides a proven business format to a franchisee, in return for initial fees and continuing royalties (see Chapter 48). Franchising involves the export of know-how or services rather than products. In a sense, franchising is a special form of licensing. Before 1970 very few franchise organizations had developed their networks internationally. Levels of international involvement were low, even among those US companies which are most often associated with franchising. Considerable development took place in the 1980s and the 'exporting' of franchising continues at a fast pace, led by but not restricted to US companies.

The growth is fuelled by strong interest in first, the franchised products/ services among foreign customers, and second, the franchise method as a business opportunity among foreign business persons. Competition is growing more intense in some markets where local franchise systems have arisen to challenge well-known 'imported' franchises. In some cases, these local franchise systems have themselves become strong enough to internationalize. Marketing know-how to foreign markets through franchising essentially involves the same steps and considerations as product exporting. Markets have to be selected, entered and decisions about standardization of the marketing programme made (Preble 1992). One difference stems from the nature of franchise channels which are contractual and characterized by overt power/dependence relations. This contrasts to the situation in channels for most exported products/services, characterized by more conventional 'buy and sell' relationships and diffused power. In the USA franchisees seem increasingly prepared to bring legal actions against abusive franchisors. Whether similar events will unfold as franchising grows internationally remains to be seen (Welch 1992).

SUCCESS IN EXPORTING

Numerous attempts have been made to discern the reasons for export success. Two main approaches have been employed, the most common of which has been to examine levels of export performance across a broad sample of companies. Researchers pursuing this approach typically attempt to explain variations in performance in terms of company characteristics and export strategies. The second approach is more focused. Rather than working with a random sample of companies, several researchers have examined only high-performance exporters. These are companies that have been recognized by governments for their export achievement and are seen as exemplars for others.

Irrespective of research approach, a fundamental question concerns how 'success' or 'high performance' should be defined. Most studies use measures for which data are relatively easy to collect, such as the export portion of total sales (or 'export intensity'), export sales volume or growth rate over a defined period. Government has employed similar success criteria in export award schemes, supplemented sometimes by others, such as entry into a difficult market or above average exports for a given industry. While convenient, these measures are not entirely satisfactory (Kirpalani and Balcome 1987).

A review of seventeen field studies of export performance is provided by Madsen (1987), along with managerial guidelines on pre-export activity; market selection; market entry; and market operations, based on the research examined. Recent studies have addressed methodological shortcomings – particularly direction of causality, specification error and interaction effects – identified by Madsen, as well as examining other determinants of export success. New research thrusts are exemplified by Axinn and Thach's (1990) study of the link between export commitment, distribution and promotion activities, and performance in the US and Canadian machine tool industries, and Dominguez and Sequeira's (1993) identification of export performance/strategy clusters for Central American companies.

Studies of export award winning companies have been undertaken in a number of countries, including Australia, Canada, the UK and the USA. These have employed either survey or clinical case methods and find consistent patterns in the export success of companies, as well as elements that vary depending on the situation faced, such as company size (Cunningham and Spigel 1971), industry sector and geographic market (Brooks et al. 1990).

SUMMARY

Exporting is one of several avenues for company expansion. Although the essentials of marketing are the same overseas as at home, exporting is a challenging activity for management. This is particularly so in the initial phase of exporting activity, when numerous barriers may have to be overcome in order to realize market opportunities abroad. Over time, management develops greater familiarity and experience with foreign customers and business practices, and export resources usually grow to support the exporting function. Beyond the initial export phase, the key tasks frequently involve managing the transition from one international business method to another, and coordinating operations in several (to many) markets.

The exporting literature has matured over the years. A good level of basic knowledge exists about export practice, although there are gaps and areas that, compared to others, are backward. More attention will be paid to theory development and testing, with more realistic conceptions of exporting and increasingly sophisticated methods being employed. Thus, whereas in the past

860

it was treated as a stand-alone function, a growing number of researchers now see exporting as being inseparable from other activities of companies (Reid 1983a). Another stream of research with potential employs the network paradigm to examine exporting (and other marketing) activity in companies (Håkansson 1982; Ford 1990). Export performance studies are increasingly emphasized, building on pioneering work of authors such as Bilkey (1982). These and other research initiatives will help improve exporting knowledge and practice.

REFERENCES

Amine, L. S. (1987) 'Toward a conceptualization of export trading companies in world markets', in S. T. Cavusgil (ed.) *Advances in International Marketing*, volume 2, Greenwich, CT: JAI Press.

Andersen, O. (1993) 'On the internationalization process of firms: a critical analysis', *Journal of International Business Studies* 24 (2): 209–31.

Ansoff, I. (1988) *The New Corporate Strategy*, New York: John Wiley.

Axinn, C. N. and Thach, S. V. (1990) 'Linking export performance to the marketing practices of machine tool exporters', in S. T. Cavusgil (ed.) *Advances in International Marketing*, volume 4, Greenwich, CT: JAI Press.

Ayal, I. and Zif, J. (1979) 'Market expansion strategies in multinational marketing', *Journal of Marketing* 43, Spring: 84–94.

Bilkey, W. J. (1982) 'Variables associated with export profitability', *Journal of International Business Studies* 13 (2): 39–55.

Bilkey, W. J. and Tesar, G. (1977) 'The export behavior of smaller-sized Wisconsin manufacturing firms', *Journal of International Business Studies* 8, Spring/Summer: 93–8.

Bonaccorsi, A. (1992) 'On the relationship between firm size and export intensity', *Journal of International Business Studies* 23 (4): 605–36.

Brooks, M. R., Patton, D. J. and Rosson, P. J. (1990) *The Export Edge: Advice from Successful Canadian Companies*, Ottawa: External Affairs and International Trade Canada.

Calof, J. (1993) 'Shifting market internationalization strategies – understanding mode change', in *Proceedings*, International Marketing Division, Administrative Sciences Association of Canada.

Cavusgil, S. T. (1983) 'Public policy implications of research on the export behavior of firms', *Akron Business and Economic Journal* 14, Summer: 16–22.

Cavusgil, S. T., Bilkey, W. J. and Tesar, G. (1979) 'A note on the export behavior of firms: exporter profiles', *Journal of International Business Studies* 10 (1): 91–7.

Cavusgil, S. T. and Czinkota, M. R. (eds) (1990) *International Perspectives on Trade Promotion and Assistance*, New York: Quorum Press.

Cavusgil, S. T. and Kirpalani, V. H. (1993) 'Introducing products into export markets: success factors', *Journal of Business Research* 27: 1–15.

Cavusgil, S. T. and Naor, J. (1987) 'Firm and management characteristics as discriminators of export marketing activity', *Journal of Business Research* 15, June: 221–35.

Cho, D.-S. (1987) *The General Trading Company*, Lexington, MA: Lexington Press.

Christensen, C. H., da Rocha, A. and Gertner, R. K. (1987) 'An empirical investigation of the factors influencing exporting success of Brazilian firms', *Journal of International Business Studies* 18 (3): 61–77.

Cunningham, M. and Spigel, R. (1971) 'A study in successful exporting', *British Journal of Marketing*, Spring: 2–12.

Czinkota, M. R. (1982) *Export Development Strategies: U.S. Promotion Policy*, New York: Praeger.

Dhawan, K. C. and Kryzanowski, L. (1978) *Export Consortia: A Canadian Study*, Montreal: DEKEMCO Ltd.

Dichtl, E., Liebold, M., Koglmayr, H.-G. and Mueller, S. (1990) 'International orientation as a precondition for export success', *Journal of International Business Studies* 21 (1): 23–41.

Dominguez, L. V. and Sequeira, C. G. (1993) 'Determinants of LDC exporters' performance', *Journal of International Business Studies* 24 (1): 19–40.

Erramilli, M. K. and Rao, C. P. (1990) 'Choice of foreign market entry modes by service firms: role of market knowledge', *Management International Review* 30 (2): 135–50.

Ford, D. (ed.) (1990) *Understanding Business Markets: Interaction, Relationships, Networks*, London: Academic Press.

Ford, D., Lawson, A. and Nicholls, J. F. (1982) 'Developing international marketing through overseas sales subsidiaries', in M. R. Czinkota and G. Tesar (eds) *Export Management: An International Context*, New York: Praeger.

Håkansson, H. (1982) *International Marketing and Purchasing of Industrial Goods: An Interaction Approach*, Chichester: Wiley.

Hirsch, S. and Lev, B. (1973) 'Foreign marketing strategies – a note', *Management International Review* 6: 81–8.

Johanson, J. and Vahlne, J.-E. (1977) 'The internationalization process of the firm – a model of knowledge development and increasing foreign market commitment', *Journal of International Business Studies* 8, Spring–Summer: 23–32.

Johanson, J. and Wiedersheim-Paul, F. (1975) 'The internationalization process of the firm: four Swedish cases', *Journal of Management Studies* 12 (3): 305–22.

Kirpalani, V. H. and Balcome, D. (1987) 'International marketing success: on conducting more relevant research', in P. J. Rosson and S. D. Reid (eds) *Managing Export Entry and Expansion: Concepts and Practice*, New York: Praeger.

Lanzara, R., Varaldo, R. and Zagnoli, P. (1991) 'Public support to export consortia: the Italian case', in F. H. R. Seringhaus and P. J. Rosson (eds) *Export Development and Promotion: The Role of Public Organizations*, Boston: Kluwer Academic Publishers.

Luostarinen, R. (1980) *Internationalization of the Firm*, Helsinki: Helsinki School of Economics.

Madsen, T. K. (1987) 'Empirical export performance studies: a review of conceptualizations and finding', in S. T. Cavusgil (ed.) *Advances in International Marketing*, volume 2, Greenwich, CT: JAI Press.

Okoroafo, S. C. (1990) 'An assessment of critical factors affecting modes of entry substitution patterns in foreign product markets', *Journal of Global Marketing* 3 (3): 87–103.

Okoroafo, S. C. (1993) 'An integration of countertrade research and practice', *Journal of Global Marketing* 6 (4): 113–27.

Organization for Economic Cooperation and Development (1964) *Export Marketing Groups for Small and Medium-Sized Firms*, Paris: OECD.

Papadopoulos, N. (1987) 'Approaches to international market selection for small- and medium-sized enterprises', in P. J. Rosson and S. D. Reid (eds) *Managing Export Entry and Expansion: Concepts and Practice*, New York: Praeger.

Papadopoulos, N. and Denis, J.-E. (1988) 'Inventory, taxonomy and assessment of methods for international market selection', *International Marketing Review*, Autumn: 47–60.

Piercy, N. (1982) *Export Strategy: Markets and Competition*, London: George Allen & Unwin.

Preble, J. F. (1992) 'Global expansion: the case of U.S. fast-food franchisors', *Journal of Global Marketing* 6 (1 & 2): 185–205.

Reid, S. D. (1981) 'The decision-maker and export entry and expansion', *Journal of International Business Studies* 12 (2): 101–12.

Reid, S. D. (1983a) 'Export research in a crisis', in M. R. Czinkota (ed.) *Export Promotion: The Public and Private Sector Interaction*, New York: Praeger.

Reid, S. D. (1983b) 'Firm internationalization, transaction costs and strategic choice', *International Marketing Review* 2, Winter: 45–56.

Rosson, P. J. (1987) 'The overseas distributor method: performance and change in a harsh environment', in P. J. Rosson and S. D. Reid (eds) *Managing Export Entry and Expansion: Concepts and Practice*, New York: Praeger.

Roy, D. A. and Simpson, C. L. (1981) 'The decision to discontinue exporting: the experience of the smaller manufacturing firm in the southeastern United States', in V. Bellur (ed.) *Proceedings*, Academy of Marketing Science Conference.

Seringhaus, F. H. R. (1993) 'Export promotion in developing countries: status and prospects', *Journal of Global Marketing* 6 (4): 7–31.

Seringhaus, F. H. R. and Rosson, P. J. (1990) *Government Export Promotion: A Global Perspective*, London: Routledge.

Seringhaus, F. H. R. and Rosson, P. J. (eds) (1991) *Export Development and Promotion: The Role of Public Organizations*, Boston: Kluwer Academic Publishers.

Sullivan, D. and Bauerschmidt, A. (1990) 'Incremental internationalization: a test of Johanson and Vahlne's thesis', *Management International Review* 30 (1): 19–30.

Terpstra, V. and Yu, C.-M. J. (1992) 'Export trading companies: an American trade failure?' *Journal of Global Marketing* 6 (3): 29–54.

Turnbull, P. W. (1987) 'A challenge to the stages theory of the internationalization process', in P. J. Rosson and S. D. Reid (eds) *Managing Export Entry and Expansion: Concepts and Practice*, New York: Praeger.

Walvoord, R. W. (1980) 'Export market research', *Global Trade Magazine*, May: 83.

Welch, L. S. (1992) 'Developments in international franchising', *Journal of Global Marketing* 6 (1–2): 81–96.

Welch, L. S. and Joynt, P. (1987) 'Grouping for export: an effective solution', in P. J. Rosson and S. D. Reid (eds) *Managing Export Entry and Expansion: Concepts and Practice*, New York: Praeger.

Welch, L. S. and Weidersheim-Paul, F. (1980) 'Initial exports – a marketing failure?', *Journal of Management Studies* 17, October: 333–44.

Wind, Y. (1979) 'From the editor', *Journal of Marketing* 43 (1): 9–12.

World Bank (1990) *Guide to International Business Opportunities*, Washington: The World Bank.

FURTHER READING

Bilkey, W. J. (1978) 'An attempted integration of the literature on the export behaviour of firms', *Journal of International Business Studies* 9, Spring–Summer: 34–46.

Buckley, P. J., Pass, C. L. and Prescott, K. (1992) *Servicing International Markets: Competitive Strategies of Firms*, Oxford: Blackwell.

Cavusgil, S. T., Zuo, S. and Naidu, G. M. (1993) 'Product and promotion adaptation in export ventures: an empirical investigation', *Journal of International Business Studies* 24 (3): 479–506.

Chang, T.-L. and Grub, P. D. (1992) 'Competitive strategies of Taiwanese PC firms in their internationalization process', *Journal of Global Marketing* 6 (3): 5–28.

Czinkota, M. R. (ed.) (1983) *Export Promotion: The Public and Private Sector Interaction*, New York: Praeger.

Czinkota, M. R. and Johnston, W. J. (1981) 'Segmenting U.S. firms for export development', *Journal of Business Research* 9 (4): 353–65.

Czinkota, M. R. and Ronkainen, I. A. (1990) *International Marketing*, 2nd edn, Chicago: Dryden Press.

Czinkota, M. R. and Tesar, G. (eds) (1982) *Export Management: An International Context*, New York: Praeger.

Denis, J.-E. (1983) 'Promoting export trade through trading houses', in V. H. Kirpalani (ed.) *International Marketing: Managerial Issues, Research and Opportunities*, Chicago: American Marketing Association.

Denis, J.-E. and Depelteau, D. (1985) 'Market knowledge, diversification and export expansion', *Journal of International Business Studies* 16 (3): 77–89.

Gripsrud, G. (1990) 'The determinants of export decisions and attitudes to a distant market: Norwegian fishery exports to Japan', *Journal of International Business Studies* 21 (3): 469–85.

Jeannet, J.-P. and Hennessey, H. D. (1988) *International Marketing Management: Strategies and Cases*, Boston: Houghton Mifflin.

Johanson, J. and Vahlne, J.-E. (1992) 'Management of foreign market entry', *Scandinavian International Business Review* 1 (3): 9–27.

Lee, W.-Y. and Brasch, J. J. (1978) 'The adoption of export as an innovative strategy', *Journal of International Business Studies* 9, Spring–Summer: 85–93.

Mattson, J. (1986) 'Initial penetration of European continental markets by small and medium-sized firms', in S. T. Cavusgil (ed.) *Advances in International Marketing*, volume 1, Greenwich, CT: JAI Press.

Paliwoda, S. J. (1993) *International Marketing*, Oxford: Butterworth Heinemann.

Reid, S. D. (1983) 'Managerial and firm influences on export behaviour', *Journal of the Academy of Marketing Science* 11 (3): 323–32.

Reid, S. D. and Burlingame, L. (1982) 'Documentation and logistics issues in exporting firms', in V. Kothari (ed.) *Proceedings*, Academy of Marketing Science Conference.

Rosson, P. J. and Ford, I. D. (1982) 'Manufacturer-overseas distributor relations and export performance', *Journal of International Business Studies* 13, Fall: 57–72.

Rosson, P. J. and Reid, S. D. (eds) (1987) *Managing Export Entry and Expansion: Concepts and Practice*, New York: Praeger.

Samiee, S. and Walters, P. G. P. (1990) 'Rectifying strategic gaps in export management', *Journal of Global Marketing* 4 (1): 7–37.

Wortzel, L. W. and Wortzel, H. V. (1981) 'Export marketing strategies for NIC & LDC based firms', *Columbia Journal of World Business*, Spring: 51–9.

Yang, S. Y., Leone, R. P. and Alden, D. L. (1992) 'A market expansion ability approach to identify potential exporters', *Journal of Marketing* 56 (1): 84–96.

Yaprak, A. (1985) 'An empirical study of the differences between small exporting and non-exporting U.S. firms', *International Marketing Review* 2, Summer: 72–8.

50

INTERNATIONAL MARKETING

Susan P. Douglas and C. Samuel Craig

INTRODUCTION

The globalization of markets is one of the most significant developments in business today. Its consequences are profound and far-reaching both for strategy development as well as for policies in all areas of business activity including marketing, manufacturing, finance and personnel. Evidence of the impact is widespread, ranging from the growing proliferation of global products and brands, to the increasingly complex systems of production logistics being developed in the automobile, electronics and computer industries, and the growing number of cooperative agreements and joint ventures among firms of different national origins.

Increased communication and interchange of people, ideas and experience between countries has stimulated the identification and targeting of global market segments. Customers with similar tastes and interests in different countries throughout the world are identified, and products, brands or services targeted to these customers worldwide. While initially such strategies tended to be confined predominantly to products and services targeted to an affluent clientele (for example, Rolex watches, Cartier watches, Gucci handbags, Hermes scarves, American Express cards), this now occurs among mass-merchandised products such as Budweiser beer or Bic razors.

Parallel to this trend, is the development of global sourcing and production logistics, facilitated by increased awareness of differential labour, production and raw material costs in different countries as well as the growing efficiency of international transportation and communication networks. Thus, Adidas sources many of its products, including textile products such as track suits and T-shirts as well as running and other sports shoes, in Asia. Similarly, Ford of Europe has sourced headlights from Lucas in the UK, transmissions in Portugal, and axles in Canada for assembly at plants in Germany and the UK.

Such developments imply that in many industries competition is taking place on a global, rather than a national or even regional scale. To compete effectively

865

companies must globalize their marketing strategy. This chapter develops a framework for viewing global marketing strategy. It begins by identifying the key parameters of strategy: business definition; and identification of the company's driving force and determining its global strategic thrust. In tandem, the firm must also assess its position in international markets, evaluating its own strengths and weaknesses as well as those of its competitors.

Formulation of global marketing strategy involves the choice of the terrain on which to compete. This defines not only the geographic scope of activities but also with whom it competes. Next is the choice of an underlying strategy (i.e. either cost leadership or differentiation or a hybrid of the two appropriate to the firm and industry). Closely linked to the choice of terrain and the underlying strategy is the level of investment required. Certain strategies require significant investment in terms of funds and other resources if they are to be successful.

Once the strategy has been established, the next step is to devise a marketing mix that effectively implements the strategy. One of the most basic considerations is whether the firm should standardize all or part of the marketing mix. This entails weighing the barriers to standardization along with the benefits of adapting elements of the marketing mix to local conditions. It is essential that a firm adopt a multi-country perspective in developing marketing strategy. By embracing a strategic approach that encompasses multiple countries, the firm is better able to develop a successful global marketing strategy. The remainder of this chapter is devoted to these issues.

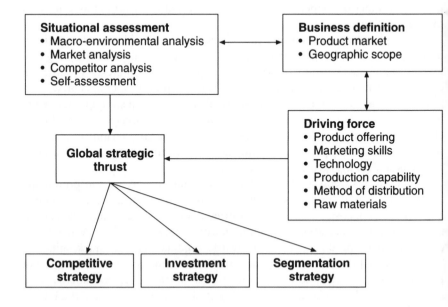

Figure 1   Strategic assessment in the international environment

GLOBAL STRATEGY PARAMETERS

The starting point for the development of global marketing strategy is the definition of the business or, in other words, the market arena in which the company will compete. While in relation to the domestic market a business is defined in terms of the specific product market or services in which the company is involved, in international markets it is important also to determine the geographic scope of the business. (See Figure 1 for an overview of this process.)

Defining the business

Defining the product market or service

The first step is to define the specific product market or markets in which the company is competing so as to determine the focus and scope of the company's activities. Often this consists of several markets. Pirelli, for example, identifies three major businesses in its operations: cable, tyre, and diversified products such as fibre optics, industrial automation, etc.

Four basic dimensions in defining the business can be identified: customer functions, technologies, customer segments and stages in the value-added system. The customer functions indicate the benefits which are to be provided, as, for example, a fast food outlet provides not only food, but speed of delivery and reliable quality standards. Technology used determines the way in which a function is provided. Thus, for example, X-ray machines may use laser or conventional technology. The segment dimension determines the specific customers to be targeted. Ryobi and Makita, for example, target small hand-powered tools to the 'do-it-yourself' amateur segment, and professionals such as repair businesses, plumbers and carpenters. The stages in the value-added system indicate the degree of vertical integration within the business. Braun, for example, markets high-priced household appliances, but production is farmed out to other companies under highly detailed design specifications.

In applying these dimensions to international markets it is important to note that these may differ from one country to another. In the first place a product or service may not necessarily be used for the same purpose in different countries or geographic regions. For example, while bicycles are predominantly used for recreation in the USA, in China they are a basic mode of transportation. This implies that the relevant product benefits vary from one country to another. While in the USA factors such as style and design may be crucial, in China benefits such as economy and durability may be more significant.

The availability of different product variants may also differ considerably from country to country. In the USA a wide variety of household detergents are available, including high sudsing and low sudsing detergents, fabric softeners with or without blue, basic bleach or colourfast bleach. In developing countries detergents also compete with rubbing washing on a ridged wooden scrub board or on rocks in the river. Consequently, the specific product benefits vary from emphasis on high sudsing versus low sudsing detergents or softness to getting the dirt out of clothes.

Differences in relative costs of labour, energy capital or other resources imply that technology varies from one country to another, again affecting the definition of the business. For example, in developing countries cash registers are often hand cranked, as compared with electronic registers or computerized systems prevalent in many industrialized countries.

Such differences imply that it may be desirable to define that product business on a country-by-country basis. Similarities between product businesses across countries can then be identified. This may in turn lead to a redefinition of the product business depending on the company's desire to target a uniform segment across countries, as opposed to responding to national differences.

Defining geographic market scope

The next step is to define the geographic scope of the business. Here four major categories of businesses may be identified based on the degree of integration of markets across countries: domestic businesses, interdomestic businesses, regional businesses, and global businesses.

1 Domestic businesses are those which are national in scope. Demand within a country is homogeneous and there are substantial barriers between countries. Many food items are typically domestic businesses. Culinary preferences with some notable exceptions tend to be localized.

2 Interdomestic businesses are those where products can be sold in other countries with marginal modifications. Many household appliances such as toasters, irons and food mixers are interdomestic as they require only minor modifications in terms of voltage and the configuration of the plugs.

3 Regional businesses span a geographic region such as Europe, Latin America and North America. The automobile market is typically regional in scope, as models are developed primarily for regional markets. Ford, for example, developed models such as the Fiesta, Granada and Sierra specifically for the European market, and a different range for the USA. At the same time economic factors are hastening an evolution toward a more global orientation. Through the development of the Mondeo, Ford is attempting to establish a world car.

4 Global businesses are those in which the market is the same worldwide, for example, tyres, fibre-optics, computers, pharmaceuticals. Such markets are highly integrated worldwide, and hence businesses operate on a global scale. Biro pens provide an example of a global consumer market.

Identifying the company's driving force

The next step is to identify the driving force of the company. This is a key determinant in strategy development, both in providing guidelines for the allocation of resources to different functional areas, and in defining its differential competitive advantage. Six different categories or areas where this may lie have been identified (Day 1984): in products offered, marketing skills, technology, production capability, method of distribution, and control of raw materials.

1 *Products offered*: if a company has certain unique or superior products or product-related advantages, it can seek to exploit these on a global scale and expand into new markets in other countries. Anita Roddick of Body Shop developed a line of environmentally friendly cosmetics, not tested on animals. Following their success in the UK, franchised stores selling the product line were established in other countries with high environmental consciousness.

2 *Marketing skills*: in this case, a company's driving force is its marketing expertise and know-how. Procter and Gamble's success in international markets stems largely from the company's mastery of mass-merchandising techniques, combining heavy media advertising with intensive distribution.

3 *Technology*: here superior technology provides the rationale for product development and identification of target markets. Siemens, for example, has been at the forefront of new technological developments in telecommunications, PBXs, digital switching.

4 *Production capability*: production-driven businesses focus on efficiency in production and the production process. Japanese competition in the car market is, for example, largely founded in superior production efficiency.

5 *Method of distribution and sale*: here, the unique characteristic of a company is its method of distribution and sales. Avon cosmetics has, for example, successfully utilized its system of employing housewives as salesladies in many different countries throughout the world.

6 *Control of raw materials*: a final category consists of companies focusing on control of raw materials. This is typically the driving force of petroleum companies such as BP, Exxon and Shell, as well as diamond-mining companies such as DeBeers. Operations in international markets are often dominated by concern with retaining control over key resources and management of conflict with host governments.

In essence, therefore, the identification of a company's driving force determines the specific aspects of strategy on which attention is focused. This does not, however, necessarily imply neglect of other areas. Focus on technology or products offered does not, for example, imply that ability to satisfy market needs and identify key target segments can be ignored. Rather it suggests priorities for allocation of management effort and resources and for the evaluation of new projects.

SITUATIONAL ASSESSMENT IN INTERNATIONAL MARKETS

A necessary preliminary to determination of a company's global strategic thrust is a situational assessment of trends and forces within the market. The business definition together with the identification of the driving force of the company provide the basic parameters for determining the scope of this assessment. Depending on the nature of the market, the analysis can be undertaken at various levels (i.e. global, regional or domestic). In general, however, it may be desirable to undertake the analysis first on a country-by-country basis, focusing on key countries and markets with an integrative and summary analysis by region and for the global market.

Macro-environmental analysis

The first step is the macro-environmental analysis. This should cover all aspects that are likely to affect the health of the product market, including economic, political, regulatory, technological, societal and cultural forces, together with elements which may impinge on the market at the global, regional and country market level. In the case of the automobile industry, for example, bilateral negotiations relating to tariff barriers and quotas imposed on automobiles of specific origins might be examined. Technological forces of relevance might include trends towards the use of robots in automobile manufacture or the replacement of steel by polymers. At the regional or continental level, economic trends influencing the purchase of automobiles and shifts towards smaller, more fuel-efficient automobiles might also be considered.

At the country level specific factors of relevance might include safety regulations and controls and requirements with regard to local content. At this level, the assessment should cover not only factors affecting the product market, but also decisions to invest in a particular country. Critical factors in this regard are country risks, including political, financial and economic. Political risk might include risks of nationalization or political instability. Financial risk might include inflation, capital flow restrictions, and foreign exchange fluctuations, while economic risk might include economic instability or decline.

Other factors that may be of concern are those which affect the costs of operation in a country, as, for example, resources and integrative networks. The types of resources to be considered include physical resources such as electricity, energy and water, human resources such as labour or management training and attitudes, and capital resources such as finance and technology. Integrative networks might include the nature of the transportation infrastructure, the distribution network, as well as the availability of mass media, TV, radio and magazines.

Market analysis

The market or industry analysis may also be undertaken at three levels. Here, it may be preferable to conduct the analysis initially on a country-by-country basis and then integrate across countries at a regional and global level, indicating major geographic growth areas as well as key customer characteristics and behaviour patterns.

The analysis should cover both quantitative and qualitative aspects of the market. This should, therefore, include examination of the size and potential of the industry in terms of units sold, or sales volume by each of the major product lines and classes. For example, in the computer industry, trends might be analysed by notebooks, personal computers, mini-computers, mainframes, and time-sharing services. Sales trends for each of these categories might then be projected for one, five or more years. Trends with regard to substitute and competing products might also be examined, together with their impact on future market developments.

In addition, customer needs, interests, purchase behaviour and characteristics should be examined. Benefits sought by customers, pricing sensitivity and purchasing behaviour, including perception of products, information sought, services required should also be considered, as well as the extent to which these vary among customers. The existence of clearly identifiable market segments might be examined as well as the degree of similarity among segments across countries. This might indicate the feasibility of pursuing a transnational segmentation strategy.

Trends with regard to resource markets also need to be examined. This includes resources such as raw materials, as well as technology, key components, capital and other inputs into the production and marketing process. Here, alternative sources of supply need to be monitored, as well as their quality, reliability and relative price. The degree of integration and collaboration among suppliers should also be assessed. This provides an important input for global sourcing strategies and production logistics.

Competitor analysis

The final element in the situational analysis is competitor analysis. It is important to assess competition at the local level, as well as the regional and global level. Local companies may enjoy a privileged position in their domestic market. This may stem from protection and support from the government or other official authorities in the form of tariff barriers, quotas, regulations restricting the entry of foreign goods or direct subsidies. Alternatively, it may arise from a strong customer franchise, and traditional ties with customers and the distributor network.

The key strengths and weaknesses of each competitor also need to be identified in relation to all the functional areas, including design, production, marketing, finance and management. Here, specific skills and resources of key competitors need to be assessed with a view not only to current situation, but also to the future competitive situation. Large multinationals, for example, often have extensive resources which enable them to build market share, sustain price wars, devote resources to establishing extensive distributor networks or to research and technological development. Smaller competitors, on the other hand, may be considerably more flexible and be able to adapt more rapidly to changes in the market situation.

Self-assessment

Once each of these aspects has been considered, a company has to assess its own resources and competencies, and its strengths and weaknesses in relation to those of key competitors. These have to be examined not only in terms of corporate resources and strategy, but also specifically relative to each country, region and in global markets. Based on this analysis, a company can then determine where its major strengths lie and in which areas of the world it appears to face strong competition.

The macro-environmental and industry analysis reveals where the best opportunities appear to lie relative to specific geographic and market areas, both currently and in the long run. Competitor analysis, on the other hand, indicates the extent to which competitors have exploited such opportunities and hence where market potential is saturated, or competition is likely to be particularly keen. These various phases of analysis provide the basic input for determining the company's global strategic thrust.

DEFINING THE GLOBAL STRATEGIC THRUST

Once a situational assessment has been conducted, the firm is ready to define its strategic thrust and formulate strategy relative to global markets. This should specify first the firm's competitive strategy, thus establishing the basis of a company differential advantage relative to competition; second, its investment strategy which determines how resources are to be allocated in order to achieve its objectives; and third, the market scope and configuration of target segments.

Competitive strategy

In international markets establishing competitive strategy requires determining, first, the terrain or geographic area in which a company is to compete; and, second, the strategy or tactics to be used in competing on this terrain. These decisions establish the boundaries or limits at which the company's efforts are to be directed, as well as providing guidelines for the allocation of those efforts.

Choice of terrain

In entering international markets, an important consideration is the choice of geographic terrain on which a company plans to compete. This requires determining the number and type of countries in which to compete, as well as the geographic scope of operations. An important element affecting this latter decision is the scope of competition – whether this takes place predominantly on a global, regional, interdomestic or domestic scale. However, it is important to note that even though competition is predominantly global or regional, a company may not necessarily choose to compete at that level. For example, it may choose to compete on a national or regional level in a global product market: Henkel and Kao compete in the detergent market on a regional scale, against global giants such as P&G, Colgate and Unilever.

In determining which countries and on what scale to compete, a key factor is the company's resources and skills relative to those of its competitors. Competing in a global market with a broad product line is likely to require extensive resources and the capacity to operate on a worldwide scale. A small company entering or operating in such a market may therefore prefer to concentrate its resources and operate on a more limited scale, focusing on national or regional markets. For example, in the automobile market, giants such as General Motors, Ford and Toyota compete on full-line basis worldwide. Others such as the Peugeot group and Fiat compete predominantly on a regional scale. Yet others such as Seat compete on a national level.

A company has to weigh its skills and resources against those required to compete effectively in the product market. Potential economies of scale in production and marketing, which may be achieved from operating on a global or regional scale, have to be weighed against transportation costs of serving markets from a central location. Recent developments in production technology facilitate introduction of minor product design changes at reduced cost so that products may be adapted to different market requirements and marketed on a broader scale. Thus products can be marketed on an interdomestic rather than a domestic scale without substantially increasing costs.

Other aspects to consider in choosing the terrain on which to compete are whether a country is a competitor's home market or neutral territory, and the degree of concentration or diversification in the choice of markets. In its home market, a competitor may benefit from a strongly entrenched position due to customer franchise and loyalty, a well-established distribution network, or protection from the home government. In addition, it is likely to be more sensitive to attacks in its home market. In Korea, for example, Hyundai benefits from a substantial customer franchise, and constitutes a major obstacle to US companies' penetration of the market. In neutral territory, where there is no major domestic competitor, competition may take place on more equal terms.

On the other hand, if such barriers to entry do not exist and there is a substantial threat of competitive entry, it may be desirable to enter as many markets as rapidly as possible in order to pre-empt competition. This may be particularly desirable if the company's products or product lines are highly innovative or have some unique advantage relative to competition.

Choice of competitive tactics

The choice of terrain determines the geographic limits in which a company chooses to operate. Next, the firm has to select the tactics with which it will compete on that terrain. Here, two strategic options are typically identified: cost leadership, and product differentiation.

1   *Cost leadership* strategy is typically grounded in operating efficiencies which enable a company to offer equivalent product quality at a lower price than competitors. This strategy is frequently followed by Japanese companies such as Casio in calculators, Seiko in watches, and more recently by Korean companies in colour TVs, video cassette recorders, etc. In pursuing such a strategy it is important to ensure that cost leadership can be sustained in the long run, and is founded in real operating efficiencies. Otherwise, it may stimulate price wars which can erode profit margins dramatically.

2   *Product differentiation* focuses on the product and on creating a perception that it is unique, offering certain advantages which are not provided by competitors. A company may, for example, offer a product which is perceived to be of superior quality, as, for example, Hewlett-Packard in measuring instruments. Alternatively, a company may be perceived as superior in terms of product reliability, service or delivery. IBM, for example, has traditionally held a worldwide reputation for product reliability and service.

   Introduction of innovative features provides another means for differentiating products. Apple Computers, for example, continually introduces new models in personal computers and notebooks, with new features such as lite pens and colour screens, in order to stay ahead of their competition. A company may also be able to develop a strong or unique brand image for its product. Coca-Cola Classic has, for example, a certain mystique which to a large extent accounts for its success worldwide. Similarly, Mercedes and Rolls Royce both convey a prestige luxury image, but each is of a somewhat different character. Fragrances are also frequently marketed based on their distinctive image; for example the heady image of Yves St Laurent's Opium, or the sporty image of Ralph Lauren's Polo and Safari.

3   *Hybrid strategies* can be pursued which combine both cost leadership and product differentiation strategies. Effectively executed, this will enable the firm to establish a strong position in global markets. Heinz, for example, has spent heavily on advertising to develop strong brand names in many country markets while at the same time managing costs by adapting purchasing and technology to local market conditions.

In essence, therefore, competitive strategy should define the firm's strategic thrust in global markets, based on its core advantage relative to its competitors. At the same time, it provides the basic parameters for its investment strategy, relative to different business functions and geographic locations.

Investment strategy

The second component of global marketing strategy relates to the commitment of resources to various business functions such as R&D, production or marketing in different countries throughout the world. How and where resources such as raw materials, technology, components and capital are obtained have also to be considered. These decisions depend in part on the relative costs associated with producing and supplying markets from alternative locations and transportation costs, as also on perceived risks such as political or economic instability, foreign exchange fluctuations, associated with a given location.

Country investment strategy

The choice of countries to enter implies commitment of resources to these countries. The level of commitment does, however, depend on the mode of operation. A company can, for example, develop licensing agreements, export via agents or through its own sales organization, enter into contract manufacturing or strategic alliances or establish a wholly-owned subsidiary. Each of these options differs in terms of the commitment of resources to overseas markets, the flexibility of that commitment, and the degree of control over operations.

Licensing agreements entail minimal commitment of financial resources to overseas markets. In this case, a company licences another company, typically local, to manufacture and market a patented product or use a trademark or brand name in a foreign market, in return for a fee or royalty. While the initial financial commitment is low, resources frequently have to be devoted to monitoring the performance of the licensee, to ensure that the product meets quality standards and royalties reflect actual sales. In addition, while the licensor receives a limited return in the form of royalties, he has little guarantee that market potential is fully exploited. Furthermore, once a licensing agreement has been established, it cannot easily be reversed for the specified period of the agreement.

Exporting provides another option limiting the level of international commitment. Since international markets are supplied from the domestic base no investment in production facilities in other countries is required. On the other hand, additional transportation, insurance and handling costs are incurred, as well as customs duties and tariffs. These additional costs have to be weighed against economies of scale achieved through centralization of production, and risks of foreign investment.

Another alternative limiting risk and financial exposure in international

875

markets is the establishment of a joint venture or strategic alliance with another company or government agency. Capital, management and other resources required for international market operations are provided in part by the partner(s). There is, however, always the possibility of potential conflict and communication problems. In particular, problems often arise with regard to decisions concerning the distribution of profits, future expansion and investment plans.

Establishment of a wholly-owned subsidiary entails a significant investment and a long-run commitment to international markets. On the other hand, it allows maximum control over the conduct of such operations and development of their potential. It also allows more flexibility for disinvestment and reallocation of resources than licensing or joint ventures.

In addition to the level of investment, its timing has also to be considered, especially where substantial investment in production facilities is entailed. Thus, the sequencing of entry and expansion in different country markets needs to be examined, and a long-run strategy for global market expansion developed, rather than making decisions on a country-by-country market basis.

Business function investment

While the choice of terrain establishes country investment priorities, competitive strategy indicates investment priorities by business function, for example, in improving production efficiencies or developing brand image.

Cost leadership strategies require that prime attention be paid to developing and maintaining a cost structure which is more efficient than the competition's. This can be achieved in a variety of ways. One alternative is to focus on production processes which are more efficient than those of competitors. Plant and equipment in the Japanese and South Korean steel industries, for example, are more technologically advanced than in the USA or Europe, thus enabling more efficient production. Similarly, production efficiencies enable the Japanese manufacturers to produce a compact car for significantly less than US manufacturers.

Cost efficiencies may also be achieved through sourcing from low labour cost countries such as Malaysia, Indonesia or China. Other measures include marketing of stripped-down models and elimination of all extras, essentially a 'no frills' policy. This can be an effective strategy in developing countries where there is a high degree of price sensitivity.

In contrast to cost leadership strategies, product differentiation strategies require investment in product development, image building, media distribution and service. The primary emphasis is on insulating the company from price competition, focusing on delivery of customer satisfaction, and building strong customer relationships.

Emphasis of product quality requires investment in product design and quality control. This strategy is popular among many US and European companies in international markets and limits vulnerability to low price competition. For example, Kodak competes in world markets, based on a strong image of quality and reliability.

Product innovation and introduction of innovative features, on the other hand, requires attention to product R&D. Here, a key danger in international markets is that competitors in low cost labour countries will rapidly introduce cut-rate imitation of product innovations. For example, in the personal computer market, IBM and Compaq encounter competition from clones produced by competitors in Taiwan, Hong Kong and Singapore.

A product differentiation strategy thus requires determination of the specific product or marketing features to be emphasized and allocation of resources accordingly. While cost leadership strategies are typically leveraged worldwide, differentiation strategies are not necessarily the same in different countries or parts of the world depending on segmentation strategies. These are next examined in more detail.

Market scope and segmentation

The third component of the firm's global strategic thrust concerns the geographic market scope and configuration of target segments. Here, two issues need to be considered: the degree of integration across geographic markets; and the breadth of the target market (see Figure 2). Both issues are closely interlinked with decisions relating to competitive strategy and investment priorities.

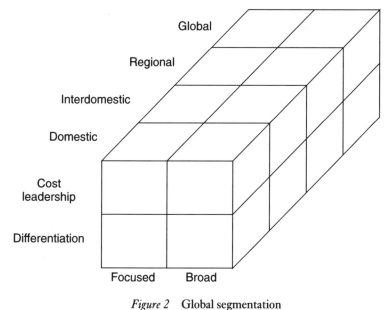

Figure 2   Global segmentation

877

Degree of integration

In considering the degree of integration across geographic markets, or whether the same customer or segments are targeted worldwide, management needs to examine the similarity of customer behaviour and response patterns across geographic markets, as well as the extent of market interconnectedness or linkages between markets. Some types of customers such as business executives, young adults and children have highly similar interests and behaviour patterns irrespective of nationality. Consequently, some products and marketing strategies are effective in targeting such customers worldwide.

Similarly, in certain industrial markets such as fibre optics, polymers, mainframe computers and CAT scanners, customer requirements are essentially the same worldwide. In some cases, separate product lines are developed for specific market segments. For example, cosmetic manufacturers market a premium line for the more affluent, acne products for teenagers, anti-wrinkle products for the middle aged, and environmentally friendly lines for the environmentally conscious. The underlying assumption is that similarity of these segments in different countries outweighs any country differences.

On the other hand, if desired customer benefits or the nature of product market vary substantially from one country to another, product lines and marketing strategy will need to be tailored to specific geographic areas or markets. Differences between countries are thus perceived as greater than those within countries. This may be an appropriate strategy for a food processing company. Findus, Nestlé's frozen food division, has separate product lines in different countries which are adapted to local food tastes. Products such as fish fingers and fishcakes are marketed in the UK, *coq au vin* and *boeuf bourguinon* in France, lasagna, cannelloni and pizza in Italy and dim sum in Singapore.

Some companies pursue hybrid strategies, marketing some products and brands globally, as well as some tailored to specific regions or local markets. Cigarette manufacturers such as Philip Morris or BAT market global brands such as Marlboro, but also develop local brands, tailored to specific preferences for different types of tobacco, length of cigarette and nicotine for tar content.

Similarly, Coca-Cola markets its Classic Coke worldwide, but also has local and regional brands of soft drinks such as Lilt, a pineapple-grapefruit soda, Georgia coffee in a can and Regal ginger ale which cater to specific local tastes.

Breadth of target market

The breadth or scope of the target market has also to be determined. Management may, for example, decide to adopt a broad-line strategy, targeting all segments or potential customers in a given market, or alternatively focus on targeting a specific segment.

In the automobile industry, for example, companies such as GM, Ford and Toyota market a broad-based product line worldwide, while others such as

Ferrari and Maserati focus on targeting the luxury sportscar segment. A broad-based strategy implies that efforts are targeted towards the entire market, irrespective of any differences in interest or market response among customers. This typically implies that any gains that might be achieved from tailoring strategies to specific individual needs are largely outweighed by economies of scale of production and efficiencies in mass distribution. This is likely to be an appropriate strategy for products targeted to mass markets. A focused strategy, on the other hand, is likely to be most appropriate for a company with relatively limited resources, facing global competition on a full product line, or where distinctive competencies are required to satisfy specific market segments as, for example, in fashion apparel and other items.

Except in the case of globally integrated industries such as aerospace or chemicals, broad-line strategies typically require some tailoring to specific geographic markets, while focused strategies are more readily leveraged worldwide.

Thus, competitive strategy determines the parameters of the company's operations and its driving thrust in global markets, investment strategy establishes priorities for how resources are to be allocated across countries and functions so as to achieve competitive objectives, while segmentation defines the spatial configuration of activities. This in turn provides guidelines for the development of the tactics to be used in international markets in relation to each of the elements of the marketing mix. These aspects are next examined in more detail.

ESTABLISHING THE MARKETING MIX

A central issue in determining marketing mix tactics in international markets is the extent to which these are standardized across countries. This depends on the scope of the market, global, regional or domestic; the basis on which the firm competes, cost leadership or differentiation; and the segmentation strategy pursued by a company. Even where the product market is global in character there may be barriers to implementation of such a strategy such as the nature of the marketing infrastructure or government regulation (see Buzzell 1968). This is affected by the choice of terrain on which to compete. These relationships are shown in Figure 3.

Furthermore, even though the overall positioning is global or regional, specific elements of the mix or the way in which they are executed may need to be adapted. For example, the product or service may be the same, but its positioning may differ somewhat from country to country, or alternatively the specific promotional theme or distribution strategy. Similarly, even though the basic promotional theme is the same, the copy execution may need to be adapted to specific national or cultural contexts. Thus, the degree of uniformity versus adaptation may vary all the way from a totally uniform strategy for all elements of the mix to uniformity with regard to some, but not others, or adaptation of all facets. This is next considered in relation to each of the elements.

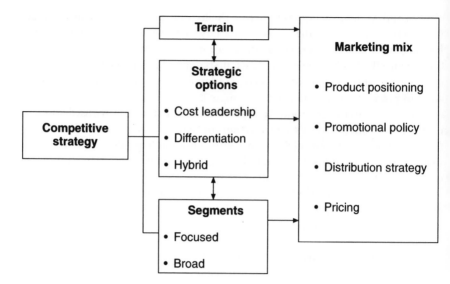

Figure 3 Global competitive strategy

Product positioning

Product positioning is the cornerstone of the marketing mix, insofar as it operationalizes the key elements of competitive strategy which differentiate the company's offering from others in a given product market. Positioning defines product market boundaries and the relevant competing product set, the specific benefits or attributes to be emphasized, and the segment whose needs and interests the company aims to satisfy.

In establishing positioning strategy, a key issue is whether or not to adopt a global position. A global positioning strategy offers a number of advantages. In the first place, it portrays a uniform image worldwide. Second, cost savings may be achieved since products do not have to be adapted nor separate advertising copy developed for specific markets. Benetton, for example, utilizes the same commercials worldwide, not only saving on production costs, but also reinforcing its global image. Good ideas and know-how, whether for products, advertising or distribution, can be transferred from one country to another, and exploited on a worldwide basis.

On the other hand, even where markets are essentially global in character and customer needs and interests are uniform worldwide, there are often a number of barriers to the adoption of a global positioning. In the first place, government regulation may require the addition of catalytic converters to automobiles, or restrict use of comparative advertising. Second, differences in the marketing infrastructure such as, for example, the absence of TV advertising, limited reach of print media, absence of supermarkets or discount outlets may limit the ability to use the same positioning strategy or to execute it in an equivalent manner. Finally, differences in local competition from one market to another may limit the effectiveness of a specific positioning strategy. If, for example, positioning emphasizes premium pricing, local competitors may be able to provide equivalent quality at a lower price.

Any of these factors may necessitate modification or adaptation of the positioning strategy, whether in relation to most or only certain countries or markets in the world. For example, the positioning strategy of the Renault 5 car was modified in the German market to emphasize engine and safety features to meet competition from Volkswagen, and in Italy to emphasize superior road handling in order to meet competition from Fiat. In some cases, even though the basic product remains the same, positioning strategies may be dramatically changed to emphasize different benefits, and targeted to different segments. Powered garden tools, for example, such as small tractors and hoes, have been positioned as light agricultural machinery in developing countries.

Promotional policy

Similarly, in the case of promotional policy, substantial benefits from standardization may be reaped in the form of cost savings, uniform image and exploitation of good ideas. However, obstacles exist in the form of regulation of promotional copy, budgets, instore promotions, availability and reach of media, as well as interpretation and translation of messages. For example, all forms of comparative advertising and mention of competitive brands are banned.

As a result of such obstacles, an intermediate solution is sometimes adopted. A prototype campaign is developed, indicating the key themes and message. This is then executed and adapted to the specific cultural context and infrastructure in each country. Guinness, for example, developed a prototype campaign to market Guinness in Europe. The scenario consisted of a table laid for two, with two glasses of Guinness. In Italy this was translated into an antipasto laid on a terrace overlooking the bay of Sorrento, in France the context was a bistro with a red check tablecloth, and in Germany a tavern with sausages and sauerkraut.

Distribution strategy

In the case of distribution strategy, the benefits of a standardized strategy are perhaps least evident. Here, there are substantial differences in the nature of distribution channels, and in the availability of certain types of distribution outlets. This frequently impedes the development of a standardized strategy. A key factor in this context is the relative importance of small independents and other forms of retailing such as kiosks, open markets, itinerants, as opposed to large-scale organized distribution. In many countries, especially developing and emerging nations, the former still account for a significant proportion of distribution.

Fragmentation of retailing has implications for the wholesale structure insofar as it typically implies that wholesalers are a key link in the distribution system. In Japan, for example, wholesalers frequently perform not only delivery and warehousing functions, but also finance retailers offering credit terms or selling goods on a consignment basis.

Such differences in the structure of distribution imply that distribution strategies frequently need to be tailored to the specific characteristics of the distribution system in order to provide the desired level of coverage and control, as well as customer service.

Pricing

The final element of the marketing mix is that of pricing. Again, especially in consumer markets, many factors impede or render sub-optimal the establishment of a uniform pricing strategy. These include, for example, differences in cost structures from one country to another, in demand response functions, in competitive prices, and in government or trade regulation of prices.

In the case of costs, differences in labour, raw materials, management or other operating costs from one country to another, as well as transportation, tariffs, customs and other charges, may result in differences in delivered market costs. Price escalation is often acute when exporting, due to transportation costs, customs and handling dues and agent margins. Retail, wholesale and dealer margins also vary, as well as local taxes, thus resulting in substantial differences in terms of costs. Differences in demand response functions and competitor prices from one country to another also suggest that it may be preferable to price differentially to be more competitive. In the automobile market, for example, prices frequently differ from country to country due not only to taxes and margins, but also to differences in prices of competitive models.

Government or trade regulation of prices, wholesale margins, sales taxes and VAT constitute a final factor hindering uniform pricing. These are often designed to restrict the use of price as a competitive tool and provide basic parameters for pricing policy. While other factors such as costs can be manipulated, these essentially constitute 'givens' within which a company has to operate.

Thus, the advantages of standardization or uniformity versus adaptation need to be weighed for each of the elements of the marketing mix. Even where the overall positioning is global, this does not necessarily imply that each mix element will or can be uniform, or executed identically in each case. It is, however, important that tactics in each area should be consistent with the overall positioning strategy. Thus, for example, a positioning strategy based on product reliability and service should be backed by reliable service, whether provided by the distributor, manufacturer or other intermediary. Similarly, a positioning based on product quality should be accompanied by premium pricing to ensure a coherent image.

SUMMARY

As markets worldwide become more competitive and more interlinked, firms hoping to compete successfully must adopt a global perspective and plan marketing strategy on an international basis. This involves a range of issues that go beyond development of strategy on a purely domestic basis. This chapter has attempted to highlight some of the key components of international marketing strategy. Because of space constraints, these issues were not covered in great depth or detail. The reader who is faced with the challenge of developing a strategy in the international arena is encouraged to consult Douglas and Craig (1995), Jeannet and Hennessey (1995) and Yip (1992) for more comprehensive treatment of the topic.

REFERENCES

Buzzell, Robert D. (1968) 'Can you standardize multinational marketing?', *Harvard Business Review*, November–December: 102–13.
Day, George S. (1984) *Strategic Market Planning: The Pursuit of Competitive Advantage*, St. Paul, MN: West Publishing Co.
Douglas, Susan P. and Craig, C. Samuel (1995) *Global Marketing Strategies*, New York: McGraw-Hill.
Jeannet, Jean-Pierre and Hennessey, Hubert D. (1995) *Global Marketing Strategies*, 3rd edn, Boston: Houghton Mifflin.
Yip, George S. (1992) *Total Global Strategy*, Englewood Cliffs, NJ: Prentice-Hall.

51

REGIONAL TRADING BLOCS

Jim Hamill

INTRODUCTION

In his seminal article on the globalization of markets, Levitt (1983) argued that a combination of technological, social and economic developments was driving the world towards a 'converging commonality' – an homogenized, unified world market in terms of consumer tastes and product preferences. The main beneficiaries of this trend towards a 'global village' would be global firms producing globally standardized products in order to achieve economies of scale. Such global firms would be able to undercut the prices of more nationally orientated competitors.

More recent authors have further developed Levitt's main argument. Ohmae (1989), for example, has argued that globalization is now 'a fact of life'; that the trend towards a single global market is unstoppable. The implication of this for corporate marketing strategy is that the 'whether' of globalization is 'yesterday's news', only the 'how' is still of interest. In other words, companies no longer have the choice of whether they should globalize their operations. The only strategic issue is the best way to achieve globalization.

Viewed from the perspective of the early 1990s, there can be little doubt that there has been a significant trend towards the globalization of many industries. An equally important development, however, has been the growing unification and economic integration of countries on a regional basis. According to several authors, the years towards the millennium will be characterized by the growing importance of regional trading blocs rather than the emergence of a unified global market. The emergence of regional trading blocs as an important phenomenon in international marketing is examined in this chapter.

The chapter comprises four main sections. The first section examines different types of regional trading blocs ranging from free trade agreements to full economic, political and monetary union. While there are numerous examples of regional trading blocs, by far the most important are the European Union, the North American Free Trade Agreement and the various attempts to create cross-country cooperation in the Pacific Asia region. Section two provides a brief commentary on each of the three major blocs. The emergence of regional trading blocs raises important issues concerning marketing strategy and marketing management in international firms and these are examined in the third section. Section four examines some of the wider international management implications of regionalization.

TYPES OF REGIONAL TRADING BLOCS

Table 1 lists the most important regional trading blocs around the world. While there is a common theme of cross-country cooperation in each bloc, they vary significantly with respect to the extent and depth of cooperation. Five main types of regional trading agreements can be identified: preferential trading arrangements; free trade areas (FTAs); customs unions; common markets; economic union. To this we may add a sixth, namely full economic, political and monetary union.

1 *Preferential trade arrangements* – in which a country applies lower tariffs to imports from a specified group of countries; or members apply lower tariffs to each other than to non-member countries.

2 *Free trade areas (FTAs)* – in a free trade area all barriers to trade among member countries are removed; goods and services are freely traded within the area although each country can maintain its own barriers with non-member countries. The two best known examples of FTAs are the European Free Trade Area (EFTA) and the North American Free Trade Agreement (NAFTA).

3 *Customs unions* – similar to FTAs (i.e. free trade among member countries) but with a common trade policy with non-member countries such as a common external tariff.

4 *Common market* – a further development of the FTA concept which covers factors of production (labour, capital and technology) as well as trade. In a common market, factors of production are freely mobile between member states in addition to the free movement of goods and services.

5 *Economic union* – in addition to the free movement of goods, services and factors of production, an economic union involves integration and coordination of economic policy among member states covering harmonization of monetary and fiscal policies, fixed exchange rates and so on. In a full economic union a common currency would be used.

6 *Full integration* – the final stage in the spectrum of regional cooperation would be full integration of member states covering the free movement of goods, services and factors of production; integration of economic policy; and, finally, political integration leading to some loss of national political sovereignty.

Table 1   Regional economic groupings

Organization	Date of establishment	Member countries
Andean Group (Acuerdo de Cartagena; Grupo Andino)	1969	Bolivia, Columbia, Ecuador, Peru, Venezuela.
ASEAN (Association of South-East Asian Nations)	1967	Brunei, Indonesia, Malaysia, Philippines, Singapore, Thailand.
CARICOM (Caribbean Community and Common Market)	1973	Antigua and Barbuda, Barbados, Belize, Dominica, Grenada, the Grenadines, Guyana, Jamaica, Montserrat, St Christopher and Nevis, St Lucia, St Vincent, Trinidad and Tobago.
Central American Common Market (Mercado Comun Centro Americano)	1960	Costa Rica, El Salvador, Guatemala, Honduras, Nicaragua.
Council of Arab Economic Unity	1964	Iraq, Jordan, Kuwait, Libya, Mauritania, Palestine Liberation Organisation, Somalia, Sudan, Syria, United Arab Emirates, Yemen Arab Republic, People's Democratic Republic of Yemen.
Council for Mutual Economic Assistance (COMECON)	1949	Bulgaria, Cuba, Czechoslovakia, German Democratic Republic, Hungary, Mongolia, Poland, Romania, USSR, Vietnam.
Economic Community of West African States (ECOWAS)	1975	Benin, Burkina Faso, Cape Verde, Gambia, Ghana, Guinea, Guinea-Bissau, Ivory Coast, Liberia, Mali, Mauritania, Niger, Nigeria, Senegal, Sierra Leone, Togo.
European Community (EC)	1957	Belgium, Denmark, France, Germany, Greece, Republic of Ireland, Italy, Luxembourg, Netherlands, Portugal, Spain, UK.
European Free Trade Association (EFTA)	1959	Austria, Finland, Iceland, Norway, Sweden, Switzerland.
Latin American Integration Association	1986	Argentina, Bolivia, Brazil, Chile, Colombia, Ecuador, Mexico, Paraguay, Peru, Uruguay, Venezuela.

Organisation Commune Africaine et Mauricienne (OCAM)	1965	Benin, Central African Republic, Ivory Coast, Mauritius, Niger, Rwanda, Senegal, Togo, Upper Volta.
North American Free Trade Agreement (NAFTA)	1994	Canada, Mexico, USA.
Asia Pacific Economic Cooperation (APEC)	Under negotiation	Australia, Brunei, Canada, China, Hong Kong, Indonesia, Japan, Malaysia, Mexico, New Zealand, Papua New Guinea, Philippines, Singapore, South Korea, Taiwan, Thailand, USA.

It should be clear that the regional groupings shown in Table 1 vary considerably in terms of the extent of cooperation. Thus, a contrast can be made between the fairly loose structures of, for example, EFTA and the Andean Group and the movement in Europe towards full economic integration (see below); and between regional groupings which already exist and those currently under negotiation (e.g. Asia Pacific Economic Cooperation).

MAJOR REGIONAL TRADING BLOCS

Table 1 lists the major regional trading blocs around the world. By far the most important of these are the European Union, the North American Free Trade Agreement (NAFTA) and the Asia Pacific Economic Cooperation (APEC).

European Union

The evolution towards European economic, political and monetary union has been a slow and often torturous one (see Table 2). The vision of a 'United States of Europe' was first put forward by Winston Churchill in 1946 in order to encourage political cooperation between European governments to reduce the threat of another war and economic cooperation to challenge the growing dominance of the US in the world economy. The first real progress, however, was made in 1951 when six countries established the European Coal and Steel Community (ECSC). As well as establishing a common market in coal and steel, the cooperation developed through ECSC led to the six countries establishing the Treaty of Rome in 1957, which established the European Economic Community.

The principal objective of the Treaty of Rome was the elimination of trade barriers which divided Europe and the establishment of a common market through:

887

Table 2   Towards European Union?

1946	A 'United States of Europe'.
1951	European Coal and Steel Community (ECSC) – Belgium, France, West Germany, Italy, Luxembourg, Netherlands.
1957–8	Six ECSC members sign Treaty of Rome establishing the European Economic Community.
1958–69	Period of transition.
1973	Enlargement of EEC to include Britain, Ireland and Denmark.
1979	Establishment of European Monetary System (EMS).
1981	Greece joins EEC.
1985	Publication of White Paper on Single European Market.
1986	Single European Act.
	Spain and Portugal join EC.
1989	Fall of communism in Eastern Europe.
1991	Maastricht Treaty on European Union.
1992–3	Establishment of Single European Market.
	European economic area extending single market legislation to non-member countries.
Future	Towards full economic, political and monetary union?

- eliminating duties and quantitative restrictions on trade between member countries;
- establishing a common external customs tariff;
- abolition of all restrictions on the free movement of goods, services, people and capital within the Community.

These objectives were to be met within a period of twelve to fifteen years. By the late 1970s substantial progress had been made towards the establishment of a European Common Market. Almost all tariff and quota restrictions on internal trade had been abolished; the Community had been enlarged in 1973 to include Britain, Ireland and Denmark; and the European Monetary System (EMS) had been established in 1979 to provide greater exchange rate stability. By the early 1980s, however, major obstacles still remained to the establishment of a truly common market and there was growing disenchantment within Europe towards the EC, especially given the deteriorating economic performance of Europe compared to the USA and Japan. The increasing pressure for change resulted in the White Paper on the Single European Market in 1985 and the Single European Act of 1986. The Act contained approximately 300 proposals for change, aimed at the 'removal, by the end of 1992, of all internal barriers to the free movement of goods, services, capital and personnel within the countries of the EC'. While the aims of the 1992 proposals were broadly similar to those of the Treaty of Rome, the contents were far more radical and had major implications for the future of Europe (see Table 3). To date, substantial progress has been made in achieving the objectives of the Single European Act although much still needs to be done.

Table 3 Single European Market proposals: major elements of the 1992 programme

In standards, testing, certification
Harmonization of standards for:
  Toys
  Automobiles, trucks, and motorcycles
    and their emissions
  Telecommunications
  Construction products
  Machine safety
  Measuring instruments
  Medical
  Gas appliances
  Cosmetics
  Quick frozen foods
  Flavourings
  Food preservatives
  Instant formula
  Fruit juices
  Food inspection
  Definition of spirited beverages and
    aromatized wines
  Tower cranes (noise)
  Tyre pressure gauges
  Detergents
  Fertilizers
  Lawn mowers (noise)
  Medicinal products and medical
    specialities
  Radio interferences

**New rules for harmonizing packing,
labelling, and processing
requirements**
  Ingredients and labels for food and
    beverages
  Nutritional labelling
  Classification, packaging, labelling of
    dangerous preparations

**Harmonization of regulations for the
health industry (including
marketing)**
  Medical specialities
  Pharmaceuticals
  Veterinary medicinal products
  High technology medicines
  Implantable electromedical devices
  Single-use devices (disposable)
  In-vitro diagnostics

**Harmonization of regulation of
services**
  Banking
  Mutual funds
  Broadcasting
  Tourism
  Road passenger transport
  Railways
  Information services
  Life and non-life insurance
  Securities
  Maritime transport
  Air transport
  Electronic payment cards

Liberalization of capital movements
  Long-term capital, stocks
  Short-term capital

Consumer protection regulations
  Misleading definitions of products
  Indication of prices

**Harmonization of laws regulating
company behaviour**
  Mergers and acquisitions
  Trademarks
  Copyrights
  Crossborder mergers
  Accounting operations across borders
  Bankruptcy
  Protection of computer programs
  Transaction taxes
  Company law

Harmonization of taxation
  Value-added taxes
  Excise taxes on alcohol, tobacco, and
    other

**Harmonization of veterinary and
phytosanitary controls**
Harmonization of an extensive list of
  rules covering items such as:
  Antibiotic residues
  Animals and meat
  Plant health
  Fish and fish products
  Live poultry, poultry meat and
    hatching eggs
  Pesticide residues in fruit and
    vegetables

Table 3 continued

Changes in government procurement regulations	Elimination and simplification of national transit documents and procedures for intra-EC trade
Coordination of procedures on the award of public works and supply contracts	Introduction of the Single Administrative Document (SAD)
Extension of EC law to telecommunications, utilities, transport	Abolition of customs presentation charges
Services	Elimination of customs formalities and the introduction of common border posts
	Harmonization of rules pertaining to the free movement of labour and the professions within the EC
	Mutual recognition of higher educational diplomas
	Comparability of vocational training qualifications
	Training of engineers and doctors
	Activities in the field of pharmacy
	Elimination of burdensome requirements related to residence permits

Source: *Business America*, 1 August 1988: 2

North American Free Trade Agreement (NAFTA)

The North American Free Trade Agreement, ratified by the US Congress in January 1994 after a long and controversial debate, aims at establishing a free trade zone by eliminating a broad array of tariff and other trade barriers between the USA, Canada and Mexico.

To a significant extent NAFTA was a reaction to the formation of the European Single Market. This was the case for two main reasons. First, the fear amongst US and Canadian firms that they would be 'shut out' of European markets due to the imposition of external tariffs. Second, concern that the large size of the European market would provide European firms with economies of scale and allow them to compete more effectively with North American firms in global markets. In addition to providing a much larger 'domestic' market, NAFTA will present opportunities for US companies to lower production costs by transferring production to Mexico for re-export back to the USA. This has created major fears in the USA regarding the possible adverse employment effects of NAFTA. Finally, it is highly likely that once NAFTA has been operationalized, it will be extended to cover other South American and Caribbean countries. It should be noted, however, that NAFTA is a less comprehensive agreement than the Single European Act. The former is confined mainly to trade. The latter covers economic, political and monetary integration as well as free trade between member countries.

Although NAFTA is still in its infancy, the early indications are that it will have a major impact on North American trade. In the first ten months after NAFTA was introduced, US exports to Mexico increased by 18 per cent and there was a similar increase in Mexican and Canadian exports to the USA. The Free Trade Agreement is also having a major impact on foreign direct investment flows and the production strategies of multinational enterprises. American and Canadian companies invested $2.4 bn in Mexico in the first nine months of 1994. Much of this was in duty-free assembly plants along the Mexican-US border (the Maquiladoras Industry) for re-export back to the US market. Some multinationals such as the Ford Motor Co. are moving towards integrated North American production strategies. Prior to NAFTA, Ford had to produce locally for the Mexican market. Following the free trade accord, the company's exports to Mexico from the USA increased from 1,200 vehicles in 1993 to 30,000 in 1994. Ford's exports of Mexican-made vehicles to the USA have also increased by 30 per cent.

Pacific Asia

In the past, the region of the world now commonly known as Pacific Asia has been described by a variety of terms including East of Suez, the Far East, East Asia, South-East Asia and so on. The increasing use of the term Pacific Asia is not simply a matter of semantics. Rather, it is a belated recognition of the rapid economic growth of the region and the fact that its global orientation is changing radically. Until World War II the region was dominated by colonial interests, mainly European. By the 1950s European influence had declined and the USA had emerged as the dominant power in the region. Since the 1970s, however, and especially over the last decade, Japan has emerged as the leading economic power. In other words, the region now looks east and has become much more conscious of its geographical position in relation to the Pacific rather than to Europe. Terms such as the Near or Far East are thus anachronisms since they describe geographical location with respect to European colonial powers (see Drakakis-Smith 1992).

Most commentators would agree that we are now entering the Pacific Asia century in terms of economic growth, market size and exports. Reflecting this, and the growing confidence in the region generally, various negotiations have taken place concerning the establishment of Asian regional trading blocs. The most developed bloc to date is the Association of South-East Asian Nations (ASEAN), established in 1967. More recently, discussions have been taking place concerning much wider cooperation in the region generally under the auspices of Asia Pacific Economic Cooperation (APEC).

APEC was founded in 1989 at the suggestion of Australia. Its aim is to increase multilateral cooperation among the countries of the Pacific Rim, given the rapid economic growth of the region and the growing interdependence of countries. Negotiations have included the USA, keen to become involved in order to head off any move to create an Asian trading bloc that excluded the USA. Membership of APEC is listed in Table 1 and the group has established ten working parties covering cooperation in investment and trade; trade promotion; investment in industrial science and technology; human resource development; energy cooperation; marine resource conservation; telecommunications; transport; tourism; and fisheries. The most recent summit of APEC member states was held in Indonesia in November 1994. Leaders of the 17 member countries agreed a target of the year 2010 for free and open trade amongst the industrialized member states and the year 2020 for free trade amongst developing country members. Although many difficult issues remain to be negotiated, APEC could emerge as the dominant regional trading bloc of the twenty-first century and this could have major implications for the global economy.

Implications for the world economy

The growing importance of regional trading blocs has generated a considerable amount of controversy concerning the impact of such agreements on international trade and the world economy. Both negative (trade diversion) and positive (trade creation) views have been expressed.

Opponents of regionalism argue that trading blocs are inward looking and lead to trade diversion rather than trade creation effects. Rather than being a step towards greater multilateral (global) free trade, regional trading blocs represent a retrogressive step. This arises for two main reasons. First, interest groups that benefit from regional agreements will oppose any further movement towards a more open multilateral (global) trading system. Second, the concentration of scarce political capital and energy on promoting regionalism will divert attention away from globalism. The over-riding fear is that the world will divide into three large and competing trading blocs – the European Union, Asia and North America. The inevitable friction that will arise could have disastrous consequences for global trade.

Supporters of regionalism, on the other hand, argue that regional trading blocs are trade creating rather than trade diverting. Furthermore, proponents argue that negotiations for a more open global trading environment (e.g. GATT) are more likely to make progress when conducted among three large blocs and that regional agreements have gone much further than the tariff cutting exercises of multilateral (GATT) negotiations.

The formation of regional trading blocs also raises important issues concerning marketing strategy and management which are examined in the following section.

MARKETING IMPLICATIONS OF REGIONALIZATION

The growing importance of regional trading blocs in international trade raises important implications concerning both marketing strategy and marketing management in international firms. The sections below summarize the emerging literature on the marketing implications of regionalization. Given that the process of economic integration has gone furthest in Europe, there is a heavy European slant to the literature.

Pan-regional marketing strategies

Several authors have examined the extent to which the process of European integration will allow the adoption of pan-European marketing strategies. Gogel and Larréché (1989), for example, have argued that competitiveness in the Single European Market will depend on two critical variables, namely, the strength of a company's products (market share) and its geographical market coverage within Europe (see Figure 1). Companies which stand to gain most from the process of market liberalization and integration are those with strong product portfolios and extended geographical market coverage across Europe (i.e. pan-European companies or 'kings', as in Figure 1). McGee and Segal-

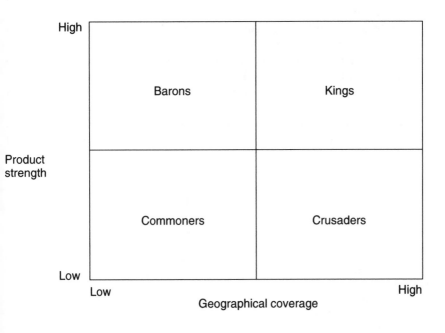

Figure 1 The international competitive posture matrix
Source: Gogel and Larréché (1989)

893

Horn (1992) develop a similar argument in relation to strategic groups in the European food processing industry, with competitive advantage being dependent on building the pan-European market coverage of key brands. One of the major ways in which companies have attempted to build pan-European scope is through crossborder mergers, acquisitions and strategic alliances (MAAs). The late 1980s and early 1990s have witnessed a wave of crossborder MAAs in Europe as companies attempt to strengthen product and market positions with the removal of internal trade barriers (Hamill 1993).

In a paper entitled 'Pan-European Marketing – Myth or Reality?', Halliburton and Hünerberg (1993b) examine whether firms should treat Europe as a single market with standardized marketing and which aspects of marketing lend themselves to a pan-European approach. The authors argue that pan-European marketing is more myth than reality, but that current trends point to greater integration. Companies, therefore, should reassess their European marketing strategies and adapt their marketing programmes and operations accordingly. The authors maintain that pan-European marketing is a myth for three reasons. First, many products are already global and mostly sold on a Europe-wide basis (e.g. Chivas Regal, Remy Martin, After Eights, Coca-Cola, McDonald's, etc.). Second, many so-called pan-European products are in reality regionalized within Europe as between, for example, the northern colder climates and the warmer Mediterranean countries. Third, many products will remain essentially national or local in scope.

Despite such constraints, Halliburton and Hünerberg (1993a) identify a number of factors contributing to closer integration – the impetus of the 1992 programme; developments towards monetary union and a single European currency; the incorporation of EFTA countries; closer cooperation between east and west Europe; the emergence of Euroconsumers; the race to form Eurocompanies. Given these trends, many companies are reassessing their European marketing programmes (see Table 4). The authors identify three generic strategic options for the Single Market namely market retreat, full

Table 4 Euromarketing reassessment

Reassess your European marketing approach	
From	*To*
Local targets	Pan-European targets
Geographic segments	Non-geographic segments
Product/country markets	Global or Europe-wide concepts
Local pricing	Crossborder pricing
Local sales/distribution	European 'key account' plus local channels
Local communications mix	Global core communication strategy
Local marketing	Transnational structures
Organizations and processes	

Source: Halliburton and Hünerberg (1993a)

894

Table 5 European strategic marketing options

Options	Strategies	Remarks
1. Market retreat	Sell out to pan-European player (example Nabisco).	May be preferable to a stuck in the middle position.
	Seek a different, less competitive market (example Nokia Data).	
2. Pan-European competition	Identify true pan-European market segments (example Perrier).	May be few true segments.
	Organic penetration from existing national markets (example Pilkington).	Excessive time required.
	Aggressive policy of acquisitions to complete European portfolio (example BSN).	Few winners.
	Cooperation with other national players to form pan-European organizations (example Carnaud-Metal Box) or alliances (example European Retailers Association).	Complex and risky but increasingly important in post-1992 Europe.
3. Niche position	Consolidate national position through realignment, merger or acquisition (example Mannesmann-VDO).	Vulnerable to standardized Euro-products if national differences are marginal.
	Identify new Euro-regions.	Information access.
	Identify segments across limited number of countries (example Campbells Biscuits).	Need to cumulate scale benefits.
	Seek economies at component level while retaining niche brands (example Electrolux).	Organizational complexity.
	Become an OEM supplier to pan-European companies.	Vulnerable to pan-European OEM suppliers.

Source: Halliburton and Hünerberg (1993a)

Europe-wide competition through growth, acquisition or alliances, and defending a niche position. These are summarized in Table 5.

Product policy

The issue of product standardization versus differentiation has been one of the most debated topics in global marketing. A large volume of literature exists on the extent to which multinationals can, should or do standardize products for global markets (Buzzell 1980; Keegan 1980; Cavusgil and Nevin 1981; Levitt 1983; Quelch and Hoff 1986; Martenson 1987; Rau and Preble 1987; Kreutzer 1988; Onkvisit and Shaw 1989; Rosen *et al.* 1989). Company examples supporting both standardization and adaptation have been quoted frequently (Gregson 1987; Herbert 1988; Espey 1989; Main 1989). In addition, there is an extensive literature on standardization of individual elements of the global marketing mix (Becker 1980; Killough 1980; Shulman 1980; Keown *et al.* 1989; Luqmani *et al.* 1989; Peebles 1989; Glaum 1990; Turnbull and Doherty-Wilson 1990).

Subsequent literature in this area has moved away from a narrow focus on product standardization versus differentiation towards a wider focus on global marketing segmentation and product positioning. The traditional approach to international marketing segmentation is to segment on a country basis in order to take account of national differences in consumer demand. However, papers by Kale and Sudharsham (1987), Day *et al.* (1988), and Perry (1988) develop an alternative approach that makes customers rather than countries the basis for global market segmentation and product positioning. The approach focuses on similarities rather than differences across groups of consumers in different countries and is compatible with the need for coordination and integration of marketing on a global basis.

The growing importance of regional trading blocs in international business has resulted in a parallel discussion concerning pan-regional products and pan-regional consumers, especially in Europe where the scope for pan-European brands has been discussed extensively.

A paper by Vandermerwe (1989) examined the impact of the Single Market on European consumers. The author dismisses the two extreme cases of a single, homogenized and integrated market, on the one hand, and completely fragmented, small specialized markets on the other. In her opinion, the most likely model is a market system consisting of regional Euro-clusters with customers geographically close but not necessarily living in the same country. They will have similar economic, demographic and lifestyle characteristics which cut across cultural and national boundaries and will exhibit similar needs and purchasing behaviour. Differences among customers will persist but will not be nationally determined. Three main clusters of Euro-consumer are identified:

896

Table 6 Euro-market groups: marketing strategy

Marketing strategy Eight Ps	Regional mass clusters	Regional niche clusters	Local niche markets
Positioning	Pan-European. Uniform corporate identity.	Pan-European. Uniformity with some differences when necessary.	Localized, adapted to suit market.
Product	Pan-European rationalized brands. Increased choice. Standard marketing names, logos, etc.	Pan-European rationalized brands. Differentiation and customization. Some adaptation.	Localized products and brands specific to area.
Pricing	Uniform Pan-Europe. Lower.	Uniform Pan-Europe, some differentiation. Lower.	Localized depending on circumstances.
Place	Uniform. Consolidated and rationalized systems.	Uniform, adapted. Some consolidation and rationalization.	To suit area. Locally based.
Promotion	Pan-European integrated sales and marketing. Some harmonization.	Pan-European. Some adaptation and integration. Some harmonization.	Local, done by locals for locals.
Public affairs	Pan-European integration with promotion. Some local activity.	Pan-European where possible. Regional activity.	Highly localized. Some Pan-European activity.
People	Pan-European cultures, people and organizations linked and integrated. Local contact.	Pan-Europe approach linkage. Regional structures and organization. Local contact.	Local people and structure.
Period	Shorter life cycles and diffusion. Simultaneous marketing Pan-Europe.	Shorter life cycles and diffusion. Simultaneous marketing in regions even Pan-European.	Local timing of strategies.

Source: Vandermerwe (1989)

897

- Groups of regional mass clusters – these are large and medium-sized groups made up of consumers with common needs; when aggregated, these groups make up the mass Euro-market in a given product or service category.
- Groups of regional niche clusters – these are large and medium-sized groups of consumers with similar but somewhat differentiated needs; when aggregated they make up the regional Euro-markets in a given product or service.
- Local and specialized clusters – these are small-sized groups with highly specialized, local needs.

The marketing strategy implications of the three main clusters of Euro-consumer are summarized in Table 6. Opportunities for a pan-European approach to product and marketing strategy are clearly greater for the regional mass cluster, but also for the regional niche cluster. For local niche markets products will continue to require local adaptation despite the move towards European integration.

An interesting paper by Paitra (1991) also addresses the 'myth or reality' of the Euro-consumer. Based on detailed sociocultural research, three 'poles of purchasing mentality' in Europe are identified:

- The Moderns – individuals whose purchasing behaviour is very flexible, open to change and cosmopolitan. They represent the 'ideal' transnational or Euro-consumer.
- The Go Betweens – individuals whose purchasing behaviour is changing rapidly, but who have not yet reached the pan-European 'ideal'.
- The Traditionals – individuals who, despite the process of European integration, cling to local or national traditions.

Promotion

As for product policy considered above, there is an extensive literature on the extent to which promotion can be coordinated on a global basis (see Mooij and Keegan 1991). The formation of regional trading blocs creates opportunities for coordinating promotion on a pan-regional, if not global basis. The principal advantages of regional coordination of promotion include (ibid. 1991):

- cost savings through economies of scale in promotion;
- promotion of a uniform brand and corporate image;
- simplified promotional planning through uniform objectives and simplified coordination and control;
- maximum use of good ideas, transmission of know-how and continuous exchange of ideas;
- better use of management abilities and resources;
- universal guidelines and quality standards;
- better access to the stored know-how and experience of other countries.

The extent to which promotion can be centrally coordinated and standardized on a pan-regional basis will be constrained by a number of factors, both external and internal to the firm. Despite regional economic cooperation, there will remain major differences between countries in terms of language and culture and these will constrain standardization. There may be equally important differences in the legal and regulatory environment and in the promotion infrastructure which will require a degree of decentralization and local adaptation. Furthermore, the company's competitive position may vary between countries, again requiring local adaptation. Finally, there may be opposition at subsidiary level to centrally determined promotional campaigns.

It should be noted that in the majority of companies, promotional decisions are not an either/or choice between complete centralization (standardization) or complete decentralization (local adaptation). The majority of companies will adopt a mixed approach where some decisions are centralized and others decentralized. Common practice is for the head office (or the regional HQs in pan-regional strategies) to be responsible for developing the core promotional objectives and core campaigns and providing advice to local affiliates. Decisions regarding detailed implementation of core campaigns in foreign markets are often left to subsidiary managers to achieve local flexibility. However, certain local decisions (e.g. expenditure) may still require the ultimate approval of the parent or regional HQs.

Pricing

Pricing is probably the most difficult of the Four Ps to coordinate either globally or regionally, given the wide range of factors influencing local price levels (e.g. income levels, market demand and market structure, competition, government policy, taxes, exchange rate factors, transport and production cost variations).

A narrowing of price differences would be an expected outcome of regional economic integration. Even in a highly developed regional trading bloc such as the EU, however, major price differentials still exist between countries. For example, a study by Nestlé (see Maucher 1991) has shown that the average price differential for consumer products across Europe is approximately 20 per cent. Much higher differences exist for some products – 115 per cent for chocolate; 65 per cent for tomato ketchup; 155 per cent for beer; 30 per cent for natural yoghurt.

One of the major effects of the lack of standardized pricing in a common market is parallel importing. Opportunities for parallel importing exist when there are significant price differentials between countries. In such circumstances, distributors, individual entrepreneurs or individuals may buy products in low price countries and re-export to high price countries, undercutting the market price in the high price country but still making a profit from the price differential. In Europe, in recent years, parallel importing has become common in the automobile and alcoholic beverages industries. For example, prices in both sectors are significantly higher in the UK than in Continental Europe. This has led to individuals buying on the Continent and re-exporting to the UK. One estimate has suggested that the UK alcoholic beverage industry is losing £1 billion per annum as a consequence of such parallel imports.

Distribution

Reference has already been made to the link between the establishment of regional trading blocs and the adoption of pan-regional marketing strategies. One of the main areas in which the adoption of pan-regional strategies is becoming common is in production and distribution. Regional integration reduces the need for a country-by-country approach towards production and distribution and creates opportunities for seeking competitive advantage through regional coordination of sourcing and logistics. In Europe, for example, many multinational enterprises (MNEs) are currently reassessing their regional production and distribution strategies. The most likely consequence of this is an increase in plant closures brought about by the relocation, rationalization and consolidation of production into a smaller number of larger, more efficient plants supplying multi-country markets and supported by a coordinated European logistics system.

This trend was first identified by Doz in a paper published in 1978. Reduced intra-European trade barriers provided MNEs with the opportunity for plant specialization and integration. Rather than having local-for-local plants, each serving its own domestic market with a broad product range, it was becoming feasible and economically attractive to rationalize production into an integrated network of large-scale, specialized plants serving multi-country markets. While not a new phenomenon, the process of plant rationalization has accelerated in recent years with the deepening of the European integration process; and many examples can be quoted. The Dutch company Philips, for instance, is currently involved in a major restructuring of its European production and logistics network involving the concentration of activity into large-scale, efficient international production centres serving multi-country markets. This represents a radical departure from the traditional strategy of local production for local markets and will result in major job losses. In the food and drink industry, the closer convergence of consumer tastes as a result of 'Europeanization' is encouraging the major multinational producers such as BSN to restructure their manufacturing and logistics systems, aimed at reducing costs and improving efficiency. This will involve plant closures and the consolidation of previously fragmented operations into fewer, more cost-effective plants to achieve economies of scale in both production and distribution. The same process is evident in the FMCG industry. Procter and Gamble have recently announced a 12 per cent reduction in their global workforce and the closure of 30 of their 147 manufacturing plants, including several in Europe.

Three recent examples illustrate the importance and topicality of this issue.

In February 1993 Hoover announced the closure of its Dijon plant in France, with production being transferred to its Glasgow facility. A day later, Nestlé announced the transfer of production from Glasgow to Dijon. Shortly after this, Digital Equipment announced the closure of its manufacturing plant in Galway, Ireland, and the transfer of production to Scotland.

Underlying these shifts in plant location is the view that coordinated regional production and logistics networks are becoming the key to competitiveness in highly integrated regional markets. De Meirlier (1991), for example, argues that plant location (and relocation) and logistics choices are key strategic decisions which have long-term implications for MNE competitiveness in global and regional markets. Competitive advantage is becoming increasingly dependent on time-based factors, including distribution and proximity to markets. An efficient, coordinated and integrated regional sourcing and distribution strategy can be an important source of competitive advantage through costs (production and transportation); control; production flexibility; market responsiveness; place; time; and information.

MANAGEMENT IMPLICATIONS OF REGIONALIZATION

Previous sections have examined the marketing strategy and marketing management implications of the growing importance of regional trading blocs, mainly from a European perspective since the EU is the most highly developed regional grouping. The trend towards greater regional integration, however, also raises a number of wider issues for management in international firms. These are largely outside the scope of this chapter, but are worth mentioning briefly. Two issues, in particular, should be identified. First, regional economic, political and monetary cooperation will be supported by increased cross-national cooperation at the level of individual firms. In Europe, for example, the years since the late 1980s have witnessed a boom in crossborder joint ventures and strategic alliances as companies attempted to consolidate their market positions in the run-up to 1992. The evidence shows, however, that inter-firm collaborative ventures suffer from a very high failure rate, especially in crossborder collaboration where there is the added problem of different management and national cultures. The implication for management is that careful attention needs to be paid to the planning, negotiation and management of crossborder collaboration in order to reduce the likelihood of failure (see Hamill 1993).

Second, the growing importance of regional trading blocs raises important implications concerning the organization and control structures of international firms. Reflecting the growth of regional cooperation and integration, many MNEs are introducing geographically based organizational structures through the establishment of regional head offices whose purpose is to coordinate and integrate corporate strategy within a region.

901

CONCLUSIONS

The emergence of regional trading blocs is one of the most important developments in international business over the last decade or so and one which will have a major impact on the world economy towards the millennium. Whether the world develops towards a global market or a series of competing regional markets remains a major question to be answered.

REFERENCES

Becker, H. (1980) 'Pricing: an international marketing challenge', in H. Thorelli and H. Becker, *International Marketing Strategy*, New York: Pergamon Press.

Buzzell, R. D. (1980) 'Can you standardise multinational marketing?', in H. Thorelli and H. Becker, *International Marketing Strategy*, New York: Pergamon Press.

Cavusgil, T. S. and Nevin, J. R. (1981) 'State-of-the-art in international marketing: an assessment', in B. M. Enis and K. J. Roering (eds) *Review of Marketing 1981*, Chicago: American Marketing Association.

Cova, B. and Halliburton, C. (1993) 'Towards the new millennium – a new perspective for European marketing', in C. Halliburton and R. Hünerberg, *European Marketing: Readings and Cases*, Wokingham: Addison-Wesley.

Day, E., Fox, R. J. and Huszagh, S. M. (1988) 'Segmenting the global market for industrial goods: issues and implications', *International Marketing Review* 5 (3), Autumn.

De Meirlier, M. (1991) 'Strategies and trends for plant location: global management', Geneva: Management Centre Europe.

Doz, Y. L. (1978) 'Managing manufacturing rationalisation within multinational companies', *Columbia Journal of World Business* 13.3.

Drakakis-Smith, D. (1992) *Pacific Asia*, London: Routledge.

Espey, J. (1989) '"The Big Four": an examination of the international drinks industry', *European Journal of Marketing* 23 (9).

Glaum, M. (1990) 'Strategic management of exchange rate risks', *Long Range Planning* 23 (4).

Gogel, R. and Larréché, J. C. (1989) 'The battlefield for 1992 : product strength and geographical coverage', *European Management Journal* 7 (2).

Gregson, J. (1987) 'How Cadbury Schwepped into worldwide markets', *Financial Weekly*, March.

Halliburton, C. and Hünerberg, R. (1993a) *European Marketing: Readings and Cases*, Wokingham: Addison-Wesley.

Halliburton, C. and Hünerberg, R. (1993b) 'Pan-European marketing – myth or reality?', *Journal of International Marketing* 3, July: 77–92.

Halliburton, C., Hünerberg, R. and Töpfer, A. (1993) 'Strategic marketing options in the Single European Market', *European Management Journal*, 20th Anniversary Issue, June.

Hamill, J. (1993) 'Managing crossborder mergers and acquisitions in Europe', in M. J. Baker (ed.) *Perspectives on Marketing Management*, Chichester: John Wiley.

Herbert, I. C. (1988) 'How coke markets to the world', *Journal of Business Strategy*, September–October.

Kale, S. H. and Sudharsham, D. (1987) 'A strategic approach to international segmentation', *International Marketing Review*, Summer.

Keegan, W. J. (1980) 'Five strategies for multinational marketing', in H. Thorelli and H. Becker, *International Marketing Strategy*, New York: Pergamon Press.

Keown, C. F., Synodinus, N. E. and Jacobs, L. W. (1989) 'Advertising practices in Northern Europe', *European Journal of Marketing*, 23 (3).

Killough, J. (1980) 'Improved payoffs from transnational advertising', in H. Thorelli and H. Becker, *International Marketing Stretegy*, New York: Pergamon Press.

Kreutzer, R. T. (1988) 'Marketing-mix standardisation: an integrated approach in global marketing', *European Journal of Marketing* 22 (10).

Levitt, T. (1983) 'The globalization of markets', *Harvard Business Review*, May–June.

Luqmani, M., Yavas, U. and Quraeshi, Z. (1989) 'Advertising in Saudi Arabia: content and regulation', *International Marketing Review* 6 (1).

McGee, J. and Segal-Horn, S. (1992) 'Will there be a European food processing industry?', in S. Young and J. Hamill (eds) *Europe and the Multinationals: Issues and Responses for the 1990s*, Cheltenham: Edward Elgar.

Main, J. (1989) 'How to go global – and why', *Fortune*, 28 August 1989.

Martenson, R. (1987) 'Is standardisation of marketing feasible in culture-bound industries? A European case study', *International Marketing Review* 4 (3).

Maucher, H. O. (1987) 'Langfristige Konzeption um zukünftige Politik in einer internationaltätigen Unternehmung, der Ernährungsindustrie', in H. Afheldt (ed.) *Zukunftsfaktor Führung*, Stuttgart.

Maucher, H. O. (1991) 'The impact of the Single European Market on regional product and price differentiation – the example of the European food industry', in C. Halliburton and R. Hünerberg (eds) *European Marketing: Readings and Cases*, Wokingham: Addison-Wesley.

Mooij, M. K. (de) and Keegan, W. (1991) *Advertising Worldwide: Concepts, Theories and Practice of International, Multinational and Global Advertising*, New York: Prentice-Hall.

Ohmae, K. (1989) 'Managing in a borderless world', *Harvard Business Review* 3, May–June.

Onkvisit, S. and Shaw, J. J. (1989) 'The international dimension of branding: strategic considerations and decisions', *International Marketing Review* 6 (3).

Paitra, J. (1993) 'The Euro-consumer, myth or reality?', in C. Halliburton and R. Hünerberg, *European Marketing: Readings and Cases*, Wokingham: Addison-Wesley.

Peebles, D. M. (1989) 'Don't write off global advertising: a commentary', *International Marketing Review* 6 (1).

Perry, M. (1988) 'Conceptual overview and applications of international marketing positioning', *European Management Journal* 6 (4), Winter.

Quelch, J. A. and Hoff, R. J. (1986) 'Customizing global marketing', *Harvard Business Review*, May–June.

Rau, P. A. and Preble, J. F. (1987) 'Standardisation of marketing strategy by multinationals', *International Marketing Review*, Autumn.

Rosen, B. N., Boddewyn, J. J. and Louis, E. A. (1989) 'US brands abroad: an empirical study of global branding', *International Marketing Review* 6 (1).

Shulman, J. S. (1980) 'Transfer pricing in the multinational firm', in H. Thorelli and H. Becker, *International Marketing Stretegy*, New York: Pergamon Press.

Turnbull, P. W. and Doherty-Wilson, L. (1990) 'The internationalisation of the advertising industry', *European Journal of Marketing* 24 (1).

Vandermerwe, S. (1989) 'Strategies for pan-European marketing', *Long Range Planning* 22 (3).

FURTHER READING

Brown, R. (1993) *Managing in the Single European Market*, Oxford: Institute of Management Foundation, Butterworth-Heinemann.

Calori, R. and Lawrence, P. (eds) (1991) *The Business of Europe: Managing Change*, London: Sage.
Halliburton, C. and Hünerberg, R. (eds) (1993) *European Marketing: Readings and Cases*, Wokingham: Addison-Wesley.
Higgott, R., Leaver, R. and Ravenhill, J. (1993) *Pacific Economic Relations in the 1990s: Cooperation or Conflict?*, London: Allen and Unwin.
Thurow, L. (1992) *Head to Head: The Coming Economic Battle Among Japan, Europe and America*, London: Nicholas Brealey Publishing.

52

MARKETING ETHICS

N. Craig Smith

Marketing ethics can be defined as both the study of the moral evaluation of marketing and the standards applied in the judgement of marketing decisions, behaviours and institutions as morally right and wrong. It refers to a discipline and the subject matter of that discipline, the 'rules' governing the appropriateness of marketing conduct. It is a subset of business ethics, which in turn is a subset of ethics or moral philosophy. More simply, marketing ethics is about the moral problems of marketing managers. It includes, for example, the ethical considerations associated with product safety, truth in advertising, and fairness in pricing. It is an integral part of marketing decision-making.

Much of the discussion of marketing ethics by academics and practitioners is centred on ethical dilemmas: issues that arise when there is an obligation to one group of people in conflict with an obligation to another, suggesting a difficult choice between alternative courses of action. For instance, a company's relationship with its customers may conflict with its relationship with its channel intermediaries when it finds opportunities to supply its customers directly. Wholesalers that may have developed the business initially could be denied margins on future transactions, though customers may be better served. Fundamentally, these ethical issues are about the incorporation of values such as honesty, trust, respect and fairness into marketing decision-making. The end result should be more consistently good marketing decisions; good in the sense of promoting the welfare and having respect for those affected by marketing decisions.

Marketing ethics is a subject area in its own right, with frameworks specific to the evaluation of marketing. Much of the work in this area has involved describing the ethics of marketing practices and formulating criteria for their evaluation. Accordingly, this article traces the origins of marketing ethics and its fit within marketing knowledge, identifies the major ethical issues in marketing and provides some answers to the question asked increasingly by marketing managers: How do I know my marketing is ethical?

ETHICS AND MARKETING

Ethics is the branch of philosophy concerned with the study of the evaluation of human conduct, particularly the criteria that may be used in judgements of what is good and right for human beings. It is also called moral philosophy. Often the terms 'ethics' and 'morality' are used interchangeably. Ethics is used here to refer to a discipline of study and to standards. There are three categories of approaches within ethics:

1 The descriptive approach, a morally neutral attempt to describe the ethics dominant in a society.
2 Meta-ethics, the analysis of the meaning and nature of moral concepts and judgements.
3 Normative ethics, a prescriptive approach identifying moral principles and methods of moral reasoning that justify rules and judgements of what is right and wrong.

Ethics may be applied to the moral problems of specific human activities, such as a profession. Accordingly, medical ethics involves the application of general ethical principles to the practice of medicine. Business ethics is also an example of applied ethics. It involves the study of the moral evaluation of business decisions, behaviours and institutions. Business ethics is primarily concerned with normative ethics applied to business.

Although most business schools now offer courses in business ethics, the discipline is relatively new. The first business ethics texts appeared in the late 1970s. However, concern about the moral problems of business is as old as business itself: Adam Smith's *The Wealth of Nations* is a moral as well as economic treatise; Roman philosopher Cicero's *De Officiis* discusses the moral duties of merchants. Prior to business ethics courses, most discussion in business schools of the moral problems of business was in business and society courses. In vogue between the late 1960s and early 1980s, both in these courses and in business itself, was the concept of corporate social responsibility.

The analysis of social responsibility in business is largely concerned with identifying the obligations of business to society. Enlightened self-interest was the rationale to which its proponents appealed, including business leaders. Firms were encouraged to practise corporate social responsibility, even where it could not be clearly justified on the basis of cost and revenue projections, because it was believed to be in their best long-term interest. Corporate social responsibility has become subsumed within the broader topic of business ethics.

A comprehensive review of marketing ethics by Murphy and Laczniak (1981) identified the earliest marketing writings on the topic emerging in the 1960s. They note that in the 1970s there was a shift from broad observations on marketing ethics to a focus on specific issues. This continued in the 1980s with an increasingly more rigorous treatment of the topic. From the mid-1980s onwards, spurred by developments in business ethics, marketing writers began to make substantial use of moral philosophy to develop descriptive and normative theories of marketing ethics, while interest in researching specific issues continued (this informs the discussion of ethical issues in marketing, below). Murphy and Laczniak (1981) included over 100 contributions on the topic. A later, selective bibliography on marketing ethics has over 200 contributions (Smith and Quelch 1993).

A major impetus for the development of the business ethics discipline was an overwhelming concern in society about business practices, particularly during the so-called 'greed decade' of the 1980s. This concern was focused on misconduct in financial institutions, such as insider trading, and unethical marketing practices, such as bribery, deceptive sales practices, and environmentally harmful products and packaging. Interest in marketing ethics has grown concurrently with business ethics.

Is marketing unethical?

Recent criticism of the ethics of marketing reflects the increased societal concern about business practices and has focused on specific issues, industries and companies. However, there has been a long-standing suspicion of marketing. Many people associate marketing activities, especially selling and advertising, with hucksterism (a term that dates back to the sixteenth century). There is the persistent belief that marketing is unethical, *per se*.

Farmer (1967) asked: 'Would you want your daughter to marry a marketing man?' Proclaiming marketing as unethical, he suggested 'too many of us have been "taken" by the tout or con-man' or 'prodded into buying all sorts of "things" we really did not need, and which we found later on we did not even want'. Ten years later he asked: 'Would you want your son to marry a marketing lady?' He remained sceptical of marketing ethics, noting that marketing essentially deals with greed, selfishness and base human desires. This position was largely unchanged in his third and posthumous 1987 critique though he did identify the beneficial consequences of marketing activities in developed countries that brought peace and prosperity to developing economies through international trade. Critics of marketing suggest it uses dubious means to sell products that people do not need. While this criticism is not entirely unwarranted, it should not amount to the view that marketing ethics is an oxymoron.

The basic response to most critics of marketing is *caveat emptor* [let the buyer beware]. Where this is insufficient there are legal safeguards to protect the vulnerable, such as laws prohibiting the sale of cigarettes and alcohol to minors. *Caveat emptor* is a more satisfactory response when it is coupled with an understanding of how markets work and how competition gives rise to the imperative of customer satisfaction that is central to the marketing concept. Accordingly, it is argued, firms must provide products of quality at fair prices, with their benefits honestly (albeit persuasively) communicated, or be at a competitive disadvantage. Should a firm resort to deception or manipulation and

907

the consumer not obtain good value, it is unlikely to stay in business because (aside from any legal remedies) it needs repeat purchases and positive word-of-mouth recommendations. This, at least, is the ideology of marketing.

Critics that suggest marketing heightens materialism, wasting scarce resources and making consumption an end in itself, often ignore the role of the consumer in this process – that marketing is a response to consumer preferences. Also ignored are the intangible benefits products may provide, especially the psycho-social benefits that more typically are the result of marketing activities such as advertising and branding. Hence, the alternative view is that marketing serves society.

These arguments may be sufficient to counter the charge that marketing is unethical, *per se*. However, they require assumptions that do not always hold. First, not all markets are competitive and not all consumers are well informed. Second, the law has limits and shortcomings; for example, not everyone can afford litigation, even within a contingency fee system. Third, marketing practices (such as advertising) reflect society, yet they also contribute to socialization with possible adverse consequences. For example, the marketing of cosmetics may create an undue concern with appearance, leading to unhappiness, if not anorexia. Finally, competitive pressures notwithstanding, marketing managers exercise discretion that by mistake or otherwise may cause harm. Accordingly, specific marketing practices may be unethical.

For these reasons, there are many instances of unethical conduct in marketing. Indeed, marketing is viewed by many as the worst offender of the business functions. (For example, Americans in Gallup's honesty and ethics polls, between 1977 and 1993, consistently ranked advertising practitioners and car salesmen last, business executives generally were ranked midway in the list of 25 professions.) Hence, marketers need to evaluate carefully their decisions, to prevent instances of bad practice, to make amends and condemn them when they do occur, and to recognize a responsibility for the sort of society they are contributing towards.

Marketing ethics, the law and other related topics

Many instances of unethical conduct in marketing are illegal; many countries have laws prohibiting deceptive advertising, price fixing, or bribery, for example. Generally, what is illegal is also unethical. Breaking the law may be regarded as unethical; more important, the law acts to proscribe unethical conduct. So deceptive advertising is unethical as well as illegal because it conflicts with the principles or code of morals of the marketing profession; it is known to be 'wrong' and, for instance, contradicts the American Marketing Association (AMA) code of ethics. More basically, deceptive advertising is lying and so conflicts with the value of honesty.

However, not all unethical conduct in marketing is illegal. Marketing managers are frequently in a position to make legal decisions that are unethical.

There are issues not yet covered by the law or, because of their complexity or uncertainty about correct conduct, the law cannot or will not prescribe. So, for example, price gouging is usually not illegal, but is often viewed as unethical; television advertising to young children is legal in many countries, yet it, too, is often criticized as unethical. The 'grey areas', where conduct may be legal but unethical or where legality and ethics are uncertain, are often the more challenging for practitioners and academics.

As well as legal restrictions on marketing, there are other topics closely related to marketing ethics. Just as corporate social responsibility has become subsumed within business ethics, social responsibility in marketing is part of marketing ethics. Marketing ethics includes consideration of the responsibilities of marketing decision-makers to various groups in society affected by marketing practices (known as stakeholders). Sometimes, social responsibility in marketing is confused with social marketing. Both are concerned with a relationship between society and marketing. However, social responsibility in marketing is concerned with the effects of marketing activities on society, whereas social marketing uses marketing to change behaviours for society and (usually) the individual's benefit. For example, advertising offensive to a group in society, such as the elderly, is an issue of social responsibility in marketing. Examples of social marketing include programmes to promote smoking cessation or to discourage drinking and driving. As in all other areas of marketing activity, ethical issues also arise in social marketing. Particularly important is the extent to which social marketing programmes involve the informed consent of participants and avoid coercion. Also closely related to marketing ethics are the topics of green marketing and quality of life and marketing.

ETHICAL ISSUES IN MARKETING

One source of information on the ethical issues in marketing is survey research of business people. Baumhart (1961) reports findings of a survey of 1,500 US executives. More than half responded to a question asking them to identify the one practice they would most like to see eliminated in their industry. Most of the practices identified involve marketing. Ranked by frequency of citation, they were:

- gifts, gratuities, bribes, and 'call girls' (23 per cent);
- price discrimination, unfair pricing (18 per cent);
- dishonest advertising (14 per cent);
- miscellaneous unfair competitive practices (10 per cent);
- cheating customers, unfair credit practices, overselling (9 per cent);
- price collusion by competitors (8 per cent);
- dishonesty in making or keeping a contract (7 per cent);
- unfairness to employees, prejudice in hiring (6 per cent).

A follow-up study, fifteen years later, identified largely similar concerns.

Chonko and Hunt (1985) surveyed marketing practitioners, asking them to describe the job situation that poses the most difficult ethical problem. The issues identified, ranked by frequency of citation, were as follows:

1 Bribery (most frequently cited; includes gifts from outside vendors, 'money under the table', payment of questionable commissions).
2 Fairness (manipulation of others, corporate interests in conflict with family interests, inducing customers to use services not needed).
3 Honesty (misrepresenting services and capabilities, lying to customers to obtain orders).
4 Price (differential pricing, meeting competitive prices, charging higher prices than firms with similar products while claiming superiority).
5 Product (products that do not benefit consumers, product and brand copyright infringements, product safety, exaggerated performance claims).
6 Personnel (hiring, firing, employee evaluation).
7 Confidentiality (temptation to use or obtain classified secret or competitive information).
8 Advertising (misleading customers, crossing the line between puffery and misleading).
9 Manipulation of data (distortion, falsifying figures or misusing statistics or information).
10 Purchasing (reciprocity in supplier selection).

Some of the issues in the Chonko and Hunt (1985) survey are not unique to the marketing function, applying to all managers. They fall more appropriately within the broader domain of business ethics; marketing ethics is concerned primarily with the ethical problems of marketing managers in their marketing decision-making. The most frequently reported ethical conflict in the Chonko and Hunt survey involved attempting to balance the corporate interest against the interests of customers (28 per cent of cases). This is in keeping with marketing's role of managing the firm's relationships with its customers. These issues of concern, and others, are discussed below.

In marketing research

Marketing research ethics has received considerable attention. This can be attributed to the emphasis on professionalism within marketing research coupled with the self-interest concerns of the industry. Consumer goodwill is vital and unethical practices lessen the likelihood of consumer cooperation. Unethical practices that harm clients bring the entire industry into disrepect, reducing confidence in the potential contribution of marketing researchers to marketing decision-making. Hunt et al. (1984), in a survey of marketing researchers, found that research integrity was cited as the most difficult ethical problem by one third of respondents. The next most frequently reported issue was treating outside clients fairly, cited by 11 per cent of respondents.

Comprehensive codes governing marketing research have been developed by

ICC/ESOMAR, the UK Market Research Society, the Council of American Survey Research Organizations, and the Professional Marketing Research Society of Canada. The codes are structured according to the rights and obligations of the different stakeholders of marketing research. The primary stakeholders (and participants) in marketing research are the research subjects (typically consumer respondents), research users (clients' sponsors), and the researcher (and his/her organization). Other stakeholders in marketing research include society, the research profession, competitors, and respondents other than consumers, such as employees, suppliers or distributors.

There are five major ethical issues involving consumer respondents:

1   Use of deception (including non-disclosure of the study procedures, purposes or sponsor; involving participants in research without their knowledge).
2   Failure to preserve respondent anonymity.
3   Causing embarrassment, hindrance, or offence.
4   Exposing participants to mental stress.
5   Use of coercion.

These ethical issues, restricted by research codes, reflect concern about the violation of the respondent's rights to choose, to safety, to be informed, to respect, and to privacy. If these rights are violated, it is suggested that the respondent has a right to be heard and to redress. Some codes include 'sugging' (selling under the guise of research), though this is more accurately viewed as an unethical practice in selling. Tybout and Zaltman (1974) show that many questionable practices involving respondents are not only unethical, but likely to bias research findings too; for example, the degree of anonymity provided may affect subject responses.

The major ethical issues involving client sponsors are largely the result of the 'researcher's dilemma', a conflict between professional/scientific aspirations and business/commercial obligations. Accordingly, codes include provisions governing research integrity and the confidentiality of the study and client. For example, the researcher must make a clear distinction between study results and any recommendations. Other issues involving client sponsors include conflicts of interests, such as research projects for competing clients, and overbilling.

Client abuse of the researcher-client relationship arises when clients attempt to exploit the researcher's business/commercial obligations or subvert the professional/scientific aspirations of the researcher. Major ethical issues include: inappropriate use of research proposals ('holding out the carrot' by requesting proposals for an initial study unlikely to lead to a major study, to fulfil corporate purchasing policies, unauthorized requests); disclosure (to other researchers) or use (in-house) of a researcher's specialized techniques and models; pressure to conduct research in ways that would support *a priori* conclusions; portrayal of research findings in a biased or distorted fashion.

In target marketing

Market selection decisions inevitably involve including some consumers and excluding others. Target marketing thus raises a variety of ethical concerns. Inclusion issues result when targeted groups are offended or victimized. Exclusion issues result when there is harm or offence to groups of consumers not targeted. Inclusion issues include the following:

1 The privacy concerns of the target market; for example, telemarketing intrusions and when consumers are included in customer profile databases.
2 Stereotyping the target market; for example, sex/race/age stereotypes in advertising.
3 Harmful products targeted at narrow segments, creating victims of those consumers; for example, US public opinion forced R. J. Reynolds to drop the Uptown cigarette targeted at blacks.

Exclusion issues include:

1 Advertising spillover effects that may frustrate or offend consumers outside the target market; for example, expensive toys advertised on Saturday morning television, female sex-role stereotypes in beer advertising aimed at men.
2 Consumers denied products or services by 'redlining' (financial services and much direct marketing, for example) and restricted distribution whereby the poor pay more (grocery retailing in inner cities, for example).

In product policy

Product policy is where marketing provides the most tangible value to consumers. Ethical issues arise in product policy throughout the product life cycle, from development to elimination. Product safety, for example, is an active consideration in all stages of the new product development process. It remains a consideration even when the product has been dropped, because products remaining in use may develop safety problems requiring a product recall. The major ethical issues in product policy are:

- product safety;
- 'questionable' products, that are harmful, in bad taste, or not considered socially beneficial;
- 'me-too' products and product counterfeiting;
- environmental impacts of products and packaging;
- deceptive practices in packaging or product quality specifications;
- planned obsolescence;
- arbitrary product elimination;
- service product delivery.

There is a legal requirement in most countries to provide products of 'merchantable' quality – that is, worthy of sale and fit for their intended purpose. This requirement encompasses product safety. In addition to this 'implied warranty', an absence of 'ordinary care' on the part of sellers (manufacturers, wholesalers and retailers) can give rise to charges of negligence under tort law, with the seller made liable for products proven defective that have caused injury. In some countries, the theory of 'strict liability' has been adopted, under which the seller is liable for injuries caused by a product without any requirement of the plaintiff to demonstrate an absence of ordinary care on the seller's part. Strict liability has resulted in substantial court awards, with consumers well compensated for injuries from products, sometimes augmented by 'punitive damages' if manufacturers clearly violated product safety standards, such as insufficient product safety testing. Product safety has improved as a consequence, but the costs of doing business have also increased; many firms purchase product liability insurance. In addition to the prospect of civil penalties, sellers must comply with safety regulations established by government agencies; for example, in many countries automobile manufacturers are required to fit seat belts in their vehicles.

There remain ethical considerations in product safety beyond those established by the law. Marketers have to ask: How safe should a product be? It is not possible to create a risk-free environment, with products incapable of causing harm, largely because product safety is a function of the consumer as well as the product's design and manufacture. Under the law, a consumer's role in causing injury from products is recognized as 'contributory negligence'. For example, many consumers injured in automobile accidents were not wearing seat belts or were driving under the influence of alcohol. However, the marketer can protect the consumer in three important areas: positioning, packaging and labelling, and product recalls. Care can be exercised in selecting target markets and developing advertising messages to reach those markets. For example, positioning a sports car to appeal to younger drivers is problematic if the advertising emphasizes the speed of the vehicle and dangerous manoeuvres when younger drivers are more prone to risk taking. Product packaging and labelling can be an important source of information on the safe use of a product. Finally, companies can plan for product recalls in anticipation of defects arising in normal use and through consumer misuse or abuse. Advance planning ensures the quickest withdrawal of the product and the maximum return of defective products that could cause harm.

Firms are often criticized for marketing 'questionable' products. Automobiles and alcohol are examples of products that may cause harm through misuse or abuse. Some products cause harm when used as intended; for example, cigarettes and handguns. The consumer's right to choose comes in conflict with the right to safety when harmful products are involved, particularly if harm is caused to others. There are many examples of products of doubtful social benefit, causing harm or in bad taste or that in other ways are controversial. There has been criticism, for example, of the abortion pill RU486, pornographic computer software, violent toys, and, because of sacrilegious content, the novel

The Satanic Verses and the film *The Last Temptation of Christ*. When markets exist for 'questionable' products, marketers have to decide if they wish to respond to that demand.

'Me-too' products also may be considered questionable. Pharmaceutical companies, for example, have been criticized for wasting resources developing me-toos instead of new drugs. Also, copying a competitor's product may be unfair and in some cases is an infringement of the competitor's product or brand. Legal remedies often exist, particularly when there is a breach of copyright and in the extreme form of product counterfeiting.

Environmental concern has pressured manufacturers to avoid non-functional packaging and provide ways to recycle necessary packaging and, in some cases, the product as well. Germany has taken the lead in this area. The environmental impact of products and packaging is joining product safety as an essential consideration in new product development. As well as the environmental concern, packaging may also raise ethical issues if it deceives customers about the quantity of product provided. Partially filled containers may be used to protect the product (such as potato crisps) or result from settling (cereals). However, sometimes slack packaging is used to allow the manufacturer to reduce quantity and avoid an increase in price; manufacturers also change quality specifications for the same reason. In either case, the practice may be unethical if a significant number of consumers are deceived.

Reasonable expectations of consumers may also be at odds with practice when firms use postponed, designed or style obsolescence or if they eliminate products prematurely. In industrial markets especially, firms often fail to notify customers of product elimination decisions and respond to their concerns, or ensure an adequate replacement parts policy. Finally, there are ethical issues in the delivery of service products. Rote-like service is one concern. Another concern is the requirement of respect for the customer and, conversely, ensuring service employees are treated with respect by customers.

In pricing

Pricing is the most regulated area of marketing. There are legal as well as ethical prohibitions governing horizontal and vertical price fixing, price discrimination, predatory pricing, deceptive pricing and markup pricing (some US state laws set the minimum amount that any product must be marked up). In some cases, unethical practices may be possible without being illegal. For example, competitors may find ways to signal prices that result in informal price fixing. In competitive bids for government contracts, for example, competitors may not collude on price but may be selective in submitting bids, effectively sharing the business among competitors to raise the average contract price. In business-to-business marketing, legal but unethical price discrimination may be encountered by smaller accounts.

Other major ethical issues in pricing relate to fairness and the use of misleading practices. Fairness in pricing requires just, honest and impartial treatment of both parties to an exchange in the determination and communication of the price governing that exchange. In practice, uncertainty about the fairness of a price often leads marketers to adopt the conventional economic model and to judge the fair price to be the market price, the price consumers choose to pay. This assumption of *caveat emptor* and price comparisons by consumers may be unwarranted. Search activities by consumers may be limited, because of 'consumer satisficing' and a requirement for 'simplification'; inadequate information makes price comparisons difficult; and consumers may trust vendors. However, Kahneman *et al.* (1986) have shown that even profit maximizing firms have an incentive to act in a manner that is perceived as fair if the individuals with whom they deal are willing to resist unfair transactions and punish unfair firms at some cost to themselves. Their studies indicate that consumers will take fairness into account.

A price may be unfair because it is too low and viewed as 'dumping' by other competitors. From the consumer's perspective, a price more typically is considered unfair when it is too high. Prices may be perceived as too high when price is used as a signal of quality, when firms practise price discrimination (not illegal at the retail level), when an oligopolistic market emphasizes non-price competition, when there is informal price fixing, and when supply constraints give rise to price gouging. Consumer ability to pay may also be a consideration; for example, with life-saving drugs. If the consumer does not receive the value expected, an expectation based perhaps on prior experience, then the price may also be judged as too high; for example, the non-price price increases involving changes in size ('downsizing') or quality, discussed above. Society and some consumers may judge prices as too low when they do not include social costs; for example, when a product causes environmental harm.

Misleading pricing issues include: non-unit pricing and an absence of item marking in retail stores; and price advertising that, through disclaimers or otherwise, fails to provide information on the full price the consumer will pay. Recently, many retailers have adopted 'high-low' pricing, setting prices at an initially high level for a limited period of time and then discounting the merchandise for the bulk of the selling season. A response to an intensely competitive retail environment, this use of fictitiously high reference ('regular' or 'original') prices can deceive consumers. The practice persists despite its doubtful legality and consumers have become uncertain about when a 'sale' is really a sale.

In distribution

Ethical issues in distribution largely involve conflicts between channel intermediaries, typically reflecting a power imbalance in channel relationships. Marketing scholars have studied the concept of channel power. Until recently, however, ethical issues arising from the exercise of that power have escaped notice. The size and market power of large retailers, wholesalers or manufacturers, give rise to an ethical obligation because they are so powerful. For example, the ethical standards of UK retailer Marks and Spencer have been widely praised but not always by its suppliers, particularly if they have been subject to its tough price or delivery demands.

The increasing power of the retailer has resulted in demands of suppliers that not all can meet; 'slotting allowances', for instance, have escalated in the grocery trade. For many years, grocery product manufacturers provided the trade with an introductory deal at the time of a new product launch, typically, temporary, off-invoice case allowances or free product. The fees demanded by some retailers have become so high as to exclude some smaller suppliers, often to the consumer's detriment as well as the supplier's. Similarly, the growth of franchising has brought with it complaints by franchisees about abuses of power by franchisors; franchise agreements do not always provide legal remedies. The problem is particularly acute in mature franchise systems where the logic for using franchising (i.e. a capital requirement or need for rapid expansion) no longer exists.

A separate issue involving channel intermediaries results when grey markets establish. A grey market involves unauthorized distribution of goods within or across markets. Within markets, the practice is called 'diverting'; across international markets it is known as 'parallel importing'. Although often of short-term benefit to consumers (providing lower prices and greater product availability), the practice can harm channel intermediaries because it may involve free-riding on the authorized intermediaries, and can damage brand and channel equity, reduce consumer protection, and reduce cooperation in channel relationships. The long-term benefit to consumers can become questionable.

Distribution issues more clearly of harm to consumers include: discrimination in distribution, such as redlining of financial services; direct marketing and privacy concerns; and lower standards in export markets, such as the aggressive marketing of infant formula in LDCs. Finally, marketers have an obligation to make products available to consumers. Ethical issues arise when availability is restricted; for example, if a company would otherwise be in violation of international trade sanctions, or if the safety of retail stores is in doubt, as in the case of bomb threats against bookstores carrying *The Satanic Verses*.

In personal selling and salesforce management

The persuasive purpose of the sales task often creates conflicts for the salesperson. In addition to challenges created by the salesperson's advocacy role, the 'boundary-spanning' position and autonomous operation of the salesperson and organizational pressures to 'make the numbers', also increase the likelihood of ethical conflicts involving the salesforce. These conflicts arise within three interfaces: the salesperson/customer, the salesperson/company, and the salesperson/competitor.

Major ethical issues in the salesperson/customer interface are:

- the use of gifts and entertainment;
- questionable/psychological sales techniques;
- overselling;
- misrepresentation;
- account discrimination/favouritism;
- conflicts of interest.

Gifts and entertainment can be construed as bribery. Although commercial bribery is generally illegal, the potential gains from this unethical practice are often so great that it can be found in many markets. It is harmful to competitors and to the organization employing the recipient of the bribe. Less obviously, it harms the economic system. In some countries, bribery is so endemic as part of a wider pattern of corruption that the economic efficiency of the country is significantly impaired. Bribery scandals involving US corporations overseas led US lawmakers to pass the Foreign Corrupt Practices Act (1977), forbidding the bribery of foreign government officials. While there is general agreement that a cash payment made to a buyer to influence a purchase decision constitutes a bribe, there is less certainty about gift giving and entertainment. Standards vary across industries and from country to country. Key considerations are timing (before or after the purchase decision), the recipients (whether spouses/friends are included), and the value of the gift or entertainment (relative to industry norms).

Some sales techniques, particularly in 'closing' a sale, are said to manipulate or trick buyers so that they agree to a purchase they might otherwise not have made. A common technique used in sales calls to a person's home is to ask on arrival for a glass of water. This minimal demand of the customer creates an obligation to at least hear the salesperson out while the glass remains full. Closing techniques often have a similar theoretical basis in social psychology. Psychological techniques and high-pressure sales tactics have resulted in laws that create a 'cooling off' period governing many industries: during a specified period the order may be cancelled.

In business-to-business as well as consumer marketing, salespeople may engage in overselling, particularly if the salesperson is substantially remunerated on commission. Overselling includes overstocking, overestimating the customer's problem, overspecifying the product requirement, and overpromising likely product performance. Overselling may amount to misrepresentation, if the salesperson exceeds the bounds of permissible puffery. Misrepresentation is generally grounds for legal action as a deceptive selling practice, fraud, or as a breach of warranty. A salesperson may also say too little rather than too much, contrary to a disclosure obligation to the customer.

Account discrimination/favouritism can take many forms, not all of which are legally restricted (price discrimination is). Reciprocity considerations, whether the company is a sole supplier to the customer, and personalities may influence the terms of a sale, resulting in preferential treatment for some customers. Conflicts of interest can occur when salespeople are on varying commission levels for different products or other incentives encourage them to push a product that may not be the best choice for the customer. While all these issues arise in the salesperson/customer interface, they are not solely at the discretion of the individual salesperson; he or she is an agent of company policies and practices too.

Major marketing ethics issues in the salesperson/company interface are:

- equity in evaluation and compensation;
- use of company assets;
- falsifying expense accounts and sales reports;
- salesperson compliance with company policy.

The allocation of sales territories, the determination of sales quotas, and methods of salesforce evaluation can significantly affect a salesperson's remuneration and other forms of compensation (such as winning a sales contest) and promotion prospects. Evenhandedness is expected of the firm in its treatment of the salesforce. Equally, the salesperson has an obligation not to misuse company assets (such as personal use of an automobile), 'pad' expense reports, falsify sales reports, or breach company policy such as 'stealing' business from other company salespeople or exposing the company to legal risk.

Major ethical issues in the salesperson/competitor interface are:

- competitive disparagement;
- tampering with a competitor's product;
- spying;
- exclusionary behaviour;
- discussing prices.

These practices, except in the most minimal form, are illegal under laws prohibiting misrepresentation and unfair competition and antitrust legislation.

In advertising and sales promotion

The visibility of advertising, coupled with its role as persuasive communication, result in it being the area of marketing most criticized. The major ethical issues in advertising and sales promotion are misleading or deceptive advertising and sales promotions and the social harm attributed to advertising. (The terms deceptive and misleading have been used synonymously in relation to advertising; they can be differentiated by ascribing intent to deception, viewing misleading advertising as unintentionally deceptive.) Other ethical issues include: fairness in agency-client relations; the independence of the media; pirating direct marketing lists; bait-and-switch in advertising and sales promotion; fraud in sales promotion.

Truth in advertising has been an ethical issue since the earliest use of

918

advertising. In most countries advertisers are subject to stringent self-regulation by industry bodies and government regulation. Advertisers must be able to substantiate claims about product performance, for example. In the USA the FTC (Federal Trade Commission) can determine that advertising is deceptive, intentionally or otherwise and without requiring evidence that consumers have been deceived. It can issue consent or cease and desist orders or require advertising substantiation, affirmative disclosure, or corrective advertising. Most major advertising agencies have compliance departments that work with legal counsel to review every advertisement produced. An advertisement is deceptive if there is a representation, omission or practice that is likely to mislead consumers, acting reasonably under the circumstances, in a material way. Identifying deceptive advertising is difficult. For example, all individual claims in an advertisement may be factually correct; however, it is deceptive if together they imply and convey a false claim. Advertisers are well advised to be honest in developing advertising campaigns and to test that consumers are not misled.

Deceptive advertising often occurs when it involves mock-ups and demonstrations, endorsements and testimonials, comparative advertising, price claims, and advertising to children. Time and content limits have been imposed on children's television advertising because it may exploit their vulnerabilities. Direct marketing and consumer promotions may also be found to be deceptive.

The persuasive intent of advertising gives rise to puffery. Levitt (1970) has suggested that 'embellishment and distortion are among advertising's legitimate and socially desirable purposes ... illegitimacy in advertising consists only of falsification with larcenous intent'. The distinction is between permissible puffery and deception. Beyond the ethical and legal restrictions on deceptive and misleading advertising, there are many criticisms of the social harm of advertising (Pollay 1986).

The forms of social harm attributed to advertising include sustaining sex/race/age stereotypes, creating false needs among consumers leading to unnecessary or harmful demand, and increasing materialism. Packard (and many others) suggested that advertising is a 'hidden persuader', manipulating or controlling behaviour. As a contributor to socialization processes, advertising is criticized because of the values and behaviours it promotes. It has been described as 'pollution' and as an offence to public decency, particularly in its appeal to base motives and use of vulgarity. In response, it is suggested that advertising is misunderstood by its critics and provides freedom of choice.

A 1987 survey of advertising agency executives asked respondents to describe the most difficult ethical problem confronting them in their work. Ranked by frequency of citation, the five most important problems were:

1 treating clients fairly (28 per cent);
2 creating honest, non-misleading, socially desirable advertisements (24 per cent);
3 representing clients whose products/services are unhealthy, unneeded,

useless, or unethical (12 per cent);
4 treating suppliers, vendors, and media fairly (9 per cent);
5 treating employees and management of agency fairly (5 per cent).

Advertising has been criticized because of its influence on the independence of the advertising and editorial sides of the media – particularly when media include 'advertorials', when the content reflects the needs of advertisers rather than its audience, and when a high proportion of advertising is needed to support media.

The three most unethical practices in direct marketing, identified in a 1989 survey of direct marketing professionals, were:

1 Misrepresentation of products, misleading advertising.
2 Pirating, theft, or unauthorized multiple use of lists.
3 No intention of fulfilling orders.

More recently, privacy has become one of the industry's biggest problems, with consumers objecting to telemarketing intrusions and breaches of confidentiality.

In sales promotion, as well as issues of deception, there are plentiful examples of fraud. Manufacturers are subject to coupon fraud in consumer promotions, most often involving retailers or their employees. Consumers are frequently subject to unfair operations of sweepstakes, contests and games, with prizes rigged or not awarded, or little of the proceeds going to the designated fund in ostensibly charitable contests. Finally, advertising and sales promotion may involve bait-and-switch. This is a tactic, generally illegal, whereby advertising or a promotion invite consumer interest in a product but due to its restricted availability or for other reasons, the seller switches the attention of the consumer to other, generally more expensive products.

NORMATIVE MARKETING ETHICS

Ethical issues arise at all stages of the marketing process, from strategy formulation to implementation. The major issues only are identified above. Also, the issues of current concern will change, though the underlying ethical principles remain constant. For example, the privacy problems arising in sharply focused target marketing are a relatively recent development reflecting the use of sophisticated database technology. Moreover, the desired end result of more consistently good marketing decisions requires more than not being unethical. It requires a concern with being ethical, where the choice is not so much between good and bad, but between different forms of good. Hence, the more fundamental problem, of which the above issues are symptomatic, is the incorporation of values into marketing decision-making. If managers were to reconcile better the ethical considerations of marketing decisions, these issues would be far less likely to arise. This section is about ethical marketing decision-making, including frameworks managers might find helpful.

Conflicting pressures for marketing managers

The increased concern about business ethics and changes in society's expectations of business have increased the pressure on marketing managers for ethical conduct. Consumers, the media, interest groups, regulators and lawyers are less tolerant of unethical marketing practices. The increased competitiveness of markets has facilitated a shift from *caveat emptor* toward *caveat venditor*. If ignored, firms risk adverse publicity and consumer boycotts that can damage hard-won reputations and hurt sales (Smith 1990), as well as litigation and government regulation.

This is not to suggest that marketing managers would otherwise choose the less ethical alternatives. A study of Machiavellianism found that marketing has its share of Machiavellians, but no more than other functions. Most marketing managers attempt to follow their conscience and do the right thing. However, this can be especially difficult given the different interests served by marketing managers, a result of marketing's boundary spanning function, agency role, and capacity for exercising economic power. Arguably, the potential and motivation

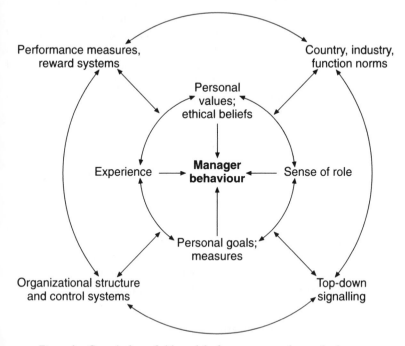

Figure 1   Corey's force field model of pressures on the marketing manager
Source: Corey (1993: 43)

for behaving unethically may 'go with the territory'. The tension between the external pressures on marketing managers' behaviour and the inner forces affecting their choices is illustrated in Corey's force field model shown in Figure 1. The challenge of resolving the conflicting pressures of the marketing function makes ethical reasoning of particular relevance to marketing decision-making.

Ethical reasoning

For thousands of years philosophers have reflected on how to determine the ethics of human conduct. Business academics have developed synopses of important theories in moral philosophy; the most useful contribution being to note the distinction between deontology and teleology. Deontological theories employ rule-based analysis: actions are inherently right or wrong, independent of their consequences, because of the kinds of actions they are or because they conform to a formal principle. Judeo–Christian morality, for example, provides a body of moral rules in the Ten Commandments. Teleological theories, in contrast, hold that an action is right because of the goodness of its consequences; hence this approach is often described as consequentialist. Under utilitarianism, for example, an action is judged as right if it produces the greatest good for the greatest number of people.

Hunt and Vitell propose a 'general theory of marketing ethics' that explains the decision-making process for problem situations having ethical content. The model describes how an individual might arrive at deontological and teleological evaluations that lead to ethical judgements, intentions, and behaviour. They do not attempt to prescribe how deontological and teleological approaches should influence marketing decision-making. Rather, their purpose is to provide a positive theory that shows how these two approaches are used. Their model is in the realm of descriptive ethics. Other models that describe how managers make ethical marketing decisions include theories of individual and organizational moral development, reasoned action, and contingency-based decision-making.

In a revised version of their model of the reasoning process, Hunt and Vitell (1993) incorporated more background factors and 'action control' (the extent to which an individual actually exerts control in the enactment of an intention in a particular situation). Reflecting recent research, the revised model includes personal characteristics such as 'religiosity', individual values and beliefs, strength of moral character, cognitive moral development, and ethical sensitivity. It also includes the norms, codes and code enforcement of the organization and factors in the broader industry, professional and cultural environment (see Figure 2).

Marketing ethics guidelines and frameworks

Normative marketing ethics provides guidelines and frameworks that managers can use in making marketing decisions. It addresses the prescriptive concern:

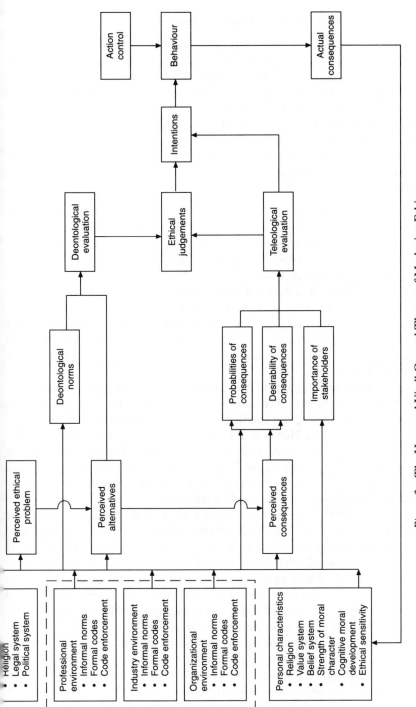

Figure 2 The Hunt and Vitell General Theory of Marketing Ethics
Source: Hunt and Vitell (1993: 776)

'How do I know my marketing is ethical?' Managers use the following maxims:

- The Golden Rule: Do unto others as you would have them do unto you.
- The Media Test: Would I be embarrassed in front of colleagues/family/ friends, if my decision was publicized in the media?
- The Invoice Test: Are payments being requested that could not be fully disclosed within company accounts?
- Good Ethics is Good Business: The belief that good ethics is in the long-term best interests of the firm.
- The Professional Ethic: Would the action be viewed as proper by an objective panel of professional colleagues?
- When in Doubt, Don't.

Some business writers have provided decision rules that incorporate major theories of moral philosophy. Laczniak (1983) discusses the theories of Ross, Garrett and Rawls, presenting a synthesis of factors to be considered. If every question he lists can be answered negatively, then the action is probably ethical. For example: Does action A violate the law? Does action A violate any general moral obligation (such as duties of fidelity, gratitude, or justice)? Are any major evils likely to result from or because of action A?

Nash (1989) offers twelve questions that draw on moral philosophy but avoid the abstraction of Laczniak's list and normally associated with formal moral reasoning (see Table 1). They illuminate decision-making, but do not suggest the 'right' decision.

Nash's questions highlight the importance of identifying stakeholders. Stakeholder analysis has been widely adopted within business ethics. It is valuable in determining the parties affected by a decision and creating a framework for analysis. However, it does not resolve dilemmas where interests of different stakeholders conflict. One solution to this problem is to incorporate normative theories of moral philosophy. The framework by Robin and Reidenbach (1986) combines utilitarianism and deontology with a systems view of marketing exchanges that identifies stakeholders.

Fritzsche (1991) has offered a model of ethical decision-making that incorporates theories of moral philosophy within a decision-tree approach. Decisions are subject first to utilitarian analysis, assessing benefits to society. If that screen is passed, the effect on individuals is assessed, requiring an examination of the deontological concerns of rights and justice (see Figure 3). In an update of Laczniak's framework, Laczniak and Murphy (1993) also propose a series of tests: the legal, duties, special obligations, motives, consequences, utilitarian, rights, and justice tests.

Smith (1993) offers a marketing-specific framework that managers can use to evaluate marketing decisions. It comprises the ethics continuum and the consumer sovereignty test. Its domain is limited to corporate impacts on customers, a limitation that conforms with the view that ethical issues in marketing largely involve company-customer relationships and conflicts. The

Table 1 Nash's twelve questions for examining the ethics of a business decision

1 Have you defined the problem accurately?
2 How would you define the problem if you stood on the other side of the fence?
3 How did this situation occur in the first place?
4 To whom and to what do you give your loyalty as a person and as a member of the corporation?
5 What is your intention in making this decision?
6 How does this intention compare with the probable results?
7 Whom could your decision or action injure?
8 Can you discuss the problem with the affected parties before you make your decision?
9 Are you confident that your position will be as valid over a long period of time as it seems now?
10 Could you disclose without qualm your decision or action to your boss, your CEO, the board of directors, your family, society as a whole?
11 What is the symbolic potential of your action if understood? If misunderstood?
12 Under what conditions would you allow exceptions to your stand?

Source: Nash (1989: 246)

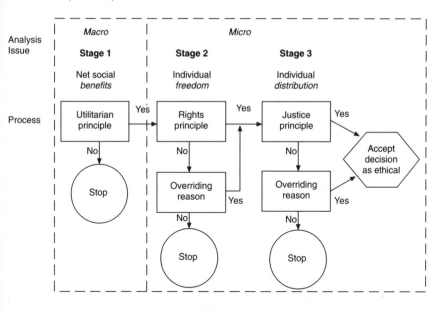

Figure 3 Fritzsche's ethical decision model
Source: Fritzsche (1991: 349)

framework does not, therefore, directly address marketing impacts on other stakeholders.

The ethics continuum suggests there are different positions – founded on different values and views of the firm's obligations to its customers – from which marketing decisions may be evaluated. This is not to suggest they carry equal

925

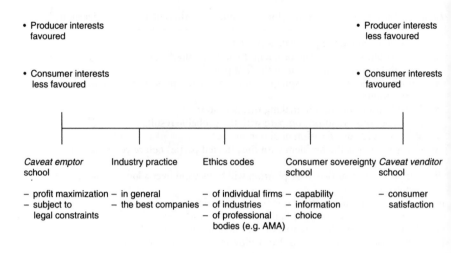

Figure 4   Smith's marketing ethics framework: an ethics continuum
Source: Smith (1993: 21)

Table 2   Marketing ethics framework: consumer sovereignty test

Dimension	*Establishing adequacy*
1 Capability – of the consumer	• Vulnerability factors (age, education, income, etc.)
2 Information – availability and quality	• Sufficient to judge whether expectations on purchase will be fulfilled
3 Choice – opportunity to switch	• Level of competition • 'Switching costs'

Source: Smith (1993: 30)

weight. Rather, the continuum presents benchmarks against which business conduct may be calibrated and understood. The continuum ranges from a position on the far left where producer interests are most favoured and consumer interests least favoured, to a position on the far right, where producer interests are least favoured and consumer interests most favoured (see Figure 4). It suggests a conflict between producer and consumer interests as the basis for different positions on the ethics of marketing practice. The continuum may be used to review marketing practices over time. Smith suggests marketing ethics are moving toward the consumer sovereignty position, which he recommends to the marketing manager wishing to pursue ethical marketing.

The consumer sovereignty test is grounded in marketing thought and practice, making it relatively straightforward for marketing managers. The test requires managers to fulfil the promise of marketing ideology, promoting as a first priority the interests of the consumer. It creates an obligation to ensure consumer capability, information and choice, even where there is an absence of market pressure. The manager would establish, for example, whether a target market was fully capable of understanding the risks associated with a product, going beyond legal requirements and perhaps to the firm's economic disadvantage by excluding some potential consumers. Table 2 summarizes the test, including a basis for determining the adequacy of performance along each dimension. In making these assessments, the manager must still exercise judgement, based on his or her values and interpretation of the facts. In particular, how much sovereignty is enough? The answer to this question is likely to change as society's expectations of business change. However, when conscience signals something is not right about a marketing decision, the manager has this and other models with which to explore its ethical dimensions and some indication of the right decision.

Ethics in the organization

An individual's good intent may be influenced or frustrated by the organization. Ferrell *et al.* (1989), in keeping with research that predicts unethical behaviour, suggest that decisions about what type of behaviour is appropriate in any given situation are influenced by the opportunity for the individual to engage in ethical/unethical behaviour. Opportunity is a function of organizational culture, professional codes, corporate policy and rewards and punishments.

Laczniak and Murphy (1993) suggest implementing marketing ethics entails policies that promote ethical decisions and a corporate culture conducive to ethical behaviour. This requires the identification of stakeholders, top management leadership, codes of ethics, ethics seminars and other programmes, and ethics audits. Because research on codes of conduct suggests limited effectiveness, Laczniak and Murphy recommend that codes be regularly communicated, specific, pertinent to the industry, enforced, and periodically revised. Research does confirm the importance of top management leadership. Accordingly, Corey (1993) suggests that to create an environment conducive to ethical behaviour, managers at all levels must send signals that clearly underscore the importance of moral conduct. In keeping with his force field model, he recommends that performance measures take account of ethical conduct and job security be clearly established.

POTENTIAL FUTURE DEVELOPMENTS

Heightened concern about ethics in public life has proven more than a fad in the US and other countries. The pressure on marketing managers for ethical conduct seems set to grow rather than dissipate. Due to cultural differences, interest in marketing ethics is likely to continue to be more explicit in the US. Responses also differ; Americans emphasize codification, be it in corporate codes or criminal and civil law, while Europeans, for example, rely on more informal guidelines and sanctions. Ethical concerns may mean that calls for greater professionalism within marketing will at last be heeded.

New issues will emerge. The continued development of information technology is likely to raise new issues for marketers involving intellectual property rights. Environmental concern will give greater impetus to green marketing. As the world becomes a global marketplace, marketers increasingly will have to deal with different values in the different countries they serve; for example, non-traditional portrayals of women in advertising now used in Western countries, may be less welcome elsewhere. Increasing world trade is likely to increase measures to combat unfair competition, especially bribery; the CIA has expressed an interest in this problem. Finally, as the former Eastern Bloc transitions to a market economy, where there is an absence of sanctity of contract it will probably discover that values, such as trust, are necessary to foster exchange, as well as the enactment and enforcement of commercial law.

Concern about marketing ethics is likely to sustain the growth in research and teaching of the topic. Researchers continue to refine descriptive and normative models of marketing ethics. With pressures on business schools to be more responsive to business, there may be greater efforts to make the theory of marketing ethics relevant to business. In the early 1990s, textbook writers started including materials on marketing ethics in introductory texts and in specialized texts on marketing research, retailing and sales management. This helps the integration of ethics into the marketing curriculum, supported by the efforts of Bol *et al.* (1991) and others. Interest may be sufficient to maintain the development of separate courses on marketing ethics, a new phase in the teaching of business ethics that aims to ground students in the ethical issues of their chosen career field while continuing to build their overall expertise in that area. With a deeper understanding of ethical issues in marketing and ethical reasoning, students should be better equipped to deal with the ethical dilemmas they will undoubtedly face in their marketing careers.

REFERENCES

Baumhart, Raymond C. (1961) 'How ethical are businessmen?', *Harvard Business Review*, July–August: 6–19, 156–76.

Bol, Jan W., Crespy, Charles T., Stearns, James M. and Walton, John R. (1991) *The Integration of Ethics into the Marketing Curriculum: An Educator's Guide*, Needham Heights, MA: Ginn Press.

Chonko, Lawrence B. and Hunt, Shelby D. (1985) 'Ethics and marketing management: an empirical investigation', *Journal of Business Research* 13: 339–59.

Corey, E. Raymond (1993) 'Marketing managers: caught in the middle', in N. Craig Smith and John A. Quelch, *Ethics in Marketing*, Homewood, IL: Richard D. Irwin.

Farmer, Richard N. (1967), 'Would you want your daughter to marry a marketing man?', *Journal of Marketing* 31, January: 1–3.

Ferrell, O. C., Gresham, Larry G. and Fraedrich, John (1989) 'A synthesis of ethical decision models for marketing', *Journal of Macromarketing* 9, Fall: 55–64.

Fritzsche, David J. (1991) 'Ethical issues in multinational marketing', in Jan W. Bol, Charles T. Crespy, James M. Stearns and John R. Walton (eds) *Readings in Marketing Ethics*, Needham Heights, MA: Ginn Press.

Hunt, Shelby D., Chonko, Lawrence B. and Wilcox, James B. (1984) 'Ethical problems of marketing researchers', *Journal of Marketing Research* 21, August: 309–24.

Hunt, Shelby D. and Vitell, Scott J. (1993) 'The general theory of marketing ethics: a retrospective and revision', in N. Craig Smith and John A. Quelch, *Ethics in Marketing*, Homewood, IL: Richard D. Irwin.

Kahneman, Daniel, Knetsch, Jack L. and Thaler, Richard H. (1986) 'Fairness and the assumptions of economics', *Journal of Business* 59 (4, pt. 2): 285–300.

Laczniak, Gene R. (1983) 'Framework for analyzing marketing ethics', *Journal of Macromarketing* 1, Spring: 7–18.

Laczniak, Gene R. and Murphy, Patrick E. (1993) *Ethical Marketing Decisions: The Higher Road*, Needham Heights, MA: Allyn and Bacon.

Levitt, Theodore (1970) 'The morality (?) of advertising', *Harvard Business Review*, July–August: 84–92.

Murphy, Patrick and Laczniak, Gene R. (1981) 'Marketing ethics: a review with implications for managers, educators and researchers', in Ben M. Enis and Kenneth J. Roering (eds) *Review of Marketing*, Chicago: American Marketing Association.

Nash, Laura (1989) 'Ethics without the sermon', in Kenneth R. Andrews (ed.) *Ethics in Practice: Managing the Moral Corporation*, Boston: Harvard Business School Press.

Pollay, Richard W. (1986) 'The distorted mirror: reflections on the unintended consequences of advertising', *Journal of Marketing* 50, April: 18–36.

Robin, Donald P. and Reidenbach, R. Eric (1986) 'A framework for analyzing issues in marketing', *Business and Professional Ethics Journal* 5 (2): 3–22.

Smith, N. Craig (1990) *Morality and the Market: Consumer Pressure for Corporate Accountability*, London and New York: Routledge.

Smith, N. Craig (1993) 'Ethics and the Marketing Manager', in N. Craig Smith and John A. Quelch, *Ethics in Marketing*, Homewood, IL: Richard D. Irwin.

Tybout, Alice M. and Zaltman, Gerald (1974) 'Ethics in marketing research: their practical relevance', *Journal of Marketing Research* 11, November: 357–68.

FURTHER READING

Bol, Jan W., Crespy, Charles T., Stearns, James M. and Walton, John R. (eds) (1991) *Readings in Marketing Ethics*, Needham Heights, MA: Ginn Press.

Laczniak, Gene R. and Murphy, Patrick E. (1985) *Marketing Ethics: Guidelines for Managers*, Lexington, MA: Lexington Books.

Smith, N. Craig and Quelch, John A. (1993) *Ethics in Marketing*, Homewood, IL: Richard D. Irwin.

Stark, Andrew (1993) 'What's the matter with business ethics?', *Harvard Business Review*, May–June: 38–48.

Tsalikis, John and Fritzsche, David J. (1989) 'Business ethics: a literature review with a focus on marketing ethics', *Journal of Business Ethics* 8, September: 695–743.

53

STRATEGIC MARKETING FOR NON-PROFIT ORGANIZATIONS

Philip Kotler and Alan R. Andreasen

INTRODUCTION

The form and layout of this chapter is determined by the necessary sequence of activities involved in the marketing planning process, combined with the specific strategic requirements of the non-profit sector. Thus, the chapter is divided into five principal sections:

1 Developing a customer orientation.
2 Strategic planning and organization.
3 Developing and organizing resources.
4 Designing the marketing mix.
5 Controlling marketing strategies.

Developing a customer orientation

Discussion commences with the issue of the cultivation of a corporate customer orientation as this is the essential starting-point and necessary mind-set for the development of an effective marketing strategy.

Strategic planning and organization

The principal need of the non-profit sector in the 1990s is not so much for techniques to implement marketing, but for assistance in strategic planning. Many non-profits face significant decline in traditional sources of revenue, dramatic changes in their customer mix, and bold new competition. Therefore, they need help in rethinking where they are going and what broad strategies they should be using to get there. Consequently, strategic marketing planning occupies a prominent and very important position in the overall marketing process.

Developing and organizing resources

If an organization's marketing programme is to make an impact both internally and externally, it must have sufficient financial and personnel resources to do so. Thus, the acquisition, development, and organization of such resources are essential forerunners to the marketing planning process.

Designing the marketing mix

All marketing activities must be realistically costed and form part of a planned and timed programme of events. Each individual element of the marketing mix must form part of a coordinated and complementary programme.

Controlling marketing strategies

Finally, evaluation and control is an essential part of a marketing programme as it provides ongoing feedback on the reactions of the targeted audience and responses to the marketing efforts of one's organization.

DEVELOPING A CUSTOMER ORIENTATION

Growth and development of the non-profit sector

Marketing is no longer considered a radical approach to solving the problems of public and non-profit organizations. It is well into its maturity as an effective management tool. Economic and social changes and a proven rate of success have led to rapidly broadened and deepened applications. In the 1990s increased privatization of public programmes, renewed interest in voluntarism, growing appreciation of the potential role of marketing in international social programmes, and decreased support from traditional sources have converged to expand dramatically the importance of non-profit marketing.

Although there is now growing interest in voluntarism, non-profits are faced with two realities. First, they cannot rely on traditional sources of support. Second, as they turn increasingly to the marketplace for this support, they find other non-profits there scratching for the same subsistence. The consequence is that in the 1990s the greatest challenges facing non-profit marketers are competitive. Non-profit marketers must therefore learn not only to find and attract new markets, they must also learn how to accommodate their efforts to a flood of competitors. This means that marketing strategy must be the dominant concern of marketing managers in the 1990s.

Thus, our focus is on approaches and techniques that can improve significantly the practice of marketing management in the non-profit sector on the part of existing and future managers. The emphasis is on the development of:

931

1 a proper philosophy of marketing;
2 a systematic approach to solving marketing problems;
3 an awareness and ability to use the very latest concepts and techniques from the private sector.

The starting point for a consideration of strategic marketing in non-profit organizations is a clear perception and understanding of the unique environment in which they operate. Non-profit organizations can be defined legally, but it is more crucial to understand the organization's environment and the specific marketing activities which constitute its mission. The major factors affecting the organization's environment are whether:

1 it is donative or commercial;
2 its performance is subject to public scrutiny;
3 marketing is perceived to be desirable;
4 the organization is largely volunteer;
5 marketing is judged by non-marketing standards.

The missions of non-profit organizations differ depending on the type of demand they seek to influence and the type of activity they are engaged in. The organization's type of activity can be defined in terms of the key concept of exchange. Target customers are asked to 'pay' economic costs; sacrifice old ideas, values, and views of the world; sacrifice old patterns of behaviour; or sacrifice time and energy. In return, they can expect products, services, social or psychological benefits, or some combination of these. Although non-profits seek to influence exchanges of money for goods and services in the same way as for-profit organizations, what makes them unique is their concentration on exchanges involving non-monetary costs on the one hand and social and psychological benefits on the other. Influencing such exchanges requires different perspectives and modified techniques.

Developing a marketing mind-set

The starting point for an effective marketing strategy is the proper marketing mind-set. Historically, marketing has passed through four stages:

• product orientation
• production orientation
• selling orientation
• customer orientation

The first three stages are characterized by management putting the organization's own needs and desires at the centre of the strategic process. It is only when management realizes that it is the customer who truly determines the long-run success of any strategy that the non-profit firm can join the ranks of the sophisticated customer-centred marketing strategists typically found in the private sector.

Several clues can be used to identify a non-profit which is still mired in an organization-centred perspective: they see their offering as inherently desirable; they see the ignorance or lack of motivation of their customers as the major barrier to the organization's success; research plays a minor role in strategy formulation; marketing tends to be defined as synonymous with promotion; marketing specialists tend to be chosen for their product knowledge or for their familiarity with communications techniques; a 'one best' strategy is typically used in approaching the market; generic competition is typically ignored in the process.

Indoctrinating a non-profit organization from top to bottom with the proper marketing philosophy is not an easy task. The experience of those who have successfully achieved this objective suggest such strategies as: recognizing the limited understanding of others about what marketing really is; allowing for other pressures on the organization that may temporarily mandate non-customer-oriented approaches; picking visible, short-term projects for the first marketing applications; and recognizing that the introduction of a new philosophy is as much a political exercise as a matter of logic and persuasion. Allies must be sought and enemies deflected. Above all, it is essential to secure top management's commitment to the new way of thinking. Without it a true marketing orientation will not be achieved and customer-centred thrusts in one area will inevitably run foul of organization-mindedness elsewhere.

STRATEGIC PLANNING AND ORGANIZATION

The strategic marketing planning process

Once management has developed the appropriate marketing mind-set, it must determine the basic direction which the organization will take over the strategic planning horizon. The means by which this is carried out is called the strategic marketing planning process and involves four steps. These are:

1 Identification of the organization's overall mission, objectives and specific goals and an understanding of its basic culture.
2 Analysis of strengths and weaknesses.
3 Analysis of the organization's external environment and identification and understanding of: its key publics; its competitors; the macro-environment.
4 Development of a specific mission, goals and objectives for the marketing department based on the information provided in the earlier steps.

Decisions about the basic mission then lead naturally to the formulation of objectives for the planning period. These can include maximizing surpluses, revenues, usage or budgets. Alternatively, the organization can set objectives in terms of usage targeting, full or partial cost recovery, or satisfaction of its own staff. These objectives must be turned into detailed goals. These goals should give direction to the organization's staff and describe pathways to its future. They should offer benchmarks for measuring progress and provide triggers for contingency plans. Goals should be motivating for staff and should provide a basis for assessing future performance. Finally, goals should communicate the organization's direction to the outside world and indicate needs for developing marketing tracking information systems.

Understanding consumer behaviour

The ultimate objective of all marketing strategy and tactics is to influence target audience behaviour. Sometimes this necessitates changing ideas and thoughts by communicating facts or changing attitudes. However, since the ultimate goal is behaviour change and the proper philosophy is customer-centred, it is essential that all strategic planning starts with customer behaviour.

The targets of the influence strategies of non-profit marketers can be extremely diverse. However, in all cases, the marketer's objective is to bring about exchanges wherein target audience members give up some costs in return for some expected positive consequences. Exchanges may involve two or multiple parties and be of fixed or continuing duration. The starting-point for understanding customer behaviour must be an understanding of the exchange relationship to be effected. Most importantly, that exchange must be seen from the target audience's perspective.

Exchanges in the non-profit sector are usually high involvement and often concern target audience behaviours where audience members have little or no experience. In such highly complex decision situations, customers begin by gathering information to form a choice set of alternative behaviours and to determine the criteria which will eventually be used to choose among them. The criteria, in turn, will be affected by the customer's own needs and wants and by the influences of significant others.

The next step in a typical process is for the customer to evaluate the chosen alternatives on the relevant criteria and to form attitudes and behavioural intentions towards each. These behavioural intentions will again be influenced by others. In a similar way, the eventual course of behaviour will be modified by situational factors such as the availability of funds or time. Finally, behaviour will result in experience and subsequent evaluations which will influence both attitudes and behavioural intentions in the future.

Marketers have several options in seeking to influence complex exchanges that are not turning out as a marketer wishes. The marketer can attempt to change the target customers' perceptions of the probable outcomes of choosing the marketer's alternative and/or the alternatives of competitors. Weightings on the criteria can be changed, although this is more difficult, or the customer can be pointed towards new or neglected favourable consequences.

With experience, customers proceed to simplify and then routinize behavoural patterns. In such cases, criteria are relatively fixed and alternatives are considerably narrowed. At the routine stage, behaviour may appear to occur with little conscious thought or even appear probabilistic. In cases of low-involvement decisions, relatively little cognition may be the norm, even when the customer has little experience.

Not all decisions of interest to non-profit marketers are individual. Where one is dealing with households or organizations, it is first necessary to understand the possible roles various members of the group can play. These roles include initiator, influencer, decider, transactor and exchanger. But even for such groups, a given decision may be much like that which occurs for individuals in that it may be complex, simplified or relatively routine.

Developing a core marketing strategy: segmenting the market

Once an organization has analysed its marketing environment and its internal strengths and weaknesses, it needs to develop a core marketing strategy. The core marketing strategy is the single most important element of the organiza-tion's strategic marketing planning process. It involves selecting key target segments, carefully positioning the organization, and then coordinating a set of marketing mix elements to implement the positioning to the target segments. The core marketing strategy must be customer-centred, visionary, differ-entiating, sustainable, easily communicated, motivating and flexible.

Four approaches to market segmentation are mass marketing, differentiated marketing, target marketing and niche marketing. Segmenting the market requires partitioning the market into subgroups which are mutually exclusive, exhaustive, measurable, accessible, substantial, and possessing differential responsiveness. Bases for segmentation are general or specific, objective or inferred. Many marketers think first of simple objective general measures such as age, income, geographic location, and marital status. Over the years more complex general objective measures such as social class and family life cycle and inferred general measures such as values and lifestyles have become more popular.

Specific bases for the segmentation apply to the specific product or service. They include objective measures such as user status, usage rate and loyalty. Inferred specific measures include beliefs, benefits and perceived sacrifices. Organization markets can be segmented by organization size, interest profile, buying process and degree of local autonomy.

Organizations can target their markets by undifferentiated, differentiated and concentrated marketing. Choices among these options depend on an organiza-tion's resources, its strengths and weaknesses, the relative homogeneity of the segments and competitive activity. The organization should focus on market segments that have intrinsic attractiveness and which it has a differential advantage in serving.

935

Developing a marketing strategy: positioning the organization

Organization positioning involves setting the organization apart from competitors to secure a lasting, defensible position in the marketplace. Positioning involves both establishing a unique set of products and services and making sure the target market perceives them (and the organization) as such. This calls for image measurement, two of the most common approaches to which are the semantic differential and direct attitude measurement.

Positioning has been said to be a largely creative exercise and might be achieved by a number of alternative strategies: building on present strengths; creating a niche; repositioning competitors. The positioning strategy chosen sets the parameters for the marketing mix and makes clear that it needs careful coordination.

In mature industries the organization must decide whether to pursue a market leader, market challenger, market follower or market nicher strategy. Market leaders have to decide further whether they will emphasize expanding the total market, protecting market share or expanding market share. Challengers must decide whom to challenge: the market leaders, other firms their own size, or firms smaller than themselves. Market followers must decide whether to follow closely, at a distance or selectively. The market nicher must decide on the basis of its niching strategy. The key idea in niching is specialization. The organization must have the required skills and resources to satisfy successfully the specialized requirements of the niche and must be able to defend its position from major competitors. In addition, the niche must be of sufficient size, offer growth potential and be of negligible interest to major competitors. For many multiple-niching is the most effective and safest strategy.

The positioning strategy makes clear what the principal elements of the organization's marketing mix must be to round out the core marketing strategy. Once the core marketing strategy is set, the strategic marketing planning process is completed by developing an organization structure and management systems to carry out the marketing strategy. Next, specific tactics are established for each element of the marketing mix, and benchmarks set by which progress towards marketing goals is assessed. The final steps then involve implementation of the plan and careful assessment of its overall effects in preparation for the next round of strategic marketing planning.

Acquiring and using marketing information

Most non-profit organizations carry out much less marketing research than they should. This is a consequence of their limited budgets, relative newness in the marketing field and limited expertise. Increasing the amount of marketing research, therefore, calls for both education and motivation, showing non-profit executives what market research can do and how to do it properly as well as encouraging them to do it more often. Non-profits have accepted certain myths:

they assume that marketing research should only be used for major decisions; that it involves big surveys and takes a long time; that it is always expensive; that it requires sophisticated researchers; and, when it is finished, that it is usually not read or used. But research using a diversity of techniques, many at low cost, can be extremely valuable to a wide range of decisions. Effective research requires that the non-profit organization have:

1 a marketing research mission;
2 a long-range strategy;
3 a budget;
4 an approach to carrying out individual projects;
5 an organization;
6 a system of evaluation and control.

Eventually, the sophisticated non-profit manager should plan to invest in a marketing information system. A marketing information system has four major sub-systems: an internal records system; a market intelligence system; a marketing research system; and an analytical marketing system.

Research can help managers by describing, explaining or predicting market characteristics. Most non-profit research is applied, and we would argue forcefully that no market research should be undertaken by a non-profit with a limited budget unless it leads directly into a decision. However, where one has a more generous budget basic or methodological research might be undertaken. The applied nature of the research provides a good framework for decisions about budgets and for designing specific research projects.

The kinds of studies that should be used most heavily by mature non-profits include: determination of market characteristics; short- and long-range forecasting; trend studies; competitive offerings studies; measurements of market potentials; market share analyses; sales analyses.

There are several approaches to budgeting research, including historical increment, percentage of revenues, competitive matching, and affordable budgeting. A cost/benefit approach is preferable, however, because it explicitly takes account of the uses to which the study's results are to be put. The actual amount to be spent would then depend on the likely quality that the expenditure could achieve.

An applied orientation also recommends a 'backward' research design process. Here the research manager first looks to the decisions to be made using the research results and then works backward to design a study that would best inform such decisions. An important step would be deciding what report format would provide the most managerially useful information. The report form would then suggest the type of analysis needed which, in turn, would specify how the data are to be collected and processed.

Research can be quantitative or non-quantitative, high cost or low cost. Qualitative research, such as in-depth interviewing or focus groups, can be useful in identifying a problem, gathering background for later quantitative studies, interpreting past studies, pretesting advertisements, product concepts, packaging and brochures, and generating ideas for new products, services and advertisements. Other techniques for keeping research costs low are experimentation, low-cost sampling designs, and use of secondary data and volunteer assistance.

Non-profit management of individual projects must involve careful attention in advance to potential biases, followed by careful evaluation of accomplishments or failures after the project has been completed. Such evaluation and control is especially essential as the organization develops a continuous programme of strategic research over several years.

Estimating and forecasting markets

Whether a non-profit should venture into a new market or whether it is getting a reasonable share of the existing market are questions that can be answered only after present and future market potential have been carefully determined. Therefore, in order to carry out their responsibilities for marketing planning, execution, and control, non-profit marketing managers need measures of current and future market size. We define a market as the set of actual and potential consumers of a market offer. The marketer's task is to distinguish various levels of the market that is being investigated, such as the potential market, available market, qualified available market, target market, and penetrated market.

The next step is to estimate the size of current demand. Total current demand can be estimated through the chain ratio method, which involves multiplying a base number by a succession of appropriate percentages to arrive at the defined market. Estimating actual industry sales requires identifying the relevant competitors and using some method of estimating the sales of each. Finally, the organization should compare its sales to industry sales to find whether its market share is improving or declining.

In the vast majority of markets, total market demand and specific organization demand are not stable from year to year, and good forecasting becomes a key factor in effective performance. This is particularly true for non-profits in which these problems are compounded by a lack of good historical data. In such cases, poor forecasting can lead to excess or insufficient personnel and supplies.

For estimating future demand, the organization can use one or any combination of six forecasting methods: buyer intentions surveys; intermediary estimates; expert estimates; market tests; time-series analysis; or statistical demand analysis. These methods vary in their appropriateness with the purpose of the forecast, the type of product, and the availability and reliability of data.

DEVELOPING AND ORGANIZING RESOURCES

Fund-raising

Fund-raising is one of the major problems of non-profit organizations and as such is an essential component of all non-profit strategies. Organizations that raise money typically pass through three stages of marketing orientation in their thinking about how to carry out effective fund-raising. Non-profit organizations have gradually been moving away from a product orientation to a sales orientation and then to a marketing orientation. A marketing orientation calls for carefully segmenting donor markets, measuring their giving potential, and assigning executive responsibility and resources to cultivate each market. Marketers assume that the act of giving is really an exchange process in which the giver also gets something that the organization can offer.

The first step in the fund-raising process is to study the characteristics of each of the four major donor markets: individuals, foundations, corporations, and government. Each donor market has its own giving motives and giving criteria, in addition to institutional and behavioural characteristics.

The second step is to organize the fund-raising operation in such a way as to cover the different donor markets, organization services, marketing tools and geographical areas.

The third step is to develop sound goals and strategies to guide the fund-raising effort. Goals are set on either an incremental basis, need basis, or opportunity basis. Strategies require selection of target markets, positioning and coordination of a full marketing mix.

The fourth step is to develop a mix of fund-raising tactics for the various donor groups. Fund-raising strategy sets the overall parameters for the fund-raising effort, which the development officer must fill with specific actions. Different tactics are effective in the four main segments considered by most fund-raising organizations: the mass anonymous small-gift market, the members-and-their-friends market, the affluent citizens market, and the wealthy donors market.

The fifth step is to conduct regular evaluations of fund-raising results in order to improve the effectiveness of strategies. A macro-evaluation consists of analysing the percentage of the goal reached, the composition of the gifts, comparison with competitors, and the expense/contributions ratio. Micro-evaluation consists of evaluating the performance of each individual fund-raiser.

Acquiring volunteer and corporate support

Non-profits have limited resources – they lack adequate time, workforce, skills and finance to achieve the mission they or society have established for them. As a consequence, they must become experts at securing these additional staffing, skills and financial resources. This, too, is a marketing task. Others must be convinced that the benefits of helping exceed the costs.

Non-profits are unique in needing volunteers to help them accomplish their basic goals. Strategies for recruiting and managing volunteers must take into account changes in the environment. Today's volunteers cover a wider spectrum of people. They are more demanding and have different motivations than they had in the past. More importantly, some groups are challenging the basic value of volunteer service. These trends are putting pressure on non-profit organizations to improve their abilities to recruit volunteers and to manage them more effectively once they are recruited.

Recruiting volunteers is simply another marketing task and should proceed in a planned strategic way. The most important element of this is undoubtedly understanding the target audience. Thus, recruiting volunteers requires getting to know the target audiences through segmentation, prospect, motivational, or image studies. The non-profit should also know how to retain volunteers. Studies of former volunteers and the satisfaction and dissatisfaction of present volunteers can be helpful in this regard. Problems that may emerge involve volunteers' expectations, training, supervision and feedback.

Managing volunteers can also be a problem if the organization is not truly professional in its approach. Many volunteers work hard and effectively with little incentive or guidance. Some hardly work at all under any circumstances. Most, however, respond best to being treated as professionals. This means matching responsibilities to skills, setting clear, achievable goals, and then holding volunteers to achieving them.

Non-profits must also secure important outside help in critical skill areas such as advertising and market research. Commercial agencies might be quite willing to help out for both altruistic and self-interested reasons. The Advertising Council is a prime example of such help. Business firms can also help by loaning space, staff, or equipment and by providing specific advice. Recently, affinity cards and cause-related marketing have been major sources of leverage from private sector firms. Faculty and students from local colleges and universities are another major source of assistance. An effective vehicle for coordinating all of these efforts is through a marketing advisory council.

Organizing for implementation

The role of marketing in a non-profit organization typically evolves through three stages. In the introductory stage there is resistance because organization members are opposed to marketing in principle or because they feel they are already doing it. If the organization wishes to proceed without a formal department, it can make use of outside resources. Should a formal marketing function be contemplated, a marketing committee should carefully consider what form it should take and how it should be introduced.

Marketing will clearly be a separate function during the growth phase. At this

940

point, a major issue is whether marketing should be established as a line or a staff function. There may also be a question of what kind of background is appropriate for marketing positions. While it may be expedient initially to use someone with an advertising or journalism background, most organizations eventually turn to individuals with formal marketing training.

Initial projects for the marketing group should have a high economic impact yet be relatively inexpensive to implement. They should be completed in a short period of time and have high visibility if successful.

Once the mature phase is reached, marketing is well established. The organizational question at this stage is what form is best. The major alternatives are a functional orientation, a product/service orientation, a customer orientation, or some mixture. While the specific form chosen should depend on the experience, market conditions, and mission of the organization, the customer-centred form most explicitly incorporates the philosophy emphasized by the authors. Even when the customer-centred form is not chosen, it is essential that the organization adopt such a perspective. This can be accomplished by careful hiring and training, explicit top management support, and a reward structure that reinforces customer-centred behaviour.

DESIGNING THE MARKETING MIX

Planning and budgeting the marketing mix

There are three tasks involved in developing and choosing cost-effective marketing mixes:

1 Choosing between alternative products or programmes: here cost/benefit analysis is helpful. The programmes with the highest benefit/cost ratio are preferred. To calculate benefits and costs, monetary and quantitative measures are preferred, although ultimately non-quantifiable benefits should be taken into account.

2 Deciding on the marketing expenditure level: organizations decide on their expenditure level using one of five methods – affordable, percentage-of-sales, competitive-based, objective-and-task, response optimization.

3 Developing an optimal marketing mix of product, price, place and promotion: the optimal marketing mix can be set if the response function for each separate marketing mix element is known. The appropriate marketing mix varies with the type of buyer (households or organizations), the communication task, the stage of the offer life cycle and the economic outlook.

Managing products and services

The mix of offerings in many ways defines an organization and establishes its position against competition. While, traditionally, offerings are categorized as products or services, a broader definition focuses on the fact that, from the customer's standpoint, an offer is simply a set of potential positive and negative consequences (benefits and costs). Consequences can be delivered by products or services or by the customer's own actions (e.g. dieting or exercising). Many non-profit organizations promote all three kinds of offerings. Three levels of the concept of the product offering can be distinguished:

1 The core product defines the needs that the product is really meeting.
2 The tangible product is the form in which the product exists. It is comprised of the product's features, styling, quality, packaging and brand names.
3 The augmented product consists of the tangible product and the additional services and benefits such as installation, after-sale service, delivery, credit and warranty.

As competition increases, organizations must carefully manage the length, width, and depth of their product offerings to compete.

Most non-profit organizations are primarily in the service business. Services can be delivered by people, places and objects or equipment. Services are especially difficult to manage because they are typically intangible, inseparable from the producer, variable in characteristics, perishable, and involve the customer in their production. Services marketers, therefore, must develop ways of making the intangible tangible, such as by using brand names and atmospherics.

Inseparability means that services are often synonymous with the people who deliver them. Service marketers must vigorously pursue internal marketing to ensure that key frontline people have a customer-first attitude and internal systems to empower frontline people to take the actions necessary to meet customer needs and wants.

Variability in service quality can be managed by good personnel selection and careful training along with as much routinization of the service itself as is possible without diminishing it. Perishability requires attention to service demand and supply which can be altered to some extent through creative pricing, marketing campaigns, adjustments of personnel and facilities, and sharing services with other organizations during peak periods. Finally, customer involvement in service delivery can enhance demand and satisfaction if marketers design services so that they are as easy as possible to use and 'train' customers themselves to be effective and appreciative coproducers.

Social marketing

Social marketing is one of the fastest growing sectors of non-profit marketing. Social marketing is the application of generic marketing to a specific class of problems where the object of the marketer is to change social behaviour primarily to benefit the target audience and the general society. Social marketing can seek to influence behaviour that is: low or high involvement; individual or group; one time or continuing. Continuing high involvement behaviour of groups or individuals is the most difficult to influence and often requires legal measures to achieve any major, long-term effect.

Good social marketers accord exchange a central role in their planning, are willing to change their offer (or consumer perceptions of it), seek to develop coordinated programmes, make extensive use of marketing research, segment their markets, have a 'bottom-line' orientation, are committed to planning and are willing to take reasoned risks. Social marketing differs from generic marketing in that it is subject to public scrutiny and extravagant expectations and often must seek to influence non-existent or negative demand of non-literate target audiences. It often deals with sensitive, hard-to-reach issues, invisible benefits or benefits to third parties that are difficult to portray and that are supposed to lead to long-term change. Social marketers, however, have less freedom to change their offerings, more limited budgets, and need to work with others who are often suspicious of marketing.

Social marketers make use of other disciplines, particularly social anthropology, education and mass communication, and behavioural analysis. Marketing is accorded the coordinating role. While social marketing can now document a significant number of successes, social marketers have recently turned their attention to the problems of sustaining the behaviour they have attempted to influence and of institutionalizing the process of social marketing itself.

Developing and launching new offerings

To be successful in today's non-profit environment, organizations must learn to launch and develop new offerings effectively and efficiently. These may involve new or existing offerings in combination with new or existing markets. Extensions into new offerings or markets may involve undertakings that are similar to or dissimilar to present marketing programmes.

To be successful in developing new offerings, the organization must be both creative and systematic. The first stage of the process is to generate ideas for new offerings. This can involve careful searching of available information or attempts to create new ideas through a variety of artificial idea generation techniques. Once the ideas have been produced, it becomes necessary to screen them to eliminate those that do not meet established organization goals.

The next stage involves elaborating the idea into a concrete concept that can be subjected to formal testing. The concept, if successful, must then generate a specific marketing strategy which, in turn, must survive a rigorous business analysis. The final stages of the development process then involve specific offer development and market testing, followed by a carefully orchestrated and timed commercialization process. Critical path techniques may be used to ensure that the project meets any crucial timing and cost objectives.

New offerings follow an S-shaped pattern over their life cycle. They move through introductory, growth, maturity and decline stages. In the introductory and growth stages, the manager must first be concerned with securing trials of the new offering. Five customer groups may be identified on the basis of when they are likely to try the new innovation.

1   *The innovators* – this group will try almost anything that is new and are often considered odd by the rest of the population. They can usually be ignored by the new offer manager.
2   *The early adopters* – they cannot be ignored because they are the opinion leaders who influence the next large group.
3   *The early majority* – they follow the opinion leaders and establish the offer's success.
4   *The late majority* – this group pays less attention to others in making their decisions to adopt and must be convinced that the new offering is not a fad.
5   *The laggards* – this last group, can typically also be ignored because they are very tradition-oriented and very slow to try anything new.

There is a clear set of stages through which individuals typically go in adopting some new pattern of behaviour.

Knowledge   Persuasion   Decision   Confirmation

Innovations that have significant relative advantages over old approaches, which are compatible with the culture, are not complex, which can be communicated easily, and tried out before full adoption will diffuse faster than other innovations.

Managing perceived costs

Non-profit marketers seek to influence exchanges. Costs are the prices that customers perceive they must pay in order to participate. In a great many of the exchanges sought by a non-profit marketer, managing the perceived costs is often much more important than managing the benefits. Furthermore, the nominal money price tag on the exchange may be the least important of the perceived costs about which the consumer is concerned; in social behaviour exchanges there usually is no price tag at all. Thus, costs can be monetary, non-monetary or mixed. Non-monetary costs include psychic pain, the need to change old habits or ideas, expenditures of time and energy and dislocations of social arrangements.

The non-profit manager has a dual task in managing these costs. Some costs must be kept reasonably high to assure continuing revenues to the organization. Other costs must be reduced as much as possible to lower barriers to customer action. The problem in managing costs rather than a cost (singular) is to figure out which of many costs to reduce and how much to reduce them. To make these decisions the marketing manager needs to know relative responses. That is, for a given amount of the marketer's expenditure, which cost or costs should be impacted to yield the largest net gain in the number of exchanges.

In developing a strategy for monetary prices, the organization must first establish objectives. It could seek:

*   surplus maximization;
*   cost recovery;
*   market size maximization;
*   social equity;
*   market disincentivization.

Its specific strategy to meet these objectives may be primarily cost-oriented, demand-oriented, or competition-oriented. Organizations that are planning to change an existing price should take into account the price elasticity of demand and perceptual factors in the target audience's response.

Managing the marketing channel

Exchanges require that offers be made at a particular time and in a particular place. Thus, the marketer's task is to create time and place utility for the customer. Often, this requires the services of other agencies, who can provide warehouse and transportation facilities and careful coordination of complex interacting systems. While channels may simply be means to facilitate consumers' time and place utilities, they have potential either significantly to augment or effectively to sabotage carefully designed marketing programmes.

To achieve an effective and efficient channel strategy, the non-profit marketer must decide what quality of service to offer and whether marketing will be direct or indirect. Then the marketer must determine the length and breadth of the channel, recruit channel members and assign functions. Finally, the marketer should put in place systems for effective coordination and control among the channel members.

Coordination and control are best achieved by judicious use of the power potentially available to the non-profit marketer. This power can be based on:

1   rewards;
2   coercion;
3   law;
4   social norms;
5   expertise;
6   prestige;
7   control of critical information.

In general, power strategies that rely on simple compliance on the part of intermediaries (for example, those based on coercion or the law), are less effective in the long run than strategies that encourage intermediaries to identify with and internalize the non-profit organization's goals.

Formulating communications strategies

Every contact a non-profit has with its various publics, whether directly or indirectly, is an occasion for influence. Influencing behaviour is largely a matter of communication. It is a matter of informing target audiences about the alternatives for action, the positive consequences of choosing a particular one, and the motivations for acting (and continuing to act) in a particular way. These contacts may be carried out by many different departments or people using diverse vehicles ranging all the way from standard paid and unpaid media to package designs, corporate publicity releases, personal sales presentations and even promotional 'gimmicks' like shopping bags and T-shirts. For programmes to be effective they must be grounded in a clear understanding of influence processes.

Influence typically involves persuasion. This requires the preparation and transmittal of specific messages. Messages must be encoded by the marketer (the sender), communicated through media, and then decoded by the receiver. At each of these stages, considerable noise can be introduced into the communications process such that the accumulated effect of the received message is very different from what was intended. In general, the more parties involved in the communications system and the less control the marketer has over them, the greater the chance for distortion. Marketers use formal and informal feedback to track these effects. Where communication is face to face, feedback can be easily obtained. Where it is not, as in media campaigns, pre- and post-tests of message strategies must always be carried out. Six steps are involved in developing effective messages:

1 Communications objectives must be determined.
2 Messages must be generated. These can be rational, emotional, moral, or they can be generated from a rewards/situations framework.
3 Thought must be given to how these communications can overcome consumers' tendencies selectively to expose themselves or attend to messages in which they are interested. The style, tone, wording, order, and format of the messages are critical to getting a message noticed.
4 Thought must be given to constructing the communications to overcome perceptual distortion, the tendency to add and reinterpret what is actually in the message based on the audience member's own experience, motives, and biases.
5 A medium must be chosen to convey the message to achieve maximum impact. Often, in the non-profit sector, this means choosing a spokesperson. If a spokesperson is used, the marketer must assure that he/she is trustworthy and that the message is so clear that it cannot be distorted by a target audience.
6 The marketer must evaluate all the possible messages and select the ones that are most desirable, exclusive, and believable.

The marketer must recognize that strategies to influence behaviour need not rely on persuasion – that is, in first changing cognitions in order to change behaviour. Other strategies, such as behaviour modification, can simply manipulate rewards. These strategies (such as shaping, the foot-in-the-door and door-in-the-face techniques) rely on a different model, in which it is assumed that changing behaviour without changing cognitions is an adequate goal in itself and that, once behaviour is changed, attitudes and other cognitions may also change.

Managing advertising and sales promotion

Advertising, non-personal communication conducted through paid media under clear sponsorship, must be planned strategically like any other element of the marketing mix. Objectives must be set, budgets determined, messages defined, media selected and a system of evaluation established.

Advertising objectives must fit with prior decisions about the target market, offer positioning, and the nature of the remainder of the marketing mix. It must be clear what response is sought from the target audience. The ultimate response, of course, is behaviour. But in highly involving and infrequent decisions, behaviour is the end result of a consumer decision-making process. Typically, the response is movement forward through six stages:

1 Awareness.
2 Knowledge.
3 Liking.
4 Preference.
5 Conviction.
6 Action.

Budgets can be set by affordable, percent-of-sales or competitive methods, but the objective-and-task method is best. Budgets must be both set in total and allocated among different market segments, geographical areas, and time periods. Budgets must also be allocated across media categories and to specific media vehicles. Choices here depend on the marketer's objectives, the intended target audience, the planned message and media costs.

Managers must also decide on media timing. Advertisements should be scheduled seasonally or cyclically to parallel changes in audience interest. Within seasons, decisions must be made on short-run timing. The major options are to advertise continuously, intermittently, or in preplanned bursts. These choices should be based on audience turnover, the frequency of the behaviour to be influenced, and forgetting rates.

Evaluation schemes involve pre-testing and post-testing advertising. Pre-testing can incorporate comprehension studies, mailed questionnaires, portfolio recall tests, physiological tests, focus group interviews, or self-administered questionnaires. Post-tests are usually based on recall, recognition, or some direct behavioural response such as enquiries or sales.

Sales promotion involves a wide range of incentives designed to have short-term effects on specific behaviours of consumers, intermediaries, or the salesforce. Sales promotion incentives can impel immediate action but there must be careful planning of objectives, recipient, inclusiveness, form, and amount and time of payment.

Managing public relations

Public relations is a well-established function in profit and non-profit organizations. However, the more recent introduction of marketing into non-profit organizations has raised the question of marketing's relationship to public relations. The authors assume that public relations is a tool used to advance the marketing purposes of the organization. As such, careful long-range and annual planning of the public relations function cannot be emphasized strongly enough.

The task of public relations is to form, maintain, or change public attitudes towards the organization or its products and services. This process consists of seven steps:

1 Identification of the organization's relevant publics.
2 Measurement of the images and attitudes held by these publics.
3 Establishment of image and attitude goals for the key publics.
4 Development of cost-effective public relations strategies.
5 Preparation for public relations crises.
6 Careful choice of specific public relations tools, such as written material, audiovisual material, organization identity media, news, events, speeches and telephone information services.
7 Implementation of actions and evaluation of results.

Just as elsewhere in the organization, a customer orientation is the best philosophy to apply to both long-term and short-term public relations strategies.

Managing personal selling

Many organizations utilize sales representatives and assign to them a pivotal role in the creation of sales. The high cost of the sales resource calls for effective sales management, consisting of six steps:

1 Establishment of salesforce objectives.
2 Design of salesforce strategy, structure, size and compensation.
3 Recruitment and selection.
4 Training.
5 Supervision.
6 Evaluation.

As an element of the marketing mix, the salesforce is capable of effectively achieving certain marketing objectives. The organization has to decide on the proper mix of the following sales activities: prospecting, communicating, selling and servicing, information gathering, and allocating.

Given the salesforce objectives, the salesforce is then designed to answer the question of what strategy would be most effective (individual selling, team selling), what type of structure would work best (territorial-, product-, customer-structured), how large a salesforce is needed and how it should be compensated.

Sales representatives must be recruited and selected carefully to avoid the high costs of hiring the wrong persons. Their training should familiarize them with the organization's history, products and policies, customer and competitor characteristics, and the art of selling. The art of selling itself calls for training in a seven-step sales process:

- prospecting and qualifying;
- preapproach;
- approach;
- presentation and demonstration;
- handling objections;
- closing;
- follow-up.

The salesperson needs supervision and continuous encouragement. Periodically, the person's performance must be evaluated formally to help him/her do a better job.

CONTROLLING MARKETING STRATEGIES

Marketing evaluation and control

The purpose of marketing control is to maximize the probability that the organization will achieve its short-run and long-run objectives in the marketplace. Non-profit managers must therefore have carefully designed measurement systems in place in order to track organizational performance and make appropriate adjustments. Marketing control systems are an intrinsic part of the marketing planning process since they permit such crucial and timely adjustments. There are two broad categories of control systems:

1 Strategic control systems monitor the organization's environment, competitors, publics, strengths and weaknesses and long run performance.
2 Tactical control systems monitor day-to-day performance for the purposes of fine-tuning current marketing efforts.

Two types of tactical control systems are those that measure organization revenues and those that measure customer satisfaction. In non-profit organizations that have some sort of revenue objective, the three main control tools are:

revenue analysis, market share analysis, and marketing expenses-to-sales analysis. The first two measures assess effectiveness, the latter efficiency. For non-profits without sales or revenue outcomes, other measures are necessary.

Customer satisfaction should be a major objective of all non-profit organizations. Complaint tracking systems provide one way of assessing this satisfaction over time. However, complaint measures are typically biased both as to types of complaints and persons affected. Periodic direct surveys of customers do not suffer from these biases. They can measure satisfaction directly as problems, indirectly as derived dissatisfaction, or as a combined measure of performance and importance. Studies of problems can be particularly helpful if they also track performance of the organization's complaint-handling activities.

Equally important as a measurement of the effectiveness of the programme is that of efficiency. An effective control system therefore also ought to track costs and relate them to the returns from the programme elements on which they are spent. Where the returns are dollar revenues, this evaluation is usually referred to as profitability analysis. Where the returns involve other measures of satisfaction or attitude change, the evaluation is usually referred to by the more general term of cost/benefit analysis.

SUMMARY

Many of the techniques and practices discussed in this chapter constitute the basic elements of the marketing planning process and are considered, in this instance, in relation to their application in the non-profit sector in order that they may be thoroughly explained and their application demonstrated. However, they are equally applicable to a wide variety of other marketing sectors, and as such, all of these topics are discussed in their own right in greater detail at other points in the Encyclopedia.

NOTE

This chapter is a summary of *Strategic Marketing for Non-profit Organizations*, 4th edn, Englewood Cliffs, NJ: Prentice-Hall, and was prepared by Ms Claire Currie of the University of Strathclyde.

VI   SPECIAL TOPICS

54

TOTAL QUALITY MANAGEMENT (TQM)

John S. Oakland

INTRODUCTION

In any chapter on the management of quality, it is first necessary to define what is meant by quality and its related concepts. Juran, one of the pioneers of quality management, first summarized a basic rule which is applicable here:

> Any widespread discipline must identify and clarify the universal concepts which underlie its very existence as a discipline. In addition it must evolve and standardise the key words and phrases through which practitioners of the discipline can communicate with each other.
>
> (Juran 1988)

Quality is not a property which has an absolute meaning and the word quality is often used for several distinct purposes. For these reasons, the meaning of quality, in terms of its management, will be explored. The remainder of the chapter will be about how to manage in a total quality way. It is structured around five parts of a model for TQM.

The core of the model is the customer-supplier interfaces, both externally and internally, and the fact that at each interface there lie a number of processes. This sensitive core must be surrounded by commitment to quality through well supported policy, communication of the quality message through effective leadership, and recognition of the need to change the culture of most organizations to create total quality. These are the 'soft foundations' of TQM, to which must be added the systems, the tools and the teams – the 'hard management necessities'.

The interfaces between quality and marketing activities and systems are clearly established and the essential steps for the successful implementation of TQM are set out. These include the development of a mission statement, identification of critical success factors (CSFs) and critical processes, all linked through a cycle of continuous improvement.

The chapter concludes with a discussion of current issues and future developments, including the results of recent research linking TQM and bottom-line results.

QUALITY

Quality is often used to signify excellence of a product or service – people talk about 'Rolls-Royce quality' and 'top quality'. In some engineering companies the word may be used to indicate that a piece of metal conforms to certain physical dimension characteristics, often set down in the form of a particularly 'tight' specification. In a hospital it might be used to indicate some sort of professionalism. If we are to define quality in a way that is useful in its management, then we must recognize the need to include in the assessment of quality the true requirements of the customer – the needs and expectations.

Quality, then, is simply meeting the customer requirements and this has been expressed in many ways by other authors:

'Fitness for purpose or use' (Juran 1988).

'The totality of features and characteristics of a product or service that bear on its ability to satisfy stated or implied needs' (BS 4778: 1987).

'Quality should be aimed at the needs of the consumer, present and future' (Deming 1982).

'The total composite product and service characteristics of marketing, engineering, manufacture and maintenance through which the product and service in use will meet the expectation by the customer' (Feigenbaum 1991).

'Conformance to requirements' (Crosby 1979).

There is another word that we should define properly – reliability. Quality and reliability are often used synonymously, sometimes in a totally confused way. Clearly, part of the acceptability of a product or service will depend on its ability to function satisfactorily over a period of time, and it is this aspect of performance which is given the name reliability. It is the ability of the product or service to continue to meet the customer requirements. Reliability ranks with quality in importance, since it is a key factor in many purchasing decisions where alternatives are being considered. Many of the general management issues related to achieving product or service quality are also applicable to reliability.

It is important to realize that the 'meeting the customer requirements' definition of quality is not restrictive to the functional characteristics of products or services. Anyone with children knows that the quality of some of the products they purchase is more associated with satisfaction in ownership than some functional property. This is also true of many items, from antiques to certain pieces of clothing. The requirements for status symbols account for the sale of some executive cars, certain bank accounts and charge cards, and even hospital

Outside organization

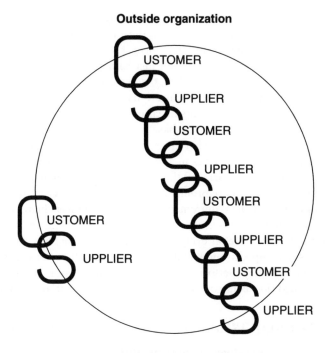

Outside organization

Figure 1   The quality chains

beds. The requirements are of paramount importance in the assessment of the quality of any product or service.

By consistently meeting customer requirements we can move to a different plane of satisfaction – delighting the customer. There is no doubt that many organizations have so well addressed their capability to meet their customers' requirements time and time again, that this has created a reputation for excellence. But within the same organization there exists in each department, each office, even each household, a series of suppliers and customers. The typist is a supplier to the boss – are his requirements being met? Does he receive error-free typing set out as he wants it, when he wants it? If so, then he has a quality typing service. Does the air hostess receive from her supplier in the airline the correct food trays in the right quantity?

Throughout and beyond all organizations, whether they are manufacturing concerns, banks, retail stores, universities, hospitals or hotels, there is a series of quality chains of customers and suppliers (Figure 1) which may be broken at any point by one person or one piece of equipment not meeting the requirements of the customer, internal or external. The interesting point is that this failure usually finds its way to the interface between the organization and its outside

955

customers, and the people who operate at that interface – like the air hostess or a sales representative – usually experience the ramifications. The concept of internal and external customers/suppliers forms the core of total quality.

Quality has to be managed – it will not just happen. Clearly it must involve everyone in the process and be applied throughout the organization. Many people in the support functions of organizations never see, experience, or touch the products or services that their organizations purchase or provide, but they do handle or produce things like purchase orders or invoices. If every fourth invoice carries at least one error, what image of quality is transmitted?

Failure to meet the requirements in any part of a quality chain has a way of multiplying. Failure in one part of the system creates problems elsewhere, leading to yet more failure, more problems and so on. The price of quality is the continual examination of the requirements and ability to meet them. This alone will lead to a 'continuing improvement' philosophy. The benefits of making sure that the requirements are met at every stage, every time, are truly enormous in terms of increased competitiveness and market share, reduced costs, improved productivity and delivery performance, and the elimination of waste. The Japanese have called this 'company-wide quality improvement' or CWQI.

MEETING THE REQUIREMENTS – THE MARKETING INTERFACE

If quality is meeting the customer requirements then this has wide implications. The requirements may include availability, delivery, reliability, maintainability and cost effectiveness, among many other features. The first item on the list of things to do is to find out what the requirements are. If we are dealing with a customer/supplier relationship crossing two organizations, then the supplier must establish a 'marketing' activity charged with this task.

The marketers must, of course, understand not only the needs of the customer, but also the ability of their own organization to meet the demands. If my customer places a requirement on me to run 1500 metres in 4 minutes, then I know I am unable to meet this demand, unless something is done to improve my running performance. Of course, I may never be able to achieve this requirement.

Within organizations, between internal customers and suppliers, the transfer of information regarding requirements is frequently poor to totally absent. How many executives really bother to find out what are the requirements of their customers – their secretaries? Can their handwriting be read, do they leave clear instructions, do the secretaries always know where the boss is? Equally, do the secretaries establish what their bosses need – error-free typing, clear messages, a tidy office? These internal supplier/customer relationships are often the most difficult to manage in terms of establishing the requirements. To achieve quality throughout an organization, each person in the quality chain must interrogate every interface as follows:

Customers

- Who are my immediate customers?
- What are their true requirements?
- How do or can I find out what the requirements are?
- How can I measure my ability to meet the requirements?
- Do I have the necessary capability to meet the requirements? If not then what must change to improve the capability?
- Do I continually meet the requirements? If not then what prevents this from happening, when the capability exists?
- How do I monitor changes in the requirements?

Suppliers

- Who are my immediate suppliers?
- What are my true requirements?
- How do I communicate my requirements?
- Do my suppliers have the capability to measure and meet the requirements?
- How do I inform them of changes in the requirements?

The measurement of capability is extremely important if the quality chains are to be formed within and without an organization. Each person in the organization must also realize that the supplier's needs and expectations must be respected if the requirements are to be fully satisfied.

MANAGING PROCESSES

As we have seen, quality chains can be traced right through the business or service processes used by any organization. A process is the transformation of a set of inputs, which can include actions, methods and operations, into desired outputs which satisfy the customer needs and expectations, in the form of products, information, services or – generally – results. Everything we do is a process, so in each area or function of an organization there will be many processes taking place. For example, a marketing group may be involved in market research processes, segmentation processes, advertising and promotion processes, pricing processes. Each process in each department or functional area can be analysed by an examination of the inputs and outputs. This will determine some of the actions necessary to improve quality.

The output from a process is that which is transferred to somewhere or to someone – the customer. Clearly to produce an output which meets the requirements of the customer, it is necessary to define, monitor and control the inputs to the process, which in turn may be supplied as output from an earlier process. At every supplier-customer interface then there resides a transformation process (Figure 2), and every single task throughout an organization must be viewed as a process in this way.

957

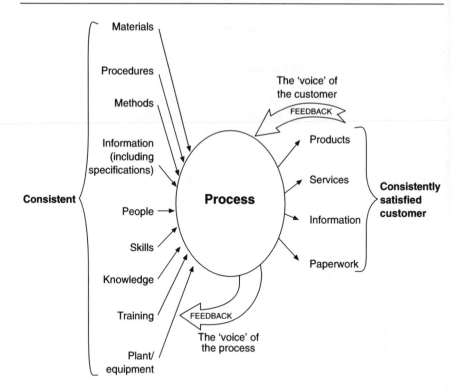

Figure 2 The systematic approach to process management

Improving the management of processes in many organizations involves replacing a strategy of detection of problems with one of prevention. This concentrates the attention on the front end of any process – the inputs – and changes the emphasis to making sure the inputs are capable of meeting the requirements of the process. This is a managerial responsibility.

These ideas apply to every transformation process, including those in marketing, which must be subject to the same scrutiny of the methods, people, skills, equipment and so on to make sure they are correct for the job. A person giving a sales presentation, whose overhead projector equipment will not focus correctly, or whose materials are not appropriate, will soon discover how difficult it is to provide a presentation which meets the requirements of the recipients.

In every organization there are some very large processes called key or critical or business processes. These are groups of smaller processes or activities which the organization must carry out especially well if its mission and objectives are to be achieved. Understanding these is crucial if the management of quality is to be integrated into the strategy for the organization.

QUALITY STARTS WITH MARKETING

The author has been asked on more than one occasion if TQM applies to marketing. The answer to the question is not remarkable – it starts there. The marketing function of an organization must take the lead in establishing the true requirements for the product or service. Having determined the need, marketing should define the market sector and demand. This will determine product or service features such as grade, price, quality, timing. Clearly a major hotel chain, before opening a new hotel or refurbishing an old one, will need to consider its location and accessibility, before deciding whether it will be predominantly a budget, first-class, business or family hotel.

Marketing will also need to establish customer requirements by reviewing the market needs, particularly in terms of unclear or unstated expectations or preconceived ideas held by customers. Marketing is responsible for identifying the key characteristics that determine the suitability of the product or service in the eyes of the customer. This may, of course, involve the use of market research techniques, data gathering, and analysis of customer complaints. If possible, quasi-quantitative methods should be employed giving proxy variables that can be used to grade the characteristics in importance, and to decide in which areas superiority over competitors exists. It is often useful to compare these findings with internal perceptions of quality.

Excellent communication between customers and suppliers is the key to total quality. This will eradicate the 'demanding nuisance/idiot' view of customers which pervades some organizations. Poor communications often occur in the supply chain between organizations, when neither party realizes how poor they are. Feedback from both customers and suppliers needs to be improved where dissatisfied customers and suppliers do not communicate their problems. In such cases, non-conformance of purchased products or services is often due to the customers' inability to communicate their requirements clearly. If these ideas are also used within an organization, then the internal supplier/customer interfaces or internal marketing will operate much more smoothly.

All efforts devoted to finding the nature and timing of the demand will be pointless if marketing fails to communicate the requirements promptly, clearly, and accurately to the remainder of the organization. The marketing function should be capable of supplying the company with a formal statement or outline of the requirements for each product or service. This constitutes a preliminary set of specifications which can be used as the basis for service or product design. The information requirements include:

1 Characteristics of performance and reliability – these must make reference to the conditions of use and any environmental factors which will be important.
2 Aesthetic characteristics such as style, colour, smell, taste, feel.
3 Any obligatory regulations or standards that govern the nature of the product or service.

Marketing must also establish systems for feedback of customer information and reaction, which should be designed on a continuous monitoring basis. Any information pertinent to the product or service should be collected and collated, interpreted, analysed, and communicated to improve the response to customer experience and expectations. These same principles must also be applied inside the organization for continuous improvement at every transformation process interface to be achieved. If for example the marketing group in a company has problems recruiting the correct sort of staff, and the personnel department have not established mechanisms for gathering, analysing, and responding to information on new employees, then frustration and conflict will replace communication and cooperation.

One aspect of the analysis of market demand that extends back into the organization is the review of market readiness of a new product or service. Items that clearly require some attention include assessment of:

- the suitability of the distribution and customer service systems;
- training of personnel in the field;
- availability of spare parts or support staff;
- evidence that the organization is capable of meeting customer requirements.

All organizations receive a wide range of information from customers through invoices, payments, requests for information, letters of complaints, responses to advertisements and promotion. An essential component of any system for the analysis of market demand is that these data are channelled quickly into the appropriate areas for action and, if necessary, response.

There are various techniques of market research that will not be described in detail here for they are well documented elsewhere in this Encyclopedia. The number of methods and techniques for researching market demand is limited only by imagination and funds. The important point to stress is that the supplier, whether the internal individual or the external organization, keeps very close to the customer. Market research, coupled with analysis of complaints data, is an essential part of finding out what the requirements are and breaking out from the obsession with inward scrutiny which bedevils quality.

QUALITY IN ALL FUNCTIONS

For an organization to be truly effective, each part of it must work properly together. Each part, each activity, each person in the organization affects and is in turn affected by others. Errors have a way of multiplying and failure to meet the requirements in one part or area creates problems elsewhere, leading to yet more errors, yet more problems and so on. The benefits of getting it right first time everywhere are enormous.

Everyone experiences – almost accepts – problems in working life. This causes people to spend a large part of their time on useless activities, correcting errors, looking for things, finding out why things are late, checking suspect information, rectifying and reworking, apologizing to customers for mistakes, poor quality and lateness. The list is endless and it is estimated that about one-third of our efforts are wasted in this way. In the service sector it can be much higher.

Quality, the way we have defined it as meeting the customer requirements, gives people in different functions of an organization a common language for improvement. It enables all the people, with different abilities and priorities, to communicate readily with one another, in pursuit of a common goal. When business and industry were local, the craftsman could manage more or less on his own. Business is now so complex and employs so many different specialist skills that everyone has to rely on the activities of others in doing their jobs.

Some of the most exciting applications of TQM have materialized from departments which could see little relevance when first introduced to the concepts. Following training, many examples from different departments of organizations show the use of the techniques. Sales staff can monitor and increase successful sales calls, office staff have used TQM methods to prevent errors in word-processing and improve inputting to computers, customer service people have monitored and reduced complaints, distribution have controlled lateness and disruption in deliveries.

It is worthy of mention that the first point of contact for some outside customers is the telephone operator, the security people at the gate, or the person in reception. Equally the paperwork and support services associated with the product, such as invoices and sales literature, must match the needs of the customer. Clearly TQM cannot be restricted to the production or operational areas without losing great opportunities to gain maximum benefit.

Managements that rely heavily on exhortation of the staff to 'do the right job right the first time', or 'accept that quality is your responsibility', will not only fail to achieve quality but will also create division and conflict. These calls for improvement infer that faults are caused only by the staff and that problems are departmental when, in fact, the opposite is true – most problems are interdepartmental. The involvement of all members of an organization is a requirement of company-wide quality improvement. It must involve everyone working together at every interface to achieve perfection. This can only happen if the top management is really committed to quality improvement.

THE TOTAL QUALITY MANAGEMENT APPROACH

What is total quality management? The answer to this question is often that it is something best left to the experts. But this response is avoiding the issue because it allows executives and managers to opt out, to avoid getting involved. Quality is too important to leave to the so-called quality professionals; it cannot be achieved on a company-wide basis if it is left to the experts. Equally dangerous, however, are the uninformed who try to follow their natural instincts because they 'know what quality is when they see it', or 'it's just basic commonsense really'. This type of intuitive approach will lead to serious attitude problems which do no more than reflect the understanding and knowledge of quality that is present in an organization.

The organization that believes that the traditional quality-control techniques, and the way they have always been used, will resolve their quality problems is wrong. Employing more inspectors, tightening up standards, developing correction, repair and rework teams does not promote quality. Traditionally, quality has been regarded as the responsibility of the QC department, and it has still not been recognized in some organizations that many quality problems originate in the marketing, sales, service and administration areas.

Total quality management (TQM) is far more than shifting the responsibility of detection of problems from the customer to the producer. It requires a comprehensive approach which must first be recognized and then implemented if the rewards are to be realized. Today's business environment is such that managers must plan strategically to maintain a hold on market share, let alone increase it. We have known for years that consumers place a higher value on quality than on loyalty to home-based producers and that price is no longer the major determining factor in consumer choice. Price has been replaced by quality and this is true in industrial, service, hospitality, and many other markets.

If definitions are needed, TQM is an approach to improving the competitiveness, effectiveness and flexibility of a whole organization. Essentially it is a way of planning, organizing and understanding each activity, and involving each individual at each level. For an organization to be truly effective, each part of it must work properly together towards the same goals, recognizing that each person and each activity affects and in turn is affected by others. TQM is also a way of ridding people's lives of wasted effort by involving everyone in the processes of improvement, increasing the effectiveness of work so that results are achieved in less time.

The methods and techniques used in TQM can be applied throughout any organization. They are equally useful in marketing, manufacturing, public service, health care, education and the hospitality industries. TQM needs to gain ground rapidly and become a way of life in many organizations.

The impact of TQM on an organization is first to ensure that the management adopt a strategic overview of quality. The approach must focus on developing a problem prevention mentality, but it is easy to underestimate the effort that is required to change attitudes and approaches. Many people will need to undergo a complete change of mind-set to unscramble their intuition which rushes into the detection/inspection mode to solve quality problems – 'we have a quality problem, we had better check every letter – take two samples out of each sack – check every widget twice'.

The correct mind-set may be achieved by looking at the sorts of barriers that exist in key areas. Staff will need to be trained and shown how to reallocate their time and energy to studying their processes in teams, searching for causes of problems, and correcting the causes, not the symptoms, hopefully once and for all. This will require of management a positive, thrusting initiative to promote the right-first-time approach to work situations. Through process improvement teams, which will need to be set up, these actions will reduce naturally the inspection-rejection syndrome. If things are done correctly first time round, the usual problems that create the need for inspection for failure will disappear.

COMMITMENT AND POLICY

To be successful in promoting business efficiency and effectiveness, TQM must be truly organization-wide and it must start at the top with the chief executive, or equivalent. The most senior directors and management must all demonstrate that they are serious about quality. The middle management have a particularly important role to play. They must not only grasp the principles of TQM, but go on to explain them to the people for whom they are responsible, and ensure that their own commitment is communicated. Only then will TQM spread effectively throughout the organization. This level of management must also ensure that the efforts and achievements of their subordinates obtain the recognition, attention and reward that they deserve.

The chief executive of an organization must accept the responsibility for and commitment to a quality policy in which he/she must really believe. This commitment is part of a broad approach extending well beyond the accepted formalities of the quality assurance function. It creates responsibilities for a chain of quality interactions between the marketing, design, production/operations, purchasing, distribution and service functions. Within each and every department of the organization at all levels, starting at the top, basic changes of attitude will be required to operate TQM. If the owners or directors of the organization do not recognize and accept their responsibilities for the initiation and operation of TQM, then these changes will not happen. Controls, systems and techniques are very important in TQM, but they are not the primary requirement. It is more an attitude of mind, based on pride in the job and teamwork, and it requires total commitment from the management, which must then be extended to all employees at all levels and in all departments.

Senior management commitment must be obsessional, not lip service. It is possible to detect real commitment: it shows in the salesforce, on the shop floor, in the offices, in the hospital wards – at the point of operation. Going into organizations sporting poster campaigning for quality instead of belief, one is quickly able to detect the falseness. The people are told not to worry if quality problems arise, 'just do the best you can', 'the customer will never notice'. The contrast of an organization where total quality means something can be seen, heard, felt. Things happen at this operating interface as a result of real commitment. Material problems are connected with suppliers, sales campaigns are properly organized, equipment difficulties are put right by improved maintenance programmes or replacement, people are trained, change takes place, partnerships are built, continuous improvement is achieved.

963

The quality policy

A sound quality policy, together with the organization and facilities to put it into effect, is a fundamental requirement if an organization is to begin to implement TQM. Every organization should develop and state its policy on quality, together with arrangements for its implementation. The contents of the policy should be made known to all employees. The preparation and implementation of a properly thought-out quality policy, together with continuous monitoring, makes for smoother production or service operation, minimizes errors and reduces waste.

Management must be dedicated to the ongoing improvement of quality, not simply a one-step improvement to an acceptable plateau. These ideas must be set out in a quality policy which requires top management to:

• establish an organization for quality;
• identify the customers' needs and perception of needs;
• assess the ability of the organization to meet these needs economically;
• ensure that bought-out materials and services reliably meet the required standards of performance and efficiency;
• concentrate on the prevention rather than detection philosophy;
• educate and train for quality improvement;
• review the quality management systems to maintain progress.

The quality policy must be publicized and understood at all levels of the organization.

EFFECTIVE LEADERSHIP FOR TQM

Some management teams have broken away from the traditional style of management, they have made a 'managerial breakthrough'. Their approach puts these organizations ahead of their competitors in the fight for sales, profits, resources, funding and jobs. Many service organizations are beginning to move in the same direction and the successful quality-market based strategy they are adopting depends very much on effective leadership.

Effective leadership starts with the chief executive's vision, capitalizing on market or service opportunities, continues through a strategy which will give the organization competitive advantage, and leads to business or service success. It goes on to embrace all of the beliefs and values held, the decisions taken and the plans made by anyone anywhere in the organization and the focusing of them into effective, value adding action.

Together effective leadership and total quality management result in the company or organization doing the right things, right first time. There are five main things which top management must do to be effective leaders.

Five key leadership points

The mission statement

Clear documented corporate beliefs must be developed and published – a mission statement. Executives must express values and beliefs through a clear vision of what they want their company or organization to be and its objectives – what they specifically want to achieve in line with the basic beliefs. Together, they define what the company or organization is all about. The senior management team will need to spend some time away from the coalface to do this and develop their programme for implementation.

Clearly defined and properly communicated beliefs and objectives, which can be summarized in the form of a mission statement, are essential if the directors, managers and other employees are to work together as a winning team. The beliefs and objectives should address:

- The definition of the business – for example, the needs that are satisfied or the benefits provided.
- A commitment to effective leadership and quality.
- Target sectors and relationships with customers, and market or service position.
- The role or contribution of the company, organization or unit – for example, profit generator, service department, opportunity seeker.
- The distinctive competence – a brief statement which applies only to that organization, company or unit.
- Indications for future direction – a brief statement of the principal plans which would be considered.
- Commitment to monitoring performance against customers needs and expectations, and continuous improvement.

The mission statement and the broader beliefs and objectives may then be used to communicate an inspiring vision for the organization of where it is going. The top management must then show total commitment to it.

Develop clear and effective strategies and supporting plans for achieving the mission and objectives

The achievement of the company or service objectives requires the development of business or service strategies, including the strategic positioning in the marketplace. Plans can then be made for implementing the strategies. Such strategies and plans can be developed by senior managers alone, but there is likely to be more commitment to them if employee participation in their development and implementation is encouraged.

Identify the critical success factors and critical processes

The next step is the identification of the critical success factors (CSFs), a term used to mean the most important subgoals of a business or organization. CSFs are what must be accomplished for the mission to be achieved. The CSFs are followed by the key or critical or business processes for the organization – the activities which must be done particularly well for the CSFs to be achieved. (This process is described in some detail in Oakland 1993).

Review the management structure

Defining the corporate objectives and strategies, CSFs and critical processes might make it necessary to review the organizational structure. Directors, managers and other employees can be fully functional only if an effective structure based on process management exists. This includes both the definition of responsibilities for the organization's management and the operational procedures they will use. These must be the agreed best ways of carrying out the critical process.

The review of the management structure should also include the establishment of process improvement teams throughout the organization.

Empowerment – encourage effective employee participation

For effective leadership, it is necessary for management to get very close to the employees. They must develop effective communications – up, down and across the organization, and take action on what is communicated. Good communications should be encouraged between all suppliers and customers.

THE FOUNDATIONS OF THE TQM MODEL

The vehicle for achieving effective leadership is total quality management. We have seen that it involves the entire organization, all the people and all the functions, including external organizations and suppliers. Several facets of TQM have been reviewed, including:

- Recognizing customers and discovering their needs.
- Setting standards that are consistent with customer requirements.
- Controlling processes, including systems, and improving their capability.
- Management's responsibility for setting the guiding philosophy and quality policy, providing motivation through leadership and equipping people to achieve quality.
- Empowerment of people at all levels in the organization to act for quality improvement.

The task of implementing TQM can be daunting and the chief executive and

966

directors faced with it may become confused and irritated by the proliferation of theories and packages. A simplification is required. The *core* of TQM must be the customer-supplier interfaces, both internally and externally, and the fact that, at each interface, there are processes which convert inputs to outputs. Clearly, there must be commitment to building-in quality through management of the inputs and processes.

How can senior managers and directors be helped in their understanding of what needs to be done to become committed to quality and implement the vision? Some American and Japanese quality gurus have each set down a number of points or absolutes – words of wisdom in management and leadership – and many organizations are using these to establish a policy based on quality. These have been distilled down and modified here to ten points for senior management to adopt.

TEN POINTS FOR SENIOR MANAGEMENT

1 The organization needs long-term commitment to constant improvement.

There must be a constancy of purpose, and commitment to it must start from the top. The quality improvement process must be planned on a truly organization-wide basis (i.e. it must embrace all locations and departments and must include customers, suppliers, and subcontractors). It cannot start in one department in the hope that the programme will spread from there.

The place to start the quality process is in the boardroom – leadership must be by example. Then progressively expand it to embrace all parts of the organization. It is wise to avoid the Blitz approach to TQM implementation, which can lead to a lot of hype but no real changes in behaviour.

2 Adopt the philosophy of zero errors/defects to change the culture to right first time.

This must be based on a thorough understanding of the customers' needs and expectations and teamwork, developed through employee participation and rigorous application of Deming's Plan-Do-Act cycle (Figure 3).

3 Train the people to understand the customer-supplier relationships.

Again the commitment to customer needs must start from the top, with the chairman or chief executive. Without that, time and effort will be wasted. Customer orientation must then be achieved for each and every employee, directors and managers. The concept of internal customers and suppliers must be thoroughly understood and used.

4 Do not buy products or services on price alone – look at the total cost.

Demand continuous improvement in everything, including suppliers. This will bring about improvements in product, service and failure rates. Continuously improve the product or the service provided externally, so that the total costs of doing business are reduced.

5 Recognize that the improvement of the systems needs to be managed.

Defining the performance standards expected and the systems to achieve

967

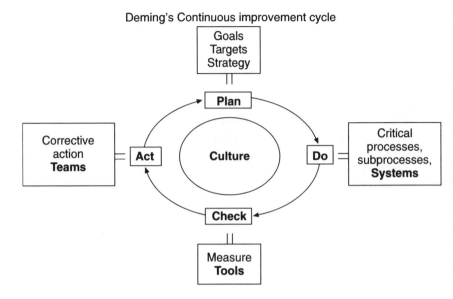

Figure 3 Deming's Continuous Improvement cycle
Source: Deming (1982)

them is a managerial responsibility. The rule has to be that the systems will be in line with the shared needs and expectations and will be part of the continuous improvement process.

6 Adopt modern methods of supervision and training – eliminate fear.

It is all too easy to criticize mistakes, but it often seems difficult to praise efforts and achievements. Recognize and publicize efforts and achievements and provide the right sort of facilitation and supervision.

7 Eliminate barriers between departments by managing the process – improve communications and teamwork.

Barriers are often created by 'silo management', in which departments are treated like containers which are separate from one another. The customers are not interested in departments – they stand on the outside of the organization and see slices through it – they see the processes. It is necessary to build teams and improve communications around the processes.

8 Eliminate:

• arbitrary goals without methods;
• all standards based only on numbers;
• barriers to pride of workmanship;
• fiction, get facts by using the correct tools.

At all times it is essential to know how well you are doing in terms of satisfying the customers' needs and expectations. Help every single employee to know how they will achieve the goals and how well they are doing.

9 Constantly educate and retrain – develop the experts in the business.

The experts in any business are the people who do the job every day of their lives. The energy that lies within them can be released into the organization through education, training, encouragement and involvement.

10 Develop a systematic approach to manage the implementation of TQM.

TQM should not be regarded as a woolly-minded approach to running an organization. It requires a carefully planned and fully integrated strategy, derived from the mission. By these means it will help any organization to realize its vision.

Summary of ten points for senior management

- Identify *Customer/Supplier* relationships
- Manage *Processes*
- Change the *Culture*
- Improve *Communication*
- Show *Commitment*

These form the basis of the first part of a model for TQM – the 'soft' outcomes of TQM (see Figure 4). The process core must be surrounded, however, by some 'hard' management necessities:

- *Systems* (based on a good international standard).
- *Tools* (for analysis, correlations, and predictions for action for continuous improvement to be taken).
- *Teams* (councils, quality improvement teams, quality circles, corrective action teams).

The model now provides a multi-dimensional TQM 'vision' against which a particular company's status can be examined, or against which a particular approach to TQM implementation may be compared and weaknesses highlighted. It is difficult to draw in only two dimensions, but Figure 4 is an attempt to represent the major features of the model.

QUALITY SYSTEMS IN MARKETING, SALES AND CUSTOMER SERVICE

Historically, formal quality systems and procedures were confined to the manufacturing aspects of industry, but in recent years they have extended rapidly into the services sector and functions as organizations seek to enhance their reputations for supplying quality products and services. Against a background of escalating international competition and customer expectations,

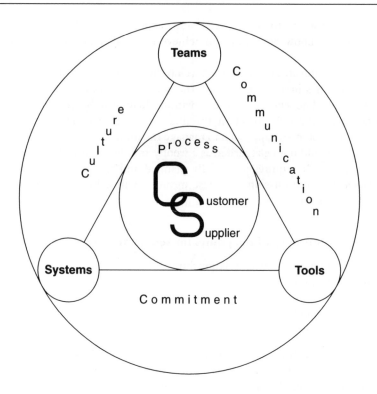

Figure 4   Total quality management model

more and more customers are demanding objective evidence of quality and consistency from their suppliers. This is increasingly taking the form of independent, third party confirmation and certification to recognized standards, in all areas of the business.

The International Standard ISO 9000 series on Quality Systems (BS EN ISO in the UK), clearly has its origins in manufacturing industry, yet the principles it embodies are common to services and to the marketing function. Having said that, however, it must be recognized that the interpretation of the standard for these areas is not so simple. It is for this reason that various Guidance Notes have been generated for various sectors, and a separate standard for Marketing Quality Assurance has been written.

Marketing Quality Assurance (MQA)

MQA is a third party certification organization which specializes in providing assessment services to organizations wishing to develop quality systems for their marketing, sales, and customer service activities; in assessing companies in the

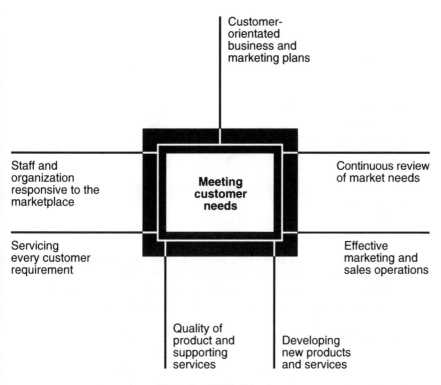

Customer-
orientated
business and
marketing plans

Staff and
organization
responsive to the
marketplace

**Meeting
customer
needs**

Continuous review
of market needs

Servicing
every customer
requirement

Effective
marketing and
sales operations

Quality of
product and
supporting
services

Developing
new products
and services

Figure 5   MQA objectives

services sector to the ISO 9000 series of Quality System Standards; and in developing third party certification guidelines for specific service areas, such as public relations.

MQA has produced a Quality Assurance Specification for marketing, sales and customer assurance. This is an associated document to the ISO 9000 series, and MQA offers registration to ISO 9001, BS EN ISO 9001 for an organization's marketing, sales and customer service activities. MQA awards a certificate of excellence and the right to use the MQA mark if companies achieve the required standard. The aim is to signal to customers, competitors and employees that the certified organization is one that has achieved independent recognition that it has marketing excellences.

The objectives of using the MQA approach may be summarized in Figure 5. Its own Quality Specification deals with systems that apply specifically to marketing, sales and customer assurance. The specification defines a marketing audit, marketing strategy, customer assurance, code of conduct, and a marketing and sales quality system. The 58 requirements of the specification are categorized under 15 areas, which clearly relate to the ISO 9000 series:

- quality policy
- business plans
- organization
- management representatives
- management review
- quality system
- marketing and sales plans
- code of conduct
- marketing and sales operations
- customer assurance
- purchasing
- resources, personnel, training, organization structure
- controls and procedures
- records
- quality audits

Briefly, the specification states that business plans must exist and marketing inputs should have contributed to their development. There should be clearly defined processes for the review of market needs which should identify and reassess customer needs and preference. The marketing and sales plans must relate to the business plans, and be understood and agreed by the contributing departments. The requirements under marketing and sales operations call for best practice in all the operational areas, including product or service development, promotion, pricing, selling, and distribution. All aspects of customer assurance should be covered to inspire confidence that the stated or implied needs are being satisfied. The specification sets down requirements, under resources, personnel, training and organization structure, for well-trained experienced staff who are responsive to the needs of the marketplace. All this and the more traditional areas are to be in a documented quality system which demonstrates the organization's capabilities in meeting customer requirements.

In 1991 Exxon Chemical International Marketing BV became the first organization to achieve registration to Marketing Quality Assurance (MQA) for the marketing, sales and customer assurance activities of its Adhesives and Sealants Sector which comprised seven offices throughout Europe. This Exxon chemical industry sector achieved registration in seven assessed European offices in Cologne, Paris, Milan, Southampton, Rotterdam, Madrid and Brussels.

The European Business Unit General Manager claimed that the MQA Quality Specification had enabled the organization to further its commitment to achieving a quality culture, and to achieve registration to ISO 9000 in 'three of the most significant areas of any business'.

CURRENT ISSUES AND FUTURE DEVELOPMENTS

We often hear expressions such as 'TQM is a journey without a destination', which highlight that the business quest for progress and advancement is never-ending. This sometimes creates, however, a dichotomous situation insofar as managing business organizations is concerned. Many managers, while not denying the need for constant improvements, are presented with a very difficult situation – they are also expected to show consistent results in the marketplace in the short term. Many managers find it difficult to reconcile the short-term benefits with the long-term opportunities for improvement.

Every book, chapter and article on TQM talks about the need for management commitment. Management commitment is, of course, essential for the introduction of TQM, but it may not be enough to generate success in the marketplace. Many failures in TQM implementation have been attributed to factors such as: the executive promotional ladder; executive bonuses and the interest in short-term results; shareholder pressures.

Senior management commitment to TQM is certainly required to overcome the first two factors, but commitment of all employees and their willingness to combat waste, reduce costs and carry out consistent improvement is essential. Commitment of shareholders and financial institutions to taking an interest in longer term business performance and sustainability, and commitment of governments to preparing the right climate for business, the right incentives and adequate protections, are also crucial for results to be consistently achieved.

The question in relation to TQM and business performance is, therefore, twofold:

1. What are the short-term benefits in enhancing profit levels and initiating growth?
2. What are the long-term benefits through ensuring sustainability and achieving repeated superior performance standards?

In order that TQM can deliver the right answers to these questions, its implementation has to be carried out in a very systematic way, without any wavering in commitment, and without hesitation and deferral in the decision-making process. The following questions must be continually addressed if TQM is to lead to pay-offs:

- Does the organization really understand its purpose?
- Is there a clear vision/mission and clear goals?
- Have the vision and TQM plan been communicated effectively?
- Have the goals been deployed effectively?
- Have the people been trained, educated, motivated and really empowered to carry out the improvement efforts?
- Is the organization really customer focused and does it truly understand its customer requirements?
- Does it understand and appreciate what takes place in the marketplace?

- Are systems, tools and teams in place and used in 'anger'?
- Do improvement efforts get measured?

We hear comments such as: 'TQM has failed to help businesses perform in the marketplace'. But what about the question: 'Did businesses fail to introduce TQM effectively, and as such fail to perform in the market?' Many poor business performances can be traced back to poor implementation of TQM. In many instances, TQM implementation has lacked strategic focus and was introduced as a bolt-on to unchanged business culture. The link between TQM and business performance can only be established if the above questions have been answered in the affirmative.

How does TQM drive business performance?

TQM is a business tool. As such it is about achievements and results. Results are the yardsticks of achievement and progress and, if they are not captured on a regular basis, it becomes very difficult to maintain momentum, commitment and, more importantly, the motivation and desire to achieve higher standards.

A study has been carried out, by the author and his colleagues, on 29 companies known to be practising TQM (Oakland *et al.* 1992). The research focused on externally reported information which is readily available and recorded continuously. This enabled the examination of patterns of behaviour and performance. One of the questions concerning the design of the research was when is it reasonable to expect TQM to start to deliver benefits? From experience and the multitude of case studies of companies that have implemented TQM, it was decided that if TQM is introduced with a sound plan, a clear mission and tangible goals and if the whole process has been deployed in the right way, then it is reasonable to expect benefits to be derived over a period of five years. The sample of 29 companies was chosen carefully, based on good knowledge and understanding of the specific TQM approaches adopted by each individual company.

Seven performance indicators were used for the analysis. The mean for each company was calculated over five years' results for each performance indicator. To establish the extent of enhancements or otherwise, performance under each indicator for each company was compared to the industry median. The results indicate that most of the 29 companies tended to exhibit positive trends in performance, in comparison with their industry average:

- *Profit margin* – 22 out of the 29 companies studied show healthier profit margins than their industry median.
- *Return on total assets* – 22 out of the 29 companies show better returns on investment than their industry median.
- *Turnover per employee* – 23 out of the 29 companies show sales (per employee) higher than their industry median.
- *Profit per employee* – 23 out of the 29 companies show positive quantums in

comparison with their industry median.

- *Total assets per employee* – 23 out of the 29 companies have at their disposal greater asset value per employee than their industry median.
- *Fixed asset trend* – 21 out of the 29 companies show a positive pattern of long-term investment in comparison to their respective industry median.
- *Average remuneration* – in 27 out of the 29 companies studied is higher than their industry median.

The seven indicators chosen for carrying out the various comparisons reflect business performance, both in short-term and long-term perspectives. They also contain 'softer' measures that are people related, such as employee remuneration. In combination, the indicators show a consistent pattern of positiveness in performance between the chosen companies and their industry median.

These patterns of positive business performance suggest that there is a positive association between TQM introduction and bottom-line results. Although the study does not conclude by suggesting direct causation, it is in line with what studies in the USA and Japan have highlighted. Clearly TQM can have a direct impact on bottom-line results, provided its implementation is properly managed and provided that there is strong commitment to sustaining the continuous effort of quality improvement that benefits the end customer.

Developing TQM

The Bradford study does not suggest that TQM leads directly to improvements in bottom-line results. TQM offers companies the opportunity to carry out improvements and presents an opportunity to get closer to customers. It is only a licence to practice. Companies must, of course, have the right strategies in place, the right products and services, the right commitment, and the right investment plans. Senior managers in many organizations recognize the need for change to deal with increasing competitiveness, but lack an understanding of how to implement the changes. Successful organizations in the future will see that change is effected, not by focusing on formal structures and systems, but by aligning process management teams. This starts with writing the mission statement, analysis of the critical success factors (CSFs) and understanding the critical or key processes.

Some of the obstacles to TQM implementation and resistance to change still need to be overcome through education, communication, participation, facilitation, and support. The 'blitz' or rapid change approach will be rejected in favour of a slow, planned purposeful one, engaging the top management and using bottom-up involvement.

Successful management teams will achieve process alignment through a self-reinforcing cycle of commitment, communication, and culture change. The main steps in this process will always be: gain commitment to change, develop a shared mission or vision of the business or desired change, and define the measurable objectives. The remaining steps will involve developing the mission, really understanding the key or critical processes, gaining ownership, breaking down the critical processes into subprocesses, activities and tasks, and monitoring and adjusting process alignment in response to difficulties in the change process.

Making quality happen requires not only commitment but a competence in the mechanics of TQM. Crucial next steps will involve development of the appropriate organization structures, collecting information including quality costs for prioritizing teamwork, quality systems, training, and self-assessment.

Managers must really understand and pursue never-ending improvement. This will involve planning and operating processes, providing inputs, evaluating outputs, examining performance, and modifying processes and their inputs. The three basic principles of continuous improvement – focus on the customer, understand the process, involve the people – will form the core of TQM in the future.

REFERENCES

BS 4778 (1987) [ISO 8402, 1986] *Quality Vocabulary: Part 1, International Terms*, London: HMSO.
Crosby, P. B. (1979) *Quality is Free*, New York: McGraw-Hill.
Deming, W. E. (1982) *Out of the Crisis*, Cambridge, Mass.: MIT.
Feigenbaum, A. V. (1991) *Total Quality Control*, 3rd edn, New York: McGraw-Hill.
Juran, J. M. (ed.) (1988) *Quality Control Handbook*, New York: McGraw-Hill.
Juran, J. M. (1989) *Juran on Leadership for Quality: An Executive Handbook*, New York: The Free Press.
Oakland, J. S. (1993) *Total Quality Management*, 2nd edn, Oxford: Butterworth-Heinemann.
Oakland, J. S., Zairi, M. and Letza, S. (1992) *TQM and Bottom Line Results*, Technical Publications.

FURTHER READING

Adair, J. (1987) *Not Bosses but Leaders: How to Lead the Successful Way*, Guildford: Talbot Adair Press.
Adair, J. (1988) *The Action-Centred Leader*, London: Industrial Society.
Adair, J. (1988) *Effective Leadership*, 2nd edn, London: Pan Books.
Atkinson, P. E. (1990) *Creating Culture Change: The Key to Successful Total Quality Management*, Bedford: IFS.
Aubrey, C. A. and Felkins, P. K. (1988) *Teamwork: Involving People in Quality and Productivity Improvement*, Milwaukee, WI: ASQC.
Bank, J. (1992) *The Essence of Total Quality Management*, Hemel Hempstead: Prentice Hall.
BS 600 (1935) *The Application of Statistical Methods to Industrial Standardisation and Quality Control*, London: HMSO.
BS 2564 (1955) *Control Chart Technique When Manufacturing to a Specification, With Special Reference to Articles Machined to Dimensional Tolerances*, London: HMSO.
BS 4891 (1972) *A Guide to Quality Assurance*, London: HMSO.

BS 5700 (1984) *Guide to Process Control Using Quality Control Chart Methods and Cusum Techniques*, London: HMSO.

BS 5701 (1980) *Guide to Number-Defective Charts for Quality Control*, London: HMSO.

BS 5703 (1980–82) [Parts 1–4] *Guide to Data Analysis and Quality Control Using Cusum Techniques*, London: HMSO.

BS 5750 (1987–91) [ISO 9001, Part 1; ISO 9002, Part 2; ISO 9003, Part 3; ISO 9004–2, Part 8; ISO 900-3, Part 13] *Quality Systems*, London: HMSO.

BS 5760 (1981–91) [Parts 0–7] *Reliability of Systems, Equipment and Components*, London: HMSO.

BS 5781 (1988) [Parts 1–2] *Measurement and Calibration Systems*, London: HMSO.

BS 6143 (1990–91) [Parts 1–2; ISO 2859–3] *Guide to the Economies of Quality*, London: HMSO.

BS 7165 (1991) *Recommendations for Achievement of Quality in Software*, London: HMSO.

BS 7229 (1991) [Parts 1–3; ISO 10011] *Guide to Quality Systems Auditing*, London: HMSO.

BS 7850 (1992) *Total Quality Management*, London: HMSO.

BS 9000 (1989–91) [Parts 1–8] *General Requirements for a System for Electronic Components of Assessed Quality*, London: HMSO.

BS (1991) [Published Document PD 3542] *The Role of Standards in Company Quality Management*, London: HMSO.

Caulcutt, R. (1989) *Data Analysis in the Chemical Industry*, vol. 1, Chichester: Ellis Horwood.

Caulcutt, R. (1991) *Statistics in Research and Development*, 2nd edn, London: Chapman and Hall.

Choppin, J. (1991) *Quality Through People: A Blue Print for Proactive Total Quality Management*, Kempston: IFS.

Ciampa, D. (1992) *Total Quality – A User's Guide for Implementation*, Reading, Mass.: Addison-Wesley.

Cook, S. (1992) *Customer Care – Implementing Total Quality in Today's Service Driven Organisation*, London: Kogan Page.

Crosby, P. B. (1984) *Quality Without Tears*, New York: McGraw-Hill.

Dale, B. G. and Cooper, C. (1992) *Total Quality and Human Resources – An Executive Guide*, Oxford: Blackwell.

Dale, B. G. and Oakland, J. S. (1991) *Quality Improvement Through Standards*, Cheltenham: Stanley Thornes.

Dale, B. G. and Plunkett, J. J. (eds) (1990) *Managing Quality*, Hemel Hempstead: Philip Allan.

Deming, W. E. (1993) *The New Economics*, Cambridge, Mass.: MIT.

Dimaxcescu, D. (1992) *The Seamless Enterprise – Making Cross Functional Management Work*, New York: Harper Business.

Francis, D. (1990) *Unblocking the Organisational Communication*, Aldershot: Gower.

Garvin, D. A. (1988) *Managing Quality: The Strategic Competitive Edge*, New York: The Free Press.

Hall, T. J. (1992) *The Quality Manual – The Application of BS 5750 ISO 9001 EN29001*, Chichester: J. Wiley.

Harrington, H. J. (1991) *Business Process Improvement*, New York: McGraw-Hill.

Hutchins, D. (1985) *The Quality Circle Handbook*, Aldershot: Gower.

Hutchins, D. (1990) *In Pursuit of Quality*, London: Pitman.

Hutchins, D. (1992) *Achieve Total Quality*, Cambridge: Director Books.

Ishikawa, K. (1985) *What is Total Quality Control? – the Japanese Way*, Englewood Cliffs, N.J.: Prentice-Hall.

Juran, J. M. and Gryna, F. M. (1980) *Quality Planning and Analysis*, 2nd edn, New York: McGraw-Hill.

King Taylor, L. (1992) *Quality: Total Customer Service*, London: Century Business.

Lash, L. M. (1989) *The Complete Guide to Customer Service*, New York: J. Wiley.

Muhlemann, A. P., Oakland, J. S. and Lockyer, K. G. (1992) *Production and Operations Management*, 6th edn, London: Pitman.

Munro-Faure, L. and Munro-Faure, M. (1992) *Implementing Total Quality Management*, London: Pitman.

Murphy, J. A. (1986) *Quality in Practice*, Dublin: Gill and MacMillan.

Neave, H. (1990) *The Deming Dimension*, Knoxville: SPC Press.

Oakland, J. S. and Followell, R. F. (1990) *Statistical Process Control: A Practical Guide*, 2nd edn, Oxford: Butterworth-Heinemann.

Popplewell, B. and Wildsmith, A. (1988) *Becoming the Best*, Aldershot: Gower.

Price, F. (1985) *Right First Time*, Aldershot: Gower.

Price, F. (1990) *Right Every Time*, Aldershot: Gower.

Robson, M. (1989) *Quality Circles: A Practical Guide*, 2nd edn, Aldershot: Gower.

Rothery, B. (1991) *ISO 9000*, Aldershot: Gower.

Scherkenbach, W. W. (1991) *Deming's Road to Continual Improvement*, Knoxville: SPC Press.

Scholtes, P. R. (1990) *The Team Handbook*, Madison, NY: Joiner Associates.

Stebbing, L. (1989) *Quality Assurance: The Route to Efficiency and Competitiveness*, 2nd edn, Chichester: J. Wiley.

Tennor, A. R. and De Toro, I. J. (1992) *Total Quality Management – Three Steps to Continuous Improvement*, Reading, Mass.: Addison-Wesley.

Townsend, P. L. and Gebhardt, J. E. (1992) *Quality in Action – 93 Lessons in Leadership, Participation and Measurement*, New York: J. Wiley Press.

Wellins, R. S., Byham, W. C. and Wilson, J. M. (1991) *Empowered Teams*, Oxford: Jossey Bass.

Zairi, M. (1991) *Total Quality Management for Engineers*, Cambridge: Woodhead.

Zeithaml, V. A., Parasuraman, A. and Berry, L. L. (1990) *Delivering Quality Service: Balancing Customer Perceptions and Expectations*, New York: The Free Press.

55

GREEN MARKETING

Heribert Meffert and Manfred Kirchgeorg

ENVIRONMENTAL PROTECTION AS A CHALLENGE TO MARKET-ORIENTED MANAGEMENT

Especially during the 1980s people recognized the need to adapt management in such a way as to take account of the problems posed by environmental protection. This marked the beginning of a far-reaching process of evolution in theory and practice. Environmental issues get into the headlines and on to the political agendas of many nations of the world. As Figure 1 shows, a poll of 16 countries (4,600 interviews) found that more than four-fifths of respondents identified with the statement: 'I am very worried about the state of the environment'. More than half concurred that 'pollution must be reduced even if it means slower growth'. So environmental issues extend more and more into mainstream in the consumer's mind.

There is now a growing tendency to stress the need to anchor pollution control as a guiding principle in enterprises (Post and Altman 1992; Schmidheiny 1992; Fischer and Schot 1993; Meffert and Kirchgeorg 1993a; Steger 1993; Welford and Gouldson 1993; Winter 1993); and to view it as a task that must be adjusted to every level of functional responsibility.

In this context, attention is focused on two aspects of market-oriented environmental management. On the one hand, commercially oriented marketing often receives a great deal of criticism because it paved the way for our throwaway consumer society. A reorientation in marketing is regarded as an essential prerequisite for transforming the consumer society into a 'sustainable society'. On the other hand, the approaches developed by marketing are considered to be valuable instruments that might be used to accelerate the necessary environmentally oriented change in society. Green marketing or environmental marketing is expected to change the customers' outlook, provide a new direction for competition, and gain market acceptance for innovative environmental solutions.

Within the framework of environment-conscious management, green or

979

I am very worried about the state of the environment.

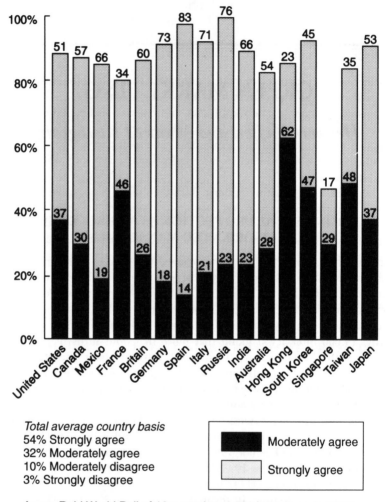

Total average country basis
54% Strongly agree
32% Moderately agree
10% Moderately disagree
3% Strongly disagree

■ Moderately agree

□ Strongly agree

Angus Reid World Poll of 16 countries, 4,600 interviews, in 1992.
Sample sizes differed; 8% margin of error for each country.

Figure 1   Worldwide environmental concern
Source: CNN/Angus Reid Group World Poll (1992) cited in Ottmann (1992)

environmental marketing has a duty to ensure that environmental pollution is avoided or reduced at every stage of market-oriented activity (planning, coordination, implementation and inspection). The aim is to achieve corporate objectives by permanently satisfying the needs of present or potential clients while exploiting competitive advantages and safeguarding social legitimacy (Meffert and Kirchgeorg 1993a).

In the long run ecologically and economically ineffective partial solutions could jeopardize the credibility and legitimacy of the enterprise in the market as well as in the community at large. To avoid this, it is essential that marketing management should develop a specific conception of green marketing. The planning procedure involves the following five steps:

1 Analysing relevant environmental problems that affect the enterprise at present or are likely to affect it at some point in the future. This analysis entails an assessment of opportunities and risks as well as advantages and disadvantages for marketing (informational aspect).
2 Broadening the enterprise's philosophy and objectives. This entails the formulation of environmental principles and goals (philosophical and teleological aspect).
3 Generating and evaluating options. This is to identify target groups and to find the right positioning and competitive strategy for green marketing concepts.
4 Modifying and integrating the utilization of marketing instruments in order to put green marketing principles into practice in horizontal and vertical competition (action and coordination aspect).
5 Supervising and regulating environment-oriented marketing activities as part of an ecological supervision scheme (control aspect).

APPROACHES TO GREEN MARKETING AND PREREQUISITES FOR ITS SUCCESS

Let us begin by considering to what extent green marketing can be implemented by a firm with some chances of success. The feasibility of such an undertaking will depend on the prevailing circumstances under which the firm must manage. As shown in Figure 2, we can distinguish four typical situations in which decisions are taken, and in which green marketing has to prove its worth (Kaas 1992; Meffert 1993).

To begin with we draw a distinction on the basis of whether an environmental benefit provides a surplus for the customer or whether the decision to buy an environment friendly product benefits the community as a whole (social benefit). Furthermore, we may make finer distinctions by considering whether environmental advantages are to be gained at a lower, identical or higher price; or at higher costs than traditional products. In addition to the price that must be paid one also has to take account of opportunity costs related to the purchase of environmentally oriented products (e.g. more time spent and more work involved in collecting information).

Provided that the consumer as an individual derives a benefit from the offer of environment friendly products, and that these goods provide better value than the traditional alternatives (field I), environmental advantages automatically result in competitive advantages, as when energy-saving electrical appliances are

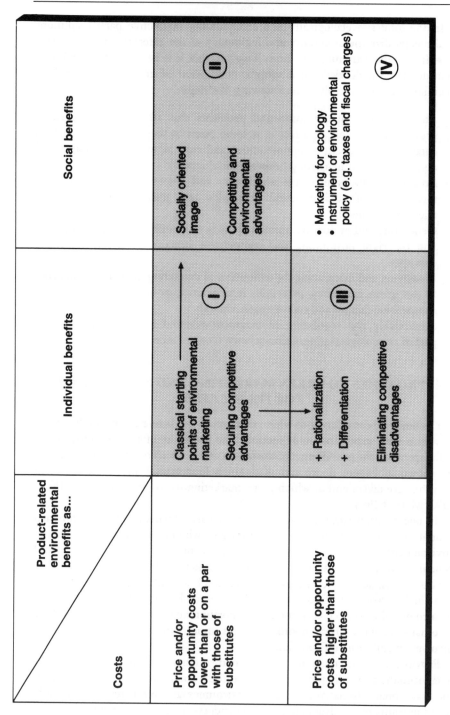

offered for sale at very reasonable prices. In addition to finding such solutions, the main task of green marketing must be to guarantee competitive advantage. If what benefits the environment provides a social benefit and not a surplus for the individual consumer but environment friendly products are cheaper than their substitutes, an entrepreneur who applies the principles of green marketing (field II) should have no difficulty in inducing the consumer to buy ecologically oriented products. All the entrepreneur has to do is to highlight the economic advantages of these goods or exploit their prestige value. Good examples of this are provided by the case of CFC-free aerosol cans or products made from reasonably priced recycled materials which are just as good as their traditional alternatives.

In reality environment friendly products are often more expensive, and their acquisition entails additional opportunity costs for the consumer (field III). More expensive recycled paper and organic food are familiar examples. If consumers associate individual benefits with environment friendly products, price-linked competitive disadvantages – provided they cannot be reduced by means of rationalization – may be offset with the aid of other green marketing instruments. Green marketing can provide a basis for successful market penetration by highlighting the notion of environmental benefit in advertising campaigns and targeting publicity on various groups of consumers according to their willingness or ability to pay.

The limits of green marketing are shown in field IV. If environment friendly products offer neither extra individual benefits nor economic incentives, we are confronted with a classical phenomenon of market failure. Traditional products are preferred to more environment friendly alternatives. In such a situation environmentally oriented behaviour may be dictated by state intervention and environmental protection acts or encouraged by tax incentives, as in the case of catalytic converters. Another solution is to exploit marketing-for-ecology concepts with a view to changing consumers' attitudes, thereby encouraging environmentally oriented behaviour through knowledge and understanding. In many cases, however, this objective cannot be achieved by the green marketing of a single enterprise. This is particularly true of waste disposal, a typical example being the purchase or use of products with expensive and bulky multi-way packing.

SITUATION ANALYSIS AS A STARTING-POINT

An ecologically oriented conception of marketing must be based on external and internal situation analysis. Green marketing lies in an area of tension between 'ecology push' (e.g. EC Directives (Bennett 1992), national environmental legislation, demands made by various social groups (Blumenfeld *et al.* 1992)) and 'ecology pull' (e.g. an increase in the demand for environment friendly products, pollution control as a factor of competition). We must study this area systematically, paying close attention to the determinants underlying the market

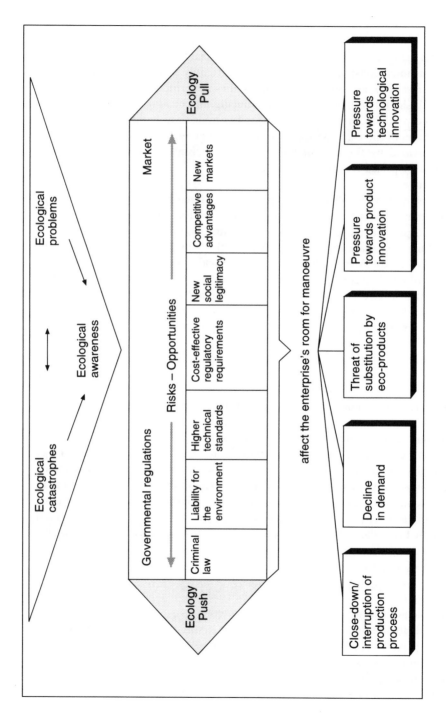

Figure 3 Environmental marketing in the tension between 'ecology push' and 'ecology pull'

Mounting pressures from four directions

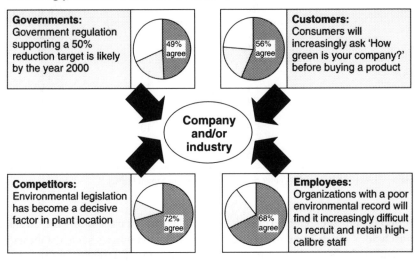

Figure 4 Empirical results about 'ecology push' and 'ecology pull' factors in worldwide industry

Source: Winsemius and Guntram (1992: 38)

forces as well as the interconnections that exist between these determinants (Figure 3).

Figure 4 shows that worldwide business leaders recognize that increased societal awareness of environmental problems is exerting ecology push and ecology pull on all sectors of industry from four directions: government regulations, customers, competitors and employees. The observation and analysis of developments in environmental legislation are an essential pre-requisite of proactive and holistic green marketing. Abidance by legal require-ments is held to be vital to legal legitimacy and cannot be exploited as a means of improving a company's public image. It is incumbent upon the environmental marketeer to take the initiative in working out solutions before environmental claims are put forward by the legislator or by various sections of the community.

Green marketing and the situation analysis is centred on the consumer. Table 1 shows the results of a multi-country study conducted in 1992 in 22 countries of the world; 81 per cent of Germans, 57 per cent of Americans and 40 per cent of Japanese have so far actively avoided products perceived as harmful. Other studies from Germany and the USA show results at lower levels. Extensive panel research as well as many opinion poll ratings reveal a well-marked north-south divide in the ecological awareness of European consumers. In the countries

Table 1 Personal environmental commitment in different countries of the world

Countries	Avoided environmentally harmful products %	Active in environment group %	Voted/worked for pro-environment candidate %
USA	57	11	19
Canada	77	12	15
Japan	40	4	14
Germany (West)	81	10	18
United Kingdom	75	10	10
Netherlands	68	7	21
Denmark	65	10	18

Source: Gallup, Health of the Planet Survey 1992, cited in Simon (1992)

bordering on the Mediterranean the ecological awareness of the average household is much less strongly developed than in countries such as Germany, Holland or Norway. Owing to such culture-specific differences in attitude, it may therefore prove quite difficult to work out a standardized strategy for green marketing which will gain acceptance throughout the countries (Simon 1992). Research has also shown that consumers in every part of Europe are more environment conscious than their actual behaviour would lead one to believe. In Germany, for instance, the percentage of environment-conscious households in 1993 was 60 per cent. Yet only 50 per cent of these households displayed consistently environment-oriented behaviour. Another consumer typology from the USA was published in 1992 by the Roper Organization. They identified five segments within the US population, each with a different level of environmental commitment: active environmentalists 25 per cent (True-Blue Greens 20 per cent and Greenback Greens 5 per cent); the swing group 31 per cent (Sprouts); not active environmentalists 44 per cent (Grousers 9 per cent; Basic Browns 35 per cent). In other words, there is a significant discrepancy between the consumers' intentions and their actual behaviour. Therefore green marketing concepts should be based on a segmentation of the target groups by ecological awareness or environmental commitment and environmentally oriented buying behaviour (McIntyre *et al.* 1993).

There are a great many different obstacles that prevent people from changing their behaviour. Empirical studies show that a reluctance to pay a higher price for pollution control is indeed a serious hindrance, but that there are many other impediments that have mainly to do with knowledge, quality, habits and motivation as well as specific situations (e.g. the availability of ecologically oriented products on the market). All these obstacles have been identified and even explained in terms of behaviour theory (see Monhemius 1992). Hence a great many decision-making situations in green marketing must be assigned to field II or field III in Figure 2.

Particular importance must be attributed to the analysis of the competitive position of the enterprise so that the risks and opportunities of competitive image building as an element of green marketing can be properly assessed. The focus of attention is on the analysis of driving forces that determine the degree of competitive intensity. These forces depend on the following factors (see Meffert and Kirchgeorg 1993a; Porter 1984):

- the risk that new competitors will enter the market;
- the threat posed by substitutes;
- suppliers' bargaining power;
- rivalry between enterprises within an industrial sector;
- buyer's bargaining power.

Distributors have assumed an increasingly active role as ecological gate-keepers (Hansen 1992). Since they have been directly affected by environmental problems as a result of their legal liability to take back bottles, packaging and the like, they have distinguished themselves as guardians of the environment in their role as intermediaries between the manufacturer and the consumer.

As a link between the manufacturer and the consumer, the distributor plays a key role within the context of the situational analysis. For the purposes of green marketing it is therefore necessary to gather information via trade-related data concerning the following elements: the ecological awareness of distributors; their environmental problems; or the extent to which distributors are prepared to cooperate in solving ecological problems.

With the aid of these criteria, a segmentation of impacted present and potential distributors may be helpful in working out appropriate vertical marketing options on the basis of channel-type-specific information.

The strategic market positions of enterprises are now also increasingly influenced by the behaviour of non-market groups like environmental stake-holders (e.g. media reporting, civic action groups and ecological campaigns) (Miles 1987; Dyllick 1989; Ottman 1992), so that classical forms of market research have to be expanded.

Opportunities and risks for the market and the environment must be balanced against corporate strengths and weaknesses. Depending on the particular situation in which an enterprise finds itself, the most relevant internal key factors will be as follows:

- the open-mindedness and flexibility of management with regard to ecological problems;
- damage to the environmental media (i.e. soil, water and air pollution) and consumption of resources associated with the procurement, production, sale, use and disposal of products;
- the proximity of the firm's range of services to environmental protection markets;
- the firm's public profile or 'visibility';

- the amount of funds available;
- the basic orientation of the marketing and corporate strategy.

Within the context of the internal situational analysis, environmental problems must be considered throughout the products' value chain and at every stage in the life cycle of the products and services offered by the enterprise. In order to develop an integrated pollution control concept we therefore need a green marketing situation analysis which cuts across functional and corporate divisions (e.g. suppliers, distributors and consumers). This makes it possible to identify potential opportunities for differentiation and competitive advantage at every stage in the value chain. Appropriate methodical instruments that might be used here include value chain analyses, product life cycle analysis or so-called eco-portfolios (see Meffert and Kirchgeorg 1993a: 104 ff.; Schaltegger and Sturm 1992; Winsemius and Hahn 1992; Linnanen et al. 1994).

STRATEGIC PLANNING IN GREEN MARKETING

On the basis of the situation analysis it is necessary to reconsider and modify corporate objectives and strategic corporate positions.

The 'sustainable development' model is often invoked in this context (Dietz and Simonis 1992; International Institute for Sustainable Development 1992; Schmidheiny 1992; Enquete-Kommission 1993; Meffert and Kirchgeorg 1993b). In accordance with this model the environmental orientation of an enterprise is to be determined by the principles of a circular flow economy; an approach involving the replacement of non-renewable by renewable resources, various forms of ecologically oriented technical progress, as well as worldwide cooperative action (Pearce and Turner 1990; Kuik and Verbruggen 1991). From these principles we must derive a number of operational environmental objectives for green marketing, objectives which can and must be achieved by a series of small but bold steps. Here are some typical examples of such objective contents:

- cutting down on the use of resources;
- reducing the energy consumption of certain products;
- giving wider publicity to innovations designed to protect the environment;
- investing more time in environmental counselling as after-sales service;
- attaining certain return rates by means of retrodistribution;
- increasing the consumer's willingness to purchase more environment friendly products.

When defining the strategic orientation of green marketing, we can draw a distinction between reactive and proactive base strategies. We speak of reactive behaviour when it is only legal requirements that induce a firm to take account of ecological demands made by limited sections of the community. In such a case the company meets minimal ecological demands, but in the long term it forfeits its chance of giving itself a clear image as an ecologically oriented enterprise.

988

Empirical studies confirm that in the long run offensive and innovative environmental strategies offer better chances of market success than passive or selectively oriented strategies. This is particularly true of psychographic success parameters such as competence and image. However, the other side of the coin is that the application of offensive and innovative strategies entails higher risks when a firm is attempting to tap a new market (Kirchgeorg 1990; Arnfalk and Thidell 1992; Meffert and Kirchgeorg 1993c).

When offensive environmental strategies are pursued, special attention must be given to the requirements of the customer and the competitive position of the enterprise in order that actions in favour of the environment can be exploited to gain customer and competitive advantage. Competitive strategies can take several generic forms: quality leadership or differentiation, cost leadership and focusing on a particular niche or submarket. The decision in favour of one of these strategies will inevitably depend on the likelihood of gaining at least an important, obvious und defendable competitive advantage.

Ecologically oriented differentiation strategies aim to outdo competitors in satisfying the customers' demands with regard to the environmental compatibility of products and manufacturing processes. A distinction may be drawn between cases in which a firm merely meets this demand within certain niches and cases where it succeeds in attaining this objective in all of the existing market segments it caters to.

Regardless of whether competitive strategies are oriented towards a global market or a submarket, it is always essential that advantages gained by differentiation should be durable and defendable. The success of ecologically oriented competitive strategies depends on the extent to which the ecological advantages of products are anchored at every stage of the corporate value chain.

Holistic eco-strategies that ensure sustainable differentiation advantages must overcome barriers between corporate functions and entities and embrace the entire cycle of production, utilization and disposal ('cradle-to-grave' approach). Differentiation strategies are particularly relevant in the cases indicated in field III of Figure 2 (i.e. in cases where the producers of environment friendly products expect consumers to pay a higher price).

If a firm pursues a cost leadership strategy, what distinguishes it from its competitors is the fact that it can whittle down its unit costs by means of consistent product and process optimization and pass this cost benefit on to the market in the form of lower prices. With regard to the prevailing conditions in green marketing the aim is to exploit cost leadership with a view to gaining a position in field I or field II (see Figure 2). The success of cost leadership strategies depends on whether the enterprise succeeds in wresting sizeable market share from its rivals, thus enabling it to exploit degression and experience curve effects. This strategy, therefore, will only be successful if customers are more responsive to price arguments than to particular utility expectations as purchasing criteria.

Ecologically oriented competitive image-building can be legitimately based on a cost and price leadership strategy if the unit costs of new environment friendly products are lower than those of comparable traditional goods. Such a situation is conceivable if ecologically harmful and expensive raw materials can be replaced by cheaper and more environment friendly raw materials or the amount of expensive raw materials used in the production process can be reduced by employing recycled material.

Most people agree that there is little chance that environment friendly product innovation will result in substantial cost benefits. As a rule, ecologically oriented innovations are accompanied by cost increases which are incompatible with the requirements of successful cost leadership strategies.

. When competitive strategies are worked out, the timing of activities with respect to competitors assumes paramount importance. The main question is whether a firm which has devised solutions to environmental problems should enter the market as a pioneer or a market follower. A number of empirical studies have shown that timing, unlike other problems associated with environmental innovation, has been submitted to exceptionally precise and subtle analysis (see Steger 1993). On the one hand, attention is drawn to the fact that eco-friendly products have to contend with considerable market resistance. This is particularly so whenever they have to be offered for sale at prices above those of traditional products. In such a case a firm's rash attempt to distinguish itself in the market may prove counterproductive if it is foiled by competitors and critical consumer groups. On the other hand, pioneers in pollution control have every prospect of creating a durable acceptable image for their products, thereby achieving a kind of success which can only be attained with the aid of a first-to-market strategy.

In green marketing the manufacturer also has to decide whether the application of an environmental strategy necessitates vertical integration in concert with distributors (Meffert and Kirchgeorg 1993a). In order to size up the situation the producer has to be informed about distributors' basic ecological options. If traders decide in favour of one particular basic eco-strategy this will largely determine the extent to which the manufacturer will be able to gain acceptance for his green marketing concepts. Figure 5 shows basic strategic attitudes which may be adopted by manufacturers and traders. If both manufacturers and traders pursue an offensive pollution control strategy, cooperation may provide further scope for innovation. It often affords opportunities for exploiting ecological know-how at every stage in the distribution process, thereby greatly facilitating the application of integrated solutions to environmental problems. However, manufacturers and distributors may come into conflict with each other in those cases where their environmental strategies diverge.

If the manufacturer pursues an offensive eco-strategy and traders apply a defensive one, pollution control will be a bone of contention between them. In this kind of situation the producer may attempt to circumvent ecologically defensive marketing intermediaries. To this end he may set up his own field

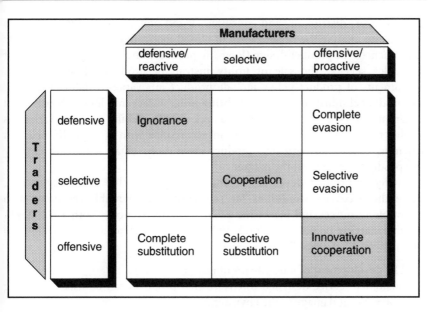

		Manufacturers		
		defensive/ reactive	selective	offensive/ proactive
T r a d e r s	defensive	Ignorance		Complete evasion
	selective		Cooperation	Selective evasion
	offensive	Complete substitution	Selective substitution	Innovative cooperation

Figure 5   Basic eco-strategies in vertical marketing

organization or look for new marketing intermediaries. If, on the other hand, it is the traders who pursue an offensive eco-strategy, their task will be greatly facilitated by the increase in the number of eco-friendly products now offered in many lines of merchandise. They will find it relatively easy to exclude certain suppliers and replace them by producers pursuing more offensive eco-strategies. This substitution process enables traders to avoid practically all kinds of marketing conflicts by selecting suppliers who share their own ecologically oriented marketing conception.

DESIGNING AN ECOLOGICALLY ORIENTED MARKETING MIX

Once due consideration has been given to customers, competitors and distributors, an ecologically oriented marketing mix has to be devised as part of a global environmental strategy (Henion and Kinnear 1976; Charter 1992; Ottman 1992; Peattie 1992; Hopfenbeck 1993; Meffert and Kirchgeorg 1993a).

Product policy

A product life cycle analysis (LCA) (Petersen 1992) can provide a sound basis for more eco-friendly solutions to the problems associated with product and packaging policies. In order to resolve product-related environmental problems, it is necessary to analyse the various spheres of responsibility of the supplier, manufacturer, distributor, and consumer. From now on marketing specialists will have to analyse the organization of closed loop value chains with all of its consequences for product design (long-life products, the growing importance of after-sales service, the sale of utility instead of products) (see Figure 6). Instruments of product policy include product innovation, product variation, and product elimination designed to bring programmes into line with ecological requirements (see Ostmeier 1990; Türck 1990). While product variations involve modifying existing products in accordance with ecologically oriented demands, ecologically oriented product innovations entail launching entirely new product concepts on the market.

Intelligent product development and closed loop value chain engineering create the necessary conditions for replacing non-renewable resources with renewable resources and increasing ecological effectiveness (Noth 1992: S.49). Possible starting points are (Türck 1990; Oliff 1991; Stahel 1991; Baram and Dillon 1993; Bhat 1993; Rushton 1993):

1 The development of long-life products.
2 Customer service designed to ensure that products can be used for a long time without damage to the environment.
3 Multiple use and utilization strategies ('product stewardship').

If it proves impossible to adapt existing product concepts to ecologically oriented requirements by means of an innovation or variation policy, a product elimination process ought to be initiated as part of a credible green marketing programme. Should any problems arise, particularly at the utilization and disposal stages, recall actions or special disposal services may be necessary.

The introduction of packaging regulation in most European countries obliges both producers and retailers to develop eco-friendly packaging and logistic alternatives as part of their packaging policy. They have to devise ways and means of reducing superfluous packaging or facilitating the recycling of packaging without jeopardizing the transport protection, dimensioning, presentation, quality or information functions of packaging.

In this context eco-friendly solutions often require a modification of the logistics and goods representation at the point of sale. The preparation of an ecological balance sheet for packaging materials and packaging systems (e.g. non-returnable and multi-way packaging) will ultimately be the only means of finding out which form of packaging can be considered the most environment friendly. Since in some cases packaging cannot be entirely eliminated, recycling and reuse must be envisaged from the outset when packaging is conceived and designed. It is particularly important to create new applications and markets for recycled products in order to ensure that packaging materials returned via retrodistribution channels are reused.

When shaping a brand policy one should consider to what extent a firm's positioning objectives may be attained by means of a different brand image or additional markings such as the German 'Blue Angel' eco-label used as a symbol

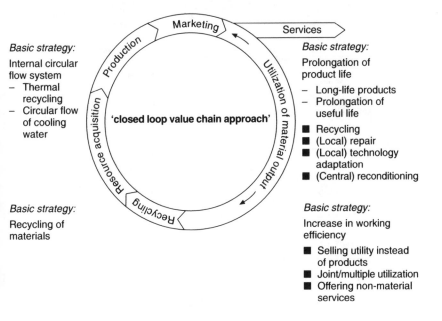

Basic strategy:
Internal circular
flow system
– Thermal
  recycling
– Circular flow
  of cooling
  water

Basic strategy:
Prolongation of
product life
– Long-life products
– Prolongation of
  useful life
■ Recycling
■ (Local) repair
■ (Local) technology
  adaptation
■ (Central) reconditioning

Basic strategy:
Recycling of
materials

Basic strategy:
Increase in working
efficiency
■ Selling utility instead
  of products
■ Joint/multiple utilization
■ Offering non-material
  services

Figure 6   Starting-points for product policy in a closed loop value chain

of environmental friendliness in Germany. The Blue Angel eco-labelling
scheme was introduced in 1978. In 1993 over 4,000 products carried the label;
80 per cent of German households are aware of the eco-label, and it receives
widespread support from manufacturers. Since 1991 there is a new EC eco-
labelling regulation in preparation. The objectives of this EC regulation are to
promote products with a reduced environmental impact throughout their entire
life cycle and to provide better information to consumers on the environmental
impacts of products. The EC eco-labelling scheme, issued as a regulation,
applies directly to all member states and is EC-wide. It is a voluntary scheme
and should be self-financing (Welford 1992).

In order to anchor the environmental utility of products as a confidence
characteristic in the consumer's mind, a company may envisage the creation of
its own eco-friendly brands or the exploitation of environmental seals or
certificates awarded by neutral institutions such as the Federal Environment
Office, technical control boards or one of the various environmental associations.
An example for helpful consumer environmental information is the consumer
guidebook *Shopping for a Better World* in the USA. The guide shows consumers
how they can help the environment and contribute to solving various social
problems by skewing purchase towards companies with outstanding rewards for
green achievement (Tasaday 1991). The shopping guide lists over 2,400 brands
of consumer products according to their manufacturers' records on 11 social

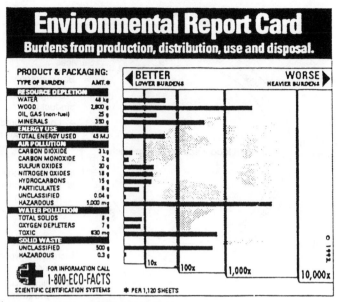

2 PLY BATH TISSUE FROM NON-INTEGRATED VIRGIN MILL
(SYSTEM BOUNDARY EXCLUDES ECOSYSTEM)

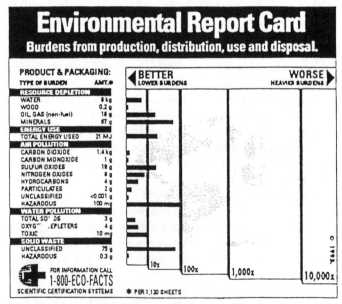

TREE-FREE 2-PLY 100% RECYCLED BATH TISSUE

Figure 7 Environmental Report Card in the USA
Source: Scientific Certification Systems

994

criteria. According to research results 78 per cent of readers have changed brands after reading the guide (Ottman 1992).

In the USA there exists also a Green Report Card (Figure 7). This card measures products on life-cycle analysis. The Scientific Certifications Systems Corp. includes subsets under five basic categories: resource, depletion, energy use, air pollution, and solid waste. How a product scores in all five areas is clearly displayed on the Green Report Card. So the consumer can get detailed information about products and the burdens from production, distribution, use and disposal (Schlossberg 1993).

In many cases a company's after-sales service offers the only chance of exerting direct or indirect influence on the way in which products are used, consumed or disposed of. Preventive customer service may provide some scope for competitive image-building, and it can help to reduce environmental pollution caused at the utilization stage by heating systems, motor vehicles and the like.

Communications policy

Activities associated with product policy should be backed up by an environmentally oriented communications policy. The integration of environmental arguments into product and corporate advertising could improve the corporate image by highlighting the firm's competence in matters relating to the environment. One of the major challenges that must be met by corporate communications experts in this domain is that information about corporate behaviour with respect to the environment is brought to public notice not only via controlled communication channels, but also to an increasing extent through reports presented by the media, environmental organizations and administrative agencies. This being so, the specialists who shape corporate communications policy must take account of such institutions and opinion leaders.

Firms ought to work out holistic, environment friendly solutions to their problems before offering information to the public. Yet even when this necessary condition is fulfilled, problems often arise when companies attempt to apply classical advertising techniques (e.g. emotional and empirically oriented sales messages) to the organization of credible, environmentally oriented communications campaigns. Taking account of a company's initial situation and environmental vulnerability, communications experts must identify the target groups to whom environmentally oriented marketing messages can, must, or ought to be transmitted. They must also determine to what extent communication in the relevant sector is dominated by environmental arguments (Peattie 1992). Content analyses of ecologically oriented advertising in print media have been made at the Marketing Institute, and the research findings show that since the middle of 1980 there has been an increase in the emotional content of advertising messages. We may therefore conclude that environmentally oriented advertising has recourse to classical activation patterns in order to attract consumers' attention to advertisements amidst the welter of information to which they are exposed on a daily basis. Traditional methods of communication may be complemented by various types of environmental sponsorship (e.g. cooperation with environmental associations demonstrating deep commitment to pollution control; Bruhn 1990).

Communications policy must also take account of statutory requirements to furnish information. In this context mention must be made of a Directive issued by the EC Council of Ministers in 1990. This Directive, which relates to free access to corporate information about the environment, is to be incorporated into the law of each European country. Third parties are to be allowed access to corporate environmental information made available to administrative bodies. This means that firms will have to check through their files to find out exactly what corporate data have been transmitted to administrative bodies. Such data may cause considerable embarrassment to the company if they are brought to public notice and it turns out that they are not concordant with the information hitherto provided by the firm as part of its communications policy. In order to avoid such embarrassing situations, companies will have to be less secretive about malfunctions, accidents and other environmental hazards associated with industrial activities. They will have to provide relevant information to all of the social groups concerned (i.e. local residents, environmental associations and the media). Empirical studies relating to the chemical industry demonstrate that confidence in a firm may even be boosted by the proactive publication of information about environmental hazards. However, this is only possible in cases where a company has already acquired a certain reputation and a certain measure of credibility in the eyes of the public. In order to reach a consensus on the acceptance of environmental hazards, industrialists ought to seek a dialogue with all of the social groups concerned, making use of concepts related to citizen participation, citizens' advisory councils, panel discussions and the like (Miles 1987; Jungermann et al. 1990).

Distribution policy

The implementation of the closed loop value chain in green marketing forces us to rethink the distribution mix. The packaging regulation, and the amendments to the Waste Disposal Law in particular, have created new conditions for the design of the distribution strategy. In many cases producers have a legal obligation to take back used packaging and products. Just as producers have traditionally had to choose between various kinds of distribution channels, so they now have to concern themselves increasingly with the task of choosing an appropriate retrodistribution channel.

In many cases solutions worked out on a sectoral basis seem to be proving quite efficient, but producers ought to consider setting up their own retro-distribution systems as a competitive strategy, and possibly also for other purposes. By integrating external organizations into retrodistributional logistics and recycling processes one may create hybrid organizations which make coordination quite difficult.

Beyond that, the logistic system ought to be expanded to take account of resource- and environment-related factors (energy and industrial pollution) in addition to cost factors, which have hitherto been the sole preoccupation of the business community. Special attention should also be given to the consequences that the overburdening of the transport systems can have for the logistics of vertical marketing. Logistic operating rates can be lowered by standardizing freight containers, changing the composition of orders (delivery of minimum quantities) or by grouping orders from firms that supply goods to the same customer.

Pricing

Decisions relating to pricing are mainly determined by the consumer's sensitivity to price, but the need to integrate the cost of legally stipulated pollution control now plays an increasingly important role in this domain. Thus, for instance, firms mapping out their pricing strategies now have to take account of the packaging regulation and the amendments to the Waste Disposal Law, which necessitate more serious consideration of the costs of recycling and environment friendly waste disposal.

Cost increases due to pollution control can often only be justified by asking environment-conscious buyers to pay a higher price. It has already been emphasized that consumers are still very reluctant to pay a higher price for pollution control. This is especially true in cases where traditional alternatives are available in the market.

Pricing is therefore a matter of paramount importance in green marketing. Pricing strategies should be based on a segmentation of actual and potential target groups classified with the aid of three criteria:

1 Ecological awareness.
2 Personal affectedness.
3 Willingness to pay a price for pollution control.

Segments displaying varying degrees of price sensitivity constitute the basis for price differentiation strategies.

As a matter of principle, lower introductory prices for eco-friendly products help customers to reorient their buyer behaviour, thereby facilitating a more rapid diffusion of eco-friendly products. Combined costing at the expense of non eco-friendly products can ensure a necessary balance here. The return of used packaging and products raises the question of pricing incentives for retrodistribution. For example, retrodistribution rates can be increased by charging deposits, but deposits may also have an inhibiting effect on buyers, thereby limiting total sales. Further points of departure should be examined

997

Table 2 Environmental best implementation practices

Component	Characteristics of management systems
Senior-level support and commitment	• Top-level commitment, direction and leadership • Senior executive to champion programmes • Adequate environmental funding and commitment
Information management and communication	• Corporate environmental policy statement • Policy goals translated into active procedures • Communication and reinforcement of environmental commitment • Management information system • Systematic feedback/learning
Regulatory knowledge and tracking	• Awareness of the full range of regulatory requirements • Systematic approach to tracking regulatory changes • Regulatory influence on upcoming requirements
Integration of environmental management into business operations	• Consideration of environmental issues in key business strategies and major investments • Consideration of environment in market-end pricing analyses • Competitive analysis on environmentally driven costs
Organizational interfaces that promote environmental effectiveness	• Organizational structure that supports effective communication and matches needs and culture of company • Clearly defined environmental roles and responsibilities • Strong horizontal and vertical reporting relationships with complete system of environmental authorities
Employee awareness and training	• Establish ownership for environmental programmes by linking efforts to performance appraisals • Training to convey environmental ethics to workforce • Focus on accident prevention training as well as worker right-to-know programmes
Risk assessment and management	• Environmental compliance audits of facilities • Assessment of raw materials/product/operations health, safety, and environmental risks • Environmental due diligence assessments for property transfers

within the context of terms policy (e.g. special annual quantity discounts or methods of financing eco-friendly product variants). Especially where consumer durables are concerned, green marketing specialists ought to draw the consumer's attention to ways of obtaining compensation through government subsidies for higher expenditure on pollution control (e.g. tax benefits, grants for regenerative power plants).

The examples illustrating various aspects of the marketing mix problem show that better environmental quality only goes hand in hand with better sales development where environmental requirements are fulfilled within the context of an integrated green marketing programme.

THE IMPLEMENTATION OF GREEN MARKETING

Green marketing must be implemented within the context of an overall concept of ecologically oriented management. In many cases implementation inevitably entails a change in values and cultural conceptions (Hoffman 1993), which affects every corporate function and necessitates a high degree of adaptability in the world of day-to-day realities. Table 2 shows practices for the implementation process.

The successful implementation of environmental concepts will depend to a large extent on a combination of the top-down and bottom-up approaches designed to gain general acceptance for new ideas and make a strong impact on all sections of the community.

Owing to the complexity and the interdisciplinary nature of environmental problems it is particularly important that the function-oriented way of thinking that predominates in many firms should be complemented by a more holistic or integrated point of view. This is closely related to the question of whether pollution control ought to be integrated as an independent organizational form into existing corporate structures. Owing to the numerous tasks and special problems that have to be coped with, it will often be necessary to set up an environmental protection organization in order not to put too great a strain on existing departments. This does not mean that the individual employee no longer shares responsibility for pollution control. He can apply to a staff unit for pollution control if he requires competent advice or information relating collectively to several functions.

In order to coordinate and supervise the implementation of environmental measures we shall have to complement classical controlling with a type of ecologically oriented controlling which will provide decision-makers with planning, regulatory and supervisory instruments for working out and applying an environmental strategy. The scope of traditional controlling will have to be widened by attributing particular importance to the recording of information on the quantity structure of corporate activities. At the implementation stage ecological controlling has to fulfil a double function: to show where information and coordination are required, and to ensure close coordination among all those concerned by means of interface management.

REFERENCES

Arnfalk, P. and Thidell, A. (1992) *Environmental Management in the Swedish Manufacturing Industry*, Lund: Lund University, Dept of Industrial Environmental Economics.

Baram, M. S. and Dillon, P. S. (1993) 'Forces shaping the development and use of product stewardship in the private sector', in K. Fischer and J. Schot (eds) *Environmental Strategies for Industries*, Washington: Island Press.

Bennett, E. (1992) 'European industry and the environment: the developing role of the EC and a strategy for industry', *European Environment* 2 (6): 2–4.

Bhat, V. N. (1993) 'A blueprint for green product development', *Industrial Management* 35 (2): 4–7.

Blumenfeld, K., Earle III, R. and Annighöfer, F. (1992) 'Environmental performance and business strategy', *PRISM* 4th Quarter: 65–85.

Bruhn, M. (1990) *Sozio- und Umweltsponsoring*, München: Gabler-Verlag.

Charter, H. (ed.) (1992) *Greener Marketing*, Sheffield: Greenleaf Publishing.

Dietz, F. J., Simonis, U. E. and Straaten, J. van der (eds) (1992) *Sustainability and Environmental Policy*, Berlin: Edition Sigma Bohn Verlag.

Dyllick, Th. (1989) *Management der Umweltbeziehungen*, Wiesbaden: Gabler-Verlag.

Enquete-Kommission 'Schutz des Menschen und der Umwelt' des Deutschen Bundestages (ed.) (1993) *Verantwortung für die Zukunft – Wege zum nachhaltigen Umgang mit Stoff- und Materialströmen*, Bonn: Enquete-Kommission.

Fischer, K. and Schot, J. (eds) (1993) *Environmental Strategies for Industries*, Washington: Island Press.

Hansen, U. (1992) 'Umweltmanagement im Handel', in U. Steger (ed.) *Handbuch des Umweltschutzes*, München: Beck Verlag.

Henion, K. E. and Kinnear, T. C. (eds) (1976) 'Ecological marketing', *Educational Workshop Series* 1, Austin: American Marketing Association.

Hoffman, A. J. (1993) 'The importance of fit between individual values and organisational culture in the greening of industry', *Business Strategy and the Environment*, Winter: 10–19.

Hopfenbeck, W. (1993) *The Green Management Revolution*, Hemel Hempstead: Verlag Moderne Industrie.

International Institute for Sustainable Development (1992) *Business Strategy for Sustainable Development*, Winnipeg, Manitoba: International Institute for Sustainable Development.

Jungermann, H., Rohrmann, B. and Wiedemann, P. M. (eds) (1990) *Risiko-Konzepte, Risiko-Konflikt, Risiko-Kommunikation, Monographien des Forschungszentrums Jülich* 3, Jülich: Forschungszentrum.

Kaas, K. P. (1992) *Marketing und Neue Institutionenlehre*, Arbeitspapier Nr. 1 aus dem Forschungsprojekt Marketing und ökonomische Theorie, Frankfurt a.M.

Kirchgeorg, M. (1990) *Ökologieorientiertes Unternehmensverhalten*, Wiesbaden: Gabler-Verlag.

Kuik, O. and Verbruggen, H. (eds) (1991) *In Search of Indicators of Sustainable Development*, Dordrecht, Boston, London: Kluwer Academic Publ.

Linnanen, L., Boström, T. and Miettinen, P. (1994) *Life Cycle Management*, Espoo: Weilin and Goos.

McIntyre, R. P., Meloche, M. S. and Lewis, S. L. (1993) 'National culture as a macro tool for environmental sensitivity segmentation', in D. W. Cravens and P. R. Dickson (eds) *Enhancing Knowledge Development in Marketing, 1993 AMA Educator's Proceedings*, Chicago: American Marketing Association.

Meffert, H. (1993) 'Umweltbewußtes Konsumentenverhalten. Ökologieorientiertes Marketing im Spannungsfeld zwischen Individual – und Sozialnutzen', *Marketing ZfP* 1: 51–4.

Meffert, H. and Kirchgeorg, M. (1993a) *Marktorientiertes Umweltmanagement*, 2nd edn, Stuttgart: Poeschel-Verlag.
Meffert, H. and Kirchgeorg, M. (1993b) 'Das neue Leitbild Sustainable Development – der Weg ist das Ziel', *Harvard Business Manager* 15 (2): 34–45.
Meffert, H. and Kirchgeorg, M. (1993c) 'Environmental protection and corporate strategy of German companies', in D. W. Cravens and P. R. Dickson (eds) *Enhancing Knowledge Development in Marketing, 1993 AMA Educator's Proceedings*, Chicago: American Marketing Association.
Miles, R. (1987) *Managing the Corporate Social Environment*, Englewood Cliffs, N.J.: Prentice Hall.
Monhemius, K. Ch. (1992) *Umweltbewußtes Kaufverhalten von Konsumenten*, Frankfurt: Lang-Verlag.
Noth, K. (1992) 'Environmental business management', *Management Development Series* 30, Geneva.
Oliff, M. D. (1991) 'Corporate challenges for an age of reconsumption', *The Columbia Journal of World Business*, Fall: 7–21.
Ostmeier, H. (1990) *Ökologieorientierte Produktinnovationen*, Frankfurt a.M.: Lang-Verlag.
Ottman, J. A. (1992) *Green Marketing*, Lincolnwood Ill.: NTL Publishing Group.
Pearce, D. and Turner, R. K. (1990) *Economics of Natural Resources and Environment*, New York: Harvester Wheatsheaf.
Peattie, K. (1992) *Green Marketing*, London: Pitman.
Petersen, B. (1992) *Environmental Assessment of Products*, Helsinki: UETP-EEE, The Finnish Association of Graduate Engineers.
Porter, M. (1984) *Wettbewerbsstrategie*, Frankfurt: The Free Press.
Post, J. E. and Altman, B. W. (1992) 'Models of corporate greening', *Markets, Politics, and Social Performance* 13: 3–29.
Rushton, B. M. (1993) 'How protecting the environment impacts R&D in the United States', *Research Technology Management* 36 (3): 13–21.
Schaltegger, S. C. and Sturm, A. J. (1992) *Ökologieorientierte Entscheidungen im Unternehmen*, Bern: Haupt-Verlag.
Schlossberg, H. (1993) 'Hardware industry understands importance of going green', *Marketing News* 27 (21): 10.
Schmidheiny, S. and the Business Council for Sustainable Development (1992) *Changing Course – A Global Business Perspective on Development and the Environment*, Cambridge: Massachusetts Institute of Technology.
Simon, F. L. (1992) 'Marketing green products in the triad', *Columbia Journal of World Business*, Fall–Winter: 269–85.
Stahel, (1991) *Langlebigkeit und Materialrecycling*, Essen: Vulkan Verlag.
Steger, U. (1993) *Umweltmanagement*, 2nd edn, Frankfurt: Gabler-Verlag.
Tasaday, L. (1991) *Shopping for a Better Environment*, New York: Meadowbrook Press.
Türck, R. (1990) *Das ökologische Produkt*, Diss., Frankfurt a.M.: Campus-Verlag.
Welford, R. (1992) 'A guide to eco-labelling and the EC eco-labelling scheme', *European Environment* 2 (6): 13–15.
Welford, R. and Gouldson, A. (1993) *Environmental Management & Business Strategy*, London: Pitman.
Winsemius, P. and Guntram, U. (1992) 'Responding to the environmental challenge', *Business Horizons*, March–April: 37–45.
Winsemius, P. and Hahn, W. (1992) 'Environmental option assessment', *The Columbia Journal of World Business*, Fall–Winter: 249–66.
Winter, G. (1993) *Business and the Environment*, München: Beck-Verlag.

FURTHER READING

Charter, H. (ed.) (1992) *Greener Marketing*, Sheffield: Greenleaf Publishing.
Fischer, K. and Schot, J. (eds) (1993) *Environmental Strategies for Industries*, Washington: Island Press.
Henion, K. E. and Kinnear, T. C. (eds) (1976) 'Ecological marketing', *Educational Workshop Series* 1, Austin: American Marketing Association.
Meffert, H. and Kirchgeorg, M. (1993) *Marktorientiertes Umweltmanagement*, 2nd edn, Stuttgart: Poeschel-Verlag.
Ottman, J. A. (1992) *Green Marketing*, Lincolnwood Ill: NTL Publishing Group.
Post, J. E. and Altman, B. W. (1992) 'Models of corporate greening', *Markets, Politics, and Social Performance* 13: 3–29.

56

THE FUTURE OF MARKETING

Michael J. Baker

INTRODUCTION

In the call for papers for the AMA's 1994 Winter Educators' Conference the organizers set the theme as 'Renaissance in Marketing Thought and Practice' and observed:

The ongoing interplay of marketing theory and practice has led to several new research areas. As a field, our agenda now features topics such as Relationship Marketing, Strategic Alliances, Managing Brand Equity, Total Quality Management and Market-oriented Management, among others.

The emergence of such topics raises at least two provocative issues for marketing scholars. First, are we reinventing the wheel? Even though the general topic headings may be new, how new are the specific research questions related to each area? ... Second, interest in many of these emerging topics extends beyond the traditional domain of marketing. Unfortunately, interdisciplinary collaboration in the conduct of research in marketing is rare.

A very similar view was expressed in the *Journal of Marketing Management* (9.2, 1993) in which the Editor wrote:

As a confirmed supporter of the concept of the product life cycle (PLC) it is interesting to speculate on its application to the study of marketing as a business discipline. While the establishment of the first chair in the subject can be dated to the 1880s most would agree that marketing only really took off in the mid 1950s to early 1960s with a number of seminal contributions by authors such as Peter Drucker, Joel Dean, Ted Levitt and Eugene McCarthy. Since that time the number of students opting to study the subject at the undergraduate and postgraduate levels has accelerated rapidly and resulted in a significant expansion in the number of academics researching and teaching the subject.

The question is, however, at what stage will growth begin to slow and the 'market' approach saturation and maturity? The question is prompted not by a concern with the quality of contributions to *JMM* but a more broadly based awareness that research and publication in marketing might be approaching a plateau. Two factors prompt this observation. The first is the decline in the incremental value added by current research/publication. The second is the trend towards increasing marketing's domain to the point when it will subsume other fields whose practitioners might legitimately consider to be quite distinct from marketing.

The decline in incremental value added is noticeable everywhere. To a marked degree it is fuelled by the feeling that one should only cite the latest work relating to one's topic. As a result earlier path breaking and insightful contributions tend to be overlooked or ignored and much of what passes for original work is a weak replication of seminal contributions published 30 or 40 years ago. The extension of marketing's domain is apparent in the flurry of publication about internal marketing and relationship marketing. To an old-fashioned marketer like myself much of this writing gives a distinct impression that the authors have just discovered the subject of human resource management, and concepts such as motivation and leadership. While I am all for this, I am not sure we are not doing marketing a disservice if we seek to take over rather than integrate these concepts. Either way both phenomena are symptomatic of the 'hunting' behaviour observed in biological life cycles when an organism perceives a limit to growth and searches frantically for a means to get round it.

Perhaps it is a symptom of advancing years that what is regarded as history by a new generation was an important element in the education and experience of the old. For the older generation nostalgia and resistance to change may cause them to cling to the old-fashioned and outmoded ways of yesteryear. For the new generation a desire to think for themselves and make their own impact on the affairs of the world may lead them to overlook, or, worse still, ignore, hard-won lessons of the past.

Such oversight or ignorance may well lead to a condition first diagnosed over thirty years ago by one of marketing's most influential scholars and authors, Ted Levitt, in his seminal 'Marketing Myopia' (1960). Levitt along with Keith (1960) is widely regarded as one of the founding fathers of the 'marketing management' model which has dominated much of marketing education and practice for the past thirty years or so. While this model has been subject to much criticism in recent years (Webster 1992; Marion 1993; Gummesson 1993; Grönroos 1993 – with its emphasis on the Four Ps of Product, Price, Place and Promotion – McCarthy 1960; Kotler 1967), one feels bound to question whether or not it is myopic to discard it in favour of a new-found enthusiasm for relationship marketing, etc.? Will our concern for recency (no citation more than ten years old is worth citing – possibly true for much of the physical sciences) blur our vision of what is relevant? In ignoring the past will we reinvent what is already known or, by taking cognisance of the past, will we see a renaissance in marketing theory and practice which properly reflects our rich inheritance?

In other words, what is the future of marketing? To answer this question it will be helpful to take stock of where we are currently.

WHERE ARE WE NOW?

In our opening paragraph we cited the AMA Conference Chairman's question concerning the possible reinvention of currently fashionable topics. To address this issue Park and Smith asserted that: 'Answers to these questions call for the benchmarks provided by state-of-the-art reviews in traditional areas of inquiry. However, there is a noticeable shortage of such progress updates'.

In and of itself this shortage is indicative of a lack of interest in the past. In building our new temple of knowledge we bury the foundations of the old with scarcely a thought as to their ability to support the new edifice. If we are wrong then, surely, the whole structure is liable to topple about our ears. Given the scope and complexity of modern marketing no single chapter could define fully the foundations of modern marketing thought. Nonetheless, it will be useful to sketch some of the outlines of our subject to establish the present *status quo* before attempting to address the more challenging question *Quo vadis?*

As a basis for answering our first question – where are we now – as good a place to begin as any is the plenary session of the 1993 AMA Winter Educators' Conference. At that meeting a distinguished panel consisting of Hal Kassarjian, Sidney Levy and Stephen Greyser under the chairmanship of Jagdish Sheth offered their 'Reflections on the Evolution of the Field of Marketing'.

Hal Kassarjian opened the session by giving a broad perspective of the evolution of marketing during this century. In his view, prior to World War II, most professors of marketing were trained as economists and research on the subject was largely of a narrative nature with some underpinning of economic theorizing. Interestingly, in his view, it was the migration of Europeans to the USA that introduced behavioural concepts into the marketing repertoire. Thus it was George Katona whose psychological analysis of economic behaviour broke the mould and paved the way for the development of media studies and motivation research associated with the names of Gallup, Nielsen, Kantril, Lazerfeld, Dichter, Hertzog, and many others.

The 1960s saw the growth of cognitive research and the migration of scientific ideas from other disciplines. Again, many of the scholars such as Bass, Levy and Silk, who were prominent in this field, were strongly linked to the positivist influence of Europeans.

During the 1970s marketing became seen as the handmaiden of the industrial/militaristic complex. This association prompted many marketing scholars to seek methods for broadening the base of their subject into other areas and saw the introduction of social marketing and marketing for non-profit organizations. Consumerism re-emerged as a potent force. However, the emphasis upon the consumers in the 1970s saw something of a counter revolution in the 1980s with many challenging the concept of the learning consumer and the emergence of ideas of low involvement and muddling through.

As for the 1990s, in Kassarjian's view it is clear that we are headed for information processing models and he speculated that Clinton's administration would lead to the return of Kennedy's 'Camelot', with a strong emphasis on consumerism.

Sid Levy echoed many of Kassarjian's themes in a presentation which strongly emphasized the need for present-day scholars to be aware of the contributions of those who had preceded them. As he observed, 'Companies tend to lack memory'. Parenthetically, he clearly believes that many marketing researchers suffer from the same problem. He certainly struck a receptive chord with the author when he observed that 'when you get this old you suffer from the disease of reminiscence'. That said, it is clear that while fashions and theory ebb and flow there is a strong central current so that most arguments are very similar but appear in different guises, reflecting the original distinctions introduced by Aristotle and Plato.

Levy, too, was of the opinion that Europeans have always been more willing to pursue a greater in-depth approach to research than their American colleagues. Finally, he identified the current hot topics as:

- consumer satisfaction (it always was);
- internationalism – with everything;
- environmentalism;
- ethics.

Steve Greyser took as his theme 'Marketing and Public Policy'. Tracing developments over the course of the century Greyser summed up by seeing the 1970s as a period of hyper-activity, the 1980s as a period of remission, and he anticipates that the 1990s will offer tremendous potential for a revival of interest in marketing and public policy as the pendulum swings yet again.

Finally, Jagdish Sheth spoke on the theme of 'Marketing Theory: A Metatheory Assessment'. In classifying marketing schools of thought Sheth argued that evolution has gone back and forth between non-interactive and interactive perspectives. Starting with an economic and non-interactive perspective in the 1950s, interest in the 1960s shifted to an interactive perspective but still underpinned by economic considerations. In turn this led, in the 1970s, to an emphasis upon non-economic factors but in a non-interactive perspective which, in the 1980s, moved into an interactive and non-economic perspective. Based on his analysis Sheth argued that today's marketing theory depends largely on borrowed constructs and depends heavily on context. In future he sees it moving towards a discipline based upon its own indigenous constructs which, in turn, represents a move from the existence of an invisible hand to the visible hand of managed competition.

Sheth concluded that marketing will not be a discipline so long as it is treated as context and relies on borrowed constructs and theories. Clearly, he sees 'relationship marketing' as providing the opportunity to develop this distinctive set of constructs which will enable marketing to emerge as a discipline.

From these presentations by distinguished marketing scholars the author drew three broad conclusions. First, marketing thought and research is largely distinguished by its micro perspective with an emphasis upon the individual and the firm. Second, from decade to decade the emphasis on firm and individual swings from one to the other with the common thread being the interaction between these parties to exchange. Third, there are some significant differences in the approach taken by North American and European researchers, a need to improve communication between these schools and considerable potential for integrating them into a single holistic approach to the subject.

It must be emphasized that the above represents the author's interpretation of what the distinguished panel said and, in the absence of a written transcript, one is conscious of the ever-present dangers of selective perception and hearing what one wants to hear. However, for an authoritative and widely accepted written statement on the current status of marketing we do not have to look far. In 'The Changing Role of Marketing in the Corporation', Fred Webster Jr. set out 'to outline both the intellectual and pragmatic roots of changes that are occurring in marketing, especially marketing *management*, as a body of knowledge, theory, and practice and to suggest the need for a new paradigm of the marketing function within the firm' (1992: 1).

Webster dates the early roots of the development of marketing as an area of academic study to around 1910 with a growing interest in the marketing of agricultural products in the mid-western land grant universities. Three separate schools may be identified:

1 Focusing on the commodities themselves.
2 Focusing on the institutions involved.
3 Focusing on the functions performed by these institutions.

All three schools tended to be descriptive rather than normative with the functional being the most analytical and providing the basis for conceptual development. Relatively little attention was given to managerial factors or orientation and 'marketing was seen as a set of social and economic processes rather than as a set of managerial activities and responsibilities' (Webster 1992: 2). This perspective began to emerge in the late 1940s and early 1950s and, in Webster's view, 'the managerial approach brought relevance and realism to the study of marketing, with an emphasis on problem solving, planning, implementation, and control in a competitive marketplace' (ibid.: 2).

The new managerial school, represented by scholars such as Howard (1957), McCarthy (1960) and Kotler (1967), looked upon marketing as a problem-solving and decision-making process and drew heavily on analytical frameworks from economics, psychology, sociology and statistics. It was during the 1950s that the marketing concept was articulated, by writers such as Drucker (1954), McKitterick (1957) and Levitt (1960), emphasizing customer satisfaction as the primary objective of the organization with profit being seen as the reward.

Unsurprisingly, proponents of the institutional/functionalist view were not ready to discard lightly the accumulation of fifty years of writing and research and the managerial approach was not received with universal enthusiasm. However, as calls for greater rigour in approaches to management education gathered momentum in the late 1950s and early 1960s so the managerial school became dominant and was to remain so for nearly three decades.

The foundation of the managerial school was the basic micro-economic paradigm emphasizing profit maximization and the nature of transactions between buyer and seller. 'Behavioural science models were used primarily to structure problem definition, helping the market researcher to define the questions that are worth asking and to identify important variables and the relationships between them' (Webster 1992: 3). To measure and analyse these relationships sophisticated statistical analysis was called for and the marketing function grew within major organizations as groupings or departments containing individuals with the requisite expertise and professionalism – a development well suited to the culture of large, divisionalized, bureaucratic and hierarchical organizations. Such organizations were the 'engines of economic activity' (Miles and Snow 1978) for more than a century and were the dominant organizations as the managerial approach to marketing developed in the 1950s and 1960s. Often marketing departments evolved from sales departments as these large organizations moved slowly to adopt the greater rigour and discipline offered by the new managerial orientation.

In the large, divisionalized corporations where size and economies of scale and experience were seen as leading to competitive success, 'the task of the marketing function was first to develop a thorough understanding of the marketplace to ensure that the firm was producing goods and services required and desired by the consumer' (Webster 1992: 4). Having done so, marketing was responsible for creating and sustaining consumer preference through manipulation of the mix variables – product, price, promotion and distribution. Centralized, corporate marketing departments were the order of the day.

During the late 1970s and early 1980s the move towards decentralization began to gather momentum as the concept of the strategic business unit (SBU) with profit and loss responsibility found favour with corporate management. Inevitably, decentralization led to duplication and excessive numbers and layers of middle management. Faced with increased competition both domestically and internationally cost containment became an imperative and 'down-sizing' the consequence. However, down-sizing was only a partial solution and more radical restructuring was clearly required.

> The new organisations emphasised partnerships between firms; multiple types of ownership and partnering within the organisation (divisions, wholly owned subsidiaries, licensees, franchises, joint ventures, etc.); teamwork among members of the organisation, often with team members from two or more co-operating firms; sharing of responsibility for developing converging and overlapping technologies; and often less emphasis on formal contracting and managerial reporting, evaluation and control systems.
>
> (Webster 1992: 4)

Various names have been coined for these more flexible and adaptable organizational forms ('networks', Miles and Snow 1978; 'value adding partnerships', Johnston and Lawrence 1988; 'alliances', Ohmae 1989; and 'shamrocks', Handy 1990).

All are characterised by flexibility, specialisation, and an emphasis on relationship

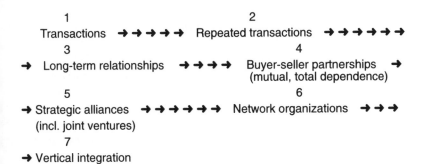

1
Transactions → → → → →   2
Repeated transactions → → → → → →
3
→ Long-term relationships → → → →   4
Buyer-seller partnerships →
(mutual, total dependence)
5
→ Strategic alliances → → → → → →   6
Network organizations → → →
(incl. joint ventures)
7
→ Vertical integration

Figure 1   The range of marketing relationships

management instead of market transactions. They depend on administrative processes but they are not hierarchies (Thorelli 1986); they engage in transactions within ongoing relationships and they depend on negotiation, rather than market-based processes, as a principal basis for conducting business and determining prices, though market forces almost always influence and shape negotiation. The purpose of these new organisation forms is to respond quickly and flexibly to accelerating change in technology, competition, and customer preferences.

(Webster 1992: 4–5)

Although Webster perceives no strong consensus in the terminology and typology for describing the new organization forms he proposes a continuum from pure transactions to fully integrated organizations, as depicted in Figure 1.

As one moves along this continuum the role of the marketing function will change and Webster describes each of these phases in some detail. Based on his analysis of the evolution of exchange relationships he states (1992: 10): 'The intellectual core of marketing management needs to be expanded beyond the conceptual framework of micro economics in order to address more fully the set of organisational and strategic issues inherent in relationships and alliances'.

To do so will require closer consideration of phenomena which, traditionally, have been 'the subject of study of psychologists, organisational behaviourists, political economists and sociologists. The focus shifts from products and firms as units of analysis to people, organisations, and the social processes that bind actors together in ongoing relationships' (ibid.).

In order to consider the role of marketing in the evolving organization Webster argues that it is essential to recognize that marketing really operates at three strategic levels – corporate, business or SBU, and the functional or operational level. He further states that it is a failure to distinguish clearly these three levels which underlies much of the misdefinition and misunderstanding of the marketing concept over the years: 'In addition to the three levels of strategy we can identify three distinct dimensions of marketing – marketing as *culture*, marketing as *strategy*, and marketing as *tactics*' (original emphasis, 1992: 10). Marketing as culture is the responsibility of corporate and SBU levels, marketing as strategy is the emphasis of the SBU level, and marketing as tactics is the focus at the operating level responsible for managing the marketing mix. Webster elaborates on each of these propositions and reiterates his view that 'the political economy and organisational behaviour models seem to be more appropriate for a *strategic* view of the marketing function as distinct from the *sales* or demand stimulation function, for which the micro-economics paradigm is still more fitting' (ibid.: 13).

In conclusion, Webster offers us a definition and an opinion. Marketing 'is the management function responsible for making sure that every aspect of the business is focused on delivering superior value to customers in the competitive marketplace' (ibid.: 14). 'Marketing can no longer be the sole responsibility of a few specialists. Rather, everyone in the firm must be charged with responsibility for understanding customers and contributing to developing and delivering value for them' (ibid.).

Clearly, there is considerable correspondence between Webster's views and those cited earlier. If nothing else it seems reasonable to accept them as the dominant and prevailing school of thought in the USA. That said it must be recognized that there are dissident voices or at least alternative perspectives within the USA while in Europe, Japan and many other countries there is a sense of some surprise that it has taken the Americans so long to reach a conclusion they had arrived at some time ago. (Perhaps it is not so surprising when one appreciates how limited is the American scholars' awareness of non-American sources. For example. Webster's 1992 article contains over 70 references. Only 6 of these are non-American and 5 of these 6 are by American authors. A clear case of acute research myopia.)

ALTERNATIVE PERSPECTIVES

One of the key tenets of the marketing management faith is that the articulation of the marketing concept and its implementation through the development of marketing management occurred with the transition from a production and sales orientation/era which had preceded the marketing era. This belief, enshrined in the traditional three eras conceptualization of marketing, was challenged seriously by Ronald A. Fullerton in his article 'How Modern is Modern Marketing?' (1988).

Fullerton attributes the source of the three eras approach to a seminal article by Keith (1960) in which he described the evolution of marketing in the Pillsbury Company as having followed a production, sales and marketing stage. While this conceptualization has pedagogical advantages in summarizing the changes in the dominant orientation of business management it is singularly deficient in analysing the much more complex processes which underlay and resulted in these changes. Such an analysis is properly the domain of the business historian following the requirements of rigorous historical research. It is this which Fullerton sets out to achieve and we summarized the key arguments in the opening chapter.

Fullerton's thesis about the evolutionary nature of marketing receives considerable support from the work of another American historian – Richard S. Tedlow (1990, 1993). He identifies three phases in the history of consumer product marketing in the USA: fragmentation (lasting until the 1880s); unification (1880s–early 1950s); and segmentation (1950s–late 1980s/early 1990s). He speculates that we are now entering a fourth phase of micro-marketing or hyper-segmentation based upon developments in information technology. Inevitably this implies the establishment of closer relationships between producers and consumers and lends support to Webster and Sheth, *inter alia*, that we are on the threshold of a new era in marketing.

It is here, however, that American scholars and researchers are seen as latecomers to a perspective of marketing which has enjoyed considerable support for decades amongst other international researchers. Indeed, as we saw in Chapter 1, in the opinion of one leading French researcher, Giles Marion, although the normative theory of marketing management may well have had a useful impact on managerial thinking and practice, 'there has been nothing new since the 1960s or even well before' (Marion 1993: 166).

Since the 1960s generations of managers have been educated in the 'marketing management' school popularized by McCarthy (1960) and Kotler (1967) and their numerous disciples. This positivist approach – analysis, planning and control – has been the dominant paradigm for over thirty years. But, because many managers have experienced difficulty in implementing the 'marketing orientation' its nature and validity have come into question (see Swartz 1990).

In Marion's view the marketing management school is founded largely on myth and rhetoric. Three essential ideas are cited as central to the contributions of Drucker, McKitterick, Keith and Levitt:

which appear as the basis of all textbooks on marketing management:

1. That it is the customer who ultimately determines the purpose of companies and even of organisations, in other words, the marketing concept;
2. That all companies, and even all organisations will eventually adopt this concept;
3. That the 'opponents' of this concept cannot and must not succeed because the company would not survive.

(Marion 1993: 157)

Marion points out that the first proposition is simply a definition of a market economy and is an idea which is axiomatic in economics and one which was articulated as long ago as 1933 by Tosdal when specifically discussing marketing management:

The first, and one of the most significant and striking changes of the last dozen years, stressed particularly since 1929, is the increased emphasis placed upon consumer wants and needs as a guide to good marketing management. While serious students of marketing have continuously recognised this viewpoint, here is good reason to agree ... that manufacturers as a whole have been giving only lip service to the consideration of consumer wants and needs.

and:

The idea that consumer needs and wants should be the starting point for business thinking is certainly not revolutionary. For a century or more, economists have made assertions that the aim of our economic and business structure and its functioning was the satisfaction of consumer needs.

(Tosdal 1933: 157)

Perhaps Tosdal had in mind the oft-quoted observation in Adam Smith's *Wealth of Nations* (1766) that 'consumption is the sole end and purpose of production'.

While few would challenge the central role of economic thinking in the development of marketing theory, proponents of the marketing management school are seen as promoting the satisfaction of consumer needs as the very *raison d'être* of the organization. But Marion, *inter alia*, rightly points out that other motivations underlie organizational and managerial behaviour which is why single factor explanations have been singlarly unsuccessful in explaining competitive performance (Baker and Hart 1989).

To overcome the failings of the normative theory of marketing management with its assumptions that needs are given so that consumer sovereignty and managerial rationality are the foundation of exchange behaviour, Marion argues that one must consider simultaneously both parties to the relationship. Doing so enables one to reconcile the views of those like Galbraith, who used the same assumption of exogenous preferences, to argue for producer sovereignty. Thus Marion (1993) is proposing a model based on interactive rationality according to which 'the origin of preferences is endogenous, they are built by the actors' interaction before becoming exogenous and growing into a set of constraints'.

Such a model is in keeping with the Scandinavian School dealing with inter-organizational exchanges in an industrial environment (the 'interaction' approach), with channel theory, and more broadly based theories of organizational behaviour such as those proposed by March and Simon (1958), Cyert and March (1963), and others.

Marion argues that 'marketing as a discipline, should show greater humility by presenting its prescriptions in a more prudent manner, and by describing more systematically the interaction between supply and demand and the organisational consequences that follow' (1993: 166). In conclusion Marion expresses the view that, while the normative theory of marketing management may well have had a useful impact on managerial thinking and practice, there has been nothing new for some decades.

As we saw in Chapter 1, while Marion's critique strikes at the very heart of the marketing management school promoted by Americans, it is comparatively mild compared with the trenchant criticisms expressed by Evert Gummesson and Christian Grönroos, leading members of the Scandinavian School.

EVOLUTION NOT REVOLUTION

At this juncture it will be helpful to summarize the arguments presented in the preceding sections, suggest some conclusions and propose at least a partial answer to the questions implicit in the title of this chapter.

Whatever their perspective, all the authorities cited appear to agree that between 1960 and 1990 the dominant paradigm in marketing theory and practice can be identified as the 'marketing management model' of which Philip Kotler has been the most influential exponent.

However, there is considerable diversity of views about the emergence of this model as the natural consequence of a shift in business orientation from a production or sales orientation to a marketing orientation. While the distinguishing of these three stages or eras is a useful pedagogical device to highlight differences in emphasis in management thinking and practice, the chronology proposed in most marketing management textbooks is severely flawed as evidenced by the work of business historians.

Further, in promoting the marketing management model as a 'new approach' its proponents have been guilty of ignoring or overlooking the roots or foundations of marketing which are to be found originally in the writings of the political economists of the nineteenth century. (This view is inferred by the author and is not made specifically by the sources quoted. In my opinion political economy was/is a behavioural theory of production, consumption and exchange and it is only the more recent preoccupation with quantification – presumably in pursuit of an unattainable 'scientific' rigour – which has disguised and distorted this fact. *Caveat* marketer!) Certainly, there is little 'new' in the marketing management model as articulated from the 1960s onwards.

The marketing management model is production orientated due to its preoccupation with what marketers 'do' to consumers. Its emphasis is essentially short term and transactional. Furthermore it is concerned primarily with the production and sale of fast-moving consumer goods which represent only a fraction of all commercial exchanges.

With its emphasis on the manipulation of the marketing mix of product, price, place and promotion (the Four Ps) the marketing management model ignores the influence and impact of numerous other factors which are involved in exchange relationships. Attempts to explain competitive performance solely in terms of marketing factors are doomed to failure.

While the marketing management model has been the dominant model, alternative explanations of marketing are to be found in the interaction, services and now relationship approaches developed in Europe from the 1960s onwards, particularly by the so-called Scandinavian School. The relationship marketing approach has been recognized and enthusiastically promoted in the USA since

Anglo Saxon	Germanic-Alpine
Basic principle	
Free competition	Controlled competition
Power centres	
The stock exchange	The Bank
Customer (as consumer)	Company over customer
	Management over shareholder
Time perspective	
Short term	Long term
The tyranny of the	Development as
quarterly report	opposed to profit
Types of business relationship	
Ad hoc transaction	Long-term relationship
Social involvement	
Weak	Strong

Figure 2　Major differences between the two models
Source: Dussart (1994)

the early 1990s (particularly by Sheth and Webster). It is now widely seen as both an alternative to and replacement for the marketing management model.

The relationship marketing model can trace its lineage directly to the work of European economists from the 1930s onwards (the Copenhagen School's parameter theory). It is also implicit in the Germanic/Alpine model of capitalism that contrasts strongly with the Anglo-Saxon model of capitalism which dominates thinking in the free market economies of the USA and UK. The essence of these two models of capitalism is summarized in Figure 2.

From the evidence presented there can be little doubt that most marketing scholars are guilty of research myopia in that they fail to consider earlier research within their own discipline, parallel research activity by scholars in other geographical areas, and complementary research by scholars in other disciplines. In large measure the failure to consider earlier research is attributable to a preoccupation with recency (you will note there are very few 'dated' references in this chapter!). It seems inevitable, therefore, that we will frequently be guilty of reinvention. For example, a major preoccupation of marketers in recent years has been 'time to market'. Robert Weigand addressed this very topic in the *Journal of Marketing* in 1962, but is seldom if ever cited. The importance of parallel processing, concurrent engineering and simultaneity are seen as vital but few researchers appear to be aware of the PERT and CPA techniques first articulated in the late 1950s. Competitiveness is of central concern to us all but how many readers are aware of, let alone have consulted the analysis by Carter and Williams (1958) of the characteristics of technically progressive firms. And so we could go on.

If these indictments are correct then the relevance of much of what we do must also be called into question. If productivity, on which academic recognition and preferment are judged, is to be measured in terms of frequency and recency rather than quality and importance then the proliferation of trivia can only gather momentum to the neglect of true knowledge.

What is called for is a renaissance in marketing thinking and research. The time may now be right for this to occur. Given that renaissance was the theme of the 1994 AMA Educators' Winter Conference, and given the widespread enthusiasm for relationship marketing in place of the marketing management model which has dominated our thinking for the past thirty years or more, the opportunity for a fundamental reappraisal of marketing thinking could not be better. Now is the time for all of us to revisit the marketing classics of the 1950s and early 1960s for it was these that influenced and challenged the senior scholars at the top of our profession today. Now is also the time to reaffirm that marketing like architecture, engineering and medicine is a synthetic discipline which draws upon contributions from many other disciplines and integrates these into a body of knowledge which is relevant to a craft or professional practice. Unlike many of the core disciplines, such as economics, psychology and sociology, on which it draws, marketing cannot afford to become enmeshed in a scientific rigour that requires one to control or assume away the complexity which is the real world of practice. As with architecture, engineering and medicine the acid test should be 'does it work?' What we need are more basic principles and rules of thumb – what at Harvard Business School in my day were called 'currently useful generalizations' (CUGs) – and fewer esoteric irrelevancies which are fit only to grace the pages of the *Journal of Obscurity*.

Further, in creating our vision of the future perhaps what we need most of all is a greater awareness of our past. Business history and the works of the political economists of the eighteenth and nineteenth centuries should be required reading for us all. That said, help is nearer to hand. As noted in the Preface to this Encyclopedia, this work represents the distilled wisdom of many of the world's leading authorities, each of whom is recognized internationally as an expert in their field. While the contributing authors have concentrated on specific topics, many of the themes addressed here are to be found in their individual chapters and it is to these that the reader should turn first for enlightenment.

Inevitably, the writing of this chapter had to be deferred until all the other contributions had been received. Given that these represent the current state of marketing knowledge and thinking as of the end of 1994 it would have been foolish not to. Thus it was that in November 1994 I received the latest Editorial for volume 10.8 of the *Journal of Marketing Management* by David Carson and Stephen Brown of the University of Ulster. David and Stephen and their colleagues were responsible for organizing the annual conference of the UK Marketing Education Group and it fell to them to select a cross-section from over 200 papers presented to provide a flavour of the Conference and its theme

'Unity in Diversity'. In their Editorial Carson and Brown echo many of the issues and themes touched on in this chapter which speculates on the current state and future development of marketing thought and practice. It offers a fitting end piece both to this chapter and to the work as a whole:

Although the marketing function has been performed since the dawn of civilization, the modern marketing concept, or philosophy, dates from the early 1950s and Peter Drucker's (1954: 36) famous contention that, 'Marketing ... is the whole business seen from the point of view of its final result, that is, from the customer's point of view'. Forty years on from Drucker's seminal insight – and the dangers of disciplinary anthropomorphism notwithstanding – it is perhaps only to be expected that marketing is in the throes of its 'mid-life crisis'. As a glance at the journals amply testifies, doubts are increasingly being cast on the veracity of the marketing concept; marketing principles no longer seem relevant to the real world of practitioners; leading figures in the field are marketing's most outspoken critics; and the sense of academic cohesion, solidarity and commitment to the marketing cause has been torn asunder by a series of bitter philosophical disputes and declarations of epistemological independence (Brady and Davis 1993; Freeling 1994; Wilson and McDonald 1994).

Rather than dwell on marketing's current crisis of relevance and representation, it may be more appropriate to remind ourselves of several salient facts. First, 'crises' in marketing are not exactly new. More than 30 years ago, for example, Bartels (1962) was discussing the then crisis in marketing. Twenty years or so ago, Bell and Emory (1971) were saying something similar. And, it is more than 10 years now since Bennett and Cooper (1981) were also crying crisis. Second, crises in marketing are not necessarily unhealthy. As the 'broadening' convulsions of the early 1970s and the philosophical 'crisis' literature of a decade ago clearly demonstrate, periods of instability impel everyone, not just the protagonists, to reflect on their own position, consider alternative approaches or embrace novel perspectives, the ultimate consequence of which is an all-round improvement in academic standards. Third, and most importantly, marketing's current bout of self-abasement should not tempt us to forget the enormous strides that it has made in the post-war era. As Baker and Hart (1989) have shown, there is considerable evidence that a marketing orientation is the key to long-term business success. The marketing concept has been enthusiastically embraced in fields as diverse as health care, public administration and the not-for-profit sector. It is rapidly colonizing the erstwhile command economies of eastern Europe, where the market is supplanting Marxism as the societal touchstone, albeit not without privation. And, the proliferation of publications, professorships, degree programmes, university departments and professional societies testifies to the fact that marketing is in the ascendant as an academic discipline.

It is important, therefore, in these uncertain times and in this the 40th anniversary of Drucker's acclaimed contribution, to remember that we have indeed come a long way baby! In today's fragmented marketing world of realism and relativism, positivism and post-positivism, micro-marketing and macro-marketing, scientists and semiologists, transactions and relationships, myths and metaphors, modernists and post-modernists, where all manner of shortcomings are being identified, putative solutions to our ills proposed and the possibility of disciplinary disintegration looms large, it is equally important to remember that marketing is a very broad church. Marketing is and always has been a remarkably diverse discipline, drawing from and, increasingly, contributing to cognate academic specialisms. Indeed, it is arguable that now, more than ever, is the time to abandon our long-standing lack of scholarly self-esteem, the utterly erroneous but depressingly widespread view that marketers cannot make an original contribution to knowledge, that we are forever condemned

1016

to live off the scraps from the tables of our academic elders and betters (Brown 1994). Despite its rich, welcome and ever-increasing diversity, marketing still possesses an underlying unity. This unity, however, does not derive from the phenomena we study, the subject matter of our investigations. Marketing does not 'own' new product development; it does not possess a monopoly on distribution channels or pricing strategies; and, only the most reactionary or recidivist scholar would consider advertising and promotion to be marketing's disciplinary preserve. Nor, for that matter, is marketing unified by a distinctive methodology, a particular scale of analysis, or, arguably, a core concept such as 'exchange'. Marketing, rather, seems to be held together by the, sometimes divergent, often overlapping, belief systems of those that consider themselves marketers. *Marketing*, to modify the venerable neologism, *is not what marketers do; marketing is what marketers perceive it to be* [my emphasis].

REFERENCES

Baker, Michael J. (ed.) (1993) *Perspectives on Marketing Management*, Vol. 3, Chichester: John Wiley & Sons.
Baker, Michael J. and Hart, Susan J. (1989) *Marketing and Competitive Success*, London: Philip Allen.
Bartels, R. (1962) *The Development of Marketing Thought*, Homewood: Richard D. Irwin.
Bell, M. L. and Emory, C. W. (1971) 'The faltering marketing concept', *Journal of Marketing* 35, October: 37–42.
Bennett, R. C. and Cooper, R. G. (1981) 'The misuse of marketing: an American tragedy', *Business Horizons* 24 (6): 51–61.
Brady, J. and Davis, I. (1993) 'Marketing's mid-life crisis', *McKinsey Quarterly* 2: 17–28.
Brown, S. (1994) 'Sources and status of marketing theory', in M. J. Baker (ed.) *Marketing: Theory and Practice*, 3rd edn, London: Macmillan.
Carson, D. and Brown, S. (1994) 'Editorial', *Journal of Marketing Management* 10.8.
Carter, C. F. and Williams, B. R. (1959) 'The characteristics of technically progressive firms', *Journal of Industrial Economics*, March.
Cyert, R. M. and March, J. G. (1963) *A Behavioural Theory of the Firm*, Englewood Cliffs, NJ: Prentice-Hall.
Drucker, Peter (1954) *The Practice of Management*, New York: Harper & Row.
Dussart, Christian (1994) 'Capitalism versus capitalism', in Michael J. Baker (ed.) *Perspectives on Marketing Management*, Vol. 4, Chichester: John Wiley & Sons.
Freeling, A. (1994) 'Marketing is in crisis – can market research help?', *Journal of the Market Research Society* 36 (2): 97–104.
Fullerton, Ronald A. (1988) 'How modern is modern marketing?', *Journal of Marketing*.
Grönroos, Christian (1993) 'Quo vadis, marketing', invited paper, European Marketing Academy, Annual Conference, Barcelona, May.
Gummesson, E. (1993) 'Broadening and specifying relationship marketing', invited paper, Monash Colloquium on Relationship Marketing, Monash University, Melbourne, Australia, 1–4 August.
Handy, Charles (1990) *The Age of Unreason*, Boston: Harvard Business School Press.
Howard, J. A. (1957) *Marketing Managemement: Analysis and Planning*, Homewood, Ill: Richard D. Irwin, Inc.
Johnston, Russell and Lawrence, Paul R. (1988) 'Beyond vertical integration – the rise of the value-adding partnership', *Harvard Business Review* 66, July–August: 94–101.
Keith, R. J. (1960) 'The marketing revolution', *Journal of Marketing* 24, January: 35–8.
Kotler, Philip (1967) *Marketing Management: Analysis, Planning and Control*, Englewood Cliffs, NJ: Prentice-Hall.

Levitt, T. (1960) 'Marketing myopia', *Harvard Business Review*, July–August.
McCarthy, E. Jerome (1960) *Basic Marketing: A Managerial Approach*, Homewood, Ill: Richard D. Irwin, Inc.
McKitterick, J. B. (1957) 'What is the marketing management concept?', in F. M. Bass (ed.) *The Frontiers of Marketing Thought and Science*, Chicago: American Marketing Association: 71–82.
March, J. G. and Simon, H. A. (1958) *Organization*, New York, NY: John Wiley.
Marion, G. (1993) 'The marketing management discourse: what's new since the 1960s?', in Michael J. Baker (ed.) *Perspectives on Marketing Management*, Vol. 3, Chichester: John Wiley & Sons.
Miles, R. E. and Snow, C. C. (1978) *Organizational Strategy, Structure and Process*, New York, NY: McGraw-Hill.
Ohmae, Kenichi (1989) 'The global logic of strategic alliances', *Harvard Business Review* 67, March–April: 143–54.
Swartz, G. S. (1990) 'Organising to become market-driven', Conference Summary, Marketing Science Institute, Cambridge, MA., 13–14 September.
Tedlow, Richard S. (1990) *New and Improved: The Story of Mass Marketing in America*, Oxford: Heinemann.
Tedlow, Richard S. and Jones, Geoffrey (eds) (1993) *The Rise and Fall of Mass Marketing*, London: Routledge.
Thorelli, Hans R. (1986) 'Networks: between markets and hierarchies', *Strategic Management Journal* 7: 37–51.
Tosdal, H. R. (1933) 'Some recent changes in the marketing of consumer goods', *Harvard Business Review* 2, January.
Webster, F. E. Jr. (1992) 'The changing role of marketing in the corporation', *Journal of Marketing*, October: 1–17.
Weigand, Robert (1962) 'How extensive is the planning and development program?', *Journal of Marketing* 3, July: 55–7.
Wilson, M. and McDonald, M. (1994) 'Marketing at the crossroads – a comment', *Marketing Intelligence and Planning* 12 (1): 41–5.

INDEX

Nash, L. 924–5
National Livestock and Meat Board,
  USA 797
National Westminster Bank 833
nations, trading *see* trading nations
needs 4–5, 8
  diffusion 453–4
  elements 452
  green marketing 980
  intensity 452–3
  Maslow's hierarchy 4
  stability 453
  TQM 959, 964
negotiation flows, distribution channels
  148
Nelson, P. 755
Nestlé, infant formula 107
Netherlands, green marketing 986
nets, firm's 206
network organization
  flexible organization 269
  hollow 268–9
  strategy implications 270–1
  value-added 269–70
  virtual 270
network position 207
network research 211
networks 96, 195–6, 202–12
  central concept 266–7
  classification 268
  customer care 763
  formation process 267
  hollow 268–9
  marketing coalition company 264–6
  marketing strategy 229, 231
  neural 124, 311
  organizational consequences 264
  services marketing 822
  telecommunications 303
neural networks 124, 311
Nevett, T. 30, 31, 32
new business selling 703–4
new entrants, market dynamics 489
new offerings, non-profit organizations
  943–4
new product forecasting 387–8
new product process
  failure factors 472–4
  five stages of 465–70
  success factors 474–6
new products
  beta tests 469

definition 464–5
development 312, 462–79
failure factors 471–4
market evolution 491–2
segment identification 399
success factors 474–6
New York Cotton Exchange 794
New Zealand Dairy Board 795, 800, 801
new-to-the-world products 464
newbuys, organizational buying
  behaviour 177–80, 183
newness, new products 464–5
news, advertising 673
niche positions, pan-European marketing
  895–6, 898
niche strategies
  core 935
  decline phase 495, 497
  product policy 450
Nigeria, cocoa 793
Nine Ps, sales promotions interaction
  690–1
  see also packaging; personal selling;
  place of purchase; position; price;
  products; promotion; promotional
  advertising; public relations
Nippon Sunhome 104–5
Nohria, N. 211
non-partitioned approaches 131–4
non-price competition 51
non-profit organizations
  development 931–2
  strategic marketing 930–50
non-renewable resources, green
  marketing 988, 992
non-store retailing 625–6
non-tariff trade barriers 790
Nordic School of Services 819
normal distribution 128
Normann, R. 759
normative marketing ethics 906–7, 920–7
norms, social 91–2
North American Free Trade Agreement
  (NAFTA) 828, 885, 887, 890–1
Norway, green marketing 986
Nylon, market extension 493–4

Oakland, J. S. 953–76
objective specification 120–2
objectives
  advertising 672–3
  budgeting 283, 297, 299